## PART VII

### Fiscal and Monetary Policy

## PART VIII

### The United States in the World Economy

## Ideas for Beyond the Final Exam

**1.** How Much Does It Really Cost?

**2.** Attempts to Repeal the Laws of Supply and Demand: The Market Strikes Back.

**3.** The Surprising Principle of Comparative Advantage.

**4.** Trade is a Win-Win Situation.

**5.** The Importance of Thinking at the Margin.

**6.** Externalities: A Shortcoming of the Market Cured by Market Methods.

**7.** Why the Costs of Education and Medical Care Keep Growing.

**8.** The Trade-off between Efficiency and Equality.

**9.** The Short-Run Trade-off between Inflation and Unemployment.

**10.** Inflation Distorts Measurements.

**11.** Why Was It Important to Reduce the Budget Deficit?

**12.** Productivity Growth is (Almost) Everything in the Long Run.

# E C O N O M I C S

# ECONOMICS

## PRINCIPLES AND POLICY

### EIGHTH EDITION

**WILLIAM J. BAUMOL**
C.V. Starr Center for Applied Economics
New York University

**ALAN S. BLINDER**
Princeton University

**THE DRYDEN PRESS**
**A DIVISION OF HARCOURT COLLEGE PUBLISHERS**
FORT WORTH   PHILADELPHIA   SAN DIEGO   NEW YORK   ORLANDO   AUSTIN   SAN ANTONIO
TORONTO   MONTREAL   LONDON   SYDNEY   TOKYO

**Vice President, Publisher**
Mike Roche

**Acquisitions Editor**
Gary Nelson

**Consulting Developmental Editor**
Trish Taylor

**Developmental Editor**
Tim Hewitt

**Market Strategist**
Debbie K. Anderson

**Project Editor**
Charles J. Dierker

**Art Director**
Linda Beaupré

**Production Manager**
Darryl King

*Address for Domestic Orders*
The Dryden Press, 6277 Sea Harbor Drive, Orlando, FL 32887-6777
800-782-4479

*Address for International Orders*
International Customer Service
The Dryden Press, 6277 Sea Harbor Drive, Orlando, FL 32887-6777
407-345-3800
(fax) 407-345-4060
(e-mail) hbintl@harcourtbrace.com

*Address for Editorial Correspondence*
The Dryden Press, 301 Commerce Street, Suite 3700, Fort Worth, TX 76102

*Web Site Address*
**http://www.harcourtcollege.com**

THE DRYDEN PRESS, DRYDEN, and the DP LOGO are registered trademarks of Harcourt Inc.

Harcourt College Publishers may provide complimentary instructional aids and supplements or supplement packages to those adopters qualified under our adoption policy. Please contact your sales representative for more information. If as an adopter or potential user you receive supplements you do not need, please return them to your sales representative or send them to:

Attention: Returns Department, Troy Warehouse, 465 South Lincoln Drive, Troy, MO 63379

Printed in the United States of America

9 0 1 2 3 4 5 6 7 8 048 10 9 8 7 6 5 4 3 2 1

The Dryden Press
Harcourt College Publishers

To my four children, Ellen, Daniel, and now Sabrina and Jim.

*W.J.B.*

To Scott and William, both now well beyond the final exam.

*A.S.B.*

# ABOUT THE AUTHORS

## *William J. Baumol*

William Baumol was born February 26, 1922, in an area of New York City that has since come to be known as Fort Apache. He received his BSS at the College of the City of New York in 1942 and his Ph.D. at the University of London in 1949.

He is Professor of Economics and Director of the C.V. Starr Center for Applied Economics at New York University and Professor Emeritus at Princeton University. He is a frequent consultant to the management of major firms in a wide variety of industries in the United States and other countries, as well as to a number of governmental agencies. In several fields, including the telecommunications and electric utility industries, current regulatory policy is based on his explicit recommendations. Among his many contributions to economics are research on the theory of the firm, the contestability of markets, the economics of the arts and other services—the "cost disease of the services" is often referred to as "Baumol's disease"—and productivity convergence among nations. In addition to economics, he taught a course in wood sculpture at Princeton for about 20 years.

He has been president of the American Economic Association, and three other professional societies. He is an elected member of the National Academy of Sciences, created by the U.S. Congress, and of the American Philosophical Society, founded by Benjamin Franklin. He is also on the board of trustees of the National Council on Economic Education, and of the Theater Development Fund. He is the recipient of nine honorary degrees.

Baumol is the author of 30 books and hundreds of journal and newspaper articles, and his writings have been translated into more than a dozen languages.

## *Alan S. Blinder*

Alan S. Blinder was born in New York City and attended Princeton University, where one of his teachers was William Baumol. After earning a master's degree at the London School of Economics and a Ph.D. at MIT, Blinder returned to Princeton, where he has taught since 1971. He is currently the Gordon S. Rentschler Memorial Professor of Economics and co-director of Princeton's Center for Economic Policy Studies, which he founded.

In January 1993, Blinder went to Washington as part of President Clinton's first Council of Economic Advisers. Then, from June 1994 through January 1996, he served as vice chairman of the Federal Reserve Board. He thus played a role in formulating both the fiscal and monetary policies of the 1990s, topics discussed extensively in this book.

For more than 10 years, Blinder wrote newspaper and magazine columns on economic policy, and his op-ed pieces still appear regularly in various newspapers.

Blinder has been vice president of the American Economic Association and is a member of both the American Philosophical Society and the American Academy of Arts and Sciences. He has two grown sons, and lives in Princeton with his wife, where he plays tennis as often as he can.

The economy changes all the time, but certain principles endure. Steadfastly, we refuse to give up the principles that have guided us through seven previous editions of this book. We still follow our original precept that practical issues and developments in the real economy should influence the content of an introductory economics course and determine how its materials are presented. So we begin most chapters with a real problem and use it as a launching pad for our analysis, rather than the reverse. We still refuse to be lured into the claim that everything contained in this volume is of extreme importance for the reader's future. Therefore, throughout the book we single out those materials that we believe to have enduring value for the student. We believe that readers who do not make some effort to understand and remember these matters after the course is ended will have shortchanged themselves.

It has been said that economics is no laughing matter, and that an economist is a person who, having observed something that works in reality, wonders whether it works in theory! This book contains its share of theoretical material. But the theory is not merely an exercise in making students miserable; it is driven by issues that are real and current. As used by physicists, biologists, and economists—indeed by all in the fields of research in colleges and universities—the word *theory* simply means a thorough and rigorous explanation. For example, economists believe that foreign trade can harm some workers but make most members of the community better off. We need theory to explain why. Or another example: Average incomes of people who live in market economies have grown far faster than those of others in countries where the economy is directed by government planners. Again, theory can explain why.

These observations also suggest two major areas in which this book has been changed since the previous edition. Although coverage of trade among nations and economic growth have always played a substantial part in this text, these subjects are now emphasized even more and are raised wherever they are appropriate. We were induced to turn in this direction by recent developments in the United States and in other industrial economies. More and more of what is produced in the typical country is sold abroad rather than to domestic consumers. Correspondingly, ever more of what consumers buy comes from other lands. At the same time, the continuing appearance of new and improved technology enables workers in all countries to produce more than they did before. Yet, despite the resulting prosperity in the United States during most of the last two decades, the earnings of less-educated workers have fallen behind those of workers with more education and higher skills.

To keep up the prosperity, to offer a better future to those who are now less educated, and to deal with the enormous economic problems of the poorer nations of the world, we need to understand the effects of international trade and of improvements in technology. Do they make most of us better off by making products cheaper, so that our incomes go further? Or do they threaten our incomes by making us more vulnerable to foreign competition and labor-saving technology? These crucial issues are addressed at several points in this book. We have provided an entirely new chapter (Chapter 15) analyzing how competition involving improved products and production techniques drives the growth in free-market economies. This chapter offers material that has not been published previously and seems to have no counterpart in other principles texts.

In addition to this new chapter, many parts of the book have been extensively rewritten and reorganized for easier comprehension. Many of these changes follow suggestions of users of the book and others whose opinions we solicited in an extensive survey. In particular, the four core microeconomics chapters were substantially modified with improved readability in mind. In each of these chapters we were careful to retain the features that readers reported as being helpful in earlier editions.

We have also added a brief treatment of the principle of comparative advantage to Chapter 4. Last, but certainly not least, these halcyon days—when neither high unemployment nor high inflation seem to threaten the U.S. economy—make it appropriate to place greater emphasis on economic growth in the macroeconomic discussion. This has been done throughout the book, but especially in Chapters 24, 33, and 34.

## NOTE TO THE STUDENT

We would like to offer one suggestion for success in your economics course. Unlike some of the other courses you may be taking, economics is cumulative: Each week's lesson builds upon what you have learned before. You will save yourself a lot of frustration and a lot of work by keeping up on a week-to-week basis. To assist you in doing so, we provide a chapter summary, a list of important terms and concepts, and a selection of questions to help you review the contents of each chapter. Making use of these learning aids will increase your chances of success in your economics course. For additional assistance, we have developed student supplements to help reinforce the concepts in this book and provide opportunity for practice and feedback. See the following list of ancillaries for learning tools that apply specifically to students.

## ANCILLARIES

As economic education incorporates new technologies, we have expanded and improved our extensive learning package to accommodate student and instructor needs.

**STUDY GUIDE**  Craig Swan of the University of Minnesota has revised the student Study Guide to make it an even more valuable tool for understanding the text's main concepts. The Study Guide, which is available in main, micro, and macro split versions, includes:

- Learning objectives

- Lists of important terms and concepts for every chapter

- Quizzes that help students test their understanding and comprehension of concepts

- Multiple-choice tests for self-understanding

- Lists of supplementary readings and study questions for every chapter

- "Economics in Action" sections that use current news articles to illustrate economic concepts

- "Economics Online," exercises that outline useful Internet and Web sources for economic data and information. Periodic updates of these sources will be provided on the Dryden/Harcourt Web page at www.harcourtcollege.com.

**INSTRUCTOR'S MANUAL**  David O'Hara of Metropolitan State University has extensively revised the Instructor's Manual. Every chapter includes detailed chapter outlines, teaching tips and suggestions, answers to end-of-chapter questions in the main text, and questions for classroom discussion.

**MICROECONOMICS TEST BANK**  The updated and revised Microeconomics Test Bank by Doug Kinnear of Colorado State University consists of more than 200 questions per chapter and covers Chapters 1–22 and 35 in the text. Every question has been checked to ensure the accuracy and clarity of the answers and painstakingly revised to address the main text revisions. The Test Bank includes true/false, multiple-choice, and short-answer questions that assess students' critical-thinking skills. Easy, medium, and difficult questions outline the process that students must use to arrive at their answers: recall, application, and integration. Questions are organized by text section to help instructors pick and choose their selections with ease.

**MACROECONOMICS TEST BANK**  The updated and revised Macroeconomics Test Bank by Edward F. Stuart of Northeastern Illinois University consists of more than

200 questions per chapter covering Chapters 23–34 and 36–37 in the text. Every question has been checked to ensure the accuracy and clarity of the answers and painstakingly revised to address the main text revisions. The Test Bank includes true/false, multiple-choice, and short-answer questions that assess students' critical-thinking skills. Easy, medium, and difficult questions outline the process that students must use to arrive at their answers: recall, application, and integration. Questions are organized by text section to help instructors pick and choose their selections with ease.

**COMPUTERIZED TEST BANKS** The computerized Test Banks, available in our easy-to-use EXAMaster program, have been enhanced significantly for this edition. EXAMaster allows instructors to add and edit their own questions, create and edit graphics, print scrambled versions of tests, and convert multiple-choice questions to open-ended questions. EXAMaster 99 now includes a more intuitive graphic interface, increased test sizes of up to 500 questions, the capacity to create up to 99 versions of any one test, online testing and grade bookkeeping, and many more features. The new software is now available on CD-ROM in Windows and Macintosh formats.

**THE WALL STREET JOURNAL EDITION** Instructors can help students relate the economic concepts in the text to everyday life by ordering the *Wall Street Journal* edition of the textbook. This special edition supplements the standard edition with a discounted 20-week *Wall Street Journal* subscription for students. Professors get a free subscription when 10 or more of their students order the *Wall Street Journal*. the *Wall Street Journal* provides an effective tie-in to the text because new examples of economic principles appear in each day's paper. Students can activate their subscriptions by simply completing and mailing the business reply card located in the back of the book. This option is available for both the main version of the book and the paperback splits. Instructors interested in finding out more about this program can contact their sales representative or simply call 800-782-4479.

**TRANSPARENCY ACETATES** Full color transparency acetates for all important figures and tables in the eighth edition are available for use on an overhead projector. They are available to adopters upon request in microeconomic and macroeconomic sets.

**POWERPOINT PRESENTATION SOFTWARE** Steven Shulman of Colorado State University has prepared a comprehensive and user-friendly PowerPoint presentation for use in classroom lectures. The presentation consists of speaking points and chapter outlines that are accompanied by graphs and tables from the main text. *PowerPoint Viewer* is provided in the package.

**ECONACTIVE STUDENT CD-ROM** A new HTML-based EconActive student CD-ROM supplement is now available and very easy to use. The look and feel is similar to that of a Web site. The CD-ROM contains chapter-review sections, automatically graded multiple choice and true/false quizzes, "cyberproblems" that launch to the World Wide Web for real-world economic analysis, and more. It also includes interactive graphs and graphing problems that require students to graph solutions.

**INSTRUCTOR'S CD-ROM** Beginning with the eighth edition, accompanying instructor's supplements are available on one CD-ROM. Included on the CD-ROM are the PowerPoint slides, Instructor's Manual, and Test Banks. The CD-ROM also displays a navigation bar that allows instructors to easily search among the microeconomics and macroeconomics versions of the supplements.

**WEB SITE** Valuable resources for both instructors and students can be found on the Internet at www.dryden.com/econ/baumol. For instructors, the PowerPoint presentations and Instructor's Manual are available on the instructors' resources section of the site. Students will find chapter-by-chapter links to economics-related Internet sites, automatically graded practice quizzes, PowerPoint slides for their review, sample chapters from the study guide and *EconActive CD-ROM*, and other resources. Also, career listings for students, leading economic indicator information, and an economic URL database can be found at www.dryden.com.

**WEBCT COURSE MANAGEMENT SOFTWARE**    Harcourt now offers HTML-based software for instructors who are interested in building Web-based learning sites for their students. This software can be utilized by nontechnical users to create entire online courses or simply to post office hours or supplementary course materials for students. Instructors can design Web sites that provide a full array of educational tools, including communications links with their students, Web testing, student grade tracking with access control, database collaboration and searching, and more. It is free of charge to adopters. For more information, call the Harcourt customer service line at 800-237-2665, or visit our home page at www.harcourtcollege.com. You can also visit www.webct.com for a "virtual" tour.

**MACROECONOMICS ONLINE**    Available for Spring 2000, *Macroeconomics Online* by Michael Lehmann and Tawni Ferrarini is a Web-based course that can serve as a supplement to the macroeconomics portion of this text. The course, which uses the Web-CT platform and is delivered online, uses the retrieval of economic data from the World Wide Web and graphical analysis to teach real-world application of economic concepts.

**INTERACTIVE COMPUTER GAMES**    *Survival II: Warrior Island* and *Inuit Hunter* are two interactive games designed by George Bohler, Professor of Economics at Florida Community College at Jacksonville. Both games teach basic economic principles through the discovery method.

- The setting of *Survival II: Warrior Island* is a remote island in the Pacific Ocean populated by 100 survivors of a shipwreck. The goal of the game is to maximize survivors' food production in their 12 months of exile. Players quickly learn that the game's objective requires the application of fundamental economic concepts including resource allocation, capital budgeting, and opportunity cost.
- *Inuit Hunter* is a game of economic strategy that endeavors to recreate the survival activities of Inuit hunter-gatherer bands of the Canadian Arctic in the early years of the 20th century. As with most games, the object is to win. The player who accumulates the highest number of fox furs by the end of the game is the winner. In order to do this, a number of economic principles—including scarcity, opportunity cost, the advantages of trade and specialization, and profit maximization—must be employed.

**GAMES MANUAL**    A games manual, in part a contribution by Charles Stull of Kalamazoo College, provides instructors with classroom games designed to illustrate and enliven important economic concepts. The games have been tremendously popular with instructors and are very useful for classroom learning.

Harcourt College Publishers may provide complimentary instructional aids and supplements or supplement packages to those adopters qualified under its adoption policy. Please contact your sales representative for more information. If, as an adopter or potential user you receive supplements you do not need, please return them to your sales representative or send them to: Returns Department, Troy Warehouse, 465 South Lincoln Drive, Troy, MO 63379.

## NOTE TO THE INSTRUCTOR

In trying to improve the book from one edition to the next, we rely heavily on our experiences as teachers. But our experience using the book is minuscule compared with that of the hundreds of instructors who use it nationwide. If you encounter problems or have suggestions for improving the book, we urge you to let us know by writing to us in care of Harcourt College Publishers, 301 Commerce Street, Suite 3700, Fort Worth, TX 76102. Such letters are invaluable, and we are glad to receive both praise and suggestions for improvement. Many such suggestions that were accumulated after publication of the seventh edition have found their way into this new book. Suggested course outlines for both one-semester and one-quarter courses follow.

**OUTLINE FOR A ONE-SEMESTER COURSE IN MICROECONOMICS**

| CHAPTER | TITLE |
|---|---|
| 1 | What is Economics? |
| 2 | The Use and Misuse of Graphs |
| 3 | The Economy: Myth and Reality |
| 4 | Scarcity and Choice: *The* Economic Problem |
| 5 | Supply and Demand: An Initial Look |
| 6 | Consumer Choice: Individual and Market Demand |
| 7 | Demand and Elasticity |
| 8 | Production, Inputs, and Cost: Building Blocks for Supply Analysis |
| 9 | Output, Price, and Profit: The Importance of Marginal Analysis |
| 10 | The Firm and the Industry Under Perfect Competition |
| 11 | The Price System and the Case for the Free Market |
| 12 | Monopoly |
| 13 | Between Competition and Monopoly |
| 14 | The Market Mechanism: Shortcomings and Remedies |
| 15 | The Microeconomics of Innovation: Prime Engine of Growth |
| 16 | Real Firms and their Financing: Stocks and Bonds |
| 17 | Pricing the Factors of Production |
| 18 | Labor: The Human Input |
| 20 | Limiting Market Power: Regulation and Antitrust |
| 21 | Taxation and Resource Allocation |

**Plus any two of the following:**

| | |
|---|---|
| 19 | Poverty, Inequality, and Discrimination |
| 22 | Externalities, the Environment, and Natural Resources |
| 35 | International Trade and Comparative Advantage |

**OUTLINE FOR A ONE-SEMESTER COURSE IN MACROECONOMICS**

| CHAPTER | TITLE |
|---|---|
| 1 | What is Economics? |
| 2 | The Use and Misuse of Graphs |
| 3 | The Economy: Myth and Reality |
| 4 | Scarcity and Choice: *The* Economic Problem |
| 5 | Supply and Demand: An Initial Look |
| 23 | The Realm of Macroeconomics |
| 24 | The Goals of Macroeconomic Policy |
| 25 | Income and Spending: The Powerful Consumer |
| 26 | Demand-Side Equilibrium: Unemployment or Inflation? |
| 27 | Changes on the Demand Side: Multiplier Analysis |
| 28 | Supply-Side Equilibrium: Unemployment *and* Inflation? |
| 29 | Managing Aggregate Demand: Fiscal Policy |
| 30 | Money and the Banking System |
| 31 | Monetary Policy and the National Economy |
| 32 | The Debate Over Monetary Policy |
| 33 | Deficits, Monetary Policy, and Growth |
| 34 | The Phillips Curve and Economic Growth |
| 35 | International Trade and Comparative Advantage |
| 36 | The International Monetary System: Order or Disorder? |
| 37 | Exchange Rates and the Macroeconomy |

**OUTLINE FOR A ONE-QUARTER COURSE ON APPLICATIONS OF BOTH MACROECONOMICS AND MICROECONOMICS**

| CHAPTER | TITLE |
|---|---|
| 19 | Poverty, Inequality, and Discrimination |
| 20 | Limiting Market Power: Regulation and Antitrust |
| 21 | Taxation and Resource Allocation |
| 22 | Externalities, the Environment, and Natural Resources |
| 24 | The Goals of Macroeconomic Policy |
| 33 | Deficits, Monetary Policy, and Growth |
| 35 | International Trade and Comparative Advantage |
| 36 | The International Monetary System: Order or Disorder? |
| 37 | Exchange Rates and the Macroeconomy |

## WITH THANKS

Finally, and with great pleasure, we turn to the customary acknowledgments of indebtedness. Ours have been accumulating now through eight editions. In these days of specialization, even a pair of authors cannot master every subject that an introductory textbook must cover. Our friends and colleagues Albert Ando, Charles Berry, Rebecca Blank, William Branson, the late Lester Chandler, Gregory Chow, Avinash Dixit, Robert Eisner, Susan Feiner, the late Stephen Goldfeld, Claudia Goldin, Ronald Grieson, Daniel Hamermesh, Yuzo Honda, Peter Kenen, Melvin Krauss, Herbert Levine, the late Arthur Lewis, Burton Malkiel, Edwin Mills, Janusz Ordover, Uwe Reinhardt, Harvey Rosen, Laura Tyson, and Martin Weitzman have all given generously of their knowledge in particular areas over the course of eight editions. We have learned much from them, and only wish we had learned more.

Many economists and students at other colleges and universities offered useful suggestions for improvements, many of which we have incorporated into this eighth edition. We wish to thank Ray Cohn, Illinois State University; George Hoffer, Virginia Commonwealth University; Kirk Kim, University of Wisconsin at Whitewater; Doug Kinnear, Colorado State University; Sang Lee, University of Florida; Robby Rosenman, Washington State University; Edward Stuart, Northeastern Illinois University; John Tiemstra, Calvin College; Hendrick Van den Berg, University of Nebraska at Lincoln; Doug Walker, Lousiana State University; and Stephan Weiler, Colorado State University, for their insightful reviews.

We also wish to thank the many economists who responded to our survey; their responses were invaluable in planning this revision: Mustafa Acar, Purdue University; Terence J. Alexander, Iowa State University; Samuel Kojo Andon, Southern Connecticut State University; B. W. Balch, Middle Tennessee State University; Donald N. Baum, University of Nebraska at Omaha; David C. Black, The University of Toledo; Morgan K. Bridge, Mesa State College; Jozell Brister, Abilene Christian University; Ted Burczak, Denison University; Anthony Chan, Santa Monica College; John E. Charalambakis, Asbury College; Jonathan Conning, Williams College; Barbara Connolly, Westchester Community College; Carrie Cornwell, Sierra College; Pati Shaw Crabb, Indiana University Southeast; Stephen Cullenberg, University of California, Riverside; Dan Dabney, St. Edward's University; Na Li Dawson, University of Connecticut; Peter C. Dawson, University of Connecticut; Justino De La Cruz, University of Texas, San Antonio; Bruce Dixon, University of Arkansas, Fayetteville; Heriberto Dixon, Milano Graduate School of Management; Michael Dowd, University of Toledo; Luoana Dulgheru, University of Connecticut; Elizabeth Elmore, The Richard Stockton College of New Jersey; Mona El Shazly, Columbia College; William C. Freund, Pace University, New York City; John B. Gabor, Lake Tahoe Community College; Yilma Gebremariam, Southern Connecticut State University; Robert Godby, University of Wyoming; Eugene W. Gotwalt, George Mason University; Richard R. Hawkins, University of West Florida; Ali Hekmat, College of Eastern Utah; Whitney Hicks, University of Missouri; Farrokh Hormozi, Pace University; John Houchens, University of Wisconsin-Marathan County; Mahmood Hussain, University of Colorado at Boulder; Young-Iob Chung,

Eastern Michigan University; John Isbister, University of California at Santa Cruz; Oded Izraeli, Oakland University; Don C. Jackson, Abilene Christian University; Ameeta Jaiswal-Dale, University of St. Thomas; Derek C. Jones, Hamilton College; Brad Kamp, University of South Florida-Tampa; Ashok K. Kapoor, Augsburg College; Mariam Khawar, Elmira College; Mohammed Khayum, University of Southern Indiana; Kamau Kinuthia, South Puget Sound Community College; Robert A. Kleinhenz, California State University-Fullerton; Aric W. Krause, Clarion University of Pennsylvania; Jeffrey A. Krautkraemer, Washington State University; Dr. Samuel M. Laposata, Muhlenberg College; Soyon Lee, Benedictine University; Martin Lefsky, Ocean Township High School; Cynthia S. McCarty, Jacksonville State University; Zagros Madjd-Sadjadi, Golden Gate University; Paul A. Mantegani, Kent School; Margaret Malixi, California State University-Bakersfield; Carrie A. Meyer, George Mason University; Hadley T. Mitchell, Taylor University; Masoud Moghaddam, St. Cloud State University; Kahn A. Mohabbat, Northern Illinois University; W. Douglas Morgan, University of California-Santa Barbara; Francis Mummery, California State University-Fullerton; Michael A. Nelson, Washington State University; Anthony O'Brien, Lehigh University; John F. O'Connell, College of the Holy Cross; David O'Hara, Metropolitan State University; Charles C. Okeke, College of Southern Nevada-Las Vegas; Theodore Paliros, Louisiana State University; Paul Pecorino, University of Alabama; Mark G. Pelletier, Winslow Senior High School, Winslow, Maine; Elida Petrella, Wheeling Jesuit University & Indian Creek High School; Arthur L. Porter, Southern Utah University; Robert C. Rogers, Wright College; Bernard Rose, Rocky Mountain College; Richard E. Rosenberg, University of Wisconsin-Parkside; Robert A. Rosenthal, Stonehill College; Steven Rundle, Biola University; Larry D. Schelhorse, San Diego State University; Stanley W. Samarasinghe, Tulane University; James A. Schloss, The Anthenian School; Calvin Siebert, University of Iowa; Kathleen C. Simmons, Gainesville College; Stefani Smith, Tulane University; Peter J. Snedecor, Northfield Mount Hermon School; Jeffrey Stewart, Miami University; Joseph F. Talarico, Rider University; Robert W. Taylor, Purdue University; Mark O. Tengesdal, Southeastern Oklahoma State University; James Thorson, Southern Connecticut State University; Robert M. Toepper, Concordia University; Robert Tokle, Idaho State University; Karen M. Travis, Pacific Lutheran University; Karen Vorst, University of Missouri-Kansas City; Lawrence A. Waldman, University of New Mexico; Pamela Whalley, Western Washington University; James A. Wilde, University of North Carolina-Chapel Hill; Art Woolf, University of Vermont; William J. Zeis, Bucks County Community College.

Obviously, the book you hold in your hands was not produced by us alone. An essential role was played by the staff at Harcourt College Publishers, including Gary Nelson, Acquisitions Editor for Economics; Trish Taylor, Consulting Senior Developmental Editor; Tim Hewitt, Developmental Editor; Charles J. Dierker, Project Editor; Linda Beaupré, Art Director; Darryl King, Production Manager; Linda Blundell, Art and Literary Rights Editor; Annette Coolidge, Photo and Literary Rights Researcher; and Debbie K. Anderson, Marketing Strategist.

We also thank our intelligent and delightful secretaries and research coworkers at Princeton University and New York University, Phyllis Durepos and Janeece Roderick, who struggled successfully with the myriad tasks involved in completing the manuscript. Above all, Professor Baumol owes an unrepayable debt to his long-standing partner in crime, Sue Anne Batey Blackman, who updated much of the materials and contributed draft paragraphs, illustrative items, and far more with her usual insight and diligence. By now, Sue Anne undoubtedly knows more about the book than the authors do.

And, finally, there are our wives, Hilda Baumol and Madeline Blinder. They have now participated and helped with this project for nearly a quarter of a century. During that period, this book has quite literally become part of our families. And both their contributions and our affection have grown.

*William J. Baumol*
*Alan S. Blinder*

# TABLE OF CONTENTS

# I
## GETTING ACQUAINTED WITH ECONOMICS

Welcome to economics! Some of your fellow students may

have warned you that "Econ is boring." Don't

believe them—or at least, don't believe them

too much. It is true that studying economics

may not be as much fun as, say, studying

literature or film. But a first course in eco-

nomics can be an eye-opening experience.

There is a vast and important world out

there—the economic world—and this book is

designed to help you understand it better.

Have you ever wondered whether jobs

will be plentiful or scarce when you graduate? Or why a college

education becomes more and more expensive?

Was the government right to sue Microsoft? Why can't pollution be eliminated? How did the U.S. economy manage to grow so rapidly in the 1990s while Japan's stagnated? If any of these questions have piqued your curiosity, read on. You may find economics to be more interesting than you had thought!

The five chapters of Part I introduce you to both the subject matter of economics and to some of the methods that economists use to study their subject.

Why does public discussion of economic policy so often show the abysmal ignorance of the participants? Why do I so often want to cry at what public figures, the press, and television commentators say about economic affairs?

Robert M. Solow

# WHAT IS ECONOMICS?

Economics is a broad-ranging discipline, both in the questions it asks and the methods it uses to seek answers. Rather than try to define the discipline in a single sentence or paragraph, we will instead introduce you to economics by letting the subject matter speak for itself.

Many of the world's most pressing problems are economic in nature. The first part of the chapter is intended to give you some idea of the sorts of issues that economic analysis helps to clarify and the kinds of solutions that economic principles suggest. The second part briefly introduces the tools that economists use—tools you are likely to find useful in your career, personal life, and role as an informed citizen, long after the course is over.

### ■ IDEAS FOR BEYOND THE FINAL EXAM

As college professors, we realize it is inevitable that you will forget much of what you learn in this course—perhaps with a sense of relief—soon after the final exam. There is not much point bemoaning this fact; elephants may never forget, but people do.

Nevertheless, some economic ideas are so important that you will want to remember them after the course is over. To help you pick out a few of the most crucial concepts, we have selected 12 from among the many contained in this book. Some offer key insights into the workings of the economy. Others bear on important policy issues that appear in newspapers. Others point out common misunderstandings that occur among even the most thoughtful lay observers. As the opening quote of this chapter suggests, many learned judges, politicians, and university administrators who have failed to understand or misused these economic principles could have made wiser decisions than they did.

Each of the *Ideas for Beyond the Final Exam* will be discussed in depth as it occurs in the course of the book and called to your attention at the time by yellow sticky notes in the margin denoting the relevant idea. In addition, we will help you see how these ideas work throughout the book by noting how each chapter topic relates to the relevant ideas in the summary for each chapter. So you should not expect to master them now, but notice how often the same ideas arise as we address economic topics throughout the book. Nonetheless, it is useful to sketch them briefly here both to introduce you to economics and to provide a preview of what is to come.

*Ideas for Beyond the Final Exam*

### IDEA 1: HOW MUCH DOES IT REALLY COST?

Despite dramatic improvements in standards of living since the Industrial Revolution, human society has not come anywhere near a state of unlimited abundance. So people must constantly make choices. If you purchase a new computer, you may have to give up that trip you had planned with friends. If a business decides to retool its factories, it may have to postpone plans for new executive offices. If a government expands its defense program, it may be forced to reduce its outlays on roads or school buildings.

Economists say that the true costs of such decisions are not the number of dollars spent on the computer, the new equipment, or the military establishment, but rather *the value of what must be given up in order to acquire the item*—the vacation trip, the new executive offices, the improved roads, and the new schools. These are called **opportunity costs** because they represent the *opportunities* the individual, firm, or government must forgo to make the desired expenditure. Economists maintain that rational decision making must be based on opportunity costs (Chapter 4).

The opportunity cost of a college education provides a vivid example that is probably close to your heart. How much do you think it costs to go to college? Most likely you would answer this question by adding together your expenditures on tuition, room and board, books, and the like, and then deducting any scholarship funds you may receive. Suppose that comes to $15,000.

Economists would keep score differently. They would first want to know how much you would be earning if you were not attending college. Suppose that is $16,000 a year. This may sound like an irrelevant piece of information. But because you give up these earnings by attending college, they must be added to your tuition bill as a cost of your education. Nor would economists accept the university's bill for room and board as a measure of your living costs. They would want to know how much more it costs you to live at school rather than at home. Economists would count only this extra cost as an expense. On balance, your college education is probably costing you much more than you think.

The **opportunity cost** of some decision is the value of the next best alternative that must be given up because of that decision (for example, working instead of going to school).

### IDEA 2: ATTEMPTS TO REPEAL THE LAWS OF SUPPLY AND DEMAND—THE MARKET STRIKES BACK

When a commodity is in short supply, its price naturally tends to rise. Sometimes disgruntled consumers badger politicians into "solving" this problem by imposing a legal ceiling on the price. Similarly, when supplies are abundant—say, when fine weather produces extraordinarily abundant crops—prices tend to fall. Falling prices naturally dismay producers, who often succeed in getting legislation to impose price floors.

But such attempts to repeal the laws of supply and demand usually backfire and sometimes produce results virtually the opposite of those that were intended. Where rent controls are adopted to protect tenants, housing grows scarce because the law makes it unprofitable to build and maintain apartments. When price floors are placed under agricultural products, surpluses pile up.

As we will see in Chapter 5 and elsewhere in this book, such consequences of interfering with the price mechanism are no accident. They follow inevitably from the way free markets work.

## IDEA 3: THE SURPRISING PRINCIPLE OF COMPARATIVE ADVANTAGE

Japan produces many products that Americans buy in huge quantities—including cars, TV sets, cameras, and electronic equipment. American manufacturers often complain about Japanese competition and demand protection from the flood of imports that, in their view, threatens American standards of living. Is this view justified?

Economists think not. They maintain that both sides must gain from international trade. But what if the Japanese were able to produce *everything* more cheaply than we can? Wouldn't Americans be thrown out of work and our nation be impoverished?

A remarkable result, called the law of *comparative advantage*, shows that, even in this extreme case, the two nations can still benefit by trading and that each can gain as a result! We will explain this principle first in Chapter 4 and then more fully in the chapter on international trade, where we will also note some potentially valid arguments in favor of providing special incentives for particular domestic industries. But for now a simple parable will make the reason clear.

Suppose Sally grows up on a farm and is a whiz at plowing. But she is also a successful country singer who earns $4,000 a performance. Should Sally turn down singing engagements to leave time for working the fields? Of course not. Instead she should hire Alfie, a much less efficient farmer, to do the plowing for her. Sally may be better at plowing. But she earns so much more by singing that it makes sense for her to specialize in that and leave the farming to Alfie. Though Alfie is a less skilled farmer than Sally, he is an even worse singer.

So Alfie earns his living in the job at which he at least has a *comparative* advantage (his farming is not as bad as his singing), and both Alfie and Sally gain. The same is true of two countries. Even if one of them is more efficient at everything, both countries can gain by producing the things they do best *comparatively*.

## IDEA 4: TRADE IS A WIN-WIN SITUATION

One of the most fundamental ideas of economics is that *both* parties must expect to gain something in a *voluntary* exchange. Otherwise why would they both agree to trade? This principle seems self-evident. Yet it is amazing how often it is ignored in practice.

For example, it was widely believed for centuries that in international trade one country's gain from an exchange must be the other country's loss (Chapter 35). Analogously, some people feel instinctively that if Ms. A profits handsomely from a deal with Mr. B, then Mr. B must have been exploited. Laws sometimes prohibit mutually beneficial exchanges between buyers and sellers—as when a loan transaction is banned because the interest rate is "too high" (Chapter 24) or when a willing worker is condemned to remain unemployed because the wage she is offered is "too low" (Chapter 18), or when the resale of tickets to sporting events ("ticket scalping") is outlawed even though the buyer is happy to get the ticket that he would not obtain at a lower price (Chapter 5).

In every one of these cases, and many more, well-intentioned but misguided reasoning blocks the mutual gains that arise from voluntary exchange—and thereby interferes with one of the most basic functions of an economic system (see Chapter 4).

### IDEA 5: THE IMPORTANCE OF THINKING AT THE MARGIN

We will devote many pages of this book to explaining and extolling a type of decision-making process called *marginal analysis* (see especially Chapters 6, 8, and 9), which we can best illustrate by an example.

Suppose an airline is told by its accountants that the full cost of transporting one passenger from Los Angeles to New York is $300. Can the airline profit by offering a reduced fare of $200 to students who fly on a standby basis? The surprising answer is, probably yes. The reason is that most of the costs will be paid whether the plane carries 20 passengers or 120 passengers.

Marginal analysis points out that costs such as maintenance, landing rights, and ground crews are irrelevant to the decision of whether to carry standby passengers for reduced rates. The only costs that *are* relevant are the *extra* costs of writing and processing additional tickets, the food and beverages these passengers consume, the additional fuel required, and so on. These costs are called *marginal costs* and are probably quite small in this example. Any passenger who pays the airline more than its marginal cost will add something to the company's profit. So it probably is more profitable to let the students ride at low fares than to let the plane fly with empty seats.

In many real cases, a failure to understand marginal analysis has led decision makers to reject advantageous possibilities like the reduced fare in our example. These people were misled by calculating in terms of *average* rather than *marginal* cost figures—an error that can be quite costly.

### IDEA 6: EXTERNALITIES: A SHORTCOMING OF THE MARKET CURED BY MARKET METHODS

Markets are very adept at producing the goods that consumers want and in just the quantities they desire. They do so by rewarding those who respond to what consumers want and who produce these products economically. Similarly, the market mechanism ferrets out waste and inefficiency by seeing to it that inefficient producers lose money.

This all works out well as long as each exchange involves only the buyer and the seller—and no one else. But some transactions affect third parties who were not involved in the decision. Examples abound. Electric utilities that generate power for Midwestern states also produce pollution—which kills freshwater fish in New York state. A farmer sprays crops with toxic pesticides, but the poison seeps into the ground water and affects the health of neighboring communities.

Such social costs are called *externalities* because they affect parties *external* to the economic transactions that cause them. Externalities escape the control of the market mechanism because no financial incentive motivates polluters to minimize the damage they do—as we will learn in Chapters 14 and 22. So business firms make their products as cheaply as possible, disregarding any environmental harm they may cause.

Yet Chapters 14 and 22 point out a way for the government to use the market mechanism to control undesirable externalities. If the electric utility and the farmer are charged for the damage they do to the air and water, just as they are charged for any coal and fertilizer they use, then they will have a financial incentive to reduce the amount of pollution they generate. Thus, in this case, economists believe that market methods are often the best way to cure one of the market's most important shortcomings.

### IDEA 7: WHY THE COSTS OF EDUCATION AND MEDICAL CARE KEEP GROWING

A distressing phenomenon is occurring throughout the industrialized world: The costs of providing many services have risen consistently faster than the rate of inflation. Perhaps the most publicized examples are medical care and education. For example, over a recent 50-year period the daily cost of a hospital stay outstripped the rate of inflation by over 800 percent.

But the phenomenon is not limited to education and health. Many public services have been deteriorating even as they grow more expensive to provide. There are fewer postal deliveries and garbage pickups and larger classes in public schools. Often the problem is blamed on greed, inefficiency, and political corruption. But this cannot be the whole story, because the scenario has been repeated in virtually every other industrialized country, despite great differences in the way public services are provided.

As we shall learn in Chapter 14, the root cause of the problem is economic. It stems, ironically, from the dazzling growth in efficiency of private manufacturing industries. Because technological improvements make workers more productive in manufacturing, wages rise. But wages must rise not only for manufacturing workers, but also for hospital workers, teachers, and other service workers, because otherwise people would leave their low-paying service jobs and compete for high-paying manufacturing jobs.

Unlike manufacturing, however, the technology of labor-intensive personal services is not easily changed. It still takes one person to drive a postal truck, one teacher to teach a class, and four musicians to play a string quartet—just as it always has. So, with wages rising, the costs of these services are forced up. This phenomenon has been called the "cost disease" of the personal services, a malady that affects services as diverse as college teaching, restaurant cooking, and automobile repair.

The cost disease is important to understand not because it excuses the financial record of our governments, but because it suggests what we should expect the future to bring and, perhaps, indicates what policies we should advocate to deal with it.

## IDEA 8: THE TRADE-OFF BETWEEN EFFICIENCY AND EQUALITY

In the United States, wages and incomes have been growing more unequal for several decades now. Highly skilled workers are pulling away from low-skilled workers. The rich have grown richer while the poor have become (relatively) poorer. Yet U. S. unemployment is low, and jobs are easy to get. In much of the European Union, things are just the reverse. Unemployment has been persistently high for years—much higher than in the United States. Yet the inequalities of wages and incomes in these countries are smaller and have not grown more extreme.

Many economists feel that these phenomena are two sides of the same coin. Europe and the United States have made different choices of how best to balance the conflicting claims of greater economic efficiency (more output and jobs) versus greater equality.

Roughly speaking, the American solution is to let markets work to promote efficiency—something they are very good at doing—with only minimal government interferences to reduce economic inequalities. (Some of these interferences are studied in Chapter 19.) If very low wages are needed to keep people employed, so be it. That is better than putting them on the dole.

Much of continental Europe takes a different view. They find it scandalous that many Americans work for less than $6 an hour, with virtually no fringe benefits and no job security. European laws prevent this: They mandate not only relatively high minimum wages but also substantial fringe benefits and employment protections. European social welfare programs to protect the poor are also more extensive and generous than the corresponding American programs. And, of course, European taxes must be much higher to pay for all this.

As economists see it, each system's virtue is also its vice. There is an agonizing *trade-off* between the *size* of a nation's output and the degree of *equality* with which that output is distributed. European-style policies designed to divide the proverbial economic pie more equally inadvertently can cause the size of the pie to shrink. American-style arrangements that promote maximal efficiency and output may permit or even breed huge inequalities. Which system is better? There is no clear answer, but we will examine the issue in detail in Chapter 19.

### IDEA 9: THE SHORT-RUN TRADE-OFF BETWEEN INFLATION AND UNEMPLOYMENT

The U.S. economy was lucky in the second half of the 1990s. A set of fortuitous events—falling energy prices, tumbling computer prices, a rising dollar, and so on—pushed inflation down even while unemployment fell to its lowest level in almost 30 years. During the 1970s and early 1980s, we were not so fortunate. Skyrocketing prices for food and, especially, energy sent both inflation and unemployment up to extraordinary heights. In both episodes, inflation and unemployment rose or fell together.

But economists maintain that neither of these two episodes was "normal." When we are not experiencing either unusually good luck (as in the 1990s) or exceptionally bad luck (as in the 1970s) there is a *trade-off between inflation and unemployment*, meaning that very low unemployment normally makes inflation rise and very high unemployment normally makes inflation fall. We will study the mechanisms underlying this trade-off in Parts VI and VIII, especially Chapter 34. It poses one of the fundamental dilemmas of national economic policy.

### IDEA 10: INFLATION DISTORTS MEASUREMENTS

It is natural to use the dollar as an economic measuring rod, and people do it all the time. It cost your grandparents $1 to buy a movie ticket, but costs you $7. That's seven times as much, right? Banks were giving mortgages at 12 percent interest in 1980, but charging only 7 percent in 1998? That's much cheaper, right? In both cases, the answer is no. And the reason is the same: When there is inflation, the dollar is a flawed standard for measuring values at different points of time.

Start with the movie ticket. Over the past 50 years, average consumer prices in the United States have increased about seven-fold. So in terms of purchasing power—what a dollar will buy—the $1 movie ticket that grandpa bought in 1949 cost about the same as the ticket you bought in 1999. Chapters 2, 23, and 24 will teach us how to make such comparisons over time more correctly.

But what about interest rates? Isn't it obvious that it is more costly to borrow money at 12 percent interest than at 7 percent? That question seems easy, even without a course in economics. But, in fact, it is not. An example will show why.

In 1998, when banks were lending money to home buyers at annual interest rates near 7 percent, inflation was below 2 percent per year. In 1980, when mortgage interest were over 12 percent, inflation was running at about 10 percent. But why is the rate of inflation relevant for deciding how costly it is to borrow?

Consider the position of a person who borrows $100 for one year at a 12 percent rate of interest when prices are rising at 10 percent per year. At the end of the year the borrower pays back her $100 plus $12 interest. But over that same year her indebtedness declines by $10 *in terms of what that money will buy*. Because the purchasing power of money declines 10 percent, it is as if $10 of her debt had been forgiven. Thus, in terms of purchasing power, the borrower really pays only $2 in interest on her $100 loan, or 2 percent.

Now consider someone who borrows $100 at 7 percent interest when inflation is only 2 percent. This borrower pays back the original $100 plus $7 in interest and sees the purchasing power of his debt decline by $2 due to inflation—for a net payment in purchasing-power terms of $5, or 5 percent. Thus, in the economically relevant sense, the 7 percent loan under 2 percent inflation is actually more expensive than the 12 percent loan under 10 percent inflation.

### IDEA 11: WHY WAS IT IMPORTANT TO REDUCE THE BUDGET DEFICIT?

The political struggle to reduce the federal budget deficit dominated the economic news for more than 15 years. First President Reagan and then President Bush argued that raising taxes would be worse than tolerating the deficit, a claim disputed by many. Critics objected that deficits hold dire consequences—including higher interest rates, more inflation, a stagnant economy, and an irksome burden on future Americans. So President Bush reluctantly accepted a large deficit-reduction package, including tax increases, which cost him dearly at the polls. Finally, during the Clinton administration, a large deficit-reduction package was enacted in 1993, and a smaller one followed in 1997. Together with rapid economic growth, they transformed the deficit into a surplus.

The conflicting claims and counterclaims in the deficit debate have left many laypersons confused. Who is right? Do large budget deficits promote or hinder economic growth? Do they burden future generations? The answers, economists insist, are so complicated that the only correct short answer is that it all depends. The precise factors on which the answers depend, and the reasons why, are important enough to merit an entire chapter (Chapter 33). There we will learn that a budget deficit may or may not burden future generations, depending on its size and on the reasons for its existence.

## IDEA 12: PRODUCTIVITY GROWTH IS (ALMOST) EVERYTHING IN THE LONG RUN

In Geneva today, a worker in a watch factory turns out more than 100 times as many mechanical watches per year as her ancestors did three centuries earlier. The *productivity* of labor (output per hour of work) in cotton production has probably gone up more than 1,000-fold in 200 years. It is estimated that rising labor productivity has increased the standard of living of a typical American worker more than sevenfold in the past century. This means that Americans now enjoy about seven times as much clothing, housewares, and luxury goods as did a typical inhabitant of the United States 100 years ago.

Economic issues such as inflation, unemployment, monopoly, and inequality are important to us all and will receive much attention in this book. But in the long run nothing has as great an effect on our material well-being and the amounts society can afford to spend on hospitals, schools, and social amenities as the rate of growth of productivity. Chapter 24 points out that what appears to be a small increase in productivity growth can have a huge effect on a country's standard of living over a long period of time because productivity compounds like the interest on savings in a bank. Similarly, a slowdown in productivity growth that persists for a substantial number of years can have a devastating effect on standards of living.

## EPILOGUE

These, then, are some of the more fundamental concepts you will find in this book—ideas that we hope you will retain beyond the final exam. There is no need to master them right now, for you will hear much more about each as you progress through the book. Instead, keep them in mind as you read—we will point them out to you as they occur—and look back over this list at the end of the course. You may be amazed to see how natural, or even obvious, they will seem then.

## ■ INSIDE THE ECONOMIST'S TOOL KIT

Now that you have some idea of the kinds of issues economists deal with, you should know something about the way they grapple with these problems.

## ECONOMICS AS A DISCIPLINE

Economics has something of a split personality. Although clearly the most rigorous of the social sciences, it nevertheless looks decidedly more "social" than "scientific" when compared with, say, physics. An economist must be a jack of several trades, borrowing modes of investigation from numerous fields.

*"I'm a social scientist, Michael. That means I can't explain electricity or anything like that, but if you ever want to know about people I'm your man."*

Mathematical reasoning is used extensively in economics, but so is historical study. And neither looks quite the same as when practiced by a mathematician or a historian. Statistical inference plays a major role in modern economic inquiry; but economists have had to modify standard statistical procedures to fit the kinds of data they analyze.

An introductory course in economics will not make you an economist; but it should help you approach social problems dispassionately. You will not find solutions to all society's economic problems in this book. But you should learn how to pose questions in ways that will help produce answers that are both useful and illuminating.

## THE NEED FOR ABSTRACTION

Some students find economics unduly abstract and "unrealistic." The stylized world envisioned by economic theory seems only a distant cousin to the world they know. There is an old joke about three people—a chemist, a physicist, and an economist—stranded on an island with an ample supply of canned food but no tools to open the cans. The chemist thinks that lighting a fire under the cans would expand their contents and cause the cans to burst. The physicist advocates building a catapult with which they could smash the cans against some nearby boulders. The economist's suggestion? "Assume we have a can opener."

Economic theory *does* make unrealistic assumptions; you will encounter many of them in the pages that follow. But this propensity to abstract from reality results from the incredible complexity of the economic world, not from any fondness economists have for sounding absurd.

| MAP 1 | **Detailed Road Map of Los Angeles** |
|---|---|

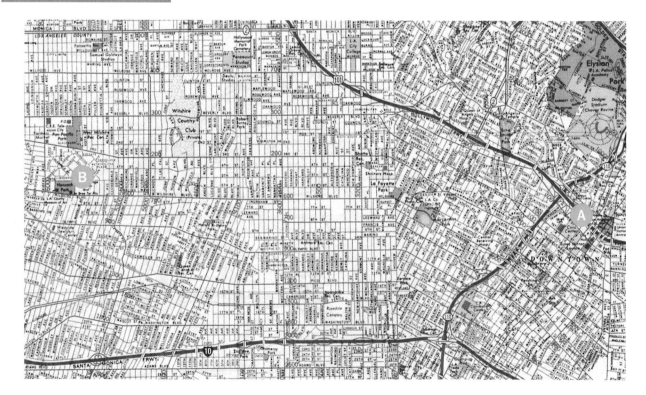

Compare the chemist's simple task of explaining the interactions of compounds in a chemical reaction with the economist's complex task of explaining the interactions of people in an economy. Are molecules motivated by greed or altruism, by envy or ambition? Do they ever emulate other molecules? Do forecasts about them influence their behavior? People, of course, do all these things, and many, many more. It is therefore vastly more difficult to predict human behavior than to predict chemical reactions. If economists tried to keep track of every aspect of human behavior, they would never get anywhere. Thus:

**Abstraction from unimportant details is necessary to understand the functioning of anything as complex as the economy.**

To appreciate why economists **abstract** from details, imagine the following hypothetical situation. You have just arrived, for the first time in your life, in Los Angeles. You are now at the Los Angeles Civic Center. This is the point marked *A* in Maps 1 and 2, which are alternative maps of part of Los Angeles. You want to drive to the Los Angeles County Museum of Art, point *B* on each map. Which map would you find more useful? You will notice that Map 1 has complete details of the Los Angeles road system. If you are like most people, you will find it hard to read and not very useful for determining how to get from the Civic Center (point *A*) to the Los Angeles County Museum of Art. For this purpose, Map 1 is far too detailed, though for some other purposes (for example, locating some small street in Hollywood) it may be the best map available.

In contrast, Map 2 shows a different perspective of Los Angeles, because it omits many minor roads—we might say they are assumed away—so that the freeways and major arteries stand out more clearly. As a result of this simplification, several routes from the Civic Center to the Los Angeles County Museum of Art emerge. For example, we can take the Hollywood Freeway west to Alvarado Boulevard, go south to Wilshire Boulevard, and then head west again. The museum is on the right. Although we *might* find a shorter route by poring over the details in Map 1, most strangers to the city would prefer Map 2. With its guidance, they are likely to find the museum in a reasonable

**Abstraction** means ignoring many details in order to focus on the most important elements of a problem.

MAP 2

**Major Los Angeles Arteries and Freeways**

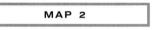

amount of time. Map 2 seems to *abstract* successfully from a lot of confusing details while retaining the essential aspects of the city's geography. Economic theories strive to do the same thing.

Map 3, which shows little more than the major interstate routes that pass through the greater Los Angeles area, illustrates a danger of which all theorists must beware. Armed only with the information provided on this map, you might never find your way to the art museum. Instead of a useful idealization of the Los Angeles road network, the map makers have produced a map that is oversimplified for our purpose. Too much has been assumed away. Of course, this map was never intended to be used as a detailed tourist guide, which brings us to an important point:

There is no such thing as one "right" degree of abstraction for all analytic purposes. The proper degree of abstraction depends on the objective of the analysis. A model that is a gross oversimplification for one purpose may be needlessly complicated for another.

Economists are constantly treading the thin line between the concept illustrated in Map 2 and Map 3, between useful generalization about complex issues and gross distortions of the pertinent facts. How can they tell when they have abstracted from reality just enough? There is no objective answer to this question, which is why applied economics is as much art as science. One of the things distinguishing good economics from bad economics is the degree to which analysts are able to find the factors that constitute the equivalent of Map 2 (rather than Maps 1 or 3) for the problem at hand. It is not always easy to do.

For example, suppose you want to learn why different people have different incomes, why some are fabulously rich while others are abjectly poor. People differ in many ways, too many to enumerate, much less to study. The economist must ignore most of these details in order to focus on the important ones. The color of a person's hair or eyes is probably not important to the problem at hand, but the color of his or her skin certainly is. Height and weight may not matter, but education probably does. Proceeding in this way, we pare Map 1 down to the manageable dimensions of Map 2. But there is a danger of going too far, stripping away some of the crucial factors, and winding up with Map 3.

**MAP 3**

**Greater Los Angeles Freeways**

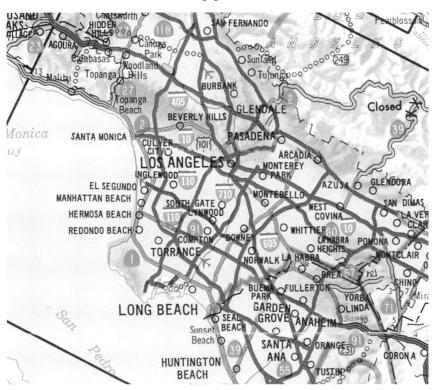

### THE ROLE OF ECONOMIC THEORY

A person "can stare stupidly at phenomena; but in the absence of imagination they will not connect themselves together in any rational way." These words of the renowned American philosopher-scientist C. S. Peirce succinctly express the crucial role of theory in scientific inquiry. What do we mean by a theory?

*A **theory** is a deliberate simplification of relationships used to explain how those relationships work.*

To an economist or natural scientist, the word **theory** means something different from what it means in common parlance. In scientific usage, a theory is *not* an untested assertion of alleged fact. The statement that aspirin provides protection against heart attacks is not a theory; it is a *hypothesis*, which will prove to be true or false once the right sorts of experiments have been completed. Instead, a theory is a deliberate simplification (abstraction) of factual relationships that attempts to explain how those relationships work. It is an *explanation* of the mechanism behind observed phenomena. Thus, gravity forms the basis of theories that describe and explain the paths of the planets. Similarly, Keynesian theory (discussed in Parts VI and VII) seeks to describe and explain how government policies affect the path of the national economy.

People who have never studied economics often draw a false distinction between *theory* and *practical policy*. Politicians and business people, in particular, often reject abstract economic theory as something that is best ignored by "practical" people. The irony of these statements is that:

It is precisely the concern for policy that makes economic theory so necessary and important.

If we could not change the economy through public policy, economics could be a historical and descriptive discipline, asking, for example, what happened in the United States during the Great Depression of the 1930s or how is it that industrial pollution got to be so serious in the 20th century. But deep concern about public policy forces economists to go beyond historical questions. To analyze policy options, they are forced to deal with *possibilities that have not actually occurred.*

For example, to learn how to prevent economic depressions, they must investigate whether the Great Depression of the 1930s could have been avoided by more astute government policies. Or to determine what environmental programs will be most effective, they must understand how and why a market economy produces pollution and what might happen if government placed taxes on industrial waste discharges and automobile emissions. Such questions require some *theorizing*, not just examination of the facts, because we need to consider possibilities that never occurred.

The facts, moreover, can sometimes be highly misleading. Data often indicate that two variables move up and down together. But this statistical **correlation** does not prove that either variable *causes* the other. For example, when it rains people drive their cars more slowly, and there are also more traffic accidents. But this correlation does not mean that slow driving causes accidents. Rather, we understand that both phenomena are caused by a common underlying factor— more rain. How do we know this? Not just by looking at the correlation (the degree of similarity) between data on accidents and driving speeds. Data alone tell us little about cause and effect. We must use some simple *theory* as part of our analysis.

Similarly, most economic issues hinge on some question of cause and effect. So simply observing correlations in data is not enough. Only a combination of theoretical reasoning and data analysis can hope to provide useful answers. We must first proceed deductively from assumptions to conclusions and then test the conclusions against data. In that way, we may hope to understand *how*, if at all, different government policies will lead to a lower unemployment rate or *how* a tax on emissions will reduce pollution.

> **Statistical correlation need not imply causation. Some theory is usually needed to interpret data.**

Two variables are said to be **correlated** if they tend to go up or down together. But correlation need not imply causation.

## WHAT IS AN ECONOMIC MODEL?

An **economic model** is a representation of a theory or a part of a theory, often used to gain insight into cause and effect. The notion of a "model" is familiar enough to children; and economists—like other scientists—use the term in much the same way that children do.

A child's model automobile or airplane looks and operates much like the real thing, but it is much smaller and much simpler, and so it is easier to manipulate and understand. Engineers for General Motors and Boeing also build models of cars and planes. Although their models are far bigger and much more elaborate than a child's toy, they use them for much the same purposes: to observe the workings of these vehicles "up close," to experiment with them in order to see how they might behave under different circumstances. ("What happens if I do this?") From these experiments, they make educated guesses as to how the real-life version will perform.

Economists use models for similar purposes. The late A. W. Phillips, the famous engineer-turned-economist who discovered the "Phillips curve" (discussed in Chapter 34), was talented enough to construct a working model of the determination of national income in a simple economy by using colored water flowing through pipes. For years this contraption has graced the basement of the London School of Economics. While we will explain the theory with words and diagrams later in the book, Phillips's engineering background enabled him to depict the theory with tubes, valves, and pumps. Most economists lack Phillips's manual dexterity, so economic

An **economic model** is a simplified, small-scale version of some aspect of the economy. Economic models are often expressed in equations, by graphs, or in words.

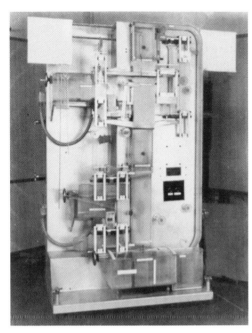

A. W. Phillips built this model in the early 1950s to illustrate Keynesian theory.

models are generally built with paper and pencil (or a laptop) rather than with wrenches and screwdrivers.

Because many of the models used in this book are depicted in diagrams, we explain the construction and use of various types of graphs in the following chapter. But sometimes economic models are expressed only in words. The statement "Business firms produce the level of output that maximizes their profits" is the basis for a behavioral model whose consequences we explore in some detail in Parts II through V. Don't be put off by seemingly abstract models. Think of them as useful road maps. And remember how hard it would be to find your way around Los Angeles without one.

## REASONS FOR DISAGREEMENTS: IMPERFECT INFORMATION AND VALUE JUDGMENTS

"If all the earth's economists were laid end to end, they could not reach an agreement," or so the saying goes. Politicians and reporters are fond of pointing out that economists can be found on both sides of many public policy issues. If economics is a science, why do economists quarrel so much? After all, astronomers do not debate whether the earth revolves around the sun or vice versa.

The question reflects a misunderstanding of the nature of science. Disputes are normal at the frontier of any science. For example, astronomers once did argue, and quite vociferously, over whether the earth revolves around the sun. Nowadays, they argue about black holes, gamma-ray bursts, young red supergiants, and other esoterica. These arguments go mostly unnoticed by the public because few of us understand what they are talking about. But economics is a *social* science, so its disputes are aired in public. All sorts of people are eager to join economic debates about inflation, pollution, poverty, and the like.

Furthermore, the fact is that economists agree on much more than is commonly supposed. Virtually all economists, regardless of their politics, agree that taxing polluters is one of the best ways to protect the environment (see Chapters 14 and 22), that rent controls can ruin a city (Chapter 5), and that free trade among nations is preferable to the erection of barriers through tariffs and quotas (see Chapter 35). The list could go on and on. It is probably true that the issues about which economists agree *far* exceed the subjects on which they disagree.

Finally, many disputes among economists are not scientific disputes at all. Sometimes the pertinent facts are simply unknown. For example, you will learn in Chapter 22 that the proper tax to levy on industrial emissions depends on quantitative estimates of the harm done by the pollutant. But, very often, good estimates of this damage are not yet available. For example, while there is reasonable scientific agreement that the earth is slowly warming, there are huge disagreements over how costly global warming may be and over whether human activities are the primary cause of the warming. Such disputes make it difficult to agree on a concrete policy proposal.

Another important source of disagreements is that economists, like other people, come in all political stripes: conservative, middle-of-the-road, liberal, radical. Each may have different values and different views of what constitutes a good society. So each may hold a different view of the "right" solution to a public policy problem, even if they will agree on the underlying analysis. Here are two examples:

1. We suggested early in this chapter that anti-inflation policies are likely to cause recessions. Many economists believe they can even measure the depth of a recession that must be endured to reduce inflation by a given amount. Is it worth having 2.6 million more people out of work for a year to cut the inflation rate by 1 percent?

2. In designing an income tax, society must decide how much of the burden to put on upper income taxpayers. Some people believe the rich should pay a dis-

proportionate share of the taxes. Others disagree, arguing that it is fairer to levy the same income tax rate on everyone.

Economists cannot answer questions like these any more than nuclear physicists could have determined whether dropping the atomic bomb on Hiroshima was a good idea. The decisions rest on moral judgments about the trade-off between inflation and unemployment, and about the importance of income inequality—judgments that can be made only by the citizenry through its elected officials.

> Although economic science can contribute the best theoretical and factual knowledge there is on a particular issue, the final decision on policy questions often rests either on information that is not currently available or on social values and ethical opinions about which people differ, or on both.

## COMMON SENSE: USEFUL BUT DANGEROUS

Many people think sound economic decisions are just a matter of "common sense." If that were so—if untrained but intelligent observers could reach the right decisions using only their instincts and intuition—there would be little reason to study economics. Unfortunately, while common sense is invaluable, it is not always a reliable guide in economics.

True, there are many cases where it is not misleading. Most people undoubtedly realize, for example, that a surge in demand for a product is likely to raise its price, at least for a while. They also understand that increases in the prices of American goods will reduce the quantity we can export to foreign countries. Such simple precepts illustrate why much of economics is just systematized common sense.

But other economic relationships are counterintuitive. Try your intuition on this one. You own a widget manufacturing company that rents a warehouse. Your landlord raises your rent by $10,000 per year. Should you raise the price of your widgets to try to recoup some of your higher costs? Or should you lower your price to try to sell more and "spread your overhead?" We shall see in Chapter 8 that both answers are probably wrong!

We will explain many more counterintuitive economic relationships in this book. By the end, you will have a better sense of when common sense works and when it fails. And you will be able to recognize common fallacies that are all too often offered as pearls of wisdom by public figures, the press, and television commentators.

---

## SUMMARY

1. To help you get the most out of your first course in economics, we have devised a list of 12 important ideas that you will want to remember *Beyond the Final Exam.* Briefly, they are as follows:

   a. Opportunity cost is the correct measure of cost.

   b. Attempts to fight market forces often backfire.

   c. Nations can gain from trade by exploiting their comparative advantages.

   d. Both parties gain in a voluntary exchange.

   e. Good decisions typically require marginal analysis that weighs incremental costs against incremental benefits.

   f. Externalities may cause the market mechanism to malfunction, but this defect can be repaired by market methods.

   g. Personal services are subject to a cost disease that drives their prices inexorably higher.

   h. There is a trade-off between efficiency and equality. Many policies that promote one damage the other.

   i. In the short run, policymakers face a trade-off between inflation and unemployment. Policies that reduce one normally increase the other.

   j. Inflation distorts many economic measurements.

   k. Budget deficits may or may not be harmful, depending on their size and the circumstances.

   l. In the long run, productivity is almost the only thing that matters for a society's material well-being.

2. Economics is a broad-ranging discipline that uses a variety of techniques and approaches to address important social questions.

3. Because of the great complexity of human behavior, economists are forced to *abstract* from many details, to make generalizations that they know are not quite true, and to organize what knowledge they have in terms of some theoretical structure called a "model."

4. *Correlation* need not imply causation.

5. Economists use simplified models to understand the real world and predict its behavior, much as a child uses a model railroad to learn how trains work.

6. Although these models, if skillfully constructed, can illuminate important economic problems, they rarely can answer the questions that confront policymakers. Value judgments are needed for this purpose, and the economist is no better equipped than anyone else to make them.

7. Common sense is often an unreliable guide to the right economic decision.

## KEY TERMS

Opportunity cost   4

Comparative advantage   5

Voluntary exchange   6

Externalities   6

Marginal analysis   6

Marginal costs   6

Productivity   9

Abstraction and generalization   11

Theory   12

Correlation versus causation   13

Economic model   13

## QUESTIONS FOR REVIEW

1. Think about how you would construct a *model* of how your college is governed. Which officers and administrators would you include and exclude from your model if the objective were one of the following:

   a. To explain how decisions on financial aid are made?

   b. To explain the quality of the faculty?

   Relate this to the map example in the chapter.

2. Relate the process of *abstraction* to the way you take notes in a lecture. Why do you not try to transcribe every word the lecturer utters? Why do you not just write down the title of the lecture and stop there? How do you decide, roughly speaking, on the correct amount of detail?

3. Explain why a government policymaker cannot afford to ignore economic theory.

Everything should be made as simple as possible,
but not more so.

Albert Einstein

# THE USE AND MISUSE OF GRAPHS[1]

In Chapter 1, we noted that economists often explain and analyze their models with the help of graphs. This book is full of them. But that is not the only reason for you to study how they work. Most of you will deal with graphs in the future, perhaps frequently. You will see them in newspapers. If you become a doctor you will use graphs to keep track of patients' progress. If you take a job in government, you may use them to keep track of the amount of money that the United States owes to foreign countries. If you join a business firm, you will use them to check profit and sales performance at a glance. If you work in a nonprofit enterprise concerned with social issues, you may use them to examine trends in ethnic composition of cities or to relate the occurrence of felonies to family income.

This chapter will introduce you to some of the techniques of graphic analysis—tools you will use throughout the book and, more important, very likely throughout your working career. Then, in the second part of the chapter, we examine some pitfalls in graphic analysis—common ways in which graphs can be misleading if not drawn and interpreted with care.

---

[1] Students who have a nodding acquaintance with geometry and feel quite comfortable with graphs can safely skip the first part of this chapter and proceed directly to the second part, which begins on page 23.

## ■ GRAPHS USED IN ECONOMIC ANALYSIS

Economic graphs are invaluable because they can display a large quantity of data quickly and because they facilitate data interpretation and analysis. They enable the eye to take in at a glance important statistical relationships that would be far less apparent from written descriptions or long lists of numbers. But badly constructed graphs can confuse and mislead.[2]

### What's Wrong with This Graph?

This figure, which will be explained fully later in this chapter, appears to show that the U.S. economy suffered a catastrophe between 1990 and 1992. From the looks of the graph, in those two years unemployment literally exploded. It suggests that between the beginning and end of the period portrayed, the percent of American workers who were jobless rose about fivefold. We will see later that actual developments in the labor force were not nearly so serious. The impression that the economy was collapsing is only the result of the

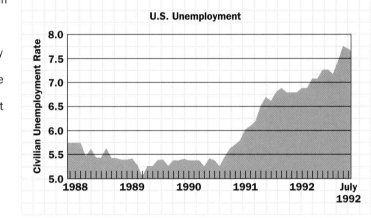

sloppy way the graph was drawn in the publication in which it appeared. This is important because it is not an isolated misuse of graphics. In fact, *most* newspapers and magazines frequently distort statistics in just this way.

### TWO-VARIABLE DIAGRAMS

Much of the economic analysis found in this and other books requires that we keep track of two **variables** simultaneously. For example, in studying how markets operate, we will want to keep one eye on the *price* of a commodity and the other on the *quantity* of that commodity that is bought and sold.

For this reason, economists frequently find it useful to display real or imaginary figures in a *two-dimensional graph*, which simultaneously represents the behavior of two economic variables. The numerical value of one variable is measured along the horizontal line at the bottom of the graph (called the *horizontal axis*), starting from the **origin** (the point labeled "0"), and the numerical value of the other is measured up the vertical line on the left side of the graph (called the *vertical* axis), also starting from the origin.

Figures 2–1(a) and 2–1(b) are typical graphs of economic analysis. They depict an imaginary *demand curve*, represented by the red dots in Figure 2–1(a) and the

A **variable** is something measured by a number; it is used to analyze what happens to other things when the size of that number changes (varies).

The "0" point in the lower left-hand corner of a graph where the axes meet is called the **origin.** Both variables are equal to zero at the origin.

---

[2] An interesting and informative book on the subject is called *How to Lie with Statistics* by Darrell Huff and Irving Geis (New York: Norton, 1954).

## A Hypothetical Demand Curve for Natural Gas in St. Louis

FIGURE 2-1

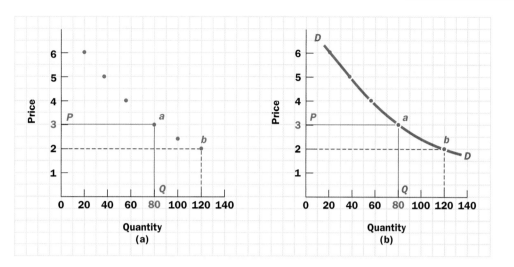

NOTE: Price is dollars per thousand cubic feet; quantity is in billions of cubic feet per year.

heavy red line in Figure 2–1(b). The graphs show the price of natural gas on their vertical axes and the quantity of gas people want to buy at each price on the horizontal axes. The dots in Figure 2–1(a) are connected by the continuous red curve labeled *DD* in Figure 2–1(b).

Economic diagrams are generally read just as one would read latitudes and longitudes on a map. On the demand curve in Figure 2–1, the point marked *a* represents a hypothetical combination of price and quantity of natural gas demanded by customers in St. Louis. By drawing a horizontal line leftward from that point to the vertical axis, we learn that the average price for gas in St. Louis is $3 per thousand cubic feet. By dropping a line straight down to the horizontal axis, we find that consumers want 80 billion cubic feet per year at this price, just as the statistics in Table 2–1 show. The other points on the graph give similar information. For example, point *b* indicates that if natural gas in St. Louis costs only $2 per thousand cubic feet, quantity demanded would be higher—it would reach 120 billion cubic feet per year.

### Quantities of Natural Gas Demanded at Various Prices

TABLE 2-1

| Price (per thousand cubic feet) | $2 | $3 | $4 | $5 | $6 |
|---|---|---|---|---|---|
| Quantity demanded (billions of cubic feet per year) | 120 | 80 | 56 | 38 | 20 |

Notice that information about price and quantity is *all* we can learn from the diagram. The demand curve will not tell us what kinds of people live in St. Louis, the size of their homes, or the condition of their furnaces. It tells us about the quantity demanded at each possible price—no more, no less. Specifically, it tells us that when price declines, consumers increase the amount of natural gas that they are willing and able to buy.

A diagram abstracts from many details, some of which may be quite interesting, in order to focus on the two variables of primary interest—in this case, the price of natural gas and the amount of gas that is demanded at each price. All the diagrams used in this book share this basic feature. They cannot tell the reader the "whole story," any more than a map's latitude and longitude figures for a particular city can make someone an authority on that city.

## THE DEFINITION AND MEASUREMENT OF SLOPE

One of the most important features of economic diagrams is the rate at which the line or curve being sketched runs uphill or downhill as we move to the right. The demand curve in Figure 2–1 clearly slopes downhill (the price falls) as we follow it to the right (that is, as consumers demand more gas). In such instances we say that *the curve has a negative slope, or is negatively sloped, because one variable falls as the other one rises.*

> The *slope of a straight line* is the ratio of the vertical change to the corresponding horizontal change as we move to the right along the line or, as it is often said, the ratio of the "rise" over the "run."

The four panels of Figure 2–2 show all the possible slopes for a straight-line relationship between two unnamed variables called $Y$ (measured along the vertical axis) and $X$ (measured along the horizontal axis). Figure 2–2(a) shows a negative slope, much like our demand curve. Figure 2–2(b) shows a positive slope, because variable $Y$ rises (we go uphill) as variable $X$ rises (as we move to the right). Figure 2–2(c) shows a *zero* slope, where the value of $Y$ is the same irrespective of the value of $X$. Figure 2–2(d) shows an *infinite* slope, meaning that the value of $X$ is the same irrespective of the value of $Y$.

| FIGURE 2–2 | Different Types of Slope of a Straight-Line Graph |

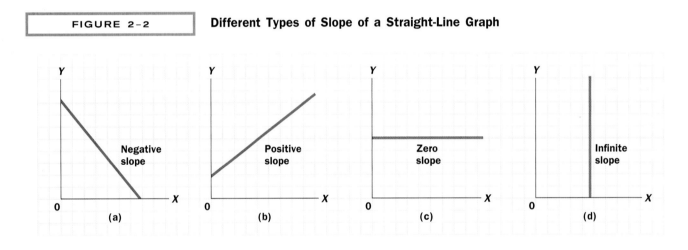

Slope is a numerical concept, not just a qualitative one. The two panels of Figure 2–3 show two positively sloped straight lines with different slopes. The line in Figure 2–3(b) is clearly steeper. But by how much? The labels should help you compute

| FIGURE 2–3 | How to Measure Slope |

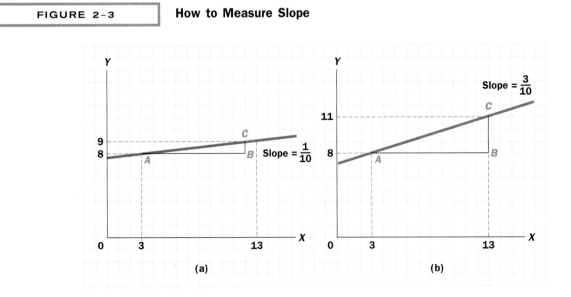

the answer. In Figure 2–3(a) a horizontal movement, *AB*, of 10 units (13 − 3) corresponds to a vertical movement, *BC*, of 1 unit (9 − 8). So the slope is *BC/AB* = 1/10. In Figure 2–3(b), the same horizontal movement of 10 units corresponds to a vertical movement of 3 units (11 − 8). So the slope is 3/10, which is larger—the rise divided by the run is greater than in Figure 2–3 (b)

By definition, the slope of any particular straight line remains the same, no matter where on that line we choose to measure it. That is why we can pick any horizontal distance, *AB*, and the corresponding slope triangle, *ABC*, to measure slope. But this is not true of curved lines.

> Curved lines also have slopes, but the numerical value of the slope differs at every point along the curve as we move from left to right.

The four panels of Figure 2–4 provide some examples of *slopes of curved lines*. The curve in Figure 2–4(a) has a negative slope everywhere, while the curve in Figure 2–4(b) has a positive slope everywhere. But these are not the only possibilities. In Figure 2–4(c) we encounter a curve that has a positive slope at first but a negative slope later on. Figure 2–4(d) shows the opposite case: a negative slope followed by a positive slope.

The **tangent** to a curve at some point, *Z*, on that curve is a straight line that touches point *Z* but does not cross the curve at that point.

**Behavior of Slopes in Curved Graphs** | **FIGURE 2–4**

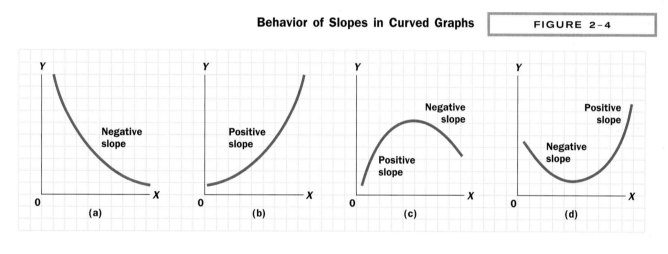

We can measure the slope of a smooth curved line numerically *at any particular point* by drawing a *straight* line that *touches*, but does not *cut*, the curve at the point in question. Such a line is called a **tangent** to the curve.

**FIGURE 2–5**

> The slope of a curved line at a particular point is defined as the slope of the straight line that is tangent to the curve at that point.

**How to Measure Slope at a Point on a Curved Graph**

Figure 2–5 shows tangents to the red curve at two points. Line *tt* is tangent at point *T*, and line *rr* is tangent at point *R*. We can measure the slope of the curve at these two points by applying the definition. The calculation for point *T*, then, is the following:

$$\text{Slope at point } T = \text{Slope of line } tt = \frac{(\text{Distance } BC)}{(\text{Distance } BA)}$$

$$= \frac{(1-5)}{(3-1)} = \frac{-4}{2} = -2.$$

A similar calculation yields the slope of the curve at point *R*, which, as we can see from Figure 2–5, must be smaller numerically; that is, the tangent line *rr* is less steep than line *tt*:

$$\text{Slope at point } R = \text{Slope of line } rr$$

$$= \frac{(5-7)}{(8-6)} = \frac{-2}{2} = -1.$$

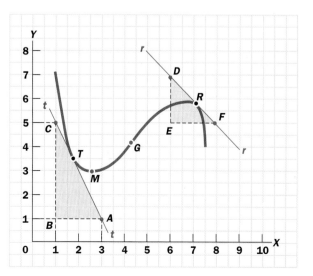

**EXERCISE**  Show that the slope of the curve at point $G$ is about 1.

What would happen if we tried to apply this graphical technique to the high point in Figure 2–4(c) or to the low point in Figure 2–4(d)? Take a ruler and try it. The tangents that you construct should be horizontal, meaning that they should have a slope exactly equal to zero. It is always true that where the slope of a smooth curve changes from positive to negative, or vice versa, there will be at least one point whose slope is zero.

Curves shaped like hills, such as Figure 2–4(c), have a zero slope at their *highest* point. Curves shaped like valleys, such as Figure 2–4(d), have a zero slope at their *lowest* point.

## RAYS THROUGH THE ORIGIN AND 45° LINES

The point at which a straight line cuts the vertical ($Y$) axis is called the *Y-intercept*. For example, the $Y$-intercept of the line in Figure 2–3(a) is a bit less than 8.

Lines whose *Y*-intercept is zero have so many special uses in economics and other disciplines that they have been given a special name: a **ray through the origin**, or a **ray**.

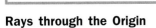

## FIGURE 2-6

**Rays through the Origin**

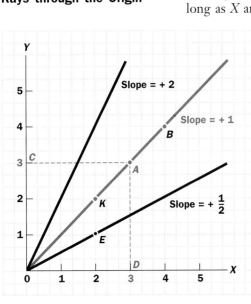

Figure 2–6 shows three rays through the origin, and the slope of each is indicated in the diagram. The ray in the center (whose slope is 1) is particularly useful in many economic applications because it marks points where $X$ and $Y$ are equal (as long as $X$ and $Y$ are measured in the same units). For example, at point $A$ we have $X = 3$ and $Y = 3$; at point $B$, $X = 4$ and $Y = 4$. A similar relation holds at any other point on that ray.

How do we know that this is always true for a ray whose slope is 1? If we start from the origin (where both $X$ and $Y$ are zero) and the slope of the ray is 1, we know from the definition of slope that:

$$\text{Slope} = \frac{\text{Vertical change}}{\text{Horizontal change}} = 1$$

This implies that the vertical change and the horizontal change are always equal, so the two variables must always remain equal. Any point along that ray (for example, point $A$) is exactly equal in distance from the horizontal and vertical axes (length $DA$ = length $CA$)—the number on the $X$-axis (the abscissa) will be the same as the number on the $Y$-axis (the ordinate).

Rays through the origin with a slope of 1 are called **45° lines** because they form an angle of 45° with the horizontal axis. A 45° line marks off points where the variables measured on each axis have equal values.[3]

If a point representing some data is above the 45° line, we know that the value of $Y$ exceeds the value of $X$. Conversely, whenever we find a point below the 45° line, we know that $X$ is larger than $Y$.

## SQUEEZING THREE DIMENSIONS INTO TWO: CONTOUR MAPS

Sometimes problems involve more than two variables, so two dimensions just are not enough. This is unfortunate, because the surface of a sheet of paper is only two-dimensional. When we study a business firm's decision-making process, for example, we may want to keep track simultaneously of three variables: how much labor it employs, how much raw material it imports from foreign countries, and how much output it creates.

A **45° line** is a **ray through the origin** with a slope of +1. It marks off points where the variables measured on each axis have equal values (assuming both variables are measured in the same units).

A **production indifference map** is a graph whose axes show the quantities of two inputs that are used to produce some output. A curve in the graph corresponds to some given quantity of that output, and the different points on that curve show the different quantities of the two inputs that are enough to produce the given output.

---

[3] The definition assumes that both variables are measured in the same units.

Luckily, economists can use a well-known device for collapsing three dimensions into two, namely a *contour map*. Figure 2–7 is a contour map of the summit of Mt. Owen in British Columbia. On some of the irregularly shaped "rings" on this map, we find numbers (like 9000) indicating the height (in feet) above sea level at that particular spot on the mountain. Thus, unlike the more usual sort of map, which gives only latitudes and longitudes, this contour map (also called a topographical map) exhibits *three* pieces of information about each point: latitude, longitude, and altitude.

**A Geographic Contour Map**

**FIGURE 2-7**

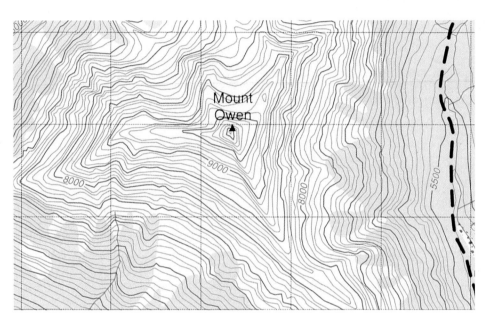

SOURCE: National Geographic Maps, Trails Illustrated,™ Lake Louise Area, Banff National Park, British Columbia, Canada.

Figure 2–8 looks more like the contour maps encountered in economics. It shows how some third variable, called $Z$ (think of it as a firm's output, for example), varies as we change either variable $X$ (think of it as a firm's employment) or variable $Y$ (think of it as the use of imported raw material). Just like the map of Mt. Owen, any point on the diagram conveys three pieces of data. At point $A$, we can read off the values of $X$ and $Y$ in the conventional way ($X$ is 30 and $Y$ is 40), and we can also note the value of $Z$ by checking to see on which contour line point $A$ falls. (It is on the $Z = 20$ contour.) So point $A$ is able to tell us that 30 hours of labor and 40 yards of cloth produce 20 units of output per day. The contour line that indicates 20 units of output shows the various combinations of labor and cloth a manufacturer can use to produce 20 units of output. Economists call such maps **production indifference maps.**

Although most of the analyses presented in this book rely on the simpler two-variable diagrams, contour maps will find their applications, especially in the appendixes to Chapters 6 and 8.

**FIGURE 2-8**

**An Economic Contour Map**

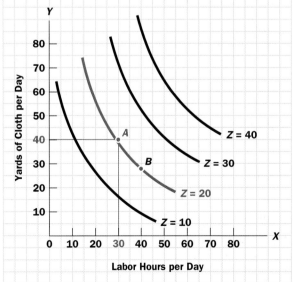

### PERILS IN THE
### ■ INTERPRETATION
### OF GRAPHS

The preceding materials contain just about all you will need in order to understand the simple graphics used in our economic models. We turn now to the second objective of this chapter: to show how statistical data are portrayed on graphs and some of the pitfalls to watch out for.

## THE INTERPRETATION OF GROWTH TRENDS

Probably the most common form of graph in empirical economics is a year-by-year (or perhaps a month-by-month) depiction of the behavior of some economic variable—the profits of a particular corporation, its annual sales to foreign customers, the number of persons unemployed in the U.S. economy, or some measure of consumer prices. They are called **time-series graphs** and you will find them in newspapers and magazines as well as in this book.

A **time-series graph** is a type of two-variable diagram in which time is the variable measured along the horizontal axis. It shows how some variable changed as time passed.

By summarizing an immense amount of data in compact and easily understandable form, time-series graphs can be invaluable, offering an instant visual grasp of trends. But if misused, they can be dangerous. Consider Figure 2–9 as an example. It shows gross domestic product (GDP) in the United States since 1959 and seems to show that the country has grown richer at an enormous rate, increasing to about 17 times its 1959 level in four decades.

| FIGURE 2-9 | **The GDP of the United States Since 1959** |

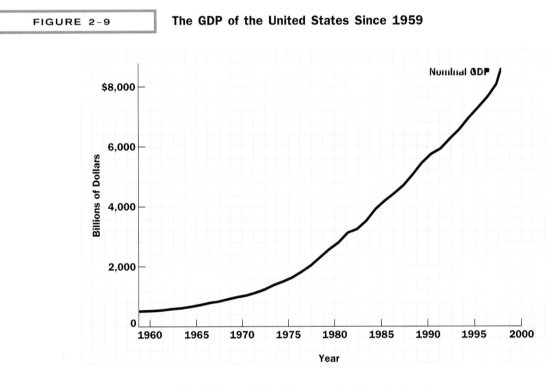

SOURCE: *Economic Report of the President* 1999 (Washington, D.C.: U.S. Government Printing Office, 1999).

However, this graph can easily mislead persons who are not experienced in dealing with such graphs. Perhaps even more dangerous are the lies perpetrated accidentally and unintentionally by people who draw graphs without sufficient care and who may innocently mislead themselves as well as their readers. Most of the spectacular GDP growth over this period is attributable to two mundane influences: inflation and population growth. First, the price of almost everything rose substantially since 1959 because of **inflation.** On average, prices in 1998 were about five times as large as in 1959. Since each dollar in 1998 bought about one-fifth what it did in 1959, the dollar makes a rather poor measuring stick for comparison of production in the two years. Most of the apparent growth in "output" suggested in Figure 2–9 is really the result of higher prices, not greater production.

**Inflation** refers to a sustained increase in the average level of prices.

Economists correct for inflation by a process called *deflating by a price index.* Proper deflation changes our original black GDP line to the lower blue line in Figure 2–10, which shows the real growth of *GDP in dollars of constant purchasing power.* Economists call this **real GDP.** By this more informative measure, we find that output in 1998 was about three and a half times as high as in 1959, not 17 times as high.

**Real GDP** is the value of all the goods and services produced by an economy in a year, evaluated in dollars of constant purchasing power. Hence, inflation does not raise real GDP.

**Nominal GDP, Real GDP, and Real GDP per Capita, 1959–1998** | FIGURE 2-10

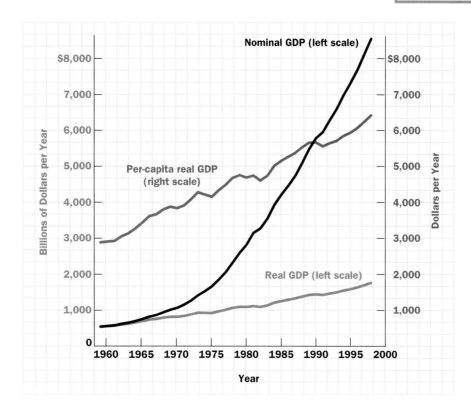

NOTE: Real GDP figures are in 1959 dollars.

SOURCE: *Economic Report of the President* 1999 (Washington, D.C.: U.S. Government Printing Office, 1999).

Second, there were many more Americans alive in 1998 than in 1959—52 percent more, to be exact. So GDP *per person* (economists usually refer to it as "per capita") rose by considerably less than even the blue line in Figure 2–10 indicates. The red line corrects *both* for inflation *and* for population growth by charting the time-series behavior of *GDP per capita* in dollars of constant purchasing power. Americans were indeed richer in 1998 than in 1959, but not nearly by as much as a naive look at Figure 2–9 may suggest. In fact, the American standard of living roughly *doubled* over this period; it did *not* rise seventeenfold, or even three-and-a-half-fold. This shows how misleading it can be simply to "look at the facts." The general conclusion is:

The facts, as portrayed in a time-series graph almost never "speak for themselves." Because almost everything grows in a growing economy, one must use good judgment and make corrections before drawing conclusions about growth trends. It is often necessary to correct for rising prices or population growth or for other distorting and misleading influences.

## DISTORTING TRENDS BY CHOICE OF THE TIME PERIOD

In addition to possible misinterpretations of growth trends, users of statistical data must guard against distortions of trends caused by unskillfully chosen (or unscrupulously chosen) first and last time periods (in other words, starting and end points) for the graph. This is best explained by an example.

Figure 2–11 shows the behavior of average stock market prices from January 1966 to June 1982. The figures have been corrected

*"Dow Jonesy enough for you?"*

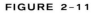

**FIGURE 2-11**    **Stock Prices, January 1966 to June 1982**

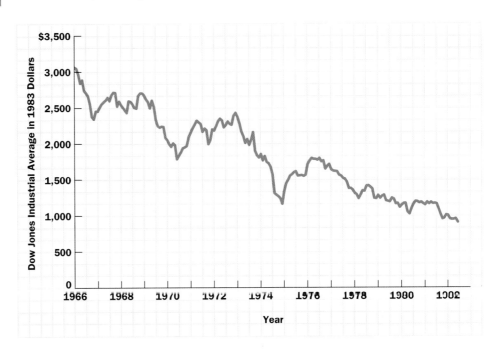

**FIGURE 2-12**

**Stock Prices, January 1993 to January 1998**

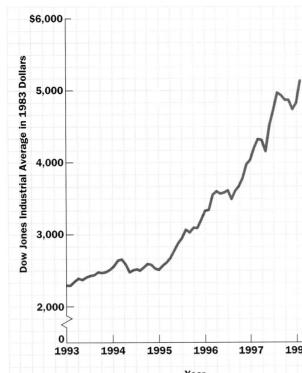

for inflation; that is, they are expressed in dollars of unchanging purchasing power. The graph displays a clear downhill movement that would suggest to anyone who does not have other information that stocks are a terrible investment.

However, an unscrupulous seller of stocks could use the same set of stock market statistics to tell exactly the opposite story by carefully selecting another group of years. Figure 2–12 shows the behavior of average stock prices from January 1993 to January 1998. The size of the increase is quite dramatic. Stocks now look like a rather good investment.

However, a much longer and less-biased choice of period (1925–1998) gives a less distorted picture (Figure 2–13). It indicates that investments in stocks are sometimes profitable and other times unprofitable.

Careful readers of economic data must constantly watch for deliberate or inadvertent distortion resulting from an unfortunate or unscrupulous choice of time period for a graph.

No rules can give absolute protection from this difficulty, but several precautions can be helpful:

■ Make sure the first date shown on the graph is not an exceptionally high or low point. In comparison with 1966, a year of unusually high stock market prices, the years immediately following are bound to give the impression of a downward trend.

■ For the same reason, make sure the graph does not end in a year that is extraordinarily high or low (although this may be unavoidable if the graph simply ends with figures that are as up-to-date as possible).

■ Make sure that (in the absence of some special justification) the graph does not depict only a very brief period, which can easily be atypical.

SOURCE: *Economic Report of the President*, Washington, D.C.: U.S. Government Printing Office, various years.

**Full History of Stock Prices, Corrected for Inflation, 1925–1998**

FIGURE 2-13

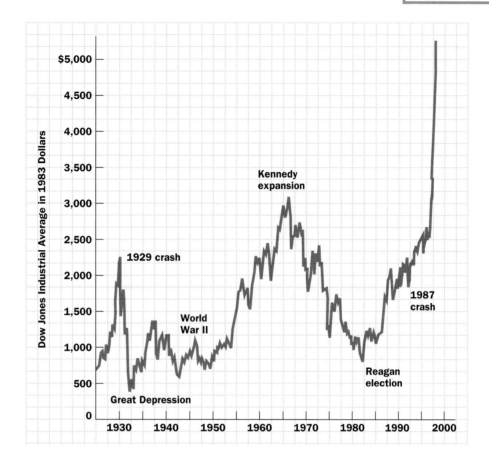

SOURCES: *The Dow Jones Averages, 1885–1985* (centennial edition), ed. Phyllis S. Pierce (Homewood, Ill.: Dow Jones-Irwin, 1986); *Citibase*; U.S. Department of Commerce, Census Bureau, *Historical Statistics of the United States* (Washington, D.C.: U.S. Government Printing Office, 1975); and *Economic Report of the President*, (Washington, D.C.: U.S. Government Printing Office, various years).

## Dangers of Omitting the Origin: The Puzzle Solved

Frequently, the value of an economic variable described by a graph does not fall anywhere near zero during the time period under consideration. For example, between 1988 and 1992 the civilian unemployment rate never fell below 5 percent. This means that a time-series graph showing unemployment over time would have a lot of wasted space between the horizontal axis (where the unemployment rate is zero) and the level of the graph representing 5 percent. There would simply be no data points to plot in that range. It is therefore tempting to *eliminate* this wasted space by beginning the graph at 5 percent, as the magazine *The International Economy* did when it published Figure 2–14 in 1992. This is the graph with which the chapter began, the one that suggests that between 1990 and 1992 unemployment in the United States exploded, increasing more than 700 percent. We will see that the actual rise was much smaller than that. It will be recalled that our puzzle question was: What is wrong with the drawing? The answer is: Nothing—so long as you read it carefully. But a *hasty* glance vastly exaggerates the rise in unemployment. Figure 2–14 makes it look like the United States experienced an economic catastrophe from 1990 to 1992. A less misleading graph, which includes the origin as well as all the "wasted space" in between, appears as Figure 2–15. Note how this alternative presentation gives a dramatically different visual impression. Although the rise in unemployment was distressingly large, it was not nearly so enormous as the previous graph suggested. It rose less than 50 percent, certainly not nearly the 700 percent that the previous figure suggests.

**FIGURE 2-14**

**A Graph Distorted by Omission of the Origin**

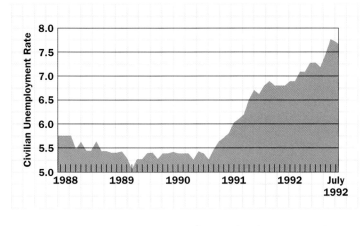

SOURCE: *The International Economy*, September/October 1992, p. 10.

Why does the actual percentage change appear to be so much smaller in Figure 2–15 than in the previous graph? The answer is that the level of unemployment at the starting point of the graph (1988) was not nearly as low as it appears to have been in Figure 2–14. Omission of the "wasted space" in the graph creates the illusion that the starting point was very low and therefore exaggerates any change in the graph. In Figure 2–15, with the zero point restored, the changes look much less dramatic. (It's like comparing a two-inch spurt of growth in an infant with a two-inch growth spurt in a tall teenager—the baby's starting point is very low, so two inches is a big change, but the teenager's starting point is much higher so the two-inch change is less dramatic.)

*Omitting the origin in a graph is dangerous because it exaggerates the magnitudes of the percentage changes that have taken place.*

Of course, sometimes it's true that the inclusion of the origin would waste so much space that it is undesirable to include it. In that case, a good practice is to put a clear warning on the graph to remind the reader that this has been done. Figure 2–16 shows one way to do so.

## UNRELIABILITY OF STEEPNESS AND CHOICE OF UNITS

The last problem we will consider has consequences similar to the one we have just discussed. We can never trust the impression we get from the steepness of an economic graph. A graph of stock market prices that moves uphill sharply (has a large

**FIGURE 2-15**

**The Same Graph as Figure 2–14 with Origin Point Included**

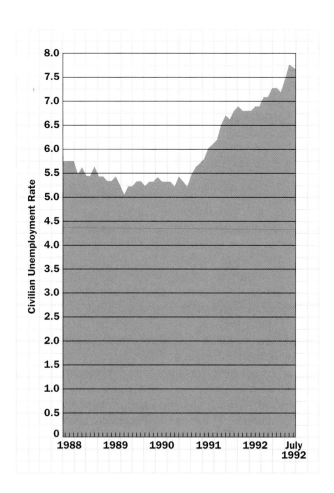

positive slope) appears to suggest that prices are rising rapidly, whereas another graph in which the rate of climb is much slower seems to imply that prices are going up sluggishly. Yet, depending on how one draws the graph, exactly the same statistics can produce a graph that is rising very quickly or very slowly.

This possibility arises because there is no universal, fixed unit of measurement in economics. Hamburger sales can be measured in number of burgers or in pounds of beef. Coal production can be measured in hundredweight (hundreds of pounds) or in tons. Prices can be measured in cents or in dollars or in millions of dollars. Time can be measured in days or in months or in years. Any of these choices is perfectly legitimate, but that choice makes all the difference in the world to the *speed* at which a graph using the resulting figures rises or falls.

An example will bring out the point. Suppose that we have the following (imaginary) data on sales of hamburgers by Daniel's Hamburger House, measuring sales by the number of quarter-pounders purchased and by the amount of beef bought:

**FIGURE 2–16**

**The Same Graph as Figure 2–14 with a Warning Break**

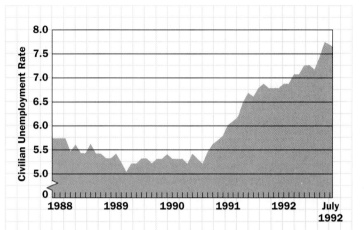

| Month | Hamburgers Purchased | Pounds of Beef Purchased |
|---|---|---|
| January | 1,000 | 250 |
| February | 1,100 | 275 |

Look at Figures 2–17(a) and 2–17(b), one graph showing the data in number of hamburgers and the other showing the data counted in pounds of beef. The line in Figure 2–17(a) seems to suggest that business is rising quite sharply. But in Figure 2–17(b), because a sales increase of 100 quarter-pound hamburgers is the same as a sales increase of 25 pounds of beef, the rise in sales looks much more modest, even though both graphs really give the same information.

Unfortunately, we cannot solve the problem by agreeing always to stick to the same measurement units. Pounds may be the right unit for measuring demand for beef, but they will not do in measuring demand for cloth or for coal. A penny may be the right monetary unit for postage stamps, but it is not a very convenient unit for the cost of airplanes or automobiles.

**FIGURE 2–17**

**Slope Depends on Units of Measurement**

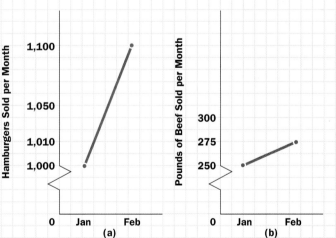

A change in units of measurement stretches or compresses the axis on which the information is represented, which automatically changes the slope of a graph. Therefore, we must never place much faith in the apparent implications of the slope of an ordinary graph in economics.

Later, in Chapter 7 on demand analysis, we will encounter a useful approach economists have adopted to deal with this problem. Instead of calculating changes in "absolute" terms—like pounds of beef or billions of dollars—economists use *percentage* increases as their common units. By using percentages rather than absolute figures, the problem can be avoided. The reason is simple. If we look at our hypothetical hamburger sales figures again, we see that no matter whether we measure the increase in output from January to February in hamburgers (from 1,000 to 1,100) or in pounds of beef (from 250 to 275), the *percentage* increase is the same. 100 is 10 percent of 1,000, and 25 is 10 percent of 250. Since a change in units affects both the numbers *proportionately*, the result is a washout—it does nothing to the percentage calculation and thus does not distort the figure.

1. Because graphs are used so often to portray economic models, it is important for students to acquire some understanding of their construction and use. Fortunately, the graphics used in economics are usually not very complex.

2. Most economic models are depicted in *two-variable diagrams*. We read data from these diagrams just as we read the latitude and longitude on a map: each point represents the values of two *variables* at the same time.

3. In some instances, three variables must be shown at once. In these cases, economists use contour maps, which, as the name suggests, show "latitude," "longitude," and "altitude" all at the same time.

4. Often, the most important property of a line or curve drawn on a diagram will be its slope, which is defined as the ratio of the "rise" over the "run," or the vertical change divided by the horizontal change. Curves that go uphill as we move to the right have *positive slopes*; curves that go downhill have *negative slopes*.

5. By definition, a *straight line* has the same *slope* wherever we choose to measure it. The *slope of a curved line* changes, but the

slope at any point on the curve can be calculated by measuring the slope of a straight line *tangent to the curve* at that point.

6. A *time-series graph* is a particular type of two-variable diagram that is useful in depicting statistical data. Time is measured along the horizontal axis, and some variable of interest is measured along the vertical axis.

7. Although time-series graphs are invaluable in helping us condense a great deal of information in a single picture, they can be quite misleading if they are not drawn and interpreted with care. For example, growth trends can be exaggerated by an inappropriate choice of units of measurement or by a failure to correct for some obvious source of growth (such as rising population). Omitting the origin can make the ups and downs in a time series appear much more extreme than they actually are. Or, by a clever choice of the starting and ending points for the graphs, the same data can be made to tell very different stories. Readers of such graphs—and this includes anyone who ever reads a newspaper—must be on guard for problems like these or they may find themselves misled by "the facts."

Variable   18

Two-variable diagram   18

Horizontal and vertical axes   18

Origin (of a graph)   18

Slope of a straight (or curved) line   20

Negative, positive, zero, and infinite slope   20

Tangent to a curve   21

*Y*-intercept   22

Ray through the origin, or ray   22

45° line   22

Contour map   23

Production indifference map   23

Time-series graph   24

Inflation   24

Deflating by a price index   24

Real GDP   24

1. Look for a graph in your local newspaper, on the financial page or elsewhere. What does the graph try to show? Is someone trying to convince you of something with this graph? Check to see if the graph is distorted in any of the ways mentioned in this chapter.

2. Portray the following hypothetical data on a two-variable diagram:

| Academic Year | Total Enrollment | Enrollment in Economics Courses |
|---|---|---|
| 1994–1995 | 3,000 | 300 |
| 1995–1996 | 3,100 | 325 |
| 1996–1997 | 3,200 | 350 |
| 1997–1998 | 3,300 | 375 |
| 1998–1999 | 3,400 | 400 |

Measure the slope of the resulting line, and explain what this number means.

3. From Figure 2–5, calculate the slope of the curve at point *M*.

4. Colin believes that the number of job offers he will get depends on the number of courses in which his grade is B+ or better. He concludes from observation that the following figures are typical:

| | |
|---|---|
| Number of grades of B+ or better | 0 1 2 3 4 |
| Number of job offers | 1 3 4 5 6 |

Put these numbers into a graph like Figure 2–1a. Measure and interpret the slopes between adjacent dots.

5. In Figure 2–6, determine the values of *X* and *Y* at point *K* and at point *E*. What do you conclude?

6. In Figure 2–8, interpret the economic meaning of points *A* and *B*. What do the two points have in common? What is the difference in their economic interpretation?

7. Suppose that between 1998 and 1999 expenditures on dog food rose from $35 million to $70 million and the price of dog food doubled. What do these facts imply about the popularity of dog food?

8. Suppose that between 1990 and 1999 the U.S. population went up 10 percent and that the number of silk neckties imported from Thailand rose from 3,000,000 to 3,100,000. What do these facts imply about the growth in popularity of Thai ties?

E pluribus unum (Out of many, one)

Motto on U.S. currency

# THE ECONOMY:
# MYTH AND REALITY

This chapter introduces you to the U.S. economy and its role in the world. It may seem that no such introduction is necessary, for you have probably lived your entire life in the United States. Every time you work at a summer or part-time job, pay your college bills, or buy a slice of pizza, you not only participate in the American economy; you also observe something about it.

But the casual impressions we acquire in our everyday lives, though sometimes correct, are often misleading. Experience shows that most Americans—not just students—either are unaware of or harbor grave misconceptions about some of the most basic economic facts. One popular myth holds that the United States is inundated with imported goods, mostly from Japan. Another is that business profits account for something like a third of the price we pay for a typical good or service. Also, "everyone knows" that federal government jobs have grown rapidly over the past few decades. In fact, none of these things is true.

So, before we begin to study elaborate theories about how the economy works, it is useful to get a more *accurate* picture of our economy as it really is.

## ■ THE AMERICAN ECONOMY: A THUMBNAIL SKETCH

The U.S. economy is the biggest national economy on earth, for two very different reasons. First, there are a lot of us. The population of the United States is more than 270 million—making it the third most populous nation on earth after China (1.2 billion) and India (969 million). That vast total includes children, retirees, full-time students, institutionalized people, and the unemployed, none of whom produce much output. But the *working population* of the United States numbers about 132 million. As long as they are reasonably productive, that many people are bound to produce vast amounts of goods and services. And they do.

But population is not the main reason why the U.S. economy is by far the world's biggest. After all, India has about three and one-half times the population of the United States, but its economy is considerably smaller than that of the state of Texas. The second reason why the U.S. economy is so large is that we are a very rich country. Because American workers are among the most productive in the world, our economy produces about $30,000 worth of goods and services for every living American. If each of the 50 states was a separate country, California would be the eighth largest national economy on earth!

**Inputs** or **factors of production** are the labor, machinery, buildings, and natural resources used to make outputs.

**Outputs** are the goods and services that consumers want to acquire.

Why are some countries (like the United States) so rich and others (like India) so poor? That is a central question facing economists. It is useful to think of an economic system as a machine that takes **inputs,** such as labor and other things we call **factors of production,** and transforms them into **outputs,** or the things people want to consume. The American economic machine performs this task with extraordinary efficiency, whereas the Indian machine runs quite inefficiently. Learning why is one of the chief reasons to study economics.

Thus, what makes the American economy the center of world attention is our unique combination of prosperity and population. There are other rich countries in the world, like Germany and Switzerland, and there are other countries with huge populations, like China and India. But no nation combines a huge population with high per-capita income the way the United States does. Japan, with an economy about 54 percent as large as ours, is the only nation that comes close.

Although the United States is a rich and populous country, the 50 states certainly were not created equal. Population density varies enormously—from a high of nearly 1,100 people per square mile in crowded New Jersey to a low of just one person per square mile in Alaska. Income variations are much less pronounced. But, still, the average income in Mississippi is only about half that in Connecticut.

### A PRIVATE-ENTERPRISE ECONOMY

Part of the secret of America's economic success is that free markets and private enterprise have flourished here. These days more than ever, private enterprise and capitalism are the rule, not the exception, around the globe. But the United States has taken the idea of the free market further than almost any other country. It remains "the land of opportunity."

Every country has a mixture of public and private ownership of property. Even in the darkest days of communism, Russians owned their own personal possessions. In our country, the post office and the electricity-producing Tennessee Valley Authority are enterprises of the federal government, and many cities and states own and operate mass transit facilities and sports stadiums. But the United States stands out among the world's nations as one of the most "privatized." Few industrial assets are publicly owned in the United States. Even many city bus companies, and almost all utilities (such as electricity, gas, and telephones), are run as private companies in the United States; in Europe, they are more often government enterprises, though there is a substantial move toward transfer of government firms to private ownership.

**Gross domestic product (GDP)** is a measure of the size of the economy or, rather, of the total amount it produces. It is, roughly speaking, the money value of all the goods and services produced in a year.

The United States also has one of the most "marketized" economies on earth. The standard measure of the total output of an economy is called **gross domestic product (or GDP),** a term which appears frequently in the news. The share of GDP

### ● THE U.S. SHARE OF WORLD GDP—IT'S NICE TO BE RICH

The nearly 6 billion people of the world produced approximately $31 trillion worth of goods and services in 1997. The United States, with only 4.6 percent of that population, turned out nearly 27 percent of total output, or almost six times the average share. As the accompanying graph shows, the United States is still the leader in goods and services, with about $30,000 worth of GDP produced per person, or per capita. Just seven major industrial economies (the United States, Japan, Germany, France, Italy, the United Kingdom, and Canada—which account for 12 percent of global population) generated 44 percent of world output and exported 48 percent of total exports.

SOURCE: International Monetary Fund, *World Economic Outlook, May 1998,* Washington, D.C., 1998.

*"And may we continue to be worthy of consuming a disproportionate share of this planet's resources."*

### 1997 GDP per Capita in 10 Industrial Countries

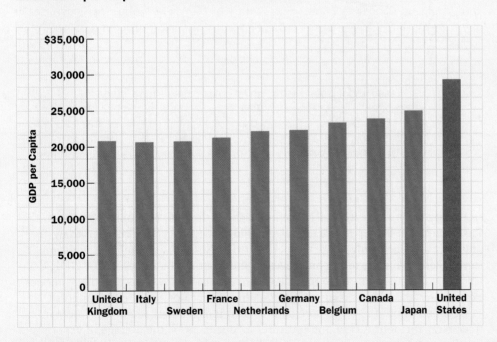

NOTE: GDP is in U.S. dollars, using purchasing-power parities.

SOURCE: Organization for Economic Cooperation and Development, Main Economic Indicators, October 1998, www.oecd.org, accessed January 1999.

that passes through markets in the United States is enormous. Although government purchases of goods and services amount to about 18 percent of GDP, much of that is purchased from private businesses. Direct government *production* of goods is extremely rare in our society, and government services amount to only about 11 percent of GDP.

## A RELATIVELY "CLOSED" ECONOMY

All nations trade with one another, and the United States is no exception. Our annual exports exceed $900 billion and our annual imports exceed $1,000 billion. That's a lot of money. But America's international trade often gets more attention than it deserves. The fact is that we produce most of what we consume and consume most of what we produce, though the share of imports and exports has been growing, as Figure 3–1 shows. In 1959 the average of exports and imports was only 4 percent of GDP, a tiny fraction of the total. It has since gone up to about 12 percent. This is no longer negligible, but it still means that over 85 percent of what Americans acquire from the economy every year is made in the U.S.A.

| FIGURE 3–1 | **Share of U.S. GDP Exported and Imported, 1959–1998** |

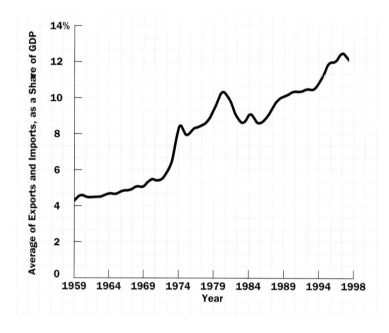

SOURCE: *Economic Report of the President* (Washington, D.C.: U.S. Government Printing Office, various years).

Among the most severe misconceptions about the U.S. economy is the myth that this country no longer manufactures anything, but rather imports everything from, say, Japan. In fact, only about 13 percent of U.S. GDP is imported, with imports from Japan making up about one-seventh of this—or about 2 percent of GDP. Contrary to a second myth, if we include *services* along with *goods* in the total, America's exports—at about 12 percent of GDP—almost (but not quite) equal imports.

Economists use the terms *open* and *closed* to indicate how important international trade is to a nation. A common measure of "openness" is the average of exports and imports, expressed as a share of GDP. Thus, the Netherlands is considered an extremely **open economy** because it imports and exports about 56 percent of its GDP. (See Table 3–1.) By this criterion, the United States stands out as among the most **closed economies** of the advanced, industrial nations. We export and import a smaller share of GDP than almost all of the countries listed in the table.

An economy is called relatively **open** if its exports and imports constitute a large share of its GDP.

An economy is considered relatively **closed** if they constitute a small share.

## A GROWING ECONOMY . . . BUT WITH INFLATION

The next salient fact about the U.S. economy is its growth; it gets bigger almost every year. Gross domestic product in 1998 was around $8.5 trillion, almost 17 times

**Openness of Various National Economies, 1998**

TABLE 3-1

|  | GDP | Exports | Imports | Openness |
|---|---|---|---|---|
| Netherlands | $   343.9 | $203.1 | $   179.1 | 56% |
| Canada | 658.0 | 208.6 | 194.4 | 31 |
| Germany | 1,740.0 | 521.1 | 455.7 | 28 |
| United Kingdom | 1,242.0 | 268.0 | 283.5 | 22 |
| Mexico | 694.3 | 110.4 | 109.8 | 16 |
| Japan | 3,080.0 | 421.0 | 339.0 | 12 |
| United States | 8,083.0 | 958.8 | 1,055.5 | 12 |
| Russia | 692.0 | 86.7 | 66.9 | 11 |

NOTE: Dollar amounts are in billions.

SOURCE: For United States, *Economic Report of the President, 1999,* (Washington, D.C.: U.S. Government Printing Office, Feb. 1999). For other countries, *CIA Factbook 1998,* www.odci.gov/cia/publications/factbook.

as much as in 1959. In Figure 3–2 the upper black curve shows that extraordinary upward march. But, as we learned in Chapter 2, a large part of this apparent growth in GDP is due to price inflation—because of higher prices, the *purchasing power* of each 1998 dollar was actually only about one-fifth of each 1959 dollar. Corrected for inflation, we see that *real GDP* (the blue curve in the figure) was only about three-and-a-half times greater in 1998 than in 1959. Another reason for the rise in GDP is the growth in U.S. population. But if a nation's GDP grows no faster than its population, we cannot say that it has become richer, because each person ends up with no more purchasing power. To see how much richer the United States has actually become, we must divide real GDP by the size of the population to obtain *real per-capita GDP* (the red curve in Figure 3–2). It turns out that real income per person in 1998 was only about twice as much as in 1959. That is, still, not a bad performance.

**Nominal GDP, Real GDP, and Real GDP per Capita Since 1959**

FIGURE 3-2

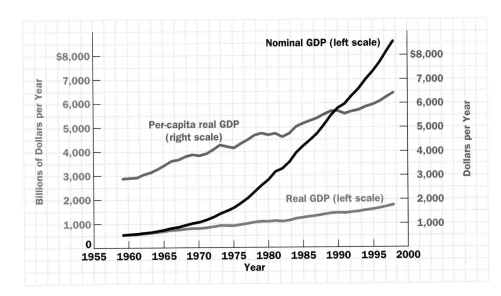

NOTE: Real GDP figures are in 1959 dollars.

SOURCE: *Economic Report of the President* (Washington, D.C.: U.S. Government Printing Office, various years).

## BUMPS ALONG THE GROWTH PATH: RECESSIONS

The bird's-eye view that Figure 3–2 offers conceals one more important fact: America's economic growth has been quite irregular. We have experienced alternating periods of good and bad times, which are called *economic fluctuations* or sometimes just *business cycles*. In some years—five since 1959, to be exact—GDP actually declined. Such periods of *declining* economic activity are called **recessions.**

A **recession** is a period of time during which the total output of the economy falls.

The bumps along the American economy's historic growth path are visible upon closer inspection of Figure 3–2 but stand out more clearly in Figure 3–3, which displays the same data in a different way. Here we plot not the *level* of real GDP each year, but rather its *growth rate*—the percentage change from one year to the next. Now the booms and busts that delight and distress people—and swing elections—stand out clearly. From 1983 to 1984, for example, real GDP grew by close to 7 percent, which helped ensure Ronald Reagan's landslide reelection. But from 1990 to 1991, real GDP actually fell by 1 percent, which helped Bill Clinton defeat George Bush.

| FIGURE 3–3 | **The Growth Rate of Real GDP in the United States Since 1959** |

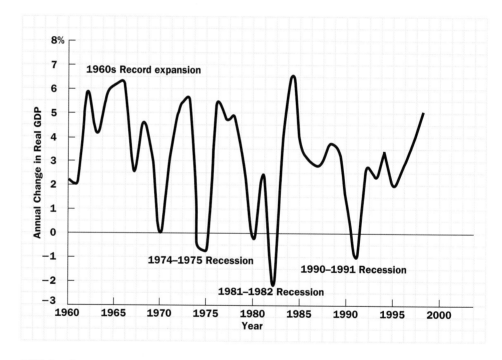

NOTE: Growth rates are for 1959–1960, 1960–1961, and so on.
SOURCE: *Economic Report of the President* (Washington, D.C.: U.S. Government Printing Office, various years).

One important consequence of these ups and downs in economic growth is that *unemployment* varies considerably from one year to the next. (See Figure 3–4) During the Great Depression of the 1930s, unemployment ran as high as 25 percent of the workforce. But it fell to barely over 1 percent during World War II. Within the past few years, the national unemployment rate has been as high as 7.7 percent (in June 1992) and as low as 4.2 percent (in March 1999). In human terms, that 3.5 percentage point difference represents more than 4.5 million fewer jobless workers. Understanding why joblessness varies so dramatically, and what we can do about it, is another major reason for studying economics.

### ● UNEMPLOYMENT RATES IN EUROPE

During most of the period after the Second World War, unemployment rates in the industrialized countries of Europe were significantly lower than those in the United States. In the mid-1970s, rates of joblessness in Europe leaped, with double digits becoming common. In April 1999, *The Economist* reported the following unemployment rates:

| | | | |
|---|---|---|---|
| Switzerland | 3.4 % | Australia | 7.4 % |
| Netherlands | 3.6 | Canada | 7.8 |
| United States | 4.2 | Germany | 11.1 |
| Austria | 4.3 | France | 11.5 |
| Japan | 4.6 | Belgium | 11.7 |
| Sweden | 5.6 | Italy | 12.3 |
| Denmark | 6.0 | Spain | 18.2 |
| Britain | 6.3 | | |

These days, the U.S. economy is the envy of Europe, and its low unemployment rate is among the main reasons.

SOURCE: *The Economist*, April 16, 1999, p. 104.

---

**The Unemployment Rate in the United States, 1929–1998**    FIGURE 3-4

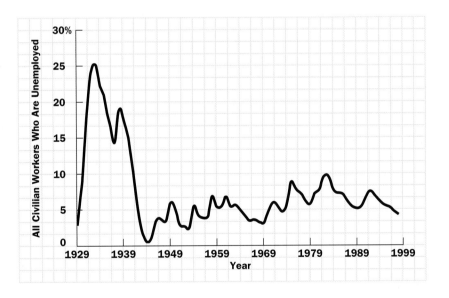

SOURCE: *Economic Report of the President* (Washington, D.C.: U.S. Government Printing Office, various years); and Bureau of the Census, *Historical Statistics of the United States, Colonial Times to 1970* (Washington, D.C.: U.S. Government Printing Office, 1975).

## ■ THE INPUTS: LABOR AND CAPITAL

Let's now return to the analogy of an economy as a machine turning inputs into outputs. The most important input is human labor: the men and women who run the machines, work behind the desks, and serve you in stores.

FIGURE 3-5

## The Composition of Employment by Sex, 1950 and 1998

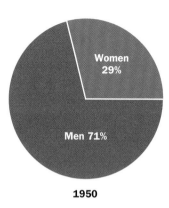

**1950**

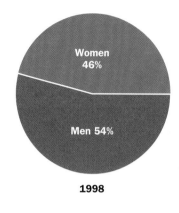

**1998**

SOURCE: *Economic Report of the President*, Washington, D.C.: U.S. Government Printing Office, various years.

FIGURE 3-6

## Working Women as a Percentage of the Labor Force, 1960 versus 1996

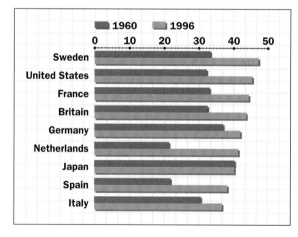

SOURCE: "A Survey of Women and Work," *The Economist*, July 18, 1998, p. 4.

## THE AMERICAN WORKFORCE: WHO IS IN IT?

We have already mentioned that about 132 million Americans hold jobs—more than two and a half times as many as the apparently ambitious goal for the country that optimists were proposing during World War II, when Henry Wallace, Franklin Delano Roosevelt's vice president during his third term, sought a goal of employing 60 million workers within the United States. Roughly 54 percent of these 132 million workers are men; 46 percent are women. This ratio represents a drastic change from a generation or two ago, when most women worked only at home (see Figure 3–5). Indeed, the massive entrance of women into the paid labor force has been one of the major social transformations of American life during the second half of the 20th century. In 1950, just 29 percent of women worked in the marketplace; now about 60 percent do. As Figure 3–6 shows, the share of women in the labor forces of other industrial countries has also been growing. The expanding role of women in the labor market has raised many controversial questions—whether they are discriminated against (the evidence suggests that they are), whether the government should compel employers to provide maternity leave, and so on.

In contrast to women, the percentage of teenagers in the workforce has dropped significantly since the mid-1970s (See Figure 3–7.) Young men and women aged 16 to 19 accounted for 8.6 percent of employment in 1974 but only 5.4 percent in 1998. As the baby boom gave way to the baby bust, people under 20 became scarce resources! Still, more than 7 million teenagers hold jobs in the U.S. economy today, and their numbers have increased in the past few years. Most fill low-wage jobs at fast-food restaurants, amusement parks, and the like. Relatively few teenagers can be found in the nation's factories.

## THE AMERICAN WORKFORCE: WHAT DOES IT DO?

What do these 132 million working Americans do? The only real answer is: almost anything you can imagine. In 1997, America had 68,000 architects, 3,000 watchmakers, 501,000 computer programmers, more than 700,000 carpenters, almost 3 million truckdrivers, 425,000 lawyers, 17,000 aircraft assemblers, 164,000 kindergarten teachers, 6,000 bookbinders, 464,000 physicians and surgeons, 30,000 oilfield roustabouts, 6,300 ship engineers, 226,000 firefighters, and 47,000 economists![1] Figure 3–8 shows the breakdown by economic sector. It holds some surprises for most people. The majority of American workers—like workers in all developed countries—produce services, not goods. In 1998, about 101 million people were employed by service industries in the United States, including 22 million in retail trade, whereas only 25 million produced goods. The popular image of the typical American worker as a blue collar worker—Homer Simpson, if you will—is really quite misleading. Manufacturing companies employ only about 18 million people, and almost a third of those work in offices rather than in the factory. Federal, state, and local governments employ about 20 million people. Contrary to another popular misconception, few of these civil servants work for the *federal* government. Federal *civilian* employment is about

---

[1] Source: U.S. Bureau of Labor Statistics, *Occupational Employment Statistics Survey 1997*, http://stats.bls.gov., accessed January 6, 1999.

**Teenage Employment as a Percentage of Total Employment, 1950–1998**

FIGURE 3–7

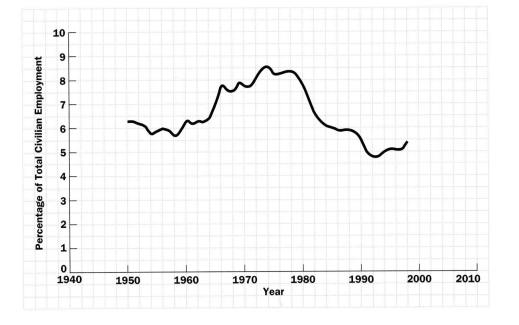

SOURCE: *Economic Report of the President* (Washington, D.C.: U.S. Government Printing Office, various years).

**Civilian Employment by Sector, 1998**

FIGURE 3–8

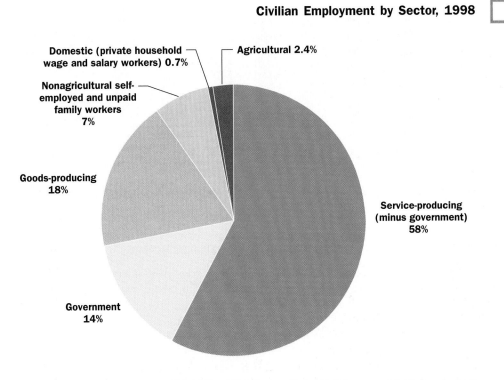

SOURCE: *Economic Report of the President, 1999;* and U.S. Bureau of Labor Statistics, www.stats.bls.gov, accessed February 1999.

2.7 million—and has fallen every year since 1990. At the same time, state and local governments provide about 17 million jobs. Finally, approximately 3.4 million Americans work on farms, and the armed forces employ about 1.5 million workers.

As Figure 3–9 shows, *all* industrialized countries have become "service economies." That is, to a considerable degree, a result of increased demand for labor by the service sector and reduced demand in manufacturing. Activities related to computers, to research, to the transmission of information by teaching and publication, and other information-related activities have provided many new jobs. This means that workers who moved into the service sector of the economy have not gone predominantly into dishwashing or housecleaning or other such low-skill jobs. Many have found employment in service areas where education and experience provide a great advantage. At the same time, technological change has made it possible to produce a given set of manufactured products using fewer and fewer workers. Such labor-saving innovation in manufacturing has moved a considerable share of the labor force out of goods-producing jobs and into the services.

FIGURE 3-9

### The Growing Share of Service Sector Jobs, 1967–1996

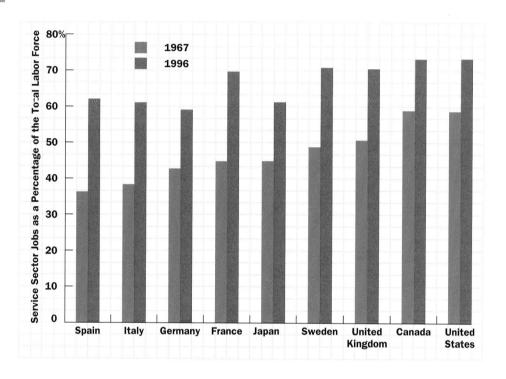

SOURCE: Organization for Economic Cooperation and Development, *Quarterly Labour Force Statistics,* various issues; and www.oecd.org, accessed February 1999.

## THE AMERICAN WORKFORCE: WHAT IT EARNS

Altogether, these workers' wages account for nearly three-quarters of the income that the production process generates. That figures up to an average hourly wage of about $13—plus fringe benefits like health insurance and pensions, which can contribute an additional 30 to 40 percent for people holding what are often called "good jobs." Because the average work week is about 35 hours long, a typical weekly pay check is about $455 before taxes. That is hardly a princely sum, and most college graduates can expect to earn more.[2] But it is typical of average wage rates in a rich country like the United States.

Wages in Japan and throughout northern Europe are similar. Indeed, workers in a number of other industrial countries receive higher compensation than American

---

[2] These days, male college graduates typically earn about 85 percent more than men with only high school diplomas, and female college grads earn more than twice what high-school-educated women earn. Source: U.S. Census Bureau, *Measuring 50 Years of Economic Change, 1947–1997* (Washington, D.C.: U.S. Government Printing Office, September 1998.)

workers do, for the first time in many decades. According to the U.S. Bureau of Labor Statistics, in 1997 workers in U.S. manufacturing sectors made less than those in Germany, Belgium, the Netherlands, and Canada (see Figure 3–10). However, U.S. compensation levels still remain well ahead of those in Japan, France, the United Kingdom, and many other countries.

**Average Hourly Compensation Rates in Manufacturing, 1997** | FIGURE 3-10

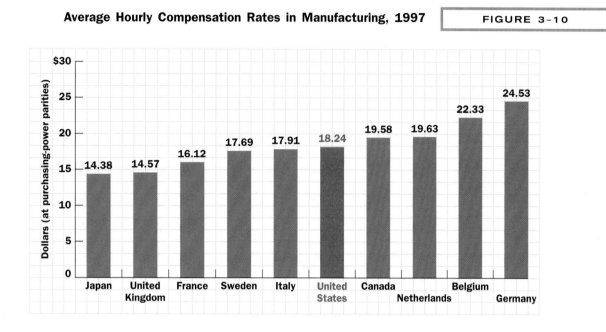

SOURCE: U.S. Bureau of Labor Statistics, http://stats.bls.gov, accessed September 1998; and Organization for Economic Cooperation and Development, www.oecd.org, accessed October 1998.

## CAPITAL AND ITS EARNINGS

The rest of national income (after deducting for the tiny sliver of income that goes to land and natural resources) mainly accrues to the owners of *capital*—the machines and buildings that make up the nation's industrial plant.

The total market value of these business assets—a tough number to estimate—is believed to be greater than $25 *trillion*. Because that capital earns an average rate of return of about 10 percent before taxes, total earnings of capital come to about $2,500 billion. Of this, profits are less than half; the rest is mainly interest.

Public opinion polls routinely show that Americans have a distorted view of the level of business profits in our society. The man and woman on the street believe that profits account for about 30 percent of the price of a typical product (see the accompanying box, "Public Opinion on Profits"). In fact, when you spend a dollar in our economy, 65 cents is for labor costs, 11 cents goes to cover the wear and tear on the capital stock,[3] 8 cents is for taxes, 5 cents is for interest, and 2 cents goes to rental income. That leaves about 10 cents for after-tax profits.

## ■ THE OUTPUTS: WHAT DOES AMERICA PRODUCE?

What does all this labor and capital produce? Consumer spending accounts for almost 70 percent of GDP. And what an amazing variety of goods and services it buys! American households spend roughly 60 percent of their budgets on services,

---

[3] Economists and accountants call this *depreciation*. It is a well-known cost of doing business.

● PUBLIC OPINION ON PROFITS

Most Americans think corporate profits are much higher than they actually are. One public opinion poll, for example, found that the average citizen thought that corporate profits *after taxes* amounted to 32 percent of sales for the typical manufacturing company. The actual profit rate at the time was closer to 4 percent!* Interestingly, when a previous poll asked how much profit was "reasonable," the response was 26 cents on every dollar of sales—more than six times as large as profits actually were.

*This poll was conducted in 1986. Corporate profit rates increased considerably in the 1990s.

SOURCE: "Public Attitudes toward Corporate Profits," *Public Opinion Index* (Princeton, N.J.: Opinion Research Corporation, June 1986).

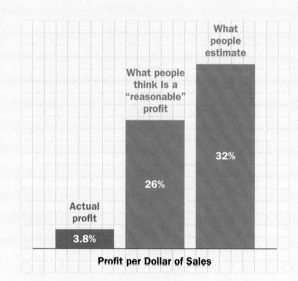

Profit per Dollar of Sales

with housing commanding the largest share. They also spend $86 billion annually on their telephone bills, $27 billion on airline tickets, and $47 billion on dentists. The other 40 percent of American budgets goes for goods—ranging from $85 billion per year on new cars to $36 billion on shoes.

This leaves close to a third of GDP for all *nonconsumption* uses. Government services take up about 17 percent, buying such things as airplanes, guns, and the services of soldiers, teachers, and bureaucrats. The rest is mainly business purchases of machinery and industrial structures (about 12 percent of GDP) and consumer purchases of new houses (about 4 percent).

## ■ THE CENTRAL ROLE OF BUSINESS FIRMS

Calvin Coolidge once said that "the business of America is business." He was largely right. When we peer inside the economic machine that turns inputs into outputs, we see mainly private companies. Astonishingly, the United States has more than 22 million business firms—about one for every 12 people!

The owners and managers of these businesses hire people, acquire or rent capital goods, and arrange to produce things consumers want to buy. Sound simple? It isn't. About 80,000 businesses fail every year. A few succeed spectacularly. Some do both. Fortunately for the U.S. economy, however, the lure of riches induces hundreds of thousands of people to start new businesses every year—against the odds.

A number of the biggest firms do business all over the world, just as foreign-based *multinational corporations* do business here. Indeed, some people claim that it is now impossible to determine the true "nationality" of a multinational corporation—which may have factories in ten or more countries, sell its wares all over the world, and have stockholders in dozens of nations. (See the accompanying box, "Is That an American Company?") Most of General Motors' profits are generated abroad, for example, and the Honda you drive was probably made in Ohio.

Firms compete with other companies in their *industry*. Most economists believe that this *competition* is the key to industrial efficiency. A sole supplier of a commodity will find it easy to make money, and may therefore fail to innovate or control costs. Its management is liable to become relaxed and sloppy. But a company

---

### ● IS THAT AN AMERICAN COMPANY?

Robert Reich, a former secretary of labor in the Clinton administration, has argued that it is almost impossible to define the nationality of a multinational company these days. Although many scholars think Reich exaggerates the point, no one doubts that he has one. Here are some examples:

What's the difference between an "American" corporation that makes or buys abroad much of what it sells around the world and a "foreign" corporation that makes or buys in the United States much of what it sells? . . . The mind struggles to keep the players straight. In 1990, Canada's Northern Telecom was selling to its American customers telecommunications equipment made by Japan's NTT at NTT's factory in North Carolina.

If you found that one too easy, try this: Beginning in 1991, Japan's Mazda would be producing Ford Probes at Mazda's plant in Flat Rock, Michigan. Some of these cars would be exported to Japan and sold there under Ford's trademark.

A Mazda-designed compact utility vehicle would be built at a Ford plant in Louisville, Kentucky, and then sold at Mazda dealerships in the United States. Nissan, meanwhile, was designing a new light truck at its San Diego, California, design center. The trucks would be assembled at Ford's Ohio truck plant, using panel parts fabricated by Nissan at its Tennessee factory, and then marketed by both Ford and Nissan in the United States and in Japan. Who is Ford? Nissan? Mazda?

SOURCE: Robert B. Reich, *The Work of Nations* (New York: Knopf, 1991), pp. 124, 131.

---

besieged by dozens of competitors eager to take its business away must constantly seek ways to innovate, cut costs, and build a better mousetrap. The rewards for business success can be magnificent. But the punishment for failure is severe.

## ■ MEASURING ECONOMIC PROGRESS

One of the American free-market economy's most noteworthy accomplishments is the abundance of growth it has fostered. Never in human history has the real income available to the average inhabitant of a country reached such heights. Studies estimate that in the 14 centuries before the American Revolution, the growth in per-capita income was, on average, approximately *zero*. In contrast, during the 20th century the real income of an average American grew by a factor of nearly 10.[4] Looked at another way, an average American family living around the last turn of the century could afford only *one-tenth* the food, clothing, housing and other amenities that constitute the standard of living today. The change is so enormous that it is difficult to grasp. Just try to imagine how your family's life would be changed if it lost nine out of ten dollars from its consumption expenditure.

The U.S. economy has achieved this remarkable progress through increased American labor *productivity*. Labor productivity is the amount of product that an average worker turns out in a given amount of time, say, per hour of labor. In the United States, over this century, labor productivity in manufacturing has grown by a factor of more than 13: that is, today, a worker turns out 13 times as much in a single hour

---

[4] Angus Maddison, *The Nature and Functioning of European Capitalism: A Historical and Comparative Perspective* (Groningen, Netherlands: University of Groningen, 1997), p. 34.

as her counterpart did around the turn of the century. That, fundamentally, is why we have so much more available to consume than our ancestors did 100 years ago.

We can look at this enormous economic progress another way: by examining what has happened to the costs of the things we purchase. This cannot be done very effectively using dollar prices, because this century has experienced a good deal of inflation, which distorts both prices and wages. Instead, we can measure what really happened to the cost of commodities by asking how many minutes an American must work in order to earn enough to purchase particular items. For example, statistics show that in 1919, in order to buy a pound of chicken an average U.S. worker had to work nearly an hour. Today, at current wages and poultry prices, less than five

| FIGURE 3-11 | **Work Time Needed to Buy Snack Foods, Earlier Dates versus 1997** |

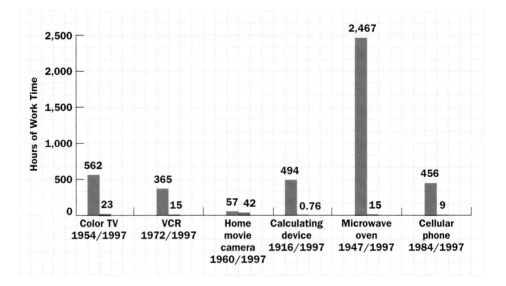

SOURCE: Federal Reserve Bank of Dallas, "Time Well Spent: The Declining *Real* Cost of Living in America," *1997 Annual Report*, 1997.

| FIGURE 3-12 | **Work Time Needed to Buy Various Items for the Home, Earlier Dates versus 1997** |

SOURCE: Federal Reserve Bank of Dallas, "Time Well Spent: The Declining *Real* Cost of Living in America," *1997 Annual Report*, 1997.

minutes of labor are required for the purpose! But it is not only chicken or only food that has become much less costly in terms of the labor time needed to pay for it. Figure 3–11 shows how much cheaper a variety of snack foods have become.

Figure 3–12 shows the great cost reductions of various types of electronic equipment—a cut of 98 percent in the cost of a color TV between 1954 and 1997, 96 percent in the cost of a VCR between 1972 and 1997, and 99 percent in the cost of a microwave oven between 1947 and 1997.

But, of course, the most sensational decrease of all is in the cost of computers. Computer capability is standardized in terms of the number of MIPS (million instructions per second) that the computer is capable of handling. To buy a computer today, it costs about 27 minutes of labor per MIPS capacity. In 1984, it cost the wages of 52 *hours* of labor; in 1970, the cost was 1.24 *lifetimes* of labor; and in 1944, the price was a barely believable 733,000 *lifetimes* of labor.

However, the magic of productivity growth has not yet succeeded in invading every sector of the U.S. economy. In particular, the process of college teaching seems to have been able to escape the cost-reducing ability of productivity

**FIGURE 3-13**

**Work Time Needed to Buy a College Education, 1965 versus 1997**

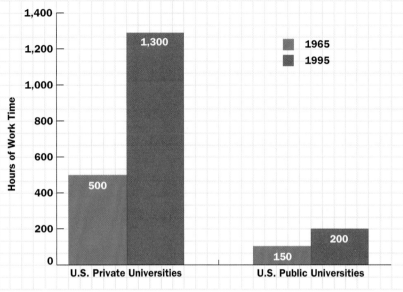

growth. Figure 3–13 shows the consequences. Between 1965 and 1995, the cost of a college education has risen 33 percent at public universities, whereas at private universities it has gone up by more than 150 percent, from 500 to 1,300 hours.

SOURCE: Federal Reserve Bank of Dallas, "Time Well Spent: The Declining *Real* Cost of Living in America," *1997 Annual Report*, 1997.

## WHAT'S MISSING FROM THE PICTURE? GOVERNMENT

Thus far we have the following capsule summary of how the U.S. economy works: About 22 million private businesses, energized by the profit motive, employ about 132 million workers and about $25 trillion of capital. These firms bring their enormously diverse wares to market, where they try to sell them to nearly 270 million consumers.

Households and businesses are linked in a tight circle, depicted in Figure 3–14. Firms use their receipts from sales to pay employee wages and interest and profits to people who provide capital. These income flows, in turn, enable consumers to purchase the goods and services that companies produce. This circular flow of money and goods lies at the center of the analysis of how the national economy works. All these activities are linked by a series of interconnected markets, some of which are highly competitive and others of which are less so.

All very well and good. But the story leaves out something important: the role of *government*, which is pervasive even in our decidedly free-market economy. Just what does government do in the U.S. economy—and why?

**FIGURE 3-14**

**The Circular Flow of Goods and Money**

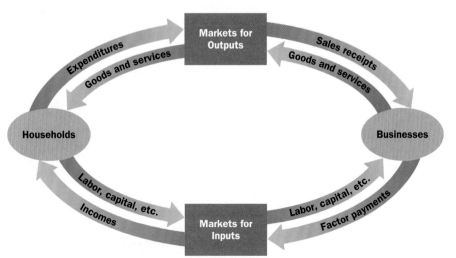

Although an increasing number of tasks seem to get assigned to the state each year, the traditional role of government in a market economy revolves around five jobs:

■ Providing certain goods and services such as national defense

■ Levying taxes to pay for these goods and services

■ Redistributing income

■ Regulating business

■ Making and enforcing the laws

Every one of these tasks is steeped in controversy and surrounded by intense political debate. We conclude this chapter with a brief look at the role of government.

## THE GOVERNMENT AS REFEREE

For the most part, power is diffused in our economy, and people "play by the rules." But, in the scramble for competitive advantage, disputes are bound to arise. Did Company A live up to its contract? Who owns that disputed piece of property? In addition, some unscrupulous businesses are liable to step over the line now and then—via misleading advertising, attempts to monopolize markets, employment of child labor, and the like.

Enter the government as rule maker, referee, and arbitrator. Congress and state and local legislatures pass the laws that define the rules of the economic game. The executive branches of all three governmental levels share the responsibility for enforcing them. And the courts interpret the laws and adjudicate disputes.

## THE GOVERNMENT AS BUSINESS REGULATOR

Nothing is pure in this world of ours. Even in "free-market" economies, governments interfere with the workings of free markets in many ways and for myriad reasons. Some government activities seek to make markets work better. For example, America's *antitrust laws* are used to protect competition against possible encroachment by monopoly. Some regulations seek to promote social objectives that unfettered markets do not foster—environmental regulations are a particularly clear case. But some economic regulations have no sensible economic rationale at all!

We mentioned earlier that the American belief in free enterprise runs deep. For this reason, the regulatory role of government is more contentious here than in most other countries. After all, Thomas Jefferson said that government is best which governs least. Two hundred years later, Presidents Reagan, Bush, and Clinton pledged to dismantle regulations—and sometimes did.

## GOVERNMENT EXPENDITURES

The most contentious political issues often involve taxing and spending because those are the government's most prominent roles. In 1995 and 1996, President Clinton and the Republican-led Congress battled fiercely over the federal budget. Differences over tax policies and spending cuts even led to some temporary shutdowns of the government. Since then, the federal government has achieved a surplus. For the first time in 30 years, its spending is less than its revenues, and the surplus is expected to continue for many years.

During fiscal year 1998, the federal government spent more than $1.6 *trillion*—a sum that is literally beyond comprehension. Figure 3–15 shows where the money went. Over one-third went for *pensions and income security* programs, which include both social insurance programs (like Social Security and unemployment compensation) and programs designed to assist the poor. About 16 percent went for *national defense*. Another 20 percent was absorbed by *health-care* expenditures, mainly on Medicare and Medicaid. Adding in *interest on the national debt*, these four functions alone accounted for about 88 percent of federal spending. The rest went for a miscellany of other purposes including education, transportation, agriculture, housing, and foreign aid.

Government spending at the state and local levels was about $1.2 trillion in 1996. Education claimed the biggest share of state and local government budgets (33 percent), with health and public welfare programs in second place (17 percent).

Despite this vast outpouring of public funds, many observers believe that serious social needs remain unmet. Critics claim that our public infrastructure (such as bridges and roads) is inadequate, that our educational system is lacking, that we do not do enough for the poor and homeless, and so on. Many people echoed these claims during the 1999 budget debate. The argument was over what should be done with the funds made available by the budget surplus. President Clinton proposed to spend part of it on financing Social Security and education. His Republican opponents argued that government already tries to do too much, and instead advocated a tax reduction.

Although government activity in the United States is substantial, it is quite moderate when we compare it to other leading economies. Figure 3–16 is a bar graph showing government expenditure as share of GDP for 10 countries. We see that the share of government in the U.S. economy is the lowest in this group of countries.

**FIGURE 3-15**

**The Allocation of Government Expenditures**

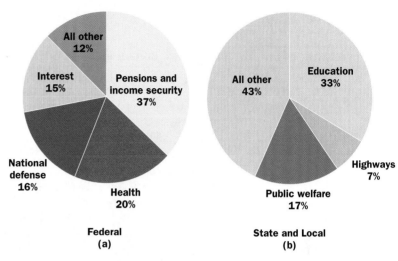

Federal
(a)

State and Local
(b)

SOURCE: *Economic Report of the President, 1999* (Washington, D.C.: U.S. Government Printing Office, February 1999).

**Government Spending as a Percentage of GDP, 1997**

**FIGURE 3-16**

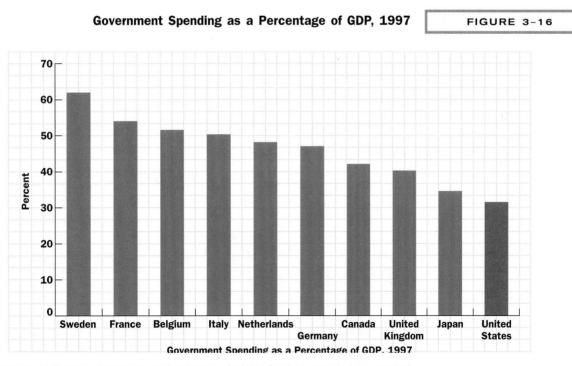

Government Spending as a Percentage of GDP, 1997

SOURCE: Organization for Economic Cooperation and Development, *Analytical Databank,* www.oecd.org, accessed January 1999.

## TAXES IN AMERICA

Taxes finance this array of goods and services, and sometimes it seems that the tax collector is everywhere. We have income and payroll taxes withheld from our paychecks, sales taxes added to our purchases, property taxes levied on our homes; we pay gasoline taxes, liquor taxes, and telephone taxes.

Americans have always felt that taxes are both too many and too high. In the 1980s and 1990s, antitax sentiment became a dominant feature of the U.S. political scene. The old slogan "no taxation without representation" gave way to the new slogan "no new taxes." Yet by international standards, Americans are among the most lightly taxed people in the world. Figure 3–17 compares the fraction of income paid in taxes in the United States with those paid by residents of other wealthy nations.

---

**FIGURE 3–17**

### The Tax Burden in Selected Countries, 1996

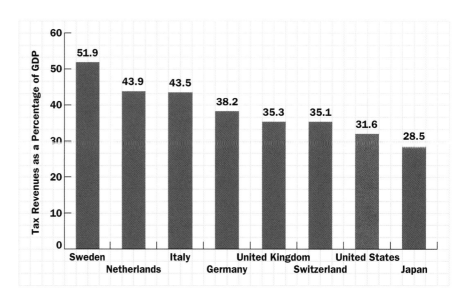

SOURCE: Organization for Economic Cooperation and Development, *Main Economic Indicators*, October 1998, www.oecd.org, accessed January 1999.

---

**FIGURE 3–18**

## Sources of Government Revenue

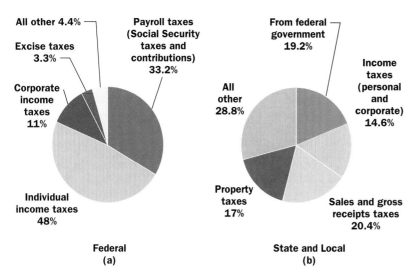

**Federal**
**(a)**

**State and Local**
**(b)**

SOURCE: *Economic Report of the President, 1999* (Washington, D.C.: U.S. Government Printing Office, February 1999).

How is this money raised? The *personal income tax* is the federal government's biggest revenue source, though the *payroll tax*—a flat-rate tax on wages and salaries up to a certain limit—is not far behind. The rest of federal revenue comes mainly from the *corporate income tax*. Most states and many large cities levy broad-based *sales taxes* on retail purchases, with certain specific exemptions (such as food and rent). Local governments generally raise revenue by levying *property taxes* on homes and business properties. Figure 3–18 shows the breakdown of revenue sources at both the federal and state and local levels.

### THE GOVERNMENT AS REDISTRIBUTOR

In a market economy, people earn incomes according to what they have to sell. Unfortunately, many people have nothing to sell but unskilled labor, which commands a paltry price. Others lack even that. Such people fare poorly in unfettered markets. In extreme cases, they are homeless, hungry, and ill. Robin Hood transferred money from the rich to the poor. Some think the government should do the same; others disagree.

If poverty amidst riches offends your moral sensibilities—a personal judgment that each of us must make—two basic remedial approaches are possible. The socialist idea is to force the distribution of income to be more equal by overriding the decisions of the market. "From each according to his ability, to each according to his needs" was Marx's ideal. In practice, things were not quite so noble under socialism. But there is little doubt that incomes in the old Soviet Union were more equally distributed than those in the United States.

The liberal idea is to let free markets determine the distribution of *before-tax* incomes, but then to use the tax system and **transfer payments** to reduce inequality—just as Robin Hood did. This is the rationale for, among other things, **progressive taxation** and the antipoverty programs colloquially known as "welfare." Americans who support redistribution line up solidly behind the liberal approach. But which ways are the best, and how much is enough? No simple answers emerge from debate on these highly contentious questions.

> **Transfer payments** are sums of money that certain individuals receive as outright grants from the government rather than as payments for services rendered.
>
> A tax is **progressive** if the ratio of taxes to income rises as income rises.

## ■ CONCLUSION: THE MIXED ECONOMY

Ideology notwithstanding, all nations at all times blend public and private ownership of property in some proportions. All rely on markets for some purposes, but all also assign some role to government. Hence, people speak of the ubiquity of **mixed economies.** But mixing is not homogenization; different countries can and do blend the state and market sectors in different ways. Even today, the Russian economy is a far cry from the Italian economy, which is vastly different from that of Hong Kong.

> A **mixed economy** is one with some public influence over the workings of free markets. There may also be some public ownership mixed in with private property.

While most of you were in elementary school, a stunning historical event occurred: Communism collapsed all over Europe. Now the formerly socialist economies are in the midst of a painful transition from a system in which private property, free enterprise, and markets played subsidiary roles to one in which they are central. These nations are changing the mix, if you will—and dramatically so. To understand why this transformation is at once so difficult and so important, we need to explore the main theme of this book: *What does the market do well, and what does it do poorly?* This task begins in the next chapter.

## SUMMARY

1. The U.S. economy is the biggest national economy on earth, both because Americans are rich by world standards and because we are a populous nation. Relative to most other advanced countries, our economy is also exceptionally "privatized" and *closed.*

2. The U.S. economy has grown dramatically over the years. But this growth is exaggerated by looking only at dollar figures, which are distorted by both *inflation* and population growth. To get a better understanding of the growth of living standards, we must look at *real GDP per capita.*

3. The growth path of the U.S. economy has been interrupted by periodic *recessions*, during which unemployment rises.

4. The United States has a big, diverse workforce whose composition by age and sex has been changing substantially. Relatively few workers these days work in factories or on farms; most work in service industries.

5. Employees take home most of the nation's income. Most of the rest goes, in the forms of interest and profits, to those who provide the capital.

6. Productivity and per-capita incomes in the United States and other industrialized countries have grown at rates and reached levels never before achieved in human history.

7. Governments at the federal, state, and local levels employ one-seventh of the American workforce. They finance their expenditures by taxes, which account for about 32 percent of GDP. This percentage is one of the lowest in the industrialized world.

8. In addition to raising taxes and making expenditures, the government in a market economy serves as referee and enforcer of the rules, regulates business in a variety of ways, and redistributes income through taxes and *transfer payments.* For all these reasons, we say that we have a *mixed economy*, which blends private and public elements.

---

### KEY TERMS

| | | |
|---|---|---|
| Factors of Production   32 | Open economy   34 | Productivity   43 |
| Inputs   32 | Closed economy   34 | Transfer payments   49 |
| Outputs   32 | Real GDP per capita   35 | Progressive tax   49 |
| Gross domestic product (GDP)   32 | Recession   36 | Mixed economy   49 |

---

### QUESTIONS FOR REVIEW

1. Which are the two biggest national economies on earth? Why are they so much bigger than the others?

2. What is meant by a "factor of production?" Have you ever sold any on a market?

3. Why do you think per-capita income in Connecticut is nearly double that in Mississippi?

4. Roughly speaking, what fraction of U.S. labor works in factories? In service businesses? In government?

5. It sounds paradoxical to say that most American businesses are small, but most of the output is produced by large businesses. How can this be true?

6. If your purchasing power were reduced by 90 percent, to a 1900 level, what purchases would you give up?

7. What is the role of government in a mixed economy?

*Our necessities are few but our wants are endless.*

Fortune cookie inscription

# SCARCITY AND CHOICE: *THE* ECONOMIC PROBLEM

Understanding what the market system does well and what it does badly is this book's central task. But to address this complex question, we must first answer a simpler one: What do economists expect the market to accomplish?

The most common answer is that the market resolves what is often called *the* fundamental economic problem: All decisions are constrained by the scarcity of available resources. A dreamer may envision a world free of want, in which everyone drives a BMW and eats caviar, but the earth lacks the resources needed to make that dream come true.

Because resources are scarce, all economic decisions involve *trade-offs.* Should you use that $5 bill to buy a hoagie or some new diskettes for your computer files? Should General Motors invest more money in assembly lines or in research? A well-functioning market system facilitates and guides such decisions, assigning each hour of labor and each kilowatt-hour of electricity to the task where, it is hoped, the input will best serve the public.

This chapter shows how economists analyze choices like these. The same basic principles, based on the concept of *opportunity cost,* apply to the decisions of business firms, governments, and society as a whole. Many of the most basic ideas of economics, such as *efficiency, division of labor, comparative advantage, exchange,* and *the role of markets* appear here for the first time.

## What to Do with the Budget Surplus?

For years, the United States government struggled to cope with a large budget deficit that illustrated all too vividly how scarce public funds really were. Existing programs had to be cut back, and new programs were extremely difficult to finance. Presidents Reagan, Bush, and Clinton all struggled with Congress over tax and spending priorities. Then, in 1997 and 1998, the budget deficit melted away like a spring snow, and a $70 billion surplus appeared. That sounds like a lot of money. At last, you might think, budget battles would become a thing of the past.

Not so. In fact, President Clinton and Congress engaged in fierce political combat during 1998 and 1999 over how to "spend" the budget surplus. Many Republican members of Congress wanted substantial tax cuts. Other legislators argued that certain long-neglected spending priorities had higher priority. But the president objected, insisting that most of the money be reserved to put Social Security on a firm financial footing. Yes, $70 billion was a tidy sum. But it was not nearly enough to accomplish all three objectives. The necessity of making hard choices had not disappeared just because the budget showed a surplus.

Even when resources are quite generous, they are never unlimited. So everyone must still make tough choices. An *optimal* decision is one that chooses the most desirable alternative *among the possibilities permitted by the available resources,* which are always scarce in this sense.

## ■ SCARCITY, CHOICE, AND OPPORTUNITY COST

**Resources** are the instruments provided by nature or by people that are used to create goods and services. Natural resources include minerals, the soil, water, and air. Labor is a scarce resource, partly because of time limitations (the day has only 24 hours) and partly because the number of skilled workers is limited. Factories and machines are resources made by people. These three types of resources are often referred to as *land, labor,* and *capital.* They are also called *inputs* or *factors of production.*

One of the basic themes of economics is scarcity: the fact that **resources** are always limited. Even Philip II, of Spanish Armada fame and ruler of one of the greatest empires in history, had to cope with frequent rebellions when he could not meet the payroll or even provide basic provisions. In more recent years, the U.S. government has been agonizing over difficult budget decisions even though it spends more than 1.7 trillion dollars annually! That's $1,700,000,000,000.

But the scarcity of *physical resources* is more fundamental than the scarcity of funds. Fuel supplies, for example, are not limitless, and some environmentalists claim that we should now be making some hard choices—such as keeping our homes cooler in winter and warmer in summer and living closer to our jobs. Although energy may be the most widely discussed scarcity, the general principle applies to all the earth's resources—iron, copper, uranium, and so on. Even goods produced by human effort are in limited supply because they require fuel, labor, and other scarce resources as inputs. We can manufacture more cars, but the increased use of labor, steel, and fuel in auto production will mean that we must cut back on something else, perhaps the production of refrigerators. This all adds up to the following fundamental principle of economics, one we will encounter again and again in this text.

Virtually all resources are *scarce,* meaning that humanity has less of them than we would like. Therefore, choices must be made among a *limited* set of possibilities, in full recognition of the inescapable fact that a decision to have more of one thing means that we will have less of something else.

In fact, one popular definition of economics is the study of how best to use *limited* means to pursue *unlimited* ends. Although this definition, like any short statement, cannot possibly cover the sweep of the entire discipline, it does convey the flavor of the economist's stock in trade.

To illustrate the true cost of an item, consider the decision to produce additional cars, and therefore fewer refrigerators. Although the production of a car may cost $15,000 per vehicle, or some other amount, *its real cost to society is the refrigerators that society must forgo to get an additional car.* If the labor, steel, and energy needed to manufacture a car are sufficient to make 30 refrigerators, the **opportunity cost** of a car is 30 refrigerators. The principle of opportunity cost is so important that we will spend most of this chapter elaborating on it in various ways.

**THE PRINCIPLE OF OPPORTUNITY COST** Economics examines the options available to households, businesses, governments, and entire societies, given the limited resources at their command. It studies the logic of how people can make **rational decisions** from among competing alternatives. One overriding principle governs this logic—a principle we introduced in Chapter 1 as one of the *Ideas for Beyond the Final Exam:*

With limited resources, a decision to have *more* of one thing is simultaneously a decision to have *less* of something else. Hence, the relevant *cost* of any decision is its *opportunity cost*—the value of the next best alternative that is given up. Rational decision making must be based on opportunity-cost calculations.

*How Much Does It Really Cost?*

## OPPORTUNITY COST AND MONEY COST

Because we live in a market economy where (almost) everything has its price, students often wonder about the connection or difference between an item's *opportunity cost* and its *market price.* What we just said seems to divorce the two concepts: The true *opportunity cost* of a car is not its market price but the value of the other things (like refrigerators) that could have been made or purchased instead.

But isn't the opportunity cost of a car related to its money cost? The normal answer is yes. The two concepts of cost are usually closely tied because of the way a market economy sets prices. Steel, for example, is used to manufacture both automobiles and refrigerators. If consumers value items that can be made with steel (such as refrigerators) highly, then economists would say that the *opportunity cost* of making a car is high. But, under these circumstances, a well-functioning price system will assign a high price to steel, which will therefore make the *money cost* of manufacturing a car high as well. In summary:

If the market functions well, goods that have high opportunity costs will also have high money costs, and goods whose opportunity costs are low will also have low money costs.

Yet it would be a mistake to treat opportunity costs and explicit monetary costs as identical. For one thing, sometimes the market does not function well, and hence assigns prices that do not accurately reflect opportunity costs.

Moreover, some valuable items may not bear explicit price tags at all. We encountered one such example in Chapter 1, where we noted that the opportunity cost of a college education may differ sharply from its explicit money cost. Why? Because one important item is typically omitted from the money-cost calculation: the *market value of your time,* that is, the wages you could earn by working instead of attending college. Because you give up these potential wages, which might amount to $15,000 a year or more, in order to acquire an education, they must be counted as a major part of the opportunity cost of going to college.

Other common examples where money costs and opportunity costs diverge are goods and services that are given away "free." For example, some early settlers of the American West destroyed natural amenities such as forests and buffalo herds, which had no market price, leaving later generations to pay the opportunity costs in terms of lost resources. Similarly, you incur no explicit monetary cost to acquire

The **opportunity cost** of any decision is the value of the next best alternative that the decision forces the decision maker to forgo.

A **rational decision** is one that best serves the objectives of the decision maker, whatever those objectives may be. Such objectives may include a firm's desire to maximize its profits, a government's desire to maximize the welfare of its citizens, or another government's desire to maximize its military might. The term *rational* connotes neither approval nor disapproval of the objective itself.

an item that is given away free. But if crowds turn up to demand the "free" commodity, you incur an opportunity cost equal to the value of the next best use of your time.

## SCARCITY AND CHOICE FOR A SINGLE FIRM

The nature of opportunity cost is perhaps clearest in the case of a single business firm that produces two outputs from a fixed supply of inputs. Given current technology and the limited resources at its disposal, the more of one good the firm produces, the less of the other it will be able to make. Unless managers explicitly weigh the desirability of each against the other, they are unlikely to make rational production decisions.

Consider the example of Farmer Jones, whose available supplies of land, machinery, labor, and fertilizer are capable of producing the various combinations of soybeans and wheat listed in Table 4–1. Obviously, devoting more resources to soybean production means that Farmer Jones will produce less wheat.

Table 4–1 indicates, for example, that if Jones grows only soybeans, the harvest will be 40,000 bushels. But, if he reduces soybean production to 30,000 bushels, he can also grow 38,000 bushels of wheat. Thus, *the opportunity cost of obtaining 38,000 bushels of wheat is 10,000 fewer bushels of soybeans.* Put another way, the opportunity cost of 10,000 more bushels of soybeans is 38,000 bushels of wheat. The other numbers in Table 4–1 have similar interpretations.

### FIGURE 4–1

**Production Possibilities Frontier for Production by a Single Firm**

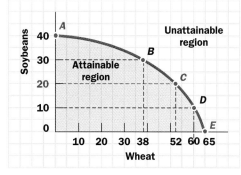

NOTE: Quantities are in thousands of bushels per year.

A **production possibilities frontier** shows the different combinations of various goods that a producer can turn out, given the available resources and existing technology.

## THE PRODUCTION POSSIBILITIES FRONTIER

Figure 4–1 presents this same information graphically. Point *A* corresponds to the first line of Table 4–1, point *B* to the second line, and so on. Curves similar to *AE* appear frequently in this book; they are called **production possibilities frontiers.** Any point *on or inside* the production possibilities frontier is attainable. Points *outside* the frontier cannot be achieved with the available resources and technology.

Because resources are limited, the production possibilities frontier always slopes downward to the right. The farmer can *increase* wheat production (move to the right in Figure 4–1) only by devoting more land and labor to growing wheat. But this simultaneously *reduces* soybean production (moves downward) because less land and labor remain available for growing soybeans.

Notice that, in addition to having a negative slope, our production possibilities frontier *AE* has another characteristic; it is "bowed outward." What does this curvature mean?

Suppose Farmer Jones initially produces only soybeans, using even land that is best suited for wheat cultivation (point *A*). Now he decides to switch some land from soybean production into wheat production. Which part of the land will he switch? If Jones is sensible, he will use the part best suited to growing wheat. As he shifts to point *B*, soybean production falls from 40,000 bushels to 30,000 bushels as wheat production rises from zero to 38,000 bushels. A sacrifice of only 10,000 bushels of soybeans "buys" 38,000 bushels of wheat.

Imagine now that the farmer wants to produce still more wheat. Figure 4–1 tells us that the sacrifice of an additional 10,000 bushels of soybeans (from 30,000 down to 20,000) will yield only 14,000 more bushels of wheat (see point *C*). Why? The main reason is *that inputs tend to be specialized.* As we noted, at point *A*, the farmer was using resources for soybean production that were actually more suitable for growing wheat. Consequently, their productivity in soybean production was low. When these resources are switched to wheat production, the yield is high.

**Production Possibilities Open to a Farmer**

TABLE 4-1

| Bushels of Soybeans | Bushels of Wheat | Label in Figure 4-1 |
|---|---|---|
| 40,000 | 0 | A |
| 30,000 | 38,000 | B |
| 20,000 | 52,000 | C |
| 10,000 | 60,000 | D |
| 0 | 65,000 | E |

But this cannot continue forever. As more wheat is produced, the farmer must utilize land and machinery that are better suited to producing soybeans and less well-suited to producing wheat. This is why the first 10,000 bushels of soybeans forgone "buys" the farmer 38,000 bushels of wheat, whereas the second 10,000 bushels of soybeans "buys" only 14,000 bushels of wheat. Figure 4-1 and Table 4-1 show that these returns continue to decline as wheat production expands: The next 10,000-bushel reduction in soybean production yields only 8,000 bushels of additional wheat, and so on.

The **principle of increasing costs** states that as the production of a good expands, the opportunity cost of producing another unit generally increases.

We can now see that the *slope* of the production possibilities frontier graphically represents the concept of *opportunity cost*. Between points C and B, for example, the opportunity cost of acquiring 10,000 additional bushels of soybeans is 14,000 bushels of forgone wheat; between points B and A, the opportunity cost of 10,000 bushels of soybeans is 38,000 bushels of forgone wheat. In general, as we move upward to the left along the production possibilities frontier (toward more soybeans and less wheat), the opportunity cost of soybeans in terms of wheat increases. Putting the same thing differently, as we move downward to the right, the opportunity cost of acquiring wheat by giving up soybeans increases.

## THE PRINCIPLE OF INCREASING COSTS

We have just described a very general phenomenon with applications well beyond farming. The **principle of increasing costs** states that as the production of one good expands, the opportunity cost of producing another unit of this good generally increases.

This principle is not a universal fact—exceptions do arise. But it does seem to be a technological regularity that applies to a wide range of economic activities. As our farming example suggests, the principle of increasing costs is based on the fact that resources tend to be at least somewhat specialized. So we lose some of their productivity when they are transferred from doing what they are relatively *good* at to what they are relatively *bad* at. In terms of diagrams such as Figure 4-1, the principle simply asserts that the production possibilities frontier is bowed outward.

Perhaps the best way to understand this idea is to contrast it with a case in which no resources are specialized. Figure 4-2 depicts a production possibilities frontier for producing black shoes and brown shoes. Because the labor and capital used to produce black shoes are just as good at producing brown shoes, the frontier is a straight line. If the firm cuts back its production of black shoes by 10,000 pairs, it gets 10,000 additional pairs of brown shoes. It loses no productivity in the switch because resources are not specialized.

More typically, however, as a firm concentrates more and more of its productive capacity on one commodity, it is forced to employ inputs that are better suited to making another commodity. The firm is forced to vary the *proportions* in which it

FIGURE 4-2

**Production Possibilities Frontier with No Specialized Resources**

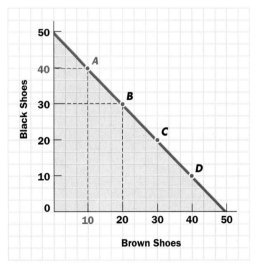

NOTE: Quantities are in thousands of pairs per week.

uses inputs because of the limited quantities of some of the inputs it uses. This fact also explains the typical curvature of the firm's production possibilities frontier.

## ■ SCARCITY AND CHOICE FOR THE ENTIRE SOCIETY

Like an individual firm, the entire economy is also constrained by its limited resources and technology. If society wants more aircraft and tanks, it will have to give up some boats and automobiles. If it wants to build more factories and stores, it will have to build fewer homes and sports arenas. In general:

The position and shape of the production possibilities frontier that constrains society's choices are determined by the economy's physical resources, its skills and technology, its willingness to work, and how much it has devoted in the past to the construction of factories, research, and innovation.

Because so many nations have debated whether to reduce or augment military strength for so long, let us illustrate the nature of society's choices by the example of choosing between military might (represented by missiles) and civilian consumption (represented by automobiles). Just like a single firm, the economy as a whole faces a production possibilities frontier for missiles and autos, determined by its technology and the available resources of land, labor, capital, and raw materials. This production possibilities frontier may look like curve *BC* in Figure 4–3. If most workers are employed in auto plants, car production will be large, but the output of missiles will be small. If society transfers resources out of auto manufacturing, it can alter the output mix toward more missiles (the move from *D* to *E*). However, something is likely to be lost in the process because physical resources are specialized. The fabric used to make car seats will not help much in missile production. The principle of increasing costs strongly suggests that the production possibilities frontier curves downward toward the axes.

We may even reach a point where the only resources left are not very useful outside of auto manufacturing. In that case, even a large sacrifice of automobiles will get the economy few additional missiles. That is the meaning of the steep segment, *FC*, on the frontier. At point *C* there is little additional output of missiles as compared to point *F*, even though at *C* automobile production has been given up entirely.

The downward slope of society's production possibilities frontier implies that hard choices must be made. Civilian consumption (automobiles) can be increased only by decreasing military expenditure, not by rhetoric nor by wishing it so. The curvature of the production possibilities frontier implies that, as defense spending increases, it becomes progressively more expensive to "buy" additional military strength ("missiles") by sacrificing civilian consumption.

**FIGURE 4-3**

**Production Possibilities Frontier for the Entire Economy**

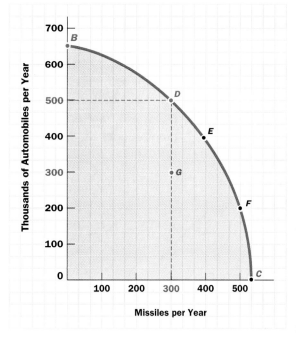

Missiles per Year

### SCARCITY AND CHOICE ELSEWHERE IN THE ECONOMY

We have emphasized that limited resources force hard choices on business managers and society as a whole. But the same type of choices arise elsewhere—in households, universities, and other nonprofit organizations, as well as the government.

The nature of opportunity cost is perhaps most obvious for a household that must decide how to divide its income among the goods and services that compete for the family's attention. If the Simpson family buys an expensive new car, it may be forced to cut back sharply on some other purchases. This fact does not make it unwise to buy the car. But it does make it unwise to buy the car until the family considers the

## ● THE MILITARY-CIVILIAN OUTPUT TRADE-OFF IN REALITY

The arms race may have ground to a halt, but space-age technology that helped keep the peace for 50 years is now being channeled in new directions. Literally hundreds of companies have had to face the new reality: Find other applications for current products, or perish.

The innovations have been spectacular. A rocket parts plant in Colorado developed a racing bike frame made from thermoplastic and reinforced carbon fiber. Composite materials, including boron filaments, graphites, and carbon fibers, have long been principal components in jet aircraft. Today, they are as likely to be found in golf club shafts, tennis rackets, ski poles, and even hockey sticks. Racecar companies are trying to take advantage of strong, lightweight materials in car designs.

Spillover benefits haven't been limited to the sports industry. E-Systems, which still does big defense business, demonstrated an innovative touch by adapting spy satellite technology to improve tumor-detection capabilities in mammograms. New uses have even been found for shuttered military bases. San Francisco's Treasure Island Naval Station, for example, is now being used as a movie studio.

SOURCES: Tim Smart, "Beating Swords into Golf Clubs?" *Business Week,* April 18, 1994, p. 85; "Uncle Sam's Fire Sales," *U.S. News & World Report,* January 9, 1995; "Aerospace and Defense," *Forbes,* January 3, 1994, p. 106.

full implications for its overall budget. If the Simpsons are to utilize their limited resources most effectively, they must explicitly acknowledge that the opportunity costs of the car are the things they will forgo as a result—perhaps a vacation and an expensive new TV set.

### Allocating the Budget Surplus

Even a rich and powerful nation like the United States must cope with the limitations implied by scarce resources. The necessity for choice imposed on governments by their limited budgets is similar in character to the problems faced by business firms and households. For the goods and services that it buys from others, a government must prepare a budget similar to that of a very large household. For the items it produces itself—education, police protection, libraries, and so on—it faces a production possibilities frontier much like a business firm does. Even though the U.S. government will spend over $1.7 trillion in 1999, some of the most acrimonious debates between President Clinton and the Congress arise from disagreements about how the government's limited resources should be allocated among competing uses. Even if unstated, the concept of opportunity cost has been central to these debates.

## APPLICATION: ECONOMIC GROWTH IN THE UNITED STATES AND THE ASIAN "TIGERS"

Any nation must make one extremely important decision that illustrates the concept of opportunity cost particularly well. This choice is embodied in the question "How fast should the economy grow?" At first, the question may seem ridiculous. Because

**Economic growth** occurs when an economy is able to produce more goods and services for each consumer.

**economic growth** means, roughly speaking, that the average citizen gets more and more goods and services, is it not self-evident that faster growth is always better?

Again, the fundamental problem of scarcity looms large. Economies do not grow by magic. Resources must be devoted to the growth process, and all resources are scarce. Cement and steel that might have been used to make swimming pools must be diverted to building factories. Wood that could have been used to make skis must be used for ladders instead. By deciding how much of its resources to devote to *future* needs rather than to *current* consumption, society in effect *chooses* (within limits) how fast it will grow.

In diagrammatic terms, economic growth means that the economy's production possibilities frontier shifts outward over time—like the move from *FF* to *GG* in Figure 4–4(a). Why? Because an outward shift means that the economy can produce more of both outputs. Thus, after growth has occurred, it is possible to produce the combination of products represented by points like *N*, which were impossible before growth. Point *N*, lying outside the economy's original production possibilities frontier, was beyond its means.

How does growth occur? That is, what shifts an economy's production frontier outward? There are many answers. For example, workers may acquire skills and training that enable them to produce more output in an hour. Or the economy may build more factories and machinery, giving up some consumption goods to free up the necessary resources. Finally, inventions like the steam engine, AC electricity, and computers can and *do* increase the economy's productive capacity, thereby shifting its production possibilities frontier outward. However, to improve its technology, the economy must devote more resources to research and development.

A **consumption good** is an item that is available for immediate use by households, one that satisfies people's wants without contributing directly to the economy's future production.

A **capital good** is an item used to produce other goods and services in the future, rather than being consumed today. Factories and machines are examples.

Figure 4–4 illustrates the nature of the choice for two different countries by depicting production possibilities frontiers for **consumption goods,** which people consume today (like food and electricity), versus **capital goods,** which can produce larger outputs for future consumption (like reapers and electricity-generating plants). Figure 4–4(a) depicts a society like the United States, which devotes a relatively small quantity of resources to growth, preferring current consumption instead. It chooses a point such as *A* on this year's production possibilities frontier, *FF.* At *A,* consumption is relatively high and production of capital is relatively low, so the production possibilities frontier shifts only to *GG* next year.

| FIGURE 4–4 | **Growth in Two Economies** |

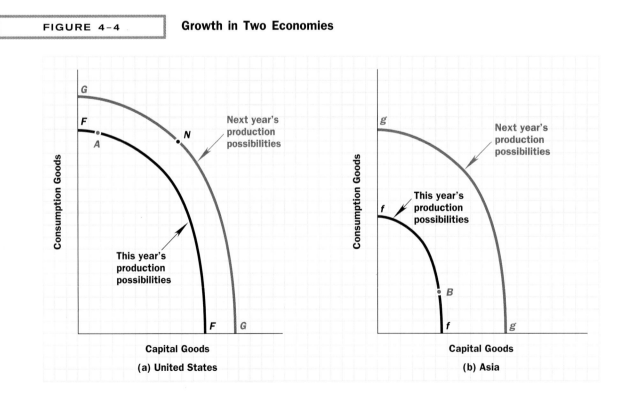

(a) United States

(b) Asia

Figure 4–4(b) depicts a society, such as one of the Asian Tiger economies (Korea, Singapore, Hong Kong, and Taiwan are good examples), that is much more enamored of growth. It selects a point like *B* on its production possibilities frontier, *ff*. At *B*, consumption is much lower and production of capital goods is much higher, so its production possibilities frontier moves all the way to *gg* by next year. Asia grows faster than the United States. But the more rapid growth has a price—an *opportunity cost:* Asian citizens must give up some of the current consumption that Americans enjoy.[1]

An economy grows by giving up some current consumption and producing capital goods for the future instead. The more capital it produces, the faster its production possibilities frontier will shift outward over time.

## ■ THE CONCEPT OF EFFICIENCY

So far our discussion of scarcity and choice has assumed that either the firm or the economy always operates on its production possibilities frontier rather than *below* it. In other words, we have tacitly assumed that, whatever the firm or economy decides to do, it does so *efficiently*.

Economists define *efficiency* as the absence of waste. An efficient economy utilizes all of its available resources and produces the maximum amount of output that its technology permits.

To see why any point on the economy's production possibilities frontier in Figure 4–3 represents an efficient decision, suppose for a moment that society has decided to produce 300 missiles. The production possibilities frontier tells us that if 300 missiles are to be produced, then the maximum number of automobiles that can be made is 500,000 (point *D* in Figure 4–3). The economy is therefore operating efficiently if it actually produces 500,000 automobiles rather than some smaller amount such as 300,000 (as at point *G*).

Point *D* is efficient, but point *G* is not, because the economy is capable of moving from *G* up to *D*, thereby producing 200,000 more automobiles without giving up any missiles (or anything else). Clearly, failure to take advantage of the option of choosing point *D* rather than point *G* constitutes a wasted opportunity—an inefficiency.

Note that the concept of efficiency does not tell us which point on the production possibilities frontier is *best*. It tells us only that any point that is *below* the frontier cannot be best, because any such point represents wasted resources. For example, should society ever find itself at a point like *G*, the necessity of making hard choices would (temporarily) disappear. It would be possible to increase production of *both* missiles *and* automobiles by moving to a point such as *E*.

Why, then, would a society ever find itself at a point below its production possibilities frontier? Why are resources wasted in real life? The most important reason in today's economy is *unemployment*. When many workers are unemployed, the economy finds itself at a point like *G*, below the frontier, because by putting the unemployed to work in both industries, the economy could produce both more missiles *and* more automobiles. The economy would then move from point *G* to the right (more missiles) and upward (more automobiles) toward a point such as *E* on the production possibilities frontier. Only when no resources are wasted is the economy on the frontier.

Inefficiency occurs in other ways, as well. One prime example is assigning inputs to the wrong task—as when wheat is grown on land best suited to soybean cultivation. Another important type of inefficiency occurs when large firms produce goods that smaller enterprises could make better because they can pay closer attention to

---

[1] A number of economists have argued that the Asian Tigers took this process too far, devoting *too many* resources to growth and not enough to current consumption.

detail, or when small firms produce outputs best suited to large-scale production. Some other examples are the outright waste that occurs because of favoritism (for example, promotion of an incompetent brother-in-law) or restrictive labor practices (for example, requiring a railroad to keep a fireman on a diesel-electric locomotive where there is nothing for him to do).

A particularly unfortunate form of waste is caused by discrimination against African-American, Hispanic, or female workers. When a job is given to a white male in preference to a more qualified African-American woman, society sacrifices potential output and the entire community is apt to be affected adversely. Every one of these inefficiencies means that the community obtains less output than it could have, given the available inputs.

## ■ THE THREE COORDINATION TASKS OF ANY ECONOMY

**Allocation of resources** refers to the society's decisions on how to divide up its scarce input resources among the different outputs produced in the economy and among the different firms or other organizations that produce those outputs.

In deciding how to **allocate its scarce resources,** every society must somehow make three sorts of decisions:

- ■ First, as we have emphasized, it must figure out *how to utilize its resources efficiently;* that is, it must find a way to reach its production possibilities frontier.
- ■ Second, it must decide *what combination of goods to produce*—how many missiles, automobiles, and so on; that is, it must select one specific point on the production possibilities frontier.
- ■ Third, it must decide *how much of each good to distribute to each person,* doing so in a sensible way that does not assign meat to vegetarians and wine to teetotalers.

Societies can and do make each of these decisions—which economists often refer to as *how, what,* and *to whom?*—in many ways. For example, a central planner might tell people how to produce, what to produce, and what to consume, as the authorities used to do, at least to some extent, in the former Soviet Union. But in a market economy, no one group or individual makes such resource allocation decisions explicitly. Rather, consumer demands and production costs allocate resources *automatically* and *anonymously* through a system of prices and markets. As the formerly socialist countries learned, markets do an impressively effective job in carrying out these tasks. To see how markets can do all this, let's consider each task in turn.

## ■ SPECIALIZATION FOSTERS EFFICIENT RESOURCE ALLOCATION

Production efficiency is one of the economy's three basic tasks, and societies pursue it in many ways. But one source of efficiency is so fundamental that we must single it out for special attention: the tremendous productivity gains that stem from *specialization*.

### THE WONDERS OF THE DIVISION OF LABOR

**Division of labor** means breaking up a task into a number of smaller, more *specialized* tasks so that each worker can become more adept at a particular job.

Adam Smith, the founder of modern economics, first marveled at how **division of labor** raises efficiency and productivity when he visited a pin factory. In a famous passage near the beginning of his monumental book, *The Wealth of Nations* (1776), he described what he saw:

> One man draws out the wire, another straightens it, a third cuts it, a fourth points it, a fifth grinds it at the top for receiving the head. To make the head requires two or three distinct operations; to put it on is a peculiar business, to whiten the pins is another; it is even a trade by itself to put them into the paper.[2]

---

[2] Adam Smith, *The Wealth of Nations* (New York: Random House, 1937), p. 4.

Smith observed that by dividing the work to be done in this way, each worker became quite skilled in a particular specialty, and the productivity of the group of workers as a whole was greatly enhanced. As Smith related it:

> I have seen a small manufactory of this kind where ten men only were employed. . . . Those ten persons . . . could make among them upwards of forty-eight thousand pins in a day. . . . But if they had all wrought separately and independently . . . they certainly could not each of them have made twenty, *perhaps not one pin in a day.*[3]

In other words, through the miracle of division of labor and specialization, ten workers accomplished what might otherwise have required thousands. This was one of the secrets of the Industrial Revolution, which helped lift humanity out of the abject poverty that had been its lot for centuries.

## THE AMAZING PRINCIPLE OF COMPARATIVE ADVANTAGE

But specialization in production fosters efficiency in an even more profound sense. Adam Smith noticed that *how* goods are produced can make a huge difference to productivity. But so can *which* goods are produced. The reason is that people (and businesses, and nations) have different abilities. Some can repair automobiles, whereas others are wizards with numbers. Some are handy with computers, and others can cook. An economy will be most efficient if people specialize in doing what they do best and then trade with one another, so the accountant gets her car repaired and the computer programmer gets to eat tasty and nutritious meals.

This much is obvious. What is less obvious—and is one of the great ideas of economics—is that two people (or two businesses, or two countries) can generally gain from trade *even if one of them is more efficient than the other in producing everything.* A simple parable will help explain why.

Some lawyers can type better than their administrative assistants. Should such a lawyer fire her assistant and do her own typing? Not likely. Even though the lawyer may type better than the assistant, good judgment tells her to concentrate on practicing law and leave the typing to a lower-paid assistant. Why? Because the *opportunity cost* of an hour devoted to typing is an hour less time spent with clients, which is a far more lucrative activity.

This example illustrates the principle of **comparative advantage** at work. The lawyer specializes in arguing cases despite her advantage as a typist because she has a *still greater* advantage as an attorney. She suffers some direct loss by leaving the typing to a less-efficient employee. But she more than makes up for that loss by the income she earns selling her legal services to clients.

One country is said to have a **comparative advantage** over another in the production of a particular good relative to other goods if it produces that good less inefficiently as compared with the other country.

Precisely the same principle applies to nations. As we shall learn in greater detail in the chapter on international trade, comparative advantage underlies the economic analysis of international trade patterns. A country that is particularly adept at producing certain items—such as aircraft manufacturing in the United States, coffee growing in Brazil, and oil extraction in Saudi Arabia—should specialize in those activities, producing more than it wants for its own use. The country can then take the money it earns from its exports and purchase from other nations items that it does not make for itself.

The underlying logic is precisely the same as in our lawyer-typist example. The United States might, for example, be better than Japan at manufacturing both computers and television sets. But if the United States is vastly more efficient at producing computers, but only slightly more efficient at making TV sets, it pays for the United States to specialize in computer manufacture, for Japan to specialize in TV production, and for the two countries to trade.[4]

---

[3] Ibid., p. 5.

[4] This particular example is considered in detail in the chapter that examines international trade.

This principle, called the *law of comparative advantage*, was discovered by David Ricardo, one of the giants in the history of economic analysis, almost 200 years ago. It is one of the *Ideas for Beyond the Final Exam* introduced in Chapter 1.

*The Surprising Principle of Comparative Advantage*

**THE LAW OF COMPARATIVE ADVANTAGE** Even if one country (or one worker) is worse than another country (or another worker) in the production of *every* good, it is said to have a *comparative advantage* in making the good at which it is *least inefficient*—compared to the other country. Ricardo discovered that two countries can gain by trading even if one country is more efficient than another in the production of *every* commodity. Precisely the same logic applies to individual workers or to businesses.

In determining the most efficient patterns of production and trade, it is comparative advantage that matters. Thus, a country can gain by importing a good from abroad even if that good can be produced more efficiently at home. Such imports make sense if they enable the country to specialize in producing goods at which it is *even more efficient*.

## ■ SPECIALIZATION LEADS TO EXCHANGE

The gains from specialization are welcome, but they create a problem: With specialization, people no longer produce only what they want to consume themselves. The workers in Adam Smith's pin factory had no use for the thousands of pins they produced each day; they wanted to trade them for things like food, clothing, and shelter. Similarly, the administrative assistant has no personal use for the legal briefs she types. Thus, specialization requires some mechanism by which workers producing pins can *exchange* their wares with workers producing such things as cloth and potatoes, and office workers can turn their typing skills into things they want to consume.

Without a system of exchange, the productivity miracle achieved by comparative advantage and the division of labor would do society little good. With it, standards of living have risen enormously. As we observed in Chapter 1, such exchange benefits *all* participants.

*Trade Is a Win-Win Situation*

**MUTUAL GAINS FROM VOLUNTARY EXCHANGE** Unless someone is deceived or misunderstands the facts, a *voluntary* exchange between two parties must make both parties better off—or else why would each party agree? Trading increases production by permitting specialization, as we have just seen. But even if no additional goods are produced as a result of the act of trading, the welfare of society is increased because each individual acquires goods that are more suited to his or her needs and tastes. This simple but fundamental precept of economics is another of our *Ideas for Beyond the Final Exam*.

Although people can and do trade goods for other goods, a system of exchange works better when everyone agrees to use some common item (such as pieces of paper with unique markings printed on them) for buying and selling things. Enter *money*. Then workers in pin factories, for example, can be paid in money rather than in pins, and they can use this money to purchase cloth and potatoes. Textile workers and farmers can do the same.

These two phenomena—specialization and exchange (assisted by money)—working in tandem led to vast improvements in humanity's well-being. But what forces induce workers to join together so that society can enjoy the fruits of the division of labor? And what forces establish a smoothly functioning system of exchange so that people can first exploit their comparative advantages and then acquire what they want to consume? One alternative is to have a central authority telling people what to do. But Adam Smith explained and extolled another way of organizing and coordinating economic activity—markets and prices can coordinate those activities.

## ■ MARKETS, PRICES, AND THE THREE COORDINATION TASKS

Smith noted that people are adept at pursuing their own self-interests, and that a **market system** harnesses this self-interest remarkably well. As he put it—with pretty clear religious overtones—in doing what is best for themselves, people are "led by an invisible hand" to promote the economic well-being of society as a whole.

Those of us who live in a well-functioning market economy like the United States tend to take the achievements of the market for granted, much like the daily rising and setting of the sun. Few bother to think about, say, what makes Florida oranges show up daily in South Dakota supermarkets. Although the process by which the market guides the economy in such an orderly fashion is subtle and complex, the general principles are well known.

The market deals with efficiency in production through the profit motive, which discourages firms from using inputs wastefully. Valuable resources (such as energy) command high prices, giving producers strong incentives to use them efficiently. The market mechanism also guides firms' output decisions, matching quantities produced to consumer preferences. A rise in the price of wheat because of increased demand for bread, for example, will persuade farmers to produce more wheat and devote less of their land to soybeans.

Finally, a price system distributes goods among consumers in accord with their tastes and preferences, using voluntary exchange to determine who gets what. Consumers spend their incomes on the things they like best (among those they can afford). But the ability to buy goods is hardly divided equally. Workers with valuable skills and owners of scarce resources can sell what they have at attractive prices. With the incomes they earn, they can purchase generous amounts of goods and services. Those who are less successful in selling what they own receive lower incomes and so can afford to buy less. In extreme cases, they may suffer severe deprivation.

This, in broad terms, is how a market economy solves the three basic problems facing any society: how to produce any given combination of goods efficiently, how to select an appropriate combination of goods to produce, and how to distribute these goods sensibly among people. As we proceed through the following chapters, you will learn much more about these issues. You will see that they constitute the central theme that permeates not only this text, but the work of economists in general. As you progress through the book, keep in mind two questions:

- ■ What does the market do well?
- ■ What does it do poorly?

There are numerous answers to both questions, as you will learn in subsequent chapters.

> Society has many important goals. Some of them, such as producing goods and services with maximum efficiency (minimum waste), can be achieved extraordinarily well by letting markets operate more or less freely.
>
> Free markets will not, however, achieve all of society's goals. For example, they often have trouble keeping unemployment low. In fact, the unfettered operations of markets may even run counter to some goals—such as protection of the environment. Many observers also believe that markets do not necessarily distribute income in accord with ethical or moral norms.
>
> But even in cases where markets do not perform at all well, there may be ways of harnessing the power of the market mechanism to remedy its own deficiencies, as you will learn in later chapters.

A **market system** is a form of economic organization in which resource allocation decisions are left to individual producers and consumers acting in their own best interests without central direction.

## ■ LAST WORD: DON'T CONFUSE ENDS WITH MEANS

Economic debates often have political and ideological overtones. So we think it important to close this chapter by emphasizing that the central theme that we have just outlined is neither a *defense of* nor an *attack on* the capitalist system. Nor is it a "conservative" position. One does not have to be a conservative to recognize that the market mechanism can be an extraordinarily helpful instrument for the pursuit of economic goals. Most of the formerly socialist countries of Europe have been working hard to "marketize" their economies, and even the communist People's Republic of China has taken huge strides in that direction.

The point is not to confuse ends with means in deciding how much to rely on market forces. Liberals and conservatives surely have different goals. But the means chosen to pursue these goals should, for the most part, be chosen on the basis of how effective they are, not on some ideological prejudgments.

Even Karl Marx emphasized that the market is remarkably efficient at producing an abundance of goods and services that had never been seen in precapitalist history. Such wealth can be used to promote conservative goals, such as reducing tax rates, or to facilitate goals favored by liberals, such as providing more generous public aid for the poor.

Certainly, the market cannot deal with every economic problem. Indeed, we have just noted that the market is the *source* of a number of significant problems. But the evidence accumulated over centuries leads economists to believe that most economic problems are best handled by market techniques. The analysis in this book is intended to help you identify both the objectives the market mechanism can reliably achieve and those that it will fail to promote, or at least not promote very effectively. We urge you to forget the slogans you have heard—whether from the left or from the right—and make up your own mind after learning the material in this book.

## S U M M A R Y

1. Supplies of all *resources* are limited. Because resources are scarce, a *rational decision* is one that chooses the best alternative among the options that are possible with the available resources.

2. With limited resources, a decision to obtain more of one item is also a decision to give up some of another. What we give up is called the *opportunity cost* of what we get. The opportunity cost is the true cost of any decision. This is one of the *Ideas for Beyond the Final Exam.*

3. When markets function effectively, firms are led to use resources efficiently and to produce the things that consumers want most. In such cases, opportunity costs and money costs (prices) correspond closely. When the market performs poorly, or when important costly items do not get price tags, opportunity costs and money costs can diverge.

4. A firm's *production possibilities frontier* shows the combinations of goods it can produce, given the current technology and the resources at its disposal. The frontier is usually bowed outward because resources tend to be specialized.

5. The *principle of increasing costs* states that as the production of one good expands, the opportunity cost of producing another unit of that good generally increases.

6. Like a firm, the economy as a whole has a production possibilities frontier whose position is determined by its technology and by the available resources of land, labor, capital, and raw materials.

7. A firm or an economy that ends up at a point below its production possibilities frontier is using its resources inefficiently or wastefully. This is what happens, for example, when there is unemployment.

8. *Economic growth* means there is an outward shift in the economy's production possibilities frontier. The faster the growth, the faster this shift occurs. But growth requires a sacrifice of current consumption—which is its opportunity cost.

9. Economists define *efficiency* as the absence of waste. It is achieved primarily by the gains in productivity brought about through *specialization* that exploits *division of labor* and *comparative advantage* and by a *system of exchange.*

10. Two countries (or two people) can gain by specializing in the activity in which each has a comparative advantage and then trading with one another. These gains from trade remain available even if one country is inferior at producing everything. This so-called *principle of comparative advantage* is one of our *Ideas for Beyond the Final Exam.*

11. If an exchange is voluntary, both parties must benefit, even if no additional goods are produced. This is another of the *Ideas for Beyond the Final Exam.*

12. Every economic system must find a way to answer three basic questions: How can goods be produced most efficiently? How much of each good should be produced? How should goods be distributed?

13. The *market system* works very well in solving some of society's basic problems, but it fails to remedy others and may, indeed, create some of its own. Where and how it succeeds and fails constitute the central theme of this book and characterize the work of economists in general.

---

### KEY TERMS

Resources   52

Scarcity   52

Choice   52

Opportunity cost   53

Rational decision   53

Outputs   54

Inputs (means of production)   54

Production possibilities frontier   54

Principle of increasing costs   55

Economic growth   58

Consumption good   58

Capital good   58

Efficiency   59

Allocation of resources   60

Three coordination tasks   60

Specialization   60

Division of labor   60

Comparative advantage   61

Exchange   62

Market system   63

---

### QUESTIONS FOR REVIEW

1. Discuss the resource limitations that affect:

    a. the poorest person on earth

    b. Bill Gates, the richest person in the United States

    c. a farmer in Kansas

    d. the government of Indonesia

2. If you were president of your college, what would you change if your budget were cut by 10 percent? By 25 percent? By 50 percent?

3. If you were to leave college, what things would change in your life? What, then, is the opportunity cost of your education?

4. A person rents a house for which she pays the landlord $12,000 a year. The house can be purchased for $100,000, and the tenant has this much money in a bank account that pays 4 percent interest per year. Is buying the house a good deal for the tenant? Where does opportunity cost enter the picture?

5. Construct graphically the production possibilities frontier for the nation of Stromboli, using the data given in the following table. Does the principle of increasing cost hold in Stromboli?

6. Consider two alternatives for Stromboli in the year 2000. In case (a), its inhabitants eat 60 million pizzas and build only 6,000 pizza ovens. In case (b), the population eats only 15 million pizzas but builds 18,000 ovens. Which case will lead to a more generous production possibilities frontier for Stromboli in 2001?

7. Sarah's Snack Shop sells two brands of potato chips. Brand X costs Sarah 60 cents per bag, and Brand Y costs Sarah $1. Draw Sarah's production possibilities frontier if she has $60 budgeted to spend on potato chips. Why is it not "bowed out"?

8. Raising chickens requires several types of feed, such as corn and soy meal. Consider a farm in the former Soviet Union. Try to describe how decisions on the number of chickens to be raised, and the amount of each feed to use in raising them, were made under the old communist regime. If the farm is now privately owned, how does the market guide the decisions that used to be made by the central planning agency?

9. The United States is one of the world's wealthiest countries. Think of a recent case in which the decisions of the U.S. government were severely constrained by scarcity. Describe the trade-offs that were involved. What were the opportunity costs of the decisions that were actually made?

**Stromboli's 2000 Production Possibilities**

| Pizzas per year | Pizza Ovens per year |
|---|---|
| 75,000,000 | 0 |
| 60,000,000 | 6,000 |
| 45,000,000 | 11,000 |
| 30,000,000 | 15,000 |
| 15,000,000 | 18,000 |
| 0 | 20,000 |

**The free enterprise system is absolutely too important to be left to the voluntary action of the marketplace.**

Florida Congressman Richard Kelly, 1979

# SUPPLY AND DEMAND: AN INITIAL LOOK

Scarcity, choice, and coordination constitute the basic problem of economics, as we saw in Chapter 4. In this chapter we study the most basic tool for investigation of these subjects: supply and demand. Whether your course concentrates on macroeconomics or microeconomics, you will find that it uses the so-called law of supply and demand as the fundamental tool of economic analysis. Economists use supply and demand analysis to study issues as diverse as inflation and unemployment, the international value of the dollar, government regulation of business, and environmental protection. So careful study of this chapter will pay rich dividends, both in this course and in any other economics courses you may take. Supply and demand curves—graphs that relate price to quantity supplied and quantity demanded, respectively—show how prices and quantities are determined in a free market.

One major theme of the chapter is that governments around the world and throughout recorded history have tampered with the price mechanism. We will see that these bouts with Adam Smith's invisible hand often have produced undesirable side effects that surprised and dismayed the authorities. The invisible hand fights back!

This chapter uses graphs such as those described in Chapter 2 extensively. If you have difficulties with these graphs, we suggest that you review the first part of that chapter before proceeding.

### What in the World Happened to Those Asian Currencies?

A worldwide financial crisis began in the last half of 1997, when the currencies of several Asian economies, including Thailand, Indonesia, Malaysia, and South Korea, plummeted in value. The most spectacular example was the fall of the Indonesian rupiah. In July 1997, it took about 2,500 rupiah to buy one U.S. dollar. By winter, it took about 10,000. This means that, relative to the dollar, the rupiah lost a stunning 75 percent of its value in just a few months.

What could have caused such a calamitous drop in the value of the rupiah? The answer is complicated, and not entirely rational. We shall have much more to say about the Asian economic crisis later in the book. But the essence of the rupiah's problem, as we shall see in this chapter, involved nothing more complex than the rudimentary law of supply and demand.

## ■ THE INVISIBLE HAND

The **invisible hand** is a phrase used by Adam Smith to describe how, by pursuing their own self-interests, people in a market system are "led by an invisible hand" to promote societal well-being.

Adam Smith greatly admired the price system. He marveled at its accomplishments—both as an efficient producer of goods and as a guarantor that consumers' preferences are obeyed. Many people since Smith's time have shared his enthusiasm for the concept of the **invisible hand,** but many have not. His contemporaries in the American colonies, for example, were often unhappy with the prices produced by free markets and thought they could do better by legislative decree. They could not,

## ● PRICE CONTROLS AT VALLEY FORGE

George Washington, the history books tell us, was beset by many enemies during the winter of 1777–1778, including the British, their Hessian mercenaries, and the merciless winter weather. But he had another enemy that the history books ignore, an enemy that meant well but almost destroyed his army at Valley Forge. As the following excerpt explains, that enemy was the Pennsylvania legislature.

In Pennsylvania, where the main force of Washington's army was quartered . . . the legislature . . . decided to try a period of price control limited to those commodities needed for use by the army. . . . The result might have been anticipated by those with some knowledge of the trials and tribulations of other states. The prices of uncontrolled goods, mostly imported, rose to record heights. Most farmers kept back their produce, refusing to sell at what they regarded as an unfair price. Some who had large families to take care of even secretly sold their food to the British who paid in gold.

After the disastrous winter at Valley Forge when Washington's army nearly starved to death (thanks largely to these well-intentioned but misdirected laws), the ill-fated experiment in price controls was finally ended. The Continental Congress on June 4, 1778, adopted the following resolution:

"Whereas . . . it hath been found by experience that limitations upon the prices of commodities are not only ineffectual for the purposes proposed, but likewise productive of very evil consequences . . . resolved, that it be recommended to the several states to repeal or suspend all laws or resolutions within the said states respectively limiting, regulating or restraining the Price of any Article, Manufacture or Commodity."

SOURCE: Robert L. Schuettinger and Eamonn F. Butler, *Forty Centuries of Wage and Price Controls* (Washington, D.C.: Heritage Foundation, 1979), p. 41. Reprinted by permission.

*Valley Forge*

as explained in the accompanying box, "Price Controls at Valley Forge." In countless other instances, the public was outraged by the prices charged on the open market, particularly in the case of housing rents, interest rates, and insurance rates.

Attempts to control interest rates (which are the price of borrowing money) go back hundreds of years before the birth of Christ, at least to the code of laws compiled under the Babylonian king Hammurabi in about 1800 B.C. Our historical legacy also includes a rather long list of price ceilings on foods and other products imposed in the reign of Diocletian, emperor of the declining Roman Empire. More recently, Americans have been offered the "protection" of a variety of price controls.

Laws have placed ceilings on some prices (such as rents) to protect buyers, whereas legislation has placed floors under other prices (such as farm products) to protect sellers. Yet, somehow, everything such regulation touches seems to end up in even greater disarray than it was before. Despite rent controls, rents in New York City have soared. Despite laws against "scalping," tickets for popular shows and sports events sell at tremendous premiums—tickets to the Super Bowl, for example, often fetch thousands of dollars on the "gray" market. Taxis cost much more in New York City (where they are tightly regulated) than in Washington, D.C. (where they are not).

To understand what goes wrong when markets are tampered with, we must first learn how they operate unfettered. This chapter takes a first step in that direction by studying the machinery of supply and demand. Then, at the end of the chapter, we return to the issue of price controls.

Every market has both buyers and sellers. We begin our analysis on the consumers' side of the market.

## ■ DEMAND AND QUANTITY DEMANDED

People commonly think of consumer demands as fixed amounts. For example, when product designers propose a new computer model, management asks: "What is its market potential?" Similarly, government bureaus conduct studies to determine how many engineers the workforce will require (demand) in subsequent years.

Economists respond that such questions are not well posed—that there is no single answer to such a question. Rather, they say, the "market potential" for computers or the number of engineers that will be "required" depends on a great number of influences, including the price charged for each.

The **quantity demanded** is the number of units of a good that consumers want to buy over a specified period of time.

> The **quantity demanded** of any product normally depends on its price. Quantity demanded also depends on a number of other determinants, including population size, consumer incomes, tastes, and the prices of other products.

Because prices play a central role in a market economy, we begin our study of demand by focusing on how quantity demanded depends on price. A little later, we will bring the other determinants of quantity demanded back into the picture. For now, we consider all influences other than price as fixed; this assumption, often stated as "other things being equal," holds for virtually any static economic analysis. Consider, as an example, the quantity of milk demanded. Almost everyone purchases at least some milk. However, if the price of milk is very high, its "market potential" may be very small. People will find ways to get along with less milk, perhaps by switching to fruit juice or soda. If the price of milk declines, people will tend to drink more milk. They may give their children larger portions or switch away from juices and sodas. Thus:

A **demand schedule** is a table showing how the quantity demanded of some product during a specified period of time changes as the price of that product changes, holding all other determinants of quantity demanded constant.

A **demand curve** is a graphical depiction of a demand schedule. It shows how the quantity demanded of some product during a specified period of time will change as the price of that product changes, holding all other determinants of quantity demanded constant.

A **shift in a demand curve** occurs when any variable other than price changes. If consumers want to buy *more* at any given price than they wanted previously, the demand curve shifts to the right (or outward). If they desire *less* at any given price, the demand curve shifts to the left (or inward).

> There is no one demand figure for milk, for computers, or for engineers. Rather, there is a different quantity demanded at each possible price, all other influences being held constant.

### THE DEMAND SCHEDULE

Table 5–1 displays this hypothetical information for milk in what we call a **demand schedule**. It indicates how much milk consumers in a particular area are willing and able to buy at different possible prices during a specified period of time, other things held equal. Specifically, the table shows the quantity of milk that will be demanded in a year at each possible price ranging from $1.50 to 90 cents per quart. We see, for example, that at a relatively low price, like $1 per quart, customers wish to purchase 70 billion quarts per year. But if the price were to rise to, say, $1.40 per quart, quantity demanded would fall to 50 billion quarts.

Common sense tells us why this happens.[1] First, as prices rise, some customers will reduce the quantity of milk they consume. Second, higher prices will induce

**TABLE 5–1**

**Demand Schedule for Milk**

| Price per Quart | Quantity Demanded | Label in Figure 5–1 |
| --- | --- | --- |
| $1.50 | 45 | A |
| 1.40 | 50 | B |
| 1.30 | 55 | C |
| 1.20 | 60 | E |
| 1.10 | 65 | F |
| 1.00 | 70 | G |
| 0.90 | 75 | H |

NOTE: Quantity is in billions of quarts per year.

---

[1] This common-sense answer is examined more fully in later chapters.

some customers to drop out of the market entirely—for example, by switching to soda or juice. On both counts, quantity demanded will decline as the price rises.

As the price of an item rises, the quantity demanded normally falls. As the price falls, the quantity demanded normally rises, all other things held constant.

## THE DEMAND CURVE

The information contained in Table 5–1 can be summarized in a graph like Figure 5–1, which is called a **demand curve.** Each point in the graph corresponds to a line in the table. This curve shows the relationship between price and quantity demanded. For example, to sell 70 billion quarts per year, the price must be one dollar. This is shown at point *G* in Figure 5–1. If, instead, the price is $1.40, consumers will demand only 50 billion quarts (point *B*). Because the quantity demanded declines as the price increases, the demand curve has a negative slope.[2]

Notice the last phrase in the definitions of the demand schedule and the demand curve: "holding all other determinants of quantity demanded constant." What are some of these "other things," and how do they affect the demand curve?

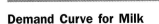

**FIGURE 5–1**

**Demand Curve for Milk**

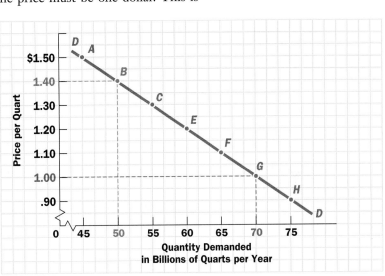

## SHIFTS OF THE DEMAND CURVE

The quantity of milk demanded is subject to a variety of influences other than the price of milk. Changes in population size and characteristics, consumer incomes and tastes, and the prices of alternative beverages such as soda and orange juice presumably change the quantity of milk demanded, even if the price of milk does not change.

Because the demand curve for milk depicts only the relationship between the quantity of milk demanded and the price of milk, holding all other factors constant, a change in any of these *other* factors produces a **shift of the entire demand curve.** More generally:

A change in the price of a good produces a movement *along* a fixed demand curve. By contrast, a change in any other variable that influences quantity demanded produces a shift of the *entire* demand curve.

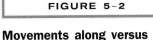

**FIGURE 5–2**

**Movements along versus Shifts of a Demand Curve**

If consumers want to buy more milk at every given price than they wanted previously, the demand curve shifts to the right (or outward). If they desire less at every given price, the demand curve shifts to the left (or inward toward the origin).

Figure 5–2 shows this distinction graphically. If the price of milk falls from $1.30 per quart to $1.10, and quantity demanded rises accordingly, we move along demand curve $D_0D_0$ from point *C* to point *F*, as shown by the blue arrow. If, on the other hand, consumers suddenly decide that they like milk better than they did formerly, or if more

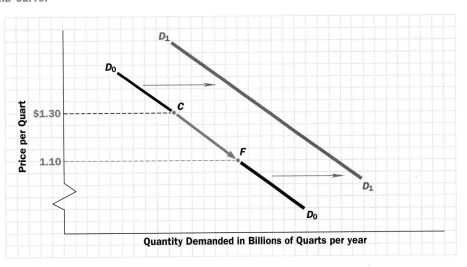

**Quantity Demanded in Billions of Quarts per year**

---

[2] If you need to review the concept of slope, refer back to Chapter 2.

children are born who need more milk, the entire demand curve shifts outward from $D_0D_0$ to $D_1D_1$, as indicated by the red arrows. To make this general idea more concrete, and to show some of its many applications, let us consider some specific examples of those "other things" that can shift demand curves.

**CONSUMER INCOMES**    If average incomes rise, consumers will purchase more of most goods, including milk, even if the prices of those goods remain the same. That is, increases in income normally shift demand curves outward to the right, as depicted in Figure 5–3(a), where the demand curve shifts outward from $D_0D_0$ to $D_1D_1$, establishing a new equilibrium price and quantity.

| FIGURE 5–3 | **Shifts of the Demand Curve** |

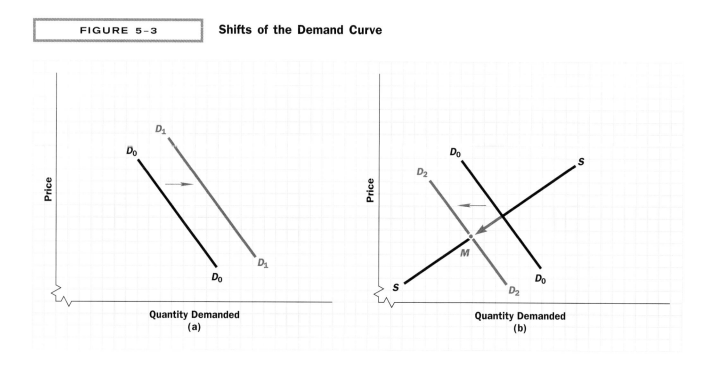

POPULATION    Population growth affects quantity demanded in more or less the same way as increases in average incomes. For instance, a larger population will presumably want to consume more milk, even if the price of milk and average incomes do not change, thus shifting the entire demand curve to the right, as in Figure 5–3(a). The equilibrium price and quantity both rise. And increases in particular population segments can elicit shifts in demand—for example, the United States in recent years has been experiencing a miniature population boom of people in their mid- to late-20s. Dubbed "Generation X," this fast-growing group has sparked higher demand for big-ticket items such as sport-utility vehicles and contemporary furniture.

In Figure 5–3(b) we see that a decrease in population should shift the demand curve for milk to the left from $D_0D_0$ to $D_2D_2$.

**CONSUMER PREFERENCES**    If the dairy industry mounts a successful advertising campaign extolling the benefits of drinking milk, families may decide to buy more at any given price. If so, the entire demand curve for milk would shift to the right, as in Figure 5–3(a). Alternatively, a medical report on the dangers of kidney stones may persuade consumers to drink less milk, thereby shifting the demand curve to the left, as in Figure 5–3(b). Again, these are general phenomena:

*If consumer preferences shift in favor of a particular item, its demand curve will shift outward to the right, as in Figure 5–3(a).*

An interesting example of this phenomenon was the mushrooming demand for Beanie Babies. Collectors snapped up these toy animals so quickly that retailers couldn't keep them in their stores.

**PRICES AND AVAILABILITY OF RELATED GOODS**  Because soda, orange juice, and coffee are popular drinks that compete with milk, a change in the price of any of these other beverages can be expected to shift the demand curve for milk. If any of these alternative drinks becomes cheaper, some consumers will switch away from milk. Thus, the demand curve for milk will shift to the left, as in Figure 5–3(b). Other price changes shift the demand curve for milk in the opposite direction. For example, suppose that cookies, which are often consumed with milk, become less expensive. This may induce some consumers to drink more milk and thus shift the demand curve for milk to the right, as in Figure 5–3(a). In general:

> Increases in the prices of goods that are substitutes for the good in question (as soda is for milk) move the demand curve to the right. Increases in the prices of goods that are normally used together with the good in question (such as cookies and milk) shift the demand curve to the left.

This is just what happened when a frost wiped out almost half of Brazil's coffee bean harvest in 1995. The three biggest U.S. coffee producers raised their prices by 45 percent, and, as a result, the demand curve for alternative beverages like tea shifted to the right. Then in 1998, coffee prices dropped about 34 percent, and this influenced the demand curve for tea to shift toward the left (or toward the origin), all other things being equal.

Although the preceding list does not exhaust the possible influences on quantity demanded, we have said enough to suggest the principles followed by demand and shifts of demand. Let us therefore turn to the supply side of the market.

## ■ SUPPLY AND QUANTITY SUPPLIED

Like quantity demanded, the quantity of milk that is supplied by business firms such as dairy farms is not a fixed number; it also depends on many things. Obviously, we expect more milk will be supplied if there are more dairy farms, or more cows per farm. Cows may give less milk if bad weather deprives them of their feed. As before, however, let's turn our attention first to the relationship between the *price* and *quantity* of milk supplied.

Economists generally suppose that a higher price calls forth a greater **quantity supplied**. Why? Remember our analysis of the principle of increasing cost in Chapter 4 (page 55). According to that principle, as more of any farmer's (or the nation's) resources are devoted to milk production, the opportunity cost of obtaining another quart of milk increases. Farmers will therefore find it profitable to increase milk production only if they can sell the milk at a higher price—high enough to cover the additional costs incurred to expand production.

In other words, it normally will take higher prices to persuade farmers to raise milk production. This idea is quite general and applies to the supply of most goods and services.[3] As long as suppliers want to make profits and the principle of increasing costs holds:

> As the price of any commodity rises, the quantity supplied normally rises. As the price falls, the quantity supplied normally falls.

### THE SUPPLY SCHEDULE AND THE SUPPLY CURVE

Table 5–2 shows the relationship between the price of milk and its quantity supplied. Tables such as this are called **supply schedules;** they show how much sellers are willing to provide during a specified period at alternative possible prices. This particular supply schedule shows that a low price like $1 per quart will induce suppliers to provide only 40 billion quarts, whereas a higher price like $1.30 will induce them to provide much more—70 billion quarts.

The **quantity supplied** is the number of units that sellers want to sell over a specified period of time.

A **supply schedule** is a table showing how the quantity supplied of some product during a specified period of time changes as the price of that product changes, holding all other determinants of quantity supplied constant.

---

[3] This analysis is carried out in much greater detail in later chapters.

## ● A 20,000 PERCENT BOUNCE: NOW THAT'S VOLATILITY

This 1998 newspaper story shows the dramatic effect on prices that can sometimes result from a shift in a demand curve.

Because no one can stockpile electricity . . . prices have proved to be extremely volatile at times of high demand like this summer's heat waves. Here is the *Cinergy-Power Markets Week* daily index, in dollars per megawatt hour. When heat waves blistered much of the country in June and July, utility customers like Juana Esparza of Dallas ran fans and air conditioners nonstop, and power demand soared.

SOURCE: *The New York Times,* Business Section, August 23, 1998, p. 4.

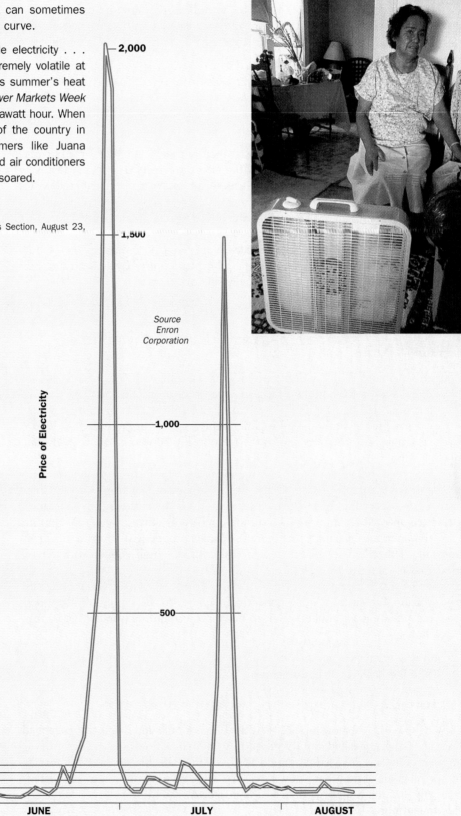

Source
Enron
Corporation

NOTE: Price is in dollars per megawatt hour.

**Supply Schedule for Milk**

TABLE 5-2

| Price per Quart | Quantity Supplied | Label in Figure 5–4 |
| --- | --- | --- |
| $1.50 | 90 | a |
| 1.40 | 80 | b |
| 1.30 | 70 | c |
| 1.20 | 60 | e |
| 1.10 | 50 | f |
| 1.00 | 40 | g |
| 0.90 | 30 | h |

A **supply curve** is a graphical depiction of a supply schedule. It shows how the quantity supplied of some product during a specified period of time will change as the price of that product changes, holding all other determinants of quantity supplied constant.

NOTE: Quantity is in billions of quarts per year.

FIGURE 5-4

As you might have guessed, when information like this is plotted on a graph, it is called a **supply curve**. Figure 5–4 is the supply curve corresponding to the supply schedule in Table 5–2, showing the relationship between the price of milk and the quantity supplied. It slopes upward because quantity supplied is higher when price is higher. Notice again the same phrase in the definition: "holding all other determinants of quantity supplied constant." What are these "other determinants"?

**Supply Curve for Milk**

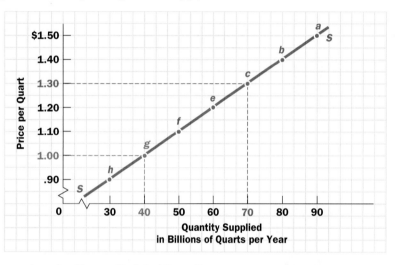

### SHIFTS OF THE SUPPLY CURVE

Like quantity demanded, the quantity supplied in a market typically responds to many influences other than price. The weather, the cost of feed, the number and size of dairy farms, and a variety of other factors all influence how much milk will be brought to market. Because the supply curve depicts only the relationship between the price of milk and the quantity of milk supplied, holding all other influences constant, a change in any of these other determinants of quantity supplied will cause the entire supply curve to shift. That is:

A change in the price of the good causes a movement *along* a fixed supply curve. But price is not the only influence on quantity supplied. If any of these other influences change, the *entire* supply curve shifts.

Figure 5–5 depicts the distinction graphically. A rise in price from $1.10 to $1.30 will raise quantity supplied by moving along supply curve $S_0S_0$ from point *f* to point *c*. But any rise in quantity supplied attributable to an influence other than price will shift the *entire* supply curve outward to the right from $S_0S_0$ to $S_1S_1$, as shown by the red arrows. Let us consider what some of these other influences are and how they shift the supply curve.

FIGURE 5-5

**Movements along versus Shifts of a Supply Curve**

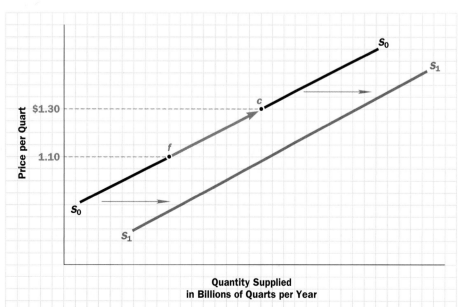

**SIZE OF THE INDUSTRY** We begin with the most obvious influence. If more farmers enter the milk industry, the quantity supplied at any given price will increase. For example, if each farm provides 600,000 quarts of milk per year at a price of $1.10 per quart, then 100,000 farmers provide 60 billion quarts, but 130,000 farmers provide 78 billion. Thus, when more farms are in the industry, the quantity of milk supplied will be greater at any given price—and hence the supply curve will move farther to the right.

Figure 5–6(a) illustrates the effect of an expansion of the industry from 100,000 farms to 130,000 farms—a rightward shift of the supply curve from $S_0S_0$ to $S_1S_1$. Figure 5–6(b) illustrates the opposite case: a contraction of the industry from 100,000 farms to 62,500 farms. The supply curve shifts inward to the left from $S_0S_0$ to $S_2S_2$. Even if no farmers enter or leave the industry, results like those depicted in Figure 5–6 can be produced by expansion or contraction of the *existing* farms.

| FIGURE 5–6 | **Shifts of the Supply Curve** |
| --- | --- |

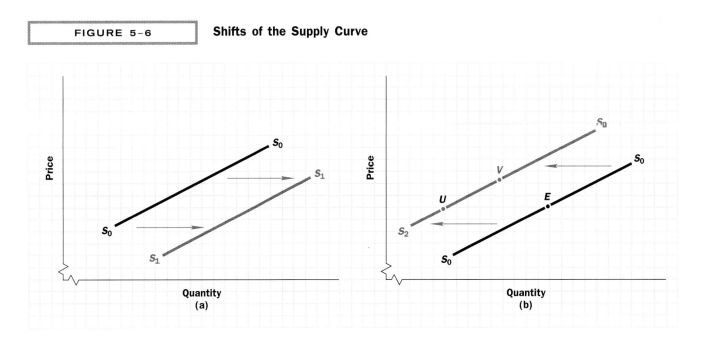

Quantity
(a)

Quantity
(b)

**TECHNOLOGICAL PROGRESS**    Another influence that shifts supply curves is technological change. Suppose some enterprising farmer discovers that cows produce more milk if they listen to Mozart during milking time. Thereafter, at any given price, farms will be able to produce more milk; that is, the supply curve will shift outward to the right, as in Figure 5–6(a). This, again, illustrates a general influence that applies to most industries:

> Technological progress that reduces costs will shift the supply curve outward to the right.

Automakers, for example, have been able to reduce production costs since industrial technology invented robots that can be programmed to work on several different car models. This technological advance has shifted the supply curve outward.

**PRICES OF INPUTS**    Changes in input prices also shift supply curves. Suppose a drought raises the price of animal feed. Farmers will have to pay more to keep their cows alive and healthy and consequently will no longer be able to provide the same quantity of milk at each possible price. This example illustrates that:

> Increases in the prices of inputs that suppliers must buy will shift the supply curve inward to the left.

**PRICES OF RELATED OUTPUTS**    Dairy farms sell products other than milk. If cheese prices rise sharply, farmers may decide to use some raw milk to make cheese, thereby reducing the quantity of milk supplied. On a supply-demand diagram, the supply curve would then shift inward, as in Figure 5–6(b).

Similar phenomena occur in other industries, and sometimes the effect goes the other way. For example, suppose that the price of beef goes up, which increases the quantity of meat supplied. That, in turn, will raise the number of cowhides supplied even if the price of leather does not change. Thus, a rise in the price of beef will lead to a rightward shift in the supply curve of leather. In general:

A change in the price of one good produced by a multiproduct industry may be expected to shift the supply curves of other goods produced by that industry.

A **supply-demand diagram** graphs the supply and demand curves together. It depicts the equilibrium price and quantity.

A **shortage** is an excess of quantity demanded over quantity supplied. When there is a shortage, buyers cannot purchase the quantities they desire.

## ■ SUPPLY AND DEMAND EQUILIBRIUM

To analyze how the free market determines price, we must compare the desires of consumers (demand) with the desires of producers (supply) to see whether the two plans are consistent. Table 5–3 and Figure 5–7 help us do this.

Table 5–3 brings together the demand schedule from Table 5–1 and the supply schedule from Table 5–2. Similarly, Figure 5–7 puts the demand curve from Figure 5–1 and the supply curve from Figure 5–4 on a single graph. Such graphs are called **supply-demand diagrams,** and you will encounter many of them in this book. Notice that, for reasons already discussed, the demand curve has a negative slope and the supply curve has a positive slope. That is generally true of supply-demand diagrams.

In a free market, price and quantity are determined by the intersection of the supply and demand curves. At only one point in Figure 5–7, point *E*, do the supply curve and the demand curve intersect. At the price corresponding to point *E*, which is $1.20 per quart, the quantity supplied and the quantity demanded are both 60 billion quarts per year. This means that, at a price of $1.20 per quart, consumers are willing to buy exactly what producers are willing to sell.

At any lower price, such as $1, only 40 billion quarts of milk will be supplied (point *g*) whereas 70 billion quarts will be demanded (point *G*). Thus, quantity demanded will exceed quantity supplied. There will be a **shortage** equal to 70 minus 40, or 30 billion quarts. Price will thus be driven up by unsatisfied demand. Alternatively, at a higher price like $1.50, quantity supplied will be 90 billion quarts (point *a*) while quantity demanded will be only 45 billion (point *A*). Quantity supplied will exceed quantity demanded—constituting a **surplus** equal to 90 minus 45, or 45 billion quarts.

**FIGURE 5-7**

**Supply-Demand Equilibrium**

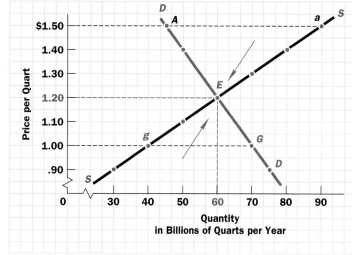

A **surplus** is an excess of quantity supplied over quantity demanded. When there is a surplus, sellers cannot sell the quantities they desire to supply.

| Determination of the Equilibrium Price and Quantity of Milk | | | | TABLE 5-3 |
|---|---|---|---|---|
| **Price per Quart** | **Quantity Demanded** | **Quantity Supplied** | **Surplus or Shortage?** | **Price Direction** |
| $1.50 | 45 | 90 | Surplus | Fall |
| 1.40 | 50 | 80 | Surplus | Fall |
| 1.30 | 55 | 70 | Surplus | Fall |
| 1.20 | 60 | 60 | Neither | Unchanged |
| 1.10 | 65 | 50 | Shortage | Rise |
| 1.00 | 70 | 40 | Shortage | Rise |
| 0.90 | 75 | 30 | Shortage | Rise |

NOTE: Quantity is in billions of quarts per year.

"Of course our problem is productivity. What else could it be?"

An **equilibrium** is a situation in which there are no inherent forces that produce change. Changes away from an equilibrium position will occur only as a result of "outside events" that disturb the status quo.

Because $1.20 is the price at which quantity supplied and quantity demanded are equal, we say that $1.20 per quart is the equilibrium price in this market. Similarly, 60 billion quarts per year is the equilibrium quantity of milk. The term **equilibrium** merits a little explanation, because it arises so frequently in economic analysis.

An equilibrium is a situation in which there are no inherent forces that produce change. Think, for example, of a pendulum resting at its center point. If no outside force (such as a person's hand) comes to push it, the pendulum will remain exactly where it is; it is therefore in equilibrium.

But if you give the pendulum a shove, its equilibrium will be disturbed and it will start to move upward. When it reaches the top of its arc, the pendulum will, for an instant, be at rest again. But this is not an equilibrium position, for the force of gravity will pull the pendulum downward. Thereafter, gravity and friction will govern its motion from side to side. Eventually, we know, the pendulum will return to its original position. The fact that the pendulum tends to return to it original position is described by saying that this position is a stable equilibrium. And that position is the only equilibrium position of the pendulum. At any other point, inherent forces will cause the pendulum to move.

The concept of equilibrium in economics is similar and can be illustrated by our supply-and-demand example. Why is no price other than $1.20 an equilibrium price in Table 5–3 or Figure 5–7? What forces will change any other price?

Consider first a low price like $1, at which quantity demanded (70 billion quarts) exceeds quantity supplied (40 billion). If the price were this low, many frustrated customers would be unable to purchase the quantities they desired. In their scramble for the available supply of milk, some would offer to pay more. As customers sought to outbid one another, the market price would be forced up. Thus, a price below the equilibrium price cannot persist in a free market because a shortage sets in motion powerful economic forces that push price upward.

Similar forces operate if the market price is above the equilibrium price. If, for example, the price should somehow get to be $1.50, Table 5–3 tells us that quantity supplied (90 billion quarts) would far exceed quantity demanded (45 billion). Producers would be unable to sell their desired quantities of milk at the prevailing price, and some would undercut their competitors by reducing price. Such competitive price cutting would continue as long as the surplus remained, that is, as long as quantity supplied exceeded quantity demanded. Thus, a price above the equilibrium price cannot persist indefinitely.

We are left with a clear conclusion. The price $1.20 per quart and the quantity 60 billion quarts per year is the only price-quantity combination that does not sow the seeds of its own destruction. It is thus the only equilibrium for this market. Any lower price must rise, and any higher price must fall. It is as if natural economic forces place a magnet at point $E$ that attracts the market, just as gravity attracts a pendulum.

The pendulum analogy is worth pursuing further. Most pendulums are more frequently in motion than at rest. However, unless they are repeatedly buffeted by outside forces (which, of course, is exactly what happens to pendulums used in clocks), pendulums gradually return to their resting points. The same is true of price and quantity in a free market. They are moved about by shifts in the supply and demand curves that we have already described. So markets are not always in equilibrium. But, if nothing interferes with them, experience shows that they normally move toward equilibrium.

## THE LAW OF SUPPLY AND DEMAND

In a free market, the forces of supply and demand generally push the price toward its equilibrium level, the price at which quantity supplied and quantity demanded are equal. Like most economic "laws," some markets will occasionally disobey the law of supply and demand. Markets sometimes display shortages or surpluses for long periods of time. Prices sometimes fail to move toward equilibrium. But the "law" is a fair generalization that is right far more often than it is wrong.

The **law of supply and demand** states that, in a free market, the forces of supply and demand generally push the price toward the level at which quantity supplied and quantity demanded are equal.

## EFFECTS OF DEMAND SHIFTS ON SUPPLY-DEMAND EQUILIBRIUM

Figure 5–3 showed how developments other than changes in price—such as increases in consumer income—can shift the demand curve. We saw that a rise in income, for example, will shift the demand curve to the right, meaning that at any given price, consumers—with their increased purchasing power—will buy more of the good than before. This, in turn, will move the equilibrium point, changing both market price and quantity sold.

This market adjustment, shown in Figure 5–8(a) adds a supply curve to Figure 5–3(a) so that we can see what happens to the supply-demand equilibrium. In the example in the graph, the quantity demanded at the old equilibrium price of $1.20 increases from 60 billion quarts per year (point $E$ on the demand curve $D_0D_0$) to 75 billion (point $R$ on the demand curve $D_1D_1$). We know that $1.20 is no longer the equilibrium price, because at this price quantity demanded (75 billion quarts) exceeds quantity supplied (60 billion). To restore equilibrium, the price must rise. The diagram shows that the new equilibrium occurs at point $T$, where the price is $1.30 per

**The Effects of Shifts of the Demand Curve**     FIGURE 5-8

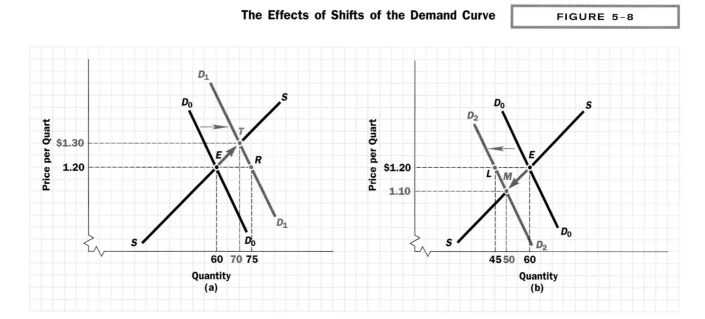

Quantity
(a)

Quantity
(b)

NOTE: Quanitity is in billions of quarts per year.

quart and both quantities demanded and supplied are 70 billion quarts per year. This illustrates a general result:

> Any influence that makes the demand curve shift outward to the right, and does not affect the supply curve, will raise the equilibrium price and the equilibrium quantity.[4]

Everything works in reverse if consumer incomes fall. Figure 5–8(b) depicts a leftward (inward) shift of the demand curve that results from a decline in consumer incomes. For example, the quantity demanded at the previous equilibrium price ($1.20) falls from 60 billion quarts (point $E$) to 45 billion (point $L$ on the demand curve $D_2D_2$). The initial price is now too high and must fall. The new equilibrium will eventually be established at point $M$, where the price is $1.10 and both quantity demanded and quantity supplied are 50 billion quarts. In general:

> Any influence that shifts the demand curve inward to the left, and that does not affect the supply curve, will lower both the equilibrium price and the equilibrium quantity.

### Application: The Fall of the Rupiah

As we observed early in the chapter, sharp drops in the values of a number of Asian currencies, especially the Indonesian rupiah, stunned the world in 1997. What happened?

The basic problem was that people lost confidence in the rupiah—which translated into a sharp leftward shift in the demand curve, like that depicted in Figure 5–3(b). Specifically, foreigners became worried about the stability of the rupiah and decided to hold less of it. Similarly, Indonesians became concerned about the large losses they would suffer if the rupiah fell, and therefore they did the same.

As we know, when the demand curve in a market shifts inward, the price normally falls. In this case, the relevant price was the exchange rate—the price of a rupiah in terms of U.S. dollars—and it dropped precipitously as the market equilibrium moved from point $E$ to point $M$.

### SUPPLY SHIFTS AND SUPPLY-DEMAND EQUILIBRIUM

A story precisely analogous to that of the effects of a demand shift on equilibrium price and quantity applies to supply shifts. Figure 5–6 described the effects on the supply curve of milk if the number of farms increase. Figure 5–9(a) now adds a demand curve to the supply curves of Figure 5–6 so that we can see the supply-demand equilibrium. Notice that at the initial price of $1.20, the quantity supplied after the shift is 78 billion quarts (point $I$ on the supply curve $S_1S_1$), which is 30 percent more than the original quantity demanded of 60 billion (point $E$ on the supply curve $S_0S_0$). We can see from the graph that the price of $1.20 is too high to be the equilibrium price; the price must fall. The diagram shows that the new equilibrium point is $J$, where the price is $1.10 per quart and the quantity is 65 billion quarts per year. In general:

> Any change that shifts the supply curve outward to the right, and does not affect the demand curve, will lower the equilibrium price and raise the equilibrium quantity.

This must always be true if the industry's demand curve has a negative slope, because the greater quantity supplied can be sold only if price is decreased to induce

---

[4] For example, when incomes rise rapidly in many developing countries, the demand curves for a variety of consumer goods shift rapidly outward to the right. In Japan, for example, the demand for used Levi's jeans and Nike running shoes from America skyrocketed in the early 1990s as status-conscious Japanese consumers searched for outlets for their rising incomes.

**Effects of Shifts of the Supply Curve**    FIGURE 5-9

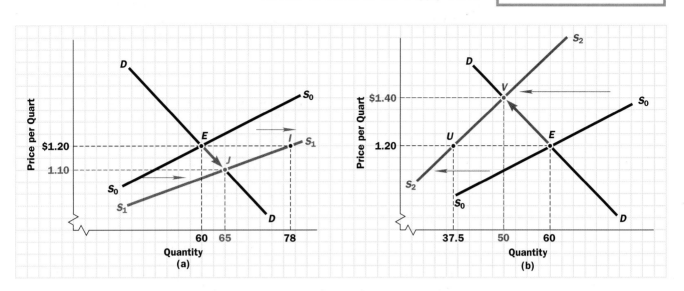

**Quantity**
**(a)**

**Quantity**
**(b)**

NOTE: Quantity is in billions of quarts per year.

customers to buy more.[5] The cellular phone industry is a case in point. As more providers have entered the industry, the cost of cellular service has plummeted. Some cellular carriers have even given away telephones as sign-up bonuses.

Figure 5–9(b) illustrates the opposite case: a contraction of the industry. The supply curve shifts inward to the left and equilibrium moves from point $E$ to point $V$, where the price is $1.40 and quantity is 50 billion quarts per year. In general:

> Any factor that shifts the supply curve to the left, and does not affect the demand curve, will raise the equilibrium price and reduce the equilibrium quantity.

Many outside forces can disturb equilibrium in a market by shifting the demand curve or the supply curve, either temporarily or permanently. In 1998, gasoline prices dropped because recession in Asia reduced demand, and a reduction in use of petroleum resulted from a mild winter. In the summer of 1998, severely hot weather and lack of rain damaged the cotton crop in the United States. Often these outside influences change the equilibrium price and quantity by shifting either the supply curve or the demand curve. If you look again at Figures 5–8 and 5–9, you can see clearly that any event that causes either the demand curve or the supply curve to shift will also change the equilibrium price and quantity.

## APPLICATION: WHO REALLY PAYS THAT TAX?

Supply and demand analysis offers insights that may not be readily apparent. Here is an example. Suppose your state legislature raises the gasoline tax by 10 cents per gallon. Service station operators will then have to collect 10 additional cents in taxes on every gallon they pump. They will consider this higher tax as an addition to their costs and will shift it to you and other consumers by raising the price of gas by 10 cents a gallon. Right? No, it's wrong—or rather, partly wrong.

The gas station owners would certainly *like* to shift the entire tax to buyers, but the market mechanism will allow them to shift only *part* of it—perhaps 6 cents per gallon. They will then be stuck with the remainder—4 cents in our example. Figure 5–10, which is just another supply-demand graph, shows why.

The demand curve is the blue curve $DD$. The supply curve before the tax is the black curve $S_0S_0$. So, before the new tax, the equilibrium point is $E_0$ and the price is $1.04. We can interpret the supply curve as telling us at what price sellers are

---

[5] Graphically, whenever a positively sloped curve shifts to the right, its intersection point with a negatively sloping curve must always move lower. Just try drawing it yourself.

**FIGURE 5-10**

**Who Pays for a New Tax on Products?**

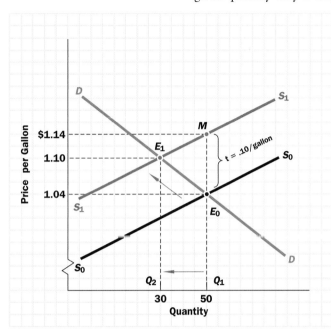

NOTE: Quantity is in millions of gallons of gasoline per year.

willing to provide any given quantity. For example, they are willing to supply quantity $Q_1 = 50$ million gallons per year if the price is $1.04 per gallon.

So what happens as a result of the new tax? Because they must now turn 10 cents per gallon over to the government, gas station owners will be willing to supply any given quantity only if they get 10 cents more per gallon than they did before. Therefore, to get them to supply quantity $Q_1 = 50$ million gallons, a price of $1.04 per gallon will no longer suffice. Only a price of $1.14 per gallon will now induce them to supply 50 million gallons. Thus, at quantity $Q_1 = 50$, the point on the supply curve will move up by 10 cents, from point $E_0$ to point $M$ on the supply curve $S_1S_1$. Because firms will insist on the same 10-cent price increase for any other quantity they supply, the *entire* supply curve will shift up (to the left) by the 10-cent tax—from the black curve $S_0S_0$ to the new red supply curve $S_1S_1$. So the supply-demand equilibrium point will move from $E_0$ to $E_1$ and the price will increase from $1.04 to $1.10.

The supply curve shift may give the impression that gas station owners have succeeded in passing the entire 10-cent increase on to consumers—the distance from $E_0$ to $M$—but look again. The *equilibrium* price has only gone up from $1.04 to $1.10. That is, the price has risen by only 6 cents, not by the full 10-cent amount of the tax. The gas station will have to absorb the remaining 4 cents of the tax.

Now this really *looks* as though we have pulled a fast one on you—a magician's sleight of hand. After all, the supply curve has shifted upward by the full amount of the tax, and yet the resulting price increase has covered only part of the tax rise. However, a second look shows that, like most apparent acts of magic, this one has a simple explanation. The explanation arises from the *demand* side of the supply-demand mechanism. The negative slope of the demand curve means that when prices rise, at least some consumers will reduce the quantity of gasoline they demand. That will force sellers to give up part of the price increase. In other words, firms absorb part of the tax—4 cents—that consumers are unwilling to absorb. But note also that the equilibrium quantity $Q_1$ has fallen from 50 million gallons to 30 million gallons—so both consumers and suppliers lose out in some sense.

This example is not an oddball case. It is almost always true. The cost of any increase in a tax on any commodity will usually be paid partly by the consumer, partly by the seller. This is true regardless of whether the legislature says that it is imposing the tax on the sellers or on the buyers. Whichever way it is phrased, the economics are the same: The supply-demand mechanism ensures that the tax will be shared by both parties.

## ■ FIGHTING THE INVISIBLE HAND: THE MARKET FIGHTS BACK

*Attempts to Repeal the Laws of Supply and Demand— The Market Strikes Back*

As we have noted in our *Ideas for Beyond the Final Exam*, lawmakers and rulers have often been dissatisfied with the outcomes of free markets. From Rome to South Dakota and from biblical times to the space age, they have battled the invisible hand. Sometimes, rather than trying to make adjustments in the workings of the market, governments have tried to raise or lower the prices of specific commodities by decree. In many such cases, the authorities felt that market prices were, in some sense, immorally low or immorally high. Penalties were therefore imposed on anyone offering the commodities in question at prices above or below those established by the authorities. Such legally imposed constraints on prices are called "price ceilings" and "price floors." To see their result, we will focus on the use of price ceilings.

## RESTRAINING THE MARKET MECHANISM: PRICE CEILINGS

A **price ceiling** is a legal maximum on the price that may be charged for a commodity.

The market has proven itself a formidable foe that strongly resists attempts to get around its decisions. In case after case where legal price ceilings are imposed, virtually the same series of consequences ensues:

1. *A persistent shortage develops because quantity demanded exceeds quantity supplied.* Queuing (people waiting in lines), direct rationing, or any of a variety of other devices, usually inefficient and unpleasant, must substitute for the distribution process provided by the price mechanism. Example: Rampant shortages in Eastern Europe and the former Soviet Union helped precipitate the revolts that ended communism.

2. *An illegal, or "black," market often arises to supply the commodity.* Usually some individuals are willing to take the risks involved in meeting unsatisfied demands illegally. Example: Although most states ban the practice, ticket "scalping" occurs at most popular sporting events and rock concerts.

3. *The prices charged on illegal markets are almost certainly higher than those that would prevail in free markets.* After all, lawbreakers expect some compensation for the risk of being caught and punished. Example: Illegal drugs are normally quite expensive. (See the accompanying Policy Debate box, "Economic Aspects of the War on Drugs.")

4. *A substantial portion of the price falls into the hands of the illicit supplier instead of going to those who produce the good or who perform the service.* Example: A constant complaint during the public hearings that marked the history of theater ticket price controls in New York City was that the "ice" (the illegal excess charge) fell into the hands of ticket scalpers rather than going to those who invested in, produced, or acted in the play.

5. *Investment in the industry generally dries up. Because price ceilings reduce the monetary returns that investors can legally earn, less capital will be invested in industries that are subject to price controls.* Even fear of impending price controls can have this effect. Example: Price controls on farm products in Zambia have prompted peasant farmers and large agricultural conglomerates alike to cut back production rather than grow crops at a loss. The result has been thousands of lost jobs and widespread food shortages.

### CASE STUDY: RENT CONTROLS IN NEW YORK CITY

These points and others are best illustrated by considering a concrete example of price ceilings. New York is the only major city in the United States that has legislated rent controls continuously since World War II. Rent controls, of course, are intended to protect the consumer from high rents. But most economists believe that rent control does not help the cities or their residents and that, in the long run, it makes almost everyone worse off. Elementary supply-demand analysis shows us why.

Figure 5–11 is a supply-demand diagram for rental units in New York. Curve DD is the demand curve and the curve SS is the supply curve. Without controls, equilibrium would be at point *E*, where rents average $2,000 per month and three million units are occupied. If rent controls are effective, they must set a ceiling price below the equilibrium price of $2,000. But with a low rent ceiling, such as $1,200, the quantity of housing demanded will be 3.5 million units (point *B*) while the quantity supplied will be only 2.5 million units (point *C*).

The diagram shows a shortage of one million apartments. This theoretical concept of a "shortage" manifests itself in New York City as an abnormally low vacancy rate—typically about half of the national urban average.

FIGURE 5-11

**Supply-Demand Diagram for Rental Housing**

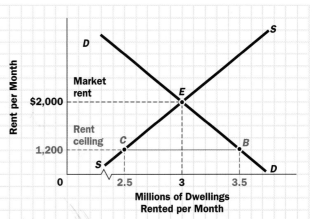

---

● **POLICY DEBATE** ▮ **ECONOMIC ASPECTS OF THE WAR ON DRUGS**

---

For years now, the U.S. government has engaged in a highly publicized "war on drugs." Billions of dollars have been spent on trying to stop illegal drugs at the border. In some sense, interdiction has succeeded: Federal agents have seized literally tons of cocaine and other drugs. Yet these efforts have made barely a dent in the flow of drugs to America's city streets. Simple economic reasoning explains why.

When drug interdiction works, it shifts the supply curve of drugs to the left, thereby driving up street prices. But that, in turn, raises the rewards for potential smugglers and attracts more criminals into the "industry," which shifts the supply curve back to the right. The net result is that increased shipments of drugs to our shores replace much of what the authorities confiscate. This is why many economists believe that any successful antidrug program must concentrate on reducing demand, which would lower the street price of drugs, not on reducing supply, which can only raise it.

Some people suggest that the government should go even further and legalize many drugs. Although this remains a highly controversial position that few are ready to endorse, the reasoning behind it is straightforward. A stunningly high fraction of all the violent crimes committed in America—especially robberies and murders—are drug-related. One major reason is that street prices of drugs are so high that addicts must steal to get the money, and drug traffickers are all too willing to kill to protect their highly profitable "businesses."

How would things differ if drugs were legal? Because South American farmers earn pennies for drugs that sell for hundreds of dollars on the streets of Los Angeles and New York, we may safely assume that legalized drugs would be vastly cheaper. In fact, according to one estimate, a dose of cocaine would cost less than 50 cents. That, proponents point out, would reduce

drug-related crimes dramatically. When, for example, was the last time you heard of a gang killing connected with the distribution of cigarettes or alcoholic beverages?

The argument against legalization of drugs is largely moral: Should the state sanction potentially lethal substances? But there is also an economic aspect. The vastly lower street prices of drugs that would surely follow legalization would increase drug use. Thus, while legalization would almost certainly reduce crime, it would also produce more addicts. The key question here is: How many more addicts? (Nobody has a good answer.) If you think the increase in quantity demanded would be large, you are unlikely to find legalization an attractive option.

---

Naturally, rent controls have spawned a lively black market in New York. The black market raises the effective price of rent-controlled apartments in many ways, including bribes, so-called key money paid to move up on a waiting list, and requirements that force prospective tenants to purchase worthless furniture at inflated prices.

According to the diagram, rent controls reduce the quantity supplied from 3 million to 2.5 million apartments. How does this show up in New York? First, some property owners, discouraged by the low rents, have converted apartment buildings into office space or other uses. Second, some apartments have been inadequately maintained. After all, rent controls create a shortage, which makes even dilapidated apartments easy to rent. Third, some landlords have actually abandoned their buildings rather than pay rising tax and fuel bills. These abandoned buildings rapidly become eyesores and eventually pose threats to public health and safety.

With all of these problems, why do rent controls persist in New York City? And why do other cities sometimes move in the same direction?

Part of the explanation is that most people simply do not understand the problems that rent controls create. Another part is that landlords are unpopular politically. But a third, and important, part of the explanation is that not everyone is hurt by rent controls—and those who benefit from controls fight hard to preserve them. In New York, for example, many tenants pay rents that are only a fraction of what their apartments would fetch on the open market. They are, naturally enough, quite happy with this situation. This last point illustrates another very general phenomenon:

> Virtually every price ceiling or floor creates a class of people that benefits from the regulations. These people use their political influence to protect their gains by preserving that status quo, which is one reason why it is so hard to eliminate price ceilings or floors.

## RESTRAINING THE MARKET MECHANISM: PRICE FLOORS

Interferences with the market mechanism are not always designed to keep prices low. Agricultural price supports and minimum wages provide two notable examples in which the law keeps prices *above* free-market levels. **Price floors** are typically accompanied by a standard series of symptoms:

A **price floor** is a legal minimum on the price that may be charged for a commodity.

1. *A surplus develops as sellers cannot find enough buyers.* Example: Surpluses of various agricultural products have been a persistent—and costly—problem for the U.S. government. The problem is even worse in the European Union (EU), where the common agricultural policy holds prices even higher. One source estimates that this policy accounts for half of all EU spending.[6]

2. *Where goods, rather than services, are involved, the surplus creates a problem of disposal.* Something must be done about the excess of quantity supplied over quantity demanded. Example: The U.S. government has often been forced to purchase, store, and then dispose of large amounts of surplus agricultural commodities.

3. *To get around the regulations, sellers may offer discounts in disguised—and often unwanted—forms.* Example: When airline fares were regulated by the government, airlines offered more and better food and stylish uniforms for flight attendants instead of lowering fares. Today, the food is worse, but tickets cost much less.

4. *Regulations that keep prices artificially high encourage overinvestment in the industry.* Even inefficient businesses whose high operating costs would doom them in an unrestricted market can survive beneath the shelter of a generous price floor. Example: This is why the airline and trucking industries both went through painful "shakeouts" of the weaker companies in the 1980s, when they were deregulated and allowed to charge market-determined prices.

Once again, a specific example is useful.

## CASE STUDY: SUGAR PRICE SUPPORTS

America's extensive program of farm price supports began in 1933 as a "temporary method of dealing with an emergency"—farmers were going broke in droves. These price supports are still with us today, even though farmers in the United States make up less than 3 percent of the workforce.[7] One of the more controversial farm price supports involves the sugar industry. Sugar producers receive low-interest loans from the federal government and a guarantee that the price of sugar will not fall below a certain level.

But in a market economy like ours, Congress cannot simply set prices by decree; it must take some action to enforce the price floor. In the case of sugar, that "something" is limiting both domestic production and foreign imports, thereby shifting

---

[6] *The Economist*, Feb. 20, 1999.

[7] Under major legislation passed in 1996, many agricultural price supports were supposed to be phased out over a seven-year period. However, in actuality, many support programs have changed little, especially for sugar.

**FIGURE 5-12**

**Supporting the Price of Sugar**

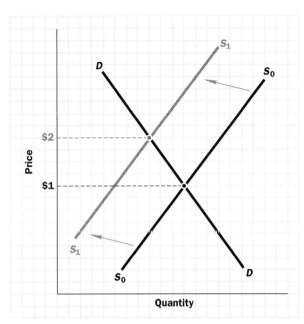

the supply curve inward to the left. Figure 5–12 displays the mechanics. Government policies shift the supply curve inward from $S_0S_0$ to $S_1S_1$ and drive the U.S. price up from \$1 to \$2 per pound. The more the supply curve shifts inward, the higher the price.

The sugar industry obviously benefits from the price-control program. But consumers pay for it in the form of higher prices for sugar and sugar-filled products such as soft drinks, candy bars, and cookies. Estimates vary, but the federal sugar price support program costs consumers somewhere around \$1.5 billion a year.

If all of this sounds a bit abstract to you, take a look at the ingredients in a U.S.-made soft drink. Instead of sugar, you will likely find "high-fructose corn syrup" listed as a sweetener. Foreign producers generally use sugar. But in the United States, sugar is simply too expensive to be used for this purpose.

### A CAN OF WORMS

Our two case studies—rent controls and sugar price supports—illustrate some of the major side effects of price floors and ceilings, but barely hint at others. Difficulties arise that we have not even mentioned, for the market mechanism is a tough bird that imposes suitable retribution on those who seek to evade it by government decree. Here is a partial list of other problems that may arise when prices are controlled.

**FAVORITISM AND CORRUPTION** When price ceilings or floors create shortages or surpluses, someone must decide who gets to buy or sell the limited quantity that is available. This can lead to discrimination along racial or religious lines, political favoritism, or corruption in government. For example, many prices were held at artificially low levels in the former Soviet Union, making queuing for certain goods quite common. But, somehow, Communist party officials and other favored groups were able to purchase the scarce commodities that others could not get.

**UNENFORCEABILITY** Attempts to limit prices are almost certain to fail in industries with numerous suppliers, simply because the regulating agency must monitor the behavior of so many sellers. People will usually find ways to evade or violate the law, and something like the free-market price will generally reappear. But there is an important difference: Because the evasion process, whatever its form, will have some operating costs, those costs must be borne by someone. Normally, that someone is the consumer.

**AUXILIARY RESTRICTIONS** Fears that a system of price controls will break down invariably lead to regulations designed to shore up the shaky edifice. Consumers may be told when and from whom they are permitted to buy. The powers of the police and the courts may be used to prevent the entry of new suppliers. Occasionally, an intricate system of market subdivision is imposed, giving each class of firms a protected sphere in which others are not permitted to operate. For example, in New York City there are laws banning conversion of rent-controlled apartments to condominiums.

**LIMITATION OF VOLUME OF TRANSACTIONS** To the extent that controls succeed in affecting prices, they can be expected to reduce the volume of transactions. Curiously, this is true regardless of whether the regulated price is above or below the free-market equilibrium price. If it is set above the equilibrium price, quantity demanded will be below the equilibrium quantity. On the other hand, if the imposed price is set below the free-market level, quantity supplied will be cut down. Because sales volume cannot exceed either the quantity supplied or the quantity demanded, a reduction in the volume of transactions is the result.[8]

---

[8] See Review Question 9 at the end of the chapter.

**MISALLOCATION OF RESOURCES**   Departures from free-market prices are likely to result in misuse of the economy's resources because the connection between production costs and prices is broken. For example, Russian farmers used to feed their farm animals bread instead of unprocessed grains because price ceilings kept the price of bread ludicrously low. In addition, just as more complex locks lead to more sophisticated burglary tools, more complex regulations lead to the use of yet more resources for their avoidance.

Economists put it this way. Free markets are capable of dealing efficiently with the three basic coordination tasks outlined in Chapter 4: deciding what to produce, how to produce it, and to whom the goods should be distributed. Price controls throw a monkey wrench into the market mechanism. Though the market is surely not flawless, and government interferences often have praiseworthy goals, good intentions are not enough. Any government that sets out to repair what it sees as a defect in the market mechanism runs the risk of causing even more serious damage elsewhere. As a prominent economist once quipped, societies that are too willing to interfere with the operation of free markets soon find that the invisible hand is nowhere to be seen.

## ■   A SIMPLE BUT POWERFUL LESSON

Astonishing as it may seem, many people in authority do not understand the law of supply and demand, or act as if it were not there. For example, a few years ago *The New York Times* carried a dramatic front page picture of the president of Kenya setting fire to a large pile of elephant tusks that had been confiscated from poachers. The accompanying story explained that the burning was intended as a symbolic act to persuade the world to halt the ivory trade.[9] One may well doubt whether the burning really touched the hearts of criminal poachers. However, one economic effect was clear. By reducing the supply of ivory on the world market, the burning of tusks forced up the price of ivory, which raised the illicit rewards reaped by those who slaughter elephants. That could only encourage more poaching—precisely the opposite of what the Kenyan government sought to accomplish.

---

### SUMMARY

1. An attempt by government regulations to force prices above or below their equilibrium levels is likely to lead to shortages or surpluses, to black markets in which goods are sold at illegal prices, and to a variety of other problems. The market always strikes back at attempts to repeal the law of supply and demand.

2. The quantity of a product that is demanded is not a fixed number. Rather, quantity demanded depends on such factors as the price of the product, consumer incomes, and the prices of other products.

3. The relationship between quantity demanded and price, holding all other things constant, can be displayed graphically on a demand curve.

4. For most products, the higher the price, the lower the quantity demanded. So the demand curve usually has a negative slope.

5. The quantity of a product that is supplied also depends on its price and many other influences. A supply curve is a graphical representation of the relationship between quantity supplied and price, holding all other influences constant.

6. For most products, the supply curves have positive slopes, meaning that higher prices lead to supply of greater quantities.

7. A change in quantity demanded that is caused by a change in the price of the good is represented by a movement *along* a fixed demand curve. A change in quantity demanded that is caused by a change in any other determinant of quantity demanded is represented by a *shift* of the demand curve.

8. This same distinction applies to the supply curve: Changes in price lead to movements along a fixed supply curve; changes in other determinants of quantity supplied lead to shifts of the whole supply curve.

9. A market is said to be in equilibrium when quantity supplied is equal to quantity demanded. The equilibrium price and quantity are shown by the point on a graph where the supply and demand curves intersect. The law of supply and demand states that price and quantity tend to gravitate to this point in a free market.

10. Changes in consumer incomes, tastes, technology, prices of competing products, and many other influences cause shifts

---

[9] *The New York Times*, July 19, 1989.

in either the demand curve or the supply curve and produce changes in price and quantity that can be determined from supply-demand diagrams.

11. A tax on a good generally leads to a rise in the price at which the taxed product is sold. However, the rise in price is generally less than the tax, so consumers usually pay less than the entire tax.

12. Consumers generally pay only part of a tax because the resulting rise in price leads them to buy less and the cut in the quantity they demand helps to keep price down.

---

## KEY TERMS

Quantity demanded   70

Demand schedule   70

Demand curve   71

Quantity supplied   73

Supply schedule   73

Supply curve   75

Supply-demand diagram   77

Shortage   77

Surplus   77

Equilibrium price and quantity   78

Equilibrium   78

Law of supply and demand   79

Shifts in versus movements along supply and demand curves   80

Price ceiling   82

Price floor   85

---

## QUESTIONS FOR REVIEW

1. How often do you rent videos? Would you do so more often if a rental cost half as much? Distinguish between your demand curve for home videos and your "quantity demanded" at the current price.

2. What shapes would you expect for demand curves for the following:

    a. A medicine that means life or death for a patient?

    b. French fries in a food court with kiosks offering many types of food?

3. The following are the assumed supply and demand schedules for hamburgers in Collegetown:

| Demand Schedule | | Supply Schedule | |
| --- | --- | --- | --- |
| Price | Quantity Demanded per Year | Price | Quantity Supplied per Year |
| $2.25 | 6,000 | $2.25 | 15,000 |
| 2.00 | 8,000 | 2.00 | 14,000 |
| 1.75 | 10,000 | 1.75 | 13,000 |
| 1.50 | 12,000 | 1.50 | 12,000 |
| 1.25 | 14,000 | 1.25 | 11,000 |
| 1.00 | 16,000 | 1.00 | 10,000 |

    a. Plot the supply and demand curves and indicate the equilibrium price and quantity.

    b. What effect would a decrease in the price of beef (a hamburger input) have on the equilibrium price and quantity of hamburgers, assuming all other things were to remain constant? Explain your answer with the help of a diagram.

    c. What effect would an increase in the price of pizza (a substitute commodity) have on the equilibrium price and quantity of hamburgers, assuming again that all other things were held constant? Use a diagram in your answer.

4. Suppose the supply and demand schedules for bicycles are as follows:

| Price | Quantity Demanded per Year | Quantity Supplied per Year |
| --- | --- | --- |
| $160 | 20,000,000 | 12,000,000 |
| 200 | 18,000,000 | 14,000,000 |
| 240 | 16,000,000 | 16,000,000 |
| 280 | 14,000,000 | 18,000,000 |
| 320 | 12,000,000 | 20,000,000 |
| 360 | 10,000,000 | 22,000,000 |

    a. Graph these curves and show the equilibrium price and quantity.

    b. Now suppose that it becomes unfashionable to ride a bicycle, so the quantity demanded at each price falls by 4 million bikes per year. What is the new equilibrium price and quantity? Show this solution graphically. Explain why the quantity falls by less than 4 million bikes per year.

    c. Suppose instead that several major bicycle producers go out of business, thereby reducing the quantity supplied by 4 million bikes at every price. Find the new equilibrium price and quantity, and show it graphically. Explain again why quantity falls by less than 4 million.

    d. What are the equilibrium price and quantity if the shifts described in Review Questions 4(b) and 4(c) happen at the same time?

5. The following table summarizes information about the market for principles of economics textbooks:

| Price | Quantity Demanded per Year | Quantity Supplied per Year |
| --- | --- | --- |
| $40 | 2,100 | 100 |
| 50 | 1,100 | 300 |
| 60 | 600 | 600 |
| 70 | 350 | 1,000 |
| 80 | 225 | 1,500 |

a. What is the market equilibrium price and quantity of textbooks?

b. In order to quell outrage over tuition increases, the college places a $50 limit on the price of textbooks. How many textbooks will be sold now?

c. While the price limit is still in effect, automated publishing increases the efficiency of textbook production. Show graphically the likely effect of this innovation on the market price and quantity.

6. Show how the following demand curves are likely to shift in response to the indicated changes:

a. The effect of a drought on the demand curve for umbrellas.

b. The effect of higher popcorn prices on the demand curve for movie tickets.

c. The effect on the demand curve for coffee of a decline in the price of Coca-Cola.

7. Discuss the likely effects of the following:

a. Rent ceilings on the market for apartments.

b. Floors under wheat prices on the market for wheat.

Use supply-demand diagrams to show what may happen in each case.

8. U.S. government price supports for milk led to a chronic surplus of milk. In an effort to reduce the surplus about a decade ago, Congress offered to pay dairy farmers to slaughter cows. Use two diagrams, one for the milk market and one for the meat market, to illustrate how this policy should have affected the price of meat. (Assume that meat is sold in an unregulated market.)

9. It is claimed in this chapter that either price floors or price ceilings reduce the actual quantity exchanged in a market. Use a diagram or diagrams to test this conclusion, and explain the common sense behind it.

10. The same rightward shift of the demand curve may produce a very small or a very large increase in quantity, depending on the slope of the supply curve. Explain with diagrams.

11. In 1981, when regulations were holding the price of natural gas below its free-market level, then-Congressman Jack Kemp of New York said the following in an interview with *The New York Times*: "We need to decontrol natural gas, and get production of natural gas up to a higher level so we can bring down the price."[10] Evaluate the congressman's statement.

12. From 1990 to 1997 in the United States, the number of working men grew by 6.7 percent; the number of working women grew 11 percent. During this time, average wages for men grew by 20 percent, while average wages for women grew 25 percent. Which of the following two explanations seems more consistent with the data?

a. Women decided to work more, raising their relative supply (relative to men).

b. Discrimination against women declined, raising the relative (to men) demand for female workers.

13. The two accompanying diagrams show supply and demand curves for two substitute commodities: tapes and compact discs (CDs).

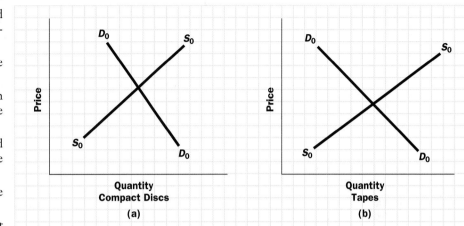

**Quantity
Compact Discs**

**(a)**

**Quantity
Tapes**

**(b)**

a. On the right-hand diagram, show what happens when rising raw material prices make it costlier to produce tapes.

b. On the left-hand diagram, show what happens to the market for CDs.

14. Consider the market for milk discussed in this chapter (Tables 5–1 through 5–3 and Figures 5–1 and 5–8). Suppose that the government decides to fight kidney stones by levying a tax of 30 cents per quart on sales of milk. Follow these steps to analyze the effects of the tax:

a. Construct the new supply schedule (to replace Table 5–2) that relates quantity supplied to the price that consumers pay.

b. Graph the new supply curve constructed in Review Question 14(a) on the supply-demand diagram depicted in Figure 5–8. What are the new equilibrium price and quantity?

c. Does the tax succeed in its goal of reducing the consumption of milk?

d. How much does the equilibrium price increase? Is the price rise greater than, equal to, or less than the 30-cent tax?

e. Who actually pays the tax, consumers or producers? (This may be a good question to discuss in class.)

15. (More difficult) The demand and supply curves for T-shirts in Touristtown, U.S.A., are given by the following equations:

$$Q = 24,000 - 500P \qquad Q = 6,000 + 1,000P$$

where $P$ is measured in dollars and $Q$ is the number of T-shirts per year.

<hr />

[10] *The New York Times*, December 23, 1981.

a. Find the equilibrium price and quantity algebraically.

b. If tourists decide they do not really like T-shirts that much, which of the following might be the new demand curve?

$$Q = 21,000 - 500P \qquad Q = 27,000 - 500P$$

Find the equilibrium price and quantity after the shift of the demand curve.

c. If, instead, two new stores that sell T-shirts open up in town, which of the following might be the new supply curve?

$$Q = 3,000 + 1,000P \qquad Q = 9,000 + 1,000P$$

Find the equilibrium price and quantity after the shift of the supply curve.

# II

## THE BUILDING BLOCKS OF DEMAND AND SUPPLY

The next four chapters describe and analyze the basic building blocks with which economists explain how markets work. The two essential elements of any market are its buyers (consumers) and its sellers (producers). As in a piece of machinery, all the parts of a market function together and simultaneously, so there is no logical place to begin the story. Furthermore, the heart of the story is not found in the individual components, but in the way they fit together. The four central micro chapters start off with the separate components, but then assemble them into a working model of how firms determine price and output simultaneously.

**Everything is worth what its purchaser will pay for it.**

Publilius Syrus (1st century B.C.)

# CONSUMER CHOICE: INDIVIDUAL AND MARKET DEMAND

Yo are about to start a new year in college, and your

favorite clothing store is having a sale. So you decide to

stock up on jeans. How do you decide how many to buy?

How is your decision affected by the price of the jeans

and the amount of money you earned in your summer

job? How can you get the most for your money? Eco-

nomic analysis provides some rational ways to make

these decisions. Do you think about your decision as an

economist would, either consciously or unconsciously?

Should you? By the end of the chapter you will be able

to consider these questions, and you will have learned a

new way to analyze purchase decisions using concepts

called "utility" and "marginal analysis."

Chapter 5 introduced you to the idea of supply and

demand and how we can use supply and demand curves

to analyze how markets determine prices and quantities

of products sold. This chapter will enable us to investigate the underpinnings of the demand curve which, as we have already seen, shows us half of the market picture.

### Paradox: Should Water Be Worth More Than Diamonds?

When Adam Smith lectured at the University of Glasgow in the 1760s, he introduced the study of demand by posing a puzzle. Common sense, he said, suggests that the price of a commodity must somehow depend on what that good is worth to consumers—on the amount of *utility* that the commodity offers. Yet, Smith pointed out, some cases suggest that a good's utility may have little influence on its price.

Smith cited diamonds and water as examples. He noted that water has enormous value to most consumers; indeed, its availability can be a matter of life and death. Yet water generally is either free or sells at a very low price, whereas diamonds sell for very high prices even though few people would consider them necessities. We will soon be in a position to see how marginal analysis, the powerful method of analysis introduced in this chapter, helps to resolve the paradox.

### ■ SCARCITY AND DEMAND

When economists use the term "demand," they do not mean mere wishes, needs, requirements, or preferences. Rather, demand refers to actions of consumers who, so to speak, put their money where their mouths are. "Demand" assumes that consumers can pay for the goods in question and that they are also willing to pay out the necessary money. Some of us may, for example, dream of owning a racehorse or a Lear jet, but only a few wealthy individuals can turn such fantasies into effective demands.

Any individual consumer's choices are subject to one overriding constraint that is at least partly beyond that consumer's control: The individual has only a limited income available to spend. This scarcity of income is the obvious reason why less affluent consumers demand fewer computers, trips to foreign countries, and expensive restaurant meals than wealthy consumers do. The scarcity of income affects even the richest of all spenders—the government. The U.S. government spends billions of dollars on the armed services, education, and a variety of other services, but governments rarely if ever have the funds to buy everything they want.

Because income is limited (and thus is a scarce resource), any consumer's purchase decisions for different commodities must be *interdependent*. The number of movies that John can afford to see depends on the amount he spends on new clothing. If Jane's parents have just sunk a lot of money into an expensive addition to their home, they may have to give up a vacation trip. Thus, no one can truly understand the demand curves for movies and clothing, or for homes and vacation trips, without considering demand curves for alternative goods.

The quantity of movies demanded, for example, probably depends not only on ticket prices but also on the prices of clothing. Thus, a big sale on shirts might induce John to splurge on several, leaving him with little or no cash to spend on movies. Therefore, an analysis of consumer demand that focuses on only one commodity at a time leaves out an essential part of the story. Nevertheless, to make the analysis easier to follow, we begin by considering products in isolation. That is, we employ what is called "partial analysis," using a standard simplifying assumption. This assumption requires that all other variables remain unchanged. Later in the chapter and in the appendix, we will tell a fuller story.

## ■ UTILITY: A TOOL TO ANALYZE PURCHASE DECISIONS

In the American economy, millions of consumers make millions of decisions every day. You decide to buy a movie ticket instead of a paperback novel. Your roommate decides to buy two tubes of toothpaste rather than one tube or three tubes. How do people make these decisions?

Economists have constructed a simple theory of consumer choice based on the hypothesis that each consumer spends her or his income in the way that yields the greatest amount of satisfaction, or *utility*. This seems to be a reasonable starting point, because it says only that people do what they prefer. To make the theory operational, we need a way to measure utility.

A century ago, economists envisioned utility as an indicator of the pleasure a person derives from consuming some set of goods, and they thought that utility could be measured directly in some kind of psychological units (sometimes called *utils*) after somehow reading the consumer's mind. Gradually, they came to realize that this was an unnecessary and, perhaps, impossible task. How many utils did you get from the last movie you saw? You probably cannot answer that question because you have no idea what a util is. Neither does anyone else.

But you may be able to answer a different question like, "How many hamburgers would you give up to get that movie ticket?" If you answer "three," no one can say how many utils you get from seeing a film, but they can say that you get more from the movie than from a single hamburger. When economists approach the issue in this manner, hamburgers, rather than the more vague "utility," becomes the unit of measurement. They can say that the utility of a movie (to you) is three hamburgers.

Early in the 20th century, economists concluded that this indirect way of measuring consumer benefit gave them all they needed to build a theory of consumer choice. One can measure the benefit of a movie ticket by asking how much of some other commodity (like hamburgers) you are willing to give up for it. Any commodity will do for this purpose, but the simplest choice, and the one that we will use in this book, is money.[1]

---

[1] Note to Instructors: You will recognize that, while not using the terms, we are distinguishing here between neoclassical *cardinal utility* and *ordinal utility*. Moreover, throughout the book, *marginal utility in money terms* (or *money marginal utility*) is simply used as a synonym for the *marginal rate of substitution* between money and the commodity.

## TOTAL VERSUS MARGINAL UTILITY

The **total utility** of a quantity of a good to a consumer (measured in money terms) is the maximum amount of money that he or she is willing to give in exchange for it.

Thus, we define the **total utility** of some bundle of goods to some consumer as *the largest sum of money that person will voluntarily give up in exchange for those goods.* For example, imagine that you love pizza and are planning to buy four pizzas for a party you are hosting. You are, as usual, a bit low on cash. Taking this into account, you decide that you are willing to buy the four pies if they cost up to $52 in total, but you're not willing to pay more than $52. As economists, we then say that the *total utility* of four pizzas to you is $52, the maximum amount you are willing to spend to have them.

Total utility measures the benefit that you derive from your total purchases of some commodity during some selected period of time. *Total* utility is all that really matters to you. But to understand which decisions most effectively promote total utility, we must consider the related concept of **marginal utility**. This concept does not measure your goal, but rather provides a tool to analyze how much of a commodity that you will buy. It refers to *the addition to total utility that an individual derives by consuming one more unit of any good.* For example, if you consumed two pizzas last month, marginal utility indicates how much additional pleasure you would have received by increasing your consumption to three pizzas instead.

The **marginal utility** of a commodity to a consumer (measured in money terms) is the maximum amount of money that she or he is willing to pay *for one more unit* of that commodity.

Table 6–1 helps to clarify the distinction between marginal and total utility and shows how the two are related. The first two columns show how much *total* utility (measured in money terms) you derive from various quantities of pizza, ranging from zero to eight per month. For example, a single pizza pie is worth (no more than) $15 to you, two are worth $28 in total, and so on. The *marginal* utility is the *difference* between any two successive total utility figures. For example, if you have consumed three pizzas (worth $40.50 to you), an additional pie brings your total utility up to $52. Your marginal utility is thus the difference between the two, or $11.50.

Remember: Whenever we use the terms *total utility* and *marginal utility*, we define them in terms of the consumer's willingness to part with *money* for the commodity, not in some unobservable (and imaginary) psychological units.

## THE "LAW" OF DIMINISHING MARGINAL UTILITY

The **"law" of diminishing marginal utility** asserts that additional units of a commodity are worth less and less to a consumer in money terms. As the individual's consumption increases, the marginal utility of each additional unit declines.

With these definitions, we can now propose a simple hypothesis about consumer tastes:

The more of a good a consumer has, the less *marginal* utility an additional unit contributes to overall satisfaction.

| TABLE 6–1 |
|---|

### Your Total and Marginal Utility for Pizza this Month

| (1) | (2) | (3) | (4) |
|---|---|---|---|
| Quantity (Q) Pizzas per month | Total Utility (TU) | Marginal Utility (MU) = ($\Delta$TU/$\Delta$Q) | Point in Figure 6–1 |
| 0 | $ 0.00 | | |
| | | $15.00 | A |
| 1 | 15.00 | | |
| | | 13.00 | B |
| 2 | 28.00 | | |
| | | 12.50 | C |
| 3 | 40.50 | | |
| | | 11.50 | D |
| 4 | 52.00 | | |
| | | 8.00 | E |
| 5 | 60.00 | | |
| | | 5.00 | F |
| 6 | 65.00 | | |
| | | 3.00 | G |
| 7 | 68.00 | | |
| | | 0.00 | H |
| 8 | 68.00 | | |

NOTE: Each entry in Column (3) is the difference between successive entries in Column (2). This is indicated by zig-zag lines.

Economists use this plausible proposition widely. The idea is based on the assertion that every person has a *hierarchy* of uses for a particular commodity. All of these uses are valuable, but some are more valuable than others. Take pizza, for example. Perhaps you consider your *own* appetite for pizza first—you buy enough pizza to satiate your own personal taste for pizza. But pizza may also provide you with an opportunity to satisfy your social needs. So, instead of eating all the pizza you buy, you decide to have a pizza party. First on your guest list, of course, is your boyfriend or girlfriend. Next priority is your roommate, and, if you feel really flush, you may even invite your economics instructor! Thus, if you buy only one pizza, you eat it yourself. If you buy a second pizza, you share it with your friend. A third is shared with your roommate, and so on.

The point is: Each pizza contributes something to your satisfaction, but each *additional* pizza contributes less (measured in terms of money) than its predecessor because it satisfies a lower-priority use. This, in essence, is the logic behind the **"law" of diminishing marginal utility.**

The third column of Table 6–1 illustrates this concept. The marginal utility (abbreviated MU) of the first pizza is $15; that is, you are willing to pay *up to* $15 for the first pie. The second is worth no more than $13 to you, the third pizza only $12.50, and so on until you are willing to pay only $5 for the sixth (the MU of that pizza is $5).

Figure 6–1, a demand curve, shows a graph of the numbers in the first and third columns of the table. For example, point *D* indicates that the MU of a fourth pizza is $11.50. So, at any higher price, you will not buy a fourth pizza.

Note that the curve for marginal utility is negatively sloped; this again illustrates how marginal utility diminishes as the quantity of the good rises. Like most laws, however, it has exceptions. Some people want even more of some good that is particularly significant to them as they acquire more, as in the case of addiction. Stamp collectors and alcoholics provide good examples. The stamp collector who has a few stamps may consider the acquisition of one more to be mildly amusing. The person who has a large and valuable collection may be prepared to go to the ends of the earth for another stamp. Similarly, an alcoholic who finds

**FIGURE 6–1**

**A Marginal Utility (or Demand) Curve: Your Demand for Pizza This Month**

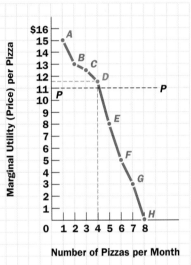

"It's been fun, Dave, but I think we're entering the diminished marginal utility phase of our relationship."

## ● DO CONSUMERS REALLY BEHAVE "RATIONALLY" AND MAXIMIZE UTILITY?

It may strike you that this chapter's discussion of the consumer's decision process—equating price and marginal utility—does not resemble the thought processes of any consumer you have ever met. Buyers may seem to make decisions much more instinctively and without any calculation of marginal utilities or anything like them. That is true, and yet it need not undermine the pertinence of the discussion.

When you give a command to your computer, you actually activate some electronic switches and start some operations in what is referred to as *binary code*. Most computer users do not know they are doing this and do not care. Yet they are doing it nevertheless, and the analysis of the computation process does not misrepresent the facts by describing this sequence. In the same way, if a shopper divides her purchasing power among various available purchase options in a way that yields the largest possible utility for her money, she *must* be following the rules of marginal analysis, even though she is totally unaware of this choice.

Still, growing experimental evidence points out some persistent deviations between reality and the picture of consumer behavior provided by marginal analysis. Experimental studies by groups of economists and psychologists have turned up many examples of behavior that seem to violate the optimal purchase rule. For example, one such study offered two groups of respondents what were really identical options, presumably yielding similar marginal utilities. Yet, depending on differences in some irrelevant information that was also provided to the respondents, the two groups made very different choices.

One group of subjects received the information in parentheses, and the other received the information in brackets. . . .
[*Problem 1*]. Imagine that you are about to purchase . . . a calculator for ($15)[$125]. The calculator salesman informs you that the calculator you wish to buy is on sale for ($10)[$120] at the other branch of the store, located a 20-minute drive away. Would you make the trip to the other store?

The responses to the two versions of this problem were quite different. When the calculator cost $125 only 29 percent of the subjects said they would make the trip, whereas 68 percent said they would go when the calculator cost only $15.

Thus, in this problem *both* groups were really being told they could save $5 on the price of a product if they took a 20-minute trip to another store. Yet, depending on an irrelevant fact, whether the product was a cheap or an expensive one, the number of persons willing to make the same trip to save the same amount of money was very different. The point is that human purchase decisions are affected by the environment in which the decision is made, and not only by the price and marginal utility of the purchase.

SOURCE: Richard H. Thaler, *Quasi Rational Economics* (New York: Russell Sage Foundation, 1992), pp. 148–150.

the first beer quite pleasant may find the fourth or fifth to be absolutely irresistible. Economists generally treat such cases of increasing marginal utility as anomalies. For most goods and most people, marginal utility declines as consumption increases.

Table 6–1 and Figure 6–1 illustrate another noteworthy relationship. Notice that as someone buys more and more units of the commodity, that is, as that person moves further down the table, the total utility numbers get larger and larger, while the marginal utility numbers get smaller and smaller. The reasons should now be fairly clear. The marginal utility numbers keep declining, as the law of diminishing marginal utility tells us. But *total* utility keeps rising so long as marginal utility remains positive. A woman who owns ten cans of tennis balls, other things being equal, is better off (she has higher total utility) than a woman who possesses only nine, as long as the MU of the tenth can is positive. In summary:

As a rule, as a person acquires more of a commodity, total utility increases and marginal utility from that good decreases, all other things being equal. In particular, when a commodity is very scarce, economists expect it to have a high marginal utility, even though it may provide little total utility because people have so little of the item.

## USING MARGINAL UTILITY: THE OPTIMAL PURCHASE RULE

Now let us use the concept of marginal utility to analyze consumer choices. As we noted, each consumer has a limited amount of money to spend. Consumers must always choose among the many commodities that compete for their dollars. How can you use the idea of utility to help you understand the purchase choices that best serve your preferences?

You can obviously choose among many different quantities of pizza, any of which will add to your total utility. But which of these quantities will yield the greatest net benefits? If pizza were all that you ever considered buying, in theory the choice would involve a simple calculation. We would need a statistical table that listed all of the alternative numbers of pizzas that you may conceivably buy. The table should indicate the *net* utility that each possible choice yields: that is, the total utility that you would get from that number of pizzas, minus the utility you would lose by having to pay for them. We could then simply read your optimal choice from this imaginary table—the number of pizzas that would give you the highest net utility number.

Even in theory, calculating optimal decisions is, unfortunately, more difficult than that. No real table of net utilities exists; an increase in expenditure on pizzas would mean less money available for clothing or movies, and you must balance the benefits of spending on each of these items against spending on the others. All of this means that we must find a more effective technique to determine optimal pizza purchases (as well as clothing, entertainment, and so on). That technique is *marginal analysis.*

To see how marginal analysis helps consumers determine their optimal purchase decisions, first recall our assumption that you are trying to maximize the total *net* utility you obtain from your pizza purchases. That is, you are trying to select the number of pies that maximizes the total utility the pizzas provide you *minus the total utility you give up with the money you must pay for them.*

We can compare the analysis of the optimal decision process to the process of climbing a hill. First, imagine that you consider the possibility of buying only one pizza. Then suppose you consider buying two pizzas, and so on. If two pizzas give you a higher total net utility than one, you may think of yourself as moving higher up the total net utility hill. Buying more pizzas enables you to ascend that hill higher and higher, until at some quantity you reach the top—*the optimal purchase quantity.* Then, if you buy any more you will have overshot the peak and begun to descend the hill.

Figure 6–2 shows such a hill and describes how your total net utility changes when you change the number of pizzas you buy. It shows the upward-sloping part of the hill, where the number of purchases has not yet brought you to the top. Then it shows the point (*M*) at which you have bought enough pizzas to make your net utility as large as possible (the peak occurs at four pizzas). At any point to the right of *M*, you have overshot the optimal purchase. You are on the downward side of the hill because you have bought more than enough pizzas to best serve your interests; you have bought too many to maximize your net utility.

How does marginal analysis help you to find that optimal purchase quantity, and how does it warn you if you are planning to purchase too little (so that you are still on the ascending portion of the hill) or too much (so that you are descending)? The numerical example in Table 6–1 will help reveal the answers. The marginal utility of, for example, a third pizza is $12.50. This means that the total utility you obtain from three pizzas ($40.50) is exactly $12.50 higher than the total utility you get from two pizzas ($28). Thus, the marginal utility of the third pizza is the amount that this pizza adds to your total utility. As long as marginal utility is a positive number, the more you purchase, the more total utility you will get.

That shows the benefit side of the purchase. But such a transaction also has a debit side—the amount you must pay for the purchase. Suppose that the price is $11 per pizza. Then the net *marginal* utility of the third pizza is marginal utility minus price, $12.50 minus $11, or $1.50. This is the amount that the third pizza adds to your total net utility. (See the third and fourth lines of Table 6–1.) So you really *are* better off with three pizzas than with two.

**FIGURE 6-2**

**Finding Your Optimal Pizza Purchase Quantity: Maximizing Total Net Utility**

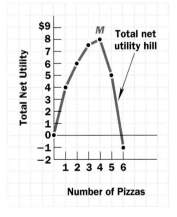

NOTE: Total Net Utility equals Total Utility minus Total Expenditure (Price × Quantity)

We can generalize the logic of the previous paragraph to show how marginal analysis solves the problem of finding the optimal purchase quantity, given the price of the commodity being purchased.

> **RULE 1:** If marginal net utility is positive, the consumer must be buying too small a quantity to maximize total net utility. Because marginal utility exceeds price, one can increase total net utility by buying one more unit of the product. In other words, a positive marginal net utility means that total net utility is still going uphill. The consumer has not yet bought enough to get to the top of the hill.

> **RULE 2:** No purchase quantity for which marginal net utility is a negative number can ever be optimal. In such a case, a buyer can get a higher total net utility by cutting back the purchase quantity. You would have climbed too far on the net utility hill, passing the topmost point and beginning to descend.

*The Importance of Thinking at the Margin*

This leaves only one option. The consumer cannot be at the top of the hill if marginal net utility (MU − P) is greater than zero, that is, if MU is greater than P. Similarly, the purchase quantity cannot be optimal if marginal net utility at that quantity (MU − P) is less than zero, that is, if MU is less than P. The purchase quantity can be optimal, giving the consumer the highest possible total net utility, only if:

$$\text{Marginal net utility} = MU - P = 0, \text{ that is, if } MU = P$$

Consequently, the hypothesis that the consumer chooses purchases to make the largest net contribution to total utility leads to the following *optimal purchase rule:*

> It always pays the consumer to buy more of any commodity whose marginal utility (measured in money) exceeds its price, and less of any commodity whose marginal utility is less than its price. When possible, the consumer should buy the quantity of each good at which price (*P*) and marginal utility (*MU*) are exactly equal, that is, at which:

$$MU = P$$

because only these quantities will maximize the *net total utility* that the consumer gains from purchases, given the fact that these decisions must divide available money among all purchases.[2]

Notice that, although the consumer really cares about maximizing total *net* utility (since marginal utility has no intrinsic interest), we have used marginal analysis as a *guide* to the optimum purchase quantity. Marginal analysis serves only as an analytic method—as a means to an end. In Chapter 9, after several other applications of marginal analysis, we will generalize the discussion to show how thinking "at the margin" allows us to make optimal decisions in a wide variety of fields besides consumer purchases.

Let's briefly review graphically how the underlying logic of the marginal way of thinking leads to the optimal purchase rule: MU = P. Refer back to the graph of marginal utilities of pizzas (Figure 6–1). Suppose that Paul's Pizza Parlor currently sells pizzas at a price of $11 (line *PP* in the graph).

At this price, five pizzas (point *E*), for example, is *not* an optimal purchase because the $8 marginal utility of the fifth pizza is less than its $11 price. You would be better off buying only four pizzas since that would save $11 with only a $8 loss in utility—a net gain of $3—from the decision to buy one fewer pizza.

You should note that, in practice, there may not exist a number of pizzas at which MU is *exactly* equal to P. In our example, the fourth pizza is worth $11.50, whereas the fifth pizza is worth $8—neither of them is *exactly* equal to their $11 price. If

---

[2] Economists can equate a dollar price with marginal utility only because they measure marginal utility in money terms (or, as they more commonly state, because they deal with the marginal rate of substitution of money for the commodity). If marginal utility were measured in some psychological units not directly translatable into money terms, a comparison of *P* and *MU* would have no meaning. However, MU could also be measured in terms of any commodity other than money. (Example: How many pizzas are you willing to trade for an additional ticket to a basketball game?)

you could purchase an appropriate (in-between) quantity (say, 4.38 pizzas), then MU would, indeed, exactly equal *P*. But Paul's Pizza Parlor will not sell you 4.38 pizzas, so you must do the best you can. You buy four pizzas, for which MU comes as close as possible to equality with *P*.

The rule for optimal purchases states that you should not buy a quantity at which MU is higher than price (points like *A*, *B*, and *C* in Figure 6–1) because a larger purchase would make you better off. Similarly, you should not end up at points *E*, *F*, *G*, and *H*, at which MU is below price, because you would be better off buying less. Rather, you should buy four pizzas (point *D*), where *P* = MU (approximately). Thus, marginal analysis leads naturally to the rule for optimal purchase quantities.

> The decision to purchase a quantity of a good that leaves marginal utility greater than price cannot maximize total net utility, because buying an additional unit would add more to total utility than it would cost. Similarly, it cannot be optimal for the consumer to buy a quantity of a good that leaves marginal utility less than price, because then a reduction in the quantity purchased would save more money than it would sacrifice in utility. Consequently, the consumer can maximize total net utility only if the purchase quantity makes marginal utility as close as possible to equality with price.

Note that price is an objective, observable figure determined by the market, whereas marginal utility is subjective and reflects consumer tastes. Because individual consumers lack the power to influence the price, they must adjust purchase quantities to make the marginal utility of each good equal to the price given by the market.

## FROM DIMINISHING MARGINAL UTILITY TO DOWNWARD-SLOPING DEMAND CURVES

We can use the optimal purchase rule to show that the "law" of diminishing marginal utility implies that demand curves typically slope downward to the right, that is, they have negative slopes.[3] To do this, we use the list of marginal utilities in Table 6–1 to determine how many pizzas you would buy at any particular price. For example, we see that at a price of $8, it pays for you to buy five pizzas, because the MU of that fifth pizza ordered is $8. Table 6–2 gives several alternative prices and the optimal purchase quantity corresponding to each price derived in just this way. (To make sure you understand the logic behind the optimal purchase rule, verify that the entries in the right-hand column of Table 6–2 are in fact correct.) This *demand schedule* appears graphically as the *demand curve* shown in Figure 6–1. This demand curve is simply the red marginal utility curve. You can see its negative slope, characteristic of demand curves.

Let's examine the logic underlying the negatively sloped demand curve a bit more carefully. If you are purchasing the optimal number of pizzas, and then the price falls, you will find that your marginal utility for that product is now *above* the newly reduced price. For example, Table 6–1 indicates that at a price of $12.50 per pizza, you would optimally buy three, because the marginal utility (MU) of the fourth pizza is only $11.50. If price falls below $11.50, it then pays to purchase the fourth pizza because its MU exceeds its price. The marginal utility of the next (fifth) pizza is only $8, and so if the price were to remain above $8, it would not pay you to buy that fifth pizza, just as prescribed in the optimal purchase rule.

Note the critical role that the law of diminishing marginal utility plays here. If *P* falls, a consumer who wishes to maximize total utility must buy more, to the point that MU falls correspondingly. According to the law of diminishing marginal utility, the only way to do this is to increase the quantity purchased.

Although this explanation is a bit abstract, we can easily rephrase it in practical terms. We have noted that individuals put commodities to various uses, each of which has a different priority. For you, buying a pizza for your date has a higher priority than using the pizza to feed your roommate. If the price of pizzas is high, it makes sense for you to buy only enough for the high-priority uses—those that

---

[3] If you need to review the concept of slope, turn back to the Chapter 2 discussion on graphic analysis.

| TABLE 6–2 |
| :---: |

**List of Optimal Quantities of Pizza for You to Purchase at Alternative Prices**

| Price | Quantity of Portions Purchased per Month |
| :--- | :---: |
| $ 3.00 | 7 |
| 5.00 | 6 |
| 8.00 | 5 |
| 11.50 | 4 |
| 12.50 | 3 |
| 13.00 | 2 |
| 15.00 | 1 |

NOTE: For simplicity of explanation the prices shown have been chosen to equal the marginal utilities in Table 6—1. In-between prices would make the optimal choices involve fractions of pizzas (say, 2.6 pizzas).

offer high marginal utilities. When price declines, however, it pays to purchase more of the good—enough for some lower-priority uses. The same general assumption about consumer psychology underlies both the law of diminishing marginal utility and the negative slope of the demand curve. They are really two different ways of describing consumers' assumed attitudes.

## ■ CONSUMER CHOICE AS A TRADE-OFF: OPPORTUNITY COST

We have expressed the optimal purchase rule as a decision about how much of *one* commodity to buy. However, we have already observed that the scarcity of income lurking in the background turns every decision into a trade-off. Given each consumer's limited income, a decision to buy a new car usually means giving up some travel or postponing furniture purchases. The money that the consumer gives up when she makes a purchase—her expenditure on that purchase—is only one measure of the true underlying cost to her.

*How Much Does It Really Cost?*

The real cost is the *opportunity cost* of the purchase—the commodities that she must give up as a result of the purchase decision. This opportunity cost calculation has already been called for in our *Ideas for Beyond the Final Exam*—we must always consider the real cost of our purchase decisions, how much of *other* things they force us to forgo. Any decision to buy implies some such trade-off because scarcity constrains all economic decisions. Though their dilemmas may not inspire much pity, even billionaires face very real trade-offs: Invest $200 million in an office building, or go for the $300 million baseball team?

This last example has one other important implication. The trade-off from a consumer's purchase decision does not always involve giving up another *consumer good*. This is true, for example, of the choice between consumption and saving. Consider a high school student deciding whether to buy a new car or to save the money to pay for college. If he saves the money, it can grow by earning interest, so that the original amount plus interest earned will be available to pay for tuition and board three years later. A decision to cut down on consumption now and put the money into the bank means that the student will be wealthier in the future because of the interest he will earn. This, in turn, will enable the student to afford more of his college expenses at the future date when those expenses arise. So the opportunity cost of a new car today is the forgone opportunity to save funds for the future. We conclude:

From the viewpoint of economic analysis the true cost of any purchase is the opportunity cost of that purchase, rather than the amount of money that is spent on it.

The opportunity cost of a purchase can be either higher or lower than its price. For example, if your computer cost you $1,800, but the purchase required you to take off two hours from your job that pays $20 per hour, the true cost of the computer—that is, the opportunity cost—is the amount of goods you could have bought with $1,840 (the $1,800 price plus the $40 in earnings that the purchase of the computer required you to give up). In this case, the opportunity cost ($,1840, measured in money terms) is higher than the price of the purchase ($1,800). (For an example in which price is higher than opportunity cost, see Review Question 8 at the end of the chapter.)

### CONSUMER'S SURPLUS: THE NET GAIN FROM A PURCHASE

The optimal purchase rule, MU (approximately) = *P*, assumes that the consumer always tries to maximize the money value of the total utility from the purchase *minus* the amount spent to make that purchase.[4] Thus, any difference between the price

---

[4] Again, in practice, the consumer can often only approximately equate MU and *P*.

consumers *actually* pay for a commodity and the price they would be *willing* to pay for that item represents a net utility gain in some sense. Economists give the name **consumer's surplus** to that difference, that is, to the net gain in total utility that a purchase brings to a buyer. The consumer is trying to make the purchase decisions that maximize:

**Consumer's surplus** is the difference between the value to the consumer of the quantity of Commodity *X* purchased and the amount that the market requires the consumer to pay for that quantity of *X*.

Consumer's surplus = Total utility (in money terms) − Total expenditure

Thus, just as economists assume that business firms maximize total profit (equal to total revenue minus total cost), they assume that consumers maximize consumer's surplus, that is, the difference between the total utility of the purchased commodity and the amount that consumers spend on it.

The concept of *consumer's surplus* seems to suggest that the consumer gains some sort of free bonus, or *surplus*, for every purchase. In many cases, this idea seems absurd. How can it be true, particularly for goods whose prices seem to be outrageous?

We hinted at the answer in Chapter 4, where we observed that both parties must gain from a voluntary exchange or else one of them will refuse to participate. The same must be true when a consumer makes a *voluntary* purchase from a supermarket or an appliance store. If the consumer did not expect a net gain from the transaction, he or she would simply not bother to buy. Even if the seller were to "overcharge" by some standard, that would merely reduce the size of the consumer's net gain, not eliminate it entirely. If the seller is so greedy as to charge a price that wipes out the net gain altogether, the punishment will fit the crime: The consumer will refuse to buy, and the greedy seller's would-be gains will never materialize. The basic principle states that every purchase that is not marginal—that is, every purchase except those about which the consumer is indifferent—must yield *some* consumer's surplus.

But how large is that surplus? At least in theory, it can be measured with the aid of a table or graph of marginal utilities (Table 6–1 and Figure 6–1). Suppose that, as in our earlier example, the price of a large pizza is $11 and you purchase four of them. Table 6–3 reproduces the marginal utility numbers from Table 6–1. It shows that the first pizza is worth $15 to you, so at the $11 price, you reap a net gain (surplus) of $15 minus $11, or $4, by buying that pizza. The second pizza also brings you some surplus, but less than the first one does, because the marginal utility diminishes. Specifically, the second pizza provides a surplus of $13 minus $11, or $2. Reasoning in the same way, the third pizza gives you a surplus of $12.50 minus $11, or $1.50. It is only the fourth serving—the last one that you purchase—that offers little or no surplus because, by the optimal purchase rule, the marginal utility of the last unit is approximately equal to its price.

We can now easily determine the total consumer's surplus that you obtain by buying four pizzas. It is simply the sum of the surpluses received from each pizza. Table 6–3 shows that this consumer's total surplus is:

$$\$4 + \$2 + \$1.50 + \$0.50 = \$8$$

This way of looking at the optimal purchase rule shows why a buyer must always gain some consumer's surplus if she buys more than one unit of a good. Note that

**Calculating Marginal Net Utility (Consumer's Surplus) from Your Pizza Purchases**

| | | | TABLE 6-3 |
|---|---|---|---|

| Quantity | Marginal Utility | Price | Marginal Net Utility (Surplus) |
|---|---|---|---|
| 0 | $15.00 | $11.00 | $4.00 |
| 1 | 13.00 | 11.00 | 2.00 |
| 2 | 12.50 | 11.00 | 1.50 |
| 3 | 11.50 | 11.00 | 0.50 |
| Total | | | $8.00 |

the price of each unit remains the same, but the marginal utility diminishes as more units are purchased. The last unit bought yields only a tiny consumer's surplus because MU (approximately) = *P*. But all prior units must have had marginal utilities farther above the MU of the last unit because of diminishing marginal utility.

We can be more precise about the calculation of the consumer's surplus with the help of a graph (Figure 6–3) showing marginal utility as a set of bars. The bars labeled *A*, *B*, *C*, and *D* come from the corresponding points on your marginal utility curve (demand curve) in Figure 6–1. Your consumer's surplus from each pizza equals the marginal utility of that pizza minus the price you pay for it. By representing consumer's surplus graphically, we can determine just how much surplus you obtain from your entire purchase by measuring the area between the marginal utility curve and the horizontal line representing the price of pizzas—in this case, the horizontal line *PP* represents the (fixed) $11 price.

In Figure 6–3, the bar whose upper, right-hand corner is labeled *A* represents the $15 marginal utility you derive from the first pizza; the same interpretation applies to the bars *B*, *C*, and *D*. Clearly, the first serving that you purchase yields a consumer's surplus of $4, indicated by the shaded part of bar *A*. The height of that part of the bar is equal to the $15 marginal utility minus the $11 price. In the same way, the next two shaded areas represent the surpluses offered by the second and third pizzas. The fourth pizza has the smallest shaded area because the height representing marginal utility is (as close as you can get to being) equal to the height representing price. Sum up the shaded areas in the graph to obtain, once again, your total consumer's surplus ($4 + $2 + $1.50 + $0.50 = $8) from your four-serving purchase.

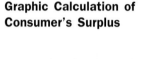

FIGURE 6–3

**Graphic Calculation of Consumer's Surplus**

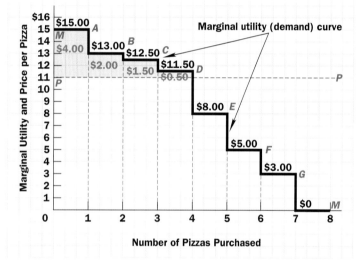

Number of Pizzas Purchased

The consumer's surplus derived from buying a certain number of units of a good is obtained graphically by drawing the person's demand curve as a set of bars whose heights represent the marginal utilities of the corresponding quantities of the good, and then drawing a horizontal line whose height is the price of the good. The sum of the heights of the bars above the horizontal line, that is, the area of the demand (marginal utility) bars above that horizontal line, measures the *total* consumer's surplus that the purchase yields.

### Resolving the Diamond-Water Paradox

We can now use marginal utility analysis to solve Adam Smith's paradox (which he was never able to explain) that diamonds are very expensive, whereas water is generally very cheap, even though water seems to offer far more utility. The resolution of the diamond-water paradox is based on the distinction between marginal and total utility.

The *total* utility of water—its role as a necessity of life—is indeed much higher than that of diamonds. But price, as we have seen, is not related directly to *total* utility. Rather, the optimal purchase rule tells us that price tends to equal *marginal* utility. We have every reason to expect the marginal utility of water to be very low, whereas the marginal utility of a diamond is very high.

Given normal conditions, water is comparatively cheap to provide, so its price is generally quite low. Consumers thus use correspondingly large quantities of water. The principle of diminishing marginal utility, therefore, pushes down the marginal utility of water for a typical household to a low level. As the consumer's surplus diagram (Figure 6–3) suggests, this also means that its *total* utility is likely to be high.

On the other hand, high-quality diamonds are scarce (partly because a monopoly keeps them so). As a result, the quantity of diamonds consumed is not large enough to drive down the MU of diamonds very far, so buyers of such luxuries must pay high prices for them. As a commodity becomes more scarce, its *marginal* utility and its market price rise higher, regardless of the size of its *total* utility. Also, as we have seen, because so little of the commodity is consumed, its *total* utility is likely to be comparatively low, despite its large *marginal* utility.

Thus, like many paradoxes, the diamond-water puzzle has a straightforward explanation. In this case, all one has to remember is that:

Scarcity raises price and *marginal* utility, but it generally reduces *total* utility. And although total utility measures the benefits consumers get from their consumption, it is marginal utility that is equal (approximately) to price.

## INCOME AND QUANTITY DEMANDED

Our application of marginal analysis has enabled us to examine the relation between the *price* of a commodity and the quantity that will be purchased. Let us next consider briefly how quantity demanded responds to changes in *income*.

As a concrete example, consider what happens to the number of ballpoint pens a consumer will buy when her real income rises. It may seem almost certain that she will buy more such pens than before, but that is not necessarily so. A rise in real income can either increase or decrease the quantity of any particular good purchased.

Why might an increase in income lead a consumer to buy fewer ballpoint pens? People buy some goods and services only because they cannot afford anything better. They may purchase used cars instead of new ones. They may use inexpensive ballpoint pens instead of finely crafted fountain pens or buy clothing secondhand instead of new. If their real income rises, they may then drop out of the used car market and buy brand-new automobiles or buy more fountain pens and fewer ballpoints. Thus, a rise in real income will reduce the quantities of cheap pens and used cars demanded. Economists have given the rather descriptive name **inferior goods** to the class of commodities for which quantity demanded falls when income rises.

An **inferior good** is a commodity whose quantity demanded falls when the purchaser's real income rises, all other things remaining equal.

The upshot of this discussion is that economists cannot draw definite conclusions about the effects of a rise in consumer incomes on quantity demanded. But for most commodities, if incomes rise and prices do not change, quantity demanded will increase. (Such an item is often called a *normal good.*)

## FROM INDIVIDUAL DEMAND CURVES TO MARKET DEMAND CURVES

So far in this chapter we have studied how *individual demand curves* are obtained from the logic of consumer choice. But to understand how the market system works, we must derive the relationship between price and quantity demanded *in the market as a whole*—the **market demand curve.**

A **market demand curve** shows how the total quantity of some product demanded by *all* consumers in the market during a specified period of time changes as the price of that product changes, holding all other things constant.

### MARKET DEMAND AS A HORIZONTAL SUM

If each individual pays no attention to other people's purchase decisions when making his or her own, we can easily derive the market demand curve from consumers' individual demand curves: Simply *add* the negatively sloping individual demand curves *horizontally* as shown in Figure 6–4. The figure gives the individual demand curves *DD* and *ZZ* for two people, Alex and Naomi, and the total (market) demand curve, *MM*. Alex and Naomi are both consumers of the product.

We can derive this market demand curve in the following straightforward way:

*Step 1*: Pick any relevant price, say, $10.

*Step 2*: At that price, determine Alex's quantity demanded (9 units) from his demand curve in Panel (a) and Naomi's quantity demanded (6 units) from her demand curve in Panel (b). Note that these quantities are indicated by the line segment labeled *AA* for Alex and that labeled *NN* for Naomi.

FIGURE 6-4

**The Relationship between Total Market Demand and the Demand of Individual Consumers within That Market**

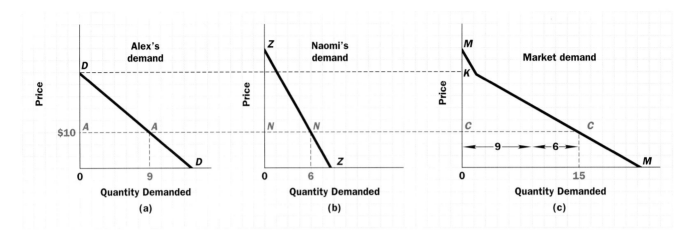

*Step 3:* Add Naomi's and Alex's quantities demanded at the $10 price (segment *AA* + segment *NN* = 9 + 6 = 15) to yield the total quantity demanded by the market at that price. This gives segment *CC*, with total quantity demanded equal to 15 units, in Panel (c).

Now repeat the process for each alternative price to obtain other points on the market demand curve until the shape of the entire curve *MM* appears. (The sharp angle at point *K* on the market curve occurs because that point corresponds to the price at which Alex, whose demand pattern is different from Naomi's, first enters the market. At any higher price, only Naomi is willing to buy anything.) That is all there is to the adding-up process. (Question: What would happen to the market demand curve if, say, another consumer entered the market?)

## THE "LAW" OF DEMAND

The **"law" of demand** states that a lower price generally increases the amount of a commodity that people in a market are willing to buy. Therefore, for most goods, market demand curves have negative slopes.

Just as for the case of an individual's demand curve, we expect the total quantity demanded by the market to move in the opposite direction from price. Economists call this relationship the **"law" of demand.**

Notice that we have put the word *law* in quotation marks. By now you will have observed that economic laws are not always obeyed, and we shall see in a moment that the "law" of demand is not without its exceptions. But first let us see why the "law" usually holds.

Earlier in this chapter, we explained that individual demand curves usually slope downward because of the "law" of diminishing marginal utility. If individual demand curves slope downward, then the preceding discussion of the adding-up process implies that market demand curves must also slope downward. This is just common sense; if every consumer in the market buys fewer pizzas when the price of pizza rises, then the total quantity demanded in the market must surely fall.

But market demand curves may slope downward even when individual demand curves do not, because not all consumers are alike. For example, if a bookstore reduces the price of a popular novel, it may draw many new customers, but few of the customers who already own a copy will buy a second one. Similarly, people differ in their fondness for pizza. True devotees may maintain their pizza purchases even at exorbitant prices, whereas others would not eat pizza even if you gave it to them free of charge. As the price of pizza rises, less enthusiastic pizza eaters drop out of the market entirely, leaving the expensive pie to the more devoted consumers. Thus, the quantity demanded declines as price rises, simply because higher prices induce more people to kick the pizza habit. Indeed, for many commodities, lower prices encourage new customers to come into the *market*, and it is these "fair weather" customers (rather than the negative slope of *individual* demand curves) that account for the law of demand.

This is also illustrated in Figure 6–4, where only Naomi will buy the product at a price higher than *D*. However, at a price below *D*, Alex will also purchase. Hence, below point *K* the market demand curve lies further to the right than it would have if Alex had not entered the market. Put another way, a rise in price from a level below *D* to a level above *D* would cut quantity demanded for two reasons: first, because Naomi's demand curve has a negative slope and, second, because it would drive Alex out of the market.

We conclude, therefore, that the law of demand stands on fairly solid ground. If individual demand curves are downward sloping, then the market demand curve surely will be, too. Further, the market demand curve may slope downward, even when individual demand curves do not.

## EXCEPTIONS TO THE LAW OF DEMAND

Nevertheless, exceptions to the law of demand have been noted. One common exception occurs when people judge quality on the basis of price—they perceive a more expensive commodity as offering better quality. For example, many people buy name-brand aspirin, even if right next to it on the drugstore shelf they see an unbranded, generic aspirin with a virtually identical chemical formula, selling at half the price. The consumers who do buy the name-brand aspirin may well use comparative price to judge the relative qualities of different brands. They may prefer Brand *X* to Brand *Y* because *X* is slightly more expensive. If Brand *X* were to reduce its price below that of *Y*, consumers might assume that it was no longer superior and actually reduce their purchases.

Another possible cause of an upward-sloping demand curve is snob appeal. If part of the reason for purchasing a Rolls Royce is to advertise one's wealth, a decrease in the car's price may actually reduce sales, even if the quality of the car remains unchanged. Other types of exceptions have also been noted by economists. But, for most commodities, it seems quite reasonable to assume that demand curves have negative slopes, an assumption that is supported by the data.

This chapter has begun to take us behind the demand curve, to discuss how it is determined by the preferences of the individual consumer. The chapter that follows will explore the demand curve further by examining what determines its shape and the implications of that shape for consumer behavior.

---

## SUMMARY

1. Economists distinguish between total and marginal utility. *Total utility*, or the benefit a consumer derives from a purchase, is measured by the maximum amount of money he or she would give up in order to have the good. Rational consumers seek to maximize (net) total utility, or *consumer's surplus:* the total utility derived from a commodity minus the value of the money spent in buying it.

2. *Marginal utility* is the maximum amount of money that a consumer is willing to pay for an additional unit of a particular commodity. Marginal utility is useful in calculating the set of purchases that maximizes net total utility. This illustrates one of our *Ideas for Beyond the Final Exam.*

3. The *"law" of diminishing marginal utility* is a psychological hypothesis stating that as a consumer acquires more and more of a commodity, the marginal utility of additional units of the commodity decreases.

4. To maximize the total utility obtained by spending money on Commodity *X*, given the fact that other goods can be purchased only with the money that remains after buying

*X*, the consumer must purchase a quantity of *X* such that the price equals (or approximately equals) the commodity's marginal utility (in monetary terms).

5. If the consumer acts to maximize utility, and if her marginal utility of some good declines when she purchases larger quantities, then her demand curve for the good will have a negative slope. A reduction in price will induce her to purchase more units, leading to a lower marginal utility.

6. Abundant goods tend to have low prices and low marginal utilities regardless of whether their total utilities are high or low. That is why water can have a lower price than diamonds despite its higher total utility.

7. An *inferior good*, such as secondhand clothing, is a commodity that consumers buy less of when they get richer, all other things held equal.

8. Consumers usually earn a surplus when they purchase a commodity voluntarily. This means that the quantity of the good that they buy is worth more to them than the money they give up in exchange. Consumer's surplus is normally positive.

9. As another of our *Ideas for Beyond the Final Exam*, "How Much Does It Really Cost?" tells us, the true economic cost of the purchase of a commodity, X, is its opportunity cost, that is, the value of the alternative purchases that the acquisition of X requires the consumer to forgo. The money value of the opportunity cost of a unit of good X can be higher or lower than the price of X.

10. A rise in a consumer's income can push quantity demanded either up or down. For normal goods, the effect of a rise in income raises the quantity demanded; for inferior goods, which are purchased in order to save money, a higher income reduces the quantity demanded.

11. The demand curve for an entire market is obtained by taking a horizontal sum of the demand curves of all of the individuals who buy or consider buying in that market. This sum is obtained by adding up, for each price, the quantity of the commodity in question that every such consumer is willing to purchase at that price.

---

### KEY TERMS

Total utility   96

Marginal utility   96

The "law" of diminishing marginal utility   96

Marginal analysis   99

Optimal purchase rule   100

Consumer's surplus   103

Scarcity and marginal utility   105

Inferior good   105

Market demand curve   105

The "law" of demand   106

---

### QUESTIONS FOR REVIEW

1. Describe some of the different things you do with water. Which would you give up if the price of water were to rise a little? If it were to rise by a fairly large amount? If it were to rise by a very large amount?

2. Which gives you greater *total* utility, 12 gallons of water per day or 20 gallons per day? Why?

3. At which level do you get greater *marginal* utility: 12 gallons per day or 20 gallons per day? Why?

4. Suppose that you wanted to measure the marginal utility of a commodity to a consumer by directly determining the consumer's psychological attitude or strength of feeling for the commodity rather than by seeing how much money the consumer would give up for the commodity. Why would you find it difficult to get such a psychological measurement?

5. Some people who do not understand the optimal purchase rule argue that if a consumer buys so much of a good that its price equals its marginal utility, she could not possibly be behaving optimally. Rather, they say, she would be better off quitting while she was ahead, that is, buying a quantity such that marginal utility is much greater than price. What is wrong with this argument? (*Hint:* What opportunity would the consumer then miss? Is it maximization of marginal or total utility that serves the consumer's interests?)

6. What inferior goods do you purchase? Why do you buy them? Do you think you will continue to buy them when your income is higher?

7. Which of the following items are likely to be normal goods for a typical consumer? Which are likely to be inferior goods?

   a. Expensive perfume

   b. Paper plates

   c. Secondhand clothing

   d. Overseas trips

8. Emily buys an air conditioner that costs her $600. Because the air in her home is cleaner, this saves her $150 in curtain cleaning costs over the lifetime of the air conditioner. In money terms, what is the opportunity cost of the air conditioner?

9. Suppose that strawberries sell for $2 per basket. Jim is considering whether to buy zero, one, two, three, or four baskets. On your own, create a plausible set of total and marginal utility numbers for the different quantities of strawberries (like we did for pizza in Table 6–1) and arrange them in a table. From your table, calculate how many baskets Jim would buy.

10. Draw a graph showing the consumer's surplus Jim would get from his strawberry purchase and check your answer with the help of your marginal utility table.

11. Consider a market with two consumers, Jasmine and Jim. Draw a demand curve for each of the two consumers and use those curves to construct the demand curve for the entire market.

---

● **APPENDIX** ▌ **ANALYZING CONSUMER CHOICE GRAPHICALLY: INDIFFERENCE CURVE ANALYSIS**

The consumer demand analysis presented in this chapter, although correct as far as it goes, has one shortcoming: By treating the consumer's decision about the purchase of each commodity as an isolated event, it conceals the fact that consumers must *choose* because of their limited budgets. The foregoing analysis does not explicitly indicate the hard choice behind every purchase decision—the sacrifice of some goods to obtain others.

The idea is included implicitly, of course, because the purchase of any commodity involves a trade-off between that good and money. If you spend more money on rent, you have less to spend on entertainment. If you buy more clothing, you have less money for food. But to represent the consumer's *choice* problem explicitly, economists have invented two geometric devices, the *budget line* and the *indifference curve*, which are described in this appendix.

## GEOMETRY OF AVAILABLE CHOICES: THE BUDGET LINE

Suppose, for simplicity, that only two commodities are produced in the world: cheese and rubber bands. The decision problem of any household is then to allocate its income between these two goods. Clearly, the more it spends on one, the less it have of the other. But just what is the trade-off? A numerical example will answer this question and also introduce the graphical device that economists use to portray the trade-off.

Suppose that cheese costs $2 per pound, boxes of rubber bands sell at $3 each, and a consumer has $12 at his disposal. He obviously has a variety of choices, as displayed in Table 6–4. For example, if he buys no rubber bands, he can go home with six pounds of cheese, and so on. Each of the combinations of cheese and rubber bands that the consumer can afford can be shown in a diagram in which the axes measure the quantities purchased of each commodity. In Figure 6–5, pounds of cheese are measured along the vertical axis, the number of boxes of rubber bands is measured along the horizontal axis, and a labeled point represents each of the combinations enumerated in Table 6–4. This budget line *AE* shows all the different combinations of cheese and rubber bands that the consumer can buy with $12 if cheese costs $2 per pound and a box of rubber bands costs $3. For example, point *A* corresponds to spending everything on cheese; point *E* corresponds to spending everything on rubber bands. At intermediate points on the budget line (such as *C*), the consumer buys some of both goods (at *C*, two boxes of rubber bands and three pounds of cheese), which together use up the $12 available.

**FIGURE 6–5**

### A Budget Line

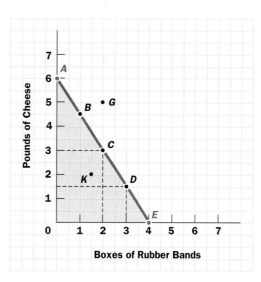

**Boxes of Rubber Bands**

If a straight line connects points *A* through *E*, the red line in the diagram, it traces all possible ways to divide the $12 between the two goods. For example, at point *D*, if the consumer buys three boxes of rubber bands, he will have only enough money left to purchase $1\frac{1}{2}$ pounds of cheese. This is readily seen to be correct from Table 6–4. Line *AE* is therefore called the *budget line*.

> The *budget line* for a household graphically represents all possible combinations of two commodities that it can purchase, given the prices of the commodities and some fixed amount of money at its disposal.

### PROPERTIES OF THE BUDGET LINE

Let us now use *r* to represent the number of boxes of rubber bands purchased by the consumer and *c* to indicate the amount of cheese that he acquires. Thus, at $2 per pound, he spends on cheese a total of $2 times the number of pounds of cheese bought, or $2c. Similarly, he spends $3r on rubber bands, making a total of $2c

## Alternative Purchase Combinations for a $12 Budget        TABLE 6–4

| Boxes of Rubber Bands (at $3 each) | Expen diture on Rubber Bands | Remaining Funds | Pounds of Cheese (at $2 each) | Label in Figure 6–5 |
|---|---|---|---|---|
| 0 | $ 0 | $12 | 6 | A |
| 1 | 3 | 9 | 4.5 | B |
| 2 | 6 | 6 | 3 | C |
| 3 | 9 | 3 | 1.5 | D |
| 4 | 12 | 0 | 0 | E |

plus $3r, which must equal $12, if he spends the entire $12 on the two commodities. Thus, $2c + 3r = 12$ is the equation of the budget line. It is also the equation of the straight line drawn in the diagram.[5]

Note also that the budget line represents the *maximum* amounts of the commodities that the consumer can afford. Thus, for any given purchase of rubber bands, it indicates the greatest amount of cheese that his money can buy. If the consumer wants to be thrifty, he can choose to end up at a point *below* the budget line, such as *K*. Clearly, then, the choices he has available include not only those points on the budget line, *AE*, but also any point in the shaded triangle formed by that line and the two axes. By contrast, points above the budget line, such as *G*, are not available to the consumer given his limited budget. A bundle of five pounds of cheese and two boxes of rubber bands would cost $16, which is more than he has to spend.

## CHANGES IN THE BUDGET LINE

The position of the budget line is determined by two types of data: the prices of the commodities purchased and the income at the buyer's disposal. We can complete our discussion of the graphics of the budget line by examining briefly how a change in either prices or income affects the location of that line.

Obviously, any increase in the income of the household increases the range of options available to it. Specifically, *increases in income produce parallel shifts in the budget line*, as shown in Figure 6–6. The reason is simple: An increase in available income of, say, 50 percent, if spent entirely on these two goods, would permit the family to purchase exactly 50 percent more of *either* commodity. Point *A* in Figure 6–5 would shift upward by 50 percent of its distance from the origin, whereas point *E* would move to the right by 50 percent.[6] Figure 6–6 shows three such budget lines corresponding to incomes of $9, $12, and $18, respectively.

Finally, we can ask what happens to the budget line when the price of some commodity changes. In Figure 6–7, when the price of the rubber bands *decreases*, the budget line moves outward, but the move is no longer parallel because the point on the cheese axis remains fixed. Once again, the reason is fairly straightforward. A 50 percent reduction in the price of rubber bands (from

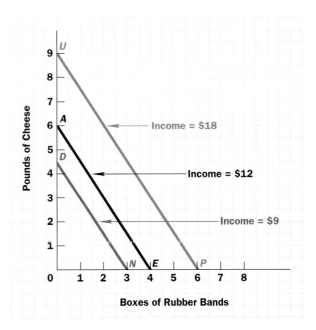

**FIGURE 6–6**

**The Effect of Income Changes on the Budget Line**

$3.00 to $1.50) permits the consumer to buy twice as many boxes of rubber bands with his $12 as before: Point *E* moves rightward to point *H*, where the buyer can obtain eight boxes of rubber bands. However, since the price of cheese has not changed from point *A*, the amount of cheese that can be bought for $12 is unaffected. This gives the general result that *a reduction in the price of one of the two commodities swings the budget line*

**FIGURE 6–7**

**The Effect of Price Changes on the Budget Line**

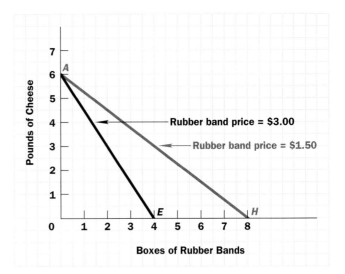

*outward along the axis representing the quantity of that item while leaving the location of the other end of the line unchanged.* Thus a fall in the price of rubber bands from $3.00 to $1.50 swings the price line from *AE* to red line *AH*. This happens because at the higher price, $12 buys only four boxes of rubber bands, but at the lower price, it can buy eight boxes.

### ■ WHAT THE CONSUMER PREFERS: PROPERTIES OF THE INDIFFERENCE CURVE

The budget line indicates what choices are *available* to the consumer, given the size of his income and the commodity prices fixed by the market. Next, we must examine the consumer's *preferences* in order to determine which of these available possibilities he will choose.

After much investigation, economists have determined what they believe to be the minimum amount of information they need about a purchaser in order to analyze his choices. Economists only need know how a consumer *ranks* alternative bundles of available commodities. Suppose, for instance, that the consumer can choose between two bundles of goods, Bundle *W*, which contains three boxes of rubber bands and one pound of cheese, and Bundle *T*, which contains two boxes of rubber bands and three pounds of cheese. The economist wants to know for this purpose only whether the consumer prefers *W* to *T* or *T* to *W*, or whether he is *indifferent* about which one he gets. Note that the analysis requires no information about *degree* of preference—whether the consumer is wildly more enthusiastic about one of the bundles or just prefers it slightly.

Graphically, the preference information is provided by a group of curves called *indifference curves* (Figure 6–8). Any point on the diagram represents a combination of cheese and rubber bands. (For example, point *T* on indifference curve *I*ᵦ represents two boxes of rubber bands and three pounds of cheese.) Any two points on the same indifference curve (for example, *S* and *W*, on indifference curve *I*ₐ) represent two combinations of the goods that the consumer likes equally well. If two points, such as *T* and *W*, lie on different indifference curves, the consumer prefers the one on the higher indifference curve.

> An *indifference curve* is a line connecting all combinations of the commodities that are equally desirable to the consumer.

But before we examine these curves, let us see how to interpret such a curve. A single point on an indifference curve says nothing about preferences. For example, point *R* on curve *I* simply represents the bundle of goods composed of four boxes of rubber bands and ½ pound of cheese. It does *not* suggest that the consumer is indifferent between ½ pound of cheese and four boxes of rubber bands. For the curve to indicate anything, one must consider at

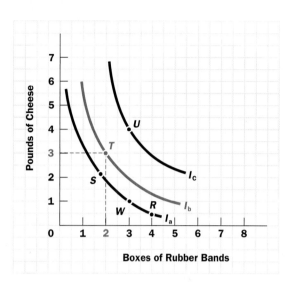

**FIGURE 6–8**

**Three Indifference Curves for Cheese and Rubber Bands**

least two of its points, for example, points *S* and *W*. An indifference curve, by definition, represents all such combinations that provide equal utility to the consumer.

We do not know yet which bundle, among all of the bundles he can afford, the consumer prefers; this analysis indicates only that a choice between certain bundles will lead to indifference. Before using indifference curves to analyze the consumer's choice, one must examine a few of its properties. Most important is the fact that:

> As long as the consumer desires *more* of each of the goods in question, *every* point on a higher indifference curve (that is, a curve farther from the origin in the graph) will be preferred to *any* point on a lower indifference curve.

In other words, among indifference curves, *higher is better*. The reason is obvious. Given two indifference curves, say, *I*ᵦ and *I*ᵤ in Figure 6–8, the higher curve will contain points lying above and to the right of some points on the lower curve. Thus, point *U* on curve *I*ᵤ lies above and to the right of point *T* on curve *I*ᵦ. This means that the consumer gets more rubber bands *and* more cheese at *U* than at *T*. Assuming that he desires both commodities, the consumer must prefer *U* to *T*.

Because every point on curve *I*ᵤ is, by definition, equal in desirability to point *U*, and the same relation holds for point *T* and all other points along curve *I*ᵦ, the consumer will prefer *every* point on curve *I*ᵤ to *any* point on curve *I*ᵦ.

This at once implies a second property of indifference curves: *They never intersect.* This is so because if an indifference curve, say, *I*ᵦ, is anywhere above another, say, *I*ₐ, then *I*ᵦ must be above *I*ₐ everywhere, since every point on *I*ᵦ is preferred to every point on *I*ₐ.

Another property that characterizes the indifference curve is its *negative slope*. Again, this holds only if the consumer wants more of both commodities. Consider two points, such as S and R, on the same indifference curve. If the consumer is indifferent between them, one point cannot represent more of *both* commodities than the other point. Since point S represents more cheese than point R, R must offer more rubber bands than S, or the consumer would not be indifferent about which she gets. This means that any movement toward the one with the larger number of rubber bands implies a decrease in the quantity of cheese. The curve will always slope downhill toward the right, a negative slope.

A final property of indifference curves is the nature of their curvature—the way *they round toward the axes*. They are drawn "bowed in"—they flatten out (their slopes decrease in absolute value) as they extend from left to right. To understand why this is so, we must first examine the economic interpretation of the slope of an indifference curve.

## THE SLOPES OF INDIFFERENCE CURVES AND BUDGET LINES

In Figure 6–9, the average slope of the indifference curve between points M and N is represented by RM/RN. RM is the quantity of cheese that the consumer gives up in moving from M to N. Similarly, RN is the

### FIGURE 6-9

**Slopes of a Budget Line and an Indifference Curve**

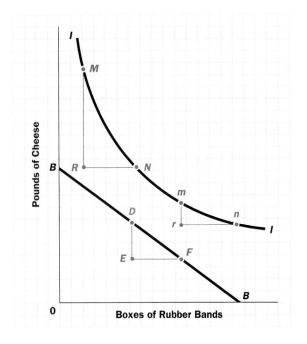

increased number of boxes of rubber bands acquired in this move. Because the consumer is indifferent between bundles M and N, the gain of RN rubber bands must just suffice to compensate him for the loss of RM pounds of cheese. Thus, the ratio RM/RN represents the terms on which the consumer is just willing—*according to his own preference*—to trade one good for the other. If RM/RN equals 2, the consumer is willing to give up (no more than) two pounds of cheese for one additional box of rubber bands.

> The *slope of an indifference curve,* referred to as the *marginal rate of substitution* between the commodities, represents the maximum amount of one commodity that the consumer is willing to give up in exchange for one more unit of another commodity.

The slope of the budget line, BB, in Figure 6–9 is also a rate of exchange between cheese and rubber bands. But it no longer reflects the consumer's subjective willingness to trade. Rather, the slope represents the rate of exchange that *the market* offers to the consumer when he gives up money in exchange for cheese and rubber bands. Recall that the budget line represents all commodity combinations that a consumer can get by spending a fixed amount of money. The budget line is thus a curve of constant expenditure. At current prices, if the consumer reduces his purchase of cheese by amount DE in Figure 6–9, he will save just enough money to buy an additional amount, EF, of rubber bands, since at points D and F he is spending the same total number of dollars.

> The *slope of a budget line* is the amount of one commodity that the market requires an individual to give up in order to obtain one additional unit of another commodity without any change in the amount of money spent.

The slopes of the two types of curves, then, are perfectly analogous in their meaning. The slope of the indifference curve indicates the terms on which the *consumer* is willing to trade one commodity for another, whereas the slope of the budget line reports the *market* terms on which the consumer can trade one good for another.

It is useful to carry our interpretation of the slope of the budget line one step further. Common sense suggests that the market's rate of exchange between cheese and rubber bands should be related to their prices, *pc* and *pr*, and it is easy to show that this is so. Specifically, the slope of the budget line is equal to the ratio of the prices of the two commodities. The reason is straightforward. If the consumer gives up one box of rubber bands, he has *pr* more dollars to spend on cheese. But at a lower price of cheese, this money will enable him to buy a greater quantity of cheese—that is, his cheese purchasing power will be inversely related to its price. Because the price of cheese is *pc* per pound, the additional *pr* dollars permit him to buy *pr/pc* more pounds of cheese. Thus, the slope of the budget line is *pr/pc*.

Before returning to our main subject, the study of consumer choice, we pause briefly and use our interpretation of the slope of the indifference curve to discuss the third of the properties of the indifference curve—its characteristic curvature—which we left unexplained earlier. The shape of indifference curves means that the slope decreases with movement from left to right. In Figure 6–9, at point $m$, toward the right of the diagram, the consumer is willing to give up far less cheese for one more box of rubber bands (quantity $rm$) than he is willing to trade at point $M$, toward the left. This is because at $M$ he initially has a large quantity of cheese and few rubber bands, whereas at $m$ his initial stock of cheese is low and he has many rubber bands. In general terms, the curvature premise on which indifference curves are usually drawn asserts that consumers are relatively eager to trade away a commodity of which they have a large amount but are more reluctant to trade goods of which they hold small quantities. This psychological premise underlies the curvature of the indifference curve.

We can now use our indifference curve apparatus to analyze how the consumer chooses among the combinations that he can afford to buy, that is, the combinations of rubber bands and cheese shown by the budget line. Figure 6–10 brings together in the same diagram the budget line from Figure 6–5 and the indifference curves from Figure 6–8.

## TANGENCY CONDITIONS

Because, according to the first of the properties of indifference curves, the consumer prefers higher curves to lower ones, he will go to the point on the budget line that lies on the highest indifference curve attainable.

**FIGURE 6-10**

**Optimal Consumer Choice**

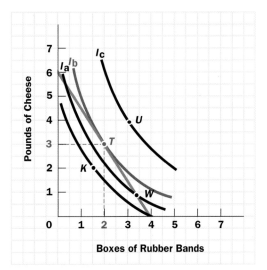

This will be point $T$ on indifference curve $I_b$. He can afford no other point that he likes as well. For example, neither point $K$ below the budget line nor point $W$ on the budget line gets him on such a high indifference curve. Further, any point on an indifference curve above $I_b$, such as point $U$, is out of the question because it lies beyond his financial means. We end up with a simple rule of consumer choice:

> Consumers will select the most desired combination of goods obtainable for their money. The choice will be that point on the budget line at which the budget line is tangent to an indifference curve.

We can see why only the point of tangency, $T$ (two boxes of rubber bands and three pounds of cheese), will give the consumer the largest utility that his money can buy. Suppose that the consumer were instead to consider buying $3\frac{1}{2}$ boxes of rubber bands and one pound of cheese. This would put him at point $W$ on the budget line and on the indifference curve $I_a$. But then, by buying fewer rubber bands and more cheese (a move upward and to the left on the budget line), he could get to another indifference curve, $I_b$, that would be higher and hence more desirable without spending any more money. It clearly does not pay to end up at $W$. Only the point of tangency, $T$, leaves no room for improvement.

At a point of tangency, where the consumer's benefits from purchasing cheese and rubber bands are maximized, the slope of the budget line equals the slope of the indifference curve. This is true by the definition of a point of tangency. We have just seen that the slope of the indifference curve is the marginal rate of substitution between cheese and rubber bands, and that the slope of the budget line is the ratio of the prices of rubber bands and cheese. We can therefore restate the requirement for the optimal division of the consumer's money between the two commodities in slightly more technical language:

> Consumers will get the most benefit from their money when they choose combinations of commodities whose marginal rates of substitution equal the ratios of their prices.

It is worth reviewing the logic behind this conclusion. Why is it not advisable for the consumer to stop at a point like $W$, where the marginal rate of substitution (slope of the indifference curve) is less than the price ratio (slope of the budget line)? Instead, by moving upward and to the left along his budget line, he can take advantage of market opportunities to obtain a commodity bundle that he likes better. This will always be true, for example, if the amount of cheese the consumer is *personally* willing to exchange for a box of rubber bands (the slope of the indifference curve) is greater than the amount of cheese for which the box of rubber bands trades *on the market* (the slope of the budget line).

## CONSEQUENCES OF INCOME CHANGES: INFERIOR GOODS

Next, consider what happens to the consumer's purchases after a rise in income. We know that a rise in income produces a parallel outward shift in the budget line, such as the shift from *BB* to *CC* in Figure 6–11. The quantity of rubber bands demanded rises from three to four boxes, and the quantity demanded of cheese also increases. This moves the consumer's equilibrium from tangency point *T* to tangency point *E* on a higher indifference curve.

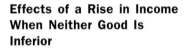

**FIGURE 6-11**

**Effects of a Rise in Income When Neither Good Is Inferior**

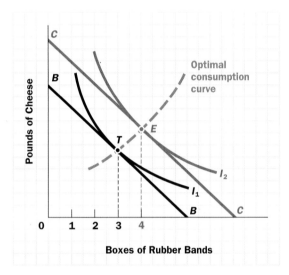

A rise in income may or may not increase the demand for a commodity. In Figure 6–11, the rise in income does lead the consumer to buy more cheese *and* more rubber bands, but indifference curves need not always be positioned in a way that yields this sort of result. In Figure 6–12, as the consumer's budget line rises from *BB* to *CC*, the tangency point moves leftward from *H* to *G*, so that when his income rises he actually buys *fewer* rubber bands. This implies that rubber bands are an *inferior good.*

## CONSEQUENCES OF PRICE CHANGES: DERIVING THE DEMAND CURVE

Finally, we come to the main question underlying demand curves: How does a consumer's choice change if the price of one good changes? We explained earlier that a reduction in the price of a box of rubber bands causes the budget line to swing outward along the horizontal axis while leaving its vertical intercept unchanged. In Figure 6–13, we depict the effect of a decline in the price of rubber

**FIGURE 6-12**

**Effects of a Rise In Income When Rubber Bands Are an Inferior Good**

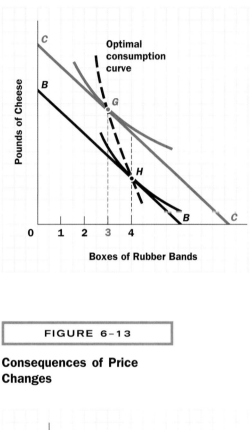

**FIGURE 6-13**

**Consequences of Price Changes**

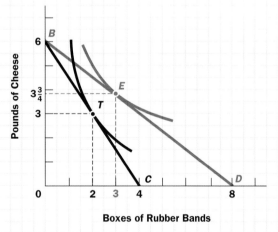

bands on the quantity of rubber bands demanded. As the price of rubber bands falls, the budget line swings from *BC* to *BD*. The tangency points, *T* and *E*, also move in a corresponding direction, causing the quantity demanded to rise from two to three boxes. The price of rubber bands has fallen, and the quantity demanded has risen, so the demand curve for rubber bands is negatively sloped. The desired purchase of rubber bands increases from two to three boxes, and the desired purchase of cheese also increases, from three pounds to $3\frac{3}{4}$ pounds.

The demand curve for rubber bands can be constructed directly from Figure 6–13. Point $T$ shows that the consumer will buy two boxes of rubber bands when the price of a box is $3.00. Point $E$ indicates that when the price falls to $1.50, quantity demanded rises to three boxes of rubber bands.[7] These two pieces of information are shown in Figure 6–14 as points $t$ and $e$ on the demand curve for rubber bands. By examining the effects of other possible prices for rubber bands (other budget lines emanating from point $B$ in Figure 6–13), we can find all the other points on the demand curve in exactly the same way. The demand curve is derived from the indifference-curve diagram by varying the price of the commodity to see the effects of all other possible prices.

The indifference curve diagram also brings out an important point that the demand curve does not show. A change in the *price of rubber bands* also has consequences for the *quantity of cheese demanded* because it affects the amount of money left over for cheese purchases. In the example illustrated in Figure 6–13, the decrease in the price of rubber bands increases the demand for cheese from 3 to $3\frac{3}{4}$ pounds.

**FIGURE 6-14**

**Deriving the Demand Curve for Rubber Bands**

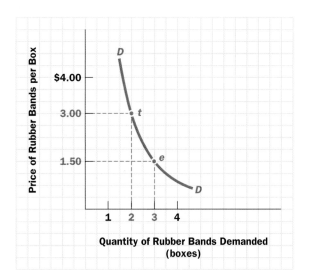

## SUMMARY

1. Indifference-curve analysis permits economists to study the interrelationships of the demands for two (or more) commodities.

2. The basic tools of indifference-curve analysis are the consumer's *budget line* and *indifference curves.*

3. A budget line shows all combinations of two commodities that the consumer can afford, given the prices of the commodities and the amount of money the consumer has available to spend.

4. The budget line is a straight line whose slope equals the ratio of the prices of the commodities. A change in price changes the slope of the budget line. A change in the consumer's income causes a parallel shift in the budget line.

5. Two points on an indifference curve represent two combinations of commodities such that the consumer does not prefer one combination over the other.

6. Indifference curves normally have negative slopes and are "bowed in" toward the origin. The *slope of an indifference curve* indicates how much of one commodity the consumer is willing to give up in order to get an additional unit of the other commodity.

7. The consumer will choose the point on her budget line that gets her to the highest attainable indifference curve. Normally this will occur at the point of tangency between the two curves. This point indicates the combination of commodities that gives her the greatest benefits for the amount of money she has available to spend.

8. The consumer's demand curve can be derived from her indifference curve.

## KEY TERMS

Budget Line    109

Indifference curve    111

Marginal rate of substitution    112

Slope of an indifference curve    112

Slope of a budget line    112

---

[7] How do we know that the price of rubber bands corresponding to the budget line *BD* is $1.50? Because the $12.00 total budget will purchase at most eight boxes (point *D*), the price per box must be $12.00/8 = $1.50.

1. John Q. Public spends all of his income on gasoline and hot dogs. Draw his budget line under several conditions:

   a. His income is $80 and one gallon of gasoline and one hot dog each cost $1.60.

   b. His income is $120 and the two prices remain the same.

   c. His income is $80, hot dogs cost $1.60 each, and gasoline costs $1.20 per gallon.

2. Draw some hypothetical indifference curves for John Q. Public on a diagram identical to the one you constructed for the preceding question.

   a. Approximately how much gasoline and how many hot dogs will Mr. Public buy?

   b. How will these choices change if his income increases to $120, as in the previous question? Is either good an inferior good?

   c. How will these choices change if gasoline prices fall to $1.20 per gallon, as in the previous question?

3. Explain the information that the *slope* of an indifference curve conveys about a consumer's preferences. Use this relationship to explain the typical U-shaped curvature of indifference curves.

A high cross elasticity of demand [between two goods indicates that they] compete in the same market. [This can prevent a supplier of one of the products] from possessing monopoly power over price.

U.S. Supreme Court, DuPont cellophane decision, 1956

# DEMAND AND ELASTICITY

In this chapter we continue our study of demand and demand curves, which we began in the previous chapter. We focus here on how we can measure the extent to which quantity demanded responds to price changes, and what such responsiveness implies about the revenue that producers will receive if they change prices. In particular, we introduce and explain an important concept called *elasticity* that economists use to examine the relationship between quantity demanded and price.

## Will Taxing Cigarettes Make Teenagers Stop Smoking?

In 1997, President Bill Clinton proposed legislation that would have forced tobacco companies to raise cigarette prices. Although this proposal was eventually rejected by Congress in 1998, public health experts believe that such increases are a major weapon in the effort to cut teenage smoking. Imagine yourself on a panel of consultants helping a congressional committee draft new legislation to deal with this issue. As the youngest member of the group, you are asked your opinion about how effective a big tax increase on cigarettes would be in getting young people to stop smoking. How would you respond? What sorts of statistical data, if any, would you use to find your answer? And how might you go about analyzing the relevant numbers?

We shed light on such questions in this chapter, where we deal with topics such as the shape of the demand curve and its implications for the effects of a price change on quantity demanded and on the amount of revenue suppliers can earn from consumers. As often happens in economics, we will see that careful investigation brings out some surprises. This is true in the case of taxes to discourage teenage smoking. A tax on cigarettes may actually benefit teenagers'—and other citizens'—health. And it will, of course, benefit government finances by bringing in more tax money. Nothing surprising so far. But the surprise is this: the more effective the tax turns out to be

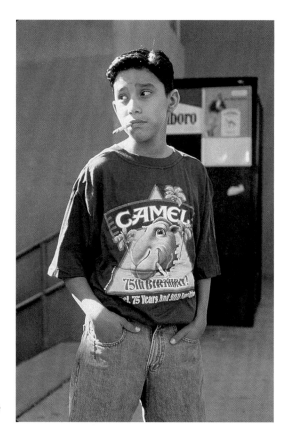

in curbing teenage smoking, the less beneficial it will be to the government's finances, and vice versa: the more it benefits the government, the less it will contribute to health.

The concept of elasticity of demand will make this and other related matters clearer.

# ■ ELASTICITY: THE MEASURE OF RESPONSIVENESS

Governments, business firms, supermarkets, consumers, and law courts need a way to measure how responsive demand is to price changes. Economists measure the responsiveness of quantity demanded to price changes via a concept called *elasticity*. Marketers sometimes use estimated elasticities to decide how to price their products, whether to add new product models, and other questions. A relatively flat demand curve like Figure 7–1(b) indicates that consumers respond sharply to a change in price—the quantity they demand falls by 2.5 units (from 4 units to 1.5 units) when price rises $10. They demand or buy much less of the product when price rises even a little bit. Such a "touchy" curve is called *elastic* or *highly elastic*. A relatively steep demand curve like Figure 7–1(a), which indicates that consumers respond hardly at all to a price change, is called *inelastic*. In this graph, a $10 price rise cuts quantity demanded by only one unit.

**Two Hypothetical Demand Curves for Film** | **FIGURE 7–1**

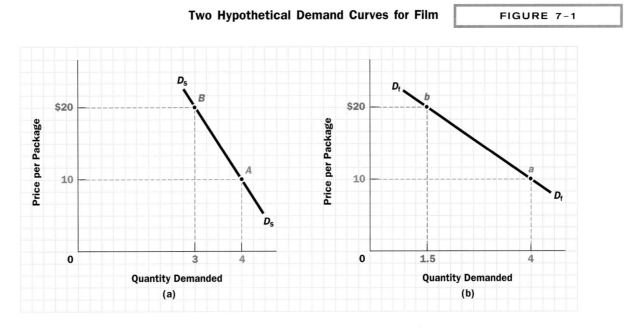

NOTE: Quantities are in millions of packages of film per year.

The precise measure used for this purpose is called the **price elasticity of demand,** or sometimes simply the **elasticity of demand.** We define elasticity of demand as the ratio of the *percentage* change in quantity demanded to the associated *percentage* change in price.

> The **(price) elasticity of demand** is the ratio of the *percentage* change in quantity demanded to the *percentage* change in price that brings about the change in quantity demanded.

Thus, demand is called *elastic* if, say, a 10 percent rise in price reduces quantity demanded by *more* than 10 percent. Demand is called *inelastic* if such a rise in price reduces quantity demanded by *less* than 10 percent.

Why do we need these definitions to analyze the responsiveness to price shown by a particular demand curve? At first, it may seem that the *slope* of the demand curve conveys the needed information: Curve $D_sD_s$ is much steeper than curve $D_fD_f$ in Figure 7–1, so any given change in price appears to correspond to a much smaller change in quantity demanded in Figure 7–1(a) than in Figure 7–1(b). For this reason, it is tempting to call demand in Panel (b) "more elastic." But slope will not do the job, because the slope of any curve depends on the particular units of measurement (as we showed in Chapter 2), and economists use no standardized units of measurement. Cloth output may be measured in yards or in meters, milk in quarts or liters, and coal in tons or hundred-weights. Figure 7–2(a) brings out the point explicitly. In this graph, we return to the pizza example from Chapter 6, measuring quantity demanded in terms of pizzas and price in dollars per pizza. A fall in price from $15 to $11 per large pizza (points *A* and *B*) raises quantity demanded at Paula's Pizza Parlor from 280 pizzas to 360 per week, that is, by 80 pizzas.

| FIGURE 7–2 | The Sensitivity of Slope to Units of Measurement at Paula's Pizza Parlor |

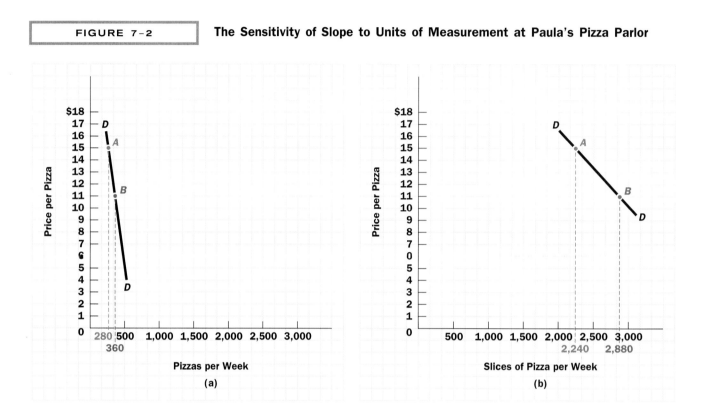

(a)

Pizzas per Week

(b)

Slices of Pizza per Week

Now look at Figure 7–2(b), which provides *exactly* the same information, but measures quantity demanded in *slices* of pizzas rather than whole pizzas (assuming one pizza yields eight slices). Thus, the same price change as before increases quantity demanded, from 8 × 280 = 2,240 slices to 8 × 360 = 2,880 slices—that is, by 640 slices, rather than by 80 pizzas.

Visually, the increase in quantity demanded looks eight times as great in Panel (b) as in Panel (a), but all that has changed is the unit of measurement. The 640-unit increase in Figure 7–2(b) represents the same increase in quantity demanded as the 80-unit increase in Figure 7–2(a). Just as you get different numbers for a given rise in temperature, depending on whether you measure it in Celsius or Fahrenheit, so the slopes of demand curves differ, depending on whether you measure quantity in pizzas or in pizza slices. Clearly, then, slope does not really measure responsiveness of quantity demanded to price, because the measure changes whenever the units of measurement change.

Economists created the elasticity concept precisely in response to this problem. Elasticity measures responsiveness on the basis of *percentage* changes in price and quantity rather than on *absolute* changes. The elasticity formula solves the units problem because percentages are unaffected by units of measurement. If the government defense budget doubles, it goes up by 100 percent, whether measured in millions or billions of dollars. If a person's height doubles between the ages of 2 and 18, it goes up 100 percent, whether measured in inches or centimeters. The elasticity formula given earlier expresses both the change in quantity demanded and the change in price as *percentages*.[1]

---

[1] The remainder of this section involves fairly technical computational issues. On a first reading you may prefer to go directly to the new section that begins at the bottom of the next page.

Further, elasticity calculates the change in quantity demanded *as a percentage of the average of the two quantities*: the quantity demanded *before* the change in price has occurred ($Q_0$) and the quantity demanded *after* the price change ($Q_1$). In our example, the number of pizzas sold per week rises by 80, which is 25 percent of the average (320) of 280 ($Q_0$) and 360 ($Q_1$), the "before" and "after" sale of pizzas. This is a useful compromise between viewing the change in quantity demanded (80 pizzas) as a percentage of the initial quantity (280) or as a percentage of the final quantity (360).

Similarly, the change in price is expressed as a percentage of the average of the "before" and "after" prices, so that, in effect, it represents elasticity at the price halfway between those two prices. That is, the price falls by $4 (from $15 to $11). Because $4 is (approximately) 31 percent of the average of $15 ($P_0$) and $11 ($P_1$) ($13), we say that in this case a 31 percent fall in price led to a 25 percent rise in quantity of pizza demanded.

To summarize, the elasticity formula has two basic attributes:

■ Each of the changes with which it deals is measured as a *percentage* change.

■ Each of the percentage changes is calculated in terms of the average values of the before and after quantities and prices.

In addition, economists usually adjust the price elasticity of demand formula a third way. Note that when the price *increases*, the quantity demanded usually *declines*. So, when the price change is a positive number, the quantity change will normally be a negative number, and when the price change is a negative number, the quantity change will normally be a positive number. This means that the ratio of the two percentage changes will be a negative number. However, we customarily express elasticity as a positive number. Hence:

■ Each percentage change is taken as an "absolute value," meaning that the calculation drops all minus signs.[2]

We can now state the formula for price elasticity of demand, keeping all three features of the formula in mind:

$$\text{Price elasticity of demand} = \frac{\text{Change in quantity demanded, expressed as a percentage of the average of the before and after quantities}}{\text{Corresponding percentage change in price}}$$

In our example:

$$\text{Elasticity of demand for pizzas} =$$

$$-\frac{(Q_1 - Q_0)/\text{average of } Q_0 \text{ and } Q_1}{(P_1 - P_0)/\text{average of } P_0 \text{ and } P_1} = -\frac{80/320}{-4/13} = \frac{25\%}{31\%} = 0.8 \text{ (approximately)}$$

## PRICE ELASTICITY OF DEMAND AND THE SHAPES OF DEMAND CURVES

We noted earlier that looks can be deceiving in some demand curves because their units of measurement are arbitrary. Economists have provided the elasticity formula to overcome that problem. Nonetheless, the shape of a demand curve does convey some information about its elasticity. Let us see what information some demand curve shapes give, with the aid of Figure 7–3.

---

[2] This third attribute of the elasticity formula—the removal of all minus signs—applies only when the formula is used to measure the responsiveness of *quantity demanded* to a change in *price*. Later in the chapter, we will show that similar formulas are used to measure the responsiveness between other pairs of variables. For example, the elasticity of supply uses a similar formula to measure the responsiveness of quantity supplied to price. In such other uses, it is not customary to drop minus signs when calculating elasticity. The reasons will become clearer later in the chapter.

| FIGURE 7–3 | **Demand Curves with Different Elasticities** |

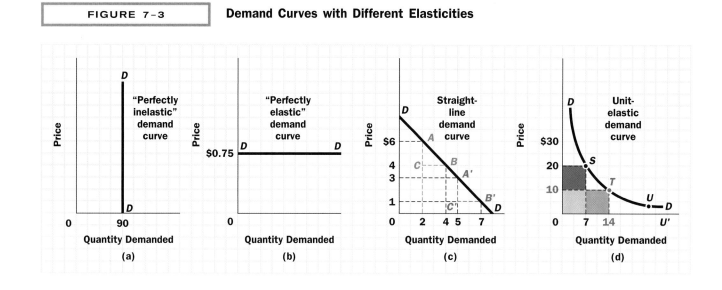

**PERFECTLY INELASTIC DEMAND CURVES**  Panel (a) depicts a completely vertical demand curve. Such a curve is called *perfectly inelastic* throughout because its elasticity is zero at every point on the curve. Because quantity demanded remains at 90 units no matter what the price, the percentage change in quantity is always zero, and hence in this case the elasticity (which equals percentage change in quantity divided by percentage change in price) is always zero. Thus, in this case, consumer purchases do not respond at all to any change in price.

Vertical demand curves like this occur when a commodity is very inexpensive. For example, you probably will not buy more rubber bands if their prices fall. The demand curve may also be vertical when consumers consider the item in question an absolute necessity. For example, if your roommate's grandfather has a heart attack, the family will buy whatever medicine the doctor prescribes, regardless of the price, and will not purchase any more even if the price falls.

**PERFECTLY ELASTIC DEMAND CURVES**  Panel (b) of Figure 7–3 shows the opposite extreme: a horizontal demand curve. This curve is said to be *perfectly elastic* (or *infinitely elastic*). At any price above $0.75, quantity demanded will drop to zero; that is, the percentage change in quantity demanded will be infinitely large. Perfect elasticity typically occurs when many producers sell a product and consumers can switch easily from one seller to another if the former raises his price. For example, suppose you and the other students in the economics class are required to buy a newspaper every day to keep up with economic events. If newsdealer X, from whom you have been buying the newspaper, raises the price from 75 cents to 80 cents, while the competitor, Y, across the street keeps the old price, then X may lose all her newspaper customers to Y. This is likely to be true whenever an acceptable rival product is available at the going price (75 cents in the diagram). In cases where no one will pay more than the going price, the seller will lose all of her customers if she raises her price by even a penny.

**(SEEMINGLY SIMPLE) STRAIGHT-LINE DEMAND CURVES**  Panel (c) of Figure 7–3 depicts a case between these two extremes: a *straight-line* demand curve that runs neither vertically nor horizontally. Though the *slope* of a straight-line demand curve remains constant throughout its length, its *elasticity* does not. For example, the elasticity of demand between points *A* and *B* in Figure 7–3(c) is as follows:

$$\frac{\text{Change in } Q \text{ as a percentage of average } Q}{\text{Change in } P \text{ as a percentage of average } P} = \frac{2/3}{2/5} = \frac{66.67\%}{40\%} = 1.67$$

But the elasticity of demand between points *A'* and *B'* is as follows:

$$\frac{2 \text{ as percentage of } 6}{2 \text{ as a percentage of } 2} = \frac{33.33 \text{ percent}}{100 \text{ percent}} = 0.33$$

The general point is that:

> Along a straight-line demand curve, the price elasticity of demand grows steadily smaller as you move from left to right. That is because the quantity keeps getting larger, so that a given *numerical* change in quantity becomes an ever smaller *percentage* change. But the price keeps going lower, so that a given numerical change in price becomes an ever larger percentage change.

**UNIT-ELASTIC DEMAND CURVES**   If the elasticity of a straight-line demand curve varies from one part of the curve to another, what does a demand curve with the same elasticity throughout its length look like? For reasons explained in the next section, it has the general shape indicated in Figure 7–3(d). That panel shows a curve with elasticity equal to 1 throughout (a *unit-elastic* demand curve). A unit-elastic demand curve bends in the middle toward the origin of the graph—at either end, it moves closer and closer to the axes but never touches or crosses them.

As we have noted, a curve with an elasticity greater than 1 is called an *elastic demand curve* (one for which the percentage change in quantity demanded will be greater than the percentage change in price); a curve whose elasticity is less than 1 is known as an *inelastic* curve. When elasticity is exactly 1, economists say that the curve is *unit-elastic*.

Real-world price elasticities of demand seem to vary considerably from product to product. Moderate luxury goods, such as expensive vacations, are generally more price elastic than goods like milk and shirts, which are considered necessities. Products with close substitutes, like Coke and Pepsi, tend to have relatively high elasticities because if one soft drink gets expensive, consumers will switch to the other. Also, the elasticities of demand for goods that business firms buy, such as raw materials and machinery, tend to be higher on the whole than those for consumers' goods. This is because competition forces firms to buy their supplies wherever they can get them most cheaply. The exception occurs when a firm requires a particular input for which no reasonable substitutes exist or the available substitutes are substantially inferior. Table 7–1 gives actual statistical estimates of elasticities for some industries in the economy.

| | Price Elasticity Estimates | TABLE 7-1 |
|---|---|---|

| Product | Price Elasticity |
|---|---|
| Industrial Chemicals | 0.4% |
| Shoe repairs and cleaning | 0.4 |
| Food, tobacco, and beverages | 0.5 |
| Newspaper and magazines | 0.5 |
| Data processing, precision and optical instruments | 0.7 |
| Medical care and hospitalization insurance | 0.8 |
| Metal products | 1.1 |
| Purchased meals (excluding alcoholic beverages) | 1.6 |
| Electricity (household utility) | 1.9 |
| Boats, pleasure aircraft | 2.4 |
| Public transportation | 3.5 |
| China, tableware | 8.8 |

SOURCES: H. S. Houthakker and Lester D. Taylor, Consumer Demand in the United States, 2d ed. (Cambridge, Mass.: Harvard University Press, 1970), pp. 153–158; and Joachim Möller, "Income and Price Elasticities in Different Sectors of the Economy—An Analysis of Structural Change for Germany, the U.K., and U.S." University of Regensburg, December 1998. Thanks to Professor Möller for the early release of his estimates.

## PRICE ELASTICITY OF DEMAND: ITS EFFECT ON TOTAL REVENUE AND TOTAL EXPENDITURE

Aside from its role as a measure of the responsiveness of demand to a change in price, elasticity serves a second very important purpose. As a real illustration at the end of this chapter will show, a firm often wants to know whether a rise in price will increase or decrease its total revenue—the money it obtains from sales to its customers. The price elasticity of demand provides a simple guide to the answer:

> If demand for the seller's product is elastic, a price increase will decrease total revenue. If demand is exactly unit-elastic, a rise in price will leave total revenue unaffected. If demand is inelastic, a rise in price will raise total revenue. The opposite changes will occur when price falls.

A corresponding story must hold true about the expenditures made by the *buyers* of the product. After all, the expenditures of the buyers are exactly the same thing as the revenues of the seller.

These relationships between elasticity and total revenue hold because total revenue (or expenditure) equals price times quantity demanded, $P \times Q$, and a fall in price has two opposing effects on that arithmetic product. It decreases $P$, and, if the demand curve is negatively sloped, it increases $Q$. The first effect *decreases revenues* by cutting the amount of money that consumers spend on each unit of the good. But the second effect *increases* revenues by raising the number of units of the good that the firm sells.

The net effect on total revenue (or total expenditure) depends on the elasticity. If price goes down 10 percent and quantity demanded increases 10 percent (a case of *unit elasticity*), the two effects just cancel out: $P \times Q$ remains constant. On the other hand, if price goes down 10 percent and quantity demanded rises 15 percent (a case of *elastic* demand), $P \times Q$ increases. Finally, if a 10 percent price fall leads to only a 5 percent rise in quantity demanded (*inelastic* demand), $P \times Q$ falls.

We can easily see the relationship between elasticity and total revenue in a graph. First, note that:

> The total revenue (or expenditure) represented by any point on a demand curve (any price-quantity combination), such as point $S$ in Figure 7–4, equals the area of the rectangle under that point (the area of rectangle $ORST$ in the figure). This is true because the area of a rectangle equals its height times width, $OR$ times $RS$. That is, clearly, price times quantity, which is exactly total revenue.

**FIGURE 7–4**

**An Elastic Demand Curve**

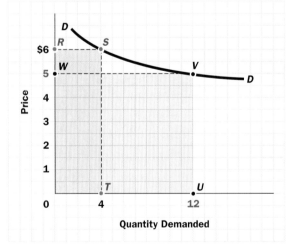

Quantity Demanded

To illustrate the connection between elasticity and consumer expenditure, Figure 7–4 shows an elastic portion of a demand curve, *DD*. In this figure, when price falls, quantity demanded rises by a greater percentage, increasing total expenditure. At a price of $6 per unit, the quantity sold is four units, so total expenditure is $4 \times \$6 = \$24$, represented by the vertical rectangle whose upper right-hand corner is point $S$. When price falls to $5 per unit, 12 units are sold. Consequently, the new expenditure ($\$60 = \$5 \times 12$), measured by the rectangle $0UVW$, exceeds the old.

In contrast, Figure 7–3(d), the unit-elastic demand curve, shows constant expenditures even though price changes. Total spending is $140 whether the price is $20 and seven units are sold (point $S$), or the price is $10 and 14 units are sold (point $T$).

This discussion also indicates why a unit-elastic demand curve must have the shape depicted in Figure 7–3(d), hugging the axes closer and closer but never touching or crossing them. When demand is unit elastic, total expenditure must be the same at every point on the curve. It must equal $140 at point $S$ and point $T$ and point $U$. Suppose that at point $U$ (or some other point on the curve), the demand curve were to touch the horizontal axis, meaning that the price would equal zero.

Then total expenditure would be zero, not $140. Therefore, if the demand curve remains unit elastic all along its length, it can never cross the horizontal axis (where $P = 0$). By the same reasoning, it cannot cross the vertical axis (where $Q = 0$). Because the slope of the demand curve is negative, the curve simply must get closer and closer to the axes as it moves away from its middle points, as illustrated in Figure 7–3(d).

All this indicates why demand elasticity is so important for business decisions. A firm should not jump to the conclusion that a price increase will automatically add to its profits, for it may find that consumers take their revenge by cutting back on their purchases. For example, when Heinz's Pet Products Co. raised the prices of its 9-Lives cat food a few years ago, its market share plummeted from 23 percent to 15 percent as customers flocked to other brands. In fact, if its demand curve is elastic, a firm that raises price will end up selling so many fewer units that its total revenue will actually fall, even though it makes more money than before on each unit it sells.

Price *cuts* can also be hazardous—if the elasticity of demand is low. For example, among adult smokers cigarettes have an estimated price elasticity of approximately 0.4, meaning that we can expect a 10 percent drop in price to induce only a 4 percent rise in demand. This may explain why, when Philip Morris cut the price of Marlboros by about 18 percent, the company's profits dropped by 25 percent within months. Thus, the strategic value to a business firm of a price rise or a price cut depends very much on the elasticity of demand for its product. But elasticity only tells us how a price change affects a firm's revenues; later, we'll consider the impact of costs on the firm's output decisions.

### So, Will a Cigarette Tax Decrease Teenage Smoking Significantly?

We're back to the issue with which we began this chapter: Will a tax on cigarettes, which increases their price, effectively reduce teenage smoking? We can express the answer in terms of the price elasticity of demand for cigarettes by teenagers. If that demand elasticity is high, the tax will be effective, because a small increase in cigarette taxes will lead to a sharp cut in purchases by teenagers. The opposite will clearly be true if this demand elasticity number is small.

Young people *are* more sensitive to price increases than adult smokers. The estimates on teenagers' price elasticity of demand for cigarettes range from about 0.7 all the way up to 1.65.[3] This means that if, for example, a tax on cigarettes raised their price 10 percent, the number of teenage smokers would fall by somewhere between 7 and 16.5 percent. If these elasticity estimates are accurate, we can expect that a significant tax on cigarettes that results in a significant price increase would cause a higher percentage of teenagers than adults to stop smoking.

We said earlier in the chapter that if a cigarette tax program failed to curb teen smoking, it would benefit the government's tax collectors a great deal. On the other hand, if the program successfully curbed teenage smoking, then government finances would benefit only a little. The logic of this should now be clear. If teen cigarette demand were inelastic, the tax program would fail to make a dent in teen smoking. That would mean that many teenagers would continue to

---

[3] Sources: *Economic Report of the President 1997*, Washington, D.C.: U.S. Government Printing Office, February 1997; David R. Francis, "Demographic Groups Differ in Response to Substance Abuse Policies," *The NBER Digest*, National Bureau of Economic Research, September 1998, www.nber.org, who cites Frank Chaloupka and Rosalie Liccardo Pacula, "An Examination of Gender and Race Differences in Youth Smoking Responsiveness to Price and Tobacco Control Policies," NBER Working Paper No. 6541; Barry Meier, "Proposed Cigarette Deal Doesn't Force Rise in Price," *New York Times*, October 9, 1998, p. A14; Daniel Seligman, "Keeping Up: A Case for the Three-Day Week, How to Really Stop Smoking, the Mob Cuts Prices, and Other Matters," *Fortune*, July 30, 1990, who cites Michael Grossman, City University of New York.

buy cigarettes and government tax revenue would grow as a result of the rise in tax rate. But when elasticity is high, a price rise *decreases* total revenue (in this case, the amount of tax revenues collected) because quantity demanded falls by a greater percentage than the price rises. That is, with an elastic demand, relatively few teen smokers will remain after the tax increase, so there will be few of them to pay the new taxes. The government will "lose out." Of course, in this case the tax seeks to change behavior, so the government would no doubt rejoice at its small revenues!

## WHAT DETERMINES DEMAND ELASTICITY?

What kinds of goods have elastic demand curves, meaning that quantity demanded responds strongly to price? What kinds of goods have inelastic demand curves? Several factors influence consumers' sensitivity to price changes.

**NATURE OF THE GOOD**   *Necessities*, such as basic foodstuffs, normally have relatively inelastic demand curves, meaning that the quantities consumers demand of these products respond very little to price changes. For example, people buy roughly the same quantity of potatoes even when the price of potatoes rises. One study estimated that the price elasticity of demand for potatoes is just 0.3, meaning that when their price rises 10 percent, the quantity of potatoes purchased falls only 3 percent. In contrast, many *luxury goods*, such as restaurant meals, have rather elastic demand curves. One estimate found that the price elasticity of demand for restaurant meals is 1.6, so that we can expect a 10 percent price rise to cut purchases by 16 percent.

**AVAILABILITY OF CLOSE SUBSTITUTES**   If consumers can easily obtain a good substitute for a product whose price increases, they will switch readily. Thus, when the market offers close substitutes for a given product, its demand will be more elastic. Substitutability is often a critical determinant of elasticity. The demand for gasoline is inelastic because we cannot easily run a car without it, but the demand for *any particular brand* of gasoline is extremely elastic, because other brands will work just as well. This example suggests a general principle: the demand for narrowly

"Why does it have to be us who prove that price elasticity really works?"

defined commodities (such as romaine lettuce) is more elastic than the demand for more broadly defined commodities (such as vegetables).

**FRACTION OF INCOME ABSORBED**   The fraction of income absorbed by the purchase of a particular item also affects its elasticity. Very inexpensive items tend to have inelastic demand curves. Who will buy fewer rubberbands if their price rises ten percent? But some families will be forced to postpone buying new cars, or will buy used cars instead, if auto prices go up by ten percent.

**PASSAGE OF TIME**   The time period is relevant because the demand for many products is more elastic in the long run than in the short run. For example, when the price of home heating oil rose in the 1970s, some homeowners switched from oil heat to gas heat. Very few of them switched immediately, however, because they needed to retrofit their furnaces to accommodate the other fuel. So the short-term demand for oil was quite inelastic. As time passed and more homeowners had the opportunity to purchase and install new furnaces, the demand curve gradually became more elastic.

## ELASTICITY AS A GENERAL CONCEPT

So far we have looked only at how quantity demanded responds to price changes— that is, the *price* elasticity of demand. But elasticity has a more general use in measuring how any one economic variable responds to changes in another. From our earlier discussion we know that a firm will be keenly interested in the price elasticity of its demand curve, but its interest in demand does not end there. As we have noted, quantity demanded depends on other things besides price. Business firms will be interested in consumer responsiveness to changes in these variables as well.

### INCOME ELASTICITY

For example, quantity demanded depends on consumer incomes. A business firm's managers will, therefore, want to know how much a change in consumer income will affect the quantity of its product demanded. Fortunately, an elasticity measure can be helpful here too. An increase in consumer incomes clearly raises the amounts of most goods that consumers will demand. To measure the response, economists use the **income elasticity of demand,** which is the ratio of the percentage change in quantity demanded to the percentage change in income. For example, foreign travel is quite income elastic, with middle and higher income people traveling abroad much more extensively than poor people do. In contrast, blue jeans, worn by rich and poor alike, show little demand increase as income increases.

> **Income elasticity of demand** is the ratio of the percentage change in quantity demanded to the percentage change in income.

### PRICE ELASTICITY OF SUPPLY

Economists also use elasticity to measure other responses. For example, to measure the response of quantity *supplied* to a change in price, we use the *price elasticity of supply*—defined as the ratio of the percentage change in quantity supplied to the percentage change in price. The logic and analysis of all such elasticity concepts are, of course, perfectly analogous to those for price elasticity of demand.

### CROSS ELASTICITY OF DEMAND

Consumers' demand for many products are substantially affected by the quantities and prices of *other* available products. Some goods make other products more desirable; some products decrease consumer demand for other goods.

Some products just naturally go together. For example, cream and sugar increase the desirability of coffee, and vice versa. The same is true of mustard or ketchup and hamburgers. In some extreme cases, neither product ordinarily has any use without the other—automobiles and tires, shoes and shoelaces, and so on. Such goods, each of which makes the other more valuable, are called **complements.**

> Two goods are called **complements** if an increase in the quantity consumed of one increases the quantity demanded of the other, all other things remaining constant.

The demand curves of complements are interrelated; specifically, a rise in the price of coffee is likely to reduce the quantity of sugar demanded. Why? When coffee prices rise, people drink less coffee and therefore demand less sugar to sweeten it. The opposite will be true of a fall in coffee prices. A similar relationship holds for other complementary goods.

At the other extreme, some goods make one another *less* valuable. These are called **substitutes.** Ownership of a motorcycle, for example, may decrease one's desire for a bicycle. If your pantry is stocked with cans of tuna fish, you are less likely to rush out and buy cans of salmon. As you may expect, demand curves for substitutes are also related, but in the opposite direction. When the price of motorcycles falls, people may demand fewer bicycles, so the quantity demanded falls. When the price of salmon goes up, people may eat more tuna.

Economists use another elasticity measure to determine whether two products are substitutes or complements: their **cross elasticity of demand.** This measure is defined much like the ordinary price elasticity of demand, only instead of measuring the responsiveness of the quantity demanded of, say, coffee, to a change in its own price, cross elasticity of demand measures how quantity demanded of one good (coffee) responds to a change in the price of another, say, sugar. For example, if a 20 percent rise in the price of sugar reduces the quantity of coffee demanded by 5 percent (a change of *minus* 5 percent in quantity demanded), then the cross elasticity of demand will be:

$$\frac{\text{Percentage change in quantity of coffee demanded}}{\text{Percentage change in sugar price}} = \frac{-5\%}{20\%} = -0.25$$

Obviously, cross elasticity is important for business firms, especially where rival firms' prices are concerned. Northwest Airlines, for example, knows all too well that it will lose customers if it does not match price cuts by Continental or United. Coke and Pepsi provide another clear case in which cross elasticity of demand is crucial. But firms other than direct competitors may well take a substantial interest in cross elasticity. For example, the prices of VCRs and video rentals may profoundly affect the quantity of theater tickets that consumers demand.

The cross elasticity of demand measure underlies the following rule about complements and substitutes:

> If two goods are substitutes, a rise in the price of one of them tends to raise the quantity demanded of the other; so their cross elasticities of demand will normally be positive. If two goods are complements, a rise in the price of one of them tends to decrease the quantity demanded of the other item, so their cross elasticities will normally be negative. Notice that, because cross elasticities can be positive or negative, we do *not* customarily drop minus signs as we do in a calculation of the ordinary price elasticity of demand.

This result is really a matter of common sense. If the price of a good rises and buyers can find a substitute, they will tend to switch to the substitute. If the price of Japanese cameras goes up and the price of American cameras does not, at least some people will switch to the American product. Thus, a *rise* in the price of Japanese cameras causes a *rise* in the quantity of American cameras demanded. Both percentage changes are positive numbers and so their ratio, the cross elasticity of demand, is also positive.

On the other hand, if two goods are complements, a rise in the price of one will discourage both its own use and use of the complementary good. Automobiles and car radios are obviously complements. A large increase in automobile prices will depress car sales, and this in turn will reduce sales of car radios. Thus, a positive percentage change in the price of cars leads to a negative percentage change in the quantity of car radios demanded. The ratio of these numbers, the cross elasticity of demand for cars and radios, is therefore negative.

In practice, courts of law often evaluate cross elasticity of demand to measure whether particular firms face strong competition that can prevent them from overcharging consumers—hence, the quote from the U.S. Supreme Court at the

---

Two goods are called **substitutes** if an increase in the quantity consumed of one cuts the quantity demanded of the other, all other things remaining constant.

The **cross elasticity of demand** for Product X to a change in the price of another product, Y, is the ratio of the percentage change in quantity demanded of X to the percentage change in the price of Y that brings about the change in quantity demanded.

opening of this chapter. The quotation is one of the earliest examples of the courts using the concept of cross elasticities. It tells us that if two rival products exhibit a high cross elasticity of demand, for example, between McDonald's and Burger King, then neither firm can raise its price much without losing customers to the other. If this is so, no one can legitimately claim that either firm has a monopoly. If a rise in Firm X's price causes its consumers to switch in droves to a competitor's product, Y, then the cross elasticity of demand for Product Y with respect to the price of X will be high. That, in turn, means that competition is really powerful enough to prevent Firm X from raising its price arbitrarily. This is why cross elasticity is used so often in litigation before courts or government regulatory agencies when the degree of competition is an important issue. The cross elasticity issue keeps coming up whenever firms are accused of acting like monopolists. For example, in 1997 a dispute arose between Litton and Honeywell, the two main manufacturers of the mechanisms that guide the flight of aircraft. In 1998 the issue reappeared in a lawsuit in which Rolite, an ash recycling firm, sued Waste Management, a waste removal company, charging monopolistic behavior by the latter.

## ■ CHANGES IN DEMAND: MOVEMENTS ALONG THE DEMAND CURVE VERSUS SHIFTS IN THE DEMAND CURVE

Demand is obviously a complex phenomenon. We have studied in detail the dependence of quantity demanded on price, and we have noted that quantity demanded depends also on *other* variables such as consumers' incomes and the prices of complementary and substitute products. Because of changes in these *other* variables (which we formerly held constant while we were studying only the impact of changes in price), demand curves often do not keep the same shape and position as time passes. Instead, they shift about. Chapter 5 showed that shifts in demand curves affect both quantity and price predictably.

Public policy and business discussions often make vague references to "changes in demand." By itself, this expression does not mean anything. Remember from our discussion in Chapter 5 that we must distinguish between a response to a price change—*which shows up as a movement along the demand curve*—and a change in the relationship between price and quantity demanded—*which produces a shift in the demand curve* (in effect, it moves the curve itself).

When price falls, quantity demanded generally rises. This is a movement *along* the demand curve. On the other hand, an effective advertising campaign may result in people buying more goods at *any given price*. This would cause a rightward *shift* of the demand curve. Such a shift can be caused by a change in the value of any of the variables other than price that affect quantity demanded. Although the distinction between a shift in a demand curve and a movement along it may at first seem trivial, the difference is very significant in practice. Let us pause for a moment to consider how changes in some of these other variables shift the demand curve.

### DEMAND SHIFTERS

As an example, consider the effect of a change in consumer income on the demand curve for sweaters. In Figure 7–5(a), the black curve $D_0D_0$ is the original demand curve for sweaters. Now suppose that parents start sending more money to their needy sons and daughters in college. If the price of sweaters remained the same, those students are likely to use some of their increased income to buy more sweaters. For example, if the price were to remain at $35, quantity demanded might rise from 40,000 sweaters (point $R$) to 60,000 (point $S$). Similarly, if price had been $28, and remained at that level, the rise in income might produce a corresponding change from $T$ to $U$. In other words, we would expect the rise in income to *shift* the entire demand curve to the right from $D_0D_0$ to $D_1D_1$. In exactly the same way, a fall in consumer income can be expected to lead to a leftward shift in the demand curve for sweaters, as shown in Figure 7–5(b).

## HOW LARGE IS A FIRM'S MARKET SHARE? CROSS ELASTICITY AS A TEST

A firm's "market share" is often a crucial element in antitrust lawsuits (see Chapter 20) for a simple reason. If the firm supplies no more than, say, 20 percent of the industry's output, courts and regulators presume that the firm is not a monopoly, as its competitors account for most of the industry's sales. On the other hand, if the defendant firm in the lawsuit accounts for 90 percent of the industry's output, courts may have good reason to worry about monopoly power (which we cover in Chapter 12).

Thus court cases often provide lively debates in which the defendant firms try to prove that they have very small market shares, while the plaintiffs seek to establish the opposite. Each side knows how much the defendant firm actually produces and sells, so what do they find to argue about? The dispute is about *the size of the total relevant market*, which clearly affects the magnitude of the firm's market *share*. Ambiguity arises here because different firms do not produce identical products. For instance, are Rice Krispies in the same market as Cheerios? And how about Quaker Oatmeal, which users eat hot? What about frozen waffles? Are all of these products part of the same market? If they are, then the overall market is big, and each seller therefore has a smaller share. But if these products are in different markets, the opposite will be true.

Many observers argue, as the Supreme Court did in the famous DuPont cellophane case (and, more recently, as was argued when Rolite sued Waste Management in 1998), that one of the proper criteria for determining the borders of the relevant market is *cross elasticity of demand*. If two products have a high and positive cross elasticity, they must be close enough substitutes to compete closely; that is, they must be in the same market. But how large must the cross elasticity be before the court decides that two products are in the same market? Although the law has established no clear elasticity benchmark to determine whether a particular firm is in a relevant market, several courts have determined that a very high cross elasticity number clearly indicates effective competition between them, meaning that the two items must be in the same market.

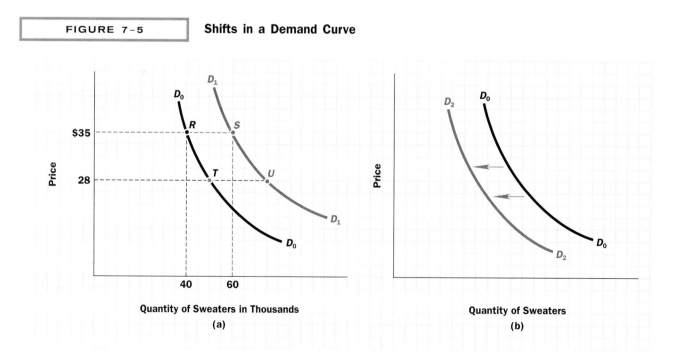

| FIGURE 7-5 | **Shifts in a Demand Curve** |

**Quantity of Sweaters in Thousands**
**(a)**

**Quantity of Sweaters**
**(b)**

We can analyze other variables that affect quantity demanded in the same way. For example, increased television advertising for sweaters may lead to a rightward (outward) shift in the demand curve for sweaters, as in Figure 7–5(a). The same thing might occur if the price of a substitute product, such as jackets, were to increase, because that would put sweaters at a competitive advantage. If two goods are substitutes, a rise in the price of one of them will tend to shift the demand curve for the other one outward (to the right). Similarly, if a complementary product (perhaps matching pants to go with the sweaters) becomes more expensive, we expect the demand curve for sweaters to shift to the left, as in Figure 7–5(b). In summary:

We expect a demand curve to shift to the right (outward) if consumer incomes rise, if tastes change in favor of the product, if substitute goods become more expensive, or if complementary goods become cheaper. We expect a demand curve to shift to the left (inward) if any of these factors goes in the opposite direction.

## THE TIME PERIOD OF THE DEMAND CURVE AND ECONOMIC DECISION MAKING

One more important feature of a demand curve does not show up on a graph. A demand curve indicates, at each possible price, the quantity of the good that is demanded *during a particular time period*. That is, all of the alternative prices considered in a demand curve must refer to the *same* time period. Economists do not compare a price for a particular item of $10 in January with a price of $8 in September.

This feature imparts a peculiar character to the demand curve and complicates statistical calculations. Actual observed historical data show different prices and quantities only for different dates. Why, then, do economists adopt this apparently peculiar approach? The answer is that the demand curve's time dimension arises inescapably from the logic of decision making.

When a business seeks to price one of its products for, say, the following six months, it must consider the range of alternative prices available for that six-month period and the consequences of each of these possible prices. For example, if management is reasonably certain that the best price for the six-month period lies somewhere between $3.50 and $5.00, it should perhaps consider each of four possibilities, $3.50, $4.00, $4.50, and $5.00, and estimate how much it can expect to sell at each of these potential prices during the six-month period. The result of these estimates may appear in a format similar to that of the following table:

| Potential Six-Month Price | Expected Quantity Demanded |
| --- | --- |
| $3.50 | 75,000 |
| 4.00 | 73,000 |
| 4.50 | 70,000 |
| 5.00 | 60,000 |

This table supplies managers with information that they need to make optimal pricing decisions. It also contains precisely the information an economist uses to draw a demand curve.

The demand curve describes a set of hypothetical quantity responses to a set of potential prices, but the firm can only actually charge one price. All of the points on the demand curve refer to alternative possibilities for the *same time* period—the period for which the decision is to be made.

Thus, a demand curve of the sort just described is not just an abstract notion that is useful primarily in academic discussions. Rather, it offers precisely the information that businesses need to make rational decisions. However, as already noted, the fact that all points on the demand curve are hypothetical possibilities for the same period of time causes problems for statistical estimation of demand curves. These problems are discussed in the appendix to this chapter.

## ■ REAL-WORLD APPLICATION: POLAROID VERSUS KODAK

Let's look at an example from the real world to show how the elasticity concept helps to resolve a concrete problem rather different from those we have been discussing.

In 1989, a lengthy trial resulted in a judgment against the photographic products manufacturing company Eastman-Kodak for patent infringement on technology that rival firm Polaroid had designed. The court then set out to determine the amount of money Kodak owed Polaroid for its patent infringement during the ten-year period (1976 to 1986) when Kodak had sold very similar instant cameras and film. The key issue was how much profit Polaroid had lost as a result of Kodak's entry into the field of instant photography. Both price elasticity of demand and cross elasticity of demand played crucial roles.

The courts needed accurate estimates of the price elasticity of demand to determine whether the explosive growth in instant camera sales from 1976 to 1979 was mainly attributable to the fall in price that resulted from Kodak's competition or was, rather, attributable to Kodak's reputation and its access to additional retail outlets. If the latter were true, then Polaroid might actually have *benefited* from Kodak's entry rather than *losing* profits, because Kodak's presence in the market would have increased the total number of potential customers aware of and eager to try instant cameras.

After 1980, instant camera and film sales began to drop sharply. On this issue, the *cross elasticity of demand* between instant and conventional (35-millimeter) cameras and film was crucial to the explanation. Why? Because the decline in the instant camera market occurred just as the prices of 35-millimeter cameras, film, developing, and printing all began to fall significantly. If the decline in Polaroid's overall sales was attributable to the decreasing cost of 35-millimeter photography, then Kodak's instant photography activity was *not* to blame. Consequently, the amount that Kodak would be required to pay to Polaroid would decrease significantly. On the other hand, if the cross elasticity of demand between conventional photography prices and the demand for instant cameras and film was low, then the cause of the decline in Polaroid's sales might well have been Kodak's patent-infringing activity— *adding* to the damage compensation payments to which Polaroid was entitled.

Yet a third elasticity issue was central to the trial. How much would Polaroid's total revenue have increased as a result of the film-price increase it claimed it *would* have adopted in the absence of illegal competition from Kodak? The crux of the matter was the price elasticity of demand for instant camera film. Polaroid tried to show that this elasticity figure was low, to support its contention that the rise in price would have raised its revenues a great deal—meaning that Kodak had damaged it quite severely. Kodak, on the other hand, offered statistical evidence suggesting that demand for instant film—then a novelty and something of a luxury good—was highly elastic, to support its own claim that a higher price would have brought in little, if any, additional revenue.

On the basis of its relevant elasticity calculations, Polaroid at one point claimed that Kodak was obligated to pay it $9 *billion* or more. Kodak claimed that it owed Polaroid only (!) something in the neighborhood of $450 million. A lot of money was at stake! The judge's verdict came out with a number very close to Kodak's figure.[4]

In this chapter we have continued our study of the demand side of the market. Rather than focusing on what underlies demand formation, as we did in the chapter before this, we sought to apply demand analysis to business decisions. Most

---

[4] William Baumol was a witness in the case, testifying on behalf of Kodak.

notably, we described and analyzed the economist's measure of the responsiveness of consumer demand to changes in price, and we showed how this determines the effect of a firm's price change on the revenues of that enterprise. We illustrated how these concepts throw light not only on business sales and revenues, but also on a number of rather different issues, such as smoking and health, the effectiveness of competition among business firms as studied by law courts, and the determination of penalties for patent infringement. In the next chapter we turn to the supply side of the market and move a step closer to completing the framework we need in order to understand how markets work.

## SUMMARY

1. To measure the responsiveness of the quantity demanded to price, economists calculate the *elasticity of demand*, which is defined as the percentage change in quantity demanded divided by the percentage change in price.

2. If demand is *elastic* (elasticity is greater than 1), then a rise in price will reduce total expenditures. If demand is *unit elastic* (elasticity is equal to 1), then a rise in price will not change total expenditures. If demand is *inelastic* (elasticity is less than 1), then a rise in price will increase total expenditure.

3. Demand is not a fixed number. Rather, it is a relationship showing how quantity demanded is affected by price and other pertinent influences. If one or more of these other variables change, the demand curve will shift.

4. Goods that make each other more desirable (hot dogs and mustard, wristwatches and watch straps) are called *comple-*

*ments*. When consumers want less of one good as they get more of another (steaks and hamburgers, Coke and Pepsi), economists call those goods *substitutes*.

5. *Cross elasticity of demand* is defined as the percentage change in the quantity demanded of one good divided by the percentage change in the price of another good. Two substitute products normally have a positive cross elasticity of demand. Two complementary products normally have a negative cross elasticity of demand.

6. A rise in the price of one of two substitute products can be expected to *shift the demand curve* of the other product to the right. A rise in the price of one of two complementary goods is apt to shift the other's demand curve to the left.

7. All points on a demand curve refer to the *same* time period—the time during which the price will be in effect.

## KEY TERMS

(Price) elasticity of demand   119

Elastic, inelastic, and unit-elastic demand curves   123

Complements   127

Substitutes   128

Cross elasticity of demand   128

Shift in a demand curve   129

## QUESTIONS FOR REVIEW

1. What variables besides price and advertising are likely to affect the quantity demanded of a product?

2. Describe the probable shifts in the demand curves for:

   a. Airplane trips when airlines' on-time performance improves

   b. Automobiles when airplane fares rise

   c. Automobiles when gasoline prices rise

   d. Electricity when the average temperature in the United States falls during a particular year

   (*Note:* The demand curve for electricity in Maine and the demand curve for electricity in Florida should respond in different ways. Why?)

3. Taxes on particular goods discourage their consumption. Economists therefore say that such taxes "distort consumer demands." In terms of the elasticity of demand for the commodities in question, what sort of goods would you choose to tax to achieve the following objectives?

   a. Collect a large amount of tax revenue

   b. Distort demand as little as possible

   c. Discourage consumption of harmful commodities

   d. Discourage production of polluting commodities

4. Explain why elasticity of demand is measured in *percentages*.

5. Explain why the elasticity of demand formula normally eliminates minus signs.

6. Give examples of commodities whose demand you expect to be elastic and some whose demand you expect to be inelastic.

7. Explain why the elasticity of a straight-line demand curve varies from one part of the curve to another.

8. A rise in the price of a certain commodity from $15 to $20 reduces quantity demanded from 20,000 to 5,000 units. Calculate the price elasticity of demand.

9. If the price elasticity of demand for gasoline is 0.3, and the current price is $1.20 a gallon, what rise in the price of gasoline will reduce its consumption by 10 percent?

10. A rise in the price of a product whose demand is elastic will reduce the total revenue of the firm. Explain.

11. Name some events that will cause a demand curve to shift.

12. Which of the following product pairs would you expect to be substitutes, and which would you expect to be complements?

   a. Shoes and sneakers

   b. Gasoline and sport utility vehicles

   c. Bread and butter

   d. Instant camera film and regular camera film

13. For each of the previous product pairs, what would you guess about the products' cross elasticity of demand?

   a. Do you expect it to be positive or negative?

   b. Do you expect it to be a large or small number? Why?

14. Explain why the following statement is true: "A firm with a demand curve that is inelastic at its current output level can always increase its profits by raising its price and selling less." (*Hint:* Refer back to the discussion of elasticity and total expenditure/total revenue on pages 124–125.)

---

### ● APPENDIX ▎ STATISTICAL ANALYSIS OF DEMAND RELATIONSHIPS

The peculiar time dimension of the demand curve, in conjunction with the fact that many variables other than price influence quantity demanded, makes it surprisingly hard to derive a product's demand curve from statistical data. Specialists can and often do derive such estimates, but the task is full of booby traps and usually requires quite advanced statistical methods and interpretation. This appendix seeks to warn you about the booby traps. It implies, for example, that if you become the marketing manager of a business firm after you graduate from college, and you need demand analysis, you will need experts to do the job. The appendix will also show you some mistakes to look for as you interpret the results, if you have reason to doubt the qualifications of the statisticians you hire to calculate or forecast your demand curve.

The most obvious way to go about estimating a demand curve statistically is to collect a set of figures on prices and quantities sold in different periods, like those given in Table 7–2. These points can then be plotted on a diagram with price and quantity on the axes, as shown in Figure 7–6. We can then draw in a line (the dotted line *TT*) that connects these points (labeled Jan., Feb., and so on) reasonably well to represent the prices and quantities sold in the months indicated. This line may appear to approximate the demand curve, but unfortunately, line *TT*, which summarizes the historical data, may bear no relationship to the true demand curve.

You may notice at once that the prices and quantities represented by the historical points in Figure 7–6 refer to different periods of time, and that each point on the graph represents an *actual* (not hypothetical) price and quantity sold at a particular period of time (for example,

January). The distinction is significant. Over the entire period covered by the historical data (January through May), the true demand curve, which is what an economist really wants, may well have shifted because of changes in some of the other variables affecting quantity demanded.

The actual events may appear as shown in Figure 7–7. In January, the demand curve was given by *JJ*, but

---

### FIGURE 7-6

**Plot of Historical Data on Price and Quantity**

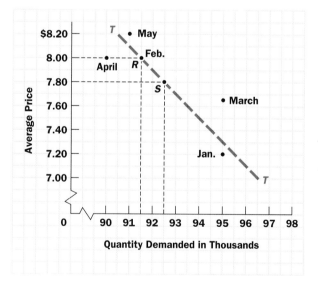

---

### TABLE 7-2

**Historical Data on Price and Quantity**

|  | January | February | March | April | May |
|---|---|---|---|---|---|
| Quantity Sold | 95,000 | 91,500 | 95,000 | 90,000 | 91,000 |
| Price | $7.20 | $8.00 | $7.70 | $8.00 | $8.20 |

FIGURE 7-7

**Plot of Historical Data and
True Demand Curves for
January, February, and March**

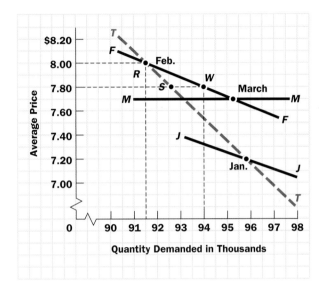

(line *FF* in Figure 7–7) indicates an increase in sales of 2,500 units (from point *R*, with sales of 91,500 units, to point *W*, with sales of 94,000 units). A manager who based her decision on the historical plot, rather than on the true demand curve, might be led into serious error. Nevertheless, it is astonishing how often people make this mistake in practice, even when using apparently sophisticated techniques.

## AN ILLUSTRATION: DID THE ADVERTISING PROGRAM WORK?

Some years ago one of the nation's largest producers of packaged foods conducted a statistical study to judge the effectiveness of its advertising expenditures, which amounted to nearly $100 million a year. A company statistician collected year-by-year figures on company sales and advertising outlays and discovered, to his delight, that they showed a remarkably close relationship to one another: quantity demanded rose as advertising rose. The trouble was that the relationship seemed just too perfect. In economics, data about demand and any one of the elements that influence it almost never show such a neat pattern. Human tastes and other pertinent influences are just too variable to permit such regularity.

by February the curve had shifted to *FF*, by March to *MM*, and so on. This figure shows a separate and distinct demand curve for each of the relevant months, and none of them need have any resemblance to the plot of historical data, *TT*.

In fact, the slope of the historical plot curve, *TT*, can be very different from the slopes of the true underlying demand curves, as is the case in Figure 7–7. This means that the decision maker can be seriously misled if she selects her price on the basis of the historical data. She may, for example, think that demand is quite insensitive to changes in price (as line *TT* seems to indicate), so she may reject the possibility of a price reduction. In fact, the true demand curves show that a price reduction would increase quantity demanded substantially, because they are much more elastic than the shape of the estimated curve in Figure 7–6 would suggest.

For example, if she were to charge a price of $7.80 rather than $8.00 in February, the historical plot would lead her to expect a rise in quantity demanded of only 1,000 units. (Compare point *R*, with sales of 91,500 units, and point *S*, with sales of 92,500 units, in Figure 7–6.) However, the true demand curve for February

Suspicious company executives asked one of the authors of this book to examine the analysis. A little thought showed that the suspiciously close statistical relationship between sales and advertising expenditures resulted from a disregard for the principles just presented. The investigator had in fact constructed a graph of *historical* data on sales and advertising expenditure, analogous to *TT* in Figures 7–6 and 7–7 and therefore not necessarily similar to the truly relevant relationship.

The stability of the relationship actually arose from the fact that, in the past, the company had based its advertising outlays on its sales, automatically allocating a fixed percentage of its sales revenues to advertising. The *historical* relationship between advertising and demand therefore described only the company's budgeting practices, not the effectiveness of its advertising program. If the firm's management had used this curve in planning future advertising campaigns, it might have made some regrettable decisions. *The moral of the story:* Avoid the use of purely historical curves like *TT* in making economic decisions.

> Of course that's only an estimate. The actual cost will be somewhat more.
>
> Auto mechanic to customer

# PRODUCTION, INPUTS, AND COST: BUILDING BLOCKS FOR SUPPLY ANALYSIS

Suppose you take a summer job working on Naomi's Natural Farm, where, among other things, she raises a small herd of hogs.[1] When you get there, you find that Naomi has bought land and built her barns, and purchased two-years' worth of all the ingredients, except corn, in the organic feed she gives the pigs. She has also purchased all the other farm supplies she needs, so she is left with only one decision about her farm input purchases: How much corn should she buy? In this chapter, we explore this kind of decision and answer the question, what input choice constitutes the most profitable way for a business firm to produce its output?

---

[1] In 1992, women operated 145,000 farms in the United States, and 50,000 of them had sales of $10,000 or more (U.S. Census Bureau, *Statistical Abstract of the United States: 1998*, 118th ed., Washington, D.C., 1998).

When firms make their supply (output) decisions, they weigh the costs of supplying their products against the expected revenue they can earn from selling the products in the marketplace. Thus, they examine the likely demand for the products they create. We have already studied demand in the last two chapters. But to understand the firm's decisions about the supply side of markets, we must also study the firm's production costs. A firm's costs depend on the quantities of labor, raw materials, machinery, and other inputs that it buys, and on the prices it pays for each input. Just how does the firm decide how much of each input to buy? This chapter examines how businesses can select optimal input combinations, that is, the combinations that enable firms to produce whatever output they decide upon at minimum cost as they seek to maximize profitability. We will discuss the firm's decisions about output and price in the next chapter.

To make the analysis of optimal input quantities easier to follow, we approach this task in two stages, based on a very important economic distinction: the short run and the long run. The first part of the chapter deals with a simpler, short-run case in which the firm can vary the quantity of only one input, while all other input quantities are already determined. This assumption vastly simplifies the analysis and enables us to answer three key questions:

■ How does the quantity of input affect the quantity of output?

■ How can the firm select the optimal quantity of an input?

■ How do these input decisions give the firm the cost information it needs?

In the second part of the chapter, we go over the same territory for the case in which the firm can vary the quantities of several inputs at once. Many new insights emerge from this multi-input analysis, but they will be easier to absorb after you have mastered the single-input analysis.[2]

### Are Larger Firms More Efficient?

Modern industrial societies enjoy cost advantages as a result of automation, assembly lines, and sophisticated machinery, all of which often reduce production costs dramatically. But if equipment with such enormous capacity requires a very large investment, small companies will be unable to reap many of these benefits of modern technology. Only large firms will be able to take advantage of the associated cost savings. Where firms can take advantage of such *economies of scale,* as economists call them, production costs per unit will decline as output expands.

But this relationship between large size and low costs does not fit every industry. Sometimes the courts must decide whether a giant firm should be broken up into smaller units. The most celebrated case of this kind involved American Telephone and Telegraph Company, which had a monopoly on the nation's phone service for nearly 50 years. In 1982, AT&T settled a government antitrust suit by agreeing to divest 22 operating units, informally known today as

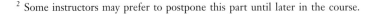

[2] Some instructors may prefer to postpone this part until later in the course.

the "Baby Bells."[3] Government agencies and analysts who urged a breakup of AT&T argued that such a giant firm has great economic power and deprives consumers of the benefits of competition. But those who opposed the breakup, including AT&T itself, pointed out that if AT&T's large size brought significant economies of scale, then smaller firms would be much less efficient producers than the larger one, so that if AT&T were replaced by several smaller companies, costs to consumers would have to be correspondingly higher. Who was right? To settle the issue, the courts needed to know whether significant economies of scale affected AT&T's business before the divestiture.

Sometimes data like those shown in Figure 8–1 are offered to the courts when they consider such cases. These data, provided by AT&T, indicate that as the volume of telephone messages rose after 1942, the capital cost of long-distance communication by telephone dropped enormously and continued to drop consistently for more than 40 years, even as demand for long-distance services increased dramatically. In fact, the dollar cost per circuit mile of long-distance calls had fallen below 8 percent of its 1942 level. Economists maintain that, while this graph may be valid evidence of efficiency and innovation in the telecommunications industry, it does *not* constitute legitimate evidence, one way or another, about the presence of economies of scale. At the end of this chapter, we will study precisely what is wrong with the evidence presented in Figure 8–1 and what sort of evidence really would prove whether a very large firm can indeed produce more efficiently as a result of economies of scale.

**FIGURE 8–1**

**Historical Costs for Long-Distance Telephone Transmissions**

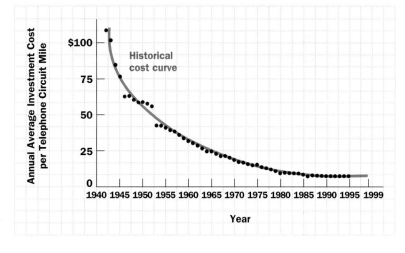

NOTE: Figures are in dollars per year.
SOURCE: AT&T. Recent figures are estimates.

## ■ SHORT-RUN VERSUS LONG-RUN COSTS: WHAT MAKES AN INPUT VARIABLE?

As firms make input and output decisions, their actions are limited by previous commitments to equipment, plant, and other production matters. At any point in time, many input choices are *precommitted* by past decisions. If, for example, a firm

---

[3] AT&T is a descendant of the original Bell Telephone Company, affectionately known as "Ma Bell." The company relinquished the use of the name Bell when it divested itself of 22 regional companies in 1982. These companies were reorganized into the "Baby Bells"—seven regional phone companies called NYNEX, Bell Atlantic, Ameritech, BellSouth, Southwestern Bell Corporation, USWest, and Pacific Telesis Group. Ironically, in the 1990s several of these "Baby Bells"—for example, Bell Atlantic and NYNEX—merged once again.

purchased machinery a year ago, it has committed itself to that production decision for the remainder of the machine's economic life, unless the company is willing to take the loss involved in replacing that equipment sooner. An economist would say that these temporarily unalterable capital commitments are not variable for the time period in question. Firms that employ unionized labor forces may also incur costs that are temporarily not variable if labor contracts commit the firms to employing a certain number of employees, or to use employees for a required number of weeks per year. Costs are not variable for some period if they are caused by a longer-term financial commitment, such as a contract to buy a raw material, lease a warehouse, or invest in equipment that cannot be resold or transferred without substantial loss of the investment. Even if the firm has not paid for these commitments ahead of time, legally it must still pay for the contracted goods or services.

## THE ECONOMIC SHORT RUN VERSUS THE ECONOMIC LONG RUN

A two-year-old machine with a nine-year economic life is an inescapable commitment and therefore represents a cost that is not variable for the next seven years. But that investment is not an unchangeable commitment in plans that extend *beyond* those seven years, because by then it may benefit the firm to replace the machine in any case. Economists summarize this notion by speaking of two different "runs" (or periods of time) for decision making: the **short run** and the **long run.**

The **short run** is a period of time during which some of the firm's cost commitments will *not* have ended.

The **long run** is a period of time long enough for all of the firm's commitments to come to an end.

These terms recur time and again throughout this book. In the short run, firms have relatively little opportunity to change production processes in order to adopt the most efficient way of producing their current outputs, because plant sizes have largely been predetermined by past decisions. Though managers may be able to hire more workers to work overtime and may be able to buy more supplies, they can't easily increase factory size, even if sales turn out to be much greater than expected. Over the long run, however, all such inputs, including plant size, become adjustable.

Consider, as an example, the case of Naomi's Natural Farm and the amount of organic corn that she feeds her hogs. Ultimately—that is, in the long run—Naomi can buy more piglets, feed them different grains, buy more land and buildings, and so on. But suppose for the moment that Naomi's only *current* choice is how much corn to feed the pigs. Once she has constructed the barn in which the animals are sheltered, she has relatively little discretion over its capacity. She can build an addition, but that project may be considerably more expensive than building a bigger barn to begin with. Cutting the size of the barn to save heating bills is even more costly. Over a somewhat longer planning horizon, however, Naomi will need to replace the original building, and she will be free to decide all over again how large a barn to construct.

Much the same is true of big industrial firms. Companies have little control over their plant and equipment capacities in the short run. But with some advance planning, they can acquire different types of machines, redesign factories, and make other choices. For instance, General Motors continued producing the Chevrolet Caprice and other big, rear-wheel drive cars at its plant in Arlington, Texas, for the 1995 and 1996 model years even though the vehicles were not selling well. That was partly because the company knew that it would need time to convert the plant to manufacture its popular full-size pickup trucks, which were in short supply. By the 1997 model year, however, GM engineers were able to convert the plant to truck production.

Note that the short run and long run do not refer to the same time periods for all firms; rather, those periods vary in length, depending on the nature of the firm's commitments. If, for example, the firm can change its workforce every week, its machines every two years, and its factory every 20 years, then 20 years will be the long run, and any period less than 20 years will constitute the short run.

## FIXED COSTS AND VARIABLE COSTS

This distinction between the short run and the long run also determines which of the firm's costs rise or fall with a change in the amount of output the firm produces. Some costs cannot be varied, *no matter how long the period in question.* These are called

Data of the sort provided in Table 8–1 do not represent a farmer's subjective opinion; rather they are objective information that an agricultural scientist can supply from experimental evidence. Now, we don't claim to be experts on hogs, and the data in Table 8–1 (and the following graphs) are not necessarily true-to-life. But we have attempted to approximate the reality of raising hogs on a small organic farm. According to the National Pork Producers Council (www.nppc.org), average hog market weight is 250 pounds, and it takes about $3\frac{1}{2}$ pounds of feed to produce one pound of live hog weight. Thus, a 250-pound porker will have eaten almost 900 pounds of feed. Since hogs are marketed at an age of about five months, this works out to about 180 pounds of feed per month, or an average of 45 pounds of feed per week. The illustrative numbers that we have used in our example of Naomi's Natural Hogs are (we hope) a reasonable approximation of this information.

**fixed costs,** and they arise when some types of inputs can be bought only in big batches or when inputs have a large productive capacity. For example, there is no such thing as a "mini" automobile assembly line capable of producing two cars a week, and except for extreme luxury models, it is impractical to turn out automobiles without an assembly line. So the fixed cost of automobile manufacturing includes the cost of the smallest (least expensive) assembly line that the firm can acquire. These costs are called *fixed* because the total amount of money spent in buying the assembly line does not vary, whether it is used to produce ten cars a day or 100, so long as the output quantity does not exceed the assembly line's capacity.

In the short run, there are other costs that behave very much as fixed costs do; in other words, they are predetermined by previous decisions and are *temporarily* fixed. But in the longer run, firms can change both their capital and labor commitments. So, in the long run, more costs become **variable.** We will have more to say about fixed and variable costs as we examine other key input and cost relationships.

A **fixed cost** is the cost of an input whose quantity does not rise when output goes up, one that the firm requires to produce any output at all. The total cost of such indivisible inputs does not change when the output changes. Any other cost of the firm's operation is called a **variable cost.**

## PRODUCTION, INPUT CHOICE, AND COST WITH ONE VARIABLE INPUT

Although, in reality, all businesses use many different inputs, we will begin our discussion with the short-run case in which there is *only a single input that is variable,* that is, in which the quantities of all other inputs will not be changed. In doing so, we are trying to replicate in our theoretical analysis what physicists or biologists do in the laboratory when they conduct a *controlled* experiment: changing just one variable at a time to enable us to see the influence of one variable in isolation. Thus, we will study the effects of variation in the quantity of one input under the assumption that all other things remain unchanged—that is, other things being equal.

### TOTAL, AVERAGE, AND MARGINAL PHYSICAL PRODUCTS

We begin the analysis with the first of the firm's three main questions: the relationship between the quantity of inputs utilized and the quantity of production. Naomi has studied how much weight her hogs gain as she uses various amounts of corn. The relevant data are displayed in Table 8–1.

**TABLE 8–1**

**Total Physical Product Schedule for Naomi's Natural Farm**

| Corn Input (100-lb. bags) | Pork Output (lbs.) |
| --- | --- |
| 0 | 0.0 |
| 1 | 14.0 |
| 2 | 36.0 |
| 3 | 66.0 |
| 4 | 100.0 |
| 5 | 130.0 |
| 6 | 156.0 |
| 7 | 175.0 |
| 8 | 184.0 |
| 9 | 185.4 |
| 10 | 180.0 |
| 11 | 165.0 |
| 12 | 144.0 |

FIGURE 8-2

**Total Physical Product with Different Quantities of Corn for Naomi's Natural Farm**

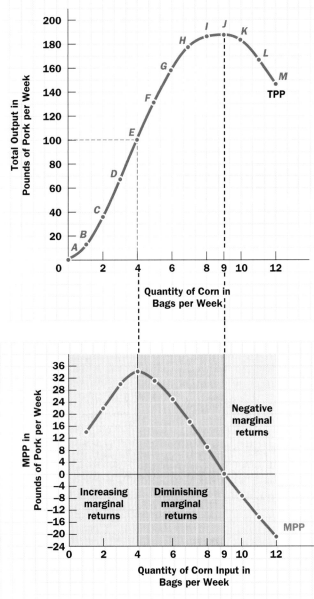

The table begins by confirming the commonsense observation that hogs cannot be raised without food. Thus, output is zero when Naomi provides zero corn input (see the first line of the table). After that, the table shows the increase in pork output that additional corn yields. After nine bags of corn per week, more corn actually reduces output.

For instance, with an input of four 100-pound bags of corn per week (for her small hog herd), output is 100 pounds. Eventually, however, Naomi will reach a saturation point beyond which additional corn will not add to the pigs' growth and actually may cause some of them to become ill.

**TOTAL PHYSICAL PRODUCT** The data in Table 8–1 appear graphically in Figure 8–2, which is called a **total physical product (TPP)** curve. This curve reports how much pork Naomi can produce with different quantities of corn, holding the quantities of all other inputs constant.

**AVERAGE PHYSICAL PRODUCT** To understand more about how the quantity of corn she feeds her hogs contributes to their growth, Naomi can use two other physical product relationships given in Table 8–2. **Average physical product (APP)** measures output per unit of input; it is simply total physical product divided by the quantity of variable input used. On Naomi's farm, it is total pork output in pounds divided by the number of bags of corn. APP is shown in Column (4) of Table 8–2. For example, since four 100-pound bags of corn yield 100 pounds of pork, the APP of four bags of corn is 100/4, or 25 pounds of pork per bag of corn.

**MARGINAL PHYSICAL PRODUCT** To decide how much corn to feed her hog herd, Naomi must know how much *additional* pork output to expect from each *additional* bag of corn. This concept is known as **marginal physical product (MPP),** and she can calculate it from the data on total physical product using the same method we introduced to derive marginal utility from total utility in Chapter 6. For example, the marginal physical product of the fourth bag of corn is the total output of pork when Naomi uses four bags of corn *minus* the total output when she uses three bags (100 − 66 = 34 pounds). We calculate the other MPP entries in the third column of Table 8–2 in exactly the same way. Figure 8–3 displays these numbers in a graph called a *marginal physical product curve.*

FIGURE 8-3

**Naomi's Marginal Physical Product (MPP) Curve**

## MARGINAL PHYSICAL PRODUCTS AND THE "LAW" OF DIMINISHING MARGINAL RETURNS

The shape of the marginal physical product curve in Figure 8–3 has important implications for Naomi's hog raising. Compare the TPP curve in Figure 8–2 with the MPP curve in Figure 8–3. The MPP curve can be described as the curve that reports the *rate* at which the TPP curve is changing—that is, it tells us how much of an increase in pork output results from each additional bag of corn she feeds the hogs. Thus, until input reaches four bags of corn, the marginal physical product of corn *increases* when Naomi feeds more corn. This means that TPP increases at an increasing rate between points *A* and *E* in Figure 8–2. Between four bags and nine bags, the MPP *decreases* but still has *positive* values throughout (that is, it lies above the

### Naomi's Schedules for Total Physical Product, Marginal Physical Product, Average Physical Product, and Marginal Revenue Product of Corn

TABLE 8-2

| (1) | (2) | (3) | (4) | (5) |
|---|---|---|---|---|
| Corn Input (bags) | Total Physical Product (pork output in lbs.) | Marginal Physical Product (lbs. of pork per bag) | Average Physical Product (lbs. of pork per bag) | Marginal Revenue Product |
| 0 | 0.0 | | | |
| | | 14.0 | | $ 10.50 |
| 1 | 14.0 | | 14.0 | |
| | | 22.0 | | 16.50 |
| 2 | 36.0 | | 18.0 | |
| | | 30.0 | | 22.50 |
| 3 | 66.0 | | 22.0 | |
| | | 34.0 | | 25.50 |
| 4 | 100.0 | | 25.0 | |
| | | 30.0 | | 22.50 |
| 5 | 130.0 | | 26.0 | |
| | | 26.0 | | 19.50 |
| 6 | 156.0 | | 26.0 | |
| | | 19.0 | | 14.25 |
| 7 | 175.0 | | 25.0 | |
| | | 9.0 | | 6.75 |
| 8 | 184.0 | | 23.0 | |
| | | 1.4 | | 1.05 |
| 9 | 185.4 | | 20.6 | |
| | | -5.4 | | -4.05 |
| 10 | 180.0 | | 18.0 | |
| | | -15.0 | | -11.25 |
| 11 | 165.0 | | 15.0 | |
| | | -21.0 | | -15.75 |
| 12 | 144.0 | | 12.0 | |

horizontal axis). Consequently, in this range, TPP is still increasing (MPP > 0), but at a decreasing rate (MPP is falling). That is, in this region, between points $E$ and $J$ in Figure 8–2, each additional bag of corn adds to pork output, but it adds less than the previous bag added. Beyond nine bags, to the right of point $J$ on Figure 8–2, the MPP of corn actually becomes *negative*: This means that the total physical product curve starts to decrease—additional corn actually makes some of the hogs sick.

Figure 8–3 is divided into three zones to illustrate these three cases. Note that the marginal returns to corn increase at first and then diminish. This is the typical pattern, and parallels what we had to say about the utility of consumption in Chapter 6. Each additional unit adds some productivity, but at a decreasing rate. In the left zone of Figure 8–3 (the region of increasing marginal returns), each additional bag of corn adds more to TPP than the previous bag did.

The "law" of diminishing marginal returns, which has played a key role in economics for two centuries, states that an increase in the amount of any one input, *holding the amounts of all others constant,* ultimately leads to lower marginal returns to the expanding input.[4]

The so-called *law* rests simply on observed facts; economists did not deduce the theorem analytically. Returns to a single input usually diminish because of the "law" of variable input proportions. When the quantity of one input increases while all others remain constant, the variable input whose quantity increases gradually becomes more and more abundant relative to the others. (For example, the proportion of corn increases and the proportions of other feed, such as soybean meal, decreases.) As Naomi uses more and more corn with fixed quantities of other feed,

The firm's **total physical product (TPP)** is the amount of output it obtains in total from a given quantity of input.

The **average physical product (APP)** is the total physical product (TPP) divided by the quantity of input. Thus, APP = TPP/$X$ where $X$ = the quantity of input.

The **marginal physical product (MPP)** of an input is the increase in total output that results from a one-unit increase in the input, holding the amounts of all other inputs constant.

---

[4] The "law" is generally credited to Anne Robert Jacques Turgot (1727–1781), one of the great comptrollers-general of France before the revolution, whose liberal policies, it is said, represented the old regime's last chance to save itself. With characteristic foresight, the king fired Turgot.

the pigs' diet becomes unbalanced so that adding yet more corn does little good and eventually harms them. At this point, the marginal physical product of corn becomes *negative*.

Many real-world cases seem to display the law of variable input proportions. In China, for instance, farmers have been using increasingly more fertilizer as they try to produce larger grain harvests to feed the country's burgeoning population. Although that country's consumption of fertilizer is four times higher than it was 15 years ago, its grain output has increased by only 50 percent. This certainly suggests that fertilizer use has reached the zone of diminishing returns.

## THE OPTIMAL QUANTITY OF AN INPUT AND DIMINISHING RETURNS

We can now address the second question that all firms must ask as they make production decisions: How can the firm select the optimal quantity of an input? For this purpose, look again at the first and third columns of Table 8–2, which show the farm's marginal physical product schedule. We will assume that a 100-pound bag of the special organic corn that the farm uses costs $10, and that Naomi can sell her hogs for 75 cents per pound (she gets top dollar for these pasture-raised, "natural" hogs).[5]

Now suppose that Naomi is considering using just one bag of corn. Is this optimal? That is, does this maximize her profits? The answer is no, because the marginal physical product of a second bag of corn is 22 pounds of pork, the second entry in marginal physical product Column (3) of Table 8–2. At a price of $0.75 per pound, this extra output would add $16.50 to revenue. Since the added revenue exceeds the $10 cost of the second bag of corn, the farm comes out ahead by $16.50 minus $10, or $6.50.

**MARGINAL REVENUE PRODUCT AND INPUT PRICES** The additional *money revenue* that a firm receives when it increases the quantity of some input by one unit is called the input's **marginal revenue product.** If Naomi's hogs sell at a fixed price of $0.75 per pound, the marginal revenue product (MRP) of the input equals its marginal physical product (MPP) multiplied by the output price:

$$\text{MRP} = \text{MPP} \times \text{Price of output}$$

For example, we have just shown that the marginal revenue product of the second bag of corn is $16.50, which we obtained by multiplying the MPP of 22 pounds by the price of $0.75 per pound. The other (MRP) entries in Column (5) of Table 8–2 are calculated in the same way. The MRP concept enables us to formulate a simple rule for the optimal use of any input. Specifically:

> When the marginal revenue product of an input exceeds its price, it pays the firm to use more of that input. Similarly, when the marginal revenue product of the input is less than its price it pays the firm to use less.

Let's test this rule in the case of Naomi's hogs. We have observed that two bags of corn cannot be enough because the MRP of a second bag ($16.50) exceeds its price ($10). What about a third bag? Table 8–2 shows that the MRP of the third bag ($0.75 × 30 = $22.50) also exceeds its price; thus, stopping at three bags also is not optimal. This remains true through the seventh bag of corn, because its MRP of $14.25 still exceeds its $10 price. The same cannot be said of an eighth

The **marginal revenue product (MRP)** of an input is the additional revenue that the producer earns from the increased sales when it uses an additional unit of the input.

---

[5] More hog facts: In 1997 the average price of hogs was $53 per hundredweight (hundred pounds). But we have assumed here that Naomi, along with many real-world farmers, raises a small herd of premium, organic pigs, so she gets at least $75 per hundredweight (75 cents per pound). Thus, she sells her 250-pound hogs for $187.50 each. In 1997, corn cost $2.42 per bushel (a bushel of corn weighs 56 pounds), or approximately five cents per pound. But Naomi's hogs eat only the best—we assume that the special, hybrid organic corn that she feeds her pampered herd costs 10 cents a pound, or $10 per 100-pound bag.

bag, however. The eighth bag is not a good idea because its MRP, only $6.75, is less than its $10 cost. Thus, the optimal quantity of corn for Naomi to purchase each week is seven bags, yielding a total output of 175 pounds of pork.

Notice the crucial role of diminishing returns in this analysis. When the marginal *physical* product of corn begins to decline, the money value of that product falls, as well; that is, the marginal *revenue* product also declines. The producer always profits by expanding input use until diminishing returns set in and reduce the MRP to the price of the input. So Naomi should stop *increasing* her corn purchases when MRP falls to the price of corn.

A common expression suggests that it does not pay to continue doing something "beyond the point of diminishing returns." As we see from this analysis, quite to the contrary, it normally *does* pay to do so! The firm has employed the proper amount of input only when diminishing returns reduce the marginal revenue product of the input to the level of its price, because then the firm will be wasting no opportunity to *add* to its total profit. Thus, the optimal quantity of an input is that at which MRP equals its price (*P*). In symbols:

$$MRP = P \text{ of input}$$

The logic of this analysis is exactly the same as in our discussion of marginal utility and price in Chapter 6. Naomi is trying to maximize *profits*—the difference between the *total* revenue her corn input yields and the *total* cost of buying that input. To do so, she must increase her corn usage up to the point where its price equals its marginal revenue product, just as an optimizing consumer keeps buying until price equals marginal utility.

## INPUT QUANTITIES AND TOTAL, AVERAGE, AND MARGINAL COST CURVES

We turn now to the third of the three main questions that a firm must ask: How do we derive the firm's cost relationships from the input decisions that we have just explained? We will need these cost relationships to analyze the firm's output and pricing decisions in Chapter 9, where we will study the last of the main components of our analysis of the market mechanism: How much of its product or service should the profit-maximizing firm produce?

The most desirable output quantity for the firm clearly depends on the way in which costs change when output varies. Economists typically display and analyze such information in the form of *cost curves*. Indeed, since we will use marginal analysis again in our discussion, we will need three different cost curves: *the total cost curve, the average cost curve, and the marginal cost curve.*

These curves follow directly from the nature of production. The technological production relationships for hog farming—hog physiology and the best animal husbandry practices—dictate the amount of corn that Naomi uses to produce a given quantity of pork. This technological relationship appears in Figure 8–2. From these data on corn usage and the price of corn, Naomi can determine how much it will cost to produce some given amount of pork. Therefore, the relevant cost relationships depend directly on the production relationships we have just discussed. The calculation of the firm's total costs from its physical product schedule assumes that the firm cannot influence the price of corn and, for simplicity, we will continue for now to assume that the quantities of all inputs other than corn are fixed.

The method is simple: For each quantity of output, record from Table 8–1 or Figure 8–2 the amount of corn required to produce it. Then multiply that quantity of corn by its price.

**TOTAL COSTS** In addition to the cost of corn, Naomi must spend money on other inputs, such as soybean meal, electricity to light the barn, and so on. Furthermore, her costs must include the *opportunity costs* of any inputs that Naomi herself contributes (such as soybeans that she grew herself, which she could have sold to other farmers instead of feeding to her pigs). Because we are simplifying matters by focusing exclusively on corn input for now, however, let us assume for the next several pages that all other inputs are free. Later, we will bring in the costs of the other inputs.

Because corn costs $10 per bag, the data in Table 8–1 lead directly to the total costs shown in Table 8–3. For example, the fourth row of Table 8–1 indicates that Naomi needs three bags of corn to produce 66 pounds of pork. At $10 per bag, this input costs $30, which is the fourth entry in Column (3) of Table 8–3.The other numbers in Table 8–3 are derived similarly. In general:

> The total product curve specifies the input quantities needed to produce any given output. From those input quantities and the prices of the inputs, we can determine the *total cost* (TC) of producing any level of output. Thus, the relationship of total cost to output is determined by the technological production relationships between inputs and outputs and by input prices.

**FIGURE 8–4**

**Naomi's Total, Average, and Marginal Costs**

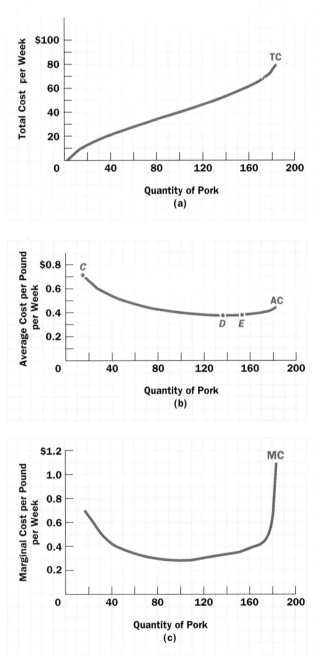

NOTE: Quantity is in pounds per week.

**TOTAL, AVERAGE, AND MARGINAL COST CURVES**   Two other cost curves—the average cost (AC) and marginal cost (MC) curves—provide information crucial for our analysis. We can calculate these curves directly from the total cost curve, just as Table 8–2 calculated average and marginal physical product from total physical product. For any given output, *average cost* is defined as total cost divided by quantity produced. For example, Table 8–3 shows that the total cost of producing 100 pounds of pork is $40, so that the average cost is $40/100, or $0.40 per pound per week.

Similarly, we define the *marginal cost* as the increase in total cost that arises from the production of an additional pound of pork. For example, the marginal cost of the 100th pound of pork is the difference between the total cost of producing 100 pounds ($40) and the total cost of producing 99 pounds (say, $39.71), although the table doesn't show this number); this difference equals approximately $0.29. Figure 8–4 shows all three curves, the total, average, and marginal cost curves. The TC curve is generally assumed to rise fairly steadily as the firm's output increases. After all, Naomi cannot expect to produce 100 pounds of pork at a lower total cost than she could produce 80 pounds. The AC curve and the MC curve both look roughly like the letter ∪—first going downhill, then gradually turning uphill again. We will explore the reason for and implications of this ∪-shape later in the chapter.

So far, we have ignored the money that Naomi must spend on inputs other than corn. Of course, she cannot obtain these other inputs free, so, because the quantities of these inputs are assumed to be fixed in the short run, their costs should be treated as constants—as positive numbers rather than as zero. In the following discussion, we will treat all of these other costs as fixed.

**TOTAL FIXED COST AND AVERAGE FIXED COST CURVES** Although variable costs are only part of total costs (which include fixed and variable costs), variable cost curves have the same general shape as the total cost curve shown in Figure 8–4(a). In contrast, the curves that record *total fixed costs* (TFC) and *average fixed costs* (AFC) have very special shapes, illustrated in Figure 8–5. By definition, TFC remains the same whether the firm produces a little or a lot—so long as it produces anything at all. As a result, any TFC curve is horizontal like the one in Figure 8–5(a). It has the same height at every output.

### ● BLAME THE USUAL SUSPECTS: SUPPLY AND DEMAND

The hog market is cyclical. The National Pork Producers Council explains: "If supplies are low and/or demand is high, prices will be high, and vice versa. When prices are high, more sows are bred and more pigs are produced. When . . . they reach market, supplies increase and prices fall." For instance, hog prices were high in 1997. Farmers responded by raising more hogs in 1998. The result, according to the *New York Times,* was that ". . . a glut in the number of hogs being raised sent hog prices plummeting to Depression-era lows." And many economists argued that the traditional forces of supply and demand largely explained the plunging prices.

To try to manage the risk inherent in these fluctuating prices, hog producers can buy what amounts to insurance contracts on the Chicago Mercantile Exchange (called Lean Hogs and Pork Bellies contracts) and the Mid-American Exchange (Lean Hogs contracts).

SOURCE: "Pork Facts 1998/1999," National Pork Producers Council (www.nppc.org), and David Barboza, "The Great Pork Gap," *The New York Times,* January 7, 1999, Business Day, pp. 1 and 17.

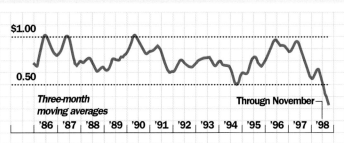

"ROBERTS, WHAT'S ALL THIS TALK I HEAR ABOUT PORK BELLIES?"

We conclude that firms can generally substitute one input for another. A firm can produce the same number of desks with less labor, *if* it is prepared to sink more money into machinery. But whether it *pays* to make such a substitution depends on the relative costs of labor and machinery. Several general conclusions follow from this discussion.

- Normally, a firm can choose among different technological options to produce a particular volume of output. Technological considerations rarely fix input proportions immutably.

- Given a target production level, a firm that cuts down on the use of one input (say, labor) will normally have to increase its use of another input (say, machinery). This is what we mean when we speak of *substituting* one input for another.

- The combination of inputs that represents the *least costly* way to produce the desired level of output depends on the relative prices of the various inputs.

## THE PRODUCTION FUNCTION AND SUBSTITUTABILITY

To help select the combination of inputs to produce the desired output at least cost, economists have invented a concept they call the **production function.** The production function summarizes the technical and engineering information about the relationship between a firm's output and *all* of its inputs. It indicates, for example, just how much pork Naomi's Natural Farm can produce with given amounts of land, labor, corn, and so on. If, as we normally assume, the firm can produce the desired amount of output in many ways, the production function lays out all input combinations that will do the job.

If a firm needs only two inputs (which are enough for our purposes to give you the idea of the basic principles), a production function can be represented graphically (which we do in the appendix to this chapter) or by a simple table. For example, such

The **production function** indicates the *maximum* amount of product that any particular collection of inputs is capable of producing.

a table can show various combinations of quantities of two inputs, say soybean meal and corn, with any combination capable of yielding 120 pounds of pork per week. In Table 8–5(b), for example, the production function can indicate that 4.7 bags of corn per week and no soy meal can produce the 120 pounds of pork on Naomi's farm, but that 3.5 bags of corn and half a bag of soy meal will also do the job. Such a table can also tell her that, at the other extreme, she can raise the 120 pounds of pork without any corn by using 3.7 bags of soy meal.

Which will she choose? Naturally, she prefers the cheapest combination. The least-cost option can be found directly with the help of such a table and the relevant input-price information (for example, that corn costs $10 per bag while soy meal is priced at $20). The total cost for each way of producing 120 pounds of pork is calculated, as before, by multiplying the input quantities by the input prices and adding them together. To illustrate, consider the three options just mentioned for the production of 120 pounds of pork:

**Option A:** 4.7 bags of corn @ $10 per bag = $47

**Option B:** 3.5 bags of corn @ $10 per bag + 0.5 bags of soybean meal @ $20 per bag = $35 + $10 = $45

**Option C:** 3.7 bags of soy meal @ $20 per bag = $74

These calculations tell us that, of the three input combinations capable of producing 120 pounds of pork, the lowest total cost, $45, is obtained by Option B, the use of 3.5 bags of corn and 0.5 bags of soy meal per week. Other possible feed combinations that produce the 120 pounds of pork can, of course, be evaluated in exactly the same way, enabling Naomi to determine the most economical way to produce that output quantity. Similar calculations (Table 8–5a) also enable Naomi to determine the least expensive way to produce 80 pounds of pork. It looks like the cheapest way Naomi can produce 80 pounds of pork is to use 2.3 bags of corn and 0.7 bags of soy meal ($10 × 2.3 + $20 × 0.7 = $37).

Of course, outputs of 80 and 120 pounds per week are not the only production levels that Naomi should consider. She also should consider, for example, the least costly way to produce 60 pounds, 180 pounds, and so on. The total cost of producing *any* given quantity of output equals the sum of the cost-minimizing quantities of each of the inputs, with each input quantity multiplied by the price of that input.

Using the procedures just outlined, Naomi can calculate the minimum cost of producing *any* quantity of output. Let's suppose now that she has done this, completing the information that she needs to plot her *total cost curve*. As before, dividing the total cost for each output by the quantity of output then gives the corresponding *average cost*, that is, the cost per unit of output. Similarly, she can derive the marginal cost curve from the total cost figures, just as we did in an earlier section.

| TABLE 8–5 | **Alternative Input Combinations for Production of Given Output Quantities** |

| (a) Ways to Produce 80 Pounds of Pork per Week | | | (b) Ways to Produce 120 Pounds of Pork per Week | | |
|---|---|---|---|---|---|
| Corn (bags per week) | Soy Meal (bags per week) | Total Cost* (per week) | Corn (bags per week) | Soy Meal (bags per week) | Total Cost* (per week) |
| 3.8 | 0 | $38 | 4.7 | 0 | $47 |
| 3.0 | 0.5 | 40 | 3.5 | 0.5 | 45 |
| 2.3 | 0.7 | 37 | 2.8 | 1.2 | 52 |
| 1.5 | 2.1 | 57 | 2.0 | 2.8 | 76 |
| 0 | 3 | 60 | 0 | 3.7 | 74 |

*Total cost is calculated from the formula TC = Price of corn × Quantity of corn + Price of soy meal × Quantity of soy meal, with corn priced at $10 per bag and soy meal at $20 per bag.

## THE MARGINAL RULE FOR OPTIMAL INPUT PROPORTIONS

Choosing the input proportions that minimize the cost of producing a given output is really a matter of common sense. To understand why, let us turn, once again, to our concrete example. As before, Naomi is considering whether to feed her hogs more corn and less soy meal, or vice versa. The two feeds are substitutes; if the pigs get more soy meal, they need less corn. *But the feeds are not perfect substitutes.* Soy meal provides more protein but fewer carbohydrates than corn, so Naomi gains a considerable benefit by providing the pigs with a balance of the two. If their diet contains too much of one feed and too little of the other, the output of pork will suffer. In other words, it is reasonable to assume *diminishing returns* to excessive substitution of either type of feed for the other.

We continue to assume that corn costs $10 per 100-pound bag, as in our earlier example, although the same size bag of soy meal costs twice as much. Given the $10 and $20 prices for corn and soy, how much of each feed should Naomi use? To answer this question, she must compare the prices of each feed with information on what each of them yields—their marginal physical products. Let's say that the marginal physical product (MPP) of a bag of corn is about 20 pounds of meat, and the marginal physical product of an additional bag of soy meal is about 30 pounds. What should Naomi do? Naomi should cut down on soy meal and increase her use of corn. Why? Because soy meal costs twice as much as corn, but its marginal yield is much less than twice as much meat—only 50 percent more. Obviously, it pays to spend more on the type of feed that yields more pork output per dollar than the other feed does. The corn provides a marginal yield of 20 pounds for $10, or two pounds per dollar. The soy yields 30 pounds of pork for $20, that is, 1.5 pounds per dollar. Clearly her marginal dollar gives her more pork if she invests it in corn than if she uses it to buy soy. So it will pay her to reduce the money she spends on the latter and use that money to buy more of the former.

MARGINAL ANALYSIS What makes this example work out the way it does is that *the ratio of the marginal product of soy meal to the price of soy meal is less than the ratio of the marginal product of corn to the price of corn.* This means, as we have seen, that Naomi gets more for her money—at the margin—by spending on corn rather than on soy meal. This illustrates one of the *Ideas for Beyond the Final Exam* that we see throughout the book: To minimize costs or maximize profits, producers must learn to examine cost relationships at the margin. To generalize, a firm can interpret the ratio:

$$\frac{\text{MPP of any input}}{\text{Price of that input}}$$

as the marginal product obtained by spending an additional $1 on the input. It always pays to reduce spending on Input A if its MPP per dollar is less than the MPP per dollar of Input B. That dollar should be spent on Input B instead. Such a move must *always* reduce the firm's cost of producing some given amount of output. By switching away from the input with the *lower* marginal product per dollar and buying more of the input with the *higher* marginal product per dollar, the firm can reduce the money it spends without reducing its output.

*The Importance of Thinking at the Margin*

We have thus derived the basic rule for determining the most economical way to produce any given output:

A firm can reduce the cost of producing a given output by using less of some input, A, and making up for it by using more of another input, B, whenever the ratio of the marginal physical product of A to the price of A is less than the ratio of the marginal physical product of B to the price of B, that is, whenever:

$$\frac{\text{MPP}_a}{P_a} < \frac{\text{MPP}_b}{P_b}$$

The opposite will be true if the MPP per dollar spent on A is higher than the MPP per dollar spent on B. Putting these two together, we conclude that input

We have just discussed how a firm can determine the most economical input combination for any given level of output. This analysis does not apply only to business enterprises. Nonprofit organizations like your own college are interested in finding the least costly ways to accomplish a variety of tasks (for example, maintaining the grounds and buildings); government agencies seek to meet their objectives at minimum costs; even in the home, we can find many ways to "skin a cat." Thus, our present analysis of *cost minimization* is widely applicable.

proportions *cannot* be optimal if the ratios of the marginal physical products to the prices for any two inputs differ, that is:

**The proportions of any two inputs, A and B, used by the firm can be optimal only if:**

$$\frac{MPP_a}{P_a} = \frac{MPP_b}{P_b}$$

This rule, as we have noted, is simply common sense. If a unit of Input A has a marginal product that is, say, three times as big as that of Input B, the firm should be willing to pay exactly three times as much money for an additional unit of A as it pays for a unit of B, no more and no less.

But what if the market happens to set input prices so that this isn't true, meaning that the two fractions are unequal at the current input prices? Suppose that the market price of A happens to be twice as large as that of B, as in our hog-raising example. What can Naomi do about it? In this case, she should buy less of A (soy meal, in our example) and more of B (corn). That will not change the market *prices* of corn and soy meal, but it will change *the marginal physical products* of the two inputs because of the law of diminishing returns. As Naomi buys more corn and less soy meal, the marginal product of corn will fall and the marginal product of soy meal will rise. When Naomi has switched just enough money from soy meal to corn, the ratio of their marginal products will rise from $30 \div 20 = 1.5$ up to, say, $36 \div 18 = 2.00$. At that point, the ratio of the prices of the two inputs will be equal to the ratio of their marginal products, satisfying the rule for cost minimization.

### CHANGES IN INPUT PRICES AND OPTIMAL INPUT PROPORTIONS

The commonsense reasoning behind the rule for optimal input proportions leads to an important conclusion. Let's say that Naomi is producing 120 pounds of output at minimum cost. But suppose that the price of corn rises, while the price of soy meal remains the same. That will cause a violation of the optimal-purchase rule:

$$\frac{MPP_{corn}}{P_{corn}} = \frac{MPP_{soy\ meal}}{P_{soy\ meal}}$$

To restore optimality, the MPP of corn must also rise to match the rise in corn price. But, by the "law" of diminishing returns, the MPP of corn is *higher* only when

## ● INPUT SUBSTITUTION IN THE FOREST

After Congress outlawed logging in much of the Redwood National Forest, Louisiana Pacific Corporation (one of the world's largest lumber producers) lost access to one of its essential inputs: old-growth timber from which the company made building materials. But CEO Harry Merlo was pragmatic about the situation, and turned his attention to trees that were not under the watchful eye of conservationists. One likely candidate, the aspen—a so-called *waste-species*—immediately came to his attention. Aspens grow quickly and they appear plentifully in forests stretching the width of North America. Fortunately, Merlo had kept himself abreast of the latest technology in the building industry.

Canadian lumber mills have long had the capability of trimming small trees into sheets and then gluing and pressing the sheets together. Merlo observed this process, and he conceived some innovative ideas of his own. He correctly figured that alternating the grain of the layered sheets would add to overall strength. The result was waferwood, which turned out to be cheaper and stronger than plywood. It could be used as siding and, when combined with other engineered lumber, used to create I-beams for floor joists and roof rafters.

Thus, when Louisiana Pacific was priced out of the market for its old input (old-growth timber), it substituted a new input, aspen wood, for one that was no longer available.

SOURCE: "Let's Go for Growth," *Fortune*, March 7, 1994, p. 60.

the use of corn is lower. Thus, a rise in the price of corn leads the farmer to use *less* corn and, if she still wants to produce 120 pounds of pork, to use *more* soy meal. In general we have the commonsense result that:

> As any one input becomes more costly relative to competing inputs, the firm is likely to substitute one input for another; that is, to use less of the input that has become more expensive and to use more of competing inputs.

This general principle of input substitution applies in industry just as it does on Naomi's farm. For some real-world applications of the analysis, see the accompanying box, "Input Substitution in the Forest."

## ■ ECONOMIES OF SCALE

We are now beginning to put together the tools we need to address the question posed at the beginning of this chapter: Does a large firm benefit from substantial **economies of scale** that allow it to operate more efficiently than smaller firms? To answer this question, we need a precise definition of this concept.

An enterprise's scale of operation arises from the quantities of the various inputs that it uses. The production function illustrates what happens when the firm doubles its scale of operations. For example, suppose that the production function for Naomi's Natural Farm indicates that with 1.5 bags of corn and 2.1 bags of soy meal, output is 80 pounds of pork (assuming soy meal and corn are the only two inputs).[9]

Production is said to involve **economies of scale,** also referred to as **increasing returns to scale,** if, when all input quantities are doubled, the quantity of output is *more* than doubled.

---

[9] This assumption is necessary because the table deals with only two inputs and the definition requires that *all* inputs be doubled simultaneously. To be true to the definition, if *labor, corn, land, and machinery* were all used by the farmer, their quantities would all have to double.

---

| POLICY DEBATE | SHOULD WATER BE PROVIDED TO WESTERN FARMERS AT SUBSIDIZED PRICES? |

---

Farmers in the western United States use a great deal of water. California alone used more than 29 billion gallons of irrigation water per day in 1995 (about 22 percent of total U.S. irrigation water).* Because most of the area's climate is high desert, agriculture there requires artificial irrigation—indeed, water is critical. Yet western farmers and ranchers pay very low prices for the water they use. For example, government controls keep the price of water used for agriculture artificially low, so that California farmers pay only about 1/30th of the price that urban residents pay for water. Even during a recent drought, farmers in that state continued to use vast quantities of water, while residents in the cities were forced to ration.

This situation has given rise to an intense debate between farmers and environmentalists. There is no question that water is scarce in the western states, and there are some predictions of a looming shortage of disastrous proportions. It is also clear that farmers pay a price that is much lower than the true marginal cost of water, particularly because that cost includes a very high *opportunity cost,* that is, the value of the other uses of water that must be forgone as a result of its extensive employment in agriculture.

As analysis from this chapter shows, a low price for an input increases the amount that producers use, and there is little doubt that the low price of water substantially increases its use by western farmers. Environmentalists and economists have joined forces in arguing

that western water users should pay prices that cover its true marginal cost. Indeed, it has been suggested that at such a price any shortage would simply disappear.

The farmers, on the other hand, say that long practice entitles them to continued low water prices and that low prices in the past induced them to invest extensively in their agricultural properties, so that a price increase now would be tantamount to confiscating their investments. Moreover, they argue that a sharp rise in the price of this critical input would destroy a way of life that is valuable for society. The politicians undoubtedly feel caught in the middle, as the debate continues.

*U.S. Geological Survey (http://water.usgs.gov, accessed April 1999).

Now suppose that Naomi were to increase both inputs by 33.33 percent—to two bags of corn and 2.8 bags of soy meal. Output would rise by 50 percent (to 120 pounds). Because output goes up by a greater percentage than the increase in each of the inputs, Naomi's production function displays *increasing returns to scale* (also known as economies of scale), at least in this range.

Economies of scale affect operations in many modern industries. Where they exist, they give larger firms cost advantages over smaller ones and thereby foster large firm sizes. Automobile production and telecommunications are two common examples of industries that enjoy significant economies of scale. Predictably, firms in these industries are, indeed, huge.

Technology generally determines whether or not a specific economic activity is characterized by economies of scale. One particularly clear example of a way in which this can happen is provided by warehouse space. Imagine two warehouses, each shaped like perfect cubes with the length, width, and height of Warehouse 2 twice as large as those of Warehouse 1. Now remember your high-school geometry. The surface area of any side of a cube is equal to the square of its length. Therefore, the amount of material needed to build Warehouse 2 will be $2^2$, or four times as great as that needed for Warehouse 1. However, because the volume of a cube is equal to the cube of its length, Warehouse 2 will have $2^3$, or eight times as much storage space as Warehouse 1. Thus, in a cubic building multiplying the inputs by four leads to eight times the storage space—an example of strongly increasing returns to scale.

This example is, of course, oversimplified. It omits such complications as the need for stronger supports in taller buildings, the increased difficulty of moving goods in and out of higher stories, and the like. Still, the basic idea is correct, and the example shows why, up to a point, the very nature of warehousing creates technological relationships that lead to economies of scale.

Our definition of economies of scale, though based on the production function, relates closely to the shape of the *long-run* average cost curve. Notice that the definition requires that a doubling of *every* input must bring about more than a doubling of output. If all input quantities are doubled, total cost must double. But if output *more* than doubles when input quantities are doubled, then cost per unit (average cost) must decline. In other words:

> Production functions with economies of scale lead to long-run average cost curves that decline as output expands.

Figure 8–7(a) depicts a decreasing average cost curve, but this is only one of three possible shapes that the long-run average cost curve can take. Panel (b) shows the curve for *constant* returns to scale. Here, if all input quantities double, both total cost (TC) and the quantity of output (Q) double, so average cost (AC = TC/Q) remains *constant*. Finally, output may increase, but less than double, when all inputs double. This is a case of *decreasing* returns to scale, which leads to a *rising* long-run average cost curve like the one depicted in Panel (c). The figure reveals a close association between the slope of the AC curve and the nature of the firm's returns to scale.

**Three Possible Shapes for the Long-Run Average Cost Curve**   FIGURE 8-7

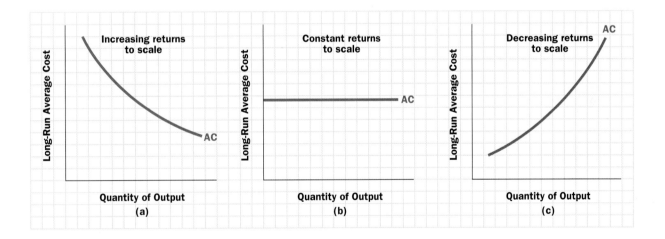

(a)       (b)       (c)

Note that the same production function can display increasing returns to scale in some ranges, constant returns to scale in other ranges, and decreasing returns to scale in yet others. This is true of all the ∪-shaped average cost curves we have shown, for example, Figure 8–4(b).

## THE "LAW" OF DIMINISHING RETURNS AND RETURNS TO SCALE

Earlier in this chapter, we discussed the "law" of diminishing marginal returns. Is there any relationship between economies of scale and the phenomenon of diminishing returns? At first, the two ideas may seem contradictory. After all, if a producer gets diminishing returns from his inputs as he uses more of each of them, doesn't it follow that by using more of *every* input, he must encounter decreasing returns to scale? In fact, the two principles do not contradict one another, for they deal with fundamentally different issues.

■ *Returns to a single input.* This analysis asks the question, how much does output expand if a firm increases the quantity of just *one* input, *holding all other input quantities unchanged?*

■ *Returns to scale.* Here the question is, how much does output expand if *all* inputs are increased *simultaneously* by the same percentage?

The "law" of diminishing returns pertains to the first question, because it examines the effects of increasing only one input at a time. It is plausible that the firm will encounter diminishing returns as this one input becomes relatively abundant. Thus, for example, the addition of too much soy meal relative to a given quantity of corn will contribute too much protein and too few carbohydrates to the pigs, yielding diminishing returns.

Returns to scale pertain to proportionate increases in *all* inputs and therefore answer the second question. If Naomi doubles the quantities of both corn and soy meal, the hogs' diet need not become unbalanced. Thus, the "law" of diminishing returns (to a single input) is compatible with *any* sort of returns to scale. In summary:

Returns to scale and returns to a single input (holding all other inputs constant) refer to two distinct aspects of a firm's technology. A production function that displays diminishing returns to *a single input* may show diminishing, constant, or increasing returns when *all input quantities are increased proportionately.*

## HISTORICAL COSTS VERSUS ANALYTICAL COST CURVES

In Chapter 6, we noted that all points on a demand curve pertain to the *same* period of time. Decision makers must use this common time period because the demand curve illustrates alternative choices *for a given period of time.* The same is true of a cost curve. All points on a cost curve pertain to exactly the same time period because the graph examines the cost of each alternative output level that the firm can choose for that period.

It follows that a graph of historical data on prices and quantities at *different points in time* is normally *not* the cost curve that the decision maker needs. This observation will help to resolve the problem posed at the beginning of the chapter about whether declining historical costs were evidence of economies of scale.

All points on any of the cost curves used in economic analysis refer to the same period of time.

One point on an auto manufacturer's cost curve may show, for example, how much it would cost the firm to produce 2.5 million cars during 1999. Another point on the same curve may show what would happen to the firm's costs if, *instead,* it were to produce 3 million cars in 1999. Such a curve is called an *analytical cost curve* or, when there is no possibility of confusion, simply a cost curve. This curve must be distinguished from a diagram of *historical costs,* which shows how costs have changed from year to year.

The different points on an analytical cost curve represent *alternative possibilities,* all for the same time period. In 1999, the car manufacturer will produce either 2.5 million or 3 million cars (or some other amount), but certainly not both. Thus, at most, only one point on this cost curve will ever be observed. The company may, indeed, produce 2.5 million in 1999 and 3 million in 2000, but the 2000 data are not relevant to the 1999 cost curve. By the time 2000 comes around, the cost curve may have shifted, so the 1999 cost figure will not apply to the 2000 cost curve either.

A different sort of graph can, of course, indicate year by year how costs and outputs have varied. Such a graph, which gathers together the statistics for a number of different periods, is not, however, a *cost curve* as that term is used by economists. An example of such a diagram of historical costs appeared in Figure 8–1.

Why do economists rarely use historical cost diagrams and instead deal primarily with analytical cost curves, which are more abstract, harder to explain, and more difficult to estimate statistically? The answer is that analysis of real policy

---

● **CLOSER TO HOME: THE DIMINISHING MARGINAL RETURNS TO STUDYING**

---

The "law" of diminishing marginal returns crops up a lot in ordinary life, not just in the world of business. Consider Jason and his study habits: He has a tendency to procrastinate and then cram for exams the night before he takes them, pulling "all-nighters" regularly. How may an economist speak of his payoff from an additional hour of study in the wee hours of the morning, relative to Colin's (who studies for two hours every night)?

problems—such as the desirability of having a single supplier of telephone services for the entire market—leaves no choice in the matter. Rational decisions require analytical cost curves. Let's see why.

## Resolving the Economies of Scale Issue

Recall the problem that we introduced early in the chapter. We examined the AT&T divestiture and concluded that in order to determine whether it made sense to break up such a large company, economists would have to know whether or not the industry provided economies of scale. Among the data offered as evidence was a graph that showed a precipitous drop in the capital cost of long-distance communications as the volume of calls rose after 1942. But we did not answer a more pertinent question: Why didn't such information constitute legitimate evidence about the presence of economies of scale?

As this section shows, to determine whether a single supplier can provide telephone service more cheaply in 1999 than a number of smaller firms can, we must compare the costs of *both large-scale and small-scale production in 1999.* It does no good to compare the cost of a large supplier in 1999 with its own costs as a smaller firm back in 1942, because that cannot possibly supply the needed information. The cost situation in 1942 is irrelevant for today's decision between large and small suppliers because no small firm today would use the obsolete techniques of 1942.

Since the 1940s, great technical progress has taken the telephone industry from ordinary open-wire circuits to microwave systems, telecommunications satellites, coaxial cables of enormous capacity, and now to fiber optics. All of this means that the *entire* analytical cost curve of telecommunications must have shifted downward quite dramatically from year to year. Innovation must have reduced not only the cost of large-scale operations *but also the cost of smaller-scale operations.* Until decision makers compare the costs of large and small suppliers *today,* they cannot make a rational choice between single-firm and multifirm production. It is the analytical cost curve, all of whose points refer to the same period, that, by definition, supplies this information.

FIGURE 8-8

**Declining Historical Cost Curve with the Analytical Average Cost Curve also Declining in Each Year**

Figures 8–8 and 8–9 show two extreme hypothetical cases, one that entails true economies of scale and one that does not. Both are based on the same historical cost data (in black) with their very sharply declining costs. (This curve is reproduced from Figure 8–1.) They also show (in red and blue) two possible average cost curves, one for 1942 and one for 1999. In Figure 8–8, the analytical AC curve has shifted downward very sharply from 1942 to 1999, as technological change reduced all costs. Moreover, both of the AC curves slope downward to the right, meaning that, in either year, a larger firm has lower average costs. Thus, the situation shown in Figure 8–8 really does entail scale economies, so that one large firm can serve the market at lower cost than many small ones.

But now look at Figure 8–9, which shows exactly the same historical costs as Figure 8–8. Here, however, both analytical AC curves are U-shaped. In particular, the 1999 AC curve has its minimum point at an output level, *A,* that is less than one-half of the current output, *B,* of the large supplier. Thus, the shape of the analytical cost curves does *not* show economies of scale. This means that, for the situation shown in Figure 8–9, a smaller company can produce more cheaply than a large one. In this case, one cannot justify domination of the market by a single large firm on the grounds that its costs are lower—despite the sharp downward trend of historical costs. In sum, the behavior of historical costs reveals nothing about the cost advantages or disadvantages of a single large firm. More generally:

**Because a diagram of historical costs does not compare the costs of large and small firms *at the same point in time,* it cannot be used to determine whether an industry provides economies of large-scale production. Only the analytical cost curve can supply this information.**

FIGURE 8-9

**Declining Historical Cost Curve with U-Shaped Analytical Cost Curves in Each Year**

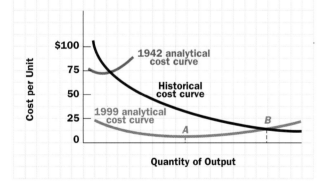

Quantity of Output

In the case of telephone service, some estimates indicate that economies of large-scale production do indeed exist. Presumably because of this, almost 20 years after the Bell telephone system breakup, the typical firm providing long-distance telephone service is still very large, with AT&T, MCI, and Sprint in the vanguard. Yet half a dozen or so other smaller firms still compete in this arena. It is perhaps ironic that some of the "Baby Bell" local telephone companies that were broken away from AT&T by the courts in 1982 have recombined, and others are seeking to merge in order to obtain cost and other advantages of larger size.

## COST MINIMIZATION IN THEORY AND PRACTICE

Lest you be tempted to run out and open a business, confident that you now understand how to minimize costs, we should point out that business decisions are a good deal more complicated than we have indicated here. Rare is the business executive who knows for sure what his or her production function looks like, or the exact shapes of his or her marginal physical product schedules, or the precise nature of his or her cost curves. No one can provide an instruction book for instant success in business. What we have presented here is, instead, a set of principles that constitutes a guide to the logic of good decision making.

Business management has been described as the art of making critical decisions on the basis of inadequate information, and our complex and ever-changing world often leaves people no alternative but educated guesses. Actual business decisions will at best approximate the cost-minimizing ideal outlined in this chapter. Certainly, practicing managers will make mistakes, but when they do their jobs well and the market system functions smoothly, the approximation may prove amazingly good. Although no system is perfect, inducing firms to produce at the lowest possible cost is undoubtedly one of the jobs the market system does best.

1. A firm's total cost curve shows its lowest possible cost of producing any given quantity of output. This curve is derived from the input combination that the firm uses to produce any given output and the prices of the inputs.

2. The *marginal physical product (MPP)* of an input is the increase in total output resulting from a one-unit increase in that input, holding the quantities of all other inputs constant.

3. The *"law" of diminishing marginal returns* states that if a firm increases the amount of one input (holding all other input quantities constant), the marginal physical product of the expanding input will eventually begin to decline.

4. To maximize profits, a firm must purchase an input up to the point at which diminishing returns reduce the input's *marginal revenue product (MRP)* to equal its price (MRP = MPP × price).

5. The *long run* is a period sufficiently long for the firm's plant to require replacement and for all of its current contractual commitments to expire. The *short run* is any period briefer than that.

6. *Fixed costs* are costs whose total amounts do not vary when output increases. All other costs are called *variable costs.* Some costs are variable in the long run but not in the short run.

7. At all levels of output, the total fixed cost (TFC) curve is horizontal and the average fixed cost (AFC) curve declines toward the horizontal axis but never crosses it.

8. TC = TFC + TVC    AC = AFC + AVC.

9. It is usually possible to produce the same quantity of output in a variety of ways by substituting more of one input for less of another. Firms normally seek the least costly way to produce any given output.

10. A firm that wants to minimize costs will select input quantities at which the ratios of the *marginal physical product* of each input to its price—its MPP per dollar—are equal for all inputs.

11. The *production function* shows the relationship between inputs and output. It indicates the maximum quantity of output obtainable from any given combination of inputs.

12. If a doubling of all the firm's inputs *just* doubles its output, the firm is said to have *constant returns to scale.* If a doubling of all inputs leads to *more than* twice as much output, it has *increasing returns to scale* (or *economies of scale*). If a doubling of inputs produces *less than* a doubling of output, the firm has *decreasing returns to scale.*

13. With increasing returns to scale, the firm's long-run average costs are decreasing; constant returns to scale are associated with constant long-run average costs; decreasing returns to scale are associated with increasing long-run average costs.

14. Economists cannot tell if an industry offers economies of scale (increasing returns to scale) simply by inspecting a diagram of historical cost data. Only the underlying analytical cost curve can supply this information.

Short run    140

Long run    140

Fixed cost    141

Variable cost    141

Total physical product (TPP)    142

Average physical product (APP)    142

Marginal physical product (MPP)    142

Marginal revenue product (MRP)    144

Production function    151

Economies of scale (increasing returns to scale)    155

1. A firm's total fixed cost is $360,000. Construct a table of its total and average fixed costs for output levels varying from zero to 6 units. Draw the corresponding TFC and AFC curves.

2. With the following data, calculate the firm's AVC and MC and draw the graphs for TVC, AVC, and MC.

| Quantity | Total Variable Costs |
|---|---|
| 1 | $ 40,000 |
| 2 | 80,000 |
| 3 | 120,000 |
| 4 | 176,000 |
| 5 | 240,000 |
| 6 | 360,000 |

3. From the figures in Review Questions 1 and 2, calculate TC and AC for each of the output levels from 1 to 6 units and draw the two graphs.

4. If a firm's commitments in 2001 include machinery that will need replacement in five years, a factory building rented for twelve years, and a three-year union contract specifying how many workers it must employ, when, from its point of view in 2001, does the firm's long run begin?

5. If the marginal revenue product of a gallon of oil used as input by a firm is $1.20 and the price of oil is $1.07 per gallon, what can the firm do to increase its profits?

6. A firm hires two workers and rents 15 acres of land for a season. It produces 150,000 bushels of crop. If it had doubled its land and labor, production would have been 325,000 bushels. Does it have constant, decreasing, or increasing returns to scale?

7. Suppose that wages are $20,000 per season per person and land rent per acre is $3,000. Calculate the average cost of

150,000 bushels and the average cost of 325,000 bushels, using the figures in Review Question 6. (Note that average costs increase when output increases.) What connection do these figures have with the firm's returns to scale?

8. Naomi has stockpiled a great deal of corn. Suppose now that she buys more piglets, but not more corn, and divides the corn she has evenly among the larger number of piglets. What is likely to happen to the marginal physical product of corn? What, therefore, is the role of input proportions in the determination of marginal physical product?

9. Labor costs $10 per hour. Nine workers produce 180 bushels of product per hour, while ten workers produce 196 bushels. Land rents for $1,000 per acre per year. With ten acres worked by nine workers, the marginal physical product of an acre of land is 1,400 bushels per year. Does the farmer minimize costs by hiring nine workers and renting

ten acres of land? If not, which input should he use in larger relative quantity?

10. Suppose that Naomi's total costs increase by $12 per week at every output level. Show in Table 8–2 how this affects her total and average costs.

11. (More difficult) A firm experiences a sudden increase in the demand for its product. In the short run, it must operate longer hours and pay higher overtime wage rates to satisfy this new demand. In the long run, however, the firm can install more machines instead of operating fewer machines for longer hours. Which do you think will be lower, the short-run or the long-run average cost of the increased output? How is your answer affected by the fact that the long-run average cost includes the new machines the firm buys, while the short-run average cost includes no machine purchases?

---

● **APPENDIX** ▮ **PRODUCTION INDIFFERENCE CURVES**

---

To describe a production function—that is, the relationship between input combinations and the size of a firm's total output—economists use a graphic device called the *production indifference curve* instead of the sort of numerical information described in Table 8–5 in the chapter.

> A *production indifference curve* (sometimes called an *isoquant*) is a curve in a graph showing quantities of inputs on its axes.

Each indifference curve indicates *all* combinations of input quantities just capable of producing a *given* quantity of output; thus, a separate indifference curve corresponds to each possible quantity of output. These production indifference curves are perfectly analogous to the consumer indifference curves discussed in the appendix to Chapter 6.

Figure 8–10 represents different quantities of labor and capital capable of producing given amounts of wheat. The figure shows three indifference curves: one for the production of 220,000 bushels of wheat, one for 240,000 bushels, and one for 260,000 bushels. The indifference curve labeled 220,000 bushels indicates that a farm can generate an output of 220,000 bushels of wheat using *any one* of the combinations of inputs represented by points on that curve. For example, it can employ ten years of labor and 200 acres of land (point *A*) or the labor-capital combination shown by point *B* on the same curve. Because it lies considerably below and to the right of point *B*, point *A* represents a productive process that uses more labor and less land.

Points *A* and *B* can be considered *technologically* indifferent because each represents a bundle of inputs just capable of yielding the same quantity of finished goods. However, the word "indifference" in this sense does not

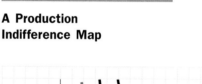

**FIGURE 8–10**

**A Production Indifference Map**

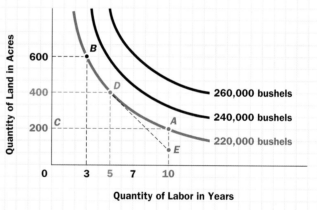

mean that the producer will be unable to decide between input combinations *A* and *B*. Input prices will permit the producer to arrive at a decision.

The production indifference curves in a diagram such as Figure 8–10 constitute a complete description of the production function. For each combination of inputs, they show how much output can be produced. Since production indifference curves are drawn in two dimensions, they represent only two inputs at a time. In more realistic situations, firms are likely to need more than two inputs, so, to study the subject, economists must conduct an algebraic analysis. Still, all the principles we need to analyze such a situation can be derived from the two-variable case.

## CHARACTERISTICS OF THE PRODUCTION INDIFFERENCE CURVES, OR ISOQUANTS

Before discussing input pricing and quantity decisions, we first examine what is known about the shapes of production indifference curves.

**Characteristic 1:** *Higher curves correspond to larger outputs.* Points on a higher indifference curve represent larger quantities of *both* inputs than the corresponding points on a lower curve. Thus, a higher curve represents a larger *output*.

**Characteristic 2:** *An indifference curve will generally have a negative slope.* It goes downhill as we move toward the right. This means that if a firm reduces the quantity of one input, and it does not want to cut production, it must use more of another input.

**Characteristic 3:** *An indifference curve is typically assumed to curve inward toward the origin near its middle.* This shape reflects the "law" of diminishing returns to a single input. For example, in Figure 8–10, points B, D, and A represent three different input combinations capable of producing the same quantity of output. At point B, the firm uses a large amount of land and relatively little labor, whereas the opposite is true at point A. Point D is intermediate between the two.

Now consider the choice among these input combinations. When the farmer considers moving from point B to point D, he gives up 200 acres of land and instead hires two additional years of labor. Similarly, the move from D to A involves giving up another 200 acres of land. This time, however, hiring an additional two years of labor does not make up for the reduced use of land. Diminishing returns to labor as the farmer hires more and more workers to replace more and more land means that the farm now needs a much larger quantity of additional labor, five person-years rather than two, to make up for the reduction in the use of land. Without such diminishing returns, the indifference curve would have been a straight line, *DE*. The curvature of the indifference curve through points D and A reflects diminishing returns to substitution of inputs.

## THE CHOICE OF INPUT COMBINATIONS

A production indifference curve describes only the input combinations that *can* produce a given output; it indicates the technological possibilities. To decide which of the available options suits its purposes best, a business needs the corresponding cost information: the relative prices of the inputs.

The budget line in Figure 8–11 represents all equally costly input combinations for a firm. For example, if farmhands are paid \$9,000 a year and land rents for \$1,000 per acre a year, then a farmer who spends \$360,000 can hire 40 farmhands but rent no land (point K), or he can rent 360 acres but have no money left for farmhands (point J). It is undoubtedly more sensible to pick some intermediate point on his budget line at which he divides the \$360,000 between the two inputs. The slope of the budget line represents the amount of land the farmer must give up if he wants to hire one more worker without increasing his budget.

| FIGURE 8–11 |
| --- |

**A Budget Line**

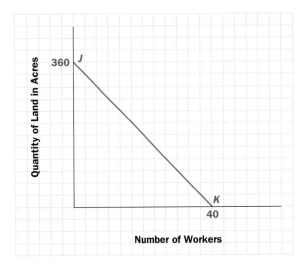

If the prices of the inputs do not change, then the slope of the budget line will not change anywhere in the graph. It will be the same at every point on a given budget line, and it will be the same on the \$360,000 budget line as on the \$400,000 budget line or on the budget line for any other level of spending. For if the price of hiring a worker is nine times as high as the cost of renting an acre, then the farmer must rent nine fewer acres to hire an additional farmhand without changing the total amount of money he spends on these inputs. Thus, the slope will be acres given up per added farmhand = −9/1 = −9.

So, with input prices given, the slope of any budget line does not change and the slopes of the different budget lines for different amounts of expenditures are all the same. Two results follow: (1) the budget lines are straight lines because their slopes remain the same throughout their length, and (2) because they all have the same slope, the budget lines in the graph will all be parallel, as in Figure 8–12.

**FIGURE 8-12**

## Cost Minimization

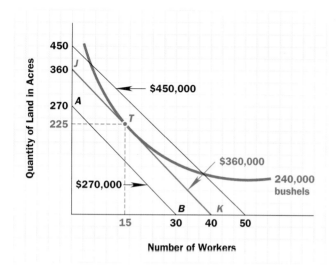

A firm that is seeking to minimize costs does not necessarily have a fixed budget. Instead, it wants to produce a given quantity of output (say, 240,000 bushels) with *the smallest possible budget*.

Figure 8–12 combines the indifference curve for 240,000 bushels from Figure 8–10 with a variety of budget lines similar to *JK* in Figure 8–11. The firm's problem is to find the lowest budget line that will allow it to reach the 240,000-bushel indifference curve. Clearly, an expenditure of $270,000 is too little; no point on the budget line, *AB*, permits production of 240,000 bushels. Similarly, an expenditure of $450,000 is too much, because the firm can produce its target level of output more cheaply. The solution is at point *T* where the farmer uses 15 workers and 225 acres of land to produce the 240,000 bushels of wheat. In general:

> The least costly way to produce any given level of output is indicated by the point of tangency between a budget line and the production indifference curve corresponding to that level of output.

COST MINIMIZATION,
EXPANSION PATH,
AND COST CURVES

Figure 8–12 shows how to determine the input combination that minimizes the cost of producing 240,000 bushels of output. The farmer can repeat this procedure exactly for any other output quantity, such as 200,000 bushels or 300,000 bushels. In each case, we draw the corresponding production indifference curve and find the lowest budget line that permits the farm to produce that much. For example, in Figure 8–13, budget line *BB* is tangent to the indifference curve for 200,000 units of

output; budget line *JK* is, again, tangent to the indifference curve for 240,000 bushels; and budget line *B'B'* is tangent to the indifference curve for 300,000 units of output. This gives us three tangency points: *S*, which gives the input combination that produces a 200,000-bushel output at lowest cost; *T*, which gives the same information for a 240,000-bushel output; and *S'*, which indicates the cost-minimizing input combination for the production of 300,000 bushels.

**FIGURE 8-13**

## The Firm's Expansion Path

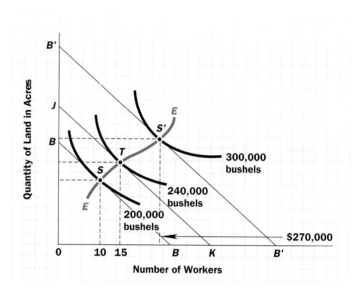

This process can be repeated for as many other levels of output as we like. For each such output we draw the corresponding production indifference curve and find its point of tangency with a budget line. Red curve *EE* in Figure 8–13 connects all these cost-minimizing points; that is, it is the locus of *S, T, S'*, and all other points of tangency between a production indifference curve and a budget line. Curve *EE* is called the firm's expansion path.

> The *expansion path* is the locus of the firm's cost-minimizing input combinations for all relevant output levels.

Point *T* in Figure 8–12 shows the quantity of output (given by the production indifference curve through that point) and the total cost (shown by the tangent budget line). Similarly, we can determine the output and total cost for every other point on the expansion path, *EE*, in Figure 8–13. For example, at point *S*, output is 200,000 and total cost is $270,000. This is precisely the sort of information we need to find the firm's total cost curve; that is, it is just the sort of information contained in Table 8–3, it is the source of the total cost curve and the average and marginal cost curves in Figure 8–4. Thus:

The points of tangency between a firm's production indifference curves and its budget lines yield its expansion path, which shows the firm's cost-minimizing input combination for each pertinent output level. This information also yields the output and total cost for each point on the expansion path, which is just what we need to draw the firm's cost curves.

## EFFECTS OF CHANGES IN INPUT PRICES

Suppose that the cost of renting land increases and the wage rate of labor decreases. This means that the budget lines will differ from those depicted in Figure 8–12. Specifically, with land now more expensive, any given sum of money will rent fewer acres, so the intercept of each budget line on the vertical (land) axis will shift *downward*. Conversely, with labor cheaper, any given sum of money will buy more labor, so the intercept of the budget line on the horizontal (labor) axis will shift to the *right*. Figure 8–14 depicts a series of budget lines corresponding to a $1,500 per acre rental rate for land and a $6,000 annual wage for labor. If input prices change, the combination of inputs that minimizes costs will normally change. In this diagram, the land rent at $1,500 per acre is more than it was in Figure 8–12, whereas labor costs $6,000 per year (less than in Figure 8–12). As a result, these budget lines are less steep than those shown in Figure 8–12, and point *E* now represents the least costly way to produce 240,000 bushels of wheat.

To assist you in seeing how things change, Figure 8–15 combines, in a single graph, budget line *JK* and tangency point *T* from Figure 8–12 with budget line *WV* and tangency point *E* from Figure 8–14. When land becomes more expensive and labor becomes cheaper, the budget lines (such as *JK*) become less steep than they were previously (see *VW*). As a result, the least costly way to produce 240,000 bushels shifts from point *T* to point *E*, at which the firm uses more labor and less land. As common sense suggests, when the price of one input rises in comparison with that of another, it will pay the firm to use less of the more expensive input and more of the other.

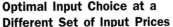

**FIGURE 8–14**

**Optimal Input Choice at a Different Set of Input Prices**

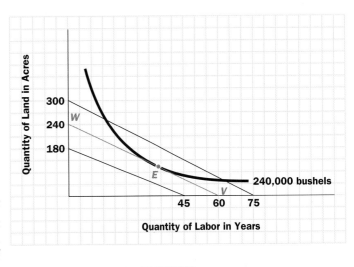

**FIGURE 8–15**

**How Changes in Input Prices Affect Input Proportions**

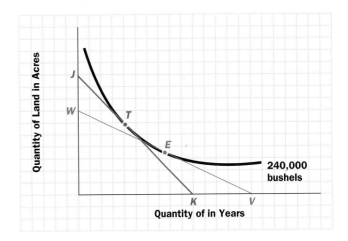

In addition to substituting one input for another, a change in the price of an input may induce the firm to alter its level of output. This is a subject that we will cover in the next chapter.

## SUMMARY

1. A production function can be described by a series of *production indifference curves*, each of which shows all the input combinations capable of producing a specified amount of output.

2. As long as each input has a positive marginal physical product, production indifference curves will have negative slopes and the higher curves will represent larger amounts of output than the lower curves. Because of diminishing returns, these curves characteristically bend toward the origin near the middle.

3. The optimal input combination for any given level of output is indicated by the point of tangency between a budget line and the corresponding production indifference curve.

4. The firm's *expansion path* shows, for each of its possible output levels, the combination of input quantities that minimizes the cost of producing that output.

5. Total cost for each output level can be derived from the production indifference curves and the budget lines tangent

to them along the expansion path. These figures can be used to determine the firm's total cost, average cost, and marginal cost curves.

6. When input prices change, firms will normally use more of the input that becomes relatively less expensive and less of the input that becomes relatively more expensive.

## KEY TERMS

Production indifference curve   162

Budget line   163

Expansion path   164

## QUESTIONS FOR REVIEW

1. Compound Consolidated Corporation (CCC) produces containers using two inputs: labor and glue. If labor costs $10 per hour and glue costs $5 per gallon, draw CCC's budget line for a total expenditure of $100,000. In this same diagram, sketch a production indifference curve indicating that CCC can produce no more than 1,000 containers with this expenditure.

2. With respect to Review Question 1, suppose that wages rise to $20 per hour and glue prices rise to $6 per gallon. How are CCC's optimal input proportions likely to change? (Use a diagram to explain your answer.)

3. What happens to the expansion path of the firm in Review Question 2?

Business is a good game. . . . You keep score with money.

Nolan Bushnell, founder of Atari
(an early video game maker)

# OUTPUT, PRICE, AND PROFIT: THE IMPORTANCE OF MARGINAL ANALYSIS

S uppose you become president of a firm that makes video games. One of your most critical decisions will be how many video games to produce and at what price to offer them for sale. The owners of the company want to make as much profit as possible. This chapter explores how to make logical decisions that help to attain that goal.

With this chapter, we cap off our discussion of the fundamental building blocks of microeconomics. Chapters 6 and 7 dealt with the behavior of consumers, the first of the two main protagonists. Then Chapter 8 introduced the other leading member of the cast: the firm. The firm's two main roles are, first, to produce its product efficiently and, second, to sell it at a profit. The previous chapter described production decisions. Now we turn to the selling decisions.

An **optimal decision** is one which, among all the decisions that are actually possible, is best for the decision maker. For example, if profit is the sole objective of some firm, the price that makes the firm's profit as large as possible is optimal for that company.

Throughout Part II, we have described how firms and consumers can make **optimal decisions,** meaning that their decisions go as far as possible, given the circumstances, to promote the consumer's and producer's goals. In this chapter, we will continue to assume that business firms seek primarily to maximize total profit, just as we assumed that consumers maximize utility.

As in the previous three chapters, marginal analysis helps us to determine what constitutes an optimal decision. Because that method of analysis is so useful, this chapter summarizes and generalizes what we have learned about the methods of marginal analysis, showing also how this analysis applies in many other situations in which optimality is an issue.

Marginal analysis leads to some surprising conclusions that show how misleading unaided "common sense" can sometimes be. Here is an example. Suppose a firm suffers a sharp increase in its rent or some other fixed cost. How should the firm react? Some would argue that the firm should raise product prices to cover the higher rent; others would argue that it should cut its price in order to increase its sales enough to pay the higher rent. We will see in this chapter that both of these answers are incorrect! A profit-maximizing firm faced with a rent increase should neither raise nor lower its price.

## Two Puzzles

Price and output decisions can sometimes perplex even the most experienced business people, as the following real-life illustrations show.[1] At the end of the chapter, we will see how marginal analysis helped solve the problems.

**Case 1: Making Profits by Selling Below Costs**   Ordinary good sense is not necessarily the best guide in business decisions. Our first illustrative case indicates that it is possible for a firm to make a profit by selling at a price that is apparently below its cost!

In a recent legal battle between two manufacturers of pocket calculators, Company B accused Company A of selling 10 million sophisticated calculators at a price of $12, which A allegedly knew was too low to cover costs. B claimed that A was doing this only to drive B out of business. At first, Company A's records, as revealed to the court, appeared to confirm B's accusations. The cost of materials, labor, advertising, and other direct costs of the calculator came to $10.30 per calculator. Company A's accountants also assigned to this product its share of the company's annual expenditure on overhead—such items as general administration, research, and the like—which amounted to $4.25 per calculator.

The $12 price clearly did not cover the $14.55 cost attributed to each calculator. Yet economists representing Company A were able to convince the court that

---

[1] The following cases are disguised to protect the confidentiality of the firms involved.

manufacturing the calculator was a profitable activity for Company A, so there was no basis on which to conclude that its only purpose was to destroy B. At the end of the chapter, we will explain just how this was possible.

**Case 2: Pricing a Six-Pack of Soda**   Managers at one of America's largest soft drink manufacturers became concerned when a rival company introduced a cheaper substitute for one of their leading products. As a result, some of the market leader's managers advocated reducing the price of a six-pack from $1.50 to $1.35. This stimulated a heated debate. Everyone agreed to the price cut if it could be shown to be unlikely to reduce the company's profits. Although some of the managers maintained that the cut made sense because of the additional sales it would stimulate, others held that the price cut would hurt the company by slashing profit per unit of output. The company had reliable information about costs, but didn't know much about the shape of its demand curve. At this point a group of consultants (including one of the authors of this book) was called in to offer suggestions. We will see how economic analysis helped them to solve the problem, even though the vital demand elasticity figures were unavailable.

## ■ PRICE AND QUANTITY: ONE DECISION, NOT TWO

When your company introduces a new line of video games, the marketing department has to decide what price to charge and the number of games to produce. These crucial decisions strongly influence the firm's labor requirements, consumer response to the product, and, indeed, the company's future success.

When the firm selects a *price* and a *quantity* of output that maximize profits, it seems that it must choose two numbers. In fact, however, the firm can pick only one. Once it has selected the *price*, the *quantity* it can sell is up to consumers. Alternatively, the firm may decide how many units it would like to sell, but then the market will determine the *price* at which this quantity can be sold. Clearly, the firm's dilemma explicitly illustrates the powerful role that consumers play in the market. Management gets two numbers by making only one decision because the firm's demand curve tells it, for any quantity it may decide to market, the highest possible price its product can bring.

To illustrate, we return to Chapter 8's hog-farming example. Naomi's Natural Farm sells organic pork to local restaurants and food markets, and Naomi is trying to figure out how to make more money on her hog operation. Now, whether or not she is aware of it, Naomi faces a demand curve for her hogs, *DD* in Figure 9–1. The curve shows the quantity demanded at each price. For example, the

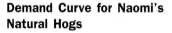

**FIGURE 9–1**

**Demand Curve for Naomi's Natural Hogs**

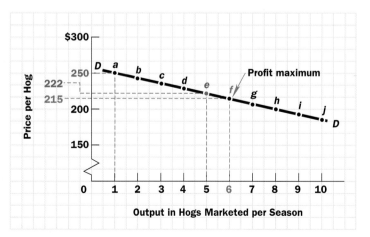

curve shows that at a price of $222 per hog (point *e*), Naomi's customers will demand five hogs. If Naomi gets greedy and tries to charge the high price of $250 per hog (point *a* on the curve), she can sell only one hog. On the other hand, if she wants to sell eight hogs, she can find the required number of customers only by offering the hogs at the lower price of $201 each (point *h*). In summary:

> Each point on the demand curve represents a price-quantity pair. The firm can pick any such pair. But it can never pick the price corresponding to one point on the demand curve and the quantity corresponding to another point, because such an output could not be sold at the selected price.

Throughout this chapter, then, we will not discuss price and output decisions separately, for they are actually two different aspects of the same decision. To analyze this decision, we will make a strong assumption about the behavior of business firms—the assumption that firms strive for the largest possible total profit to the exclusion of any other goal. Although not literally correct, this seems to be a useful simplification of a much more complex reality. As with other chapters, we will present this theoretical and intentionally simplified case first, and then we will let some of those "other things being equal" variables change.

We will therefore assume throughout this chapter (and for most of the book) that the firm has only one objective. It wants to make its total profit as large as possible. Our analytic strategy will seek to determine what output level (or price) achieves this goal. But you should keep in mind that many of our results depend on this simplifying assumption, so the conclusions will not apply to every case. Our decision to base the analysis on the profit-maximizing assumption gives us sharper insights, but we pay with some loss of realism.

## ■ TOTAL PROFIT: KEEP YOUR EYE ON THE GOAL

The **total profit** of a firm is its net earnings during some period of time. It is equal to the total amount of money the firm gets from sales of its products (the firm's total revenue) minus the total amount that it spends to make and market those products (total cost).

**Total profit,** then, is the firm's goal. By definition, total profit is the difference between what the company earns in the form of sales revenue and what it pays out in the form of costs:

> Total profit = Total revenue − Total costs

**OPPORTUNITY COST** Total profit defined in this way is called **economic profit** to distinguish it from an accountant's definition of profit. The two concepts of profit differ because an economist's total cost counts the *opportunity* cost of any capital, labor, or other inputs supplied by the firm's owner. For example, let's say that Alex, who owns a small business, earns just enough to pay him the money that his labor and capital could have earned if they had been sold to others (say, $60,000 per year). Then, as we saw in **Chapter 4**, economists say that he is earning zero economic profit. (Alex is just covering all his costs, including his opportunity costs.) In contrast, most accountants would say his profit is $60,000, referring to the difference between his gross receipts and his gross costs.

*How Much Does It Really Cost?*

**Economic profit** equals net earnings, in the accountants sense, minus the *opportunity costs* of capital and of any other inputs supplied by the firm's owners.

To see how total profit depends on output, we must study how the two components of total profit, total revenue (TR) and total cost (TC), behave when output changes. It should be obvious that both total revenue and total cost depend on the output-price combination the firm selects; we study these relationships next.

### TOTAL, AVERAGE, AND MARGINAL REVENUE

We can calculate total revenue directly from the demand curve because, by definition, it is the product of price times the quantity that consumers will buy at that price:

$$TR = P \times Q$$

Table 9–1 shows how we derive the total revenue schedule from the demand schedule for Naomi's natural hogs. The first two columns simply express Figure

**TABLE 9–1**

## Demand for Naomi's Natural Hogs, Her Total Revenue Schedule, and Her Marginal Revenue Schedule

| Number of Hogs per Season | Price = Average Revenue per Hog | Total Revenue per Season | Marginal Revenue per Hog |
|---|---|---|---|
| 0 | — | $      0 | $250 |
| 1 | $250 | 250 | 236 |
| 2 | 243 | 486 | 222 |
| 3 | 236 | 708 | 208 |
| 4 | 229 | 916 | 194 |
| 5 | 222 | 1,110 | 180 |
| 6 | 215 | 1,290 | 166 |
| 7 | 208 | 1,456 | 152 |
| 8 | 201 | 1,608 | 138 |
| 9 | 194 | 1,746 | 104 |
| 10 | 185 | 1,850 | |

## Total Revenue Curve for Naomi's Natural Hogs

**FIGURE 9–2**

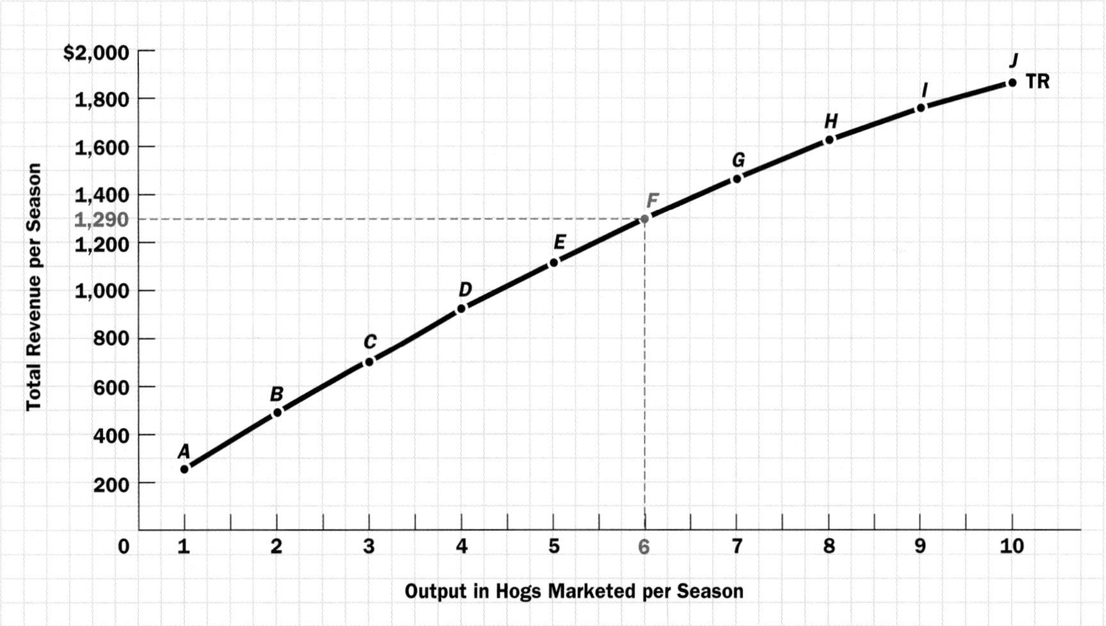

9–1's demand curve in tabular form. The third column gives, for each quantity, the product of price times quantity. For example, if Naomi sells seven hogs at a price of $208 per hog, her seasonal sales revenue will be 7 hogs × $208 per hog = $1,456.

Figure 9–2 displays Naomi's total revenue schedule in graphical form as the black TR curve. This graph shows precisely the same information as the demand curve in Figure 9–1, but in a somewhat different form. For example, point *f* on the demand curve in Figure 9–1, which shows a price-quantity combination of *P* = $215 per hog and *Q* = 6 hogs per season, appears as point *F* in Figure 9–2 as a total revenue of $1,290 per season ($215 per hog times 6 hogs). Similarly, each point on the TR curve in Figure 9–2 corresponds to the similarly labeled point in Figure 9–1.

We can speak of the relationship between the demand curve and the TR curve in a slightly different and more useful way. Because the product price is the revenue

FIGURE 9-3

## Cost Curves for Naomi's Natural Hogs

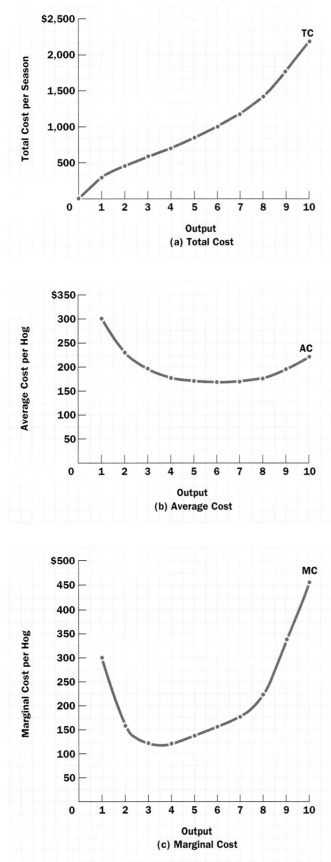

(a) Total Cost

(b) Average Cost

(c) Marginal Cost

NOTE: Output is in hogs per season.

per unit that the firm receives, we can view the demand curve as an **average revenue (AR)** curve. Average revenue and total revenue (TR) are related to one another in a simple way.[2] Specifically:

$$AR = TR/Q = P \times Q/Q = P$$

Therefore, average revenue and price are two names for the same thing. The reason should be clear. If a supermarket sells candy bars at the same price, say, $1, to each and every customer who wants one, then the average revenue that the store derives from the sale of all these candy bars must also be $1.

Finally, the last column of Table 9–1 shows the **marginal revenue (MR)** for each level of output. Marginal revenue provides us with an analytic tool that we will explain presently. This concept (analogous to marginal utility and marginal cost) refers to the addition to total revenue that results from raising output by one unit. Thus, in Table 9–1, we see that when output rises from two to three hogs, total revenue goes up from $486 to $708, so marginal revenue is $708 minus $486, or $222.

### TOTAL, AVERAGE, AND MARGINAL COST

The revenue side is, of course, only half of the firm's profit picture. We must turn to the cost side for the other half. As we saw in the previous chapter, average cost (AC) and marginal cost (MC) are obtained directly from total cost (TC) in exactly the same way that average and marginal revenue were calculated from total revenue.

Figure 9–3 plots the numbers in Table 9–2 and thus shows the total, average, and marginal cost curves for the hog operation. As we learned in the previous chapter, the shapes of the curves depicted here are considered typical. The shapes mean that, in any given industry, there is some size of firm that is most efficient in producing the output. Smaller enterprises lose any advantages that derive from a large volume of production, and so their average cost (the cost per unit of output) will be greater than that of a firm operating at the most efficient size of output. Similarly, firms that are too large will suffer from difficulties of supervision and coordination, and perhaps from bureaucratic controls, so that their costs per unit of output will also be higher than those of a firm of the most efficient size.

### MAXIMIZATION OF TOTAL PROFIT

We now have all the tools we need to answer our central question: What combination of output and price will yield the largest possible total profit? To study how total profit depends on output, we bring together in Table 9–3 the total revenue and total cost schedules from the two previous tables. The last column in Table 9–3—called, appropriately enough, total profit—is just the difference between total revenue and total cost at each level of output.

---

[2] See the appendix to this chapter for a general discussion of the relationship between totals and averages.

## Naomi's Total, Average, and Marginal Costs

TABLE 9-2

| Hogs per Season | Total Cost per Season | Marginal Cost per Hog | Average Cost per Hog |
|---|---|---|---|
| 0 | $ 0 | | — |
| | | $ 300 | |
| 1 | 300 | | $300 |
| | | 159 | |
| 2 | 459 | | 229 |
| | | 123 | |
| 3 | 582 | | 194 |
| | | 123 | |
| 4 | 705 | | 176 |
| | | 141 | |
| 5 | 847 | | 169 |
| | | 159 | |
| 6 | 1,006 | | 168 |
| | | 180 | |
| 7 | 1,185 | | 169 |
| | | 226 | |
| 8 | 1,411 | | 176 |
| | | 335 | |
| 9 | 1,746 | | 194 |
| | | 459 | |
| 10 | 2,205 | | 220 |

NOTE: Numbers in the table are rounded for simplicity, and thus may not add up exactly.

The **average revenue (AR)** is total revenue (TR) divided by quantity.

**Marginal revenue,** often abbreviated MR, is the addition to total revenue resulting from the addition of one unit to total output. Geometrically, marginal revenue is the slope of the total revenue curve. Its formula is $MR_1 = TR_1 - TR_0$, and so on.

Because we assume that Naomi's objective is to maximize profits, it is simple enough to determine the level of production she will choose. By producing and selling six hogs per season, Naomi's hog operation earns the highest level of profits it is capable of earning—$285 per season. Any higher or lower rate of production would lead to lower profits. For example, profits would drop to $271 if output were increased to seven hogs. If Naomi were to make the mistake of producing 10 hogs per season, she would actually suffer a net loss.

**MARGINAL ANALYSIS** You will likely have noticed a recurrent theme in this chapter, which is a cornerstone of any economic analysis and thus one of our *Ideas for Beyond the Final Exam.* In any decision about whether to expand an activity, it is always the marginal cost and marginal benefit that are the relevant factors. A calculation based on average figures is likely to lead the decision maker to miss all sorts of opportunities, some of them critical.

More generally, if one wants to make optimal decisions, marginal analysis should be used in the planning calculations. This is true whether the decision applies to a business firm seeking to maximize total profit or minimize the cost of the output it has selected, to a consumer trying to maximize utility, or to a less developed country striving to maximize per-capita output. It applies as much to decisions on input

*The Importance of Thinking at the Margin*

## Total Revenues, Costs, and Profit for Naomi's Natural Hogs

TABLE 9-3

| Hogs per Season | Total Revenue (TR) | Total Cost (TC) | Total Profit (TP) |
|---|---|---|---|
| 0 | $ 0 | $ 0 | $ 0 |
| 1 | 250 | 300 | −50 |
| 2 | 486 | 458 | 28 |
| 3 | 708 | 582 | 126 |
| 4 | 916 | 705 | 211 |
| 5 | 1,110 | 846 | 264 |
| 6 | 1,290 | 1,005 | 285 |
| 7 | 1,456 | 1,185 | 271 |
| 8 | 1,608 | 1,410 | 198 |
| 9 | 1,746 | 1,746 | 0 |
| 10 | 1,850 | 2,204 | −354 |

NOTE: Numbers are rounded for simplicity, and thus may not match some numbers in Table 9-2.

proportions and advertising as to decisions about output levels and prices. Indeed, this is such a general principle of economics that it is one of the *Ideas for Beyond the Final Exam.*

**Profit Maximization: A Graphical Interpretation**

## PROFIT MAXIMIZATION: A GRAPHICAL INTERPRETATION

We can present the same information on a graph. In Panel (a) of Figure 9–4, we bring together into a single diagram the relevant portion of the total revenue curve from Figure 9–2 and the total cost curve from Figure 9–3. Total profit, which is the difference between total revenue and total cost, appears in the diagram as the vertical distance between the TR and TC curves. For example, when output is four units, total revenue is $916 (point *A*), total cost is $705 (point *B*), and total profit is the distance between points *A* and *B*, or $211.

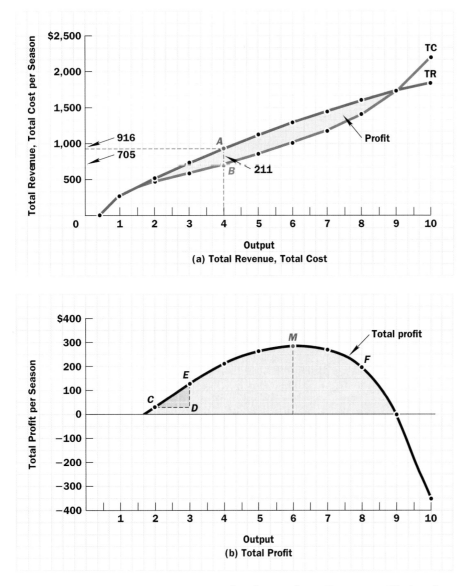

NOTE: Output is in hogs per season.

In this graphical view of the problem, Naomi wants to maximize total profit, which is the vertical distance between the TR and TC curves. Panel (b) of Figure 9–4 shows the curve of total profit—that is, TR minus TC. We see that it reaches its maximum value, about $285, at an output level of six units per week. This is the same conclusion we reached by looking at Table 9–3.

The total profit curve in Figure 9–4(b) is shaped like a hill. Though such a shape is not inevitable, we expect a hill shape to be typical for the following reason: if a firm produces nothing, it certainly earns no profit. At the other extreme, a firm can produce so much output that it swamps the market, forcing price down so low that it loses money. Only at intermediate levels of output—something between zero and the amount that floods the market—will the company earn a positive profit. Consequently, the total profit curve will rise from zero (or negative) levels at a very small output to positive levels at intermediate outputs; finally, it will fall to negative levels when output gets too large.

## ■ MARGINAL ANALYSIS AND MAXIMIZATION OF TOTAL PROFIT

We see from Figure 9–4 and Table 9–3 that many levels of output may yield a positive profit, but the firm is not aiming for just any level of profit. It wants the largest possible profit. If management knew the exact shape of its profit hill, that is, if it had Table 9–3, choosing the optimal level of output would be a simple task indeed.

It would only have to locate the point, such as *M* in Figure 9–4(b), that defined the top of its profit hill. However, management rarely if ever has so much information, so a different technique for finding the optimum is required. That technique is marginal analysis—the same set of tools we used to analyze the firm's input purchase decisions in Chapter 8 and the consumer's buying decisions in Chapters 6 and 7.

This time we will use a concept known as **marginal profit** to solve Naomi's problem. Referring back to Table 9–3, we see that an increase in Naomi's output from two to three hogs would raise total profit from $28 to $126; that is, it would generate $98 in additional profit. We call this the marginal profit resulting from the addition of the third unit. Similarly, marginal profit from the seventh unit would be:

> **Marginal profit** is the addition to total profit resulting from one more unit of output.

Total profit from 7 units − Total profit from 6 units = $271 − $285 = −$14.

The marginal rule for finding the optimal level of output is easy to understand:

**If the marginal profit from increasing output by one unit is positive, then output should be increased. If the marginal profit from increasing output by one unit is negative, then output should be decreased. Thus, an output level can maximize total profit only if marginal profit is neither positive nor negative, that is, if it equals zero at that output.**

On Naomi's Natural Farm, the marginal profit from the third unit of output (a third hog) is $98. This means that going from the second to the third unit adds $98 to profit, so it pays to produce the third unit. But marginal profit from the seventh unit is $271 − $285, or −$14, so the farm should not produce the seventh hog because that would reduce total profit by $14. Only where marginal profit is neither positive nor negative (as is approximately true for the sixth unit of output) can total profit be as big as possible, because neither increasing nor reducing output can add to total profit.

The profit hill in Figure 9–4(b) is a graphical representation of the condition that marginal profit should be as close to zero as possible. Marginal profit is defined as the additional profit that accrues to the firm when output rises by one unit. So when output is increased, say, from two units to three units, the distance *CD* in Figure 9–4(b), total profit rises by $98 (the distance *DE*) and marginal profit is therefore *DE/CD* (see the blue triangle in the graph). This is precisely the definition of the slope of the total profit curve between points *C* and *E*. In general:

**Marginal profit is the slope of the total profit curve.**

With this geometric interpretation in hand, we can easily understand the logic of the marginal profit rule. At a point such as *C*, where the total profit curve is rising, marginal profit (which equals slope) is positive. Profit cannot be maximal at such a point, because we can increase profits by moving farther to the right. A firm that decided to stick to point *C* would be wasting the opportunity to increase profits by increasing output. Similarly, the firm cannot be maximizing profits at a point like *F*, where the slope of the curve is negative, because there marginal profit (which, again,

*"Basic economics—sometimes the parts are worth more than the whole."*

equals slope) is negative. If it finds itself at a point like *F*, the firm can raise its profit by decreasing its output.

Only at a point such as *M*, where the total profit curve is neither rising nor falling, can the firm possibly be at the top of the profit hill rather than on one of the sides of the hill. Point *M* is precisely where the slope of the curve—and hence the marginal profit—is zero, or as near as possible to zero. Thus:

> An output decision cannot be optimal unless the corresponding marginal profit is zero.

The firm is not interested in marginal profit for its own sake, but rather for what it implies about total profit. Marginal profit is like the needle on the temperature gauge of a car: the needle itself is of no concern to anyone, but failure to watch it can result in serious consequences.

One common misunderstanding of marginal analysis is the idea that it seems foolish to go to a point where marginal profit is zero. "Isn't it better to earn a positive marginal profit?" This notion springs from a confusion between the quantity one is seeking to maximize (total profit) and the gauge that indicates whether such a maximum has in fact been attained (marginal profit). Of course, it is better to have a positive total profit than a zero total profit. In contrast, a zero value on the marginal profit gauge merely indicates that all is well, that total profit is at its maximum.

## MARGINAL REVENUE AND MARGINAL COST: GUIDES TO OPTIMIZATION

An alternative version of the marginal analysis of profit maximization can be derived from the cost and revenue components of profit. For this purpose, refer back to Figure 9–4, where we used total revenue (TR) and total cost (TC) curves to construct the profit hill. There is another way of finding the profit-maximizing solution.

We want to maximize the firm's profit, which is measured by the vertical distance between the TR and TC curves. This distance, we see, is not maximal at an output level such as two units, because there the two curves are growing farther apart. If we move farther to the right, the vertical distance between them (which is total profit) will increase. Conversely, we have not maximized the vertical distance between TR and TC at an output level such as eight units, because there the two curves are coming closer together. We can add to profit by moving farther to the left (reducing output). The conclusion from the graph, then, is that total profit—the vertical distance between TR and TC—is maximized only when the two curves are neither growing farther apart nor coming closer together, that is, when their slopes are equal.

Marginal revenue and marginal cost curves, which we learned about earlier in the chapter, will help us understand this concept better. For precisely the same reason that marginal profit is the slope of the total profit curve, marginal revenue is the slope of the total revenue curve, because it represents the increase in total revenue resulting from the sale of one additional unit. Again, for the same reason, marginal cost is equal to the slope of the total cost curve. This interpretation of marginal revenue and marginal cost, respectively, as the slopes of the total revenue and total cost curves permits us to restate the geometric conclusion we have just reached in an economically significant way:

> Profit can be maximized only at an output level at which marginal revenue is (approximately) equal to marginal cost. In symbols:

$$MR = MC$$

The logic of the MR = MC rule for profit maximization is straightforward.[3] When MR is not equal to MC, profits cannot possibly be maximized because the

---

[3] You may have surmised by now that just as Total profit = Total revenue − Total cost, it must be true that Marginal profit = Marginal revenue − Marginal cost. This is, in fact, correct. It also shows that when Marginal profit = 0, we must have MR = MC.

firm can increase its profits either by raising its output or by reducing it. For example, if MR = $236 and MC = $159, an additional unit of output adds $236 to revenues but only $159 to costs. Hence, the firm can increase its net profit by $77 by producing and selling one more unit. Similarly, if MC exceeds MR, say, MR = $152 and MC = $226, then the firm loses $74 on its marginal unit, so it can add $74 to its profit by reducing output by one unit. Only when MR = MC (or comes as close as possible to equaling MC), is it impossible for the firm to add to its profit by changing its output level.

Table 9–4 reproduces marginal revenue and marginal cost data for Naomi's Natural Farm from Tables 9–1 and 9–2. The table shows, as must be true, that the MR = MC rule leads us to the same conclusion as Figure 9–4 and Table 9–3. If she wants to maximize her profits, Naomi should produce and sell six hogs per season. The marginal revenue of the sixth hog is $180 ($1,290 from the sale of six hogs less $1,110 from selling five) whereas the marginal cost is only $159 ($1,006 − $847). Therefore, the firm should produce the sixth unit. The seventh hog, however, brings in only $166 in marginal revenue while its marginal cost is $180—clearly a losing proposition. Only at six units of output does MR come closest to equaling MC (MR equals MC *exactly* at an output level of about 6.5 hogs, but in the real world Naomi can't produce half a hog!).

Because the graphs of marginal analysis will prove so useful in later chapters, Figure 9–5(a) shows the MR = MC condition for profit maximization graphically. The black curve labeled MR in the figure is the marginal revenue schedule from Table 9–4. The red curve labeled MC is the marginal cost schedule. They intersect at point *E*, which is therefore the point where marginal revenue and marginal cost are equal. The optimal output for Naomi is six units.[4] Figures 9–5(b) and 9–5(c), respectively, are reproductions of the TR and TC curves from the upper panel of Figure 9–4 and the total profit curve from the lower panel of that figure. Note how MC and MR intersect near the same output at which the distance of TR above TC is greatest, which is also the output at which the profit hill reaches its peak.

## FINDING THE OPTIMAL PRICE FROM OPTIMAL OUTPUT

At the start of this chapter, we set two goals: to determine the profit-maximizing output and also the profit-maximizing price. So far, we have found the profit-maximizing output, the output level at which MR = (approximately) MC (six hogs per season in our example). That leaves us with the task of determining the profit-maximizing price.

Fortunately, this requires only one more easy step. As we said at the beginning of the chapter, once the firm has selected the output it wants to produce and sell, the demand curve determines the price it must charge to induce consumers to buy that amount of product. Consequently, if we know that the profit-maximizing output is six hogs, the demand curve in Figure 9–1 tells us what price Naomi must charge to sell that profit-maximizing output. To sell an average of six hogs per season, she must price them at $215 (point *f*). The demand curve tells us that this is the only price at which this quantity will be demanded by customers.

> Once the profit-maximizing output quantity has been determined with the help of the MR = MC rule, it is easy to find the profit-maximizing price with the help of the demand curve. Just use that curve to find out at what price the optimal quantity will be demanded.

| TABLE 9-4 |
| --- |

**Naomi's Marginal Revenue and Marginal Cost**

| Hogs per Season | Marginal Revenue | Marginal Cost |
| --- | --- | --- |
| 0 | — | — |
| 1 | $250 | $300 |
| 2 | 236 | 159 |
| 3 | 222 | 124 |
| 4 | 208 | 124 |
| 5 | 194 | 141 |
| 6 | 180 | 159 |
| 7 | 166 | 180 |
| 8 | 152 | 226 |
| 9 | 138 | 335 |
| 10 | 104 | 459 |

NOTE: Marginal revenue and marginal costs are per hog, per season.

---

[4] We must note one important qualification. Sometimes marginal revenue and marginal cost curves do not have the nice shapes depicted in Figure 9–5(a), and they may intersect more than once. In such cases, although it remains true that MR = MC at the output level that maximizes profits, there may be other output levels at which MR is also equal to MC but at which profits are not maximized.

FIGURE 9–5

**Profit Maximization: Another Graphical Interpretation**

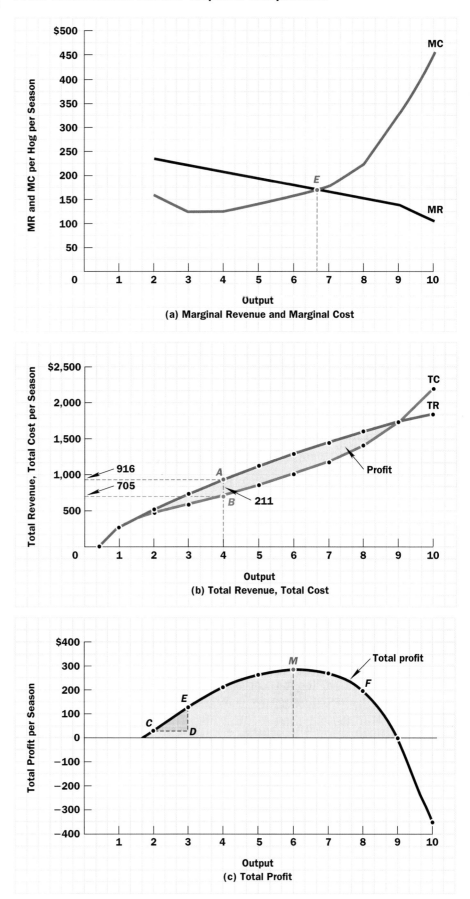

(a) Marginal Revenue and Marginal Cost

(b) Total Revenue, Total Cost

(c) Total Profit

NOTE: Output is in hogs per season.

---

**● POLICY DEBATE    ▌ PROFIT AND THE NEW MARKET ECONOMIES**

---

The collapse of communism after its catastrophic failure to produce economic abundance has led the nations of eastern Europe and elsewhere to turn to the market mechanism. They hope that the market will soon bring them the sort of prosperity achieved by the industrialized countries.

The market, as we know, is driven by the profit motive, and in a free market, profits are not determined by a government agency but by demand and cost conditions, as described by the demand and cost curves. Many citizens of these new market economies are appalled by the sizes of the profits that the free market affords to successful businesspeople, and they are upset by the greed that these entrepreneurs display. There are pressures to put limits on these profits.

The same thing has happened in Great Britain and elsewhere as firms formerly owned by the government have been sold to private individuals and returned to the market. In Britain, a number of the privatized firms were initially monopolies, and the government has chosen to protect consumers by putting ceilings on prices but not on profits in order to provide the firms with appropriate incentives. Yet when some of these firms proved to be quite profitable, the British government agencies reduced the price ceilings

in order to cut those profits, a move that was attacked sharply not only by the firms themselves but also by some British economists. The debate in the United Kingdom and elsewhere amounts to this: Should severe limits be placed on profits as a matter of fairness and to improve the ethical climate of society, or should this be avoided because ceilings on profits undermine the incentives for business success and therefore prevent the market mechanism from delivering the economic abundance of which it is capable?

---

## GENERALIZATION: THE LOGIC OF MARGINAL ANALYSIS AND MAXIMIZATION

The logic of marginal analysis of profit maximization that we have just studied can be generalized, because essentially the same argument was already used in Chapters 6 and 8 and it will recur in a number of the chapters that follow. To avoid having to master the argument each time all over again, it is useful to see how it can be applied in problems other than the determination of the firm's profit-maximizing output.

The general issue is this: Decision makers often are faced with the problem of selecting the magnitude of some variable, such as how much to spend on advertising, or how many bananas to buy, or how many school buildings to construct. Each of these acts brings benefits, so that the larger the number selected by the decision maker, the larger the total benefits that will be derived. But, unfortunately, as larger numbers are selected, the associated costs also grow. The problem is to take the trade-off properly into account and calculate at what point the net gain—the difference between the total benefit and the total cost—will be greatest. Thus, we have the following general principle:

If a decision is to be made about the quantity of some variable, then to maximize:

Net benefit = Total benefit − Total cost

the decision maker must select a value of the variable at which:

Marginal benefit = (approximately) Marginal cost

For example, if a community were to determine that the marginal benefit from building an additional school was greater than the cost of an additional school, it would clearly be better off if it built another school. On the other hand, if it were building so many schools that the marginal benefit was less than the marginal cost, it would be better off with a more limited construction program. Only if the marginal benefit and cost are as close as possible to being equal will the community have the optimal number of schools.

We will apply this same concept in later chapters. Again and again, we analyze a quantitative decision that brings together both benefits and costs and we always conclude that the optimal decision occurs at the point where the marginal benefit equals the marginal cost. The logic is the same whether we are considering the net gains to a firm, to a consumer, or to society as a whole.

## APPLICATION: FIXED COST AND THE PROFIT-MAXIMIZING PRICE

We can now use our analytic framework to offer a surprising insight. Suppose there is a rise in the firm's fixed cost; say, that the property taxes on Naomi's Natural Farm double. What will happen to the profit-maximizing price and output? Should she raise her price to cover the increased cost, or should she produce a larger output even if that requires a drop in price? The answer is surprising: Neither!

> When a firm's fixed cost increases, its profit-maximizing price and output remain completely unchanged, so long as it pays the firm to stay in business.

In other words, there is nothing that the firm's management can do to offset the effect of the rise in fixed cost. Management must just put up with it. This is surely a case where common sense is not a reliable guide to the right decision.

Why is this so? Remember that, by definition, a fixed cost does not change when output changes. The increase in Naomi's fixed costs is the same whether business is slow or booming, whether production is two hogs or 200. This is illustrated in Table 9–5, which also reproduces Naomi's total profits from Table 9–3. The third column of the table shows that total fixed cost has risen from zero to $100 per season. As a result, total profit is $100 less than it would have been otherwise—no matter what the firm's output. For example, when output is four units, we see that total profit falls from $211 (second column) to $111 (last column).

Now, because profit is reduced by the same amount at every output level, whatever output was most profitable before the increase in fixed costs must still be

| TABLE 9-5 |
|-----------|

**Total Profit before and after a Rise in Fixed Cost**

| Hog Output per Season | Total Profit without Fixed Costs | Total Fixed Costs per Season | Total Profit with Fixed Costs |
|:---:|:---:|:---:|:---:|
| 0 | $     0 | $100 | $ −100 |
| 1 | −50 | 100 | −150 |
| 2 | 28 | 100 | −72 |
| 3 | 126 | 100 | 26 |
| 4 | 211 | 100 | 111 |
| 5 | 264 | 100 | 164 |
| 6 | 285 | 100 | 185 |
| 7 | 271 | 100 | 171 |
| 8 | 198 | 100 | 98 |
| 9 | 0 | 100 | −100 |
| 10 | −354 | 100 | −454 |

most profitable. In Table 9–5, we see that $185 is the largest entry in the last column, which shows profits after the rise in fixed cost. This highest possible profit is attained, as it was before, when output is at six units. In other words, the firm's profit-maximizing price and quantity will remain exactly as they were before.

All of this is shown in Figure 9–6, which displays the firm's total profit hill before and after the rise in fixed cost (reproducing Naomi's initial profit hill from Figure 9–4). We see that the cost increase simply moves the profit hill straight downward by $100, so the highest point on the hill is just lowered from point *M* to point *N*. But the top of the hill is shifted neither toward the left nor toward the right. It remains at the six-hog output level, just as Table 9–5 indicated.

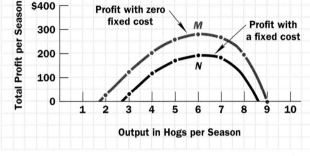

**FIGURE 9–6**

**Fixed Cost Does Not Affect Profit-Maximizing Output**

## Marginal Analysis in Real Decision Problems

We can now put the marginal analysis of profit determination to work to unravel the puzzles with which we began this chapter. These are both examples drawn from reality, and reality never works as neatly as a textbook illustration. In particular, neither example involves a mechanical application of the MR = MC rule. However, as these cases show, the underlying reasoning does shed useful light on real problems.

**Case 1: The "Unprofitable" Calculator**   Our first case study concerned a firm that was apparently losing money on calculator sales because its $12 price was less than the $14.55 average cost that the company's accountants assigned to the product. This $14.55 figure included $10.30 of costs caused directly by manufacture and marketing of the calculators plus a $4.25 per-calculator share of the company's overall general expenses ("overhead"). Accused of deliberately selling below cost in order to drive a competitor out of business, the company turned to marginal analysis to show that this was not true. The calculators were indeed a profitable line of business.

To demonstrate this fact, the company's witness explained that if the sales were really unprofitable, the company would have been able to raise its net earnings by *ceasing* production and sale of the calculators. A moment's consideration shows, however, that the opposite would have happened: profits would have decreased if the company gave up its annual sale of 10 million calculators.

The company's revenues would have been reduced by $12 for each of the 10 million units sold—a (marginal) revenue reduction of $120 million. But how much cost would it have saved? The answer is that the cost outlay actually caused by the production of each calculator was only the $10.30 in direct cost. The company president would not have been fired if the product were discontinued, and general expenditures on new product research probably would even have increased. Thus, none of the company's overhead would have been saved by ending calculator production. Rather, the (marginal) cost saving would have been the direct cost of $10.30 per calculator times the 10 million calculator output—a total cost saving of $103 million.

Thus, elimination of the product would have reduced total profit by $17 million per year—the $103 million cost saving minus the $120 million in revenue forgone. In other words, continued production of the calculators was not causing losses; on the contrary, it was contributing $17 million in profits every year. The court concluded that this reasoning was correct and used this conclusion in its decision.

This case illustrates a point that is encountered frequently. The calculator producer was selling its product at a price that appeared not to cover costs but really did. The same sort of issue frequently faces a firm considering the introduction of a new product or the opening of a new branch office. In many such cases, the new operation may not cover average costs, as measured by standard accounting methods. Yet to follow the apparent implications of those cost figures would amount to throwing away a valuable opportunity to add to the net earnings of the firm (because added [or marginal] revenues exceed added [or marginal] costs) and, perhaps, to contribute to the welfare of the economy. Only marginal analysis can reveal whether the contemplated action is really worthwhile.

**Case 2: The Soda-Pricing Problem**   Our second problem dealt with a firm's choice between keeping the price of a brand of soda at $1.50 per six-pack or reducing it to $1.35 when a competitor entered the market. The trouble was that to know what to do, the firm needed to know its demand curve (and hence its marginal revenue curve). However, the firm did not have enough data to determine the shape of its demand curve. How, then, could a rational decision be made?

As we indicated, the debate among the firm's managers finally reached agreement on one point: the price should be cut if, as a result, profits were not likely to decline, that is, if marginal profit were not negative. Fortunately, the firm was able to obtain the data needed to determine whether marginal profit was positive. Initial annual sales were 10 million units, and the firm's engineers maintained emphatically that marginal costs were very close to constant at $1.20 per six-pack over the output range in question. Instead of trying to determine the actual increase in sales that would result from the price cut, the team of consultants decided to try to determine the minimum increase in quantity demanded that would be required to avoid a decrease in profits.

It was clear that, if profits were not to decline, the firm needed additional revenue at least as great as the additional cost of supplying the added volume. That is, MR had to exceed MC. The consultants knew that total revenues at the initial price of $1.50 per six-pack were $15 million ($1.50 per unit times 10 million units). Letting $Q$ represent the (unknown) quantity of six-packs that would be sold at the proposed new price of $1.35, the economists compared the added revenue with the added cost of providing the $Q$ new units. Because MC was constant at $1.20 per unit, the added cost amounted to:

$$\text{Added cost} = \$1.20 \times (Q - 10 \text{ million})$$

This was to be compared with the added revenue:

$$\text{Added revenue} = \text{New revenue} - \text{Old revenue} = \$1.35Q - \$15 \text{ million}$$

No loss would result from the price change if the added revenue was greater than or equal to the added cost. The minimum $Q$ necessary to avoid a loss therefore was that at which added revenue equaled added cost, or:

$$1.35Q - 15 \text{ million} = 1.2Q - 12 \text{ million}$$

or:

$$0.15Q = 3 \text{ million}$$

This would be true if, and only if, $Q$, the quantity sold at the lower price, would be:

$$Q = 20 \text{ million units.}$$

In other words, this calculation showed that the firm could break even from the 15-cent price reduction only if the quantity of its product demanded rose at least 100 percent (from 10 million to 20 million units). Because past experience indicated that such a rise in quantity demanded was hardly possible, the price reduction proposal was quickly abandoned. Thus, the logic of the MR = MC rule, plus a little ingenuity, enabled the consultants to deal with a problem that at first seemed baffling—even though they had no estimate of marginal revenue.

## CONCLUSION: THE FUNDAMENTAL ROLE OF MARGINAL ANALYSIS

We saw in Chapter 8 how marginal analysis helps us to understand the firm's input choices. Similarly, in Chapters 6 and 7, it cast indispensable light on the consumer's purchase decisions. In this chapter, it enabled us to analyze output and pricing decisions. The logic of marginal analysis applies not only to economic decisions by consumers and firms but also to those of governments, universities, hospitals, and other organizations. In short, the analysis applies to any individual or group that must make optimal choices about the use of scarce resources. Thus, one of the most important conclusions that can be drawn from this chapter, a conclusion brought out vividly by the two examples we have just discussed, is the importance of thinking "at the margin"—one of our *Ideas for Beyond the Final Exam*.

*The Importance of Thinking at the Margin*

A real-life example far removed from profit maximization will illustrate how marginal criteria are useful in decision making. For some years before women were admitted to Princeton University (and to several other colleges), administrators cited the cost of the proposed admission of women as a major obstacle. They had decided in advance that any women coming to the university would constitute a net addition to the student body because, for a variety of reasons involving relations with alumni and other groups, it was not feasible to reduce the number of male students. Presumably on the basis of a calculation of average cost, some critics spoke of cost figures as high as $80 million.

To economists it was clear, however, that the relevant figure was the *marginal cost*, the addition to total cost that would result from the admission of the additional students. The women students would, of course, bring to Princeton additional tuition fees (marginal revenues). If these fees were just sufficient to cover the amount that they would add to costs, the admission of the women would leave the university's financial picture unaffected.

A careful calculation showed that the admission of women would add far less to the university's financial problems than the average cost figures indicated. One reason was that women's course preferences then were characteristically different from men's, and hence women frequently selected courses that were undersubscribed in exclusively male institutions. Therefore, the admission of 1,000 women to a formerly all-male institution could be expected to require fewer additional classes than if 1,000 more men had been admitted.[5] More important, it was found that a number of classroom buildings were underutilized. The cost of operating these buildings was nearly fixed—their total utilization cost would be changed only slightly by the influx of women. The marginal cost for classroom space was therefore almost zero and certainly well below the average cost (the cost per student).

For all of these reasons, it turned out that the relevant marginal cost was much smaller than the figures that had been bandied about earlier. Indeed, this cost was something like a third of the earlier estimates. There is little doubt that this careful marginal calculation played a critical role in the admission of women to Princeton and to some other institutions that subsequently made use of the calculations in the Princeton analysis. More recent data, incidentally, confirmed that the marginal calculations were amply justified.

## THE THEORY AND REALITY: A WORD OF CAUTION

We have now completed two chapters describing how business managers can make optimal decisions. Can you go to Wall Street or Main Street and find executives calculating marginal cost and marginal revenue to decide how much to produce? Not

---

[5] See Gardner Patterson, "The Education of Women at Princeton," *Princeton Alumni Weekly* 69 (September 24, 1968).

## ● DO FIRMS REALLY MAXIMIZE PROFITS?

Naturally, many people question whether firms really try to maximize profits to the exclusion of all other goals. Japanese companies, for instance, often promote well-known corporate priorities such as lifetime employment for workers and a preference for doing business with other Japanese companies.

Besides, businesspeople are like other human beings: Their motives are varied and complex. Given the choice, many executives may prefer to control the *largest* firm rather than the most profitable one. Some may be fascinated by technology and therefore may spend so much on R&D that it cuts down on profit. Some may want to conduct business in the most environmentally benign manner. Others may be motivated by a desire to "do good" and therefore may give away some of the stockholders' money to hospitals and colleges. Different managers within the same firm may not always agree with one another on goals, so that it may not even make sense to speak about "the" goal of the firm. Thus, any attempt to summarize the objectives of management in terms of a single number (profit) is bound to be an oversimplification.

In addition, the exacting requirements for maximizing profits are tough to satisfy. In deciding how much to invest, what price to set for a product, or how much to allocate to the advertising budget, the range of available alternatives is enormous. Also, information about each alternative is often expensive and difficult to acquire. As a result, when a firm's management decides on, say, an $18 million construction budget, it rarely compares the consequences of that decision in any detail with the consequences of all the possible alternatives—such as budgets of $17 million or $19 million. But unless all the available possibilities are compared, management cannot be sure that it has chosen the one that brings in the highest possible profit.

Often, management's concern is whether the decision's results are likely to be acceptable—whether its risks will be acceptably low, whether its profits will be acceptably high—so that the company can live satisfactorily with the outcome. Such analysis cannot be expected to bring in the maximum possible profit. The decision may be good, but some unexplored alternative may be even better.

Decision making that seeks only solutions that are acceptable has been called *satisficing,* to contrast it with optimizing (profit maximization). Some analysts, such as Nobel Prize winner Herbert Simon of Carnegie-Mellon University, have concluded that decision making in industry and government is often of the satisficing variety.

But even if this is true, it does not necessarily make profit maximization a bad assumption. Recall our discussion of abstraction and model-building in Chapter 1. A map of Los Angeles that omits hundreds of roads is no doubt "wrong" if interpreted as a literal description of the city. Nonetheless, by capturing the most important elements of reality, it may help us understand the city better than a map that is cluttered with too much detail. Similarly, we can learn much about the behavior of business firms by assuming that they try to maximize profits, even though we know that not all of them act this way all of the time.

*"It's true that more is not necessarily better, Edward, but it frequently is."*

very often—though in some important applications they do. Nor can you find consumers in stores using marginal analysis to decide what to buy. Like consumers, successful businesspeople often rely heavily on intuition and "hunches" that cannot be described by any set of rules. In fact, in a 1993 survey of CEOs conducted by *Inc.* magazine, nearly 20 percent of the respondents admitted to using guesswork to price their first product or service.

However, we have not sought a literal description of business behavior but rather a model to help us analyze and predict this behavior. The four chapters that we have just completed constitute the core of microeconomics. We will find ourselves returning again and again to the principles learned in these chapters.

## SUMMARY

1. A firm can choose the quantity of its product that it wants to sell or the price that it wants to charge. But it cannot choose both because price affects the quantity demanded.

2. In economic theory, we usually assume that firms seek to maximize profits. This should not be taken literally but rather interpreted as a useful simplification of reality.

3. Marginal revenue is the additional revenue earned by increasing sales by one unit. Marginal cost is the additional cost incurred by increasing production by one unit.

4. Maximum profit requires the firm to choose the level of output at which marginal revenue is equal to (or most closely approximates) marginal cost.

5. Geometrically, the profit-maximizing output level occurs at the highest point on the total profit curve. There the slope of the total profit curve is zero (or as close to zero as possible), meaning that marginal profit is zero.

6. A change in fixed cost will not change the profit-maximizing level of output.

7. It may pay a firm to expand its output if it is selling at a price greater than marginal cost, even if that price happens to be below average cost.

8. Optimal decisions must be made on the basis of marginal cost and marginal revenue figures, not average cost and average revenue figures. This is one of the *Ideas for Beyond the Final Exam.*

## KEY TERMS

| | | |
|---|---|---|
| Optimal decision   168 | Total revenue (TR)   170 | Profit maximization   174 |
| Total profit   170 | Average revenue (AR)   170 | Marginal analysis   174 |
| Economic profit   170 | Marginal revenue (MR)   170 | Marginal profit   175 |

## QUESTIONS FOR REVIEW

1. "It may be rational for the management of a firm not to try to maximize profits." Discuss the circumstances under which this statement may be true.

2. Suppose that the firm's demand curve indicates that at a price of $12 per unit, customers will demand two million units of its product. Suppose that management decides to pick both price and output; the firm produces 3 million units of its product and prices them at $20 each. What will happen?

3. Suppose that a firm's management would be pleased to increase its share of the market, but if it expands its production the price of its product will fall. Will its profits necessarily fall? Why or why not?

4. Why does it make sense for a firm to seek to maximize total profit rather than to maximize marginal profit?

5. A firm's marginal revenue is $133 and its marginal cost is $90. What amount of profit does the firm fail to pick up by refusing to increase output by one unit?

6. Calculate average revenue (AR) and average cost (AC) in Table 9–3. How much profit does the firm earn at the output at which AC = AR? Why?

7. A firm's total cost is $800 if it produces one unit, $1,400 if it produces two units, and $1,800 if it produces three units of output. Draw up a table of total, average, and marginal costs for this firm.

8. Draw an average and marginal cost curve for the firm in the preceding question. Describe the relationship between the two curves.

9. A firm has the demand and total cost schedules given in the following table. If it wants to maximize profits, how much output should it produce?

| Quantity | Price | Total Cost |
|:---:|:---:|:---:|
| 1 | $6 | $ 1.00 |
| 2 | 5 | 2.50 |
| 3 | 4 | 6.00 |
| 4 | 3 | 7.00 |
| 5 | 2 | 11.00 |

---

● **APPENDIX**   ▌ **THE RELATIONSHIPS AMONG TOTAL, AVERAGE, AND MARGINAL DATA**

---

You may have surmised that there is a close connection between the average revenue curve and the marginal revenue curve and that there must be a similar relationship between the average cost curve and the marginal cost curve. After all, we derived our average revenue figures from the total revenues and also calculated our marginal revenue figures from the total revenues at the various possible output levels; a similar relationship applied to costs. In fact:

Marginal, average, and total figures are inextricably bound together. From any one of the three, the other two can be calculated. The relationships among total, average, and marginal figures are exactly the same for any variable—such as revenue, cost, or profit—to which the concepts apply.

To illustrate and emphasize the wide applicability of marginal analysis, we switch our example from profits, revenues, and costs to a noneconomic variable. As we are about to see, the same concepts can also be applied to human body weights. We switch to this example because calculation of weights is more familiar to most people than calculation of profits, revenues, or costs, and we can use it to illustrate several fundamental relationships between average and marginal figures.

In Table 9–6, we begin with an empty room. (The total weight of occupants is equal to zero.) A person weighing 100 pounds enters; total, marginal and average weight are all, then, 100 pounds. If the person is followed by a person weighing 140 pounds (marginal weight equals 140 pounds), the total weight increases to 240 pounds, average weight rises to 120 pounds (240/2), and so on.[6]

| **TABLE 9-6** |
| --- |

**Weights of Persons in a Room**

| Number of Persons in a Room | Total Weight | Average Weight | Marginal Weight |
| --- | --- | --- | --- |
| 0 | 0 | — | |
| 1 | 100 lbs | 100 lbs | 100 lbs |
| 2 | 240 | 120 | 140 |
| 3 | 375 | 125 | 135 |
| 4 | 500 | 125 | 125 |
| 5 | 600 | 120 | 100 |
| 6 | 660 | 110 | 60 |

---

[6] Note that in this illustration "persons in room" is analogous to units of output, "total weight" is analogous to total revenue or cost, and "marginal weight" is analogous to marginal revenue or cost in the discussions of marginal analysis in the body of the chapter.

The rule for converting totals to averages, and vice versa, is:

Rule 1a. Average weight equals total weight divided by number of persons.

Rule 1b. Total weight equals average weight times number of persons.

This rule naturally applies equally well to cost, revenue, profit, or any other variable.

We calculate marginal weight from total weight using the same subtraction process already used to calculate marginal cost and marginal revenue. Specifically:

Rule 2a. The marginal weight of, say, the third person equals the total weight of three people minus the total weight of two people.

For example, when the fourth person enters the room, total weight rises from 375 to 500 pounds, and hence the corresponding marginal weight is 500 − 375 = 125 pounds, as is shown in the last column of Table 9–6. We can also do the reverse—calculate total from marginal weight—through an addition process.

Rule 2b. The total weight of, say, three people equals the (marginal) weight of the first person who enters the room plus the (marginal) weight of the second person, plus the (marginal) weight of the third person.

You can verify Rule 2b by referring to Table 9–6 which shows that the total weight of three persons, 375 pounds, is indeed equal to 100 + 140 + 135 pounds, the sum of the preceding marginal weights. A similar relation holds for any other total weight figure in the table, as you should verify.

In addition to these familiar arithmetic relationships, there are two other useful relationships.

Rule 3. With an exception (fixed cost) discussed in the previous chapter, the marginal, average, and total figures for the first person must all be equal.

This rule holds because when there is only one person in the room whose weight is $X$ pounds, the average weight will obviously be $X$, the total weight must be $X$, and the marginal weight must also be $X$ (because the total must have risen from zero to $X$ pounds). Put another way, when the marginal person is alone, he or she is obviously also the average person and also represents the totality of all relevant persons.

Our final and very important relationship is:

Rule 4. If marginal weight is lower than average weight, then average weight must fall when the number of persons increases. If marginal weight exceeds average weight, average weight must rise when the number of persons increases. If marginal and average weight are equal, the average weight must remain constant when the number of persons increases.

These three possibilities are all illustrated in Table 9–6. Notice, for example, that when the third person enters the room, the average weight rises from 120 to 125 pounds. That is because this person's (marginal) weight is 135 pounds, which pulls up the average, as Rule 4 requires. Similarly, when the sixth person—who is a 60-pound child—enters the room, the average falls from 120 to 110 pounds because marginal weight, 60 pounds, is below average weight.

It is essential to avoid a common misunderstanding of this rule. It does not state, for example, that if the average figure is rising, the marginal figure must be rising. When the average rises, the marginal figure may rise, fall, or remain unchanged. The arrival of two persons, both well above average, will push the average up in two successive steps even if the second new arrival is lighter than the first. We see such a case in Table 9–6, where average weight rises successively from 100 to 120 to 125, while the marginal weight falls from 140 to 135 to 125.

## GRAPHICAL REPRESENTATION OF MARGINAL AND AVERAGE CURVES

We have shown how, from a curve of total profit (or total cost or total anything else), one can determine the corresponding marginal figure. We noted several times in the chapter that the marginal value at any particular point is equal to the slope of the corresponding total curve at that point. But for some purposes, it is convenient to use a graph that records marginal and average values directly rather than deriving them from the curve of totals.

We can obtain such a graph by plotting the data in a table of average and marginal figures, such as Table 9–6. The result looks like the graph shown in Figure 9–7. Here we have indicated the number of persons in the room on the horizontal axis and the corresponding average and marginal figures on the vertical axis. The solid dots represent average weights; the small circles represent marginal weights. Thus, for example, point *A* shows that when two persons are in the room, their average

weight is 120 pounds, as recorded on the third line of Table 9–6. Similarly, point *B* on the graph represents information provided in the next column of the table, that is, that the marginal weight of the third person who enters the room is 135 pounds. We have connected these points into a marginal curve and an average curve, represented, respectively, by the solid and the broken curves in the diagram. This is the representation of marginal and average values economists most frequently use.

Figure 9–7 illustrates two of our rules. Rule 3 says that for the first unit, the marginal and average values will be the same; that is precisely why the two curves start out together at point *C*. The graph also depicts Rule 4 between points *C* and *E*, where the average curve is rising, the marginal curve lies above the average. (Notice, however, that over part of this range, the marginal curve falls even though the average curve is rising; Rule 4 says nothing about the rise or fall of the marginal curve.) We see also that over range *EF*, where the average curve is falling, the marginal curve is below the average curve, again in accord with Rule 4. Finally, at point *E*, where the average curve is neither rising nor falling, the marginal curve meets the average curve: the average and marginal weights are equal at that point.

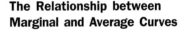

**FIGURE 9–7**

**The Relationship between Marginal and Average Curves**

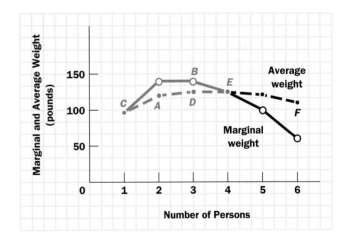

---

## QUESTIONS FOR REVIEW

1. Suppose that the following table is your record of exam grades in your Principles of Economics course:

| Exam Date | Grade | Comment |
|-----------|-------|---------|
| September 30 | 65 | A slow start |
| October 28 | 75 | A big improvement |
| November 26 | 90 | Happy Thanksgiving! |
| December 13 | 85 | Slipped a little |
| January 24 | 95 | A fast finish! |

Use these data to make up a table of total, average, and marginal grades for the five exams.

2. From the data in your table, illustrate each of the rules mentioned in this appendix. Be sure to point out an instance where the marginal grade falls but the average grade rises.

# III

## MARKETS, FROM COMPETITION TO MONOPOLY: VIRTUES AND VICES

So far, we have talked only about firms in general without worrying about the sorts of markets in which they operate. To understand the different types of competition a firm can face, it is necessary, first, to explain clearly what we mean by the word "market." Economists do not reserve the term only to mean an organized exchange operating in a specific location. In its more general and abstract usage the word *market* refers to a set of sellers and buyers whose activities affect the price at

which a *particular commodity* is sold. For example, two separate sales of General Motors stock in different parts of the country can be considered to take place in the same market, whereas sales of bread in one stall of a market square and sales of carrots in the next stall, may, in our sense, occur in totally different markets.

Economists distinguish among different kinds of markets according to how many firms they include, whether the products of the different firms are identical or somewhat different, and how easy it is for new firms to enter the markets. *Perfect competition* is at one extreme (many small firms selling an identical product, with easy entry), and *pure monopoly* (a single firm) is at the other extreme. In between are hybrid forms—called *monopolistic competition* (many small firms each selling slightly different products) and *oligopoly* (a few large rival firms)—that share some of the characteristics of both perfect competition and monopoly.

Perfect competition is far from the typical market form in the U.S. economy. Indeed, it is quite rare. Pure monopoly—literally *one* firm—is also infrequently encountered. Most of the products you buy are no doubt supplied by oligopolies or monopolistic competitors—terms that we will define precisely in Chapter 13.

Competition . . . brings about the only . . . arrangement of social production which is possible. . . . [Otherwise] what guarantee [do] we have that the necessary quantity and not more of each product will be produced, that we shall not go hungry in regard to corn and meat while we are choked in beet sugar and drowned in potato spirit, that we shall not lack trousers to cover our nakedness while buttons flood us in millions?

Friedrich Engels

# THE FIRM AND THE INDUSTRY UNDER PERFECT COMPETITION

Industries differ dramatically in the number and typical sizes of their firms. Some, such as commercial fishing, encompass a great many very small firms. Others, like automobile manufacturing, are composed of a few industrial giants. This chapter deals with a very special type of market structure—called *perfect competition*—in which firms are numerous and small. We begin by comparing alternative market forms and defining perfect competition precisely. But first, once again, we set out our puzzle.

### Pollution Reduction Incentives That Actually Increase Pollution

Many economists and other citizens concerned about the environment believe that society can obtain cleaner air and water cheaply and effectively by requiring polluters to pay for the damages they cause. (See Chapter 22 for more details.) Yet people often view pollution charges as just another tax, and that word can spell political poison. Some politicians—reasoning that they can get a donkey to move just as effectively by offering it a carrot as by poking it with a stick—have proposed *paying* firms to cut down polluting emissions.

At least some theoretical and statistical evidence indicates that such a system of bribes (or subsidies) does work, *at least up to a point.* Individual polluting firms will, indeed, respond to government payments for decreased emissions by reducing their pollution. But, over the long haul, it turns out that society will end up with more pollution than before! Subsidy payments to the firms actually exacerbate pollution problems. How is it possible that subsidies induce each firm to pollute less but in the long run lead to a rise in total pollution? The analysis in this chapter will supplement your own common sense sufficiently to supply the answer.

## ■ PERFECT COMPETITION DEFINED

**Perfect competition** occurs in an industry when that industry is made up of many small firms producing homogeneous products, when information is perfect, and when there is no impediment to the entry or exit of firms.

You can appreciate just how special perfect competition is by considering this comprehensive definition. A market is said to operate under **perfect competition** when the following four conditions are satisfied:

■ *Numerous small firms and customers.* Competitive markets contain so many buyers and sellers that each one constitutes a negligible portion of the whole: so small, in fact, that each player's decisions have no effect on price. This requirement rules out trade associations or other collusive arrangements in which firms work together to influence price.

■ *Homogeneity of product.* The product offered by any seller is identical to that supplied by any other seller. (For example, No. 1 red winter wheat is a homogeneous product; different brands of toothpaste are not.) Because products are homogeneous, consumers do not care from which firm they buy, so competition is more powerful.

■ *Freedom of entry and exit.* New firms desiring to enter the market face no impediments that previous entrants can avoid. So new firms can easily come in and compete with older firms. Similarly, if production and sale of the good proves unprofitable, no barriers prevent firms from leaving the market.

■ *Perfect information.* Each firm and each customer is well informed about available products and prices. They know whether one supplier is selling at a lower price than another.

These exacting requirements are rarely if ever found in practice. One example that comes close to the perfectly competitive standard is a market for common stocks. On any given day, literally millions of buyers and sellers trade AT&T stock; all of the shares are exactly alike; anyone who wishes to sell his or her AT&T stock can enter the market easily, and most relevant company and industry information is readily available (and virtually free of charge) in the daily newspapers or on the Internet. Many farming and fishing industries also approximate perfect competition. But it is hard to find many other examples. Our interest in the perfectly competitive model surely does not lie in its ability to describe reality.

Why, then, do we spend time studying perfect competition? The answer takes us back to the central theme of this book. Only under perfect competition does the market mechanism perform best. If we want to learn what markets do well, we can put the market's best foot forward by beginning with perfect competition.

As Adam Smith suggested some two centuries ago, perfectly competitive firms use society's scarce resources with maximum efficiency. Also, as Friedrich Engels (Karl Marx's closest friend and coauthor) suggested in the opening quotation of this chapter, only perfect competition can ensure that the economy turns out just those varieties and relative quantities of goods that match consumer preferences. By studying perfect competition, we can learn just what an *ideally functioning* market system can accomplish. This is the topic of this chapter and the next one. Then, in Chapters 12 and 13, we will consider other market forms and see how they deviate from the perfectly competitive ideal. Still later chapters (especially Chapter 14 and the chapters in Parts IV and V) will examine many important tasks that the market does *not* perform at all well, even under perfect competition. These chapters combined should provide a balanced assessment of the virtues and vices of the market mechanism.

## ■ THE COMPETITIVE FIRM

To discover what happens in a perfectly competitive market, we must deal separately with the behavior of *individual firms* and the behavior of the *industry* that is constituted by those firms. One basic difference between the firm and the industry under competition relates to *pricing*:

> Under perfect competition, the firm has no choice but to accept the price that has been determined in the market. We say that it is a **price taker**.

Under perfect competition, the firm is a **price taker.** It has no choice but to accept the price that has been determined in the market.

The idea that no firm in a perfectly competitive market can exert any control over product price follows from our stringent definition of perfect competition. The presence of a vast number of competitors, each offering identical products, forces each firm to meet but not exceed the price charged by the others. With two important exceptions, the firm under perfect competition behaves exactly as we described and analyzed in Chapters 8 and 9. The two exceptions are the special shape of the competitive firm's demand curve and the freedom of entry and exit, along with their effects on the firm's profits. We will consider each of these special features of perfect competition in turn, beginning with the demand curve.

### THE FIRM'S DEMAND CURVE UNDER PERFECT COMPETITION

In Chapter 9, we always assumed that the firm faced a downward-sloping demand curve; if a firm wished to sell more (without increasing its advertising or changing its product specifications), it had to reduce product price. The competitive firm is an exception to this general principle.

> A perfectly competitive firm faces a *horizontal* demand curve. This means that it can sell as much as it wants at the prevailing market price. It can double or triple its sales without reducing the price of its product.

How is this possible? The answer is that the competitive firm is so insignificant relative to the market as a whole that it has absolutely no influence over price. The farmer who sells his corn through a commodities exchange in Chicago must accept the current quotation his broker reports to him. Because there are thousands of farmers, the Chicago price per bushel will not budge because Farmer Al decides he doesn't like the price and stores a truckload of corn rather than taking it to the grain elevator.

## ● THE GARDEN STATE: FARM INCOME IN A COMPETITIVE MARKET

Because farmers are *price takers,* they simply have to live with the price that is determined by the market's supply and demand. Here is an example.

With the month's first drops of rain on Monday, many farmers relaxed a bit about the year's longest and most intense dry spell, and got back to the problem that plagues them rain or shine: earning enough from their crops to stay afloat.

And that boils down to the farmer's golden rule: entwined as they are, prices are still far more variable than weather.

"The quality of the produce does not have anything to do with your income," explained Mark Malench, a 38-year-old farmer who grows lettuce, peppers, eggplant and more than a dozen other crops on his family's 60-acre spread in Vineland [New Jersey]. "It's supply and demand." . . . [And] it was competition, not weather, that almost ruined the blueberry market. . . . "There were just a lot of people out there with berries at the same time," said Dennis G. Doyle, the general manager of the Tru-Blu Cooperative in New Lisbon, where nearly half of New Jersey's 145 blueberry farmers sell. But, he said, that's just part of the high-risk business of farming. "We're near Atlantic City and people ask me if I go much," Mr. Doyle said. "I say no. The risk isn't great enough."

The bottom line for farmers is the price they sell their crops for, which varies not only because of the weather, but also according to competition from other growers.

SOURCE: *The New York Times,* August 16, 1998.

Thus, the demand curve for Farmer Al's corn is as shown in Figure 10–1(a); the price he is paid in Chicago will be $3 per bushel whether he sells one truckload (point *A*) or two (point *B*) or three (point *C*). This is because that $3 price is determined by the intersection of the *industry's* supply and demand curves shown in the right-hand portion of the graph, Panel (b).

Notice that, in the case of perfect competition, the downward-sloping industry demand curve in Figure 10–1(b) leads to the horizontal demand curve for the individual firm in Figure 10–1(a). Also notice that the height of that horizontal firm demand curve will be the height of the intersection point, *E,* of the industry supply and demand curves. And the firm's demand will generally not resemble the demand curve for the industry.

### SHORT-RUN EQUILIBRIUM FOR THE PERFECTLY COMPETITIVE FIRM

We already have sufficient background to study the decisions of a firm operating in a perfectly competitive market. Remember from Chapter 9 that profit maximization requires the firm to pick an output level that makes its *marginal cost equal to its marginal*

---

### FIGURE 10–1

**Demand Curve for a Firm under Perfect Competition**

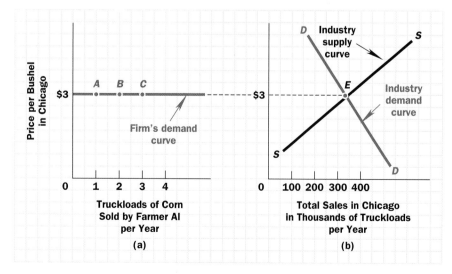

*revenue:* MC = MR. The only feature that distinguishes the profit-maximizing equilibrium for the competitive firm from that of any other type of firm is its horizontal demand curve. We know from Chapter 9 that the firm's demand curve is also its average revenue curve because the average revenue a firm gets from selling a commodity is equal to the price of the commodity. Because the demand curve is horizontal, the competitive firm's marginal revenue curve is a horizontal straight line that coincides with its demand curve; hence, MR = Price *(P)*. It is easy to see why this is so.

If the price does not depend on how much the firm sells (which is exactly what a horizontal demand curve means), then each *additional* unit sold brings in an amount of revenue (the *marginal* revenue) exactly equal to the market price. So marginal revenue always equals price under perfect competition because the firm is a price taker. Once we know the shape and position of a firm's marginal revenue curve, we can use this and the marginal cost curve to determine its optimal output and profit, as shown in Figure 10–2. As usual, the profit-maximizing output is that at which MC = MR (point *B*). The demand curve, *D*, is horizontal because the firm's output is too small to affect market price. This particular competitive firm produces 50,000 bushels of corn per year—the output level at which MC and MR both equal the market price, $3. Thus:

**FIGURE 10–2**

**Short-Run Equilibrium of the Competitive Firm**

> Because it is a price taker, the *equilibrium* of a profit-maximizing firm in a perfectly competitive market must occur at an output level at which marginal cost equals price. This is because a horizontal demand curve makes price and MR equal and, therefore, both must equal marginal cost according to the profit maximizing principle. In symbols:

$$MC = P$$

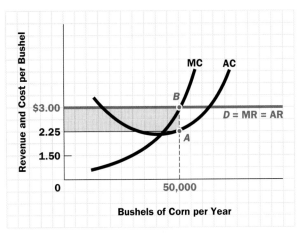

This idea is illustrated in Table 10–1, which gives the firm's total and marginal revenue, total and marginal cost, and total profit for different output quantities. We see from Column (6) that total profit is maximized at an output of about 50,000 bushels where total profit is $37,500. An increase in output from 40,000 to 50,000 bushels incurs a marginal cost ($26,500) that approximately equals the corresponding marginal revenue ($30,000), confirming that 50,000 bushels is the profit-maximizing output.[1]

**Revenues, Costs, and Profits of a Competitive Firm** | **TABLE 10–1**

| (1) Total Quantity | (2) Total Revenue | (3) Marginal Revenue | (4) Total Cost | (5) Marginal Cost | (6) Total Profit |
|---|---|---|---|---|---|
| 0 | $ 0 | | | | |
| | | $30 | | | |
| 10 | 30 | | $ 32 | | $ −2 |
| | | 30 | | $ 24 | |
| 20 | 60 | | 56 | | 4 |
| | | 30 | | 11.5 | |
| 30 | 90 | | 67.5 | | 22.5 |
| | | 30 | | 18.5 | |
| 40 | 120 | | 86 | | 34 |
| | | 30 | | 26.5 | |
| 50 | 150 | | 112.5 | | 37.5 |
| | | 30 | | 56.5 | |
| 60 | 180 | | 169 | | 11 |
| | | 30 | | 93 | |
| 70 | 210 | | 262 | | −52 |

NOTE: Quantity is in thousands of bushels; dollars are in thousands.

---

[1] To calculate marginal costs and marginal revenues accurately, we should increase output one bushel at a time instead of proceeding in leaps of 10,000 bushels. But that would require too much space! In any event, our failure to make a more careful calculation in terms of individual bushels explains why we are unable to find the output at which MR and MC are *exactly* equal.

## SHORT-RUN PROFIT: GRAPHIC REPRESENTATION

Our analysis so far tells us how a firm can pick the output that maximizes its profit. But even if it succeeds in doing so, the firm may conceivably find itself in trouble. If the demand for its product is weak or its costs are high, even the firm's most profitable option may lead to a loss. In the short run, the demand curve can either be high or low relative to costs. To determine whether the firm is making a profit or incurring a loss, we must compare *total* revenue (TR $= P \times Q$) with *total* cost (TC $=$ AC $\times Q$). Because $Q$ is common to both of these, this equation tells us that the process is equivalent to comparing $P$ with AC.

We can therefore show the firm's profit in Figure 10–2, which includes the firm's *average cost* (AC) curve. By definition, profit per unit of output is revenue per unit *(P)* minus cost per unit (AC). We see in Figure 10–2 that average cost at 50,000 bushels per year is only $2.25 per bushel (point *A*), whereas *average revenue* (AR) is $3 per bushel (point *B*). The firm makes a profit of AR − AC = $0.75 per bushel, which appears in the graph as the vertical distance between points *A* and *B*.

Notice that in addition to showing the *profit per unit*, Figure 10–2 can be used to show the firm's *total profit*. Total profit is the profit per unit ($0.75 in this example) times the number of units (50,000 per year). Therefore, total profit is represented by the *area* of the shaded rectangle whose height is the profit per unit ($0.75) and whose width is the number of units (50,000).[2] In this case, profits are $37,500 per year. In general, total profit at any output is the area of the rectangle whose base equals the level of output and whose height equals AR − AC.

> The MC = *P* condition gives us the output that maximizes the perfectly competitive firm's profit. It does not, however, tell us whether the firm is making a profit or incurring a loss. To determine this, we must compare price (average revenue) with average cost.

## THE CASE OF SHORT-TERM LOSSES

The market is obviously treating the farmer in Figure 10–2 rather nicely. But what if the corn market were not so generous in its rewards? What if, for example, the market price were only $1.50 per bushel instead of $3? Figure 10–3 shows the equilibrium of the firm under these circumstances. The cost curves are the same in this diagram as they were in Figure 10–2, but the demand curve has shifted down to correspond to the market price of $1.50 per bushel. The firm still maximizes profits by producing the level of output at which marginal cost is equal to price—point *B* in the diagram. But this time "maximizing profits" really means minimizing losses, as shown by the shaded rectangle.

At the optimal level of output (30,000 bushels per year), average cost is $2.25 per bushel (point *A*), which exceeds the $1.50 per bushel price (point *B*). The firm therefore runs a loss of $0.75 per bushel times 30,000 bushels, or $22,500 per year. This loss, which is represented by the area of the gold rectangle in Figure 10–3, is the best the firm can do. If it selected any other output level, its loss would be even greater.

---

**FIGURE 10–3**

**Short-Run Equilibrium of the Competitive Firm with a Lower Price**

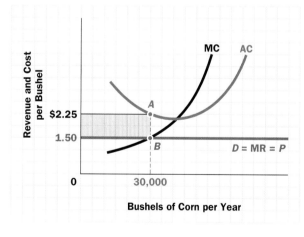

Bushels of Corn per Year

---

## SHUTDOWN AND BREAK-EVEN ANALYSIS

Of course, any firm will accept only a limited amount of loss before it stops production. If losses get too big, the firm can simply go out of business. To understand the logic of the choice between shutting down and remaining in operation, we must return to the distinction between costs that are variable in the short run and those that are not. Remember from Chapter 8 that costs are not variable if the

---

[2] Recall that the formula for the area of a rectangle is area $=$ height $\times$ width.

firm cannot escape them in the short run, either because of a contract (say, with the landlord or a union) or because it has already bought the item whose cost is not variable (for example, a machine).

If the firm stops producing, its revenue will fall to zero. Its short-run variable costs will also fall to zero. But its costs that are not variable will remain. If the firm is losing money, sometimes it will be better off continuing to operate until its obligations to pay the nonvariable costs expire; sometimes it will do better by shutting down and producing nothing. Two rules govern the decision:

*Rule 1.* The firm will make a profit if total revenue (TR) exceeds total cost (TC). In that case, it should not plan to shut down, either in the short run or in the long run.

*Rule 2.* The firm should continue to operate in the short run if TR exceeds total short-run variable cost (TVC). It should nevertheless plan to close in the long run if TR is less than TC.

The first rule is self-evident. If the firm's revenues cover its total costs, then it does not lose money. The second rule is a bit more subtle. Suppose that TR is less than TC. If our unfortunate firm continues in operation, it will lose the difference between total cost and total revenue, that is:

$$\text{Loss if the firm stays in business} = \text{TC} - \text{TR}.$$

However, if the firm stops producing, both its revenues and short-run variable costs become zero, leaving only the *nonvariable* costs to be paid:

$$\text{Loss if the firm shuts down} = \text{Nonvariable costs} = \text{TC} - \text{TVC}$$

Hence, it is best to keep operating as long as:

$$\text{TC} - \text{TR} < \text{TC} - \text{TVC}$$

or

$$\text{TVC} < \text{TR}$$

That is Rule 2.

We can illustrate Rule 2 by the two cases in Table 10–2. Case A deals with a firm that loses money but is better off staying in business in the short run. If it shuts down, it will lose its entire $60,000 worth of short-run nonvariable cost. But if it continues to operate, total revenue of $100,000 exceeds total variable cost (TVC = $80,000) by $20,000. That means continuing operation contributes $20,000 toward meeting nonvariable costs and reduces losses to $40,000. In Case B, on the other hand, it pays the firm to shut down because continued operation only adds to its losses. If the firm operates, it will lose $90,000 (the last entry in Table 10–2), whereas if it shuts down, it will lose only the $60,000 in nonvariable costs, which it must pay whether it operates or not.

We can also analyze the shutdown decision graphically. In Figure 10–4, the firm will run a loss whether the price is $P_1$, $P_2$, or $P_3$, because none of these prices is

**The Shutdown Decision**  | TABLE 10-2

|  | Case A | Case B |
|---|---|---|
| Total revenue (TR) | $100 | $100 |
| Total variable cost (TVC) | 80 | 130 |
| Fixed cost (FC) | 60 | 60 |
| Total cost (TC) | 140 | 190 |
| Loss if firm shuts down (= FC) | 60 | 60 |
| Loss if firm does not shut down | 40 | 90 |

NOTE: Figures are in thousands of dollars.

FIGURE 10-4

**Shutdown Analysis**

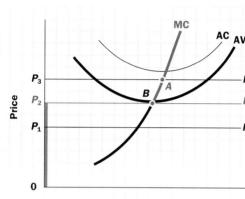

Quantity Supplied

high enough to reach the minimum level of average cost (AC). We can show the *lowest* price that keeps the firm from shutting down by introducing one more short-run cost curve: the average variable cost (AVC) curve. Why is this curve relevant? Because, as we have just seen, it pays the firm to remain in operation if its total revenue (TR) exceeds its total short-run variable cost (TVC). If we divide both TR and TVC by quantity $(Q)$, we get $TR/Q = P$ and $TVC/Q = AVC$. So, we can state the condition for continued operation equivalently as the requirement that price must exceed AVC. The conclusion is:

The firm will produce nothing unless price lies above the minimum point on the AVC curve.

In Figure 10–4, price $P_1$ is below the minimum average variable cost. With this price, the firm cannot even cover its variable costs and is better off shutting down (producing zero output). Price $P_3$ is higher. Although the firm still runs a loss if it sets $MC = P$ at point *A* (because AC exceeds $P_3$), it allows the firm to at least cover its short-run variable costs, and so it pays to keep operating in the short run. Price $P_2$ is the borderline case. If the price is $P_2$, the firm is indifferent between shutting down and staying in business and producing at a level where $MC = P$ (point *B*). $P_2$ is thus the *lowest* price at which the firm will produce anything. As we see from the graph, $P_2$ corresponds to the minimum point on the AVC curve.

## THE COMPETITIVE FIRM'S SHORT-RUN SUPPLY CURVE

Without realizing it, we have now derived the supply curve of the competitive firm in the short run. Why? Recall that a supply curve summarizes in a graph the answers to questions such as, "If the price is so and so, how much output will the firm offer for sale?" We have now discovered two possibilities:

■ In the short run, if the price exceeds the minimum AVC, it pays a competitive firm to produce the level of output at which MC equals P. Thus, for any price above point *B*, we can read the corresponding quantity supplied from the firm's MC curve.

■ If the price falls below the minimum AVC, then it pays the firm to produce nothing. Quantity supplied falls to zero, as indicated by vertical line $0P_2$, in Figure 10–4.

Putting these two observations together, we conclude that:

The short-run supply curve of the perfectly competitive firm is that portion of its marginal cost curve that lies above the point where it intersects the average (short-run) variable cost curve, that is, above the minimum level of AVC. If price falls below this level, the firm's quantity supplied drops to zero.

## ■ THE COMPETITIVE INDUSTRY

Having completed the analysis of the competitive *firm's* supply decision, we turn our attention next to the competitive *industry*.

### THE COMPETITIVE INDUSTRY'S SHORT-RUN SUPPLY CURVE

Again we need to distinguish between the short run and the long run, but the distinction is different here. The short run for the *industry* is defined as a period of time too brief for new firms to enter the industry or for old firms to leave, so the number of firms is fixed. By contrast, the long run for the industry is a period of time long enough for any firm to enter or leave as it desires. In addition, in the long run each firm in the industry can adjust its output to its own long-run costs.[3] We begin our analysis of industry equilibrium in the short run.

With the number of firms fixed, it is a simple matter to derive the supply curve of the competitive industry from those of the individual firms. At any given price, we simply *add up* the quantities supplied by each of the firms to arrive at the industry-wide quantity supplied. For example, if each of 1,000 identical firms in the corn industry supplies 45,000 bushels when the price is $2.25 per bushel, then the quantity supplied by the industry at a $2.25 price will be 45,000 bushels per firm × 1,000 firms = 45 million bushels.

This process of deriving the *market* supply curve from the *individual* supply curves of firms is perfectly analogous to the way we derived the *market* demand curve from the *individual* consumers' demand curves in Chapter 7. Graphically, what we are doing is *summing the individual supply curves horizontally*, as illustrated in Figure 10–5. At a price of $2.25, each of the 1,000 identical firms in the industry supplies 45,000 bushels—point *c* in Panel (a)—so the industry supplies 45 million bushels—point *C* in Panel (b). At a price of $3, each firm supplies 50,000 bushels—point *e* in Panel (a)—and so the industry supplies 50 million bushels—point *E* in Panel (b). We can carry out similar calculations for any other price. By adding up the quantities supplied by each firm at each possible price, we arrive at the industry supply curve *SS* in panel (b).

| Derivation of the Industry Supply Curve from the Supply Curves of the Individual Firms | FIGURE 10-5 |
| --- | --- |

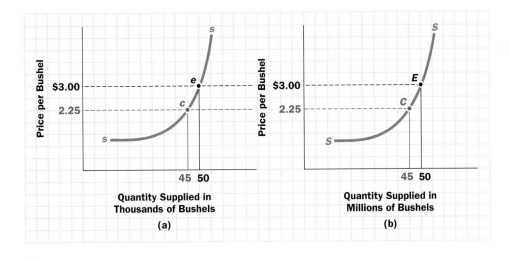

The supply curve of the competitive industry in the short run is derived by *summing* the short-run supply curves of all the firms in the industry *horizontally*.

This adding-up process indicates, incidentally, that the supply curve of the industry will shift to the right whenever a new firm enters the industry.

Notice that if the short-run supply curves of individual firms slope upward, then the short-run supply curve of the competitive industry will slope upward as well. We have seen that the firm's supply curve is its marginal cost curve (above the level of minimum average variable cost), so it follows that rising marginal costs lead to an upward-sloping short-run *industry* supply curve.

---

[3] The relationship between short-run and long-run cost curves for the firm was discussed in Chapter 8, pages 149–150.

## INDUSTRY EQUILIBRIUM IN THE SHORT RUN

Now that we have derived the industry supply curve, we need only add a market demand curve to determine the price and quantity that will emerge in equilibrium. We do this for our illustrative corn industry in Figure 10–6, where the blue industry supply curve, carried over from Figure 10–5(b), is *SS* and the demand curve is *DD*. The only equilibrium combination of price and quantity is a price of $3 and a quantity of 50 million bushels, at which the supply curve, *SS*, and the demand curve, *DD*, intersect (point *E*). At any lower price, such as $2.25, quantity demanded (72 million bushels, as shown by point *A* on the demand curve) will be higher than the 45-million-bushel quantity supplied (point *C*). Thus, the price will be bid up toward the $3 equilibrium. The opposite will happen at a price such as $3.75, which is above equilibrium.

Note that for the competitive industry, unlike the competitive firm, the demand curve normally slopes downward. Why? Each firm by itself is so small that if it alone were to double its output the effect would hardly be noticeable. But if *every* firm in the industry were to expand its output, that would make a substantial difference. Customers can be induced to buy the additional quantities arriving at the market only if the price of the good falls.

Point *E* is the equilibrium point for the competitive industry, because only at a price of $3 are sellers willing to offer exactly the amount that consumers want to purchase (in this case, 50 million bushels).

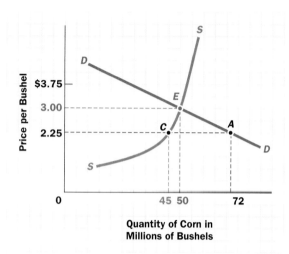

**FIGURE 10-6**

**Supply-Demand Equilibrium of a Competitive Industry**

Should we expect price actually to reach, or at least to *approximate*, this equilibrium level? The answer is yes. To see why, we must consider what happens when price is not at its equilibrium level. Suppose that the price is lower, say, $2.25. This low price will stimulate customers to buy more; it will also lead firms to produce less than they would at a price of $3. Our diagram confirms that at a price of $2.25, quantity supplied (45 million bushels) is lower than quantity demanded (72 million bushels). Thus, unsatisfied buyers will probably lead sellers to raise their prices, which will force the price *upward* in the direction of its equilibrium value, $3.

Similarly, if we begin with a price higher than the equilibrium price, we may readily verify that quantity supplied will exceed quantity demanded. Under these circumstances, frustrated sellers are likely to reduce their prices, so price will be forced downward. In the circumstances depicted in Figure 10–6, then, in effect, a magnet at the equilibrium price of $3 will pull the actual price in its direction, if for some reason the actual price starts out at some other level.

In practice, in most competitive markets, over a long period of time prices do move toward equilibrium levels. Matters eventually appear to work out as depicted in Figure 10–6. Of course, numerous transitory influences can jolt any real-world market away from its equilibrium point—a workers' strike that cuts production, a sudden change in consumer tastes, and so on.

Yet, as we have just seen, powerful forces push prices back toward equilibrium—toward the level at which the supply and demand curves intersect. These forces are fundamentally important for economic analysis. If no such forces existed, prices in the real world would bear little resemblance to equilibrium prices, and there would be little reason to study supply-demand analysis. Fortunately, the required equilibrating forces do step in as appropriate to bring markets back toward equilibrium.

## INDUSTRY AND FIRM EQUILIBRIUM IN THE LONG RUN

The equilibrium of a competitive industry in the long run may differ from the short-run equilibrium that we have just studied for two reasons. First, the number of firms in the industry (1,000 in our example) is not fixed in the long run. Second, as we saw in Chapter 8 (pages 139–141), in the long run firms can vary their plant size and change other commitments that were unchangeable in the short run. Hence, the firm's (and the industry's) long-run cost curves are not the same as the short-run cost curves.

What will lure new firms into the industry or encourage old ones to leave? In a word: *profits*—economic profits that exceed the economy average. Remember that when a firm selects its optimal level of output by setting MC = P, it may wind up with either a profit, as in Figure 10–2, or a loss, as in Figure 10–3. Such profits or losses must be *temporary* for competitive firms, because new firms are free to enter the industry if profits greater than the average are available. For the same reason, old firms will leave if they cannot cover their costs in the long run. Suppose that firms in the industry earn very high profits, in excess of the normal rates of return currently available. Then new companies will find it attractive to enter the business, and expanded production will force the market price to fall from its initial level. Why? Recall that the industry supply curve is the horizontal sum of the supply curves of individual firms. Under perfect competition, new firms can enter the industry *on the same terms as existing firms*. Thus new entrants will have the *same* individual supply curves as old firms. If the market price did not fall, entry of new firms would lead to an increased number of firms, with no change in output *per firm*. Consequently, the total quantity supplied to the market would be higher, and it would exceed quantity demanded—which, of course, would also drive prices down. Thus, the entry of new firms *must* push the price down.

**FIGURE 10-7**

**A Shift in the Industry Supply Curve Caused by the Entry of New Firms**

Figure 10–7 shows how the entry process works. In this diagram, the demand curve DD and the original (short-run) supply curve $S_0S_0$ are carried over from Figure 10–6. The entry of new firms seeking high profits *shifts the industry's short-run supply curve outward to the right*, to $S_1S_1$. The new market equilibrium at point A (rather than at point E), indicates that price is $2.25 per bushel and that 72 million bushels are produced and consumed. The entry of new firms reduces price and raises total output.

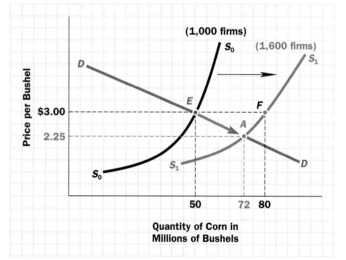

If the price had not fallen, quantity supplied after entry would have been 80 million bushels—point F. Why must the price fall in this case? Because the demand curve for the industry slopes downward: consumers will purchase the increased output only at a reduced price.

To see the point at which new entrants stop seeking high profits, we must consider how new firm entry affects existing firms' behavior. At first glance, this notion may seem to contradict the idea of perfect competition; perfectly competitive firms are not supposed to be affected by what competitors do, because no individual firm can influence the industry. Indeed, these corn farmers don't care. But they *do* care very much about the market price of corn and, as we have just seen, the entry of new firms into the corn-farming industry lowers the price of corn.

In Figure 10–8, we juxtapose the diagram of competitive firm equilibrium (Figure 10–2) with the competitive industry equilibrium diagram (Figure 10–7). Before entry, the market price was $3, point E in Figure 10–8(b), and each of the 1,000 firms produced 50,000 bushels—the point where marginal cost and price were equal, point e in Figure 10–8(a). Each firm faced the horizontal demand curve $D_0$ in Figure 10–8(a). Firms within the industry enjoyed profits because average costs (AC) at 50,000 bushels per firm were less than price.

Now suppose that 600 new firms are attracted by these high profits and enter the industry. Each faces the cost structure indicated by the AC and MC curves in Figure 10–8(a). As a result of the new entrants' production, the industry supply curve in Figure 10–8(b) shifts to the right, and price falls to $2.25 per bushel. Because the height of the firm's horizontal demand curve is, as we have seen, equal to the industry price, the firm's demand curve must now move down to the red line $D_1$ *corresponding to the reduced market price*. Firms in the industry react to this demand

**The Competitive Firm and the Competitive Industry**

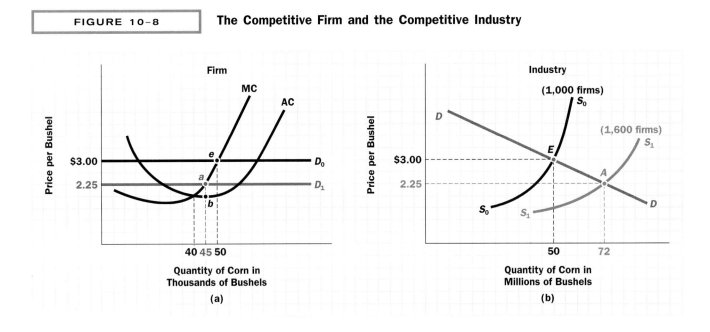

shift and its associated lower price. As we see in Figure 10–8(a), each firm reduces its output to 45,000 bushels (point *a*). But now there are 1,600 firms, so total industry output is 45,000 × 1,600 = 72 million bushels, point *A* in Figure 10–8(b).

At point *a* in Figure 10–8(a), some profits remain available because the $2.25 price exceeds average cost (point *b* is below point *a*). Thus, the entry process is not yet complete. New firms will stop appearing only when all profits have been competed away. The two panels of Figure 10–9 show the competitive firm and the competitive industry in long-run equilibrium. Only when entry shifts the industry supply curve so far to the right—$S_2S_2$ in Figure 10–9(b)—that each individual firm faces a demand curve that has fallen to the level of minimum average cost—point *m* in Figure 10–9(a)—will all profits be eradicated and entry cease.[4]

**Long-Run Equilibrium of the Competitive Firm and Industry**

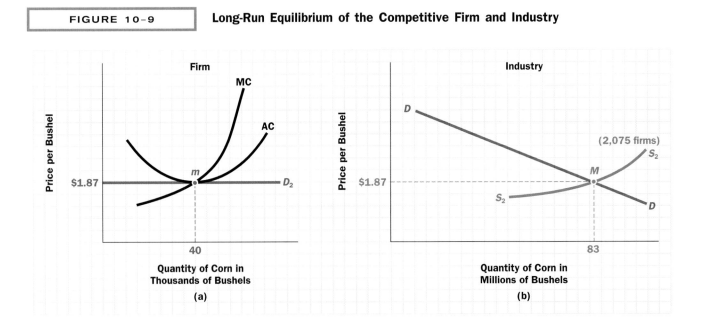

--------

[4] If the original short-run equilibrium had involved losses instead of profits, firms would have exited from the industry, shifting the industry supply curve inward, until all losses were eradicated, and we would end up in a position exactly like Figure 10–9. *Exercise:* To test your understanding, draw the version of Figure 10–8 that corresponds to this case.

Notice that at the equilibrium point, *m* in Panel (a), each firm picks its own output level to maximize its profit. This means that for each firm $P = MC$. But free entry also forces AC to equal *P* in the long run—point *M* in Panel (b) of the graph—because if *P* were not equal to AC, firms would either earn profits or suffer losses. That would mean, in turn, that firms would find it profitable to enter or leave the industry, which is not compatible with industry equilibrium. Thus:

> When a perfectly competitive industry is in long-run equilibrium, firms maximize profits so that $P = MC$, and entry forces the price down until it is tangent to the long-run average cost curve ($P = AC$). As a result, in long-run competitive equilibrium it is always true that for each firm:
>
> $$P = MC = AC$$

Thus, even though every firm earns zero profit, profits are at the maximum that is sustainable.[5]

## ZERO ECONOMIC PROFIT: THE OPPORTUNITY COST OF CAPITAL

Why would there be any firms in the industry *at all* if in the long run they could make no profits? The answer is that the zero profit concept used in economics does not mean the same thing that it does in ordinary, everyday usage.

We have noted repeatedly that when economists measure average cost, they include the cost of *all* of the firm's inputs, *including the opportunity cost of the capital (the funds) or any other inputs, such as labor, provided by the firm's owners.* Because the firm may not make explicit payments to some of the people who provide it with capital, this element of cost may not be picked up by the firm's accountants. So what economists call zero **economic profit** will correspond to a positive amount of profit as measured by conventional accounting techniques. For example, if investors can earn 15 percent by lending their funds elsewhere, then the firm must earn a 15 percent rate of return to cover its opportunity cost of capital.

> **OPPORTUNITY COST** Because economists consider this 15 percent opportunity cost to be the *cost of the firm's capital*, they include it in the AC curve. If the firm cannot earn at least 15 percent on its capital, funds will not be made available to it, because investors can earn greater returns elsewhere. In order to break even—to earn zero *economic profit*—a firm must earn enough not only to cover the cost of labor, fuel, and raw materials but also the cost of its funds, including the opportunity cost of any funds supplied by the owners of the firm.

**Economic profit** equals net earnings, in the accountant's sense, minus the opportunity costs of capital and of any other inputs supplied by the firm's owners.

*How Much Does It Really Cost?*

An example will illustrate how economic profit and accounting profit differ. Suppose that U.S. government bonds pay 8 percent interest, and the owner of a small shop earns 6 percent on her business investment. The shopkeeper might see a 6 percent profit, but an economist would see a 2 percent loss on every dollar she has invested in her business. By keeping her money tied up in her firm, she gives up the chance to buy government bonds and receive an 8 percent return. With this explanation of economic profit, we can understand the logic behind the zero-profit condition for the long-run industry equilibrium.

> Zero profit in the economic sense simply means that firms are earning the normal, economy-wide rate of profit in the accounting sense. This result is guaranteed, in the long run, under perfect competition by freedom of entry and exit.

## THE LONG-RUN INDUSTRY SUPPLY CURVE

We have now seen basically what lies behind the supply-demand analysis that we first introduced in Chapter 5. Only one thing remains to be explained. Figures 10–5

---

[5] *Exercise:* Show what happens to the equilibrium of the firm and of the industry in Figure 10–9 if there is a rise in consumer income that leads to an outward shift in the industry demand curve.

through 10–8 depicted short-run industry supply curves and short-run equilibrium. However, because Figure 10–9 describes long-run competitive equilibrium, its industry supply curve must also, of course, pertain to the long run.

How does the long-run industry supply curve relate to the short-run supply curve? The answer is implicit in what we have just discussed. The long-run industry supply curve evolves from the short-run supply curve via two simultaneous processes. First, new firms enter or some existing ones exit, which shifts the short-run industry supply curve toward its long-run position.

Second, and concurrently, as each firm in the industry is freed from its fixed commitments, the cost curves pertinent to its decisions become its long-run cost curves rather than its short-run cost curves. For example, consider a company that was stuck in the short run with a plant designed to serve 20,000 customers, even though it is now fortunate enough to have 25,000 customers. When it is time to replace the old plant, management will want to build a new plant that can serve the larger number of customers more conveniently, efficiently, and cheaply. The reduced cost that results from the larger plant is the pertinent cost to both the firm and the industry in the long run.

Finally, let us note that the long-run supply curve of the competitive industry ($S_2S_2$ in Figure 10–9) must be identical to the industry's long-run *average* cost curve. This is because in the long run, as we have seen, economic profit must be zero. The price the industry charges cannot exceed the long-run average cost (LRAC) of supplying that quantity because any excess of price over LRAC would constitute a profit opportunity that would attract new firms. Similarly, price cannot be below LRAC because firms would then refuse to supply that output at this price. Therefore, for each possible long-run quantity supplied, the price must equal the industry's long-run average cost. Thus, this long-run industry supply curve is the cost curve relevant for determination of long-run equilibrium price and quantity in a standard supply-demand diagram.

**FIGURE 10–10**

**Short-Run Industry Supply and Long-Run Industry Average Cost**

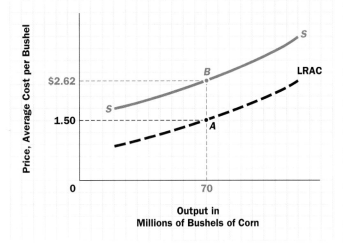

Output in Millions of Bushels of Corn

These ideas are illustrated in Figure 10–10, in which the short-run industry supply curve, *SS*, lies above and to the left of the long-run average cost curve, LRAC. Consider any industry output: say, 70 million bushels of corn per year. At that output, the long-run average cost is $1.50 per bushel (point *A*). But if the price charged by farmers were given by the short-run supply curve for that output—that is, $2.62 per bushel (point *B*)—then the firms would earn $1.12 in economic profit on each and every bushel they sold.

Such economic profits would induce other firms to enter the industry, which would force prices downward as the industry supply curve shifted outward. So long as this shift did not take *SS* all the way down to LRAC, some economic profits would remain, and so entry would continue. Thus, *SS* must continue to fall until it reaches the position of the long-run average cost curve. Then and only then will entry cease and long-run equilibrium be attained.

**The long-run supply curve of the competitive industry is also the industry's long-run average cost curve. The industry is driven to that supply curve by the entry or exit of firms and by the adjustment of firms already in the industry.**

## PERFECT COMPETITION AND ECONOMIC EFFICIENCY

Economists have long admired perfect competition as a thing of beauty, like one of King Tutankhamen's funerary masks. (And it's just as rare!) Adam Smith's invisible hand produces results that are considered *efficient* in a variety of senses that we will

---

● **POLICY DEBATE** | **SHOULD GOVERNMENT REGULATORS USE PERFECT COMPETITION AS A GUIDE?**

As we have seen here and will discuss further in the next chapter, perfect competition displays the market mechanism at its best. It prevents firms from earning excess profits, it forces firms to produce the output quantity at which AC is as low as possible, and it has other virtues besides.

As we will see in Chapters 12 and 13, markets where monopoly or oligopoly prevail are very different from perfect competition. In monopolistic or oligopolistic markets a few large firms may charge high prices that yield large profits, and they may produce output quantities that do not match consumer preferences. Consequently (see Chapter 20), such industries are often *regulated* by government agencies.

But just what should regulation force monopoly or oligopoly firms to do? Should it force them to behave like perfectly competitive firms? Should it force their prices to equal marginal costs? Should it try to break them up into thousands of tiny enterprises?

No one believes that government regulation should go quite that far. Indeed, there are economists and others who argue that perfect competition is an undesirable and, indeed, impossible goal for such regulated industries. For example, if those industries are characterized by economies of scale, then breaking them into small firms will raise their costs and consumers will have to pay more, not less. Moreover, as we saw in Chapter 8, where there are economies of scale, the average cost curve must go downhill—the larger the firm's output, the lower its average cost. So marginal cost must be below average cost (see the appendix to Chapter 8 for review), and a price equal to marginal cost must also be below average cost. Thus, where there are economies of scale, if the firm is forced to charge a price equal to marginal cost it will be forced to go bankrupt!

Still, many regulators, economists, and others believe that perfect competition is so desirable a state of affairs that regulated firms should be required to come as close to it as possible in their behavior.

examine carefully in the next chapter. But one aspect of the great efficiency of perfect competition follows immediately from the analysis we have just completed.

We saw earlier that when the firm is in long-run equilibrium, it must have $P = MC = AC$, as indicated by Figure 10–9(a). This implies that the long-run competitive equilibrium of the firm will occur at the lowest point on its long-run AC curve, which is also where that curve is tangent to the firm's horizontal demand curve.

In long-run competitive equilibrium, every firm produces at the minimum point on its average cost curve. Thus, the outputs of competitive industries are produced at the lowest possible cost to society.

An example will show why it is most efficient if each firm in a competitive industry produces at the point where AC is as small as possible. Suppose the industry is producing 12 million bushels of corn. This amount can be produced by 120 farms each producing 100,000 bushels, or by 100 farms each producing 120,000 bushels, or by 200 farms each producing 60,000 bushels. Of course, the job can also be done instead by other numbers of farms, but for simplicity let us consider only these three possibilities.

| TABLE 10–3 | **Average Cost for the Firm and Total Cost for the Industry** |
|---|---|

| (1)<br>Firm's<br>Output | (2)<br>Firm's<br>Average<br>Cost | (3)<br>Number of<br>Firms | (4)<br>Industry<br>Output | (5)<br>Total<br>Industry<br>Cost |
|---|---|---|---|---|
| 60,000 | $0.90 | 200 | 12,000,000 | $10,800,000 |
| 100,000 | 0.70 | 120 | 12,000,000 | 8,400,000 |
| 120,000 | 0.80 | 100 | 12,000,000 | 9,600,000 |

NOTE: Output is in bushels.

Suppose that the AC figures for the firm are as shown in Table 10–3. Suppose, moreover, that an output of 100,000 bushels corresponds to the lowest point on the AC curve, with an AC of 70 cents per bushel. Which is the cheapest way for the industry to produce its 12-million-bushel output? In other words, what is the cost-minimizing number of firms for the job? Looking at Column (5) of Table 10–3, we see that the industry's total cost of producing the 12-million-bushel output is as low as possible if 120 firms each produce the cost-minimizing output of 100,000 bushels.

Why is this so? The answer is not difficult to see. For any *given* industry output, $Q$, since $Q$ is constant, *total* industry cost (= AC × $Q$) will be as small as possible if and only if AC (for *each* firm) is as small as possible, that is, if the number of firms doing the job is such that each is producing the output at which AC is as low as possible.

That this kind of cost efficiency characterizes perfect competition in the long run can be seen in Figures 10–8 and 10–9. Before full long-run equilibrium is reached (Figure 10–8), firms may not be producing in the least costly way. For example, the 50 million bushels being produced by 1,000 firms at points *e* and *E* in Figures 10–8(a) and 10–8(b) could be produced more cheaply by more firms, each producing a smaller volume, because the point of minimum average cost lies to the left of point *e* in Figure 10–8(a). This problem is rectified, however, in the long run by entry of new firms seeking profit. We see in Figure 10–9 that after the entry process is complete, every firm is producing at its most efficient (lowest AC) level—40,000 bushels.

As Adam Smith might have put it, even though each farmer cares only about his or her own profits, the corn-farming industry as a whole is *guided by an invisible hand* to produce the amount of corn that society wants at the lowest possible cost.

### Which Is Better to Cut Pollution— The Carrot or the Stick?

We end by returning to the puzzle with which the chapter began, because we now have all the tools needed to resolve it. Remember that we asked: Should polluters be *taxed* on their emissions, or should they, instead, be offered *subsidies* to cut emissions? A subsidy—that is, a government payment to the firms that comply— would indeed induce firms to cut their emissions. Nevertheless, the paradoxical result is likely to be an *increase* in total pollution. Let us see now why this is so.

In Figure 10–11, we have drawn the industry long-run average cost curve (LRAC), *XX*. We now know that this must also be the industry's long-run supply curve, because if the supply curve lies above (to the left of) LRAC, then economic profits will be earned and entry will drive the supply curve to the right. The opposite would occur if the supply were below and to the right of LRAC.

Now, a tax on business firms clearly raises the long-run average costs of the industry. Suppose that it shifts the LRAC, and thus the long-run supply curve, upward from *XX* to *TT* in the graph. This will move the equilibrium point from *E* to *B* and reduce polluting output from $Q_e$ to $Q_b$. Similarly, a subsidy reduces average

"So <u>that's</u> where it goes! Well, I'd like to thank you fellows for bringing this to my attention."

cost, and so it shifts the LRAC and the long-run supply curve downward and to the right (from *XX* to *SS*). This moves the equilibrium point from *E* to *A and raises polluting output to $Q_a$.*

Our paradoxical result follows from the presumption that the more output a polluting industry produces, the more pollution it will emit. Under the tax on emissions, equilibrium moves from *E* to *B,* and so the polluting output falls from $Q_e$ to $Q_b$. Thus, emissions will fall—just as common sense leads us to expect. But, with the subsidy, industry output will *rise* from $Q_e$ to $Q_a$. Thus, contrary to intuition and despite the fact that each firm emits less, the industry must pollute more!

What explains this strange result? The answer is *entry.* The subsidy will initially bring economic profits to the polluters, and that will attract even more polluters into the industry. In essence, a subsidy encourages more polluters to open up for business. But our graph takes us one step beyond this simple observation. It is true that we end up with more polluting firms, but each will be polluting less than before. Thus, we have one influence leading to more pollution and another influence leading to less pollution. Which of these forces will win out? The graph tells us that if a rise in the polluting good's output always increases pollution, then, in a perfectly competitive industry, subsidies *must* lead to increased pollution on balance.

FIGURE 10-11

**Taxes versus Subsidies as Incentives to Cut Pollution**

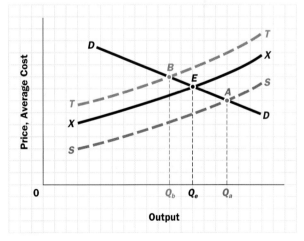

---

# S U M M A R Y

1. *Markets* are classified into several types depending on the number of firms in the industry, the degree of similarity of their products, and the possibility of impediments to entry.

2. The four main market structures discussed by economists are monopoly (single-firm production), oligopoly (production by a few firms), monopolistic competition (production

by many firms with somewhat different products), and *perfect competition* (production by many firms with identical products and free entry and exit).

3. Few, if any, industries satisfy the conditions of perfect competition exactly, although some come close. Perfect competition is studied because it is easy to analyze and because it represents a case in which the market mechanism works well, so that it is useful as a yardstick to measure the performance of other market forms.

4. The demand curve of the perfectly competitive firm is horizontal because its output is so small a share of the industry's production that it cannot affect price. With a horizontal demand curve, price, average revenue, and marginal revenue are all equal.

5. The short-run equilibrium of the perfectly competitive firm is at the level of output that maximizes profits; that is, where MR = MC = price. This equilibrium may involve either a profit or a loss.

6. The short-run supply curve of the perfectly competitive firm is the portion of its marginal cost curve that lies above its average variable cost curve.

7. The industry's short-run supply curve under perfect competition is the horizontal sum of the supply curves of all of its firms.

8. In the long-run equilibrium of the perfectly competitive industry, freedom of entry forces each firm to earn zero *economic profit*, that is, no more than the firm's capital could earn elsewhere (the opportunity cost of the capital).

9. Industry equilibrium under perfect competition is at the point where the industry supply and demand curves intersect.

10. In long-run equilibrium under perfect competition, the firm chooses output such that average cost, marginal cost, and price are all equal. Output is at the point of minimum average cost. The firm's demand curve is tangent to its average cost curve at its minimum point.

11. The competitive industry's long-run supply curve coincides with its long-run average cost curve.

12. Both a tax on the emission of pollutants and a subsidy payment for reductions in those emissions induce firms to cut emissions. However, under perfect competition, a subsidy leads to the entry of more polluting firms and the likelihood of a net increase in emissions by the industry.

## KEY TERMS

Market   189
Pure monopoly   190
Monopolistic competition   190
Oligopoly   190
Perfect competition   192

Price taker   193
Horizontal demand curve   193
Short-run equilibrium   194
Variable cost   197
Firm's supply curve   198

Long-term equilibrium   202
Economic profit   203
Opportunity cost   203
Industry supply curve   203

## QUESTIONS FOR REVIEW

1. Explain why a perfectly competitive firm does not expand its sales without limit if its horizontal demand curve indicates that it can sell as much as it wants to at the current market price.

2. Explain why a demand curve is also a curve of average revenue. Recalling that when an average revenue curve is neither rising nor falling, marginal revenue must equal average revenue, explain why it is always true that $P = MR = AR$ for the perfectly competitive firm.

3. Under what circumstances might you expect the demand curve of the firm to be:
   a. Vertical
   b. Horizontal
   c. Negatively sloping
   d. Positively sloping

4. Explain why $P = MC$ in the short-run equilibrium of the perfectly competitive firm, whereas in long-run equilibrium $P = MC = AC$.

5. Regarding the four attributes of perfect competition—many small firms, freedom of entry, standardized product, and perfect information:
   a. Which is primarily responsible for the fact that the demand curve of a perfectly competitive firm is horizontal?

   b. Which is primarily responsible for the firm's zero economic profits in long-run equilibrium?

6. We indicated in this chapter that the MC curve cuts the AVC (average variable cost) curve at the *minimum* point of the latter. Explain why this must be so. (*Hint:* Because marginal costs are, by definition, entirely composed of variable costs, the MC curve can be considered the curve of *marginal variable costs.* Apply the general relationships between marginals and averages explained in Chapter 9.)

7. Explain why it is not sensible to close a business firm if it earns zero economic profits.

8. If the firm's lowest average cost is $48 and the corresponding average variable cost is $24, what does it pay a perfectly competitive firm to do if:
   a. The market price is $49?
   b. The price is $30?
   c. The price is $8?

9. If the market price in a competitive industry were above its equilibrium level, what would you expect to happen?

10. (More difficult) In this chapter we stated that the firm's MC curve goes through the lowest point of its AC curve and also through the lowest point of its AVC curve. Because the AVC curve lies below the AC curve, how can both of these statements be true? Why are they true? (*Hint:* See Figure 10–4.)

If there existed the universal mind that . . . would register simultaneously all the processes of nature and of society, that could forecast the results of their inter-reactions, such a mind . . . could . . . draw up a faultless and an exhaustive economic plan. . . . In truth, the bureaucracy often conceives that just such a mind is at its disposal; that is why it so easily frees itself from the control of the market.

Leon Trotsky, a leader of the Russian Revolution

# THE PRICE SYSTEM AND THE CASE FOR FREE MARKETS

Our study of microeconomics focuses on two crucial questions: What does the market do well, and what does it do poorly? By applying what we learned about demand in Chapters 6 and 7, supply in Chapters 8 and 9, and ideal market functioning in Chapter 10, we can provide a fairly comprehensive answer to the first part of this question. This chapter describes the tasks that the market carries out well—some, indeed, with spectacular effectiveness.

We begin by recalling two important themes from Chapters 4 and 5. First, because all resources are *scarce*, a society must use them efficiently; second, an economy must somehow coordinate the many individual consumers' and producers' actions. Specifically, society must somehow choose:

■ How much of each good to produce.

■ What input quantities to use in the production process.

■ How to distribute the resulting outputs among consumers.

As suggested by the opening quotation (by someone who was certainly in a position to know), these tasks are exceedingly difficult for a centrally planned economy. That overwhelming difficulty surely contributed to the fall of communism in the late 1980s, and the same difficulty shows up in the few remaining centrally planned economies, such as North Korea and Cuba. But for the most part those same tasks appear to be rather simple for a market system. This is why observers with philosophies as diverse as those of Adam Smith and the Russian Revolution's Leon Trotsky have admired the market, and why even those countries that maintain very strong central governments have now moved toward market economies.

Do not misinterpret this chapter as a piece of salesmanship. Here we study the market mechanism at its theoretical very best—when every good is produced under the exacting conditions of perfect competition. Some industries in our economy are reasonable approximations of perfect competition, but many others are as different from this idealized world as the physical world is from a frictionless vacuum tube. Just as the physicist uses the vacuum tube to study the laws of gravity, the economist uses the theoretical concept of a perfectly competitive economy to analyze the virtues of the market. We will spend plenty of time in later chapters studying its vices.

## How Should CalTrans Set the Price to Cross the San Francisco–Oakland Bay Bridge?

Appropriate pricing ensures efficient resource allocation in a market economy. In California, the San Francisco–Oakland Bay Bridge is very heavily traveled. The large volume of toll-paying traffic has probably long since paid for the cost of building this bridge, although that is probably less likely for the nearby San Mateo–Hayward and

Dumbarton bridges, which are less crowded. Yet economists argue that the price charged to use the San Francisco–Oakland Bay Bridge should be higher than the prices for the second two. Why may that make sense? Before you have finished reading this chapter, you may even agree with this seemingly unfair proposition.

## ■ EFFICIENT RESOURCE ALLOCATION AND PRICING

The fundamental fact of scarcity limits the volume of goods and services that any economic system can produce. In Chapter 4, we illustrated the concept of scarcity with a graphic device called a production possibilities frontier, which we repeat here for convenience as Figure 11–1. The frontier, curve *BC*, depicts all combinations of missiles and milk that a hypothetical society can produce given the limited resources at its disposal. For example, if it decides to produce 300 missiles, it will have enough resources left over to produce no more than 500 billion quarts of milk (point *D*). Of course, it is always possible to produce fewer than 500 billion quarts of milk—at a point, such as *G*, below the production possibilities frontier. But if a society does this, it is wasting some of its output potential; that is, it is not operating efficiently.

In Chapter 4, we defined efficiency rather loosely as the absence of waste. Because this chapter discusses primarily how a competitive market economy allocates resources efficiently, we now need a more precise definition. It is easiest to define an **efficient allocation of resources** by saying what it is not. For example, suppose that we could rearrange our resource allocation so that one group of people would get more of the things it wanted, while no one else would have to give up anything. Then, the failure to change the allocation of resources to take advantage of this opportunity would surely be wasteful— that is, inefficient. When society has taken advantage of every such opportunity for improvement, so that no such possibilities remain for making some people better off without making others worse off, we say that the allocation of resources is efficient.

Because point *G* in Figure 11–1 is below the frontier, there must be points like *E* on the frontier that lie above and to the right of *G*. This means that at *E* we get more of *both* outputs without any increase in input, making it possible to make some people better off without harming anyone. Thus, no point below the frontier can represent an efficient allocation of resources. By contrast, every point on the frontier is efficient because, no matter where on the frontier we start, we cannot get more of one good without giving up some of the other.

This discussion also shows that, normally, many particular allocations of resources will be efficient; in the example, every combination of outputs that is represented by a point on frontier *BC* can be efficient. As a rule, the concept of efficiency cannot tell us which of these efficient allocations is best for society. Yet, as we shall see in this chapter, we can use the concept of efficiency to formulate surprisingly detailed rules to steer us away from situations in which resources would be wasted.

**FIGURE 11–1**

**Production Possibilities Frontier and Efficiency**

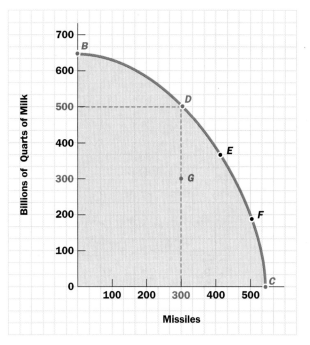

## PRICING TO PROMOTE EFFICIENCY: AN EXAMPLE

We can use the real example in our opening puzzle about the San Francisco–Oakland Bay Bridge to illustrate the connection between efficiency and the way prices can guide efficient choices. Prices can make all the difference between efficiency and inefficiency. The prices (tolls) that the California Department of Transportation charges drivers to use San Francisco Bay area bridges can make drivers' commutes shorter and safer—that is, more efficient. We will see that people nonetheless may well reject the efficient solution.

Figure 11–2 shows a map of the San Francisco Bay area, featuring the five bridges that serve most of the traffic in and around the bay. A traveler going from a location north of Berkeley (point *A*) to Palo Alto (point *B*) can choose among at least three routes:

**Route 1:** Over the Richmond–San Rafael Bridge, across the Golden Gate Bridge, through San Francisco, and on southward on Highway 101.

**Route 2:** Across the bay on the San Francisco–Oakland Bay Bridge and on southward on Highway 101 as before.

**Route 3:** Down the eastern shore of the bay, across the San Mateo–Hayward Bridge or the Dumbarton Bridge, and then on to Palo Alto (shown in red in Figure 11–2).

Let's consider which of these three choices uses society's resources—commuter time, gasoline, and so on—most efficiently. The San Francisco–Oakland Bay Bridge is clearly the most crowded of the five bridges, followed by the Golden Gate Bridge. The first carries 270,000 vehicles per day, and the second 125,000. During rush hours (when more than 20,000 vehicles per hour cross the San Francisco–Oakland

An **efficient allocation of resources** is one that takes advantage of every opportunity to make some individuals better off in their own estimation while not worsening the lot of anyone else.

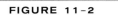

**FIGURE 11-2**

**Toll Bridges of the San Francisco Bay Area**

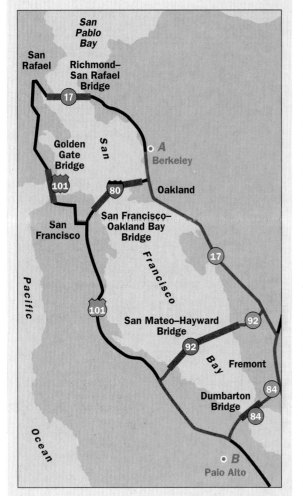

Bay Bridge), delays are frequent and traffic barely crawls across both bridges. In other words, space is scarce, and every car that uses these bridges makes it that much harder for others to get across.

On the other hand, the San Mateo–Hayward and Dumbarton bridges carry approximately 85,000 and 65,000 vehicles per day, respectively. To achieve efficiency, any driver who is indifferent about the two routes should take the one using the least crowded bridges. This would help reduce the amount of travel time wasted by the population as a whole. Specifically, in our illustration, Route 1, using the Golden Gate Bridge, is not a socially desirable way for our driver to get to Palo Alto because it adds too many miles to the trip and because it requires two bridge crossings. Route 2, with its use of the San Francisco–Oakland Bay Bridge, is even worse because of the added delays it causes for everyone else. Route 3, for drivers who are indifferent about these options, is the best choice from the viewpoint of the public interest. This does not mean that it is socially efficient to equalize the traffic among the routes, but it certainly would help travelers get where they are going faster if CalTrans could induce some drivers to leave the most crowded routes and switch over to some less crowded ones.

Appropriate prices can promote this sort of efficiency in bridge utilization. Specifically, if higher prices (very likely *substantially* higher prices) were charged for drivers to cross the most crowded bridges (on which space is a scarce resource), balanced by lower prices on the uncrowded bridges, then more drivers could be induced to use the uncrowded bridges. This is just the same reasoning that leads economists to advocate low prices for abundant minerals and high prices for scarce ones.

## CAN PRICE INCREASES EVER SERVE THE PUBLIC INTEREST?

This discussion raises a point that people untrained in economics always find extremely difficult to accept: Low prices may not always serve the public interest! The reason is pretty clear. If a price, such as the price of crossing a crowded bridge or the price of gasoline, is set "too low," then consumers will receive the "wrong" market signals. Low prices will encourage them to crowd the bridge even more or to consume more oil, thereby squandering society's precious resources.

A striking historical illustration brings out this point. In 1834, a professor of economics at the University of Dublin named Mountifort Longfield lectured about the price system. He offered the following example:

> Suppose the crop of potatoes in Ireland was to fall short in some year one-sixth of the usual consumption. If [there were no] increase of price, the whole . . . supply of the year would be exhausted in ten months, and for the remaining two months a scene of misery and famine beyond description would ensue. . . . But when prices [increase] the sufferers [often believe] that it is not caused by scarcity. . . . They suppose that there are provisions enough, but that the distress is caused by the insatiable rapacity of the possessors . . . [and] they have generally succeeded in obtaining laws against [the price increases] . . . which alone can prevent the provisions from being entirely consumed long before a new supply can be obtained. [1]

You may be intrigued to know that this talk was given some 10 years before the great potato famine, which caused unspeakable misery and death by starvation and

---

[1] Mountifort Longfield, *Lectures on Political Economy Delivered in Trinity and Michaelmas Terms* (Dublin: W. Curry, Jr., and Company, 1834), pp. 53–56.

brought many people from Ireland to the United States. The story of the actual potato famine in Ireland is much more complex than Longfield's discussion indicates. Still, the implications of his lecture about the way the price system works are entirely valid.

We can perhaps rephrase Longfield's reasoning more usefully. If the crop fails, potatoes become scarcer. If society is to use its scarce resources efficiently, stretching out the potato supply to last until the next crop arrives, it must cut back on the consumption of potatoes during earlier months—which is just what rising prices will do automatically if free-market mechanisms are allowed to work. However, if the price is held artificially low, consumers will use society's resources inefficiently. In this case, the inefficiency shows up in the form of famine and suffering when people deplete this year's crop months before the next one is harvested.

It is not easy to accept the notion that higher prices can serve the public interest better than lower ones. Politicians who voice this view are in the position of the proverbial parent who, before spanking a child, announces, "This is going to hurt me much more than it hurts you!" Because advocacy of higher prices courts political disaster, the political system often rejects the market solution when resources suddenly become more scarce.

The way that airport officials price landing privileges at crowded airports offers a good example. Airports become particularly congested at "peak hours," just before 9 A.M. and just after 5 P.M. This is when passengers most often suffer long delays. But many airports continue to charge bargain landing fees throughout the day, even at those crowded hours. That makes it attractive for small corporate jets or other planes carrying only a few passengers to arrive and take off at those hours, worsening the delays. Higher fees for peak-hour landings can discourage such overuse, but they are politically unpopular, and many airports are run by local governments. So we continue to experience late arrivals as a normal feature of air travel.

**THE MARKET STRIKES BACK** As we saw in our *ideas,* keeping prices low when a rise is appropriate can have serious consequences indeed. We have seen that it can worsen the effects of shortages of food and other vital goods. We know that inappropriately low prices caused nationwide chaos in gasoline distribution after the sudden drop in Iranian oil exports in 1979. In times of war, constraints on prices have even contributed to the surrender of cities under military siege, deterring those who would otherwise have risked smuggling food supplies through enemy lines. Low prices have also discouraged housing construction in cities where rent controls made building a losing proposition. Of course, in some cases it is appropriate to resist price increases—when unrestrained monopoly would otherwise succeed in gouging the public, when taxes are imposed on products capriciously and inappropriately, and when rising prices fall so heavily on poor people that rationing becomes the more acceptable option. But before tampering with the market mechanism we must carefully evaluate the potentially serious and even tragic consequences that artificial restrictions on prices can produce.

*Attempts to Repeal the Laws of Supply and Demand: The Market Strikes Back*

## SCARCITY AND THE NEED TO COORDINATE ECONOMIC DECISIONS

Efficiency becomes a particularly critical issue when we concern ourselves with the workings of the economy as a whole, rather than narrower topics such as choosing among bridge routes or deciding on the output of a single firm. We can think of an economy as a complex machine with literally millions of component parts. If this machine is to function efficiently, we must find some way to make the parts work in harmony.

A consumer in Peoria, Illinois, may decide to purchase two dozen eggs, and on the same day thousands of shoppers throughout the country make similar decisions. None of these purchasers knows or cares about the decisions of the others. Yet scarcity requires that these demands must somehow be coordinated with the production process so that the total quantity of eggs demanded does not exceed the total quantity supplied. Consumers, supermarkets, wholesalers, shippers, and

## ● AFTER "SHOCK THERAPY," THE POLISH ECONOMY IS THRIVING

Ten years ago, communism collapsed all over eastern Europe and the former Soviet Union, ending economic central planning and heralding the emergence of a free market in these countries. Nowhere were these changes as dramatic as in Poland, where reforms constituted no less than economic "shock therapy."

Poland's transformation into a market economy, though far from complete, has been nearly as radical as the first post-communist government hoped. Poland began the decade saddled with a legendarily incompetent, old-fashioned, and badly managed economy, which in its depths managed to run out of things like matches and salt, its paltry living standards bequeathed by a centrally controlled economy. It reached out to the West for help in creating monetary, budget, trade, and legal regimes. It now ranks among Europe's fastest-growing economies, with an annual GDP growth rate of more than 5 percent. Economic liberalization has freed thousands of entrepreneurs to sell, within loose limits, anything they want at whatever price they can get. Today, more than 65 percent of GDP comes from the private sector (up from just 16 percent in 1989), and more than half of Polish workers are employed in private enterprise.

The new, free-market mechanisms are clearly visible on Warsaw streets. Once-empty shelves are now overflowing with goods. Stores sell the latest fashions from Levi Strauss and Benetton. Glitzy billboards symbolize the battle over the consumer's pocketbook.

Despite all the good news, Poland still has much work to do. Many of its publicly owned industries are still backward, business and personal life remains hampered by bureaucratic red tape, and agriculture is 50 years behind the rest of Europe, with 27 percent of Polish workers engaged in farming.

SOURCES: "Survey of Business in Eastern Europe," *The Economist,* November 22, 1997; "Russia Is Not Poland, and That's Too Bad," Week in Review, *New York Times,* August 30, 1998, p. 5; and "Poland and the European Union," *The Economist,* February 28, 1998.

chicken farmers must somehow arrive at mutually consistent decisions; otherwise the economic process will deteriorate into chaos, as will millions of other such decisions. A machine cannot run with a few missing parts.

In a planned or centrally directed economy, we can easily imagine how such coordination takes place—though implementation is far more difficult than conception. Central planners set production targets for firms and sometimes tell firms how to meet these targets. In extreme cases, consumers may even be told, rather than asked, what they want to consume.

In contrast, a market system uses *prices* to coordinate economic activity. High prices discourage consumption of the most scarce resources, whereas low prices encourage consumption of comparatively abundant resources. In this way, Adam Smith's invisible hand uses prices to organize the economy's production.

The invisible hand has an astonishing capacity to handle enormously complex coordination problems—even those that remain beyond computer capabilities. Like any mechanism, this one has its imperfections, some of them rather serious. But we should not lose sight of the tremendously demanding task that the market constantly does accomplish—unnoticed, undirected, and in some respects, amazingly well. Let's look at just how the market goes about coordinating economic activity.

### THREE COORDINATION TASKS IN THE ECONOMY

We noted in Chapter 4 that any economic system, whether planned or unplanned, must find answers to three basic questions of resource allocation:

■ *Output selection.* How much of each commodity should be produced?

■ *Production planning.* What quantities of each of the available inputs should be used to produce each good?

■ *Distribution.* How should the resulting products be divided among consumers?

These coordination tasks may at first appear to be tailor-made for a regime of government planning like the one that the former Soviet Union used to employ. Yet most economists (even, nowadays, those in the formerly centrally planned economies) believe that it is in exactly these tasks that central direction performs most poorly and, paradoxically, the undisciplined free market performs best.

To understand how the unguided market manages the miracle of creating order out of what might otherwise be chaos, let's look at how each of these questions is answered by a system of free and unfettered markets—the method of economic organization that 18th-century French economists named **laissez faire.** Under laissez faire, the government acts to prevent crime, enforce contracts, and build roads and other types of public works; but it does not set prices and interferes as little as possible with the operation of free markets. How does such an unmanaged economy solve the three coordination problems?

**Laissez faire** refers to the practice of minimal government interference with the workings of the market system. The term means that people should be left alone in carrying out their economic affairs.

**OUTPUT SELECTION**    A free-market system decides what should be produced via what we have called the "law" of supply and demand. Where there is a shortage (that is, where quantity demanded exceeds quantity supplied), the market mechanism pushes the price upward, thereby encouraging more production and less consumption of the commodity that is in short supply. Where a surplus arises (that is, where quantity supplied exceeds quantity demanded), the same mechanism works in reverse: the price falls, discouraging production and stimulating consumption.

As an example, suppose that millions of people wake up one morning with a particular craving for omelets. As a result, for the moment, the quantity of eggs demanded exceeds the quantity supplied. But, within a few days, the market mechanism swings into action to meet this sudden change in demand. The price of eggs rises, which stimulates egg production. At first, farmers will simply bring more eggs to market by taking them out of storage. Over a somewhat longer time period, chickens that otherwise would have been sold for meat are kept in the chicken coops laying eggs. Finally, if the high price of eggs persists, farmers begin to increase their flocks, build more cages, and so on. Thus, a shift in consumer demand leads to a shift in society's resources; more eggs are wanted, and so the market mechanism sees to it that more of society's resources are devoted to egg production and marketing.

Similar reactions follow if a technological breakthrough reduces the input quantities needed to produce some item. Electronic calculators are a marvelous example. Just 25 years ago, calculators were so expensive that they could be found only in business firms and scientific laboratories. Then advances in science and engineering reduced their cost dramatically, and the market went to work. With costs sharply reduced, prices fell and the quantity demanded skyrocketed. Electronics firms flocked into the industry to meet this demand, which is to say that more of society's resources were devoted to producing the calculators that were suddenly in such great demand. These examples lead us to conclude that:

Under laissez faire, the allocation of society's resources among different products depends on consumer preferences (demands) and the production costs of the goods demanded. Prices (and the resulting profitability of the different products) vary so as to bring the quantity of each commodity produced into line with the quantity demanded.

Notice that no bureaucrat or central planner arranges resource allocation. Instead, an unseen force guides allocation—the lure of profits, which is the invisible hand that guides chicken farmers to increase their flocks when eggs are in greater demand and guides electronics firms to build new factories when the cost of electronic products falls.

**PRODUCTION PLANNING**    Once the market has decided on output composition, the next coordination task is to determine just how those goods are going to be produced. The production-planning problem includes, among other things, the division

CORPORATE LEADERS GATHER IN A FIELD OUTSIDE DARIEN, CONNECTICUT, WHERE ONE OF THEM CLAIMS TO HAVE SEEN THE INVISIBLE HAND OF THE MARKETPLACE.

of society's scarce inputs among enterprises. Which farm or factory will get how much of which materials? Of the labor force? Of the produced inputs such as plant and machinery? Such decisions can be crucial. If a factory runs short of an essential input, the entire production process may grind to a halt.

As a matter of fact, no economic system can select inputs and outputs separately. The input distribution between the production of cars and the manufacture of washing machines determines the quantities of cars and washing machines that society can obtain. However, it is simpler to think of input and output decisions as if they occur one at a time.

Once again, under laissez faire it is the price system that apportions fuels and other inputs among different industries in accord with those industries' requirements. The firm that needs a piece of equipment most urgently will be the last to drop out of the market for that product when prices rise. If millers demand more wheat than is currently available, the price will rise and bring quantity demanded back into line with quantity supplied, always giving priority to those users who are willing to pay the most for grain. Thus:

> In a free market, inputs are assigned to the firms that can make the most productive (most profitable) use of them. Firms that cannot make a sufficiently productive use of some input will be priced out of the market for that item.

This task, which sounds so simple, is actually almost unimaginably complex. It is so complex that it has helped to bring down many centrally planned systems. We will return to it shortly, as an illustration of how difficult it is to replace the market by a central planning bureau. But first let us consider the third of our three coordination problems.

**DISTRIBUTION OF PRODUCTS AMONG CONSUMERS**    The third task of any economy is to decide which consumer gets each of the goods that has been produced. The objective is to distribute the available supplies to match differing consumer preferences as well as possible. Coffee lovers must not be flooded with tea while tea drinkers are showered with coffee.

The price mechanism solves this problem by assigning the highest prices to the goods in greatest demand and then letting individual consumers pursue their own self-interests. Consider our example of rising egg prices. As the price of eggs rises, those whose craving for omelets is not terribly strong will begin to buy fewer eggs. In effect, the price acts as a rationing device that apportions the available eggs among consumers who are willing to pay the most for them.

Thus, the price mechanism has an important advantage over other rationing devices: it can respond to individual consumer preferences. If a centrally planned economy rations eggs by distributing the same amount to everyone (say, two eggs per week to each person), then everyone ends up with two eggs whether he likes eggs or detests them. The price system, on the other hand, permits each consumer to set her own priorities. Thus:

**THE TRADE-OFF**  The price system carries out the distribution process by rationing goods on the basis of preferences and relative incomes. Notice the last three words of the previous sentence. The price system *does* favor the rich, and this is a problem that market economies must confront.

However, we may still want to think twice before declaring ourselves opposed to the price system. If equality is our goal, might not a more reasonable solution be to use the tax system to equalize incomes and then let the market mechanism distribute goods in accord with preferences? We take this idea up in Chapter 21, where we discuss tax policy.

*The Trade-off between Efficiency and Equality*

We have just seen, in broad outline, how a laissez-faire economy addresses the three basic issues of resource allocation: what to produce, how to produce it, and how to distribute the resulting products. Because it performs these tasks quietly, without central direction, and with no apparent concern for the public interest, many radical critics have predicted that such an unplanned system must degenerate into chaos. Yet unplanned, free-market economies are far from chaotic. Quite ironically, it is the centrally planned economies that have often ended up in economic disarray while the invisible hand seems to go on about its business seamlessly. Perhaps the best way to appreciate the free market's accomplishments is to consider how a centrally planned system must cope with the coordination problems we have just outlined. Let us examine just one of them: production planning.

## INPUT-OUTPUT ANALYSIS: THE NEAR IMPOSSIBILITY OF PERFECT CENTRAL PLANNING

Of the three coordination tasks of any economy, the assignment of input to specific industries and firms has claimed the most attention of central planners. Why? Because the production processes of the various industries are interdependent. Industry X cannot operate without Industry Y's output, but Industry Y, in turn, needs Industry X's product. The whole economy can grind to a halt if planners do not solve the production-planning problem satisfactorily. In recent years, failure to adapt to this kind of interdependence has had graphic consequences in North Korea, one of the last remaining centrally planned economies. Breakdowns of key economic activities such as the electric supply grid, transportation systems, and other basic industries have each exacerbated the others' failures and created a terrible cycle of economic disaster, contributing to severe famine.

A simple example will further illustrate the point. Unless economic planners allocate enough gasoline to the trucking industry, products will not get to market. And unless they allocate enough trucks to haul gasoline to gas stations, consumers will not be able to get around. Thus, trucking activity depends on gasoline production but gasoline production also depends on trucking activity. We seem to be caught in a circle. Planners must decide both truck and gasoline outputs together, not separately.

Because the output required from any one industry depends on the output from every other industry, planners can be sure that the production of the various outputs is sufficient to meet both consumer and industrial demands only by taking explicit account of the interdependencies among industries. If they change the output target for one industry, they must also adjust every other industry's output target.

For example, if planners decide to provide consumers with more electricity, then more steel must be produced in order to build more electric generators. But an increase in steel output requires more coal to be mined. More mining, in turn, means

## ● INPUT-OUTPUT EQUATIONS: AN EXAMPLE

Imagine an economy with only three outputs: electricity, steel, and coal, and let *E, S,* and *C* represent the dollar values of their respective outputs. Suppose that to produce every dollar's worth of steel, $0.20 worth of electricity is used, so that the total electricity demand of steel manufacturers is 0.2*S*. Similarly, assume that coal manufacturers use $0.30 of electricity in producing $1 worth of coal, or a total of 0.3*C* units of electricity. Because *E* dollars of electricity are produced in total, the amount left over for consumers, after subtraction of industrial demands for fuel, will be *E* (available electricity) minus 0.2*S* (used in steel production) minus 0.3*C* (used in coal production). Suppose further that the central planners have decided to supply $15 million worth of electricity to consumers. We end up with the electricity output equation:

$$E - 0.2S - 0.3C = 15$$

The planner will also need such an equation for each of the two other industries, specifying for each of them the net amount intended to be left for consumers after the industrial uses of the product. The full set of equations will then be similar to the following:

$$E - 0.2S - 0.3C = 15$$
$$S - 0.1E - 0.06C = 7$$
$$C - 0.15E - 0.4S = 10$$

These are typical equations in an input-output analysis. In practice, however, such an analysis has dozens and sometimes hundreds of equations with similar numbers of unknowns. This, then, is the logic of input-output analysis.

**Input-output analysis** is a mathematical procedure that takes account of the interdependence among the economy's industries and determines the amount of output each industry must provide as inputs to the other industries in the economy.

that still more electricity is needed to light the mines, to run the elevators, perhaps to operate some of the trains that carry the coal, and so on and on. Any single change in production sets off a chain of adjustments throughout the economy that require still further adjustments.

To decide how much of each output an economy must produce, the planner must use statistics to form a set of equations, one equation for each product, and then solve those equations simultaneously. The simultaneous solution process prevents the circularity of the analysis—electricity output depends on steel production, but steel output depends on electricity production—from becoming a vicious circle. The technique used to solve these complicated equations—**input-output analysis**—was invented by the late economist Wassily Leontief, who won the 1973 Nobel Prize for his work.

The equations of input-output analysis illustrated in the accompanying box, "Input-Output Equations: An Example," take explicit account of the interdependence among industries by describing precisely how each industry's target output depends on every other industry's target. Only by solving these equations simultaneously for the required outputs of electricity, steel, coal, and so on can planners ensure a consistent solution that produces the required amounts of each product—including the amount of each product needed to produce every other product.

The example of input-output analysis that appears in the box is not provided so that you can learn how to apply the technique yourself. Its real purpose is to help you imagine how very complicated the problems facing a central planner can become. Their task, although analogous to the one in the box, is enormously more complex. In any real economy, the number of commodities is far greater than the three outputs in the example. In the United States, some large manufacturing companies deal in hundreds of thousands of items, and the armed forces keep several million different items in inventory.

— Наверное, в проекте произошла неувязка...

Рисунок В. ТИЛЬМАНА

In this cartoon from a Soviet humor magazine, one construction worker comments to another, "A slight mistake in the plans, perhaps." It is interesting that there were many cartoons making fun of the inefficiencies of the Soviet economy in the humor magazines of the USSR before the collapse of communism.

Planners must thus ultimately make calculations for each single item. It is not enough to plan the right number of bolts in total; they must make sure that the required number of each size is produced. (Try putting 5 million large bolts into 5 million small nuts!) To be sure that their plans will really work, they need a separate equation for every size of bolt and one for every size and type of nut. But then, to replicate the analysis described in the box, they would have to solve several million equations simultaneously! This task would strain even the most powerful computer's capability, if it could do the job at all.

Worse still is the data problem. Each of our three equations requires three pieces of statistical information, making $3 \times 3$, or 9 numbers in total. The equation for electricity must indicate how much electricity is needed in steel production, how much in coal production, and how much is demanded by consumers, all on the basis of statistical information that is itself subject to error. Therefore, in a five-industry analysis, $5 \times 5$, or 25 pieces of data are needed; a 100-industry analysis requires $100^2$, or 10,000 numbers, and a million-item input-output study might need one trillion pieces of information. Solving data-gathering problems is, therefore, no easy task, to put it mildly. Still other complications arise, but we have seen enough to conclude that:

A full, rigorous central-planning solution to the production problem is a tremendous task, requiring an overwhelming quantity of information and some incredibly difficult calculations. Yet this very complex job is carried out automatically and unobtrusively by the price mechanism in a free-market economy.

## WHICH BUYERS AND WHICH SELLERS GET PRIORITY?

Because the supplies of all commodities are limited, some potential customers of a product will end up with none of it. And because demand is not infinite, some potential suppliers of a commodity will find no market available for them. So, which consumers get the scarce commodity, and which firms get to supply the goods? Again, the price mechanism comes to the rescue.

Other things being equal, the price mechanism ensures that those consumers who want a scarce commodity most will receive it, and that those sellers who can supply it most efficiently will get to supply the commodity.

To illustrate, let's look at Figure 11–3, an ordinary supply-demand graph. For simplicity, suppose we are dealing here with a commodity such as a best-selling novel. We assume also that no one buys more than one copy of the book. The

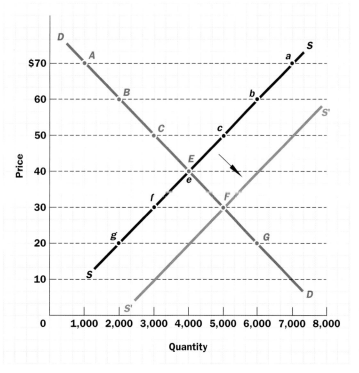

demand curve, *DD*, represents the preferences of 6,000 potential customers with widely differing preferences. The first 1,000 of them are willing to pay as much as $70 for the book, as shown by point *A* on the demand curve (though they would, of course, prefer to pay less). Point *B* shows a second group of 1,000 buyers who will purchase the book at a price of $60, but refuse to spend $70 on it (because they care less about the book than the point *A* consumers). Similarly, point *C* represents the demand of a third group of consumers, to whom the book is even less important, so that they are willing to spend only $50 for a copy. And points *E*, *F*, and *G* represent sets of consumers with successively lower desires for the book, until at point *G*, consumers are only willing to pay $20 for the book.

With *SS* the supply curve, the equilibrium point is *E*, where *SS* and *DD* intersect. Under perfect competition, the market price of the book will be $40. Buyers at point *A*, to whom the book is worth $70, will be delighted to buy it for only $40. Similarly, buyers at points *B*, *C*, and *E* will also buy the book. But the consumers at points *F* and *G*, to whom the book is worth less than $40, will not buy the book. We can see in this example that the book will go to the consumers who value it most (in terms of money), and only those who value it least will be deprived of it.

*The price mechanism always ranks potential consumers of a good in the order of the intensity of their preference for the good, as indicated by the amount they are willing to spend for it.*

The price system's priority to those consumers who assign most importance to a good goes one step further. Suppose that supply increases, with the supply curve shifting to the right, from *SS* to *S'S'* in the figure. Which consumers will get the increased quantity supplied? Answer: Of those consumers in the group of people who were previously denied the commodity, those who want it most intensely will acquire the product. In the graph, the shift in supply moves the equilibrium point from *E* to *F*, so point *F* consumers will now be included in the group of buyers of the book (along with point *A*, *B*, *C*, and *E* consumers), but the point *G* consumers still do not purchase the book. The book is worth more to point *F* consumers ($30) than it is to point *G* consumers, who value it only at $20.

The price system seems to set the right priorities in deciding which prospective consumers of some specific good do receive some of it, and which do not. Only one major imperfection arises in this argument, to which we will return in a moment.

First, however, let's look at Figure 11–3 again, this time from the supplying firm's point of view. Assume that *SS* is the long-run industry supply curve. Point *g* on this curve represents the amount that the industry will supply if the price is $20—that is, it is the amount that will be supplied by firms whose average cost is no higher than $20, so that the price will cover their cost. Similarly, point *f* represents the output of all firms whose average cost is no higher than $30, so that the group of suppliers now includes some firms that are less efficient (they have higher average cost) than those at point *g*. And at point *e* some of the suppliers will have average costs of $40, but none of suppliers will have an average cost higher than that. Using the same reasoning, as we move further along *SS* to points *c*, *b*, and *a*, increasingly inefficient firms will be included among the suppliers.

Now, we examine the supply-demand equilibrium point *e*, at which price is $40. Which suppliers will be able to market their products at this point? Answer: Those at points *g*, *f*, and *e*, but not firms at points *c*, *b*, and *a*, because no firm in the last three groups can cover its costs at the equilibrium price. Once again, the price mechanism does its job. It ranks firms in order of their efficiency, as measured by long-run average costs, and brings business to the more efficient firms, leaving out the least efficient potential suppliers.

All this illustrates yet another of the many desirable features of the price mechanism. But there is one fly in the ointment—at least on the demand side of the story. We saw that consumers in group G were likely to be denied the scarce commodity we are discussing, because they wanted it less than the other consumers. Group G consumers were willing to spend only $20 for the book, whereas the others were willing to spend more for it. But what if some consumers in group G want the book very badly, but are also very poor? This is an important question—one we will encounter again and again. The price mechanism is like a democracy, but one in which the rule is not "one person, one vote," but rather, "one dollar, one vote." In other words, under the price mechanism rich consumers' preferences get much more attention than poor consumers' desires do.

## ■ HOW PERFECT COMPETITION ACHIEVES EFFICIENCY

We have indicated how the market mechanism solves the three basic coordination problems of any economy—what to produce, how to produce it, and how to distribute the goods to consumers. Also, we have suggested that these same tasks pose almost insurmountable difficulties for central planners. One critical question remains. Is the allocation of resources that the market mechanism selects *efficient*, according to the precise definition of efficiency presented at the start of this chapter?

### EXAMPLE: EFFICIENT RESOURCE ALLOCATION IN OUTPUT SELECTION

The answer, under perfect competition's idealized circumstances, is yes. Because a detailed proof of this assertion for all three coordination tasks is long and time-consuming, we will present the proof only for the first of the three tasks—*output selection*. We will show that, at least in theory, perfect competition does guarantee efficiency in determining the relative quantities of the different commodities that the economy produces.

The proof comes in two steps. First, we derive a criterion for efficient output selection, that is, a test that tells us whether or not production is being carried out efficiently. Second, we show that the prices that emerge from the market mechanism under perfect competition automatically pass this test.

**STEP 1: RULE FOR EFFICIENT OUTPUT SELECTION**    We begin by stating the rule for efficient output selection:

MARGINAL ANALYSIS    Efficiency in the choice of output quantities requires that, for each of the economy's outputs, the marginal cost (MC) of the last unit produced be equal to the marginal utility (MU) of the last unit consumed.[2] In symbols:

$$MC = MU$$

This rule is yet another example of the basic principle of marginal analysis that we learned in Chapter 9.

The efficient decision about output quantities is the one that maximizes the total benefit (total utility) to society, minus the cost to society of producing the output quantities that are chosen. In other words, the goal is to maximize the surplus that society gains—total utility minus total cost. But, as we saw in Chapter 9, to maximize the difference between total utility and total cost, we must find the outputs

*The Importance of Thinking at the Margin*

---

[2] Recall from Chapter 6 that we measure marginal utility in money terms, that is, the amount of money that a consumer is willing to give up for an additional unit of the commodity. Economists usually call this the marginal rate of substitution between the commodity and money.

that equalize the corresponding marginal figures—marginal utility and marginal cost—to one another, as the preceding efficiency rule tells us.

An example will help us to see explicitly why resource allocation must satisfy this rule to be deemed efficient. Suppose that the marginal utility of an additional pound of beef to consumers is $8, but its marginal cost is only $5. Then the value of the resources that would have to be used up to produce one more pound of beef (its MC) would be $3 less than the money value that consumers would willingly pay for that additional pound (its MU). By expanding the output of beef by one pound, society could get more (in MU) out of the economic production process than it was putting in (MC). We know that the output at which MU exceeds MC cannot be optimal, because society would be better off with an increase in that output level. The opposite is true if the MC of beef exceeds the MU of beef.

We have therefore shown that, if any product's MU is not equal to MC—whether MU exceeds MC or MC exceeds MU—the economy must be wasting an opportunity to achieve a net improvement in consumers' welfare. This is exactly what we mean by saying society is using resources inefficiently. Just as was true at point G in Figure 11–1, if MC does not equal MU for any commodity, it is possible to rearrange production to make some people better off while harming no one else. It follows, then, that efficient output choice occurs only when MC equals MU for every good.[3]

**STEP 2: THE PRICE SYSTEM'S CRITICAL ROLE**    Next, we must show that under perfect competition, the price system automatically leads buyers and sellers to behave in a way that equalizes MU and MC.

To see this, recall from the previous chapter that under perfect competition it is most profitable for each beef-producing firm to produce the quantity at which the marginal cost equals the price *(P)* of beef:

$$MC = P$$

This must be so because, if the marginal cost of beef were less than the price, the farmer could add to profits by increasing the size of the herd (or the amount of grain fed to the animals). The reverse would be true if the marginal cost of beef were greater than its price. Thus, under perfect competition, the lure of profits leads each producer of beef (and of every other product) to supply the quantity that makes MC = P.

We also learned, in Chapter 6, that each consumer will purchase the quantity of beef at which the marginal utility of beef in money terms equals the price of beef:

$$MU = P$$

If consumers did not do this, either an increase or a decrease in their beef purchases would leave them better off.

Putting these last two equations together, we see that the invisible hand enforces the following string of equalities:

$$MC = P = MU$$

But if the MC of beef and the MU of beef both equal the same price, *P*, then they must equal each other. That is, it must be true that the quantity of beef produced and consumed in a perfectly competitive market satisfies the equation:

$$MC = MU$$

This is precisely our rule for efficient output selection. Because the same must be true of every other product supplied by a competitive industry:

Under perfect competition, producers and consumers will make uncoordinated decisions that we can expect automatically (and amazingly) to produce exactly the

---

[3] *Warning:* As shown in Chapter 14, markets sometimes perform imperfectly because the decision maker faces a different marginal cost from the marginal cost to society. This occurs when the individual who creates the cost can make someone else bear the burden. Example: Firm X's production causes pollution emissions that increase nearby households' laundry bills. In such a case, Firm X will ignore the cost and produce inefficiently large outputs and emissions. We study such problems, called externalities, in Chapters 14 and 22.

quantity of each good that satisfies the MC = MU rule for efficiency. That is, under the idealized conditions of perfect competition, the market mechanism, without any government intervention and without anyone else directing it or planning for it, is capable of allocating society's scarce resources efficiently.

## THE INVISIBLE HAND AT WORK

This is truly a remarkable result. How can the price mechanism automatically satisfy all of the exacting requirements for efficiency (that marginal utility equals marginal cost for each and every commodity)—requirements that no central planner can hope to handle because of the masses of statistics and the enormous calculations they entail? This seems analogous to a magician suddenly pulling a rabbit out of a hat!

But, as always, rabbits come out of hats only if they were hidden there in the first place. What really is the mechanism by which our act of magic works? The secret is that the price system lets consumers and producers pursue their own best interests—something they are probably very good at doing. Prices are the dollar costs of commodities to consumers, so in pursuing their own best interests, consumers will buy the commodities that give them the most satisfaction per dollar. But the price the consumer pays is also equal to MC.

Because MC measures the resource cost (in every firm) of producing one more unit of the good, this means that consumers will buy the commodities that give them the most satisfaction for the resources used up in producing them. In other words, the market mechanism leads consumers to squeeze the greatest possible benefit out of the social resources used up in making the goods and services they buy. So, if resources are priced appropriately (P = MC), when consumers make the best use of their money they must also be making the best use of society's resources. That is the way the market mechanism ensures economic efficiency.

> When all prices are set equal to marginal costs, the price system gives correct cost signals to consumers. It has set prices at levels that induce consumers to use society's resources with the same care they devote to watching their own money, because the money cost of a good to the consumer has been set equal to the opportunity cost of the good to society. A perfectly analogous explanation applies to the decisions of producers.

This is the magic of the invisible hand. Unlike central planners, consumers need not know how difficult it is to manufacture a certain product or how scarce the inputs required by the production process are. Everything consumers need to know to make their decisions is embodied in the market price, which, under perfect competition, accurately reflects marginal costs. Similarly, producers do not need to know anything about the psychology and tastes of their individual customers—price movements tell them all they need to know when consumer preferences change.

## OTHER ROLES OF PRICES: INCOME DISTRIBUTION AND FAIRNESS

So far we have stressed the role of prices that economists emphasize most: Prices guide resource allocation. But prices also command the spotlight in another role: Prices influence the distribution of income between buyers and sellers. For example, high rents often make tenants poorer and landlords richer.

This rather obvious role of prices draws the most attention from the public, politicians, and regulators, and we should not lose sight of it.[4] Markets serve only those demands that are backed up by consumers' desire and *ability to pay*. The market system may do well in serving poor families, because it gives them more food and clothing than a less efficient economy would provide. But the market system offers far more to wealthy families. Many people think that such an arrangement represents a great injustice, however efficient it may be.

---

[4] Income distribution is the subject of Part IV.

---

● **POLICY DEBATE** █ **USER CHARGES FOR PUBLIC FACILITIES**

---

At a time when budget cutting is the way to popularity for a politician, the notion of charging users for the services that government once gave away free is under debate. Economists have often advocated such charges for the use of roads, bridges, museums, educational facilities, and the like. Of course, it's true that if the services are provided "free," the public has to pay for them anyhow, though more indirectly through taxes. But if people are asked to pay directly for such services, it can make a big difference.

For example, let's say a road is financed out of general taxes. In this circumstance, it does not matter how many times Sabrina, the owner of an independent trucking firm, uses the road. She pays the same amount whether she uses it twice a year or every day. But if Sabrina has to pay a toll every time she uses the road, she will have a strong incentive to avoid unnecessary use. That is why advocates of pricing to promote economic efficiency propose more substantial *user charges,* not only for roads and bridges but also for admission to national parks, for the use of publicly owned grazing lands, and for the use of the television and radio spectrum by broadcasters.

Opponents of user charges contend that these fees are unfair to poor people. Besides, it is argued, the use of public facilities like libraries, museums, and schools should be encouraged rather than impeded by user charges. For instance, in New York there is no charge to cross the three deteriorating bridges that connect Brooklyn and Queens with Manhattan. But each time user charges are proposed, they are met with the cry, "Should I have to pay an admission fee into my own city?!"

Often, people oppose economists' recommendations for improving the economy's efficiency on the grounds that these proposals are *unfair.* For example, economists frequently advocate higher prices for transportation facilities at the times of day when the facilities are most crowded. Economists propose a pricing arrangement called "peak, off-peak pricing" under which prices for public transportation are higher during rush hours than during other hours.

The rationale for this proposal should be clear from our discussion of efficiency. A seat on a train is a much scarcer resource during rush hours than it is during other times of the day when the trains run fairly empty. Thus, according to the principles of efficiency outlined in this chapter, seats should be more expensive during rush hours to discourage those consumers with no set schedule from riding the trains during peak periods. The same notion applies to other services. Charges for long-distance telephone calls made at night are sometimes lower than those in the daytime. And in some places, electricity is cheaper at night, when demand does not strain the supplier's generating capacity.

Yet the proposal that transportation authorities should charge higher fares for public transportation during peak hours—say, from 8:00 A.M. to 9:30 A.M. and from 4:30 P.M. to 6:00 P.M.—often runs into stiff opposition. Opponents say that most of the burden of such higher fares will fall on lower-income working people who have no choice about the timing of their trips. For example, a survey in Great Britain of economists and members of Parliament found that, while high peak-period fares were favored by 88 percent of the economists, only 35 percent of the Conservative Party members of Parliament and just 19 percent of the Labour Party members of Parliament approved of this arrangement (see Table 11–1). We may surmise that these members of the British Parliament reflected the views of the public more accurately than did the economists. In this case, people simply found the efficient solution unfair, and so they refused to adopt it.

### YET ANOTHER FREE-MARKET ACHIEVEMENT: GROWTH VERSUS EFFICIENCY

This chapter has followed the economist's standard approach in evaluating the market mechanism. Economists usually stress efficiency in resource allocation and the role of the market in ensuring such efficiency—that resources are divided among alternative uses to maximize consumer net benefits.

---

● **PEAK/OFF-PEAK PRICES WORK ON THE ISLAND OF SINGAPORE**

---

With incomes per head of $23,000, a population of 3 million, and an area of just 650 square kilometers, Singapore is a very rich, very small country. People want to cruise around in style. Their 370,000 cars (plus 310,000 buses, lorries, vans, and motorbikes) translate into 220 vehicles per road-kilometer, one of the highest densities in the world. If nothing were done, the result would be endless traffic jams.

For the past 20 years, to enter the central restricted zone, covering about seven square kilometers, drivers have had to display a license [which costs] . . . $2 in the morning peak hour, falling to $1.30 at off-peak times. In 1989 authorities extended the peak surcharge to the evening rush hour as well. That reduced evening traffic sharply (see chart) and raised average speeds inside the restricted zone by 20 percent. Some drivers have switched to off-peak travel and now take buses or trains; through-traffic has declined.

SOURCE: "Singapore's Plan," *The Economist*, December 6, 1997, p. 22.

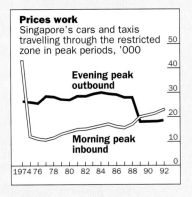

**Prices work**
Singapore's cars and taxis travelling through the restricted zone in peak periods, '000

SOURCE: John Polak, Piotr Olszewski, and Yiik-diew Wong.

---

However, other viewpoints are less likely to emphasize the free market's efficiency accomplishments. A very diverse group, including businesspeople, politicians, economic historians, leaders in formerly communist economies such as Mikhail Gorbachev, and even Marxists, admire the market primarily for a very different reason— the extraordinary growth in output which market economies have achieved and the historically unprecedented abundance that has resulted.

Historians have estimated that before the arrival of the capitalistic market mechanism, output per person grew with glacial slowness. But today, an average American can afford almost *ten* times the quantity of goods and services that an individual's income bought 100 years ago. Undoubtedly, the failure to achieve substantial growth and prosperity (and not just inefficiencies in allocating goods) helped to bring about the fall of communism in eastern Europe. Even Karl Marx stressed this role of the market mechanism and waxed lyrical in his description of its accomplishments. Chapter 15 will return to this subject, indicating what a free market economy can accomplish in terms of economic growth.

---

**Replies to a Questionnaire** | **TABLE 11–1**

| Question: In order to make the most efficient use of a city's resources, how should subway and bus fares vary during the day? | Economists | Conservative Party Members of Parliament | Labor Party Members of Parliament |
|---|---|---|---|
| a. They should be relatively low during rush hour to transport as many people as possible at lower costs. | 1% | 0% | 40% |
| b. They should be the same at all times to avoid making travelers alter their schedules because of price differences. | 4 | 60 | 39 |
| c. They should be relatively high during rush hour to minimize the amount of equipment needed to transport the daily travelers. | 88 | 35 | 19 |
| d. Impossible to answer on the data and alternatives given. | 7 | 5 | 2 |

SOURCES: Adapted from Samuel Brittan, *Is There an Economic Consensus?* (London: Curtis Brown, Ltd., 1973), p. 93. Copyright Samuel Brittan, 1973. Reproduced by permission of Curtis Brown Ltd.

## ● EARTHQUAKE, BRIDGE CONGESTION, AND ROUTE SUBSTITUTION

Bridge congestion and route substitution took on graphic proportions after the partial collapse of the San Francisco-Oakland Bay Bridge during the Loma Prieta earthquake that shook the San Francisco area on October 17, 1989. According to one newspaper report:

> The bridge closure forced commuters . . . [who] used it to cross the bay some other way. While many people stayed home the week after the disaster, they now appear to be rejoining the ranks of the daily rush. . . . The result has been major delays on alternative routes, such as the Golden Gate, San Mateo and San Rafael-Richmond bridges.

Just a little over four years later, the Northridge earthquake in Los Angeles decimated that city's massive freeway system, with the worst damage to bridges on the nation's most heavily traveled road, the Santa Monica Freeway. Many of the more than 300,000 commuters who travel that highway daily switched over to the city's rail system, where average ridership shot up from 8,000 commuters per day to peaks of 30,000 per day.

SOURCES: *The Boston Globe,* October 31, 1989, p. 15; "New Technology Cuts Time for Bridge Repair," *American City and County,* December 1994, p. 42; "Working Together to Unclog Road," *Public Relations Journal,* May 1994.

### San Francisco Bridge Pricing Revisited

Our earlier example of the San Francisco Bay area bridges also raises fairness issues. Recall that we concluded from our analysis that efficient bridge use requires higher tolls on the more crowded bridges. Because this principle seems so clear and rational, it may be interesting to see what the actual bridge tolls were in 1998. Travel on the privately owned Golden Gate Bridge required a $3 toll for a round trip. But the publicly owned San Francisco-Oakland Bay, Dumbarton, Richmond-San Rafael, and San Mateo-Hayward bridges all carried a uniform $2 toll even though, as we saw earlier, average daily traffic on these bridges varies widely, with the San Francisco-Oakland Bay Bridge by far the most crowded.[5]

From an efficiency point of view, the pattern of tolls on the four publicly owned bridges seems quite irrational. The least crowded bridges were assigned the same tolls as the most crowded bridge! The explanation lies in some widely held notions of fairness.

Many people feel that it is fair for those who travel on a particular bridge to pay for its costs. In this view, it would be unjust for those who use the crowded San Francisco-Oakland Bay Bridge to pay more, in order to subsidize the least-crowded Dumbarton Bridge. Naturally, a heavily traveled bridge recoups its building, maintenance, and operating costs more quickly. On the other hand, it is felt that the relatively few users of a less crowded bridge should make a fair contribution toward its costs.

---

[5] Toll schedule and traffic volumes for the San Francisco Bay area bridges from California Department of Transportation, www.dot.ca.gov., October 1998. We should note that CalTrans has encouraged additional efficiency by instituting faster carpool lanes for buses and cars with three or more passengers; such vehicles cross the four publicly owned bridges free of charge between 5 and 10 A.M. and between 3 and 6 P.M.

An economically irrational pattern of tolls does nothing to ease congestion on overcrowded bridges, and thereby contributes to inefficiency. But one cannot legitimately conclude that advocates of such prices are "stupid." Whether this pattern of tolls is or is not desirable must be decided, ultimately, on the basis of the public's sense of what constitutes fairness and justice in pricing. It also depends on the amount that people are willing to pay in terms of delays, inconvenience, and other inefficiencies in order to avoid apparent injustices.

Economics alone cannot decide the appropriate trade-off between fairness and efficiency. It cannot even pretend to judge which pricing arrangements are fair and which are unfair. But it can and should indicate whether a particular pricing decision, proposed because it is considered fair, will impose heavy inefficiency costs on the community. Economic analysis also can and should indicate how to appraise these costs, so that the issues can be evaluated on a rational, factual basis.

## ■ TOWARD ASSESSMENT OF THE PRICE MECHANISM

We do not mean to imply in our discussion of the case for free markets that the free-enterprise system is an ideal of perfection, without flaw or room for improvement. In fact, it has a number of serious shortcomings that we will explore in subsequent chapters. But recognition of these imperfections should not conceal the price mechanism's enormous accomplishments.

We have shown that, given the proper circumstances, prices are capable of meeting the most exacting requirements of allocative efficiency: requirements that go well beyond any central planning bureau's capacities. Even centrally planned economies use the price mechanism to carry out considerable portions of the task of allocation, most notably in the distribution of consumer goods. No one has invented an instrument for directing the economy that can replace the price mechanism, which no one ever designed or planned for, but which simply grew by itself, a child of the processes of history.

## SUMMARY

1. Economists consider an allocation of resources inefficient if it wastes opportunities to change the use of the economy's resources in any way that makes at least some consumers better off without harming anyone. Resource allocation is called efficient if there are no such wasted opportunities.

2. Under perfect competition, the free-market mechanism adjusts prices so that the resulting resource allocation is efficient. It induces firms to buy and use inputs in ways that yield the most valuable outputs per unit of input. It distributes products among consumers in ways that match individual preferences. Finally, it produces commodities whose value to consumers exceeds the cost of producing them and assigns the task of production to the potential suppliers who can produce most efficiently.

3. Resource allocation involves three basic coordination tasks:

   a. How much of each good to produce.

   b. What quantities of available inputs to use in producing the different goods.

   c. How to distribute the goods among different consumers.

4. Efficient decisions about what goods to produce require that the marginal cost (MC) of producing each good be equated to its marginal utility (MU) to consumers. If the MC of any good differs from its MU, then society can improve resource allocation by changing the amount produced.

5. Because the market system induces firms to set MC equal to price, and it induces consumers to set MU equal to price, it automatically guarantees satisfaction of the condition that MC should equal MU.

6. Improvements in efficiency occasionally require some prices to increase in order to stimulate supply or to prevent waste in consumption. This is why price increases can sometimes be beneficial to consumers.

7. In addition to resource allocation, prices also influence income distribution between buyers and sellers.

8. The price mechanism can be criticized on the grounds that it is unfair because it accords wealthy consumers preferential treatment.

## QUESTIONS FOR REVIEW

1. What possible social advantages of price increases accrue in each of the following two cases?

    a. Charging higher prices for electrical power on very hot days when many people use air conditioners.

    b. Raising water prices in drought-stricken areas.

2. Discuss the fairness of the two preceding proposals.

3. Using the concepts of marginal cost (MC) and marginal utility (MU), discuss the nature of the inefficiency in each of the following cases:

    a. An arrangement that offers relatively little coffee and much tea to people who prefer coffee and does the reverse for tea lovers.

    b. An arrangement in which skilled mechanics are assigned to ditch digging and unskilled laborers to repairing cars.

    c. An arrangement that produces a large quantity of trucks and few cars, assuming that both cost about the same amount to produce and to run, but that most people in the community prefer cars to trucks.

4. In reality, which of the following circumstances might give rise to each of the preceding problem situations?

    a. Regulation of output quantities by a government.

    b. Rationing of commodities.

    c. Assignment of soldiers to different jobs in an army.

5. We have said that the economy's three coordination tasks are output selection, production planning, and product distribution. Which of these is done badly in the case described in Review Questions 3a, 3b, and 3c?

6. In a free market, how will the price mechanism deal with each of the inefficiencies described in Review Question 3?

7. Suppose that a given set of resources can be used to make either handbags or wallets, and the MC of a handbag is $19 while the MC of a wallet is $10. If the MU of a wallet is $10 and the MU of a handbag is $30, what can be done to improve resource allocation? What can you say about the gain to consumers?

8. In the early months after the end of communism in eastern Europe, there seems to have been an almost superstitious belief that the free market could solve all problems. What sorts of problems do you think the leaders and the citizens of those countries had in mind? Which of those problems is there good reason to believe the market mechanism actually can deal with effectively? What disappointments and sources of disillusionment should have been expected? Which disappointments have resulted?

**The price of monopoly is upon every occasion the highest which can be got.**

Adam Smith[1]

# MONOPOLY

In Chapters 10 and 11, we described an idealized market system in which all industries are perfectly competitive, and we extolled the beauty of that system. In this chapter, we turn to one of the blemishes—the possibility that some industries may be monopolized—and to the consequences of such a flaw in the market system.

We will indeed find that monopolized markets do not match the ideal performance of perfectly competitive markets. Under monopoly, the market mechanism no longer allocates society's resources efficiently. This suggests that government actions to constrain monopoly may sometimes be able to improve the workings of the market—a possibility that we will study in detail in Chapter 20.

But first, as usual, we start with a real-life puzzle.

---

[1] But Adam Smith's statement is incorrect! See Review Question 7 at the end of the chapter.

## Competition in Local Telephone Service Markets?

We are all keenly aware of the strong competition in the market for long-distance telephone service. How can we miss it? Representatives of the firms offering this service—some with familiar names like MCI and Sprint, and some newer and smaller firms with less familiar names—interrupt countless dinners with their telephone sales pitches. But, though vigorous competition has occurred in the market for long-distance phone service since the late 1970s, most areas of the United States still treat *local* telephone service markets as regulated monopolies. People in northern Colorado, however, see a new and innovative trend in telecommunications: competitive local phone markets. The residents in this region can now choose between US West, the established provider, and a new firm, McleodUSA.

The markets for local phone service in northern Colorado and a relatively small number of other areas around the nation currently contain competing firms, and this phenomenon is on the rise. Soon all consumers may be able to choose from two or more providers of local phone service. This competition potentially promises lower rates, better service, and a wider range of options for phone service. Why is competition possibly arising now in this market? What has allowed this industry, which until recently had been considered by some as a classic example of "natural monopoly," to suddenly offer the beginnings of competition? In this chapter you will learn about the causes and consequences of monopoly and, in the process, learn the answers to these questions.

## ■ *MONOPOLY* DEFINED

A **pure monopoly** is an industry in which there is only one supplier of a product for which there are no close substitutes and in which it is very hard or impossible for another firm to coexist.

Requirements to meet the definition of **pure monopoly** are quite stringent. First, only one firm may exist in the industry—the monopolist must be "the only game in town." Second, no close substitutes for the monopolist's product may exist. Thus, even a city's sole provider of natural gas is not considered a pure monopoly, because other firms offer close substitutes like heating oil and electricity. Third, some reason must make entry and survival of potential competitors extremely unlikely. Otherwise monopolistic behavior and its excessive economic profits could not persist.

These rigid requirements make pure monopoly a rarity in the real world. The local telephone company and the post office in some small towns may be examples of one-firm industries that face little or no effective competition. But most firms face at least a degree of competition from substitute products. If only one railroad serves a particular town, it still must compete with bus lines, trucking companies, and airlines. Similarly, the producer of a particular brand of beer may be the only supplier of that specific product, but the firm is not a monopolist by our definition. Because many other beers are close substitutes for its product, the firm will lose much of its business if it tries to raise its price far above the prices of other brands. Even the local phone company and the post office face competition in more populous areas.

There is another reason why the unrestrained pure monopoly of economic theory is rarely found in practice. We will learn in this chapter that pure monopoly can have a number of undesirable features. So in markets where pure monopoly might otherwise prevail, the government has intervened to prevent monopolization or to limit the discretion of the monopolist to set its price.

If we do not study pure monopoly for its descriptive realism, why do we study it? Because, like perfect competition, pure monopoly is a market form that is easier to analyze than the more common market structures that we will consider in the next chapter. Thus, pure monopoly is a stepping stone toward more realistic models. Also, we will understand the possible evils of monopoly most clearly if we examine monopoly in its purest form.

## SOURCES OF MONOPOLY: BARRIERS TO ENTRY AND COST ADVANTAGES

The key requirement for preservation of a monopoly is exclusion of potential rivals from the market. One way to achieve this is by means of some specific impediment that prevents the establishment of a new firm in the industry. Economists call such impediments *barriers to entry*. Some examples follow.

**LEGAL RESTRICTIONS**    The U.S. Postal Service has a monopoly position because Congress has given it one. Private companies that may want to compete with the postal service directly are prohibited from doing so by law. Local monopolies of various kinds are sometimes established either because government grants some special privilege to a single firm (for example, the right to operate a food concession in a municipal stadium) or prevents other firms from entering the industry (for instance, by licensing only a single cable television supplier).

**PATENTS**    Some firms benefit from a special, but important, class of legal impediments to entry called patents. To encourage inventiveness, the government gives exclusive production rights for a period of time to the inventors of certain products. As long as a patent is in effect, the firm has a protected position and holds a monopoly. For example, Xerox for many years had (but no longer has) a monopoly in plain-paper copying. Most pharmaceutical companies also get monopolies on the drugs they develop. The drug maker Eli Lilly, for instance, has a patent on Prozac, the world's best-selling antidepressant. However, the patent expires in 2003.

**CONTROL OF A SCARCE RESOURCE OR INPUT**    If a certain commodity can be produced only by using a rare input, a company that gains control of the source of that input can establish a monopoly position for itself. Real examples are not easy to find, but the South African diamond syndicate is one.

**DELIBERATELY ERECTED ENTRY BARRIERS**    A firm may deliberately attempt to make entry difficult for others. One way is to start costly lawsuits against new rivals, sometimes on trumped-up charges. Another is to spend exorbitant amounts on advertising, thus forcing any potential entrant to match that expenditure.

**LARGE SUNK COSTS**    Entry into an industry will, obviously, be very risky if it requires a large investment, especially if that investment is sunk—meaning that it cannot be recouped for a considerable period of time. Thus, the need for a large sunk investment discourages entry into an industry. Many analysts therefore consider sunk costs to be the most important type of "naturally imposed" barrier to entry. For example, the high sunk costs involved in jet airplane building helped Boeing enjoy a monopoly in the top end of the long-range, wide-body jet airliner market for many years after the launch of the 747 jumbo jet. But Airbus, which, with European governments' sponsorship has been able to afford the high investments, has encroached on Boeing's territory.

Such barriers can keep rivals out and ensure that an industry is monopolized. But monopoly can also occur in the absence of barriers to entry if a single firm has substantial cost advantages over potential rivals. Two examples of this are technical superiority and economies of scale.

**TECHNICAL SUPERIORITY**     A firm whose technological expertise vastly exceeds that of any potential competitor can, for a period of time, maintain a monopoly position. For example, IBM for many years had little competition in the computer business mainly because of its technological virtuosity. Eventually, however, competitors caught up. More recently, Microsoft has established a commanding position in the software business, especially for operating systems, through a combination of inventiveness and marketing wizardry.

**ECONOMIES OF SCALE**     If mere size gives a large firm a cost advantage over a smaller rival, it is likely to be impossible for anyone to compete with the largest firm in the industry.

## NATURAL MONOPOLY

This last type of cost advantage is important enough to merit special attention. In some industries, economies of large-scale production or economies of scope (from simultaneous production of a large number of related items, for example, car motors and bodies, truck parts, and so on) are so extreme that the industry's output can be produced at far lower cost by a single firm than by a number of smaller firms. In such cases, we say there is a **natural monopoly.** Once a firm gets large enough relative to the size of the market for its product, its natural cost advantage may well drive the competition out of business whether or not anyone in the relatively large firm has evil intentions.

A monopoly need not be a large firm if the market is small enough. *What matters is the size of a single firm relative to the total market demand for the product.* Thus, a small bank in a rural town or a gasoline station at a lightly traveled intersection may both be monopolies, even though they are very small firms.

Figure 12–1 shows the sort of average cost (AC) curve that leads to natural monopoly. It has a negative slope throughout, meaning that the more a firm in this industry produces, the lower its average cost will be. Suppose that any firm producing video games has this AC curve and that, initially, there are two firms in the industry. Suppose also that the larger firm is producing 2 million games at an average cost of $2.50 (red point *A*), and the smaller firm is producing 1 million games at an average cost of $3.00 (blue point *B*). Clearly, the larger firm can drive the smaller firm out of business if it offers its output for sale at a price below $3.00 (so the smaller firm can match the price only by running a loss) but above $2.50 (so it can still make a profit). Hence, a monopoly may arise "naturally," even in the absence of barriers to entry.

Once the monopoly is established (producing, say, 2.5 million video games—point *C*) the economies of scale act as a very effective deterrent to entry because no new entrant can hope to match the low average cost ($2.00) of the existing monopoly firm. Of course, the public interest may be well served if the natural monopolist uses its low cost to keep its prices low. The danger, however, is that the firm may raise its price once rivals have left the industry.

Many public utilities operate as *regulated* monopoly suppliers for exactly this reason. It is believed that the technology of producing or distributing their output enables them to achieve substantial cost reductions by producing large quantities. It is therefore often considered preferable to permit these firms to achieve lower costs by having the entire market to themselves, and then to subject them and their prices to regulatory supervision, rather than to break them up into a number of competing firms. We will examine the issue of regulating natural monopolies in detail in Chapter 20. To summarize this discussion:

There are two basic reasons why a monopoly may exist: barriers to entry, such as legal restrictions and patents, and cost advantages of superior technology or large-scale operation that lead to natural monopoly. It is generally considered undesirable to break up a large firm whose costs are low because of scale

A **natural monopoly** is an industry in which advantages of large-scale production make it possible for a single firm to produce the entire output of the market at lower average cost than a number of firms each producing a smaller quantity.

**FIGURE 12–1**

**Natural Monopoly**

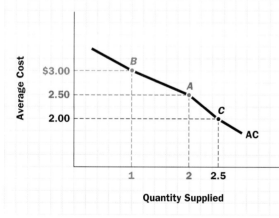

NOTE: Average cost is in dollars per unit; quantity is in millions.

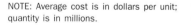

economies. But barriers to entry are usually considered to be against the public interest except where they are believed to offer offsetting advantages, as in the case of patents.

The rest of this chapter analyzes how a monopoly can be expected to behave if its freedom of action is not limited by the government.

## ■ THE MONOPOLIST'S SUPPLY DECISION

A monopoly firm does not have a "supply curve," as we usually define the term. Unlike a perfect competitor, a monopoly is not at the mercy of the market; the firm does not have to accept the market's price as beyond its control and adjust to it. Instead, it has the power to set the price, or rather to select the price-quantity combination on the demand curve that suits its interests best.

Put differently, a monopolist is not a *price taker* that must simply adapt to whatever price the forces of supply and demand decree. Rather, a monopolist is a *price maker* that can, if so inclined, raise the product price. For any price that the monopolist chooses, the demand curve for the product indicates how much consumers will buy. Thus, the standard supply-demand analysis described in Chapter 5 does not apply to the determination of price or output in a monopolized industry.

The demand curve of a monopoly, unlike that of a perfect competitor, is normally downward sloping, not horizontal. This means that a price rise will not cause the monopoly to lose *all* of its customers. But any increase will cost it *some* business. The higher the price, the less the monopolist can expect to sell.

> The market cannot impose a price on a monopolist as it imposes a price on the price-taking competitive firm. But the monopolist cannot select both price and the quantity it sells. In accord with the demand curve, the higher the price it sets, the less it can sell.

In deciding what price best serves the firm's interests, the monopolist must consider whether profits can be increased by raising or lowering the product's price. Because of the downward-sloping demand curve, the sky is not the limit in pricing by a monopolist. Some price increases are not profitable.

In our analysis, we shall assume that the monopolist wants to maximize profits. That does not mean that a monopoly is guaranteed a positive profit. If the demand for its product is low, or if the firm is inefficient, even a monopoly may lose money and eventually be forced out of business. However, if a monopoly firm does earn a positive profit, it may be able to keep on doing so in the long run because there will be no entry that competes the profits away.

We can use the methods of Chapter 9 to determine which price the profit-maximizing monopolist will prefer. To maximize profits, the monopolist must compare marginal revenue (the addition to total revenue resulting from a 1-unit rise in output) with marginal cost (the addition to total cost resulting from that additional unit). Figure 12–2 shows a marginal cost (MC) curve and a marginal revenue (MR) curve for a typical monopolist. Recall that the firm's demand curve (DD) is also its average revenue (AR) curve. That is because if a firm sells *Q* units of output, selling every unit of output at the price *P*, then the average revenue brought in by a unit of output must be the price, *P*, because the average of a bunch of equal numbers must be that same number. Because the demand curve gives the price at which any particular quantity can be sold, it also automatically indicates the AR (= price) yielded by that quantity.

**FIGURE 12-2**

**Profit-Maximizing Equilibrium for a Monopolist**

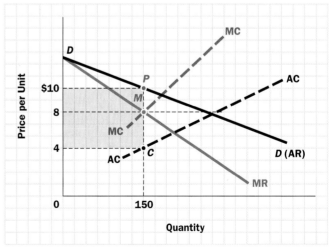

NOTE: Price is in dollars per unit.

---

### IS THE SOFTWARE INDUSTRY A NATURAL MONOPOLY?

Some leading economists believe the software industry is prone to monopoly. Three influences may incline the industry in this direction, as an article in *InfoWorld* describes:

"One factor is diminishing costs: while the first copy of a software program costs millions to produce, the cost to produce subsequent copies is negligible. The second factor is the network effect in which the value of software increases by the number of people using it and developers creating applications for it. The third factor is the lock-in effect, in which the cost of switching to another system (installation, training, application compatibility) persuades users to stick with current systems. . . . These forces create natural barriers to entry for newcomers, and Microsoft's operating-system dominance is a prime example."

SOURCE: Lynda Radosevich, "Top of the News: How the Software Industry Creates Monopolies," *InfoWorld* 20 (May 25, 1998).

Notice that the marginal revenue curve is always below the demand curve, meaning that MR is always less than price (*P*). This important fact is easy to explain. The monopoly firm charges the same price to all of its customers. If the firm wants to increase sales by 1 unit, it must decrease the price somewhat to all of its customers. When it cuts the price to attract new sales, all previous customers also benefit. Thus, the additional revenue that the monopolist takes in when sales increase by 1 unit (*marginal revenue*) is the price the firm collects from the new customer *minus the revenue it loses by cutting the price paid by all of its old customers.* This means that MR is necessarily less than price; graphically, it implies that the MR curve is below the demand curve, as in Figure 12–2.

### DETERMINING THE PROFIT-MAXIMIZING OUTPUT

Like any other firm, the monopoly maximizes its profits by setting marginal revenue (MR) equal to marginal cost (MC). It selects point *M* in Figure 12–2, where output is 150 units. But point *M* does not tell us the monopoly price because, as we have just seen, price exceeds MR for a monopolist. To learn what price the monopolist charges, we must use the demand curve to find the price at which consumers are willing to purchase the profit-maximizing output of 150 units. The answer, we see, is given by point *P* directly above *M*. The monopoly price is $10 per unit. Not surprisingly, it exceeds both MR and MC (which are equal at $8).

The monopolist depicted in Figure 12–2 is earning a tidy profit. This profit is shown in the graph by the shaded rectangle whose height is the difference between price (point *P*) and average cost (point *C*) and whose width is the quantity produced (150 units). In the example, profits are $6 per unit, or $900.

To study the decisions of a profit-maximizing monopolist:

1. Find the output at which MR = MC to select the profit-maximizing output level.

2. Find the height of the demand curve at that level of output to determine the corresponding price.

3. Compare the height of the demand curve with the height of the AC curve at that output to see whether the net result is an economic profit or a loss.

We can also show a monopolist's profit-maximization calculation numerically. In Table 12–1, the first two columns show the quantity and price figures that constitute the monopolist's demand curve. Column (3) shows total revenue (TR) for each output, which is the product of price times quantity. Thus, for 3 units of output, we have TR = $92 × 3 = $276. Column (4) shows marginal revenue (MR). For example, when output rises from 3 to 4 units, TR increases from $276 to $320, so MR is $320 − $276 = $44. Column (5) gives the monopolist's total cost for each level of output. Column (6) derives marginal cost (MC) from total cost (TC) in the usual way. Finally, by subtracting TC from TR for each level of output, we obtain total profit in Column (7).

The table brings out a number of important points. We note first in Columns (2) and (3) that a cut in price may increase or decrease total revenue. When output rises from 1 to 2 units, P falls from $140 to $107 and TR rises from $140 to $214. But when (between 5 and 6 units of output) P falls from $66 to $50, TR falls from $330 to $300. Next we observe, by comparing Columns (2) and (4), that after the first unit, price always exceeds marginal revenue. Finally, from Columns (4) and (6) we see that MC = MR = $44 when Q is between 3 and 4 units, indicating that this is the level of output that maximizes the monopolist's total profit. That is confirmed in Column (7) of the table, which shows that at those outputs profit reaches its highest level, $110, for any of the output quantities considered in the table.

## COMPARING MONOPOLY AND PERFECT COMPETITION

This completes our analysis of the monopolist's price-output decision. At this point it is natural to wonder whether there is anything distinctive about the monopoly equilibrium. But to find out, we need a standard of comparison. Perfect competition provides this standard because, as we learned in Chapters 10 and 11, it is a theoretical benchmark of ideal performance against which other market structures can be judged. By comparing the results of monopoly with those of perfect competition, we will see why economists since Adam Smith have condemned monopoly as inefficient.

**A MONOPOLIST'S PROFIT PERSISTS**   The first difference between competition and monopoly is a direct consequence of barriers to entry in monopoly. Profits such as those shown in Figure 12–2 would be competed away by free entry in a perfectly

**A Profit-Maximizing Monopolist's Price-Output Decision**              TABLE 12-1

| | | Revenue | | Cost | | Total Profit |
|---|---|---|---|---|---|---|
| (1) Q | (2) P | (3) TR = P × Q | (4) MR | (5) TC | (6) MC | (7) TR − TC |
| 0 | | $ 0 | | $ 10 | | $−10 |
| | | | $140 | | $60 | |
| 1 | $140 | 140 | | 70 | | 70 |
| | | | 74 | | 50 | |
| 2 | 107 | 214 | | 120 | | 94 |
| | | | 62 | | 46 | |
| 3 | 92 | 276 | | 166 | | 110 |
| | | | 44 | | 44 | |
| 4 | 80 | 320 | | 210 | | 110 |
| | | | 10 | | 43 | |
| 5 | 66 | 330 | | 253 | | 77 |
| | | | −30 | | 45 | |
| 6 | 50 | 300 | | 298 | | 2 |

competitive market, because a positive profit would attract new competitors into the business. A competitive firm must earn *zero economic profit* in the long run; that is, it can earn only enough to cover its costs, including the opportunity cost of the owner's capital and labor. But higher profit *can* persist under monopoly—if the monopoly is protected from the arrival of new competitors by barriers to entry. Fate can allow monopolists to grow wealthy at the expense of their consumers. But because people find such accumulations of wealth objectionable, monopoly is widely condemned. As a result, monopolies are regulated by government, which often limits the profits they can earn.

**MONOPOLY RESTRICTS OUTPUT TO RAISE SHORT-RUN PRICE**    Excess monopoly profit can be a problem. But economists believe that the second difference between competition and monopoly is even more worrisome:

> Compared with the perfectly competitive ideal, the monopolist restricts output and charges a higher price.

**FIGURE 12-3**

**Comparison of a Monopoly and a Competitive Industry**

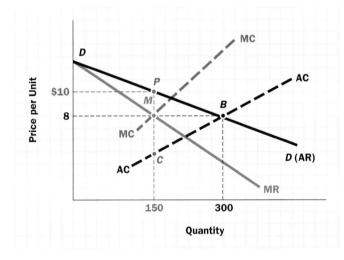

To see that this is so, let us conduct the following thought experiment. Imagine that a court order breaks up the monopoly firm depicted in Figure 12–2 (and reproduced as Figure 12–3) into a large number of perfectly competitive firms. Suppose further that the industry demand curve is unchanged by this event and that the MC curve in Figure 12–3 is also the (horizontal) sum of the MC curves of all the newly created competitive firms. These may be unrealistic assumptions, as we will soon explain. However, they make it easy to compare the output-price combinations that would emerge in the short run under monopoly and perfect competition.

Before making our comparison, we must note that under monopoly, the firm and the industry are exactly the same entity. But under perfect competition, any one firm is just a small portion of the industry. So when we measure the performance of monopoly against that of perfect competition, we should compare the monopoly with the entire competitive industry, not with an individual competitive firm. In Figure 12–3, the monopolist's output is point *M* at which MC = MR. The long-run competitive output (point *B*) is greater than the monopoly's because it must be sufficiently large to yield zero economic profit (*P* = AR = AC).

It is self-evident and not very interesting to observe that the output of the monopolist is virtually certain to be larger than that of a tiny competitive *firm*. The interesting issue is how much product gets into the hands of consumers under the two market forms, that is, how much output is produced by a monopoly as against the quantity provided by a comparable competitive *industry*.

**MONOPOLY RESTRICTS OUTPUT TO RAISE LONG-RUN PRICE**    As we have seen, monopoly output is determined by the profit-maximization requirement that MC = MR (point *M*). But as we learned in Chapter 10, long-run competitive equilibrium occurs at point *B* in Figure 12–3, where price and average cost are equal and economic profit is zero.

By comparing point *B* with the monopolist's equilibrium (point *M*), we see that the monopolist produces fewer units of output than would a competitive industry with the same demand and cost conditions. Because the demand curve slopes downward, producing less output means charging a higher price. The monopolist's price, indicated by point *P* on the demand curve and directly above *M*, exceeds the price that would result from perfect competition at point *B*. This is the essence of the truth behind the popular view that unregulated monopolists "gouge the public."

We should note that matters will always turn out that way if the average cost curve has a positive slope between the monopoly output level and the competitive output level. That is because we know, in this case, that the MC curve must lie above the AC curve (to review why, see pages 172–180 of Chapter 9). We have also just seen that the MR curve must lie below the demand (AR) curve. It is clear, then, that the point where the MR curve meets the MC curve (the monopoly output) must always lie to the left of the output at which AC and AR meet (the competitive industry output). Consequently, monopoly output will always be the smaller of the two when the curves of the competitive and monopoly industries are identical. With monopoly output lower, its price will always be higher.

**MONOPOLY LEADS TO INEFFICIENT RESOURCE ALLOCATION** We conclude, then, that a monopoly will charge a higher price and produce a smaller output than will a competitive industry with the same demand and cost conditions. Why do economists find this situation so objectionable? Because, as we learned in Chapter 11, a competitive industry devotes "just the right amount" of society's scarce resources to the production of its particular commodity. Therefore, if a monopolist produces less than a competitive industry, it must be producing too little.

Remember from Chapter 11 that efficiency in resource allocation requires that the marginal utility (MU) of each commodity be equal to its marginal cost. Also, perfect competition guarantees that:

$$MU = P \text{ and } MC = P, \text{ so } MU = MC$$

Under monopoly, consumers continue to maximize their own welfare by setting MU equal to $P$. But the monopoly producer sets MC equal to MR. Because MR is *below* the market price, $P$, we conclude that in a monopolized industry:

$$MU = P \text{ and } MC = MR < P \text{ so that } MC < MU$$

Because MU exceeds MC, too small a share of society's resources is being used to produce the monopolized commodity. Consumers would have a net benefit of $MU - MC > 0$ if output were increased above the monopoly level by one unit. Adam Smith's invisible hand is sending out the wrong signals. Consumers are willing to pay an amount for an additional unit of the good (its MU) that exceeds what it costs to produce that unit (its MC). But the monopoly refuses to increase production, because if it raises output by one unit, the revenue it will collect (MR) will be less than the price the consumer will pay for the additional unit ($P$). The monopolist does not increase production, and resources are allocated inefficiently. To summarize this discussion of the consequences of monopoly:

> Because it is protected from entry, a monopoly firm may earn profits in excess of the opportunity cost of capital. At the same time, monopoly breeds inefficiency in resource allocation by producing too little output and charging too high a price. For these reasons, some of the virtues of laissez-faire evaporate if an industry becomes monopolized.

## ON BALANCE, CAN ANYTHING GOOD BE SAID ABOUT MONOPOLY?

Except for the case of natural monopoly—where a single firm offers important cost advantages—or the case of a monopoly obtained through an inventor's patent, which is designed to encourage innovation, it is not easy to find arguments in favor of monopoly. However, the preceding comparison of monopoly and perfect competition is very artificial. It assumes that all other things will remain the same, even though that is unlikely to happen in reality.

### MONOPOLY IS LIKELY TO SHIFT DEMAND

For one thing, we have assumed that the market demand curve is the same whether the industry is competitive or monopolized. But is this usually so? The demand curve will be the same if the monopoly firm does nothing to expand its market, but that is hardly plausible.

Under perfect competition, purchasers consider the products of all suppliers in an industry to be identical, and so no single supplier has any reason to advertise. But if a monopoly takes over from a perfectly competitive industry, it may very well pay to advertise. If management believes that the touch of the advertising agency can make consumers rush to the market to purchase the product whose virtues have been extolled on television, then the firm will allocate a substantial sum of money to accomplish this feat. Take Kodak, for example. It enjoyed a near monopoly on U.S. film sales from the turn of the century until the 1980s, but that did not stop the company from spending a good deal on advertising. This type of expenditure should shift the demand curve outward. The monopoly's demand curve and that of the competitive industry will then no longer be the same.

The higher demand curve for the monopoly's product may induce it to expand production and therefore reduce the difference between the competitive and the monopolistic output levels indicated in Figure 12–3. But it may also make it possible for the monopoly to charge even higher prices, so the increased output may not constitute a net gain for consumers.

## MONOPOLY IS LIKELY TO SHIFT COST CURVES

The advent of a monopoly may also shift the average and marginal cost curves. One reason for higher costs is the advertising we have just been discussing. Another reason is the sheer size of the monopolist's organization, which may lead to bureaucratic inefficiencies, coordination problems, and the like.

On the other hand, a monopolist may be able to eliminate certain types of duplication that are unavoidable for a number of small, independent firms: One purchasing agent may do the input-buying job where many buyers were needed before; a few large machines may replace many small items of equipment in the hands of the competitive firms. In addition, the large scale of the monopoly firm's input purchases may permit it to take advantage of quantity discounts not available to small competitive firms.

If the consolidation achieved by a monopoly does shift down the marginal cost curve, monopoly output will tend to move up closer to the competitive level. The monopoly price will then tend to move down closer to the competitive price.

## MONOPOLY MAY AID INNOVATION

Some economists have argued that it is misleading to compare the cost curves of a monopoly and a competitive industry *at a single point in time*. Because it is protected from rivals and therefore sure to capture the benefits from any cost-saving methods and new products it can invent, a monopoly has particularly strong motivation to invest in research, these economists argue. If this research bears fruit, the monopolist's costs will be lower than those of a competitive industry in the long run, even if they are higher in the short run. Monopoly, according to this view, may be the handmaiden of innovation. Although the argument is an old one, it remains controversial. The statistical evidence is decidedly mixed.

## NATURAL MONOPOLY: WHERE SINGLE-FIRM PRODUCTION IS CHEAPEST

Finally, we must remember that the monopoly depicted in Figure 12–2 is not a natural monopoly, because its average costs increase rather than decrease when its output expands. But some of the monopolies you find in the real world are natural ones. Where a monopoly is natural, costs of production would, by definition, be higher—possibly much higher—if the single large firm were broken up into many smaller firms. (Refer back to Figure 12–1.) In such cases, it may serve society's interests to allow the monopoly to continue because consumers benefit from the economies of large-scale production. But then it may be appropriate to regulate the monopoly by placing legal limitations on its ability to set its prices.

## ■ PRICE DISCRIMINATION UNDER MONOPOLY

So far we have assumed that a monopoly charges the same price to all of its customers, but that is not always true. In reality, monopoly firms can sell the same product to different customers at different prices, even if that price difference is unrelated to any special costs that affect some customers but not others. Such a practice is called **price discrimination.** Pricing is also said to be discriminatory if it costs more to supply a good to Customer A than to Customer B, but A and B are nonetheless charged the same price.

We are all familiar with cases of price discrimination. For example, suppose that Matt and Emily both mail letters from Philadelphia, but his goes to New York while hers goes to Seattle. Both pay the same 33-cent postage even though Seattle is much farther than New York from Philadelphia. Bargain airline fares are another example. Passenger C may find herself seated next to Passenger D, who has paid 25 percent more for the same flight.

The airline example shows that price discrimination occurs in industries that are not monopolies. Still, it is far easier for a monopolist to charge discriminatory prices than it is for a firm that is affected by competition, because price discrimination means that sales to some customers are more profitable than sales to others. Such discrepancies in profitability tempt rivals, including new entrants into the industry, to charge the more profitable consumers somewhat lower prices in order to lure them away from the firm that is "overcharging" them. Price discriminators sneeringly call this type of targeted entry *cream skimming*, meaning that entrants go after the best paying customers, leaving the low payers (the "skimmed milk") to the discriminator. But, whether desirable or not, such entry certainly makes it harder to charge higher prices to the more profitable customers.

**Price discrimination** is the sale of a given product at different prices to different customers of the firm, when there is no difference in the cost of supplying different customers. Prices are also discriminatory if it costs more to supply one customer than another, but they are charged the same price.

Why do firms sometimes engage in price discrimination? You may already suspect the answer: to increase their profits. To see why, let us consider a simple example. Imagine a town with 100 rich families and 1,000 poor ones. The poor families are each willing to buy one video game but cannot afford to pay more than $25. The rich, however, are prepared to buy one per family as long as the price is no higher than $75.

If it cannot price-discriminate, the best the firm can do is to set the price at $25 for everyone, yielding a total revenue of $25 × 1,100 = $27,500. If it charged more, say, $75, it would sell only to the rich and earn just $7,500. If the added cost of producing the 1,000 games for the poorer families is less than the $27,500 − $7,500 = $20,000 in added revenues from the sales to the poor, then the $25 price must be more profitable than the $75 price.

But what if the game maker can charge different prices to the rich and to the poor—and can prevent the poor from reselling their low-priced merchandise to the rich at a markup? Then the revenue obtainable by the firm from the same 1,100 video game output becomes $25 × 1,000 = $25,000 from selling to the poor plus $75 × 100 = $7,500 from selling to the rich, for a total of $32,500. This is clearly a better deal for the firm than the $27,500 revenue obtainable without price discrimination. Profits are $5,000 higher. In general:

> When a firm charges discriminatory prices, profits are normally higher than when the firm charges nondiscriminatory (uniform) prices.

We have constructed our simple example to make the two profit-maximizing prices obvious. In practice, that is not so; the monopolist knows that if it sets a price too high, quantity demanded and hence profits will be too low. The discriminating monopolist's problem is determining the profit-maximizing prices to charge to different customer groups. The answer is given by another rule of marginal analysis. For simplicity, suppose that the seller proposes charging two different prices to two customer groups, A and B. Profit maximization requires that the price to Group A and the price to Group B are such that they yield the same *marginal* revenue, that is:

> The marginal revenue from a sale to a Group A customer must be the same as that from a sale to a Group B customer:

$$MR_a = MR_b$$

The reasoning is straightforward. Suppose that the sale of an additional video game to a Group A customer brings in $MR_a = \$18$ in revenue although the corresponding sale to a Group B customer adds only $MR_b = \$15$. Such an arrangement cannot possibly be a profit-maximizing solution. By switching 1 unit of sales from B customers to A customers the firm gives up $15 in revenue to gain $18—a net gain of $3 from the same total sales. Because a similar argument holds for any other pair of marginal revenues that are unequal, profit maximizing clearly requires that the marginal revenue from each group of customers be equal.

The equal-marginal-revenue rule enables us to determine the profit-maximizing prices and sales volumes for the two groups of customers diagrammatically. The two panels of Figure 12–4 show the demand curves and corresponding marginal revenue curves for customer groups A and B. Suppose that the firm is selling the quantity $Q_a$ to Group A customers. How much must the firm then sell to Group B customers in order to maximize profits? Our rule gives the answer. The marginal revenue from selling to Group A is equal to $M$—point $V$ directly above $Q_a$ on the MR curve in Panel (a). The rule tells us that the firm must charge a price to Group B customers that induces them to buy the quantity that yields the same marginal revenue, $M$. We find this quantity by drawing a horizontal line $MM$ from Panel (a) to Panel (b). The marginal revenues of the two customer groups will clearly be equal where $MM$ cuts the Group B marginal revenue curve—at point $W$. The profit-maximizing sales volume to Group B will be $Q_b$, directly below point $W$.

Unfortunately, that is not quite the end of the story because we have not yet said anything about costs, and we know that profit maximization must take account of costs as well as revenues. But we can deal with the cost issue quite easily, at least if

**Prices and Quantities under Price Discrimination**  FIGURE 12–4

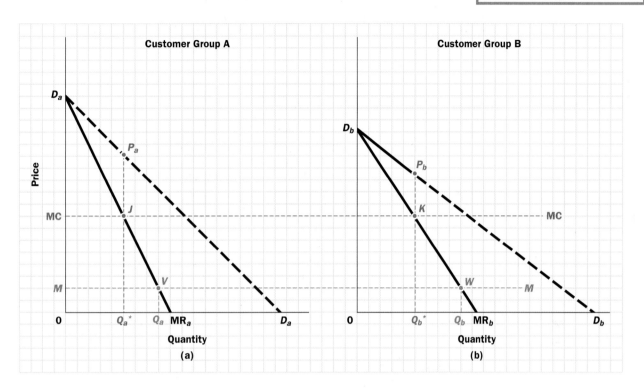

the marginal cost of a video game is the same whether supplied to an A customer or a B customer. Even under price discrimination, we still have the fundamental MR = MC rule for profit maximization in each market segment (see page 179 of Chapter 9). The extended profit-maximization rule under price discrimination must be:

$$MR_a = MR_b = MC$$

Going back to our graph, assume for simplicity that the firm's marginal cost is a fixed number—indicated by the height of the red horizontal marginal cost curve MCMC. Then $MR_a = MR_b = MC$ when the firm sells the quantity $Q_a^*$ to A customers (point $J$) and the quantity $Q_b^*$ to B customers (point $K$). Moreover, the demand curve for A customers tells us that selling quantity $Q_a^*$ to this group requires a price of $P_a$—the red point on demand curve $D_aD_a$ directly above $Q_a^*$. Similarly, the profit-maximizing price to B customers is $P_b$ on the B demand curve in Figure 12–4(b).

> To determine the profit-maximizing outputs and prices under price discrimination, do the following:
>
> 1. Draw the demand and marginal revenue curves for the different customer groups side by side.
>
> 2. Draw in the pertinent marginal cost as a horizontal line if MC is constant.
>
> 3. Find the profit-maximizing sales quantity for each customer group where the horizontal MC line cuts the MR curve for that group, so that MC = MR for each group.
>
> 4. Determine each customer group's profit-maximizing price by locating the point on the demand curve corresponding to the profit-maximizing quantity.

## IS PRICE DISCRIMINATION ALWAYS UNDESIRABLE?

The word *discrimination* is generally used to refer to an undesirable practice. However, *price* discrimination may not always be bad. Most people feel strongly that it is appropriate for the post office to charge the same price for all first-class letters going between two points in the United States, regardless of the differences in delivery costs. Similarly, most people approve of discounts on theater tickets sold to students or to senior citizens, even though those prices are obviously discriminatory. The same is widely agreed about lower doctor's fees for needy patients.

Other reasons, in addition to some standard of fairness or justice, may provide a defense for price discrimination in certain cases. One such case arises when it is impossible without price discrimination for a private firm to supply a product that customers want. For an illustration, go back to our first numerical example of price discrimination. Suppose that the total cost of producing 100 video games is $8,000, and the total cost of producing 1,100 video games is $30,000. Then our firm cannot cover its costs with a uniform, nondiscriminatory price. If it charged $75 to the 100 rich customers willing to pay that much, its $7,500 total revenue would fall short of its $8,000 total cost. Similarly, charging the uniform price of $25 to all 1,100 customers would yield total revenue of only $27,500, which is less than the $30,000 total cost. Thus, *any* uniform price would drive the firm out of business, depriving customers of the consumers' surplus from purchasing the product. But with discriminatory prices, we saw that the firm would earn, $32,500, enabling the firm to cover the $30,000 cost of supplying the requirements of both sets of customers.

It is even possible that price discrimination can make a product cheaper than it would otherwise be for all customers—even those who pay the higher prices. As you may imagine, this can be true only if there are significant economies of scale in the production of the commodity. Thus, suppose that price discrimination permits the firm to offer lower prices to certain customers, thereby attracting some business that it would not otherwise have. The firm's output will therefore increase. But scale economies will then reduce the firm's marginal costs. If marginal cost falls enough, even the "high-priced" customer group may end up paying less than it would in the absence of price discrimination.

The conclusion from this discussion is not that price discrimination is always a good thing. However, it does follow that it is sometimes desirable. In particular, we must recognize that a firm may be unable to cover its costs without price discrimination—a situation that some observers consider to be relatively common.

### The Puzzle Resolved: Competitive Local Telephone Service

We conclude our discussion of monopoly by returning to the puzzle that began this chapter: Why are local phone services around the country threatened by competition in an industry that was once considered the very definition of a natural monopoly? The answer is that there has been a change in the way that the federal government proposes to treat this industry.

Until recently, the market for local telephone service was considered a natural monopoly. Local and state governments disallowed competition in these markets because they believed that it would lead to wasteful duplication of large fixed costs and hence to higher prices. Instead, local utility commissions regulated these monopolies to ensure adequate service and reasonable prices. Recent changes in communications technology, however, combined with legislative action, have ripened this market for competition. Computers and satellite technology have reduced the investment costs of providing phone service, and the federal government has improved the prospects for competition with the enactment of the Telecommunications Act of 1996.

The act overturns state restrictions on competition in local and long-distance telephone service and removes barriers to entry that once kept new firms from entering these markets. Specifically, the act requires existing phone companies to allow new competitors access to their phone lines that connect customers, essentially turning these lines into a *shared* network available to all firms offering phone service. The new competitors must pay an access fee to route their customers' calls over the existing lines, but if the price is not too high, the access

will permit competition without requiring new firms to reproduce already existing plants and equipment.

The federal government has taken a legislative approach, turning an industry with huge start-up costs and economies of scale into one that firms may enter with much smaller investments. Thus, these new firms may be able to offer better service at lower rates. For now the issue is in the courts, with the established local monopolies battling prospective entrants over the price to be charged to entrants for access to local facilities.

Your own community may still have a monopoly providing local phone service, but, wherever you live, competition may be on the way. Soon, in addition to those annoying phone calls from long-distance providers, you may also be getting calls from local phone companies attempting to lure you onto their client lists.

## S U M M A R Y

1. A *pure monopoly* is a one-firm industry producing a product for which there are no close substitutes.

2. Monopoly can persist only if there are important cost advantages to single-firm operation or barriers to free entry. These barriers may be legal impediments (patents, licensing), the special risks faced by a potential entrant resulting from the need to incur large sunk investments, or the result of "dirty tricks" designed to make things tough for an entrant.

3. One important case of cost advantages is *natural monopoly:* instances where only one firm can survive because of important economies of large-scale production.

4. A monopoly has no supply curve. It maximizes its profit by producing an output at which its marginal revenue equals its marginal cost. Its price is given by the point on its demand curve corresponding to that output.

5. In a monopolistic industry, if demand and cost curves are the same as those of a competitive industry, and if the demand curve has a negative slope and the supply curve a positive slope, then monopoly output will be lower and price will be higher than those of the competitive industry.

6. Economists consider the fact that monopoly output tends to be below the competitive level to constitute an (undesirable) inefficiency.

7. Advertising may enable a monopoly to shift its demand curve above that of a comparable competitive industry's. Through economies such as large-scale input purchases, a monopoly may be able to shift its cost curves below those of a competitive industry.

8. A monopoly may be able to increase its profits by engaging in *price discrimination*—charging higher prices for the same goods to those of its customers who are less resistant to price increases, or failing to charge higher prices to customers whom it costs more to serve.

9. The profit-maximizing discriminatory prices, and corresponding sales volumes, for a firm with several different customer groups can be determined with the help of an extended rule for profit maximization: that the marginal revenue from sales to each customer group must equal the firm's marginal cost.

10. Price discrimination can sometimes be damaging to the public interest, but at other times it can be beneficial. Some firms cannot survive without it, and price discrimination may reduce prices to all customers if there are substantial economies of scale.

11. Any rise in costs generally hurts a monopolist. Because of the negatively sloping demand curve, a monopolist cannot simply pass on cost increases entirely to consumers.

## QUESTIONS FOR REVIEW

1. Which of the following industries are pure monopolies?

   a. The only supplier of heating fuel in an isolated town

   b. The only supplier of IBM notebook computers in town

   c. The only supplier of instant cameras

   Explain your answers.

2. Suppose that a monopoly industry produces less output than a similar competitive industry. Discuss why this may be considered socially undesirable.

3. If competitive firms earn zero economic profits, explain why anyone would invest money in them. (*Hint:* What is the role of the opportunity cost of capital in economic profit?)

4. The following are the demand and total cost schedules for Company Town Water, a local monopoly:

| Output in Gallons | Price per Gallon | Total Cost |
|---|---|---|
| 50,000 | $0.28 | $ 6,000 |
| 100,000 | 0.26 | 15,000 |
| 150,000 | 0.22 | 22,000 |
| 200,000 | 0.20 | 32,000 |
| 250,000 | 0.16 | 46,000 |
| 300,000 | 0.12 | 64,000 |

   How much output will Company Town Water produce, and what price will it charge? Will it earn a profit? How much? (*Hint:* You will first have to compute its MR and MC schedules.)

5. Show from the preceding table that for the water company, marginal revenue (per 50,000-gallon unit) is always less than price.

6. Suppose that a tax of $24 is levied on each item sold by a monopolist, and as a result, she decides to raise her price by exactly $24. Why may this decision be against her own best interests?

7. Use Figure 12–2 to show that Adam Smith was wrong when he claimed that a monopoly would always charge "the highest price which can be got."

8. MCI and Sprint have invested vast amounts of money in their fiber-optic networks, which are costly to construct but relatively cheap to operate. If both of them were to go bankrupt, why might this *not* result in a decrease in the competition facing AT&T? (*Hint:* At what price would the assets of the bankrupt companies be offered for sale?)

9. What does your answer to the preceding question tell you about ease or difficulty of entry into telecommunications?

10. A monopoly sells Frisbees to two customer groups. Group A has a downward-sloping straight-line demand curve, whereas the curve for Group B is infinitely elastic. Draw the graph determining the profit-maximizing discriminatory prices and sales to the two groups. What will be the price of Frisbees to Group B? Why? How is the price to Group A determined?

11. A firm cannot break even by charging uniform (nondiscriminatory) prices, but with price discrimination it can earn a small profit. Explain why in this case consumers *must* be better off if the firm is permitted to charge discriminatory prices.

12. It can be proved that, other things being equal, under price discrimination the price charged to some customer group will be higher the less elastic the demand curve of that group is. Why is that result plausible?

Neither fish nor fowl.

# BETWEEN COMPETITION AND MONOPOLY

Most productive activity in the United States, as in any advanced industrial society, falls somewhere between the two extreme market forms we have considered so far. So, if we want to understand the workings of the market mechanism in a real, modern economy, we must look somewhere between perfect competition and pure monopoly, at the hybrid market structures: *monopolistic competition* and *oligopoly*. Monopolistic competition is a market structure characterized by many small firms selling somewhat different products. Here each firm's output is so small relative to the total output of closely related and, hence, rival products that the firm does not expect its competitors to respond to or even to *notice* any changes in its own behavior.

Monopolistic competition or something close to it is widespread in retailing: shoe stores, restaurants, and gasoline stations are good examples. Most firms in our economy can be classified as monopolistic competitors, because even though they are small, such enterprises are abundant. We begin the chapter by using the theory of the firm described in Chapter 9 to analyze a monopolistically competitive firm's price-output decisions, then we consider the role of entry and exit, as we did in Chapter 10.

Finally we turn to oligopoly, a market structure in which a few large firms dominate the market. The steel, automobile, and airplane manufacturing industries are good examples of oligopolies, despite the increasing number of strong foreign competitors. Probably the largest share of U.S. economic output comes from oligopolists. Although they are fewer in number than monopolistic competitors, many oligopoly firms are extremely large, with annual sales exceeding the total outputs of most countries in the world and even of some of the smaller industrial European countries (see the accompanying box, "A Global Colossus That Is Richer Than Most Nations").

One critical feature distinguishing an oligopolist from either a monopolist or a perfect competitor is that oligopolists care very much about what other firms in the industry do. The resulting *interdependence* of decisions, we will see, makes oligopoly very hard to analyze, and results in a wide range of behavior patterns. Consequently, economic theory uses not just one but many models of oligopoly (some of which we will review in this chapter), and it is often hard to know which model to apply in any particular situation.

We will also see that the case for free markets is weakened where monopolistic competition or oligopoly occur.

### Some Puzzling Observations

We need to study the hybrid market structures considered in this chapter because we cannot explain many economic phenomena via theories of perfect competition or pure monopoly. Here are three examples:

**Case 1: Why Are There So Many Retailers?**  You have seen road intersections with gasoline stations on each corner. Often, two or three of them have no customers at the pumps. There seem to be more gas stations than the number of cars warrant, with a corresponding waste of labor, time, equipment, and other resources. Why—and how—do they all stay in business?

**Case 2: Why Do Oligopolists Advertise More Than "More Competitive" Firms?**  Although some advertising is primarily designed to inform (for example, help-wanted ads), much of the advertising on television, in magazines, and elsewhere is part of a competitive struggle for our business. Many big companies use advertising as a principal weapon as they battle for customers, and advertising budgets can constitute very large shares of their expenditures. Such firms spend literally hundreds of millions of dollars per year on advertising, seeking to leap ahead of rivals. Indeed, in 1997 Procter & Gamble, Philip Morris, and Chrysler each spent more than a billion dollars on ads, and General Motors spent more than two billion. Yet critics often accuse oligopolistic industries containing only a few giant firms of being "uncompetitive." Farming, on the other

## ● A GLOBAL COLOSSUS THAT IS RICHER THAN MOST NATIONS

General Motors (GM) is the world's largest company in sales and share of global economic output. When strikes shut down its North American operations, as happened in the summer of 1998, the entire American economy feels the blow.

SOURCE: "Keith Bradsher, "Forget Microsoft. G.M. Is Still the Biggest Kid on the Block," *The New York Times,* July 26, 1998, section 4, p. 4.

**The World's Biggest Company ...**

The revenues of the world s biggest corporations and six other selected companies, with their global rank and number of employees, in 1997.

| Company | (rank) | Revenue | Employees |
|---|---|---|---|
| GM | (1) | $178 billion | 698,000 |
| Ford | (2) | 154 | 364,000 |
| Mitsui | (3) | 143 | 40,000 |
| Mitsubishi | (4) | 129 | 36,000 |
| Shell | (5) | 128 | 105,000 |
| Wal-Mart | (8) | 119 | 825,000 |
| GE | (12) | 91 | 276,000 |
| AT&T | (32) | 53 | 128,000 |
| Boeing | (39) | 46 | 239,000 |
| Intel | (125) | 25 | 64,000 |
| Microsoft | (400) | 11 | 22,000 |

**... Produces More Than Many Nations**

GM s revenue and the gross domestic product of 10 nations, ranked globally in 1997.

| Nation | (rank) | GDP |
|---|---|---|
| Sweden | (20) | $250 billion |
| Austria | (21) | 226 |
| Indonesia | (22) | 226 |
| Thailand | (23) | 185 |
| Turkey | (24) | 181 |
| *GM Revenue* | | 178 |
| Denmark | (25) | 174 |
| Norway | (26) | 158 |
| Hong Kong | (27) | 155 |
| Poland | (28) | 134 |
| Saudi Arabia | (29) | 126 |

hand, is considered as close to perfect competition as any industry in our economy, but few, if any, individual farmers spend anything at all on advertising.[1] Why do these allegedly "uncompetitive" oligopolists make such heavy use of combative advertising whereas very competitive farmers do not?

**Case 3: Why Do Oligopolists Seem to Change Their Prices So Infrequently?** Many prices in the economy change from minute to minute. Every day, newspapers and other media publish the latest prices of commodities such as soybeans, pork bellies, and copper. If you want to buy one of these commodities at 11:45 A.M. today, you cannot use yesterday's price—or even the price from 11:44 A.M. today—because it has probably changed already. Yet prices of products

[1] But farmers associations, such as Sunkist and various dairy groups, do spend money on advertising

such as cars and refrigerators generally change only a few times a year at most, even during fairly rapid inflation. Firms that sell cars and refrigerators know that product and input market conditions change all the time. Why don't they adjust their prices more often? This chapter will offer answers to each of these questions.

## ■ MONOPOLISTIC COMPETITION

**Monopolistic competition** refers to a market in which products are heterogeneous but which is otherwise the same as a market that is perfectly competitive.

For years, economic theory told us little about market forms in between the two extreme cases of pure monopoly and perfect competition. Then, during the 1930s, Edward Chamberlin of Harvard University and Joan Robinson of Cambridge University (working separately) partially filled this gap and helped to make economic theory more realistic. The market structure they analyzed is called **monopolistic competition.**

### CHARACTERISTICS OF MONOPOLISTIC COMPETITION

A market is said to operate under conditions of monopolistic competition if it satisfies four requirements, three of which are the same as those for perfect competition:

- *Numerous participants*—that is, many buyers and sellers, all of whom are small
- *Freedom of exit and entry*
- *Perfect information*
- *Heterogeneous products*—as far as the buyer is concerned, each seller's product differs at least somewhat from every other's

Notice that monopolistic competition differs from perfect competition in only the last respect. Perfect competition assumes that the products of different firms in an industry are identical, but under monopolistic competition products differ from seller to seller—in quality, packaging, supplementary services offered (such as windshield washing at a gas station), or merely in terms of consumers' perceptions. The attributes that differentiate products need not be "real" in any objective or directly measurable sense. For example, differences in packaging or in associated services can and do distinguish otherwise identical products. On the other hand, two products may perform quite differently in quality tests, but if consumers know nothing about this difference, it is irrelevant.

In contrast to a perfect competitor, a monopolistic competitor's demand curve is negatively sloped. Because each seller's product is different, each caters to a set of customers who vary in their loyalty to the particular product. If the firm raises its price somewhat, it will drive *some* of its customers to competitors' offerings, but customers who strongly favor the firm's product will not switch. If one monopolistic competitor lowers its price, it may expect to attract some trade from rivals. But, because different products are imperfect substitutes, it will not attract away *all* of the rivals' business.

Thus, if Harriet's Hot Dog House reduces its price slightly, it will attract those customers of Sam's Sausage Shop who were nearly indifferent between the two. If Harriet were to cut her prices further, she would gain some customers who have a slightly greater preference for Sam's product. But even a big cut in Harriet's price will not bring her the hard-core sausage lovers who hate hot dogs. Therefore, monopolistic competitors face a negatively sloped demand curve, like that of a monopolist, rather than horizontal, like that of a perfect competitor who will lose all his business if he insists on a higher price than a rival's.

Because consumers see each product as distinct from all others, a monopolistically competitive firm appears to have something akin to a small monopoly. Can we therefore expect it to earn more than zero economic profit? As with a perfect competitor, perhaps monopolistic competitors will obtain economic profits in the short run. But in the long run, high economic profits will attract new entrants into a monopolistically competitive market—not with products *identical* to an existing firm's, but with products sufficiently similar to absorb the excess economic profits.

If McDonald's is thriving at a particular location, it can confidently expect Burger King or some other fast-food outlet to open a franchise nearby shortly. When one seller adopts a new, attractive package, rivals will soon follow suit with slightly different designs and colors of their own. For example, when Coke brought back its curved glass bottle in 1994, Pepsi countered with a new cube-shaped package that fits easily into the refrigerator. In this way, freedom of entry ensures that the monopolistically competitive firm earns no higher return on its capital in the long run than that capital could earn elsewhere: in other words, the firm earns no excess economic profits. Just as under perfect competition, competition will drive price down to equal average cost, including the opportunity cost of capital. In this sense, though its product differs somewhat from everyone else's offering, the firm under monopolistic competition has no more monopoly *power* than one operating under perfect competition.

Let us now examine the process that ensures that competition will drive economic profits down to zero in the long run, even under monopolistic competition, and see what prices and outputs that process fosters.

## PRICE AND OUTPUT DETERMINATION UNDER MONOPOLISTIC COMPETITION

The *short-run* equilibrium of the firm under monopolistic competition differs little from equilibrium under monopoly. Because the firm faces a downward-sloping demand curve (labeled *D* in Figure 13–1), its marginal revenue (MR) curve will lie below its demand curve. Like any firm, a monopolistic competitor maximizes profits by producing the output at which marginal revenue equals marginal cost (MC). In Figure 13–1, the profit-maximizing output for a hypothetical gas station is 12,000 gallons per week, and it sells this output at a price of $1 per gallon (point *P* on the demand curve). The firm makes 10 cents per gallon in profits, as depicted by the vertical distance from *C* to *P*.

This analysis, you will note, looks much like Figure 12–2 for a monopoly. The main difference is that monopolistic competitors are likely to face a much flatter demand curve than pure monopolists do, because many products serve as close substitutes for the monopolistic competitor's product. If our gas station raises its price to $1.30 per gallon, most of its customers will go across the street. If it lowers its price to 70 cents, it will have long lines at its pumps.

The gas station depicted in Figure 13–1 is enjoying economic profits. Because average cost at 12,000 gallons per week is only 90 cents per gallon (point *C*), the station makes a profit of 10 cents per gallon on gasoline sales, or $1,200 per week in total, shown by the shaded rectangle. Under monopoly, such profits can persist. But under monopolistic competition they cannot, because economic profits will entice new firms to enter the market. Although the new gas stations will not offer the identical product, they will offer products that are close enough to take away some business from our firm. (For example, they may sell Conoco or Shell gasoline instead of Exxon.)

When more firms enter the market, each firm's demand curve will shift downward (to the left). But how far will it shift? The answer is basically the same as it was under perfect competition. Market entry will cease only when the most that the firm can earn is zero economic profit—exactly the same return the firm can earn elsewhere.

**FIGURE 13–1**

**Short-Run Equilibrium of the Firm under Monopolistic Competition**

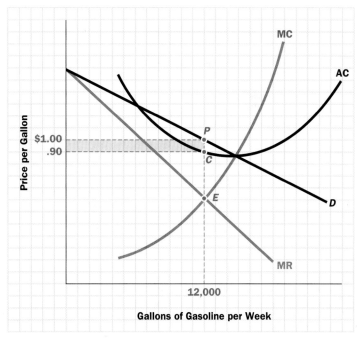

FIGURE 13-2

**Long-Run Equilibrium of the Firm under Monopolistic Competition**

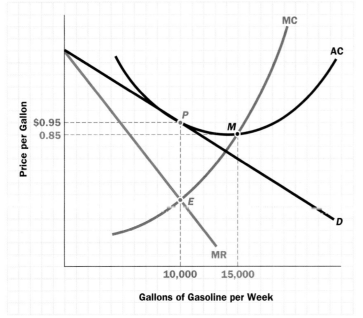

Figure 13–2 depicts the same monopolistically competitive firm as in Figure 13–1 *after* the adjustment to the long-run equilibrium is complete. The demand curve—and hence also the MR curve—has been pushed down so far by the entry of new rivals that when the firm equates MC and MR in order to maximize profits (point *E*), it simultaneously equates price *(P)* and average cost (AC) so that profits are zero (point *P*). As compared to the short-run equilibrium depicted in Figure 13–1, price in long-run equilibrium is *lower* (95 cents per gallon versus $1), *more firms* participate in the industry, and each firm is producing a *smaller* output (10,000 gallons versus 12,000) at a *higher* average cost per gallon (95 cents versus 90 cents).[2] In general:

*Long-run equilibrium under monopolistic competition requires that the firm's demand curve be tangent to its average cost curve.*

Why? Because if the two curves intersected, firms could produce output quantities at which price would exceed average cost, which means that participants would be earning economic profits that would draw an influx of new close-substitute products. Similarly, if the average cost curve failed to touch the demand curve altogether, the firm would incur an economic loss—it would be unable to obtain returns equal to those that its capital can get elsewhere, and firms would leave the industry.

This analysis of entry is quite similar to the perfectly competitive case. Moreover, the notion that firms under monopolistic competition earn exactly zero economic profits seems to correspond fairly well to what we see in the real world. Gas station operators, whose markets fit the characteristics of monopolistic competition, do not earn notably higher profits than do small farmers, who operate under conditions closer to perfect competition.

## THE EXCESS CAPACITY THEOREM AND RESOURCE ALLOCATION

One economically significant difference arises between perfect and monopolistic competition. Look at Figure 13–2 again. The tangency point between the average cost and demand curves, point *P*, occurs along the *negatively sloping portion* of the average cost curve, because *P* is the only point where the AC curve has the same (negative) slope as the demand curve. If the AC curve is ∪-shaped, the tangency point must therefore lie above and to the left of the *minimum point* on the average cost curve, point *M*. In other words, under monopolistic competition, the demand curve hits the average cost curve in a region where average costs are still declining. Average costs have yet to reach their lowest point. By contrast, the perfectly competitive firm's demand curve is horizontal, so tangency must take place at the minimum point on the average cost curve You can easily confirm this by referring back to Figure 10–9(a). This difference leads to the following important conclusion:

*Under monopolistic competition in the long run, the firm will tend to produce an output lower than that which minimizes its unit costs, and hence unit costs of the monopolistic competitor will be higher than necessary. Because the level of output that corresponds to minimum average cost is naturally considered to be the firm's optimal capacity, this result has been called the excess capacity theorem of monopolistic competition. Thus, monopolistic competition tends to lead firms to have unused or wasted capacity.*

---

[2] *Exercise:* Show that if the demand curve fell still further, the firm would incur a loss. What would then happen in the long run?

It follows that if every firm under monopolistic competition were to expand its output, cost per unit of output would be reduced. But we must be careful about jumping to policy conclusions from that observation. It does *not* follow that *every* monopolistically competitive firm *should* produce more. After all, such an overall increase in industry output means that a smaller portion of the economy's resources will be available for other uses; from the information at hand, we have no way of knowing whether that leaves us better or worse off in terms of social benefits.

Yet the situation depicted in Figure 13–2 probably still represents a substantial *inefficiency*. Although it is not clear that society would gain if *every* firm were to achieve lower costs by expanding its production, society *can* save resources if firms combine into a smaller number of larger companies that produce the same total output. For example, suppose that in the situation shown in Figure 13–2, 15 monopolistically competitive firms each sell 10,000 gallons of gasoline per week. The total cost of this output, according to the figures given in the diagram, would be:

Number of firms × Output per firm × Cost per unit = 15 × 10,000 × \$.95 = \$142,500

If, instead, the number of stations were cut to 10 and each sold 15,000 gallons, total production would be unchanged. But total costs would fall to 10 × 15,000 × \$.85 = \$127,500, a net saving of \$15,000 *without any cut in total output.*

This result does not depend on the particular numbers that we used in our illustration. It follows directly from the observation that lowering the cost per unit must always reduce the total cost of producing *any* given industry output. Society must gain in the sense of getting the same total output as before but at a lower cost. After all, which do you prefer—a dozen cans of soda for 60 cents each or a dozen cans of soda for 35 cents each?

### Explaining the Abundance of Retailers

The excess capacity theorem explains one of the puzzles mentioned at the start of this chapter. The highway intersection with four gas stations, where two could serve the available customers with little increase in customer delays and at lower costs, is a real-world example of excess capacity.

The excess capacity theorem seems to imply that too many sellers participate in monopolistically competitive markets and that society would benefit from a reduction in their numbers. However, such a conclusion may be a bit hasty. Even if a smaller number of larger firms can reduce costs, society may not benefit from the change because it will leave consumers a smaller range of choice. Because all products differ at least slightly under monopolistic competition, a reduction in the number of *firms* means that the number of different *products* falls, as well. We achieve greater efficiency at the cost of greater standardization.

"Why have we come? Because only Earth offers the rock-bottom prices and wide selection of men's, women's, and children's clothing in the styles and sizes we're looking for."

In some cases, consumers may agree that this trade-off represents a net gain, particularly if the variety of products available was initially so great that it only served to confuse them. But for some products, most consumers would probably agree that the diversity of choice is worth the extra cost involved. After all, we would probably save money on clothing if every student were required to wear a uniform. But because the uniform is likely to be too hot for some students, too cool for other students, and aesthetically displeasing to almost everyone else, would the cost saving really be a net benefit?

## ■ OLIGOPOLY

An **oligopoly** is a market dominated by a few sellers, at least several of which are large enough relative to the total market to be able to influence the market price.

An **oligopoly** is a market dominated by a few sellers, at least several of which are large enough relative to the total market that they may well be able to influence the market price.

In highly developed economies, it is not monopoly, but *oligopoly*, that is virtually synonymous with "big business." Any oligopolistic industry includes a group of giant firms, each of which keeps a watchful eye on the actions of the others. Under oligopoly, rivalry among firms takes its most direct and active form. Here one encounters such actions and reactions as frequent new product introductions, free samples, and aggressive—if not downright nasty—advertising campaigns. A firm's price decision may elicit cries of pain from its rivals, and firms are often engaged in a continuing battle in which they plan strategies day by day and each major decision induces direct responses by rival firms.

Notice that the definition of oligopoly does not mention the degree of product differentiation. Some oligopolies sell products that are essentially identical (such as steel plate from different steel manufacturers), whereas others sell products that are quite different in consumers' eyes (for example, Chevrolets, Fords and Hondas). Some oligopolistic industries also contain a considerable number of smaller firms (example: soft drink manufacturers), but they are nevertheless considered oligopolies because a few large firms carry out the bulk of the industry's business, and smaller participants must follow their larger rivals' lead to survive at the margins of the industry. As shown in the accompanying box, "The Mad Scramble to Differentiate the Product," oligopolistic firms often seek to create unique products—unique, at least, in consumers' perceptions. To the extent that an oligopolistic firm can create a unique product in terms of features, location, or appeal, it protects itself from the pressures of competition that will force down its prices and eat into its sales.

Managers of large, oligopolistic firms who have occasion to study economics are somewhat taken aback by the notion of perfect competition, because it is devoid of all harsh competitive activity as they know it. Remember that under perfect competition, firm managers make no price decisions—they simply accept the prices dictated by market forces and adjust their output accordingly. As we observed at the beginning of the chapter, a perfectly competitive firm does not advertise; it adopts no sales gimmicks; it does not even know who most of its competitors are. But because oligopolists have some degree of influence on market forces, they do not enjoy such luxurious anonymity. They worry about prices, spend fortunes on advertising, and try to understand or even predict their rivals' behavior patterns.

### Why Oligopolists Advertise but Perfectly Competitive Firms Generally Do Not

The two reasons for such divergent behavior should be clear, and they explain the puzzling fact that oligopolists advertise far more than the supposedly far more competitive firms in perfectly competitive markets. First, a perfectly competitive firm can sell all it wants at the current market price, so why should it waste money on advertising? By contrast, General Motors (GM) and Toyota cannot sell all the cars

---

### ● THE MAD SCRAMBLE TO DIFFERENTIATE THE PRODUCT

---

Competition is fierce in the world of business, and it's not easy to lure customers away from your rivals. McDonald's hit upon a good thing:

Liberal, Kan.—One recent evening after 9 P.M., Jody Hibbert stopped by the only McDonald's in this west Kansas town for the fourth time that day. She wasn't there for the food.

Like a multitude of Americans, Mrs. Hibbert is hooked on Teenie Beanie Babies. She didn't want to miss getting all 12 of the critters starring in a promotion that is shaping up as one of the most successful marketing campaigns ever. . . . McDonald's Corp. is striking gold by simply repeating a Teenie Beanie Babies promotion that was a hit last spring. This year's babyfest began just two weeks ago and was supposed to last a month. But many metropolitan-area McDonald's were cleaned out of the toys days ago, and even rural pockets like Liberal expect to sell their last ones this weekend. . . .

All this is putting happy faces on McDonald's executives and the company's 2,772 franchisees. "Our cash flow has just been super," says Mark Benzinger, owner of the burger chain's outlet in Liberal. He credits the toys with pushing his sales up more than 30% from a year ago. Other franchisees report similar results.

Last year, the initial Teenie Beanie giveaway overwhelmed McDonald's and its famed marketing department. . . . It didn't anticipate the scramble miniatures would cause. At some restaurants police had to control crowds. Almost overnight about 80 million toys were gobbled up.

SOURCE: The *Wall Street Journal*, June 5, 1998, pp. B1 and B8.

they want at the current price. Because they face negatively sloped (and thus less than perfectly elastic) demand curves, if they want to sell more, they must either reduce prices (to move along the demand curve toward greater quantities) or advertise more (to shift their demand curves outward).

Second, because the public believes that the products supplied by firms in a perfectly competitive industry are identical, if Firm A advertises its product, the advertisement is just as likely to bring customers to Firm B. Under oligopoly, however, consumer products are often *not* identical. Ford advertises to convince consumers that its automobiles are better than Chrysler's or Subaru's. If the advertising campaign succeeds, Chrysler and Subaru will be hurt and probably will respond with more advertising of their own. Thus, the firms in an oligopoly with differentiated products must compete via advertising, whereas perfectly competitive firms gain little or nothing by doing so.

## WHY OLIGOPOLISTIC BEHAVIOR IS SO HARD TO ANALYZE

Firms in an oligopolistic industry, in particular the largest of those firms, thus have some latitude in choosing product prices and outputs. Further, to survive and thrive in an oligopolistic environment, firms must take direct account of rivals' responses. Both of these features complicate the analysis of the oligopolistic firm's behavior and prevent unambiguous conclusions about resource allocation under oligopoly. Oligopoly is much more difficult to analyze than other forms of economic organization, because oligopolistic decisions are, by their very nature, *interdependent*. Oligopolists *recognize* that the outcomes of their decisions depend on rivals' responses. For example, Ford managers know that their actions will probably lead to reactions by General Motors, which in turn may require a readjustment in Ford's plans, thereby modifying GM's response, and so on. Where such a sequence of moves and countermoves may lead is difficult enough to ascertain. But the fact that Ford executives know all this in advance, and may try to second-guess or predict GM's reactions as they initially decide on a marketing tactic, makes even that first step difficult, if not impossible, to analyze and predict.

Truly, almost anything can and sometimes does happen under oligopoly. The early railroad kings went so far as to employ gangs of hoodlums who fought pitched battles to prevent rival lines' operations. At the other extreme, oligopolistic firms have employed overt or covert forms of collusion to avoid rivalry altogether—to transform an oligopolistic industry, at least temporarily, into a monopolistic one. In other instances, oligopolistic firms seem to have arranged to live and let live, via price leadership (discussed later) or geographic allocations, dividing up customers by agreement among the firms.

Because of this rich variety of behavior patterns, it should not be surprising that economists use a number of oligopoly models. Because oligopolies in the real world are so diverse, oligopoly models in the theoretical world should also come in various shapes and sizes. Oligopoly theory contains some really remarkable pieces of economic analysis, a few of which we will review in the following sections.

## A SHOPPING LIST

An introductory course cannot hope to explain all of the different oligopoly models. This section offers a quick general review of some oligopolistic behavior models. In the remainder of the chapter, we turn our attention to a particularly interesting set of models that use methods such as game theory to predict firm behavior under oligopoly.

**IGNORING INTERDEPENDENCE**   One simple approach to the problem of oligopolistic interdependence is to assume that the oligopolists themselves ignore it—that they behave as if their actions will not elicit reactions from their rivals. Perhaps an oligopolist, finding the "if they think that we think that they think" chain of reasoning too complex, will decide to ignore rivals' behavior. The firm may then just seek to maximize profits, assuming that its decisions will not affect its rivals' strategies. In this case, economists can analyze oligopoly in the same way they look at monopoly, which we described in Chapter 12. Probably no oligopolist totally ignores all of its major rivals' decisions. But many of them seem to do so as they make their more routine decisions, which are nevertheless often quite important.

**STRATEGIC INTERACTION**   Although *some* oligopolists may ignore interdependence *some* of the time, models based on such behavior probably do not offer a general explanation for *most* oligopoly behavior *most* of the time. The reason is simple. Because they operate in the same market, the price and output decisions of soap makers Brand X and Brand Y *really are* interdependent.

Suppose, for example, that Brand X, Inc., managers decide to cut its price to $1.05, on the assumption that Brand Y, Inc., will continue to charge $1.12 per box. X decides to manufacture 5 million boxes per year and to spend $1 million per year on advertising. It may find itself surprised when Brand Y, Inc., cuts its price to $1 per box, raises production to 8 million boxes per year, and sponsors the Super Bowl! If so, Brand X's profits will suffer, and the company will wish it had not cut its price in the first place. Most important for our purposes, Brand X managers will learn not to ignore interdependence in the future.

For many oligopolies, then, competition may resemble military operations involving tactics, strategies, moves, and countermoves. Thus, we must consider models that deal explicitly with oligopolistic interdependence.

**CARTELS**   The opposite of ignoring interdependence occurs when all firms in an oligopoly try to do something about their interdependence and agree to set price and output, acting as a monopolist would. In a **cartel,** firms collude directly to coordinate their actions to transform the industry into a giant monopoly.

A **cartel** is a group of sellers of a product who have joined together to control its production, sale, and price in the hope of obtaining the advantages of monopoly.

---

### ● VENEZUELAN ACCUSATION AGAINST IRAN HITS OIL PRICES

World oil prices slipped yesterday after Venezuela accused Iran of breaking the Riyadh pact on production.

Luis Giusti, president of Petroleos de Venezuela, said Iran was producing 250,000 barrels a day above the level agreed at the emergency meeting of Saudi Arabia, Mexico and Venezuela in March.

The cuts—ratified by the Organization of Petroleum Exporting Countries but also involving producers from outside the organization—were an attempt to support the oil price. However, the markets have appeared skeptical that the production limits will have a real impact on long-term oil supplies. . . . At the close of trading on London's International Petroleum Exchange, the benchmark August contract for Brent crude was $12.95 a barrel, compared with Friday's close of $13.55.

SOURCE: *Financial Times*, Commodities and Agriculture, July 7, 1998, p. 34.

A notable cartel is the Organization of Petroleum Exporting Countries (OPEC), which first began making joint decisions in the 1970s. For a while, OPEC was one of the most spectacularly successful cartels in history. By restricting output, the member nations managed to quadruple the price of oil between 1973 and 1974. Then, unlike most cartels, which come apart in internal bickering or for other reasons, OPEC held together through two worldwide recessions and a variety of unsettling political events. It struck again with huge price increases between 1979 and 1980. In the mid-1980s its members began to act in ways that did not promote the interest of the entire industry and oil prices tumbled, but OPEC still dominates the world oil market. (See the accompanying box, "Venezuelan Accusations against Iran Hit Oil Prices," for more recent news of OPEC and oil prices.)

OPEC's early success is hardly the norm. Cartels are difficult to organize and are even more difficult to enforce. Firms find it hard to agree on such things as the amount by which each will reduce its output in order to help push up the price. For a cartel to survive, each member must agree to produce no more output than that assigned to it by the group. Yet once the cartel drives up the price and increases profitability, each member faces the temptation to offer secret discounts that lure some of the very profitable business away from other members. When this happens, or even when members begin to suspect one another of doing so, collusive agreement often begins to come apart. Each member begins suspecting the others and is tempted to cut price first, before the others beat it to the punch.

Cartels, therefore, usually adopt elaborate policing arrangements. In effect, they spy on each member firm to make sure it does not sell more than it is supposed to or shave the price below that chosen by the cartel. This means that cartels are unlikely to succeed or to last very long if the firms sell many, varied products whose prices are difficult to compare and whose outputs are difficult to monitor. In addition, if firms frequently negotiate prices on a customer-by-customer basis and often offer special discounts, a cartel may be almost impossible to arrange.

Many economists consider cartels to be the worst form of market organization, in terms of efficiency and consumer welfare. A successful cartel may end up charging the monopoly price and obtaining monopoly profits. But because the firms do not actually combine operations, cartels offer the public no offsetting benefits in the form of economies of large-scale production. For these and other reasons, open collusion among firms is illegal in the United States, as we will see in Chapter 20, and outright cartel arrangements rarely occur within the United States, though cartels

Antitrust laws unequivocally prohibit price fixing—collusion among competitors in which they agree on their pricing policies (see Chapter 20). But suppose that the firms in an industry, recognizing their interdependence, simply decide to "go along with" each other's decisions? Is this collusion by long distance? Should it be declared illegal? Should the government require such a firm to "make believe" that it does not know how competitors will respond to its price moves? Must firms act as if they were not interdependent? If such requirements make no sense, what should the government require of oligopolistic firms?

The airline industry constantly illustrates this issue and its complexities. In 1992, American Airlines decided that the vast number of different airline fares and discounts hurt all airlines and that the industry needed a simplified fare structure. American offered a new, simplified pricing plan called "value pricing," in the hope that other airlines would copy that structure widely. But a few weeks later, Northwest Airlines introduced a special vacation travel deal that undercut American's pricing. This led to a price war, and American had to withdraw its plan, losing considerable money in the process. In this case, American's rivals did not go along with a price leader's decision.

In a more recent set of events, matters worked out differently. The airlines, which have lost money for years, have been seeking ways to cut costs by reducing wages, firing employees, and so on. As part of these cost-cutting efforts, Delta Airlines announced in early 1995 that it was capping

payments to travel agents for each ticket sold. As it moved first to make the first such cut in 10 years, Delta feared (as we know from its internal memoranda) that if the other airlines did not do the same, travel agents would stop booking passengers on Delta. Everything depended on whether other airlines would support Delta's new policy. They did. Within a week of Delta's announcement, the seven largest airlines each announced (apparently without consulting one another) that they would adopt Delta's ceiling on payments to travel agents. The travel agents sued, charging tacit collusion. The case was settled out of court with a compromise.

are common in some other countries. Only one major exception occurs in the United States: Government regulations have sometimes forced industries such as railroads and gas pipeline transportation to behave as cartels. Regulations prohibit these firms from undercutting the prices set by the regulatory agencies—an exception that we will discuss in Chapter 20.

**PRICE LEADERSHIP AND TACIT COLLUSION**    Overt collusion—in which firms meet to decide on prices and outputs—is quite rare. But some observers think that *tacit collusion*—where firms, without meeting together, do unto their competitors as they hope their competitors will do unto them—occurs quite commonly among oligopolists in our economy. Oligopolists who do not want to rock a very profitable boat may seek to find some indirect way of communicating with one another, signaling their intentions and managing the market accordingly. Each tacitly colluding firm hopes that if it does not make things too difficult for its competitors, its rivals will return the favor. For example, the three main makers of infant formula—Abbott Laboratories, Bristol-Myers Squibb Co., and American Home—were accused of conspiring against competitors by keeping their wholesale prices only a few cents apart. The formula makers denied any wrongdoing. (See the accompanying Policy Debate box, "Acting on Recognized Interdependence versus 'Tacit Collusion'," for another example.)

One common form of tacit collusion is **price leadership,** an arrangement in which one firm in the industry, in effect, makes pricing decisions for the entire group. Other firms are expected to adopt the prices set by the price leader, even

Under **price leadership,** one firm sets the price for the industry and the others follow.

though no explicit agreement exists, only tacit consent. Often, the price leader will be the largest firm in the industry. But in some price-leadership arrangements, the leadership role may rotate from one firm to another. For example, analysts suggested that for many years the steel industry conformed to the price-leadership model, with U.S. Steel and Bethlehem Steel assuming the leadership role at different times.

Price leadership *does* overcome some problems that result from oligopolistic inter-dependence, although it does not provide the only possible way of doing so. If Brand X, Inc., acts as price leader for the soap suds industry, it can predict how Brand Y, Inc., will react to any price increases it announces: Brand Y will match the increases. Similarly, Brand Z executives will be able to predict Brand Y's behavior as long as the price-leadership arrangement holds up.

One problem besetting price leadership is that, although the oligopolists as an industry may benefit by avoiding a damaging **price war,** the *firms* may not benefit equally. The price leading firm may be able to enhance its own profits more easily than any of the other firms in the group can. But if the price leader does not con-sider its rivals' welfare as it makes price decisions, it may find itself dethroned! Like cartels, such arrangements can easily break down.

In a **price war,** each competing firm is determined to sell at a price that is lower than the prices of its rivals, usually regardless of whether that price covers the pertinent cost. Typically, in such a price war, Firm A cuts its price below Firm B's; then B retaliates by undercutting A, and so on and so on until one or more of the firms surrender and let themselves be undersold.

## SALES MAXIMIZATION: AN OLIGOPOLY MODEL WITH INTERDEPENDENCE IGNORED

Early in our analysis of the firm we discussed the profit maximization hypothesis, and we noted that firms have other possible objectives. Among these alternative goals, one has attracted much attention: *sales maximization.*

Modern industrial firms are managed by people who are not the owners of the companies. Paid executives manage the firms, working for the company on a full-time basis. These managers may begin to believe that whatever is good for them as individuals must be good for the company. The owners may be a large and diffuse group of stockholders, most of whom own only a tiny fraction of the outstanding stock. They may take little interest in the company's day-to-day operations and may feel no real sense of ownership. In such a situa-tion, managers' goals may influence company decisions more heavily than the owners' goal of profit maximization.

Some statistical evidence, for example, sug-gests that management's compensation often relates more directly to company *size*, as mea-sured by sales volume, than to *profit.* The pres-ident of a large firm generally fetches a much higher salary—and bigger incentive rewards—than the president of a tiny company. Therefore, firm managers may select price-output combi-nations that maximize *sales* rather than profits. But does sales maximization lead to different outcomes than profit maximization? We shall see shortly that the answer is yes.

The diagram in Figure 13–3 should be famil-iar by now. It shows the marginal cost (MC) and average cost (AC) curves for a soap suds firm—in this case Brand X, Inc.—along with its demand and marginal revenue (MR) curves. We have used such diagrams before and thus know that if the company wants to maximize profits, it will select point *A*, where MC = MR. Brand X will produce 2.5 million boxes of soap suds

**FIGURE 13-3**

**Sales-Maximization Equilibrium**

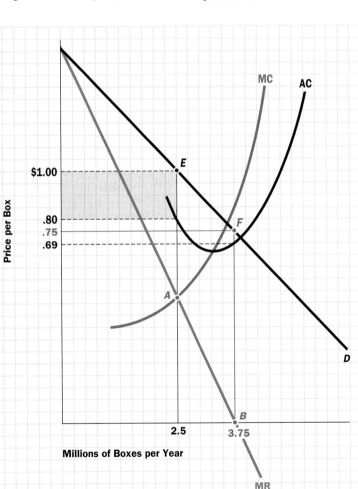

per year and sell them at $1 each (point *E* on the demand curve above *A*). Because average cost at this level of output is only 80 cents per box, X earns 20 cents profit per unit. Total profits are therefore $.20 × 2,500,000 = $500,000 per year. This is the highest attainable profit level for Brand X, Inc.

Now what if Brand X wants to maximize sales revenue instead? In this case, it will want to keep producing until MR falls to *zero*; that is, it will select point *B*. Why? By definition, MR is the *additional* revenue obtained by raising output by 1 unit. If the firm wishes to maximize revenue, then whenever MR is positive, it will want to increase output further, and any time that MR becomes negative, X management will want to decrease output. Only when MR = 0 can management possibly have maximized sales revenue.[3]

Thus, if Brand X, Inc., is a sales maximizer, it will produce 3.75 million boxes of soap suds per year (point *B*), and charge 75 cents per box (point *F*). Because average costs at this level of production are only 69 cents per box, profit per unit is 6 cents and, with 3.75 million units sold, total profit is $225,000. Naturally, this profit is substantially less than what the firm can achieve if it reduces output to the profit-maximizing level. But this is not the goal of X's management. Its sales revenue at point *B* is 75 cents per unit times 3.75 million units, or $2,812,500, whereas at point *A* it was only $2,500,000 (2.5 million units at $1.00 each). We conclude that:

> If a firm is maximizing sales revenue, it will produce more output and charge a lower price than it would if it were maximizing profits.

Figure 13–3 clearly shows that this result holds for Brand X, Inc. But does it always hold? The answer is yes. Look again at Figure 13–3, but ignore the numbers on the axes. At point *A*, where MR = MC, marginal revenue must be positive because it equals marginal cost (which, we may assume, is *always* positive—output can never be increased at zero additional cost). At point *B*, MR is equal to zero. Because the marginal revenue curve slopes negatively, the point where it reaches zero (point *B*) must necessarily correspond to a higher output level than does the point where it cuts the marginal cost curve (point *A*). Thus, sales-maximizing firms always produce more than profit-maximizing firms and, to sell this greater volume of output, they must charge lower prices. *Exercise:* In the graph how much below maximum profit is total profit under sales maximization?

## The Kinked Demand Curve Model[4]

Another oligopoly analysis model accounts for the alleged "stickiness" in oligopolistic pricing, meaning that prices in oligopolistic markets change far less frequently than do competitive market prices—one of the puzzling phenomena with which we began this chapter. The prices of corn, soybeans, pork bellies, and silver, all commodities that trade in markets with large numbers of buyers and sellers, change second by second. But products supplied by oligopolists such as cars, televisions, and refrigerators usually change prices only every few months or even more rarely. These products seem to resist frequent price changes, even in inflationary periods.

One reason for such "sticky" prices may be that when an oligopolist cuts its product's price, it can never predict how its rivals will react. One extreme possibility is that Firm Y will ignore Firm X's price cut; that is, Y's price will not change. Alternatively, Y may reduce its price, precisely matching that of Firm X. Accordingly, the model of oligopolistic behavior we discuss next uses two different

---

[3] The logic here is exactly the same as the logic that led to the conclusion that a firm maximized profits by setting *marginal profit* equal to zero. If you need to review, consult Chapter 9, especially pages 175–176.

[4] Variants of this model were constructed by Hall and Hitch in England and by Sweezy in the United States. See R. L. Hall and C. J. Hitch, "Price Theory and Business Behavior," *Oxford Economic Papers 2* (May 1939): pp. 12–45; and P. M. Sweezy, "Demand under Conditions of Oligopoly," *Journal of Political Economy 47* (August 1939): pp. 568–573.

demand curves. One curve represents the quantities a given oligopolistic firm can sell at different prices *if competitors match its price moves,* and the other demand curve represents what will happen if competitors stubbornly *stick to their initial price levels.*

Point *A* in Figure 13–4 represents our firm's initial price and output: 1,000 units at $10 each. Two demand curves, *DD* and *dd,* pass through point *A. DD* represents our company's demand if competitors keep their prices fixed, and *dd* indicates what happens when competitors match our firm's price changes.

**FIGURE 13-4**

**The Kinked Demand Curve**

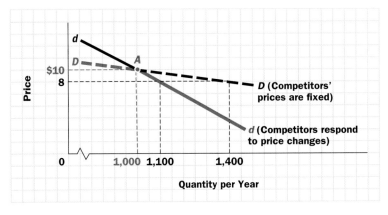

The *DD* curve is the more elastic (flatter and more responsive) of the two, and a moment's thought indicates why this should be so. If our firm cuts its price from its initial level of $10 to, say, $8, and if competitors do not match this cut, we would expect our firm to get a large number of new customers—perhaps its quantity demanded will jump to 1,400. However, if its competitors respond by also reducing their prices, its quantity demanded will rise by less—perhaps only to 1,100 (more inelastic demand curve *dd*). Similarly, when it raises its price, our firm may expect a larger sales flight if its rivals fail to match its increase, as indicated by the relative flatness (elasticity) of the curve *DD* in Figure 13–4, as compared to *dd,* the firm's demand curve when rivals do match our firm's price changes.

How does this relate to sticky oligopolistic prices? The economists who designed this model hypothesized that a typical oligopolistic firm has good reason to fear the worst. If it lowers its prices and its rivals do not, its sales will seriously cut into its competitors' volume, and so the rivals will *have* to match the price cut in order to protect themselves. The inelastic demand curve, *dd,* will therefore apply if our firm decides on a price reduction (points below and to the right of point *A*).

On the other hand, if our company chooses to *increase* its price, management will fear that its rivals will continue to sit at their old price levels, calmly collecting customers as they flee from X's higher prices. Thus, the relevant demand curve for price increases (above *A*) will be *DD.*

In sum, our firm will figure that it will face a segment of the elastic demand curve *DD* if it raises its price and a segment of the inelastic demand curve *dd* if it decreases its price. Its true demand curve will then be given by the heavy red line, *DAd.* For obvious reasons, this is called a *kinked demand curve.*

The kinked demand curve represents a "heads you lose, tails you lose" proposition in terms of any potential price changes. If a firm raises its price, it will lose many customers (because in that case its demand is elastic); if it lowers its price, the sales increase will be comparatively small (because then its demand is inelastic). In these circumstances, management will vary its price only under extreme provocation, that is, only if its costs change enormously.

Figure 13–5 illustrates this conclusion graphically. The two demand curves, *dd* and *DD,* are carried over precisely from Figure 13–4. The dashed line labeled MR is the marginal revenue curve associated with *DD,* while the solid line labeled mr is the marginal revenue curve associated with *dd.* The marginal revenue curve relevant to the firm's decision making is MR for any output level below 1,000 units, but mr for any output level above 1,000 units. Therefore, the composite marginal revenue curve facing the firm is shown by the yellow-highlighted line DBCmr with two angles.

**FIGURE 13-5**

**The Kinked Demand Curve and Sticky Prices**

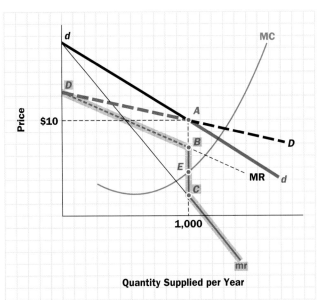

The marginal cost curve drawn in the diagram cuts this composite marginal revenue curve at point *E,* which indicates the profit-maximizing combination of output and price for this oligopolist. Specifically, the quantity supplied at point *E* is 1,000 units, and the price is $10, which we read from demand curve *DAd.*

The unique aspect of this diagram is that the kinked demand curve leads to a marginal revenue curve that takes a sharp plunge between points *B* and *C.* Consequently, even if the MC curve shifts moderately upward or downward, it will still intersect the marginal revenue curve somewhere between *B* and *C* and thus will *not* lead the firm to change its output decision. Therefore, *the firm's price will remain unchanged.* (Try this for yourself in Figure 13–5.) Oligopoly prices are "sticky," then, in the sense that they do not respond to minor cost changes. Only cost changes large enough to push the MC curve out of the *BC* range will lead to price changes.

If this is, in fact, the way oligopolists view their competitors' behavior, we can easily see why they may be reluctant to make frequent price changes. We can also understand why price leadership may arise. The price leader firm can raise prices at will, confident that the firm will not be left out on a limb (a kink?) by other firms' unwillingness to follow. (See the accompanying box, "Will the Internet End 'Sticky Prices'?" for more on price flexibility.)

## THE GAME-THEORY APPROACH

In 1944, mathematician John von Neumann (1903–1957) and economist Oskar Morgenstern (1902–1977) contributed a new approach to oligopoly analysis called *game theory.* Game theory is now economists' most widely used approach to analyze oligopoly behavior. The theory approaches the issue of interdependence directly by assuming, for the most part, that each firm's managers proceed on the assumption *that their rivals are extremely ingenious strategic decision makers.* In this model, each oligopolist acts as a competing player in a strategic game.

Game theory uses two fundamental concepts: *strategy* and the *payoff matrix.* A strategy represents a participant's operational plan. In its simplest form, it may refer to just one possible decision, such as "I will add a new car to my product line that features a TV set for the passengers," or "I will cut the price of my car to $19,500." For simplicity's sake, game-theory analysis often focuses on an oligopoly of two firms—a *duopoly.* We illustrate the payoff matrix for a two-person game in Table 13–1.

This matrix reports the profits that each of two rival firms, Firm A and Firm B, can expect to earn—depending on the pricing strategy that each adopts (not knowing the price that the other will offer to customers). The choice open to each firm is either to charge a "high price" or a "low price." The payoff matrix reports the profits that each

---

**TABLE 13–1**

**A Payoff Matrix**

|  |  | Firm B's Strategy | | | |
|---|---|---|---|---|---|
|  |  | High Price | | Low Price | |
| Firm A's Strategy | High Price | A gets $10 | B gets $10 | A gets $−2 | B gets $12 |
|  | Low Price | A gets $12 | B gets $−2 | A gets $3 | B gets $3 |

NOTE: Figures are in millions of dollars.

---

### ● WILL THE INTERNET END "STICKY PRICES?"

People all over the world have access to the Internet, and companies large and small maintain Internet Web sites. The following excerpt from the British magazine *The Economist* discusses the prospect of more flexible prices that the Internet may offer.

As shares are bought and sold, the prices on trading screens flicker red and black. Most other prices are far less jumpy. Petrol-pump prices don't change every time the oil price moves, holiday prices and standard hotel rates are fixed for months, and doctors seldom alter their fees. Some claim the Internet could change all that. Prices could flick at the click of a computer mouse. And, they argue, the economy would run more efficiently as a result.

Will the Internet really make prices more flexible? The answer depends on why prices fail to fluctuate with every shift in supply and demand now. Simply put, prices change only when the cost of leaving them unchanged becomes bigger than the expense of adjusting them. In financial markets, prices move all the time because the cost of quoting the "wrong" price can be huge. If market makers failed to raise prices when they were too low, for instance, they would make hefty losses because they would be obliged to sell unlimited amounts of securities on the cheap. And on a market stall, a fruit trader who didn't lower prices when they were too high would have to throw away unsold produce at the end of the day.

The Internet is unlikely to increase the cost of leaving prices unchanged. . . . But it *will* make it cheaper to change *some* prices. Electronic price-tags can be altered almost costlessly. Digital holiday brochures do not need reprinting. And the Internet makes finding out and comparing prices much easier. Rates for hotel rooms in Honolulu can now be checked from a laptop in London. That, some argue, will make booking a room more like buying shares, where investors plump for the broker quoting the best price, which changes all the time.

SOURCE: *The Economist*, May 16, 1998, p. 86.

firm can expect to earn, given its own pricing choice and that of its rival. We read Table 13–1 much like a mileage chart. For example, the upper, left-hand cell indicates that if both firms decide to charge high prices, both A and B will earn $10 million.

We also see that if either firm succeeds in charging a low price when the other does not, the price cutter will actually raise its profit to $12 million (presumably by capturing more sales) and drive its rival to a $2 million loss. However, if *both* firms offer low prices, each will be left with a modest $3 million profit.

How does game theory analyze optimal strategic choice? We may envision the management of Firm A reasoning as follows: "If I choose a high-price strategy, the worst that can happen to me is that my competitor will select the low-price counterstrategy, which will cut my return to −$2 million (the blue number in the first row of the payoff matrix). Similarly, if I select a low-price strategy, the worst possible outcome for me is a $3 million profit (the blue minimum payoff in the second row of the matrix)."

**THE MAXIMIN STRATEGY AND THE PRISONERS' DILEMMA** How can the managers of Firm A best protect their company from trouble in these circumstances? Game theory suggests that it may be rational to select a strategy based on its *minimum* payoff, just as described earlier. They should pick the strategy that will guarantee them the *highest* minimum payoff (in other words, the best of the bad outcomes). This is called the **maximin criterion,** in which one seeks the *max*imum of the *min*imum payoffs to the various available strategies. In this case, the maximin strategy for each firm is to offer a low price and earn a profit of $3 million (the red-shaded boxes in Table 13–1).

The **maximin criterion** requires you to select the strategy that yields the maximum payoff on the assumption that your opponent does as much damage to you as he or she can.

Notice that each firm's fear of what its rival will do virtually forces it to offer a low price and to forgo the high ($10 million) profit that each could earn if it could trust the other to stick to a high price. This example illustrates why many observers conclude that, particularly where the number of firms is small, firms should not be permitted to confer or exchange information on prices, because consumers would pay for the additional profits provided by successful collusion. The same sort of analysis also helps to explain how competition limits profits and benefits consumers, and why price cartel arrangements are fragile.

A payoff matrix with a pattern like that in Table 13–1 has many other interesting applications. It can show how people can get trapped into making each other (and themselves) worse off. For example, it applies to people driving polluting cars in the absence of laws requiring emission controls. Each does so because she does not trust other drivers to install emission controls voluntarily. (*Exercise:* Make up a payoff matrix that tells this story.)

Still another interpretation applies, one which gave this matrix the name by which it is known to game theorists: "the prisoners' dilemma." Here, instead of a two-firm industry, the underlying scenario is that of two burglary suspects who are captured by the police and interrogated in separate rooms. Each suspect has two strategy options: to deny the charge or to confess. If both deny it, both go free, for the police have no other evidence. But if one confesses and the other does not, the silent prisoner can expect the key to his cell to be thrown away. The *maximin* solution, then, is for both to confess and receive the moderate sentence that this elicits.

**OTHER STRATEGIES: THE NASH EQUILIBRIUM**    We can interpret the maximin strategy as a pessimist's way to deal with uncertainty. A player who adopts this strategy assumes that the worst will always happen: no matter what move he makes, his opponent will adopt the countermove that does him the most damage. The maximin strategy neglects the possibility that opponents will not have enough information to find out the most damaging countermove. It also ignores the possibility of finding common ground, as when two competitors collude to extract monopoly profit from consumers.

> A **Nash equilibrium** results when each player adopts the strategy that gives her the highest possible payoff if her rival sticks to the strategy he has chosen.

Other strategies are less pessimistic, yet still rational. One of the most analytically useful strategies leads to what is called a **Nash equilibrium.** Mathematician John Nash devised this strategy, for which he won the Nobel Prize in economics in 1994. The basic idea is simple. In a two-player game, suppose that each firm is trying to decide whether to adopt a red or a blue package for its product. Assume that each firm earns a higher profit if it selects a package color that differs from the other's. Then, if Firm X happens to select a blue package, it will obviously be most profitable for Y to select a red package. Moreover, it will pay each firm to stick with that choice, because red is Y's most profitable response to X's choice of blue, and vice versa.

In general, a Nash equilibrium describes a situation in which both players adopt moves such that each player's move is its most profitable response to the other's move. Often, no such mutually accommodating solution is possible. But where it is possible, if both players realize this and act accordingly, they may both be able to benefit. Thus, note how much worse off both firms would be in the preceding example if Firm Y were determined to damage X, whatever the cost to itself, and adopted a blue package, just like X's.

**REPEATED GAMES**    The scenarios described so far involve one-time transactions, as when a tourist passes through a city and makes a purchase at a store that she will never visit again. Most business transactions are different. A firm usually sells its products day after day, often to repeat buyers. It must continuously review its pricing decisions, knowing that its rivals are likely to respond to any change.

> A **repeated game** is one that is played over again a number of times.

**Repeated games** give players the opportunity to learn something about each other's behavior patterns and, perhaps, to arrive at mutually beneficial arrangements. By adopting some fairly clear pricing behavior pattern, each firm can attain a reputation that elicits desired responses from competitors.

We return to the example of the price war between Firm A and Firm B to show how this works. When we studied the payoff matrix for that game, we saw that in a single play in which neither player knew anything about the other's behavior pattern, each player was likely to feel forced to adopt the maximin strategy. In other words, each firm set a low price for fear that if it adopted the potentially more profitable high price, its rival would adopt a low price and take customers away. In that way, both firms would end up with low prices and low profits.

But when games are repeated, the players may be able to escape such a trap. For example, Firm A can cultivate a reputation for playing a strategy called *"tit for tat."* Each time Firm B charges a high price, Firm A responds by charging a high price next time. Firm A follows a similar strategy if B's price is low. After a few repetitions, B will learn that A always matches its decisions. B will then see that it is better off sticking to a high price. Firm A, too, benefits from its tit-for-tat approach, which will also lead it, eventually, to set permanently high prices.

**THREATS AND CREDIBILITY**    A player can also use *threats* to induce rivals to change their behavior. The trouble is that, if carried out, the threat may well damage both parties. For example, a retailer can threaten to double its output and drive prices down near zero if a rival imitates its product. However, the rival is unlikely to believe the threat, because such a low price harms the threatener as much as the threatened. Such a threat is simply not *credible*, with one exception.

The possibility can become a **credible threat** if the threatener takes steps that commit it to carry out the action. For example, if Firm A signed an irrevocable contract committing it to double its output if Firm B copied A's product, then the threat would become credible, and B would be forced to believe it. But A can make other commitments that make its threat credible. For example, it can build a large plant with plenty of excess capacity. The factory may be very expensive to build, but once built, that cost is irrevocable. If the additional cost of turning out the product, once the plant has been built, is very low, then it will pay A to expand its output of the product even at a very low price (if that price exceeds the marginal cost of the item).

This last possibility leads directly to an important application of game theory: how firms inside an industry ("old firms") can decide strategically how to prevent *new* firms from entering into the industry. To create a credible threat to potential entrants, the old firm may well consider building a bigger factory than it would otherwise want.

Some hypothetical numbers and a typical game theory graph will make the story clear. The old firm faces two options: to build a small factory or a big one. Potential new firms also face two options: open for business (that is, enter the industry) or do not enter. Figure 13–6 shows the four resulting possible decision combinations and the corresponding profits or losses that the two firms may expect in each case.

The graph shows that the best outcome for the old firm is if it builds a small factory and the new firm decides not to enter. In that case, the old firm will earn $6 million, whereas the new firm will earn nothing, because it never starts up.

However, if the old firm *does* decide to build a small factory, it can be pretty sure that the new firm most likely *will* open up for business, because the new firm can then earn $2 million (rather than zero), as shown by the dashed lines. In the process, the old firm's profit will be reduced to $2 million.

On the other hand, if the old firm builds a big factory, its increased output will depress prices and profits. The old firm will now earn only $4 million if the new firm stays out, as shown by the asterisk line, whereas *each* firm will *lose* $2 million if the new firm enters. Obviously, if the old firm builds a big factory, the new firm will be better off staying out of the business rather than subjecting itself to a $2 million loss.

A **credible threat** is a threat that does not harm the threatener if it is carried out.

**FIGURE 13-6**

**Entry and Entry-Blocking Strategy**

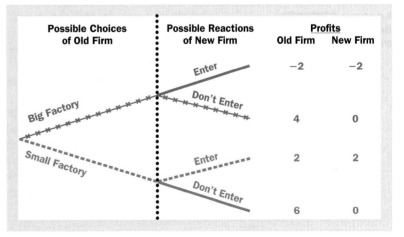

What size factory, then, should the old firm build? When we consider the firms' interactions, the old firm should clearly build the large factory with its excess capacity—because this decision will keep the new firm out of the industry, leaving the old firm a $4 million profit. The moral of the story: "Wasting" money on excess capacity may not be wasteful to the oligopolist firm if it protects the firm's long-term interest.

Of course, game theory is a much richer topic than we have explained here. For example, game theory also provides tools for economists and business managers to analyze coalitions. It indicates, for cases involving more than two firms, which firms would do well to align themselves together against which others. People other than economists have also used game theory to analyze a variety of complicated problems outside the realm of oligopoly theory. Management training programs employ its principles, as do a number of government agencies (see the accompanying box, "Billion-Dollar Application: Game Theory and FCC Auctions"). Political scientists and military strategists use game theory to formulate and analyze strategy.

## MONOPOLISTIC COMPETITION, OLIGOPOLY, AND PUBLIC WELFARE

How well or poorly do monopolistically competitive or oligopolistic firms perform, from the viewpoint of the general welfare?

We have seen that their performance *can* leave much to be desired. For example, the excess capacity theorem showed us that monopolistic competition can lead to inefficiently high production costs. Similarly, because market forces may not sufficiently restrain their behavior, oligopolists' prices and outputs may differ substantially from socially optimal levels. In particular, when oligopolists organize themselves into a successful cartel, prices will be higher and outputs lower than their perfectly competitive counterparts. Moreover, some people believe that misleading advertising by corporate giants often distorts consumer judgments, leading them to buy things they do not need and would otherwise not want. Many social critics feel that such corporate giants wield political power, economic power, and power over the minds of consumers—power that undermines the benefits of Adam Smith's invisible hand.

Because oligopoly behavior varies so widely, the social welfare implications differ from case to case. But some recent economic analysis provides one theoretical case in which oligopolistic behavior and performance quality can be predicted and judged unambiguously.[5] The analysis can also serve as a model for government agencies that are charged with the task of preventing harmful anticompetitive behavior by oligopolistic firms. In this theoretical case, called a **perfectly contestable market,** entry into or exit from the market is costless and unimpeded. Here, the constant threat of the possible entry by new firms forces even the largest existing firm to behave well—to produce efficiently and never to overcharge. Otherwise, the firm will be threatened with replacement by an entrant who offers to serve customers more cheaply and efficiently.

A market is **perfectly contestable** if entry and exit are costless and unimpeded.

We define a market as perfectly contestable if firms can enter it and, if they choose, exit it without losing the money they invested. The crucial issue here is not the amount of capital required to enter the industry, but whether or not an entrant can withdraw the investment if it wishes. For example, if market entry requires investing in highly *mobile* capital (like airplanes, trucks, or river barges—which can be moved around easily), the entrant may be able to exit quickly and cheaply.[6] For

---

[5] See William J. Baumol, John C. Panzar, and Robert D. Willig, *Contestable Markets and the Theory of Industry Structure*, rev. ed. (San Diego: Harcourt Brace Jovanovich, 1988).

[6] Earlier it was thought that air transportation could be classed as a highly contestable industry, but recent evidence suggests that although this judgment is not entirely incorrect, it requires considerable reservations.

## ● BILLION-DOLLAR APPLICATION: GAME THEORY AND FCC AUCTIONS

When the Federal Communications Commission announced plans to auction off radio spectrum wavelengths for such "personal communications services" as cell phones and pagers, many large companies scrambled to hire game theorists to advise them about strategy in this extremely high-stakes undertaking. The FCC used game theory to design the on-line auction of these so-called *rights to the airways,* and the bidding companies themselves had to figure out how much to pay for the right to service a particular region.

By any measure, the game theorists had their work cut out for them. Each bidder sent its information through its computer, so the FCC had a difficult task in checking out the number and size distribution of the competition. Also, because the commodity being purchased was the latest generation of wireless technology, it was nearly impossible to understand the buying decision completely. Knowing competitors' cost and revenue structures was another hard one, as was gauging future demand for the service. This enormous uncertainty made nimble strategies all important.

The FCC might simply have priced the licenses for the various available regions itself. But by conducting an auction, it placed the decision-making onus on the bidding companies and their hired game theorists. Each bidder had to decide what sectors it could serve most efficiently, and each had to

anticipate competitiors' most likely moves and countermoves. As it turned out, the FCC auctioned off more than 1,000 PCS licenses in nearly 500 cities or regions between August 1996 and January 1997, raising more than $20 billion.

SOURCE: "FCC Plans Spectrum Auction Conference," June 16, 1998, and "Consent in Bid-Rigging Case," November 10, 1998, CNN Financial Network, June 16, 1998 *http://cnnfn.com.*

instance, if a barge operation decides to serve the lower Mississippi River but finds business disappointing, it can easily transfer its boats to, say, the Ohio River.

A profitable market that is also contestable therefore attracts *potential* entrants. Because no barriers to entry or exit exist, firms undertake little risk by going into such a market. If their entry turns out to have been a mistake, they can move to another market without loss.

Because perfect competition requires a large number of firms, all of them small relative to the size of the industry, no industry with economies of large-scale production can be perfectly competitive. However, markets that contain a few relatively large firms may be highly contestable, though they are certainly not perfectly competitive. But no real-world industry is in fact *perfectly* contestable, just as no industry is perfectly competitive.

The constant threat of entry forces oligopolists to perform well. Even monopolists must perform well if they do business in a highly contestable market. In particular, perfectly contestable markets have at least two socially desirable characteristics.

First, freedom of entry eliminates any excess economic profits so that in this respect contestable markets resemble perfectly competitive markets. For example, if the current opportunity cost of capital is 12 percent while the firms in a contestable market are earning a return of 18 percent, then new firms will enter the market, expand the industry's outputs, and drive down the prices of its products to the point at which no firm earns any excess profit. To avoid this outcome, established firms must expand output to a level that precludes excess profit.

Second, inefficient enterprises cannot survive in a perfectly contestable industry because cost inefficiencies invite replacement of the existing firms by entrants who can provide the same outputs at lower cost and lower prices. Only firms operating at the lowest possible cost can survive. In sum, firms in a perfectly contestable market will be forced to operate as efficiently as possible and to charge prices as low as long-run financial survival permits.

The theory of contestable markets has been widely used by courts and government agencies concerned with the performance of business firms (for a recent example, see Chapter 20) and provides workable guidelines for improved or acceptable behavior in industries in which economies of scale mean that only a small number of firms can or should operate.

## ■ A GLANCE BACKWARD: COMPARING THE FOUR MARKET FORMS

We have now completed the set of chapters that has taken us through the four main market forms: perfect competition, monopoly, monopolistic competition, and oligopoly. You have probably absorbed a lot of information about the workings of these market forms as you read through Chapters 10 through 13, but you may be confused by the details. Table 13–2 presents an overview of the main attributes of each of the market forms for comparison. It shows that:

■ Perfect competition and pure monopoly are concepts useful primarily for *analytical* purposes—we find neither very often in reality. There are very many monopolistically competitive firms, and oligopoly firms account for the largest share of the economy's output.

■ Profits are zero in long-run equilibrium under perfect competition and monopolistic competition because entry is so easy that high profits attract new rivals into the market.

■ Consequently, AC = AR in long-run equilibrium under these two market forms. In equilibrium, MC = MR for the profit-maximizing firm under any market form. However, under oligopoly, firms may adopt the strategies described by game theory or they may pursue goals other than profits; for example, they may be sales maximizers. Therefore, in the equilibrium of the oligopoly firm, MC may be unequal to MR.

■ The behavior of the perfectly competitive firm and industry theoretically leads to an efficient allocation of resources that maximizes the benefits to consumers, given the resources available to consumers. Monopoly, however, can misallocate resources by restricting output in order to raise prices and profits. Under monopolistic competition, excess capacity and inefficiency are apt to result. And under oligopoly, almost anything can happen, so it is impossible to generalize about its vices or virtues.

**Attributes of the Four Market Forms**

TABLE 13-2

| Market Form | Number of Firms in the Market | Frequency in Reality | Entry Barriers | Public Interest Results | Long-Run Profit | Equilibrium Conditions |
|---|---|---|---|---|---|---|
| Perfect competition | Very many | Rare (if any) | None | Good | Zero | MC = MR = AC = AR = P |
| Pure monopoly | One | Rare | Likely to be high | Misallocates resources | May be High | MR = MC |
| Monopolistic competition | Many | Widespread | Minor | Inefficient | Zero | MR = MC AR = AC |
| Oligopoly | Few | Produces large share of GDP | Varies | Varies | Varies | Vary |

1. Under *monopolistic competition*, there are numerous small buyers and sellers; each firm's product is at least somewhat different from every other firm's product—that is, each firm has a partial "monopoly" of some product characteristics, and thus a downward-sloping demand curve; there is freedom of entry and exit; and there is perfect information.

2. In long-run equilibrium under monopolistic competition, free entry eliminates economic profits by forcing the firm's demand curve into a position of tangency with its average cost curve. Therefore, output will be below the point at which average cost is lowest. This is why monopolistic competitors are said to have "excess capacity."

3. An oligopolistic industry is composed of a few large firms selling similar products in the same market.

4. Under *oligopoly*, each firm carefully watches the major decisions of its rivals and often plans counterstrategies. As a result, rivalry is often vigorous and direct, and the outcome is difficult to predict.

5. One model of oligopoly behavior assumes that the oligopolists ignore interdependence and simply maximize profits or sales. Another assumes that they join together to form a *cartel* and thus act like a monopoly. A third possibility is *price leadership*, where one firm sets prices and the others follow suit.

6. A firm that maximizes sales will continue producing up to the point where marginal revenue is driven down to zero. Consequently, a sales maximizer will produce more than a profit maximizer and will charge a lower price.

7. If a firm thinks that its rivals will match any price cut but fail to match any price increase, its demand curve becomes "kinked" and its price will be sticky—in other words, it will be adjusted less frequently than would be true under either perfect competition or pure monopoly.

8. *Game theory* provides new tools for the analysis of business strategies under conditions of oligopoly.

9. In a *maximin strategy*, the player takes the strongest possible precautions against the worst possible outcome of any move it selects.

10. A *Nash equilibrium* is one in which each player adopts the move that yields the highest possible payoff to itself, given the move selected by the other player.

11. In *repeated games*, a firm can seek to acquire a reputation that induces the other player to make decisions that do not damage its interests. It may also promote its goals by means of *credible threats*.

12. Monopolistic competition and oligopoly can be harmful to the general welfare. But because behavior varies widely, the implications for social welfare also vary from case to case.

Monopolistic competition   248

Excess capacity theorem   250

Oligopoly   252

Oligopolistic interdependence   253

Cartel   254

Price leadership   256

Price war   257

Sales maximization   257

Kinked demand curve   258

Sticky price   259

Game theory   260

Maximin criterion   261

Prisoners' dilemma   261

Nash equilibrium   262

Repeated game   262

Credible threat   263

Perfectly contestable market   264

1. How many real industries can you name that are oligopolies? How many that operate under monopolistic competition? Perfect competition? Which of these is hardest to find in reality? Why do you think this is so?

2. Consider some of the products that are widely advertised on television. By what kind of firm is each produced—a perfectly competitive firm, an oligopolistic firm, or what? How many major products can you think of that are *not* advertised on TV?

3. In what ways may the small retail sellers of the following products differentiate their goods from those of their rivals to make themselves monopolistic competitors: hamburgers, radios, cosmetics?

4. Pricing of securities on the stock market is said to be carried out under conditions in many respects similar to perfect competition. The auto industry is an oligopoly. How often do you think the price of a share of Ford Motor Company's common stock changes? How about the price of a Ford Taurus? How would you explain the difference?

5. Suppose that Chrysler hires a popular singer to advertise its compact automobiles. The campaign is very successful, and the company increases its share of the compact-car market substantially. What is Ford likely to do?

6. Using game theory, set up a payoff matrix similar to one Chrysler's management might employ in analyzing the problem presented in Review Question 5.

7. Review Question 4 at the end of Chapter 12 presented cost and demand data for a monopolist and asked you to find the profit-maximizing solution. Use these same data to find the sales-maximizing solution. Are the answers different? Explain.

8. A new entrant, Bargain Airways, cuts air fares between Eastwich and Westwich by 20 percent. Biggie Airlines,

which has been operating on this route, responds by cutting fares by 35 percent. What does Biggie hope to achieve?

9. If air transportation were perfectly contestable, why would Biggie Airlines fail to achieve the ultimate goal of its price cut?

10. Which of the following industries are most likely to be contestable?

   a. Aluminum production

   b. Barge transportation

   c. Automobile manufacturing

   Explain your answers.

11. Since the deregulation of air transportation, a community served by a single airline is no longer protected by a regulatory agency from monopoly pricing. What market forces, if any, restrict the ability of the airline from raising prices as a pure monopolist would? How effective do you think those market forces are in keeping air fares down?

12. Explain, for a repeated game:

   a. Why it may be advantageous to have the reputation of a tough guy who always takes revenge against anyone who harms your interests.

   b. Why it may be advantageous to have a reputation of irrationality.

> When she was good
>
> She was very, very good,
>
> But when she was bad
>
> She was horrid.

Henry Wadsworth Longfellow

# THE MARKET MECHANISM: SHORTCOMINGS AND REMEDIES

What does the market do well, and what does it do poorly? This is the focus of our microeconomic analysis, and we are well on our way toward answers. In Chapters 10 and 11 we explained the workings of Adam Smith's invisible hand, the instrument by which a perfectly competitive economy allocates resources efficiently without any guidance from government. Of course, that perfectly competitive model is just a theoretical ideal, but our observations of the real world confirm the extraordinary accomplishments of the market mechanism. Free-market economies have achieved levels of output, productive efficiency, variety in available consumer goods, and general prosperity that are unprecedented in history—and are now the envy of the formerly planned economies. We will discuss that phenomenal record of production and growth in detail in Chapter 15.

Yet the market mechanism has its weaknesses. In Chapters 12 and 13, we examined one of these defects—the free market's vulnerability to exploitation by large and powerful business firms, which can lead to both an inappropriate concentration of wealth and resource misallocation. Now we take a more comprehensive view of market failures and of some of the things that can be done to remedy them. Clearly, the market does not do everything we want it to do. Amid the vast outpouring of products, we also find appalling poverty, cities choked by traffic and pollution, and hospitals, educational institutions, and artistic organizations in serious financial trouble. Though our economy produces an overwhelming abundance of material wealth, it seems far less capable of reducing social ills and environmental damage. We will examine the reasons for these failings and indicate why the price system *by itself* may not be able to deal with them.

However, recognition of the market's limitations does not imply that the public interest calls for its abandonment. As we will see, many of the imperfections of this economic system are treatable within the market environment, sometimes even making use of the market mechanism to cure its own deficiencies.

### Why Are Health-Care Costs in Canada Rising?

Long before the U.S. government made a serious attempt to grapple with the costs of health care, Canada adopted a universal health-care program intended to solve the same problem in that country. For this purpose, the Canadian government imposed strong controls over prices and fees. Each province has one insurance plan that reimburses doctors according to a uniform fee schedule; hospitals are put on predetermined overall budgets; and patients pay very low direct, out-of-pocket costs.

Many observers believe that Canada has created an efficient, user-friendly system, though some critics disagree. But Canadians clearly have not succeeded in containing costs. Despite price controls, Canadian health-care costs have been rising persistently faster than the general inflation rate, just as they have in the United States, where there are no such national rules to rein in rising health-care prices. Does this mean that Canadian health services are especially inefficient or corrupt? There is no evidence for such suspicions. Then why have the Canadians been unable to brake their health care costs? The materials in this chapter will help you to understand the answer, with its important implications for U.S. policy.

## ■ WHAT DOES THE MARKET DO POORLY?

Although we cannot list all of the market's imperfections, we can list some major areas in which it has been accused of failing:

- Market economies suffer from severe business fluctuations.
- The market distributes income unequally.
- Where markets are monopolized, they allocate resources inefficiently.

- The market deals poorly with the side effects of many economic activities.
- The market cannot readily provide public goods, such as national defense.
- The market may do a poor job of allocating resources between the present and the future.
- The market mechanism makes public and personal services increasingly expensive and this often induces socially damaging countermeasures by government.

We discuss the first three items in the list elsewhere in this book. This chapter deals with the remaining four. To help us analyze these cases, we will first briefly review the concept of efficient resource allocation, discussed in detail in Chapter 11.

## ■ EFFICIENT RESOURCE ALLOCATION: A REVIEW

The basic problem of resource allocation is deciding how much of each commodity the economy should produce. At first glance, the solution may seem simple: the more, the better! But this is not necessarily so, as one of our *ideas* indicates.

**TRUE COST** Outputs are not created out of thin air. We produce them from scarce supplies of fuel, raw materials, machinery, and labor. If we use these resources to produce, say, more jeans, then we must take resources away from some other products, such as backpacks. To decide whether increasing the production of jeans is a good idea, we must compare the utility of that increase with the loss of utility in producing fewer backpacks. This, as you recall, means we must consider the opportunity cost of increased output. It is *efficient* to increase the output of jeans only if society considers the additional jeans more valuable than the forgone backpacks.

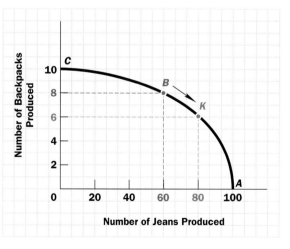

*How Much Does It Really Cost?*

To illustrate this idea, we repeat a graph you have seen several times in earlier chapters—a *production possibilities frontier*—but we put it to a somewhat different use. Curve *ABC* in Figure 14–1 is a production possibilities frontier showing the alternative combinations of jeans and backpacks that the economy can produce by reallocating its resources between production of the two goods. Suppose that point *B*, representing the production of 8 million backpacks and 60 million pairs of jeans, constitutes the *optimal* resource allocation. We assume this is the only combination of outputs that best satisfies society's wants among all the possibilities that are *attainable* (given the technology and resources as represented by the production frontier). Two questions are pertinent to our discussion of the price system:

**FIGURE 14–1**

**The Economy's Production Possibilities Frontier for the Production of Two Goods**

- What prices will get the economy to select point *B;* that is, what prices will yield an *efficient* allocation of resources?
- How can the wrong set of prices lead to a misallocation of resources?

We discussed the first question in detail in Chapter 11, where we saw that:

An efficient allocation of resources requires that each product's price be equal to its marginal cost; that is:

$$P = MC$$

The reasoning, in brief, goes like this: In a free market, the price of any good reflects the money value to consumers of an additional unit, that is, its *marginal utility* (MU). Similarly, if the market mechanism is working well, the *marginal cost* (MC) measures the value (the opportunity cost) of the resources needed to produce an additional unit of the good. That is, MC is the resources cost *caused* by producing another unit of the commodity. Hence, if prices are set equal to marginal costs, then consumers, by using *their own money* in the most effective way to maximize *their own* satisfaction, will automatically be using *society's resources* in the most effective way. In other words, as long

Number of Backpacks Produced

Number of Jeans Produced

NOTE: Numbers are in millions per year.

as it sets prices equal to marginal costs, the market mechanism automatically satisfies the MC = MU rule for efficient resource allocation that we studied in Chapter 11.[1] In terms of Figure 14–1, this means that if $P$ = MC for both goods, the economy will automatically gravitate to point $B$, which we assumed to be the optimal point.

This chapter is devoted mainly to the second question: How can the "wrong" prices cause a *mis*allocation of resources? The answer to this question is not too difficult, and we can use the case of monopoly as an illustration.

The "law" of demand tells us that a rise in a commodity's price normally will reduce the quantity demanded. Suppose, now, that the backpack industry is a monopoly, so the price of backpacks exceeds their marginal cost.[2] This will decrease the quantity of backpacks demanded below the 8 million that we have assumed to be socially optimal (point $B$ in Figure 14–1). The economy will move from point $B$ to a point such as $K$, where too few backpacks and too many pairs of jeans are being produced for maximal consumer satisfaction. By setting the "wrong" prices, then, the market prevents the most efficient use of the economy's resources.

> If a commodity's price is above its marginal cost, the economy will tend to produce less of that item than would maximize consumer benefits. The opposite will occur if an item's price is below its marginal cost.

In the rest of this chapter, we will encounter several other instances in which the market mechanism may set the "wrong" prices.

## ■ EXTERNALITIES: GETTING THE PRICES WRONG

We start with the fourth item on our list of market failures (since we have studied the first three in previous chapters): The market deals poorly with the *incidental* side effects of economic activities. This flaw is one of the least obvious yet most consequential of the price system's imperfections.

Many economic activities provide incidental *benefits* to others for whom they are not specifically intended. For example, homeowners who plant beautiful gardens in front of their homes incidentally and unintentionally provide pleasure to neighbors and passers-by, though they receive no payment in return. Economists say that their activity generates a **beneficial externality.** Similarly, some activities incidentally and unintentionally impose *costs* on others. For example, the owners of a motorcycle repair shop create a lot of noise for which they pay no compensation to their neighbors. Economists say these owners produce a **detrimental externality.** Pollution is the classic illustration of a detrimental externality.

To see why externalities cause the price system to misallocate resources, you need only recall that the price system achieves efficiency by rewarding producers who serve consumers well—that is, at the lowest possible cost. This argument breaks down, however, as soon as some of the costs and benefits of economic activities are left out of the profit calculation.

When a firm pollutes a river, it uses up some of society's resources just as surely as when the firm burns coal. However, if the firm pays for coal but not for the use of clean water, we can expect the firm's management to be economical in its use of coal and wasteful in its use of water. By the same token, a firm that provides unpaid benefits to others is unlikely to be generous in allocating resources to the activity, no matter how socially desirable it may be.

In an important sense, the source of the market mechanism's difficulty here lies in society's rules about property rights. Coal mines are *private property;* their owners will not let anyone take coal without paying for it. Thus, coal is costly and

An activity is said to generate a **beneficial** or **detrimental externality** if that activity causes incidental benefits or damages to others not directly involved in the activity and no corresponding compensation is provided to or paid by those who generate the externality.

---

[1] If you need review, consult pages 221–223.

[2] To review why price under monopoly may be expected to exceed marginal cost, you may want to reread pages 236–238.

so is not used wastefully. But waterways are not private property. Because they belong to everyone in general, they belong to no one in particular. Therefore, anyone can use waterways as free dumping grounds for wastes. Because no one pays for the use of the socially valuable dissolved oxygen in a public waterway, people will use that oxygen wastefully. The fact that waterways are exempted from the market's normal control procedures is therefore the source of a detrimental externality.

## EXTERNALITIES AND INEFFICIENCY

Using these concepts, we can see precisely why an externality has undesirable effects on the allocation of resources. In discussing externalities, it is crucial to distinguish between *social* and *private* marginal cost. We define **marginal social cost (MSC)** as the sum of two components: (1) **marginal private cost (MPC),** which is the share of an activity's marginal cost that is paid for by the persons who carry out the activity, and (2) *incidental cost,* which is the share paid by others.

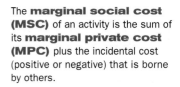

The **marginal social cost (MSC)** of an activity is the sum of its **marginal private cost (MPC)** plus the incidental cost (positive or negative) that is borne by others.

If an increase in a firm's output also increases the smoke its factory spews into the air, then, in addition to direct private costs (as recorded in the company accounts), the expansion of production imposes incidental costs on others. These costs take the form of increased laundry bills, medical expenditures, outlays for air conditioning and electricity, as well as the unpleasantness of living in a cloud of noxious fumes. These are all part of the activity's marginal *social* cost.

Where the firm's activities generate detrimental externalities, its marginal social cost will be greater than its marginal private cost. In symbols, MSC > MPC. Therefore, the firm's output must be too big because, in equilibrium, the market will yield an output at which consumers' marginal utility (MU) is equal to the firm's marginal private cost (MU = MPC). So where there are detrimental externalities, the marginal utility is *smaller* than marginal *social* cost. Society would then necessarily benefit if output of that product were *reduced.* It would lose the marginal utility but save the greater marginal social cost. We conclude that:

> Where a firm's activity causes detrimental externalities, marginal benefits will be less than marginal social costs in a free market. Smaller outputs than those that maximize profits will be socially desirable.

This is because private enterprise has no motivation to take into account any costs to others for which it does not have to pay. In fact, competition *forces* firms to produce at as low a cost as possible, because if they don't, rivals will be able to take their customers away. Thus, competition *compels* firms to make extensive use of resources for which they are not required to pay. This means that goods that cause externalities will be produced in undesirably large amounts, because they have social costs that are not paid by the supplier firms.

These principles can be illustrated with the aid of Figure 14–2. This diagram repeats the two basic curves needed for analysis of the firm's equilibrium: a marginal revenue curve and a marginal cost curve (see Chapter 9). These curves represent the *private* costs and revenues of a particular firm (in this case, a paper mill). The mill maximizes profits by providing 100,000 tons of output, corresponding to the intersection between the marginal private cost and marginal revenue curves (point *A*).

Now suppose that the factory's wastes pollute a nearby waterway, so that its production creates a detrimental externality for which the owners do not pay. Then marginal social cost must be higher than marginal private cost, as shown in the diagram. The output of paper, which is governed by private costs, will be 100,000 tons (point *A*)—an excessive amount from the viewpoint of the public interest, given its environmental consequences.

**FIGURE 14-2**

**Equilibrium of a Firm, the Output of which Produces a Detrimental Externality (Pollution)**

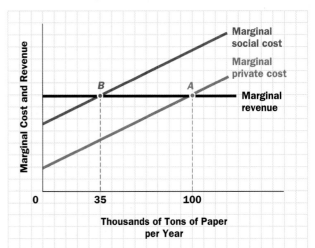

If, instead of being able to impose the external costs on others, the paper mill's owners were forced to pay them, then their private marginal cost curve would correspond to the higher of the two cost curves. Paper output would then fall to 35,000 tons, corresponding to point *B*, the intersection between the marginal revenue curve and the marginal *social* cost curve.

The same sort of diagram shows that the opposite relationship will hold when the firm's activity produces beneficial externalities. The firm will produce less of its beneficial output than it would if it were rewarded fully for its activities' benefits. Beneficial externalities arise when the activities of Firm A create incidental benefits for Firm B or Individual C (and perhaps for many others as well), or when A's activities *reduce* the costs of others' activities. For example, Firm A's research laboratories, while making its own products better, may also incidentally discover new research techniques that reduce other firms' research costs. Thus:

> Where the firm's activity generates beneficial externalities, free markets will produce too little output. Society would be better off with larger output levels.

We can also see these results with the help of a production possibilities frontier diagram similar to that in Figure 14–1. In Figure 14–3, we see the frontier for two industries: electricity generation, which causes air pollution (a detrimental externality), and tulip growing, which makes an area more attractive (a beneficial externality). We have just seen that detrimental externalities make marginal social cost greater than marginal private cost. Hence, if the electric company charges a price equal to its own marginal (private) cost, that price will be less than the true marginal social cost. Similarly, in tulip growing, a price equal to marginal private cost will be above the true marginal cost to society.

We saw earlier in the chapter that an industry that charges a price above marginal social cost will reduce quantity demanded through this high price, and so it will produce an output too small for an efficient allocation of resources. The opposite will be true for an industry whose price is below marginal social cost. In terms of Figure 14–3, suppose that point *B* again represents the efficient allocation of resources, involving the production of *E* kilowatt hours of electricity and *T* dozen tulips.

Because the polluting electricity-generation company charges a price below marginal social cost, it will sell more than *E* kilowatt hours of electricity. Similarly, because tulip growers generate external benefits, and so charge a price above marginal social cost, they will produce less than *T* dozen tulips. The economy will end up with the resource allocation represented by point *K* rather than that at point *B*. There will be too much smoky electricity production and too little attractive tulip growing. More generally:

> An industry that generates detrimental externalities will have a marginal social cost higher than its marginal private cost. If the price is equal to a firm's own marginal private cost, it will therefore be below the true marginal cost to society. The market mechanism thereby tends to encourage inefficiently large outputs of products that cause detrimental externalities. The opposite is true of products that cause beneficial externalities—private industry will provide inefficiently small quantities of these products.

## EXTERNALITIES ARE EVERYWHERE

Externalities occur throughout the economy. Many are beneficial. A factory that hires unskilled or semiskilled laborers gives them on-the-job training and provides the external benefit of better workers to future employers. Benefits to others are also generated when firms invent useful but unpatentable products, or even patentable products that can be imitated by others to some degree. We will discuss the externalities of innovation further in the next chapter.

### FIGURE 14-3

**Externalities, Market Equilibrium, and Efficient Resource Allocation**

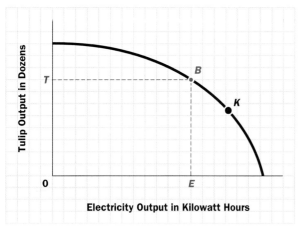

Detrimental externalities are also widespread. Pollution by factories, cars, and trucks cause some of our most pressing environmental problems. The abandonment of buildings causes the quality of neighborhoods to deteriorate and is the source of serious externalities for cities.

Although the market mechanism, acting on its own, does nothing to cure externality problems, there's more to the story. Market economies often have dirty air and rivers and suffer from the effects of improperly disposed toxic wastes, but that does not mean that *non*market economies do any better. The communist countries of eastern Europe and the Soviet Union long were known to have a dismal environmental record. But when communism fell apart in those countries, the horrors of environmental degradation that were revealed were difficult to believe. It became abundantly clear that central planning is not a guaranteed cure for environmental difficulties.

Moreover, the market mechanism does offer us one effective way of dealing with such difficulties. Although markets hardly can be claimed to protect the environment automatically, they do offer us a powerful tool for doing so.

## GOVERNMENT POLICY AND EXTERNALITIES

Because of the market's inability to cope with externalities, governments support activities that are believed to generate external benefits. Governments subsidize education, not only because they know it helps promote equal opportunity for all citizens, but also because they believe it generates beneficial externalities. For example, educated people normally commit fewer crimes than uneducated people, so the more we educate people, presumably, the less we will need to spend on crime prevention. Also, academic research that is a by-product of the educational system has often benefited the entire population and has, indeed, been a major contributor to the nation's economic growth. Biotechnology and advanced computing are just two major scientific breakthroughs that have stemmed from university research. We consequently believe that, if education were offered only by profit-making institutions, the outputs of these beneficial services would be provided at less than optimal levels.

Similarly, governments have recently begun to increase fines on companies that contribute heavily to air and water pollution. In recent years, the U.S. Environmental Protection Agency has levied more criminal fines and civil penalties against violators than ever before.

**EXTERNALITIES**  Our *ideas* suggest that standard economic analysis shows the effects of externalities on resource allocation. Externalities are really just failures to price resources such that markets can allocate them efficiently. One effective way to deal with externalities may be to use taxes and subsidies, making polluters pay for the costs they impose on society and paying the generators of beneficial externalities for the incidental benefits of their activities (which can be considered as an offset or deduction from the social cost of the activity).

*Externalities: A Shortcoming of the Market Cured by Market Methods*

For example, firms that generate beneficial externalities should be given *subsidies* per unit of their output equal to the difference between their marginal social costs and their marginal private costs. Similarly, detrimental externalities should be *taxed* so that the firm will have to pay the entire marginal social cost. In terms of Figure 14–2, after paying the tax, the firm's marginal private cost curve will shift up until it coincides with its marginal social cost curve, so the market price will be set in a manner consistent with efficient resource allocation.

Although this approach works well in principle, it is often difficult to carry out. Social costs are rarely easy to estimate, partly because they are so widely diffused throughout the community (everyone is affected by pollution) and partly because it is difficult to assess many of the costs and benefits (effects on health, unpleasantness of living in smog) in monetary terms. In Chapter 22 on environmental problems, we will continue our discussion of the pros and cons of the economist's approach to externalities and will outline alternative policies for their control.

## ■ PROVISION OF PUBLIC GOODS

A **public good** is a commodity or service whose benefits are *not depleted* by an additional user and from which it is generally difficult or *impossible to exclude* people, even if the people are unwilling to pay for the benefits.

A **private good** is a commodity characterized by both excludability and depletability.

A commodity is **depletable** if it is used up when someone consumes it.

A commodity is **excludable** if someone who does not pay for it can be kept from enjoying it.

A second area in which market failure occurs is the provision of what economists call **public goods.** These are socially valuable commodities whose provision, for reasons we will explain, cannot be financed by private enterprise, or at least not at socially desirable prices. Thus, government must pay for public goods if they are to be provided at all. Standard examples of public goods range from national defense to coastal lighthouses.

It is easiest to explain the nature of public goods by contrasting them with **private goods,** which are at the opposite end of the spectrum. *Private goods are characterized by two important attributes.* One can be called **depletability.** If you eat an apple or use a gallon of gasoline, there is that much less fruit or fuel in the world available for others to use. Your consumption depletes the supply available for other people, either temporarily or permanently.

But a pure public good is like the legendary widow's jar of oil, which always remained full no matter how many people used it. For example, once snow has been removed from a street, improved driving conditions are available to every driver who uses that street, whether ten or 1,000 cars pass that way. One passing car does not make the road less snow free for the next driver. The same is true of spraying swamps near a town to kill disease-carrying mosquitoes. The cost of spraying is the same whether the town contains 10,000 or 20,000 persons. A resident of the town who benefits from this service does not deplete its advantages to others.

The other property that characterizes private goods but not public goods is **excludability,** meaning that anyone who does not pay for the good can be excluded from enjoying its benefits. If you do not buy a ticket, you are excluded from the basketball game. If you do not pay for an electric guitar, the storekeeper will not give it to you.

But some goods or services, once provided to anyone, automatically become available to many others whom it is difficult, if not impossible, to exclude from the benefits. When the street is cleared of snow, everyone who uses the street benefits, regardless of who paid for the snowplow. If a country provides a strong military, every citizen receives its protection, even persons who do not want it.

A public good is defined as a good that lacks depletability. Very often, it also lacks excludability. Notice two important implications.

First, because nonpaying users usually cannot be excluded from enjoying a public good, suppliers of such goods will find it *difficult or impossible to collect fees* for the benefits they provide. This is the so-called free-rider problem. How many people, for example, will *voluntarily* cough up $4,400 a year to support our national defense establishment? Yet this is roughly what it costs per American family. Services such as national defense and public health, which are not depletable and where excludability is simply impossible, *cannot* be provided by private enterprise because people will not pay for what they can get free. Because private firms are not in the business of giving services away, the supply of public goods must be left to government authorities and nonprofit institutions.

The second implication we notice is that, because the supply of a public good is not depleted by an additional user, *the marginal (opportunity) cost of serving an additional user is zero.* With marginal cost equal to zero, the basic principle of optimal resource allocation (price equal to marginal cost) calls for provision of public goods and services to anyone who wants them *at no charge.* In other words, not only is it often *impossible* to charge a market price for a public good, it is often *undesirable* as well. Any nonzero price would discourage some users from enjoying the public good; but this would be inefficient, because one more person's enjoyment of the good costs society nothing. To summarize:

It is usually *not possible* to charge a price for a pure public good because people cannot be excluded from enjoying its benefits. It may also be *undesirable* to charge a price for it because that would discourage some people from benefiting, even though using a public good does not deplete its supply. For both of these reasons, government supplies many public goods. Without government intervention, public goods simply would not be provided.

Referring back to our example in Figure 14–1, if backpacks were a public good and their production were left to private enterprise, the economy would end up at point *A*, with zero production of backpacks and a far greater output of jeans than is called for by efficient allocation (point *B*). Usually, communities have not let that happen; today they devote a substantial proportion of government expenditure, indeed the bulk of municipal budgets, to financing of public goods or services believed to generate substantial external benefits. National defense, public health, police and fire protection, and research are among the services governments provide because they offer beneficial externalities or are public goods.

## ■ ALLOCATION OF RESOURCES BETWEEN PRESENT AND FUTURE

A third area in which market failure occurs is the division of benefits between today and tomorrow. When a society invests, more resources are devoted to expanding its capacity to produce consumer goods in the future. But if we devote inputs to building new plants and equipment that will add to production tomorrow, those resources then become unavailable for consumption now. Fuel used to make steel for a factory cannot be used to heat homes or drive cars. Thus, the allocation of inputs between current consumption and investment—their allocation between present and future—determines how fast the economy grows.

In principle, the market mechanism should be as efficient in allocating resources between present and future uses as it is in allocating resources among different outputs at any one time. If future demands for a particular commodity, say, personal computers, are expected to be higher than they are today, it pays manufacturers to plan now to build the necessary plant and equipment so they will be ready to turn out the computers when the market expands. More resources are thereby allocated to future consumption.

We can analyze the allocation of resources between present and future with the aid of a production possibilities frontier diagram, such as the one in Figure 14–1. The question now is how much labor and capital to devote to producing consumer goods and how much to devote to construction of factories to produce output in the future. Then, instead of jeans and backpacks, the graph will show consumer goods and number of factories on its axes, but otherwise it will be exactly the same as Figure 14–1.

The profit motive directs the flow of resources between one time period and another, just as it handles resource allocation among different industries in a given period. The lure of profits directs resources to those products *and those time periods* in which high prices promise to make output most profitable. But at least one feature of the process of resource allocation among different time periods distinguishes it from the process of allocation among industries. This is the special role that the *interest rate* plays in allocation among time periods.

### THE ROLE OF THE INTEREST RATE

If receipt of a given amount of money is delayed until some future time, the recipient incurs an *opportunity cost*—the interest that the money could have earned if it had been received earlier and invested. For example, if the prevailing interest rate is 9 percent and you can persuade someone who owes you $100 to make that payment one year earlier than originally planned, you come out $9 ahead (because you can take the $100 and invest it at 9 percent). Put another way, if the interest rate is 9 percent and the payment of $100 is postponed for one year, you lose the opportunity to earn $9. Thus, the interest rate determines the opportunity cost to a recipient who gets money at some future date instead of now—the lower the interest rate, the lower the opportunity cost. For this reason, as we will see in greater detail in Chapter 16:

> Low interest rates will persuade people to invest more now in factories and equipment, because these investments yield a large portion of their benefits in the future. Thus, more resources will be devoted to the future if interest rates are low. Similarly, high interest rates make durable investment, with future benefits, less attractive. Therefore, high interest rates tend to increase the use of resources for current output at the expense of reduced future outputs.

On the surface, it seems that the price system can allocate resources among different time periods in the way consumers prefer, because the supply of and demand for loans (see Chapter 16), which determine the interest rate, reflect the public's preferences between present and future. Suppose, for example, that the public suddenly became more interested in future consumption (say, people wanted to save more for their retirement years). People would save more money, the supply of funds available for borrowing would increase, and interest rates would tend to fall. This would stimulate investment and add to the future output of goods at the expense of current consumption.

But economists have raised several questions about how effectively the market mechanism allocates resources among different time periods in practice.

## HOW DOES IT WORK IN PRACTICE?

One thing that makes economists uneasy is that the interest rate (which is the price that controls resource allocation over time) is also used for a variety of *other* purposes. For instance, sometimes the interest rate is used to deal with business fluctuations. It plays an analogous role in international monetary relations. As a result, governments frequently manipulate interest rates. In doing so, policymakers seem to give little thought to the effects on resource allocation between present and future, so we may well worry whether the resulting interest rates are the most appropriate.

Second, some economists have suggested that, even when the government doesn't manipulate the interest rate, the market may devote too large a proportion of the economy's resources to immediate consumption. One British economist, A. C. Pigou, argued that people suffer from "a defective telescopic faculty"—that they are too shortsighted to give adequate weight to the future. A "bird in the hand" point of view leads people to spend too much on today's consumption and commit too little to tomorrow's investments.

A third reason why the free market may not invest enough for the future is that investment projects, like the construction of a new factory, are much greater risks to the individual investor than to the community as a whole. Even if the original investor goes bankrupt and the factory falls into someone else's hands, it can still go on turning out goods. But the profits will not go to the original investor or his or her heirs. Therefore, the loss to the individual investor will be far greater than the loss to society. For this reason, individual investment for the future may fall short of the socially optimal amounts. Investments too risky to be worthwhile to any group of private individuals may nevertheless be advantageous to society as a whole.

Fourth, our economy shortchanges the future when it despoils irreplaceable natural resources, exterminates whole species of plants and animals, floods canyons, "develops" attractive areas into acres of potential slums, and so on. Worst of all, industry, the military, and individuals bequeath a ticking time bomb to the future when they leave behind lethal and slow-acting toxic residues. For example, nuclear wastes may remain dangerous for hundreds or even thousands of years, but their disposal containers are likely to fall apart long before their contents lose their lethal qualities. Such actions are essentially *irreversible*. If a factory is not built this year, the deficiency in facilities provided for the future can be remedied by building it next year. But a natural canyon, once destroyed, can never be replaced. For this reason:

> Many economists believe that *irreversible decisions* have a special significance and must *not* be left entirely to the decisions of private firms and individuals, that is, to the market.

However, some writers have questioned the general conclusion that the free market will not invest enough for the future. They have pointed out that our economy's prosperity has increased fairly steadily from one decade to the next, and that there is reason to expect future generations to have far greater real average incomes and an abundance of consumer goods. Pressures to increase future investment then may be like taking from the poor to give to the rich—a sort of backward Robin Hood redistribution of income.

## ■ MARKET FAILURE AND GOVERNMENT FAILURE

We have pointed out some of the invisible hand's most noteworthy failures. We seem forced to the conclusion that a market economy, if left entirely to itself, is likely to produce results that are, at least in some respects, far from ideal. We have noted in our discussion, either directly or by implication, some of the things that government can do to correct these deficiencies. But the fact that government often *can* intervene in the economy's operation in a constructive way does not always mean that it actually *will* succeed in doing so. Governments cannot be relied on to behave ideally, any more than business firms can be expected to do so.

It is difficult to make this point in a suitably balanced way. Commentators too often stake out one extreme position or the other. Some people think the market mechanism is inherently unfair and biased by the greed of those who run its enterprises and look to the government to cure all economic ills. Others deplore government intervention and consider the public sector to be the home of every sort of inefficiency, graft, and bureaucratic stultification. The truth, as usual, lies somewhere in between.

Governments, like humans, are inherently imperfect. The political process leads to compromises that sometimes bear little resemblance to rational decisions. For example, legislators' versions of the policies suggested by economic analysis are sometimes mere caricatures of the economists' ideas. (For a satirical editorial illustrating this point, see the accompanying box, "The Politics of Economic Policy.")

Yet often the problems engendered by an unfettered economy are too serious to be left to the free market. The problems of inflation, environmental decay, and the provision of public goods are cases in point. In such instances, government intervention is likely to yield substantial benefits to the general public. However, even when *some* government action is clearly warranted, it may be difficult or impossible to calculate the *optimal* degree of governmental intervention. There is, then, the danger of intervention so excessive that the society might have been better off without it.

But in other areas the market mechanism is likely to work reasonably well, and small imperfections do not constitute adequate justification for government intervention. In any event, *even where government action is appropriate, we must consider marketlike instruments to correct market mechanism deficiencies.* The tax incentives described earlier in our discussion of externalities are an outstanding example of what we have in mind.

## ■ THE COST DISEASE OF THE SERVICE SECTOR

Next, we consider a problem that is not strictly a *failure* of the market mechanism. But it *is* a case where the market's behavior creates that illusion and often leads to ill-advised *government* action that threatens the general welfare.

### DETERIORATING PERSONAL SERVICES

Over the years, general standards of living have increased and our material possessions have multiplied. But at the same time, our communities have experienced a decline in the quality of a variety of public and private services. Not just in the United

---

● **THE POLITICS OF ECONOMIC POLICY**

---

In 1978, Alfred Kahn, a noted economist who served in the administration of President Jimmy Carter, advocated reducing pollution by raising the tax on leaded gasoline and lowering the tax on unleaded gasoline. *The Washington Post,* in an editorial excerpted below, agreed that Kahn's idea was a sound one but worried about what might emerge from Congress:

> If the administration adopts the Kahn plan, recent history offers a pretty clear view of the rest of the story. Mr. Kahn will draft a one-page bill to raise the tax on the one kind of gas and lower it on the other. But the White House political staff will immediately point out that his draft fails to address profound questions of social equity. What about the poor, who buy leaded gas because it's cheaper? What about young people driving old cars? What about the inhabitants of lower Louisiana, who need their outboard motors to get around the swamps and bayous? There will have to be a rebate formula. It will take into account each family's income, the number and ages of its various automobiles and the distance from its front doorstep to the bus stop. The legislative draftsmen at the Energy Department have had a lot of experience with that kind of formula and eventually the 53-page bill will be sent to Congress. . . .
>
> The real fun will start when it arrives at the Senate Finance Committee. First the committee will add tuition tax credits for families with children in private schools. Then, warming to its work, it will vote import quotas on straw hats from Hong Kong, beef from Argentina and automobiles from Japan. . . . [I]t will then add several obscure but pregnant provisions that seem to refer to the tax treatment of certain oil wells in the Gulf states. When the 268-page bill comes to the Senate floor, the administration will narrowly manage to defeat an amendment to improve business confidence by repealing the capital-gains tax and returning to the gold standard.
>
> When the bill gets back to the House, liberal Democrats will denounce it as an outrage and declare all-out war. They will succeed in getting all references to gasoline taxes and the environment stricken—but not, unfortunately, the import quotas or the obscure tax changes for the oil wells. By the time the staff of the Joint Committee on Taxation has straightened out a few technical difficulties, the bill will run to 417 pages and Ralph Nader will be calling on President Carter to veto it. But the feeling at the White House will be that Congress has worked so long and hard on the bill that he has no choice but to sign it. By the time the bill is finally enacted, Mr. Kahn might well wish he had chosen some other instrument of policy.

SOURCE: *The Washington Post,* December 26, 1978. © *The Washington Post.*

SOURCE: William Gropper, *The Senate* (1935). Collection, The Museum of Modern Art, New York. Gift of A. Conger Goodyear.

---

States, but throughout the world, streets and subways have grown increasingly dirty. Bus, train, and postal services have all been reduced. Amazingly enough, in the 1800s in suburban London, there were twelve mail deliveries per day on weekdays and one on Sundays! We all know what has happened to postal services since then.

Parallel cutbacks have occurred in the quality of private services. Doctors almost never visit patients at home anymore. In many areas a house call, which only 50 years ago was a commonplace event, now occurs only in a life-and-death emergency, if then. Another example, though undoubtedly a matter for less general concern, is the quality of food served in restaurants. Even some of the most elegant and expensive restaurants serve frozen and reheated meals—charging high prices for what amounts to little more than TV dinners.

### PERSONAL SERVICES ARE GETTING MORE EXPENSIVE

Perhaps most distressing of all, and closely connected with the problems just described, is the persistent and dramatic rise in the *cost* of personal services such as education and health care. You are painfully aware of the speed at which college tuitions have been increasing. The cost of a hospital stay has been going up even more rapidly. Worse still, the cost of health care has denied adequate health services to a substantial portion of our population—the poor and even some members of the middle class. These cost increases have made health care a prime subject of debate in political contests, not only in the United States but in virtually every other industrialized country.

Consider these facts: between 1948 and 1999, the Consumer Price Index (an official measure of *overall* price rises in the economy) increased at an average rate of about 3.8 percent per year, whereas the price of physicians' services rose 5.4 percent per year. This difference seems tiny, but compounded over those 51 years it had the effect of increasing the price of a doctor visit 125 percent, measured in dollars of constant purchasing power. During this same period, the price of hospital care skyrocketed: The average price of a hospital room increased at an annual rate of 8.2 percent compounded. This amounts to an almost 900 percent increase since 1948, measured in constant dollars.[3]

Virtually every major industrial nation has tried to prevent health-care costs from rising faster than its economy's rate of inflation, but none has succeeded, as Panel (a) of Figure 14–4 shows. In this graph the bar for each country shows its average yearly rate of increase in real (inflation-adjusted) health-care costs per person between 1960 and 1996. In some countries, real health-care cost has grown even faster than in the United States.

The cost of education has a similar record—costs per pupil in the United States have increased an average of 7.5 percent per year in the past 50 years. And during the approximately 30-year period 1965–1994, U.S. increases in education costs have been *lower* than education cost increases for four of the six top industrial countries, as shown in Panel (b) of Figure 14–4.

These are remarkable statistics, particularly because doctors' earnings barely kept up with the economy's overall inflation rate during this period, and teachers' salaries actually fell behind. Persistent cost increases have also plagued other services such as postal delivery, libraries, and theater tickets. The soaring costs of education, health care, and police and fire protection place a terrible financial burden on municipal budgets.

## WHY ARE PERSONAL SERVICES GETTING WORSE BUT COSTING MORE?

What accounts for the ever-increasing costs? Are they attributable to inefficiencies in government management or to political corruption? Perhaps in part to both. But another reason exists—one that cannot be avoided by any municipal administration no matter how pure and efficient—and one that affects the private service industry just as severely as it does the public sector. The common influence underlying all

**FIGURE 14-4**

**International Comparison: Growths Rates of Real per-Capita Health-Care Costs and Real per-Pupil Education Costs**

**(a) Real per-Capita Health-Care Costs, 1960–1996**

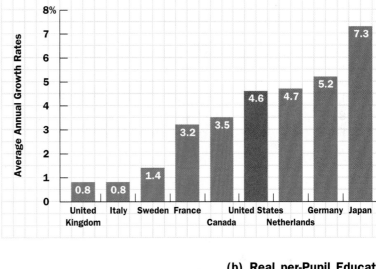

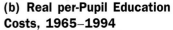

**(b) Real per-Pupil Education Costs, 1965–1994**

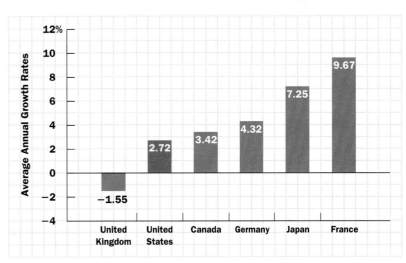

SOURCE: Organization for Economic Cooperation and Development, *OECD Health Data 1997*, CD-ROM (Paris: OECD, 1998); United Nations Educational, Scientific, and Cultural Organization, *Statistical Yearbook* (Paris: UNESCO, various years); and U.S. Department of Education, *Digest of Education Statistics*, http://nces.ed.gov, accessed March 1999.

---

[3] These figures were derived from data provided by the U.S. Department of Labor, Bureau of Labor Statistics, *CPI Detailed Report*, Washington, D.C., http://stats.bls.gov, accessed March 1999; and U.S. Department of Education, *Digest of Education Statistics*, http://nces.ed.gov, accessed March 1999.

BY ROSE FOR BYRD NEWSPAPERS, FREDERICKSBURG, VA.

of these problems of rising cost and deterioration in service quality, which is *economic* in character and expected to grow even more serious with time, has been called the *cost disease of the personal services.*

This "cost disease" stems from the basic nature of personal services. Most such services are *handicrafts*—they require direct contact between those who provide the service and those who consume it. Doctors, teachers, and librarians all engage in activities that require direct, person-to-person contact. Moreover, the quality of the service deteriorates if less time is provided by doctors, teachers, and librarians to each user of their services.

## UNEVEN LABOR PRODUCTIVITY GROWTH IN THE ECONOMY

But in other parts of the economy, like manufacturing, no direct personal contact between the consumer and the producer is required. For instance, the buyer of an automobile usually has no idea who worked on it and could not care less how much labor time went into its production. A labor-saving innovation in auto production need not imply a reduction in product quality. As a result, over the years it has proved far easier for technological change to save labor in manufacturing than to save labor in providing services. Labor productivity (output per worker) in U.S. manufacturing and agriculture has increased at an average rate of something like 2 percent a year since World War II, but the productivity of college teaching (crudely measured by number of students taught per teacher) has increased at a rate of only 1 percent per year during that period. And, in elementary and secondary education labor productivity has actually *declined*—the average number of pupils per teacher has fallen from about 27 pupils per teacher in 1955 to 17 pupils per teacher in 1994, partly because classes have become smaller.[4]

These disparate productivity performances have grave consequences for prices. When manufacturing wages rise 2 percent, the cost of manufactured products need not rise because increased output per worker can make up for the rise in wages. But the nature of many services makes it very difficult to introduce labor-saving devices

---

[4] U.S. Department of Education, ibid.

in those parts of the service sector. A 2 percent wage increase for teachers or police officers is not offset by higher productivity and must lead to an equivalent rise in municipal budgets. Similarly, a 2 percent wage increase for hairdressers must lead beauty salons to raise their prices.

In the long run, wages for all workers throughout the economy tend to go up and down together, for otherwise the activity whose wage rate falls seriously behind will tend to lose its labor force. So autoworkers and police officers will see their wages rise at roughly the same rate in the long run. But if productivity on the assembly line advances, even though productivity in the patrol car does not, then police protection must grow ever more expensive, relative to manufacturing, as time goes on. Because productivity improvements are very difficult for most personal services, their costs can be expected to rise faster, year in and year out, than the cost of manufactured products. Over a period of several decades, this difference in the growth rate of costs of the two sectors adds up, making services enormously more expensive compared with manufactured goods. In this way, personal services have grown steadily more expensive compared to goods, and they are likely to continue to do so.

## A FUTURE OF MORE GOODS BUT FEWER SERVICES: IS IT INEVITABLE?

If some services continue to get ever more expensive in comparison to goods, the implications for life in the future are profound indeed. The cost disease analysis portends a world in which the typical home contains an abundance of goods—luxuries and furnishings that we can hardly imagine. But it is a home surrounded by garbage and perhaps by violence. The cost disease analysis portends a future in which the services of doctors, teachers, and police officers are increasingly mass produced and impersonal, and in which arts and crafts are increasingly supplied only by amateurs because the cost of professional work in these fields is too high.

If this is the shape of the economy a hundred years from now, it will differ significantly from our own, and some persons will undoubtedly question whether the quality of life has increased in step with greater material prosperity. Some may even ask whether it has increased at all.

Is there anything that can be done to escape this future? The answer is that it is by no means inevitable. To see why, we must first recognize that the problem's source, paradoxically, is the growth in our economy's productivity—or rather, the *unevenness* of that growth. Trash removal costs go up, *not* because garbage collectors become less efficient but because labor in automobile manufacturing becomes *more* efficient, thus enhancing the sanitation worker's potential value on the automotive assembly line. The sanitation worker's wages must go up to keep him at his garbage removal job.

But increasing productivity in goods manufacturing does *not* make a nation poorer. It does *not* make us unable to afford things that we could afford in the past. Indeed, increasing productivity (i.e., more output from each work-hour) means that we can afford more of *all* things—televisions, electric toothbrushes, cell phones, *and* medical care, education, and other services.

> The role of services in our future depends on how we order our priorities. If we value services sufficiently, we can have more and better services—at some sacrifice in the growth rate of manufactured goods. Whether that is a good choice for society is not for economists to say. But society *does* have a choice, and if we fail to exercise it, matters may proceed relentlessly toward a world in which material goods are abundant and many things that most people now consider primary requisites for a high quality of life are scarce.

## GOVERNMENT MAY MAKE THE PROBLEM WORSE

How does the cost disease relate to the central topic of this chapter—the market's performance and its implications for the government's economic role? Here the problem is that the market *does* give the appropriate price signals, but government is likely to misunderstand these signals and to make decisions that do not promote the public interest most effectively.

Health care is a good example. The cost disease itself is capable of causing health-care costs (say, per hospital room) to rise faster than the economy's inflation rate because medical care cannot be standardized enough to share the productivity gains offered by automation and assembly lines. As a result, if we want to maintain standards of care in public hospitals, it is not enough to keep health-care budgets growing at the economy's prevailing inflation rate. Those budgets must actually grow *faster* to prevent a decline in quality. For example, when the inflation rate is 4 percent per year, hospitals' budgets may need to increase by 6 percent annually.

In these circumstances, something may seem amiss to a state legislature that increases its hospitals' budgets by only 5 percent per year. Responsible legislators will doubtless be disturbed by the fact that the budget is growing steadily, outpacing the inflation rate, and yet standards of quality at public hospitals are constantly slipping. If the legislators do not realize that the cost disease is causing the problem, they will look for villains—greedy doctors or corrupt or inefficient hospital administrators and so on. The net result, all too often, is a set of wasteful rules that hamper the freedom of action of hospitals and doctors inappropriately or that tighten hospital budgets below the levels that demands and costs would require if they were determined by the market mechanism rather than by government.

In many cases, *price controls* are proposed for sectors of the economy affected by the cost disease—for medical services, insurance services, and the like. But as we know, price controls can, at best, only eliminate the symptoms of the disease, and they often create problems that are sometimes more serious than the disease itself.[5]

### Explaining the Rising Costs of Canadian Health Care

The medical care system in Canada, as in every other industrial country, struggles with the effects of the cost disease. As we have just seen, legislative fiat cannot abolish the productivity-growth patterns that force health-care costs to rise persistently and universally faster than the overall inflation rate. The government-imposed price controls on doctors' fees and hospital budgets have, in fact, led to long waiting lists for Canadians who need high-tech medical procedures and have reduced patients' access to high-priced specialists. The Canadian government has been forced to ease up somewhat on price controls, allowing health-care prices to adapt more closely to costs in order to prevent more serious erosion of medical-care services. The overall quality of service apparently remains high, but the costs have risen persistently faster than the overall inflation rate, just as in the United States.

Panel (a) of Figure 14–4 shows that the U.S. record of health-care costs is not out of line with other industrialized countries. After correcting for differences in the overall inflation rates in the various countries (the U.S. record looks even better if this correction is omitted), we see that our performance is somewhere in the middle—by no means the best, but far from the worst in this sample of nine countries for the 36-year period from 1960 to 1996. (In Panel [b], we see that the same is true of education cost increases—the U.S. growth rate over the 29-year period, 1965 to 1994, falls in the middle of this group of six countries.) The conclusion is that, although a modification in our health-care system may or may not be desirable for other reasons, it is hardly a promising cure for the cost disease. Congress can declare both heart disease and the cost disease of the services to be illegal, but that will do little to cure either disease, and such a law may well impede more effective approaches to the problem.

In sum, the cost disease is not a case where the market performs badly. But it is a case in which the market *appears* to misbehave by singling out certain sectors for particularly large cost increases. Because the market *seems* to be working badly here, government reactions that can be highly damaging to the public interest are likely. That is, "government failure" may occur.

---

[5] See Chapter 5, pages 69–70 and 84–87.

"What really makes this heaven is our great healthcare plan."

## ■ SOME OTHER SOURCES OF MARKET FAILURE

We have now surveyed the most important imperfections of the market mechanism. But our list is not complete, and it can never be. In this imperfect world, nothing ever works out ideally, and by examining anything with a sufficiently powerful microscope, one can always detect more blemishes. However, some important items were omitted from our list. We will conclude with a brief description of three of them.

### IMPERFECT INFORMATION

In our analysis of the virtues of the market mechanism in Chapter 11, we assumed that consumers and producers have all the information they need to make their decisions. But in reality, this is not always the case. When buying a house or second-hand car or selecting a doctor, consumers are vividly reminded of how little they know about what they are purchasing. The old motto "Let the buyer beware" applies. Obviously, if participants in the market are ill-informed, they will not always make the optimal decisions described in our theoretical models. (For more on this issue, see the accompanying box, "Asymmetric Information, Lemons, and Agents.")

Yet not all economists agree that imperfect information is really a failure of the market mechanism. They point out that information, too, is a commodity that costs money to produce. Neither firms nor consumers have complete information because it would be irrational for them to spend the enormous amounts needed to get it. As always, the optimum is a compromise. One should, ideally, stop buying information at the point where the marginal utility of further information is no greater than its marginal cost. With this amount of information, the business executive or the consumer is able to make what we call "optimally imperfect" decisions.

### RENT SEEKING

An army of lawyers, expert witnesses, and business executives crowd our courtrooms and pile up enormous costs. Business firms seem to sue each other at the slightest provocation, wasting vast resources and delaying business decisions. Why? Because it is possible to make money by such seemingly unproductive activities—through legal battles over profit-making opportunities.

For example, suppose that a municipality awards a contract to produce electricity to Firm A, offering $20 million in profit. It may be worthwhile for Firm B to spend $5 million in a lawsuit against the municipality and Firm A, hoping that the courts will award it the contract (and thus the $20 million profit) instead.

In general, any source of unusual profit, such as a monopoly, is a temptation for firms to waste economic resources in an effort to obtain control of that source of profit. This process, called **rent seeking** (meaning that the firms hope to obtain earnings without contributing to production), is judged by some observers to be a

**Rent seeking** refers to unproductive activity in the pursuit of economic profit—in other words, profit in excess of competitive earnings.

## ● ASYMMETRIC INFORMATION, LEMONS, AND AGENTS

Have you ever wondered why a six-month-old car sells for so much less than a brand-new one? Economists offer one explanation, having to do with *imperfect information.* The problem is that some small percentage of new automobiles are "lemons" that are plagued by mechanical troubles. The new-car dealer probably knows no more than the buyer whether a particular car is a lemon. The information known to the two parties, therefore, is said to be *symmetric,* and there is a low probability that a car purchased from a new-car dealer will turn out to be a lemon.

In the used-car market, however, information is *asymmetric.* The person selling the used car knows very well whether the car is a lemon, but the buyer does not. Moreover, a seller who wants to get rid of a relatively new car is likely to be doing so only because it *is* a lemon. Potential buyers realize that. Hence, if a person is forced to sell a good new car because of an unexpected need for cash, he too will be stuck with a low price because he cannot *prove* that his car really works well. The moral is that asymmetric information also tends to harm the honest seller.

In addition, asymmetric information leads to what are called *principal-agent problems,* whose analysis is a major concern of recent economic research. The issue arises because many critical tasks must be delegated to others. For instance, people who own stock in a corporation delegate the running of the firm to its management team.* U.S. citizens delegate lawmaking to Congress. Union members delegate many decisions to the union leadership. In such cases, the persons who give away part of their decision-making powers are called the *principals,* and those who exercise those powers are called the *agents,* who are, in effect, hired by the principals to perform the jobs in question.

Asymmetric information is crucial here. The principals know only *imperfectly* whether their agents are serving their interests faithfully and efficiently or are instead neglecting or even acting against the principals' interests to pursue selfish interests of their own. Misuse of the principals' property, embezzlement, and political corruption are extreme examples of such dereliction of duty by agents and, unfortunately, they seem to occur often. Among other things, economic analysis studies ways of curing or at least alleviating such problems by arranging for the kind of compensation for agents that bring the agents' interests more closely into line with those of the principals. For example, if the salaries of corporate management are linked to company profits or based on the

market value of company shares, then by promoting the welfare of stockholders, managers will make themselves better off. Shareholders, even though they know only imperfectly what management is doing, can have a fair degree of confidence that management will try to serve their interests well.

*This is an important issue in *takeover battles,* where some outside group tries to gain control of a corporation by buying up a large share of its stock. Because the new owners will be likely to fire the firm's current management, this latter group may fight hard to prevent the takeover even if it is in the interest of the company's stockholders. For more discussion of takeovers, see Chapter 16, page 320.

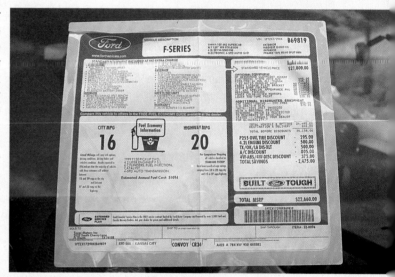

major source of inefficiency in our economy. (For more on rent seeking, see pages 342–343 of Chapter 17.)

### MORAL HAZARD

Another widely discussed problem for the market mechanism is associated with insurance. Economists view insurance—which is the provision of protection against risk—

as a useful commodity, like shoes or information. But insurance also encourages the very risks against which it provides protection. For example, if an individual has a valuable stamp collection that is fully insured against theft, she has little motivation to protect it against burglars. She may, for example, fail to lock it up in a safe-deposit box. This problem—the tendency of insurance to encourage the source of risk—is called **moral hazard,** and it makes a free market in insurance hard to operate.

**Moral hazard** refers to the tendency of insurance to discourage policyholders from protecting themselves from risk.

## ■ THE MARKET SYSTEM ON BALANCE

This chapter, like Chapter 11, has deliberately offered a rather unbalanced assessment of the market mechanism. We spent Chapter 11 extolling the market's virtues and spent this chapter cataloguing its vices. We come out, as in the nursery rhyme, concluding that the market is either very, very good or it is horrid.

There seems to be nothing *moderate* about the quality of performance of a market system. As a means of achieving efficiency in the production of ordinary consumer goods and responding to changes in consumer preferences, it is unparalleled. It is, in fact, difficult to overstate the accomplishments of the price system in these areas. On the other hand, the market has proven itself unable to cope with business fluctuations, income inequality, or the consequences of monopoly. It has proved to be a very poor allocator of resources among outputs that generate external costs and external benefits, and it has shown itself to be completely incapable of arranging for the provision of public goods. Some of the most urgent problems that plague our society—the deterioration of services in the cities, the despoliation of our atmosphere, the social unrest attributable to poverty—can be ascribed in part to one or another of these market system shortcomings.

Most economists conclude from these observations that although the market mechanism is virtually irreplaceable, the public interest nevertheless requires considerable modifications in the way it works. Proposals designed to deal directly with the problems of poverty, monopoly, and resource allocation over time abound in economic literature. All of them call for the government to intervene in the economy, either by supplying directly those goods and services that, it is believed, private enterprise does not supply in adequate amounts, or by seeking to influence the workings of the economy more indirectly through regulation. We discussed many of these programs in earlier chapters; we will explain others in future chapters.

## ■ EPILOGUE: THE UNFORGIVING MARKET, ITS GIFT OF ABUNDANCE, AND ITS DANGEROUS FRIENDS

As we said at the end of Chapter 11, economists' analysis of the free market's accomplishments, although valid enough, may fail to emphasize its central contribution. The same can be said of their analysis of the market's shortcomings.

The market's major contribution to the general welfare may well be its stimulation of *productivity*, which has yielded an abundance of consumer goods, contributed to increases in human longevity, created new products, expanded education, and raised standards of living to levels undreamed of in earlier societies. The main shortcoming of the market, in the view of many observers, lies in the arena of justice and injustice, a subject that economists are no more competent to address than anyone else. The perception that markets are cruel and unjust springs from the very heart of the mechanism. The market mechanism has sometimes been described appropriately as the profit system, because it works by richly rewarding those who succeed in introducing attractive new products or in increasing efficiency sufficiently to permit sharp price reductions of other items. At the same time, it is unforgiving to those who fail, subjecting them to bankruptcy and perhaps to poverty.

Both the wealth awarded to those who succeed and the drastic treatment accorded those who fail are main sources of the markets' productive power. But they also generate disenchantment and opposition. This has been true in the newly "marketized" countries of eastern Europe. Predictably, as enterprise in these countries was freed from government control, a number of wildly successful entrepreneurs have earned high incomes, leading to widespread resentment among the populace and calls for restrictions on entrepreneurial earnings. But critics do not seem to realize that a market without substantial rewards to successful entrepreneurs is a market whose engine has been weakened, if not altogether removed.

Indeed, efficient and effectively competitive markets often elicit support from groups who, at the same time, do their best to undermine that competition. For example, regulators who seek to prevent "excessive competition," and politicians in other countries who arrange for the sale of government enterprises to private owners only to constrain decision making by the new owners at every turn, are, in fact, doing their best to keep markets from working. When the general public demands price controls on interest rates, rents, and health-care services, it is expressing its unwillingness to accept the free market's decisions. Businesspeople who are tireless in proclaiming their support for the market system, but who seek to acquire the monopoly power that can distort its activities, are doing the same thing. In short, the market has many professed supporters who genuinely believe in its virtues, but whose behavior poses a constant threat to its effectiveness.

We cannot take for granted the success of the newly introduced market mechanism in eastern Europe. As this book is being written the Russian economy is in turmoil, as are other economies in eastern Europe and several countries in the Far East. Even in the older free-enterprise economies, we cannot just assume that the market will survive unscathed from the dangerous embrace of its most vocal supporters.

---

## S U M M A R Y

1. There are at least seven major imperfections associated with the market mechanism:

   a. Inequality of income distribution

   b. Fluctuations in economic activity (inflation and unemployment)

   c. Monopolistic output restrictions

   d. *Beneficial* and *detrimental externalities*

   e. Inadequate provision of public goods

   f. Misallocation of resources between present and future

   g. Deteriorating quality and rising costs of personal services

2. Efficient resource allocation is basically a matter of balancing the benefits of producing more of one good against the benefits of devoting the required inputs to some other good's production.

3. A detrimental externality occurs when an economic activity incidentally does harm to others who are not directly involved in the activity; a beneficial externality occurs when an economic activity incidentally creates benefits for others.

4. When an activity causes a detrimental externality, the activity's *marginal social cost* (including the harm it does to others) must be greater than the *marginal private cost* to those who carry on the activity. The opposite will be true when a beneficial externality occurs.

5. If a product's manufacture causes detrimental externalities, its price will generally not include all of the marginal social cost it causes, because part of the cost will be borne by others. The opposite is true for beneficial externalities.

6. The market will therefore tend to overallocate resources to the production of goods that cause detrimental externalities and underallocate resources to the production of goods that create beneficial externalities. This is one of the *Ideas for Beyond the Final Exam.*

7. A *public good* is defined by economists as a commodity (like the guiding beam of a coastal lighthouse) that is not depleted by additional users. In addition, it is often difficult to exclude anyone from the benefits of a public good, even those who refuse to pay for it. A *private good*, in contrast, is characterized by both *excludability* and *depletability*.

8. Free-enterprise firms generally will not produce a public good, even if it is extremely useful to the community, because they cannot charge money for the use of the good.

9. Many observers believe that the market often shortchanges the future, particularly when it makes *irreversible decisions* that destroy natural resources.

10. Because personal services—such as education, medical care, and police protection—are handicraft activities that are therefore not amenable to labor-saving innovations, they suffer from a *cost disease*. That is, their costs tend to rise persistently and considerably faster than costs in the economy as a whole, where more rapid productivity increases offset rising input costs. The result can be a distortion in the supply of services by government or the imposition of unwise price controls because the rising cost is misattributed to greed and mismanagement. This *cost disease of the service sector* is another of our *Ideas for Beyond the Final Exam.*

## KEY TERMS

Resource misallocation 270

Production possibilities 271

Externalities (detrimental and beneficial) 272

Marginal social cost (MSC) 273

Marginal private cost (MPC) 273

Public good 276

Private good 276

Depletability 276

Excludability 276

Opportunity cost 277

Irreversible decision 278

Cost disease of the personal services 279

Rent seeking 285

Asymmetric information 286

Principals 286

Agents 286

Moral hazard 286

## QUESTIONS FOR REVIEW

1. Specifically, what is the opportunity cost to society of a 100-mile trip of a truck? Why may the price of the gasoline used by the truck not adequately represent that opportunity cost?

2. Suppose that, because of a new disease that attacks coffee plants, far more labor and other inputs are required to harvest a pound of coffee than before. How might that affect the efficient allocation of resources between tea and coffee? Why? How would the prices of coffee and tea react in a free market?

3. Give some examples of goods whose production causes detrimental externalities and some examples of goods that create beneficial externalities.

4. Compare cleaning a dormitory room with cleaning the atmosphere of a city. Which is a public good and which is a private good? Why?

5. Give some other examples of public goods. Discuss in each case why additional users do not deplete them and why it is difficult to exclude people from using them.

6. Think about the goods and services that your local government provides. Which of these are "public goods" as economists use the term?

7. Explain why the services of a lighthouse are sometimes given as an example of a public good.

8. Explain why education is not a very satisfactory example of a public good.

9. In recent decades, college tuition costs have risen faster than the general price level even though the wages of college professors have failed to keep pace with the price level. Can you explain why?

10. A firm holds a patent that is estimated to be worth $20 million. The patent is repeatedly challenged in the courts by a large number of (rent-seeking) firms, each hoping to grab away the patent. In what sense may the rent seekers be "competing perfectly" for the patent? If so, how much will end up being spent in the legal battles? (*Hint:* Under perfect competition, should firms expect to earn any economic profit?)

The Bourgeoisie [i.e., capitalism] cannot exist without constantly revolutionizing the instruments of production. . . . The bourgeoisie, during its rule of scarce one hundred years has created more massive and more colossal productive forces than have all preceding generations together.

*Karl Marx and Friedrich Engels*
*The Communist Manifesto, 1847*

# MICROECONOMICS OF INNOVATION: PRIME ENGINE OF GROWTH

Human history in the last two centuries has been unlike anything ever experienced before. In the world's industrial countries, the quantity and quality of food, clothing, and comforts have reached levels that were never before dreamed possible. The change has been so revolutionary that it is difficult to grasp. What accounts for this transformation? The answer is growth in *labor productivity*—the fact that the hourly production of a person in the United States today is perhaps 20 times as high as it was in 1800. Just two figures will suggest the magnitude of the achievement. In 1800 about 90 percent of America's labor force had to work on farms, but

**Labor productivity** refers to the amount of output a worker turns out in an hour (or a week or a year) of labor. It can be measured as gross domestic product (GDP) in a given year divided by the total number of paid work hours during that year. That is, labor productivity is defined as GDP per hour of labor.

all that farm labor barely managed to produce enough food to feed the country adequately. Today less than 3 percent of U.S. workers earn their livings on farms. Yet those relatively few farm workers provide an outpouring of surpluses, which the U.S. government constantly struggles to contain.

Figure 15–1 shows, for five industrialized countries, the impressive growth of **labor productivity** over the past century. It is this spectacular growth in productivity that has transformed living standards. Productivity growth is what has made all the difference and, over the long haul, is what counts most in raising living standards.

| FIGURE 15–1 |
|---|

**The Growth of Labor Productivity, 1870 to 1996**

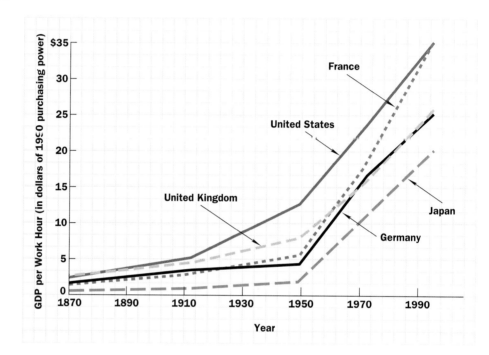

SOURCE: Angus Maddison, "The Nature and Functioning of European Capitalism: A Historical and Comparative Perspective," University of Groningen, Belgium, Oct. 1, 1997, mimeo.

*Productivity Growth Is (Almost) Everything in the Long Run*

**PRODUCTIVITY GROWTH** As we pointed out in our *ideas* in Chapter 1, only rising productivity can raise standards of living in the long run. Over long periods of time, small differences in rates of productivity growth compound like interest in a bank account and can make an enormous difference to a society's prosperity. Nothing contributes more to reduction of poverty, to increases in leisure, and to the country's ability to finance education, public health, environmental improvement, and the arts. By the same token, a slowdown in productivity growth that persists for a substantial number of years can have a devastating effect on living standards.

**Innovation** is the process by which new products or new methods of production are introduced, including all the steps from the inventor's idea to bringing the new item to market.

Many factors contribute to productivity growth. Most often cited are (1) the education and experience of the labor force that enable the worker to produce more and better goods in a given amount of time; (2) investment in plant and equipment that gives the worker more and better tools with which to do the job; and, above all, **innovation,** the discovery and introduction of new production methods and new products that offer workers productive powers never before imagined. This chapter discusses the economic influences that affect the flow of new products and new technology. In particular, we will investigate what underlies the explosion of the technical change that occurred in the past few centuries in the industrialized countries of the world.

Although we have devoted a lot of attention to the virtues and vices of the market system in earlier chapters, we have barely mentioned what may be its greatest strength. It is the one at which Marx and Engels marveled: Free-market capitalism has proven to be the most powerful engine of economic growth and innovation ever known.

Although the process of *innovation* has yet to be analyzed completely by economists, we can understand some of its crucial features using concepts you have learned in previous chapters—such as marginal cost (Chapter 8), marginal revenue (Chapter 9), and externalities (Chapter 14). Thus, though this chapter deals with a new and critically vital subject, it does not require any new analytic concepts or methods. Indeed, the chapter will help you to review those tools and their uses.

## The *Big* Puzzle: Why Do All Rival Economic Systems Trail So Far behind Free Market Growth Rates?

Undoubtedly, the spectacular and unmatched growth rates of the industrialized free-market economies (also called **capitalist** economies) distinguishes them most from *all* other economic systems. In no other system, current or past, has the general public's average income risen anywhere nearly as much or as quickly as it has in North America, western Europe, and Japan. Though the Soviet Union planned its economy and forced its population to invest heavily in factories and hydroelectric dams, its failure to raise the people's standard of living to the level enjoyed by members of the free-market economies undoubtedly played a major role in the USSR's downfall. Great civilizations have amassed extraordinary records of invention and engineering—medieval China and ancient Rome are clear examples. But none has approached the growth record of modern free-market economies. What is the secret of their extraordinary success? Resolution of this economic puzzle is undoubtedly critical to the future prosperity of our planet. The truth is that this puzzle has not yet been solved. But this chapter will offer some clues.

**Capitalism** is an economic system in which most of the production process is controlled by private firms operating in markets with minimal government control. The investors in these firms (called "capitalists") own the firms.

## ■ THE FREE MARKET'S GROWTH RECORD

Growth in per-capita income and productivity in free-market economies has been so enormous that we can hardly comprehend its magnitude. In contrast, average growth rates of per-capita incomes probably approximated *zero* for about 1,500 years before the **Industrial Revolution** (around the time of George Washington). In 1776, even the wealthiest consumers in England, then the world's richest country, could purchase only a half-dozen consumers' goods that were not also available in ancient Rome. These new products included (highly inaccurate) hunting guns, (highly inaccurate) watches, paper, window glass, and very little else. And Roman citizens enjoyed a number of amenities, such as hot baths and paved roads, that had practically disappeared long before the American Revolution. In contrast, in the past two centuries, per-capita incomes in the typical capitalist economy have risen by amounts ranging from several hundred to several thousand percent. Recent decades have yielded an unmatched outpouring of new products and services: color television, the computer, jet aircraft, the VCR, the microwave, the hand-held calculator, the cellular telephone, and so on and so on. And the flood of new products continues. Surely part of the reason for the collapse of most of the world's communist regimes was their citizens' desire to participate in the growth miracle of the capitalist economies, the very miracle that Marx and Engels—those high priests of anti-capitalist movements—were among the first economists to discern.

The **Industrial Revolution** is the stream of new technology and the resulting growth of output that began in England toward the end of the 18th century.

We must seek an explanation for this miracle in the activities of industries and the business firms of which they are constituted, for firms produce the increasing flow of goods and services that constitute the capitalist economies' amazing growth. Yet standard microeconomic theory of firms and industries that we discussed in earlier chapters provides no suggestion as to the forces underlying the business decisions that foster such explosive growth. Indeed, as we will see, standard microeconomic theory offers several reasons to expect much less than optimal growth performance in a capitalist economy.

In contrast, this chapter describes some features of competitive markets that literally force businesses to do all they can to contribute to growth.

## INNOVATION AND THE GROWTH PROCESS

A primary source of the growth miracle of the past two centuries, undoubtedly, was "the wave of new gadgets,"[1] the surge of innovation that first reached a substantial pace in Britain between 1800 and 1830. Improved education and infrastructure (the combination of facilities, factories, roads and other influences that enable firms to do business more easily) surely made substantial contributions. But innovation clearly was crucial for the explosive growth from 1800 to the present. The Industrial Revolution's inventions helped to end the incredible poverty of earlier centuries that previously prevented societies from spending much on education or on building of infrastructure, plant, and machinery.

We cannot easily grasp the magnitude of that poverty. The following passage from a noted historian suggests how serious the problem was as recently as the 1600s:

> The poor in the towns and countryside lived in a state of almost complete deprivation. Their furniture consisted of next to nothing. . . . Inventories made after death . . . testify almost invariably to the general destitution . . . a few old clothes, a stool, a table, a bench, the planks of a bed, sacks filled with straw. Official reports for Burgundy [in France] between the sixteenth and the eighteenth centuries are full of references to people [sleeping] on straw . . . with no bed or furniture, who were only separated from the pigs by a screen. . . . Paradoxically the countryside sometimes experienced far greater suffering [from famines than the townspeople]. The peasants . . . had scarcely any reserves of their own. They had no solution in case of famine except to turn to the town where they crowded together, begging in the streets and often dying in public squares.[2]

Innovation permitted growing outputs, first in agriculture and mining and then in manufacturing and transportation, that enabled society to invest increasingly in productive plant and equipment and in education. These investments themselves contributed greatly to economic growth. Thus, innovation allowed us to embark on a growth process that itself contributed to further growth.

Two of today's leading analysts of economic growth conclude:

> As yet, no empirical study proves that technology has been the engine of modern-day growth. Still, we ask the reader to ponder the following: What would the century's growth performance have been like without the invention and refinement of methods for generating electricity and using radio waves to transmit sound, without Bessemer's discovery of a new technique for refining iron, and without the design and development of products like the automobile, the airplane, the transistor, the integrated circuit, and the computer?[3]

## WHAT IS DIFFERENT ABOUT FREE-MARKET ECONOMIES?

Yet invention alone does not completely answer the great puzzle—why free-market growth has never been rivaled. Some earlier societies had spectacular invention

---

[1] According to the late British economist, T. S. Ashton, "the wave of new gadgets" is how one schoolboy (quite appropriately) described the Industrial Revolution.

[2] Fernand Braudel, *The Structures of Everyday Life: Civilization and Capitalism, 15th–18th Century, Vol. 1* (New York: Harper & Row, 1979), pp. 73–75 and 284–286.

[3] Gene M. Grossman and Elhanan Helpman, "Endogenous Innovation in the Theory of Growth," *Journal of Economic Perspectives* 8 (Winter 1994): p. 32.

records. The Chinese are the outstanding example. Centuries before Columbus came to the New World, the Chinese had invented printing, the compass, complex clockworks, gunpowder, spinning machinery, cotton gins, porcelain, matches, toothbrushes, playing cards, and much more. Other countries in history also achieved a considerable record of new products and new technology. Moreover, Chinese culture and others placed a high value on education, though much of the population was uneducated. Yet, economically, these inventions and this education never produced economic growth anything like that in modern market economies.

We know that substantial markets exist, and have existed, in virtually every economy in the world throughout recorded history. How, then, do modern markets differ, so that they exhibit the capacity to produce growth miracles in a seemingly unending stream? There is no simple answer. Indeed, any proposed answer may well leave out key influences, including political changes, religious beliefs, even historical accidents. However, two features of our economy seem to have played especially crucial roles. The first is free competition—that is, competition not handicapped by tight government regulations or tightly enforced customary rules (like the rules governing the medieval guilds, which prevented gloves-off combat among rival firms). Second, in today's economy, many rival firms use *innovation* as their main weapon with which to battle actual and potential competitors. As in an arms race between two countries, each firm fears that the other will introduce new successful products and therefore it must match the other firm's research and development expenditures. Each feels that at least matching its rival's efforts and spending on innovation is a matter of economic life or death. In such an economy, we can expect a constant stream of innovations, because firms do not dare relax their innovation activities.

## INNOVATION VERSUS PRICE AS THE PRIME COMPETITIVE WEAPON

It is quite clear that innovation is the weapon of choice for competitive battles in substantial sectors of the economy. Price does, of course, matter. But process and product improvements really capture the attention of management. Product lines as diverse as computers and computer software, automobiles, cameras, and machinery all feature constant improvements, which are instantly and widely advertised. Any firm that can come up with a better model than its rivals have will gain an advantage that its competitors cannot match as quickly and easily as a price cut. Dramatic new products also provide substantially greater market advantages than slightly lower prices. Many high-tech industries gain market advantages in exactly this way: computers, medical equipment, aeronautics, automobiles, and so forth.

Of course, not all industries compete via innovation. In fact, most innovations derive from a very few industries in a very few countries. About 80 percent of industrial outlays on new product **research and development**—the means by which firms create new products and prepare them for market, also known as **R&D**—comes from the chemical or machinery and equipment industries. Yet, even in industries where product and process development do not act as the leading instruments of competition, management cannot afford to neglect research and development activities. For if one firm fails to adopt the latest technology—even technology created by others—then rivals can easily take the lead and make disastrous inroads into slower firms' sales.

Thus, especially in high-tech sectors, firms dare not leave innovation to chance. Rather, competitive markets force firms to systematize the innovation process and (in the immortal words of W. C. Fields) "to remove all elements of chance" from the undertaking.[4] Many business firms today routinely budget for R&D, systematically decide how to promote and price their innovations, and even systematically determine what kinds of products the company's laboratories should invent. (See the

**Research and development (R&D)** is the activity of firms, universities, and government agencies that seeks to invent new products and processes and to improve those inventions so that they are ready for the market or other uses.

---

[4] This phrase is uttered when Fields seeks to lure a novice into a card game, whereupon his intended victim questions the morality of "games of chance." Fields hastens to reassure him: "Young man, when you play with me, all elements of chance have been removed!"

---

> ● **DO NEW IDEAS COME ONLY FROM LONE GENIUSES WORKING IN THEIR GARAGES OR BASEMENTS?**

Thousands of police can attest to the value of Stephanie Kwolek's breakthrough research in para-aramid fibers. The fruits of her inventiveness can be found in mooring ropes, fiber-optic cables, aircraft parts, canoes, and—most important—in lightweight bullet-resistant vests. Born in New Kensington, Pennsylvania, Kwolek received her B.S. in chemistry from the Carnegie Institute of Technology in 1946. That same year she went to work as a chemist at the Buffalo, New York, operations of E. I. Du Pont de Nemours & Company. "I really wanted to study medicine," Kwolek recalled, "but I didn't have enough money to enter medical school. I joined Du Pont as a temporary measure, but the work turned out to be so interesting that I stayed on."

Kwolek's earliest work, together with that of colleagues, pioneered low-temperature processes for the preparation of condensation polymers. These processes made possible the preparation of hundreds of new polymers and found applications in the future preparation of Lycra® spandex fiber and Nomex® and Kevlar® aramid fibers.

Later, as she searched for a fiber to reinforce radial tires, she unexpectedly discovered a new class of polymers—the liquid crystalline polyamides. This technology, which involved the formation and spinning of liquid crystalline solutions of extended-chain aromatic polyamides into fibers with very high strength and very high stiffness, became the foundation of the Kevlar® fiber. The latter fiber, which is five times stronger than steel on an equal weight basis, is the fiber of choice for bullet-resistant vests. The many unique applications of Kevlar® generate hundreds of millions of dollars in sales worldwide each year.

Kwolek moved to the Pioneering Research Laboratory at Du Pont's Experimental Station in Wilmington, Delaware, in 1950. She retired in 1986 as a research associate but continues to consult for Du Pont and has served on the committees of the National Research Council of the National Academy of Sciences. Her name appears on 17 patents issued between 1961 and 1986.

SOURCE: "Inventure Place," National Inventors Hall of Fame, www.invent.org, accessed on November 10, 1998.

---

accompanying box, "Do New Ideas Come Only from Lone Geniuses Working in Their Garages or Basements?" for an example of the fruits of such routinized R&D efforts in big firms.)

Of course, we can analyze this kind of orderly business-firm innovation activity using the standard tools of the theory of the firm much more easily than we can the "Eureka! I have found it!" process, in which the classic lone inventor working in a basement or garage happens to come up with a brilliant invention. Business-firm innovation is easier to analyze because R&D budgets and decisions look a lot like other business decisions, such as how much to produce or how much to spend on advertising. We can study all of these standard business decisions using the same tools of marginal analysis.

## HOW MUCH WILL THE PROFIT-MAXIMIZING FIRM SPEND ON INNOVATION?

So, competition forces many firms in the economy to keep up their R&D expenditures. Some of the money spent on R&D will lead to spectacular successes. Other such spending will yield only modest advances, and some R&D outlays will fail outright. Taken as a whole, we can expect that the more money firms spend on R&D, the more innovation will take place and the faster the economy will grow. The key questions are, how much can we expect firms to spend on R&D, and how will competition affect that amount?

We have encountered the general answer to these questions over and over again when we studied how basic marginal analysis addresses business decisions in Chapters 8, 9, and 10.

> If the firm seeks to maximize its profits, it will expand its spending on R&D up to the point at which its anticipated marginal cost of R&D equals its anticipated marginal revenue from R&D.

A level of R&D spending (call it $X$ dollars) at which marginal revenue is, for example, *greater* than marginal cost cannot possibly represent the profit-maximizing amount for the company to spend on R&D. If MR exceeds MC, the company can increase profits by spending more than $X$ dollars on R&D. The opposite will be true if MR < MC. Then the firm can increase its profit by decreasing R&D spending. So $X$ dollars cannot be the optimal level of spending if either MR > MC or MR < MC. It follows that the profit-maximizing level of spending on R&D can only be an amount, say $Y$ dollars, at which MR = MC. You will recognize this argument, for we have repeated it many times when we discussed other business decisions, such as those on price and quantity of output, in earlier chapters.

This analysis tells us everything, and nothing, about the R&D decision. It tells us everything, because its conclusion is correct. If the firm is a profit maximizer, and if we know its MR and its MC curves for R&D investment, then the MR = MC rule does, in theory, tell us exactly how much the firm must invest in R&D to attain its objective. But the discussion so far tells us nothing about the shape of "typical" marginal revenue and marginal cost curves for R&D. Nor does it tell us how competitive pressures affect these curves—the competition that plays such an important role in R&D decisions. Nor have we discussed how business behavior contributes to economic growth. Before dealing with these crucial matters, however, let us first apply the standard theory of the firm and the industry to see what such tools tell us about innovation.

## THE PROFITS OF INNOVATION

Many discussions of innovation start off with the assumption that innovators expect to earn very high profits. And huge rewards do accrue to those who introduce unusually successful innovations. We have all heard of innovators like Thomas Edison, Alexander Graham Bell, and, more recently, Bill Gates, Steven Jobs, and others in the computer industry, who have acquired great riches from their ability to invent, or bring innovations to market and sell their products. But for every successful innovator, many others have plowed their family savings into new gadgets and lost all they have spent. Quite possibly, inventors on average earn zero economic profits, or even lose money.

This possibility appears even more clearly when we consider business investment in R&D, which is the focus of this chapter. We have just seen that profit-maximizing firms earn zero *marginal* profit (where, by definition, marginal profit = MR − MC), because the firm will invest to the point at which MR = MC. But we can take the analysis further if new firms can enter freely into invention activity, as must be true if the industry is perfectly competitive.

As we saw in Chapter 10, an industry under perfect competition entry will occur until economic profits are zero in equilibrium. Said another way, perfectly competitive industries permit firms to earn just what they need to pay investors for the funds they provide. This must be so because if a typical firm in one industry earns more than firms in other industries, investors will put more money into the more profitable industry. Any excess (economic) profit will expand industry output, thereby driving prices down and eliminating economic profits.

Because there are some barriers to entry into innovation, we cannot be certain that economic profits to invention will tend *exactly* toward zero. But we can still expect them to be very low on average. In other words, although inventive activity sometimes pays off enormously well, large R&D investments also can fail spectacularly, so that the average comes out close to zero. In particular, a large firm with a big R&D division may work simultaneously on many possible innovations. The "law of averages" suggests that some of these efforts will fail and some will succeed. So we can expect zero economic profit even in industries with a great deal of innovative activity.

Does this conclusion fit the facts? Although we have no systematic study of all inventive activities, high-tech industries provide a useful illustration—especially the computer industry, where many founders have made fortunes and received much publicity. According to one recent assessment, however:

> "The computer industry hasn't made a dime. . . . Intel and Microsoft make money, but look at all the people who were losing money all the world over. It is doubtful the industry has yet broken even," said Peter Drucker in a recent interview . . . but is it true? Paul Gompers

"You will never catch up with the new technology."

of the Harvard Business School and Alon Brav of the University of Chicago . . . looked at companies that went public from 1975 to 1992, most of which were high-tech firms, and found their rate of return to be about average [i.e., zero economic profit], once they adjusted for risk and company size.[5]

## REDUCING RISK BY SHARING TECHNOLOGY

Low average profits from innovation arise largely from the inherent riskiness of the activity—the high likelihood that investments in apparently promising innovations will go down the drain. Recent marketing literature suggests that only about 6 to 7 percent of new products ever make it all the way to the marketing stage. We would expect firms to try to minimize their risks, and they do. For example, management may not fund research in their laboratories on inventions that they judge to be impractical. However, managers have also proven amazingly shortsighted in some cases, as when the Western Union Telegraph Company turned down the newly invented telephone.

Firms also try to protect themselves by joining together to share risks. After all, each partner in a five-firm partnership has to supply only one-fifth of the funds needed to bring an innovation to completion. Such partnerships are called "research joint ventures," and there are many of them (see the accompanying box, "Collaboration, Rather Than Competition, in Innovation," for an example).

A lesser-known phenomenon occurs when many firms try to reduce their risks by **trading technology.** It may seem to you that when a business firm succeeds in producing a promising new invention, it will do all it can to bar its competitors' access to the new technology in order to retain its competitive advantage over rivals. But this is often not true. Fearing that their own laboratories may conceivably fail in all R&D undertakings in a particular period, while competitors may possibly have better luck, firms often enter into agreements with their competitors to *share* all successful future innovations for a specified time period—say, the next five years. Such agreements reduce risk for *both* technology-sharing firms.

In photography, for example, one camera manufacturer may introduce an improved automatic focus device, another an automatic light adjustment, and a third may invent a way to make the camera more compact. Each of these three firms can keep its invention to itself. But if two of them get together and agree to produce cameras combining both their new features, then they will be able to market a product clearly superior to what either could have produced alone. They will also be in a far better position to meet competition from the third camera manufacturer.

Many firms and industries engage in this practice of **cross licensing.** For example, the Perkin-Elmer Corporation manufactures and sells scientific instruments (notably those using precision optics such as microscopes) throughout the world. Since World War II, Perkin-Elmer has entered into technology-transfer agreements with domestic and foreign firms. In 1960, for example, Perkin-Elmer agreed to share technology with the Hitachi Corporation, and a modified version of that agreement continued for decades. The contract required the two firms to supply *a full menu* of their technical developments periodically. Either firm was authorized to produce any product designed in this way, with full technical assistance from the other. Each firm agreed to pay a royalty rate of 6 to 7.5 percent for items invented by the other firm. The agreement required reciprocal technical training as well, although the company requesting such training paid its own employees' travel and living expenses.

In another example, IBM cross-licenses patents with *each* of its major competitors. Such a contract usually covers some well-defined field, such as semiconductors or input-output devices. In the negotiation of such a contract the firms compare what prospective technological changes each has to offer and agree to make up any difference in patent value via a monetary "balance payment," bargaining over the amount. Contracts normally run over several years and entitle

**Technology trading** is an arrangement in which a firm voluntarily makes its privately owned technology available to other firms either in exchange for access to the technology of the second company or for an agreed-upon fee.

**Cross licensing** of patents occurs when each of two firms agrees to let the other use some specified set of its patents, either at a price specified in their agreement or in return for access to the other firm's patents.

---

[5] "The Rewards of Investing in High Tech," *Federal Reserve Bank of Boston Regional Review* 6 (Fall 1996): p. 14.

---

### ● COLLABORATION, RATHER THAN COMPETITION, IN INNOVATION

Even some of the largest companies in the world find that collaboration, rather than competition, can sometimes give them an advantage in the global economy. Cargill and Monsanto, two firms that are active in the global market for agricultural products, recently announced a joint venture that will produce and market better animal feeds around the world.

Cargill is a producer and marketer of agricultural products, pharmaceuticals, and food ingredients with 79,000 employees in 72 countries. Monsanto is a global marketer of agricultural, food, and industrial products with 21,000 employees around the world. Even though both of these companies are large by any measure, they decided to pool their strengths: Monsanto has relatively greater expertise in genomics and biotechnology, and Cargill has a comprehensive distribution and marketing network. Together they plan to use the latest in biotechnology research to create and market better animal feeds around the world.

The Monsanto-Cargill joint venture will allow the two firms to develop new products and introduce them more rapidly to the market, perhaps reducing hunger around the world—and earning greater profits, too.

SOURCE: "Cargill and Monsanto Announce Global Feed and Processing Biotechnology Joint Venture," www.asgrow.com/corporate/cargill.html, accessed January 11, 1999.

each firm to use the other firm's current patents in a particular field, as well as any other patents obtained during the life of the contract.

One technology-exchange study looked at a sample of 11 American steel minimills of the 40 U.S. firms that are now world leaders in steel productivity. It found that *all but one* of the sample firms regularly and routinely exchanged information with the others: "sometimes, workers of competing firms were trained (at no charge), firm personnel were sent to competing facilities to help set up unfamiliar equipment, and so on."[6] The trade in know-how often included exchanges between direct rivals and, though engineers and technicians normally carried out the exchanges, upper management knew about and approved the technology transfers.[7]

Indeed, business firms provide their technology to others for a profit so commonly that MIT runs an annual seminar that teaches firms how they can earn more from their technology-rental business.

## A KINKED REVENUE CURVE MODEL OF SPENDING ON INNOVATION

Our discussion thus far leaves one basic question unanswered. If innovation takes so much effort and money, if it is so risky, and if the economic profits expected from innovation approach zero, why do firms do it? Why doesn't every firm refuse to participate in this unattractive game? The answer, at least in part, is that competitive markets leave them no choice. If firms do not keep up with competitors in terms of product attractiveness and improved process efficiency that lowers costs, they will

---

[6] Eric Von Hippel, *The Sources of Innovation* (New York: Oxford University Press, 1988), p. 79.

[7] In fields such as aircraft and semiconductor production, the U.S. Department of Defense has reportedly played an important role in encouraging automatic cross licensing. See Robert Merges and R. R. Nelson, "On Limiting or Encouraging Rivalry in Technical Progress: The Effect of 'Patent-Scope Decisions,'" in R. R. Nelson, *The Sources of Economic Growth* (Cambridge, Mass.: Harvard University Press, 1996, pp. 134–137.

---

● **BETTING ON INNOVATION**

In the world of business, the word "innovation" usually refers to a product that contains *new* capabilities and features. Apple Computer has turned this conventional wisdom on its head with the new iMac.

The iMac computer has received much attention for its appearance. With its smoothly rounded corners, translucent shell, and lollipop colors, the iMac appeals to anyone who is tired of the boxy beige machines that sit on everyone's desk. Certainly, the iMac's low price is important to most computer buyers. Beyond the price and outward appearances, though, one of the most significant differences between the iMac and virtually every other computer on the market is in the floppy disk drive: the iMac doesn't have one! Apple had good reasons for leaving out a floppy drive, but some industry analysts thought the company was taking a big risk.

The gamble seems to have paid off. Almost as soon as it hit the market, to almost universal praise, the iMac has sold like hotcakes.

SOURCES: Henry Bortman, "Does the Floppy Have a Future?" *Macworld Online,* September 1998, http://macworld.zdnet.com; Adam Engst, "With the iMac, Apple Shows It's Thinking Different," *MacWEEK,* June 1, 1998, http://www.zdnet.com; and Andrew Gore, "iMac: Groundbreaking Consumer Offering Lives Up to Its Hype," *Macworld Online,* November 1998, http://macworld.zdnet.com.

---

A **ratchet** is an arrangement that permits some economic variable, such as investment or advertising, to increase, but prevents that variable from subsequently decreasing.

lose out to their rivals and end up losing money. Clearly, firms prefer zero economic profits—profits that yield normal competitive returns to investors—to negative profits and investor flight.

We can make the technological scenario more explicit with the help of a microeconomic model very similar to one we encountered in Chapter 13—the kinked demand curve model that we used to explain why prices tend to "stick" in oligopoly markets. We saw the underlying mechanism: an asymmetry in the firm's expectations about its competitors. The firm hesitates to lower its price for fear that its rivals will match the price cut, so that the firm will end up with a few new customers, but dramatically reduced revenues. On the other hand, it fears that if it increases its price, the others will *not* follow suit, so that it will be left all by itself with an overpriced product. Thus, such a firm normally will set its price at the industry level, no more and no less, and leave it there unless the competitive situation changes drastically.

The innovation story is similar. Think about an industry with, say, five firms of roughly equal size. Company X sees that each of the other firms spends about $20 million a year on R&D. Company X will not dare to spend much less than $20 million on its own R&D because if it does so its next product model may lack new features as attractive as those of rival products. On the other hand, Company X sees little point in raising the ante to, say, $30 million because it knows the others will simply follow suit.

The story is described graphically in Figure 15–2, which shows an MC curve and two MR curves. For simplicity, we have drawn the MC curve as a straight line. The MR curves, however, reflect two possible competitor responses. If each time Company X expands its spending, *its rivals do the same*, then any improvements in X's product is likely to face comparable competitive products. Thus, the MR resulting from X's enhanced R&D will be quite low (curve *mAr*), because Company X will fail to pull ahead of its rivals. On the other hand, if competitors let X increase its R&D spending *without increasing their own*, then X can expect its increased product quality to put it well ahead of the others, and so its MR from R&D spending will be relatively high (curve *MCR*).

In Figure 15–2, Company X expects mixed reactions from its competitors. They will follow its lead in *increasing* R&D but will not follow any decreases. The result will be the Z-shaped red curve, *MCAr*, with a vertical break between points *A* and *C* at the current level of R&D investment ($20 million in the example). The explanation is simple. If each firm in the industry spends $20 million a year, and Company X were suddenly to decrease R&D spending—say, to $7 million per year—it has good reason to fear that competitors would *not* match that cut. With its product quality declining (because it is spending so much less on R&D) and no competitor's product doing so (because competitors are still spending $20 million), Company X can expect to lose a good deal of revenue. It will find itself moving backward along the "not matched" MR curve *MCR*, to point *S*. However, if Company X decides to increase its R&D spending above $20 million, it will not gain much revenue (it will move along the low "matched" MR curve *mAr*), because its rivals will feel threatened and will match the increase.

But that's not the end of the story. All five firms in the industry will continue to invest the same amount until one of them enjoys a research breakthrough leading to a wonderful new product (as happens from time to time, particularly in high-tech industries). That fortunate firm will then expand its investment in the breakthrough product, because doing so will pay off even if the other firms in the industry match the increase. The MR curve for the breakthrough firm will rise, and its MC = MR point will move to the right, to an amount larger than $20 million. Now Company X's Z-shaped marginal revenue curve will have shifted to the right, from its original position, $M_1B_1R_1$, to $M_2B_2R_2$ in Figure 15–3. Other companies in the industry will follow to some degree. So now the industry norm will no longer be a $20 million investment per year but may instead be something like $25 million per firm. No firm will dare to drop back to the old level, fearing that no other company will follow such a retrenchment move. Again, the common story of armaments races among countries parallels the story of innovation battles among firms. The MR = MC equilibrium point will now be $B_2$, at $25 million of R&D spending.

The process we have just described assumes that competition forces firms in the industry to keep up with one another in their R&D investment. But once they have caught up, the investment level remains fairly level until one firm breaks ranks and increases its spending, and all other firms follow behind. Such an arrangement is described as a **ratchet,** in analogy to the mechanical device that prevents a wound-up spring from suddenly unwinding. This arrangement holds technological spending steady, permits it under certain circumstances to move forward, but generally does not allow it to retreat. Thus, we can expect R&D spending to expand from time to time, but once the new level is reached, the ratchet—enforced by the competitive market—prevents firms from retreating to the previous lower level.

Such ratcheting acts as a critical part of the mechanism that produces the extraordinary growth records of free enterprise economies and differentiates them from all other known economic systems. Competitive pressures force firms to run as fast as they can in the innovation race just to keep up with the others.

FIGURE 15-2

**Competition and R&D Investment**

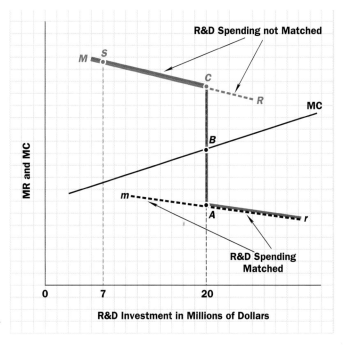

FIGURE 15-3

**Competition and R&D Investment after a Research Breakthrough by One Firm**

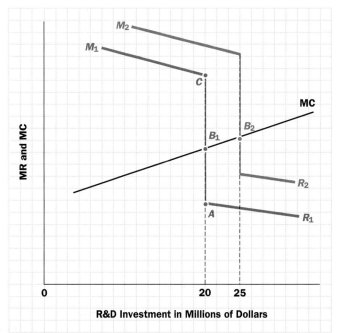

## ■ THREE GROWTH-CREATING PROPERTIES OF INNOVATION

Thus, we expect the market mechanism to force firms to devote at least a steady stream of resources to innovative activities. With luck, such level R&D efforts will yield a fairly constant flow of innovations within industries. But a steady flow of innovation does not mean that GDP remains constant. Rather, *an unchanging rate of innovation* can be expected to result in *steady growth of the economy's output.* Here we must take note of three critical features of innovation that can, so to speak, magnify the contribution that technical change makes to an economy's GDP:

- *Many innovations create cumulative changes.* Rather than merely replacing older technology, many innovations *add* to what was previously available. Thus, they increase an economy's store of technical knowledge, as when computers improve the precision of chemical processes, the new invention supplementing the old.

- *Innovation offers a public good.* An innovation, once created, usually does not contribute only to the output of the firm that discovered the breakthrough. At little or no additional cost, the new technology can also add to the outputs produced by other enterprises, often in other industries. This public-good property of technical knowledge enables those who adopt the innovation (with or without the inventor's permission) to adopt it more cheaply.

- *Innovations enjoy an accelerator feature.* A level stream of innovation usually means that output will not stay level but will grow. Like stepping on the accelerator of a car, a steady unchanging pressure makes an automobile move forward more rapidly.

Let's look at each of these growth-creating properties in turn.

### CUMULATIVE INNOVATION

Some innovation merely replaces older technology, as the automobile replaced the horse and buggy. But probably more often innovation creates new features or applications for the previous technology. Computers' new features, which constantly appear on the market, do not merely replace previous technology; those features make computers faster, more reliable, and more versatile. CD-ROM drives supplement floppy disk drives and hard drives but do not make them obsolete. Automatic focus devices became part of an older camera design rather than replacing the entire device.

The economy's stock of technical knowledge keeps expanding as new information is added to old. A steady stream of innovations accumulates and builds the volume of technical knowledge, as society discovers new applications for the new developments. Both coal and technical knowledge contribute to output. But when a ton of coal is used to create a product, it cannot be used over again. A second ton of coal must be mined and used up to make more of the product. But once technical knowledge is created, it can be used over and over again without ever being depleted.

### THE PUBLIC GOOD PROPERTY OF INNOVATION

In Chapter 14, we used the term "public good" to describe any good—that is, any input or output—that is not depleted when used once, but rather can be used over and over with little or no additional cost.[8] Such goods are available to the entire public, not just to a single individual. For instance, Thomas Edison and his colleagues worked for many months and used up much material before they finally found a way to create a viable light bulb. They did not have to repeat that outlay to produce a second light bulb. If Edison licensed the technology to another firm, that firm would not need to repeat the expensive research that yielded the first light bulb. R&D expenses need not be repeated when the firms use knowledge repeatedly to produce output. Innovation is like the oil lamp in the ancient Hanukkah

---

[8] For review of the concept of public goods, see Chapter 14, pages 274–275.

legend that dates from the second century B.C.E.: a lamp that miraculously replenished its fuel and could provide light day after day without any additional oil.

## THE ACCELERATOR PROPERTY OF INNOVATION

Each successful innovation adds to the nation's GDP, either by permitting firms to create more products with a given quantity of resources (a **process innovation**) or by making new and more valuable products available (a **product innovation**). Thus, an economy in which R&D produces a steady output of one innovation per month will obtain a GDP that is higher each month than it was in the previous month. The economy's ability to produce output will *grow constantly*, even though the innovation flow that fuels output growth remains *steady* at one invention per month.[9] This acceleration relationship applies to innovation generally, so that if the competitive market mechanism described in the previous figures leads firms to devote a constant *level* of resources to R&D, we would expect continued *growth* of GDP to result.

Of course, as noted, the ratchet principle encourages firms to *increase* expenditures on innovation, not just to leave them level. The acceleration principle tells us about the effects of this too. It says that if the level of R&D spending were to increase just once, for example, and then stay at that new higher level forever, the *growth rate* of GDP would also move upward. GDP would then grow at a faster rate forever. This process is illustrated in Figure 15–4, where we imagine that in the 21st century the level of R&D spending had been expected to be constant at the moderate level indicated by horizontal line, $R_1$. With this amount of R&D, GDP growth appears as the upward slope of the GDP line, $Y_1$. But if it turns out that R&D spending is at the higher level rate $R_2$ instead, then GDP will follow the path $Y_2$. The upward slope of $Y_2$ is greater than that of $Y_1$, meaning that with a higher *level* of expenditure on R&D we will get faster *growth* of GDP.

All of this reinforces the role of the competitive market mechanism and its stimulation of innovation as a contributor to the extraordinary growth that characterizes the world's free-enterprise economies.

A **process innovation** is an innovation that changes the way in which a commodity is produced.

A **product innovation** is the introduction of a good or service that is entirely new or involves major modifications of earlier products.

**FIGURE 15–4**

**Higher R&D Spending Accelerates GDP Growth**

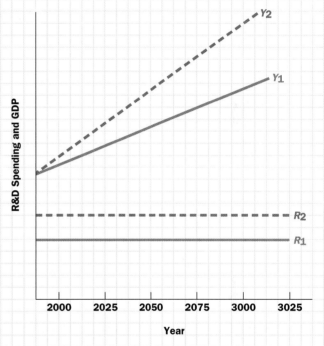

## ■ DO FREE MARKETS SPEND ENOUGH ON R&D ACTIVITIES?

Business firms, the U.S. government, universities, and others spend a good deal on research and innovation. In 1997 more than $200 billion (about 2.5 percent of total GDP) was spent on these activities, with business firms spending three-quarters of that amount (about $151 billion, or 2.2 percent of total business GDP). Is this too small or too large a share of GDP? That is, would the general public benefit or lose if more resources were devoted to innovation?

As usual, a trade-off arises. If we devote more resources to innovation this year, smaller amounts will be left over to produce cars, build dormitories, or expand movie theaters. With smaller supplies of these items, their prices will rise and they will cost us more. On the other hand, if we devote more resources to innovation, we will probably get better and cheaper products in the future. So, as with any investment,

---

[9] Note, however, that in the nearly 40-year period, 1950–1987, while the number of scientists and engineers engaged in R&D increased fivefold (from less than 200,000 to nearly 1 million), real GDP per capita only doubled. (See Charles Jones, "R&D-based models of Economic Growth," *Journal of Political Economy*, Vol. 103, No. 4, August 1995, pages 759–784.)

R&D investment entails a trade-off between the present and the future. More R&D spending means that consumers get less to consume this year, but they will get more and better products in the future. The question is, how much is enough?

It surely would be irrational to spend no resources on innovation. It would be even more irrational to devote all of GDP to this activity because that would leave nothing for consumption and everyone would starve. But these are silly extremes. What intermediate figure is best for the nation, and does the free market automatically approximate this level of expenditure?

## INNOVATION AS A POSITIVE EXTERNALITY

Many economists believe private enterprise does *not* devote enough resources to innovation, because the acquisition of new technical knowledge generates large *externalities*. Recall that an externality is an effect of a business transaction that benefits or hurts persons other than those who directly take part in the transaction.[10] For example, if some manufacturer decides to buy a lot more electric power from the local public service utility, you may have to breathe dirtier air and spend more money on laundry. Here, the electric utility company and its customer firm are the participants in the transaction, and you are among the people who suffer from the damaging externality. A detrimental externality is part of the true social cost of producing a commodity—the electricity in this example. This means that the utility will not pay all the costs its electricity generation causes because, inadvertently or deliberately, it can shift part of the cost over to you—which you pay in the form of higher doctor or laundry bills. Because lower costs lead firms to produce higher outputs, the ability to escape part of the cost of its operation will lead the utility to overproduce electricity. The result is excessive electricity production and too much pollution in the air.

But sometimes externalities *benefit* innocent third parties, so that those who carry out the transaction do not reap all the benefits. For example, suppose your roommate, an advanced engineering student, comes up with a more efficient battery that turns out to benefit laptop computer manufacturers, the makers of electric cars, and many others. Your roommate may get a prize for her work, or may even receive a royalty payment from the companies that license her innovation. But she will not get all of the benefits. This is true of most innovations: They benefit the innovator to some degree, but large parts of the benefits also go to others. Such beneficial externalities mean that a firm that invests in R&D can expect less of the profits than it would if it could keep all of the benefits of the innovation.

Consequently, many economists believe that the free market does not induce private firms to invest the socially optimal amount in innovation. They believe that many innovations whose benefits would exceed their costs are never carried out because any firm that spent the money to produce the innovation would get only part of the benefit, and that part would be insufficient to cover its costs. Thus, governments finance a good deal of innovation and research activity, carried out by research institutions such as universities.

**Basic research** refers to research that seeks to provide scientific knowledge and general principles rather than coming up with any specific marketable inventions.

**Applied research** is research whose goal is to invent or improve particular products or processes, often for profit, though the military and health industries provide examples of not-for-profit applied research.

The externality problem is probably most severe for what is called **basic research,** that is, research that deals with science and general principles rather than with improvement of a specific product. (Research of the latter sort, which is directly related to commercial or other uses, is called **applied research.**) For example, research on the nature of electricity and magnetism may yield enormous economic benefits in the near or distant future, but for the moment it only satisfies physicists' curiosity. Few business firms will finance such research. But the economy would be much less productive in the long run if no one conducted such research. That is why the governments of the United States and a number of other industrial countries provide money to finance such basic research, and why economists generally favor such funding.

So what is the bottom line? Do externalities make spending on R&D in market economies lower than it should be to promote the public interest best? Economists are still debating this issue and no settled answer has appeared.

---

[10] For review, see Chapter 14, pages 271–273.

## EFFECTS OF PROCESS RESEARCH ON AMOUNTS OF GOODS PRODUCED AND ON THEIR PRICES

As a last example of how microeconomic analysis can deal with innovation, let's consider the effects of innovation on outputs and prices. We will consider a single monopoly firm that makes decisions independently of other enterprises' activities and decisions.

Innovation, as we saw, is often divided into two types: product innovations, which consist of the introduction of a new item such as a photocopying machine or a video camera, and process innovations, which entail an improvement in the way in which commodities are produced, making them cheaper to buy. Here we will discuss only process innovations because, it turns out, they are easier to analyze.

A successful *process* innovation can be expected to expand the output of the product that uses the process, and to reduce the price of that product, for a very simple reason: A process innovation can be expected to lead to a downward shift in the firm's marginal and average cost curves. But because it involves no change in the product, it will not cause any change in the demand curve.

A standard graph familiar from earlier chapters can demonstrate these results. Figure 15–5 shows MR and *DD* (demand), the firm's marginal revenue and demand (average revenue) curves for the production of widgets. The graph also shows $MC_1$, the marginal cost curve of widgets *before* the process innovation, and $MC_2$, the new marginal cost curve *after* the innovation is adopted. $MC_2$ is naturally lower than $MC_1$ because the innovation has reduced the cost of making widgets. We see that before the innovation the quantity produced by our profit-maximizing firm is $Q_1$, the quantity at which MR = $MC_1$ (at point $E_1$). Price at this output is $P_1$, the point on the *DD* curve (the demand curve) above quantity $Q_1$. After the process innovation, the marginal cost curve shifts downward to $MC_2$. That new marginal cost curve meets the downward-sloping MR curve at point $E_2$, which lies to the right of $E_1$. This means that the profit-maximizing output quantity must increase from $Q_1$ to $Q_2$, and therefore, because of the downward slope of the demand curve, price must fall from $P_1$ to $P_2$. Thus, we have shown, as suggested earlier, that:

FIGURE 15-5

**Effect of Process Innovations on Prices and Outputs**

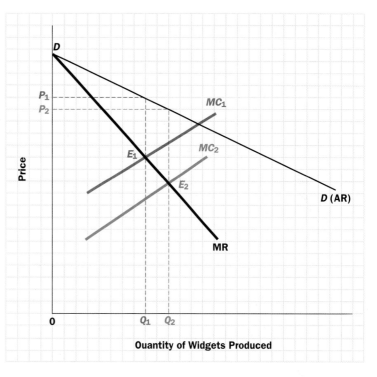

A cost-cutting process innovation increases the output and decreases the price of the product a profit-making firm supplies with the help of the innovation.

### The Puzzle Revisited: Extraordinary Growth in Free-Market Economies

In this chapter we have seen that innovation is a large part of the reason for the extraordinary productivity and growth of free-market economies. We have traced the economy's stream of innovation to the tough competition among business firms, in which those firms use new products and new processes as their most powerful weapons in their battle to win customers. Certainly, this stream of innovations sheds light on what is probably the most spectacular feature of free-enterprise economies—their unparalleled growth and the unprecedented standards of living they provide. And, as one of our *Ideas for Beyond the Final Exam* notes, that explosive growth of productivity is (almost) all that counts in the long run.

## SUMMARY

1. The growth records and per-capita incomes achieved by market economies far exceed those attained by any other form of economic organization. Innovation is one of the main sources of that economic growth.

2. *Innovation* in free-market economies is stimulated by competition among business firms, which try to outdo one another in the attractiveness of their new and improved products and in the efficiency of their productive processes. Firms pursue these goals through investment in *research and development (R&D)*.

3. As in any other decision, a profit-maximizing firm will invest in R&D up to the point at which the expected MR equals the MC of that expenditure.

4. Competition can force firms to set their R&D spending at levels corresponding to those of their rivals.

5. The typical level of R&D spending in an industry will sometimes increase, but it will rarely decline because no firm dares to be the firm to cut back on such spending.

6. Firms often seek to reduce the risks of their R&D activities by making agreements with other firms to share one another's technology. They also often sell their technology to others.

7. If new inventions appear at a constant, steady rate we can expect steady growth of the economy's productive capacity.

8. Many economists believe that private investment in innovation will be below the socially optimal level, because the externalities from innovation mean inventors do not obtain all the benefits of their innovations. However, some economists believe that these externalities, which are largely made up of improvements in the living standards of society's noninventors, are a good thing. This may mean that private investment in innovation is, in fact, not far from the socially optimal level.

9. Process innovations can be shown by MR = MC analysis to increase outputs and decrease prices, even in monopoly firms.

## KEY TERMS

Labor productivity    292

Innovation    292

Capitalism    293

Industrial Revolution    293

Research and development (R&D)    295

Technology trading    298

Cross licensing    298

Ratchet    301

Process innovation    303

Product innovation    303

Basic research    304

Applied research    304

## QUESTIONS FOR REVIEW

1. To understand how much the free-enterprise economy has increased living standards, try to envision the daily life style of a middle-class family in a major American city just after the Civil War, when the average purchasing power is estimated to have been less than one-ninth of today's. What do you think they ate? How much clothing did they own? What were their living quarters like? What share of their budgets was available for vacations and entertainment?

2. Name five common products introduced since you were born.

3. Name some companies that advertise that their products are "new" or "improved."

4. Explain why firms in an industry that spends a large amount of money on advertising may feel locked into their current advertising budgets, with no one firm daring to cut its expenditure. Describe the analogy with competition in innovation.

5. Alexander Graham Bell beat Elisha Grey to the patent office by several hours, so that Bell obtained the patent on the telephone. Imagine how much that patent turned out to be worth. How much do you think Grey got for his effort and expenditure on development of the invention? How does that help explain the possibility that *average* economic profits from innovation are close to zero?

6. If average economic profits from investment in innovation are close to zero, why would many people be anxious to invest in innovation?

7. Explain how firms that share their technology with competitors benefit by improving their ability to compete against new entrants.

8. What are the possible advantages to the general welfare when firms make their technology automatically available to others (while, of course, charging a price for use of the technology)?

9. Why may it be unprofitable for a firm to spend much more on R&D than its competitors do?

10. Define the following terms:

    a. externality

    b. public good

    c. ratchet

    Explain the applicability of these concepts to innovation.

11. From the point of view of the general welfare, do you think spending on R&D in the United States is too low? Too high? Just about right? Why?

# CHAPTER

**16**

The action of the stock market must necessarily be puzzling at times since otherwise everyone who studies it only a little bit would be able to make money in it.

B. Graham, D. L. Dodd, and S. Cottle,
authors of the classic textbook on securities analysis

# REAL FIRMS AND THEIR FINANCING: STOCKS AND BONDS

A firm does more than select inputs, outputs, and prices, the topics of previous chapters. In this chapter we discuss how real firms finance their activities—notably with stocks and bonds—from the viewpoint of both firms and investors. The latter may be of special interest to you, because a very large proportion of the nation's college graduates invest money in the stock and bond markets, and you may well do so too.

But before describing these markets, we will offer our usual opening puzzle and a broad picture of the different types of firms that make up U.S. business, focusing on individually owned enterprises, partnerships, and corporations.

**307**

## The Stock Market's Unpredictability

The stock market is something of an enigma. No other economic activity is reported in such detail in so many newspapers and followed with such concern by so many people. Yet few activities have so successfully eluded prediction of their future. There is no shortage of well-paid "experts" prepared to forecast the future of the market or a particular stock. But there are real questions about what these experts deliver.

For example, a famous study of leading analysts' predictions of company earnings (on which they based their stock-price forecasts) reports:

> [W]e wrote to 19 major Wall Street firms . . . among the most respected names in the investment business.
>
> We requested—and received—past earnings predictions on how these firms felt earnings for specific companies would behave over both a one-year and a five-year period. These estimates . . . were . . . compared with actual results to see how well the analysts forecast short-run and long-run earnings changes. . . .
>
> Bluntly stated, the careful estimates of security analysts (based on industry studies, plant visits, etc.) do very little better than those that would be obtained by simple extrapolation of past trends. . . .
>
> For example . . . the analysts' estimates were compared [with] the assumption that every company in the economy would enjoy a growth in earnings approximating the long-run rate of growth of the national income. It often turned out that . . . this naïve forecasting model . . . would make smaller errors in forecasting long-run earnings growth than . . . [did] the professional forecasts of the analysts. . . .
>
> When confronted with the poor record of their five-year growth estimates, the security analysts honestly, if sheepishly, admitted that five years ahead is really too far in advance to make reliable projections. They protested that, although long-term projections are admittedly important, they really ought to be judged on their ability to project earnings changes one year ahead.
>
> Believe it or not, it turned out that their one-year forecasts were even worse than their five-year projections.[1]

It has been said that an investor may as well pick stocks by throwing darts at the stock market page—it is far cheaper to buy a set of darts than to obtain the apparently useless advice of a professional analyst. Indeed, there have been at least two experiments, one by a U.S. senator and one by *Forbes* magazine, in which stocks picked by dart-throwing actually outperformed the mutual funds, the stocks of which are selected by experts.

Later in this chapter we will suggest an explanation for this poor performance.

## ■ FIRMS IN THE UNITED STATES

Firms are typically divided into three groups: *individual proprietorships* (businesses with one owner), *partnerships,* and *corporations.* Corporations play a crucial role in the U.S. economy. Revenues of the top 500 corporations totaled almost $6 trillion in 1998, two-thirds of the country's gross domestic product (GDP). Almost all large American firms are corporations. General Motors alone raised $161 billion in revenues in 1998, and Ford and Wal-Mart took in $144 billion and $139 billion, respectively. The combined revenues of just these three firms amount to considerably more than the GDPs of Australia, Austria, Belgium, the Netherlands, Sweden, Switzerland,

---

[1] Burton G. Malkiel, *A Random Walk Down Wall Street* (New York: W. W. Norton, 1990), pp. 140–141.

and many, many other countries. With some exceptions, these giant firms are primarily found in industries that are *oligopolies*, a market form we analyzed in Chapter 13.

But although a huge chunk of America's output comes from corporations, less than 20 percent of American firms are incorporated, because most firms are small. Even corporations are often quite small—almost 40 percent have business receipts of less than $100,000. But by far the greatest number of firms (counting all firms large and small, and including the corner grocery store and shoe repair shop) are individual or family proprietorships. Of the 22.5 million business firms in the United States, about 16.4 million are proprietorships, 4.5 million are corporations, and 1.6 million are partnerships.[2]

The nation's small business firms have a disproportionately small share of U.S. GDP. The earnings of these small firms are also very risky. The average new firm is reported to last less than seven years. When making economic decisions, the buyer is not the only one who must beware!

Let's take a closer look at the three forms of business organization and what leads those who organize a firm to choose one form rather than another.

## PROPRIETORSHIPS

Most small retail firms, farms, and many small factories are **proprietorships.** A proprietorship involves fewer legal complications than any other form of business organization. To start a proprietorship, an individual simply decides to go into business and opens a new firm or takes over an existing one. This is a major advantage of the proprietorship form of organization.

> A **proprietorship** is a business firm owned by a single person.

But the main attraction of the proprietorship is probably the owner's ability to be his or her own boss and the firm's sole decision maker. The owner does not have to consult any partners or stockholders when he or she wants to expand or change the company's product line or modify its advertising policy. A proprietorship also has tax advantages, particularly compared with a corporation. A proprietor's income is taxed only once. If the same firm were to incorporate, its income would be taxed twice—once as the firm's income (the corporate income tax) and again as the owner's income. (We'll discuss corporate taxation in detail later in this chapter).

On the other hand, a major disadvantage makes it almost impossible to organize large-scale enterprises as proprietorships: The owner of a proprietorship has **unlimited liability** for the debts of the firm. If the company goes out of business, leaving unpaid bills, the former owner can be forced to pay them out of personal savings. The owner may have to sell the family home, private collections of stamps or paintings, or any other personal assets (even those unrelated to the business) so that the proceeds can be used to pay off the company's debts.

> **Unlimited liability** is a legal obligation of a firm's owner(s) to pay back company debts with whatever resources he or she owns.

**SUMMARY**   There are three main advantages of the individual proprietorship:

- Full control remains in the hands of the owner.
- The proprietorship is subject to few legal complications.
- Owners generally pay fewer taxes.

Its two main disadvantages are that:

- The owner has unlimited liability for the debts of the company.
- Raising substantial funds for the firm can be difficult.

## PARTNERSHIPS

In terms of amount of capital, **partnerships** tend to be larger than proprietorships but smaller than corporations. However, the largest partnerships greatly exceed the smallest corporations in financing and influence. For example, some of the most prestigious law firms and investment banks are partnerships.

> A **partnership** is a firm whose ownership is shared by a fixed number of proprietors.

---

[2] U.S. Bureau of the Census, *Statistical Abstract of the United States: 1998*, 118th ed. (Washington, D.C.: U.S. Government Printing Office, 1998).

The partnership's advantage over a proprietorship is that it combines a number of people's funds and expertise to form a company larger than any single owner could have financed or managed alone. A partnership may also bring together a variety of specialists, as often happens in a medical practice. In addition, partnership, like proprietorship, offers freedom from double taxation.

But the partnership has disadvantages, too—some of them substantial. Decision making in a partnership may be harder than in any other type of firm. The sole proprietor need consult no one before acting; the corporation appoints officers who are authorized to make decisions for the company. But in a partnership, it may be necessary for *every* partner to agree before any steps are taken, and that is the primary difficulty of this form of enterprise. A partnership has been compared to two people in a horse costume, each supplying two of the legs, each prepared to go in a different direction, and each unable to move without the other.

Furthermore, partners, like sole proprietors, have unlimited liability. They can lose personal possessions to pay off company debts. Finally, the partnership suffers from unique legal complications. A partnership agreement is like a marriage contract entered into exclusively for the financial advantage of the participants, so considerable haggling about the terms can take place. Also, under the law, if a partner dies or decides to leave the firm, the partnership may have to be dissolved and haggling about the contract may begin anew.

**SUMMARY**     The benefits of the partnership to the owners of the firm are that:

- They gain access to larger quantities of capital.
- They enjoy protection from double taxation.

Its disadvantages are that:

- Many if not all partners must agree to major decisions.
- Partners share unlimited liability for the company's obligations.
- Legal complications, including automatic dissolution of the partnership, arise when *any* change in ownership occurs.

## CORPORATIONS

A **corporation** is a firm that has the legal status of a fictional individual. This fictional individual is owned by a number of persons, called its *stockholders,* and is run by a set of elected officers and a board of directors, whose chairman is often also in a powerful position.

Most big firms are **corporations,** a form of business organization whose legal status differs significantly from that of a proprietorship or a partnership. Though it seems strange, a corporation is an *individual* in the eyes of the law. Therefore, its earnings, like those of other individuals, are taxed. This leads to double taxation of the stockholders. That is, corporate earnings are taxed twice, once when they are earned by the company and a second time when they go to investors in the form of dividends (and are subject to personal income tax).

But this disadvantage is counterbalanced by an important advantage: any corporate debt is regarded as that fictitious individual's obligation, not any one stockholder's liability. So stockholders benefit from the protection of **limited liability**— they can lose no more money than they have invested in the firm.

**Limited liability** is a legal obligation of a firm's owners to pay back company debts only with the money they have already invested in the firm.

Limited liability is the main secret of the success of the corporate organizational form. Thanks to that provision, individuals throughout the world are willing to invest money in firms whose operations they do not understand and whose management personnel they do not know. Each shareholder receives in return a claim on the firm's profits, and, at least in principle, a portion of the company's ownership.

Corporations are directed by hired managers: a chairman of the board of directors, a president, various vice presidents, and so on. These executives are, legally, employees of the firm's owners—the people who, as we will see, hold stock in the corporation. This arrangement has a great advantage: It prevents the quarrels and indecision that are often problems for partnerships. On the other hand, because the managers are hired personnel, they cannot always be trusted to do what is best for the owners. Managers are often accused of looking after their own interests even if that means sacrificing those of the stockholders (the owners). This problem has recently received much attention in discussions of *takeovers*—that is, purchase of control of a corporation by outsiders—a subject we will examine later in this chapter.

Corporations escape one other problem that troubles partnerships. As we saw, if one partner wants to leave a firm, the remaining owners may have to reorganize the entire enterprise. But in a corporation, any owner who wants to quit just sells her stock, and the corporation goes on exactly as before. In this way, at least in theory, a corporation can continue forever.

**SUMMARY**  Benefits of the corporate form to the owners are that:

- They benefit from limited liability.
- They gain access to large quantities of capital.
- They enjoy ease of operation with the help of hired management.
- Permanence: The firm is not dissolved or reorganized each time an owner leaves.

Its disadvantages are that:

- Double taxation: The owners' income is taxed twice.
- Hired managers may act in their own interests rather than the owners'.

## THE EFFECT OF DOUBLE TAXATION ON CORPORATE EARNINGS

Does a person end up earning less by investing in a corporation than in a company that is equally risky but not subject to double taxation? Paradoxically, the answer is that investors, on average, will *not* lose anything by choosing the corporation. The tax will not and cannot put one type of investment at a disadvantage in comparison with any other.

How is this possible? How does the effect of the additional tax on a corporate stock disappear before it reaches the stockholder? Two processes achieve this act of magic.

First, corporations must avoid some investment opportunities that partnerships and proprietorships can afford to take on. For example, suppose that the market rate of interest to firms is 9 percent, and a new product is expected to bring a 12 percent return to a manufacturer. An individual proprietor can afford to produce the new item—borrowing the necessary funds at 9 percent and keeping the 3 percent additional return on the new item for himself. But a large corporation *cannot* afford to produce the new item. To compete for funds with the proprietorship, it must also pay investors 9 percent, which means that it will have to choose investments that promise to earn at least 14 percent—because about 35 percent of the 14 percent return will be siphoned off in corporate taxes.

Thus, double taxation keeps corporate business out of economic activities that offer real, but limited, earnings. This may cause economic inefficiency, because many firms will avoid activities that can benefit society. For instance, corporations may find it too costly to open retail outlets in slum areas or to run trains to isolated rural areas—activities that may be profitable in the absence of the tax.

A second fail-safe mechanism protects investors in corporate stocks from earning lower returns than they would on other equally risky *securities*.[3] Suppose that two otherwise identical securities, A and B, each offer a return of $60 per year, but A is subject to a 50 percent tax whereas B is not. *Question:* If the market price of Security B is $1,000, what will the market price of A be? *Answer:* The price of A will be only $500, exactly half the price of Security B. Why? Because it brings in only $30 per year after taxes, exactly half of what Security B returns, investors will pay only half as much for A as they will for the untaxed security. But at $500 and $1,000 respectively, investors in either security will earn the same rate of return after taxes. That is, $30 is 6 percent of $500 and $60 is 6 percent of $1,000 so either firm provides the same 6 percent return on investment.

---

[3] Stocks and bonds are also called securities.

Double taxation of corporate earnings tends to restrict corporations' activities, keeping them out of relatively low-profit operations. However, double taxation does not mean that the individual investor earns less by putting money into a corporation than by putting it into other businesses.

## ■ FINANCING CORPORATE ACTIVITY

When a corporation needs money to add to its plant or equipment, or to finance other types of real investment, it may reinvest its own earnings (rather than paying them out as dividends to stockholders), print and sell new stock certificates or new bonds, or take out a loan. We will consider each of these three options in detail (in reverse order of their actual use by corporations).

### LOANS

A company can obtain money by borrowing it from banks, insurance companies, or other private firms. It may also sometimes obtain assistance from a U.S. government agency, which will either lend funds directly to the corporation or serve as guarantor, promising to make sure a loan is repaid. For example, loans may be arranged with the help of the national defense agencies if they want a private firm to undertake the design and production of an expensive new weapons system. Small business firms, too, are eligible for various forms of assistance in borrowing.

### STOCKS AND BONDS

Stocks and bonds are a subject of interest to millions of Americans. How can a firm obtain money in exchange for such printed paper? Doesn't the process seem a bit like counterfeiting? If done improperly, there are grounds for the suspicion. But, carried out appropriately, it is a perfectly reasonable economic process. First, let's define our terms.

> A **common stock** of a corporation is a piece of paper that gives the holder of the stock a share of the ownership of the company.

**Common stock** represents partial ownership of a corporation. For example, if a company issues 100,000 shares, then a person who owns 1,000 shares owns 1 percent of the company and is entitled to 1 percent of the company's *dividends*, the corporation's annual payments to stockholders. This shareholder's vote counts for 1 percent of the total votes in an election of corporate officers or in a referendum on corporate policy.

> A **bond** is simply an IOU by a corporation that promises to pay the holder of the bond a fixed sum of money at the specified *maturity* date and some other fixed amount of money (the *coupon* or the *interest payment*) every year up to the date of maturity.

**Bonds** differ from stocks in several ways. First, the purchaser of a corporation's stock *buys* a share of its ownership and some control over its affairs, whereas a bond purchaser simply *lends* money to the firm and obtains no part of its ownership. Second, whereas stockholders have no idea how much they will receive when they sell their stocks, or how much they will receive in dividends each year, bondholders know with a high degree of certainty how much money they will be paid if they hold their bonds to maturity (the date the firm has promised to repay the loan). For instance, a bond with a face value of $1,000 and an $80 *coupon* (the firm's annual interest payment to the bondholder) that matures in 2007 will provide $80 per year every year until 2007, and the firm will repay the bondholder's $1,000 in 2007. Unless the company goes bankrupt, this repayment schedule is guaranteed. Third, bondholders legally have a *prior claim* on company earnings, which means the stockholders receive no money until the firm has paid its bondholders. For all these reasons, bonds are considered less risky investments than stocks.

An important exception are so-called junk bonds—very risky bonds that became popular in the 1980s. They were used heavily by people trying to purchase enough of a corporation's stock to acquire control of that firm. We will say more later about such "takeover" activities and the use of junk bonds to finance them.

To return to our question at the beginning of this section, a new issue of stocks and bonds is generally not like counterfeiting. As long as the funds obtained from the sale of the new securities are used effectively to increase a firm's profit-earning capacity, these funds will automatically yield any required repayment and appropriate interest and dividends to purchasers. But occasionally this does not happen. One of the favorite practices of the more notorious 19th-century market manipulators was "watering" company stocks—issuing stocks with little or nothing to back them up. The term is originally derived from the practice of some cattle dealers who would force their animals to drink large quantities of water just before bringing them to be weighed for sale.

**SIMILARITIES BETWEEN STOCKS AND BONDS**   In reality, the differences between stocks and bonds are not as clear-cut as just described. Two relevant misconceptions are worth noting. First, the ownership represented by a few shares of a company's stock may be more symbolic than real. A person who holds 0.002 percent of AT&T stock—which, by the way, is a *very large* investment—exercises no real control over AT&T's operations.

In fact, many economists believe that the ownership of large corporations is so diffuse that stockholders or stockholder groups rarely have *any* effective control over management. In this view, a corporation's management is a largely independent decision-making body; as long as it keeps enough cash flowing to stockholders to prevent discontent and *organized* rebellion, management can do anything it wants within the law. Looked at in this way, stockholders, like bondholders, merely provide loans to the company. The only real difference between the two groups, according to this interpretation, is that stockholders' loans are riskier and therefore entitled to higher payments.

Second, contrary to appearance, bonds actually *can* be a very risky investment. Persons who try to sell their bonds before maturity may find that the market price happens to be low; so if they need to raise cash in a hurry, they may incur substantial losses. Also, bondholders may be exposed to losses from inflation. Whether the $1,000 promised to the bondholder at the 2007 maturity date represents substantial (or very little) purchasing power depends on what happens to the general price level in the meantime (i.e., how much price inflation occurs). No one can predict the price level this far in advance with any accuracy. Finally, a firm can issue bonds with little backing; that is, the firm may own little valuable property that it can use as a guarantee of repayment to the lender—the bondholder. This was often true of the junk bonds of the 1980s, and it helps to explain their high risk.

**BOND PRICES AND INTEREST RATES**   What makes bond prices go up and down? A straightforward relationship exists between bond prices and *interest rates:* whenever one goes up, the other *must* go down.

For example, suppose that Sears Roebuck issued some 15-year bonds when interest rates were comparatively low, so the company had to pay only 6 percent to sell the bonds. People who invested $1,000 in those Sears bonds received a contract that promised them $60 per year for 15 years plus the return of their $1,000 at the end of that period. Suppose, however, that interest rates *rise*, so new 15-year bonds of similar companies now pay 12 percent. An investor with $1,000 can now buy a bond that offers $120 per year. Obviously, no one will now pay $1,000 for a bond that promises only $60 per year. Consequently, the market price of the old Sears bonds must fall.

This example is not entirely hypothetical. Until a few years ago, bonds issued much earlier—at interest rates of 6 percent or lower—were still in circulation. In the 1980s' markets, when interest rates were well *above* 6 percent, such bonds sold for prices far below their original values.

> When interest rates *rise,* the prices of previously issued bonds with lower interest earnings must fall. For the same reason, when interest rates *fall,* the prices of previously issued bonds must rise.

It follows that as interest rates change because of changes in monetary policy or other reasons, bond prices fluctuate. That is one reason why bonds can be a risky investment.

**CORPORATE CHOICE BETWEEN STOCKS AND BONDS**   If a corporation chooses to finance the construction of new factories and equipment through the issue of new stocks or bonds, how does it determine whether bonds or stocks suit its purposes?

Two considerations are of prime importance. Although issuing bonds generally exposes a firm to more risk than issuing stocks, the corporation usually expects to pay more money to stockholders over the long run. In other words, to the firm that issues them, bonds are cheaper but riskier. The decision about which is better for the firm therefore involves a trade-off between the two considerations of expense and risk.

Why are bonds risky to a corporation? When it issues $20 million in new bonds at 10 percent, a company commits itself to pay out $2 million every year of the bond's life, whether business is booming or the firm is losing money. If the firm is unable to meet its obligation to bondholders in some year, bankruptcy may result.

Stocks do not burden the company with any such risk, because the firm does not promise to pay stockholders *any* fixed amount. Stockholders simply receive whatever is left of the company's net earnings after payments to bondholders. If nothing is left to pay the new stockholders in some years, legally speaking, that is just their bad luck. The higher risk faced by stockholders is the reason they normally obtain higher average payments than bondholders.

> To the firm that issues them, bonds are riskier than stocks because they commit the firm to make a fixed annual payment, even in years when it is losing money. For the same reason, stocks are riskier than bonds to the buyers of securities. Therefore, stockholders expect to be paid more money than bondholders.

## PLOWBACK, OR RETAINED EARNINGS

The final major source of funds for corporations, in addition to loans and the issue of stocks and bonds, is **plowback** or **retained earnings.** For example, if a company earns $30 million after taxes and decides to pay only $10 million in dividends and reinvest the remaining $20 million in the firm, that $20 million is called "plowback."

When business is profitable, corporate managers will often prefer plowback to other sources of funding. For one thing, plowback usually involves lower risk. Also, plowback, unlike other sources of funding, does not come under the scrutiny of the Securities and Exchange Commission (SEC), the government agency that regulates stocks.[4] And, of course, plowback does not depend on the availability of eager customers for new company stocks and bonds. An issue of new securities can be a disappointment if there is little public demand when they are offered. But plowback runs no such risk.

Above all, a plowback decision generally does not call attention to the degree of success of management's operations, as a new stock issue does. When stock is issued, the SEC, potential buyers, and their professional advisers may all scrutinize the company carefully. No management has a perfect record, and the process may reveal things management would prefer to be overlooked.

Another reason for plowback's attractiveness is that issuing new stocks and bonds is usually an expensive and lengthy process. The SEC requires companies to gather masses of data in a *prospectus*—a document that describes a company's financial condition—before any new issue is approved.

Figure 16–1 shows the relative importance of each of the different funding sources to U.S. corporations. It indicates that plowback is by far the most important source of corporate financing, constituting about 62 percent of total corporate financing in 1996. New bond issues and other forms of borrowing supplied about 15 percent of the total, and stock sales actually contributed a *negative* amount of funding (−9 percent), because corporations reduced the number of their stocks in the public's hands by buying some back.

**Plowback** (or **retained earnings**) is the portion of a corporation's profits that management decides to keep and invest back into the firm's operations rather than paying dividends to stockholders. Corporations may also buy back shares from stockholders.

---

| FIGURE 16–1 |

**Sources of New Funds, U.S. Corporations, 1996**

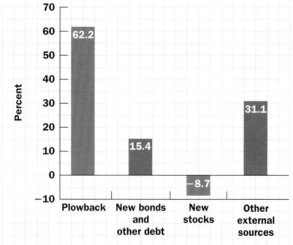

SOURCE: U.S. Bureau of the Census, *Statistical Abstract of the United States 1998* 118th ed. (Washington, D.C.: U.S. Government Printing Office, October 1998).

---

[4] The Securities and Exchange Commission, established in 1934, protects the interests of people who buy securities. It requires firms that issue stock and other securities to provide information about their financial condition, and it regulates the issue and trading of securities.

## ■ FROM THE INVESTOR'S VIEWPOINT: BUYING STOCKS AND BONDS

Although investors can purchase stocks and bonds through any brokerage firm, not all brokers charge the same fees. Bargain brokerage houses advertise in the newspapers' financial pages, offering investors very little service—no advice, no research, no other frills—other than merely buying or selling what the customer wants them to, at lower fees than those charged by higher-service brokerage firms.

Many investors are not aware of the various ways in which they can purchase (or sell) stocks. Two noteworthy arrangements are (a) a *market order* purchase, which simply tells the broker to buy a specified quantity of stock at the best price the market currently offers, and (b) a *limit order*, which is an agreement to buy a given amount of stock when its price falls to a specified level. If the investor offers to buy at $18, then the broker will purchase shares if and when the market price falls to $18 per share or less.

The most recent shareowners survey by the *New York Stock Exchange* (NYSE) estimated that in 1995 there were 69.3 million individual stockholders in the United States (about one out of every four Americans). Of these 69.3 million, just under 40 percent (27.4 million) held stock directly. The rest had a more indirect stake in the market, with their money invested through various *institutional investors*, such as mutual funds, pension plans, and employer-based savings accounts.[5]

### SELECTING A PORTFOLIO: DIVERSIFICATION

A person or organization's holdings of securities from several different corporations is called a *portfolio* of investments. A portfolio tends to be far less risky than any of the individual securities it contains. The secret is **portfolio diversification:** not putting all of your eggs in one basket.

If, for example, Alex divides his holdings among Companies A, B, and C, then his portfolio may perform satisfactorily even if Company A goes broke. Moreover, suppose that Company A specializes in producing luxury items, which do well in prosperous periods but very badly during recessions, whereas Company B sells cheap clothing, whose cyclical demand pattern differs greatly from that of Company A. If Alex holds stock in both companies, his overall risk is less than if he owned stock in only one. All other things being equal, a portfolio containing many different types of securities tends to be less risky than a portfolio with fewer types of securities.

Increasingly, institutional investors, such as **mutual funds,** have adopted portfolios composed of broad ranges of stocks typifying those offered by the entire stock

> **Portfolio diversification** means including a number and variety of stocks, bonds, and other such items in an individual's portfolio. If the individual owns airline stocks, for example, diversification requires the purchase of a stock or bond in a very different industry, such as a breakfast cereal producer.

> A **mutual fund,** in which individual investors can buy shares, is a private investment firm that holds a portfolio of securities. Investors can choose among a large variety of different mutual funds, such as stock funds, bond funds, and so forth.

"To hell with a balanced portfolio. I want to sell my Fenwick Chemical and sell it _now_."

---

[5] New York Stock Exchange, *Shareownership 1998*, www.nyse.com, accessed March 1999.

An **index fund,** is a mutual fund that chooses a particular stock market index and then buys the stocks (or most of the stocks) that are included in the index. The value of an investment in an index fund depends on what happens to the prices of all the stocks in that index.

market. Mutual funds now are among the largest U.S. investors of securities. They offer portfolios of various groups of domestic stocks, foreign stocks, and bonds. Small investors can easily put their money into these funds, thereby reducing the risks of owning individual stocks and ensuring that the overall market does not significantly outperform their portfolios. Mutual fund transactions can be carried out by telephone or over the Internet, and investors can also easily check on the past performance of the different funds and obtain other pertinent information.

One kind of mutual fund, called an **index fund,** buys the securities used in one of the standard **stock price indexes** (such as Standard & Poor's 500 or the broader Wilshire 5000 Index). A stock price index is an average of the prices of a group of stocks—weighted by the size of each company—that are believed to be representative of the overall stock market. When you invest in an index fund, the return on your money will therefore reflect the performance of the whole market, rather than any one or a few securities that you or your broker might have selected instead.

Institutional money managers increasingly use computers to decide on their portfolios and to buy or sell huge portfolios of stocks simultaneously and rapidly. Since 1982, some traders have also allowed their computers to decide when to jump in and make massive sales or purchases. This is called *program trading*. In 1998 program trading accounted for about 16 percent of total NYSE volume and a considerable amount elsewhere. Program trading is controversial, and some observers have argued that it has aggravated price fluctuations, especially during the stock market crash of October 1987.

## FOLLOWING A PORTFOLIO'S PERFORMANCE

Newspapers carry daily information on stock and bond prices. Figure 16–2 is an excerpt from the stock market page of the *Wall Street Journal*. We have highlighted the stock listing for the clothing retailer, Gap Inc. In the first two columns, before the company name, the report gives the stock's highest and lowest price in the last year. Gap Inc. stock is reported to have ranged between $32 and $68. After the stock's name and symbol (GPS), the annual dividend per share ($.20) appears. Following that is the yield, or the dividend as a percentage of the closing price (.4 percent).

The next column reports the *price earnings* (P/E) ratio (30 for Gap Inc.). This figure is the price per share divided by the company's net earnings per share in the previous year, and it is often taken as a basic measure indicating whether the stock's current price overvalues or undervalues the company. However, no simple rule enables us to interpret the P/E figures—for example, a very risky firm or a slowly growing firm with a low P/E may be considered overvalued, although a safe, rapidly growing firm with a high P/E may still be a bargain.

The next column indicates the number of shares traded on the previous day (1,683,500), an indication of whether that stock is actively traded. Finally, the last four figures indicate yesterday's highest price ($51\frac{1}{8}$), lowest price ($48), the price of the last transaction of the day ($48\frac{3}{16}$), and the change in that price from the previous day ($-4\frac{9}{16}$).

Figure 16–3, this time from *The New York Times*, gives similar information about bonds. Notice that a given company may have several different bonds differing in maturity date and coupon (annual interest payment). For example, AT&T offers five different bonds. The highlighted one is labeled ATT $7\frac{1}{2}$ 06, meaning that these bonds pay an annual interest rate of 7.5 percent (the coupon) on their face value and that their maturity (redemption) date is 2006. Next, the current yield is reported as 6.8 percent. This is simply the coupon divided by the price. Because that yield, 6.8 percent, is lower than the coupon, 7.5 percent, the bond must be selling at a price above its face value, so the return per dollar is correspondingly lower. The remaining information in the table, as in the previous figure, tells us the trading volume for the bond, the previous day's closing price, and the change in price from the day before.

---

### FIGURE 16-2

**Excerpt from a Stock-Price Table**

**-G-G-G-**

| 52 Weeks Hi | Lo | Stock | Sym | Div | Yld % | PE | Vol 100s | Hi | Lo | Close | Net Chg |
|---|---|---|---|---|---|---|---|---|---|---|---|
| 47⅞ | 30³⁄₁₆ | GATX | GMT | 1.00 | 3.2 | dd | 536 | 33⁷⁄₁₆ | 31³⁄₁₆ | 31¹¹⁄₁₆ | −1⅝ |
| 21¾ | 14½ | G&L Rlty | GLR | 1.56 | 9.8 | 17 | 26 | 15¹⁵⁄₁₆ | 15⅞ | 15¹⁵⁄₁₆ | +¹⁄₁₆ |
| 26¹⁵⁄₁₆ | 23¾ | G&L Rlty pfA | | 2.56 | 10.8 | ... | 5 | 23⅞ | 23¾ | 23¾ | −³⁄₁₆ |
| 26¹¹⁄₁₆ | 22¼ | G&L Rlty pfB | | 2.45 | 10.8 | ... | 1 | 22¾ | 22¾ | 22¾ | +½ |
| 53 | 36 | GC Cos | GCX | ... | ... | 62 | 41 | 38⅝ | 38¼ | 38⅝ | ... |
| 17¹¹⁄₁₆ | 9⅛ | GP Strategs | GPX | ... | ... | 17 | 149 | 10 | 9⅞ | 10 | ... |
| 44¹¹⁄₁₆ | 35³⁄₁₆ | GPU Inc | GPU | 2.06 | 4.8 | 17 | 6404 | 43½ | 42⅞ | 43⁹⁄₁₆ | +1³⁄₁₆ |
| 11¾ | 4⅝ | GRC Int | GRH | ... | ... | 4 | 1141 | 4¾ | 4¼ | 4⁷⁄₁₆ | −³⁄₁₆ |
| 64⅝ | 40½ | GTE | GTE | 1.88 | 3.4 | 23 | 25531 | 56¹⁄₁₆ | 53¹⁵⁄₁₆ | 55 | ... |
| 27⅛ | 25¾ | GTE DE MIPS A | | 2.31 | 8.9 | ... | 262 | 26 | 25⅞ | 26 | +¼ |
| 27⁹⁄₁₆ | 25³⁄₁₆ | GTE DE MIPS B | | 2.19 | 8.4 | ... | 220 | 26¼ | 26¹⁄₁₆ | 26⁹⁄₁₆ | ... |
| 11½ | 9⅜ | GabelliConv | GCV | .80 | 7.9 | ... | 19 | 10⅛ | 10¹⁄₈ | 10⅜ | ... |
| 28¹¹⁄₁₆ | 25⁷⁄₁₆ | GabelliConv pf | | 2.00 | 7.7 | ... | 12 | 26⅜ | 26¼ | 26⅜ | −¼ |
| 12⅜ | 9½ | GabelliTr | GAB | 1.08 | 10.7 | ... | 1341 | 10¹⁄₁₆ | 10¹⁄₁₆ | 10⅛ | −¼ |
| 26⅜ | 24⁹⁄₁₆ | GabelliTr pf | | ... | ... | ... | 263 | 25¹³⁄₁₆ | 25⁷⁄₁₆ | 25¾ | +⅝ |
| 11⅛ | 7¾ | GabelliMlti | GGT | .85e | 10.0 | ... | 57 | 8⅜ | 8½ | 8½ | −¼ |
| 27¾ | 25³⁄₁₆ | GabelliMlti pf | | 2.11e | 8.3 | ... | 8 | 25½ | 25½ | 25½ | ... |
| 28⅝ | 22 | GblsRsdntl | GBP | 2.00 | 7.5 | 21 | 270 | 26¹⁵⁄₁₆ | 26½ | 26⅝ | −⅜ |
| 25¾ | 22¹⁵⁄₁₆ | GblsRsdntl pfA | | 2.08 | 8.5 | ... | 58 | 24⁷⁄₁₆ | 24¼ | 24⁷⁄₁₆ | +⅜ |
| 10¾ | 5¾ | Gainsco | GNA | .07 | 1.0 | dd | 83 | 7⅝ | 7¾ | 7¹⁄₁₆ | −⅛ |
| 28⅞ | 8³⁄₄ | GaleyLord | GNL | ... | ... | 13 | 346 | 11¹¹⁄₁₆ | 11¹¹⁄₁₆ | 11¾ | −³⁄₁₆ |
| 46⅛ | 22 | GalileoInt | GLC | .30 | .8 | 24 | 1746 | 36¾ | 35⅛ | 35½ | −2¼ |
| 46¾ | 33¹⁄₁₆ | Gallagr | AJG | 1.40 | 3.5 | 13 | 290 | 40⁷⁄₁₆ | 39⅞ | 39¹⁵⁄₁₆ | −1⁹⁄₁₆ |
| 31¼ | 18 | GsllaherGp | GLH | 1.36e | 4.8 | ... | 591 | 29 | 28⅛ | 28⅛ | −1¹⁄₁₆ |
| 17⅝ | 6⅝ | GaloobToys | GAL | ... | ... | dd | 2934 | 11⅜ | 11¼ | 11⅛ | −³⁄₁₆ |
| 75¼ | 49 | Gannett | GCI | .76 | 1.4 | 16 | 22430 | 53¹⁵⁄₁₆ | 51⅞ | 52⅜ | −¹⁵⁄₁₆ |
| **68** | **32** | **Gap Inc** | **GPS** | **.20** | **.4** | **30** | **16835** | **51⅛** | **48** | **48³⁄₁₆** | **−4⁹⁄₁₆** |
| 30¹¹⁄₁₆ | 13²³⁄₃₂ | GardnrDenvr | GDI | ... | ... | 7 | 219 | 14⅛ | 13¾ | 13⅞ | −¼ |
| 41³⁄₄ | 19¹⁵⁄₁₆ | GartnerGp | IT | ... | ... | 24 | 10886 | 20¼ | 19¹⁄₄ | 19¹⁵⁄₁₆ | −¹⁵⁄₁₆ |
| 68¾ | 25¹⁄₁₆ | Gateway 2000 | GTW | ... | ... | 64 | 18513 | 53 | 49⁵⁄₁₆ | 49⅝ | −2¹¹⁄₁₆ |
| 37½ | 25¼ | GaylEnt | GET | .60 | 2.1 | 31 | 273 | 29¼ | 28⅝ | 28⅝ | −1⅜ |
| 31¾ | 18¹⁄₄ | GenCorp | GY | .60 | 3.3 | 10 | 531 | 19¹⁄₁₆ | 17¹³⁄₁₆ | 17¹¹⁄₁₆ | −1¹⁄₁₆ |
| 73¾ | 57¹⁄₂ | Genentech | GNE | ... | ... | 57 | 1750 | 71⅜ | 69⁹⁄₁₆ | 69½ | −2⅜ |
| 28⅝ | 10½ | Gener ADS | CHR | 1.27e | 8.9 | ... | 380 | 14¹³⁄₁₆ | 14¼ | 14¼ | −¹¹⁄₁₆ |
| 32 | 23⅜ | GenAmInv | GAM | 3.16e | 11.2 | ... | 112 | 29 | 28¼ | 28⅜ | −¹¹⁄₁₆ |
| 26⅜ | 25¹⁄₁₆ | GenAmInv pf | | .47p | ... | ... | 88 | 26¹⁄₁₆ | 25¹³⁄₁₆ | 25¹⁵⁄₁₆ | −¼ |
| 32⅞ | 13 | GenlCbl | GCN | .20 | 1.2 | 10 | 982 | 18¼ | 17¼ | 17¼ | −1¼ |
| 33⅛ | 16⅞ | GenChmGp | GCG | .20 | 1.1 | 8 | 294 | 19 | 18⅝ | 18⅝ | −¼ |
| 34 | 5½ | GenCigar | MPP | ... | ... | 5 | 248 | 6½ | 6 | 6⅛ | −⅝ |
| 7¼ | 2½ | GenDatacm | GDC | ... | ... | dd | 255 | 2¹⁵⁄₁₆ | 2¹³⁄₁₆ | 2⅞ | −⅛ |
| 55 | 37¹⁵⁄₁₆ | GenDynam | GD | .88 | 1.7 | 19 | 5458 | 51½ | 50 | 50½ | +¼ |
| 96⅞ | 59 | GenElec | GE | 1.20 | 1.6 | 29 | 99339 | 78⁷⁄₁₆ | 74⅝ | 75¾ | −4 |
| 39¼ | 31¹⁵⁄₁₆ | GenGrthProp | GGP | 1.88 | 5.4 | 21 | 242 | 35⅛ | 34⁹⁄₁₆ | 34¾ | −⅜ |
| 25⅞ | 23 | GenGrthProp pf | | .56p | ... | ... | 102 | 24⅝ | 24⅜ | 24⁷⁄₁₆ | −¹⁄₁₆ |
| 29½ | 12⅝ | GenInstr | GIC | ... | ... | ... | 17425 | 21¾ | 19⁷⁄₁₆ | 19¹⁵⁄₁₆ | −1¹¹⁄₁₆ |
| 78¼ | 59³⁄₁₆ | GenMills | GIS | 2.12 | 3.0 | 26 | 7036 | 71 | 69⅝ | 69¹¹⁄₁₆ | −⁵⁄₁₆ |
| 76¹¹⁄₁₆ | 54⁷⁄₁₆ | GenMotor | GM | 2.00 | 3.7 | 8 | 41342 | 55½ | 52¼ | 54⅜ | −1¹⁄₁₆ |
| 57¾ | 31¹⁄₂ | GenMotor H | GMH | ... | ... | ... | 2980 | 38⅛ | 36½ | 36⅝ | −⅜ |
| 29⅝ | 27⅞ | GenMotor pfG | | 2.28 | 8.1 | ... | 6 | 28⅝ | 28¾ | 28⅛ | +⅜ |
| 27⅜ | 25⅞ | GenMotor pfQ | | 2.28 | 9.1 | ... | 600 | 25⅜ | 25¼ | 25⅛ | −¹⁄₁₆ |
| 28 | 25½ | GenMot TOPRS D | | 2.17 | 8.3 | ... | 6 | 26¹⁄₁₆ | 25⅝ | 26¹⁄₁₆ | +¹⁄₁₆ |
| 30¼ | 27⁵⁄₁₆ | GenMot TOPRS G | | 2.47 | 8.9 | ... | 28 | 27¹³⁄₁₆ | 27⅝ | 27¾ | −¹⁄₁₆ |
| 275 | 191 | GenRe | GRN | 2.36 | 1.2 | 16 | 3438 | 203 | 197½ | 199 | −4 |
| 15¾ | 5⅞ | GenSemi | SEM | ... | ... | 16 | 279 | 5¹⁵⁄₁₆ | 5¹³⁄₁₆ | 5¹⁵⁄₁₆ | −¹⁄₁₆ |
| 47¼ | 31½ | GenSignl | GSX | 1.08 | 3.1 | 13 | 3399 | 35 | 33¹¹⁄₁₆ | 34¾ | +1³⁄₁₆ |
| 18⅞ | 4⅞ | Genesco | GCO | ... | ... | 11 | 1434 | 5¹¹⁄₁₆ | 5⅝ | 5⅝ | −¹⁄₁₆ |
| 21¼ | 13¹¹⁄₁₆ | GenesisEngy | GEL | 2.00 | 13.2 | 21 | 133 | 15½ | 15⅜ | 15½ | −¼ |
| 39¾ | 11⅛ | GenesisHlth | GHV | ... | ... | 8 | 1630 | 12½ | 11⅝ | 11⅞ | −⅜ |
| 4¼ | 1¾ | GenevaStl | GHV | ... | ... | dd | 137 | 1⅞ | 1¼ | 1¼ | ... |
| **34** | **10³⁄₄** | **GenRad** | **GEN** | ... | ... | **86** | **337** | **15¼** | **13⅝** | **13¾** | **−1¾** |
| 38¼ | 29⅞ | GenuinePart | GPC | 1.00 | 3.3 | 15 | 3584 | 30⁵⁄₁₆ | 29¹³⁄₁₆ | 29⅞ | −³⁄₁₆ |
| 26 | 17⁷⁄₁₆ | Geon | GON | .50 | 2.8 | 17 | 182 | 17⅞ | 17¾ | 17⅞ | +⅛ |

# STOCK EXCHANGES AND THEIR FUNCTIONS

The New York Stock Exchange—"The Big Board"—is perhaps the world's most prestigious stock market. Located on Wall Street in New York City, it is "*the* establishment" of the securities industry. The NYSE deals with only the best-known and most heavily traded securities—more than 3,000 companies in all. Approximately 1,300 of the leading brokerage firms hold "seats" on the stock exchange, which enable them to trade directly on the exchange floor. (In the NYSE's early years, members sat in assigned seats during roll call; the term lost its literal meaning with the advent of continuous trading in 1871.) Seats are traded on the open market; in February of 1999, for example, a seat on the exchange went for $2 million.

Someone who wants to buy a stock on the New York Stock Exchange must use a broker, who will in turn deal with a firm that has a seat on the exchange. Suppose that you live in Florida and want to buy 200 shares of General Motors stock. The broker you approach may be employed by a firm that holds a seat on the exchange, or he may work through another firm that holds one. The exchange broker who is to fill your order then contacts a third person called a *specialist*, who also works on the exchange floor and handles GM stock.

The specialist usually owns some GM stock of her own which she will offer to sell if no other sellers are available at the moment. In addition, the specialist usually receives a number of *limit orders* from investors offering to sell specified quantities of GM stock at specified prices. There may, for example, be one offer to sell 5,000 shares at any price above $75 and another offer to sell 1,200 shares at any price above $90. Similarly, the specialist is likely to have several limit orders to buy at various specified prices.

The floor broker brings your order to the specialist, who determines a price that she believes more or less balances supply and demand as indicated by her recent sales and purchases and her limit orders. At this price, the specialist will fill your order from one of the limit orders to sell (she must do so whenever possible) or from her personal inventory of General Motors stock. The price determination process we have just described is sometimes called the *auction market* process. The New York Stock Exchange expedites this "auction" by using an elaborate electronic system to link member firms directly to the appropriate specialists or floor brokers.

The New York Stock Exchange handles a little over half of all stock market transactions in the United States (measured in *dollar* volume). A number of *regional* exchanges—such as the Chicago, Pacific, Philadelphia, Boston, and Cincinnati Stock Exchanges—deal in many of the stocks handled on the NYSE but mainly serve large institutional customers such as banks, insurance companies, and mutual funds. These regional exchanges together handle about 9 percent of the total stock traded. The *American Stock Exchange*, another traditional stock market exchange located a few blocks away from the NYSE, carries out about 1 percent of total stock market transactions.

The remainder (about 42 percent) of all stock transactions are carried out "over the counter" via the institution called *NASDAQ* (the automated quotation system of the National Association of Securities Dealers). NASDAQ, which has become a major force in the industry since its inception in 1971, deals with stocks that are not listed on the traditional exchanges; it has no physical trading floor and all transactions are carried out on a computer network. NASDAQ handles the stocks of nearly 5,400 companies, including such giants as Intel and Microsoft.[6]

NASDAQ is a "dealer market" in which a number of securities dealers compete with one another in stock sales and purchases. More than 500 such dealer firms are active "market makers" on NASDAQ, buying and selling for their own accounts. The dealers charge no commissions and post (electronically) the prices at which they are willing to buy and sell a given stock. The market makers earn the excess of the

## FIGURE 16-3

### Excerpt from a Bond-Price Table

| Company | Cur. Yld | Vol | Price | Chg |
|---|---|---|---|---|
| AMR 8.10s98 | 8.1 | 75 | 100¹/₁₆ | ... |
| AMR 9s16 | 7.4 | 30 | 121 | − 1 |
| ATT 6s00 | 6.0 | 10 | 100¹/₄ | + ¹/₈ |
| ATT 6³/₄04 | 6.3 | 24 | 107³/₈ | + 1¹/₈ |
| ATT 7¹/₂06 | 6.8 | 35 | 110¹/₂ | + ¹/₄ |
| ATT 7³/₄07 | 6.9 | 20 | 113 | + 1⁵/₈ |
| ATT 8¹/₈22 | 7.5 | 124 | 107⁷/₈ | ... |
| AlldC zr07 | ... | 15 | 61 | + 1¹/₈ |
| AlldC zr09 | ... | 30 | 49³/₈ | ... |
| Allwst 7¹/₄14 | cv | 48 | 26 | ... |
| Alza 5s06 | cv | 134 | 121³/₄ | + 3³/₄ |
| Amoco 8⁵/₈16 | 8.1 | 23 | 105⁷/₈ | ... |
| Amresco 10s03 | 12.7 | 67 | 79 | + 6¹/₈ |
| Amresco 10s04 | 13.7 | 60 | 72⁷/₈ | + 2⁷/₈ |
| Anhr 8⁵/₈16 | 8.4 | 10 | 102¹/₂ | ... |

SOURCE: *The New York Times*, September 22, 1998, p. C17.

A **stock price index,** such as the S&P 500, is an average of the prices of a large set of stocks. These stocks are selected to represent the price movements of the entire stock market, or some specified segment of the market, and the chosen set is rarely changed.

---

[6] *Wall Street Journal Almanac 1999* (New York: Ballantine Books, 1998), p. 288; and NASDAQ, www.nasdaq.com, accessed March 1999.

You are standing on the trading floor of the New York Stock Exchange, a crowded and noisy set of rooms cluttered with people, hundreds of computer monitors, and other paraphernalia. It is a high-tech space in a 93-year-old architectural relic of bygone days. Around the floor are 17 stations, or "trading posts," presided over by *specialists,* each assigned responsibility for trading a particular set of stocks.

Suddenly the floor's frenetic activity focuses on one specialist's post. News has just come in that one of the companies whose stock she handles has earned more in the previous quarter than was expected. Brokers crowd around her, calling out orders to buy and sell the company's stock, as its price rises rapidly in the wake of the good news. Deals are completed verbally, as clerks record the trades and enter them into the computerized tape, making the information instantly available all over the globe.

SOURCE: Murray Teitelbaum, Communications Division, New York Stock Exchange.

selling price over the buying price, called *the spread.* They also may profit from changes in the prices of the securities they hold.

In the last few years, the established stock markets have faced competition from another source. With the rapid growth of the Internet, people are beginning to buy and sell stocks directly through their home computers. Some observers predict that such trading, though currently very limited in volume, will grow by leaps and bounds.

## REGULATION OF THE STOCK MARKET

Both the government and the industry itself regulate the U.S. securities markets. At the base of the regulatory pyramid, stock brokerage firms maintain compliance departments to oversee their own operations. At the next level, the New York Stock Exchange, the American Stock Exchange, NASDAQ, and the regional exchanges are responsible for monitoring their member firms' business practices, funding adequacy, compliance, and integrity. They also use sophisticated computer surveillance systems to scrutinize trading activity. The *Securities and Exchange Commission* (SEC) is the federal government agency that oversees the market's self-regulation.

One example of these self-imposed rules is the steps markets adopted after the October 1987 stock market crash to cushion future price falls. In 1988 the NYSE and other stock markets adopted a series of rules called *circuit breakers,* which halted all equities trading for one hour if the Dow Jones Industrial Average fell 250 points from the previous day's level and an additional two hours if the Dow Jones fell another 150 points on the same day. These levels were later increased and the duration of the trading halts shortened to half an hour for a 350-point drop and one hour for a 550-point drop on the same day. Circuit breakers were designed to head off a panic among market participants and forestall a crash like the one in 1987, but when they were finally tested during the October 1997 stock market plunge, they were criticized as out of date and more disruptive than helpful. A new series of circuit breakers, inaugurated in April 1998, are based on *percentage* drops in the Dow Jones, rather than point drops. Under the new rules, much steeper drops are required to activate the circuit breakers.

## STOCK EXCHANGES AND CORPORATE CAPITAL NEEDS

Although corporations often raise needed funds by selling stock, they do not normally do so through the stock exchanges. New stock issues usually are handled by a special type of bank called an *investment bank*. In contrast, the stock markets trade almost exclusively in "secondhand securities"—stocks in the hands of individuals and others who bought them earlier and now wish to sell them.

Thus, the stock market does not provide funds to corporations needing financing to expand their productive activities. The markets provide money only to persons who already hold previously issued stocks.

Yet stock exchanges have two critically important functions for corporate financing. First, by providing a secondhand market for stocks, they make individual investment in a company much less risky. Investors know that if they need the money, they can always sell their stocks to other investors or to the specialist at the current market price. This reduction in risk makes it far easier for corporations to issue new stocks.

Second, the stock market determines the current price of the company's stocks. That, in turn, determines whether it will be hard or easy for a corporation to raise money by selling new stocks.

Some people believe that a company's stock price is closely tied to its operational efficiency, its effectiveness in meeting consumer demands, and its diligence in going after profitable innovation. In this view, firms that use funds effectively will usually have comparatively high stock prices. In this way the stock market tends to channel the economy's funds to the firms that can make best use of the money. In sum:

If a firm has a promising future, its stock will tend to command a high price on the stock exchanges. Its high stock price will increase the firm's ability to raise capital by permitting it to amass a large amount of money through the sale of a comparatively small number of new stock shares. Thus, *the stock market helps to allocate the economy's resources to firms that can best use those resources.*

However, other people are skeptical about the claim that the price of a company's stock is closely tied to efficiency. These observers believe that the demand for stock is disproportionately influenced by short-term developments in a company's profitability and that the market pays little attention to management decisions affecting the company's long-term earnings growth. These critics sometimes suggest that the stock market is similar to a gambling casino in which hunch, rumor, and superstition have a critical influence on prices. (We will see more about this later in the chapter.)

Whether or not stock prices are an accurate measure of a company's efficiency, if a company's stock price is very low in comparison with the value of its plant, equipment, and other assets, or when a company's earnings seem low compared to their potential level, that company becomes a tempting target for a **takeover** attempt. This may be because the firm's current management is believed not to be very competent or perhaps because the demand for a company's stocks is inordinately influenced by short-term developments, such as temporarily low profits.

A *takeover* occurs when a group of outside financiers buys a sufficient amount of company stock to gain control of the firm. Often, the new controlling group will simply fire the current management and substitute a new chairman, president, and other top officers (see the accompanying box, "The Surge in Takeovers").

A **takeover** is the acquisition by an outside group (the raiders) of a controlling proportion of a company's stock. When the old management opposes the takeover attempt, it is called a *hostile takeover attempt.*

## ■ SPECULATION

Securities dealings are sometimes viewed with suspicion because they are thought to be an instrument of **speculation.** When something goes wrong in the stock market—when, say, prices suddenly fall—observers often blame speculators. Editorial writers, for example, often use the word *speculators* as a term of strong disapproval, implying that those who engage in the activity are parasites who produce no benefits for society and often cause considerable harm. (See the accompanying box, "How

Individuals who engage in **speculation** deliberately invest in risky assets, hoping to obtain profits from future changes in the prices of these assets.

---

## ● THE SURGE IN TAKEOVERS

Small groups of individuals or enterprises sometimes buy enough stock to gain control or take over a company. When the purchaser is another firm, this process is called a "merger" or "acquisition." Periodically, bursts of takeover activity have resulted in a very large rise in the number of mergers and acquisitions (there have been five such merger "waves" in the 20th century). For example, corporate "raiders" shook up the stock market and the managements of a number of corporations in the 1980s by trying to take over firms. This boom in takeovers slackened during the recession of the early 1990s, but has since surged again. In 1998 a record $1.6 trillion in mergers took place, with such headline-making deals as the $73.7 billion takeover of Mobil Oil by Exxon, a deal that created one of the largest corporations in the world (and put back together two of the biggest pieces from the 1911 breakup of John D. Rockefeller's Standard Oil). As this book was being written, takeover activity was still on a hot streak.*

An attempt to acquire a company by a group of "raiders" that is unfriendly to current management is called a *hostile takeover.* Naturally, the officers of that corporation will try to fight the takeover, because they do not want to lose their high-paying jobs. They can fight back in many ways, for example, by trying to arrange for a "friendly takeover" by a group of investors they like better. They may also deliberately sabotage the company—often by selling some of its most valuable parts in order to make what is left of the firm less attractive to the takeover group. Management may seek to bribe the takeover group to go away by offering a very high price for the already-acquired stock. Indeed, groups often attempt takeovers in the hope that management will be forced to offer them such a bribe (called *greenmail*).

In the 1980s, when a large number of takeover battles broke out, the issue received a good deal of publicity and set off a heated debate over the pros and cons of legal restrictions on such activity. People who argue against strong legal restrictions point out that takeover is the most effective means to rid companies of incompetent managements, thus keeping the economy at peak efficiency. They also argue that this activity helps "create stockholder value," or drive the price of an undervalued company's stock up to its true economic value.

But advocates of stricter regulations or restrictions upon takeovers argue that the process can hurt bystander stockholders, as when management pays a large bribe to the takeover group or sells off a valuable part of the company. Moreover, those seeking to buy a large percentage of the company's shares will try to do so as secretly as possible, hoping to obtain the stock cheaply. Critics claim that in the process, the raiders, in effect, cheat those who sell them stock.

Opponents of takeovers also point out that the time bright, talented people take in planning and carrying out the strategies and counterstrategies uses up a valuable

resource that could be better used elsewhere. In this view, takeover activity absorbs some of the nation's most capable individuals in financial manipulation rather than productive and innovative activity. These critics are wrong, however, when they argue that the billions of dollars changing hands in a takeover battle tie up the nation's capital wastefully or "use up" the economy's credit supply. A takeover process in fact ties up little or no capital (machinery, factories, and the like). The money and credit used are simply transferred from one group of persons to another.

Sometimes, takeovers are financed by "junk bonds," that is, the raiders issue bonds to raise the money they need to acquire control of the target corporation. These bonds are frequently backed only by the profits that the raiders *expect* to grow out of their acquisition. Such profits may arise from more efficient management. The new owners may also sell off valuable portions of the corporation's activities (one of its successful products, for example) which they purchased cheaply because the corporation's stock price was low before the takeover.

Junk bonds backed only by such earnings prospects after the takeover are risky because those promised profits may never materialize. A takeover financed in this way is called a "leveraged buyout" because the raider risks little of his or her own money in the process. Instead, the raider's limited resources are levered upward with other people's money, supplied by junk bond purchasers. Critics of leveraged buyouts note that they may leave firms saddled with burdensome financial obligations to these junk bond purchasers.

Most of the very recent mergers have not been hostile contests that resulted in heavy debt. Corporate mergers in the mid to late 1990s seem more often to have had the goal of creating bigger companies that were believed to be better able to face increasing global competition. Recent deals have been financed to a greater extent with corporate stock of the acquiring company, rather than borrowed money.

*Economic Report of the President, 1999* (Washington, D.C.: U.S. Government Printing Office, February 1999).

April 9, 2011:   Microsoft-Citibank-Exxon-Time Warner
merges with
RJR Nabisco-AT&T-Archer Daniels Midland.

May 14, 2011:   The Edible Laptop is introduced.

to Lose Billions: Betting on Derivatives" for a description of a particularly risky speculative instrument, the *derivative*.)

Economists disagree vehemently with this judgment. They argue that speculators perform two vital economic functions:

■ Speculators sell *protection from risk* to other people, much as a fire insurance policy offers protection from risk to a homeowner.

■ Speculators help to smooth out price fluctuations by purchasing items when they are abundant (and cheap) and holding them and reselling them when they are scarce (and expensive). In that way, speculators play a vital economic role in helping to alleviate and even prevent shortages.

Some examples from outside the securities markets will help clarify the role of speculators. Say a Broadway ticket broker attends a preview of a new musical comedy and suspects it will be a hit. He decides to speculate by buying a large block of tickets for future performances. In that way, he takes over part of the producer's risk, while the comedy's producer reduces her inventory of risky tickets and receives some hard cash. If the show opens and is a flop, the broker will be stuck with the tickets. If the show is a hit, he can sell them at a premium, if the law allows (and be denounced as a speculator or a "scalper").

Similarly, speculators enable farmers (or producers of metals and other commodities whose future price is uncertain) to decrease their risk. Let's say Jasmine and Jim have planted a large crop of wheat but fear its price may fall before harvest time. They can protect themselves by signing a contract with a speculator for future delivery of the crop at an agreed-upon price. If the price then happens to fall, the speculator, not Jasmine and Jim, will suffer the loss. Of course, if the price rises, the speculator will reap the gain—but that is the nature of risk bearing. The speculator who has agreed to buy the crop at a preset price, regardless of market conditions at the time of the sale, has, in effect, sold an insurance policy to Jasmine and Jim. Surely this is a useful function.

**THE WALL STREET JOURNAL**

"Don't laugh—she's called the last five Dow Jones turnarounds right on the nose."

---

● **HOW TO LOSE BILLIONS: BETTING ON DERIVATIVES**

---

Derivatives, one of the fastest growing areas of finance, are complex financial instruments so named because they "derive" their value from the price movements of an underlying investment, such as a group of stocks, bonds, or commodities. Businesses buy these very risky contracts in an effort to hedge or ensure against sudden changes in interest rates or currency values. They also can be used to speculate in the markets.

A number of recent spectacular financial failures have been closely tied to the use of derivatives. First was the nearly $2 billion loss and resulting bankruptcy of Orange County, California. Then came the collapse of a 233-year-old British investment bank, Barings PLC, after one of its employees (a 28-year-old "rogue" futures trader named Nicholas Leeson) "bet the ranch" on the movement of the Japanese stock market (and lost $1.46 billion). The latest astounding near-meltdown involved a private investment fund called Long-Term Capital Management, the management of which

happens to include two Nobel Prize–winning economists. The firm is a so-called hedge fund that uses derivatives to place (or hedge) million- and billion-dollar bets on movements in such financial instruments as Russian treasury bonds and Danish mortgages. In the fall of 1998 the firm was reported to have lost upwards of $4 billion (and had to be bailed out by its bankers) when its statistical models failed to predict the movement of global markets.

SOURCE: "Wall Street Struggles to Save Big Fund," *Washington Post*, September 24, 1998.

---

The speculators' second role is perhaps even more important. In effect, they accumulate and store goods in periods of abundance and make goods available in periods of scarcity. Suppose that a speculator has reason to suspect that next year's crop of a storable commodity will not be nearly as abundant as this year's. She will buy some now, when it is cheap, for resale when it becomes scarce and expensive. In the process, she will smooth out the swing in prices by adding her purchases to the total market demand in the low-price period (which tends to bring the price up), and bringing in her supplies during the high-price period (which tends to push the price down).[7]

Thus, the successful speculator will help to relieve matters during periods of extreme shortage. Speculators have sometimes even helped to relieve famine by releasing supplies they had deliberately hoarded for such an occasion. Of course, speculators are cursed for their high prices on such occasions. But those who curse them do not understand that prices would have been even higher if the speculators' foresight and avid pursuit of profit had not provided for the emergency. On the securities market, famine and severe shortages are not an issue, but the fact remains that successful speculators tend to reduce price fluctuations by increasing demand for stocks when prices are low and contributing to supply when prices are high.

> Far from aggravating instability and fluctuations, to earn a profit speculators *iron out* fluctuations by buying when prices are low and selling when prices are high.

### Unpredictable Stock Prices as "Random Walks"

The beginning of this chapter cited evidence that the best professional securities analysts have a forecasting record so miserable that investors may do as well predicting earnings by hunch, superstition, or any purely random process as they would by following professional advice. (See the accompanying box, "Football and Financial Forecasting" to learn about one crazy way of predicting the stock market's performance: the outcome of the Super Bowl.)

---

[7] For a diagrammatic analysis of this role of speculation, see Review Question 7 at the end of the chapter.

## ● FOOTBALL AND FINANCIAL FORECASTING

The following excerpt from Floyd Norris' column in the business section of *The New York Times* suggests some of the gimmicks that stock market analysts turn to in a desperate effort to predict stock prices.

In years gone by, when people thought that stocks went both up and down and that market timing was therefore important, market seers searched for indicators that would point the way to determining whether a certain time was a good one to be in the market.

There were indicators based on dividends and on profits, on Federal Reserve actions and on bond yields. Even skirt lengths were tried. (In very speculative markets, hem lines rise along with share prices.) But the indicator that seemed to work the best was one that was so clearly irrelevant that no one could take it seriously: the Super Bowl indicator.

Now, investors are far less interested in market timing than they were 20 years ago—a time when stock prices were below where they had been more than a decade earlier and when few thought that stocks were sure to rise over long periods of time. Now, after the best 20 years in stock market history, the general belief is that one need not pay attention to much of anything regarding value. If you buy and hold for a long period, you will do well. As a result, indicators receive far less attention.

But the Super Bowl indicator has continued to perform, albeit with less publicity. It holds—in its current version, for like many indicators it has been tweaked along the way—that if a team from the old National Football League wins the Super Bowl, stocks will rise over the next year. But if a team from the old American Football League prevails, the stock market is in trouble.

In 1998, the Super Bowl indicator got it wrong: The Denver Broncos (from the old AFL) beat the Green Bay Packers (an original NFL team), but the stock market went ahead and had a fantastic year anyway. The following year, the Broncos did it again—beating the Atlanta Falcons, 34–19. The Super Bowl indicator has never been wrong two years in a row, so is the stock market in trouble for 1999? Stay tuned.

SOURCE: Floyd Norris, "Market Place," *The New York Times,* January 22, 1998.

Does this mean that analysts are incompetent people who do not know what they are doing? Not at all. Rather, there is fairly strong evidence that they have undertaken a task that is basically impossible.

How can this be so? The answer is that to make a good forecast of *any* variable—be it GDP, population, fuel usage, or stock market prices—there must be something in the past whose behavior is closely related to the future behavior of the variable whose path we wish to predict. If a 10 percent rise in this year's consumption always produces a 5 percent rise in next year's GDP, this fact can help us predict future GDP on the basis of current observations. But if we want to forecast the future of a variable whose behavior is completely unrelated to the behavior of *any* current or past variable, there is no objective evidence that can help us make that forecast. Throwing darts or gazing into a crystal ball are no less effective than analysts' calculations.

There is a mass of statistical evidence that the behavior of stock prices is largely unpredictable. In other words, the behavior of stock prices is essentially *random;* the paths they follow are what statisticians call **random walks.** A random walk is like the path followed by a sleepwalker. All we know about his position after his next step is that it will be given by his current position plus whatever random direction his next haphazard step will carry him. The relevant feature of randomness, for our purposes, is that it is by nature *unpredictable,* which is just what the word *random* means.

The time path of a variable such as the price of a stock is said to constitute a **random walk** if its magnitude in one period (say, May 2, 2000) is equal to its value in the preceding period (May 1, 2000) plus a completely random number. That is: Price on May 2, 2000 = Price on May 1, 2000 + Random number, where the random number (positive or negative) can be obtained by a roll of dice or some such procedure.

If the evidence that stock prices approximate a random walk stands up to research in the future as it has so far, it is easy enough to understand why stock market predictions are as poor as they are. Analysts are trying to forecast behavior that is basically random; in effect, they are trying to predict the unpredictable.

Two questions remain. First, does the evidence that stock prices follow a random walk mean that investment in stocks is a pure gamble and never worthwhile? Second, how does one explain the random behavior of stock prices?

To answer the first question, it is false to conclude that investment in stocks is generally not worthwhile. The statistical evidence is that, over the long run, stock prices *as a whole* have had a fairly marked upward trend, perhaps reflecting the long-term growth of the economy. Thus, the random walk does not proceed in just any direction—rather, it represents a set of erratic movements *around a basic upward trend in stock prices.*

Moreover, it is not in the *overall* level of stock prices that the most pertinent random walk occurs, but in the performance of one company's stock compared with another's. For this reason, professional advice may be able to predict that investment in the stock market is likely to be a good thing over the long haul. But, if the random walk evidence is valid, there is no way professionals can tell us *which* of the available stocks is most likely to go up—that is, which combination of stocks is best for the investor to buy.

The only appropriate answer to the second question is that no one is sure of the explanation. There are two widely offered hypotheses—each virtually the opposite of the other. The first asserts that stock prices are random because clever professional speculators are able to foresee almost perfectly every influence that is *not* random. For example, suppose that a change occurs that makes the probable earnings of some company higher than had previously been expected. Then, according to this view, the professionals will instantly become aware of this change and immediately buy enough to raise the price of the stock accordingly. Then the only thing for that stock price to do between this year and next is wander randomly, because the professionals cannot predict random movements, and hence they cannot force current stock prices to anticipate them. The other explanation of random behavior of stock prices is at the opposite pole from the view that all nonrandom movements are wiped out by supersmart professionals. This view is that people who buy and sell stocks have learned that they cannot predict future stock prices. As a result, they react to *any* signal, however irrational and irrelevant it appears. If the president catches cold, stock prices fall. If an astronaut's venture is successful, prices go up. According to this view, investors are, in the last analysis, trying to predict not the prospects of the economy or of the company whose shares they buy, but the supply and demand behavior of other investors, which will ultimately determine the course of stock prices. Because all investors are equally in the dark, their groping can only result in the randomness that we observe.

Just a normal day at the nation's most important financial institution...

The classic statement of this view of stock market behavior was provided in 1936 by English economist John Maynard Keynes, a successful professional speculator himself:

> Professional investment may be likened to those newspaper competitions in which the competitors have to pick out the six prettiest faces from a hundred photographs, the prize being awarded to the competitor whose choice most nearly corresponds to the average preferences of the competitors as a whole; so that each competitor has to pick not those faces which he himself finds prettiest, but those which he thinks likeliest to catch the fancy of the other competitors, all of whom are looking at the problem from the same point of view. It is not a case of choosing those which, to the best of one's judgment, are really the prettiest, nor even those which average opinion genuinely thinks the prettiest. We have reached the third degree where we devote our intelligences to anticipating what average opinion expects the average opinion to be. And there are some, I believe, who practice the fourth, fifth and higher degrees.[8]

This may help to explain the impressive rise of the stock market from a Dow Jones index of 800 in 1982 to 2,700 in 1987, a 700-point fall in two consecutive trading days in October 1987, then several sharp fluctuations followed by a remarkably sustained upward trend since then.

## SUMMARY

1. The three basic types of firms are *corporations, partnerships,* and individual *proprietorships.* Most U.S. firms are individual proprietorships, but most U.S. manufactured goods are produced by corporations.

2. Individual proprietorships and partnerships have tax advantages over corporations. But corporate investors have greater risk protection because they have *limited liability*— they cannot be asked to pay more of the company's debts than they have invested in the firm.

3. Higher taxation of corporate earnings tends to limit the things in which corporations can invest and may lead to inefficiency in resource allocation.

4. A *common stock* is a share in a company's ownership. A *bond* is an IOU for money lent to a company by the bondholder. Many observers argue that a stock purchase also really amounts to a loan to the company—a loan that is riskier than a bond purchase.

5. If interest rates rise, bond prices will fall. In other words, if some bond amounts to a contract to pay 8 percent and the market interest rate goes up to 10 percent, people will no longer be willing to pay the old price for that bond.

6. Corporations finance their activities mostly by *plowback* (that is, by retaining part of their earnings and putting it back into the company). They also obtain funds by sales of stocks and bonds and through more traditional loans.

7. If stock prices correctly reflect the future prospects of different companies, it is easier for promising firms to raise money because they are able to sell each stock they issue at favorable prices.

8. Bonds are relatively risky for the firms that issue them, but they are fairly safe for their buyers, because they are a commitment by those firms to pay fixed annual amounts to the bondholders whether or not the companies make money that year. But stocks, which do not promise any fixed payment, are relatively safe for the companies and risky for their owners.

9. A portfolio is a collection of stocks, bonds, and other assets of a single owner. The greater the number and variety of securities and other assets a portfolio contains, the less risky it is.

10. A corporation is said to be taken over when an outside group buys enough stock to get control of the firm's decisions. *Takeovers* are a useful way to get rid of incompetent management or to force management to be efficient. However, the process is costly and leads to wasteful defensive and offensive activities.

11. *Speculation* affects stock market prices, but (contrary to widespread belief) speculation actually tends to *reduce* the frequency and size of price fluctuations. Speculators are also useful to the economy because they undertake risks that others wish to avoid, thereby, in effect, providing others with insurance against risk.

12. Statistical evidence indicates that individual stock prices behave randomly (in other words, unpredictably).

[8] John Maynard Keynes, *The General Theory of Employment, Interest, and Money* (New York: Harcourt Brace, 1936), p. 156.

QUESTIONS FOR REVIEW

1. Why would it be difficult to run General Motors as a partnership or an individual proprietorship?

2. Do you think it is fair to tax a corporation more than a partnership doing the same amount of business? Why or why not?

3. If you hold shares in a corporation and management decides to plow back the company's earnings some year instead of paying dividends, what are the advantages and disadvantages to you?

4. Suppose that interest rates are 6 percent in the economy and a safe bond promises to pay $3 a year in interest forever. What do you think the price of the bond will be? Why?

5. Suppose in the economy in the previous example, interest rates suddenly fall to 3 percent. What will happen to the price of the bond that pays $3 per year?

6. If you want to buy a stock, when might it pay you to use a market order? When will it pay to use a limit order?

7. Show in diagrams that if a speculator were to buy when price is high and sell when price is low, he would increase price fluctuations. Why would it be in his best interest *not* to do so? (*Hint:* Draw two supply-demand diagrams, one for the high-price period and one for the low-price period. How would the speculator's activities affect these diagrams?)

8. If stock prices really are a random walk, can you nevertheless think of good reasons for getting professional advice before investing?

9. Hostile takeovers often end up in court when managements attempt to block them and raiders accuse the managements of selfishly sacrificing the stockholders' interests. The courts often look askance at "coercive" offers by raiders—an offer to buy, say, 20 percent of the company's stock by a certain date from the first stockholders who offer to sell. By contrast, they take a more favorable attitude toward "noncoercive" offers to buy any and all stock supplied at announced prices. Do you think the courts are right to reject "coercive offers" but prevent management from blocking "noncoercive" offers? Why?

10. In "program trading," computers decide when to buy or sell stocks on behalf of large, institutional investors. The computers then carry out those transactions with electronic speed. Critics claim that this is a major reason why stock prices rose and fell sharply in the 1980s. Is this plausible? Why or why not?

# IV

## THE DISTRIBUTION OF INCOME

In Part IV we examine how a market economy distributes its income. As we will see, the market works through the price mechanism, with the prices of the inputs of the production process—the land, the labor, the capital—determined by supply and demand. We will see that the market also assigns a central role to marginal productivity.

In Chapter 17, we will study the payments made for the use of capital (interest), land (rent), and the reward to entrepreneurs (profits). Because most people earn their incomes primarily from wages and salaries, and because these payments constitute nearly three-quarters of U.S. national income, our analysis of the payments

327

to labor (wages) merits a separate chapter (Chapter 18). In Chapter 19 we turn to some important problems in the distribution of income—poverty, inequality, and discrimination. We save the discussion of the pricing of exhaustible natural resources, as part of the income of land, for Chapter 22 in Part V.

Rent is that portion of the produce of the earth which is paid to the landlord for use of the original and indestructible powers of the soil.

David Ricardo (1772–1823)

# PRICING THE FACTORS OF PRODUCTION

In Chapter 14 we saw that the market mechanism cannot be counted on to distribute income in accord with ethical notions of "fairness," and we listed this as one of the market's shortcomings. There is much more to say about how income is distributed in a market economy, and we turn to that subject in this chapter.

The market mechanism distributes income through its payments to the factors of production. Everyone owns some *factors of production*—which are simply the inputs used in the production process. Many of us have only our own labor; but some of us also have funds that we can lend, land that we can rent, or natural resources that we can sell. We sell these factors on markets at prices determined by supply and demand. So the distribution of

**Factors of production** are the broad categories, land, labor, capital, exhaustible natural resources, and entrepreneurship, into which we divide the economy's different productive inputs.

**Entrepreneurship** is the act of starting new firms, introducing new products and technological innovations, and, in general, taking the risks that are necessary in seeking out business opportunities.

income in a market economy is determined by the prices of the **factors of production** and by the amounts that are employed. For example, if wages are low and unequal and unemployment is high, then many people will be poor.

It is useful to group the factors of production into five broad categories: land, labor, capital, exhaustible natural resources, and a rather mysterious input called **entrepreneurship.** In this chapter, we will look at three of them—the interest paid to capital, the rent of land, and the profits earned by entrepreneurs—saving labor for Chapter 18 and natural resources for Chapter 22.

But first, because there is a great deal of misperception about the distribution of income among workers, capitalists, and landlords, let's see how much these three groups actually earn. In 1998, interest payments in the United States accounted for about 6.5 percent of national income; land rents were minuscule, making up only 2 percent; corporate profits accounted for about 12 percent; and income of other business proprietors made up about 8 percent.[1] In total, the returns to all the factors of production that we deal with in this chapter amounted to about one-quarter of national income. Where did the rest of it go? The answer is that close to three-quarters of national income was composed of employee compensation—wages and salaries. The huge share of labor in national income is one of the reasons why the next chapter is devoted entirely to this subject.

There are many other serious misunderstandings about the nature of income distribution and about what government can do to influence it, and discussions of the subject are often emotional. That's because the distribution of income is the one area in economics in which any one individual's interests almost inevitably conflict with those of someone else. By definition, if I get a larger slice of the total income pie, then you end up with a smaller slice.

## ■ THE PRINCIPLE OF MARGINAL PRODUCTIVITY

The **marginal physical product (MPP)** of an input is the increase in output that results from a one-unit increase in the use of the input, holding the amounts of all other inputs constant.

The **marginal revenue product (MRP)** of an input is the money value of the additional sales that a firm obtains by selling the marginal physical product of that input.

By now it will not surprise you to learn that economists analyze factor prices in terms of supply and demand. The supply sides of the markets for the various factors differ enormously, so we must discuss each factor market separately. But we can use one basic principle, the *principle of marginal productivity*, to explain how much of any input a profit-maximizing firm will *demand*, given the price of that input. To review the principle, we must first recall two concepts from Chapter 8: **marginal physical product (MPP)** and **marginal revenue product (MRP).**[2]

Table 17–1 helps us review these two concepts by recalling Naomi's Natural Farm, which has to decide how much corn to feed the hogs. The *marginal physical product* (MPP) column tells us how many additional pounds of pork each additional bag of corn will yield. For example, according to the table, the fourth bag increases output by 34 pounds. The *marginal revenue product* (MRP) column tells us how many dollars this marginal physical product is worth. In Table 17–1, we assume Naomi's prized, natural hogs sell at 75 cents a pound, so the marginal revenue product of the fourth bag of corn is $0.75 per pound times 34 pounds, or $25.50 (last column of the table).

> The marginal productivity principle states that in competitive factor markets, the profit-maximizing firm will hire or buy the quantity of any input at which the marginal revenue product equals the price of the input.

The basic logic behind this principle is both simple and powerful. We know that the firm's profit from acquiring an additional unit of an input is the input's marginal revenue product minus its marginal cost (the price of the additional unit of

[1] National income and product tables, U.S. Department of Commerce, Bureau of Economic Analysis, www.bea.doc.gov., accessed May 1999.
[2] Instructors may prefer to postpone the multi-input analysis until later in the course.

**Naomi's Natural Farm Schedules for TPP, MPP, APP, and MRP of Corn**

TABLE 17-1

| (1) Input of Corn in 100-Pound Bags | (2) TPP: Total Physical Product Hog Output | (3) MPP: Marginal Physical Product per Bag | (4) APP: Average Physical Product per Bag | (5) MRP: Marginal Revenue Product per Bag |
|---|---|---|---|---|
| 0 | 0.0 lbs. | | | |
| | | 14.0 lbs. | | $10.50 |
| 1 | 14.0 | | 14.0 lbs. | |
| | | 22.0 | | 16.50 |
| 2 | 36.0 | | 18.0 | |
| | | 30.0 | | 22.50 |
| 3 | 66.0 | | 22.0 | |
| | | 34.0 | | 25.50 |
| 4 | 100.0 | | 25.0 | |
| | | 30.0 | | 22.50 |
| 5 | 130.0 | | 26.0 | |
| | | 26.0 | | 19.50 |
| 6 | 156.0 | | 26.0 | |
| | | 19.0 | | 14.25 |
| 7 | 175.0 | | 25.0 | |
| | | 9.0 | | 6.75 |
| 8 | 184.0 | | 23.0 | |
| | | 1.4 | | 1.05 |
| 9 | 185.4 | | 20.6 | |
| | | −5.4 | | −4.05 |
| 10 | 180.0 | | 18.0 | |
| | | −15.0 | | −11.25 |
| 11 | 165.0 | | 15.0 | |
| | | −21.0 | | −15.75 |
| 12 | 144.0 | | 12.0 | |

input). If the input's marginal revenue product is greater than its price, it will pay the profit-seeking firm to hire more of that input because an additional unit of input brings the firm revenue over and above its cost. The firm should purchase that input up to the amount at which diminishing returns reduce the MRP to the level of the input's price. By similar reasoning, if MRP is less than price, then the firm is using too much of the input. We see in Table 17–1 that about seven bags is the optimal amount of corn for Naomi to use each week, because an eighth bag brings in a marginal revenue product of only $6.75, which is less than the $10 cost of buying the bag.

One corollary of the principle of marginal productivity is obvious: the quantity of any input demanded depends on its price. The lower the price of corn, the more it pays the farm to buy. In our example, it pays Naomi to use between seven and eight bags when the price per bag is $10. But if corn were more expensive, say, $20 per bag, that high price would exceed the value of the marginal product of either the sixth or seventh bag. It would, therefore, pay the firm to stop at five bags of corn. Thus, *marginal productivity analysis shows that the quantity demanded of an input normally declines as the input price rises.* The "law" of demand applies to inputs just as it applies to consumer goods.

## INPUTS AND THEIR DERIVED DEMAND CURVES

We can, in fact, be much more specific about how much of each input a profit-maximizing firm will demand, for the marginal productivity principle tells us precisely how to derive the demand curve for any input from its marginal revenue product (MRP) curve.

Figure 17–1 graphs the MRP schedule from Table 17–1, showing the marginal revenue product for corn ($MRP_c$) rising and then declining as Naomi feeds more and more corn to her hogs. In the figure, we focus on three possible prices for a bag of corn: $20, $15, and $10. The optimal purchase rule requires Naomi to keep increasing the use of corn until its MRP is reduced to the price of corn. At a price of $20 per bag, we see that the quantity demanded is about 5.6 bags of corn per

FIGURE 17–1

**Marginal Revenue Product Schedule for Naomi's Natural Farm**

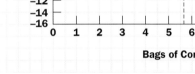

Bags of Corn per Week

week (point *A*) because at that point, MRP equals price. Similarly, if the price of corn is \$15 per bag, quantity demanded is about 6.8 bags per week (point *B*). Finally, at a price of \$10 per bag, the quantity demanded would be about 7.7 bags per week (point *C*). Points *A*, *B*, and *C* are therefore three points on the demand curve for corn. By repeating this exercise for any other price, we learn that:

> The demand curve for any input is the downward-sloping portion of its marginal revenue product curve.[3]

The demand for corn or labor (or for any other input) is called a **derived demand** because it is derived from the underlying demand for the final product (hogs in this case). For example, suppose that a surge in demand drives organic hog prices to \$1.50 per pound. Then, at each level of corn usage, the marginal revenue product will be twice as large as when hogs brought 75 cents a pound. This effect appears in Figure 17–2 as an upward shift of the (derived) demand curve for corn, from $D_0 D_0$ to $D_1 D_1$, even though the marginal physical product curves have not changed. Thus, an outward shift in demand for pork leads to an outward shift in the demand for corn.[4] We conclude that, in general:

> An outward shift in the demand curve for any commodity causes an outward shift of the derived demand curve for all factors utilized in the production of that commodity.

Similarly, an inward shift in the demand curve for a commodity leads to inward shifts in the demand curves for factors used in producing that commodity.

This completes our discussion of the *demand* side of the analysis of input pricing. The most noteworthy feature of the discussion is the fact that the same marginal productivity principle serves as the foundation for the demand schedule for each and every type of input. In particular, as we will see in the next chapter, the marginal productivity principle serves as the basis for the determination of the demand for *labor*—that crucial input whose financial reward plays so important a role in an economy's standard of living. On the demand side, one analysis fits all.

The supply side for each input, however, entails a very different story. Here we must deal with each of the main production factors individually. We must do this in order to see how each input's earnings depend on the interaction of demand *and* supply. We begin with *interest payments*, which is what we call the return on capital. First, we must define a few key terms.

FIGURE 17–2

**A Shift in the Demand Curve for Corn**

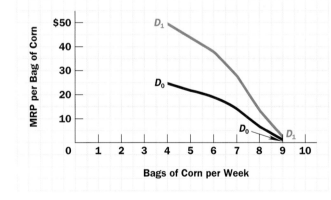

Bags of Corn per Week

---

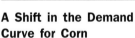

The **derived demand** for an input is the demand for the input by producers as determined by the demand for the final product that the input is used to produce.

[3] Why is the demand curve restricted to only the *downward-sloping portion* of the MRP curve? The logic of the marginal productivity principle dictates this. For example, if the price of corn were \$15.00 per bag, Figure 17–1 shows that there are two input quantities for which MRP = *P*: (approximately) 1.5 bags (point *D*) and 6.8 bags (point *B*). But point *D* cannot be the optimal stopping point because the MRP of a second bag (\$16.50) is greater than the cost of the third bag (\$15.00), so that the firm makes more money by expanding its input use beyond 1.5 bags per week. A similar profitable opportunity for expansion occurs any time the MRP curve slopes upward at the current price, because that means that an increase in the quantity of input used by the firm will raise MRP above the input's price. It follows that a profit-maximizing firm will always demand an input quantity that is in the range where MRP is diminishing.

[4] To make the diagram easier to read, the (irrelevant) upward-sloping portion and the negative portion of each curve have been omitted.

# ■ INVESTMENT, CAPITAL, AND INTEREST

Though people sometimes use the words *investment* and *capital* as if they were interchangeable, the distinction between them is important. Economists define **capital** as the inventory (or stock) of plant, equipment, and other productive resources held by a business firm, an individual, or some other organization. **Investment** is the amount by which capital *grows*. So, when economists use the word investment, they do not mean just the transfer of money. The higher the level of investment, the *faster* the amount of capital that the investor possesses grows. We can describe the relation between investment and capital by the analogy of filling a bathtub: The accumulated water in the tub is analogous to the *stock* of capital, whereas the flow of water from the faucet (which adds to the tub's water) is like the *flow* of investment. Just as the faucet must be turned on for more water to accumulate, the capital stock increases only when investment continues. If investment ceases, the capital stock stops growing (but does not disappear). In other words, if investment is zero, the capital stock does not fall to zero but remains constant (just as when you turn off the faucet the tub doesn't suddenly empty, but rather the level of the water stays the same).

The process of building up capital by investing and then using this capital in production can be divided into five steps. They are listed below and are summarized in Figure 17–3.

**Capital** refers to an inventory (*a stock*) of plant, equipment, and other (generally durable) productive resources held by a business firm, an individual, or some other organization.

**Investment** is the *flow* of resources into the production of new capital. It is the labor, steel, and other inputs devoted to the *construction* of factories, warehouses, railroads, and other pieces of capital during some period of time.

**The Investment Production Process**    | FIGURE 17-3 |

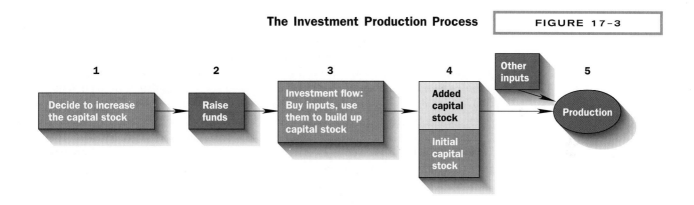

*Step 1.* The firm decides to enlarge its stock of capital.

*Step 2.* It raises the funds to finance its expansion, either from outside sources such as banks or by holding onto some of its own earnings rather than paying them out to company owners.

*Step 3.* The firm uses these funds to hire the inputs to build factories, warehouses, and the like. This step is the act of *investment*.

*Step 4.* After the investment is completed, the firm ends up with a larger stock of capital.

*Step 5.* The firm uses the capital (along with other inputs) either to expand production or to reduce costs. At this point, the firm starts earning *returns* on its investment.

Notice that investors put *money* into the investment process, either their own or funds they borrow from others. Then, through a series of steps, firms transform the funds into physical inputs suitable for production use. If investors borrow the funds, they must someday return those amounts to the lender with some payment for their use. This payment is called **interest,** and it is calculated as an annual percentage of the amount borrowed. For example, if an investor borrows $1,000 at an interest rate of 12 percent per year, the annual interest payment is $120.

**Interest** is the payment for the use of funds employed in the production of capital; it is measured as a percentage per year of the value of the funds tied up in the capital.

"I can't sleep. I just got this incredible craving for capital."

## THE DEMAND FOR FUNDS

The rate of interest is the *price* at which funds can be rented (borrowed). Just like other factor prices, interest rates are determined by supply and demand.

On the demand side of the market for loans are borrowers—people or institutions that, for one reason or another, wish to spend more than they currently have. Individuals or families borrow to buy homes or automobiles or other expensive products. Sometimes, as we know, they borrow because they want to consume more than they can afford, which can get them into financial trouble. But often, borrowing makes good sense as a way to manage their finances when they experience a temporary drop in income. It also makes sense to borrow money to buy an item like a home that will be used for many years; this long product life makes it appropriate for people to pay for the item as it is used, rather than all at once when it is purchased.

Businesses use loans primarily to finance investment. To the business executive who borrows funds to finance an investment and pays interest in return, the funds really represent an intermediate step toward the acquisition of the machines, buildings, inventories, and other forms of physical capital that the firm will purchase.

The marginal productivity principle governs the quantity of funds demanded, just as it governs the quantity of corn demanded for hog feed. Specifically:

**Firms will demand the quantity of borrowed funds that makes the marginal revenue product of the investment financed by the funds just equal to the interest payment charged for borrowing.**

One noteworthy feature of capital distinguishes it from other inputs, like corn, for example. When Naomi feeds corn to her hogs, it is used once and then it is gone. But a blast furnace, which is part of a steel company's capital, normally lasts many years. The furnace is a *durable* good; and because it is durable, it contributes not only to today's production but also to future production. This fact makes calculating the marginal revenue product more complex for a capital good than for other inputs.

To determine whether the MRP of a capital good is greater than the cost of financing it (that is, to decide whether an investment is profitable), we need a way to compare money values received at different times. To make such comparisons, economists and business people use a calculation procedure called *discounting*. We will explain discounting in detail in the appendix to this chapter, but you need not master this technique in an introductory course. There are really only two important attributes of discounting to learn here:

- **A sum of money received at a future date is worth less than the same sum of money received today.**

- **This difference in values between money today and money in the future is greater when the rate of interest is higher.**

We can easily understand why this is so. To illustrate our first point, consider what you could do with a dollar that you received today rather than a year from today. If the annual rate of interest were 10 percent, you could lend it out (for example, by putting it in a savings account) and receive $1.10 in a year's time—your original $1.00 plus 10 cents interest. For this reason, money received today is worth more than the same number of dollars received later.

Now for our second point. Suppose the annual rate of interest was 15 percent instead. In this case, $1.00 invested today would grow to $1.15 (rather than $1.10) in a year's time, which means that $1.15 received a year from today would be equivalent to $1.00 received today, and so $1.10 a year in the future must now be worth less than $1.00 today. But when the interest rate is 10 percent per year, $1.10 to be received a year from today is equivalent to $1 of today's money. This illustrates the second of our two points.

The rate of interest is a crucial determinant of the economy's level of investment. That is, it strongly influences the amount of current consumption that consumers will choose to forgo in order to use the resources to build machines and factories that can increase the output of consumers' goods in the future. The interest rate is crucial in determining the allocation of society's resources between present and future—an issue that we discussed in Chapter 14 (pages 277–279). Let us see, then, how the market sets interest rates.

## THE DOWNWARD-SLOPING DEMAND CURVE FOR FUNDS

The two attributes of discounting discussed above are all we need to explain why the quantity of funds demanded declines as interest rates rise, that is, why the demand curve for funds has a negative slope.

Remember that the demand for borrowed funds, like the demand for all inputs, is a *derived demand*, derived from the desire to invest in capital goods. But firms will receive part—perhaps all—of a machine or factory's marginal revenue product in the future. Hence, the value of the MRP *in terms of today's money* shrinks as the interest rate rises. Why? Because future returns to investment in a machine or factory must be *discounted* more when the rate of interest rises, as our illustration of the second point about discounting showed. The consequence of this shrinkage is that a machine that appears to be a good investment when the interest rate is 10 percent may look like a terrible investment if interest rates rise to 15 percent. That is, the higher the interest rate, the fewer machines a firm will demand, because investing in the machines would use up money that could earn more interest in a savings account. Thus, the demand curve for machines and other forms of capital will have a negative slope— the higher the interest rate, the smaller the quantity that firms will demand.

As the interest rate on borrowing rises, more and more investments that previously looked profitable start to look unprofitable. The demand for borrowing for investment purposes, therefore, is lower at higher rates of interest.

Note that, although this analysis clearly applies to a firm's purchase of capital goods such as plant and equipment, it may also apply to the company's land and labor purchases. Firms often finance both of these expenditures via borrowed funds, and these inputs' marginal revenue products may accrue only months or even years after the inputs have been bought and put to work. (For example, it may take quite some time before newly acquired agricultural land will yield a marketable crop.) Thus, just as in the case of capital investments, a rise in the interest rate will reduce the quantity demanded of investment goods like land and labor, just as it cuts the derived demand for investment in plant and equipment.

**FIGURE 17–4**

**The Derived Demand Curve for Loans**

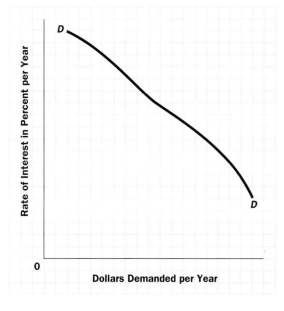

Figure 17–4 depicts a derived demand schedule for loans, with the interest rate on the vertical axis as the loan's cost to a borrower. Its negative slope illustrates the conclusion we have just stated:

The higher the interest rate, the less people and firms will want to borrow to finance their investments.

## THE SUPPLY OF FUNDS

Somewhat different relationships arise on the supply side of the market for funds—where the suppliers or *lenders* are consumers, banks, and other business firms. Funds lent out are usually returned to the owner (with interest) only over a period of time. Loans will look better to lenders when they bear higher interest rates, so the supply schedule for loans rather naturally may be expected to slope upward—at higher rates of interest, lenders supply more funds. Such a supply schedule appears as the curve *SS* in Figure 17–5, where we also reproduce the demand curve, *DD*, from Figure 17–4. Here, the free-market interest rate is 12 percent.

However, not all supply curves for funds slope uphill to the right like curve *SS*. Suppose, for example, that Mario is saving to buy a $10,000 boat in three years, and that if he lends money out at interest in the interim, he must save $3,000 a year to reach his goal. If interest rates were higher, he could get away with saving less than $3,000 each year and still reach his $10,000 goal. (The higher interest payments would, of course, contribute the difference.) So his saving (and lending) may decline as a result of the rise in interest

**FIGURE 17–5**

**Equilibrium in the Market for Loans**

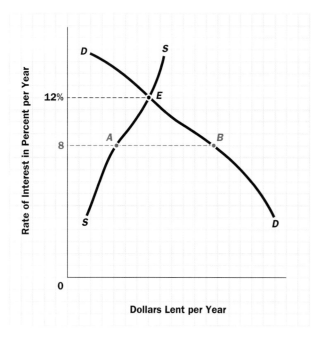

rate. This argument only applies fully to savers, like Mario, with a fixed accumulation goal. But similar considerations affect the calculations of other savers.

Generally, we expect the quantity of loans supplied to rise at least somewhat when the interest reward rises, so the supply curve will have a positive slope, like *SS* in Figure 17–5. However, for reasons similar to those indicated in Mario's example, the increase in the economy's saving that results from a rise in the interest rate is usually quite small. That is why we have drawn the supply curve so steep. The rise in the amount supplied by some lenders is partially offset by a decline in the amounts lent by savers with fixed goals (like Mario, who is putting money away to buy a boat, or Kathryn, who is saving for a mountain bike).

Having examined the relevant demand and supply curves, we are now in a position to discuss the determination of the equilibrium rate of interest. This is summed up in Figure 17–5, in which the equilibrium is, as always, at point *E*, where quantity supplied equals quantity demanded. We conclude, again, that the equilibrium interest rate on loans is 12 percent in the example in the graph.

## THE ISSUE OF USURY LAWS: ARE INTEREST RATES TOO HIGH?

People have often been dissatisfied with the market mechanism's determination of interest rates. Fears that interest rates, if left unregulated, would climb to exorbitant levels have made usury laws (which place upper limits on money-lending rates) quite popular in many times and places. Attempts to control interest payments date back to biblical days, and in the Middle Ages the influence of the church even led to total prohibition of interest payments in much of Europe. In the United States, the patchwork of state usury laws was mostly dismantled during the 1980s when the banking industry was deregulated.

Unscrupulous lenders often manage to evade usury laws by charging interest rates even higher than the free-market equilibrium rate. But even when usury laws are effective, they interfere with the operation of supply and demand and, as we will demonstrate, they often harm economic efficiency.

Look at Figure 17–5 again, but this time assume it depicts the supply of bank loans to consumers. Consider what happens if a usury law prohibits interest rates higher than 8 percent per year on consumer loans. At 8 percent, the quantity supplied (point *A* in Figure 17–5) falls short of the quantity demanded (point *B*). This means that many applicants for consumer loans are being turned down even though banks consider them to be creditworthy.

Who gains and who loses from this usury law? The gainers are the lucky consumers who get loans at 8 percent even though they would have been willing to pay 12 percent. The losers come on both the supply side and the demand side: the consumers who would have been willing and able to get credit at 12 percent but who are turned down at 8 percent, and the banks that could have made profitable loans at rates of up to 12 percent if there were no interest-rate ceiling.

This analysis explains why usury laws can be politically popular. Few people sympathize with bank stockholders; and the consumers who get loans at lower rates are, naturally, pleased with the result of usury laws. Other consumers, who would like to borrow at 8 percent but cannot because quantity supplied is less than quantity demanded, are likely to blame the bank for refusing to lend, rather than blaming the government for outlawing mutually beneficial transactions.

Yet concern over high interest rates can be rational. It may, for example, be appropriate to combat homelessness by making financing of housing cheaper for poor people. But it may be much more rational for the government to subsidize the interest on housing for the poor rather than declaring high interest rates illegal, in effect pretending that those costs can simply be legislated away, as a usury ceiling tries to do.[5]

## ■ THE DETERMINATION OF RENT

The second main factor of production is land. Rent, the payment for the use of land, is another price which, when left to the market, often seems to settle at politically unpopular levels. Rent controls are a popular solution. We discussed the effects of rent controls in Chapter 5 (pages 83–85), and we will say a bit more about them later in this chapter. But our main focus here is the determination of rents by free markets.

The market for land is characterized by a special feature on the supply side. Land is a factor of production whose quantity supplied is (roughly) unchanging: the same quantity is available at every possible price. Indeed, classical economists used this notion as the working definition of land. And the definition seems to fit, at least approximately. Although people may clear land, drain swamps, fertilize it, build on it, or convert it from one use (a farm) to another (a housing development), human effort cannot change the total land supply, or at least not very much.

What does this fact tell us about how the market determines land rents? Figure 17–6 helps to provide an answer. The vertical supply curve *SS* means that no matter what the level of rents, there are only 1,000 acres of land in a small hamlet called Littleville. The demand curve *DD* slopes downward and is a typical marginal revenue product curve, predicated on the notion that the use of land, like everything else, is subject to diminishing returns. The free-market price is determined, as usual, by the intersection of the supply and demand curves at point *E*. In this example,

---

[5] The law also sometimes concerns itself with discrimination in lending against women or members of ethnic minority groups. Strong evidence suggests sex and race discrimination in lending. For example, married women have been denied loans without the explicit permission of their husbands, even where the women had substantial independent incomes.

**Determination of Land Rent in Littleville**

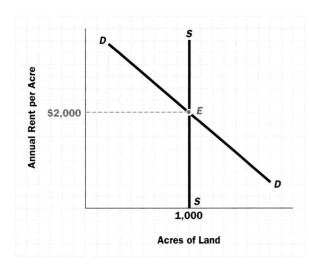

Acres of Land

each acre of land in Littleville rents for $2,000 per year. The interesting feature of this diagram is that, because quantity supplied is rigidly fixed at 1,000 acres whatever the price:

*The market level of rent is entirely determined by the market's demand side.*

If, for example, a major university relocates to Littleville, attracting more people who want to live there, the *DD* curve will shift outward, as depicted in Figure 17–7. Equilibrium in the market will shift from point *E* to point *A*. The same 1,000 acres of land will be available, but now each acre will command a rent of $2,500 per acre. The landlords will collect more rent, though society gets no more of the input—land—from the landlords in return for its additional payment.

The same process also works in reverse, however. If the university shuts its doors and the demand for land declines as a result, the landlords will suffer even though they did not contribute to the decline in the demand for land. (To see this, simply reverse the logic of Figure 17–7. The demand curve begins at $D_1D_1$ and shifts to $D_0D_0$.)

This discussion shows the special feature of rent that leads economists to distinguish it from payments to other factors of production. An **economic rent** is an "extra" payment for a factor of production (such as land) that does not change the amount of the factor that is supplied. Society is not compensated for a rise in its rent payments by any increase in the quantity of land it obtains. Economic rent is thus that portion of the factor payment that exceeds the minimum payment necessary to induce any of that factor to be supplied.

**A Shift in Demand with a Vertical Supply Curve**

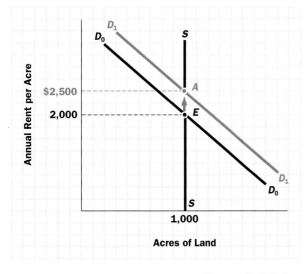

Acres of Land

As late as the end of the 19th century, the idea of economic rent exerted a powerful influence far beyond technical economic writings. An American journalist, Henry George, was nearly elected mayor of New York in 1886, running on the platform that all government should be financed by a "single tax" levied on landlords who, he said, are the only ones who earn incomes without contributing to the productive process. George said that landlords reap the fruits of economic growth without contributing to economic progress. He based his logic on the notion that landowners do not increase the supply of their factor of production—the quantity of land—when rents increase.

## LAND RENTS: COMPLICATED VERSION

If all plots of land were identical, our previous discussion would be virtually all there is to the theory of land rent. But plots of land *do* differ—in geographical location, topography, nearness to marketplaces, soil quality, and so on. The classical economists took this into account in their analysis of rent determination—a remarkable 19th-century piece of economic logic still considered valid today.

The basic notion is that capital invested on any piece of land must yield the same return as capital invested on any other piece that is actually in use. Why? If it were not so, capitalists would bid against one another for the more profitable pieces of land. This would go on until the rents they would have to pay for these parcels were driven up to a point that eliminated their advantages over other parcels.

Suppose that a farmer produces a crop on one piece of land for $160,000 per year in labor, fertilizer, fuel, and other nonland costs, while a neighbor who is no more efficient produces the same for $120,000 on a second piece of land. The rent on the second parcel must be *exactly* $40,000 per year higher than the rent on the first, because otherwise production on one plot would be cheaper than on the other. If, for example, the rent difference were only $30,000 per year, it would be $10,000

**Economic rent** is the portion of the earnings of a factor of production that exceeds the minimum amount necessary to induce any of that factor to be supplied.

cheaper to produce on the second plot of land. No one would want to rent the first plot and every grower would instead bid for the second plot. Rent on the first plot would be forced down by lack of customers, and rent on the second would be driven up by eager bidders. These pressures would come to an end only when the rent difference reached $40,000, so that both plots became equally profitable.

At any given time, some low-quality pieces of land are so inferior that it does not pay to use them at all—remote deserts are a prime example. Any land that is exactly on the borderline between being used and not being used is called **marginal land**. By this definition, marginal land earns no rent because if its owner charged any for it, no one would willingly pay to use it.

We now combine these two observations—that the difference between the costs of producing on any two pieces of land must equal the difference between their rents and that zero rent is charged on marginal land—to conclude that:

> **Rent on any piece of land will equal the difference between the cost of producing the output on that land and the cost of producing it on marginal land.**

That is, competition for the superior plots of land will permit landlords to charge prices that capture the full advantages of their superior parcels.

This analysis helps us to understand more completely the effects of an outward shift in the demand curve for land. Suppose population growth raises demand for land. Naturally, rents will rise. But we can be more specific than this. In response to an outward shift in the demand curve, two things will happen:

- *It will now pay to employ some land whose use was formerly unprofitable.* The land that was previously on the zero-rent margin will no longer be on the borderline, and some land that is so poor that it was formerly not even worth considering will now just reach the borderline of profitability. The settling of the American West illustrates this process strikingly. Land that once could not be given away is now quite valuable.

- *People will begin to exploit already-used land more intensively.* Farmers will use more labor and fertilizer to squeeze larger amounts of crops out of their acreage, as has happened in recent decades. Urban real estate that previously held two-story buildings will now be used for high-rise buildings.

These two events will increase rents predictably. Because the land that is considered marginal *after* the change must be inferior to the land that was marginal previously, rents must rise by the difference in yields between the old and new marginal lands. Table 17–2 illustrates this point. We deal with three pieces of land: A, a very productive piece; B, a piece that was initially considered only marginal; and C, a piece that is inferior to B but nevertheless becomes marginal when the demand curve for land shifts upward and to the right.

**Marginal land** is land that is just on the borderline of being used, i.e., any land the use of which would be unprofitable if the farmer had to pay even a penny of rent.

### Nonrent Costs and Rent on Three Pieces of Land

TABLE 17–2

| Type of Land | Nonland Cost of Producing a Given Crop | Total Rent | |
|---|---|---|---|
| | | Before | After |
| a. A tract that was better than marginal before and after | $120,000 | $80,000 | $ 92,000 |
| b. A tract that was marginal before but is attractive now | 200,000 | 0 | 12,000 |
| c. A tract that was previously not worth using but is now marginal | 212,000 | 0 | 0 |

The crop costs $80,000 more when produced on B than on A, and $12,000 more when produced on C than on B. Suppose, initially, that demand for the crop is so low that Farmer Jones does not plant crops in C. Farmer Jones is on the fence about whether to plant crops in field B; it is just on the margin between being used and left idle. Because field B is marginal, it will command no rent. We know that the rent on A will be equal to the $80,000 cost advantage of A over B. Now suppose demand for the crop increases enough so that plot C is just brought into use. Plot C is now marginal land, and field B now commands a rent of $12,000, the cost advantage of B over C. Plot A's rent now must rise from $80,000 to $92,000, the size of its cost advantage over C, the newly marginal land.

In addition to the quality differences among pieces of land, a second influence pushes land rents up: increased intensity of use of land that is already under cultivation. As farmers apply more fertilizer and labor to their land, the marginal productivity of land increases, just as factory workers become more productive when more is invested in their equipment. Once again, the landowner can capture this productivity increase in the form of higher rents. (If you do not understand why, refer back to Figure 17–7 and remember that the demand curves are marginal revenue product curves—that is, they indicate the amount that capitalists are willing to pay landlords to use their land.) Thus, we can summarize the theory of rent as follows:

> As the use of land increases, landlords receive higher payments from two sources:
>
> ■ Increased demand leads the community to employ land previously not good enough to use; the advantage of previously used land over the new marginal land increases, and rents go up correspondingly.
>
> ■ Land is used more intensively; the marginal revenue product of land rises, thus increasing the ability of the producer who uses the land to pay rent.

## GENERALIZATION: ECONOMIC RENT SEEKING

Economists refer to the payments to land as "rents," but land is not the only scarce input with a fixed supply, at least in the short run. Toward the beginning of this century some economists realized that the economic analysis of rent can be applied to inputs *other* than land. As we will see, this extension yielded some noteworthy insights.

The concept of rent can be used to analyze such common phenomena as lobbying in the U.S. Congress by industrial groups, lawsuits between rival firms, and battles over exclusive licenses (as for a television station). Such interfirm battles can waste very valuable economic resources—for example, the time that executives, bureaucrats, judges, lawyers, and economists spend preparing and trying cases. Because this valuable time could have been used in production, such activities entail large *opportunity costs*. Rent analysis offers insights into the reasons for these battles and provides a way to assess what *quantity* of resources people waste as they seek economic rents for scarce resources.

How is economic rent—which is a payment to a factor of production above and beyond the amount necessary to get the factor to make its contribution to production—relevant in such cases? Gordon Tullock, an economist also trained in legal matters, coined the phrase "rent seeking" to describe the search and battle for opportunities to charge or collect those payments above and beyond the amount necessary to create the source of the income.

An obvious source of such rents is a monopoly license. For example, a license to operate the only television station in town will yield enormous advertising profits, far above the amount needed for the station to operate. No wonder rent seekers swoop down when such licenses become available. Similarly, the powerful lobby for U.S. sweetener producers, including corn and beet growers as well as sugar cane farmers, pressures Congress to impede cane sugar imports, because free importation would cut prices (and rents) substantially.

How much of society's resources will be wasted in such a process? Rent seeking theory can give us some idea. Consider a race for a monopoly cable TV license

---

## ● LAND PRICES AROUND THE WORLD

Supply and demand do not equalize prices when the commodity, such as land, cannot be transferred from one geographic market to another. For instance, in the late 1980s, when property values in Japan hit their peak, the average price of residential land in Tokyo was $3,000 per square meter (about 11 square feet), compared to $110 in Toronto and $70 in Washington, D.C. The world's highest rents on commercial property can be found in Hong Kong, where a square meter of office space will cost you over $1,200, compared to $800 in New York, $400 in Stockholm, and $300 in Istanbul.

SOURCE: Steven K. Mayo, "Land Prices, Land Markets, and the Broader Economy," *Land Lines,* March 1998, Lincoln Institute of Land Policy, www.lincolninst.edu; and *The Economist,* September 12, 1998, p. 116.

---

which, once awarded, will keep competing stations from operating. But nothing prevents *anyone from entering the race* to grab the license. Anyone can hire the lobbyists and lawyers or offer the bribes needed in the battle. Thus, although the cable business itself may not be competitive, the process of fighting for the license is competitive.

Of course, we know from the analysis of long-run equilibrium under perfect competition (Chapter 10, pages 200–203) that in such markets, economic profits approximate zero—in other words, revenues just cover costs. So, if owners expect a cable license to yield, say, $900 million over its life in rent, rent seekers (i.e., companies competing to gain the license in the first place) are likely to waste something near that amount as they fight for the license.

Why? Suppose ten bidders each have an equal chance at winning the license. To each bidder, that chance should be worth about $90 million—one chance in ten of getting $900 million. If the average bidder spends, say, only $70 million on the battle, each will still value the battle for the license at $90 million minus $70 million. This will tempt an 11th bidder to enter and raise the ante to, say, $80 million in lobbying fees, hoping to grab the rent. This process stops only when all of the excess rent available has been wasted on the rent-seeking process.

We can use the concept of economic rent, then, to divide the payment for any input into two parts. The first part is simply the minimum payment needed to acquire the input: for example—the cost of producing a ball bearing or the compensation people require in exchange for the unpleasantness, hard work, and loss of leisure involved in performing labor. The owner needs at least this first part of the factor payment to supply any amount of the input willingly. If workers do not receive at least this first part, they will not supply any of their labor.

The second part of the payment is a *bonus* that does not go to every input, but only to inputs of particularly high quality. Payments to workers with exceptional natural skills are a good example. These bonuses are like the extra payment for a better piece of land and so are called *economic rents.* Indeed, like the rent of land, an increase in the amount of economic rent paid to an input may not increase the *quantity* of that input supplied. This second part of the payment—the economic rent—is pure gravy. The skillful worker is happy to have it as an extra. But it is not a deciding consideration in the choice of whether or not to work.

Shaquille O'Neal

## AN APPLICATION OF RENT THEORY: SHAQUILLE O'NEAL'S SALARY

A basketball player like Shaquille O'Neal (star center for the Los Angeles Lakers) would seem to have little in common with a plot of farmland. Yet to an economist, the same analysis—the theory of economic rent—explains how the market arrives at the amounts paid to each of these "factors of production." To understand why, we first note that there is only one Shaquille O'Neal. That is, he is a scarce input whose supply is fixed just like the supply of land. Because he is in fixed supply, the price of his services is determined in a way similar to that of land rents. Hence, economists have arrived at the definition of economic rent as any payment made to a factor of production that is above the amount necessary to induce *any* of that factor to be supplied.

A moment's thought shows how the general notion of economic rent applies both to land and to O'Neal. The total quantity of land available for use is the same whether rent is high, low, or zero; only limited payments to landlords are necessary to induce them to supply land to the market. So, by definition, a considerable proportion of the payments to landholders for their land is economic rent—payments above and beyond those necessary for landlords to provide land to the economy. O'Neal is (almost) similar to land in this respect. His athletic talents are somewhat unique and cannot be reproduced. What determines the payment to such a factor? Because the quantity supplied of such a unique, nonreproducible factor is absolutely fixed, and therefore unresponsive to price, the analysis of rent that we summarized in Figure 17–6 applies: *The position of the demand curve alone determines the price.*

Figure 17–8 portrays a hypothetical "Shaquille O'Neal market." The (mostly) vertical supply curve *TUR* represents the fact that no matter what wage he is paid, there is only one Shaquille O'Neal. Demand curve *DD* is a marginal productivity curve of sorts, but not quite the kind we encountered earlier in the chapter. Because the question, "What would be the value of a second unit of Shaquille

O'Neal?" is nonsensical, we construct the demand curve by considering only the *portion* of his time demanded at various wage levels. The curve indicates that at an annual salary of $50 million no employer can afford even a little bit of Shaq. At a lower salary of, say, $35 million per year, however, two-thirds of his time will be demanded. At $30 million per year, O'Neal's full time is demanded; and at lower wage rates, like $25 million, the demand for his time exceeds the amount of it that is for sale.

Equilibrium is at point *E* in the diagram, where the supply of and demand for his time are equal. His annual salary here is $30 million. Now we can ask: How much of that salary is economic rent? According to the economic definition of rent, the answer is: only part of it. Because the supply schedule is only partly vertical, part of O'Neal's financial reward is necessary to get him to supply his services, as is undoubtedly true in reality. Thus, it is not true that every penny he earns is rent.

This is why we said that top athletes such as O'Neal are *almost* good examples of pure rent. For, in fact, if his salary were low enough, O'Neal might well prefer to live off his savings rather than work. Suppose, for example, that $250,000 per year is the lowest salary at which Shaq would offer even one minute of his services, and that his labor supply then increases with his wage up to an annual salary of $1,500,000, at which point he is willing to work full time. Then, although his equilibrium salary will still be $30 million per year, not all of it will be rent, because some of it (at least $250,000) is required to get him to supply any services at all.

The portion of O'Neal's compensation that is not pure rent corresponds to the upward-sloping portion, *TU*, of his labor-supply curve. Thus, only part of the supply curve, *TUR* in Figure 17–8, is vertical— that portion above the $1,500,000 salary that will lead him to supply all his available time. And his equilibrium compensation level, *E*, will consist partly of rent (portion *UE*) and partly of a payment, *SU*, that is not rent.

This same analysis applies to any factor of production whose supply curve is not horizontal, as in Figure 17–9, in which we see that at any price above $5, suppliers are willing to provide some units of the input, that is, at any price above point *S*, quantity supplied is greater than zero. Yet the supply-demand equilibrium point yields a price of $7—well above the minimum price at which some input supply would be forthcoming. The difference must constitute a rent to the input suppliers, who get paid more than the minimum amount required to induce them to supply it.

Almost all employees earn some rent. What sorts of factors earn no rent? Only those factors that can be reproduced by a number of producers at constant cost earn no rents. For instance, no ball bearing supplier will ever receive any rent on a ball bearing, at least in the long run, because any desired number of them can be produced at (roughly) constant costs—say, one cent each. If one supplier tried to charge a price above one cent, another manufacturer would undercut the first supplier and take its customers away. Hence, the competitive price includes no rent.

## RENT CONTROLS: THE MISPLACED ANALOGY

Why is the analysis of economic rent important? Because only economic rent can be taxed away without reducing the quantity of the input supplied. And here common English gets in the way of sound reasoning. Many people feel that the *rent* they pay to their landlord is economic rent. After all, their apartments will still be there if they pay $1,500 per month, or $500, or $100. This view, although true in the short run, is quite myopic.

FIGURE 17-8

**Hypothetical Market for Shaquille O'Neal's Labor**

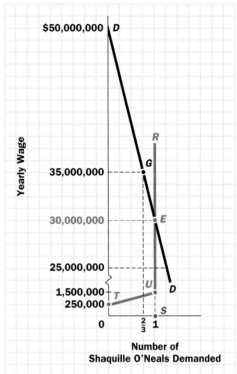

Number of Shaquille O'Neals Demanded

FIGURE 17-9

**Rent When the Supply Curve Is Not Vertical**

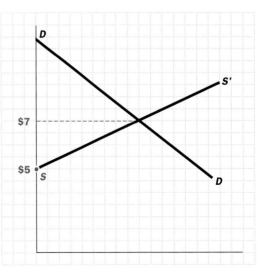

Like the ball-bearing producer, the owner of a building cannot expect to earn *economic rent* because too many other potential owners whose costs of construction are roughly the same as her own will also offer apartments. If the market price temporarily included some economic rent—that is, if price exceeded production costs plus the opportunity cost of the required capital—other builders would start new construction that would drive the price down. Thus, far from being in perfectly *inelastic* (vertical) supply, like raw land, buildings come rather close to being in perfectly *elastic* (horizontal) supply, like ball bearings. As we have learned from the theory of rent, this means that builders and owners of buildings cannot collect economic rent in the long run.

Because apartment owners collect very little economic rent, payments by tenants in a free market must be just enough to keep those apartments on the market. (This is the definition of zero economic rent.) If rent controls push these prices down, the apartments will start disappearing from the market.[6] Among other unfortunate results, we can therefore expect rent controls to contribute to homelessness—though it is, of course, not the only influence behind this distressing phenomenon.

## PAYMENTS TO ENTREPRENEURSHIP: ARE PROFITS TOO HIGH OR TOO LOW?

We turn next to business profits, the discussion of which often seems to elicit more passion than logic. With the exception of some economists, almost no one thinks that profit rates are at about the right level. Critics point accusingly at some giant corporations' billion-dollar profits and argue that they are unconscionably high. They call for much stiffer profits taxes. On the other hand, the Chambers of Commerce, National Association of Manufacturers, and other business groups complain that regulations and "ruinous" competition keep profits too low, and they constantly petition Congress for tax relief.

The public has many misconceptions about the nature of the U.S. economy, but probably none is further from reality than popular perceptions of what American corporations earn in profits. Try the following experiment. Ask five of your friends who have never had an economics course what fraction of the nation's income they imagine is pure profit to companies. Although the correct answer varies from year to year, business profits in 1998 made up about 10 percent of gross domestic product (GDP) (before taxes).[7] A comparable percentage of the prices you pay represents before-tax profit. Most people think this figure is much, much higher—as we saw in the box in Chapter 3 on page 42.

As you have no doubt noticed by now, economists are reluctant to brand factor prices as "too low" or "too high" in some moral or ethical sense. Rather, they are likely to ask first: What is the market equilibrium price? Then they will ask whether there are any good reasons to interfere with the market solution. This analysis, however, is not so easily applied to the case of *profits*, because it is hard to use supply and demand analysis when you do not know what factor of production earns profit.

In both a bookkeeping and an economic sense, *profits are the residual.* They are what remains from the selling price after all other factors have been paid.

But what production factor earns this reward? What factor's marginal productivity constitutes the profit rate?

---

[6] None of this is meant to imply that temporary rent controls in certain locations cannot have desirable effects in the short run. In the short run, the supply of apartments and houses really is fixed, and large shifts in demand can hand windfall gains to landlords—gains that are true economic rents. Controls that eliminate such windfalls should not cause serious problems. But knowing when the "short run" fades into the "long run" can be tricky. "Temporary" rent control laws have a way of becoming rather permanent.

[7] *Economic Report of the President 1999* (Washington, D.C.: U.S. Government Printing Office, February 1999).

---

### ● A FISTFUL OF DOLLARS: ENTREPRENEURSHIP IN POLAND

It would be rare in Western Europe, but in the continent's post-communist half it is commonplace; entrepreneurs start off with a fistful of dollars and become multi-millionaires a few years later. . . .

Take Univex, a Polish firm established in 1990 to import consumer electronics. It had practically no starting capital, but managed to persuade its customers to pay in advance. Univex now employs 500 people, including a bunch of managers "head-hunted" from western multinationals, and has annual sales of probably more than $50 million. . . . Its line of business has been transformed, too. The founders, two Polish engineers, have developed a range of ingenious products, sold widely in the West, including a tiny digital voice recorder that transfers its contents to a computer, allowing voicemail to be sent easily over the Internet. The company's shambolic-looking assembly line is reminiscent of an East Asian sweat shop, but its "brain room," where the product developers work, feels like Silicon Valley. This combination of low labor costs and technical ingenuity is the secret of Univex's success.

Start-ups are the engine of Poland's post-communist boom. . . . [By one calculation] private firms have trebled their share in industrial output since the transition began, from 16 percent of gross sales at the end of 1989 to 45 percent in 1995—an annual growth rate of more than a fifth.

SOURCE: "Survey of Business in Eastern Europe, *The Economist,* November 22, 1997, p. 10.

## WHAT ACCOUNTS FOR PROFITS?

**Economic profit,** as we learned in Chapter 10, is the amount a firm earns *over and above the payments for all inputs*, including the interest payments for the capital it uses and the opportunity cost of any capital provided by the owners of the firm. The payment that firm owners receive to compensate them for the opportunity cost of their capital (that in common parlance is considered profit) is closely related to interest rates. In an imaginary (and dull) world in which everything was certain and unchanging, capitalists who invested money in firms would simply earn the market rate of interest on their funds. Profits beyond this level would be competed away. Payment for capital below this level could not persist, because capitalists would withdraw their funds from firms and deposit them in banks. Capitalists in such a world would be mere moneylenders.

> **Economic profit** is the total revenue of a firm minus all of its costs including the interest payments and opportunity costs of the capital it obtains from its investors.

But the real world is not at all like this. Some capitalists are much more than moneylenders, and the amounts they earn often exceed going interest rates by a huge margin (see the accompanying box, "A Fistful of Dollars: Entrepreneurship in Poland"). These active capitalists who seek out or even create earnings opportunities are called *entrepreneurs.* We can credit such creative individuals for the constant change that characterizes business firms and for preventing operations of the firm from stagnating. Because entrepreneurs constantly seek to do something new, it is difficult to provide a general description of their activities. However, we can list three primary ways in which entrepreneurs can and do drive profits above "normal" interest rate levels.

**MONOPOLY POWER** If entrepreneurs can establish monopolies with some or all of their products, even for a short while, they can use that monopoly power to earn monopoly profits. We analyzed the nature of these monopoly earnings in Chapter 12.

**RISK BEARING** Entrepreneurs often engage in financially risky activities. For example, when a firm prospects for oil, it must drill exploratory wells hoping to find petroleum at the bottom. But many such exploratory wells only end up as dry holes, and the costs then bring no return. Of course, lucky investors do find oil and are rewarded handsomely—more than the competitive return on the firm's capital. The extra income thus pays the firm for bearing risk.

A few lucky individuals make out well in this process, but many suffer heavy losses. How well can we expect risk takers to do, on the average? If, on the average, one exploratory drilling out of ten pays off, do we expect its return to be exactly 10 times as high as the interest rate, so that the *average* firm will earn exactly the normal rate of interest? The answer is that the payoff will be *more* than 10 times the interest rate if investors dislike gambling, that is, if they prefer to avoid risk. Why? Because investors who are risk averse will not be willing to put their money into a business that faces such odds—10 to 1—unless the market provides compensation for the financial peril.

In reality, however, nothing guarantees that things always work out this way. Some people love to gamble and tend to be overly optimistic. They may plunge into projects to a degree unjustified by the odds. Average payoffs to such gamblers in risky undertakings may end up below the interest rate. The successful investor will still make a good profit, just like the lucky winner in Las Vegas. But the average participant will have to pay for the privilege of bearing risk.

**RETURNS TO INNOVATION**   The third major source of profits is perhaps the most important of all for social welfare. The first entrepreneur able to innovate and market a desirable new product or employ a new cost-saving machine will garner a higher profit than what an uninnovative (but otherwise similar) business manager would earn. Innovation differs from invention, because whereas **invention** generates new ideas, **innovation** takes the next step by putting the new idea into practical use. Businesspeople are rarely inventors, but they are often innovators.

When an entrepreneur innovates, even if her new product or new process is not protected by patents, she will be one step ahead of her competitors. She will be able to capture much of the market, either by offering customers a better product or by supplying the product more cheaply. In either case, she will temporarily find herself with some monopoly power as her competitors weaken, and she will receive monopoly profit for her initiative.

However, this monopoly profit, the reward for innovation, will only be temporary. As soon as the idea's success becomes evident to the world, other firms will find ways of imitating it. Even if they cannot turn out precisely the same product or the same process, they must find close substitutes in order to survive. In this way, new ideas spread through the economy, and in the process the innovator's special profits come to an end. The innovator can only resume earning special profits by finding still another promising idea.

The market system forces entrepreneurs to keep searching for new ideas, to keep instituting innovations, and to keep imitating new ideas even if they did not originate those innovations or ideas. This process lies at the heart of the growth of the capitalist system. It is one of the secrets of its extraordinary dynamism.

We explored these issues of innovation and growth performance in free markets more fully in Chapter 15.

## TAXING PROFITS

Thus, we can consider profits in excess of market interest rates as the return on entrepreneurial talent. But this is not really very helpful, because no one can say exactly what entrepreneurial talent is. Certainly we cannot measure it; nor can we teach it in a college course, though business schools may try. We do not know whether the observed profit rate provides more than the minimum reward necessary to attract entrepreneurial talent into the market. This relationship between observed profit rates and minimum necessary rewards is crucial when we start to consider the policy ramifications of taxes on profits—a contentious issue, indeed.

Consider a profits tax on oil companies. If oil companies earn profits well above the minimum required to attract entrepreneurial talent, those profits contain a large element of economic rent. In that case, we could tax away these excess profits (rents) without fear of reducing oil production. On the other hand, if oil company profits do not include economic rents, then a windfall profits tax can seriously curtail oil exploration and, hence, production.

This example illustrates the general problem of deciding how heavily governments should tax profits. Critics of big business who call for high, if not confiscatory, profits taxes seem to believe that profits are mostly economic rent. But if they are wrong—if, in fact, most of the observed profits are necessary to attract people into entrepreneurial roles—then a high profits tax can be dangerous. Such a tax

*(margin notes)*

**Invention** is the act of generating an idea for a new product or a new method for making an old product.

**Innovation,** the next step, is the act of putting the new idea into practical use.

would threaten the very lifeblood of the capitalist system. Business lobbying groups claim, predictably enough, that current tax policy creates precisely this threat. Unfortunately, neither group has offered much evidence for its conclusion.

## ■ CRITICISMS OF MARGINAL PRODUCTIVITY THEORY

The theory of factor pricing described in this chapter once again uses supply-demand analysis. Factor pricing theory also relies heavily on the principle of marginal productivity to derive the shape and position of the demand curve for various inputs. Indeed, some economists often refer to the analysis (rather misleadingly) as *the marginal productivity theory of distribution*, when it is, at best, only a theory of the demand side of the pertinent market.

Over the years, factor pricing analysis has been subject to attack on many grounds. One frequent accusation, which is largely (but not entirely) groundless, is the assertion that marginal productivity theory merely attempts to justify the income distribution that the capitalist system yields—in other words, that it is a piece of pro-capitalist propaganda. According to this argument, when marginal productivity theory claims that each factor is paid exactly its marginal revenue product, this is only a sneaky way of saying that each factor is paid exactly what it deserves. These critics claim that the theory legitimizes the gross inequities of the system—the poverty of many and the great wealth of the few.

The argument is straightforward but wrong. Payments are made not to factors of production, but rather to the people who happen to own them. If an acre of land earns $2,000 because that is its marginal revenue product, this does not mean, nor is it meant to imply, that the landlord *deserves* any particular payment, because he may even have acquired the land by fraud.

Second, an input's marginal revenue product (MRP) does not depend only on "how hard it works" but also on how much of it happens to be employed—because, according to the "law" of diminishing returns, the more that is employed, the lower its MRP. Thus, a factor's MRP is not and cannot legitimately be interpreted as a measure of the intensity of its "productive effort." In any event, what an input deserves, in some moral sense, may depend on more than what it does in the factory. For example, workers who are sick or have many children may be considered more deserving, even if they are no more productive.

On these and other grounds, no economist today claims that marginal productivity analysis shows that distribution under capitalism is either just or unjust. It is simply wrong to claim that marginal productivity theory is pro-capitalist propaganda. The marginal productivity principle is just as relevant to organizing production in a socialist society as it is in a capitalist one.

Other critics have attacked marginal productivity theory for using rather complicated reasoning to tell us very little about the really urgent problems of income distribution. In this view, it is all very well to say that everything depends on supply and demand and to express this in terms of many complicated equations (many of which appear in more advanced books and articles). But these equations do not tell us what to do about such serious distribution problems as malnutrition among the indigenous populations in Latin America or poverty among minority groups in the United States.

Though it does exaggerate somewhat, there is some truth to this criticism. We have seen in this chapter that the theory does provide some insights on real policy matters, though not as many as we would like. Later in the book we will see that economists do have useful things to say about the problems of poverty and under-development. But very little of what we can say about these issues arises out of marginal productivity analysis.

Perhaps, in the end, what should be said for marginal productivity theory is this: As the best model we have at the moment, marginal productivity theory offers us *some* valuable insights into the way the economy works, and until we find a more powerful model, we are better off using the tools that we do have.

---

## SUMMARY

1. A profit-maximizing firm purchases the quantity of any input at which the price of the input equals its *marginal revenue product (MRP)*. Consequently, the firm's demand curve for an input is the downward-sloping portion of that input's MRP curve.

2. Investment in a firm is the amount that is added to the firm's capital, which is its plant, equipment, inventory, and other productive inputs that tie up the company's money.

3. Interest rates are determined by the supply of and demand for funds. The demand for funds is a derived demand, because these funds are used to finance business *investment*. Thus, the demand for funds depends on the marginal productivity of *capital*.

4. A dollar obtainable sooner is worth more than a dollar obtainable later because of the *interest* that can be earned on that dollar in the interim.

5. Increased demand for a good that needs land to produce it will drive up the prices of land either because inferior land will be brought into use or because land will be used more intensively.

6. Rent controls do not significantly affect the supply of land, but they do tend to reduce the supply of buildings.

7. *Economic rent* is any payment to the supplier of a factor of production that is greater than the minimum amount needed to induce any of the factor to be supplied.

8. Factors of production that are unique in quality and difficult or impossible to reproduce will tend to be paid relatively high economic rents because of their scarcity.

9. Factors of production that are easy to produce at a constant cost and that are provided by many suppliers will earn little or no economic rent.

10. Economic profits over and above the cost of capital are earned (a) by exercise of monopoly power, (b) as payments for bearing risk, and (c) as the earnings of successful *innovation*.

11. The desirability of increased taxation of profits depends on its effects on the supply of entrepreneurial talent. If most profits are economic rents, then higher profits taxes will have few detrimental effects. But if most profits are necessary to attract *entrepreneurs* into the market, then higher profits taxes can weaken the capitalist system.

---

## KEY TERMS

Factors of production   330

Entrepreneurship   330

Marginal productivity principle   330

Marginal physical product (MPP)   330

Marginal revenue product (MRP)   330

Derived demand   332

Capital   333

Investment   333

Interest   333

Discounting   334

Usury law   336

Economic rent   338

Marginal land   339

Entrepreneurs   345

Risk bearing   345

Profit   344

Economic profit   345

Invention versus innovation   346

---

## QUESTIONS FOR REVIEW

1. A profit-maximizing firm expands its purchase of any input up to the point where diminishing returns have reduced the marginal revenue product so that it equals the input price. Why does it not pay the firm to "quit while it is ahead," buying so small a quantity of the input that the input's MRP remains greater than its price?

2. Which of the following inputs do you think include relatively large economic rents in their earnings?

   a. Nuts and bolts

   b. Petroleum

   c. A champion racehorse

   Use supply-demand analysis to explain your answer.

3. Three machines are employed in an isolated area. They each produce 2,000 units of output per month, the first requiring $20,000 in raw materials, the second $25,000, and the third $28,000. What would you expect to be the monthly charge for the first and second machines if the services of the third machine can be hired at a price of $9,000 a month? What parts of the charges for the first two machines are economic rent?

4. Economists conclude that a tax on the revenues of firms will be shifted in part to consumers of the products of those firms in the form of higher product prices. However, they believe that a tax on the rent of land usually cannot be shifted and must be paid entirely by the landlord. What explains the difference?

5. Many economists argue that a tax on apartment buildings is likely to reduce the supply of apartments, but that a tax on all land, including the land on which apartment buildings stand, will not reduce the supply of apartments. Can you explain the difference? How is this answer related to the answer to Review Question 4?

6. Distinguish between investment and capital.

7. If you have a contract under which you will be paid $10,000 two years from now, why do you become richer if the rate of interest falls?

8. What is the difference between interest and profit? Who earns interest, in return for what contribution to production? Who earns economic profit, in return for what contribution to production?

9. Do you know any entrepreneurs? How do they earn a living? How do they differ from managers?

10. Explain the difference between an invention and an innovation. Give an example of each.

11. "Marginal productivity does not determine how much a worker will earn—it determines only how many workers will be hired at a given wage. Therefore, marginal productivity analysis is a theory of demand for labor, not a theory of distribution." What, then, do you think determines wages? Does marginal productivity affect their level? If so, how?

12. (More difficult) American savings rates are among the lowest of any industrial country. This has caused concern about our ability to finance new plants and equipment for U.S. industry. Some politicians and others have advocated lower taxes on saving as a remedy. Do you expect such a program to be very effective? Why?

13. If rent constitutes only 2 percent of the incomes of Americans, why may the concept nevertheless be significant?

14. Litigation in which one company sues another often involves costs for lawyers and other court costs literally amounting to hundreds of millions of dollars per case. What does rent have to do with the matter?

---

## ● APPENDIX ▮ DISCOUNTING AND PRESENT VALUE

Frequently, in business and economic problems, it is necessary to compare sums of money received (or paid) at different dates. Consider, for example, the purchase of a machine that costs $11,000 and will yield a marginal revenue product of $14,520 two years from today. If the machine can be financed by a two-year loan bearing 10 percent interest, it will cost the firm $1,100 in interest at the end of each year, plus $11,000 in principal repayment at the end of the second year. (See the table that follows.) Is the machine a good investment?

COSTS AND BENEFITS OF INVESTING IN A MACHINE

| | End of Year 1 | End of Year 2 |
|---|---|---|
| Benefits | | |
| Marginal revenue product of the machine | $   0 | $14,520 |
| Costs | | |
| Interest | 1,100 | 1,100 |
| Repayment of principal on loan | 0 | 11,000 |
| Total Cost | 1,100 | 12,100 |

The total costs of owning the machine over the two-year period ($1,100 + $12,100 = $13,200) are less than the total benefits ($14,520). But this is clearly an invalid comparison, because the $14,520 in future benefits are not worth $14,520 in terms of today's money. Adding up dollars received (or paid) at different dates is a bit like adding apples and oranges. The process that has been invented for making the magnitudes of payments at different dates comparable to one another is called *discounting*, or *computing the present value* of a future sum of money.

To illustrate the concept of present value, let us ask how much $1 received a year from today is worth *in terms of today's money*. If the rate of interest is 10 percent, the answer is about 91 cents. Why? Because if we invest 91 cents today at 10 percent interest, it will grow to 91 cents plus 9.1 cents in interest = 100.1 cents in a year. That is, at the end of a year a payment of $100 will leave the recipient about as well off as he would have been if he had instead received $91 now. Similar considerations apply to any rate of interest. In general:

If the rate of interest is *i*, the present value of $1 to be received in a year is:

$$\frac{\$1.00}{(1 + i)}$$

This is so, because in a year

$$\frac{\$1.00}{(1 + i)}$$

will grow to

$$\frac{\$1.00}{1 + i} \times (1 + i) = \$1$$

What about money to be received two years from today? Using the same reasoning, and supposing the interest rate is 10 percent so that $1 + i = 1.1$, $1.00 invested today will grow to $1.00 times (1.1) = $1.10 after one year and will grow to $1.00 times (1.1) times (1.1) = $1.00 times $(1.1)^2$ = $1.21 after two years. Consequently, the present value of $1.00 to be received two years from today is:

$$\frac{\$1.00}{(1 + i)^2} = \frac{\$1.00}{1.21} = 82.64 \text{ cents}$$

A similar analysis applies to money received three years from today, four years from today, and so on.

The general formula for the present value of $1.00 to be received *N* years from today when the rate of interest is *i* is:

$$\frac{\$1.00}{(1 + i)^N}$$

The present value formula is based on the two variables that determine the present value of any future flow of money: the rate of interest $(i)$ and how long you have to wait before you get it $(N)$.

Let us now apply this analysis to our example. The present value of the $14,520 revenue is easy to calculate because it all comes two years from today. Since the rate of interest is assumed to be 10 percent $(i = 0.1)$ we have:

$$\text{Present value of revenues} = \frac{\$14,520}{(1.1)^2}$$

$$= \frac{\$14,520}{1.21}$$

$$= \$12,000$$

The present value of the costs is a bit trickier in this example because costs occur at two different dates.

The present value of the first interest payment is:

$$\frac{\$1,100}{(1 + i)} = \frac{\$1,100}{1.1} = \$1,000$$

And the present value of the final payment of interest plus principal is:

$$\frac{\$12,100}{(1 + i)^2} = \frac{\$12,100}{(1.1)^2} = \frac{\$12,000}{1.21} = \$10,000$$

Now that we have expressed each sum in terms of its present value, it is permissible to add them up. So the present value of all costs is:

$$\text{Present value of costs} = \$1,000 + \$10,000$$

$$= \$11,000$$

Comparing this figure to the $12,000 present value of the revenues clearly shows that the machine really is a good investment. We can use the same calculation procedure for all investment decisions.

---

## SUMMARY

1. To determine whether a loss or a gain will result from a decision whose costs and returns will come at several different periods of time, we must discount all the figures represented by these gains and losses to obtain their present value.

2. For this, we use the present value formula for $X$ dollars receivable $N$ years from now:

$$\text{Present value} = \frac{X}{(1 + i)^N}$$

3. We then combine the present values of all the returns and all the costs. If the sum of the present values of the returns is greater than the sum of the present values of the costs, then the decision to invest will promise a net gain.

---

## KEY TERMS

Discounting   349
Present value   349

---

## QUESTIONS FOR REVIEW

1. Compute the present value of $1,000 to be received in three years if the rate of interest is 11 percent.

2. A government bond pays $100 in interest each year for three years and also returns the principal of $1,000 in the third year. How much is it worth in terms of today's money if the rate of interest is 8 percent? If the rate of interest is 12 percent?

Octavius (a wealthy young Englishman):

"I believe most intensely in the dignity of labor."

The chauffeur: "That's because you never done any."

George Bernard Shaw, *Man and Superman*, Act II

# LABOR: THE HUMAN INPUT

Labor costs account, by far, for the largest share of gross domestic product (GDP). As noted in the previous chapter, the earnings of labor amount to almost three-quarters of national income. Wages also represent the primary source of personal income to the vast majority of Americans. For more than a century, wages were the centerpiece of the American dream. In almost every decade, the purchasing power of a typical worker's earnings grew substantially, and the U.S. working class evolved into a comfortable middle class—the envy of the world and an irresistible lure for millions of immigrants. Then, something changed fundamentally in ways economists do not yet fully understand.

Figure 18-1 shows that average real wages (adjusted for inflation) stopped their upward march around

"But if I haven't given you a raise in five years, Pottsburg,
why should you think I'd give you one now?"

**Index of Long-Run Trends in Real (Inflation-Adjusted) Wages, Real Compensation (Wages Plus Benefits), and Hours Worked per Week, 1909–1998**

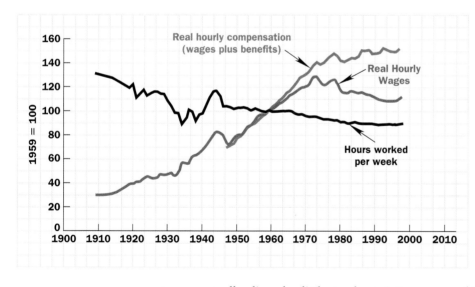

SOURCES: Constructed by the authors from data in U.S. Census Bureau, *Historical Statistics of the United States, Colonial Times to 1970* (Washington, D.C.: U.S. Government Printing Office, 1975); and *Economic Report of the President* (Washington, D.C.: U.S. Government Printing Office, various years).

1973 and, by some (disputed) calculations, even declined. In contrast, *total compensation* did not fall, as shown by the blue line in the graph, which represents wages *plus fringe benefits*—including such things as health insurance, retirement payments, and education subsidies that employers provide to their employees). But compensation *growth* did slow markedly.[1] The graph also shows that average hours worked per week have declined by about 30 percent during this century, even when wages and compensation were increasing. (The big drop in hours worked during the 1930s was a consequence of the Great Depression, and the sharp rise in hours worked during the 1940s was caused by World War II.)

Slowing wage growth has been accompanied by an expanding *income gap* between the rich and the poor. Today, high-income families in the United States earn almost fourteen times as much as low-income families—and the disparity is rising. Figure 18–2 shows how dramatically the disparity has grown. Back in 1967, the richest one-fifth of American households accounted for nearly 44 percent of all household income generated in the United States, while the poorest one-fifth accounted for only 4 percent. By 1997, the income share of the lowest fifth of households had actually slipped a little to about 3.6 percent, while the richest fifth's income share had risen to nearly 50 percent.[2]

In Germany, by contrast, the ratio between low-wage and high-wage families is only 2.5. As one economist recently said of the United States, "We are the most unequal industrialized country in terms of income and wealth, and we're growing

---

[1] The sharp increases in compensation over the years reflect, at least in part, the rising cost of services such as health care, rather than an increase in the quantity and quality of benefits provided to workers. We explored the reasons for the rising costs of services in Chapter 14, and they form the basis of one our central *Ideas for Beyond the Final Exam* (why the costs of education and health care keep growing).

[2] U.S. Census Bureau, www.census.gov, accessed on November 6, 1998.

the demand curve for labor are determined by labor's marginal revenue product. Such a demand curve is shown as blue curve DD in Figure 18–3. The figure also includes a red supply curve, labeled SS. In a competitive labor market, equilibrium will be established at the wage that equates the quantity supplied with the quantity demanded. In this figure, equilibrium occurs at point E, where demand curve DD crosses supply curve SS. The equilibrium wage is $300 per week and equilibrium employment is 500,000 workers.

If nothing interferes with the free labor market operation (such as minimum wages or unions—which we will consider later), equilibrium will be at point E, where the supply and demand curves intersect. In this example, because 500,000 workers will be employed at a wage of $300 per week, the total income of the workers will be $300 × 0.5 million = $150 million.

## INFLUENCES ON MRP$_L$: SHIFTS IN THE DEMAND FOR LABOR

The conclusion that the demand curve for labor is one and the same as labor's MRP curve is only the beginning of the story. The next question is: What influences affect MRP$_L$? The answers cast light on a number of important developments in the labor market.

Some obvious factors can change labor's MRP. For example, increased education can improve the ability of the labor force to follow complex instructions and to master difficult technology, thus raising a worker's MRP. Economists use the term **investment in human capital** to refer to spending on increased education and on other means to increase the knowledge and skills of the labor force. Such spending is analogous to investment in the firm's plant and equipment because both of them are outlays today that lead to more production.

Workers can also improve their skills through experience, called *on-the-job training*, and in a variety of other ways that add to the information they possess and increase their mental and physical dexterity.

Because the demand for labor is a *derived demand*, anything that improves the market for the goods and services that labor produces can shift the labor demand curve upward. In particular, in a period of economic prosperity consumers will have more to spend; their demand for products will shift upward and this in turn will raise the price of the worker's product, thereby shifting the MRP curve upward. The result will be a rise in the demand for labor. That, of course, is why unemployment is always low when the economy is undergoing a period of prosperity.

## TECHNICAL CHANGE, PRODUCTIVITY GROWTH, AND THE DEMAND FOR LABOR

Another critical influence upon the MRP$_L$ is the quality and quantity of the *other* inputs used in the workers' productive activity. Especially important is the technology of the workers' equipment. Innovation that improves machinery, power sources, and other productive instruments adds to the amount that can be produced by a given amount of labor. Thus, technical change that increases labor productivity plays a crucial role in determining the level of wages and the level of employment.

Technical change that increases the worker's productivity has two effects that work in opposite directions. First, increased productivity clearly implies an increase in the worker's marginal physical product—the quantity of widgets that an additional worker can produce will rise. On the other hand, because of the resulting reduction in labor cost and the increased output of widgets, we can expect that when productivity rises, widget prices will fall. Now recall that:

Marginal revenue product of labor in widget production = price of widgets multiplied by the worker's marginal widget output, that is:

$$MRP = P(\text{of widgets}) \times MPP.$$

**FIGURE 18-3**

**Equilibrium in a Competitive Labor Market**

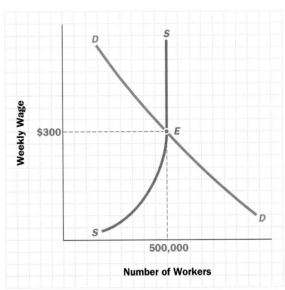

**Investment in human capital** is any expenditure on an individual that increases that person's future earning power or productivity.

Because a rise in productivity raises MPP but reduces $P$ we cannot be sure of the net effect on MRP, that is, the net effect on the demand curve for labor.

However, experience shows us how a rise in productivity will affect both wages and the demand for labor. In the very short run, a rise in labor productivity (that is, of labor-saving technology) often causes a downward shift in the demand for labor, which holds down wages. If firms can meet the current demand for their products with 10 percent fewer workers than they needed last year, they will be tempted to "downsize," which is a polite way of saying that they will fire some workers. This does not always happen, but it does sometimes occur, so workers' widespread fear of labor-saving technology is, to some degree, justified.

*Productivity Growth Is (Almost) Everything in the Long Run*

**PRODUCTIVITY GROWTH** However, in the long run, rising productivity has always improved the standard of living for both workers and the owners of other factors of production. As we indicated in one of our *Ideas for Beyond the Final Exam*, in the long run nothing contributes more to the economic well-being of the nation than rising productivity. Today workers enjoy far longer lives, better health, more education, and more luxury goods than they did a century ago or in any previous period in history. The fact that an hour of labor today can produce a large multiple of what our ancestors could create in an hour increases everyone's average income, including the workers who constitute so large a part of it. In the short run, labor-saving technological change sometimes cuts employment and holds down wages. But, historically, in the long run it has not reduced employment. It has raised workers' incomes and increased real wages spectacularly since the Industrial Revolution.

## THE SERVICE ECONOMY AND THE DEMAND FOR LABOR

Although productivity growth has not led to any long-term upward trend in unemployment, it *has* cut jobs drastically in some parts of the economy, sending the labor force to other economic sectors for employment. Agriculture is the prime example. At the time of the American Revolution, probably more than 90 percent of the U.S. labor force had agricultural jobs and eked out what today would be considered a meager standard of living. In Europe only a century earlier, farm productivity was so low that famines and starvation were frequent occurrences. Yet today, with less than 3 percent of the nation's labor working on farms, the United States produces such a surplus of products that it sometimes seems unmanageable. It is this dramatic increase in farm productivity that has forced farm employment to drop from about 90 percent to less than 3 percent of the labor force. At first, farm workers shifted to manufacturing, as growing U.S. incomes led to a sharp rise in demand for industrial products. Then productivity in manufacturing took off, and workers again had to go elsewhere for their jobs.

Now, in its turn, increased productivity in manufacturing has moved workers into the service sector of the economy. Indeed, it has transformed the United States into a "service economy," meaning that nearly three-quarters of the labor force is employed in services such as telecommunications, software design, health care, teaching, and restaurant services.

Some observers have argued that this has happened to the United States because other countries are stealing away our manufacturing business base. But the facts show that this is simply untrue. As Figure 18–4 reports, the service sector has become dominant in *all* the major industrial economies. No industrial economy has been able to avoid this development by stealing manufacturing markets away from the others. More relevant to our concerns here is another worry: that the workers driven from manufacturing into the service sector of the economy have predominantly become low-paid dishwashers and hamburger flippers That is true in some cases, but the majority of new service jobs created in the past half-century are in the information sector of the economy, which includes computation, research, and teaching, among other jobs, requiring education and specialized skills. Many economists attribute the rising relative compensation of college-educated workers to such developments.

## The Growing Share of Service Sector Jobs in Nine Countries, 1967–1996

FIGURE 18-4

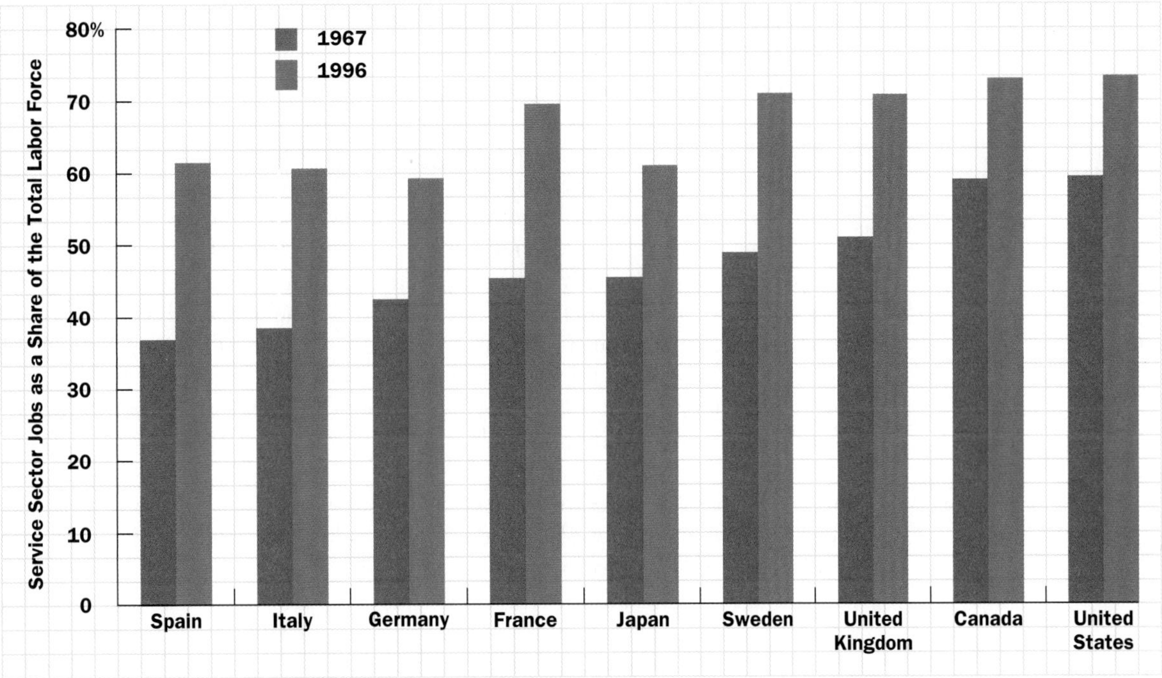

SOURCES: Organization for Economic Cooperation and Development, *Quarterly Labour Force Statistics,* various issues; and www.oecd.org, accessed November 12, 1998.

## ■ THE SUPPLY OF LABOR

Having discussed the demand for labor, we turn next to its supply. Several significant labor supply trends have characterized recent decades in the United States. First, there has been a continuation of the expansion of the total labor force that has been going on throughout the country's history. Much of this is ascribable to sheer growth of the nation's population through birth and immigration. With more people living in the country the number of job seekers and jobholders has grown—from about 60 million jobholders right after the Second World War to more than 132 million today. Second, the proportion of the population with jobs has also grown (from about 58 percent after World War II to 67 percent today). This is referred to as a rise in *labor force participation.* Third, new groups of workers have entered the labor force. This is particularly true of women, who today hold proportionately more jobs (46 percent of the workforce) than they did in earlier decades (except during wartime). Finally, in addition to the trends in sheer numbers of workers, the labor supply picture has been affected by a protracted and substantial relative decline in union membership. That is, there has been a significant fall in the share of American workers who belong to unions, the organizations whose stated purpose is to protect their interests. Because unions seek to bargain for all the workers in a firm or industry, thus eliminating competition among workers over jobs and wages, we will consider them later in the chapter, after we have finished our discussion of wage determination in labor markets that are fully competitive. First, we consider some other supply-side influences.

### RISING LABOR-FORCE PARTICIPATION

One significant development in the supply of labor in the industrial countries is the increase in the number of family members who hold jobs. For instance, in 1997, 66 percent of American married-couple families had *two* wage earners, compared with only 40 percent in 1970.[7] It used to be that the "head of the household" (usually the husband) was ordinarily the only breadwinner. Today, married women also hold jobs. This phenomenon is in part attributable to lagging wages, so that both heads of the family are forced to seek gainful employment if the household's economic aspirations are to be realized. Rapidly rising medical costs and costs of education add to these financial pressures.

But participation in the labor force has increased for other reasons: the moves toward the liberation of women from their traditional role in the family, along with progress in the education of minorities that has increased their job opportunities. Not so long ago, an African American executive in a major business firm was unheard of, and an employed wife was considered disgraceful because it implied that her husband could not support her properly. Today this has changed drastically, though discrimination is by no means a thing of the past. In many firms top jobs, beyond the "token black" and the "token woman," have gone to members of these groups. It is not unusual for women and minorities to hold positions superior to those of many employees who are white and male.

These changes have affected the labor market in several ways that, some observers have suggested, may have held back wages, at least for a time. First, the sheer increase in supply of workers tends to depress wages. This is, of course, an implication of standard supply-demand analysis. Just draw the usual supply-demand graph for a labor market and you will readily confirm that when the supply curve of labor shifts to the right, the price of labor (that is, the wage) can be expected to fall. Second, it has been argued that a combination of discrimination and the initial lack of experience of these new entrants into the labor market (which temporarily reduced their $MRP_L$) had a similar effect. Discrimination against women or black or Hispanic workers in the labor market means that in order to get jobs workers from these groups must offer special incentives to prospective employers. This can force them to accept wages lower than those paid to white male employees with comparable ability for the performance of similar tasks. Lack of experience can have a similar effect, but for a reason that is less objectionable. If workers acquire skill through experience on the job (on-the-job

---

[7] U.S. Census Bureau, *Current Population Survey*, www.census.gov, accessed February 1999.

training) then, on the average, inexperienced workers can be expected to have lower productivity than more experienced workers. Because their $MRP_L$ is comparatively low, the demand curve for the inexperienced will also be low, and lower wages will tend to follow.

## AN IMPORTANT LABOR SUPPLY PUZZLE

For most commodities, increases in their prices leads to an increase in the quantities supplied, and price declines reduce amounts supplied: that is, supply curves slope upward. But the striking historical trends in labor supply tell a very different story. Supply has tended to fall when wages rose and to rise when wages fell. Throughout the first three-quarters of this century, real wages rose, as Figure 18–1 clearly showed. Yet labor asked for and received *reductions* in the length of the workday and workweek. At the beginning of the century, the standard workweek was 50 to 60 hours (with virtually no vacations). Since then, labor hours have generally declined to an average workweek of about 35 hours.

But in the two most recent decades, as real wages have fallen, the number of family members who leave the home each day to earn wages has increased. And, in the last few years there has been a rise in overtime work, that is, workers laboring more than the standard number of hours in their firms. Thus, reduced real wages appear to have induced people to increase the quantity of labor they supply.

Where has the commonsense view of this matter gone wrong? Why, as hourly wages rose for 75 years, did workers not sell more of the hours they had available instead of pressing for a shorter and shorter workweek? And why, in recent years, have they sold more of their labor time as real wage rates stopped rising?

To answer these questions it is helpful to follow the economic analysis of labor supply and make use of a simple observation: Given the fixed amount of time in a week, a person's decision to *supply labor* to firms is simultaneously a decision to *demand leisure* time for himself. Assuming that, after deducting the necessary time for eating and sleeping, a worker has 90 usable hours in a week, then a decision to spend 40 of those hours working is simultaneously a decision to demand 50 of them for other purposes.

The supply curve of labor, like that of any other input or commodity, tells us how the quantity supplied is affected by the market price of the item in question. Here we are investigating how the quantity of labor supplied is affected by its price, that is, by the level of wages. The interpretation of the supply of labor as the opposite of the worker's demand for leisure offers us a very substantial insight into the relation between wage and labor supply. Economists say that a rise in wages has two effects on the worker's demand for leisure: the substitution effect and the income effect. We will see that they tell us a good deal about the labor market.

**SUBSTITUTION EFFECT**   The substitution effect of a rise in the price of any good is the resulting switch of customers to a substitute product whose price has not risen. A rise in the price of fish, for example, can lead consumers to buy more meat. The same is true of wages and the demand for leisure. When the wage rate rises, leisure becomes more expensive relative to other commodities that consumers can buy. For instance, if you decide not to work overtime this weekend, the price you pay for that increase in leisure (the opportunity cost) is the wage you have to give up as a result of the decision. So a rise in wages makes leisure more expensive. This leads us to expect that a wage increase will induce workers to buy *less* leisure time (and *more* of other things). Thus:

The substitution effect of higher wages leads most workers to want to work more.

**INCOME EFFECT**   A rise in the price of any good, other things equal, clearly increases the real incomes of sellers of the good and reduces the real incomes of buyers of the good. That change in income affects the amount of the good (as well as the amounts of other items) that the individual demands. This *indirect* effect of a price change on demand is called the income effect of the price change and it is especially important in the case of wages. Higher wages make consumers richer. We expect this increased wealth to raise the demand for most goods, *including leisure.* So:

> The income effect of higher wages leads most workers to want to work less (i.e., demand more leisure), whereas the income effect of lower wages make them want to work more.

Putting these two effects together, we conclude that some workers may react to an increase in their wage rate by working more, whereas others may react by working less. Still others will have little or no discretion over their work hours. In terms of the market as a whole, therefore, higher wages can lead to either a larger or a smaller quantity of labor supplied.

Statistical studies of this issue in the United States have arrived at the following conclusions:

- The response of labor supply to wage changes is not very strong for most workers.

- For low-wage workers, the substitution effect seems clearly dominant, so they work more when wages rise.

- For high-wage workers, the income effect just about offsets the substitution effect, so they do not work more when wages rise.

| FIGURE 18-5 |

**A Typical Labor Supply Schedule**

Income effects outweigh substitution effects

• *B*

Income effects balance substitution effects

• *A*

Substitution effects outweigh income effects

**Wage Rate**

**Quantity of Labor Supplied**

Figure 18–5 depicts these approximate "facts." It shows labor supply rising (slightly) as wages rise up to point *A*, *as substitution effects outweigh income effects.* Thereafter, labor supply is roughly constant as wages rise and income effects become just as important as substitution effects up to point *B*. At still higher wages, above point *B*, income effects may overwhelm substitution effects, so that rising wages can even cut the quantity of labor supplied.

Thus, it is even possible that when wages are raised high enough, further wage increases will lead workers to purchase more leisure and therefore to work less (see the accompanying box, "Is Time More Precious Than Money?"). The supply curve of labor is then said to be *backward-bending*, as illustrated by the broken portion of the curve above point *B*.

Does this theory of labor supply apply to college students? A study of the hours worked by students at Princeton University found that it does.[8] Estimated substitution effects of higher wages on the labor supply of Princeton University students were positive and income effects were negative, just as the theory predicts. Apparently, substitution effects outweighed income effects by a slim margin, so that higher wages attracted a somewhat greater supply of labor. Specifically, a 10 percent rise in wages increased the hours of work of the Princeton student body by about 3 percent.

### THE LABOR SUPPLY PUZZLE RESOLVED

We can now answer our earlier question: Why is it that, historically, rising wages have reduced labor supply and falling wages have increased it? We know that any wage increase sets in motion *both* a substitution effect *and* an income effect. If only the substitution effect operated, then rising wages would indeed cause people to work longer hours because the high price of leisure makes leisure less attractive. But this reasoning leaves out the income effect.

Rising wages enable the worker to provide for the family with fewer hours of work. So the worker can afford to purchase more leisure without a cut in living standards.

---

[8] Mary P. Hurley, "An Investigation of Employment among Princeton Undergraduates during the Academic Year," senior thesis submitted to the Department of Economics, May 1975.

---

### ● THE INCOME EFFECT: IS TIME MORE PRECIOUS THAN MONEY?

Plagued by stress, a growing number of people say they think time is becoming more precious than money and they're trying to slow down. . . . Five years before the end of what has been called the American Century, Americans say they have become worn down. But the exhaustion represents a paradox. They are extraordinarily stressed out even though they make more money, have more leisure time, spend more on recreation and enjoy more time-saving and efficient technology than adults did a generation or two ago. The reasons underlying this paradox are varied. Many Americans, especially married women, are working longer at their jobs now than they were then—although they have cut back on the amount of work they do around their homes. The anxieties wrought by the increasingly competitive global economy also have put many on edge, not to mention the fact that work-related intrusions via fax, E-mail or cellular phones can take place anywhere, from a kitchen to the family minivan.

In addition, . . . there's the thesis of economist Steffan Linder, whose book called *The Harried Leisure Class* argued that affluence itself engendered "an increasing scarcity of time." His argument: Productivity increases the "value" of time spent at work, and folks who want to maximize their worth then feel they should work more.

Now, though, a growing number of citizens have begun to unplug their lives from a system they feel leaves them little or no time to recharge. They have begun to retreat . . . into their private corners and demand at least some quiet time. In a comprehensive new quality-of-life poll conducted by U.S.

News and the advertising agency Bozell Worldwide Inc., half of all Americans say they have taken steps in the past five years that could simplify their lives—steps as dramatic as moving to communities with a less hectic way of life, cutting back their hours at work, lowering their commitments or expectations and declining promotions.

SOURCE: Excerpted from John Marks, "Time Out: Plagued by Stress, a Growing Number of People Say They Think Time Is Becoming More Precious Than Money and They're Trying to Slow Down," *U.S. News and World Report,* December 11, 1995, pp. 84–96.

Thus, the income effect of increasing wages induces workers to work fewer hours. Similarly, falling wages reduce the worker's income. To preserve the family's living standard, the worker must seek additional hours of work; and the worker's spouse may have to leave their children in day care and take a job.

Thus, it is the strong income effect of rising wages that may account for the fact that labor supply has responded in the "wrong" direction, with workers working ever-shorter hours as real wages rose and longer hours as wages fell.

### ■ WHY DO WAGES DIFFER?

Earlier in the chapter, we saw how wages are determined in a free-market economy: In a competitive labor market the equilibrium wage occurs where quantity supplied equals quantity demanded (refer back to Figure 18–3). In reality, of course, no single wage level applies to all workers. Some workers are paid very well, whereas others are forced to accept meager earnings. We all know that certain groups in our society (the young, the disadvantaged, the uneducated) earn relatively low wages and that some of our most severe social ills (poverty, crime, drug addiction) are related to this fact. But why are some wages so low while others are so high? The explanation is important, because it can help us determine what to do to help poorly paid workers increase their earnings and move up toward the income levels of the more fortunate suppliers of labor. Because the issue is so significant, we will discuss it in some detail.

In the most general terms, the explanation of wage differences is the fact that there is not one labor market but many—each with its own supply and demand curves and its own equilibrium wage. Supply-demand analysis implies that wages are relatively high in markets where demand is high relative to supply, as in Figure 18–6(a). This can happen if qualified workers are scarce or if the demand for a product is great (because labor demand is a derived demand). On the other hand, wages are comparatively low in markets where labor supply is high relative to demand, as in Figure 18–6(b). This can also be true if product demand is weak or if workers are not very productive. This is hardly startling news and doesn't tell us what we need to know about wage differentials. To make the analysis useful, we must breathe some life into the supply and demand curves.

| FIGURE 18–6 | **Wage Differentials** |

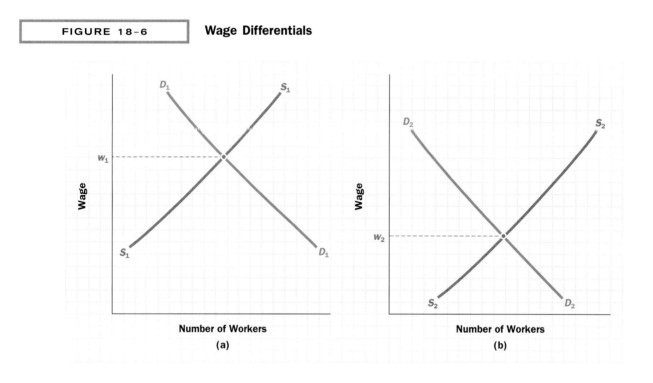

### LABOR DEMAND IN GENERAL

We start with demand. Why is the demand for labor greater in some markets than in others? Because the marginal revenue product of workers depends on their *marginal physical product* (MPP), variables that influence $MPP_L$ will influence wages. Each worker's marginal physical product depends, of course, on his or her own *abilities* and *degree of effort* on the job. But, as we have seen, the influence of these characteristics is supplemented by the *other factors of production* that workers use to produce output. Workers in American industry are more productive than workers in many other countries at least partly because they have generous supplies of machinery, natural resources, and technical know-how with which to work. As a consequence, they earn high wages. In other words, the marginal product of labor is raised by an abundance of efficient machinery and other inputs that increase the worker's effectiveness.

The marginal product of some workers can also be increased relative to that of others by superior education, training, and experience. We will go into greater detail later about the role of education in wage determination.

### LABOR SUPPLY IN GENERAL

Turning next to differences in the supply of labor to different areas, industries, or occupations, it is clear that *the size of the available working population* relative to the magnitude of industrial activity in a given area is of major importance. This helps explain why wages rose so high in sparsely populated Alaska when the Alaskan oil pipeline created many new jobs, and why wages have been and remain so low in Appalachia, where industry is dormant.

Second, the *nonmonetary* attractiveness of any job will also clearly influence the supply of workers to it. (The monetary attractiveness is the wage itself, which governs movements *along* the supply curve.) Jobs that people find pleasant and satisfying—such as teaching in suburban schools—will attract a large supply of labor and will consequently pay a relatively low wage. In contrast, a premium will have to be paid to attract workers to jobs that are onerous, disagreeable, or dangerous—such as washing the windows of skyscrapers.

Finally, the amount of ability and training needed to enter a particular job or profession is relevant to its supply of labor. Brain surgeons and professional ice skaters earn generous incomes because there are few people as highly skilled as they, and because it is time-consuming and expensive to acquire these skills even for those who have the ability.

## ABILITY AND EARNINGS: THE RENT COMPONENT OF WAGES

In considering the effects of ability on earnings, it is useful to distinguish between skills that can be duplicated easily and skills that cannot. If Jill Jones has an ability that Sandra Smith cannot acquire, even if she undergoes extensive training, then the wages that Jones earns will contain an element of *economic rent*. We saw this to be true in the case of basketball star Shaquille O'Neal's earnings in Chapter 17.[9]

Indeed, the salaries of professional athletes provide particularly clear examples of how economic rents can lead to huge wage differentials. Virtually anyone with moderate athletic ability can be taught to jump and shoot a basketball. But in most cases, no amount of training will teach the player to play basketball like Shaq. His high salary is a reward for his unique ability.

But many of the abilities that the market rewards generously—such as those of doctors and lawyers—clearly can be duplicated. Here the theory of rent does not apply, and we need a different explanation of the high wages that these skilled professionals earn. Once again, however, part of our analysis from Chapter 17 finds an immediate application because the acquisition of skills, through formal education and other forms of training, has much in common with business investment decisions. Why? Because the decision to gain more education in the hope of increasing future earnings involves a sacrifice of *current* income for the sake of *future* gain—precisely the hallmark of an investment decision.

## INVESTMENT IN HUMAN CAPITAL

The idea that education is an investment is likely to be familiar even to students who have never thought explicitly about it. You made a conscious decision to go to college rather than to enter the labor market, and you are probably acutely aware that this decision is now costing you money—lots of money. Your tuition payments may be only a minor part of the total cost of going to college. Think of a high school friend who chose not to go to college and is now working. The salary that he or she is earning could, perhaps, have been yours. You are deliberately giving up this possible income in order to acquire more education.

In this sense, your education is an *investment* in yourself—a *human investment*. Like a firm that devotes some of its money to building a plant that will yield profits at some future date, you are investing in your own future, hoping that your college education will help you earn more than your high school-educated friend or enable you to find a more pleasant or prestigious job when you graduate. Economists call activities such as going to college investments in human capital because such activities give the human being many of the attributes of a capital investment.

Doctors and lawyers earn such high salaries partly because of their many years of training. That is, part of their wages can be construed as a *return on their (educational)*

---

[9] See the previous chapter, pages 342–343.

*investments*, rather than as economic rent. Unlike the case of Shaquille O'Neal, any number of people conceivably *could* become surgeons if they found the job sufficiently attractive to endure the long years of training that are required. Few, however, are willing to make such large investments of their own time, money, and energy. Consequently, the few who do become surgeons earn very generous incomes.

Economists have devoted quite a bit of attention to the acquisition of skills through human investment. An entire branch of economic theory—called *human capital theory*—analyzes an individual's decisions about education and training in exactly the same way as we analyzed a firm's decision to buy a machine or build a factory in the previous chapter. Though educational decisions can be influenced by love of learning, desire for prestige, and a variety of other factors, human capital theorists find it useful to analyze a schooling decision as if it were made purely as a business plan. The optimal length of education, from this point of view, is to stay in school until the marginal revenue (in the form of increased future income) of an additional year of schooling is exactly equal to the marginal cost.

One implication of human capital theory is that college graduates should earn substantially more than high school graduates to compensate them for their extra investments in schooling. Do they? Will your college investment pay off? Many generations of college students have supposed that it would, and recent data strongly confirm they were right. Indeed, as we noted earlier, the gap between the wages of workers with a college degree and those with a high school education has been widening. College graduates now earn at least 85 percent more than their high school-educated peers.

> The large income differentials earned by college graduates provide an excellent "return" on the tuition payments and sacrificed earnings that they "invested" while in school.

Human capital theory emphasizes that jobs that require more education *must* pay higher wages if they are to attract enough workers, because people insist on a financial return on their human investments. But the theory does not address the other side of the question: What is it about more-educated people that makes firms willing to pay them higher wages? Put differently, the theory explains why the supply of educated people is limited, but does not explain why the *demand* is substantial even at high wages.

Most human capital theorists complete their analyses by assuming that students in high schools and colleges acquire particular skills that are productive in the marketplace, thereby raising the marginal revenue products of those workers. In this view, educational institutions are factories that take less productive workers as their raw materials, apply doses of training, and create more productive workers as outputs. This view of what happens in schools makes educators happy and accords well with common sense. However, a number of social scientists doubt that this is quite how schooling raises earning power.

## EDUCATION AND EARNINGS: DISSENTING VIEWS

Just why do jobs with stiffer educational requirements typically pay higher wages? The commonsense view that educating people makes them more productive is not universally accepted.

**EDUCATION AS A SORTING MECHANISM** One alternative view denies that the educational process teaches students anything directly relevant to their subsequent performance on jobs. In this view, people differ in ability when they enter the school system and differ in more or less the same way when they leave. What the educational system does, according to this theory, is to *sort* individuals by ability. Skills like intelligence and self-discipline that lead to success in schools, it is argued, are closely related to the skills that lead to success in jobs. As a result, the abler individuals stay in school longer and perform better. Prospective employers know this, and consequently seek to hire those whom the school system has suggested will be the most productive workers.

**THE DUAL LABOR MARKET THEORY**   Another view of the linkages among education, ability, and earnings is part of a much broader theory of how the labor market operates—the theory of *dual labor markets*. Proponents of this theory suggest that there are two very different types of labor markets with relatively little mobility between them.

The "primary labor market" is where most of the economy's "good jobs" are—jobs like business management, computer programming, and skilled crafts that are interesting and offer considerable possibilities for career advancement. The educational system helps decide which individuals get assigned to the primary labor market and, for those who make it, greater educational achievement does indeed offer financial rewards.

The privileged workers who wind up in the primary labor market are offered opportunities for additional training on the job; they augment their skills by experience and by learning from their fellow workers; and they progress in successive steps to more responsible, better-paying positions. Where jobs in the primary labor market are concerned, dual labor market theorists believe that education really is productive. But they also think that admission to the primary labor market depends in part on social position, and that firms probably care more about steady work habits and punctuality than about reading, writing, and arithmetic.

Everything is quite different in the "secondary labor market"—where we find all the "bad jobs." Jobs like cleaning and fast-food services, which are often the only ones inner-city residents can find, offer low pay, few fringe benefits, and virtually no training to improve the workers' skills. They are dead-end jobs with little or no hope for promotion or advancement. As a result, lateness, absenteeism, and pilferage are expected as a matter of course, so that workers in the secondary labor market tend to develop the bad work habits that confirm the prejudices of those who assigned them to inferior jobs in the first place.

In the secondary labor market, increased education leads neither to higher wages nor to increased protection from unemployment—benefits generally offered elsewhere in the labor market. For this reason, workers in the secondary market have little incentive to invest in education.

In sum, we have a well-established fact—that people with more education generally earn higher wages—but little agreement on what accounts for this fact. Probably, there is some truth to all of the proposed explanations.

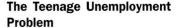

**The Teenage Unemployment Problem**

## THE EFFECTS OF MINIMUM WAGE LEGISLATION

As we have observed, the "labor market" is really composed of many submarkets for labor of different types, each with its own supply and demand curves. One particular labor market always seems to have higher unemployment than the labor force as a whole: the job market for teenagers.

Figure 18–7 shows that teenage unemployment rates have consistently been much higher than the overall unemployment rate, and black teenagers have fared worse than white teenagers. For the most part, however, the three unemployment rates have moved up and down

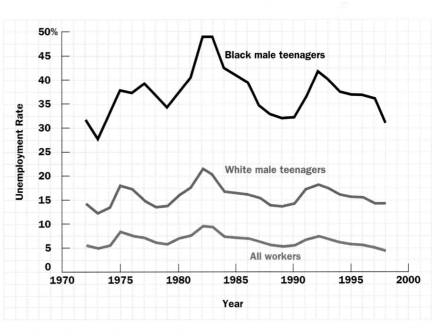

together, as this chart shows. It indicates that whenever the unemployment rate for all workers goes up or down, the teenage (defined here as a person aged 16 to 19 years) unemployment rate almost always moves in the same direction, but

SOURCE: *Economic Report of the President* (Washington, D.C.: U.S. Government Printing Office, various years).

more dramatically. Thus, when things are generally bad, things are much, much worse for teenage workers, and especially for black teenage workers. Despite social and legislative pressures against race discrimination, efforts to improve the quality of education available to children in the inner cities, and many related programs, there has been no relative improvement in black teenage unemployment in recent years.

One reason is that teenagers generally have not completed their educations and have little job experience, hence their marginal revenue products tend to be relatively low. Until recently, many economists argued that this fact, together with minimum wage laws that prevent teenagers from accepting wages commensurate with their low marginal revenue products, is the main cause of high teenage unemployment. The reasoning is that legally imposed high wages make it too expensive to hire teenagers. Recent studies of the data suggest, however, that a rise in minimum wage produces little, if any, cut in demand for teen labor.

We should also note that inflation has eaten into the real value of the minimum wage over the years. Figure 18–8 shows clearly that after 48 years of sporadic increases in the nominal minimum wage rate, the real (inflation-adjusted) rate has remained virtually unchanged.

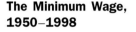

**FIGURE 18–8**

**The Minimum Wage, 1950–1998**

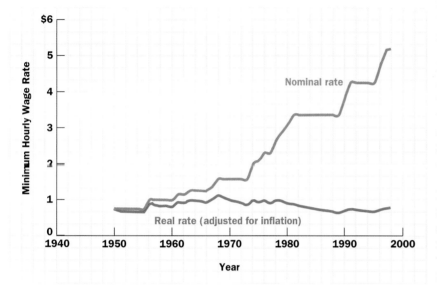

NOTE: Nominal rates deflated by CPI (1950 = 100).

SOURCE: U.S. Bureau of the Census, *Statistical Abstract of the United States,* (Washington, D.C.: U.S. Government Printing Office, various years), and U.S. Bureau of Labor Statistics, http://stats.bls.gov/, accessed May 1999.

"As far as I'm concerned, they can do what they want with the minimum wage, just as long as they keep their hands off the maximum wage."

# ■ UNIONS AND COLLECTIVE BARGAINING

Our analysis of competitive labor markets has so far not dealt with one rather distinctive feature of the markets for labor: The supply of labor is not at all competitive in many labor markets; instead it is controlled by a labor monopoly, a **labor union.**

Although they are significant, unions in the United States are not nearly as important as is popularly supposed. For example, most people who are unfamiliar with the data are astonished to learn that less than 14 percent of American workers belong to unions. This percentage is much lower than it was in the heyday of unionism in the mid-1950s, when about a quarter of all workers were union members. Figure 18–9 shows that in 1930, unions had enrolled just under 7 percent of the U.S. labor force, and by 1933 this figure had slipped to barely above 5 percent. Unionization took off with President Franklin D. Roosevelt's New Deal, reaching almost 16 percent of the labor force by 1939. It then drifted irregularly upward to a peak of about 25 to 26 percent of all workers in the mid-1950s, from which it has since fallen more or less steadily back to just under 14 percent in 1998. Since the 1950s, the unionization rate has fallen with few interruptions.

Why has the extent of unionization in the United States been declining? One reason is the shift of the U.S. labor force (like that of every other industrial country) into service industries and out of manufacturing, where unions traditionally had their base. In addition, deregulation forced airlines, trucking companies, and firms in other industries to compete more intensely, and it may thus have influenced the firms to hire less expensive nonunion labor.

In addition, American workers' preferences seem to have shifted away from unions. The increasing share of women in the labor force may have contributed to this trend, because women have traditionally been less prone than men to join unions.

Finally, American unions have been under increasing pressure in the 1990s owing to stronger competition both at home and from abroad. In response, firm after firm has closed plants and eliminated jobs. The downsizing trend has made it even more difficult for unions to win concessions that improve the economic positions of their members. That, in turn, has reduced the attractiveness of union membership.

Unionization is much less prevalent in the United States than it is in most other industrialized countries. For example, 33 percent of German workers and 90 percent of Swedish workers belong to unions.[10] The differences are quite striking and doubtless have something to do with our tradition of "rugged individualism."

The main sector of the U.S. economy in which the unions are still fairly healthy is government employment. City, state, and federal employees join unions in relatively large numbers (about 37 percent of public-sector workers are union members). Perhaps this higher union participation arises because the job opportunities for public-sector employees are controlled by political forces, and politicians find it far harder to resist the unions than private firms do.[11] However, here too, the

A **labor union** is an organization made up of a group of workers (usually with the same specialization, such as plumbing or costume design, or in the same industry). The unions represent the workers in negotiations with employers over issues such as wages, vacations, and sick leave.

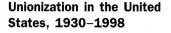

**FIGURE 18-9**

**Unionization in the United States, 1930–1998**

SOURCES: U.S. Department of Labor, Bureau of Labor Statistics, *Employment and Earnings* (Washington, D.C.: U.S. Government Printing Office, January issues, various years); and http://stats.bls.gov, accessed December 1998.

---

[10] Unpublished data provided by William McMichael, Division of Foreign Labor Statistics, U.S. Department of Labor, February 1998.

[11] U.S. Census Bureau, *Statistical Abstract of the United States: 1998*, 118th ed. (Washington, D.C.: U.S. Government Printing Office, 1998).

### ● THE WAY IT WAS

The calamitous Triangle Shirtwaist Factory fire of 1911, in which 146 women and girls lost their lives, was a landmark in American labor history. It galvanized public opinion behind the movement to improve conditions, hours, and wages in the sweatshops. Pauline Newman went to work in the factory, located on what is now New York University's campus, at the age of eight. Many of her friends lost their lives in the fire. She went on to become an organizer and executive of the newly formed International Ladies Garment Workers' Union. In her words:

> We started work at seven-thirty in the morning, and during the busy season we worked until nine in the evening. They didn't pay you any overtime and they didn't give you anything for supper money. . . .
>
> The employers didn't recognize anyone working for them as a human being. You were not allowed to sing. . . . We weren't allowed to talk to each other. . . . If you went to the toilet and you were there longer than the floor lady thought you should be, you would be laid off for half a day and sent home. And, of course, that meant no pay. You were not allowed to have your lunch on the fire escape in the summertime. The door was locked to keep us in. That's why so many people were trapped when the fire broke out. . . .
>
> You were expected to work every day if they needed you and the pay was the same whether you worked extra or not.
>
> Conditions were dreadful in those days. We didn't have anything. . . . There was no welfare, no pension, no unemployment insurance. There was nothing. . . . There was so much feeling against unions then. The judges, when one of our girls came before him, said to her: "You're not striking against your employer, you know, young lady. You're striking against God," and sentenced her to two weeks.
>
> I wasn't at the Triangle Shirtwaist Factory when the fire broke out, but a lot of my friends were. . . . The thing that bothered me was the employers got a lawyer. How anyone could have *defended* them! Because I'm quite sure that the fire was planned for insurance purposes. And no one is going to convince me otherwise. And when they testified that the door to the fire escape was open, it was a lie! It was never open. Locked all the time. One hundred and forty-six people sacrificed, and the judge fined Blank and Harris seventy-five dollars!

#### THE PROBLEM PERSISTS

The following excerpt from *Time* magazine shows that unsafe working conditions continue to produce tragedies, even in this day and age:

unions are under siege as more and more government services are contracted out to private businesses. For example, the state of New Jersey used the threat of turning highway toll collection over to private enterprise as an effective bargaining chip in 1995 negotiations with the toll-collectors' union.

### THE DEVELOPMENT OF UNIONISM IN AMERICA

Serious unionism in the United States is not much more than a century old. The current union structure began to take shape in 1881 with the founding of the American Federation of Labor (AFL) by Samuel Gompers. Working conditions then were incredibly bad by today's standards, and unscrupulous practices by many employers fostered the growth of unions (see the accompanying box, "The Way It Was").

Gompers strongly believed that unions should be nonpolitical organizations seeking more pay, better working conditions, longer vacations, and so on. He also believed that unions should be organized along craft lines—carpenters in one union, plumbers in another—rather than trying to include all types of workers within a given industry. The AFL grew steadily from about 1900 until the 1920s, went into decline during the Roaring Twenties, but then grew rapidly thanks to the favorable legislation of the Roosevelt administration in the 1930s. The National

Nobody who worked at the Imperial Food Products plant in Hamlet, North Carolina, had much love for the place. The job—cooking, weighing and packing fried chicken parts for fast-food restaurants—was hot, greasy and poorly paid. The conveyor belts moved briskly, and the rest breaks were so strictly timed that going to the bathroom at the wrong moment could lead to dismissal. But in the sleepy town of 6,200 there was not much else in the way of work. So most of the plant's 200 employees, predominantly black and female, were thankful just to have the minimum-wage job. Until last week, that is.

The morning shift had just started when an overhead hydraulic line ruptured, spilling its volatile fluid onto the floor. Gas burners under the frying vats ignited the vapors and turned the 30,000-sq.-ft. plant into an inferno of flame and thick, yellow smoke. Panicked employees rushed for emergency exits only to find several of them locked. "I thought I was gone, until a man broke the lock off," says Letha Terry, one of the survivors. Twenty-five of Terry's fellow employees were not so lucky. Their bodies were found clustered around the blocked doorways or trapped in the freezer.

The disaster brought to light the mostly invisible body count of the American workplace. By some estimates, more than 10,000 workers die each year from on-the-job injuries—about 30 every day. Perhaps 70,000 more are permanently disabled. The fire also exposed the weaknesses of measures for ensuring job safety. The 11-year-old Imperial Food Products plant had never been inspected. Like a lot of American workplaces, it fell through the gaping cracks of a system in which there are too few inspectors, penalties are mostly trifling and the procedures for reporting dangerous conditions can leave workers to choose between risking their jobs and risking their lives.

SOURCE: Excerpted from Joan Morrison and Charlotte Fox Zabusky, *American Mosaic: The Immigrant Experience in the Words of Those Who Lived It* (New York: E. P. Dutton, 1980), reprinted by permission of the publisher, E. P. Dutton, Inc.; and Richard Lacayo, "Death on the Shop Floor: A Murderous Fire in a North Carolina Poultry Plant Underscores the Dangers of America's Workplaces," *Time,* September 16, 1991, p. 28.

Labor Relations Act (Wagner Act) in 1935 guaranteed workers the right to form unions and to choose unions to represent them in collective bargaining. It also set up the National Labor Relations Board (NLRB) to protect labor from "unfair labor practices" by employers. Today the NLRB oversees elections in firms to determine which union will represent the workers. It can also force employers to take back workers who it considers to have been fired unjustly.

The favorable public attitude toward unions soured somewhat after World War II, perhaps because of the rash of strikes that took place in 1946. One result of these strikes was the Taft-Hartley Act of 1947, which specified and outlawed certain "unfair labor practices" by unions and which sought to shift some of labor's power back to management. Specifically, the act severely limited **closed shops** that hire only union members; permitted state governments to ban the **union shop,** an arrangement that *requires* employees to join the union; and provided for court injunctions to delay strikes that threaten the national interest for an 80-day "cooling-off" period.

Today, the character of American unionism is still somewhat unsettled. Unions are struggling very hard to make inroads into labor markets that by tradition have not been unionized—such as the agricultural and white-collar office markets. They have achieved notable successes in organizing teachers, government employees, and many other types of white-collar workers. Between 1983 and 1997, the number of

A **closed shop** is an arrangement that permits only union members to be hired.

A **union shop** is an arrangement under which nonunion workers may be hired, but then must join the union within a specified period of time.

managerial and professional workers belonging to unions increased from 20 million to 32 million.[12]

U.S. labor unions are very different from those in Europe and Japan. For one thing, U.S. unions are strongly committed to capitalism and have rarely espoused socialism—unlike their western European counterparts. American unions also often see themselves as adversaries of management, unlike Japanese unions. This country's century-long tradition of hostile labor-management relations has impeded current attempts to emulate the Japanese model of labor-management cooperation. However, several U.S. plants that are owned and run by Japanese companies reportedly have achieved an unprecedented degree of trust and support between the labor force and management. There are other cases though in which such firms have had extremely poor labor relations. In general, U.S. labor still seems to feel that American employers are all too likely to adopt unfair practices unless they are restrained by powerful unions.

## UNIONS AS LABOR MONOPOLIES

Unions require that we alter our economic analysis of the labor market in much the same way that monopolies required us to alter our analysis of the goods market (see Chapter 12). Remember that a monopoly seller of goods selects the point on its demand curve that maximizes its profits. Much the same idea applies to a union, which is, after all, a monopoly seller of labor. It too faces a demand curve—derived this time from the marginal revenue product schedules of firms—and can choose the point on that curve that suits it best.

The problem for the economist trying to analyze union behavior—and perhaps also for the union leader trying to select a course of action—is how to decide which point on the demand curve is "best." There is no obvious single goal analogous to profit maximization that clearly delineates what a union should do. Instead there are a number of *alternative* goals that sound plausible.

**ALTERNATIVE UNION GOALS**    The union leadership may, for example, decide that the size of the union is pretty well fixed and try to force employers to pay the highest wage they will pay without firing any of the union members. But this is a high-risk strategy for a union. Firms forced to pay such high wages will be at a competitive disadvantage compared with firms that have nonunion labor, and they may even be forced to shut down. Alternatively, union leaders may assign priority to increasing the size of their union. They may even try to make employment as large as possible by accepting a wage just above the competitive level. One way, but certainly not the only way, to strike a balance between the conflicting goals of maximizing wages and maximizing employment is to maximize the product of the two—which is the total earnings of all workers taken together.

The basic conclusion of these alternative possible goals for unions is this: Even if unions, as monopoly sellers of labor, have the power to push wages above the competitive level, they can normally only achieve such wage increases by reducing the number of jobs, because the demand curve for labor is downward sloping. Just as monopolists must limit their outputs to push up their prices, so unions must restrict employment to push up wages.

In some exceptional cases, however, a union may be able to achieve wage gains without sacrificing employment. To do this, the union must be able to exercise effective control over the demand curve for labor. Figure 18–10 illustrates such a possibility. Union actions push the demand curve outward from $D_0D_0$ to $D_1D_1$, simultaneously raising both wages and employment. Typically, this is difficult to do. One way to do it is by *featherbedding*—forcing

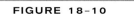

**FIGURE 18-10**

**Union Control over the Demand Curve**

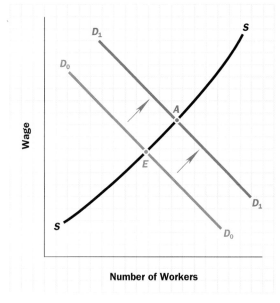

**Number of Workers**

[12] U.S. Census Bureau, *Statistical Abstract of the United States*, various years (Washington, D.C.: U.S. Government Printing Office).

management to employ more workers than it really needs.[13] Quite the opposite technique is to institute a campaign to raise worker productivity, which some unions seem to have been able to do. Alternatively, the union can try to raise the demand for the company's product either by flexing its political muscle (for example, by obtaining legislation to reduce foreign competition) or by appealing to the public to buy union products.

### Foreign Competition, Technology, and American Jobs: Are Union Fears Justified?

Unions have actively taken up the issues we discussed at the beginning of this chapter. Early in the 1990s trade agreements worldwide seemed to threaten U.S. workers' jobs—union jobs in particular. But historical evidence raises questions about these union fears.

First, we must recognize that although one effect of cheap foreign products may be to hold down American dollar wages, these inexpensive products also help to raise *real* wages. Lower product prices also mean that U.S. wages command more goods per dollar. If cars, televisions, and foods become cheaper because of imports, a given wage can buy larger quantities of these items. Besides, in comparison with most other industrial economies, the U.S. imports a relatively small proportion of its GDP, yet wages in those other countries have risen faster than those in the United States for many decades. Indeed, historically, real wages in the United States grew most rapidly when wages in the countries from which the United States received many of its imports were much further behind U.S. wages than they are now. In other words, when foreign labor was really cheap, U.S. wages were growing most rapidly.

The second part of the story, related to technological progress, also raises questions. Labor-saving innovation has played a leading role in the economic history of the United States. In the course of the past century, the productivity of the U.S. labor force has grown more than 12-fold. This means that 11 out of 12 U.S. workers could have been fired without any loss in production. Yet unemployment in the United States has shown no rising trend over this period. As we write this book, the U.S. unemployment rate is the lowest it has been in 30 years. Evidently, technological progress, which has stimulated the demand for products, has not cut the demand for the workers who turn out those products. That is because, by making goods and services cheaper and better, technical progress has always stimulated the demand for the improved commodities. But increased demand for goods and services translates into a demand for labor. Thus, in terms of demand for labor, there are two sides to technical progress. And in the long run, throughout our history, its effects have generally included rising real wages, but no trend toward increased unemployment.

**HAVE UNIONS REALLY RAISED WAGES?**     To what extent do union members actually earn higher wages than nonmembers? The consensus would probably surprise most people. Economists estimate that most union members' wages are about 15 percent above those of nonmembers who are otherwise identical (in skills, geographical locations, and so on). Though certainly not negligible, we can hardly consider this a huge differential. Narrowing the gap even further is the fact that nonunion workers do not have to pay the dues that are required of union members.

---

[13] The best-known example of featherbedding involved the railroad unions, which for years forced management to keep "firemen" in the cabs of diesel engines, in which there were no burning fires. Similarly, the musicians' union in New York City forces Broadway producers who use certain theaters to employ a minimum number of musicians—whether or not they actually play music. Of course, it is not only unionized labor that has tried to create an artificial demand for its services. Lawyers, doctors, and business firms, among others, have sought ways to induce consumers to buy more of their products and services. *Exercise:* Can you think of ways in which they have done this?

This 15 percent differential does not mean, however, that unions have raised wages no more than 15 percent. Some observers believe that union activity has also raised wages of nonunion workers by forcing nonunion employers to compete harder for their workers. If so, the differential between union and nonunion workers will be less than the amount by which unions raised wages overall.

## MONOPSONY AND BILATERAL MONOPOLY

Our analysis thus far oversimplifies matters in several important respects. For one thing, it envisions a market situation in which one powerful union is dealing with many powerless employers: We have assumed that the labor market is monopolized on the selling side but competitive on the buying side. Some industries more or less fit this model. The giant Teamsters' union negotiates with a trucking industry consisting of thousands of firms, most of them quite small and powerless. Similarly, most of the unions within the construction industry are much larger than the firms with which they bargain.

But many cases simply do not fit the model. The huge auto manufacturing corporations do not stand idly by while the United Automobile Workers (UAW) picks its favorite point on the demand curve for auto workers. Nor does the steelworkers' union sit across the bargaining table from representatives of a perfectly competitive industry. In these and other industries, although the union certainly has a good deal of monopoly power over labor supply, the firms also have some **monopsony** power over labor demand. This means that the firms may deliberately reduce the quantity of labor they demand as a way to force down the equilibrium level of wages. We can calculate the profit-maximizing restriction in the quantity of labor the same way we determined a monopolist's profit-maximizing restriction of output in Chapter 12.

Analysts find it difficult to predict the wage and employment decisions that will emerge when both the buying and selling side of a market are monopolized—a situation called **bilateral monopoly.** The difficulties here are similar to those we encountered in considering the behavior of oligopolistic industries in Chapter 13. Just as one oligopolist is acutely aware that rivals are likely to react to anything the oligopolistic employer does, a union dealing with a monopsony employer knows that any move it makes will elicit a countermove by the firm, and this knowledge makes the first decision that much more complicated. In practice, the outcome of bilateral monopoly depends partly on economic logic, partly on the relative power of the union and management, partly on the skill and preparation of the negotiators, and partly on luck. (For an example of the bargaining process that can occur in a bilateral monopoly in the real world, see the accompanying box, "Bargaining in a Bilateral Monopoly: Millionaires versus Billionaires.")

Still, we can be a bit more concrete about the outcome of the wage determination process under bilateral monopoly. A monopsonist employer unrestrained by a union will use its market power to force wages down below the competitive level, just as a monopoly seller uses its market power to force prices higher. It accomplishes this by reducing its demand for labor below what would otherwise be the profit-maximizing amount, thereby cutting both wages and the number of workers employed.

However, a union may be in a position to prevent this from happening. It can deliberately set a floor on wages, pledging its members not to work at all at any wage level below this floor. So, a union may force the monopsony employer to pay higher wages and, simultaneously, to hire more workers than the employer otherwise would.

Even though we can hardly find examples of industries that are pure monopsonists in their dealings with labor, these conclusions do bear some importance in reality. The fact is that large, oligopolistic firms do often engage in one-on-one wage bargaining with the unions of their employees, and there is reason to believe that the resulting bargaining process closely resembles the workings of the bilateral monopoly model that we just described.

A **monopsony** is a market situation in which there is only one buyer.

A **bilateral monopoly** is a market situation in which there is both a monopoly on the selling side and a monopsony on the buying side.

## ● BARGAINING IN A BILATERAL MONOPOLY: MILLIONAIRES VERSUS BILLIONAIRES

The 1998–1999 labor dispute between the National Basketball Association and the National Basketball Players Association lasted 191 days before the two sides reached a settlement—and it seems that the owners, not the players, won the match in "sudden death overtime."

The relationship between professional basketball players and the owners' association is classic example of *bilateral monopoly*—a market with a monopoly on the selling side and a monopsony on the buying side. The players' union controls the sale of professional basketball talent, and the owners have a virtual monopsony on the purchase of that talent.* A labor dispute in a bilateral monopoly market is often won by the side with the craftiest negotiator and the greatest ability to wait for the right deal. In the case of pro basketball, the owners seem to have held those advantages. With only hours to go before the entire season was to be canceled, NBA commissioner David Stern and Billy Hunter, the executive director of the player's union, reached an agreement that allowed them to salvage an abbreviated season. While Stern claimed that he had given too many concessions to the players, *Sports Illustrated* believes that Stern was the shrewdest negotiator. The agreement makes the NBA the only professional sports league with a maximum salary: under the new agreement, the maximum salary in the first year of a new contract will be $14 million, and only players with ten seasons of experience will be eligible. For the average NBA player, who earns much less than superstars like Shaquille O'Neal or Scottie Pippen, the agreement spells out a pay scale based on seniority, preventing 22-year-old newcomers from negotiating eight-figure salaries. The team owners won other victories, such as the ability to retain their draft choices for longer periods before those players became eligible for free agency and a reduction in total league revenues paid to players.

Although the players' union won a few concessions, such as an increase in the minimum salary that is paid to league benchwarmers, the team owners seem to have gotten a better bargain. It is not surprising that the players were more eager to settle the dispute, because they collectively sacrificed a half billion in salary during the strike, while the team owners saved the same amount by not paying their players. The owners were further emboldened by their television contracts, which guaranteed that they were paid, even while the season was on hold.

*But not a pure monopsony, because American basketball players can join teams in other countries.

SOURCE: Steve Springer, "Season's Greetings: How Much They're Losing; Owners Get TV Money, But Might Not Keep It," *Los Angeles Times*, December 18, 1998; Phil Taylor and Jackie MacMullan, "Pro Basketball: To The Victor Belong the Spoils," *Sports Illustrated*, January 18, 1999; and United Press International, "Report: NBA Labor Impasse Resolved," January 6, 1999.

## COLLECTIVE BARGAINING AND STRIKES

The process by which unions and management settle on the terms of a labor contract is called *collective bargaining*. Unfortunately, nothing as straightforward as a supply-demand diagram can tell us what wage level will emerge from a collective bargaining session.

Furthermore, actual collective bargaining sessions range over many more issues than wages. For example, fringe benefits such as pensions, health and life insurance, overtime pay, seniority privileges, and work conditions are often crucial issues. Many labor contracts specify in great detail the rights of labor and management to set work conditions—and also provide elaborate procedures for resolving grievances and disputes. This list could go on and on. The final contract that emerges from collective bargaining may well run to many pages of fine print.

With the issues so varied and complex, and with the stakes so high, it is no wonder that both labor and management employ skilled professionals who specialize in preparing for and carrying out these negotiations. The bargaining in these sessions is often heated, with outcomes riding as much on personalities and the skills of the negotiators as on cool-headed logic and economic facts. Negotiations may last well into the night, with each side making threats and seeming to try to wear out the other side. Unions, for their part, generally threaten strikes or work slowdowns. Firms counter that they would rather face a strike than give in, or they may even threaten to close the plant without a strike. (This is called a *lockout.*)

**MEDIATION AND ARBITRATION**    When the public interest is seriously affected, or when the union and firm reach an impasse, government agencies may well send in a *mediator,* whose job is to try to speed up the negotiation process. As an impartial observer, the mediator sits down with both sides separately to discuss their problems and then tries to persuade each to make concessions. At some stage, when an agreement looks possible, she or he may call them back together for another bargaining session in the mediator's presence. Mediators, however, have no power to force a settlement. Their success hinges on their ability to smooth ruffled feathers and to find common ground.

Sometimes in cases in which unions and firms simply cannot agree but neither wants a strike, differences are finally settled by *arbitration*—the appointment of an impartial individual empowered to settle the issues that negotiation could not resolve. This happens often, for example, in wage negotiations in professional sports or for municipal jobs such as police and firefighters. For instance, a federal arbitrator was called in to resolve the labor dispute between American Airlines and its flight attendants' union. In fact, in some vital sectors in which a strike is too injurious to the public interest, the labor contract or the law may stipulate that there must be *compulsory arbitration* if the two parties cannot agree. However, both labor and management are normally reluctant to accept this procedure.

**STRIKES**    Most collective bargaining situations do not lead to strikes. But the right to strike, and to take a strike, remain fundamentally important tools in the bargaining process. Imagine, for example, a firm bargaining with a union that was prohibited from striking. The union's bargaining position would probably be quite weak. On the other hand, a firm that always capitulated rather than suffer a strike would be virtually at the mercy of the union. So strikes—or, more precisely, the possibility of strikes—serve an important economic purpose.

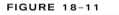

**FIGURE 18-11**

**Work-Time Lost in the United States because of Strikes, 1948–1998**

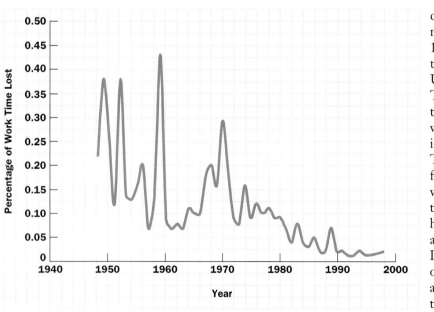

Fortunately, however, the incidence of strikes is not nearly so common as many people believe. Figure 18–11 reports the percentage of work time lost as a result of strikes in the United States from 1948 to 1998. This fraction varies greatly from year to year, but is never very large. The worst year for strikes was 1946, and it is probably no coincidence that the Taft-Hartley law was enacted the following year. The fraction of total work time lost has been under one-tenth of 1 percent since 1970 and has now dwindled to insignificance at about *one-hundredth of 1 percent.* Despite the headline-grabbing nature of major national strikes, the total amount of work time lost to strikes is truly trivial—far less, for example, than the time lost to coffee breaks!

SOURCE: U.S. Department of Labor, Bureau of Labor Statistics, *Monthly Labor Review,* various issues, and http://stats.bls.gov.

Compared with other nations, the United States suffers more from strikes than, say, Japan, but it has many fewer strikes than such countries as Italy and Canada (see Figure 18–12).

## The Incidence of Strikes in Eight Industrial Countries, 1991–1995

FIGURE 18-12

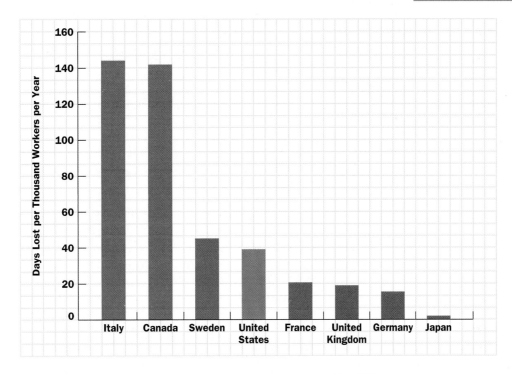

NOTE: Five-year averages (1991–1995), except for Italy (1991–1994) and the United Kingdom (1992–1995).

SOURCE: International Labour Office, *1996 Yearbook of Labour Statistics*, Geneva: 1996.

## SUMMARY

1. In a free market, the wage rate and the level of employment are determined by the interaction of supply and demand. Workers in great demand or short supply command high wages. Conversely, low wages go to workers who are in abundant supply or to workers who have skills that are not in great demand.

2. The demand curve for labor, like the demand curve for any factor of production, is derived from the marginal revenue product curve. It slopes downward because of the "law" of diminishing marginal returns.

3. The demand curve for labor can be shifted upward by an increase in education or on-the-job training that raise the workers' marginal physical products or by a rise in demand for those products that raises their price and therefore also increases labor's MRP.

4. Labor-saving innovations may either raise or lower worker's wages and available jobs in the short run. But because they are tantamount to increased productivity, in the long run they generally raise the incomes of workers along with those of other members of the community.

5. The supply of labor is determined by free choices made by individuals. The supply curve can be shifted so that more labor is supplied at any given wage level if there are developments such as increased labor force participation, as when women find it more desirable to hold jobs.

6. Because of conflicting *income and substitution effects*, the quantity of labor supplied may rise or fall as a result of an increase in wages. Historical data show that hours of work per week have fallen as wages have risen, suggesting that income effects may be dominant in the long run.

7. Some valuable skills are virtually impossible to duplicate. People who possess such skills will earn *economic rents* as part of their wages.

8. But most skills can be acquired by means of *investment in human capital*, such as education.

9. *Human capital theory* assumes that people make educational decisions in much the same way as businesses make investment decisions, and it tacitly assumes that people learn things in school that increase their productivity in jobs.

10. Other theories of the effects of education on earnings deny that schooling actually raises productivity. For example, one view is that the educational system primarily sorts people according to their abilities.

11. According to the theory of *dual labor markets*, there are two distinct types of labor markets, with very little mobility between them. The primary labor market contains the "good" jobs where wages are high, prospects for advancement are good, and higher education pays off. The secondary labor market contains the "bad" jobs with low wages, little opportunity for promotion, and little return to education.

12. Less than 14 percent of all American workers belong to *unions*, which we can think of as monopoly sellers of labor.

Compared with many other industrialized countries, unions in the United States are younger, less widespread, and less political.

13. For the most part, unions probably force wages to be higher and employment to be lower than they would be in a competitive labor market.

14. *Collective bargaining* agreements between labor and management are complex documents covering much more than employment and wage rates.

15. Strikes play an important role in collective bargaining as a way of dividing the fruits of economic activity between big business and big labor. Fortunately, strikes are not nearly so common as is often supposed.

16. For about two decades Americans have experienced three noteworthy trends: (a) a decline in union membership of more than 30 percent, (b) a steady fall in real wages partly offset by rising fringe benefits, and (c) a rise in the income gap between well-paid and poorly paid workers.

## K E Y   T E R M S

Marginal revenue product of labor (MRP$_L$)   354

Investment in human capital   355

Income and substitution effects   359

Backward-bending supply curve   360

Economic rent   363

Human capital theory   364

Dual labor markets   365

Minimum wage law   366

Labor union   367

Taft-Hartley Act (1947)   369

Closed shop   369

Union shop   369

Monopsony   372

Bilateral monopoly   372

Collective bargaining   373

Mediation   374

Arbitration   374

## Q U E S T I O N S   F O R   R E V I E W

1. Colleges are known to pay rather low wages for student labor. Can this be explained by the operation of supply and demand in the local labor markets? Is the concept of monopsony of any use? How might things differ if students formed a union?

2. College professors are highly skilled (or at least highly educated!) laborers. Yet their wages are not very high. Is this a refutation of the marginal productivity theory?

3. The following table shows the number of pizzas that can be produced by a large pizza parlor employing various numbers of pizza chefs.

| Number of Chefs | Number of Pizzas per Day |
|---|---|
| 1 | 40 |
| 2 | 64 |
| 3 | 82 |
| 4 | 92 |
| 5 | 100 |
| 6 | 92 |

   a. Find the marginal physical product schedule of chefs.

   b. Assuming a price of $9 per pizza, find the marginal revenue product schedule.

   c. If chefs are paid $100 per day, how many chefs will this pizza parlor employ? How would your answer change if chefs' wages rose to $125 per day?

   d. Suppose the price of pizza rises from $9 to $12. Show what happens to the derived demand curve for chefs.

4. Discuss the concept of the financial rate of return to a college education. If this return is less than the return on a bank account, does that mean you should quit college? Why

might you wish to stay in school anyway? Are there circumstances under which it might be rational not to go to college, even when the financial returns to college are very high?

5. It seems to be a well-established fact that workers with more years of education typically receive higher wages. What are some possible reasons for this?

6. Approximately what fraction of the American labor force belongs to unions? (Try asking this question of a person who has never studied economics.) Why do you think this fraction is so low?

7. What are some reasonable goals for a union? Use the tools of supply and demand to explain how a union might pursue its goals, whatever they are. Consider a union that has been in the news recently. What was it trying to accomplish?

8. "Strikes are simply intolerable and should be outlawed." Comment on this statement.

9. In which of the following industries is wage determination most plausibly explained by the model of perfect competition? The model of pure monopoly? The model of bilateral monopoly?

   a. Odd-job repairs in private homes

   b. Manufacture of low-priced clothing for children

   c. Steel manufacturing.

10. In a bitter strike battle between Eastern Airlines and several of its unions, it was clear from the beginning that the airline was in serious financial trouble. The airline was, indeed, eventually forced to close down at the cost of many jobs. Discuss what might nevertheless have led the unions to hold out so tenaciously.

11. Can you think of some types of workers whose marginal products probably were raised by computerization? Are there any whose marginal products were probably reduced? Can you characterize the difference between the two types of jobs in general terms?

12. European labor unions have traditionally had a strong socialistic orientation. How would you guess this is likely to be affected by the movement of countries in eastern Europe toward market economies?

13. What, if anything, do you think is the effect of long-term unemployment on crime rates? What about short-term unemployment?

14. Since about 1980, GDP per capita (that is, the average real income per person) in the United States has risen fairly substantially. Yet real wages have failed to rise. What do you think may explain this?

The white man knows how to make everything,
but he does not know how to distribute it.

Sitting Bull

# POVERTY, INEQUALITY, AND DISCRIMINATION

The last two chapters analyzed how factor prices—wages, rents, and interest rates—are determined in a market economy. One reason for concern with this issue is that these payments determine the *incomes* of the people who own the factors, and income is a primary determinant of well-being. The study of factor pricing is, therefore, an indirect way to learn about how the market *distributes income* among individuals.

In this chapter, we turn to the problem of income distribution more directly. Specifically, we seek answers to the following questions: How unequal are incomes in the United States, and why? How can society decide rationally on how much equality it wants? And, once this decision is made, what policies are available to pursue this goal?

## Ending Welfare As We Know It

For decades, America's main programs for the poor were widely decried as "the welfare mess," a vague term indicating that the programs were too bureaucratic, too expensive, and too ineffective. Some critics went so far as to claim that welfare hurts the very people it was designed to help by, for example, encouraging out-of-wedlock births and fostering a culture of dependence on the state. When candidate Bill Clinton campaigned on a promise to "end welfare as we know it" in 1992, many Americans shared his dissatisfaction with the system.

About four years later, Clinton's campaign pledge turned into reality when Congress passed and the president signed into law a complete overhaul of the federal welfare system. This so-called welfare reform abolished Aid to Families with Dependent Children (AFDC), which had been the main program providing cash grants to poor families since the 1930s. Its replacement, called Temporary Assistance to Needy Families (TANF), limits a family's eligibility for welfare checks to two years at a time and five years over a lifetime. Before recipients reach these time limits, they are supposed to have found jobs. The former federal guarantee of a minimum income is, therefore, now a thing of the past. The new law also gives states much greater freedom to design their own welfare systems as they see fit, thereby greatly reducing federal influence over welfare.

The new welfare law is highly controversial. Critics argue that it will throw many needy families to the wolves when their benefits run out. Supporters argue that it will give them "a hand up, instead of a handout"—and will save the taxpayers money to boot.

Are the criticisms of the new welfare law justified? Or would criticism be more aptly directed at the old system? As we shall see in this chapter, the debate over welfare reform is a classic example of the trade-off between equality and efficiency that we introduced in Chapter 1. Some liberals argue that society should adopt extremely generous programs to reduce discrimination, increase income equality, or eradicate poverty regardless of the potential side effects these policies might have. Some conservatives, on the other hand, seem so obsessed with these undesirable side effects, whether real or imagined, that they ignore the benefits of redistribution or of antidiscrimination programs.

Economists prefer to avoid absolutes and to think in terms of trade-offs: To reap gains on one front, society often must make sacrifices on another. A policy is not necessarily ill conceived simply because it has an undesirable effect on income

*The Trade-off between Efficiency and Equality*

inequality, *if* it makes a sufficiently important contribution to efficiency. But policies with very bad distributive consequences may deserve to be rejected, even if they would raise the nation's total output.

Admitting that there is a trade-off between equality and efficiency, that welfare spending may alleviate poverty but reduce economic efficiency, may not be the best way to win votes. But it does face the facts. And in that way, it helps us make the inherently political decisions about what should be done. If we are to understand these complex issues, a good place to start is, as always, with the facts.

## ■ THE FACTS: POVERTY

In 1962, social critic Michael Harrington published a little book called *The Other America*, which had a profound effect on American society. Harrington's "other Americans" were the poor who lived in the land of plenty. Ill-clothed in the richest country on earth, inadequately nourished in a nation where obesity was a problem, infirm in a country with some of the world's highest health standards, these people lived an almost unknown existence in their dilapidated hovels, according to Harrington. To make matters worse, this deprivation often condemned the children of the "other Americans" to repeat the lives of their parents. There was, Harrington argued, a "cycle of poverty" that could be broken only by government action.

The work of Harrington and others touched the hearts of many Americans who, it seemed, really had no idea of the abominable living conditions of some others in the country. Within a few years, the growing outrage over the plight of the poor had crystallized into a "War on Poverty," which President Lyndon Johnson declared in 1964.

## COUNTING THE POOR: THE POVERTY LINE

The **poverty line** is an amount of income below which a family is considered "poor."

As part of this program, the government adopted an official definition of poverty: The poor were those families with incomes below $3,000 in 1964. This dividing line between the poor and nonpoor was called the **poverty line**, and a goal was established: to get all Americans above the poverty line by the nation's bicentennial in 1976. (The goal was not met.) The poverty line was subsequently modified to account for differences in family size and other considerations, and it is now also adjusted each year to reflect changes in the cost of living. In 1997, the poverty line for a family of four was $16,400, and 13.3 percent of all Americans remained in poverty by official definitions.

Who are the poor? Relative to their proportions in the overall population, they are more likely to be black than white and female than male. They are less educated and in poorer health than the population as a whole. About 40 percent of the poor are children.

America made substantial progress toward eliminating poverty in the decade from 1963 to 1973; the percentage of people living below the poverty line dropped from 20 percent to 11 percent (see the red line in Figure 19–1). But thereafter, slower economic growth and cutbacks in social welfare programs reversed the trend. By 1983, the poverty rate was back to what it had been in the 1960s. Since then, the poverty rate has increased and decreased with no clear trend, but it is still well above its 1970s low.

The rise in poverty since the 1970s worries many people, especially because poverty nowadays seems often to be associated with homelessness, illegitimacy, drug

| FIGURE 19–1 | **Progress in the War on Poverty** |

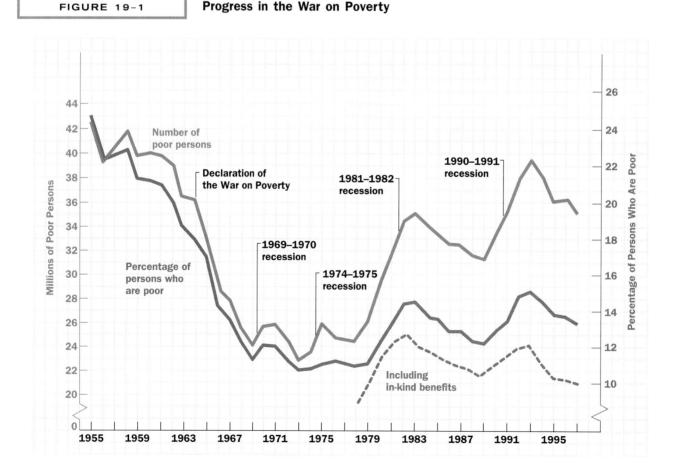

SOURCE: For 1959–1997, U.S. Bureau of the Census. For 1955–1958, estimates kindly provided by Gordon M. Fisher.

---

● **THE POOREST PLACE IN AMERICA**

---

The town has no public parks or swimming pools, no movie theaters, no shopping malls, not even a McDonald's or a Wal-Mart. In fact, business in Lake Providence, Louisiana, is so bad that even the pawnshop has shut down. "The only recreation we have," says a resident, "is poor people's fun: drinking, drugs, fighting, and sex." Restless teenagers mill around narrow streets lined with burned-out houses and dilapidated trailer parks. . . . If there is a poorer place in America, the Census Bureau cannot find it. . . .

The 1990 census found that the median annual household income in Block Numbering Area 9903, which covers the southern two-thirds of Lake Providence and three-quarters of its population, was only $6,536—less than half the official poverty level of $14,764 for a family of four and the lowest in the United States. Two years later, a Children's Defense Fund study found that in East Carroll Parish, where Lake Providence is located, 70.1 percent of children younger than 18, or 2,409, were living in poverty, the highest rate in the nation—and this amid staggeringly high rates of infant mortality, teenage pregnancy, and drug use.

Meanwhile, jobs are scarce, low paying, and seasonal. For most of the year, hundreds of families subsist on welfare: A single mother with one child gets $123 a month. . . . For many the only available work is backbreaking minimum-wage jobs in the nearby cotton fields. . . .

Inevitably, almost everyone who can escape from Lake Providence does so. "I'd rather shoot myself than stay here. It would be a wasted life," says Karva Henderson, who graduated from Lake Providence's High School in June. She plans to go to college and wants never to return.

SOURCE: Jack E. White, "The Poorest Place in America," *Time*, August 15, 1994, pp. 35–36.

---

dependency, and ill health—all symptoms of a growing underclass whose lives are no better, and are in many respects worse, than the people Harrington wrote about in 1962.

However, some critics argue that the official data badly overstate the number of poor persons. Some even go so far as to claim that poverty would be considered a thing of the past if the official definition (based on cash income) were amended to include the many goods that the poor receive in kind: public education, public housing, health care, food, and the like.

These criticisms prompted the Census Bureau to develop several experimental measures of poverty that include the value of goods given in kind. If these new measures are accepted as valid, fewer people are classified as poor, but the basic patterns of recent years are the same: Poverty has gone up and down since the late 1970s with no clear trend. (See the broken red line in Figure 19–1.)

### ABSOLUTE VERSUS RELATIVE POVERTY

This debate raises a fundamental question: How do we define "the poor"? Continuing economic growth will eventually pull almost everyone above any arbitrarily established poverty line. Does this event mark the end of poverty? Some would say yes. But others would insist that the biblical injunction is right: "The poor ye have always with you" (Deuteronomy 15:11).

We can define poverty two ways. The more optimistic definition uses an *absolute concept of poverty:* If you fall short of a certain minimum standard of living, you are poor; once you pass this standard, you are no longer poor. The second definition relies on a *relative concept of poverty:* The poor are those who fall too far behind the average income.

Each definition has its pros and cons. The basic problem with the absolute poverty concept is that it is arbitrary. Who sets the line? Most of the people of Bangladesh would be delighted to live a bit below the U.S. poverty line and would consider themselves quite prosperous. Similarly, the standard of living that we now call "poor" would probably not have been considered so in America in 1900, and certainly not in Europe during the Middle Ages. Different times and different places apparently call for different poverty lines.

Because the concept of poverty seems to be culturally, not physiologically, determined, it must be a relative concept. For example, the European Union places the poverty line at one-half the national average income. Under this definition, the poverty line automatically rises as a nation grows richer.

Once we move from an absolute to a relative concept of poverty, any sharp distinction between the poor and the nonpoor starts to evaporate. Instead, we begin to think of a parade of people from the poorest soul to the richest billionaire. The "poverty problem" then becomes an issue of disparities in income that are "too large." At least in part, the poor are so poor because the rich are so rich. If we follow this line of thought far enough, we are led away from the narrow problem of *poverty* toward the broader problem of *income inequality.*

## ■ THE FACTS: INEQUALITY

Nothing in the market mechanism guarantees equality of incomes. On the contrary, the market system tends to breed inequality, because the basic source of its great efficiency is its system of rewards and penalties. The market is generous to those who succeed in operating efficient enterprises that respond to consumer demands; it ruthlessly penalizes those who are unable or unwilling to satisfy consumer demands efficiently.

Its financial punishment of those who try and fail can be particularly severe. At times the market even brings down the great and powerful. Robert Morris, once perhaps the wealthiest resident of the American colonies, ended up in a debtors prison. In more recent decades, the financial travails of the Hunt brothers of Texas and Donald Trump of New York, once among America's richest people, have been highly publicized.

Most people have a pretty good idea that the gulf between the rich and the poor is wide. But few have any concept of where they stand in the income distribution. For example, during the 1995 congressional debate over cutting taxes for "the middle class," one member of Congress with an annual income in excess of $150,000 declared himself a member of the "middle class," if not indeed of the "lower-middle class"!

Table 19–1 offers some statistics on the 1997 income distribution in the United States. But before looking at them, try the following experiment. First, write down what you think your family's before-tax income was in 1997. (If you do not know, take a guess.) Next, try to guess what percentage of American families had incomes *lower* than this. Finally, if we divide America into three broad income classes—rich, middle class, and poor—to which group do you think your family belongs?

Now that you have written down answers to these three questions, look at the income distribution data for 1997 in Table 19–1. If you are like most college students, these figures may surprise you. First, if we adopt the tentative definition that the lowest 20 percent are the "poor," the highest 20 percent are the "rich," and the middle 60 percent are the "middle class," many fewer of you belong to the celebrated "middle class" than thought they did. In fact, the cut-off point that defined membership in the "rich" class in 1997 was only about $82,000 before taxes, an income level exceeded by the parents of many college students. (Your parents may be shocked to learn that they are rich!)

Next, use Table 19–1 to estimate the fraction of U.S. families that have incomes lower than your family's. (The caption has instructions to help you do this.) Most students who come from households of moderate prosperity feel instinctively that they stand somewhere near the middle of the income distribution; so they estimate about half, or perhaps a little more. In fact, the median income among American families in 1997 was only about $44,500.

## Distribution of Family Income in the United States in 1997

TABLE 19-1

| Income Range | All Families in This Range | Families in This and Lower Ranges |
|---|---|---|
| Less than $5,000 | 2.7% | 2.7% |
| $5,000 to $9,999 | 4.1 | 6.8 |
| $10,000 to $14,999 | 5.7 | 12.5 |
| $15,000 to $24,999 | 13.1 | 25.6 |
| $25,000 to $34,999 | 12.8 | 38.4 |
| $35,000 to $49,999 | 17.4 | 55.8 |
| $50,000 to $74,999 | 21.3 | 77.1 |
| $75,000 to $99,999 | 11.1 | 88.2 |
| $100,000 or more | 11.8 | 100.0 |

NOTE: If your family's income falls close to one of the end points of the ranges indicated here, you can approximate the fraction of families with income *lower* than yours by just looking at the last column. If your family's income falls within one of the ranges, you can interpolate the answer. Example: Your family's income was $60,000. This is 40 percent of the way from $50,000 to $75,000, so your family was richer than roughly 0.40 × 21.3 percent = 8.5 percent of the families in this class. Adding this to the percentage of families in lower classes (55.8 percent in this case) gives the answer—about 64.3 percent of all families earned less than yours.

SOURCE: U.S Bureau of the Census.

This exercise has perhaps brought us down to earth. America is not nearly as rich as Madison Avenue would like us to believe. Let us now look past the average level of income and see how the pie is divided. Table 19–2 shows the shares of income accruing to each fifth of the population in 1997, and several earlier years. In a perfectly equal society, all the numbers in this table would be "20 percent," because each fifth of the population would receive one-fifth of the income. In fact, as the table shows, this is far from true. In 1997, for example, the poorest fifth of all households had under 4 percent (3.6%) of the total income, whereas the richest fifth had 49.4 percent, almost 14 times as much.

## DEPICTING INCOME DISTRIBUTIONS: THE LORENZ CURVE

Statisticians and economists use a convenient tool to portray data graphically like those in Table 19–2. The device, called a *Lorenz curve*, appears in Figure 19–2. To construct a Lorenz curve, we first draw a square whose vertical and horizontal dimensions both represent 100 percent. Then we record the percentage of households (or persons) on the horizontal axis and the percentage of income that

### Income Shares in Selected Years

TABLE 19-2

| Income Group | 1997 | 1990 | 1980 | 1970 |
|---|---|---|---|---|
| Lowest fifth | 3.6 | 3.9 | 4.3 | 4.1 |
| Second fifth | 8.9 | 9.6 | 10.3 | 10.8 |
| Middle fifth | 15.0 | 15.9 | 16.9 | 17.4 |
| Fourth fifth | 23.2 | 24.0 | 24.9 | 24.5 |
| Highest fifth | 49.4 | 46.6 | 43.7 | 43.3 |

SOURCE: U.S Bureau of the Census.

FIGURE 19-2

**A Lorenz Curve for the
United States**

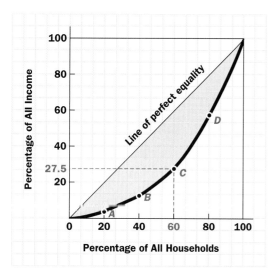

**Percentage of All Income** (vertical axis): 100, 80, 60, 40, 27.5, 20

**Percentage of All Households** (horizontal axis): 0, 20, 40, 60, 80, 100

Line of perfect equality

Points: A, B, C, D

these households (or persons) receive on the vertical axis, using all the data that we have. For example, point *C* in Figure 19–2 depicts the fact (known from Table 19–2) that in 1997, the bottom 60 percent (the three lowest fifths) of American families received 27.5 percent of the total income. Similarly, points *A*, *B*, and *D* represent the other information contained in Table 19–2. We can list four important properties of a Lorenz curve:

- It begins at the origin because zero families naturally have zero income.
- It always ends at the upper-right corner of the square because 100 percent of the nation's families must receive all of the nation's income.
- If income were distributed equally, the Lorenz curve would be a straight line connecting these two points (the thin, solid line in Figure 19–2). This is because, with everybody equal, the bottom 20 percent of the families would receive 20 percent of the income, the bottom 40 percent would receive 40 percent, and so on.
- In a real economy, with significant income differences, the Lorenz curve will "sag" downward from this line of perfect equality. It is easy to see why this is so. If there is any inequality at all, the poorest 20 percent of families must get less than 20 percent of the income. This corresponds to a point below the equality line, such as point *A*. Similarly, the bottom 40 percent of families must receive less than 40 percent of the income (point *B*), and so on.

By itself, the Lorenz curve tells us little. To interpret it, we must know what it looked like in earlier years or what it looks like in other countries. The historical data in Table 19–2 on the previous page show that:

The distribution of income in the United States has grown substantially more unequal since about 1980.

"The poor are getting poorer, but with the rich getting richer it all averages out in the long run."

Specifically, the share of the poorest fifth is now the lowest, and the share of the richest fifth is now the highest since the government began collecting data in 1947. America is not a very class-conscious society, and for years only specialists paid much attention to data like those in Table 19–2. But income inequality has recently become a big social issue, as more and more American families sense that they are losing ground to the people at the top. There is particular, and well-justified, concern that the real earnings of wage earners below the middle have fallen dramatically in the past two decades.

Comparing the United States with other countries is much harder because no two nations use precisely the same definition of income distribution. The Luxembourg Income Study is the leading international effort to produce comparable data for many countries. In its latest comparison of the income distributions of 19 (mostly European) countries, Finland and Austria had the most equal income distributions, with Sweden, Norway, and Belgium close behind. The United States stood out as having the most inequality. Thus, it appears that:

**The United States has rather more income inequality than most other industrialized countries.**

## ■ SOME REASONS FOR UNEQUAL INCOMES

Let us now formulate a list of the *causes* of income inequality. Here are some that come to mind.

**DIFFERENCES IN ABILITY** Everyone knows that people have different capabilities. Some can run faster, ski better, calculate figures more quickly, type more accurately, and so on. Hence, it should not be surprising that some people are more adept at earning income. Precisely what sort of ability is relevant to earning income is a matter of intense debate among economists, sociologists, and psychologists. The talents that make for success in school seem to have some effect, but hardly an overwhelming one. The same is true of innate intelligence—"IQ" (see the accompanying box, "How Important Is the Bell Curve?"). It is clear that some types of inventiveness are richly rewarded by the market, as is that elusive characteristic called "entrepreneurial ability." Also, it is obvious that poor health often impairs earning ability.

**DIFFERENCES IN INTENSITY OF WORK** Some people work longer hours than others, or labor more intensely when they are on the job, leading to income differences that are largely voluntary.

**RISK TAKING** Most people who acquire large sums of money do so by taking risks—by investing their money in the stock market, in a small start-up company, or in some other uncertain venture. Those who gamble and succeed become wealthy. Those who try and fail go broke. Most others prefer not to take such chances and end up somewhere in between. This is another way in which income differences arise voluntarily.

**COMPENSATING WAGE DIFFERENTIALS** Some jobs are more arduous than others, or more dangerous, or more unpleasant for other reasons. To induce people to take these jobs, some sort of financial incentive normally must be offered. For example, factory workers who work the night shift normally receive higher wages than those who work during the day.

**SCHOOLING AND OTHER TYPES OF TRAINING** Chapter 18 analyzed schooling and other types of training as "investments in human capital." The term refers to the idea that workers can sacrifice *current* income in order to improve their skills so that their *future* incomes will be higher. When this is done, income differentials naturally rise. Although it is generally agreed that differences in schooling are an important cause of income differentials, this particular cause has both voluntary and involuntary aspects. Young men or women who *choose* not to go to college have made

---

### HOW IMPORTANT IS THE BELL CURVE?

In 1994, social critic Charles Murray and the late Richard Herrnstein, a psychologist, created a furor with a book claiming that genetically inherited intelligence is an overwhelmingly important determinant of economic success. The book's title, *The Bell Curve*, was a reference to the shape of the distribution of observed test scores on conventional IQ tests (see chart), which show most people clustered near the middle of the distribution, with small minorities on either end.

Critics of government antipoverty programs were quickly attracted to the book's central message: that the poor are poor in large measure because they are not very smart. Among the most stunning claims made by Herrnstein and Murray was that much of the observed economic gap between blacks and whites could be attributed to the fact that blacks' IQs were, on average, lower than those of whites.

Although *The Bell Curve* received a blitz of media attention, social scientists generally ignored it or gave the analysis low marks. No one seriously doubts that intelligence contributes to economic success, nor that genetics has some bearing on intelligence. But the scientific evidence on the strength of each link is in great dispute. Many experts on IQ, for example, argue that environmental factors may be more important than genetics in determining intelligence and that "true" intelligence may differ from measured IQ. Furthermore, few if any economists believe that cognitive ability is the main ingredient in economic success.

The bottom line, according to most scholars, is that the black-white IQ gap does not go very far in explaining racial income inequalities. Nor can we be certain that much of the measured IQ gap is biologically, rather than culturally, determined.

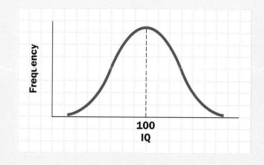

---

voluntary decisions that affect their incomes. But many never get the choice: Their parents simply cannot afford to send them. For them, the resulting income differential is not voluntary.

**WORK EXPERIENCE** It is well-known to most people and well-documented by scholarly research that more experienced workers earn higher wages.

**INHERITED WEALTH** Not all income is derived from work. Some is the return on invested wealth, and part of this wealth is inherited. Although this cause of inequality applies to few people, many of America's super-rich got that way through inheritance. And financial wealth is not the only type of capital that can be inherited; so can human capital. In part this happens naturally through genetics: High-ability parents tend to have high-ability children, although the link is an imperfect one. But it also happens partly for economic reasons: Well-to-do parents send their children to the best schools, thereby transforming their own *financial* wealth into *human* wealth for their children. This type of inheritance may be much more important than the financial type.

**LUCK** No observer of our society can fail to notice the role that chance plays. Some of the rich and some of the poor got there largely by good or bad fortune. A farmer digs for water, but strikes oil instead. A construction worker is unemployed for a whole year because of a recession that he had no part in creating. Two skilled programmers work hard, but only one develops the "killer app" that makes him rich. The list could go on and on. Many large income differentials arise purely by chance.

## THE FACTS: DISCRIMINATION

Some of the factors we have just listed lead to income differentials that are widely accepted as "just." For example, most people believe it is fair for people who work harder to receive higher incomes. Other factors on our list ignite heated debates. For example, some people view income differentials that arise purely by chance as perfectly acceptable. Others find these same differentials intolerable. However, almost no one is willing to condone income inequalities that arise from discrimination.

The facts about discrimination are not easy to come by. **Economic discrimination** occurs when equivalent factors of production receive different payments for equal contributions to output. But this definition is hard to apply in practice because we cannot always tell when two factors of production are "equivalent."

Few people would call it "discrimination" if a woman with only a high school diploma receives a lower salary than a man with a college degree. Even if a man and a woman have the same education, the man may have 10 more years of work experience than the woman. If they receive different wages for this reason, is that discriminatory?

In principle, we should compare men and women whose *productivities* are equal. If women receive lower wages than men who do the same work, we would then attribute the difference to discrimination. But discrimination normally takes much more subtle forms than paying unequal wages for equal work. For instance, employers can simply relegate women to inferior jobs, thus justifying lower salaries.

One clearly *incorrect* way to measure discrimination is to compare the different groups' typical incomes. Table 19–3 displays such data for white men, white women, black men, and black women in 1997. Virtually everyone agrees that the amount of discrimination is less than these differentials suggest, but far greater than zero. Precisely how much is a topic of continuing economic research. Several studies suggest that about half of the observed wage differential between black and white men, and at least half of the differential between white women and white men, arises from discrimination in the labor market (though more might be due to discrimination in education, and so on). Other studies have reached somewhat different conclusions. Although no one denies the existence of discrimination, its quantitative importance is a matter of ongoing controversy and research.

**Economic discrimination** occurs when equivalent factors of production receive different payments for equal contributions to output.

## ■ THE ECONOMIC THEORY OF DISCRIMINATION[1]

Let us see what economic theory tells us about discrimination. In particular, consider the following two questions:

1. Must *prejudice*, which we define as arising when one group dislikes associating with another group, lead to *discrimination* (unequal pay for equal work)?

2. Do "natural" economic forces tend either to erode or to exacerbate discrimination over time?

**Median Incomes in 1997**                    TABLE 19-3

| Population Group | Median Income | Percentage of White Male Income |
|---|---|---|
| White males | $26,115 | 100 |
| Black males | 18,096 | 69 |
| White females | 13,792 | 53 |
| Black females | 13,048 | 50 |

NOTE: For persons 15 years old and older.
SOURCE: U.S. Bureau of the Census.

[1] This section may be omitted in shorter courses.

As we shall see now, the analysis we have provided in previous chapters sheds light on both these issues.

## DISCRIMINATION BY EMPLOYERS

Most attention seems to focus on discrimination by employers, so let us start there. What happens if, for example, some firms refuse to hire blacks? Figure 19–3 will help us find the answer. Panel (a) pertains to firms that discriminate; panel (b) pertains to firms that do not. There are supply and demand curves for labor in each market, based on the analysis of Chapter 18. We suppose the two demand curves to be identical.

| FIGURE 19–3 | **Wage Discrimination** |

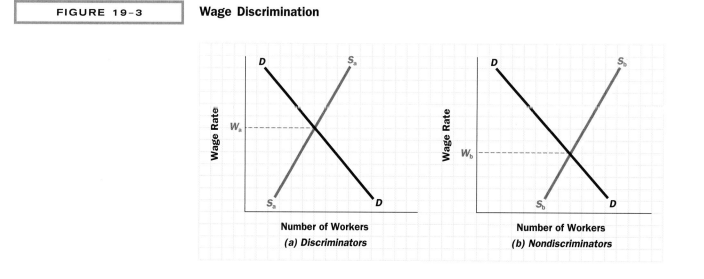

(a) Discriminators  (b) Nondiscriminators

However, the supply curve in market (b) must be farther to the right than the supply curve in market (a) because both whites *and* blacks can work in market (b), whereas only whites can work in market (a). The result is that wages will be lower in market (b) than in market (a). Because all the blacks are forced into market (b), we conclude that employers discriminate against them.

But now consider the situation from the *employers'* point of view. Firms in market (a) of Figure 19–3 pay more for labor ($W_a$ is greater than $W_b$), so they pay for the privilege of discriminating. The nondiscriminatory firms in market (b) have a cost advantage. As we learned in earlier chapters, in the face of effective competition, these nondiscriminatory firms will tend to capture more and more customers. The discriminators will gradually be driven out of business. If, on the other hand, many of the firms in market (a) have protected monopolies, they will be able to remain in business. But they will pay for the privilege of discriminating by earning lower monopoly profits than they otherwise could (because they pay higher wages than they need to).

## DISCRIMINATION BY FELLOW WORKERS

Thus, competitive forces tend to reduce discrimination over time *if* employers are the source of discrimination. Such optimistic conclusions do not follow, however, if workers, rather than employers, are prejudiced. Consider what happens, for example, if men object to having women as their supervisors. If male workers do not give their full cooperation, female supervisors will be less effective than male supervisors and hence will earn lower wages. Here prejudice does lead to discrimination. Furthermore, in this case, firms that put women into supervisory positions will be at a competitive disadvantage relative to firms that do not. So market forces will not erode discrimination.

## ● ARE WOMEN BETTER WORKERS?

Economist Audrey Freedman argues that female employees can be a better bargain than male employees, even though only women request pregnancy leaves and it is mainly women who miss workdays for child-care reasons.

It is undeniable . . . that women, not men, take pregnancy leaves. It is also undeniable that women are the primary nurturers in a family. They are the most likely to be responsible for the care and support of children, as well as their elderly parents. If we stop there . . . women in business are more costly than men.

But the built-in bias of that analysis is the failure to account for far more costly drains on corporate productivity from behavior that is more characteristic of men than of women.

For example, men are more likely to be heavy users of alcohol. This gender-related habit causes businesses to suffer excessive medical costs, serious performance losses, and productivity drains. Yet, the male-dominated corporate hierarchy most often chooses to ignore these "good old boy" habits.

Drug abuse among the fast-movers of Wall Street seems to be understood as a normal response to the pressures of taking risks with other people's money. The consequences in loss of judgment are tolerated. They are not calculated as a male-related cost of business.

Apart from performance problems at high levels, alcohol and drug abuse cause costly accidents. We never think of them, however, as risks primarily associated with male employees. In addition, in our culture, lawlessness and violence are found far more often among men than women. The statistics on criminals and prison population are obvious, yet we seem to be unable to recognize these as primarily male behaviors.

A top executive of a major airline once commented to me that his company's greatest problem is machismo in the cockpit—pilots and copilots fighting over the controls. There is an obvious solution: Hire pilots from that half of the population that is less susceptible to the attacks of rage that afflict macho males.

SOURCE: Audrey Freedman, "Those Costly 'Good Old Boys,'" *The New York Times,* July 12, 1989, p. A23. Copyright, 1989 by the New York Times Company. Reprinted by permission.

## STATISTICAL DISCRIMINATION

A final type of discrimination, called **statistical discrimination,** may be the most stubborn of all and can exist even when there is no prejudice. Here is an important example. It is, of course, a biological fact that only women can give birth. It is also a fact that most working women who have babies leave their jobs for a while to care for their newborns. Employers know this. What they cannot know, however, is *which* women of child-bearing age will leave the labor force for this reason.

**Statistical discrimination** is said to occur when the productivity of a particular worker is estimated to be low just because that worker belongs to a particular group (such as women).

Suppose three candidates apply for a job that requires a long-term commitment. Susan plans to quit after a few years to raise a family. Jane does not plan to have any children. Jack is a man. If he knew all the facts, the employer might not want Susan, but would be equally happy with Jane or Jack. But the employer cannot differentiate between Susan and Jane. He therefore presumes that either one, being a young woman, is more likely than Jack to quit to raise a family. So he hires Jack, even though Jane is just as good a prospect. Jane is discriminated against.

Lest it be thought that this example actually justifies discrimination against women on economic grounds, it should be noted that most women return to work within six months after childbirth. Furthermore, women typically have less absenteeism and job turnover for nonpregnancy health reasons than men do. The accompanying box, "Are Women Better Workers?" argues that employers often fail to take these other sex-related differences into account and thus mistakenly favor men.

### THE ROLES OF THE MARKET AND THE GOVERNMENT

In terms of the two questions with which we began this section, we conclude that different types of *discrimination* lead to different answers. Prejudice will often, but not always, lead to economic discrimination, and discrimination may occur even in the absence of prejudice. Finally, the forces of competition tend to erode some, but not all, of the inequities caused by discrimination.

However, the victims of discrimination are not the only losers. Society also loses whenever discriminatory practices impair economic efficiency. Hence, most observers believe that we should not rely on market forces *alone* to combat discrimination. The government has a clear role to play.

## ■ THE OPTIMAL AMOUNT OF INEQUALITY

We have seen that substantial income inequality exists in America, and we have noted some reasons for it. Let us now ask a question that is loaded with value judgments, but to which economic analysis can contribute nonetheless: *How much inequality is the ideal amount?* We shall not, of course, be able to answer this question definitively. Rather, our objective is to see the type of analysis that is relevant. We begin in a simple setting in which we can easily obtain the answer. Then we shall see how the real world differs from this simple model.

Consider a society in which two people, Smith and Jones, are to divide $100 between them. The objective is to maximize *total utility*. Suppose Smith and Jones are alike in their ability to enjoy money; technically, we say that their *marginal utility* schedules are identical.[2] This identical marginal utility schedule is depicted in Figure 19–4. We will now prove the following result: *The optimal distribution of income is to give $50 to Smith and $50 to Jones,* which is represented by point E in Figure 19–4.

We prove it by showing that, if the income distribution is unequal, we can improve things by moving closer to equality. So suppose that Smith has $75 (point S in the figure) and Jones has $25 (point J). Then we can see that Smith's *marginal utility* (which is s) is *less* than Jones's (which is j). This is a simple consequence of the law of diminishing marginal utility: Because Smith has more money, his marginal utility of money is lower.

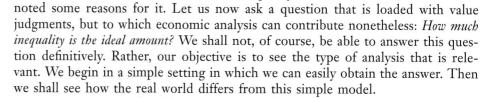

**FIGURE 19–4**

**The Optimal Distribution of Income**

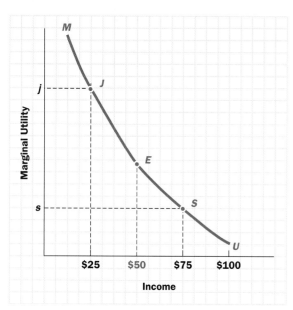

_____

[2] If you need to refresh your memory about marginal utility, see Chapter 6, especially pages 96–98.

"There is a perfect example of what is wrong with this country today."

"There is a perfect example of what is wrong with this country today."

If we take $1 away from Smith, he *loses* the low marginal utility, *s*, that a dollar gives him. When we transfer that dollar to Jones, he *gains* the high marginal utility, *j*, that a dollar gives him. On balance, society's total utility rises by *j* − *s* because Jones's gain exceeds Smith's loss. Therefore, a distribution with Smith getting only $74 is better than one in which he gets $75. Because the same argument shows that a $73/$27 distribution is better than $74/$26, and so on, we have proven our result: a $50/$50 distribution—point *E*—is best.

Now in this example there is nothing special about the fact that we assumed only two people or that exactly $100 was available. Any number of people and dollars would do as well. What really *is* crucial is our assumption that the same amount of money would be available no matter how we chose to distribute it. Thus, we have proved the following general result:

> To maximize total utility, the best way to distribute any *fixed* amount of money among people with identical marginal utility schedules is to divide it equally.

## ■ THE TRADE-OFF BETWEEN EQUALITY AND EFFICIENCY

As soon as we seek to apply this analysis to the real world, two major difficulties arise. First, people have different marginal utility schedules. Thus, *some* inequality can probably be justified. The second problem is much more formidable.

> The total amount of income in society is *not* independent of how we try to distribute it.

To see why, consider an extreme example. Ask yourself what would happen if we tried to achieve perfect equality by putting a 100 percent income tax on all workers and then dividing the tax receipts equally among the population. No one would have any incentive to work, to invest, to take risks, or to do anything else to earn money, because the rewards for all such activities would disappear. The nation's total production would fall drastically. Although the example is extreme, the principle is universal; indeed, it is the basic idea behind supply-side economics.

**THE TRADE-OFF**  Policies that redistribute income reduce the rewards of high-income earners while raising the rewards of low-income earners. Hence, they reduce the incentive to earn high income. This gives rise to a trade-off that is one of the most fundamental in all of economics, and one of our *Ideas for Beyond the Final Exam.*

When we take measures to increase the amount of economic equality, we normally reduce economic efficiency—that is, we reduce society's total output. In trying to divide the pie more equally, we may inadvertently reduce its size.

*The Trade-off between Equality and Efficiency*

Because of this trade-off, equal incomes are not optimal in practice. On the contrary:

The optimal income distribution will always involve *some* inequality.

But this stark fact does not mean that attempts to reduce inequality are misguided. We should learn two things from this analysis:

1. There are better and worse ways to promote equality. In pursuing further income equality (or fighting poverty), we should seek policies that do the least possible harm to incentives.

2. Equality is bought at a price. Thus, like any commodity, we must rationally decide how much to "purchase." We will probably want to spend some of our potential income on equality, but certainly not all of it.

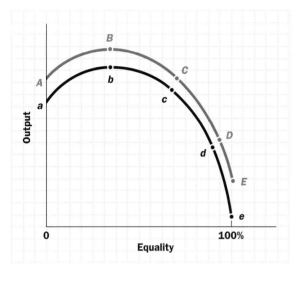

**FIGURE 19-5**

**The Trade-off between Equality and Efficiency**

Figure 19–5 illustrates both of these lessons. The curve *abcde* represents possible combinations of total output and income equality that are obtainable under the present system of taxes and transfers. If, for example, point *c* is the current position of the economy, raising taxes on the rich to finance more transfers to the poor, which is one of the things President Clinton did in 1993, might move us downward to the right toward point *d*. Equality then increases, but the nation's output falls as the rich react to higher marginal tax rates by producing less. Similarly, reducing the tax rate on capital gains, as the Republican Congress did in 1997, might move us upward to the left toward point *b*. Notice that, to the left of point *b*, output falls as inequality rises. Here there is no trade-off, perhaps because very poorly paid workers are less productive due to inadequate investment in human capital, poor nutrition, or just a general sense of disaffection.

The curve *ABCDE* represents possible combinations of output and equality under some new, more efficient redistributive policy. It is more efficient in the sense that for any desired level of equality, we can get more output with the policy represented by *ABCDE* than with the policy represented by *abcde*. The movements from points *C* and *c* toward points *D* and *d* represent two alternative policies for equalizing income distribution. The policy that leads to *D* is better because it is more efficient.

The first lesson is obvious: We should stick to the higher of the two curves. If we find ourselves at any point on curve *abcde*, we can always improve things by moving up to the corresponding point on curve *ABCDE*, that is, by changing policies. By picking the most efficient redistributive policy, we can have more equality *and* more output. In the rest of this chapter, we discuss alternative policies and try to indicate which ones damage incentives least.

The second lesson is that neither point *B* nor point *E* would normally be society's optimal choice. At point *B*, we are seeking the highest possible output with utter disregard for whatever inequality might accompany it. At point *E*, we are forcing complete equality, even if work incentives vanish and a minuscule total output is the result.

It is astonishing how much confusion is caused by a failure to understand these two lessons. Proponents of greater equality often feel obliged to deny that the programs they advocate will hurt incentives at all. Sometimes these vehement denials are so patently unrealistic that they undermine the very case the egalitarians are trying to make. Conservatives who oppose such policies also undercut the strength of their case by making outlandish claims about the efficiency losses from redistribution.

Neither side, it seems, is willing to acknowledge the fundamental trade-off between equality and efficiency depicted in Figure 19–5. As a result, the debate generates more heat than light. Because these debates will likely continue for the rest of your lives, we hope that some understanding of this trade-off stays with you well *Beyond the Final Exam.*

But merely understanding the trade-off will not tell you what to do. Look at Figure 19–5. We know that the optimal amount of equality lies between points *B* and *E*, but we do not know what it actually is. Is it more like point *D*, with greater equality and less output than we now have? Or is it more like a movement back toward point *B*? Everyone will have a different answer to this question, because it is basically one of value judgments. Just how much is more equality worth to you?

Arthur Okun, onetime chairman of the Council of Economic Advisers, put the issue graphically. Imagine that money is liquid, and that you have a bucket to use to transport money from the rich to the poor. But the bucket leaks. (These are the efficiency losses from redistribution.) As you move the money, some gets lost. Will you use the bucket if only 1 cent is lost for each $1 you move? Probably everyone would say yes. But what if each $1 taken from the rich results in only 10 cents for the poor? Only the most extreme egalitarians will still say yes. Now try the hard questions. What if 20 to 40 cents is lost for each $1 that you move? If you can answer questions like these, you can decide how far down the hill from point *B* you think society should travel, for you will have expressed your value judgments in quantitative terms.

## ■ POLICIES TO COMBAT POVERTY

Let us take it for granted that the nation has a commitment to reduce poverty. What policies can promote this goal? Which of these does the least harm to incentives, and hence is most efficient?

### EDUCATION AS A WAY OUT

Education is often advertised as one of the principal ways to escape from poverty. No doubt many people have used this route successfully, and still do.[3]

However, delivering quality education to poor children is no simple matter. Many of them, especially in the inner cities, are ill-equipped to learn and attend schools that are ill-equipped to teach. Despite some gratifying progress in recent years, dropout rates remain dismayingly high. An astonishing number of youths leave the public school system without even acquiring basic literacy. All of these problems are familiar; none is easy to solve.

In truth, our educational system must serve many goals, and the alleviation of poverty is not the major one. If it were, we would almost certainly spend more money on preschool and inner-city kids and less on college education than we do today. Furthermore, education is not a particularly effective way to lift *adults* out of poverty. Its effects are delayed for a generation or more.

### THE WELFARE DEBATE

By contrast, a variety of programs collectively known as "welfare" are specifically designed to alleviate poverty, meant to help adults as well as children, and intended to have quick effects. As mentioned at the start of this chapter, the best known and most heavily criticized of these programs used to be *Aid to Families with Dependent Children*. AFDC provided direct cash grants to families that had children but no breadwinner, generally because the father was absent or unknown and the mother could not or did not work.

AFDC was attacked as a classic example of an inefficient redistributive program. Why? One major reason was that it provided no incentive for these mothers to earn income. Once monthly earnings passed a few hundred dollars, welfare payments

---

[3] The role of education as a determinant of income was considered at length in the previous chapter.

were reduced by $1 for each $1 that the family earned as wages. Thus, if a member of the family got a job, the family was subjected to a 100 percent marginal tax rate! Little wonder, then, that many welfare recipients did not look very hard for work.

**TEMPORARY ASSISTANCE TO NEEDY FAMILIES (TANF)**    The 1996 welfare reform tackled the work-incentive problem by using a stick rather than a carrot. Instead of reducing the marginal tax rate on earnings, the new system—*Temporary Assistance to Needy Families*, or *TANF*—compels welfare recipients to work by cutting off their benefits after two years. Effective marginal tax rates under TANF vary tremendously both by income level and by state, because the 50 states have a great deal of flexibility in designing their own programs.

It is far too early to tell how successful this new approach will be. Early results have been favorable, but the years since welfare reform have seen a booming economy with plentiful jobs. Critics worry about how well the TANF program will work when jobs are less easy to find.

**FOOD STAMPS**    Another welfare program that burgeoned in the 1970s and was cut back several times in the 1980s and 1990s is *food stamps*, under which poor families can buy stamps which they can exchange for food. The dollar amount of the stamps they receive, and how much they pay for them, depends on the family's income. The poorer the family, the less it must pay for the stamps. The program made headlines in 1993 when newspapers reported that a stunning 10 percent of all Americans were receiving food stamps. That percentage has fallen in the economic boom since the early 1990s, but the program was nonetheless cut back in 1996 to save money.

**TRANSFERS IN KIND**    In addition to TANF and food stamps, the government provides many poor people with a number of important goods and services, either at no charge or at prices that are well below market levels. Medical care under the Medicaid program and subsidized public housing are two notable examples.[4] These programs significantly enhance the living standards of the poor. However, most of them offer benefits that decline as family income rises. Taken as a whole, all the antipoverty programs put some poor families in a position where they are taxed extremely heavily if their earnings rise. When this occurs, the incentive not to work becomes quite powerful.

## WELFARE REFORM AND THE TRADE-OFF

The debate over welfare reform is a good illustration of the two questions that are central to the trade-off between equality and efficiency

First come value judgments: How much equality should society buy? Congressional backers of the 1996 welfare reform argued that the government was spending too much money to reduce inequality, and so America should move from a point like *c* to a point like *b* in Figure 19–5. Opponents of welfare cutbacks argued that we were spending too little and allowing excessive amounts of inequality to persist.

The second question pertains more to means than to ends. Critics of the old welfare system argued that it was a terribly inefficient way to redistribute income, for reasons like those we have just discussed. It was more like *abcde* in Figure 19–5 than *ABCDE*. They believe that the new TANF system will do a better job. Time will tell.

## THE NEGATIVE INCOME TAX

How can we do the job better? Can we design a simple structure that gets income into the hands of the poor without destroying their incentives to work? The solution suggested most frequently by economists is called the *negative income tax (NIT)*.

Table 19–4 illustrates how an NIT works. A particular NIT plan is defined by picking two numbers: a minimum income level below which no family is allowed to

---

[4] The *Medicaid* programs pay for the health care of low-income people; *Medicare* is available to all seniors, regardless of income.

fall (the "guarantee") and a rate at which benefits are "taxed away" as income rises. The table considers a plan with a $6,000 guaranteed income and a 50 percent tax rate. Thus, a family with no earnings (top row) would receive a $6,000 payment (a "negative tax") from the government. A family earning $2,000 (second row) would have the basic benefit reduced by 50 percent of its earnings. Thus, because half its earnings is $1,000, it would receive $5,000 from the government plus the $2,000 earned income for a total income of $7,000.

Notice in Table 19–4 that, with a 50 percent tax rate, the increase in total income as earnings rise is always *half* of the increase in earnings. Thus, families always have some incentive to work. Notice also that there is a level of income at which benefits cease—$12,000 in this example. This "break-even" level is not a third number that policymakers can select freely. Rather, it is dictated by the choices of the guarantee and the tax rate. In our example, $6,000 is the maximum possible benefit, and benefits are reduced by 50 cents for each $1 of earnings. Hence, benefits will be reduced to zero when 50 percent of earnings is equal to $6,000—which occurs when earnings are $12,000. The general relation is:

$$\text{Guarantee} = \text{Tax rate} \times \text{Break-even level}$$

The fact that the break-even level is completely determined by the guarantee and the tax rate creates a vexing problem. To make a real dent in the poverty problem, the guarantee must be placed fairly close to the poverty line. But then any moderate tax rate will push the break-even level way above the poverty line. This means that families who are not considered "poor" (though they are certainly not rich) will also receive benefits. For example, a low tax rate of $33\frac{1}{3}$ percent means that some benefits are paid to families whose income is as high as three times the guarantee level.

The solution seems obvious: raise the tax rate to bring the guarantee and the break-even level closer together. But then the incentive to work shrinks, and with it the principal rationale for the NIT in the first place. So the NIT is no panacea. Difficult choices must still be made.

**THE NEGATIVE INCOME TAX AND WORK INCENTIVES** The NIT should increase work incentives for welfare recipients. However, we have just seen that a number of families who are now too well off to collect welfare inevitably would become eligible for NIT payments. For these people, the NIT imposes work disincentives by subjecting them to the relatively high NIT tax rate. Government-sponsored experiments in the 1960s found that recipients of NIT benefits did in fact work less than nonrecipients, but only slightly.

Largely because of its superior work incentives, economists believe that an NIT is a more efficient way to redistribute income than the existing welfare system. In terms of Figure 19–5, the NIT is curve *ABCDE*, whereas the present system is curve *abcde*. If this view is correct, then replacing the current welfare system with an NIT would lead to both more equality *and* more efficiency. But this does not mean that equalization would become cost free. The curve *ABCDE* still slopes downward: By increasing equality, we still diminish the nation's output.

**THE NEGATIVE INCOME TAX AND REALITY** The NIT is often mistakenly viewed as an "academic" idea that does not exist in practice. But, in fact, America has two important programs that strongly resemble an NIT. One is the Food Stamp program. Food stamp benefits decline as earnings rise, and food stamps are used like cash in many poor neighborhoods. Hence food stamp benefits look very much like the NIT plan illustrated in Table 19–4.

The second program is an important feature of the income tax code called the Earned Income Tax Credit (EITC). It works as follows. As earnings rise from zero to some upper limit ($9,350 in 1998), the federal government supplements the earnings of the working poor by giving them what amounts to a grant that is proportional to their earnings. But once earnings pass a second threshold, the government starts taking this grant back, just as an NIT would. The EITC was made substantially more generous in 1993, and it is now America's biggest income-support program.

**TABLE 19-4**

**Illustration of a Negative Income Tax Plan**

| Earnings | Benefits Paid | Total Income |
|---:|---:|---:|
| $     0 | $6,000 | $  6,000 |
| 2,000 | 5,000 | 7,000 |
| 4,000 | 4,000 | 8,000 |
| 6,000 | 3,000 | 9,000 |
| 8,000 | 2,000 | 10,000 |
| 10,000 | 1,000 | 11,000 |
| 12,000 | 0 | 12,000 |

## ■ OTHER POLICIES TO COMBAT INEQUALITY

If we take the broader view that society's objective is not just to eliminate poverty but to reduce income disparities, then the fact that many nonpoor families would receive benefits under an NIT is perhaps not a serious drawback. After all, unless the plan is outlandishly generous, these families' incomes will still fall well below the average. Still, the NIT is largely thought of as an antipoverty program, not as a tool for general income equalization.

### THE PERSONAL INCOME TAX

By contrast, the federal personal income tax is thought to promote equality. Indeed, it is probably given far more credit for this than it actually deserves. Because the income tax is *progressive*, it takes a larger share of income from the rich than from the poor. Thus, incomes *after* tax are distributed more equally than incomes *before* tax.[5] This point is illustrated by the two Lorenz curves in Figure 19–6, which show a slight equalization due to the progressive income tax. These curves, however, are not drawn accurately to scale. If they were, they would lie almost on top of each other because research shows that the degree of equalization attributable to the tax is rather modest.

### DEATH DUTIES AND OTHER TAXES

Taxes on inheritances and estates levied by both states and federal government also equalize incomes. In this case they seem clearly aimed at limiting the incomes of the rich, or at least at limiting their ability to transfer this largesse from one generation to the next. But the amount of money involved is too small to make much difference to the overall income distribution. Total receipts from estate and gift taxes by all levels of government provide well under 1 percent of total tax revenues.

Most experts agree that the many other taxes in the U.S. system—including sales taxes, payroll taxes, and property taxes—are decidedly regressive as a group. On balance, the evidence seems to suggest that:

The U.S. tax system as a whole is only slightly progressive.

---

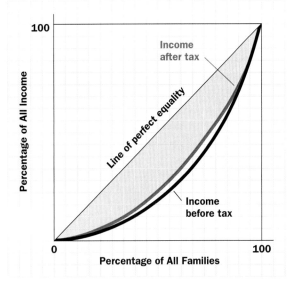

**FIGURE 19-6**

**The Effect of Progressive Income Taxation on the Lorenz Curve**

---

## ■ POLICIES TO COMBAT DISCRIMINATION

The policies we have just considered are all based on taxes and transfer payments—on moving dollars from one set of hands to another. A quite different approach has been used to fight discrimination: governments have made it *illegal* to discriminate.

Perhaps the major milestone in the war against discrimination was the *Civil Rights Act of 1964*, which outlawed many forms of discrimination and established the *Equal Employment Opportunity Commission (EEOC)*. When you read in a want ad that the company is "an equal opportunity employer," the firm is proclaiming its compliance with this and related legislation.

Originally, policymakers thought that they could attack the problem by outlawing discrimination in rates of pay and in hiring standards, and by devoting resources to enforcing these provisions. Although progress in reducing discrimination by race and sex undoubtedly was made between 1964 and the early 1970s, many people felt the pace was too slow. One reason was that discrimination in the labor market proved to be more subtle than was first thought. Officials rarely could find proof

---

[5] For definitions of progressive, proportional, and regressive taxes, see Chapter 21, page 435.

---

● **POLICY DEBATE** | **SHOULD AFFIRMATIVE ACTION BE ABOLISHED?**

---

Affirmative action has always been controversial. But it became a particularly hot political issue in the mid 1990s, as conservative politicians reacted to what they perceived to be one of the chief grievances of the "angry white male."

A number of critics believe that affirmative action has outlived its usefulness. It is time, they say, to rely on "race blind" standards that judge each person on his or her individual merits. Any other system of selection is unfair, they insist, especially when affirmative action programs devolve into rigid quotas by race or sex—as they frequently do.

Although no federal laws were changed, an important 1995 Supreme Court ruling in *Adarand v. Pena* set new and tougher standards for federal affirmative action programs. This ruling prompted President Clinton to order a comprehensive review of federal programs that favored minorities in such matters as hiring and awarding contracts. Although a few programs were cut back or eliminated, the review generally concluded that the United States was still so far from being a "color blind" society that affirmative action was still needed, and the president continued to defend affirmative action against Republican efforts to eliminate it.

Some state governments, however, went much farther than the federal government. California and Texas, for example, abolished several affirmative action programs at their state universities. (In California, this action followed a contentious statewide referendum on the matter.) When they did, minority enrollments plummeted so dramatically that a few opponents of affirmative action had well-publicized second thoughts.

The issue remains open. Few people actually like affirmative action—it offends many peoples' sense of fairness. But a majority of Americans continue to believe it is necessary to redress a centuries-long imbalance.

that unequal pay was being given for equal work, because determining when work was "equal" turned out to be a formidable task.

So a new approach was added to the antidiscrimination arsenal. Firms and other organizations with suspiciously small representations of minorities or women in their workforces were required not just to end discriminatory practices but also to demonstrate that they were taking **affirmative action** to remedy this imbalance. That is, they had to *prove* that they were making efforts to locate members of minority groups and females and then to hire them if they proved to be qualified.

This approach to fighting discrimination was controversial from the start, and remains so to this day. Critics claim that affirmative action really means quotas and compulsory hiring of unqualified workers simply because they are black or female. If this is so, it exacts a toll on economic efficiency. Proponents counter

**Affirmative action** refers to active efforts to locate and hire members of underrepresented groups.

that without affirmative action, discriminatory employers would simply claim they were unable to find qualified minority or female employees.

The difficulty revolves around the impossibility of deciding who is "qualified" and who is not based on *purely objective criteria*. What one person sees it as government coercion to hire an unqualified applicant to fill a quota, another sees as a discriminatory employer being forced to mend his or her ways. Nothing in this book, or anywhere else, will teach you which view is correct in any particular instance.

The controversy over affirmative action is another excellent example of the trade-off between equality and efficiency. Putting more women and members of minority groups into high-paying jobs would certainly make the income distribution more equal. Supporters of affirmative action seek this result. But if affirmative action disrupts industry and requires firms to replace "qualified" white males with other, "less qualified" workers, the nation's productivity will suffer. Opponents of affirmative action are disturbed by these potential efficiency losses. How far should these programs be pushed? A good question, but one without a good answer.

■  **A LOOK BACK**

We have now completed three chapters on the distribution of income. So this may be an opportune moment to pause and see how this analysis relates to our central theme: *What does the market do well, and what does it do poorly?*

We have learned that a market economy relies on the marginal productivity principle to assign an income to each individual. In so doing, the market attaches high prices to scarce factors and low prices to abundant ones, and therefore guides firms to use society's resources *efficiently*. This is one of the market's great strengths.

However, by attaching high prices to some factors and low prices to others, the market mechanism often creates a distribution of income that is quite unequal. Some people wind up fabulously rich, whereas others wind up miserably poor. For this reason, the market has been widely criticized for centuries for doing a rather poor job of distributing income in accord with commonly held notions of *fairness* and *equity*.

On balance, most observers feel that the criticism is justified: The market mechanism is extraordinarily good at promoting efficiency but not very good at promoting equality. As we said at the outset, the market has both virtues and vices.

---

**S U M M A R Y**

1. President Lyndon Johnson declared the War on Poverty in 1964, and within a decade the fraction of families below the official *poverty line* had dropped substantially. However, the poverty rate is higher today that it was in the early 1970s.

2. In the United States today, the richest 20 percent of households receive about 49 percent of the income, while the poorest 20 percent of households receive under 4 percent. These numbers reflect a considerable increase in inequality since about 1980. The U.S. income distribution also appears to be more unequal than those of most other industrial nations.

3. Individual incomes differ for many reasons. Differences in native ability, in the desire to work hard and to take risks, in schooling and experience, and in inherited wealth all account for income disparities. Discrimination also plays a role. All of these factors, however, explain only part of the inequality that we observe. A portion of the rest is due simply to good or bad luck, and the balance is unexplained.

4. Prejudice against a minority group may lead to discrimination in rates of pay, or to segregation in the workplace, or to both. However, discrimination may also arise even when there is no prejudice (this is called *statistical discrimination*).

5. There is *a trade-off between the goals of reducing inequality and enhancing economic efficiency:* Policies that help on the equality front normally harm efficiency, and vice versa.

6. Because of this trade-off, there is an *optimal degree of inequality* for any society. Society finds this optimum in the same way that a consumer decides how much to buy of different commodities: the trade-off tells us how costly it is to "purchase" more equality, and preferences then determine how much should be "bought." However, because people have different value judgments about the importance of equality, they disagree over the ideal amount of equality.

7. Whatever goal for equality is selected, society can gain by using more efficient redistributive policies because such

policies let us buy any given amount of equality at a lower price in terms of lost output. Economists claim, for example, that a *negative income tax* is preferable to our current welfare system on these grounds.

8. But the negative income tax is no panacea. Its primary virtue lies in the way it preserves incentives to work. But if this is done by keeping the tax rate low, then either the minimum guaranteed level of income will have to be low or many non-poor families will become eligible to receive benefits.

9. The goal of income equality is also pursued through the tax system, especially through the progressive federal income tax and death duties. But other taxes are typically regressive, so the tax system as a whole is only slightly progressive.

10. *Economic discrimination* has been attacked by making it illegal, not through the tax and transfer system. But simply declaring discrimination to be illegal is much easier than actually ending discrimination. The trade-off between equality and efficiency applies once again: Strict enforcement of *affirmative action* will certainly reduce discrimination and increase income equality, but it may do so at a cost in terms of economic efficiency.

---

## KEY TERMS

Poverty line   382

Absolute and relative concepts of poverty   383

Lorenz curve   385

Economic discrimination   389

Statistical discrimination   391

Optimal amount of inequality   392

Trade-off between equality and efficiency   393

Temporary Assistance to Needy Families (TANF)   396

Food stamps   396

Negative income tax (NIT)   396

Earned income tax credit (EITC)   397

Civil Rights Act of 1964   398

Equal Employment Opportunity Commission (EEOC)   398

Affirmative action   399

---

## QUESTIONS FOR REVIEW

1. Discuss the "leaky bucket" analogy (page 395) with your classmates. What maximum amount of income would you personally allow to leak from the bucket in transferring money from the rich to the poor? Explain why people differ in their answers to this question.

2. Continuing the leaky bucket example, explain why economists believe that replacing the present welfare system with a negative income tax would help reduce the leak.

3. Suppose you were to design a negative income tax system for the United States. Pick a guaranteed income level and a tax rate that seem reasonable to you. What break-even level of income is implied by these choices? Construct a version of Table 19–4 for the plan you have just devised.

4. Following is a complete list of the distribution of income in Disneyland. From these data, construct a Lorenz curve for Disneyland.

| | |
|---|---|
| Donald Duck | $ 100,000 |
| Mickey Mouse | 172,000 |
| Minnie Mouse | 68,000 |
| Pluto | 44,000 |
| Ticket taker | 16,000 |

How different is this from the Lorenz curve for the United States (Figure 19–2)?

5. Take a piece of graph paper and construct Lorenz curves for the United States for 1997 and 1980. (The data are in Table 19–2.) What do you learn from comparing these two curves?

6. Suppose the War on Poverty were starting anew and you were part of a presidential commission assigned the task of defining the poor. Would you choose an absolute or a relative concept of poverty? Why? What would be your specific definition of poverty?

7. Discuss the concept of the "optimal amount of inequality." What are some of the practical problems in determining how much inequality really is optimal?

8. A number of conservative politicians and economists advocate replacing the progressive income tax with a "flat tax" that would apply the same, low tax rate to all income above a certain exempt amount. One argument against making this change is that the distribution of income has grown much more unequal since the 1970s. Does the evidence support that view? Is it a decisive argument against a flat tax? How is the trade-off between equality and efficiency involved here?

# V

---

## THE GOVERNMENT AND THE ECONOMY

We come now to the ways in which governments seek to manage market processes. As we saw in Chapter 11, we have good reason to believe that the market mechanism generally promotes the public interest and does so very effectively. But Chapters 12 and 14 pointed out that the invisible hand does not always work perfectly. Some market failures may justify some governmental attempts to correct market operations. In Part V, we describe some kinds of governmental intervention and the logic that underlies them. You should keep in mind that governments can also make mistakes—we can find examples of governmental failure as well as market failures. When this happens, the government's cure for a market imperfection can sometimes prove worse than the disease. In other cases, however, there is reason to believe that government intervention does promote society's interests.

Three imperfections of the market mechanism drive the governmental actions described in this part. The first type of market failure results when some firm possesses market power that allows it to obtain monopoly profits (as we described in Chapter 12), generally by restricting output and charging higher prices than those firms would earn in otherwise similar competitive markets. If the government doesn't intervene, these firms can use their monopoly power to distort prices and outputs in ways that undermine economic efficiency and harm consumers. Externalities arise as a second major source of market imperfection—the benefits that firms generate for which they are not compensated, or the damage they do for which they do not have to pay. Environmental degradation—as when a firm faces no penalty even if it pours pollutants into the water we drink or fouls the air we breathe—is one clear consequence of such externalities. The government may intervene for yet a third major reason: the income inequality and widespread poverty that can occur in a free-market economy.

In Part V, we discuss what governments *can* do, and what, in fact, they *do* about these market weaknesses. We will even discuss a set of problems for which the economists' solution is to *extend* the market's role rather than constrain it—in other words, to help the market to cure itself.

The one law you can't repeal is supply and demand.

William Safire
*The New York Times*, July 13, 1998

# LIMITING MARKET POWER: REGULATION AND ANTITRUST

To protect the interests of the public when industries are, or threaten to become, monopolistic or oligopolistic, government in the United States uses two basic tools. *Antitrust policy* seeks to prevent acquisition of *monopoly power* and to ban certain monopolistic practices. All business firms are subject to the antitrust laws. In addition, some industries are also *regulated* by rules that constrain firms' pricing and other decisions. Generally, only firms suspected of having the power to act like monopolists are regulated.

## THE PUBLIC INTEREST ISSUE: MONOPOLY POWER VERSUS MERE SIZE

**Economies of scale** are savings that are obtained through increases in quantities produced. Scale economies occur when an X percent increase in input use raises output by *more than* X percent, so that the more the firm produces, the lower its per-unit costs become.

**Monopoly power** (or market power) is the ability of a business firm to raise the prices of its products above competitive levels and to keep those prices high for a substantial amount of time.

We learned in Chapters 12 and 13 that when an industry is a monopoly or an oligopoly, the result may not be as desirable in terms of the public interest as it would be if the industry were perfectly competitive. Yet for many industries anything like perfect competition is an impossible goal. This is true, notably, when the industry's technology provides **economies of scale**, meaning, you will remember, that the more of its product that a firm supplies the lower the cost of supplying a unit of that product will be. Scale economies therefore mean that in competition between a large firm and a small one, the big one can usually win. As a result, industries with scale economies usually end up having a small number of firms, each of which has a large share of the industry's sales. In other words, such an industry is usually fated to be a monopoly or an oligopoly.

But what is so bad about that? The answer is that sometimes it is not bad at all, but in other cases the public interest will be threatened because some or all of the firms in the industry will possess **monopoly power.** Monopoly power (or market power) is usually defined as the ability of a firm to raise and keep the prices of its products substantially above the levels at which those products would be priced in competitive markets. That is, if a firm has monopoly power it can charge high prices and get away with it—the market will not punish it for doing so. In a competitive industry, in contrast, the market will punish a high-price firm by the loss of its customers to rivals with lower prices. Thus, monopoly power is undesirable for several reasons, some of them obvious:

■ *High prices reduce the wealth of consumers.* The use of monopoly power is obviously undesirable to consumers because no one likes to pay high prices for purchased commodities. Such high prices may make the firm with monopoly power rich and make the consumers of its products poor. Such effects on the distribution of wealth are generally considered undesirable.

■ *High prices lead to resource misallocation.* Economists give greater emphasis to a second undesirable effect of prices that exceed the competitive level. As we saw in Chapter 14, such prices tend to reduce the quantities of the products that consumers demand. This means that smaller quantities of labor, raw materials, and other inputs will be devoted to production of these high-priced products relative to the quantities that would *best* serve consumer interests. More of those inputs will therefore be transferred to the products of competitive industries. The result will be *underproduction* of the products priced at monopoly levels and *overproduction* of the products of competitive industries. So, as a result of the exercise of monopoly power, the economy does not produce the mix of outputs that best serves the public interest.

■ *Monopoly power creates an obstacle to efficiency and innovation.* In addition, a firm with monopoly power is a firm that does not face much effective competition. It does not have as much reason to fear loss of business to others. Where this is so, there is little incentive for management to make the effort to produce efficiently with a minimum of waste or to undertake the expenses and risks of innovation. The result is that products may have poorer quality than they would if the company possessed no monopoly power, and there will be waste in the production process.

Because of the efficiency problems inherent in monopoly power, governmental intervention aims to control business firms' behavior and other attributes. The critical problem is control of monopoly power and prevention of acts by firms that are designed either to give them (or enhance) monopoly power, or to curb the use of that power to exploit the public.

A widespread misconception assumes that all big firms have monopoly power, so that the primary purpose of antitrust or regulatory activity should be to break up as many large firms and to constrain the pricing of all large firms that cannot be broken into smaller ones. But this is an invalid conclusion. It is true that firms that have a very small share of their industry's sales cannot wield market power. For reasons studied in Chapter 11, such small firms are price takers, not price makers. They must simply accept the price determined by supply and demand in a competitive market, or the prices determined by larger firms in their industry if those large firms do have market power. But though firms with small market shares never have market power, the converse is untrue. Large firms do not always have market power.

This may be true for many reasons. In an oligopoly with fierce rivalry, each firm may be prevented by the actions of its competitors from raising price above competitive levels. For example, Coca-Cola and Pepsi each have a very large share of the soft drink market. But it is well known that there is no love between the two companies. So neither dares to raise its prices substantially for fear of driving customers into the arms of its unloved competitor.

Even a monopoly may have little or no monopoly power if entry into its industry is cheap and easy. Such a firm knows that it can only retain its monopoly *if its behavior is not monopolistic.* If it tries to raise its price to monopoly levels for any substantial period of time, then its rivals will have an opportunity to come in and take some or all of its business away. So in industries where entry is very easy, a large firm will have no monopoly power because the perpetual threat of potential entry will keep it from misbehaving. For this reason government agencies concerned with monopoly issues explicitly avoid interfering with the actions of firms in industries where entry is cheap and easy.

**The primary threat of monopoly and oligopoly to the public interest is monopoly power. This power can lead to excessive prices that exploit consumers, misallocation of resources, and inefficient and noninnovative firms. But firms that are big do not necessarily have market power.**

In Part 1 of this chapter, we will begin our discussion of these issues with regulation and its history in the United States. In Part 2 of the chapter, we turn to antitrust policy.

## ■ PART 1: REGULATION

### HOW AND WHY DID REGULATION ARISE?

**Regulation** of industry in the United States began when indignation over abuse of market power by the nation's railroads led to the establishment of the Interstate Commerce Commission (ICC) in 1887. There was a public outcry over the support the railroads gave to John D. Rockefeller Sr. in the battle of his Standard Oil Company against its rivals. This, along with other railroad abuses, invited government intervention. But for several decades afterward, there was little attempt to expand regulation to other industries. Then the Federal Power Commission (FPC) was established in 1920 and the Federal Communications Commission (FCC) in 1934; many of the remaining regulatory agencies were formed during the 1930s under President Franklin D. Roosevelt's New Deal.

Today, several federal regulatory agencies control prices. Until it was abolished in 1995, the ICC regulated railroads, barges, pipelines, and some categories of trucking. Its regulatory tasks are now performed by the Department of Commerce. The FCC regulates broadcasting and telecommunications. The Federal Energy Regulatory Commission (FERC) regulates interstate transmission of electric power and sales of natural gas. The Securities and Exchange Commission (SEC) regulates sales of securities (stocks and bonds). A number of agencies, led by the Federal Reserve System, control banking operations. The work of these agencies is complemented by a variety of state agencies that regulate intrastate activities.

Despite good intentions, regulation has been criticized as a cause of inefficiency and excessive costs to the consuming public. The basic fact about regulation and

**Regulation** of industry is a process established by law that restricts or controls some specified decisions made by the affected firms, and is designed to protect the public from exploitation by firms with monopoly power. Regulation is usually carried out by a special government agency assigned the task of administering and interpreting the law. That agency also acts as a court in enforcing the regulatory laws.

"Won't all these new rules impact adversely on the viability of small businesses with fewer than fifty employees?"

other forms of government intervention that are designed to affect the operations of markets is that *neither* markets *nor* governmental agencies always work perfectly. In an uncontrolled market, for example, monopoly power can damage the public interest, but excessive or poorly conceived regulations or antitrust decisions can also be harmful.

## WHAT IS REGULATED? BY WHOM?

The regulatory agencies in the United States can be divided, roughly, into two classes: those that limit the market power of regulated firms and those devoted to consumer and worker protection and safety. In a recent count, at least 14 federal regulatory agencies dealt with restraint of market power and about 30 handled issues such as environmental protection and product safety. An example of the latter is the Food and Drug Administration (FDA), which protects the public from harmful, impure, infected, or adulterated foods, drugs, and cosmetics by preventing their sale to the public.

The federal government also regulates the safety of automobiles and mines and the use of dangerous substances such as pesticides. Such regulation affects an enormous proportion of the nation's economic activity, including the drug industry, agriculture, auto manufacturing, and the chemical and power industries. Virtually every manufacturing industry is affected by environmental regulations.

Regulations designed to limit market power, on which this chapter focuses, affect industries that together provide perhaps 10 percent of the gross domestic product (GDP) of the United States. The list includes telecommunications, railroads, electric utilities, and oil pipelines.

### Why Do Regulators Often *Raise* Prices?

Regulation sometimes forces consumers to pay *higher* prices than they would pay in its absence. For instance, before the airline industry was deregulated, the flight between New York City and Washington, D.C. (an interstate trip that was controlled by the federal government) used to cost *more* than the longer flight between San Francisco and Los Angeles (which was not controlled by the federal government, because it's entirely within the state of California). The California trip was nearly *twice* as long as the East Coast trip, and it did not have a substantially lower cost per passenger mile. So why did regulators, whose job is to protect the public interest, deliberately price the New York–Washington hop about 25 percent higher? Later in the chapter, you will be able to answer this question.

## ■ SOME OBJECTIVES OF REGULATION

Economists recognize a number of reasons that may justify the regulation of an industry.

### CONTROL OF MARKET POWER RESULTING FROM ECONOMIES OF SCALE AND SCOPE

As we learned at the beginning of this chapter, a main reason for regulation of industry is to prevent the use of or acquisition of market power by regulated firms. In some industries, it is far cheaper to have production carried out by one firm than by many, and the relatively large firms that result may gain market power. One cause is economies of large-scale production. Railroad tracks are a particularly good example of such *economies of scale*. The total cost of building and maintaining the tracks when 100 trains traverse them every day is not much higher than when only one train uses them. So substantial savings in average cost result when rail traffic increases. As we saw in Chapter 8, scale economies lead to an average cost curve that goes downhill as output increases (see Figure 20–1). This means that a firm with a large output can cover its costs at a price lower than a firm whose output is smaller. In the figure, point *A* represents the larger firm whose AC is $5, whereas point *B* is the smaller firm with an AC of $7.

A single, large firm may also have a cost advantage over a group of small firms when it is cheaper to produce a number of different commodities together rather than making each separately in a different firm. Savings made possible by simultaneous production of many different products by one firm are called **economies of scope.** One clear example of economies of scope is the manufacture of both cars and trucks by the same producer. The techniques employed in producing both commodities are similar, which provides a cost advantage to firms that produce both.

In industries where there are great economies of scale and scope, costs will be much higher if government intervenes to preserve a large number of small, and therefore costly, firms. Moreover, where economies of scale and scope are strong, society will not be able to preserve free competition, even if it wants to. The large, multiproduct firm will have so great a cost advantage over its rivals that the small firms simply will be unable to survive.

> Where monopoly production is cheapest, so that free competition is not sustainable, the industry is a natural monopoly. When monopoly is cheaper, society may not want to have competition; if free competition is not sustainable, it will not even have a choice in the matter.

But even if society reconciles itself to monopoly in such cases, it will generally not want to let the monopoly firm wield its market power without limits. Therefore, it will consider regulating the company's decisions on matters such as pricing.

### MONOPOLY POWER AND THE PRICES OF "BOTTLENECK" FACILITIES

**BOTTLENECK FACILITIES** Monopoly power can arise for reasons other than economies of scale and scope. One source that is currently a center of attention in regulatory discussion is the possession by a single firm of facilities that other firms

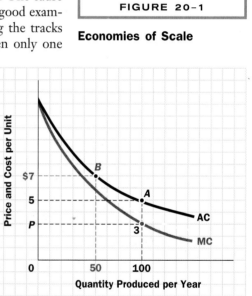

**FIGURE 20-1**

**Economies of Scale**

**Economies of scope** are savings that are obtained through simultaneous production of many different products and occur if a firm that produces many commodities can supply each good more cheaply than a firm that produces fewer commodities.

must use if they are to compete successfully with the owner of that facility. Such a facility owned by a single firm and needed for the activities of rival firms is called a **bottleneck facility.** How to price the use of these bottleneck facilities is a critical regulatory problem.

Picking up our previous railroad example, let's suppose that several competing railroads need to go over a single mountain pass, but that access to the pass is owned by one of those railroads. That pass is, then, a bottleneck facility, because no railroad can compete in that particular market without using the resource.

The same situation arises in the telecommunications and electricity industries. For instance, most long-distance telephone calls to or from points in Ohio or Illinois (whether carried by AT&T, MCI, or Sprint) must at some point get to homes or businesses via the local telephone network (called "the local loop" in regulatory parlance), which is owned by a telecommunications company called Ameritech. Now, Ameritech is hoping to get into some of the long-distance business itself. But if it does, then it, along with AT&T, MCI, and Sprint, will have to make use of its own bottleneck local loop. Here's another example: In the electric power industry, rival generators of electricity must all use the bottleneck transmission facilities (the wires, poles, and so on) owned by the utility that also generates electricity of its own.

If competition is to be maintained in both these cases, the rival firms that do not own the bottleneck facility must clearly be permitted to use the facility—after, of course, paying an appropriate price. But what price is appropriate? This issue has become central in litigation and negotiation with regulatory agencies throughout the industrial world. Clearly, if the owner of the bottleneck is able to use monopoly power in setting the price of the bottleneck facility, then that price may well end up far above the competitive price level. But if the price the owner is allowed to charge rivals for use of the bottleneck facility is too high, it can drive the competitors out of business. On the other hand, if regulators force the bottleneck owner to charge a price that is too low to cover its costs, it will be subsidizing its rivals and will find it difficult or impossible to compete with them.

What price, then, is neither too high nor too low? The answer provided by one group of economists is suggested by analogy with a simpler situation. Suppose, in our railroad example, that two railroads, A and B, need to use the bottleneck mountain

Ameritech Web site

## ● THE PRIVY COUNCIL APPROVES "PARITY-PRINCIPLE" ACCESS PRICING

New Zealand Telecom, the formerly monopoly telephone company of New Zealand, faced competition from an entrant called Clear Communications. Clear offers long-distance service and hopes to provide local service as well. For Clear's long-distance messages to reach their intended recipients, however, it is generally necessary to make use of NZ Telecom's local facilities (the local "loop"). After negotiations over the price for this *bottleneck* service broke down, Clear sued Telecom. Telecom offered to adopt the parity-principle price for access to its local loop, but Clear refused.

The High Court of New Zealand, with some reservations, decided that the parity-principle offer was appropriate, but this decision was overturned by the court of appeal on grounds related to special features of New Zealand law. That decision then was reviewed by the final appeals body, the Privy Council in London. In October 1994, the council issued its judgment, fully supporting the parity principle and holding that there were no difficulties in New Zealand law of the sort cited by the court of appeal. The decision of the Privy Council stated in part:

> Both the High Court and the Court of Appeal proceeded on the basis, with which their Lordships [that is, the judges of the Privy Council] agree, that if the terms Telecom was seeking to extract were no higher than those which a hypothetical firm would seek in a perfectly contestable market, Telecom was not using its

dominant position [that is, it was not behaving as a monopolist]. . . . The [parity principle] rule is a closely reasoned economic model which seeks to show how the hypothetical firm would conduct itself. . . . [T]he underlying object [of the relevant New Zealand law] will be achieved if the [parity principle] rule is applied.

SOURCE: Privy Council Appeal No. 21 of 1994, Judgment of the Lords of the Judicial Committee of the Privy Council, pp. 21 and 27.

pass, but the owner of the pass is not itself a railroad. To provide what regulators call a "level playing field" for the two rival railroads, it is necessary for the owner of the mountain pass to charge the same toll to Railroad A that it charges to Railroad B. Then, both railroads will be paying the same fee to use the pass. As a result, the railroad that has the lower *remaining* cost in carrying the traffic from origin to destination can clearly afford to charge a lower freight rate for the route and capture the traffic that goes over it.

**THE PARITY-PRICING PRINCIPLE** Next, suppose that the owner of the mountain pass decides to enter the rail-transport business in competition with Railroad A and Railroad B. How does that affect the proper price to charge for the use of the pass? The answer is that all three railroads should now pay the same price. This is called the *parity-pricing principle*, though it still leaves a calculation problem: that of determining exactly what price the owner of the pass really pays to *itself* for use of it. (For confirmation of the legitimacy of the parity-pricing rule by the judges of the Privy Council in London, see the accompanying box, "The Privy Council Approves 'Parity-Principle' Access Pricing.")

### UNIVERSAL SERVICE AND RATE AVERAGING

A third objective of regulation of the prices and other choices of firms in a regulated industry is the desire for "universal service." By this we mean the availability of service to everyone at "reasonable prices," particularly to impoverished consumers and small communities where the limited scale of operations may make costs extremely high. In such cases regulators may encourage or require a public utility (such as an electric power supplier) to serve some consumers at a financial loss. But a loss on some sales is financially feasible only when the regulated firm is permitted to make up for it by obtaining higher profits on its other sales. Charging higher prices to one set of customers to finance lower prices to another customer group is called **cross-subsidization.**

**Cross-subsidization** means selling one product at a loss, which is balanced by higher profits on another product.

But this sort of cross-subsidization is possible only if the regulated firm is protected from price competition and free entry of new competitors in its other, more profitable markets (in which it charges the higher prices that subsidize the financing of the mandated low prices). If no such protection is provided, potential competitors will sniff out these profit opportunities in the markets where service is supplied at prices well above cost. Many new firms will enter the business and drive prices down in those markets—a practice referred to as *cream skimming.* The entrants choose to enter only the profitable markets and skim away the "cream" of the profits for themselves, leaving the unprofitable markets (the skimmed milk?) to the supplier who had attempted to provide universal service. This phenomenon is one reason why regulatory rules, until recently, made it very difficult or impossible for new firms to enter when and where they saw fit.

Airlines and telecommunications are two industries in which these issues have arisen. In both cases, it was feared that without regulation of entry and rates, or special subsidies, less populous communities would effectively be isolated, losing their airline services and obtaining telephone service only at cripplingly high rates. Many economists question the validity of this argument for regulation, which, they say, calls for hidden subsidies of rural consumers by everyone else. The airline deregulation act provided for government subsidies to help small communities attract airline service. In fact, this market has since been taken over to a considerable extent by specialized "commuter" airlines flying much smaller aircraft than the major airlines, which have withdrawn from many such routes.

A similar issue affects the U.S. Postal Service, which charges the same price to deliver a letter anywhere within the United States, regardless of the distance or the special difficulties and costs of a particular route. To maintain this pricing scheme, the law must protect the Postal Service from direct competition in many of its activities—otherwise, its extreme form of uniform pricing would soon deprive it of its most profitable routes. Thus, the goal of providing universal service leads to the regulation of entry into and exit from the affected industry, and not just price control.

## ■ TWO KEY ISSUES THAT FACE REGULATORS

Regulators around the world face (at least) two critical issues that are of fundamental importance for economic policy. They are at the heart of recent legal battles before regulatory agencies almost everywhere.

### HOW CAN REGULATORS SET PRICES THAT BEST PROTECT CONSUMERS' INTERESTS BUT ENABLE REGULATED FIRMS TO COVER THEIR COSTS?

When governments regulate prices they usually want to prevent those prices from being so high that they bring monopoly profits to the firm. But at the same time governments want to set prices at levels that are "compensatory." That is, the prices must be sufficiently high to enable the firms to cover their costs and, consequently, to survive financially. Regulators also are asked to select prices that best serve the public interest. But these goals, as we will see next, can often be at odds.

■ *Prices intended to promote the public interest may cause financial problems for firms.* We saw in Chapters 10 and 11 that the consumer's welfare is most effectively promoted by setting the price of a product equal to that product's marginal cost. But we will see presently that such a rule would condemn many regulated firms to bankruptcy. What should the regulator do in such a case?

■ *Preventing firms with monopoly power from earning excessive profits without elimi-nating all incentive for efficiency and innovation may prove difficult.* The firm's incentive and reward for the effort and expenditure needed to improve effi-ciency and to innovate is the higher profit that it expects to obtain if it suc-ceeds. But a frequent objective of regulation is to put a ceiling on profit in order to prevent monopoly earnings. How can monopoly profits be prevented without destroying incentives?

Let's now analyze these issues, which arise frequently in today's crucial regulatory policy debates.

## MARGINAL VERSUS AVERAGE COST PRICING

Regulatory agencies often have the task of controlling the prices of regulated firms. Acrimonious debate over the proper levels for those prices has filled hundreds of thou-sands of pages of regulatory-hearing records and has involved literally hundreds of millions of dollars of expenditures in fees for lawyers, expert witnesses, and research. The question has been: What constitutes the proper formula to set these prices?

Where it is feasible, most economists favor setting price equal to marginal cost because, as was shown in Chapter 11, this pricing policy provides the incentive for firms to produce output quantities that serve consumers' wants most efficiently. However, a serious practical problem often prevents use of marginal-cost pricing. The problem is that, in many regulated industries, the firms would go bankrupt if all prices were set equal to marginal costs!

This seems a startling conclusion, but it follows inescapably from three simple facts:

*Fact 1.* In many regulated industries, there are significant economies of large-scale production. As we pointed out earlier, economies of scale are one of the main reasons why certain industries were regulated in the first place.

*Fact 2.* In an industry with economies of scale, the long-run average cost curve is downward sloping. This means that the long-run average cost falls as the quan-tity produced rises, as was illustrated by the AC curve in Figure 20–1. Fact 2 is something we learned back in Chapter 8. The reason, to review briefly, is that where there are economies of scale, if all input quantities are doubled, output will *more than double.* But costs will obviously only double if input quantities double. Thus, costs will rise more slowly than output and cost per unit of output must fall. That is, because average cost (AC) is simply total cost (TC) divided by quan-tity *(Q)* with economies of scale, AC = TC/Q must decline when all input quantities are doubled.

*Fact 3.* If average cost is declining, then marginal cost must be below average cost. This fact follows directly from one of the general rules relating marginal and average data that were explained in the appendix to Chapter 9. Once again, the logic is simple enough to review briefly. If, for example, your average quiz score is 90 percent but the next quiz pulls your average down to 87 percent, then the grade on this most recent test (the marginal grade) must be below both the old and the new average quiz scores. That is, it takes a marginal grade (or cost) that is below the average to pull the average down.

Putting these three facts together, we conclude that in many regulated industries, marginal cost (MC) will be below average cost, as depicted in Figure 20–1. Now suppose that regulators set the price at the level of marginal cost. Because *P* then equals MC, *P* must be below AC and the firm must lose money, so "*P* equals MC" is simply not an acceptable option. What, then, should be done? One possibility is to set price equal to marginal cost and to make up for the deficit out of public funds. However, subsidies to large regulated firms are not very popular politically and may also not be sensible.

A second option, which is quite popular among regulators, is to (try to) set price equal to average cost. But this method of pricing is neither desirable nor possible to carry out except on the basis of arbitrary decisions. The problem is that almost no firm produces only a single commodity. Almost every company produces a number of different varieties and qualities of some product, and many produce thousands of different products, each with its own price. Even General Motors, a fairly specialized firm that produces many makes and sizes of cars and trucks, also sells home mortgages and quite a few other things. In a multiproduct firm, we cannot even define AC = TC/Q, because to calculate Q (total output), we would have to add up all the apples and oranges (and all of the other different items) that the firm produces. But we know that one cannot add up apples and oranges. Because we cannot calculate AC for a multiproduct firm, it is hardly possible for the regulator to require P to equal AC for each of the firm's products, though regulators sometimes think they can do so.

**THE RAMSEY PRICING RULE**    Economists have been attracted to an imaginative, alternative approach to the problem of pricing in regulated industries that produce many products. This approach derives its name from its discoverer, Frank Ramsey, a brilliant English mathematician who died in 1930 at the age of 26 after making several enduring contributions to both mathematics and economics.

The **Ramsey pricing rule** is a rule for determining prices that promote consumer welfare while covering the producer's cost.

The basic idea of the **Ramsey pricing rule** can be explained in a fairly straightforward manner. We know that prices must be set above marginal costs if a firm with scale economies is to break even, but how much above? Suppose the firm makes two products, A and B, and the demand for A is much more elastic than that of B. This means that a given percentage price rise will induce consumers to cut their purchases of A much more than those of B. It then makes sense to raise price most above marginal cost for product B—the one with the less elastic demand. Why? Because a given price increase for B will interfere less with consumers' purchase decisions than a similar rise in the price of A. This insight is the essence of the Ramsey pricing rule:

> In a multiproduct, regulated firm in which prices must exceed marginal cost in order to permit that firm to break even, other things being equal, the ratios of *P* over MC should be largest for those of the firm's products whose elasticities of demand are the smallest.

Economists accept this pricing rule as the correct conclusion on theoretical grounds. It has even been proposed for postal and telephone pricing, and various regulatory commissions have used it as a general guide for the regulation of prices.

## PREVENTING MONOPOLY PROFIT BUT KEEPING INCENTIVES FOR EFFICIENCY AND INNOVATION

Opponents of regulation claim that it seriously impairs the efficiency of American industry and reduces the benefits of free markets. One obvious source of inefficiency is the endless paperwork and complex legal proceedings that prevent the firm from responding quickly to changing market conditions.

In addition, economists believe that regulatory interference in pricing causes economic inefficiency. By forcing prices to differ from those that would prevail in a free, competitive market, regulations lead consumers to demand a quantity of the regulated product that does not maximize consumer benefits from the quantity of resources available to the economy. (This resource misallocation issue was discussed in Chapter 14.)

But there is a third source of inefficiency that may be even more important. It occurs because regulators often are required to prevent the regulated firm from earning excessive profits, while at the same time offering it financial incentives for maximum efficiency of operation and allowing it enough profit to attract the capital it needs when growing markets justify expansion. It would seem to be ideal if the regulator would permit the firm to earn just the amount of revenue that covers its costs, including the cost of its capital. Thus, if the current rate of profits in competitive markets is 10 percent, the regulated firm should recover its costs plus 10 percent on its investment and not a penny more or less. The trouble with such a rule is that it removes all profit incentive for efficiency, responsiveness to consumer demand, and innovation. It, in effect, guarantees just one standard rate of profit to the firm, no more and no less—regardless of whether its management is totally incompetent or extremely talented and hardworking.

Competitive markets do not work this way. Although under perfect competition the average firm will earn just the illustrative 10 percent, a firm with an especially ingenious and efficient management will do better, and a firm with an incompetent management is likely to go broke. It is the possibility of great rewards and harsh punishments that gives the market mechanism its power to cause firms to strive for high efficiency and productivity growth.

When firms are guaranteed fixed returns no matter how well or how poorly they perform, gross inefficiencies often result. For example, many contracts for purchases of military equipment have prices calculated on a so-called cost-plus basis, meaning that the supplier is guaranteed that its costs will be covered and that, in addition, it will receive some prespecified profit. Studies of such cost-plus arrangements have confirmed enormous supplier inefficiencies. A regulatory arrangement that in effect guarantees a regulated firm its cost plus a "fair rate of return" on its investment obviously has much in common with a cost-plus contract. Fortunately, there are also substantial differences between the two, and so regulatory profit ceilings need not always have serious effects on the firm's incentives for efficiency.

Curiously, the much-criticized delay that characterizes many regulatory procedures, known as *regulatory lag*, is perhaps the main reason that profit regulation has not eliminated all rewards for efficiency and all penalties for inefficiency. Suppose, for example, that the regulatory commission approves some prices expected to yield exactly the fair rate of return to the company, say, 10 percent. If management then successfully reduces its costs, the effective rate of return under the old prices may rise to, say, 12 percent. If it takes three years for the regulators to adjust the prices they previously approved to the new cost levels, the company will earn a 2 percent bonus as a reward for its efficiency during the three years of regulatory lag. Similarly, if management makes a series of bad decisions that reduce the company's return to 7 percent, the firm may ask the regulator for price increases to recoup its losses. If the regulator takes 18 months to act, the firm suffers a penalty for its inefficiency. But regulatory lag penalizes inefficiency and rewards superior performance very imperfectly. It still leaves provision of incentives for efficiency as one of the fundamental problems of regulation. How can one prevent regulated firms from earning excessive profits, but also permit them to earn enough to attract the capital they need and, above all, still allow rewards for superior performance and penalties for poor performance?

**PRICE CAPS AS INCENTIVES FOR EFFICIENCY** A regulatory innovation designed to prevent monopoly profits while offering incentives for the firm to improve its efficiency is now in use in many countries—for electricity, telephones, and airport services in Great Britain, for example, and for telephone rates in the United States and elsewhere. The basic idea is a planned extension of the incentive for efficiency provided by regulatory lag.

Under this program, the regulators assign ceilings (called *price caps*) for the *prices* (not the profits) of the regulated firms. However, the price caps (which are measured in real, inflation-adjusted terms) are reduced each year at a rate based on the rate of cost reduction (productivity growth) previously achieved by the regulated firm. Thus, if the regulated firm subsequently achieves cost savings (by innovation or other means) greater than those it obtained in the past, the firm's real costs will fall faster than its real prices, and it will be permitted to keep the resulting profits as its reward. Of course, there is a catch. If the regulated firm reduces its costs only by, say, 2 percent per year whereas in the past its costs fell 3 percent per year, the price cap will also be falling at a 3 percent rate. The firm will therefore lose profits, though consumers will continue to benefit from falling real prices.

Thus, under price-cap regulation management is constantly forced to look for ever more economical ways of doing things. This approach clearly gives up any attempt to limit the profit of the regulated firm—leaving the possibility of higher profits as an incentive for efficiency. But it protects the consumer nonetheless by controlling the firm's prices. Indeed, it makes those prices lower and lower, in real terms.

## ■ THE PROS AND CONS OF "BIGNESS"

We have described several goals for regulation, including control of monopoly power, increased availability of bottleneck facilities, and the provision of universal service. Is it desirable, in addition to these regulatory goals, to try to make big firms become smaller? In other words, are the effects of "bigness" always undesirable? We have already seen that only relatively big firms have any likelihood of possessing monopoly power. We have also seen that monopoly power can cause a number of problems, including undesirable effects on income distribution, misallocation of resources, and inhibition of efficiency and innovation.

But we have also seen that big firms at least sometimes do not possess monopoly power. More generally, there is another side of the picture. Bigness in industry can also, at least sometimes, benefit the general public. Again, this is true for a number of reasons.

### ECONOMIES OF LARGE SIZE

Probably the most important advantage of bigness is found in industries where technology makes small-scale operation inefficient. One can hardly imagine the costs if automobiles were produced in little workshops rather than giant factories. The notion of a small firm operating a long-distance railroad does not even make sense, and a multiplicity of firms replicating the same railroad service would clearly be incredibly wasteful.

On these grounds, most policymakers have never even considered any attempt to eliminate bigness. Of course, it does not follow that every industry in which firms happen to be big is one in which big firms are best. Some observers argue that many firms, in fact, exceed the sizes required for cost minimization.

### REQUIRED SCALE FOR INNOVATION

Some economists have argued that only large firms have the resources and the motivation for really significant innovation. Many inventions are still contributed by individuals. But, because it is often an expensive, complex, and large-scale undertaking to put a new invention into commercial production, usually only large firms can afford the funds and bear the risks that such an effort demands. In addition, according to this view of the matter, only a large firm has the motivation to lay out the funds required for the innovation process because it gets to keep a considerable share of the benefits. A small company, on the other hand, will find that its innovative idea is soon likely to be followed by close imitations, which enable competitors to profit from its research outlays.

There have been many studies of the relationships among firm size, industry competitiveness, and the level of expenditure on research and development (R&D). Although the evidence is far from conclusive, it does indicate that highly competitive industries composed of very small firms tend not to spend a great deal on research. Up to a point, R&D outlays and innovation seem to increase with size of the firm and the concentration of the industry. However, some of the most significant innovations introduced in this century have been contributed by firms that started very small. Examples include the electric light, alternating current (AC) electricity, the photocopier, the electronic calculator, and the desktop computer.

The bottom line here is that bigness in business firms receives a mixed score. It can produce undesirable results, but in other cases it is necessary for efficiency and low costs and offers other benefits to the public. A rule requiring regulators to combat bigness per se, wherever it occurs, is likely to have undesirable results, and would, in any event, be unworkable.

---

### ● THE TELECOMMUNICATIONS ACT OF 1996

After much debate and argument by the affected firms, Congress passed the Telecommunications Act of 1996. This act was intended to increase competition among cable television suppliers and telecommunications firms. Of course, there already is vigorous price rivalry among suppliers of long-distance services, as we see in their television ads almost every evening, but other telecommunications services are often provided by monopolies.

The Telecommunications Act of 1996 was designed to permit telephone companies to enter into cable television service, thus providing competitors to the cable companies, which now rarely have rivals in a given geographic area. The act was also designed to permit and make it easy for the long-distance firms—AT&T, MCI, Sprint, and others—to carry local telephone calls, in competition with the current local phone monopolies. Finally, it permitted the local phone companies to compete in the long-distance business for the first time. However, the act provided that the largest local companies could invade the long-distance business only after entry had occurred in local service—that is, when the local monopoly was effectively ended.

A number of problems have since emerged. For one thing, entry into cable service has been slow to materialize because it turns out to be quite costly. Even though telephone equipment can be used to transmit cable programs through telephone wires into homes, those facilities have to be modified for that purpose at considerable expense. Competition from satellite and wireless service providers is also making entry by telephone companies into the cable business less profitable than had been hoped.

The entry of long-distance firms into local telephone service has involved even greater frustration. It is enormously costly for new entrants to construct new local facilities that replicate those of the monopolies already in place. Moreover, the facilities already available have plenty of excess capacity for them to carry many more calls. It has therefore been proposed that the local companies be required to rent space on these *bottleneck* facilities to firms that want to enter the market. This has led to battles over the *price* the local companies would be allowed to charge Sprint, MCI, AT&T, and the others for use of their facilities. (See the discussion of bottleneck pricing on pages 409–411.) The local companies claim that the prices offered by the long-distance firms are too low, whereas the long-distance firms maintain that the prices advocated by local firms are far too high. As it stands now, all these issues are tied up in court litigation, and some observers have concluded that the 1996 Act is a total failure. Others believe that the act has led to *some* progress in introducing competition into the business and that, with luck, the court decisions will yet enable most of the goals of the legislation to be attained.

---

## ■ DEREGULATION

Because regulators have sometimes adopted rules and made decisions that were ill-advised and were demonstrably harmful to the public interest, and because the bureaucracy that is needed to enforce regulation is costly and raises business costs, there have long been demands for reduced regulation. Beginning in the mid-1970s, Congress responded to such arguments by deregulating several industries, such as airlines and trucking, eliminating most of the powers of the relevant regulatory agencies. In other industries, such as railroads and telecommunications, rule changes now give regulated firms considerably more freedom in decision making. This process is still under way. For instance, Congress engaged in a major—and highly charged—debate over telecommunications regulation in 1995, ending in a major piece of legislation in 1996 (see the accompanying box, "The Telecommunications Act of 1996").

### THE EFFECTS OF DEREGULATION

One way to deal with the regulation difficulties just discussed is to shut regulation down—simply leave everything to the free market and get rid of the regulators. Many observers think that would be a good idea in a number of cases, but sometimes it would be unacceptable, as in markets that are virtually pure monopolies. Thus, the move toward deregulation has proceeded slowly, eliminating regulation in some fields, reducing it in others. Deregulation's effects in the United States are still being debated, but several conclusions seem clear:

**EFFECTS ON PRICES**   There seems little doubt that deregulation has generally led to lower prices. Airline fares, railroad freight rates, and telephone rates have all declined on the average (in real, inflation-adjusted terms) after total or partial deregulation. At least in the case of the airlines, however, the rate of decline slowed abruptly toward the end of the 1980s. Still, observers conclude that most of these prices are well below the levels that would have prevailed under regulation.

**EFFECTS ON LOCAL SERVICES**   At first it was widely feared, even by supporters of deregulation, that smaller and more isolated communities would be deprived of services because small numbers of customers would make those services unprofitable. It was feared that airlines, railroads, and telephone companies would withdraw from such communities once there was no longer any regulation to force them to stay. These worries have proved largely groundless. Although larger airlines have left smaller communities, they have usually been replaced by smaller commuter airlines that have often provided more frequent service.

**EFFECTS ON ENTRY**   As a result of deregulation, older airlines invaded one another's routes, several dozen new airlines sprang up, and about 10,000 new truck operators entered the market, though many of them have since dropped out, as profits and wages were driven down by competition. Almost all of the new airlines also ran into trouble and were sold to the older airlines. But since 1990, many small airlines have been launched. A battle is now shaping up over whether the small airlines need special protection from tough competition by the larger airlines.

**EFFECTS ON UNIONS**   Deregulation has badly hurt unions such as the Teamsters (of the trucking industry) and the Airline Pilots Association. In the new, competitive climate firms have been forced to make sharp cuts in their workforces and to resist wage increases and other costly changes in working conditions. Indeed, there has been strong pressure for retrenchment on all of these fronts. It should not be surprising, then, that unions often oppose deregulation.

**EFFECTS ON CONCENTRATION AND MERGERS**   Particularly in aviation and rail freight transportation, deregulation was followed by a wave of mergers in which two firms agreed to join together or in which one firm agreed to be bought out by another. As a result, the sizes of the largest companies in the affected industries have expanded. That this has happened should not be surprising because, as we saw earlier in the chapter, industries with substantial economies of scale are the most likely targets for regulation. Once freed from regulatory constraints, one could expect firms in such industries to take advantage of opportunities to achieve cost reductions through rapid expansion or by mergers.

---

| FIGURE 20-2 |
| --- |

**A "Hub and Spoke" Airline Routing Pattern**

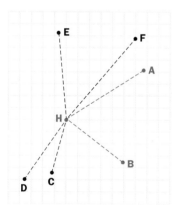

**EFFECTS ON PRODUCT QUALITY**   The public has been unpleasantly surprised by another effect of deregulation. At least in the case of aviation, increased price competition has been accompanied by sharp reductions in "frills." To cut costs, airlines have made meals less elaborate (to put it mildly) and have limited the number of flights to avoid empty seats—which has increased crowding. To fill planes with more passengers, many airlines turned to "hub and spoke" systems (see Figure 20–2). Instead of running a flight directly from a low-demand airport, A, to another low-demand airport, B, the airline flies all passengers from Airport A to its "hub" at Airport H, where all passengers bound for destination Airport B are asked to reboard an airplane flying to B. This clearly saves money and gives passengers more options as the number of flights between hubs and spokes increases. But it is less convenient for passengers than a direct flight from origin to destination. Critics of deregulation have placed a good deal of emphasis on the reductions in passenger comfort. But economists argue that competition would not bring such results unless passengers as a group prefer the reduction in fares to the greater standards of luxury that preceded them.

**EFFECTS ON SAFETY**   Also in the case of airline deregulation (though the issue can well arise elsewhere), some observers have been concerned that cost cutting after deregulation would lead to skimping on safety measures. As Figure 20–3 shows, deregulation seems not to have produced any increase in the rate of airline accidents. Still, deregulation may require special vigilance to guard against neglect of safety as a cost-cutting measure. Some observers suggest that the reduced profits that competition has caused in truck transportation has led truckers to cut corners in terms of safety.

**U.S. Airline Accident Rates, 1960–1998**    FIGURE 20-3

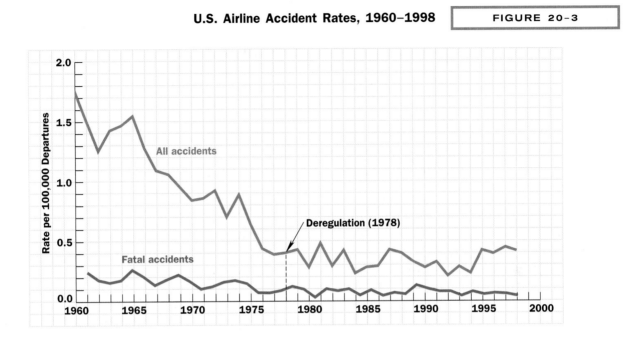

SOURCE: National Transportation Safety Board, www.ntsb.gov. Data are compiled from various news releases from January 1971 through January 1999 and are for scheduled service of all U.S. airlines operating under 14 CFR 121.

**EFFECTS ON PROFITS AND WAGES**    As the previous discussion suggested, deregulation has generally strengthened competition, and the increased power of competition has, in turn, tended to depress profits and wages. This, of course, is just the other side of reduced prices to consumers. In some cases, the profit and wage cuts were very substantial and had significant consequences. The financial problems that result for airlines and trucking firms have already been noted, and the pressures for decreases in the very high earnings of airline pilots has led to frequent confrontations with the airlines, as in the battle between American Airlines and its pilots in February 1999.

The general conclusion is that deregulation has usually worked out well, but not perfectly in promoting the welfare of consumers. But the battle for deregulation is far from over. Even if those who wish for a return to the good old days of regulation (and there are some) do not succeed, many areas exist in which regulation of the old-time variety still continues its grip or has been reintroduced in disguised form.

## The Reason Why Regulators Often Push Prices Upward

We can now return to the puzzle we posed earlier: Why would regulators, who are supposed to protect the interests of the public, raise prices? As we will see now, the answer is that regulators sometimes push for higher prices when they want to prevent the demise of any existing firms in an industry. We saw earlier that strong economies of scale and economies of scope may make it impossible for a number of firms to survive. The largest firm in an industry may have such a big cost advantage over its competitors that it will be able to drive them out of the market while still operating at a profit.

Firms that are hurt by such competitive pressures often complain to regulatory commissions that the prices charged by a rival are "unfairly low." These commissions, afraid that unrestrained pricing will reduce the number of firms in the industry, then attempt to "equalize" matters by imposing price floors (below which prices cannot be set). Such price floors are designed to permit *all* the firms in the industry to operate profitably, even those that operate inefficiently and incur costs far higher than their competitors' costs.

But many economists maintain that this approach to pricing is a perversion of the idea of competition. The virtue of competition is that, where it occurs, firms force one another to supply consumers with products of high quality at low prices. Any firm that cannot do this is driven out of business by market forces. A regulatory arrangement may allow efficient and inefficient firms to coexist only by preventing them from competing with one another, but this only preserves the appearance of competition while destroying its substance, and forces consumers to pay the higher prices necessary to keep the inefficient firms alive.

## ■ PART 2: ANTITRUST LAWS AND POLICIES

**Antitrust policy** refers to programs and laws that preclude the deliberate creation of monopoly and prevent powerful firms from engaging in related "undesirable practices."

In Part 1 of this chapter we described the process of regulation, which governments use to control monopoly or oligopoly firms that are deemed to have dangerous power to control their markets. In Part 2 we will analyze the second of government's instruments for protecting competition: **antitrust policy**. Antitrust policy (often referred to, simply, as "antitrust") refers to programs that preclude the deliberate creation of monopoly and prevent powerful firms from engaging in related "undesirable practices." Firms accused of violating the U.S. antitrust laws are likely to be sued by the federal government or other private firms. Antitrust suits seek to prevent such undesirable behavior from recurring, provide compensation to the victims, and punish offenders via fines or even imprisonment.

What justifies investment of so much power in such government agencies as the Department of Justice or the Federal Trade Commission? What are the purposes of the antitrust laws? How well has antitrust policy succeeded? These are the issues that we will discuss in the remainder of the chapter.

## ■ THE PUBLIC IMAGE OF BUSINESS WHEN THE ANTITRUST LAWS WERE BORN

Congress was first led to interfere with freedom of business enterprise in response to widely publicized and criticized business practices during the half-century following the Civil War. No doubt, many businesses in that era were beyond reproach. But the more daring breed of entrepreneurs called "robber barons" made the headlines, and tales of their exploits competed with those of the Wild West. The story of John D. Rockefeller Sr. and his Standard Oil Company is a prime example. In 1870, about five years after entering into the oil-refining business with an investment of $4,000, Rockefeller and his partners created the Standard Oil Company. The company soon combined with or bought out a number of refineries and shippers, becoming powerful enough to force the railroads to provide discounts to members of the group and not to its competitors. It even forced the railroads to give the group "drawbacks"—that is, payments on every shipment of oil refined by a rival firm. By 1879, Standard Oil and its associated companies were producing some 90 percent of the nation's refined oil and controlled all of its pipelines.

Then, in 1882, to lock in its powers, the 40 associated firms formed the Standard Oil Trust (from which the word *antitrust* derives). The trust closed down "excessive" and inefficient refinery operations, involving more than half of its plants, in order to limit output, raise prices, and earn monopoly profits.

Other trusts soon followed in the sugar, whiskey, lead, and cottonseed and linseed oil industries. In 1892, the Supreme Court of Ohio ordered the dissolution of the Standard Oil Trust, which nevertheless survived as a cooperating set of firms, with directors of the major refining companies serving on each other's boards.

Other, more lurid tales of business practices in this period are easy to find: J. P. Morgan hired an army of toughs to engage literally in pitched battle for a contested section of railroad outside Binghamton, New York. Philip Armour and his confederates obtained control of meat processing by an understanding with their rivals that each day a different one of them would offer a low bid for the morning shipment of cattle and no one would enter a higher bid. Advocates of control measures warned the public that it faced a country "in which the citizen was born to drink the milk furnished by the milk trust, eat the beef of the beef trust, illuminate his home by grace of the oil trust and die and be carried off by the coffin trust."[1] The circumstances were clearly propitious for some legislative action.

## ■ THE ANTITRUST LAWS

Five acts of Congress constitute the basis of the federal government's antitrust policy. Major provisions of these acts are summarized in Table 20–1. Congress passed the Sherman Act, the first of the U.S. antitrust laws, in 1890, soon after the trust-creating activity reached its peak. The act is brief and very general, containing two main provisions: Section 1 of the act prohibits all contracts, combinations, and conspiracies in restraint of trade, and Section 2 bans monopolization in interstate and foreign trade.

**Basic Antitrust Laws**   TABLE 20–1

| Name | Date | Major Provisions |
| --- | --- | --- |
| Sherman Act | 1890 | Prohibits "all contracts, combinations and conspiracies in restraint of trade" (Section 1) and monopolization in interstate and foreign trade (Section 2). |
| Clayton Act | 1914 | Prohibits price discrimination, "exclusive contracts" under which sellers prevent buyers from purchasing goods from the sellers' competitors, and "tying contracts" under which a customer who wants to buy some product from a given seller is required as part of the price to agree to buy some other product or products from that same seller. Prohibits acquisition by one corporation of another's shares if the act is likely to reduce competition or tend to create monopoly. Prohibits directors of one company from sitting on the board of a competitor's company. |
| Federal Trade Commission Act | 1914 | Established the FTC as an independent agency with authority to prosecute unfair competition and to prevent false and misleading advertising. |
| Robinson-Patman Act | 1936 | Prohibits special discounts and other discriminatory concessions to large purchasers unless based on differences in cost or "offered in good faith to meet an equally low price of a competitor." |
| Celler-Kefauver Antimerger Act | 1950 | Prohibits any corporation from acquiring the assets of another where the effect is to reduce competition substantially or to tend to create a monopoly. |

---

[1] Matthew Josephson, *The Robber Barons, The Great American Capitalists, 1861–1901* (New York: Harcourt Brace, 1934), p. 358.

---

### ● THE SIZE AND SCOPE OF AN ANTITRUST CASE

Alleged violations of the antitrust laws are usually dealt with by bringing the accused firm to court or by threatening to sue it in hope that the accused firm will surrender and accept a compromise. Antitrust suits are frequently well-publicized affairs because the accused firms are often the giants of industry involving such names as Standard Oil, U.S. Steel, the Aluminum Company of America (Alcoa), General Electric, International Business Machines (IBM), American Telephone and Telegraph (AT&T), and Microsoft. Even some of the nation's most prestigious colleges and universities have been accused of engaging in a pricing conspiracy.

The magnitude of an antitrust suit is difficult to imagine. After the charges have been filed, it is not unusual for more than five years to elapse before the case even comes to trial. The parties spend this period laboriously preparing their cases. Dozens of lawyers, scores of witnesses, and hundreds of researchers are likely to participate in this process. The trial itself also can run for years. A major case produces literally thousands of volumes of material, and it can easily cost the defendant several hundred million dollars. In addition, if it loses, the defendant may have to pay billions of dollars in fines.

Thus, the power of the government or another firm to haul a company into court on antitrust charges is an awesome one. Win, lose, or draw, such a case is a very heavy burden on the accused firm, draining its funds, taking the time and attention of its management, and delaying business decisions until the outcome of the legal proceedings is determined.

### SHERMAN ACT

**"PER SE" ISSUES UNDER THE SHERMAN ACT**  From the inception of the Sherman Act, Section 1 has been invoked primarily against price-fixing agreements—that is, agreements under which several ostensibly competing firms coordinate their pricing decisions. In interpreting Section 1, the courts have held that such agreements are illegal *per se;* in other words, they have held that no excuses or exonerating circumstances can make a price-fixing agreement legal.

**"RULE OF REASON" ISSUES UNDER THE SHERMAN ACT**  Section 2 of the Sherman Act deals with individual decision makers, rather than with groups of conspirators, focusing on attempts to create monopolies. In dealing with Section 2, the courts formulated the troublesome *rule of reason*, which held that monopolizing trade restraints are not necessarily illegal *per se*. According to this rule, a restraint is against the law only if it is "unreasonable." For example, one court ruled (and many economists agree) that size, by itself, does not constitute an offense—that a firm must commit objectionable overt acts to be guilty of violating Section 2 of the Sherman Act.

Because many people believed that the Sherman Act did not provide adequate protection to the public, in 1914 Congress passed two supplemental laws: the Clayton Act and the Federal Trade Commission Act.

### CLAYTON ACT OF 1914

**PRICE DISCRIMINATION IN RESTRAINT OF TRADE**  The Clayton Act deals with certain specific practices thought to facilitate the encroachment of monopoly. First, it prohibits price discrimination (see Chapter 12), which it defines as the act, by a seller, of charging different prices to different buyers of the same product. This provision would, for example, have banned the railroad rebates that Rockefeller used to squeeze out his rivals.

**EXCLUSIVE CONTRACTS AND TYING CONTRACTS**  Second, the Clayton Act prohibits *exclusive contracts,* arrangements under which sellers prevent buyers from purchasing goods from the sellers' competitors, and *tying contracts,* arrangements under which a customer who wants to buy some product from a given seller is required as part of the price to agree to buy some other product or products from that same seller.

**STOCK PURCHASES AND INDEPENDENCE**  Third, the Clayton Act prohibits one firm from purchasing the stock of another if that acquisition tends to reduce competition by ending the independence of its rivals. This provision was later strengthened by the Celler-Kefauver Antimerger Act of 1950.

---

● **PROTECTION OF COMPETITION, NOT PROTECTION OF COMPETITORS**

The courts have repeatedly emphasized that the antitrust laws are not intended to make life easier for individual firms that encounter difficulties coping with competitive market pressures. The following quotation from a recent decision of the U.S. Supreme Court makes this clear:

"The purpose of the Sherman Act is not to protect businesses from the working of the market, it is to protect the public from the failure of the market."

SOURCE: *Spectrum Sports Inc.* v. *McQuillan*, US 122 L.Ed 2d 247 [1993], p. 506.

---

**INTERLOCKING DIRECTORATES**    Finally, the Clayton Act prohibits interlocking directorates between competitors, under which some individuals are members of the boards of directors of two rival firms.

## FTC ACT

The Federal Trade Commission Act created a commission to investigate "unfair" and "predatory" competitive practices and declared illegal all "unfair methods of competition and commerce." The Federal Trade Commission (FTC) was a rather ineffective agency during its first quarter-century. In 1938, however, it was given the task of preventing false and deceptive advertising, to which it has since devoted much of its effort.

## ROBINSON-PATMAN ACT

In 1936, Congress passed the Robinson-Patman Act to protect independent sellers—both wholesalers and retailers (primarily those who sold groceries and drugs)—from the "unfair competition" of chain stores and mass distributors. The Robinson-Patman Act differed from other antitrust laws, because it sought to *restrain* competition by protecting small firms from the competition of larger ones.

## ■ MEASURING MARKET POWER: CONCENTRATION

In enforcing these laws, one piece of evidence that the U.S. Department of Justice and the Federal Trade Commission use to test whether a firm under investigation for antitrust violations is likely to possess monopoly power is the *concentration* of the markets in which the firm carries out its activities. A market or an industry is said to be "highly concentrated" if it contains only a few firms, most or all of which sell a large share of the industry's products. In contrast, an industry with many small firms is said to be "unconcentrated." Thus, concentration is a useful index of the relative bigness of the firms in the industry. Now, we have seen that big firms do not always have market power, though relatively small firms never (or almost never) do. Still, concentration is one useful piece of evidence in deciding whether market power exists in any case under investigation.

Concentration is measured in a number of ways. The most straightforward method is to calculate what share of the industry's output is sold by some selected number of the industry's firms. Most often a *four-firm* **concentration ratio** is used for this purpose. Thus, if the four largest firms in an industry account for, say, 58 percent of the industry's sales, we say that the four-firm concentration ratio is 0.58. Other formulas are used to measure concentration, but they are all designed to evaluate the same thing—how much of the industry's sales are carried out by its largest firms.

Ultimately, we care about concentration ratios if they are a good measure of market power. The question, then, is this: If an industry becomes more concentrated, will the firms necessarily increase their ability to price their products above

A **concentration ratio** is the percentage of an industry's output produced by its four largest firms. It is intended to measure the degree to which the industry is dominated by large firms.

---

The charming courtroom is old but recently refurbished, and the air conditioning is inadequate. It is often difficult to hear what is happening. The defendant firm has been accused of predatory pricing, that is, of charging very low prices in order to drive a competitor out of the market, and is defending itself against a judgment that could run into billions of dollars.

For the past two months, both sides have called up many witnesses—company executives, accountants, statisticians. The female lawyers are dressed in conservative outfits, the men in somewhat seedy two-piece matching suits. It would not do to appear too wealthy, for this is a jury trial, and the nine men and women wear casual attire including sneakers, jeans, and sports clothes. Although determined to see justice done, they are having a hard time staying awake under a hurricane of technical arguments and contradictory figures.

The judge follows the proceedings closely, often interrupting with questions of her own. Sometimes she jokes with the witnesses.

The lawyers call in an expert witness who is a specialist in the field—in this case an economist who has written on predatory pricing. He explains to the court and the jury the current thinking of the economics profession on the definition of predatory pricing and the standards by which one judges whether or not it has occurred. He is persuasive.

But the judge and jury have already heard from another economist, equally distinguished, representing the other side. Their analyses, which were quite technical, reached opposite conclusions. Which one are the jurors to believe, and on what basis?

---

competitive levels? Many economists have, in fact, concluded that although increased concentration *often* facilitates or increases market power, it does not *always* do so. Specifically, the following three conclusions are now widely accepted:

- If, after an increase in concentration, an industry still has a very low concentration ratio, then its firms are very unlikely to have any market power either before or after the rise in concentration.

- If circumstances in the industry are in other respects favorable for successful price collusion, a rise in concentration will facilitate market power. It will do so by reducing the number of firms that need to be consulted in arriving at an agreement and by decreasing the number of firms that have to be watched to make sure they do not betray the collusive agreement.

- Where entry into and exit from the industry are easy and quite inexpensive, that is, where the market is highly *contestable*, then even when concentration increases, market power will not be enhanced because an excessive price will attract new entrants who will soon force the price down.

### THE EVIDENCE ON CONCENTRATION IN REALITY

Still, concentration data may be the best evidence that we have on the effectiveness of antitrust programs. Table 20–2 shows concentration ratios in a number of industries in the United States. We see that concentration varies greatly from industry to industry: automobiles, breakfast cereals, and aircraft are produced by highly concentrated industries, whereas the jewelry, clothing, and soft-drink industries show very little concentration.

Since the beginning of this century, concentration ratios in the United States have, on the average, remained remarkably constant. It has been estimated that, at the turn of the century, 32.9 percent of manufactured goods were produced by industries in which the concentration ratios were 50 percent or more (meaning that at least 50 percent of industry output was produced by the four largest firms). By 1963, the figure had risen only to 33.1 percent, and by 1992, it had actually fallen to 26.4 percent. These figures and those for other years are shown in Table 20–3. Over the course of the 20th century, concentration in individual U.S. industries has shown no tendency to increase.

## Concentration Ratios for Representative Industries, 1992 | TABLE 20-2

| Industry | Four-Firm Ratio | Industry | Four-Firm Ratio |
|---|---|---|---|
| Electric lamps, bulbs, and tubes | 86 | Bottled and canned soft drinks | 37 |
| Cereal breakfast foods | 85 | Motors and generators | 36 |
| Motor vehicles and car bodies | 84 | Dolls and stuffed toys | 34 |
| Hard surface floor coverage | 83 | Boat building and repairing | 32 |
| Aircraft | 79 | Pharmaceutical preparations | 26 |
| Rubber tires and inner tubes | 70 | Musical instruments | 25 |
| Primary aluminum | 59 | Brooms and brushes | 23 |
| Fabricated metal cans | 56 | Fluid milk | 22 |
| Ship building and repairing | 53 | Bolts, nuts, rivets, and washers | 17 |
| Fasteners, buttons, needles, and pins | 41 | Jewelry, precious metal | 16 |
| Prerecorded records and recorded tapes | 40 | Apparel: women's, misses', juniors' dresses | 11 |
| Apparel: men's and boys' suits and coats | 39 | | |

NOTE: Ratios are percent of output produced by the four largest firms in each industry.

SOURCE: U.S. Bureau of the Census, "Concentration Ratios in Manufacturing," *1992 Census of Manufactures.* Thanks to Andrew W. Hait, Special Reports Branch, U.S. Bureau of the Census.

## The Trend in Concentration in Manufacturing Industries, 1901–1992 | TABLE 20-3

| | Around 1901 | 1947 | 1954 | 1958 | 1963 | 1966 | 1970 | 1972 | 1982 | 1987 | 1992 |
|---|---|---|---|---|---|---|---|---|---|---|---|
| Percentage of value added in industries with four-firm concentration ratios over 50 percent | 32.9 | 24.4 | 29.9 | 30.2 | 33.1 | 28.6 | 26.3 | 29.0 | 25.2 | 27.9 | 26.4 |

SOURCES: P.W. McCracken and T.G. Moore, "Competitive and Market Concentration in the American Economy," Subcommittee on Antitrust and Monopoly, U.S. Senate, March 29, 1973; F.M. Scherer, *Industrial Market Structure and Economic Performance* (Boston: Houghton Mifflin, 1980), p. 68; F.M. Scherer and David Ross, *Industrial Market Structure and Economic Performance*, 3rd ed. (Boston: Houghton Mifflin, 1990), p. 84; Personal communication with Professor F.M. Scherer, March 10, 1993; and personal communication with Andrew W. Hait, Special Reports Branch, U.S. bureau of the census, January 18, 1996.

Such information may suggest that the antitrust laws have to some degree been effective in inhibiting whatever trend toward bigness may in fact exist. But even this very cautious conclusion has been questioned by some observers, who argue that the size of firms has been held down by market forces and technical developments (such as declining computer costs that make it easier for small firms to increase their efficiency, or the takeover of much of freight traffic from large railroads by small trucking firms). These observers argue that antitrust laws have made virtually no difference in the size and the behavior of American business.

## A CRUCIAL PROBLEM FOR ANTITRUST: THE RESEMBLANCE OF MONOPOLIZATION AND VIGOROUS COMPETITION

One problem that haunts most antitrust litigation and lies at the heart of the sensational Microsoft case (discussed in detail later in the chapter), among many others, is that vigorous competition may look very similar to acts that *undermine* competition and support monopoly power. The resulting danger is that the courts will prohibit, or the antitrust authorities will prosecute, acts that *appear* to be anticompetitive but that really are the opposite.

The difficulty is that effective competition by a firm is always tough on its rivals. It forces rivals to charge lower prices, to improve product quality, and to spend money on innovations that will cut their costs and improve their products. Competition will legitimately force rivals out of business if they are inefficient and therefore cannot keep their prices low or provide products of acceptable quality. But when competition destroys a rival in this way it is difficult to tell whether it was, so to speak, murdered or died of natural causes. In both cases the surviving competitor bears some responsibility. But if the cause of the rival's demise is legitimate competition, consumers will benefit; if, however, the end of the rival was part of a process of monopoly creation, then the public will end up paying. This is a very real issue that constantly recurs in today's antitrust litigation.

## ANTICOMPETITIVE PRACTICES AND ANTITRUST

A central purpose of the antitrust laws is to prevent "anticompetitive practices," actions by a powerful firm that threaten to destroy competitors, to force them to compete less vigorously, or to prevent the entry of new rivals.

### PREDATORY PRICING

**Predatory pricing** is pricing that threatens to keep a competitor out of the market. It is a price that is so low that it will be profitable for the firm that adopts it only if a rival is driven from the market.

Typical of such accusations of anticompetitive behavior is the claim, frequent in antitrust cases, that the defendant has adopted unjustifiably low prices in order to force other firms to lose money, thereby driving competitors out of business. This practice is called **predatory pricing.** Deciding whether pricing is "predatory" is difficult, both for economists and for courts of law, because low prices generally benefit consumers. Therefore, the courts do not want to discourage firms from cutting prices by being too eager to declare that lower prices are intended to destroy a rival.

One principle widely followed by the courts holds that prices are predatory only if they are below either marginal or average variable costs. The logic of this criterion as a test for whether prices are "too low" is that even under perfect competition, prices will not, in the long run, fall below that level, but will equal marginal costs. But even in cases where prices are below marginal or average variable costs, they may be held to be predatory only under two conditions:

- If there is evidence that the low price would have been profitable *only* if it succeeded in destroying a rival or in keeping it out of the market.
- When there is a real probability that the allegedly predatory firm could raise prices to monopoly levels after the rival was driven out, thereby profiting from its venture in crime.

Many successful firms—including AT&T, American Airlines, and Microsoft— have been accused of predatory pricing. The defendants typically argue that their low prices cover both marginal and average variable costs, that the prices are low because of superior efficiency, and that the lawsuit was brought to prevent the defendants from competing effectively. The courts have generally accepted these arguments. There have been many predatory pricing cases, but few convictions.

### OTHER POSSIBLY ANTICOMPETITIVE PRACTICES: BOTTLENECK PRICING AND BUNDLING

The litigation involving Microsoft Corporation illustrates two other practices that can conceivably be anticompetitive. Microsoft is the enormously successful software supplier of computer operating systems that enable you to communicate with and control your computer; it also supplies other very popular computer programs. Microsoft's sales are huge, and it is clearly a tough and energetic competitor. The difficulty of distinguishing vigorously competitive behavior from anticompetitive acts is illustrated by the Microsoft antitrust case now before the courts, in which the U.S. Department of Justice has accused the firm of various anticompetitive practices. The Microsoft case raises many issues, two of which are discussed here as illustrations.

**BOTTLENECK PRICING**   Microsoft *Windows*, an operating system that runs about 90 percent of all personal computers, is a prime example of a bottleneck, which we discussed earlier in this chapter. To reach any substantial proportion of personal computer customers, the producer of any word processor, spreadsheet, or graphics program must use *Windows*. And there is no near-term likelihood that any alternative to *Windows* will arise and capture a large share of customers. In part, this is because *Windows* is widely considered a good program, but even more because of the desire for *user* compatibility—computer users communicate with one another, and communicating is easier if all these users employ the same operating system. The bottleneck problem arises because Microsoft itself supplies not only *Windows* but also many applications (such as *Word*, a word-processing program, *Excel*, a spreadsheet program, and *Explorer*, an Internet browser software). The worry is that Microsoft will use *Windows* in a way that favors its own programs and handicaps programs that its competitors develop.

**BUNDLING: LEGITIMATE AND ILLEGITIMATE**   Microsoft promotes its own products by providing them more cheaply to computer manufacturers if these makers buy a *bundle* of Microsoft programs, not just *Windows* alone. But this means that rival producers of word processors, spreadsheets, and Internet browsers are handicapped in selling their products to PC owners. The question is whether Microsoft's low bundle price is legitimate or if it constitutes a case of predatory pricing whose only purpose is to destroy competitors. Economists often take the position that a **bundling** discount is legitimate if it is cheaper for the firm to supply several products at once than to supply them one at a time, and if the price cut corresponds to the cost saving. However, they question the legitimacy of the bundle discount if the cost saving is considerably less than the difference between the bundled price and the sum of the prices of the included products (when bought individually).

> **Bundling** refers to a pricing arrangement under which the supplier offers substantial discounts to customers if they buy several of the firm's products, so that the price of the bundle of products is less than the sum of the prices of the products if they were bought separately.

## ■ MERGERS AND COMPETITION

**HORIZONTAL MERGERS**   **Mergers** have long been an object of suspicion by the antitrust authorities. This is particularly true when a merger is *horizontal*, meaning that the merging firms compete directly by supplying products that are identical or very similar. In these cases, it is often feared that competition will decline because there will be fewer firms in the industry.

> A **merger** refers to unification of two previously independent firms, as when one purchases the other or the two simply decide to combine into a single enterprise.

The Department of Justice and the Federal Trade Commission are both concerned with mergers. They do not wish to impede mergers that seem likely to increase efficiency. But the antitrust agencies do want to prevent mergers that threaten to reduce competition.

To help firms decide whether a proposed merger will get them into trouble, and for other reasons as well, the Department of Justice and the FTC together issue guidelines indicating when they are (or are not) likely to try to block a merger. For example, they generally will not oppose mergers in industries in which concentration is low or into which entry is very easy. However, in industries that are highly concentrated and where entry is difficult, the merger of two large firms will often be opposed.

**RECENT SURGES IN MERGER ACTIVITY**   During the early 1980s, the Justice Department issued several sets of new, more permissive guidelines. This loosening of the anti-merger rules, coupled with the Reagan administration's view that mergers were generally good for the economy, spawned a much-publicized increase in merger activity. In total, about $1.5 trillion was spent on "deal-making" activity (including mergers, acquisitions, and leveraged buyouts) during the decade of the 1980s. After a brief slowdown in the early 1990s, the merger pace picked up again. In 1998 *alone*, a record $1.6 trillion in mergers took place, with such headline-making deals as the

$77 billion takeover of Mobil Oil by Exxon, and the merger of Citibank and Travelers Group, forming the world's largest financial services company.[2]

This rash of mergers has given rise to much controversy. Some observers believe that it increases the likelihood of monopoly power, whereas others believe that it serves largely to make the merged firms more efficient. In any event, defenders argue that mergers have not historically increased the market share of big business in the United States. For example, in 1998 the share of the labor force employed by the corporations listed in the *Fortune 500* was about 16 percent, lower than its 17 percent share in 1970.[3]

**ARE MERGERS ANTICOMPETITIVE?**    Though by no means unanimous on the subject, many economists agree that mergers sometimes reduce competition, particularly in markets that are not contestable, so that threats of entry do not prevent the merged firms from raising prices above competitive levels.[4] On the other hand, where there is reason to believe that mergers will *not* reduce competition, most economists oppose impediments to them. Many economists believe that mergers that are not undertaken to reduce competition can have only one purpose—to achieve greater efficiency. For example, the larger firm that results from the merger may enjoy substantial economies of scale not available to smaller firms. Or the two merging companies may learn special skills from one another or offset one another's risks.

**DO MERGERS IMPROVE PERFORMANCE?**    Mergers have sometimes proved disappointing and brought limited cost savings; a number have subsequently been dissolved. Several studies have found that more than one-third of acquisitions are eventually divested. But economists who defend freedom to merge when there is no demonstrated threat to competition pose a challenging question: Who can judge better than the firms involved whether their marriage is likely to make their activities more efficient? Indeed, a number of recent studies of merger activity during the 1980s have all reported significant productivity increases following mergers.[5]

## ■ USE OF ANTITRUST LAWS TO PREVENT COMPETITION

Finally, let us turn to an issue that some observers consider very serious: the *misuse* of the antitrust laws to prevent competition. Many firms that have been unable to compete effectively on their own merits have turned to the courts to seek protection from their successful competitors—and some have succeeded.

Firms that try to protect themselves in this way always claim that their rivals have not achieved success through superior ability but, rather, by means that they call "monopolization." Sometimes the evidence is clear-cut, and the courts can readily discern whether an accused firm has violated the antitrust laws or whether it has simply been too efficient and innovative for the complaining competitors' tastes. In other cases, however, the issues are complicated, and only a long and painstaking legal proceeding offers any prospect of resolving them.

Various steps have been suggested to deal with the misuse of U.S. antitrust laws. In one proposal, if the courts decide that a firm has been falsely accused by another of violating the antitrust laws, then (as is done in other countries) the *accuser* should pay the legal costs of the innocent defendant. Another proposal is to subject such

[2] *Economic Report of the President 1999* (Washington, D.C.: U.S. Government Printing Office, February 1999) and "The Year of the Merger," BBC News online network, December 26, 1998, http://news.bbc.co.uk/.

[3] *Fortune*, May 1971 and April 26, 1999.

[4] See Chapter 13, pages 264–266, for a definition and discussion of contestable markets.

[5] See, for example, Frank Lichtenberg, *Corporate Takeovers and Productivity* (Cambridge, Mass.: MIT Press, 1992); Paul M. Healy, Krishna G. Palepu, and Richard S. Ruback, "Does Corporate Performance Improve After Mergers?" *Journal of Financial Economics* 31 (1992): 135–175; and Robert H. McGuckin and Sang V. Nguyen, "On Productivity and Plant Ownership Change: New Evidence from the Longitudinal Research Database," *RAND Journal of Economics* 26, no. 2 (Summer 1995): 257–276.

---

### ● CAN ANTITRUST LAWS BE USED TO *PREVENT* COMPETITION?

Many observers are concerned that the antitrust laws are often used by inefficient firms to protect themselves from the competition of more efficient rivals. When they are unable to win out in the marketplace, the argument goes, firms simply file lawsuits against their competitors claiming that those rivals have achieved success by means that violate the antitrust laws.

Not only do they seek protection from the courts against what they describe as "unfair competition" or "predatory practices," but they often sue for compensation which, under the law, can sometimes be three times as large as the damages that they claim to have suffered. Moreover, even if the defendant is found innocent, it must normally pay the very high costs of the litigation itself. Aside from the enormous waste that such lawsuits entail, observers worry that this is a perversion of the antitrust laws, which were, after all, designed to promote competition, not to prevent it.

Two recent examples illustrate the nature of such litigation.* These cases also show that the courts are often wise enough to throw out such attempts to use the antitrust laws to prevent competition.

#### AMI VERSUS IBM

Allen-Myland Inc. (AMI) is a small firm that specialized in the upgrading of computers, an activity that had earned it handsome profits in a period of time when expanding a computer's capacity was very laborious. However, technological progress by IBM then transformed what was once a labor-intensive task requiring considerable skill into the routine installation of a small and highly reliable part. This rendered obsolete many of the services offered by AMI. So AMI sued IBM, seeking to persuade the court to impose an artificial and expensive market niche for upgrading services, with AMI permanently protected from competitive pressures. The court's decision completely rejected AMI's position (Eastern District of Pennsylvania, 1988).

#### SEWELL PLASTICS VERSUS COCA-COLA, SOUTHEASTERN CONTAINER, ET AL.

The Sewell Plastics Company once had a preponderant market share in the manufacture of plastic soft-drink bottles in the United States, selling 2-liter bottles for more than 30 cents each. A group of Coca-Cola bottlers in the Southeast considered the price too high and formed a cooperative firm (Southeastern Container) to manufacture their own plastic bottles.

Within five years, Southeastern had reduced its cost below 14 cents per bottle, and real retail prices of soft drinks also fell. Despite rising national sales and profits, Sewell sued Southeastern, seeking to force its owners to sell the firm to Sewell or, as a possible alternative, to force Southeastern's customers to sign exclusive purchasing contracts with Sewell. In the spring of 1989, the judge dismissed Sewell's claims, holding that there was no need for a trial (U.S. District Court, Western District, North Carolina, April 1989).

*One of the authors of this book, William Baumol, was involved as an expert witness in both cases.

---

suits to prescreening by a government agency, as is done in Japan. But these issues are hardly open-and-shut, for there is no such thing as a perfect legal system. Anything that restricts anticompetitive, private antitrust suits will almost certainly also inhibit legitimate attempts by individual firms to defend themselves from genuine acts of monopolization by rival enterprises (for more on this issue, see the accompanying box, "Can Antitrust Laws Be Used to *Prevent* Competition?").

## ■ CONCLUDING OBSERVATIONS

As we noted at the beginning of this chapter, monopoly and monopoly power are rightly judged to cause market failure—they prevent the market from serving consumer interests most effectively by providing the products the public desires at the lowest possible prices. But the alternative is government intervention, and governments, too, sometimes make imperfect decisions. Thus, before deciding whether to regulate more or deregulate, whether to toughen antitrust laws or loosen them, informed citizens should carefully weigh the prospects for market failure against the possibility of government failure in terms of the contemplated change. Monopolists have sometimes succeeded in preventing the introduction of useful new products. They have raised prices to consumers and held down product quality. But large firms have also sometimes been innovative and their service to customers has in some cases been considered of high quality. Government has also had its missteps.

It has initiated costly lawsuits, sometimes on questionable grounds. It has forced regulated firms to adopt pricing rules that were clearly not beneficial to consumers, and it has handicapped the operations of industries, for example, arguably almost destroying the nation's railroads. Yet government, too, has done useful things in influencing industry behavior, preventing various monopolistic practices, protecting consumers from impure foods and medications, and so on. Most economists believe that by the 1970s government intervention had clearly gone too far in some respects and that deregulation was, consequently, in the public interest. However, the general issue is hardly settled.

## SUMMARY

1. *Regulation* has two primary purposes: to put brakes on the decisions of industries with monopoly power and to contribute to public health and safety.

2. In the United States, regulation of prices and other economic decisions is generally applied only to large firms, including railroads, telecommunications, and gas and electricity supply.

3. In recent years there has been a major push toward reduction of regulation. Among the industries that have been deregulated in whole or in part are air, truck, and rail transportation.

4. Among the major reasons given for regulation are (a) *economies of scale* and *economies of scope*, which make industries into natural monopolies, and (b) the *universal service* goal, which refers to the provision of service to poor people and isolated areas where supply is unprofitable.

5. Regulators often reject proposals by regulated firms to cut their prices, and sometimes the regulators even force firms to *raise* their prices. The purposes of such actions are to prevent "unfair competition" and to protect customers of some of the firm's products from being forced to *cross-subsidize* customers of other products. Many economists disagree

with most such actions and argue that the result is usually to stifle competition and make all customers pay more than they otherwise would pay.

6. Economists generally argue that a firm should be permitted to cut its price as long as it covers its marginal cost. However, in many regulated industries, firms would go bankrupt if all prices were set equal to marginal costs.

7. By putting ceilings on profits to prevent monopoly earnings, regulation can eliminate the firm's incentive for efficiency and innovation. *Price caps*, which put (inflation-adjusted) ceilings on prices, rather than profits, are used widely to deal with this problem.

8. To prevent the undermining of competition, the owner of a (monopoly) *bottleneck facility* must charge all users of the facility (including itself) the same price for access.

9. *Antitrust policy* refers to policies and programs designed to control the growth of monopoly and to prevent big business from engaging in "anticompetitive" practices.

10. The *Sherman Act* is the oldest U.S. antitrust law. It prohibits contracts, combinations, and conspiracies in restraint of trade, and it also prohibits monopolization.

11. Collusion among horizontal competitors to fix prices is *illegal per se* under the Sherman Act. Acts of monopolization—that is, acts that attempt to acquire monopoly power—are tested under the *rule of reason.*

12. Several other important antitrust laws exist, including the *Clayton Act,* which prohibits price discrimination that tends to reduce competition or create monopoly; the *Federal Trade Commission Act,* which created the commission as an independent antitrust agency; and the *Robinson-Patman Act,* which generally prohibits discriminatory price discounts.

13. *Predatory pricing* is pricing that is low relative to the marginal or average variable costs of the firm and so threatens to drive a competitor out of the market. There must also be a likelihood that if the prices do destroy a competitor the firm will acquire market power enabling it to charge prices well above competitive levels.

14. *Bundling* refers to a price reduction given to customers who purchase several of the firm's products simultaneously.

It is considered unobjectionable if it is cheaper for the firm to bundle its products and the price cut merely passes the savings on to customers. However, bundling can be used to destroy competitors who sell only some of the bundled products.

15. The evidence indicates that there has been no significant increase in the *concentration* of individual U.S. industries into fewer, relatively larger firms during the 20th century. Evidence as to whether antitrust laws have been effective in preventing monopoly is inconclusive, and observers disagree on the subject.

16. Unregulated monopoly is apt to distribute income unfairly, produce undesirably small quantities of output, and provide inadequate motivation for innovation.

17. However, sometimes only large firms may have funds sufficient for effective research, development, and innovation; where economies of scale are available, large firms can serve customers more cheaply than can small ones.

---

### KEY TERMS

Economies of scale   406

Monopoly power   406

Regulation   407

Economies of scope   409

Bottleneck facilities   409

Parity-pricing principle   411

Cross-subsidization   412

Marginal versus average cost pricing   413

Ramsey pricing rule   414

Regulatory lag   415

Price cap   415

Deregulation   417

Antitrust policy   420

Rule of reason   422

Concentration of industry   423

Concentration ratios   423

Predatory pricing   426

Bundling   427

Mergers   427

---

### QUESTIONS FOR REVIEW

1. Why is an electric company in a city often considered to be a natural monopoly? What would happen if two competing electric companies were established? How about telephone companies? How can changes in technology affect your answer?

2. Suppose that a 20 percent cut in the price of coast-to-coast telephone calls brings in so much new business that it permits a long-distance telephone company to cut its charges for service from Chicago to St. Louis, but only by 2 percent. In your opinion, is this equitable? Is it a good idea or a bad one?

3. In some regulated industries, regulatory agencies prevented prices from falling, and as a result many firms opened for business in those industries. In your opinion, is this competitive or anticompetitive? Is it a good idea or a bad one?

4. Regulators are much concerned about the prevention of "predatory pricing." The U.S. Court of Appeals has, however, noted that "the term probably does not have a well-defined meaning, but it certainly bears a sinister connotation." How might one distinguish "predatory" from "nonpredatory" pricing? What would you do about it?

5. Do you think that it is fair or unfair for rural users of telephone service to be cross-subsidized by other telephone users?

6. Suppose that a firm in a regulated industry is prohibited from earning profits higher than it is getting and it begins selling a

*new* product at a price above its long-run marginal cost. Explain why the prices of other company products will, very likely, have to be reduced.

7. To provide incentives for increased efficiency, several regulatory agencies have eliminated ceilings on the profits of regulated firms but instead put caps on their prices. Suppose that a regulated firm manages to cut its prices in half, but in the process, it doubles its profits. Should rational consumers consider this to be a good or a bad development? Why?

8. A shopkeeper sells his store and signs a contract that restrains him from opening another store in competition with the new owner. The courts have decided that this contract is a reasonable restraint of trade. Can you think of any other types of restraint of trade that seem reasonable? Can you think of any that seem unreasonable?

9. Which of the following industries do you expect to have high concentration ratios: automobile production, aircraft manufacture, hardware production, railroads, production of expensive jewelry? Compare your answers with the numbers in Table 20–2.

10. Why do you think the specific industries you selected in Review Question 9 are highly concentrated?

11. Do you think it is in the public interest to launch an antitrust suit that costs $1 billion? What leads you to your conclusion?

12. In Japan and a number of European countries, the antitrust laws are much less severe than those in the United States. Do you think that this helps or harms American industry in its efforts to compete with foreign producers? Why?

13. Can you think of some legal rules that can discourage the use of antitrust laws to prevent competition while at the same time not interfering with legitimate antitrust actions?

14. Do you think that the antitrust authorities should interfere more than they do now in corporate mergers? What are some pros and cons?

15. During the oil crisis in the 1970s, long lines at gas stations disappeared soon after price controls were removed and gas prices were permitted to rise. Should this be interpreted as evidence that the oil companies have monopoly power? Why or why not?

16. Some economists believe that firms rarely attempt predatory pricing because it would be a very risky act even if it were legal. Why may this be so?

17. Firm X cuts its prices and soon competing firm Y goes out of business. How would you judge whether this price cut was an act of legitimate and vigorous competition or an anticompetitive act?

18. Increasingly, the electric utility companies, which used to be the sole generators of electricity in their assigned areas, will face the competition of other electricity generators. However, electric utilities are generally the sole owners of the transmission lines needed to carry the electricity from the generating plant to the user, so that transmission lines are a bottleneck facility. If you were the regulator, how would you determine the price the utility will be allowed to charge a competitor for use of the transmission lines? Or would you leave that price to the free market? Why or why not?

The taxing power of the government must be used to provide revenues for legitimate government purposes. It must not be used to regulate the economy or bring about social change.

Ronald Reagan

# TAXATION AND RESOURCE ALLOCATION

"Nothing is certain but death and taxes," proclaims an old adage. In recent decades, however, American politics has turned this aphorism on its head. Nowadays, it seems, the surest route to political death is to raise taxes.

Tax-cutting fever came out of California in the late 1970s and swept the nation during the presidency of Ronald Reagan—who won two landslide elections. After pledging not to raise taxes, President George Bush agreed to some small tax increases in 1990—a decision that some think cost him the 1992 election. Next came President Bill Clinton, who made income-tax increases for upper-income taxpayers a major component of his deficit-reduction plan in 1993. The next year, the Democrats were annihilated at the polls by a Republican party pledging to cut taxes.

Politicians watch election returns carefully. So it was no wonder that the bipartisan balanced-budget program, which passed Congress in 1997, reduced the deficit entirely through spending cuts, not tax hikes.

Antitax sentiment is nothing new in America, where taxes have never been very popular. Indeed, our country was born, in part, out of a tax revolt. But taxes are inevitable in any modern, mixed economy, as we noted in Chapter 3. Although the vast majority of economic activities in the United States is left to the private sector, some—such as provision of national defense and highways—are reserved for the government. And any such government spending requires tax revenues to pay the bills. So do transfer programs like Social Security and unemployment insurance.

In addition, the government sometimes deliberately interferes with the workings of the market in order to promote some social goal. Often, these interferences involve levying taxes. For example, we will see in the next chapter that policymakers can use taxes to correct misallocations of resources caused by externalities.

This chapter discusses the types of taxes that are used to raise what President Reagan called "revenues for legitimate government purposes," the effects of taxes on resource allocation and income distribution, and the principles that distinguish "good" taxes from "bad" ones.

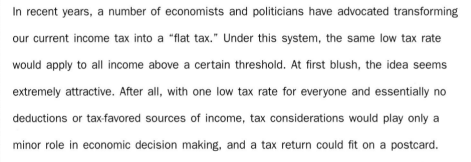

### Should We Flatten the Income Tax?

In recent years, a number of economists and politicians have advocated transforming our current income tax into a "flat tax." Under this system, the same low tax rate would apply to all income above a certain threshold. At first blush, the idea seems extremely attractive. After all, with one low tax rate for everyone and essentially no deductions or tax-favored sources of income, tax considerations would play only a minor role in economic decision making, and a tax return could fit on a postcard.

But the issue is actually a good deal more complicated than that—which is why flat-tax proposals have been so controversial. In this chapter, we will learn the principles by which tax systems are judged, and then we will apply these principles to appraising the flat tax.

## ■ THE LEVEL AND TYPES OF TAXATION

Many Americans believe that taxes have been gobbling up an ever-increasing share of the U.S. economy. Figure 21–1, however, shows that this is not true. By charting the behavior of both federal and state and local taxes *as a percentage of gross domestic product (GDP)* since 1929, we see that the share of federal taxes in GDP has been rather steady since the early 1950s. It climbed from less than 4 percent in 1929 to 20 percent during World War II, fell back to 15 percent in the immediate postwar period, and has fluctuated in the 18 to 21 percent range ever since. (It is now about 21 percent.)

The share of GDP taken by state and local taxes climbed substantially from World War II until the early 1970s. But since then it, too, has remained remarkably stable—at about 11 percent. Whether these shares are too high or too low is a matter of some debate. But:

> The shares of GDP taken in taxes by the federal, state, and local governments have been approximately constant for nearly 30 years.

**Taxes as a Percentage of Gross Domestic Product** | FIGURE 21-1

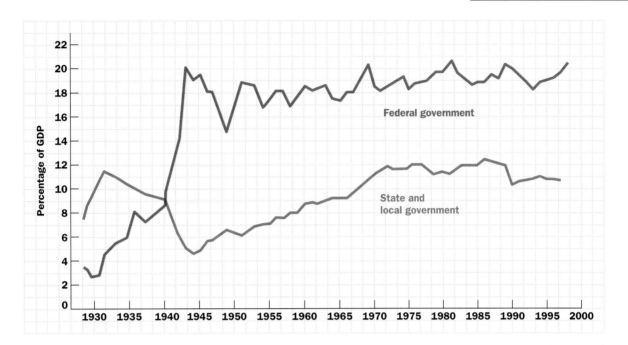

SOURCE: *Economic Report of the President, 1999* (Washington, D.C.: U.S. Government Printing Office, 1999).

As we noted in Chapter 3 (see, especially, page 48), the tax share is considerably lower in the United States than it is in most other industrial countries.

## PROGRESSIVE, PROPORTIONAL, AND REGRESSIVE TAXES

Economists classify taxes as *progressive*, *proportional*, or *regressive*. Under a **progressive tax** like the personal income tax, the fraction of income paid in taxes *rises* as a person's income increases. Under a **proportional tax** like the payroll tax, this fraction is constant. And under a **regressive tax** like the notorious *head tax*, which charges every person the same amount, the fraction of income paid to the tax collector *declines* as income rises.[1] Because the fraction of income paid in taxes is called the **average tax rate,** we can reformulate these definitions as they appear in the margin.

Often, however, the *average* tax rate is less interesting than the **marginal tax rate,** which is the fraction of each *additional* dollar that is paid to the tax collector. The reason, as we will see, is that the *marginal* tax rate, not the *average* tax rate, most directly affects economic incentives.

## DIRECT VERSUS INDIRECT TAXES

Another way to classify taxes is to classify them as either **direct taxes** or **indirect taxes.** Direct taxes are levied directly on *people:* primary examples are *income taxes* and *inheritance taxes*. In contrast, indirect taxes are levied on particular activities, such as buying gasoline, using the telephone, or owning a home.

The federal government raises revenues mainly by direct taxes, whereas states and localities rely more heavily on indirect taxes. *Sales taxes* and *property taxes* are the most important indirect taxes in the United States, although many other countries including the members of the European Union (EU) rely heavily on the *value-added tax*—or VAT, a tax that has often been discussed, but never adopted, in the United States. In fact, as a broad generalization, the U.S. government relies more heavily on direct taxes than do the governments of most other countries.

A **progressive tax** is one in which the average tax rate paid by an individual rises as income rises.

A **proportional tax** is one in which the average tax rate is the same at all income levels.

A **regressive tax** is one in which the average tax rate falls as income rises.

The **average tax rate** is the ratio of taxes to income

The **marginal tax rate** is the fraction of each *additional* dollar of income that is paid in taxes.

**Direct taxes** are taxes levied directly on people.

**Indirect taxes** are taxes levied on specific economic activities.

---

[1] In 1990, Prime Minister Margaret Thatcher caused riots in the United Kingdom by instituting a head tax.

## ■ THE FEDERAL TAX SYSTEM

**FIGURE 21-2**

**Sources of Federal Revenue**

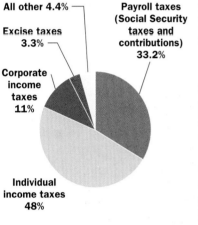

All other 4.4%

Excise taxes 3.3%

Corporate income taxes 11%

Payroll taxes (Social Security taxes and contributions) 33.2%

Individual income taxes 48%

SOURCE: *Economic Report of the President, 1999* (Washington, D.C.: U.S. Government Printing Office, 1999).

A **tax loophole** is a special provision in the tax code that reduces taxation below normal rates (perhaps to zero) if certain conditions are met.

A particular source of income is **tax exempt** if income from that source is not taxable.

A **tax deduction** is a sum of money that may be subtracted before the taxpayer computes his or her taxable income.

The *personal income tax* is the biggest source of revenue to the federal government. Few people realize that the *payroll tax*—a tax levied on wages and salaries up to a certain limit and paid by employers and employees—is the next biggest source. Furthermore, payroll taxes have been growing more rapidly than income taxes for decades. In 1960, payroll tax collections were just 36 percent of personal income tax collections; today this figure is about 71 percent. In fact, most Americans pay more in payroll taxes than they do in income taxes.

The rest of the federal government's revenues come mostly from the *corporate income tax* and from various excise (sales) taxes. Figure 3–18, which is reproduced here for convenience as Figure 21–2, shows the breakdown of federal revenues for the fiscal year 1999 budget. Let us now look at these taxes in more detail.

### THE FEDERAL PERSONAL INCOME TAX

The tax on individual incomes traces its origins to the 16th Amendment to the Constitution in 1913, but it was inconsequential until the beginning of World War II. Washington then raised the tax substantially to finance the war, and it has been the major source of federal revenue ever since.

Many taxpayers have little or no additional tax to pay when the annual April 15th day of reckoning comes around because employers withhold income taxes from payrolls and forward those funds to the U.S. Treasury. In fact, many taxpayers are "over-withheld" during the year and receive refund checks from Uncle Sam. Nevertheless, most taxpayers dread the arrival of their Form 1040 because of its legendary complexity.

The personal income tax is *progressive.* That fact is evident in Table 21–1, which shows that average tax rates rise as income rises. Ignoring a few complications, the current tax law has five basic marginal rates, each of which applies within a specific tax bracket. As income rises above certain points, the marginal tax rate increases from 15 percent to 28 percent, to 31 percent, and then finally to 36 percent and 39.6 percent on very high incomes (more than $275,000 of taxable income for a married couple).

But the income tax is actually less progressive than it seems, owing to a variety of **tax loopholes.** Let us examine a few major ones.

**TAX-EXEMPT STATUS OF MUNICIPAL BOND INTEREST**   To help state and local governments and certain public authorities raise funds, Congress has made interest on their bonds **exempt** from federal income tax. Whether or not it was Congress' intent, this provision has turned out to be one of the biggest loopholes for the very rich, who invest much of their wealth in tax-free municipal bonds. Such tax-conscious investing has long been the principal reason why some multimillionaires pay virtually no income tax.

**TAX BENEFITS FOR HOMEOWNERS**   Among the sacred cows of our income tax system is the deductibility of payments that homeowners make for mortgage interest and property taxes. These **tax deductions** substantially reduce homeowners' tax bills and give them preferential treatment compared to renters. Clearly, Congress' intent is to encourage home ownership. However, because homeowners are, on the average, richer than renters, this loophole also erodes the progressivity of the income tax.

But why call this a "loophole" when other interest expenses and taxes (such as those paid by shopkeepers, for example) are considered legitimate deductions? The answer is that, unlike shopkeepers, homeowners do not pay taxes on the income they earn by incurring these expenses. This is because the "income" from owning a home accrues not in cash, but in the form of living without paying rent.

An example will illustrate the point. Jack and Jill are neighbors. Each earns $30,000 a year and lives in a $100,000 house. The difference is that Jack owns his home, while Jill rents. Most observers would agree that Jack and Jill *should* pay the same income tax. Will they? Suppose Jack pays $2,000 a year in local property taxes

## Federal Personal Income Tax Rates in 1998 for a Married Couple Filing Jointly

TABLE 21-1

| Taxable Income | Tax | Average Tax Rate | Marginal Tax Rate |
|---|---|---|---|
| $ 10,000 | $ 1,500 | 15.0% | 15.0% |
| 25,000 | 3,750 | 15.0 | 15.0 |
| 50,000 | 8,495 | 17.0 | 28.0 |
| 100,000 | 22,495 | 22.5 | 28.0 |
| 150,000 | 37,926 | 25.3 | 31.0 |
| 250,000 | 73,628 | 29.5 | 36.0 |
| 1,000,000 | 369,604 | 37.0 | 39.6 |

and has an $80,000 mortgage at an 8 percent interest rate, which costs him about $6,400 a year in interest. Both property taxes and mortgage interest are tax deductible, so he gets to deduct $8,400 in housing expenses. But Jill, who may pay $8,400 a year in rent, does not. Thus, Jill's tax burden is higher than Jack's.

We could go on listing more tax loopholes, but enough has been said to illustrate the main point:

> Every tax loophole encourages particular patterns of behavior and favors particular types of people. Furthermore, because most loopholes mainly benefit the rich, they erode the progressivity of the income tax.

This problem was much more serious in the United States before the major tax reform of 1986, when the tax code was thoroughly rewritten. But it has by no means disappeared. Indeed, making the tax code simpler and fairer by closing more loopholes is one of the chief arguments for adopting a flat tax.

### THE PAYROLL TAX

The second most important tax in the United States is the payroll tax, whose proceeds are earmarked to be paid into various "trust funds." These funds, in turn, are used mainly to pay for Social Security, Medicare, and unemployment benefits. The payroll tax is levied at a fixed percentage rate (now about 16 percent), shared about equally between employees and employers. This means that a firm paying an employee a gross monthly wage of, say, $5,000 will deduct $400 (8 percent of $5,000) from that worker's check, add an additional $400 of its own funds, and send the $800 to the government.

On the surface, this seems like a *proportional* tax, but it is actually highly *regressive* for two reasons. First, only wages and salaries are subject to the tax; interest and dividends are not. Second, because Social Security benefits are subject to upper limits, earnings above a certain level (which changes each year) are exempted from the tax. In 1999, this level was $72,600 per year. Above this limit, the *marginal payroll tax rate* is zero.[2]

### THE CORPORATE INCOME TAX

The tax on corporate profits is also considered a "direct" tax, because corporations are fictitious "people" in the eyes of the law. All large corporations currently pay a basic marginal tax rate of 35 percent. (Firms with smaller profits pay a lower rate.) Because the tax applies only to *profits*—not to income—all wages, rents, and interest paid by corporations are deducted before the tax is applied. Since World War II, corporate income-tax collections have accounted for a declining share of federal revenue—now just 12 percent.

---

[2] This is not quite true. The portion of the payroll tax that pays for Medicare is applied to all earnings, without limit.

## EXCISE TAXES

An excise tax is a sales tax on the purchase of a particular good or service. Though sales taxes are mainly reserved for state and local governments in the United States, the federal government does levy excise taxes on a hodgepodge of miscellaneous goods and services, including cigarettes, alcoholic beverages, gasoline, and tires.

Although these taxes constitute a minor source of federal government revenue, raising revenue is not the only goal. Some taxes seek to discourage consumption of a good by raising its price. For example, Congress and the president engaged in pitched political battles in both 1998 and 1999 over raising the cigarette tax. The avowed purpose of the proposed sharp tax hike was not to raise revenue—it was to discourage teenage smoking.

## THE PAYROLL TAX AND THE SOCIAL SECURITY SYSTEM

In government statistical documents, the payroll tax euphemistically appears as "contributions for social insurance," although these "contributions" are far from voluntary. The term signifies the fact that, unlike other taxes, the proceeds from this particular tax are set aside in "trust funds" to pay benefits to Social Security recipients and others.

But the standard notion of a trust fund does not apply. Some private pension plans *are* trust funds. You pay money into them while you are working, the trustees invest those savings for you, and you withdraw it bit by bit in your retirement years. But the Social Security system does not function that way. For most of its history, the system has simply taken the payroll tax payments of current workers and handed them over to current retirees. The benefit checks that your grandparents receive each month are not, in any real sense, dividends on the investments they made while they worked. Instead these checks are paid out of the payroll taxes that you or your parents pay each month.

For many years, this "pay as you go" system managed to give every generation of retirees more in benefits than it had contributed in payroll taxes. Social Security "contributions" were indeed a good investment! How was this miracle achieved? It relied heavily on growth: both population growth and economic growth. As long as the population grows, there will always be more and more young people to tax in order to pay the retirement benefits of senior citizens. Similarly, as long as wages keep rising, the same payroll tax *rates* permit the government to pay benefits to each generation in excess of that generation's contributions. Ten percent of today's average wage is, after all, a good deal more money than 10 percent of the wages your grandfather earned 50 years ago.

Unfortunately, the growth magic stopped working in the 1970s. First, the growth in real wages slowed dramatically, as we saw in Chapter 18. But Social Security benefits continued to grow rapidly, and in 1975 they became fully protected from inflation by *indexing*, whereas wages were not. So the burden of financing Social Security grew more onerous.

Second, population growth slowed significantly in the United States. Birthrates in this country were very high from the close of World War II until about 1960 (the postwar baby boom) and fell thereafter. As a result, the fraction of the U.S. population that is over 65 has climbed from only 7.5 percent in 1945 to 12.7 percent today, and it is certain to go much higher in the next century as baby boomers retire. Thus, there will be fewer working people to support each retired person.

Third, life expectancy keeps rising. Although this fact is undoubtedly good news for Americans, it is bad news for the financial soundness of the Social Security system. The reason is simple: as people live longer, they spend more years in retirement. When Congress set the normal Social Security retirement age at 65, many Americans did not live that long. Nowadays most do, and many live 20 years or more beyond retirement.

With the growth magic over and the long-run funding of Social Security clearly at risk, the government trimmed Social Security benefits and raised payroll taxes in 1983 to shore up the system's finances. Furthermore, and most significantly, Social

According to the government's long-range projections, Social Security benefits that have already been promised exceed expected future payroll tax receipts by a wide margin. So although Social Security faces no immediate financial problem, something must be done eventually to put the system on a sound financial footing.

For years, experts assumed that some combination of higher payroll taxes and lower Social Security benefits—two politically unpalatable alternatives—would be needed to do the job. But when large federal budget surpluses emerged in the late 1990s, President Bill Clinton saw an opportunity to "fix" Social Security with far less political pain. Specifically, his January 1999 State of the Union address proposed assigning almost two-thirds of the looming budget surpluses to the Social Security Trust Fund. In addition, the president suggested that the trust fund augment its receipts by investing part of its money in the stock market. (The fund now invests exclusively in special government bonds which, though perfectly safe, pay low interest rates.)

Many Republicans in Congress and elsewhere readily accepted the president's first suggestion—that most of the surpluses be devoted to Social Security. But the second proposal—that the Trust Fund invest in common stocks—set off a vigorous political debate that was still raging when this book went to press.

Republican critics argued that political interference with private business decisions would be inevitable if the U.S. government (via the Social Security Trust Fund) owned part of corporate America. How could anyone expect politicians to keep "hands off," they asked, if part of Social Security's money

was invested in tobacco companies, or gun manufacturers, or firms that did business with unfriendly nations? It would be far better, they argued, to establish personal investment accounts in which ordinary citizens, not the government, made the investment decisions.

The administration and its supporters worried that unsophisticated investors—many of whom do not know the difference between a stock and a bond—were in no position to make important financial decisions that would affect their retirement security. Besides, they claimed, authority over investment decisions could and would be lodged in nonpolitical hands, where neither Congress nor the president could interfere.

What do you think?

Security abandoned its tradition of pay-as-you-go financing. Congress decided instead to start accumulating funds in advance so that the Social Security Administration (SSA) would be able to pay the baby boomers' retirement benefits.

Since then, the trust fund has taken in more money than it has paid out. The annual Social Security surplus is now running at about $100 billion. If current projections of population, real wages, and retirement behavior prove reasonably accurate, these annual surpluses will accumulate into a huge trust fund balance 10 to 12 years from now and then start to be drawn down. But the long-run funding problem has not been solved, for those same projections show the trust fund running out of money by about 2032. It is therefore clear that some combination of lower Social Security benefits and higher payroll taxes loom on the long-run horizon. (See the accompanying box, "Saving Social Security.")

## ■ THE STATE AND LOCAL TAX SYSTEM

Indirect taxes are the backbone of state and local government revenues, although most states also levy income taxes. Sales taxes are the principal source of revenue

FIGURE 21-3

**Sources of State and Local Revenue**

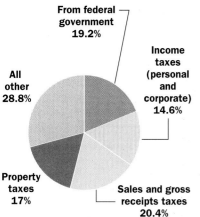

From federal government 19.2%

Income taxes (personal and corporate) 14.6%

All other 28.8%

Property taxes 17%

Sales and gross receipts taxes 20.4%

SOURCE: *Economic Report of the President, 1999* (Washington, D.C.: U.S. Government Printing Office, 1999).

to the states, whereas cities and towns rely heavily on property taxes. Figure 21–3, which repeats a portion of Figure 3–18, shows the breakdown of state and local government receipts for 1999 by source.

### SALES AND EXCISE TAXES

These days, almost all states and many large cities levy broad-based sales taxes on purchases of goods and services, with certain specific exemptions. For example, food is exempted from sales tax in many states. Overall sales tax rates typically run in the 5 to 8 percent range. In addition, most states impose special excise taxes on such things as tobacco products, liquor, gasoline, and luxury items.

### PROPERTY TAXES

Municipalities raise revenue by taxing properties, such as houses and office buildings. Educational and religious institutions are normally exempt from property tax levies. The procedure is generally to assess each taxable property based on its market value and then to place a tax rate on the community's total assessed value that yields enough revenue to cover expenditures on local services. Property taxes generally run between 1 and 3 percent of true market value.

Considerable political controversy surrounds the property tax. Because local property taxes provide the main source of financing for public schools, wealthy communities with expensive real estate are able to afford higher-quality schools than poor communities. A simple arithmetical example will clarify why. Suppose real estate holdings in Richtown average $150,000 per family, while real estate holdings in Poortown average only $50,000 per family. If both towns levy a 2 percent property tax to pay for their schools, Richtown will generate $3,000 per family in tax receipts, while Poortown will generate only $1,000.

Glaring inequalities like this have led courts in many states to declare unconstitutional the financing of public schools by local property taxes, because doing so deprives children in poorer districts of an equal opportunity to receive high-quality education. These legal decisions, in turn, have created considerable political turmoil as states scrambled to find ways to fund their schools while complying with court rulings.

### FISCAL FEDERALISM

Figure 21–3 points out that federal grants provide a major source of revenue to state and local governments. In addition, grants from the states are vital to local governments. This system of transfers from one level of government to the next, which has a long history, is referred to as **fiscal federalism.**

**Fiscal federalism** refers to the system of grants from one level of government to the next.

Aid from this source has come traditionally in the form of *restricted grants*, that is, money given from one level of government to the next on the condition that it be spent for a specific purpose. For example, the U.S. government may grant funds to a state *if* that state will use the money to build highways. Or a state government may give money to a school district to spend on a specified program or facility.

The system of grants from the federal government to the states, in particular, has been in the political spotlight of late. For years, state governments complained that Congress was saddling them with "unfunded mandates"—legal obligations to provide certain services, but without the money needed to pay the bills. In 1995, Congress responded by passing legislation to end the practice of unfunded mandates.

But that was just the beginning. Acting on the belief that state governments are more attuned to local circumstances and needs, Congress made "devolution"—the transfer of powers from the federal government to the states—a major rallying cry after the 1994 election. For example, state governments have been given much more freedom to determine the rules for programs like welfare and Medicaid.

Is devolution a good idea? Supporters see state governments as more flexible and closer to the people. They also view the states as "laboratories of democracy," where creative solutions can be developed to make government more efficient. But critics argue that the history of state government gives little reason to see them as efficient providers of public services. These people worry that minimum national standards in welfare and health care might be sacrificed as states husband their limited financial resources.

## ■ THE CONCEPT OF EQUITY IN TAXATION

Taxes are judged on two criteria: *equity* (Is the tax fair?) and *efficiency* (Does the tax interfere unduly with the workings of the market economy?). Although economists are mostly concerned with the latter, public discussions about tax proposals focus almost exclusively on the former. Let us, therefore, begin our discussion by investigating the concept of equitable taxation.

### HORIZONTAL EQUITY

There are three distinct concepts of tax equity. The first, **horizontal equity,** simply asserts that equally situated individuals should be taxed equally. Few would quarrel with that principle. But it is often difficult to apply in practice, so violations of horizontal equity can be found throughout the tax code.

> **Horizontal equity** is the notion that equally situated individuals should be taxed equally.

Consider, for example, the personal income tax. Horizontal equity calls for two families with the same income to pay the same tax. But what if one family has eight children and the other has one child? Well, you answer, we must define "equally situated" to include equal family sizes, so only families with the same number of children can be compared on grounds of horizontal equity. But what if one family has unusually high medical expenses, and the other has none? Are they still "equally situated"? By now the point should be clear: determining when two families are "equally situated" is no simple task. In fact, the U.S. tax code lists dozens of requirements that must be met before two families are construed as "equal."

### VERTICAL EQUITY

The second concept of fair taxation seems to flow naturally from the first. If equals are to be treated equally, it appears that unequals should be treated unequally. This precept is known as **vertical equity.**

> **Vertical equity** refers to the notion that differently situated individuals should be taxed differently in a way that society deems to be fair.

Just saying this, however, does not get us very far, for vertical equity is a slippery concept. Often it is translated into the **ability-to-pay principle,** according to which those most able to pay should pay the highest taxes. But this still leaves a definitional problem similar to the problem of defining "equally situated": How do we measure ability to pay? The nature of each tax often provides a straightforward answer. In income taxation, we measure ability to pay by income; in property taxation, we measure it by property value, and so on.

> The **ability-to-pay principle** of taxation refers to the idea that people with greater ability to pay taxes should pay higher taxes.

A thornier problem arises when we try to translate the notion into concrete terms. Consider the three alternative income-tax plans listed in Table 21–2. Families with higher incomes pay higher taxes under all three plans. So they all can be said to follow the ability-to-pay principle. Yet the three plans produce radically different distributive consequences. Plan 1 is a progressive tax, like the individual income tax in

### Three Alternative Income-Tax Plans

TABLE 21-2

| | Plan 1 | | Plan 2 | | Plan 3 | |
|---|---|---|---|---|---|---|
| Income | Tax | Average Tax Rate | Tax | Average Tax Rate | Tax | Average Tax Rate |
| $ 10,000 | $ 300 | 3% | $ 1,000 | 10% | $1,000 | 10% |
| 50,000 | 8,000 | 16 | 5,000 | 10 | 3,000 | 6 |
| 250,000 | 70,000 | 28 | 25,000 | 10 | 7,500 | 3 |

the United States: The average tax rate is higher for richer families. Plan 2 is a proportional tax: Every family pays 10 percent of its income. Plan 3 is regressive: Because tax payments rise more slowly than income, the average tax rate for richer families is lower than that for poorer families.

Which plan comes closest to the ideal notion of vertical equity? Many people find that Plan 3, the regressive tax, offends their sense of "fairness," for it makes the distribution of income *after taxes* more unequal than the distribution *before taxes*. But people agree much less over the relative merits of progressive versus proportional taxation. Often, in fact, the notion of vertical equity is taken to be synonymous with progressivity. Other things being equal, progressive taxes are seen as "good" taxes in some ethical sense, whereas regressive taxes are seen as "bad." On these grounds, advocates of greater equality of incomes support progressive income taxes and oppose sales taxes.

## THE BENEFITS PRINCIPLE

The **benefits principle** of taxation holds that people who derive benefits from a service should pay the taxes that finance it.

Whereas the principles of horizontal and vertical equity, for all their ambiguities and practical problems, at least do not conflict with one another, the final principle of fair taxation often violates commonly accepted notions of vertical equity. According to the **benefits principle** of taxation, those who reap the benefits from government services should pay the taxes.

The benefits principle is often used to justify earmarking the proceeds from certain taxes for specific public services. For example, receipts from gasoline taxes typically go to finance construction and maintenance of roads. Thus, those who use the roads pay the taxes roughly in proportion to their usage. Most people seem to find this system fair. But in other contexts—such as public schools, hospitals, and libraries—the body politic has been loath to apply the benefits principle because it clashes so dramatically with common notions of fairness. So these services are normally financed out of general tax revenues rather than by direct charges for their use.

## ■ THE CONCEPT OF EFFICIENCY IN TAXATION

*Economic efficiency* is among the most central concepts of economics. The economy is said to be *efficient* if it has used every available opportunity to make someone better off without making someone else worse off. In this sense, taxes almost always introduce *inefficiencies*. That is, if the tax were removed, some people could be made better off without anyone being harmed.

However, that is not a terribly pertinent comparison. The government does, after all, need revenue to pay for the services it provides. So when economists discuss the notion of "efficient" taxation, they are usually seeking taxes that cause the *least* amount of inefficiency for a given amount of tax revenue. In the more colorful words of Jean-Baptiste Colbert, treasurer to King Louis IV of France, "The art of taxation consists in so plucking the goose to obtain the largest amount of feathers, with the least possible amount of hissing."

The **burden of a tax** to an individual is the amount one would have to be given to be just as well off with the tax as without it.

To explain the concept of efficient taxation, we need to introduce one new term. Economists define the **burden of a tax** as the amount the taxpayer would have to be given to be just as well off in the presence of the tax as in its absence. An example will clarify this notion and also make clear why:

**The burden of a tax normally exceeds the revenue raised by the tax.**

Suppose the government, in the interest of energy conservation, levies a high tax on the biggest gas-guzzling cars, with progressively lower taxes on smaller cars.[3] For example, a simple tax schedule might be the following:

---

[3] A tax like this has been in effect since 1984.

| Car Type | Tax |
|---|---|
| Cadillac Catera | $1,000 |
| Chrysler 300 | 500 |
| Ford Escort | 0 |

Harry has a taste for big cars and has always bought Cadillacs. (Harry is clearly no pauper.) Once the new tax takes effect, he has three options. He can still buy a Cadillac Catera and pay $1,000 in tax; he can switch to a Chrysler 300 and avoid half the tax, or he can switch to a Ford Escort and avoid the entire tax.

If Harry sticks with the Caddy, we have a case in which the burden of the tax is exactly equal to the tax he pays. Why? Because if someone gave Harry $1,000, he would be exactly as well off as he was before the tax was enacted. In general:

> When a tax induces no change in economic behavior, the burden of the tax is measured accurately by the revenue collected.

However, this is not what we normally expect to happen, and it is certainly not what the government intends by levying a tax on big cars. Normally, we expect taxes to induce some people to alter their behavior in ways that reduce or avoid tax payments. So let us look into Harry's other two options.

If Harry decides to purchase a Chrysler, he pays only $500 in tax. But $500 understates his burden because Harry is greatly chagrined by the fact that he no longer drives a Cadillac. How much money would it take to make Harry just as well off as he was before the tax? Only Harry knows for sure. But we do know that it is more than the $500 tax that he pays. Why? Because if someone gave Harry the $500 needed to pay his tax bill, he would still be less happy than he was before the tax was introduced, owing to his switch from a Cadillac to a Chrysler. Whatever the (unknown) burden of the tax is, the amount by which it exceeds the $500 tax bill is called the **excess burden** of the tax.

Harry's final option makes the importance of understanding excess burden even more clear. If he switches to an Escort, Harry will pay no tax. Are we therefore to say he has suffered no burden? Clearly not, for he longs for the Cadillac that he no longer has. The general principle is:

> Whenever a tax induces people to change their behavior—that is, whenever it "distorts" their choices—the tax has an *excess burden*. This means that the revenue collected systematically understates the true burden of the tax.

The excess burdens that arise from tax-induced changes in economic behavior are precisely the inefficiencies we noted at the outset of this section. The basic precept of efficient taxation is to try to devise a tax system that *minimizes* these inefficiencies. In particular:

> In comparing two taxes that raise the same total revenue, the one that produces less excess burden is the more efficient.

Notice the proviso that the two taxes being compared must yield the *same* revenue. We are really interested in the *total* burden of each tax. Because:

$$\text{Total burden} = \text{Tax collections} + \text{Excess burden}$$

we can unambiguously state that the tax with less *excess* burden is more efficient only when tax collections are equal.

Excess burdens arise when consumers and firms alter their behavior on account of taxation. So this precept of sound tax policy can be restated in a way that sounds consistent with President Reagan's statement at the beginning of this chapter:

> In devising a tax system to raise revenue, try to raise any given amount of revenue through taxes that induce the smallest changes in behavior.

The **excess burden** of a tax to an individual is the amount by which the burden of the tax exceeds the tax that is paid.

---

### ● EXCESS BURDEN AND MR. FIGG

Humorist Russell Baker discussed the problem of excess burden in the newspaper column reproduced here. It seems that every time his mythical Mr. Figg took a step to avoid paying taxes and to satisfy the tax man, he became less and less happy.

NEW YORK—The tax man was very cross about Figg. Figg's way of life did not conform to the way of life several governments wanted Figg to pursue. Nothing inflamed the tax man more than insolent and capricious disdain for governmental desires. He summoned Figg to the temple of taxation.

"What's the idea of living in a rental apartment over a delicatessen in the city, Figg?" he inquired. Figg explained that he liked urban life. In that case, said the tax man, he was raising Figg's city sales and income taxes. "If you want them cut, you'll have to move out to the suburbs," he said.

To satisfy his local government, Figg gave up the city and rented a suburban house. The tax man summoned him back to the temple.

"Figg," he said, "you have made me sore wroth with your way of life. Therefore, I am going to soak you for more federal income taxes." And he squeezed Figg until beads of blood popped out along the seams of Figg's wallet.

"Mercy, good tax man," Figg gasped. "Tell me how to live so that I may please my government, and I shall obey."

The tax man told Figg to quit renting and buy a house. The government wanted everyone to accept large mortgage loans from bankers. If Figg complied, it would cut his taxes.

Figg bought a house, which he did not want, in a suburb where he did not want to live, and he invited his friends and relatives to attend a party celebrating his surrender to a way of life that pleased his government.

The tax man was so furious that he showed up at the party with blood-shot eyes. "I have had enough of this, Figg," he declared. "Your government doesn't want you entertaining friends and relatives. This will cost you plenty."

Figg immediately threw out all his friends and relatives, then asked the tax man what sort of people his government wished him to entertain. "Business associates," said the tax man. "Entertain plenty of business associates, and I shall cut your taxes."

To make the tax man and his government happy, Figg began entertaining people he didn't like in the house he didn't want in the suburb where he didn't want to live.

Then was the tax man enraged indeed. "Figg," he thundered, "I will not cut your taxes for entertaining straw bosses, truck drivers, and pothole fillers."

"Why not?" said Figg. "These are the people I associate with in my business."

"Which is what?" asked the tax man.

"Earning my pay by the sweat of my brow," said Figg.

"Your government is not going to bribe you for performing salaried labor," said the tax man. "Don't you know, you imbecile, that tax rates on salaried income are higher than on any other kind?"

And he taxed the sweat of Figg's brow at a rate that drew exquisite shrieks of agony from Figg and little cries of joy from Washington, which already had more sweated brows than it needed to sustain the federally approved way of life.

"Get into business, or minerals, or international oil," warned the tax man, "or I shall make your taxes as the taxes of 10."

Figg went into business, which he hated, and entertained people he didn't like in the house he didn't want in the suburb where he did not want to live.

At length the tax man summoned Figg for an angry lecture. He demanded to know why Figg had not bought a new plastic factory to replace his old metal and wooden plant. "I hate plastic," said Figg. "Your government is sick and tired of metal, wood, and everything else that smacks of the real stuff, Figg," roared the tax man, seizing Figg's purse. "Your depreciation is all used up."

There was nothing for Figg to do but go to plastic, and the tax man rewarded him with a brand new depreciation schedule plus an investment credit deduction from the bottom line.

SOURCE: Russell Baker, *International Herald Tribune*, April 13, 1977, p. 14. © 1977 by *The New York Times* Company. Reprinted by permission.

---

Sometimes, however, a tax is levied not primarily as a revenue raiser, but as a way to induce individuals or firms to alter their behavior—in contrast to President Reagan's dictum. For example, we mentioned earlier that President Clinton sought to use higher taxes on cigarettes to reduce teen smoking. The possibility of using taxes to change consumer behavior will be discussed in a few pages.

## TAX LOOPHOLES AND EXCESS BURDEN

We noted earlier that loopholes make the income tax less progressive than it appears to be on paper. Having learned that tax-induced changes in behavior lead to excess burdens, we can now understand the second reason why tax specialists condemn tax loopholes: loopholes make the income tax less *efficient* than it could be. Why? Because most loopholes involve imposing different tax rates on different types of income. Given a choice between paying, say, a 40 percent marginal tax rate on one type of income and a 20 percent rate on another, most rational taxpayers will favor the latter. Thus:

When different income-earning activities are taxed at different marginal rates, economic choices are distorted by tax considerations, and this impairs economic efficiency.

One major objective shared by tax reformers, including both contemporary advocates of a flat tax and many of their opponents, is to enhance both the equity and efficiency of the personal income tax by closing loopholes and lowering tax rates. The Tax Reform Act of 1986 represented a giant step in this direction. By roughly doubling the personal exemption, the law removed about 6 million households from

"LOOK AT THIS FEDERAL BUDGET. BILLIONS OF DOLLARS ARE BEING WASTED. I'D REALLY BE FURIOUS IF WE WERE PAYING TAXES."

the tax rolls. For most other taxpayers, progressivity—as measured by *average* tax rates—was left nearly unchanged even though *marginal* tax rates dropped sharply. This was accomplished by closing many important tax loopholes. Tax rates on different sources of income were equalized. The new code reduced or eliminated many deductions and exemptions. Abusive tax shelters such as special real estate deals were a particular target of tax reformers, though the details are best left to more advanced courses on taxation.

On balance, most observers believe we have a much better tax code today than we did in 1985. But it is far from perfect. In fact, since 1986 Congress has allowed a number of tax loopholes to reappear and has created some new ones. Proponents of a flat tax believe the time is ripe for another thorough-going reform.

## ■ SHIFTING THE TAX BURDEN: TAX INCIDENCE

The **incidence of a tax** is an allocation of the burden of the tax to specific individuals or groups.

The **flypaper theory of tax incidence** holds that the burden of a tax always sticks where the government puts it.

When economists speak of the **incidence of a tax,** they are referring to who actually bears the burden of the tax. In discussing the tax on gas-guzzling autos, we adhered to what has been called the **flypaper theory of tax incidence:** that the burden of any tax sticks where the government puts it. In this case, the burden stays on Harry, our luxury car fan. But often things do not work out this way.

Consider, for example, what will happen if the government levies a $1,000 tax on luxury cars like Cadillacs. We learned how to deal with such a tax in a supply-and-demand diagram back in Chapter 5: The supply curve shifts up by the amount of the tax, in this case, $1,000. Fig. 21–4 shows such a shift by the movement from $S_0S_0$ to $S_1S_1$. If the demand curve $DD$ does not shift, the market equilibrium shifts from point $A$ to point $B$. The quantity of luxury cars declines as Harrys all over America react to the higher price by buying fewer luxury cars. Notice that the price rises from $40,000 to $40,600, an increase of $600. So people who continue buying luxury cars bear a burden of only $600—less than the tax that they pay!

**FIGURE 21–4**

**The Incidence of an Excise Tax**

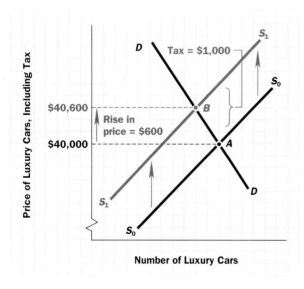

Does this mean that the tax imposes a *negative* excess burden? Certainly not. What it means is that consumers who refrain from buying the taxed commodity manage to *shift* part of the tax burden away from consumers as a whole, including those who continue to buy luxury cars. Who are the victims of this **tax shifting?** There are two main candidates. First are the automakers or, more precisely, their stockholders. To the extent that the tax reduces auto sales and profits, stockholders bear the burden. The other principal candidates are auto workers. To the extent that reduced production leads to layoffs or lower wages, the automobile workers bear part of the tax burden.

People who have never studied economics almost always believe in the flypaper theory of incidence, which holds that sales taxes are borne by consumers, property taxes are borne by homeowners, and taxes on corporations are borne by stockholders. Perhaps the most important lesson of this chapter is that:

The flypaper theory of incidence is often wrong.

**Tax shifting** occurs when the economic reactions to a tax cause prices and outputs in the economy to change, thereby shifting part of the burden of the tax onto others.

Failure to grasp this basic point has led to all sorts of misguided tax legislation in which members of Congress or state legislatures, *thinking* they were placing a tax burden on one group of people, inadvertently placed it squarely on another. Of course, there are cases where the flypaper theory of incidence is roughly correct. So let us consider some specific examples of tax incidence.

## THE INCIDENCE OF EXCISE TAXES

Excise taxes have already been covered by our automobile example, because Figure 21–4 could represent any commodity that is taxed. Our basic finding is that *part* of the burden will fall on consumers of the taxed commodity (including those who stop buying it because of the tax), and part will be borne by the firms and workers who produce the commodity.

How is the burden shared between buyers and sellers? It all depends on the slopes of the demand and supply curves. Intuitively speaking, if consumers are very loyal to the taxed commodity, they will continue to buy almost the same quantity regardless of price. In that case, they will get stuck with most of the tax bill because they leave themselves vulnerable to it. Thus:

**The more inelastic the demand for the product, the larger the share of the tax that consumers will pay.**

Similarly, if suppliers are determined to supply the same amount of the product no matter how low the price, then they will wind up paying most of the tax. That is:

**The more inelastic the supply curve, the larger is the share of the tax that suppliers will pay.**

One extreme case arises when no one stops buying luxury cars when their prices rise. The demand curve becomes vertical, like the demand curve *DD* in Figure 21–5. Then no tax shifting can take place. When the supply curve shifts upward by the amount of the tax ($1,000), the price of a luxury car (inclusive of tax) rises by the full $1,000—from $40,000 to $41,000. So consumers bear the entire burden.

The other extreme case arises when the supply curve is totally inelastic, as depicted by the vertical line *SS* in Figure 21–6. Because the number of luxury cars supplied is the same at any price, the supply curve will not shift when a tax is imposed. Consequently, automakers must bear the full burden of any tax that is placed on their product. Figure 21–6 shows that the tax does not change the market price (including tax), which, of course, means that the price received by sellers must fall by the full amount of the tax.

Demand and supply schedules for most goods and services are not as extreme as those depicted in Figures 21–5 and 21–6, so buyers and sellers share the burden. Precisely how it is shared depends on the elasticities of the supply and demand curves.[4]

## THE INCIDENCE OF THE PAYROLL TAX

We can view the payroll tax as an excise tax on the employment of labor. As we mentioned earlier, the U.S. payroll tax comes in two parts: Half is levied on employees (via payroll deductions) and half on employers. A fundamental point, which people who have never studied economics often fail to grasp, is that:

**The ultimate incidence of a payroll tax is the same whether it is levied on employers or on employees.**

A simple numerical example will illustrate why this must be so. Consider an employee earning $100 a day with a 16 percent payroll tax that is shared equally between the employer and the employee, as under our present law. How

[4] For a concrete example, see Review Questions 7 and 8 at the end of the chapter.

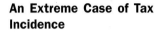

**FIGURE 21-5**

**An Extreme Case of Tax Incidence**

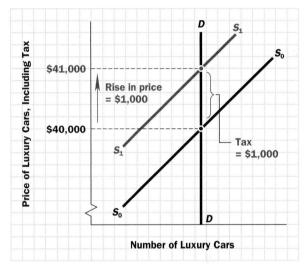

**FIGURE 21-6**

**Another Extreme Case of Tax Incidence**

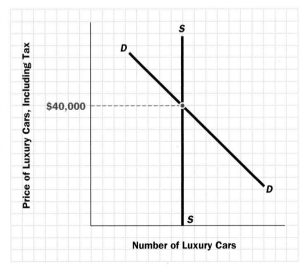

much does it cost the firm to hire this worker? It costs $100 in wages paid to the worker plus $8 in taxes paid to the government, for a total of $108 a day. How much does the worker receive? He gets $100 in wages paid by the employer less $8 deducted and sent to the government, or $92 a day. The difference between wages paid and wages received is $108 − $92 = $16, the amount of the tax.

Now suppose Congress tries to "shift" the burden of the tax entirely onto firms by raising the employer's tax to $16 while lowering the employee's tax to zero. At first, the daily wage is fixed at $100, so firms' total labor costs (including tax) rise to $116 per day and workers' net income rises to $100 per day. Congress seems to have achieved its goal.

But the achievement is fleeting, for what we have just described is not an equilibrium situation. With the daily cost of labor at $116 for firms, the quantity of labor *demanded* will be *less* than when labor cost only $108 per day. Similarly, with take-home pay up to $100 for workers, the quantity of labor *supplied* will be *more* than when the after-tax wage was only $92. Therefore, a *surplus of labor* on the market will arise (an excess of quantity supplied over quantity demanded), and this surplus will place downward pressure on wages.

How far will wages have to fall? We can easily see that an after-tax wage of $92 will restore equilibrium. If daily take-home pay is $92, the same as it was before the tax change, quantity supplied will be the same. From the firm's perspective, labor now costs $108 per day, just as it did before the tax change. So they will demand the same quantity as they did when the payroll tax was shared. Thus, in the end, the market will completely frustrate the intent of Congress.

The payroll tax is an excellent example of a case in which Congress, misled by the flypaper theory of incidence, thinks it is "taxing firms" when it raises the employer's share and "taxing workers" when it raises the employee's share. In truth, who really pays in the long run depends on the incidence of the tax. But no lasting difference results from a change in the employee's and the employer's shares.

Who, then, really bears the burden of the payroll tax? Like any excise tax, the incidence of the payroll tax depends on the elasticities of the supply and demand schedules. In the case of labor supply, a large body of empirical evidence points to the conclusion that the quantity of labor supplied is not very responsive to price for most population groups. The supply curve is almost vertical, like that shown in Figure 21–6. The result: Workers as a group can shift little of the burden of the payroll tax to employees.

But employers *can* shift it in most cases. Firms view their share of the payroll tax as an additional cost of using labor. So when payroll taxes go up, firms try to substitute cheaper factors of production (capital) for labor wherever they can. This reduces the quantity of labor demanded, lowering the wage received by workers. And this is how market forces shift part of the tax burden from firms to workers.

To the extent that the supply curve of labor has some positive slope, the quantity of labor supplied will fall when the wage goes down, and in this way workers can shift some of the burden back onto firms. But firms, in turn, can shift that burden onto consumers by raising their prices. As we know from Part III, prices in competitive markets generally rise when costs (like labor costs) increase. It is doubtful, therefore, that firms bear much of the payroll tax burden. The flypaper theory of incidence could not be further from the truth. Even though the tax is collected by the firm, it is really borne by workers and consumers.

## ■ WHEN TAXATION CAN IMPROVE EFFICIENCY

We have spent much of this chapter discussing the kinds of inefficiencies and excess burdens that arise from taxation. But, before we finish this discussion, we must point out two things.

First, economic efficiency is not society's only goal. For example, a tax on energy causes inefficiencies if it changes people's behavior patterns. But this, presumably, is exactly what the government intends. The government wants to conserve energy and is willing to tolerate some economic inefficiency to accomplish this goal. We can, of course, argue whether that is a good idea—whether the conservation achieved is worth the efficiency loss. But the general point is that:

> **Some taxes that introduce economic inefficiencies are nonetheless good social policy because they help achieve some other goal.**

We have already mentioned the excise tax on cigarettes, which aims to change behavior. Another important example is the high tax on alcoholic beverages.

A second, and more fundamental, point is that:

> **Some taxes that change economic behavior may lead to efficiency gains, rather than to efficiency *losses*.**

As you might guess, this can happen only when the system has an inefficiency prior to the tax. Then an appropriate tax may help set things right. One important example of this phenomenon came up in Chapter 14 and will occupy much of the next chapter. Because firms and individuals who despoil clean air and water often do so without paying any price, these precious resources are used inefficiently. A corrective tax on pollution can remedy this problem.

## ■ EQUITY, EFFICIENCY, AND THE OPTIMAL TAX

In a perfect world, the ideal tax would raise the revenues the government needs, reflect society's views on equity in taxation, and induce no changes in economic behavior—and so have no excess burden. Unfortunately, no one has ever been able to devise such a tax.

Sometimes, in fact, the taxes with the smallest excess burdens are the most regressive. For instance, a head tax, which charges every person the same number of dollars, is incredibly regressive. But it is also perfectly efficient. Because no change in economic behavior will enable anyone to avoid it, no one has any reason to change behavior. As we have noted, the regressive payroll tax also seems to have small excess burdens.

Fortunately, however, there is a tax that, though not ideal, still scores highly on both the equity and efficiency criteria: a comprehensive personal income tax with few loopholes.

Although it is true that income taxes can be avoided by earning less income, we have already observed that in reality the supply of labor changes little because of tax policies. People can also reduce their tax bills by investing in relatively safe assets (like government bonds) rather than riskier ones (like common stocks), because safer assets pay lower rates of return. But it is not clear that the income tax actually induces such behavior. Why? Because, although the government shares in the profits when investments turn out well, it also shares in the losses when investments turn sour. Finally, because an income tax reduces the return on saving, many economists have worried that it would discourage saving and thus retard economic growth.[5] But empirical evidence does not suggest that this happens to any great extent.

On balance, then, although unresolved questions remain and research is continuing:

> **Most of the studies that have been conducted to date suggest that a comprehensive personal income tax with no loopholes induces few of the behavioral reactions that would reduce consumer well-being, and thus has a rather small excess burden.**

On the equity criterion, we know that personal income taxes can be made as progressive as society deems desirable, though if marginal tax rates on rich people get

---

[5] For this reason, some economists prefer a tax on consumption to a tax on income.

extremely high, some of the potential efficiency losses might get more serious than they now seem to be. On both grounds, then, many economists—including both liberals and conservatives—view a comprehensive personal income tax as one of the best ways for a government to raise revenue.

### Conclusion: The Pros and Cons of a Flat Tax

How does the flat tax stack up against these criteria? Quite well on most, at least in its ideal form.

- A *low* tax rate for everyone would mean that taxes would create only small tax distortions. Excess burdens would be minimal.

- A *uniform* tax rate on all types of income would eliminate tax loopholes.

- If the exemption is large enough, the income tax can maintain progressivity at the bottom of the income distribution. For example, some plans would exempt the first $30,000 or more of income from taxation.

- As noted at the start of this chapter, filing your income-tax return under a flat tax would be extremely simple, thereby saving millions of taxpayer hours (and making many CPAs unhappy).

These are all notable virtues, which explains why the flat tax has attracted many adherents. But once we leave the realm of the *ideal* and confront the *real,* some serious problems arise:

- Some flat-tax plans would tax only *earnings,* leaving all income from capital free of tax. This would not only create strong incentives to evade the tax by transforming labor income into capital income, but it would also erode progressivity.

- It seems unlikely that Congress would eliminate *all* tax preferences. Among other things, they would have to tax the value of employer-provided fringe benefits (like health insurance) and eliminate the deductibility of home mortgage interest—two steps that would surely be politically unpopular.

"I've been thinking about the flat tax and how it would inflict hardship on the poor, and I can live with that."

■ If large tax preferences like these remain, or if income from capital is tax free, a higher tax rate will be needed to raise the required revenue. Thus, under a realistic flat tax, most Americans might actually face a *higher* marginal tax rate than they do now.

■ No flat tax can maintain progressivity at the top. Under the current tax code, the very rich pay taxes equal to about 40 percent of their taxable incomes. Under, say, a 22 percent flat tax, they would pay just 22 percent. Some Americans wonder why the very rich should get such a large tax break.

Where does this partial accounting of the pros and cons of the flat tax leave us? As usual in a serious public policy debate, with plenty of room for reasonable people to disagree! As we said back in Chapter 1, economics is not supposed to give you all the *answers*. It is supposed to teach you how to ask the right *questions*.

## SUMMARY

1. Taxes in the United States have been quite constant as a percentage of gross domestic product since the early 1970s.

2. The federal government raises most of its revenue by *direct taxes*, such as the personal and corporate *income taxes* and the payroll tax. Of these, the payroll tax is increasing most rapidly.

3. The Social Security system relied successfully on pay-as-you-go financing for decades. In recent years, however, it has been accumulating a large trust fund to be used to pay benefits to the baby boom generation when it retires. But experts do not think that trust fund will be enough.

4. State and local governments raise most of their tax revenues by *indirect taxes*. States rely mainly on sales taxes, whereas localities depend on property taxes.

5. There is controversy over whether local property taxes are an equitable way to finance public education.

6. In our multilevel system of government, the federal government makes various sorts of grants to state and local governments, and states in turn make grants to municipalities and school districts. This system of intergovernmental transfers is called *fiscal federalism* and is highly controversial these days.

7. The three concepts of fair, or "equitable," taxation occasionally conflict. *Horizontal equity* simply calls for equals to be treated equally. *Vertical equity*, which calls for unequals to be treated unequally, has often been translated into the *ability-to-pay principle*—that people who are better able to pay taxes should be taxed more heavily. The *benefits principle* of tax equity ignores ability to pay and seeks to tax people according to the benefits they receive.

8. The *burden of a tax* is the amount of money an individual would have to be given to be as well off with the tax as without it. This burden normally exceeds the taxes that are paid, and the difference between the two is called the *excess burden* of the tax.

9. Excess burden arises whenever a tax induces some people or firms to change their behavior. Because excess burdens signal *economic inefficiencies*, the basic principle of efficient taxation is to utilize taxes that have small excess burdens.

10. When people change their behavior on account of a tax, they often shift the burden of the tax onto someone else. This is why the *"flypaper theory of incidence"*—the belief that the burden of any tax sticks where Congress puts it— is often incorrect.

11. The burden of a sales or *excise tax* normally is shared between the suppliers and the consumers. The manner in which it is shared depends on the elasticities of supply and demand.

12. The *payroll tax* is like an excise tax on labor services. Because the supply of labor is much less elastic than the demand for labor, workers bear most of the burden of the payroll tax. This includes both the employer's and the employee's share of the tax.

13. Sometimes, "inefficient" taxes—that is, taxes that cause a good deal of excess burden—are nonetheless desirable because the changes in behavior they induce further some other social goal.

14. When there are inefficiencies in the system for reasons other than the tax system (for example, externalities), taxation can conceivably improve efficiency.

## KEY TERMS

Progressive, proportional, and regressive taxes   435

Average and marginal tax rates   435

Direct and indirect taxes   435

Personal income tax   436

Payroll tax   437

Corporate income tax   437

Excise tax   438

Tax loopholes   436

Tax exempt   436

Tax deductions   436

Social Security system   438

Property tax   440

Fiscal federalism   440

Horizontal and vertical equity   441

Ability-to-pay principle   441

Benefits principle of taxation   442

Economic efficiency   442

Burden of a tax   442

Excess burden 443

Incidence of a tax 446

Flypaper theory of incidence 446

Tax shifting 446

---

### QUESTIONS FOR REVIEW

1. "If the federal government continues to raise taxes as it has been doing, it will ruin the country. Americans are already overtaxed." Comment.

2. Soon after taking office in 1993, President Clinton proposed a package of tax increases, including higher income tax rates for wealthy taxpayers and higher taxes on energy. Critics argued that these taxes would harm the economy. Why did they say this?

3. Using the following hypothetical income tax table, compute the marginal and average tax rates. Is the tax progressive, proportional, or regressive?

| Income | Income Tax |
|--------|-----------|
| $20,000 | $2,000 |
| 30,000 | 2,700 |
| 40,000 | 3,200 |
| 50,000 | 3,500 |

4. Which concept of tax equity, if any, seems to be served by each of the following:
   a. The progressive income tax
   b. The flat income tax
   c. The excise tax on cigarettes
   d. The gasoline tax

5. Use the example of Mr. Figg (see the box, "Excess Burden and Mr. Figg" on page 444) to explain the concepts of efficient taxes and excess burden.

6. Think of some tax that you personally pay. What steps have you taken or could you take to reduce your tax payments? Is there an excess burden on you? Why or why not?

7. Suppose the supply and demand schedules for cigarettes are as follows:

| Price per Carton | Quantity Demanded | Quantity Supplied |
|-----|-----|-----|
| $3.00 | 360 | 160 |
| 3.25 | 330 | 180 |
| 3.50 | 300 | 200 |
| 3.75 | 270 | 220 |
| 4.00 | 240 | 240 |
| 4.25 | 210 | 260 |
| 4.50 | 180 | 280 |
| 4.75 | 150 | 300 |
| 5.00 | 120 | 320 |

NOTE: Quantity is in millions of cartons per year.

   a. What is the equilibrium price and equilibrium quantity?
   b. Now the government levies a $1.25 per carton excise tax on cigarettes. What is the equilibrium price paid by consumers, the price received by producers, and the quantity now?
   c. Explain why it makes no difference whether Congress levies the $1.25 tax on the consumer or the producer. (Relate your answer to the discussion of the payroll tax in the text.)
   d. Suppose the tax is levied on the producers. How much of the tax are producers able to shift onto consumers? Explain how they manage to do this.
   e. Will there be any excess burden from this tax? Why? Who bears this excess burden?
   f. By how much has cigarette consumption declined on account of the tax? Why might the government be happy about this outcome, despite the excess burden?

8. Now suppose the supply schedule is instead:

| Price per Carton | Quantity Supplied |
|-----|-----|
| $3.00 | 60 |
| 3.25 | 105 |
| 3.50 | 150 |
| 3.75 | 195 |
| 4.00 | 240 |
| 4.25 | 285 |
| 4.50 | 330 |
| 4.75 | 375 |
| 5.00 | 420 |

NOTE: Quantity is in millions of cartons per year.

   a. What are the equilibrium price and equilibrium quantity in the absence of a tax?
   b. What are the equilibrium price and equilibrium quantity in the presence of a $1.25 per carton excise tax?
   c. Explain why your answer to part b differs from part b of the previous question, and relate this difference to the discussion of the incidence of an excise tax in this chapter.

9. The country of Taxmania produces only two commodities: rice and caviar. The poor spend all their income on rice, while the rich purchase both goods. Both demand for and supply of rice are quite inelastic. In the caviar market, both supply and demand are quite elastic. Which good would be heavily taxed if Taxmanians cared mostly about efficiency? What if they cared mostly about vertical equity?

10. Discuss President Reagan's statement on taxes quoted on the first page of the chapter. Do you agree with him?

11. Use the criteria of equity and efficiency in taxation to evaluate the idea of taxing capital gains at a lower rate than other sources of income.

> Environmental taxes are perhaps the most powerful tool
> societies have for forging economies that protect
> human and environmental health.
>
> David Malin Roodman,
> Worldwatch Institute

# EXTERNALITIES, THE ENVIRONMENT, AND NATURAL RESOURCES

W e learned in Chapter 14 that *externalities* (which

are the incidental benefits or damages imposed on peo-

ple not directly involved in an economic activity) can cause

the market mechanism to malfunction. The first half of

this chapter studies a particularly important application:

externalities as a way to explain environmental problems.

We will consider the extent to which the price mechanism

bears responsibility for these problems and how that same

mechanism can help remedy them. In the second half of

the chapter we address a closely related subject: natural

resource depletion. We will discuss fears that the world is

quickly using up many of its vital resources and how, here

too, the price mechanism can help.

## ■ PART 1: THE ECONOMICS OF ENVIRONMENTAL PROTECTION

Environmental problems are not new. What *is* new and different is the attention we now give them. Much of the increased interest stems from rising incomes, which have reduced our concerns about our most basic needs of food, clothing, and shelter and have allowed us the luxury of concentrating on the *quality* of life.

Economic thought on the subject of environmental degradation preceded the outburst of public concern by nearly half a century. In 1911, the British economist Arthur C. Pigou wrote a remarkable book called *The Economics of Welfare*, which for the first time explained these problems in terms of externalities. He also outlined an approach to environmental policy that is still favored by most economists today and gradually seems to be winning over lawmakers, bureaucrats, and even cautious environmentalists (as the opening quotation suggests). Pigou's analysis indicated that a system of *pollution charges* can be an effective means to control pollution. In this way, the price mechanism can remedy one of its own shortcomings!

## ■ EXTERNALITIES: A CRITICAL SHORTCOMING OF THE MARKET MECHANISM

An activity is said to generate a beneficial or detrimental **externality** if that activity causes incidental benefits or damages to others not directly involved in the activity, and no corresponding compensation is provided to or paid by those who generate the externality.

Throughout this book we have sought to provide a balanced view of the private enterprise economy, carefully pointing out both its vast accomplishments and its failings. Chapter 14 listed externalities as a primary shortcoming of the market mechanism.

We also emphasized that externalities are found in many places. For example, another car's entry onto an overcrowded highway adds to delays that other travelers must endure, thereby causing those others to suffer a *detrimental* **externality.** But externalities can also be *beneficial* to third parties. In Chapter 15, on the microeconomics of innovation and growth, we emphasized that innovations usually provide beneficial externalities to persons who neither invest in an innovation nor purchase any of its products.

**EXTERNALITIES** Because those who create harmful externalities do not pay for the damage done to others, they have little incentive to desist. In this way the market tends to create an undesired *abundance* of damaging externalities. Similarly, because those who create *beneficial* externalities are not compensated for doing so, they will have little incentive to supply as large a quantity as will serve the interests of society best. Therefore, the market tends to supply an undesirably *small* amount of such beneficial externalities. In sum, economists conclude that unless something is done about it, the market will provide an overabundance of harmful externalities and an undersupply of desirable ones. Either case is far from ideal.

You may remember that externalities are one of our *Ideas for Beyond the Final Exam* because they are so important for the welfare of society and the efficient functioning of the economy. They play a crucial role in environmental deterioration, affecting the health of the population and threatening our natural resource heritage. This chapter discusses the character and magnitude of the problem and the methods that can be used to contain its harmful consequences.

*Externalities: A Shortcoming of the Market Cured by Market Methods*

In this chapter we focus on one of the most publicized externalities—pollution. Toxic fumes from a chemical plant affect not only the plant's employees and customers, but other people as well. Because the firm does not pay for this *incidental* damage, the firm's owners have no financial incentive to limit their emissions of pollution, particularly because pollution controls cost money. Instead, the owners of the polluting firm will find it profitable to continue their toxic emissions as though the fumes caused no external damage to the community.

### THE FACTS: IS EVERYTHING REALLY GETTING STEADILY WORSE?

First, let's see what the facts really are. The popular press often gives the impression that environmental problems have been growing steadily worse and that *all* pollution is attributable to modern industrialization and the profit system. The problems are, indeed, serious and some of them are extremely urgent. But it is nevertheless possible to exaggerate the situation.

For one thing, pollution is nothing new. Medieval cities were pestholes; streets and rivers were littered with garbage and the air stank of rotting wastes—a level of filth that was accepted as normal. And early in the 20th century, the automobile was hailed for its major *improvement* in the cleanliness of city streets, which until then had fought a losing battle against the proliferation of horse dung.

Since World War II, there has been marked progress in solving a number of pollution problems. Air quality has improved in U.S. cities during the past two decades, and concentrations of most air pollutants are still declining. Most dramatic has been the nearly 100 percent decrease in ambient concentrations of lead since the 1970s. Figure 22–1 portrays the encouraging trends in national air pollution levels. With the exception of ozone, average concentrations are well below the national ambient air quality standards (NAAQS). Rapid declines in automobile pollution have played a large role in this improvement, along with decreases in emissions from power plants. There have also been some spectacular gains in water quality. In the Great Lakes region, where the Cuyahoga River once caught fire because of its toxic load and where Lake Erie was pronounced dead, tough pollution controls have gradually effected a recovery.

**U.S. National Air Quality Trends, 1975–1997**   FIGURE 22-1

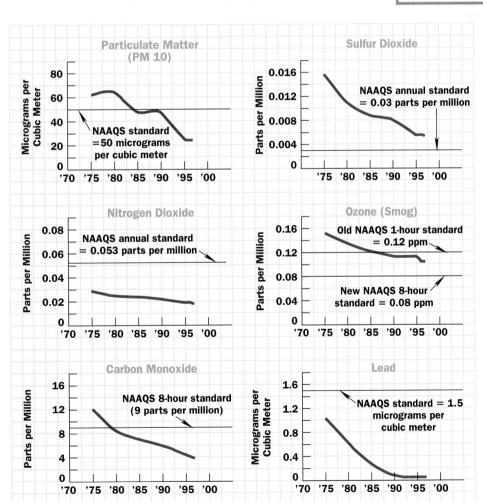

NOTE: Measures are average ambient concentrations of six pollutants. After 1987, particulate matter is measured by PM10 only, an indicator of those particles smaller than 10 micrometers.

SOURCE: Council on Environmental Quality, *Environmental Quality 1993, 24th Annual Report of the CEQ*, Washington, D.C., April 1995; and U.S. Environmental Protection Agency, *National Air Quality and Emissions Trends Report 1997*, January 1998, www.epa.gov.

**● CHINA OFFICIALLY LIFTS FILTER ON STAGGERING POLLUTION DATA**

**For the Record**

## No Silver Lining

China's major cities have some of the highest concentrations of air pollutants in the world, far exceeding international safety guidelines.

*1995 Concentrations of air pollutants in micrograms per cubic meter; annual mean concentration*

| | Total suspended particles | Sulfur dioxide |
|---|---|---|
| | *Maximum safe range under World Health Organization guidelines* | |
| Beijing | 370 | 94 |
| Shanghai | 246 | 53 |
| Chongqing | 322 | 338 |
| Taiyuan | 568 | 424 |
| Bangkok | 200 | 13 |
| Los Angeles | 76 | 8 |
| New York | 59 | 26 |
| Tokyo | 55 | 22 |

*Sources: China's Environmental Protection Agency; World Health Organization; World Bank*

SOURCE: Elisabeth Rosenthal, "China Officially Lifts Filter on Pollution Data," *The New York Times*, June 14, 1998. The article cites China's Environmental Protection Agency, the World Health Organization, and the World Bank.

The Europeans are making progress as well. For example, the infamous killing fogs of London, once the staple backdrop of British mystery fiction, are a thing of the past because of the air quality improvement since 1950. The Thames River has been cleaned up enough to allow large-scale fishing of giant conger eels to resume after a 150-year hiatus. The point is that pollution problems are not a uniquely modern phenomenon, nor is every part of the environment deteriorating relentlessly.

Free-market economies certainly have no monopoly on pollution. Though it may seem that a centrally planned economy should be able to cope much better with the environmental problems caused by externalities, such economies have in reality been the *biggest* environmental disasters. China, the last large communist society, has some of the world's worst air pollution, mainly from the burning of low-quality, high-sulfur coal and an almost complete lack of even rudimentary pollution control devices. Urban smog levels in China are far greater than those in Los Angeles, a place that Americans tend to think invented smog. (The accompanying box, "China Officially Lifts Filter on Staggering Pollution Data," compares such problems in Chinese cities with those in Los Angeles, New York, and Tokyo.)

Grave environmental problems also plague eastern Europe and the countries of the former Soviet Union. Poland, for example, is one of the most polluted industrialized countries in the world, with 11 percent of its land (on which 40 percent of its population lives) now declared "ecologically hazardous." High pollution levels contribute to severe health problems in these countries. The collapse of communism in the former Soviet Union revealed a staggering array of environmental horrors, including massive poisoning of air, ground, and water in the vicinity of industrial plants. This has resulted in widespread illness and countless premature deaths. The Soviet Union produced monumental ecological disasters. For example, the Aral Sea, once the world's fourth largest inland sea, has been reduced to less than half of its original volume.[1]

---

[1] "The Former Soviet Bloc: Environmental Crises Caused by Communist Rule," National Center for Policy Analysis, www.ncpa.org, accessed November 1998; Piotr Skubala, "Both Threats and Hopes in Upper Silesia," *The Baltic Sea Project Newsletter*, Stockholm 1997, www.skolverket.se, accessed November 1998; Murray Feshbach and Alfred Friendly, Jr., *Ecocide in the USSR: Health and Nature under Siege* (New York: Basic Books, 1992).

---

**● UNSCENELY**

Pardon the pun, but the future is unclear for scenic viewpoints in some national parks. . . .

National parks are reporting high ozone rankings this summer from Cape Cod National Seashore, Mass., to Indiana Dunes National Lakeshore. Air-quality experts say ozone levels at some parks actually are higher than those of nearby cities; the ozone-pollution levels over the Great Smoky Mountains are twice those of cities, such as Knoxville, Tenn., at lower elevations.

So far this summer, the Great Smoky Mountains National Park has already experienced 14 unhealthy days because of ozone problems. Acadia National Park in Maine has had seven unhealthy days, and Shenandoah National Park in Virginia has reported three.

SOURCE: Michelle Higgins, "Takeoffs & Landings," *The Wall Street Journal*, July 31, 1998, p. W4.

---

Yet our own environment here in the United States is hardly free from problems. Despite improvements, many U.S. urban areas still suffer many days of unhealthful air quality, particularly during summer months. According to the U.S. Environmental Protection Agency (EPA), 107 million Americans live in areas where pollution levels in 1997 still exceeded at least one national air quality standard.[2] Ozone (the presence of which 12 miles up in the stratosphere protects humans from the fiercest part of the sun's ultraviolet radiation) is the most important component of serious ground-level urban air pollution—smog. And formerly pristine wilderness areas are threatened by air pollution too (see the accompanying box, "Unscenely").

Our world is frequently subjected to new pollutants, some far more dangerous than those we have reduced, although less visible and less malodorous. Improperly dumped toxic substances—such as PCBs (polychlorinated biphenyls), chlorinated hydrocarbons, dioxins, heavy metals, and radioactive materials—can cause cancer and threaten life and health in other ways. The danger presented by some of these substances can persist for thousands of years, causing all but irreversible damage.

But even these problems pale when compared to an uncertain, but very real, environmental threat—the long-term warming of the earth's atmosphere. Many researchers (including scientists at the National Aeronautics and Space Administration) believe that the documented global warming of the past century, and especially in the past decade, is at least partly a consequence of human activities that have increased "greenhouse gases" in the atmosphere. Carbon dioxide buildup from the burning of fossil fuels such as oil, natural gas, and coal is suspected of being a significant contributor. Figure 22–2 charts the warming trend. Though sometimes disputed, forecasts of future warming range from 1.8° to 6.3° Fahrenheit by the year 2100, a dramatic change that may shift world rain patterns, disrupt agriculture, threaten coastal cities with inundation, and expand deserts.

**Although environmental problems are neither new nor confined to capitalist, industrialized economies, we continue to inflict damage on ourselves and our surroundings.**

**THE FAR SIDE**    By GARY LARSON

"The picture's pretty bleak, gentlemen. ... The world's climates are changing, the mammals are taking over, and we all have a brain about the size of a walnut."

---

[2] Source: U.S. Environmental Protection Agency, *National Air Quality and Emissions Trends Report 1997*, December 1998, www.epa.gov.

| FIGURE 22-2 | **Annual Mean Global Surface Air Temperature, 1880–1998** |

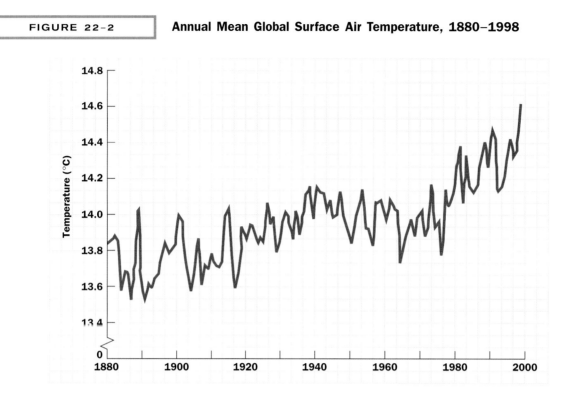

SOURCE: National Aeronautics and Space Administration, Goddard Institute for Space Studies, www.giss.nasa.gov.

## THE LAW OF CONSERVATION OF MATTER AND ENERGY

The physical law of conservation of matter and energy tells us that objects cannot disappear—at most they can be changed into something else. Petroleum, for instance, can be transformed into heat (and smoke) or into plastic—but it will never vanish. This means that after a raw material has been used, either it must be used again (recycled) or it becomes a waste product that requires disposal.

> If it is not recycled, any input used in production must ultimately become a waste product. It may end up in some municipal dump, it may literally go up in smoke, contributing to atmospheric pollution, or it may be transformed into heat, warming up adjacent waterways and killing aquatic life. But the laws of physics tell us nothing can be done to make used inputs disappear altogether.

We create an extraordinary amount of solid waste—each American discards an average of 4.5 pounds of trash every *day*, despite our efforts to reduce this waste. Fortunately, in the face of this rising tide of garbage, recycling rates for many commonly used materials (like aluminum, paper, and glass) are rising in the United States and many other industrial countries. In the United States recycling has increased substantially—according to the EPA, Americans recycled or composted 27 percent of municipal solid waste in 1995, up from under 10 percent in 1980. Switzerland recycles more than 20 percent of its municipal solid waste, and the statistics for Japan, Sweden, the Netherlands, Germany, and Spain are all in the 15 to 20 percent range.[3]

---

[3] U.S. Environmental Protection Agency, "Characterization of Municipal Solid Waste in the United States, 1997 Update," Report No. EPA530-R-98–007, May 1998, www.epa.gov; and "International Solid Waste Practices," MSW Factbook, www.epa.gov, accessed January 1999.

We should point out that recycling is not always as benign as it seems. The very process of preparing materials for reuse often can produce dangerous emissions. The recycling of waste oil is a clear example, because used petroleum products are often combined with toxic chemicals that can be released in the recycling process.

## THE ROLE OF INDIVIDUALS AND GOVERNMENTS IN ENVIRONMENTAL DAMAGE

Many people think of industry as the primary villain in environmental damage. But:

**Although business firms do their share in harming the environment, private individuals and government are also major contributors.**

Individual car owners are responsible for much of the air pollution in cities; wood-burning stoves and fireplaces are a source of particulate pollution, and wastes from flush toilets and residential washing machines also cause significant harm.

Governments, too, add to the problem. Municipal treatment plant wastes are a major source of water pollution. Military aircraft create exhaust and cause noise pollution. Obsolete atomic materials and by-products associated with chemical and nuclear weapons are among the most dangerous of all wastes, and their disposal remains an unsolved problem.

Governments also construct giant dams and reservoirs that flood farmlands and destroy canyons, often causing salt to seep into the earth and render surrounding soil unusable. Swamp drainage has altered local ecology irrevocably; canal building has diverted the flow of rivers. The U.S. Army Corps of Engineers has been accused of acting on the basis of a so-called *edifice complex*. But this kind of grandiose construction reached its greatest heights in the communist states under Stalin, whose pride in enormous (but environmentally destructive) hydroelectric installations and huge canals was well publicized in the Soviet press.

## ENVIRONMENTAL DAMAGE AS AN EXTERNALITY

Our very existence makes some environmental damage inevitable. In order to eat and protect ourselves from the elements, people must use up the earth's resources and generate wastes.

**Environmental damage cannot be reduced to zero. As long as the human race survives, eliminating such damage completely is impossible.**

Why do economists believe that though environmental damage cannot be reduced to zero, the *public interest* requires it to be reduced below its free-market level? Why do economists conclude that the market mechanism, which is so good at providing about the right number of running shoes and refrigerators, generates too much pollution? Pollution is an externality, which means that it results from a price mechanism malfunction that prevents the market from doing its usual effective job of carrying out consumers' wishes.

Here, the *failure of the pricing system* is caused by a pollution-generating firm's ability to use up some of the community's clean air or water without paying for the privilege. Just as the firm would undoubtedly use oil and electricity wastefully if they were available at no charge, the firm will use "free" air wastefully, despoiling it with chemical fumes far beyond the level justified by the public interest. The problem is that *price* has not been permitted to play its usual role here. Instead of having to pay for the pure air that it uses up, a polluting firm gets that valuable resource free of charge.

**Externalities play a crucial role affecting the quality of life. They show why the market mechanism, which is so efficient in supplying consumers' goods, has a much poorer record in terms of environmental effects. The problem of pollution illustrates the importance of externalities for public policy.**

## SUPPLY-DEMAND ANALYSIS OF ENVIRONMENTAL EXTERNALITIES

We can use basic supply-demand analysis to explain both how externalities lead to environmental problems and how these problems can be cured. As an illustration, consider the environmental damage caused by massive garbage generation.

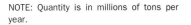

**Free Dumping of Pollutants as an Inducement to Environmental Damage**

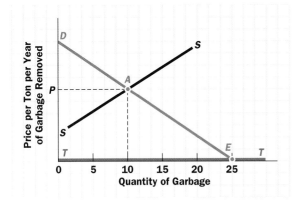

NOTE: Quantity is in millions of tons per year.

Figure 22–3 shows a hypothetical demand curve, *DE*, for garbage removal. As usual, this curve has a negative slope, meaning that if garbage removal prices rise, people will demand less removal. They may take more waste to recycling centers, repair broken items rather than throwing them out, and so on.

The graph also shows the supply curve, *SS*, of an ideal market for garbage removal. As we saw in our analysis of competitive industries (Chapter 10), the position of the market's long-run supply curve is the average cost of garbage removal. If suppliers had to pay the full costs of removal—including costs (like laundry and doctor's bills) of pollution caused when garbage is burned at the dump—the supply curve would be comparatively high (as drawn in the graph). For the community depicted in the graph, the price of garbage removal is *P* dollars per ton, and 10 million tons are generated (point *A*).

But what if the community's government decides to remove garbage "for free"? Of course, the consumer still really pays for garbage removal through taxes, but not in a way that makes each household pay for the quantity of garbage it actually produces. The supply curve is then no longer *SS*. Rather it becomes the red line *TT*, which lies along the horizontal axis, because any household can increase the garbage it throws away at no cost to itself. Now the intersection of the supply and demand curve is no longer point *A*. Rather it is point *E*, at which the price is zero, and the quantity of garbage generated is 25 million tons—a substantially greater amount.

Similar problems occur if a community offers the dissolved oxygen in its waterways and its atmosphere's purity without charge. The amount wasted and otherwise used up is likely to be enormously greater than if users had to pay for the cost of their actions to society. That is a key reason for the severity of our environmental problems.

> The magnitude of our pollution problems is largely attributable to the fact that the market lets individuals, firms, and government agencies deplete such resources as clean water and pure air without charging them any money for using up those resources.

It follows that one way of dealing with pollution problems is to charge those who emit pollution, and those who despoil the environment in other ways, a price commensurate with the costs they impose on society.

"IT'S HARD TO BELIEVE THAT HER BIGGEST PASSION IS FOR A CLEANER ENVIRONMENT."

## ● FOILED BY THE "SEATTLE STOMP"

If rubbish disposal is free, people will produce too much rubbish. The obvious economic solution is to make households pay the marginal cost of disposing of their waste. That will give them an incentive to throw out less and recycle more. . . . But as Don Fullerton and Thomas Kinnaman, two American economists, have found, this seemingly easy application of economic sense to an everyday problem has surprisingly intricate and sometimes disappointing results.

In the past few years several American towns and cities have started charging households for generating rubbish. The most common system is to sell stickers or tags which householders attach to rubbish bags or cans. . . . The price of a sticker or tag is, in effect, the marginal price the household pays for creating another bag of rubbish.

In a paper published last year Messrs Fullerton and Kinnaman studied the effects of one such scheme, introduced in July 1992 in Charlottesville, Virginia, a town of about 40,000. Residents were charged 80 cents for each sticker.

. . . [T]he number of bags or cans collected did fall sharply, by 37 percent between May and September 1992. But this was largely thanks to the "Seattle Stomp," a frantic dance first noticed when that city introduced rubbish pricing. Rather than buy more tags, people simply crammed more garbage— about 40 percent more—into each container. . . . The weight of rubbish collected in Charlottesville (a better indicator of disposal costs than volume) fell by a modest 14 percent. In 25 other Virginian cities where no pricing scheme was in place, and which were used as a rough-and-ready control group, it fell by 3.5 percent.

Less pleasing still, some people resorted to illegal dumping rather than pay to have their rubbish removed. [The authors guessed] that illegal dumping may account for 30–40 percent of the reduction in collected rubbish. The one bright spot in all this seems to have been a 15 percent increase in the weight of materials recycled, suggesting that people chose to recycle free rather than pay to have their refuse carted away.

SOURCE: *The Economist,* June 7, 1997, p. 80, which cites Don Fullerton and Thomas Kinnaman, "Household Responses to Pricing Garbage by the Bag," *American Economic Review,* September 1996, and "Garbage and Recycling in Communities with Curbside Recycling and Unit-Based Pricing," NBER Working Paper No. 6021, April 1997.

## ■ BASIC APPROACHES TO ENVIRONMENTAL POLICY

In broad terms, there are three ways to control activities that damage the environment:

■ *Voluntary efforts,* such as nonmandatory investment in pollution-control equipment by firms motivated by social responsibility, or voluntary recycling of solid wastes by consumers.

■ *Direct controls,* which either (a) impose legal ceilings on the amount any polluter is permitted to emit or (b) specify how particular activities must be carried out—for example, direct controls may prohibit backyard garbage incinerators or high-sulfur coal burning or require smokestack "scrubbers" to capture the emissions of power plants.

■ *Taxes on pollution,* or the use of other monetary incentives or penalties to make it unattractive financially for pollution emitters to continue to pollute as usual.

All of these methods have useful roles. Let's consider each of them in turn.

**VOLUNTARISM** Voluntarism often has proved weak and unreliable. Some well-intentioned business firms, for example, have voluntarily made sincere attempts to adopt environmentally beneficial practices. Yet competition has usually prevented them from spending more than token amounts for this purpose. No business, whatever its virtues, can long afford to spend so much on "good works" that rivals can easily underprice it. As a result, voluntary business programs sometimes have been more helpful to the companies' public relations activities than to the environment.

Yet voluntary measures do have their place. They are appropriate where surveillance and, consequently, enforcement is impractical, as in the prevention of littering by campers in isolated areas, where appeals to people's consciences are the only alternative. And in brief but serious emergencies, which do not allow for time to plan and enact a systematic program, voluntary compliance may be the only viable approach.

Several major cities have, for example, experienced episodes of temporary but dangerous concentrations of pollutants, forcing the authorities to appeal to the public for drastic emissions cuts. Public response to appeals requiring cooperation for short periods often has been enthusiastic and gratifying, particularly when civic pride was a factor. During the 1984 Summer Olympic Games, for example, Los Angeles city officials asked motorists to carpool, businesses to stagger work hours, and truckers to restrict themselves to essential deliveries and to avoid rush hours. The result was an extraordinary decrease in traffic and smog, such that the 6,000-foot San Gabriel Mountains suddenly became visible behind the city.

**DIRECT CONTROLS** Direct controls have been the chief instrument of environmental policy in the United States (the so-called command and control approach). The federal government, through the Environmental Protection Agency, formulates standards for air and water quality and requires state and local governments to adopt rules that will ensure achievement of those goals. For example, the standards for automobile emissions require new automobiles to pass tests showing that their emissions do not exceed specified amounts. As another example, localities sometimes prohibit industry's use of particularly "dirty" fuels or require firms to adopt processes to "clean" those fuels.

**TAXES ON POLLUTION EMISSIONS** Most economists agree that relying exclusively on direct controls is a mistake and that, in most cases, *financial penalties* on polluters can do the same job more dependably, effectively, and economically.

The most common suggestion is that governments permit firms to pollute all they want but be forced to pay a tax for the privilege, in order to make them *want* to pollute less. Under such a plan, the quantity of the polluter's emissions is metered just like the use of electricity. At the end of the month the government sends the polluter a bill charging a stipulated amount for each gallon (or other unit) of emissions. (The amount can also vary with the emissions' quality—a higher tax rate being imposed on emissions that are more dangerous or unpleasant.) Thus, in such a scheme, the more environmental damage done, the more the polluter pays. Emissions taxes are deliberately designed to *encourage* polluters to take advantage of the tax loophole—by polluting less, the polluter can reduce the amount of tax owed.

In terms of Figure 22–3, if the tax is used to increase the payment for waste emissions from zero (red supply line *TT*) and instead forces the polluter to pay its true cost to society (line *SS*), then emissions will automatically be reduced from 25 million to 10 million tons.

Businesses *do* respond to such taxes. One widely publicized example is the Ruhr River basin in Germany, where emissions taxes have been used for many years. Though the Ruhr is one of the world's most concentrated industrial centers, the rivers that are protected by taxes are clean enough for fishing and other recreational purposes. Firms have also found it profitable to avoid taxes by extracting pollutants from their liquid discharges and recycling them. (See the accompanying box, "Making the Polluter Pay," for another example of the response to taxes.)

## EMISSIONS TAXES VERSUS DIRECT CONTROLS

It is important to see why taxes on emissions may prove more effective and reliable than direct controls. Direct controls rely on the criminal justice system for enforcement. But a polluter who violates the rules must first be caught. Then the regulatory agency must decide whether it has enough evidence to prosecute. Next, it must win its case in court.

### ● MAKING THE POLLUTER PAY

In the Netherlands, a set of charges originally intended only to cover the costs of wastewater treatment has produced a classic demonstration of the pollution-preventing power of charges themselves. Since 1970, gradually rising fees for emissions of organic material and heavy metals into canals, rivers, and lakes have spurred companies to cut emissions, but without dictating how. Between 1976 and 1994, emissions of cadmium, copper, lead, mercury, and zinc plummeted 86–97 percent, primarily because of the charges, according to statistical analyses. . . . And demand for pollution control equipment has spurred Dutch manufacturers to develop better models, lowering costs and turning the country into a global leader in the market. The taxes have in effect sought the path of least economic resistance—of least cost—in cleaning up the country's waters.

SOURCE: David Malin Roodman, "Getting the Signals Right: Tax Reform to Protect the Environment and the Economy," Worldwatch Paper 134, May 1997, pp. 10–12.

### Industrial Discharges of Selected Heavy Metals into Surface Waters of the Netherlands, 1976–1994

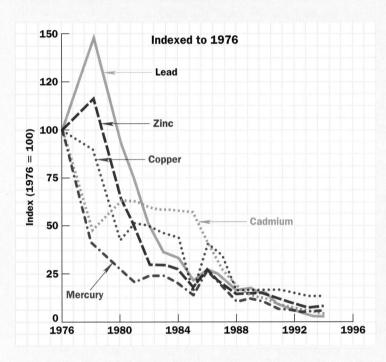

Finally, the court must impose a penalty strong enough to matter. If any *one* of these does not occur, the polluter gets away with the environmentally damaging activities.

**ENFORCEMENT ISSUES**  Enforcement of direct controls requires vigilance and enthusiasm by the regulatory agency, which must assign the resources and persons needed to carry out enforcement. But in many cases the resources devoted to enforcement are pitifully small. The effectiveness of direct controls also depends on the speed and rigor of the court system. Yet the courts are often slow and lenient. In the notorious case of the Reserve Mining Company, more than a decade of litigation was required to stop this company from pouring its wastes (which contain asbestos-like fibers believed to cause cancer) into Lake Superior, the drinking water source for a number of communities.

Finally, direct controls work only if the legal system imposes substantial penalties on violators. Lately, judges have imposed significant penalties in several cases (for instance, in 1998 Louisiana Pacific Corporation was fined a record $37 million for violations of the Clean Air Act), and some polluters have even served prison terms for their misdeeds. But much more often large firms have been convicted of polluting and fined amounts beneath the notice of even a relatively small corporation. Even the $37 million fine just cited looks small next to the company's $2.5 billion in sales.[4]

In contrast, pollution taxes are automatic and certain. No one need be caught, prosecuted, convicted, and punished. The tax bills are sent out automatically by the untiring tax collector. The only sure way for the polluter to avoid paying pollution charges is to pollute less.

**EFFICIENCY IN CLEANUP**   A second important advantage of emissions taxes is that they tend to cost less than direct controls. Statistical estimates for several pollution-control programs suggest that the cost of doing the job through direct controls can easily be twice as high as under the tax alternative. Why should there be such a difference? Under direct controls, emissions cutbacks are usually *not* apportioned among the various firms on the basis of ability to reduce pollution cheaply and efficiently.

Suppose it costs Firm A only 3 cents a gallon to reduce emissions whereas Firm B must spend 20 cents a gallon to do the same job. If each firm spews out 2,000 gallons of pollution a day, authorities can achieve a 50 percent reduction in pollution by ordering both firms to limit emissions to 1,000 gallons a day. This may or may not be fair, but it is certainly not efficient. The social cost will be 1,000 × 3 cents (or $30) to Firm A, and 1,000 × 20 cents (or $200) to Firm B, a total of $230. If the government had instead imposed a tax of 10 cents a gallon, Firm A would have done all the work at a lower cost. Why? Firm A would have eliminated its emissions altogether, paying the 3-cents-a-gallon cost to avoid the 10-cents-a-gallon tax. Firm B would have gone on polluting as before, because the tax would be cheaper than the 20-cents-a-gallon cost of controlling its pollution. In this way, under the tax, *total daily emissions would still be cut by 2,000 gallons a day.* But the total daily cost of the program would be $60 (3 cents × 2,000 gallons) as opposed to $230 under direct controls.

The secret of a pollution tax's efficiency is straightforward. Only polluters who can reduce emissions cheaply and efficiently can afford to take advantage of the built-in loophole—the opportunity to save on taxes by reducing emissions. The tax approach therefore assigns the job to those who can do it most effectively—and rewards them by letting them escape the tax.

**ADVANTAGES AND DISADVANTAGES**   Given all these advantages of the tax approach, why would anyone want to use direct controls?

In three important situations, direct controls have a clear advantage:

■ *Where an emission is so dangerous that it must be prohibited altogether.*

■ *Where a sudden change in circumstances—for example, a dangerous air-quality crisis—calls for prompt and substantial changes in conduct, such as temporary reductions in use of cars.* Tax rule changes are difficult and time-consuming, so direct controls will usually do a better job here. The mayor of a city threatened by a dangerous air-quality crisis can, for example, forbid use of private passenger cars until the crisis passes.

■ *Where effective and dependable pollution metering devices have not been invented or are prohibitively costly to install and operate.* In such cases authorities cannot operate an effective tax program because they cannot determine the emissions levels of an individual polluter and so cannot calculate the tax bill. The only effective option may be to *require* firms to use "clean" fuel or install emissions-purification equipment.

## ANOTHER FINANCIAL DEVICE TO PROTECT THE ENVIRONMENT: EMISSIONS PERMITS

The basic idea underlying the emissions-tax approach to environmental protection is that financial incentives induce polluters to reduce their environmental damage. But at least one other form of financial inducement deserves our consideration:

---

[4] "$37 Million Fine Levied for Clean Air Violation," *The New York Times*, May 28, 1998, p. A22.

## ● FOOD FOR THOUGHT: ARE EMISSIONS PERMITS JUST "LICENSES TO POLLUTE"?

In the following excerpt from *The New York Times,* Harvard University professor Michael J. Sandel addresses the morality of emissions trading.

> Despite the efficiency of international emissions trading, such a system is objectionable for three reasons.
>
> First, it creates loopholes that could enable wealthy countries to evade their obligations. Under the Kyoto formula [for trading in greenhouse gas emissions], for example, the United States could take advantage of the fact that Russia has already reduced its emissions 30 percent since 1990, not through energy efficiencies but through economic decline. The United States could buy excess credits from Russia, and count them toward meeting our obligations under the treaty.
>
> Second, turning pollution into a commodity to be bought and sold removes the moral stigma that is properly associated with it. If a company or a country is fined for spewing excessive pollutants into the air, the community conveys its judgment that the polluter has done something wrong. . . .
>
> The distinction between a fine and a fee for despoiling the environment is not one we should give up too easily. Suppose there were a $100 fine for throwing a beer can into the Grand Canyon, and a wealthy hiker decided to pay $100 for the convenience. Would there be nothing wrong in his treating the fine as if it were simply an expensive dumping charge? . . .
>
> A third objection to emission trading among countries is that it may undermine the sense of shared responsibility that increased global cooperation requires.

SOURCE: Michael J. Sandel, "It's Immoral to Buy the Right to Pollute," *The New York Times,* December 15, 1997, p. A23.

requiring polluters to buy *emissions permits* that authorize the emission of a specified quantity of pollutant. Such permits can be offered for sale in limited quantities fixed by the government authorities at prices set by demand and supply.

Under this arrangement, the environmental agency decides what quantity of emissions per unit of time (say, per year) is tolerable and then issues a batch of permits authorizing (altogether) just that amount of pollution. The permits are sold to the highest bidders, with the price determined by demand and supply. The price will be high if the number of permits offered for sale is small and a lot of firms need permits to carry out their industrial activities. Similarly, the price of a permit will be low if authorities issue many permits but the quantity of pollution firms demand is small.

Emissions permits in many ways work like a tax—they make it too expensive for firms to continue polluting as much as before. However, the permit approach has some advantages over taxes. For example, it reduces *uncertainty* about the *quantity* of pollution that will be emitted. Under a tax, we cannot be sure about this in advance, because that depends on polluters' response to a given tax rate. In the case of permits, environmental authorities decide on an emissions ceiling in advance, then issue permits authorizing just that quantity of emissions.

Many people react indignantly to the notion of emissions permits, calling them "licenses to pollute" (as evidenced in the accompanying box, "Food for Thought: Are Emissions Permits Just 'Licenses to Pollute'?"). Yet the EPA has introduced some compromise measures that seem politically palatable and can be regarded as approximations to a market in emissions permits. The accompanying box, "Using the Market to Protect the Environment: Emissions Trading," describes the successful "acid rain" market for sulfur dioxide pollution permits, which has cut both $SO_2$ emissions and polluter costs.

---

● **USING THE MARKET TO PROTECT THE ENVIRONMENT: EMISSIONS TRADING**

To reduce the damage that acid rain causes to lakes, streams, buildings, and visibility throughout the eastern United States and Canada, the 1990 Clean Air Act established the largest market ever devised for trading in emissions permits. The following excerpts from an Environmental Defense Fund news release demonstrate the success of the sulfur dioxide emissions trading program and also how the economist's way of doing things has been embraced wholeheartedly by environmentalists.

> The Environmental Defense Fund today released *More Clean Air for the Buck: Lessons from the Acid Rain Emissions Trading Program,* a report detailing the unprecedented success, to date, of the Clean Air Act acid rain reduction program in cutting emissions of sulfur dioxide ($SO_2$), a principal cause of acid rain. Highlighting the report is the finding that the program, which caps power plant $SO_2$ emissions at reduced levels while permitting companies to trade any extra $SO_2$ reductions they make, has resulted in about 1/3 more cuts in $SO_2$ throughout the Eastern U.S. than mandated by law.
>
> The report also reveals that the highest-emitting plants in the Midwest have been foremost among those making the extra reductions. At the same time, the cost of those cuts appears to be dramatically lower than predicted when Congress adopted the program in 1990. While analysts and industry put costs anywhere from $350 to $1,000 per ton, the price of extra reductions being traded actually ranges from $62 to $170 per ton.

SOURCE: "Acid Rain Cuts Hold Important, Affordable Lessons for Global Warming," Environmental Defense Fund, www.edf.org, 1997.

A principal broker of $SO_2$ pollution permits, the private firm Cantor Fitzgerald Environmental Brokerage Services, publishes advertisements like this one on the Internet—bids to buy $SO_2$ permits, offers to sell nitrogen oxide (NOx) permits, and the like.
SOURCE: Cantor Fitzgerald EBS, www.cantor.com, 1998.

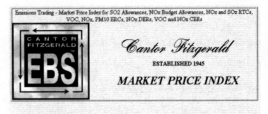

---

■ **TWO CHEERS FOR THE MARKET**

In the first part of this chapter, we have learned that environmental protection cannot be left to the free market. Because of the large externalities involved, the market will systematically allocate insufficient resources to the job. However, this market failure does not imply that we should disregard the price mechanism. On the contrary, we have seen that a legislated market solution based on pollution charges may often be the best way to protect the environment. At least in this case, the market mechanism's power can be harnessed to correct its own failings.

We turn now, in the second half of the chapter, to the issue of natural resources, where the market mechanism also plays a crucial role.

## ■ PART 2: THE ECONOMICS OF NATURAL RESOURCES

> Since Fuel is become so expensive, and will of course grow scarcer and dearer; any new Proposal for saving the [fuel] . . . may at least be thought worth Consideration.
>
> *Benjamin Franklin, 1744*

One of the most significant forms of environmental damage is the waste of natural resources. We saw earlier in this chapter that externalities can lead to just this sort of waste—as when governments, individuals, or business firms use up clean air and clean water without cost or penalty. There is a close analytic connection between the economics of environmental protection that we have just investigated and the economics of natural resources, to which we now turn.

Twenty-five years ago the world was rocked by a sudden "energy crisis." Oil prices shot up and consumers found themselves waiting in long lines to buy gasoline. This event had profound effects throughout the world and ended the widespread assumption that the stock of natural resources was unlimited and simply ours for the taking. Indeed, back in the late 1970s and early 1980s there was near-panic about the threatened exhaustion of many natural resources. The front page of a leading magazine even asked, "Are we running out of *everything*?"

Natural resources have always been scarce, and they have often been used wastefully. Nevertheless, we are *not* about to run out of the most vital resources. In many cases substitutes are available, and many of the shortages of the 1970s can largely be ascribed to the folly of government programs rather than the imminent exhaustion of natural resources.

### Those Resilient Resource Supplies

It is a plain fact that the earth is endowed with only finite quantities of such vital resources as oil, copper, tin, and coal. This reality underlies many worried forecasts about the inevitable, and imminent, exhaustion of one resource or another. For instance, the accompanying box, "The Permanent Fuel Crisis," lists a number of bleak prophecies about oil production in the United States, all of which proved far off the mark.

In fact, far from running out, available supplies of many key minerals and fuels are *growing*. In recent decades, known supplies of most minerals have grown at least as fast as production, and in many cases have far outstripped it. For example, in 1995 world reserves of tin were estimated at 7 million metric tons (mmt). During 1996, 196,000 metric tons of tin were mined from the earth. Nonetheless, by 1997 world reserves of tin had *risen* to 8 mmt. For bauxite (the ore used to produce aluminum), known reserves in 1995 were 23,000 mmt and production in 1996 amounted to 120 mmt, but 1997 reserves were still estimated at 23,000 mmt. A similar odd story is true for zinc, copper, and many more.[5] How is this possible? Aren't the quantities of these resources finite? Economic principles, as we will see, help to clear up these mysteries.

## ■ ECONOMIC ANALYSIS: THE FREE MARKET AND PRICING OF DEPLETABLE RESOURCES

If statistics on known mineral reserves behave as peculiarly as those we have just seen, we may begin to doubt their ability to tell us whether we are running out of certain resources. Is another indicator more reliable? Most economists say there is one—*the price of the resource.*

---

[5] U.S. Geological Survey, *Minerals Yearbook*, various years, www.minerals.er.usgs.gov.

---

### ● THE PERMANENT FUEL CRISIS

Humanity has a long history of panicking about the imminent exhaustion of natural resources. In the 13th century a large part of Europe's forests was cut down, primarily for use in metalworking (much of it for armor). Wood prices rose, and there was a good deal of talk about depletion of fuel stocks. People have been doing it ever since, as the accompanying table illustrates.

SOURCE: William M. Brown, "The Outlook for Future Petroleum Supplies," in Julian L. Simon and Herman Kahn, eds., *The Resourceful Earth: A Response to Global 2000* (Oxford, England: Basil Blackwell, 1984), p. 362, who cite Presidential Energy Program, Hearings before the Subcommittee on Energy and Power of the Committee on Interstate and Foreign Commerce, House of Representatives, 1st session on the implication of the President's proposals in the Energy Independence Act of 1975, Serial No. 94–20, p. 643. February 17, 18, 20, and 21, 1975.

#### Past Petroleum Prophecies (and Realities)

| Date | U.S. Production Rate | Prophecy | Reality |
|---|---|---|---|
| 1866 | 0.005 | Synthetics are available if oil production should end. *U.S. Revenue Commission* | In the next 82 years, the U.S. produces 37 billion barrels with no need for synthetics. |
| 1891 | 0.05 | Little or no chance for oil in Kansas or Texas *U.S. Geological Survey* | Production exceeds 14 billion barrels in these two states since 1891. |
| 1914 | 0.27 | Total future production only 5.7 billion barrels. *Official of U.S. Bureau of Mines* | More than 34 billion barrels produced since 1914, six times the prediction. |
| 1920 | 0.45 | U.S. needs foreign oil and synthetics: Peak domestic production almost reached. *Director, U.S. Geological Survey* | U.S. production in 1948 exceeds consumption and is more than four times the 1920 output. |
| 1939 | 1.3 | U.S. oil supplies will last only 13 years. *Interior Department* | New oil found since 1939 exceeds the 13 years' supply known at that time. |
| 1947 | 1.9 | Sufficient oil cannot be found in U.S. *Chief of Petroleum Division, State Department* | Some 4.3 billion barrels found in 1948, the largest volume in history and twice U.S consumption. |
| 1949 | 2.0 | End of U.S. oil supply almost in sight *Secretary of the Interior* | Recent industry data show ability to increase U.S. production by more than 1 million barrels daily in the next five years. |

NOTE: U.S. oil production rate in billions of barrels per year.

---

### SCARCITY AND RISING PRICES

As a resource becomes scarcer, we expect its price to rise for several reasons. One is that we do not deplete a resource simply by gradually using up a homogeneous product, every unit of which is equally available. Rather, we generally use up the most accessible and highest-quality resource deposits first and then turn to less accessible supplies that are more costly to retrieve or deposits of lower purity or quality. Oil is a clear example. First, Americans relied primarily on the most easily found domestic oil. Then they turned to imports from the Middle East with their higher transport costs. At that point it was not yet profitable to embark on the dangerous and extremely costly process of bringing up oil from the floor of the North Sea. We know that the United States still possesses a tremendous amount of petroleum embedded in shale (rock), but so far this has been too difficult and, therefore, too costly to extract.

> **Increasing scarcity of a resource such as oil is not usually a matter of imminent and total disappearance. Rather, it involves exhaustion of the most accessible and cheapest sources so that new supplies become more costly.**

Growing scarcity also raises resource prices for the usual supply-demand reason. As we know, goods in short supply tend to become more expensive. To see just how this works for natural resources, imagine a mythical mineral, "economite," consistent in quality, which has negligible extraction and transportation costs. How quickly will the reserves of this mineral be used up, and what will happen to its price as time passes?

If the market for economite is perfectly competitive, we can provide remarkably concrete answers, discovered by the American economist Harold Hotelling. They tell us that as long as the supply of the mineral lasts, its price must rise at a rate equal to the prevailing interest rate. That is, if in 1999 the price of economite is $100 per ounce and the interest rate is 10 percent, then its price in 2000 must be $110.

> **Under perfect competition, the price of a depletable resource whose transportation and extraction costs are negligible must rise at the interest rate. If the interest rate is 10 percent, the price of the resource must rise 10 percent every year.**

Why is this so? The reason is simple. People who are considering tying up money in inventories of economite must earn exactly as much per dollar of investment as they would by putting their money into, say, a government bond. Suppose instead that $100 invested in bonds would next year rise in value to $112, whereas $100 in economite would grow only to $110, and suppose the two investments were equally risky. What would happen? Investors would obviously find it unprofitable to buy the mineral and would put their money into bonds instead. But because economite lacked demand, its *current* price would then fall. The economite that would be worth $110 one year in the future would now cost less than $100. This fall in current price would continue until the return on economite equaled the return on bonds—the interest rate.

The same process, working in reverse, would apply if economite prices were rising faster than the interest rate. Investors would switch from bonds to economite, and current prices of the mineral would rise.

This fundamental principle tells us what will happen to the price of $100 worth of economite over, say, four years:

| Initial Date | 1 Year Later | 2 Years Later | 3 Years Later | 4 Years Later |
|---|---|---|---|---|
| $100 | $110 | $121 | $133.10 | $146.41 |

These prices follow from the fact that $110 is 10 percent higher than $100, $121 is 10 percent higher than $110, and so on. Note that, because of compounding, the dollar price grows faster each year. Economite's price rises $10 in the first year, $11 in the second year, $12.10 in the third, $13.31 in the fourth, and so on indefinitely.

> **The basic law of pricing of a depletable resource tells us that as its stocks are used up, its price in a perfectly competitive market will rise every year by greater and greater dollar amounts.**

## SUPPLY-DEMAND ANALYSIS AND CONSUMPTION

Although we can predict the price of economite without knowing anything about its supply or consumer demand for it, we do need to know something about supply and demand to determine what will happen to economite's consumption—the rate at which it will be used up.

Figure 22–4(a) is a demand curve for economite, *DD*, which shows the amount people want to use up *per year* at various price levels. On the vertical axis, we show how the price must rise from year to year in the pattern we have just calculated—from $100 per ton in the initial year to $110 in the next year and so on. Because of the demand curve's negative slope, it follows that consumption of this mineral will fall each year. That is, *if there is no shift in the demand curve, as in Panel (a)*, consumption will fall from 100,000 tons initially to 95,000 tons the next year and so on.

| FIGURE 22-4 | **Consumption over Time of a Depletable Resource** |

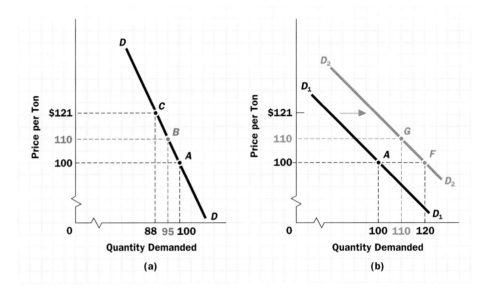

NOTE: Quantity is in thousands of tons per year.

But in reality such demand curves rarely stay still. As the economy grows and population and incomes increase, demand curves shift outward, and this has probably been true for most scarce resources. Such shifts in the demand curve will offset at least part of the reduction in quantity demanded that results from rising prices. Nevertheless, rising prices do cut consumption growth relative to what it would have been if price had remained unchanged. In Figure 22–4(b) we depict an outward shift in demand from curve $D_1D_1$ in the initial period to curve $D_2D_2$ a year later. If price had remained constant at the initial value, $100 per ton, quantity consumed per year would have risen from 100,000 tons to 120,000 tons. But because, in accord with the basic principle, price must rise to $110, quantity demanded will increase only to 110,000 tons. Thus, whether or not the demand curve shifts, we conclude:

> The ever-rising prices accompanying increasing scarcity of a depletable resource discourage consumption (encourage conservation). Even if quantity demanded grows, it will grow less rapidly than if prices were not rising.

## ■ ACTUAL RESOURCE PRICES IN THE 20TH CENTURY

How do the facts match up with this theoretical analysis? As we will see now, their correspondence is very poor indeed. Figure 22–5 shows the behavior of the prices of three critical metals—lead, zinc, and copper—since the beginning of the 20th century. This graph shows the prices of these three resources relative to other prices in the economy (in other words, the *real* prices, after adjustment for any inflation or deflation). What we find is that instead of rising steadily, as the theory leads us to expect, lead and zinc prices actually remained amazingly constant, even though they are gradually being used up. The price of copper has been all over the map but also has shown no upward trend.

Figure 22–6 shows the real price of crude oil in the United States since 1949 (again, adjusted for inflation). It gives price at the wellhead, that is, at the point of production, with no transportation cost included. Notice how constant these prices were until the first "energy crisis" in 1973, when oil prices rose precipitously. A second dramatic increase occurred in the late 1970s and early 1980s, but since then (with a temporary spike during the war with Iraq) real oil prices have fallen all the way back to their level in the early 1970s and even lower.

FIGURE 22–5

**Real Prices of Copper, Zinc, and Lead, 1900–1998**

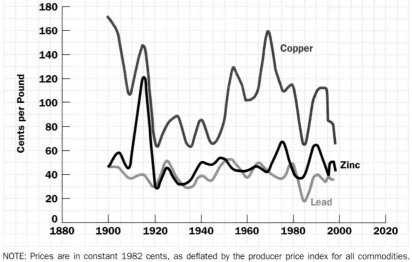

NOTE: Prices are in constant 1982 cents, as deflated by the producer price index for all commodities.
SOURCES: U.S. Bureau of the Census, *Historical Statistics of the United States, Colonial Times to 1970,* Washington, D.C.: 1975; *Statistical Abstract of the United States,* Washington, D.C., various issues; U.S. Department of Labor, Bureau of Labor Statistics, *Producer Price Index,* http://stats.bls.gov; and U.S. Geological Survey, *Minerals Yearbook,* various years, www.minerals.er.usgs.gov.

### INTERFERENCES WITH PRICE PATTERNS

How does one explain this strange behavior in the prices of finite resources, which surely are being used up, even if only gradually? Although many things can interfere with the price patterns that theory leads us to expect, we will mention only three:

FIGURE 22–6

**Real Price of Domestic Oil at the Wellhead, 1949–1998**

1. *Unexpected discoveries of reserves whose existence was previously not suspected.* If we were to stumble upon a huge and easily accessible reserve of economite, which came as a complete surprise to the market, the price of economite would obviously fall. This is illustrated in Figure 22–7, where we see that people originally believed that the $S_1S_1$ curve represented available supply. The discovery of the new economite reserves leads them to recognize that the supply is much larger than they had thought. This causes a rightward shift of the supply curve (curve $S_2S_2$), because the suppliers' cost of any given quantity is reduced by the discovery, so it will pay them to supply a larger quantity at any given price. Like any outward shift in a supply curve, this can be expected to cause a price decrease (from $P_1$ to $P_2$). A clear historical example was the Spaniards' 16th-century discovery of gold and silver in Mexico and South America,

NOTE: Price is in constant 1992 dollars, as deflated with implicit GDP price deflators.
SOURCE: U.S. Department of Energy, Energy Information Administration, www.eia.doe.gov; and Department of Commerce, Bureau of Economic Analysis, www.bea.doc.gov.

**FIGURE 22-7**

**Price Effects of a Discovery of Additional Reserves**

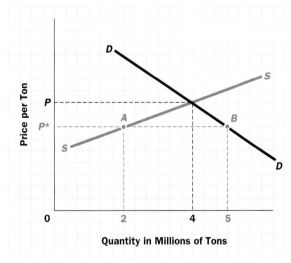

Quantity in Millions of Tons

**FIGURE 22-8**

**Controls on the Price of a Resource**

which led to substantial drops in European prices of these precious metals. The same effect can result from innovations that use the resources more efficiently. If a new invention doubles the number of miles one can travel on a gallon of gasoline, that is tantamount to doubling the supply of petroleum that still remains in the ground.

2. *The invention of new methods of mining or refining that may significantly reduce extraction costs.* This, too, can lead to a rightward shift in the supply curve as suppliers are able to deliver a larger quantity at any given price. The situation is therefore again represented by a diagram like Figure 22–7, only now a reduction in cost, not a new discovery of reserves, shifts the supply curve to the right. (See the accompanying box, "Innovation Can Increase Resources," for a real-world example.)

3. *Price controls that hold prices down or decrease them.* A legislature can pass a law prohibiting the sale of the resource at a price higher than $P^*$ (see Figure 22–8). Sometimes this doesn't work; in many cases an illegal black market emerges, where suppliers charge very high prices more or less secretly. But when price controls do work, shortages usually follow. Because the objective is to make the legal ceiling price, $P^*$, lower than the market equilibrium price, $P$, then at price $P^*$ quantity demanded (5 million tons in the figure) will be higher than the free-market level (4 million tons). Similarly, we may expect quantity supplied (2 million tons in the figure) to be less than its free-market level (again, 4 million tons). Thus, as always happens in these cases, quantity supplied is less than quantity demanded, and a shortage results (measured in Figure 22–8 by the length of *AB*, or 3 million tons).

Many economists believe that this is exactly what happened after 1971 when President Nixon decided to experiment with price controls. It was then that the economy experienced a plague of shortages, and we seemed to be "running out of nearly everything." After price controls ended in 1974, most of the shortages disappeared.

We can explain each of our examples of minerals whose price did not rise by one or more of these influences. For example, copper and zinc have benefited from technological changes that lowered extraction costs. In addition, the development of direct electroplating techniques has made copper production much more efficient. In the case of lead, new mines in Missouri held abundant quantities of ore that were much easier to extract and much cheaper to refine than what had been available before. Obviously, real events are more complex than a naïve reading of theoretical models might lead us to believe.

## IS PRICE INTERFERENCE JUSTIFIED?

Despite these influences, if a resource does become very scarce and costly to obtain, its price must ultimately rise unless government interferes. Moreover:

In a free market, quantity demanded can never exceed quantity supplied, even if a finite resource is undergoing rapid depletion. The reason is simple: In any free market, price will automatically adjust to eliminate any difference between quantity supplied and quantity demanded.

### ● INNOVATION CAN INCREASE RESOURCES

This advertisement in a British magazine illustrates technological innovation's ability to increase our natural resources.

More than a quarter of the petrol you buy owes its existence to an idea and to late night scribbles in the notebooks of two Mobil scientists. They discovered that a synthetic catalyst (crystals the size of a speck of flour) could make crude oil yield far more petrol than ever before. Their breakthrough led to a process that is now being used in nearly every major refinery in the world. It has saved consumers billions of pounds a year and has greatly extended the Earth's precious oil reserves. It has also caused Charles Plank and Edward Rosinski, who together hold 159 U.S. patents and whose careers epitomise Mobil's commitment to science and technology, to be inducted into the U.S. National Inventors Hall of Fame.

SOURCE: "©1996 Mobil Corporation," *The Economist,* October 17, 1998.

28% of the world's petrol was discovered here.

> In theory, any shortage—any excess of quantity demanded over quantity supplied—must be artificial, ascribable to a decision to prevent the price mechanism from doing its job.

To say that the cause is artificial, of course, does not settle the basic issue—whether freedom of price adjustments is desirable when resources are scarce, or whether interference with the pricing process is justified.

Many economists believe that this is a case in which the disease—shortages and their resulting economic problems—is far worse than the cure—deregulation of prices. They hold that the general public is misguided in regarding these price rises as the problem, when in fact they are part of the (admittedly rather painful) cure.

It is, of course, easy to understand why no consumer loves a price rise. It is also easy to understand why many consumers attribute any such price increase to a plot—a conspiracy by greedy suppliers who somehow deliberately arrange shortages to force prices upward. Sometimes, this view is even correct. For example, the members of the Organization of Petroleum Exporting Countries (OPEC) have openly and frankly tried to influence the flow of oil in order to increase its price. But it is important to recognize from the principles of supply and demand that when a resource grows scarce its price will tend to rise automatically, even without any conspiracies or plots.

## ON THE VIRTUES OF RISING PRICES

Rising prices help to control resource depletion in three basic ways:

- They discourage consumption and waste and provide an inducement for conservation.

- They stimulate more efficient resource use by industry, providing incentives for employment of processes that are more sparing in their use of the resource or that use substitute resources.

- They encourage innovation—the discovery of other, more abundant resources that can serve the same role and of new techniques that permit these other resources to be used economically.

### Growing Reserves of Exhaustible Resources: Our Puzzle Revisited

Earlier in Part 2 of this chapter we saw, strangely enough, that reserves of many mineral resources have actually been increasing, despite growing world production. This paradox has a straightforward economic explanation: rising mineral reserves are a tribute to the success of pricing and exploration activity. Minerals are not discovered by accident. Exploration and discovery entail costly work requiring geologists, engineers, and expensive machinery. Industry does not consider this money worth spending when reserves are high and mineral prices are low.

In the 20th century, every time some mineral's known reserves fell and its price tended to rise, exploration increased until the decline was offset. The law of supply and demand worked. In the 1970s, for example, the rising price of oil led to very substantial increases in oil exploration, which helped to build up reserves. Although, to protect ourselves from OPEC, it may not be wise for us to *consume* more oil from American sources, it certainly does seem prudent for us to increase our reserves through exploration. Increased profitability of exploration is perhaps the most effective way to get that done.

---

## S U M M A R Y

1. Pollution is as old as human history and, contrary to popular notions, some forms of pollution were actually decreasing even before government programs were initiated to protect the environment.

2. Both planned and market economies suffer from substantial environmental problems.

3. The production of commodities *must* cause waste disposal problems unless everything is recycled, but even recycling processes cause pollution (and use up energy).

4. Industrial activity causes environmental damage, but so does the activity of private individuals (as when they drive cars that emit pollutants). Government agencies also damage the environment (as when military airplanes emit noise and exhaust or a hydroelectric project floods large areas).

5. Pollution is an *externality*—when a factory emits smoke, it dirties the air in nearby neighborhoods and may damage the health of persons who neither work for the factory nor buy its products. Hence, the public interest in pollution control is not best served by the free market. This is another of our *Ideas for Beyond the Final Exam*.

6. Pollution can be controlled by voluntary programs, *direct controls, emissions taxes*, or other monetary incentives for emissions reduction.

7. Most economists believe that the monetary incentives approach is the most efficient and effective way to control damaging externalities.

8. The quantity demanded of a scarce resource can exceed the quantity supplied only if something prevents the market mechanism from operating freely.

9. As a resource grows scarce on a free market, its price will rise, inducing increased conservation by consumers, increased exploration for new reserves, and increased substitution of other items that can serve the same purpose.

10. In fact, in the 20th century the relative prices of many resources have remained roughly constant, largely because of the discovery of new reserves and cost-saving innovations.

11. In the 1970s, OPEC succeeded in raising petroleum's relative price, but the price increase led to a substantial decline in world demand as well as to an increase in production in countries outside OPEC.

12. *Known reserves* of depletable scarce resources have not tended to fall with time because as the price of the resource rises with increasing scarcity, increased exploration for new reserves becomes profitable.

---

## K E Y   T E R M S

Externality   453

Direct controls   462

Pollution charges (taxes on emissions)   462

Emissions permits   464

Known reserves   467

Organization of Petroleum Exporting Countries (OPEC)   473

Paradox of growing reserves of finite resources   474

1. What sorts of pollution problems would you expect in a small African village? In a city in India? In communist China? In New York City?

2. Suppose you are assigned the task of drafting a law to impose a tax on smoke emission. What provisions would you put into the law?

   a. How would you decide the size of the tax?

   b. What would you do about smoke emitted by a municipal electricity plant?

   c. Would you use the same tax rate in densely and sparsely settled areas?

   What information will you need to collect before determining what you would do about each of the preceding provisions?

3. Production of Commodity X creates 10 pounds of emissions for every unit of X produced. The demand and supply curves for X are described by the following table:

| Price | Quantity Demanded | Quantity Supplied |
|---|---|---|
| $10 | 80 | 100 |
| 9 | 85 | 95 |
| 8 | 90 | 90 |
| 7 | 95 | 85 |
| 6 | 100 | 80 |
| 5 | 105 | 75 |

   What is the equilibrium price and quantity, and how much pollution will be emitted?

4. If the price of X to consumers is $9, and the government imposes a tax of $2 per unit, show that because suppliers get only $7, they will produce only 85 units of output, not the 95 units of output they would produce if they received the full $9 per unit.

5. With this tax, how much pollution will be emitted?

6. Compare your answers to Review Questions 3 and 5 and show how large a reduction in pollution emissions occurs because of the $2 tax on the polluting output.

7. Discuss some valid and some invalid objections to letting rising prices eliminate shortages of supplies of scarce resources.

8. Why may a rise in fuel prices lead to more conservation after several years have passed than it does in the months following the price increase? What does your answer imply about the relative size of the long-run elasticity of demand for fuel and its short-run elasticity?

# VI

---

## THE MACRO-ECONOMY: AGGREGATE SUPPLY AND DEMAND

Macroeconomics is the headline-grabbing part of economics.

When economic news appears on the front page of your daily newspaper or is reported on the nightly television news, you are most likely reading or hearing about some macroeconomic development in the national or world economy. The Federal Reserve has just lowered interest rates. Inflation remains low. Jobs are plentiful in the United States, but scarce in Japan. The federal government's budget is in surplus. The Indonesian rupiah, or the Russian ruble, or the Brazilian real are falling in value. These are all macroeconomic news stories. But what do they mean?

477

Part VI is your introduction to macroeconomics. It will first acquaint you with some of the major concepts of macroeconomics—things that you hear about every day, such as gross domestic product (GDP), inflation, unemployment, and economic growth (Chapters 23 and 24). Then it will introduce you to the basic theory that we use to interpret and understand macroeconomic events (Chapters 25 through 28). By the time you finish Chapter 28—which is only six chapters away—those newspaper articles should make a lot more sense.

# CHAPTER

## 23

Where the telescope ends, the microscope begins.
Which of the two has the grander view?

Victor Hugo

# THE REALM OF
# MACROECONOMICS

B y time-honored tradition, economics is divided into

two fields: *microeconomics* and *macroeconomics*. These

inelegant words are derived from the Greek, where *micro*

means something small and *macro* means something

large. Chapters 4 and 5 introduced you to microeconom-

ics. This chapter does the same for macroeconomics.

How do the two branches of the discipline differ?

It is not a matter of using different tools. Supply and

demand provide the basic organizing framework for con-

structing macroeconomic models, just as they do for

microeconomic models. Rather, the distinction is based

on the issues addressed. Here is an example of a macro-

economic question.

## How did we grow so fast?

From 1996 to 1998, the U.S. economy confounded financial and economic experts by growing at an annual rate of 3.9 percent. That performance was not only faster than in the preceding two years (about 2.9 percent), it was also markedly superior to the average growth record of the previous 20 to 25 years—about 2.5 percent per annum. What happened?

Some observers believe that the nature of our economy—including its ability to grow—has changed fundamentally. They claim that we now live in a "New Economy" that no longer follows the old rules. Most economists, however, think they saw something more conventional at work in 1996–1998. The fabulous growth performance was surprising, but not inexplicable. Although we will be learning much more about the determinants of economic growth in coming chapters, this chapter offers the conventional explanation.

## DRAWING A LINE BETWEEN MACROECONOMICS AND MICROECONOMICS

In microeconomics, the spotlight is on *how individual decision-making units behave*. For example, the dairy farmers of Chapter 5 are individual decision makers; so are the consumers who purchase milk. How do they decide what actions are in their own best interests? How are these millions of decisions coordinated by the market mechanism, and with what consequences? Questions like these lie at the heart of microeconomics.

Although Plato and Aristotle might wince at the abuse of their language, microeconomics applies to the decisions of some astonishingly large units. AT&T and IBM, for instance, have annual sales that exceed the total production of many nations. Yet someone who studies the pricing policies of AT&T is a microeconomist, whereas someone who studies inflation in Monaco is a macroeconomist. The micro-versus-macro distinction in economics is certainly not based solely on size. What, then, is the basis for this long-standing distinction? The answer is that, whereas microeconomics focuses on the decisions of individual units, no matter how large, macroeconomics concentrates on *the behavior of entire economies*, no matter how small. Whereas microeconomists might look at a single company's pricing and output decisions, macroeconomists study the overall price level, unemployment rate, and other things that we call *economic aggregates*.

### AGGREGATION AND MACROECONOMICS

An "economic aggregate" is nothing but an *abstraction* that people use to describe some salient feature of economic life. For example, although we observe the prices of gasoline, telephone calls, and movie tickets every day, we never actually see "the price level." Yet many people—not just economists—find it meaningful to speak of "the cost of living." In fact, the government's attempts to measure it are widely publicized by the news media each month.

Among the most important of these abstract notions is the concept of *domestic product*, which represents the total production of a nation's economy. The process by which real objects like hairpins, baseballs, and theater tickets get combined into an abstraction called total domestic product is **aggregation,** and it is one of the foundations of macroeconomics. We can illustrate it by a simple example.

Imagine a nation called Agraria, whose economy is far simpler than the U.S. economy: Business firms in Agraria produce nothing but foodstuffs to sell to consumers. Rather than deal separately with all the markets for pizzas, candy bars, hamburgers, and so on, macroeconomists group them all into a single abstract "market for output." Thus, when macroeconomists announce that output in Agraria grew 10 percent last year, are they referring to more potatoes or hot dogs, more soybeans or green peppers? The answer is: They do not care. In the aggregate measures of macroeconomics, output is output, no matter what form it takes.

**Aggregation** means combining many individual markets into one overall market.

## THE FOUNDATIONS OF AGGREGATION

Amalgamating many markets into one means ignoring distinctions among different products. Can we really believe that no one cares whether the national output of Agraria consists of $800,000 worth of pickles and $200,000 worth of ravioli rather than $500,000 each of lettuce and tomatoes? Surely this is too much to swallow! Macroeconomists certainly do not believe that no one cares; instead, they rest the case for aggregation on two foundations:

> 1. While the *composition* of demand and supply in the various markets may be terribly interesting and important for *some* purposes (such as how income is distributed and what kinds of diets people enjoy or endure), it may be of little consequence for the economy-wide issues of growth, inflation, and unemployment—the issues that concern macroeconomists.

> 2. During economic fluctuations, markets tend to move up or down together. When demand in the economy rises, there is more demand for potatoes *and* tomatoes, more demand for artichokes *and* pickles, more demand for ravioli *and* hot dogs.

Although there are exceptions to these two principles, both seem serviceable enough as approximations. In fact, if they were not, there would be no discipline called macroeconomics, and a full-year course in economics could be reduced to a half-year. Lest this cause you a twinge of regret, bear in mind that many people feel that unemployment and inflation would be far more difficult to control without macroeconomics—which would be even more regrettable.

## THE LINE OF DEMARCATION REVISITED

These two principles—that the composition of demand and supply may not matter for some purposes and that markets normally move together—enable us to draw a different kind of dividing line between microeconomics and macroeconomics.

> In macroeconomics, we typically assume that most details of resource allocation and income distribution are relatively unimportant to the study of the overall rates of inflation and unemployment. In microeconomics, we typically ignore inflation and unemployment and focus instead on how individual markets allocate resources and distribute income.

To use a well-worn metaphor, a macroeconomist analyzes the size of the economic "pie," paying scant attention to what is inside it or to how it gets divided among the dinner guests. A microeconomist, on the other hand, assumes that the pie is of the right size and shape, and frets over its ingredients and its division. If you have ever baked or eaten a pie, you will realize that either approach alone is a trifle myopic.

Economics is divided into macroeconomics and microeconomics largely for the sake of pedagogical clarity. In reality, the crucial interconnection between macroeconomics and microeconomics is with us all the time. There is, after all, only one economy.

### SUPPLY AND DEMAND REINTERPRETED THROUGH A MACROECONOMIC LENS

Whether you are taking a course that concentrates on macroeconomics or one that focuses on microeconomics, the discussion of supply and demand in Chapter 5 serves as an invaluable introduction. Supply and demand analysis is just as fundamental to macroeconomics as it is to microeconomics.

| FIGURE 23–1 | **Two Interpretations of a Shift in the Demand Curve** |

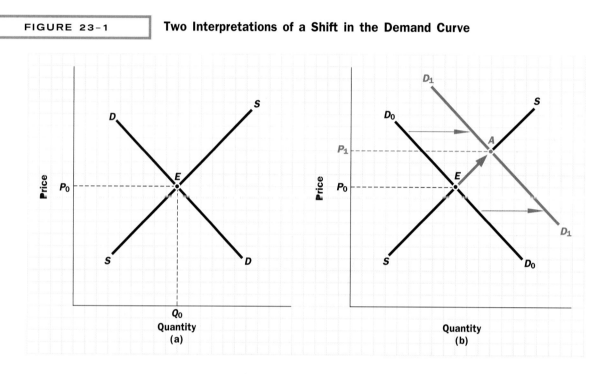

### A QUICK REVIEW

The **aggregate demand curve** shows the quantity of domestic product that is demanded at each possible value of the price level.

The **aggregate supply curve** shows the quantity of domestic product that is supplied at each possible value of the price level.

**Inflation** refers to a sustained increase in the general price level.

A **recession** is a period of time during which the total output of the economy declines.

**Gross domestic product (GDP)** is the sum of the money values of all final goods and services produced in the domestic economy and sold on organized markets during a specified period of time, usually a year.

Figure 23–1 shows two diagrams that should look familiar from Chapter 5. In Figure 23–1(a), we find a downward-sloping demand curve, labeled *DD*, and an upward-sloping supply curve, labeled *SS*. The axes labeled "Price" and "Quantity" do not specify any particular commodity because this is a multipurpose diagram. To start on familiar terrain, first imagine that this is a picture of the market for milk, so the price axis measures the price of milk whereas the quantity axis measures the quantity of milk demanded and supplied. As we know, if nothing interferes with the operation of a free market, equilibrium will be at point $E$ with a price $P_0$ and a quantity of output $Q_0$.

Next, suppose something happens to shift the demand curve outward. For example, we learned in Chapter 5 that an increase in consumer incomes might have this effect. Figure 23–1(b) shows this shift as a rightward movement of the demand curve from $D_0D_0$ to $D_1D_1$. Equilibrium shifts from E to A, so both price and output rise.

### MOVING TO MACROECONOMIC AGGREGATES

Now let's switch from microeconomics to macroeconomics. To do so, reinterpret Figure 23–1 as representing the abstract market for "domestic product." This is one of those abstractions—an economic aggregate—that we described earlier. No one has ever seen, touched, or eaten a unit of domestic product, but these kinds of abstractions provide a foundation for macroeconomic analysis.

Consistent with this reinterpretation, think of the price measured on the vertical axis as being another abstraction—the overall price index, or "cost of living."[1] Then

---

[1] The appendix to Chapter 24 explains how such price indexes are calculated.

the curve *DD* in Figure 23–1(a) is called an **aggregate demand curve,** and the curve *SS* is called an **aggregate supply curve.** We will develop an economic theory to derive these curves explicitly in Chapters 25 through 28. As we shall see there, the curves are rather different from the microeconomic counterparts we encountered in Chapter 5.

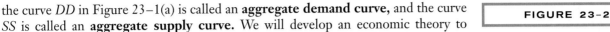

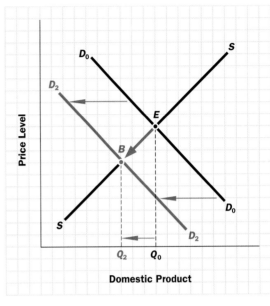

FIGURE 23-2

An Economy Slipping into a Recession

## INFLATION

With this macroeconomic reinterpretation, Figure 23–1(b) depicts the problem of **inflation.** We see from the figure that the outward shift of the aggregate demand curve, whatever its cause, pushes the price level up. If aggregate demand keeps shifting out month after month, the economy will suffer from inflation, that is, a sustained increase in the general price level.

## RECESSION AND UNEMPLOYMENT

The second principal issue of macroeconomics, recession and unemployment, also can be illustrated on a supply-demand diagram, this time by shifting the demand curve in the opposite direction. Figure 23–2 repeats the supply and demand curves of Figure 23–1(a) and in addition depicts a leftward shift of the aggregate demand curve from $D_0D_0$ to $D_2D_2$. Equilibrium now moves from point E to point *B* so that domestic product (total output) declines. This is what we normally mean by a **recession**—a period of time during which production falls and people lose jobs.

FIGURE 23-3

Economic Growth

## ECONOMIC GROWTH

Finally, turn to Figure 23–3, which illustrates macroeconomists' third area of concern: the process of economic growth. Here the original aggregate demand and supply curves are—once again—$D_0D_0$ and $S_0S_0$, which intersect at point E. But now we consider the possibility that both curves shift to the right over time, moving to $D_1D_1$ and $S_1S_1$ respectively. The new intersection point is C, and the red arrow running from point E to point C shows the economy's growth path. Over this period of time, domestic product grows from $Q_0$ to $Q_1$.

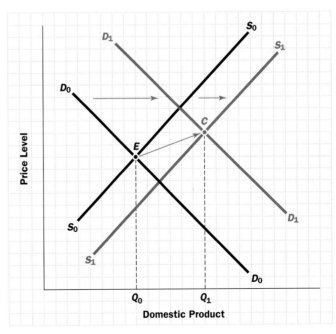

## ■ GROSS DOMESTIC PRODUCT

Up to now, we have been somewhat cavalier in using the phrase "domestic product." Let's now get more specific. Of the various ways to measure an economy's total output, the most popular choice by far is the **gross domestic product,** a term you have probably encountered in the news media. The gross domestic product, or GDP for short, is the most comprehensive measure of the output of all the factories, offices, and shops in the United States. Specifically, it is the sum of the *money values* of all *final* goods and services *produced* in the *domestic* economy within the year.

Several features of this definition need to be underscored.[2] First, you will notice that:

> We add up the *money values* of things.

## MONEY AS THE MEASURING ROD: REAL VERSUS NOMINAL GDP

The GDP consists of a bewildering variety of goods and services: computer chips and potato chips, tanks and textbooks, ballet performances and rock concerts. How can we combine all of these into a single number? To an economist, the natural way to do this begins by converting every good and service into *money* terms. If we want to add 10 apples and 20 oranges, we first ask: How much *money* does each cost? If apples cost 20 cents and oranges cost 25 cents, then the apples count for $2 and the oranges for $5, so the sum is $7 worth of "output." The market *price* of each good or service is used as an indicator of its *value* to society for a simple reason: *Someone is willing to pay that much money for it.*

**Nominal GDP** is calculated by valuing all outputs at current prices.

This decision raises the question of what prices to use in valuing different outputs. The official data offer two choices. First, we can value each good and service at the price at which it was actually sold during the year. If we do this, the resulting measure is called **nominal GDP,** or *money GDP,* or *GDP in current dollars.* This seems like a perfectly sensible choice. But as a measure of output, it has one serious drawback: Nominal GDP rises when prices rise, even if there is no increase in actual production. For example, if hamburgers cost $2.00 this year but cost only $1.50 last year, then 100 hamburgers will contribute $200 to this year's nominal GDP though they contributed only $150 to last year's. But 100 hamburgers are still 100 hamburgers—output has not grown.

**Real GDP** is calculated by valuing outputs of different years at common prices. Therefore, real GDP is a far better measure than nominal GDP of changes in total production.

For this reason, government statisticians have devised alternative measures that correct for inflation by valuing goods and services produced in *different* years at *the same* set of prices. For example, if the hamburgers were valued at $1.50 each in both years, $150 worth of hamburger output would be included in GDP *in each year.* In practice, such calculations are done in several ways, and the details are quite complicated. But such details need not detain us in an introductory course. Suffice it to say that, when the calculations are done, we obtain **real GDP** or *GDP in constant dollars.* The news media often refer to it as "GDP corrected for inflation." Throughout most of this book, and certainly whenever we are discussing the nation's output, we will be concerned with *real* GDP.

The distinction between nominal and real GDP leads us to a working definition of a *recession* as a period in which *real* GDP declines. For example, between 1990 and 1991 (our last recession year), nominal GDP rose from $5,744 billion to $5,917 billion, but real GDP *fell* from $6,136 billion to $6,079 billion.

## WHAT GETS COUNTED IN GDP?

The next important aspect of the definition of GDP is that:

> The GDP for a particular year includes only goods and services produced within the year. Sales of items produced in previous years are explicitly excluded.

For example, suppose you buy a perfectly beautiful 1965 Thunderbird next week and are overjoyed by your purchase. The national income statistician will not share your glee because she had counted your car in the GDP in 1965, when it was first produced and sold. The car will never be counted again. The same is true of houses. The resale values of houses do not count in GDP because they were already counted in the years they were built.

---

[2] Certain exceptions to the definition are dealt with in the appendix to Chapter 25. Some instructors may prefer to take up that material here.

Third, you will note from the definition of gross domestic product that:

Only **final goods and services** count in the GDP.

The adjective *final* is the key word here. For example, when a supermarket buys milk from a farmer, the transaction is not included in the GDP because the supermarket does not want the milk for itself. It buys milk only to resell it to consumers. Only when the milk is sold to consumers is it considered a final product. When the supermarket buys it, economists consider it an **intermediate good.** The GDP excludes sales of intermediate goods and services because, if they were included, we would wind up counting the same outputs several times.[3] For example, if milk sold to grocers were included in GDP, we would count the same container of milk when it was sold to the store and then again when it was sold to a consumer.

**Final goods and services** are those that are purchased by their ultimate users.

An **intermediate good** is a good purchased for resale or for use in producing another good.

Fourth:

The adjective *domestic* in the definition denotes production within the geographic boundaries of the United States.

Some Americans work abroad, and many American companies have offices or factories in foreign countries. All of these people and businesses produce valuable outputs, but none of this is counted in the GDP of the United States. (It is counted, instead, in the GDPs of the other countries.) On the other hand, quite a number of foreigners and foreign companies produce goods and services in the United States. All of this activity does count in our GDP.[4]

Finally, the definition notes that:

For the most part, only goods and services that pass through organized markets count in the GDP.

This restriction, of course, excludes many economic activities. For example, illegal activities are not included in the GDP. Thus, gambling services in Atlantic City are part of GDP, but gambling services in Chicago are not. Garage sales, though sometimes lucrative, are not included either. The definition reflects the statisticians' confession that they cannot possibly measure the value of many of the economy's most important activities, such as housework, do-it-yourself repairs, and leisure time. Although these are certainly economic activities that result in currently produced goods or services, they all lack that important measuring rod—a market price.

This omission results in certain oddities. For example, suppose that each of two neighboring families hires the other to clean house, generously paying $1,000 a week for the services. Each family can easily afford such generosity because it collects an identical salary from its neighbor. Nothing real has changed, but GDP goes up by $104,000 a year. If this example seems trivial, you may be interested to know that, according to one estimate, America's GDP would be a stunning 44 percent higher if unpaid housework were valued at market prices.[5]

## LIMITATIONS OF THE GDP: WHAT GDP IS NOT

Having seen in some detail what the GDP *is*, let's examine what it *is not*. In particular:

Gross domestic product is not a measure of the nation's economic well-being.

The GDP is not intended to measure economic well-being and does not do so for several reasons:

---

[3] Actually, there is another way to add up the GDP by counting a portion of each intermediate transaction. This is explained in the appendix to Chapter 25.

[4] There is another concept, called gross *national* product, which counts the goods and services produced by all Americans, regardless of where they work. For consistency, the outputs produced by foreigners working in the United States are not included in GNP. In practice, the two measures—GDP and GNP—are very close.

[5] Ann Chadeau, "What Is Households' Non-market Production Worth?" *OECD Economic Studies*, No. 18.

**ONLY MARKET ACTIVITY IS INCLUDED IN GDP**    As we have just seen, a great deal of work done in the home contributes to the nation's well-being but is not measured in the GDP because it has no price tag. One important implication of this exclusion arises when we try to compare the GDPs of developed and less developed countries. Americans are always surprised to learn that the per-capita GDPs of the poorest African countries are less than $250 a year. Surely, no one could survive in America on $5 a week. How can Africans do it? Part of the answer, of course, is that these people are terribly poor. But another part of the answer is that:

> International GDP comparisons are vastly misleading when the two countries differ greatly in the fraction of economic activity that each conducts in organized markets.

This fraction is relatively large in the United States and relatively small in the less developed countries, so when we compare their respective measured GDPs, we are not comparing the same economic activities at all. Many things that get counted in the U.S. GDP are not counted in the GDPs of less developed nations because they do not pass through markets. It is ludicrous to think that these people, poor as they are, survive on what to Americans would amount to $5 a week.

A second implication is that GDP statistics take no account of the so-called underground economy—a term that includes not just criminal activities, but also a great deal of legitimate business activity that is conducted in cash or by barter to escape the tax collector. Naturally, we have no good data on the size of the underground economy, but some observers think that it may amount to 10 percent or more of U.S. GDP. In some foreign countries, it is surely a much bigger share than this.

**GDP PLACES NO VALUE ON LEISURE**    As a country gets richer, its citizens normally take more and more leisure time. If that is true, a better measure of national well-being that includes the value of leisure time would display faster growth than conventionally measured GDP. For example, the length of the typical workweek in the United States fell steadily for many decades, which means that growth in GDP systematically *underestimated* the growth in national well-being. But some scholars claim that this trend has stopped, and may even have reversed. (See the accompanying box, "Are Americans Working More?")

**"BADS" AS WELL AS "GOODS" GET COUNTED IN GDP**    However, there are also reasons why the GDP *overstates* how well-off we are. Suppose there is a natural disaster—such as the devastating wildfires that ravaged central Florida in the summer of 1998. Surely the well-being of the United States was diminished by this catastrophe. People were injured; many homes, businesses, and much woodland were destroyed. Yet the disaster probably raised U.S. GDP. Consumers spent more to clean up and replace lost homes and possessions. Businesses spent more to rebuild and repair damaged buildings. The government spent more for disaster relief and cleanup. Yet no one would think America was better off for this additional GDP.

Wars represent an extreme example. Mobilization for a war fought on some other nation's soil always causes a country's GDP to rise rapidly. But men and women serving in the military could be producing civilian output instead. Factories assigned to produce armaments could instead be making cars, washing machines, and televisions. A country at war is surely worse off than a country at peace, but this fact will not be reflected in its GDP.

**ECOLOGICAL COSTS ARE NOT NETTED OUT OF THE GDP**    Many of the activities in a modern industrial economy that produce goods and services also have undesirable side effects on the environment. Automobiles provide enjoyment and a means of transportation, but they also despoil the atmosphere. Factories pollute rivers and lakes while manufacturing valuable commodities. Almost everything seems to produce garbage, which creates serious disposal problems. None of these ecological costs are deducted from the GDP in an effort to give us a truer measure of the *net* increase in economic welfare that our economy produces. Is this foolishness? Not if

According to conventional wisdom, the workweek in the United States is steadily shrinking, leaving Americans with more and more leisure time to enjoy. But, in a 1991 book, economist Juliet Schor argued that this view is wrong: Americans are really working longer and longer hours. Her findings are both provocative and controversial.

In the last twenty years the amount of time Americans have spent at their jobs has risen steadily. . . . Americans report that they have only sixteen and a half hours of leisure a week, after the obligations of job and household are taken care of. . . . If present trends continue, by the end of the century Americans will be spending as much time at their jobs as they did back in the nineteen twenties.

The rise in worktime was unexpected. For nearly a hundred years, hours had been declining. . . . Equally surprising, but also hardly recognized, has been the deviation from Western Europe. After progressing in tandem for nearly a century, the United States veered off into a trajectory of declining leisure, while in Europe work has been disappearing. . . . U.S. manufacturing employees currently work 320 more hours [per year]—the equivalent of over two months—than their counterparts in West Germany or France. . . . We have paid a price for prosperity. . . . We

are eating more, but we are burning up those calories at work. We have color televisions and compact disc players, but we need them to unwind after a stressful day at the office. We take vacations, but we work so hard throughout the year that they become indispensable to our sanity.

SOURCE: Juliet B. Schor, *The Overworked American* (New York: Basic Books, 1991), pp. 1–2, 10–11.

we remember the job that national income statisticians are trying to do: They are measuring the economic activity conducted through organized markets, not national welfare. (But see the accompanying box, " 'Green' GDP.")

## ■ THE ECONOMY ON A ROLLER COASTER

Having defined several of the basic concepts of macroeconomics, let us breathe some life into them by perusing the economic history of the United States.

### GROWTH, BUT WITH FLUCTUATIONS

As we observed in Chapter 2, the most prominent feature is *growth*—the economy gets bigger year after year. Figure 23–4 charts the growth rate of U.S. real GDP since 1870. It is almost always positive. In fact, the average annual growth rate over this period was about 3.3 percent. This growth of GDP, which is substantially faster than population growth, is the fundamental source of the ever-higher living standards that have been such a conspicuous feature of American history.

If aggregate supply and demand grow smoothly from one year to the next, as was depicted in Figure 23–3, the economy will expand at some normal rate. But not every year is normal! Figure 23–4 shows that there have been occasional setbacks—periods of falling real GDP—along the way. Such *recessions*, and their attendant problem of unemployment, have been a persistent feature of American economic performance. Especially before the Korean War, the graph gives the impression of

● **"GREEN" GDP**

GDP as conventionally measured does not net out the costs of pollution or the depletion of renewable resources like forests, nor does it "charge" for using up non-renewable mineral resources. The consequence, some critics argue, is that GDP *overstates* economic well-being. A few years ago, the U.S. government embarked on a project to develop experimental measures that would adjust for each of these factors—so-called green GDP. Unfortunately, this effort proved to be politically controversial. Although environmentalists supported it, the Republican Congress elected in 1994 to cut off funding.

Politics aside, the first phase of the research turned up a surprising result: Making an adjustment for the depletion of mineral resources hardly changed the official GDP numbers. Specifically, when government statisticians tabulated the U.S. ctook of mineral resources to estimate how much had been consumed from 1958 to 1991, they found that proven supplies had barely declined.

How can this be? In a purely physical sense, of course, it cannot be. America certainly had fewer actual mineral deposits in the ground in 1991 than in 1958. However, new discoveries of minerals and new technologies compensated for all the mining, so that *proven* reserves barely fell over the 33-year period.

| FIGURE 23-4 | **The Growth Rate of U.S. Real Gross Domestic Product, 1870–1998** |

Does the growth rate look smoother to the right of the shaded area?

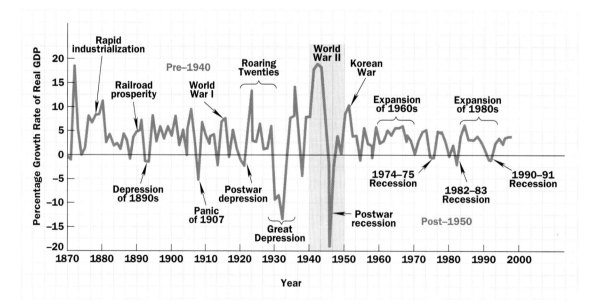

SOURCE: Constructed by the authors from Commerce Department data for 1929–1998. Data for 1869–1928 are based on research by Professor Christina Romer.

an economy on a roller coaster. The ups and downs that are apparent in Figure 23–4 are called *economic fluctuations*, or sometimes *business cycles*.

## INFLATION AND DEFLATION

The history of the inflation rate displayed in Figure 23–5 also shows more positive numbers than negative ones—more inflation than **deflation**. Although the price level has risen about 14-fold since 1869, the upward trend is of rather recent vintage. Prior to World War II, Figure 23–5 shows periods of inflation and deflation, with little or no tendency for one to be more common than the other. Indeed, prices in 1940 were barely higher than those at the close of the Civil War. However, the figure does show some large gyrations in the inflation rate, including sharp bursts of inflation during and right after the two world wars and dramatic deflations in the 1870s, the 1880s, 1921 to 1922, and 1929 to 1933.

**Deflation** refers to a sustained decrease in the general price level.

In sum, although both real GDP, which measures the economy's output, and the price level have grown a great deal over the past 130 years, neither has grown smoothly. The ups and downs of both real growth and inflation have been important economic events that need to be explained. Part VI, which develops a model of aggregate supply and demand, and Part VII, which addresses monetary and fiscal policy, will build a macroeconomic theory designed to do precisely that.

## THE GREAT DEPRESSION

As you look at these graphs, the Great Depression of the 1930s is bound to catch your eye. The decline in economic activity from 1929 to 1933 indicated in Figure 23–4 was the most severe in our nation's history, and the rapid deflation in Figure 23–5 was most unusual. The Depression is but a dim memory now, but those who lived through it—including some of your grandparents—will never forget it.

**HUMAN CONSEQUENCES** Statistics usually conceal the human consequences and drama of economic events. But this is not so of the Great Depression—instead they

**The Inflation Rate in the United States, 1870–1998**

**FIGURE 23-5**

SOURCE: Constructed by the authors from Commerce Department data for 1929–1998. Data for 1869–1928 were kindly provided by Professor Christina Romer.

---

● **LIFE IN "HOOVERVILLE"**

---

During the worst years of the Great Depression, unemployed workers often congregated in shantytowns on the outskirts of many major cities. Conditions in these slums were deplorable. With a heavy dose of irony, these communities were known as "Hoovervilles," in honor of the president of the United States who preached rugged individualism. A contemporary observer described a Hooverville in New York City as follows:

It was a fairly popular "development" made up of a hundred or so dwellings, each the size of a dog house or chickencoop, often constructed with much ingenuity out of wooden boxes, metal cans, strips of cardboard or old tar paper. Here human beings lived on the margin of civilization by foraging for garbage, junk, and waste lumber. I found some splitting or sawing wood with dull tools to make fires; others were picking through heaps of rubbish they had gathered before their doorways or cooking over open fires or battered oilstoves. Still others spent their days improving their rent-free homes, making them sometimes fairly solid and weatherproof. . . . Most of them, according to the police, lived by begging or trading in junk; when all else failed they ate at the soup kitchens or public canteens. They were of all sorts, young and old, some of them rough-

looking and suspicious of strangers. They lived in fear of being forcibly removed by the authorities, though the neighborhood people in many cases helped them and the police tolerated them for the time being.

SOURCE: Mathew Josephson, *Infidel in the Temple* (New York: Knopf, 1967), pp. 82–83.

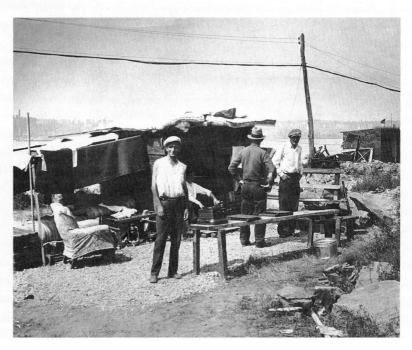

---

stand as bitter testimony to its severity. The production of goods and services dropped an astonishing 30 percent, business investment almost dried up entirely, and the unemployment rate rose ominously from about 3 percent in 1929 to 25 percent in 1933—one person in four was jobless! From the data alone, you can conjure up pictures of soup lines, beggars on street corners, closed factories, and homeless families. (See the accompanying box, "Life in 'Hooverville'.")

The Great Depression was a worldwide event; no country was spared its ravages. It literally changed the histories of many nations. In Germany, it facilitated the ascendancy of Nazism. In the United States, it enabled Franklin Roosevelt's Democratic party to engineer one of the most dramatic political realignments in our history and to push through a host of political and economic reforms.

**A REVOLUTION IN ECONOMIC THOUGHT**   The worldwide depression also caused a much-needed revolution in economic thinking. Until the 1930s, the prevailing economic theory held that a capitalist economy occasionally misbehaved but had a natural tendency to cure recessions or inflations by itself. The roller coaster bounced around but did not normally run off the tracks. This optimistic view was not confined to academia. Most political and business leaders shared it. As the great American humorist Will Rogers remarked with characteristic sarcasm:

It's almost been worth this depression to find out how little our big men knew. Mayby [sic] this depression is just "normalcy" and we don't know it. It's made a dumb guy as smart as a smart one. . . . Depression used to be a state of mind, now it's a state of coma, now it's permanent. Last year we said, "Things can't go on like this," and they didn't, they got worse.[6]

The stubbornness of the Great Depression shook almost everyone's faith in the ability of the economy to correct itself. In Cambridge, England, this questioning attitude led John Maynard Keynes, one of the world's most reknowned economists, to write *The General Theory of Employment, Interest, and Money* (1936). Probably the most important economics book of the 20th century, it carried a rather revolutionary message. Keynes rejected the idea that the economy naturally gravitated toward smooth growth and high levels of employment, asserting instead that if a pessimistic outlook led business firms and consumers to curtail their spending plans, the economy might be condemned to years of stagnation.

John Maynard Keynes

Thought of in terms of our aggregate demand—aggregate supply framework, Keynes suggested that there were times when the aggregate demand curve shifted inward by large amounts—as depicted in Figure 23–2. As that figure showed, the consequence would be declining output and deflation.

Although this doleful prognosis sounded all too realistic at the time, Keynes closed his book on a hopeful note. For he showed how government actions might prod the economy out of its depressed state. The lessons he taught the world then are among the lessons we will be learning in Parts VI and VII (along with many qualifications that economists have learned since). These lessons show how governments can manage their economies so that recessions will not turn into depressions and depressions will not last as long as the Great Depression.

While Keynes was working on *The General Theory*, he wrote his friend George Bernard Shaw that "I believe myself to be writing a book on economic theory which will largely revolutionize . . . the way the world thinks about economic problems." In many ways he was right, though parts of the Keynesian message remain controversial to this day.

## FROM WORLD WAR II TO 1973

The Great Depression finally ended when the United States mobilized for war in the early 1940s. As government spending rose to extraordinarily high levels, it gave aggregate demand a big boost. The economy boomed, and the unemployment rate fell as low as 1.2 percent during the war.

As Figure 23–1(b) suggested, wartime spending of this magnitude usually leads to inflation. But much of the potential inflation during World War II was contained by price controls. With prices held below the levels at which quantity supplied equaled quantity demanded, shortages of consumer goods were common. Sugar, butter, gasoline, cloth, and a host of other goods were strictly rationed. These shortages ended with a burst of inflation when controls were lifted after the war.

The period from the end of the war until the early 1960s was one of strong growth marred by several short recessions. Moderate but persistent inflation also became a fact of life. When the economy emerged from recession in 1961, it entered a period of unprecedented—and noninflationary—growth that was widely credited to the success of what came to be called "The New Economics," a term the media created for the economic policies that Keynes had prescribed in the 1930s. For a while, it looked as if we could avoid both unemployment and inflation, as aggregate demand and aggregate supply expanded in approximate balance. (Refer back to Figure 23–3.) But the optimistic verdicts were premature on both counts.

Inflation came first, beginning about 1966. Its major cause was high levels of wartime spending, as it had been so many times in the past. This time the Vietnam war pushed aggregate demand up too fast. Unemployment followed when the

---

[6] From *Sanity Is Where You Find It* by Will Rogers, edited by Donald Day; copyright 1955 by Rogers Company; reprinted by permission of Houghton Mifflin Company; pages 120–121.

economy ground to a halt in 1969. Despite a short and mild recession, inflation continued at 5 to 6 percent a year. Faced with persistent inflation, President Richard Nixon stunned the nation by instituting wage and price controls in 1971, the first time this had ever been done in peacetime. The controls program held inflation in check for a while. But inflation worsened dramatically in 1973, mainly because of an explosion in food prices caused by poor harvests around the world.

### THE GREAT STAGFLATION, 1973–1980

Then things began to get much worse, not only for the United States, but for all oil-importing nations. A 1973 war between Israel and the Arab nations precipitated a quadrupling of oil prices by the Organization of Petroleum Exporting Countries (OPEC). At the same time, continued poor harvests in many parts of the globe pushed world food prices higher. Prices of other raw materials also skyrocketed. Naturally, higher costs of fuel and other materials soon were reflected in the prices of manufactured goods.

By unhappy coincidence, these events came just as the Nixon administration was lifting wage and price controls. Just as had happened after World War II, the elimination of controls led to a temporary acceleration of inflation as prices that had been held artificially below equilibrium levels were allowed to rise. For all of these reasons, the inflation rate in the United States soared to above 12 percent during 1974.

**FIGURE 23-6**

**The Effects of an Adverse Supply Shift**

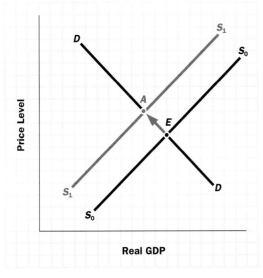

Meanwhile, the U.S. economy was slipping into what was, up to then, its longest and most severe recession since the 1930s. Real GDP fell between late 1973 and early 1975, and the unemployment rate rose to nearly 9 percent. With both inflation and unemployment unusually virulent in 1974 and 1975, the press coined a new term—**stagflation**—to refer to the simultaneous occurrence of economic *stag*nation and rapid in*flation*. Conceptually, what was happening in this episode is that the economy's aggregate supply curve, which normally moves outward from one year to the next, shifted *inward* instead. When this happens, the economy moves from a point like *E* to a point like *A* in Figure 23–6. Real GDP declines as the price level rises.

Thanks partly to government actions, but mostly to natural economic forces, a sustained recovery from recession began in 1975. Inflation tumbled rapidly as the adjustment to the end of price controls ended and food and energy prices stopped soaring. The severity of the recession also put a brake on inflation, just as it had in the past. In total, the inflation rate tumbled from over 12 percent back down to the 6 percent range.

But the price of oil soared again in 1979 following a revolution in Iran, bringing stagflation back. This time, inflation hit the astonishing rate of 16 percent during the first half of 1980 and the Carter administration clamped on credit controls. The controls broke the U.S. economy's back, and output fell at an extraordinarily rapid pace. But credit controls remained in effect for only a few months, and by late 1980 recovery was under way.

### REAGANOMICS AND ITS AFTERMATH

When President Ronald Reagan assumed office in January 1981, the U.S. economy was showing signs of reviving, but the inflation rate seemed stuck near 10 percent. The new president promised to change things with a package of policies called "supply-side economics" that, he claimed, would boost growth and reduce inflation.[7]

At first, things did change dramatically—but not in the way President Reagan wanted. Although inflation fell remarkably to only about 4 percent in 1982, the economy slumped into its worst recession since the Great Depression. When the 1981–1982 recession hit bottom, the unemployment rate was approaching 11 percent,

**Stagflation** is inflation that occurs while the economy is growing slowly ("stagnating") or in a recession.

---

[7] Supply-side economics is discussed further in Chapter 29.

"More and more, I ask myself what's the point of pursuing the meaning of the universe if you can't have a rising GNP."

the financial markets were in disarray, and the word *depression* had reentered the American vocabulary. The U.S. government also had a huge budget deficit, bigger than anyone had dreamed possible only a few years before. This problem, as we shall see in subsequent chapters, remained with us for about 15 years.

However, the recovery that began in the winter of 1982–1983 proved to be one of the most vigorous and long-lasting in our history. Unemployment fell more or less steadily for about six years, eventually dropping below 5.5 percent. Meanwhile, inflation remained tame. All of this provided an ideal economic platform on which George Bush ran to succeed President Reagan—and to continue his policies.

Unfortunately for President Bush, the good times did not keep rolling. Shortly after he took office, inflation began to accelerate a bit, economic growth began to sputter, and Congress enacted a deficit-reduction package (including a tax increase) not entirely to the president's liking. Then, in 1990–1991, the U.S. economy slumped into another recession—precipitated, according to some observers, by yet another spike in oil prices before the Persian Gulf War.

By the time of the 1992 election, the U.S. economy had still not recovered from the 1990–1991 recession. In fact, the growth rate during the Bush presidency was the weakest of any four-year period since World War II. This fact was not lost on candidate Bill Clinton, who hammered away at the lackluster economic performance of the period from 1989 to 1992. Most observers believe that the weak economy was the main factor behind George Bush's electoral defeat.

## CLINTONOMICS: DEFICIT REDUCTION AND "THE BEST ECONOMY IN 30 YEARS"[8]

President Clinton ran on a detailed economic platform that concentrated on two objectives: spurring economic growth and increasing public investment. But even before his inauguration in January 1993, the yawning budget deficit forced him to de-emphasize new spending and concentrate on deficit reduction instead. A politically

---

[8] One of the authors of this book was a member of President Clinton's original Council of Economic Advisers.

contentious package of substantial tax increases and major spending cuts barely squeaked through Congress in August 1993 without a single Republican vote, and a second deficit-reduction package passed with bipartisan support in 1997. Indeed, turning the huge federal budget deficit into a surplus has been the crowning achievement of the Clinton economic policy.

Whether by cause or coincidence, the national economy improved dramatically during President Clinton's first term. Business perked up, unemployment fell rapidly, and inflation remained remarkably well contained. By the middle of 1996, macroeconomic conditions were the best in a generation: The economic expansion was more than 5 years old, unemployment was at about 5.5 percent, and inflation was still below 3 percent. It was a wonderful backdrop for an incumbent running for reelection.

Then things got even better! As we noted at the start of this chapter, economic growth actually accelerated from 1996 to 1998, surprising most forecasters. With such rapid growth, the unemployment rate fell to 4.3 percent, its lowest level since 1970. And, to top it all off, inflation dropped to below 2 percent. Why did all these wonderful things happen at once? As we mentioned earlier, many journalists and a few economists have concluded that the basic macroeconomic rule book has changed. A revolutionary combination of globalization and computerization, they declare, has created an exciting "New Economy" that naturally performs better than it did in the past.

This is an alluring vision. But is it true? Most mainstream economists think not. They offer instead a simpler and more mundane explanation: A variety of transitory factors pushed the economy's aggregate supply curve outward at an unusually rapid pace between 1996 and 1998. When this happens, the expected result is faster economic growth and lower inflation.

To see why, look at Figure 23–7—which takes the graphical analysis of economic growth from Figure 23–3 and adds a new aggregate supply curve, $S_2S_2$, which lies to the right of $S_1S_1$. With supply curve $S_2S_2$ instead of $S_1S_1$, the economy moves from point $E$ not just to point $C$, as in the earlier figure, but all the way to point $B$. Comparing $B$ to $C$, we see that the economy winds up both further to the right (that is, it grows faster) and lower (that is, it experiences less inflation).

That, in a nutshell, is how our simple aggregate demand-aggregate supply framework explains recent U.S. history. There is much more to say, and we will return to this episode in Chapter 34, where we will explain just what factors pushed the aggregate supply curve out.

**FIGURE 23-7**

**The Effects of a Favorable Supply Shift**

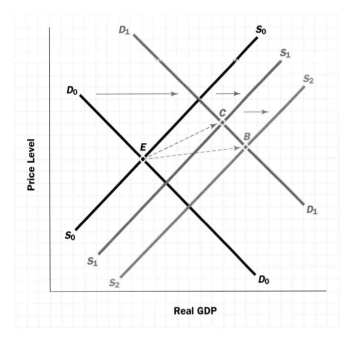

# THE PROBLEM OF MACROECONOMIC STABILIZATION: A SNEAK PREVIEW

This brief look at the historical record shows that our economy has not generally produced steady growth without inflation. Rather, it has been buffeted by periodic bouts of unemployment or inflation, and sometimes has been plagued by both. There was also a hint that government policies may have had something to do with this performance. Let us now expand briefly upon this hint—a subject that will be developed further in subsequent chapters.

**Stabilization policy** is the name given to government programs designed to prevent or shorten recessions and to counteract inflation (that is, to *stabilize* prices).

We can provide a preliminary analysis of **stabilization policy,** the name given to government programs designed to prevent or shorten recessions and to counteract inflation, by once again using the basic tools of aggregate supply and demand analysis. To facilitate this, we have reproduced as Figures 23–8 and 23–9 two diagrams found earlier in this chapter, but we now give them slightly different interpretations.

## COMBATING UNEMPLOYMENT

Figure 23–8 offers a simplified view of government policy to fight unemployment. Suppose that, in the absence of government intervention, the economy would reach an equilibrium at point $E$, where the aggregate demand curve $D_0D_0$ crosses the aggregate supply curve $SS$. Now if the output corresponding to point $E$ is so low that many workers are unemployed, *the government can reduce unemployment by increasing aggregate demand.* Chapter 29 will consider in detail how the government might do this. In the diagram, such an action would shift the demand curve to $D_1D_1$, causing equilibrium to move to point $A$. In general:

> Recessions and unemployment are often caused by insufficient aggregate demand. When this occurs, government policies that successfully augment demand—such as increases in government spending—can be an effective way to increase output and reduce unemployment. But they also normally increase prices.

A prime example of such a policy came when military spending soared during World War II, adding greatly to aggregate demand. This surge in spending, we noted earlier, brought the Great Depression to an end.

## COMBATING INFLATION

The opposite type of demand management is called for when inflation is the main macroeconomic problem. Figure 23–9 illustrates this case. Here again, point $E$, the intersection of the aggregate demand curve $D_0D_0$ and the aggregate supply curve $SS$, is the equilibrium that the economy would reach in the absence of government policy. But now we suppose that the price level corresponding to point $E$ is considered "too high," meaning that the price level would rise too rapidly from the previous period to this one if the economy moved to point $E$. A government program that reduces demand from $D_0D_0$ to $D_2D_2$ (for example, a reduction in government spending) can keep prices down and thereby reduce inflation. Thus:

> Inflation is frequently caused by aggregate demand racing ahead too fast. When this is the case, government policies that reduce aggregate demand can be effective anti-inflationary devices. But such policies also decrease real GDP and raise unemployment.

This, in brief, summarizes the intent of stabilization policy. When aggregate demand fluctuations are the source of economic instability, the government can limit both recessions and inflations by pushing aggregate demand ahead when it would otherwise lag, and restraining it when it would otherwise grow too quickly.

## DOES IT REALLY WORK?

Can the government actually stabilize the economy as these simple diagrams suggest? That is a matter of some debate, a debate we will take up in Part VII. But a look back at Figures 23–4 and 23–5 may be enlightening right now. First, cover the portions of Figures 23–4 and 23–5 that deal with the period after 1940, the portions from the shaded area rightward in each figure. The picture that emerges for the 1870 to 1940 period is of an economy with frequent and sometimes quite pronounced fluctuations.

Now do the reverse. Cover the data before 1950 and look only at the postwar period. There is, indeed, a difference. Instances of negative real GDP growth are less common and business fluctuations look less severe. Although government policies have not achieved perfection, things do look much better.

FIGURE 23-8

**Stabilization Policy to Fight Unemployment**

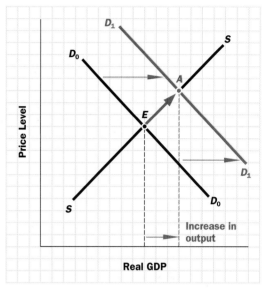

**FIGURE 23-9**

**Stabilization Policy to Fight Inflation**

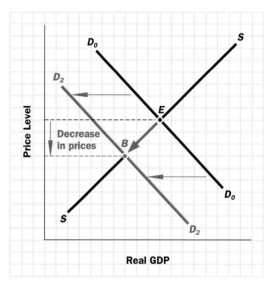

When we turn to inflation, however, things look rather worse. Gone are the periods of deflation and price stability that occurred before World War II. Prices now seem only to rise.

This quick tour through the data suggests that something has changed. The U.S. economy behaved differently from 1950 to 1998 than it did from 1870 to 1940. Although controversy over this point continues, many economists attribute this shift in the economy's behavior to lessons the government has learned about managing the economy—lessons we will be learning in Part VII.

When you look at the prewar data, you are looking at an unmanaged economy that went through booms and recessions for "natural" economic reasons. The government did little about either. When you examine the postwar data, on the other hand, you are looking at an economy that has been increasingly managed by government policy—sometimes successfully and sometimes unsuccessfully. Although the recessions are less severe, this improvement has come at a cost: The economy appears to be more inflation prone than it was in the more distant past. These two changes in our economy may be connected. But to understand why, we will have to provide some relevant economic theory.

We have, in a sense, spent much of this chapter running before we have learned to walk—that is, we have been using aggregate demand and aggregate supply curves extensively before developing the theory that underlies them. That is the task for the rest of Part VI.

---

## SUMMARY

1. *Microeconomics* studies the decisions of individuals and firms, how these decisions interact, and how they influence the allocation of society's resources and the distribution of income. *Macroeconomics* looks at how entire economies behave and studies the pressing social problems of economic growth, inflation, and unemployment.

2. Although they focus on different *subjects*, microeconomics and macroeconomics rely on virtually identical *tools*. Both use the supply and demand analysis introduced in Chapter 5.

3. Macroeconomic models use abstract concepts like "the price level" and "gross domestic product" that are derived by amalgamating many different markets into one. This process is known as *aggregation*; it should not be taken literally but rather viewed as a useful approximation.

4. The best specific measure of the nation's economic output is *gross domestic product (GDP)*, which is obtained by adding up the money values of all *final goods and services* produced in a given year. These outputs can be evaluated year by year at current market prices (to get *nominal GDP*) or at some common set of prices (to get *real GDP*). Neither *intermediate goods* nor transactions that take place outside organized markets are included in GDP.

5. GDP is meant to measure an economy's *production*, not the increase in its *well-being*. For example, the GDP places no value on housework and other do-it-yourself activities or on leisure time. On the other hand, even commodities that might be considered as "bads" rather than "goods" are counted in the GDP (for example, activities that harm the environment).

6. America's economic history shows steady *growth* punctuated by periodic *recessions*, that is, periods in which real GDP declined. Although the distant past included some periods of falling prices *(deflation)*, more recent history shows only rising prices *(inflation)*.

7. The Great Depression of the 1930s was the worst in our country's history. It profoundly affected both our nation and countries throughout the world. It also led to a revolution in economic thinking, thanks largely to the work of John Maynard Keynes.

8. From World War II to the early 1970s, the American economy exhibited much steadier growth than it had shown in the past. Many observers attributed this more stable performance to the implementation of the *stabilization policies* that Keynes suggested. At the same time, however, the price level seems only to rise, never to fall, in the modern economy. The economy seems to have become more "inflation prone."

9. Between 1973 and 1991, the U.S. economy suffered through several serious recessions. In the first part of that period, inflation was also unusually virulent. This unhappy combination of economic stagnation with rapid inflation was nicknamed *stagflation*. Since 1982, however, inflation has been low and fairly steady.

10. U.S. economic performance has been generally good since 1992, and especially so in the last few years. One possible explanation is that the aggregate supply curve has shifted out unusually rapidly.

11. One major cause of inflation is that *aggregate demand* may grow more quickly than *aggregate supply*. In such a case, a government policy that reduces aggregate demand may be able to stem the inflation.

12. Similarly, recessions often occur because aggregate demand grows too slowly. In this case, a government policy that stimulates demand may be an effective way to fight the recession.

---

### KEY TERMS

Microeconomics   479

Macroeconomics   479

Aggregation   481

Aggregate demand curve   482

Aggregate supply curve   482

Inflation   482

Recession   482

Gross domestic product (GDP)   482

Nominal GDP   484

Real GDP   484

Final goods and services   485

Intermediate good   485

Deflation   489

Stagflation   492

Stabilization policy   494

Unemployment   495

---

### QUESTIONS FOR REVIEW

1. Which of the following problems are likely to be studied by a microeconomist and which by a macroeconomist?

   a. The rapid growth of Intel

   b. Why unemployment in the United States fell in 1996 and 1997

   c. Why Japan's economy grew so much faster than the U.S. economy for several decades but has failed to do so in the 1990s

   d. Why college tuition costs have risen so rapidly in recent years

2. You probably use "aggregates" frequently in everyday discussions. Try to think of some examples. (Here is one: Have you ever said, "The students at this college generally think . . . "? What, precisely, did you mean?)

3. Use an aggregate supply and demand diagram to study what would happen to an economy in which the aggregate supply curve never moved while the aggregate demand curve shifted outward year after year.

4. Try asking a friend who has not studied economics in which year he or she thinks prices were higher: 1870 or 1900? 1920 or 1940? (In both cases, prices were higher in the earlier year.) Most young people think that prices have always risen. Why do you think they have this opinion?

5. Which of the following transactions are included in gross domestic product, and by how much does each raise GDP?

   a. Smith pays a carpenter $15,000 to build a garage.

   b. Smith purchases $3,000 worth of materials and builds himself a garage, which is worth $15,000.

   c. Smith goes to the woods, cuts down a tree, and uses the wood to build himself a garage that is worth $15,000.

   d. The Jones family sells its old house to the Reynolds family for $100,000. The Joneses then buy a newly constructed house from a builder for $150,000.

   e. You purchase a used computer from a friend for $200.

   f. Your university purchases a new mainframe computer from IBM, paying $200,000.

   g. You win $1,000 in an Atlantic City casino.

   h. You make $1,000 in the stock market.

   i. You sell a used economics textbook to your college bookstore for $25.

   j. You buy a new economics textbook from your college bookstore for $50.

6. Give some reasons why gross domestic product is not a suitable measure of the well-being of the nation. (Have you noticed newspaper accounts in which journalists seem to use GDP for this purpose?)

When men are employed, they are best contented.

Benjamin Franklin

Inflation is repudiation.

Calvin Coolidge

# THE GOALS OF MACROECONOMIC POLICY

Among the many trials faced by Odysseus, the hero of Homer's *Odyssey*, one of the most difficult was to steer his fragile boat through a narrow strait. On one side lay the rock of the monster Scylla, which threatened to break his craft into pieces; on the other was the menacing whirlpool of Charybdis. The makers of national economic policy face a similarly difficult task in trying to chart a middle course between the Scylla of unemployment and the Charybdis of inflation as they pursue their goal of healthy economic growth. If they steer the economy far from the rocks of unemployment, they run the risk of growing too fast and being swept up in the swift currents of inflation. But if they maintain a safe distance from inflation, they may slow the economy too much and smash against the rocks of unemployment.

Much of Part VI is devoted to building an economic theory that we can use to see how economic planners attempt to steer this delicate course, keeping economic growth high enough to ensure low unemployment but not so high that it spills over into high inflation. We will explain why these goals cannot be attained with machine-like precision, and why improvement on one front often spells deterioration on the other. Along the way, we will pay a great deal of attention to both the *causes* of and *cures* for inflation and unemployment.

But before getting involved in such weighty issues of theory and policy, we pause in this chapter to take a close look at the goals of macroeconomic policy themselves. How fast can—or should—the economy grow? Why does a rise in unemployment cause such social distress? Why is inflation so loudly deplored? The answers to some of these questions may seem obvious at first. But, as you will see, there is more to them than meets the eye.

The chapter is divided into three parts: The first deals with growth, the second with unemployment, and the third with inflation. An appendix explains how inflation is measured.

## ■ PART 1: THE GOAL OF ECONOMIC GROWTH

How fast should our economy, or any economy, grow? At first, the question may seem silly. Isn't it obvious that we should grow as fast as we can. For the most part, economists agree; faster growth is generally preferred to slower growth. But further thought suggests that the apparently naive question is not quite as silly as it sounds.

### Is More Growth Always Better?

For openers, some social critics have questioned the desirability of faster economic growth as an end in itself, at least in the rich countries. Faster growth surely brings more wealth, and to most people the desirability of wealth is beyond question. "I've been rich and I've been poor. Believe me, honey, rich is better," singer Sophie Tucker is said to have told an interviewer. Most people seem to share that sentiment. To those who hold this belief, a healthy economy is one that is capable of producing vast quantities of jeans, pizzas, cars, and computers.

Yet the desirability of further economic growth for a society that is already quite wealthy has been questioned on several grounds. Environmentalists worry that the sheer increase in the volume of goods imposes enormous costs on society in the form of pollution, crowding, and proliferation of wastes that need disposal. It has, they argue, dotted our roadsides with junkyards, filled our air with pollution, and poisoned our food with dangerous chemicals. Some psychologists and social critics argue that the never-ending drive for more and better goods has failed to make people happier. Instead, industrial progress has transformed the satisfying and creative tasks of the artisan into the mechanical and dehumanizing routine of the assembly-line worker. The question is whether the vast outpouring of material goods in worth all the stress and environmental damage.

Most economists answer: probably, yes. For one thing, slower growth would make it extremely difficult to finance programs that improve the quality of life—including efforts to protect the environment. Such programs tend to be expensive, and growth is what makes available the additional resources needed to pay the bills. Second, it would be difficult to prevent further economic growth even if we were so inclined. Mandatory controls are abhorrent to most Americans; we cannot order people to stop being inventive and hard working. Third, slower economic growth would seriously hamper efforts to eliminate poverty—both within our own country and throughout the world. Much of the earth's population still lives in a state of extreme want. These unfortunate people are far less interested in clean air and fulfillment in the workplace than they are in more food, better clothing, and sturdier shelters.

That said, economists concede that faster growth is not *always* better. One important reason will occupy our attention throughout Parts VI and VII: An economy that grows too fast may generate inflation. Why is that? You were introduced to the answer at the end of the last chapter: Inflation arises when aggregate demand races ahead of aggregate supply. In plain English, an economy will become inflationary when people's demands for goods and services expand faster than its capacity to produce them. So, when we think about how rapidly an economy should grow, we are left with a critical question: *How fast can the economy increase its productive capacity?*

## ■ THE CAPACITY TO PRODUCE: POTENTIAL GDP

Questions like that require quantitative answers. Economists have invented the concept of **potential GDP** to measure the economy's normal capacity to produce goods and services, that is, the real gross domestic product (GDP) we *could* produce if the **labor force** were fully employed. Note the use of the word *normal* in the preceding sentence. Just as it is possible to push a factory beyond its normal operating capacity (by, for example, adding a night shift), it is possible to push an economy beyond its normal full-employment level by working it very hard. For example, we observed in the last chapter that the unemployment rate dropped as low as 1.2 percent under abnormal conditions during World War II.

Conceptually, we estimate potential GDP in two steps. First, we take a census of the available supplies of labor, capital, and other productive resources. Then we estimate how much *output* these *inputs* could produce if they were fully utilized. This second step—the transformation of inputs into outputs—involves an assessment of the economy's *technology*. The more technologically advanced an economy, the more output it will be able to produce from any given bundle of inputs—as we emphasized in Chapter 4's discussion of the production possibilities frontier.

**Potential GDP** is the real GDP that the economy would produce if its labor and other resources were fully employed.

The **labor force** is the number of people holding or seeking jobs.

So, in short, potential GDP depends on the size of the economy's labor force, the amount of capital and other resources it has, and its technology. It therefore follows that the *growth rate* of potential GDP depends on:

- The growth rate of the labor force
- The growth rate of the nation's capital stock
- The rate of technical progress

**Labor productivity** is the amount of output a worker turns out in an hour (or a week, or a year) of labor. If output is measured by GDP, it is GDP per hour of work.

To sharpen this point, observe that real GDP is, by definition, the product of the total hours of work in the economy times the amount of output produced per hour:

GDP = hours of work × output per hour.

This second factor, output per hour, is called **labor productivity.** For example, in the United States today, using very rough numbers, GDP is about $9 trillion and total hours of work per year are about 225 billion, meaning that labor productivity is roughly: $9 trillion/225 billion hours = $40 per hour.

Now recall the question we started with: *How fast can the economy increase its productive capacity?* By transforming the preceding equation into growth rates, we have our answer: The growth rate of potential GDP is the *sum* of the growth rates of labor input (hours of work) and labor productivity:[1]

Growth rate of potential GDP = growth rate of labor input + growth rate of labor productivity

In the contemporary United States, both labor input and labor productivity have been increasing at a bit more than 1 percent per year, leading to an estimated growth rate of potential GDP in the 2 to $2\frac{1}{2}$ percent range.

Do the growth rates of potential GDP and actual GDP match up? The answer is an important one to which we will return often in this book:

Over long periods of time, the growth rates of actual and potential GDP are normally quite similar. But the two often diverge sharply over short periods.

Table 24–1 illustrates this point with some recent U.S. data. In the past decade, GDP growth rates over two-year periods have ranged from as low as 0.9 percent to as high as 3.9 percent. But over the entire 1988–1998 period, GDP growth averaged 2.6 percent—more or less in line with the growth of potential GDP.

**TABLE 24–1**

**Recent Growth Rates of Real GDP in the United States**

| Years | Growth Rate per Year |
|---|---|
| 1988–1990 | 2.3% |
| 1990–1992 | 0.9 |
| 1992–1994 | 2.9 |
| 1994–1996 | 2.4 |
| 1996–1998 | 3.9 |
| 1988–1998 | 2.6 |

SOURCE: U.S. Department of Commerce.

## ■ ALTERNATIVE MEASURES OF ECONOMIC GROWTH

There are three basic measures of economic growth, two of which have already been mentioned. The right one to use depends on the purpose.

**REAL GDP** If the objective is to track the *size* of an expanding economy, *real GDP* is the natural choice, and international growth comparisons normally focus on that. But size per se may be of limited interest. For example, India's GDP is slightly bigger than Switzerland's. But with a population more than 130 times as large, India remains a poor country whereas the Swiss are rich.

**GDP PER CAPITA** If, instead, the objective is to indicate how rapidly a country's *standard of living* is rising, a different measure—*GDP per capita*, that is, total GDP divided by the population—makes more sense because it automatically (by definition) ignores the growth that occurs simply because there are more people.

**LABOR PRODUCTIVITY** Finally, if our interest is in how much more *productive* an economy is becoming, the natural choice is the measure we have just discussed—the growth rate of *labor productivity*, which is GDP per hour of work.

---

[1] You may be wondering about what happened to capital. The answer is that one of the main determinants of labor productivity is the amount of capital each worker has to work with. The reason is simple: Workers equipped with more and better capital will produce more output.

These last two measures of economic progress differ only in their denominators: One divides GDP by population, the other by hours of work. So each will give a different reading whenever *hours of work per person* changes. That has indeed been the case in the United States in recent decades. With more of our population working, GDP *per hour* has increased about 1 percent per year over the past 20 years whereas GDP *per capita* has increased about 1.6 percent.

## THE U.S. PRODUCTIVITY SLOWDOWN: IS AMERICA ON THE DECLINE?

The growth rate of productivity in the United States has declined sharply since the early 1970s. Between 1947 and 1973, labor productivity grew at an average rate of 2.8 percent per year, which is probably faster than it had ever grown before over such a long period. But since 1973 labor productivity has plodded along at a sluggish 1.1 percent annual rate. (See Figure 24–1.)

This marked productivity slowdown is a matter of some concern. A quarter-century of growth at 1.1 percent raises productivity by a cumulative 31 percent. But a quarter-century at 2.2 percent growth, which is a more normal historical figure for the United States, would boost productivity some 72 percent. The stakes are obviously high, especially over long periods, as a look back at history will testify.

Think about the relative positions of three major nations—the United States, the United Kingdom, and Japan—at two points in history: 1870 and 1979. In 1870, the United States was a young, upstart nation. Although already among the most prosperous nations on earth in terms of per capita GDP, the United States was in no sense yet a major power. The United Kingdom, by contrast, was the preeminent economic and military power on earth. The Victorian era was at its height, and the sun never set on the British Empire. Meanwhile, somewhere across the Pacific was an inconsequential island nation called Japan. In 1870, Japan had only recently opened up to the West and was economically backward.

Now fast-forward 109 years. By 1979, the United States had become the world's preeminent economic power. But Japan had emerged as the clear number two, while the United Kingdom had retreated into the second rank of nations. It is obvious that the Japanese economy grew faster than the U.S. economy during this century while the British economy grew more slowly, or else this stunning transformation of relative positions would not have occurred. But the magnitudes of the differences in growth rates may astound you.

Labor productivity in the United States grew at a 2.3 percent compound annual rate while the United Kingdom's growth rate was 1.8 percent—a difference of merely 0.5 percent per annum, but compounded for more than a century. And what of Japan? What growth rate propelled it from obscurity into the front rank of nations? The answer is just 3 percent, a mere 0.7 percent per year faster than the United States. These numbers show vividly what a huge difference a 0.5 or 0.7 percentage point change in the growth rate makes—*eventually*.

As we pointed out in our list of *Ideas for Beyond the Final Exam,* only rising productivity can raise standards of living in the long run. Over long periods of time, small differences in rates of productivity growth compound like interest in a bank account and can make an enormous difference to a society's prosperity. Nothing contributes more to material well-being, to the reduction of poverty, to increases in leisure time, and to a country's ability to finance education, public health, environmental improvement, and the arts than its productivity growth rate.

Some observers have worried that the United States may be losing its economic leadership in both productivity and living standards. But these fears are exaggerated for several reasons.

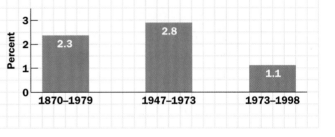

SOURCE: Data on the nonfarm business sector, from Bureau of Labor Statistics.

*Productivity Growth Is (almost) Everything in the Long Run*

**FIGURE 24-2**

**The Productivity Slowdown In Five Countries**

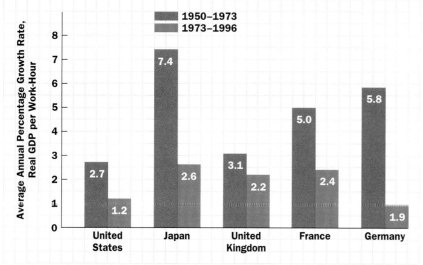

SOURCE: Angus Maddison, "The Nature and Functioning of European Capitalism," Valedictory Lecture, University of Groningen, October 1997.

First, it is important to remember that we are talking about declining *growth rates*. Throughout this period, the *level* of U.S. productivity continued to rise. Second, the United States is still by far the world's largest economy in terms of total production, wealth, and other factors such as spending on research and development.

Third, the productivity slowdown is not just an American problem. The same phenomenon has afflicted virtually every industrial country. Figure 24–2 compares productivity growth rates for five industrial countries from 1950 to 1973 with those from 1973 to 1996. While the U.S. growth rate fell by 1.5 percentage points, the growth rates of Japan, France, and Germany fell by even more.

In addition, very-long-run data on U.S. productivity growth exhibit no downward trend. Productivity plunged during the Great Depression of the 1930s and then leaped upward after World War II. When this catch-up period came to an end, the growth rate fell back. Thus, part of the deceleration after the 1970s was a return toward normalcy after a period of extraordinary growth. Moreover, as noted earlier, per-capita income has fared considerably better than productivity.

Finally, whereas those who see American economic leadership slipping away often focus on manufacturing, the surprising truth is that U.S. manufacturing industries have experienced no decline in productivity growth over the period since World War II. In fact, growth rates of manufacturing productivity in Japan and Germany are no longer higher than our own. Furthermore, recent data have some observers speculating that productivity growth may be on the rise again.

In sum, the slowdown in productivity growth does indeed pose a serious problem for the United States. But the problem is mainly that our living standards are not rising as fast as they might, not that we are falling behind the rest of the world.

## ■ EXPLANATIONS FOR THE PRODUCTIVITY SLOWDOWN

Why did productivity growth slow down? Although many explanations have been offered, a definitive answer has eluded economists—despite years of research.

### LAGGING INVESTMENT

For years, many people suggested that inadequate investment was behind America's productivity problem. Countries like Germany and Japan, these critics observed, saved and invested far more than Americans did, thereby equipping their workers with more modern equipment. Naturally, all that new capital boosted labor productivity. American tax policy, they argued, should create stronger incentives for business to invest and households to save.

The argument sounds logical, but the facts have not been kind to it. For example, the quite notable investment boom in the United States during the 1990s seems to have produced only a small boost to productivity.

### HIGH ENERGY PRICES

A second explanation begins with a tantalizing fact: The productivity slowdown started around 1973, just when the Organization of Petroleum Exporting Countries (OPEC) jacked up the price of oil. As a matter of logic, higher oil prices should reduce business use of energy, which should make labor less productive.

Furthermore, energy prices rose all over the world at exactly the same time, which helps explain why productivity growth fell everywhere.

The argument sounds persuasive—until you remember one other important fact: Energy prices dropped sharply in the mid 1980s and then again in the mid 1990s, but productivity growth did not revive.

## WORKFORCE SKILLS

More highly skilled and better trained workers are more productive on the job. That, presumably, is why college graduates earn more than high school graduates and high school grads earn more than dropouts. Could it be that the skills of the American labor force are not keeping pace? Although workforce skills are notoriously difficult to measure, there is a widespread feeling that the *quality* of education in the United States has declined. For example, SAT scores peaked in the late 1960s and then declined for about 20 years.[2]

## A TECHNOLOGICAL SLOWDOWN?

We noted early in this chapter that the upward march of *technology* is a major source of productivity growth. Today's industrial workers are vastly more productive than their counterparts were a century or two ago because of the technological wonders they work with every day. If innovation slows down, productivity growth will surely decline. Can this have happened in the last quarter of the 20th century?

Many people answer emphatically, no. After all, the microchip and the personal computer were invented in the 1970s, opening the door to what can only be called a revolution in computing and information technology. Workplaces were consequently transformed beyond recognition. Entirely new industries (like Internet services) have been created. Haven't these technological marvels raised productivity enormously? If the data do not show rapid progress, these critics argue, the numbers must be wrong. Maybe the whole alleged productivity slowdown is a myth perpetuated by bad data.

---

■ **PART 2: THE COSTS OF UNEMPLOYMENT**

We noted earlier that actual GDP growth can differ sharply from potential GDP growth over periods as long as several years. This fact has major implications for employment and unemployment.

> When the economy grows more *slowly* than its potential, it fails to generate enough new jobs for its ever-growing labor force. Hence, *the unemployment rate rises.* Conversely, GDP growth *faster* than potential leads to a *falling unemployment rate.*
>
> High unemployment is socially wasteful. When the economy does not create enough jobs to employ all the people who are willing to work, a valuable resource is lost. Potential goods and services that might have been produced and enjoyed by consumers are lost forever. This lost output is the central economic cost of high unemployment, and we can measure it by comparing actual and potential GDP.

The **unemployment rate** is the number of unemployed people, expressed as a percentage of the labor force.

That cost is considerable. Table 24–2 summarizes the idleness of workers and machines, and the resulting loss of national output, for some of the years of lowest economic activity in recent decades. The second column lists the civilian unemployment rate, and thus measures unused labor resources. The third lists the percentage of industrial capacity that U.S. manufacturers were actually using, which indicates the extent to which plant and equipment went unused. The fourth column estimates the shortfall between potential and actual real GDP. For comparison, the bottom line shows the situation in 1998, a year of above-normal utilization of

---

[2] As you probably know, the SAT was rescaled a few years ago to reflect this decline in average scores.

| TABLE 24-2 | **The Economic Costs of High Unemployment** | | |
|---|---|---|---|

| Year | Civilian Unemployment Rate | Capacity Utilization Rate | Real GDP Lost Due to Idle Resources |
|---|---|---|---|
| 1958 | 6.8% | 75.0% | 4.4% |
| 1961 | 6.7 | 77.3 | 3.3 |
| 1975 | 8.5 | 72.3 | 4.6 |
| 1982 | 9.7 | 70.3 | 7.4 |
| 1992 | 7.5 | 79.5 | 1.6 |
| 1998 | 4.5 | 80.8 | -1.6 |

SOURCES: Bureau of Labor Statistics; Federal Reserve System and the authors' calculation.

resources. We see that unemployment has cost the people of the United States as much as a $7\frac{1}{2}$ percent reduction in their real incomes.

Although Table 24–2 shows extreme examples, our inability to utilize all of the nation's available resources was a persistent economic problem from 1973 to 1993. The red line in Figure 24–3 shows actual real GDP in the United States from 1954 to 1998, while the black line shows potential GDP. The graph makes it clear that actual GDP has fallen short of potential GDP more often than it has exceeded it, especially during the 1973–1993 period. In fact:

A conservative estimate of the cumulative gap between actual and potential GDP over the years 1974 to 1993 (all evaluated in 1992 prices) is over $1,600 billion.

| FIGURE 24-3 | **Actual and Potential GDP in the United States, 1954–1999** |
|---|---|

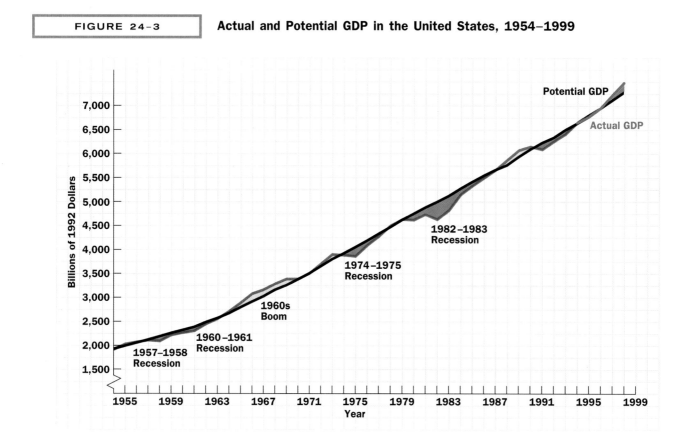

SOURCE: U.S. Department of Commerce and the authors' calculations.

At 1999 levels, this loss in output as a result of unemployment would be about $2\frac{1}{2}$ months' worth of production. And there is no way to redeem those losses. The labor wasted in 1991 cannot be utilized in 1999.

## ■ THE HUMAN COSTS OF HIGH UNEMPLOYMENT

If these numbers seem a bit dry and abstract, think about the human costs of being unemployed. Years ago, job loss meant not only enforced idleness and a catastrophic drop in income, it often led to hunger, cold, ill health—even death. Here is how one unemployed worker during the Great Depression described his family's plight in a mournful letter to the governor of Pennsylvania:

> I have been out of work for over a year and a half. Am back almost thirteen months and the landlord says if I don't pay up before the 1 of 1932 out I must go, and where am I to go in the cold winter with my children? If you can help me please for God's sake and the children's sakes and like please do what you can and send me some help, will you, I cannot find any work. . . . Thanksgiving dinner was black coffee and bread and was very glad to get it. My wife is in the hospital now. We have no shoes to were [sic]; no clothes hardly. Oh what will I do I sure will thank you.[3]

Nowadays, unemployment does not hold quite such terrors for most families, although its consequences remain dire enough. Our system of unemployment insurance (discussed later in the chapter) has taken part of the sting out of unemployment, and other social welfare programs support the incomes of the poor. Yet most families still suffer painful losses of income and, often, severe noneconomic consequences when a breadwinner becomes unemployed.

Even families that are well protected by unemployment compensation suffer when joblessness strikes. Ours is a work-oriented society. A man's place has always been in the office or shop, and lately this has become true for many women as well. A worker forced into idleness by a recession endures a psychological cost that is no less real for our inability to measure it. Martin Luther King Jr. put it graphically: "In our society, it is murder, psychologically, to deprive a man of a job. . . . You are in substance saying to that man that he has no right to exist."[4] High unemployment has been linked to psychological and even physical disorders, divorces, suicides, and crime.

It is important to realize that these costs, whether large or small in total, are distributed most unevenly across the population. In 1998, for example, the unemployment rate among all workers averaged just 4.5 percent. But, as Figure 24–4 shows, 8.9 percent of black workers were unemployed, as were 7.2 percent of women who maintained families. For teenagers, the situation was worse still, with unemployment at 14.6 percent, and that of black teenagers 27.6 percent. Married men had the lowest rate—about 2.4 percent. Overall unemployment varies from year to year, but these relationships are typical:

In good times and bad, married men suffer the least unemployment and teenagers suffer the most; nonwhites are unemployed much more often than whites; blue-collar workers have above-average rates of unemployment; well-educated people have below-average unemployment rates.

It is worth noting that the overall unemployment rate in the United States has for many years been much lower than those of most other industrialized countries. For example, during 1997, when the U.S. unemployment rate averaged 4.9 percent, the corresponding rates were 9.2 percent in Canada, 12.4 percent in France, 12.3 percent in Italy, and 7.8 percent in western Germany.

---

[3] From *Brother, Can You Spare a Dime? The Great Depression 1929–1933*, by Milton Meltzer, p. 103. Copyright 1969 by Milton Meltzer. Reprinted by permission of Alfred A. Knopf, Inc.

[4] Quoted in Coretta Scott King (ed.), *The Words of Martin Luther King* (New York: Newmarket Press, 1983), p. 45.

| FIGURE 24-4 | **Unemployment Rates for Selected Groups, 1998** |

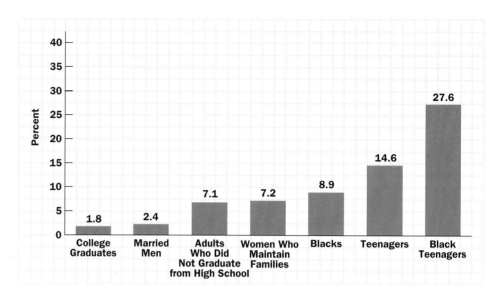

SOURCE: Bureau of Labor Statistics.

## COUNTING THE UNEMPLOYED: THE OFFICIAL STATISTICS

We have been using unemployment figures without considering where they come from or how accurate they are. The basic data come from a monthly survey of more than 50,000 households conducted for the Bureau of Labor Statistics (BLS). The census taker asks several questions about the employment status of each member of the household and, on the basis of the answers, classifies each person as *employed*, *unemployed*, or *not in the labor force*.

**THE EMPLOYED**  The first category is the simplest to define. It includes everybody currently at work, including part-time workers. Although some part-timers work less than a full week by choice, others do so only because they cannot find suitable full-time jobs. Nevertheless, these workers are counted as employed, even though many would consider them "underemployed."

"The rise in unemployment, however, which was somewhat offset by an expanding job market, was countered by an upturn in part-time dropouts, which, in turn, was diminished by seasonal factors, the anticipated summer slump, and, over-all, a small but perceptible rise in actual employment."

**THE UNEMPLOYED**   The second category is a bit trickier. For those not currently working, the BLS first determines whether they are temporarily laid off from a job to which they expect to return. If so, they are counted as unemployed. The remaining workers are asked whether they actively sought work during the previous four weeks. If they did, they are also counted as unemployed.

**OUT OF THE LABOR FORCE**   But if they failed to look for a job, they are classified as *out of the labor force* rather than unemployed. This seems a reasonable way to draw the distinction—after all, we do not want to count college students who work during the summer months as unemployed between September and May. Yet there is a problem: Research has shown that many unemployed workers give up looking for jobs after a time. These so-called **discouraged workers** are victims of poor job prospects, just like the officially unemployed. But when they give up hope, measured unemployment declines!

Involuntary part-time work, loss of overtime or shortened work hours, and discouraged workers are all examples of "hidden" or "disguised" unemployment. People concerned about such phenomena argue that we should include them in the official unemployment rate because, if we do not, the magnitude of the problem will be underestimated. Others, however, argue that measured unemployment overestimates the problem because, to count as unemployed, potential workers need only *claim* to be looking for jobs, even if they are not really interested in finding them.

A **discouraged worker** is an unemployed person who gives up looking for work and is therefore no longer counted as part of the labor force.

## ■ TYPES OF UNEMPLOYMENT

Providing jobs for those willing to work is one principal goal of macroeconomic policy. How are we to define this goal? One clearly *incorrect* answer would be "a zero measured unemployment rate." Ours is a dynamic, highly mobile economy. Households move from one state to another. Individuals quit jobs to seek better positions or retool for more attractive occupations.

These and other decisions produce some minimal amount of unemployment—people who are literally between jobs. Economists call this the level of **frictional unemployment.** The critical distinguishing feature of frictional unemployment is that it is short-lived. A frictionally unemployed person has every reason to expect to find a new job soon.

People tend to think of frictional unemployment as irreducible, but that is not true. During World War II, for example, unemployment in this country fell substantially below the frictional level. Frictional unemployment is irreducible only in the sense that—under normal circumstances—it is socially undesirable to do so. Geographic and occupational mobility play important roles in our market economy, enabling people to search for better jobs. Similarly, waste is avoided by replacing inefficient firms, or firms producing items no longer in demand, by new firms. But the operation of these normal market mechanisms will always produce some temporarily unemployed workers and some firms with unfilled positions. This is the genesis of frictional unemployment.

A second type of unemployment can be difficult to distinguish from frictional unemployment but has very different implications. **Structural unemployment** arises when jobs are eliminated by changes in the economy, such as automation or permanent changes in demand. The crucial difference between frictional and structural unemployment is that, unlike frictionally unemployed workers, structurally unemployed workers cannot realistically be considered "between jobs." Instead, they may find their skills and experience unmarketable in the changing economy in which they live. They are thus faced with either prolonged periods of unemployment or the necessity of making major changes in their skills or occupations. For older workers, learning a new trade may be nearly impossible.

The remaining type of unemployment, **cyclical unemployment,** will occupy most of our attention. Cyclical unemployment rises when the level of economic

**Frictional unemployment** is unemployment that is due to normal turnover in the labor market. It includes people who are temporarily between jobs because they are moving or changing occupations, or are unemployed for similar reasons.

**Structural unemployment** refers to workers who have lost their jobs because they have been displaced by automation, because their skills are no longer in demand, or because of similar reasons.

**Cyclical unemployment** is the portion of unemployment that is attributable to a decline in the economy's total production. Cyclical unemployment rises during recessions and falls as prosperity is restored.

activity declines, as it does in a recession. Thus, when macroeconomists speak of maintaining "full employment," they do not mean achieving zero measured unemployment, but rather limiting unemployment to its frictional and structural components—that is, keeping cyclical unemployment to a minimum. A key question, therefore, is: How much measured unemployment is frictional and structural?

## ■ HOW MUCH EMPLOYMENT IS "FULL EMPLOYMENT"?

President John F. Kennedy was the first to commit the federal government to a specific numerical goal for unemployment. Looking at experience in the prosperous early 1950s, he picked a 4 percent target. But that goal was rejected as too ambitious during the 1970s for three major reasons.

First, some economists argued that the 4 percent target had to be raised because the composition of the labor force had changed. Specifically, many more young workers entered the labor force in the 1970s than in the 1950s, and teenagers always have higher rates of unemployment than adults.

Second, they suggested, the increased generosity of unemployment compensation (which is discussed next) had reduced the incentive to get off the unemployment rolls. The logic here is simple. Because unemployment insurance reduces the income gap between those who work and those who collect unemployment benefits, it must therefore dull the incentive to seek and accept a job. And the more generous the benefits, the weaker the incentive.

A third reason stems from the short-run *trade-off between inflation and unemployment*, a notion we mentioned in Chapter 1 and which we will study in depth in Chapter 34. Economic research in the 1970s suggested that the original 4 percent unemployment target was too low in a very specific sense: Inflation will rise if unemployment remains this low.

Since the government abandoned the 4 percent unemployment target, no new number has been put in its place. Instead, we have had a long-running debate over exactly how much measured unemployment corresponds to *full employment*. In the early 1990s, some economists argued that full employment came at a measured unemployment rate above 6 percent. Others pointed out that the main factors that had raised the full-employment unemployment rate in the 1970s were reversed in the 1980s. For example, the teenage labor force dwindled, and unemployment benefits went to a smaller percentage of the unemployed.

As is so often the case, actual events helped settle the issue—though not definitively. Measured unemployment dropped below 6 percent in the fall of 1994 and below 5 percent in the summer of 1997. And, despite these low unemployment rates, inflation failed to accelerate. This conjunction of events persuaded most economists that full employment comes at an unemployment rate below 6 percent, perhaps well below. In fact, many leading economists have now adopted a number in the 5 to 5.5 percent range as their working definition of full employment. And some prefer a lower number, below 5 percent.

## ■ UNEMPLOYMENT INSURANCE: THE INVALUABLE CUSHION

One main reason why America's unemployed workers no longer experience the complete loss of income that devastated so many during the 1930s is our system of *unemployment insurance*—one of the most valuable institutional innovations to emerge from the trauma of the Great Depression.

Each of the 50 states administers an unemployment insurance program under federal guidelines. Although the precise amounts vary, the average weekly benefit check in 1998 was about $200, which amounted to about 45 percent of average earnings. Though a 55 percent drop in earnings still poses serious problems, the importance

---

**● POLICY DEBATE    DOES THE MINIMUM WAGE CAUSE UNEMPLOYMENT?**

---

Elementary economic reasoning—summarized in the simple supply-demand diagram below—suggests that setting a minimum wage (*W* in the graph) above the free-market wage (*w* in the graph) must cause unemployment. In the graph, unemployment is the horizontal gap between the quantity of labor supplied (point *B*) and the quantity demanded (point *A*) at the minimum wage. Indeed, the conclusion seems so elementary that generations of economists took it for granted. Earlier editions of this book, for example, confidently told students that a higher minimum wage must lead to higher unemployment.

But some surprising economic research published in the 1990s casts serious doubt on this conventional wisdom.* For example, economists David Card and Alan Krueger compared employment changes at fast-food restaurants in New Jersey and nearby Pennsylvania after New Jersey, but not Pennsylvania, raised its minimum wage in 1992. To their surprise, the New Jersey stores did more net hiring than their Pennsylvania counterparts. Similar results were found for fast-food stores in Texas after the federal minimum wage was raised in 1991, and in California after the statewide minimum wage was increased in 1988.

In none of these cases did a higher minimum wage seem to reduce employment—in contrast to the implications of simple economic theory. Thus, a policy question previously deemed closed now seems to be open: Does the minimum wage cause unemployment?

Resolution of this debate is of more than academic interest. In 1996, President Clinton recommended and Congress passed an increase in the federal minimum wage—justifying its action, in part, by the new research suggesting that unemployment would not rise as a result. Results since 1996 seem to indicate that few jobs were lost. (And another minimum wage increase was being considered as this book went to press.) Partly for this reason, the British government enacted a brand new minimum wage in 1998. Research can have consequences.

*See David Card and Alan Krueger, *Myth and Measurement: The New Economics of the Minimum Wage* (Princeton, N.J.: Princeton University Press, 1995).

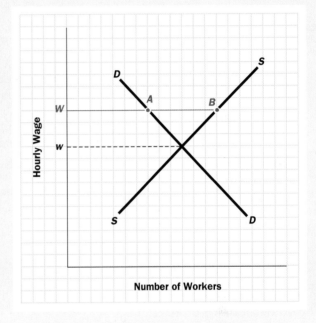

of this 45 percent income cushion can scarcely be exaggerated, especially because it may be supplemented by funds from other welfare programs. Families that are covered by unemployment insurance rarely go hungry or are dispossessed from their homes when they lose their jobs.

Eligibility for benefits varies by state, but some criteria apply quite generally. Only experienced workers qualify, so persons just joining the labor force (such as recent graduates of high schools and colleges) or reentering after prolonged absences (such as women returning to the job market after years of child rearing) cannot collect benefits. Neither can those who quit their jobs, except under unusual circumstances. Also, benefits end after a stipulated period of time, normally six months. For all of these reasons, only about one-third of the 6 million people who were unemployed in an average week in 1998 actually received benefits.

The importance of unemployment insurance to the unemployed is obvious. But significant benefits also accrue to citizens who never become unemployed. During recessions, billions of dollars are paid out in unemployment benefits, and because recipients probably spend most of their benefits, unemployment insurance limits the severity of recessions by providing additional purchasing power when and where it is most needed.

The unemployment insurance system is one of several cushions built into our economy since 1933 to prevent another Great Depression. By giving money to those who become unemployed, the system helps prop up aggregate demand during recessions.

Although the U.S. economy is now probably "depression proof," this should not be a cause for too much rejoicing, for the many recessions we have had since the 1950s amply demonstrate that we are far from "recession proof."

The fact that unemployment insurance and other social welfare programs replace a significant fraction of lost income has led some skeptics to claim that unemployment is no longer a serious problem. But the fact is that unemployment insurance is just what the name says—an *insurance* program. And insurance can never prevent a catastrophe from occurring; it can only spread the costs among many people instead of letting all the costs fall on the shoulders of a few unfortunate souls. As we noted before, unemployment robs the economy of output it could have produced, and no insurance policy can insure society against such losses.

> Our system of payroll taxes and unemployment benefits spreads the costs of unemployment over the entire population. But it does not eliminate the basic economic cost.

## ■ PART 3: THE COSTS OF INFLATION

Both the human and economic costs of inflation are less obvious than the costs of unemployment. But this does not necessarily make them any less real, for if one thing is crystal clear about inflation, it is that people do not like it.

Nowadays, inflation barely registers as a problem in national public opinion polls. But when inflation is high, it often heads the list—generally even ahead of unemployment. Surveys also show that inflation, like unemployment, causes a deterioration in consumers' sense of well-being—it makes people unhappy. Finally, studies of elections suggest that voters penalize the party that occupies the White House when inflation is high.

The fact is beyond dispute: People consider inflation to be something bad. The question is, why?

## ■ INFLATION: THE MYTH AND THE REALITY

The **purchasing power** of a given sum of money is the volume of goods and services that it will buy.

The **real wage rate** is the wage rate adjusted for inflation. It indicates the volume of goods and services that money wages will buy.

At first, the question may seem ridiculous. During inflationary times, people pay higher prices for the same quantities of goods and services they had before. So more and more income is needed just to maintain the same standard of living. Is it not obvious that this erosion of **purchasing power**—that is, the decline in what money will buy—makes everyone worse off?

### INFLATION AND REAL WAGES

This would indeed be the case were it not for one very significant fact. The wages that people earn are also prices—prices for labor services. During a period of inflation, wages also rise, and, in fact, the average wage typically rises more or less in step with prices. Thus, contrary to popular myth, workers as a group are not usually victimized by inflation.

> The purchasing power of wages—what is called the **real wage rate**—is not systematically eroded by inflation. Sometimes wages rise faster than prices, and sometimes prices rise faster than wages. The fact is that, in the long run, wages tend to outstrip prices as new capital equipment and innovation increase output per worker.

Figure 24–5 illustrates this simple fact. The red line shows the rate of increase of prices in the United States for each year since 1948, and the black line shows the rate of increase of wages. The difference between the two, shaded in blue, indicates the rate of growth of *real* wages. Generally, wages rise faster than prices, reflecting the steady advance of labor productivity; therefore, real wages rise. (But this is not always the case; the graph shows that real wages fell several times in the 1980s.)

"Sure, you're raising my allowance. But am I actually gaining any purchasing power?"

The feature of Figure 24–5 that virtually jumps off the page is the way the two lines dance together. Wages normally rise rapidly when prices rise rapidly, and they rise slowly when prices rise slowly. But you should not draw any hasty conclusions from this association. It does not, for example, tell us whether rising prices *cause* rising wages or rising wages *cause* rising prices. Remember the warnings given in Chapter 1 about trying to infer causation just by looking at data. But analyzing cause and effect is not our purpose right now. We merely want to dispel the myth that inflation inevitably erodes real wages.

Why is this myth so widespread? Imagine a world without inflation in which wages are rising 2 percent a year because of the increasing productivity of labor. Now imagine that, all of a sudden, inflation sets in and prices start rising 3 percent a year but nothing else changes. Figure 24–5 suggests that, with perhaps a small delay, wage increases will accelerate to 2 + 3 = 5 percent a year.

Will workers view this change with equanimity? Probably not. To each worker, the 5 percent wage increase will be seen as something he earned by the sweat of his brow. In his view, he *deserves* every penny of his 5 percent raise. In a sense, he is right because "the sweat of his brow" earned him a 2 percent increment in real wages that, when the inflation rate is 3 percent, can only be achieved by increasing his money wages by 5 percent. An economist would divide the wage increase in the following way:

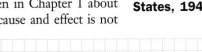

FIGURE 24-5

**Rates of Change of Wages and Prices in the United States, 1948–1998**

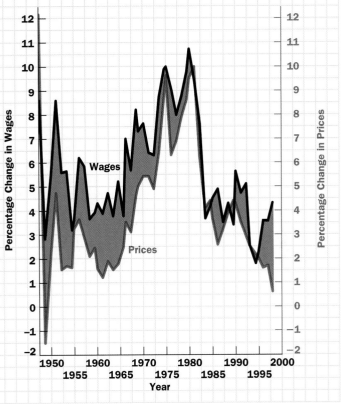

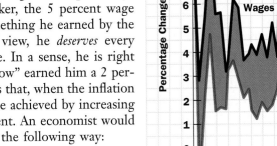

| Reasons for Wages to Increase | Amount |
|---|---|
| Higher productivity | 2% |
| Compensation for higher prices | 3 |
| Total | 5% |

But the worker will probably keep score differently. Feeling that he earned the entire 5 percent by his own merits, he will view inflation as having "robbed" him of three-fifths of his just desserts. The higher the rate of inflation, the more of his raise the worker will feel has been stolen from him.

Of course, nothing could be further from the truth. Basically, the economic system rewards the worker with *the same 2 percent real wage increment for higher productivity, regardless of the rate of inflation.* The "evils of inflation" are often exaggerated because people fail to understand this point.

## THE ILLUSION OF TRADITIONAL "FAIR" PRICES

A second reason for misunderstanding the effects of inflation is that people tend to think in terms of the number of dollars it takes to buy something rather than in terms of the *purchasing power* of these dollars. For example, if both prices and wages double, people will have to work exactly the same amount of time as before to earn the price of a loaf of bread. But because they now pay $2 a loaf instead of $1, they feel that the price of bread is scandalously high. In fact, nothing really has changed, but people cling to an outmoded idea of what bread *should* cost.

## THE IMPORTANCE OF RELATIVE PRICES

A third misperception results from failure to distinguish between a *rise in the general price level* and a change in **relative prices,** that is, a rise in one price relative to another. To see the distinction most clearly, imagine first a *pure inflation* in which *every* price rises by 10 percent during the year, so that relative prices do not change. Table 24–3 gives an example in which movie tickets go up from $6.00 to $6.60, candy bars from 50 cents

SOURCE: Data on both wages and prices pertain to the private business sector, from Bureau of Labor Statistics.

An item's **relative price** is its price in terms of some other item rather than in terms of dollars.

TABLE 24-3

**Pure Inflation**

| Item | Last Year's Price | This Year's Price | Increase |
| --- | --- | --- | --- |
| Candy bar | $0.50 | $0.55 | 10% |
| Movie ticket | 6.00 | 6.60 | 10 |
| Automobile | 9,000 | 9,900 | 10 |

to 55 cents, and automobiles from $9,000 to $9,900. After the inflation, just as before, it will still take 12 candy bars to buy a movie ticket, 1,500 movie tickets to buy a car, and so on. A person who manufactures candy bars in order to purchase movie tickets is neither helped nor harmed by the inflation. Neither is a car dealer with a sweet tooth.

But real inflations are not like this. When there is 10 percent general inflation—meaning that the "average price" rises by 10 percent—some prices may jump 20 percent or more while others actually fall.[5] Suppose that, instead of the price increases shown in Table 24–3, prices rise as shown in Table 24–4. Movie prices go up by 25 percent, but candy prices do not change. Surely, candy manufacturers who love movies will be disgruntled because it now costs 15 candy bars instead of 12 to get into the theater. They will blame inflation for raising the price of movie tickets, even though their real problem stems from the *increase in the price of movies relative to candy*. (They would have been hurt as much if movie tickets had remained at $6 while the price of candy fell to 40 cents.)

Because car prices have risen by only 5 percent, theater owners in need of new cars will be delighted by the fact that an auto now costs only 1,260 movie admissions—just as they would have cheered if car prices had fallen to $7,560 while movie tickets remained at $6. However, they are unlikely to attribute their good fortune to inflation. Indeed, they should not. What has actually happened is that *cars became cheaper relative to movies*.

Because real-world inflations proceed at uneven rates, relative prices change all the time. There are gainers and losers, just as some would gain and others lose if relative prices were to change without any general inflation. Inflation, however, gets a bad name because losers often blame inflation for their misfortune whereas gainers rarely credit inflation for their good luck.

These three kinds of misconceptions help explain why respondents to public opinion polls often cite inflation as a major national issue, why higher inflation rates depress consumers, and why voters express their ire at the polls when inflation is high.

Inflation does not systematically erode the purchasing power of wages. Nor does it lead to "unfair" prices. Nor is it usually to blame when some goods become more expensive relative to others.

But not all of the costs of inflation are mythical. Let us now turn to some of the real costs.

TABLE 24-4

**Real Inflation**

| Item | Last Year's Price | This Year's Price | Increase |
| --- | --- | --- | --- |
| Candy bar | $0.50 | $0.50 | 0% |
| Movie ticket | 6.00 | 7.50 | 25 |
| Automobile | 9,000 | 9,450 | 5 |

[5] The way statisticians figure out "average" price increases is discussed in the appendix to this chapter.

## ■ INFLATION AS A REDISTRIBUTOR OF INCOME AND WEALTH

We have just seen that the *average* person is neither helped nor harmed by inflation. But almost no one is exactly average! Some people gain from inflation and others lose. It is hard to say anything more systematic about the effects of inflation on particular prices and wages.

But inflation does have systematic effects on the distribution of income and wealth. Senior citizens trying to scrape by on pensions or other fixed incomes suffer badly from inflation. Because they earn no wages, it is little solace to them that wages keep pace with prices. Their pension incomes do not.[6]

This example illustrates a more general problem. Think of pensioners as people who "lend" money to an organization (the pension fund) when they are young in order to be "paid back" with interest when they are old. Because of the rise in the price level during the intervening years, the unfortunate pensioners get paid back in less valuable dollars than those they originally loaned. In general:

**Those who lend money are apt to be victimized by inflation.**

Although lenders may lose heavily, borrowers may do quite well. For example, homeowners who borrowed money from banks in the form of mortgages back in the 1950s, when interest rates were 3 or 4 percent, gained enormously from the surprisingly virulent inflation of the 1970s. They paid back dollars of much lower purchasing power than those they had borrowed. The same is true of other borrowers.

**Borrowers often gain from inflation.**

Because the redistribution caused by inflation generally benefits borrowers at the expense of lenders,[7] and because both lenders and borrowers can be found at every income level, we conclude that:

**Inflation does not always steal from the rich to aid the poor, nor does it always do the reverse.**

Why, then, is the redistribution caused by inflation so widely condemned? Because its victims are selected capriciously. Nobody legislates the redistribution. Nobody enters into it voluntarily. The gainers do not earn their spoils, and the losers do not deserve their fate. Moreover, inflation systematically robs particular classes of people of purchasing power year after year—people living on private pensions, families who save money and "lend" it to banks, and workers whose wages and salaries do not adjust. Even if the average person suffers no damage from inflation, that offers little consolation to those who are its victims. This is one fundamental indictment of inflation.

**Inflation redistributes income in an arbitrary way. Society's income distribution should reflect the interplay of the operation of free markets and the purposeful efforts of government to alter that distribution. Inflation interferes with and distorts this process.**

## ■ REAL VERSUS NOMINAL INTEREST RATES

But wait. Must inflation always rob lenders to bestow gifts upon borrowers? If both parties see inflation coming, won't lenders demand that borrowers pay a higher interest rate as compensation for the coming inflation? Indeed they will.

---

[6] This is not, however, true of Social Security benefits, which are automatically increased to compensate recipients for changes in the price level.

[7] By the same token, *deflation* generally benefits lenders at the expense of borrowers, because the borrowers must pay back money of greater purchasing power.

For this reason, economists draw a sharp distinction between inflation that is *expected* and inflation that is *unexpected*.

What happens when inflation is fully expected by both parties? Suppose Diamond Jim wants to borrow $1,000 from Scrooge for one year, and both agree that, in the absence of inflation, a fair rate of interest would be 3 percent. This means that Diamond Jim would pay back $1,030 at the end of the year for the privilege of having $1,000 now.

If both men expect prices to increase by 6 percent, Scrooge may reason as follows: "If Diamond Jim pays me back $1,030 a year from today, that money will buy less than what $1,000 buys today. Thus, I'll really be *paying him* to borrow from me! I'm no philanthropist. Why don't I charge him 9 percent instead? Then he'll pay back $1,090 at the end of the year. With prices 6 percent higher, this will buy roughly what $1,030 is worth today. So I'll get the same 3 percent increase in purchasing power that we would have agreed on in the absence of inflation and won't be any worse off. That's the least I'll accept."

Diamond Jim may follow a similar chain of logic. "With no inflation, I was willing to pay $1,030 a year from now for the privilege of having $1,000 today, and Scrooge was willing to lend it. He'd be crazy to do the same with 6 percent inflation. He'll want to charge me more. How much should I pay? If I offer him $1,090 a year from now, that will have roughly the same purchasing power as $1,030 today, so I won't be any worse off. That's the most I'll pay."

This kind of thinking may lead Scrooge and Diamond Jim to write a contract with a 9 percent interest rate—3 percent as the increase in purchasing power that Diamond Jim pays to Scrooge and 6 percent as compensation for expected inflation. Then, if the expected 6 percent inflation actually materializes, neither party will be made better or worse off by inflation.

This example illustrates a general principle. The 3 percent increase in purchasing power that Diamond Jim agrees to hand over to Scrooge is called the **real rate of interest.** The 9 percent contractual interest charge that Diamond Jim and Scrooge write into the loan agreement is called the **nominal rate of interest.** The nominal rate of interest is arrived at by adding the *expected rate of inflation* to the real rate of interest. Expected inflation is added to compensate the lender for the loss of purchasing power that the lender expects to suffer as a result of inflation. Because of this:

> Inflation that is accurately predicted need not redistribute income between borrowers and lenders. If the *expected* rate of inflation that is embodied in the nominal interest rate matches the *actual* rate of inflation, no one gains and no one loses. However, to the extent that expectations prove incorrect, inflation will still redistribute income.[8]

It need hardly be pointed out that errors in predicting the rate of inflation are the norm, not the exception. Published forecasts bear witness to the fact that economists have great difficulty in predicting the rate of inflation. The task is no easier for businesses, consumers, and banks. This is another reason why inflation is so widely condemned as unfair and undesirable. It sets up a guessing game that no one likes.

The **real rate of interest** is the percentage increase in purchasing power that the borrower pays to the lender for the privilege of borrowing. It indicates the increased ability to purchase goods and services that the lender earns.

The **nominal rate of interest** is the percentage by which the money the borrower pays back exceeds the money that he borrowed, making no adjustment for any fall in the purchasing power of this money that results from inflation.

## INFLATION DISTORTS MEASUREMENTS

So inflation imposes costs on society because it is hard to predict. But other costs arise even when inflation is predicted accurately. Many such costs stem from the fact that people are simply unaccustomed to thinking in inflation-adjusted terms and so make errors in thinking and calculation. Many laws and regulations that were designed for an inflation-free economy malfunction when inflation is high. Here are some important examples.

---

[8] *Exercise:* Who gains and who loses if the inflation turns out to be only 4 percent instead of the 6 percent that Scrooge and Diamond Jim expected? What if the inflation rate is 8 percent?

## CONFUSING REAL AND NOMINAL INTEREST RATES

As we noted in Chapter 1's list of *Ideas for Beyond the Final Exam*, people frequently confuse *real* and *nominal* interest rates. For example, most Americans viewed the 12 percent mortgage interest rates that banks charged in 1980 as scandalously high although they saw the 7 percent mortgage rates of 1998 as a great bargain. In truth, however, the real interest rate in 1998 (about 5 percent) was well above the bargain-basement real rates in 1980 (about 2 percent).

## PUBLIC UTILITY REGULATION

A similar problem arose in regulating public utilities. When utilities asked their regulatory agencies to permit them to earn a rate of return closer to 11 percent—a *negative* real rate of return!—there was a public uproar. The companies frequently found their "exorbitant" requests for rate hikes rejected by the commissions. One consequence was that many utilities could no longer afford to borrow the money needed to build new generating capacity. Subsequent power shortages were among the predictable results.

## THE MALFUNCTIONING TAX SYSTEM

The tax system is probably the most important example of inflation illusion at work. The law does not recognize the distinction between *nominal* and *real* interest rates; it simply taxes nominal interest regardless of how much real interest it represents. Similarly, **capital gains**—the difference between the price at which an investor sells an asset and the price that she paid for it—are taxed in nominal, not real, terms. As a result, our tax system can do strange things when inflation is high. An example will show why. Between 1979 and 1999, the price level rose by roughly 125 percent. Consider some stock that was purchased for $10,000 in 1979 and sold for $20,000 in 1999. The investor actually *lost* purchasing power in the transaction because $20,000 in 1999 could purchase less than $10,000 in 1979. Yet because the law levies taxes on nominal capital gains, with no correction for inflation, the investor would be taxed on the $10,000 nominal capital gain as though she had made a profit rather than a loss.

A **capital gain** is the difference between the price at which an asset is sold and the price at which it was bought.

Many economists have proposed that this, presumably unintended, feature of the law be changed by taxing only capital gains in excess of inflation. But up to now Congress has not agreed. This little example illustrates a pervasive and serious problem:

Because it fails to recognize the distinction between nominal and real capital gains, our tax system levies high, and presumably unintended, tax rates on capital income when there is high inflation. Similar problems arise in the taxation of interest, corporate profits, and other items. Thus the laws that govern our financial system can become counter-productive in an inflationary environment, causing problems that were never intended by the legislators. Some economists feel that the high tax rates caused by inflation discourage saving, lending, and investing—and therefore retard economic growth.

## USURY LAWS

Our last example of how inflation can make a law malfunction is *usury laws*, which set *maximum* permissible interest rates on particular types of loans. Such laws, which date back to biblical days, can have strange and unintended consequences under inflation because they place ceilings on *nominal* interest rates rather than on *real* interest rates. In effect, limits on nominal interest rates make some activities that are perfectly legal at low or zero inflation illegal in inflationary environments. In fact, usury laws created so much havoc during the period of double-digit inflation in 1979–1980 that Congress took drastic action to curtail them.

Thus, failure to understand that high *nominal* interest rates can signify low *real* interest rates has been known to make the tax code misfire, to impoverish savers, to inhibit borrowing and lending, and to make it nearly impossible for public utilities to raise the capital they need to serve rising consumer demands. It is important to note that *these costs of inflation are not purely redistributive.* Society as a whole loses when mutually beneficial transactions are prohibited by dysfunctional legislation.

Why, then, do such laws stay on the books? One reason is a general lack of understanding of the difference between real and nominal interest rates. People fail to understand that it is normally the *real* rate of interest that matters in an economic transaction because only that rate reveals how much borrowers pay and lenders receive *in terms of the goods and services that money can buy.* They focus on the high *nominal* interest rates caused by inflation, even when these rates correspond to low real interest rates.

The difference between real and nominal interest (and profit) rates, and the fact that the real rate matters economically whereas the nominal rate is politically significant, are matters that are of the utmost importance and yet are understood by very few people—including many who make public policy decisions. Furthermore, this is just one example of how inflation distorts measurements in economics.

The distinction between *real* and *nominal* magnitudes is one of our *Ideas for Beyond the Final Exam,* and if you remember it 10 years from now, you will truly have gotten a great deal out of studying economics.

*Inflation Distorts Measurements*

## ■ OTHER COSTS OF INFLATION

Another cost of inflation is that rapidly changing prices make it risky to enter into long-term contracts. In an extremely severe inflation, the "long term" may be only a few days. But even moderate inflations can have remarkable effects on long-term loans. Suppose that a corporation wants to borrow $1 million to finance the purchase of some new equipment and needs the loan for 20 years. If inflation averages 2 percent over this period, the $1 million it repays at the end of 20 years will be worth $672,971 in today's purchasing power. But if inflation averages 5 percent instead, it will be worth only $376,889.

Lending or borrowing for this long a period is obviously a big gamble. With the stakes so high, the outcome may be that neither lenders nor borrowers want to get involved in long-term contracts. But without long-term loans, business investment may become impossible. The economy may stagnate.

Inflation also makes life difficult for the shopper. You probably have a group of stores that you habitually patronize because they carry the items you want to buy at (roughly) the prices you want to pay. This knowledge saves you a great deal of time and energy. But when prices are changing rapidly, your list quickly becomes obsolete. You return to your favorite clothing store to find that the price of jeans has risen drastically. Should you buy? Should you shop around at other stores? Will they have also raised their prices? Business firms have precisely the same problem with their suppliers. Rising prices force them to shop around more, which imposes costs on the firms and, more generally, reduces the efficiency of the whole economy.

Shopping costs may sound frivolous and unimportant, but they are not. Arthur Okun, who chaired the Council of Economic Advisers under President Johnson, suggested an ingenious mental exercise that illustrates the importance of shopping costs. Ask yourself how much you would have to be paid to promise never again to buy anything from any of the stores you have patronized in the past. When you ponder this for a while, you realize the great value of having normal places to shop. Inflation takes some of this value away.

## ■ THE COSTS OF LOW VERSUS HIGH INFLATION

The preceding litany of the costs of inflation alerts us to one very important fact: *Predictable inflation is far less burdensome than unpredictable inflation.* When is inflation most predictable? When it proceeds year after year at a modest and more or less steady rate. Thus, the *variability of the inflation rate* is a crucial factor. Inflation of 3 percent a year for three consecutive years will exact lower social costs than inflation that is 2 percent in the first year, zero in the second, and 7 percent in the third. In general:

**Steady inflation is more predictable than variable inflation and therefore has smaller social and economic costs.**

But the *average level of the inflation rate* is also important. Partly because of the inflation illusions mentioned above and partly because of the more rapid breakdown in normal customer relationships that we have just mentioned, a steady inflation of 6 percent a year does more damage than a steady inflation of 3 percent a year.

Economists distinguish between *low inflation*, which is a modest economic problem, and *high inflation*, which can be a devastating one, partly on the basis of the average level of inflation and partly on its variability. If inflation remains steady and low, prices may rise for a long time, but at a moderate and fairly constant pace, allowing people to adapt. From 1982 to 1996 in the United States, for example, prices climbed a total of 58 percent, for an average annual inflation rate of 3.3 percent. And the pace of inflation was remarkably steady, never dropping below 2.1 percent or rising above 4.4 percent.

Very high inflations typically last for shorter periods of time and are often marked by highly variable inflation rates from month to month or year to year. In recent decades, for example, countries ranging from Argentina to Israel to Russia have experienced bouts of inflation exceeding 100 percent or even 1,000 percent per year. (See the following box, "Hyperinflation and the Piggy Bank.") Each of these episodes severely disrupted the country's economy.

The German hyperinflation after World War I is perhaps the most famous episode of runaway inflation. Between December 1922 and November 1923, when a hard-nosed reform finally broke the spiral, wholesale prices in Germany increased by almost 100 million percent! But even this experience was dwarfed by the great Hungarian inflation of 1945–1946, the greatest inflation of them all. For a period of one year, the *monthly* rate of inflation averaged about 20,000 percent. In the final month, the price level skyrocketed 42 quadrillion percent!

If you review the costs of inflation that have been discussed in this chapter, you will see why the distinction between low and high inflation is so fundamental. Many economists think we can live rather nicely in an environment of steady, low inflation. No one believes we can survive very well under extremely high inflation.

When inflation is steady and low, the rate at which prices rise is relatively easy to predict. It can therefore be taken into account in setting interest rates. Under high inflation, especially if prices are rising at ever-increasing or highly variable rates, this is extremely difficult, and perhaps impossible, to do. The potential redistributions become monumental, and lending and borrowing may cease entirely.

Any inflation makes it difficult to write long-term contracts. Under low, creeping inflation, the "long term" may be 20 years, or 10 years, or 5. But under high, galloping inflation, the "long term" may be measured in days or weeks. Restaurant prices may change daily. Air fares may go up while you are in the middle of your journey. When it is impossible to enter into contracts of any duration longer than a few days, economic activity becomes paralyzed. We conclude that:

**The horrors of hyperinflation either are absent in low, steady inflations or are present in such muted forms that they can scarcely be considered horrors.**

## LOW INFLATION DOES NOT NECESSARILY LEAD TO HIGH INFLATION

We noted earlier that inflation is surrounded by a mythology that bears precious little relation to reality. It seems appropriate to conclude this chapter by disposing of one particularly persistent myth: that low inflation is a slippery slope that invariably leads to high inflation.

## ● HYPERINFLATION AND THE PIGGY BANK

Whereas mild inflations are barely noticeable in everyday life, hyperinflation makes all sorts of normal economic activities more difficult and transforms a society in strange and unexpected ways. This article, excerpted from *The New York Times,* illustrates some of the problems that hyperinflation created for Nicaraguans in 1989.

> For generations, Nicaraguans have guarded their savings in piggy banks. . . . But no longer. In a country where inflation recently reached 161 percent for a 2-week period, a penny saved is a penny spent. "No one wants a bank now," said a potter who has given over his kilns to making beer mugs. "We've given up even making them."
>
> The demise of the piggy bank is only the least of the complications that have vexed the public as inflation and Government efforts to combat it have sent the value of the Nicaraguan córdoba fluctuating wildly.
>
> After inflation became unbearable, the Government replaced all of its currency in February 1988 at a new rate of 10 córdobas to a dollar. But by December, the new money had reached 4,500 to the dollar, and despite months of harsh austerity measures, it has now surged upward again, reaching 26,250 to the dollar.
>
> That kind of uncertainty has left the banking system in shambles, despite savings accounts that offer up to 70 percent interest a month. . . . And it has left a legacy of quirks that now extends throughout the country's daily life. . . .
>
> In many parts of the country, enterprising mechanics have converted the nation's once-precious stock of coins into something more valuable: metal washers to fit the nuts and bolts of rapidly deteriorating machinery. . . .
>
> In Managua, it is still necessary to deposit a copper-colored 1-córdoba coin to make a pay phone call. But . . . not everybody even remembers what a 1-córdoba coin

> looks like, and fewer still actually own one. That is probably just as well for the phone system, because if anyone bothered to carry the coins, they could make about 26,250 phone calls for a dollar. . . .
>
> Beating the exchange rates is particularly trying for restaurant owners who must have any price increases approved by the Government Institute of Tourism. Since that process consumes precious amounts of time, restaurant owners must aim high with their requests in the anticipation that new inflation will make their prices competitive, but still profitable, at some future date.
>
> When exchange rates are changing, therefore, prices at a given restaurant can shoot far out of sight, emptying it of patrons for days or weeks. Then, as has happened recently, a new devaluation can make the same prices absurdly low in dollar terms. A steak dinner for two at one of Managua's leading restaurants on a recent weekend cost a little over $3, if you could get a table.

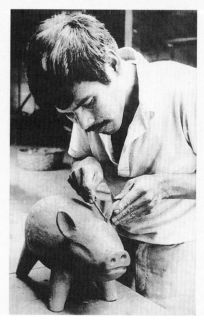

SOURCE: Mark A. Uhlig, "Is Nicaraguan Piggy Bank an Endangered Species?" *New York Times,* June 24, 1989.

These children in Germany during the hyperinflation of the 1920s are building a pyramid with cash, worth no more than the sand or sticks used by children elsewhere.

There is neither statistical evidence nor theoretical support for the belief that low inflation inevitably leads to high inflation. To be sure, inflations sometimes accelerate. But at other times they slow down.

Although creeping inflations have many causes, runaway inflations have occurred only when the government has printed incredible amounts of money, usually to finance wartime expenditures. In the German inflation of 1923, the government finally found that its printing presses could not produce enough paper money to keep pace with the exploding prices. Not that it did not try. By the end of the inflation, the *daily* output of currency was over 400 quadrillion marks! The Hungarian authorities in 1945 to 1946 tried even harder. The average growth rate of the money supply was more than 12,000 percent *per month*. Needless to say, these are not the kind of inflation problems that are likely to face industrialized countries in the foreseeable future.

But that does not mean there is nothing wrong with low inflation. Much of this chapter has been spent analyzing the very real costs of any inflation, no matter how low. A case against even moderate inflation can indeed be built, but it does not help this case to shout foolish slogans like "Creeping inflation always leads to galloping inflation." Fortunately, it is simply not true.

## SUMMARY

1. Although some psychologists, environmentalists, and social critics question the merits of faster economic growth, economists generally assume that faster growth of *potential GDP* is socially beneficial.

2. The growth rate of potential GDP is the sum of two things: the growth rate of the labor force and the growth rate of *labor productivity*. The latter depends, among other things, on technological change and investment in new capital.

3. Only rising productivity can raise standards of living in the long run. And seemingly small differences in productivity growth rates can compound to enormous differences in living standards. This is one of our *Ideas for Beyond the Final Exam*.

4. Productivity growth has slowed markedly in the United States and elsewhere since about 1973, but the reasons are not well understood.

5. Unemployment exacts heavy financial and psychological costs from those who are its victims, costs that are borne quite unevenly by different groups in the population.

6. *Frictional unemployment* arises when people are between jobs for normal reasons. Thus, most frictional unemployment is desirable.

7. *Structural unemployment* is due to shifts in the pattern of demand or to technological change that makes certain skills obsolete.

8. *Cyclical unemployment* is the portion of unemployment that rises when real GDP grows slower than potential GDP and falls when the opposite is true.

9. Most economists nowadays think that *full employment* comes at an unemployment rate between 5 and 5.5 percent.

10. *Unemployment insurance* replaces nearly one-half of the lost income of unemployed persons who are insured. But only about one-third of the unemployed collect benefits, and no insurance program can bring back the lost output that could have been produced had these people been working.

11. People have many misconceptions about inflation. For example, many people believe that inflation systematically erodes *real wages*, are appalled by rising prices even when wages are rising just as fast, and blame inflation for any unfavorable changes in *relative prices*. All of these are myths.

12. Other costs of inflation are real, however. For example, inflation often redistributes income from lenders to borrowers.

13. This redistribution is ameliorated by adding the *expected rate of inflation* to the interest rate. But expectations often prove to be inaccurate.

14. The *real rate of interest* is the *nominal rate of interest* minus the expected rate of inflation.

15. Since the real rate of interest indicates the command over real resources that the borrower surrenders to the lender, it is of primary economic importance.

16. Yet public attention often is riveted on nominal rates of interest, and this confusion can lead to costly policy mistakes. This is an application of another of our *Ideas for Beyond the Final Exam*: Inflation distorts measurements.

17. Because nominal, not real, capital gains and interest are taxed, our tax system levies heavy taxes on income from capital when inflation is high.

18. Low inflation that proceeds at moderate and fairly predictable rates year after year carries far lower social costs than high or variable inflation. But even low, steady inflations entail costs.

19. The notion that low inflation inevitably accelerates into high inflation is a myth with no foundation in economic theory and no basis in historical fact.

## KEY TERMS

Economic growth 500

Potential GDP 501

Labor force 501

Labor productivity 502

GDP per capita 502

Productivity slowdown 503

Unemployment rate 505

Discouraged workers 509

Frictional unemployment 509

Structural unemployment 509

Cyclical unemployment 509

Full employment 510

Unemployment insurance 510

Purchasing power 512

Real wage rate 512

Relative prices 513

Redistribution by inflation 515

Real rate of interest 516

Nominal rate of interest 516

Expected rate of inflation 516

Capital gain 517

## QUESTIONS FOR REVIEW

1. Two countries start with equal GDPs. But Country A grows at an annual rate of 2 percent while Country B grows at an annual rate of 2.5 percent. After 25 years of this, how much larger than Country A is Country B?

2. If the growth rate of GDP per capita exceeds the growth rate of productivity (GDP per hour of work), are people working more or fewer hours per year?

3. Most economists believe that from 1993 to 1998, actual GDP in the United States grew faster than potential GDP. What, then, should have happened to the unemployment rate? (Check the data on the inside back cover of this book to see what actually happened.)

4. Why may it not be as terrible to become unemployed nowadays as it was during the Great Depression?

5. "Unemployment is no longer a social problem because unemployed workers receive unemployment benefits and other benefits that make up for most of their lost wages." Comment.

6. Using what you learned about aggregate demand and aggregate supply in the last chapter, try to explain why the U.S. economy has often failed to produce up to its potential. (You will learn more about this question in later chapters, so don't worry if you find the question difficult now.)

7. Why is it so difficult to define *full employment*? What unemployment rate should the government be shooting for today?

8. Show why each of the following complaints is based on a misunderstanding about inflation:

   a. "Inflation must be stopped because it robs workers of their purchasing power."

   b. "Inflation is a terrible social disease. It leads to unconscionably high prices for basic necessities."

   c. "Inflation makes it impossible for working people to afford many of the things they were hoping to buy."

   d. "Inflation must be stopped today, for if we do not stop it, it will surely accelerate to ruinously high rates and lead to disaster."

9. What is the *real interest rate* paid on a credit-card loan bearing 11 percent nominal interest per year, if the rate of inflation is

   a. zero?          d. 12 percent?

   b. 2 percent?     e. 15 percent?

   c. 6 percent?

10. Suppose you agree to lend money to your friend on the day you both enter college at what you both expect to be a zero *real* rate of interest. Payment is to be made at graduation, with interest at a fixed *nominal* rate. If inflation proves to be *lower* during your college years than what you both had expected, who will gain and who will lose?

---

 **APPENDIX** ▌ **HOW STATISTICIANS MEASURE INFLATION**

### INDEX NUMBERS FOR INFLATION

Inflation is generally measured by the change in some index of the general price level. For example, between 1973 and 1998, the Consumer Price Index (CPI) rose from 44.4 to 163, an increase of 267 percent. The meaning of the *change* is clear enough. But what are the meanings of the 44.4 figure for 1973 and the 163 figure for 1998? These numbers are *index numbers*.

An *index number* expresses the cost of a market basket of goods *relative to its cost in some "base" period.*

Because the CPI currently uses 1982–1984 as its base period, the CPI of 163 for 1998 means that it costs $163 to purchase the same basket of goods and services that cost $100 in 1982–1984.

Now, the particular basket of consumer goods and services under scrutiny really did not cost $100 in 1982–1984. When constructing index numbers, it is conventional to set the index at 100 in the base period. How is this conventional figure used in obtaining index numbers of other years? Very simply. Suppose that the budget needed to buy the roughly 250 items included in the CPI was $2,000 per month in 1982 to 1984 and $3,260 per month in 1998. Then the index is defined by the following rule:

$$\frac{\text{CPI in 1998}}{\text{CPI in 1982–1984}} = \frac{\text{Cost of the market basket in 1998}}{\text{Cost of the market basket in 1982–1984}}$$

Because the CPI in 1982–1984 is set at 100:

$$\frac{\text{CPI in 1998}}{100} = \frac{\$3,260}{\$2,000} = 1.63$$

or

$$\text{CPI in 1998} = 163$$

Exactly the same sort of equation enables us to calculate the CPI in any other year. We have the rule:

$$\text{CPI in given year} = \frac{\text{Cost of market basket in given year}}{\text{Cost of market basket in base year}} \times 100$$

Of course, not every combination of consumer goods that cost $2,000 in 1982–1984 rose to $3,260 by 1998. For example, a color TV set that cost $400 in 1983 might still have cost $400 in 1998, but a $400 hospital bill in 1983 might have ballooned to $1,400.

Because no two families buy precisely the same bundle of goods and services, no two families suffer precisely the same increase in their cost of living unless all prices rise at the same rate. Economists refer to this phenomenon as the *index number problem.*

When relative prices are changing, there is no such thing as a "perfect price index" that is correct for every consumer. Any statistical index will understate the increase in the cost of living for some families and overstate it for others. At best, the index can represent the situation of an "average" family.

### THE CONSUMER PRICE INDEX

The *Consumer Price Index (CPI)*, which is calculated and announced each month by the Bureau of Labor Statistics (BLS), is surely the most closely watched price index.

When you read in the newspaper or see on television that the "cost of living rose by 0.3 percent last month," chances are the reporter is referring to the CPI.

**The *Consumer Price Index (CPI)* is measured by pricing the items on a list representative of a typical urban household budget.**

To know what items to include and in what amounts, the BLS conducts an extensive survey of spending habits roughly once every decade. (The last one was done in the early 1990s.) This means that the *same* bundle of goods and services is used as a standard for 10 years or so, whether or not spending habits change.[9] Of course, spending habits do change, and this introduces a small error into the CPI's measurement of inflation.

A simple example will help us understand how the CPI is constructed. Imagine that college students purchase only three items—hamburgers, jeans, and movie tickets—and that we want to devise a cost-of-living index (call it SPI, or "student price index") for them. First, we would conduct a survey of spending habits in the base year. (Suppose it is 1983.) Table 24–5 represents the hypothetical results. You will note that the frugal students of that day spent only \$100 per month: \$56 on hamburgers, \$24 on jeans, and \$20 on movies.

Table 24–6 presents hypothetical prices of these same three items in 1999. Each price has risen by a different amount, ranging from 25 percent for jeans up to 50 percent for hamburgers. By how much has the SPI risen? Pricing the 1983 student budget at 1999 prices, we find that what once cost \$100 now costs \$142, as the calculation in Table 24–7 shows. Thus, the SPI, based on 1983 = 100, is

$$\text{SPI} = \frac{\text{Cost of budget in 1999}}{\text{Cost of budget in 1983}} \times 100$$

$$= \frac{\$142}{\$100} \times 100 = 142$$

TABLE 24–5

**Results of Student Expenditure Survey, 1983**

| Item | Average Price | Average Quantity Purchased per Month | Average Expenditure per Month |
|---|---|---|---|
| Hamburger | \$0.80 | 70 | \$56 |
| Jeans | 24.00 | 1 | 24 |
| Movie ticket | 5.00 | 4 | 20 |
| | | | Total \$100 |

[9] Economists call this a *base-period weight index* because the relative importance it attaches to the price of each item depends on how much money consumers actually chose to spend on the item during the base period.

FIGURE 24–6

**Prices in 1999**

| Item | Price | Increase over 1983 |
|---|---|---|
| Hamburger | \$1.20 | 50% |
| Jeans | 30.00 | 25 |
| Movie ticket | 7.00 | 40 |

FIGURE 24–7

**Cost of 1983 Student Budget in 1999 Prices**

| | |
|---|---|
| 70 Hamburgers at \$1.20 | \$84 |
| 1 pair of jeans at \$30 | 30 |
| 4 movie tickets at \$7 | 28 |
| | Total \$142 |

So the SPI in 1999 stands at 142, meaning that students' cost of living has increased 42 percent over the 16 years.

## HOW TO USE A PRICE INDEX TO "DEFLATE" MONETARY FIGURES

One of the most common uses of price indexes is in the comparison of monetary figures relating to two different points in time. The problem is that, if there has been inflation, the dollar is not a good measuring rod because it can buy less now than it did in the past.

Here is a simple example. Suppose the average student spent \$100 per month in 1983 but \$130 per month in 1999. If there was an outcry that students had become spendthrifts, how would you answer the charge?

The obvious answer is that a dollar in 1999 does not buy what it did in 1983. Specifically, our SPI shows us that it takes \$1.42 in 1999 to purchase what \$1 would purchase in 1983. To compare the spending habits of students in the two years, we must divide the 1999 spending figure by 1.42. Specifically, *real* spending per student in 1999 (where "real" is defined by 1983 dollars) is:

$$\text{Real spending in 1999} = \frac{\text{Nominal spending in 1999}}{\text{Price index of 1999}} \times 100$$

Thus:

$$\text{Real spending in 1999} = \frac{\$130}{142} \times 100 = \$91.55$$

This calculation shows that, despite appearances to the contrary, the change in nominal spending from $100 to $130 actually represented a *decrease* in real spending.

This calculation procedure is called *deflating by a price index*, and it serves to translate noncomparable monetary figures into more directly comparable real figures.

*Deflating* is the process of finding the real value of some monetary magnitude by dividing by some appropriate price index.

A good practical illustration is the real wage, a concept we have discussed in this chapter. Average hourly earnings in the U.S. economy were $8.02 in 1983 and $12.77 in 1998. Since the CPI in 1998 was 163 (with 1982–1984 as the base period), the real wage in 1998 (expressed in 1982–1984 dollars) was:

$$\text{Real wage in 1998} = \frac{\text{Money wage in 1998}}{\text{Price index of 1998}}$$

$$= \frac{\$12.77}{163} \times 100 = \$7.83$$

Thus, by this measure, the real wage fell 2.4 percent over the 15 years.

## ■ THE GDP DEFLATOR

In macroeconomics, one of the most important of the monetary magnitudes that we have to deflate is the nominal gross domestic product (GDP).

The price index used to deflate GDP is called the *GDP deflator*.

Our general principle for deflating a nominal magnitude tells us how to go from nominal GDP to real GDP:

$$\text{Real GDP} = \frac{\text{Nominal GDP}}{\text{GDP deflator}} \times 100$$

As with the CPI, the 100 simply serves to establish the base of the index as 100, rather than 1.00.

Some economists consider the GDP deflator to be a better measure of overall inflation in the economy than the Consumer Price Index. The main reason is that the GDP deflator is based on a broader market basket. As already mentioned, the CPI is based on the budget of a typical urban family. By contrast, the GDP deflator is constructed from a market basket that includes *every* item in the GDP—that is, every final good and service produced by the economy. Thus, in addition to prices of consumer goods, the GDP deflator includes the prices of airplanes, lathes, and other goods purchased by businesses—especially computers, which fall in price every year. It also includes government services.

For this reason, the two indexes rarely give the same measure of inflation. Usually the discrepancy is minor. But sometimes it can be substantial, as in 1990 when the CPI recorded a 6.1 percent inflation rate over 1989 while the GDP deflator recorded only 4.3 percent.

---

### S U M M A R Y

1. Inflation is measured by the percentage increase in an *index number* of prices, which shows how the cost of some basket of goods has changed over a period of time.

2. Because relative prices change all the time, and because different families purchase different items, no price index can represent precisely the experience of every family.

3. The *Consumer Price Index (CPI)* tries to measure the cost of living for an average urban household by pricing a typical market basket every month.

4. Price indexes like the CPI can be used to *deflate* monetary figures to make them more comparable. Deflation amounts to dividing the monetary magnitude by the appropriate price index.

5. The *GDP deflator* is a broader measure of economy-wide inflation than the CPI because it includes the prices of all goods and services in the economy.

---

### K E Y   T E R M S

## QUESTIONS FOR REVIEW

1. Just below, you will find the yearly average values of the Dow Jones Industrial Average, the most popular index of stock market prices, for four different years. The Consumer Price Index for each year (on a base of 1982–1984 = 100) can be found on the inside back cover of this book. Use these numbers to deflate all four stock market values. In which year were stocks worth the most?

| Year | Dow Jones Industrial Average |
|------|------------------------------|
| 1965 | 911 |
| 1972 | 951 |
| 1987 | 2,276 |
| 1994 | 3,794 |

2. Just below you will find nominal GDP and the GDP deflator for 1978, 1988, and 1998.

   a. Compute real GDP for each year.

   b. Compute the percentage change in nominal and real GDP from 1978 to 1988, and from 1988 to 1998.

   c. Compute the percentage change in the GDP deflator over these two periods.

| GDP Statistics | 1978 | 1988 | 1998 |
|----------------|------|------|------|
| Nominal GDP (billions of dollars) | 2,291 | 5,050 | 8,511 |
| GDP deflator | 50.9 | 86.1 | 112.7 |

3. Fill in the blanks in the following table of GDP statistics:

| | 1992 | 1993 | 1994 |
|---|------|------|------|
| Nominal GDP | 6,244 | | 6,947 |
| Real GDP | 6,244 | 6,390 | |
| GDP deflator | | 102.6 | 105.1 |

4. Use the following data to compute the College Price Index for 1999 using the base 1972 = 100.

| Item | Price in 1972 | Quantity per Month in 1972 | Price in 1999 |
|------|---------------|----------------------------|---------------|
| Button-down shirts | $10 | 1 | $25 |
| Loafers | 25 | 1 | 55 |
| Sneakers | 10 | 3 | 35 |
| Textbooks | 12 | 12 | 40 |
| Jeans | 12 | 3 | 30 |
| Restaurant meals | 5 | 11 | 14 |

5. Average hourly earnings in the U.S. economy during several past years were as follows:

| 1965 | 1974 | 1984 | 1994 |
|------|------|------|------|
| $2.46 | $4.24 | $8.32 | $11.13 |

Use the CPI numbers provided on the inside back cover to calculate the real wage (in 1982–1984 dollars) for each of these years. Which decade had the fastest growth of money wages? Which had the fastest growth of real wages?

6. The example in the appendix showed that the Student Price Index (SPI) rose by 42 percent from 1983 to 1999. You can understand the meaning of this better if you do the following:

   a. Use Table 24–5 to compute the fraction of total spending accounted for by each of the three items in 1983. Call these the "expenditure weights."

   b. Compute the weighted average of the percentage increases of the three prices shown in Table 24–6, using the expenditure weights you have just computed.

   c. You should get 42 percent as your answer. This shows that "inflation," as measured by the SPI, is a weighted average of the percentage price increases of all the items that are included in the index.

**Men are disposed, as a rule and on the average, to increase their consumption as their income increases, but not by as much as the increase in their income.**

John Maynard Keynes

# INCOME AND SPENDING: THE POWERFUL CONSUMER

I n Chapter 23, we noted that the strength of aggregate demand influences the performance of the economy. When aggregate demand is growing briskly, the economy is likely to be booming, though it may also be having trouble with inflation. When aggregate demand stagnates, a recession may follow.

This chapter begins our detailed study of the theory of income determination, the tool economists use to analyze issues like these. The theory is based on the concepts of aggregate demand and supply. In this and the next two chapters, we construct a simplified model of aggregate demand and learn where the *aggregate demand curve* of Chapter 23 comes from and what may make it shift. Then Chapter 27 completes the model by adding the *aggregate supply curve.*

This initial model of the macroeconomy can teach us much about the causes of unemployment and inflation. But it is too simple to deal with policy issues, because the government and the financial system are largely ignored. We remedy these omissions in Part VII, where we give government spending, taxation, and interest rates appropriately prominent roles. The influence of the exchange rate between the U.S. dollar and foreign currencies is considered in Part VIII.

## Demand Management and the Ornery Consumer

We suggested in Chapter 23 that the government sometimes wants to shift the aggregate demand curve. It can try to do so a number of ways. One direct approach is to alter its own spending, becoming extravagant when private demand is weak and miserly when private demand is strong. But the government can also take a more indirect route by using taxes and other policy tools to influence *private* spending decisions. Because consumer expenditures constitute about two-thirds of gross domestic product, the consumer presents the most tempting target to policymakers.

Although it can do many things to alter consumer spending, the government's principal weapon is the personal income tax. You may have already encountered Form 1040, the unwelcome New Year's greeting that every taxpayer receives from the federal government each January. If not, you have probably been on a payroll and seen a share of your wages deducted and sent to the Internal Revenue Service. It should be no mystery, then, how changes in personal taxes affect consumer spending. Any reduction in personal taxes leaves consumers with more after-tax income to spend. Any tax increase leaves less.

The linkage from taxes to spendable income to consumer spending seems direct and unmistakable, and, in a certain sense, it is. But a look at the history of some major tax changes aimed at altering consumer spending raises an intriguing question.

**Case 1: The 1964 Tax Cut**   Nineteen sixty-four was a good year for economists. For years they had proclaimed that a cut in personal income taxes would be a fine way to stimulate a stagnating economy. But their plea fell on deaf ears until President John F. Kennedy was persuaded of the basic logic of the argument and his successor, Lyndon Johnson, pushed the legislation through Congress. The 1964 tax cut was designed to spur consumer spending, and so it did. Consumers reacted just about as the textbooks of the day predicted, the economy improved rapidly and markedly, and economists smiled knowingly.

**Case 2: The 1975 Tax Cut**   The next major attempt to stimulate the economy by cutting taxes met with much less success. In the spring of 1975, as the economy hit a recessionary bottom, President Gerald Ford and Congress agreed on a temporary, one-year tax cut to spur consumer spending. But consumers confounded the wishes of the president and Congress by saving a good deal of their tax cuts rather than spending them.

**Case 3: The 1981–1984 Tax Cuts**  When President Ronald Reagan was elected in 1980, one of the first things he did was to push a series of reductions in personal income tax rates through Congress. Tax rates fell by about 23 percent between 1981 and 1984, and consumer spending increased by more or less the amounts that economists predicted, thereby contributing to a long economic expansion during the 1980s.

Thus, tax policy did more or less what it was expected to do in 1964 and 1981–1984, but was far less effective in 1975. Why? This chapter attempts to provide some answers. But before getting involved in such complicated issues, we must build some vocabulary and learn some basic concepts. Then, at the end of the chapter, we will see what went wrong in 1975.

## ■ AGGREGATE DEMAND, DOMESTIC PRODUCT, AND NATIONAL INCOME

First, the vocabulary. We have already introduced the concept of *gross domestic product* as the standard measure of the economy's total output.[1]

For the most part, firms produce goods in a market economy only if they think they can sell them. **Aggregate demand,** another concept from Chapter 23, is the total amount that all consumers, business firms, government agencies, and foreigners wish to spend on all U.S. final goods and services.

The downward-sloping aggregate demand curve of Chapter 23 alerted us to the fact that *aggregate demand is a schedule, not a fixed number.* The actual numerical value of aggregate demand depends on the price level; several reasons for this dependence will emerge in coming chapters.

But the level of aggregate demand also depends on a variety of other factors like consumer incomes, various government policies, and events in foreign countries. We can understand the nature of aggregate demand best if we break it up into its major components.

**Consumer expenditure** (*consumption* for short) is simply the total demand for all consumer goods and services. This is the focus of the current chapter, and we represent it by the letter *C*. Consumer expenditures constitute about two-thirds of total spending.

**Investment spending,** represented by the letter *I*, is the amount that firms spend on factories, machinery, and the like, plus the amount that families spend on new houses. Notice that this usage of the word *investment* differs from common parlance. Most people speak of *investing* in the stock market or in a bank account. But that kind of investment merely swaps one form of financial asset (such as money) for another form (such as a share of stock). When economists speak of *investment*, they mean instead the purchase of some *new, physical* asset, like a drill press or a computer or a house. Only these kinds of investments lead directly to additional demand for newly produced goods and, subsequently, to greater productive capacity.

**Aggregate demand** is the total amount that all consumers, business firms, and government agencies are willing to spend on final goods and services.

**Consumer expenditure,** symbolized by the letter *C*, is the total amount spent by consumers on newly produced goods and services (excluding purchases of new homes, which are considered investment goods).

**Investment spending,** symbolized by the letter *I*, is the sum of the expenditures of business firms on new plant and equipment and households on new homes. Financial "investments" are not included, nor are resales of existing physical assets.

---

[1] See Chapter 23, pages 483–487.

**Government purchases,** symbolized by the letter *G,* refer to the goods (such as airplanes and paper clips) and services (such as school teaching and police protection) purchased by all levels of government.

**Net exports,** symbolized by ($X - IM$), is the difference between U.S. exports and U.S. imports. It indicates the difference between what we sell to foreigners and what we buy from them.

**National income** is the sum of the incomes that all individuals in the economy earned in the forms of wages, interest, rents, and profits. It excludes government transfer payments and is calculated before any deductions are taken for income taxes.

**Disposable income** is the sum of the incomes of all the individuals in the economy after all taxes have been deducted and all transfer payments have been added.

The third major component of aggregate demand, **government purchases** of goods and services, includes items like paper, computers, airplanes, ships, and labor bought by all levels of government. We use the symbol *G* for this variable.

The final component of aggregate demand, **net exports,** are simply defined as U.S. exports *minus* U.S. imports. The reasoning here is simple. Part of the demand for American goods and services originates beyond our borders—as when foreigners buy our wheat, our software, and our banking services. So these goods and services must be added to U.S. domestic demand. Similarly, some items included in *C* and *I* are not American made. Think, for example, of German beer, Japanese cars, and Korean textiles. So these must be subtracted if we want to measure total spending on U.S. products. The addition of exports, which we represent by the symbol *X*, and the subtraction of imports, *IM*, leads us to the following shorthand definition of aggregate demand:

Aggregate demand is the sum $C + I + G + (X - IM)$.

The last concept we need for our vocabulary is a way to measure the total *income* of all individuals in the economy. It comes in two versions: one for before-tax incomes, called **national income,** and one for after-tax incomes, called **disposable income.**[2] The term *disposable income*, which we will abbreviate *DI*, is meant to be descriptive. Because it tells us how many dollars consumers actually have available to spend or to save, it will play a prominent role in this chapter and subsequent discussions.

## THE CIRCULAR FLOW OF SPENDING, PRODUCTION, AND INCOME

Enough definitions. How do these three concepts—domestic product, total expenditure, and national income—interact in a market economy? We can answer this best with a rather elaborate diagram (Figure 25–1). For obvious reasons, Figure 25–1 is called a *circular flow diagram.* It depicts a large, circular tube in which an imaginary fluid circulates in a clockwise direction. At several breaks in the tube, some of the fluid leaks out or additional fluid is injected in.

**FIGURE 25-1**

**The Circular Flow of Expenditures and Income**

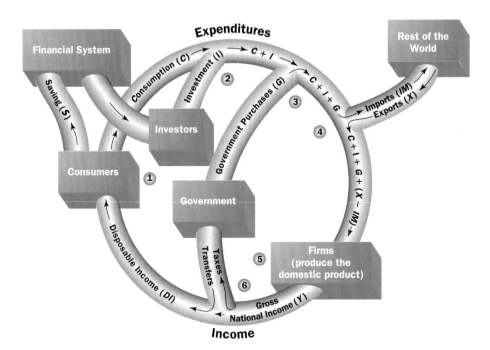

2 More detailed information on these and other concepts is provided in the appendix to this chapter.

Let's examine this system, beginning on the far left. At point 1 on the circle, we find consumers. Disposable income *(DI)* flows into their pockets, and two things flow out: consumption *(C)*, which stays in the circular flow, and saving *(S)*, which "leaks out." This depicts the fact that consumers normally spend less than they earn, and save the balance. The "leakage" to saving, of course, does not disappear; it flows into the financial system via banks, mutual funds, and so on. We postpone consideration of what happens within the financial system until Chapter 30.

The upper loop of the circular flow represents expenditures, and as we move clockwise to point 2, we encounter the first "injection" into the flow: investment spending *(I)*. The diagram shows this injection as coming from "investors"—a group that includes both business firms and home buyers.[3] As the circular flow moves past point 2, it is bigger than it was before: Total spending has increased from *C* to *C + I*.

At point 3, there is yet another injection. The government adds its demand for goods and services *(G)* to those of consumers and investors *(C + I)*. Now aggregate demand is up to *C + I + G*.

The final leakage and injection come at point 4. Here we see export spending entering the circular flow from abroad and import spending leaking out. The net effect of these two forces may increase or decrease the circular flow, depending on whether net exports are positive or negative. In either case, by the time we pass point 4, we have accumulated the full amount of aggregate demand, *C + I + G + (X − IM)*. The circular flow diagram shows this aggregate demand for goods and services arriving at the business firms, which are located at point 5. Responding to this demand, firms produce the domestic product. As the circular flow emerges from the firms, however, we rename it *gross national income*. Why? The reason is that, except for some complications explained in the appendix:

National income and domestic product must be equal.

Why is this so? When a firm produces and sells $100 worth of output, it pays most of the proceeds to its workers, to people who have lent it money, and to the landlord who owns the property on which the plant is located. All of these payments represent *income* to some individuals. But what about the rest? Suppose, for example, that the firm pays wages, interest, and rent totaling $90 million and it sells its output for $100 million. What happens to the remaining $10 million? The firm's owners receive it as *profits*. Because these owners are citizens of the country, their incomes also count in national income.[4] Thus, when we add up all the wages, interest, rents, *and profits* in the economy to obtain the national *income*, we must arrive at the *value of output*.

The lower loop of the circular flow diagram traces the flow of income by showing national income leaving firms and heading for consumers. But some of the flow takes a detour along the way. At point 6, the government does two things. First, it siphons off a portion of the national income in the form of taxes. Second, it adds back government **transfer payments**, like unemployment compensation and Social Security benefits, which government agencies give to certain individuals as outright *grants* rather than as payments for goods or services rendered.

By subtracting taxes from gross domestic product (GDP) and adding transfer payments, we obtain disposable income:[5]

**Transfer payments** are sums of money that the government gives certain individuals as outright *grants* rather than as payments for services rendered to employers. Some common examples are Social Security and unemployment benefits.

$$DI = GDP − \text{Taxes} + \text{Transfer payments}$$
$$= GDP − (\text{Taxes} − \text{Transfers})$$
$$= Y − T$$

where *Y* represents GDP and the symbol *T* represents taxes *net of transfers*. Disposable income flows unimpeded to consumers at point 1, and the cycle repeats.

---

[3] You are reminded that expenditure on housing is part of *I*, not part of *C*.

[4] Some of the income paid out by American companies goes to noncitizens. Similarly, some Americans earn income from foreign firms. This complication is dealt with in the appendix.

[5] This definition omits a few minor details, which are explained in the appendix.

"When I refer to it as disposable income, don't get the wrong idea."

Figure 25–1 raises several complicated questions, which we pose now but will not try to answer until subsequent chapters.

■ Does the flow of spending and income grow larger or smaller as we move clockwise around the circle? Why?

■ Is the output that firms produce at point 5 (the GDP) equal to aggregate demand? If so, what makes these two quantities equal? If not, what happens?

The next chapter provides the answers to these two questions.

■ Do the government's accounts balance, so that what flows in at point 6 (taxes minus transfers) is equal to what flows out at point 3 (government purchases)? What happens if they do not balance?

This important question is first addressed in Chapter 29 and then recurs many times, especially in Chapter 33, which discusses budget deficits.

■ Is our international trade balanced, so that exports equal imports? More generally, what factors determine net exports and what consequences arise from trade deficits or surpluses?

We take up these questions in the next two chapters and then deal with them more fully in Part VIII.

However, we cannot dig very deeply into any of these issues until we first understand what goes on at point 1, where consumers make decisions. We turn next, therefore, to determinants of consumer spending.

## CONSUMER SPENDING AND INCOME: THE IMPORTANT RELATIONSHIP

A **scatter diagram** is a graph showing the relationship between two variables (such as consumer spending and disposable income). Each year is represented by a point in the diagram. The coordinates of each year's point show the values of the two variables in that year.

Recall that we started the chapter with a puzzle: Why did consumers respond more or less as expected to tax changes in 1964 and the early 1980s, but not in 1975? An economist interested in predicting how consumer spending will respond to a change in personal income tax payments must first ask how $C$ (consumption) relates to disposable income, for tax increases decrease after-tax income, and tax reductions increase after-tax income. This section, therefore, examines what we know about how consumer spending responds to changes in disposable income.

Figure 25–2 depicts the historical paths of $C$ and $DI$ for the United States since 1929. The association is obviously close and certainly suggests that consumption will rise whenever disposable income does and fall whenever income falls. The vertical distance between the two lines represents personal saving. Notice how little saving consumers did during the Great Depression of the 1930s, where the two lines are very close together, and how much they did during World War II, when many consumer goods were either unavailable or rationed, leaving consumers with little on which to spend money.

Of course, knowing that consumer expenditures, *C*, will move in the same direction as disposable income, *DI*, is not enough for policy planners. They need to know *how much* one variable will go up when the other rises a given amount. Figure 25–3 presents the same data as in Figure 25–2, but in a way designed to help answer the "how much" question.

Economists call such pictures **scatter diagrams.** Such diagrams are very useful in predicting how one economic variable (in this case, consumer spending) will change in response to a change in another economic variable (in this case, disposable income). Each dot in the diagram represents the data on *C* and *DI* corresponding to a particular year. For example, the point labeled

FIGURE 25-2

**Consumer Spending and Disposable Income**

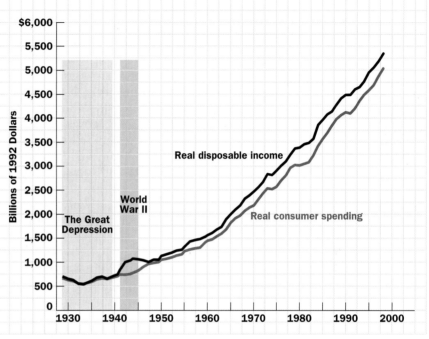

**Scatter Diagram of Consumer Spending and Disposable Income**          FIGURE 25-3

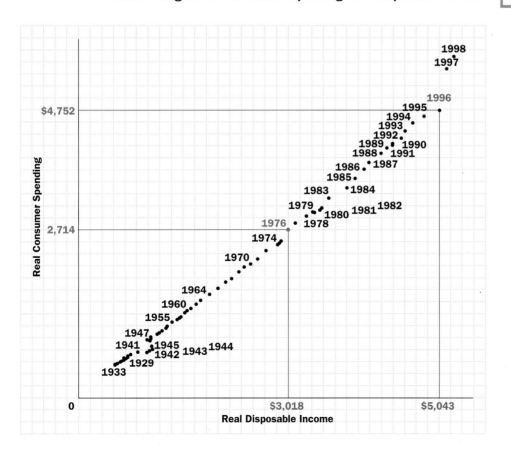

NOTE: Figures are in billions of 1992 dollars.

"1976" shows that real consumer expenditures in 1976 were $2,714 billion (which we read off the vertical axis), while real disposable incomes amounted to $3,018 billion (which we read off the horizontal axis). Similarly, each year from 1929 to 1998 is represented by its own dot in Figure 25–3.

How can such a diagram assist fiscal policy planners? Imagine that this is 1963 and you must decide whether to recommend to Congress a tax cut of $5 billion, $10 billion, or $15 billion. You have forecasts of what consumer expenditures are expected to be if taxes are not reduced. This, plus other forecasts of investment, government spending, and net exports has led you to conclude that aggregate demand in 1964 will be insufficient if the government does not reduce taxes.

To assist your imaginary decision, another scatter diagram appears in Figure 25–4. This one removes the points for 1964 through 1998, which appear in Figure 25–3; after all, these were unknown in 1963. Years prior to 1947 have also been removed because, as Figure 25–2 showed, both the Great Depression and wartime rationing seriously disturbed the normal relationship between *DI* and *C* during that period. With no more training in economics than you have right now, what would you suggest?

One rough-and-ready approach is to get a ruler, set it down on Figure 25–4, and sketch a straight line that comes as close as possible to hitting all the points. That has been done for you in the figure, and you can see that it comes remarkably close to touching all of the points. The line summarizes, in a very rough way, the consumption-income relationship that is the focus of this chapter. The two variables do indeed appear to be closely related.

The *slope* of the straight line in Figure 25–4 is very important.[6] Specifically, we note that it is:

$$\text{Slope} = \frac{\text{Vertical change}}{\text{Horizontal change}} = \frac{\$90 \text{ billion}}{\$100 \text{ billion}} = 0.90$$

Because the horizontal change involved in the move from *A* to *B* represents a rise in disposable income of $100 billion (from $1,300 billion to $1,400 billion), and the corresponding vertical change represents the associated $90 billion rise in consumer spending (from $1,200 billion to $1,290 billion), the slope of the line indicates how consumer spending responds to changes in disposable income. In this case, we see that each additional $1 of income leads to 90 cents of additional spending.

In terms of the 1964 policy issue, this line can therefore help provide an answer to the question: How much more consumer spending will be induced by tax cuts of $5 billion, $10 billion, or $15 billion, if consumers react roughly the same way they did in the past? First, we need to keep in mind that each dollar of tax cut increases disposable income by $1. Then we apply the finding from Figure 25–4 that each additional dollar of disposable income increases consumer spending by 90 cents to conclude that proposed tax cuts of $5 billion, $10 billion, or $15 billion would be expected to increase consumer spending by $4.5 billion, $9.0 billion, and $13.5 billion, respectively. Similar questions addressed by economists in 1964 led to a decision to cut taxes by about $9 billion.

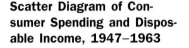

**FIGURE 25–4**

**Scatter Diagram of Consumer Spending and Disposable Income, 1947–1963**

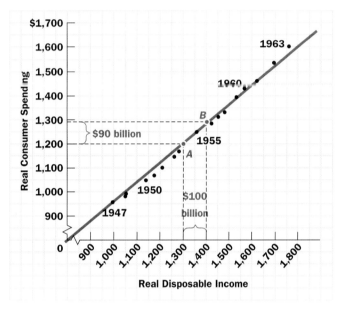

NOTE: Figures are in billions of 1992 dollars.

## THE CONSUMPTION FUNCTION AND THE MARGINAL PROPENSITY TO CONSUME

It has been said that economics is just systematized common sense. Let us, then, try to organize and generalize what has been a completely intuitive discussion thus far. One thing we have discovered is the close and apparently reliable relationship

---

[6] To review the concept of *slope*, turn back to Chapter 2, page 20.

between consumer spending, *C*, and disposable income, *DI*. Economists call this relationship the **consumption function.**

A second fact we have gleaned from these figures is that the *slope* of the consumption function is fairly constant. We infer this from the fact that the straight line drawn in Figure 25–4 comes so close to touching every point. If the slope of the consumption function had varied widely, we could not have done so well with a single straight line.[7] Because of its importance in such applications as the tax-cut example, economists have given a special name to this slope—the **marginal propensity to consume,** or **MPC** for short. The MPC tells us how much more consumers will spend if disposable income rises by $1.

$$\text{MPC} = \frac{\text{Change in } C}{\text{Change in } DI \text{ that produces the change in } C}$$

The MPC is best illustrated by an example, and for this purpose we turn away from U.S. data for a moment and look at consumption and income data of a hypothetical country whose data resemble those for the United States, except that they happen to be nice round numbers, which facilitates computation.

Columns (1) and (2) of Table 25–1 show annual consumer expenditure and disposable income from 1994 to 1999. These two columns constitute the consumption function and are plotted in Figure 25–5. Column (3) in the table shows the marginal propensity to consume (MPC), which is the slope of the line in Figure 25–5; it is derived from the first two columns. We can see that between 1996 and 1997, *DI* rose by $400 billion (from $4,000 billion to $4,400 billion) while *C* rose by $300 billion (from $3,300 billion to $3,600 billion). Thus, the MPC was:

$$\frac{\text{Change in } C}{\text{Change in } DI} = \frac{\$300}{\$400} = 0.75$$

As you can easily verify, the MPC between any other pair of years in Table 25–1 is also 0.75. This explains why the slope of the line in Figure 25–4 was so crucial in estimating the effect of a tax cut. This slope, which we found to be 0.90, is simply the MPC for the United States. The MPC tells us how much *additional* spending will be induced by each dollar *change* in disposable income. For each $1 of tax cut, economists expect consumption to rise by $1 times the marginal propensity to consume.

The **consumption function** shows the relationship between total consumer expenditures and total disposable income in the economy, holding all other determinants of consumer spending constant.

The **marginal propensity to consume (MPC)** is the ratio of changes in consumption relative to changes in disposable income that produce the change in consumption. On a graph, it appears as the slope of the consumption function.

**FIGURE 25–5**

**A Consumption Function**

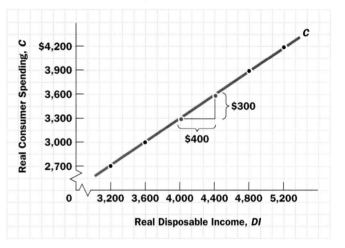

NOTE: Figures are in billions of dollars per year.

**Consumption and Income in a Hypothetical Economy**  |  **TABLE 25–1**

| Year | (1) Consumption, *C* | (2) Disposable Income, *DI* | (3) Marginal Propensity to Consume, MPC |
|------|------|------|------|
| 1994 | $2,700 | $3,200 | |
| 1995 | 3,000 | 3,600 | 0.75 |
| 1996 | 3,300 | 4,000 | 0.75 |
| 1997 | 3,600 | 4,400 | 0.75 |
| 1998 | 3,900 | 4,800 | 0.75 |
| 1999 | 4,200 | 5,200 | 0.75 |

NOTE: Amounts are in billions of dollars.

---

[7] Figure 25–4 is limited to 17 years of data, but try fitting a single straight line to all the data in Figure 25–3. You will find that you can do remarkably well.

To estimate the *initial* effect of a tax cut on consumer spending, economists must first estimate the MPC and then multiply the amount of the tax cut by the estimated MPC. But because they never know the true MPC with certainty, their prediction is always subject to some margin of error.[8]

In 1963, for example, government economists multiplied the anticipated $9 billion tax cut by the estimated MPC of 0.90 and concluded that consumer spending would rise initially approximately $8 billion. Their estimate seems to have been quite accurate.

## MOVEMENTS ALONG VERSUS SHIFTS OF THE CONSUMPTION FUNCTION

Unfortunately, this sort of calculation does not always yield such precise results. Among the most important reasons is that the consumption function does not always stand still.

You will recall from Chapter 5 the important distinction between a *movement along* a demand curve and a *shift* of the curve. A demand curve depicts the relationship between quantity demanded and *one* of its many determinants—price. Thus, a change in price causes a *movement along the demand curve*, but a change in any other factor that influences quantity demanded causes a *shift of the entire demand curve.*

Because factors other than disposable income influence consumer spending, a similar distinction is vital to understanding real-world consumption functions. Look back at the definition of the consumption function in the margin of the previous page. A change in disposable income leads to a *movement along the consumption function* precisely because the consumption function depicts the relationship between $C$ and $DI$. Such movements, which are just what we have been considering so far, are indicated by the red arrows in Figure 25–6.

But consumption also has other determinants, and a change in any of them will *shift the entire consumption function*—as indicated by the blue arrows in Figure 25–6. Such shifts account for many of the errors in forecasting consumption. To summarize:

Any change in disposable income moves us *along* a given consumption function. But a change in any of the other determinants of consumption *shifts* the entire consumption schedule (see Figure 25–6).

Let us now list some of these "other determinants" that can shift the consumption function.

---

FIGURE 25-6

**Shifts of the Consumption Function**

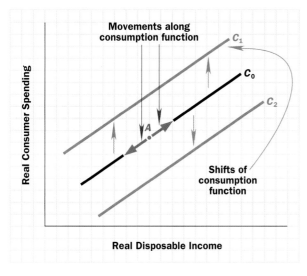

### OTHER DETERMINANTS OF CONSUMER SPENDING

**CONSUMER WEALTH**   One factor affecting consumption is consumers' *wealth*, which is a source of purchasing power in addition to income. Wealth and income are different things. For example, a retiree with a large bank balance may earn little current *income* but may have quite a bit of wealth. But a high-flying investment banker who spends every penny she earns will not accumulate wealth.

To appreciate the importance of the distinction, think about two consumers, each of whom earn $40,000 a year. If one of them has $100,000 in the bank, while the other has no assets at all, who do you think will spend more? Presumably the one with the big bank account. The general point is that current income is not the only source of spendable funds; households can also finance spending by withdrawals from their bank accounts or by cashing in other forms of wealth.

One important application of this analysis is the effect of the stock market on consumer spending. A stock market boom will raise the consumption function, as

---

[8] The word *initial* in the first sentence is an important one. Later chapters explain why the effects discussed in this chapter are only the beginning of the story.

depicted in the shift from $C_0$ to $C_1$ in Figure 25–6. That is just what economists think happened in 1997 and 1998, when the stock market boomed and American consumers went on a spending spree. Conversely, a collapse of stock prices should shift the consumption function down (see the shift from $C_0$ to $C_2$).

**THE PRICE LEVEL**    But stocks are hardly the only form of wealth. People hold much household wealth in forms with values that are fixed in money terms. Cash itself is the most obvious example, but government bonds, bank accounts, and corporate bonds have fixed face values in money terms. The purchasing power of such a *money-fixed asset* obviously declines whenever the price level rises, which means that the asset can buy less. For example, if the price level rises by 10 percent, a $1,000 government bond will buy about 10 percent less than it could when prices were lower. Consequently:

> Higher prices decrease the demand for goods and services because they erode the purchasing power of consumer wealth.

This is no trivial matter. Consumers in the United States hold money-fixed assets worth over $5 *trillion*, so that each 1 percent rise in the price level reduces the purchasing power of consumer wealth by over $50 billion, a tidy sum. The process, of course, operates equally well in reverse, because a decline in the price level increases the purchasing power of money fixed assets:

> Lower prices increase the demand for goods and services by enhancing the purchasing power of consumer wealth.

For these reasons, a change in the price level will shift the entire consumption function. Specifically:

> A higher price level leads to lower real wealth and therefore to less spending *at any given level of real income.* Thus, a higher price level leads to a lower consumption function (such as $C_2$ in Figure 25–6), and a lower price level leads to a higher consumption function (such as $C_1$ in Figure 25–6).

Because students often get confused on this point, it is worth repeating that the depressing effect of the price level on consumer spending works through real *wealth*, not through real *income*. The consumption function relates *real consumer income* to *real consumer spending*. Thus, any decline in real income, regardless of its cause, moves the economy leftward *along a fixed consumption function;* it does not shift the consumption function.[9] By contrast, any decline in *real wealth* will *shift the whole consumption function downward*, meaning that people spend less at any given level of real income.

**THE INFLATION RATE**    Prices may be high and rising slowly, or they may be low but rising rapidly. Therefore, we must distinguish between the depressing effect that a high *price level* has on real consumer spending and any effect that the *inflation rate* (that is, the rate at which the price level is *rising*) might have.

If inflation has any effect on consumer spending, it must be small. Economists are not even sure whether inflation stimulates or depresses spending. It used to be thought that high inflation rates induce consumers to spend faster to "beat" the higher prices that loom on the horizon. But actual consumer behavior seems to belie this notion. Consumers have actually spent a *higher* fraction of their disposable incomes in the 1990s, when inflation has been very low, than they did in the inflationary 1970s.

Because no strong evidence suggests that the rate of inflation shifts the consumption function systematically in one direction or the other, we shall assume that the position of the consumption function is influenced by the *price level*, but not by the *inflation rate*.

**THE REAL INTEREST RATE**    A higher real rate of interest raises the rewards for saving. For this reason, many people believe it is "obvious" that higher real interest

---

[9] This is true even if a rise in the price level lies behind the decline in real income. However, wages and prices normally move together, so there is no reason to expect real wages to fall when the price level rises.

---

● **POLICY DEBATE** ▌ **USING THE TAX CODE TO SPUR SAVING**

---

Compared to the citizens of most industrial nations, Americans save rather little. In fact, household saving dropped to zero in late 1998! Many policymakers consider this lack of savings a serious problem, so they have proposed numerous changes in the tax laws to increase incentives to save. In 1997, for example, Congress expanded Individual Retirement Accounts (IRAs), which allow taxpayers to shelter some earnings from income tax by saving it, and reduced the tax rate on capital gains.

Both of these tax changes, and others like them, increased the after-tax return on saving. For example, under the current tax system, if you put away money in a bank at a 6 percent rate of interest and your income is taxed at a 30 percent rate, your after-tax rate of return on saving is just 4.2 percent (70 percent of 6 percent). But if the interest is earned tax-free in an IRA, you get to keep the full 6 percent. Over long periods of time, this seemingly small interest differential compounds to an enormous difference in returns. For example, $100 invested for 20 years at 4.2 percent interest grows to $227.70. But at 6 percent, it grows to $320.71. Members of Congress who advocate tax incentives for saving argue that lower tax rates will induce Americans to save more.

The idea is eminently reasonable and has many supporters. Unfortunately, the evidence runs squarely against it. Economists have conducted many studies of the effect of higher rates of return on saving. With very few exceptions, they detect little or no effect. Although the evidence fails to support the "commonsense" solution to the undersaving problem, the debate goes on. Many people, it seems, refuse to believe the evidence.

---

rates must encourage saving and therefore discourage spending. Statistical studies of this relationship suggest otherwise, however. With very few exceptions, they show that interest rates have virtually no effect on consumption decisions in the United States. Hence, in developing our model of the economy, we will assume that changes in real interest rates do not shift the consumption function. (See the accompanying Policy Debate box, "Using the Tax Code to Spur Saving.")

**FUTURE INCOME EXPECTATIONS** It is hardly earth shattering to suggest that consumers' expectations about their future incomes may affect how much they spend today. This final determinant of consumer spending turns out to hold the key to resolving the puzzle posed at the beginning of the chapter: Why did tax policy succeed so well in 1964 and the early 1980s but fail to alter consumer spending much in 1975?

### Why Tax Policy Failed in 1975

To understand how expectations of future incomes affect current consumer expenditures, consider the abbreviated life histories of three consumers given in Table 25–2. (The reason for giving our three imaginary individuals such odd names will be apparent shortly.) The consumer named "No Change" earned $100 in each of the years considered in the table. The consumer named "Temporary Rise" earned $100 in three of the four years, but had a good year in 1975. The consumer named

---

| TABLE 25–2 | **Incomes of Three Consumers** |

**Incomes of Three Consumers**

| Consumer | Incomes in Each Year | | | | |
|---|---|---|---|---|---|
| | **1974** | **1975** | **1976** | **1977** | **Total Income** |
| No Change | $100 | $100 | $100 | $100 | $400 |
| Temporary Rise | 100 | 120 | 100 | 100 | 420 |
| Permanent Rise | 100 | 120 | 120 | 120 | 460 |

"Permanent Rise" enjoyed a permanent increase in income in 1975 and was therefore clearly the richest.

Now let us use our common sense to figure out how much each of these consumers might have spent in 1975. Temporary Rise and Permanent Rise had the same income that year. Do you think they spent the same amount? Not if they had some ability to foresee their future incomes, because Permanent Rise was richer in the long run.

Now compare No Change and Temporary Rise. Temporary Rise had 20 percent higher income in 1975 ($120 versus $100), but only 5 percent more over the entire four-year period ($420 versus $400). Do you think his spending in 1975 was closer to 20 percent above No Change's, or closer to 5 percent above it? Most people guess the latter.

The point of this example is that consumers very reasonably decide on their *current* consumption spending by looking at their *long-run* income prospects. This should come as no surprise to a college student. Are you spending only what you earn this year? Probably not. But that does not make you a foolish spendthrift. On the contrary, you know that your college education gives you a strong expectation of a much higher incomes in the future, and you are spending with that in mind.

Now let us see what all this has to do with the failure of the 1975 income tax cut. For this purpose, imagine that the three rows in Table 25–2 now represent the entire economy under three different government policies. Recall that 1975 was the year of the temporary tax cut. The first row (No Change) shows the unchanged path of disposable income in the absence of any tax cut. The second (Temporary Rise) shows an increase in disposable income attributable to a tax cut *for one year only*. The bottom row (Permanent Rise) shows a policy that increases *DI* in *every future year* by cutting taxes permanently in 1975. Which of the two lower rows do you imagine would have generated more consumer spending in 1975? The bottom row (Permanent Rise), of course. What we have concluded, then, is this:

**Permanent cuts in income taxes cause greater increases in consumer spending than do temporary cuts of equal magnitude.**

The application of this analysis to the case of the 1975 tax cut is immediate. The temporary tax cuts were clearly one-time increases in income like that experienced by Temporary Rise in Table 25–2. No future income was affected, so consumers did not increase their spending as much as government officials had hoped.

We have, then, what appears to be a general principle, backed up both by historical evidence and common sense. Permanent changes in income taxes have more significant impacts on consumer spending than do temporary changes. Though it may seem obvious, this is not a lesson you would have learned from an introductory textbook 25 years ago. It is one that we learned the hard way, through bitter experience. Indeed, not all policymakers seem to have learned this lesson. In 1997, the Japanese government tried to stimulate its moribund economy by enacting a one-year income tax cut. The policy failed.

## ■ HOW PREDICTABLE IS CONSUMER BEHAVIOR?

We have now learned enough to see why the economist's problem in predicting how consumers will react to an increase or decrease in taxes is not nearly as simple as suggested earlier in this chapter.

One principal problem seems to be anticipating how taxpayers will view any changes in the income tax law. If the government *says* that a tax cut is permanent, will consumers take the government at its word and increase their spending accordingly? Perhaps not, if the government has a history of raising taxes after promising to keep them low. Similarly, when (as in 1975) the government explicitly announces that a tax cut is temporary, will consumers always believe the announcement? Or might they greet it with a hefty dose of skepticism? Such a reaction is quite possible if there is a history of "temporary" tax changes that stayed on the books indefinitely.

Thus, the effectiveness of any *future* tax policy move may well depend on the government's *past* track record. A government that repeatedly uses a succession of so-called "permanent" tax cuts and tax increases for short-run stabilization purposes may find consumers beginning to ignore the tax changes entirely. The story of the boy who cried wolf should probably be required reading for fiscal policy planners.

Nor is this the only problem. Consumer spending may be influenced by large and rapid accumulations of wealth (as happened when the stock marked soared between 1995 and 1998) or by sizable losses of wealth (such as in the stock market crash of 1987). Poor forecasts of future prices may lead consumption forecasts astray. Also, other hazards arise that we have not even mentioned here. Economic predictions are inexact, and predictions of consumption illustrate this well.

We could say much more about the determinants of consumption, but it is best to leave the rest to more advanced courses. For we are now ready to apply our knowledge of the consumption function to the construction of the first model of the whole economy. Although it is true that income determines consumption, the consumption function in turn helps to determine the level of income. If that sounds like circular reasoning, read the next chapter!

## SUMMARY

1. *Aggregate demand* is the total volume of goods and services purchased by consumers, businesses, government units, and foreigners. It can be expressed as the sum $C + I + G + (X - IM)$, where $C$ is *consumer spending*, $I$ is *investment spending*, $G$ is *government purchases*, and $X - IM$ is *net exports*.

2. Aggregate demand is a schedule: the aggregate quantity demanded depends (among other things) on the price level. But, for any given price level, aggregate demand is a number.

3. Economists reserve the term *investment* to refer to purchases of newly produced factories, machinery, and houses.

4. Gross domestic product is the total volume of final goods and services produced in the country.

5. *National income* is the sum of the *before-tax* wages, interest, rents, and profits earned by all individuals in the economy. By necessity, it must be approximately equal to domestic product.

6. *Disposable income* is the sum of the incomes of all individuals in the economy *after taxes and transfers*. It is the chief determinant of consumer expenditures.

7. All of these concepts, and others, can be depicted in a *circular flow diagram* that shows expenditures on all four sources flowing into business firms and national income flowing out.

8. The close relationship between consumer spending, $C$, and disposable income, $DI$, is called the *consumption function*. Its slope, which is used to predict the change in consumption that will be caused by a change in income taxes, is called the *marginal propensity to consume (MPC)*.

9. Changes in disposable income move us *along a given consumption function*. Changes in any of the other variables that affect $C$ *shift the entire consumption function*. Among the most important of these other variables are total consumer wealth, the price level, and expected future incomes.

10. Because consumers hold so many money fixed assets, they lose purchasing power when prices rise, which leads them to reduce their spending.

11. The government often has tried to manipulate aggregate demand by influencing private consumption decisions, usually through changes in the personal income tax. Although this policy seemed to work well in 1964 and 1981, it did not work well in 1975.

12. Future income prospects help explain these disparate events. The 1975 tax cut was temporary and therefore left future incomes unaffected. By contrast, the 1964 and 1981–1984 tax cuts were permanent and affected future as well as current incomes. It is no surprise, then, that the 1964 and 1981 actions had stronger effects on spending than did the 1975 action.

## KEY TERMS

1. What are the four components of aggregate demand? Which of these is the largest? Which is the smallest?

2. What is the difference between *investment* as the term is used by most people and *investment* as defined by an economist? Which of the following acts constitute investment according to the economist's definition?

   a. Intel builds a new factory to manufacture semiconductors.

   b. You buy 100 shares of Intel stock.

   c. A small chip maker goes bankrupt, and Intel purchases its factory and equipment.

   d. Your family buys a newly constructed home from a developer.

   e. Your family buys an older home from another family. (*Hint:* Are any *new* products demanded by this action?)

3. What would the circular flow diagram (Figure 25–1) look like in an economy with no government? Draw one for yourself.

4. The marginal propensity to consume (MPC) for the nation as a whole is roughly 0.90. Explain in words what this means. What is your personal MPC at this stage in your life? How might that change by the time you are your parents' age?

5. Look at the scatter diagram in Figure 25–3. What does it tell you about what was going on in this country in the years 1942 to 1945?

6. What is a consumption function, and why is it a useful device for government economists planning a tax cut?

7. On a piece of graph paper, construct a consumption function from the data given below and determine the MPC.

| Year | Consumer Spending | Disposable Income |
|------|-------------------|-------------------|
| 1995 | $1,200 | $1,500 |
| 1996 | 1,440 | 1,800 |
| 1997 | 1,680 | 2,100 |
| 1998 | 1,920 | 2,400 |
| 1999 | 2,160 | 2,700 |

8. In which direction will the consumption function shift if the price level rises? Show this on your graph.

9. Explain why permanent tax cuts are likely to lead to bigger increases in consumer spending than are temporary tax cuts.

10. (More difficult) Between 1990 and 1991, real disposable income (in 1992 dollars) actually fell from $4,490 billion to $4,484 billion, owing to a recession. Use the data on real consumption expenditures given on the inside front cover of this book to compare the change in *C* to the change in *DI*. Explain why dividing the two does *not* give a good estimate of the marginal propensity to consume.

11. In 1997, Congress enacted several tax incentives designed to promote saving. If such saving incentives had been successful, how would the consumption function have shifted?

---

### ● APPENDIX   ▌ NATIONAL INCOME ACCOUNTING

The type of macroeconomic analysis presented in this book dates from the publication of John Maynard Keynes's *The General Theory of Employment, Interest, and Money* in 1936. But at that time there was really no way to test Keynes's theories because the necessary data did not exist. It took some years for the theoretical notions used by Keynes to find concrete expression in real-world data.

> The system of measurement devised for expressing macroeconomic data is called *national income accounting*.

The development of this system of accounts ranks as a great achievement in applied economics, perhaps as important in its own right as Keynes's theoretical work. Without it, the practical value of Keynesian analysis would be severely limited. Economists spent long hours wrestling with the many difficult conceptual questions that arose as they translated the theory into numbers, but they had one acknowledged leader: the late Professor Simon Kuznets, who was subsequently awarded the Nobel Prize in economics for his contributions to economic measurement techniques. Along the way some more-or-less arbitrary decisions and conventions had to be made. You may not agree with all of them, but the accounting framework that was devised is eminently serviceable, though, inevitably, it has some limitations that must be understood.

### ▌ DEFINING GDP: EXCEPTIONS TO THE RULES

We first encountered the concept of gross domestic product (GDP) in Chapter 3.

> Gross domestic product (GDP) is the sum of the money values of all final goods and services produced during a specified period of time, usually one year.

However, the definition of GDP has certain exceptions that we have not yet noted.

First, the treatment of government output involves a minor departure from the principle of using market prices. Outputs of private industries are sold on markets, so we can observe and record their prices. But "outputs" of government offices are not sold; indeed, it is sometimes even difficult to define what those outputs are. Lacking prices for outputs, national income accountants fall back on the only prices they have: prices for the inputs from which the outputs are produced. Thus:

> Government outputs are valued at the cost of the inputs needed to produce them.

This means, for example, that if a clerk at the Department of Motor Vehicles earns $16 an hour and spends one-half hour torturing you with explanations of why you cannot get a driver's license, that particular government "service" is worth $8—it increases GDP by that amount.

Second, some goods that are produced during the year but not sold are nonetheless counted in that year's GDP. Specifically, goods that firms add to their *inventories* count in the GDP even though they do not pass through markets.

> National income statisticians treat inventories as if they were "bought" by the firms that produced them, even though these "purchases" do not actually take place.

Finally, the treatment of investment goods runs slightly counter to the rule that GDP includes only final goods. In a broad sense, factories, generators, machine tools, and the like might be considered as intermediate goods. After all, their owners want them only for use in producing other goods, not for any innate value that they possess. But this would present a real problem. Because factories and machines normally are never sold to consumers, when would we count them in GDP? National income statisticians avoid this problem by defining investment goods as final products demanded by the *firms* that buy them.

Now that we have a more complete definition of what the GDP is, let us turn to the problem of actually measuring it. National income accountants have devised three ways to perform this task, and we consider each in turn.

## GDP AS THE SUM OF FINAL GOODS AND SERVICES

The first way to measure GDP seems to be the most natural, because it follows so directly from the circular flow diagram (Figure 25–1) in this chapter. It also turns out to be the most useful definition for macroeconomic analysis. We simply add up the final demands of all consumers, business firms, government, and foreigners. Using the symbols $Y$, $C$, $I$, $G$, and $(X - IM)$ just as we did in the text, we have:

$$Y = C + I + G + (X - IM)$$

The $I$ that appears in the actual U.S. national accounts is called *gross private domestic investment*. We will explain the word *gross* presently. *Private* indicates that government investment is considered part of $G$, and *domestic* just means that machinery sold by American firms to foreign companies is included in exports rather

than in $I$ (investment). Gross private domestic investment in the United States has three components:

- Business investment in plant and equipment
- Residential construction (home building)
- Inventory investment

We repeat again that *only* these three things are *investment* in national income accounting terminology.

> As defined in the national income accounts, *investment* includes only newly produced capital goods, such as machinery, factories, and new homes. It does not include exchanges of existing assets.

The symbol $G$, for government purchases, represents the *volume of current goods and services purchased by all levels of government*. Thus, all government payments to its employees are counted in $G$, as are all of its purchases of goods.

Few citizens realize, however, that *the federal government spends most of its money, not for purchases of goods and services, but rather on transfer payments*—literally, giving away money—either to individuals or to other levels of government.

The importance of this conceptual distinction lies in the fact that $G$ represents the part of the national product that government uses up for its own purposes—to pay for armies, bureaucrats, paper, and ink—whereas transfer payments merely represent shuffling of purchasing power from one group of citizens to another group. Except for the administrators needed to run the programs, real economic resources are not used up in this process.

In adding up the nation's total output as the sum of $C + I + G + (X - IM)$, we sum the shares of GDP that are used up by consumers, investors, government, and foreigners, respectively. Because transfer payments merely give someone the capability to spend on $C$, it is logical to exclude transfers from our definition of $G$, including in $C$ only the portion of these transfer payments that consumers spend. If we included transfers in $G$, the same spending would get counted twice: once in $G$ and then again in $C$.

The final component of GDP is net exports, which are simply exports of goods and services minus imports of goods and services. Table 25–3 shows GDP for 1998, in both nominal and real terms, computed as the sum of $C + I + G + (X - IM)$. You will note that the numbers for net exports in the table are actually negative. We will say much more about America's trade deficit in Part VIII.

## GDP AS THE SUM OF ALL FACTOR PAYMENTS

We can count up the GDP another way: by *adding up all the incomes in the economy*. Let's see how this method handles some typical transactions. Suppose that General

## TABLE 25-3

**Gross Domestic Product in 1998 as the Sum of Final Demands**

| Item | Nominal Amount* | Real Amount† |
|---|---|---|
| Personal consumption expenditures (C) | $5,807.9 | $5,153.3 |
| Gross private domestic investment (I) | 1,367.1 | 1,330.1 |
| Government purchases of goods and services (G) | 1,487.1 | 1,296.9 |
| Net exports (X – IM) | −151.2 | −238.2 |
| Exports (X) | 959.0 | 984.7 |
| Imports (IM) | 1,110.2 | 1,222.9 |
| Gross domestic product (Y) | $8,511.0 | $7,551.9 |

NOTE: *In billions of current dollars.

†In billions of 1992 dollars.

SOURCE: U.S. Department of Commerce. Totals do not add up precisely due to rounding and method of deflating.

Electric builds a generator and sells it to General Motors for $1 million. The first method of calculating GDP simply counts the $1 million as part of *I*. The second method asks: What incomes resulted from the production of this generator? The answer might be something like this:

| | |
|---|---|
| Wages of GE employees | $400,000 |
| Interest to bondholders | 50,000 |
| Rentals of buildings | 50,000 |
| Profits of GE stockholders | 100,00 |

The total is $600,000. The remaining $400,000 is accounted for by inputs that GE purchased from other companies: steel, circuitry, tubing, rubber, and so on. But if we traced this $400,000 back further, we would find that it is accounted for by the wages, interest, and rentals paid by these other companies, *plus* their profits, *plus* their purchases from other firms. In fact, for *every* firm in the economy, there is an accounting identity that says:

$$\text{Revenues from sales} = \begin{array}{l}\text{Wages paid +}\\ \text{Interest paid +}\\ \text{Rentals paid +}\\ \text{Profits earned +}\\ \text{Purchases from other firms}\end{array}$$

Why must this always be true? Because profits are the balancing item; they are what is *left over* after the firm has made all other payments. In fact, this accounting identity is really just a reorganization of the definition of profits: sales revenue less all production costs.

Now apply this accounting identity to *all firms in the economy*. Total purchases from other firms are precisely

what we call *intermediate goods*. What, then, do we get if we subtract these intermediate transactions from both sides of the equation?

$$\begin{array}{l}\text{Revenues from sales } minus\\ \text{Purchases from other firms}\end{array} = \begin{array}{l}\text{Wages paid +}\\ \text{Interest paid +}\\ \text{Rentals paid +}\\ \text{Profits earned}\end{array}$$

On the right-hand side, we have the sum of all factor incomes: payments to labor, land, and capital. On the left-hand side, we have total sales minus sales of intermediate goods. This means that we have only sales of *final* goods, which is precisely our definition of GDP. Thus, the accounting identity for the entire economy can be rewritten as:

**GDP = Wages + Interest + Rents + Profits**

and this gives national income accountants another way to measure the GDP.

Table 25–4 shows 1998's GDP measured by the sum of all incomes. Once again, we have omitted a few details in our discussion. The sum of wages, interest, rents, and profits actually adds up to only $6,995 billion (whereas GDP is $8,511 billion). We call this sum *national income* because it is the sum of all factor payments.

But the actual selling prices of goods include another category of expense that we have ignored so far: sales taxes, excise taxes, and the like. National income statisticians call these taxes *indirect business taxes*, and when we add them to national income, we obtain the *net national product (NNP)*.

Notice here the use of the adjective *national* rather than *domestic*. When we add up all the wages, interest, rents, and profits received by Americans, we will inevitably include some payments derived from production in other countries. Similarly, some of the factor payments made by American businesses go to citizens of other countries. If we subtract the former and add back the latter, we change net *national* product into net *domestic product (NDP)*.

Now we are almost to GDP. The only difference between GDP and NDP is depreciation of the nation's capital stock.

> **Depreciation** is the value of the portion of the nation's capital equipment that is used up within the year. It tells us how much output is needed just to maintain the economy's capital stock.

The difference between gross and net simply refers to whether depreciation is included or excluded. We add depreciation to NDP to get GDP. Thus, GDP is a measure of all final output, taking no account of the capital used up in the process (and therefore in need of replacement). NDP deducts the required replacements to arrive at a *net* production figure.

From a conceptual point of view, most economists feel that NDP is a more meaningful indicator of the economy's output than GDP. After all, the depreciation component of GDP represents the output that is needed just to repair

## TABLE 25-4

## Gross Domestic Product in 1998 as the Sum of Incomes

| Item | Amount |
|---|---|
| Compensation of employees (wages) | $4,981.1 |
| plus | |
| Net interest | 449.3 |
| plus | |
| Rental income | 162.6 |
| plus | |
| Profits | 1,401.8 |
| Corporate Profits | 824.6 |
| Proprietors' income | 577.2 |
| equals | |
| **National income** | 6,994.7 |
| plus | |
| Indirect business taxes and misc. items | 587.8 |
| equals | |
| **National net product** | 7,582.6 |
| minus | |
| Income received from other countries | 269.2 |
| plus | |
| Income paid to other countries | 289.6 |
| equals | |
| Net domestic product | 7,603.0 |
| plus | |
| Depreciation | 908.0 |
| equals | |
| **Gross domestic product** | $8,511.0 |

NOTE: Amounts are in billions of dollars.
SOURCE: U.S. Department of Commerce. Totals do not add up precisely due to rounding.

and replace worn-out factories and machines; it is not available for anybody to consume.[10] Therefore, NDP seems to be a better measure of well-being than GDP.

But, alas, GDP is much easier to measure because depreciation is a particularly tricky item. What fraction of his tractor did Farmer Jones "use up" last year? How much did the Empire State Building depreciate during 1999? If you ask yourself these difficult questions, you will understand why most economists feel that we can measure GDP more accurately than we can NDP. For this reason, most economic models are based on GDP.

In Table 25–4, you can hardly help noticing the preponderant share of employee compensation in total national income—more than 71 percent. Labor is by far the most important factor of production. The return on

---

[10] If the capital stock is used for consumption, it will decline, and the nation will wind up poorer than before.

land is just over 2 percent of national income, and interest accounts for under 7 percent. Profits account for the remaining 20 percent, though the size of corporate profits (less than 12 percent of GDP) is much less than the public thinks. If, by some magic stroke, we could eliminate all corporate profits without upsetting the economy's performance, the average worker would get a raise of about 16 percent!

## ■ GDP AS THE SUM OF VALUES ADDED

It may strike you as strange that national income accountants include only *final* goods and services in GDP. Aren't *intermediate* goods part of the nation's product? Of course they are. The problem is that, if all intermediate goods were included in GDP, we would wind up double and triple counting certain goods and services and therefore get an exaggerated impression of the actual level of economic activity.

To explain why, and to show how national income accountants cope with this difficulty, we must introduce a new concept, called *value added*.

The *value added* by a firm is its revenue from selling a product minus the amount paid for goods and services purchased from other firms.

The intuitive sense of the concept is clear: If a firm buys some inputs from other firms, does something to them, and sells the resulting product for a price higher than it paid for the inputs, we say that the firm has "added value" to the product. If we sum up the values added by all the firms in the economy, we must get the total value of all final products. Thus:

GDP can be measured as the sum of the values added by all firms.

To verify this, look back at the second accounting identity on the previous page. The left-hand side of this equation, sales revenue minus purchases from other firms is precisely the firm's value added. Thus:

Value added = Wages + Interest + Rents + Profits

Because the second method we gave for measuring GDP is to add up wages, interest, rents, and profits, we see that the value-added approach must yield the same answer.

The value-added concept is useful in avoiding double counting. Often, however, intermediate goods are difficult to distinguish from final goods. Paint bought by a painter, for example, is an intermediate good. But paint bought by a do-it-yourselfer is a final good. What happens, then, if the professional painter buys some paint to refurbish his own garage? The intermediate good becomes a final good. You can see that the line between intermediate goods and final goods is a fuzzy one in practice.

If we measure GDP by the sum of values added, however, we need not make such subtle distinctions. In this method, *every* purchase of a new good or service counts, but we do not count the entire selling price, only the portion that represents value added.

To illustrate this idea, consider the data in Table 25–5 and how they would affect GDP as the sum of final products. Our example begins when a farmer who grows soybeans sells them to a mill for $3 a bushel. This transaction does *not* count in the GDP, because the miller does not purchase the soybeans for his own use. The miller then grinds up the soybeans and sells the resulting bag of soy meal to a factory that produces soy sauce. The miller receives $4, but GDP still has not increased because the ground beans are also an intermediate product. Next, the factory turns the beans into soy sauce, which it sells to your favorite Chinese restaurant for $8. Still no effect on GDP.

But then the big moment arrives: The restaurant sells the sauce to you and other customers as a part of your meals, and you eat it. At this point, the $10 worth of soy sauce becomes a final product and *does* count in the GDP. Notice that if we had also counted the three intermediate transactions (farmer to miller, miller to factory, factory to restaurant), we would have come up with $25—$2\frac{1}{2}$ times too much.

Why is it too much? The reason is straightforward. Neither the miller, the factory owner, nor the restaurateur values the product we have been considering *for its own sake*. Only the customers who eat the final product (the soy sauce) have increased their material well-being, so only this last transaction counts in the GDP. However, as we shall now see, value-added calculations enable us to come up with the right answer ($10) by counting only *part* of each transaction. The basic idea is to count at each step only the contribution to the value of the ultimate final product that is made at that step, excluding the values of items produced at other steps.

Ignoring the minor items (such as fertilizer) that the farmer purchases from others, the entire $3 selling price of the bushel of soybeans is new output produced by the farmer; that is, the whole $3 is value added. The miller then grinds the beans and sells them for $4. He has added $4 minus $3, or $1 to the value of the beans. When the factory turns this soy meal into soy sauce and sells it for $8, it has added $8 minus $4, or $4 more in value. Finally, when the restaurant sells it to hungry customers for $10, a further $2 of value is added.

The last column of Table 25–6 shows this chain of creation of value added. We see that the total value added by all four firms is $10, exactly the same as the restaurant's selling price. This is as it must be, for only the restaurant sells the soybeans as a final product.

### TABLE 25-5

**An Illustration of Final and Intermediate Goods**

| Item | Seller | Buyer | Price |
|---|---|---|---|
| Bushel of soybeans | Farmer | Miller | $3 |
| Bag of soy meal | Miller | Factory | 4 |
| Gallon of soy sauce | Factory | Restaurant | 8 |
| Gallon of soy sauce used as seasoning | Restaurant | Consumers | 10 |
| | | **Total:** | **$25** |

Addendum: Contribution to GDP $10

### TABLE 25-6

**An Illustration of Value Added**

| Item | Seller | Buyer | Price | Value Added |
|---|---|---|---|---|
| Bushel of soybeans | Farmer | Miller | $3 | $3 |
| Bag of soy meal | Miller | Factory | 4 | 1 |
| Gallon of soy sauce | Factory | Restaurant | 8 | 4 |
| Gallon of soy sauce used as seasoning | Restaurant | Consumers | 10 | 2 |
| | | **Total:** | **$25** | $10 |

Addendum: Contribution to GDP

| | |
|---|---|
| Final products | $10 |
| Sum of values added | $10 |

## SUMMARY

1. Gross domestic product (GDP) is the sum of the money values of all final goods and services produced during a year and sold on organized markets. There are, however, certain exceptions to this definition.

2. One way to measure the GDP is to add up the final demands of consumers, investors, government, and foreigners: GDP = $C + I + G + (X - IM)$.

3. A second way to measure the GDP is to start with all the factor payments—wages, interest, rents, and profits—that constitute the national income and then add indirect business taxes and depreciation.

4. A third way to measure the GDP is to sum up the values added by every firm in the economy (and then once again add indirect business taxes and depreciation).

5. Except for possible bookkeeping and statistical errors, all three methods must give the same answer.

---

## KEY TERMS

National income accounting  541

Gross domestic product (GDP)  541

Gross private domestic investment (*I*)  542

National income  543

Net national product (NNP)  543

Net domestic product (NDP)  543

Depreciation  543

Value added  544

---

## QUESTIONS FOR REVIEW

1. Which of the following transactions are included in the gross domestic product, and by how much does each raise GDP?

   a. You buy a new Honda, made in the USA, paying $12,000.

   b. You buy a new Toyota, imported from Japan, paying $17,000.

   c. You buy a used Chevrolet, paying $3,000.

   d. America OnLine spends $100 million to increase its Internet capacity.

   e. Your grandmother receives a government Social Security check for $1,200.

   f. Chrysler manufactures 1,000 automobiles at a cost of $12,000 each. Unable to sell them, it holds them as inventories.

   g. Mr. Black and Mr. Blue, each out for a Sunday drive, have a collision in which their cars are destroyed. Black and Blue each hire a lawyer to sue the other, paying the lawyers $3,000 each for services rendered. The judge throws the case out of court.

   h. You sell a used computer to your friend for $100.

2. Explain the difference between final goods and intermediate goods. Why is it sometimes difficult to apply this distinction in practice? In this regard, why is the concept of value added useful?

3. Explain the difference between government spending and government purchases of goods and services (*G*). Which is larger?

4. Explain why national income and gross domestic product would be essentially equal if there were no depreciation and no indirect business taxes.

5. The following outline provides a complete description of all economic activity in Trivialand for 1999. Draw up versions of Tables 25–3 and 25–4 for Trivialand showing GDP computed in two different ways.

   a. There are thousands of farmers but only two big business firms in Trivialand: Specific Motors (an auto company) and Super Duper (a chain of food markets). There is no government and no depreciation.

   b. Specific Motors produced 1,000 small cars, which it sold at $6,000 each, and 100 trucks, which it sold at $8,000 each. Consumers bought 800 of the cars, and the remaining 200 cars were exported to the United States. Super Duper bought all the trucks.

   c. Sales at Super Duper markets amounted to $14 million, all of it sold to consumers.

   d. All the farmers in Trivialand are self-employed and sell all their wares to Super Duper.

   e. The costs incurred by all the businesses were as follows:

   |  | Specific Motors | Super Duper | Farmers |
   | --- | --- | --- | --- |
   | Wages | $3,800,000 | $4,500,000 | $2,000,000 |
   | Interest | 100,000 | 200,000 | 700,000 |
   | Rent | 200,000 | 1,000,000 | 2,000,000 |
   | Purchases of food | 0 | 7,000,000 | 0 |

6. (More difficult) Now complicate Trivialand in the following ways and answer the same questions. In addition, calculate national income and disposable income.

   a. The government bought 50 cars, leaving only 150 cars for export. In addition, the government spent $800,000 on wages and it made $1,200,000 in transfer payments.

   b. Depreciation for the year amounted to $600,000 for Specific Motors and $200,000 for Super Duper. (The farmers had no depreciation.)

   c. The government levied sales taxes amounting to $500,000 on Specific Motors and $200,000 on Super Duper (none on farmers). In addition, the government levied a 10 percent income tax on all wages, interest, and rental income.

   d. In addition to the food and cars mentioned in Question 5, consumers in Trivialand imported 500 computers from the United States at $2,000 each.

Investment . . . is a flighty bird, which needs to be controlled.

J. R. Hicks

# DEMAND-SIDE EQUILIBRIUM: UNEMPLOYMENT OR INFLATION?

Let's briefly review where we have just been. In Chapter 23, we learned that the interaction of aggregate demand and aggregate supply determines whether the economy will stagnate or prosper, whether our labor and capital resources will be fully employed or unemployed. And in Chapter 25, we learned that aggregate demand has four components: consumer expenditure ($C$), investment ($I$), government purchases ($G$), and net exports ($X - IM$). It is now time to start building a theory that puts all the pieces together so we can see where the aggregate demand and aggregate supply curves originate.

Our approach is sequential. Because it is best to walk before you try to run, we imagine for most of this chapter and the next that the price level, the rate of interest, and the international value of the dollar are all constant. None of these assumptions are true, of course, and we will eventually dispense with each. But we reap two important benefits from making these unrealistic assumptions now. First, they enable us to construct a simple but useful model of how the strength of aggregate demand influences the level of gross domestic product (GDP)—a model we will use to derive specific numerical solutions. Second, this model will give us an initial answer to a question of great importance to policymakers: Can we expect the economy to achieve full employment if the government does not intervene?

Subsequent chapters will drop the three unrealistic assumptions in turn. In Chapter 28, we bring aggregate supply back into the picture, which enables us to treat the price level as a variable rather than a constant. In Chapter 31, we will see how interest rates—and hence investment—are determined. Finally, Chapters 36 and 37 add the exchange rate to the story and study the determinants of net exports.

## Why Does the Market Permit Unemployment?

Economists are fond of pointing out—with some awe—the amazing achievements of free markets. Without central direction, they somehow get businesses to produce just the goods and services that consumers want—and to do so cheaply and efficiently. If consumers want less meat and more fish, markets respond; if people subsequently change their minds, markets respond again. Free markets seem to coordinate literally millions of decisions effortlessly and seamlessly.

Yet for hundreds of years and all over the globe, market economies have stumbled over one particular coordination problem: the periodic bouts of mass unemployment that we call *recessions* and *depressions*. Widespread unemployment represents a failure to coordinate economic activity in the following sense. If the unemployed were hired, they would be able to buy the goods and services that businesses cannot sell. The revenues from those sales would, in turn, allow firms to pay the workers. So a seemingly straightforward "deal" offers jobs for the unemployed and sales for the firms. But somehow this deal is not made. Workers remain unemployed and firms get stuck with unsold output.

Thus, free markets, which somehow manage to get rough diamonds dug out of the ground in South Africa and turned into beautiful rings that grooms buy for brides in Los Angeles, cannot seem to solve the coordination problem posed by unemployment. Why not? For centuries, economists puzzled over this question. By the end of the chapter, you will be well on the way toward providing an answer.

---

● **INVESTMENT AND GROWTH**

---

A country builds capacity for future production by investing. One commonly used indicator of how well a nation is providing for its future is the share of GDP devoted to business investment. A clear statistical association between this investment share and the rate of economic growth is apparent in the accompanying chart, which is a scatter diagram covering 42 countries.

During the investment boom of the 1990s, the share of business investment in GDP in the United States rose from about 9 percent to more than 12 percent. This augurs well for our future.

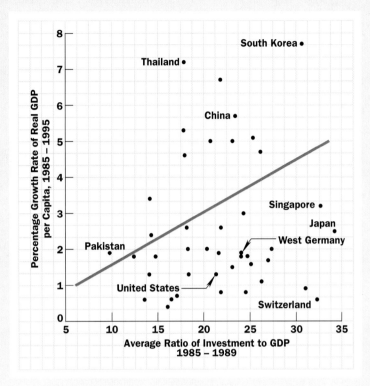

---

■ **THE EXTREME VARIABILITY OF INVESTMENT**

But first things first. We begin by examining the most volatile component of aggregate demand: investment spending.[1] In Chapter 25, we learned that consumer spending closely follows movements in disposable income. Investment spending, by contrast, swings from high to low levels with astonishing speed. For example, when the U.S. economy declined a scant 1 percent (as measured by real GDP) between 1990 and 1991, real investment spending dropped by a hefty 9.7 percent. Then, when the overall economy "boomed" at a 3.9 percent rate from 1997 to 1998, investment rose 10.3 percent. What accounts for these wide swings in investment spending?

**BUSINESS CONFIDENCE AND EXPECTATIONS ABOUT THE FUTURE**

Although many factors influence business people's desires to invest, Keynes stressed the importance of the *state of business confidence*, which in turn depends on *expectations about the future*.

Though tricky to measure, it does seem obvious that businesses will build more factories and purchase more new machines when they are optimistic. Conversely, their investment plans will be very cautious if the economic outlook appears bleak. Keynes pointed out that psychological perceptions like these are subject to abrupt shifts, so that fluctuations in investment can be a major cause of instability in aggregate demand. Hence the analogy to a "flighty bird" in the chapter's opening quotation.

---

[1] We repeat the warning given in the previous chapter about the meaning of the word *investment*. It *includes* spending by businesses and individuals on *newly produced* factories, machinery, and houses. But it *excludes* sales of used industrial plants, equipment, and homes. It *also excludes* purely financial transactions, such as the purchases of stocks and bonds.

Unfortunately, neither economists nor, for that matter, psychologists have many good ideas about how to *measure*—much less *control*—business confidence. So economists usually focus on several more objective determinants of investment—determinants that are easier to quantify and, perhaps even more important, are more easily influenced by government policy.

### THE LEVEL AND GROWTH OF DEMAND

Firms have strong incentives to invest when demand presses against capacity. Under these circumstances, business executives are likely to feel that new factories and machinery can be employed profitably. So, for example, Internet carriers like Sprint and MCI have recently been investing heavily in new capacity to meet burgeoning demand. By contrast, if a great deal of machinery, empty factories, and the like go unused—as is common nowadays in Southeast Asia—managers may not find investment opportunities very attractive.

Because it takes a substantial amount of time to order machinery or to build a factory, *businesses make investment plans with an eye on the future.* Even when pressures on current capacity are not particularly severe, a firm that expects rapid sales growth may start investing now in order to ensure adequate capacity for the future. Furthermore, briskly growing sales are likely to make business people more optimistic. Conversely, slow growth of demand and output will discourage investment. In sum:

High levels of sales relative to current capacity and expectations of rapid economic growth create an atmosphere conducive to investment. Low levels of sales and slow anticipated growth are likely to discourage investment.

Government stabilization policies can thus affect investment spending indirectly. By stimulating aggregate demand, the government can induce business firms to invest more, though the precise amount may be hard to predict.

### TECHNICAL CHANGE AND PRODUCT INNOVATION

Technology drives some investments. New investment opportunities suddenly appear when a new product like the mobile telephone is invented, or when a technological breakthrough makes an existing product much cheaper or better, as happened with microcomputers in the 1980s and Internet services in the 1990s. In our capitalist market system, entrepreneurs seize such opportunities quickly, building new factories, stores, and offices. These new investments need not be "high tech." The VCR, for example, spawned an entire service industry of video rental shops that now dot the American landscape. Two decades ago, such stores did not even exist.

### THE REAL RATE OF INTEREST

The real interest rate is the determinant of investment that will play the pivotal role in later chapters. When interest rates rise, investment falls, and it is not hard to see why. Businesses must borrow to finance most investment, and the interest rate indicates how much firms must pay for that privilege. Some investment projects that yield a profit at an interest rate of 6 percent will be money losers if the firm has to pay 10 percent.

The amount that businesses will want to invest depends on the real interest rate they must pay to borrow funds. The lower the real rate of interest, the more investment spending there will be.

In Chapter 31, we will study in some detail how the government can influence the rate of interest. Because interest rates affect investment, they provide policymakers with another handle on aggregate demand—a handle they do not hesitate to use. The point is that—unlike business confidence, expectations, and technology—governments can manipulate interest rates to some extent. Therefore, even if investment is much more sensitive to changes in confidence than to changes in interest rates, interest rates are nonetheless a more important instrument of government policy. But this is a topic for later in the book.

## ● INVESTMENT IN WHAT?

In 1998, American businesses spent more than $900 billion on new plant and equipment—a tidy sum. What were they buying? Quite a few different things. But the fastest-growing category of investment spending by far has been computers and related office equipment. From only 5 percent of business investment in 1990, computers have risen to account for over 36 percent of investment in 1998. And the share is still rising.

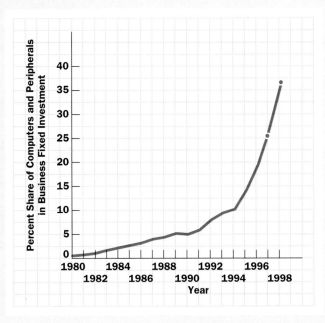

NOTE: Percentages are based on 1992 dollars.

## TAX PROVISIONS

The government has yet another important way to influence investment spending—by altering various tax law provisions. For example, as we mentioned in earlier chapters, President Clinton and Congress agreed in 1997 to reduce the tax rate on *capital gains*—the profit earned by selling an asset for more than you paid for it. Perhaps the principal argument supporting that policy change was that lower capital gains taxes would lead to greater investment spending.

In addition, the U.S. *taxes corporate profits* and can reduce that tax to spur investment—as it did in 1986. There are other, more complicated, tax provisions, as well. To summarize:

> The tax law gives the government several ways to influence business spending on investment goods. But influence is far from control. Investment remains a "flighty bird."

## ■ THE DETERMINANTS OF NET EXPORTS

Another highly variable source of demand for U.S. products is foreign purchases of U.S. goods—our *exports*. However, as we learned in Chapter 25, to obtain the net contribution of foreigners to U.S. aggregate demand, we must subtract *imports*, which is the portion of domestic demand that is satisfied by foreign producers.

## NATIONAL INCOMES

Although both exports and imports depend on many factors, the predominant one is *national income*. When consumption and investment spending by American consumers and firms rise, they spend some of the increase on foreign goods. Therefore:

> Our imports rise when our GDP rises and fall when our GDP falls.

Similarly, our *exports* are the *imports* of other countries, so it is natural to assume that our exports depend on *their* GDPs, not on our own. Thus:

**Our exports are relatively insensitive to our own GDP, but are quite sensitive to the GDPs of other countries.**

Putting these two ideas together leads to a clear implication: When our economy grows faster than those of our trading partners, our net exports tend to shrink. Conversely, when foreign economies grow faster than ours, our net exports tend to rise. Events during the 1990s illustrated this point dramatically. The U.S. economy stagnated between 1990 and 1992, and our net exports rose from –$62 billion to –$30 billion. (Remember, –30 is a larger number than –62!) Then, when growth here outstripped growth abroad from 1992 to 1998, U.S. net exports plummeted from –$30 billion to –$238 billion.

## RELATIVE PRICES AND EXCHANGE RATES

Although GDP levels at home and abroad are important influences on a country's net exports, they are not the only relevant factors. International price differences matter, too. To make things concrete, let's focus on trade between the United States and Japan. Suppose the prices of American goods rise while Japanese prices fall. Then U.S. products become more expensive *relative to Japanese goods*. If American consumers react to the new relative prices by buying more Japanese goods, our *imports rise*. If Japanese consumers react to the same relative price changes by buying fewer American products, our *exports fall*. Both reactions reduce America's *net* exports.

Naturally, a decline in American prices (or a rise in Japanese prices) does precisely the opposite: Exports are stimulated and imports are discouraged, so net exports rise. Thus:

**A rise in the prices of a country's goods will lead to a reduction in that country's net exports. Analogously, a fall in the prices of a country's goods will raise that country's net exports. Conversely, price increases abroad raise a country's net exports whereas price decreases abroad have the opposite effect.**

This simple idea holds the key to understanding how exchange rates among the world's currencies influence exports and imports—a topic we will consider in depth in Chapters 36 and 37. The reason is that exchange rates translate foreign prices into terms that customers are familiar with—their own currencies.

Consider, for example, Americans interested in buying British sweaters that cost £30. If the British pound is worth $1.50, the sweaters cost potential American buyers $45 each. But if the pound is worth $2.00, those same sweaters cost Americans $60, and consumers are likely to buy fewer. These sorts of responses help explain why American automakers won back market share from Japanese imports when the yen soared in the mid-1990s—and then lost some share back when the yen fell in the late 1990s.

## ■ EQUILIBRIUM ON THE DEMAND SIDE OF THE ECONOMY

The preceding discussion accounts for three of the four main components of total spending. The fourth, government purchases of goods and services (*G*), is determined in the political arena by our elected representatives. Let's now put the four pieces together and see how they interact, using as our organizing framework the circular flow diagram from the last chapter. Our objective is to see how total spending is determined.

In doing so, we will at first ignore the possibility—raised in Chapter 23—that the government might vary its taxes (*T*) and spending (*G*) to steer the economy in some desired direction. Aside from pedagogical simplicity, we have an important reason for doing this. One of the crucial questions surrounding government stabilization policy is whether the economy would *automatically* gravitate toward full employment if the government would simply leave it alone. Keynes, contradicting the teachings of generations of economists before him, claimed that it would not. But Keynes's views remain controversial to this day. We can study the issue best by imagining an economy in which the government never tried to manipulate aggregate demand. This is just what we do in this chapter.

Look now at Figure 26–1, which repeats Figure 25–1 from the last chapter. We can use this circular flow diagram to begin to construct a simple model of the determination of national income. But first we must understand what we mean by *equilibrium income.*

**The Circular Flow Diagram**

**FIGURE 26–1**

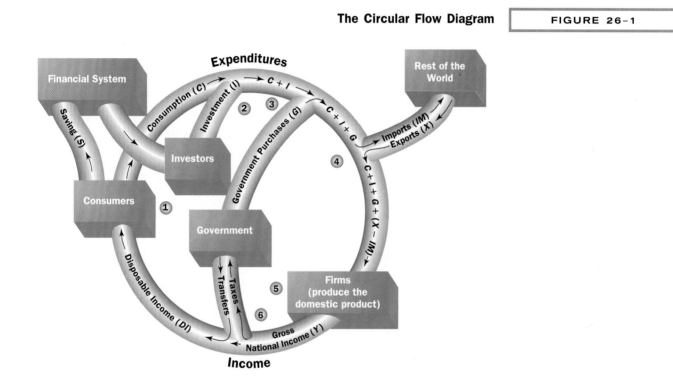

## THE MEANING OF EQUILIBRIUM GDP

As we explained in the last chapter, total *production* and total *income* must, of necessity, be equal. But the same need not be true of total *spending.* Imagine that, for some reason, the total expenditures, $C + I + G + (X - IM)$, made after point 4 in the figure exceed the value of the output produced by the business firms at point 5.

Two things may happen in such a situation. Because consumers, businesses, government, and foreigners together are buying more than firms are producing, businesses will take goods out of their warehouses to meet customer demand. Thus, inventory stocks will fall. Such inventory reductions serve as a signal to retailers that they need to increase their orders and to manufacturers that they need to step up production. Consequently, production is likely to rise.

At some later date, if evidence indicates that the high level of spending is not just a temporary aberration, either manufacturers or retailers (or both) may also respond to buoyant sales performances by raising their prices. Economists therefore say that neither output nor the price level is in **equilibrium** when total spending exceeds current production.

The definition of *equilibrium* tells us that the economy cannot be in equilibrium when total spending exceeds production, for falling inventories demonstrate to firms

**Equilibrium** refers to a situation in which neither consumers nor firms have any incentive to change their behavior. They are content to continue with things as they are.

that their production and pricing decisions were not quite appropriate.[2] Thus, because we normally use GDP to measure output:

> The equilibrium level of GDP cannot be one at which total spending exceeds the value of output because firms will notice that they are depleting their inventory stocks. Firms may first decide to increase production sufficiently to meet the higher demand. Later they may decide to raise prices, as well.

Now imagine the other case, in which the flow of spending reaching firms falls short of current production. Some output cannot be sold and winds up as additional inventories. The inventory pile-up signals firms that either their pricing or output decision was wrong. Once again, they will probably react first by cutting back on production, causing GDP to fall (at point 5 in Figure 26–1). If the imbalance persists, they may also lower prices to stimulate sales. But they certainly will not be happy with things as they are. Thus:

> The equilibrium level of GDP cannot be one at which total spending is less than the value of output, because firms will not allow inventories to continue to pile up. They may decide to decrease production, or they may decide to cut prices in order to stimulate demand. Normally, firms are reluctant to cut prices until they are certain that the low level of demand is not a temporary phenomenon, so they rely more heavily on output reductions.

We have now determined, by process of elimination, the level of output that is consistent with people's desires to spend. We have reasoned that GDP will *rise* whenever it is below total spending, $C + I + G + (X - IM)$, and that GDP will *fall* whenever it is above $C + I + G + (X - IM)$. Equilibrium can occur, then, only when there is just enough spending to absorb the current level of production. Under such circumstances, producers conclude that their price and output decisions are correct. They therefore have no incentive to change those decisions. We conclude that:

> The *equilibrium level of GDP on the demand side* is the one at which total spending equals production. In such a situation, firms find their inventories remaining at desired levels, so they have no incentive to change output or prices.

Thus, the circular flow diagram has helped us to understand the concept of equilibrium GDP on the demand side. It has also shown us how the economy is driven toward this equilibrium. It leaves unanswered, however, three important questions:

- How large is the equilibrium level of GDP?
- Will the economy suffer from unemployment, inflation, or both?
- Is the equilibrium level of GDP on the demand side also consistent with firms' desires to produce? That is, is it also an equilibrium on the *supply* side?

The first two questions will occupy our attention in this chapter; the third question is reserved until Chapter 28.

## CONSTRUCTING THE EXPENDITURE SCHEDULE

Our first objective is to determine precisely the equilibrium level of GDP and to see on what factors it depends. To make the analysis more concrete, we turn to a numerical example. Specifically, we examine the relationship between total spending and GDP in the hypothetical economy we introduced in the last chapter.

Columns (1) and (2) of Table 26–1 repeat the consumption function that we first encountered in Table 25–1. They show how consumer spending, $C$, depends on GDP, which we symbolize by the letter $Y$. Columns (3) to (5) provide the other three components of total spending, $I$, $G$, and $X - IM$, through the simplifying assumptions that each is just a fixed number regardless of the level of GDP. Specifically, we

---

[2] All the models in this book assume, strictly for simplicity, that firms seek constant inventories. Deliberate inventory changes are treated in more advanced courses.

**The Total Expenditure Schedule**

TABLE 26-1

| (1)<br>GDP<br>(Y) | (2)<br>Consumption<br>(C) | (3)<br>Investment<br>(I) | (4)<br>Government<br>Purchases<br>(G) | (5)<br>Net<br>Exports<br>(X – IM) | (6)<br>Total<br>Expenditure |
|---|---|---|---|---|---|
| 4,800 | 3,000 | 900 | 1,300 | −100 | 5,100 |
| 5,200 | 3,300 | 900 | 1,300 | −100 | 5,400 |
| 5,600 | 3,600 | 900 | 1,300 | −100 | 5,700 |
| 6,000 | 3,900 | 900 | 1,300 | −100 | 6,000 |
| 6,400 | 4,200 | 900 | 1,300 | −100 | 6,300 |
| 6,800 | 4,500 | 900 | 1,300 | −100 | 6,600 |
| 7,200 | 4,800 | 900 | 1,300 | −100 | 6,900 |

FIGURE 26-2

**Construction of the Expenditure Schedule**

assume that investment spending is $900 billion, government purchases are $1,300 billion, and net exports are –$100 billion—meaning that in this hypothetical economy, as in the United States at present, imports exceed exports.

By adding Columns (2) through (5), we calculate $C + I + G + (X – IM)$, or total expenditure, which we display in Column (6). Columns (1) and (6) are highlighted in blue to show how total expenditure depends on income. We call this relationship the **expenditure schedule.**

Figure 26–2 shows the construction of the expenditure schedule graphically. The black line labeled $C$ is the consumption function; it plots on a graph the numbers given in Columns (1) and (2) of Table 26–1.

The blue line, labeled $C + I$, displays our assumption that investment is fixed at $900 billion, regardless of the level of GDP. It lies a fixed distance (corresponding to $900 billion) above the $C$ line. If investment were not always $900 billion, the two lines would either move closer together (at income levels at which investment was below $900 billion) or grow farther apart (at income levels at which investment was above $900 billion). For example, our list of determinants of investment spending suggested that $I$ might be larger at higher levels of GDP. Because of this added investment—which we call **induced investment**—the resulting $C + I$ line would have a steeper slope than the $C$ line.

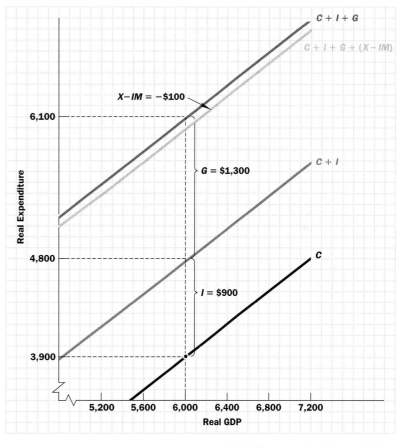

The red line, labeled $C + I + G$, adds government purchases. Because they are assumed to be $1,300 billion regardless of the size of GDP, the red line is parallel to the blue line and $1,300 billion higher.

Finally, the gold line labeled $C + I + G + (X – IM)$ adds in net exports. It is parallel to the red line and $100 billion lower, reflecting our assumption that net exports are always –$100 billion. Once again, if imports depended on GDP, as our previous discussion suggested, the $C + I + G$ and $C + I + G + (X – IM)$ lines would not be parallel.

NOTE: Figures are in billions of dollars per year.

An **expenditure schedule** shows the relationship between national income (GDP) and total spending.

**Induced investment** is the part of investment spending that rises when GDP rises and falls when GDP falls.

| TABLE 26-2 | | The Determination of Equilibrium Output | | |
|---|---|---|---|---|
| **(1)** Output (Y) | **(2)** Total Spending [C + I + G + (X − IM)] | **(3)** Balance of Spending and Output | **(4)** Inventory Status | **(5)** Producer Response |
| 4,800 | 5,100 | Spending exceeds output | Falling | Produce more |
| 5,200 | 5,400 | Spending exceeds output | Falling | Produce more |
| 5,600 | 5,700 | Spending exceeds output | Falling | Produce more |
| 6,000 | 6,000 | Spending = output | Constant | No change |
| 6,400 | 6,300 | Output exceeds spending | Rising | Produce less |
| 6,800 | 6,600 | Output exceeds spending | Rising | Produce less |
| 7,200 | 6,900 | Output exceeds spending | Rising | Produce less |

NOTE: Amounts are in billions of dollars.

## THE MECHANICS OF INCOME DETERMINATION

We are now ready to determine demand-side equilibrium in our hypothetical econ-omy. Look first at Table 26–2, which presents the logic of our circular flow argu-ment in tabular form. The first two columns of this table reproduce the expenditure schedule that we just constructed in Table 26–1. The other columns explain the process by which the economy approaches equilibrium. Let us see why a GDP of $6,000 billion must be the equilibrium level.

Consider first any output level below $6,000 billion. For example, at output level Y = $5,200 billion, total expenditure is $5,400 billion—Column (2)—which is $200 billion more than production. With spending greater than output—Column (3)—inventories will fall—Column (4). As the table suggests, this will signal producers to raise their output—Column (5). Clearly, then, no output level below Y = $6,000 billion can be an equilibrium. Output is too low.

A similar line of reasoning eliminates any output level above $6,000 billion. Con-sider, for example, Y = $6,800 billion. The table shows that total spending would be $6,600 billion if national income were $6,800 billion, so $200 billion of the GDP would go unsold. This would raise producers' inventory stocks and signal them that their rate of production was too high.

Just as we concluded from our circular flow dia-gram, equilibrium will be achieved only when total spending, C + I + G + (X − IM), exactly equals GDP (Y). In symbols, our condition for equilibrium GDP is:

$$Y = C + I + G + (X − IM)$$

The table shows that this occurs only at a GDP of $6,000 billion. This, then, must be the equilibrium level of GDP.

Figure 26–3 displays this same conclusion graphi-cally, by adding a 45° line to Figure 26–2. Why a 45° line? Recall from Chapter 2 that a 45° line marks all points on a graph at which the value of the variable measured on the horizontal axis equals the value of the variable measured on the vertical axis. In this convenient graph of the expenditure schedule, gross domestic prod-uct (Y) is measured on the horizontal axis and total expenditure, C + I + G + (X − IM), is measured on the vertical axis. So the 45° line shows all the points at which output and spending are equal—that is, where Y = C + I + G + (X − IM). *The 45° line therefore displays all the points at which the economy can possibly be at*

| FIGURE 26-3 |
|---|

**Income-Expenditure Diagram**

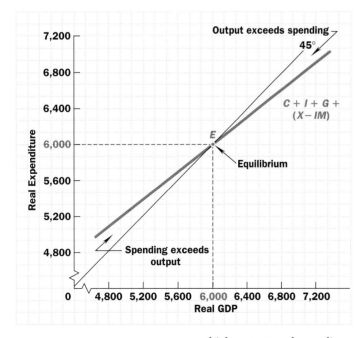

NOTE: Figures are in billions of dollars per year.

*equilibrium,* for firms will be content with current output levels only if total spending equals production.

Now we must compare these *potential* equilibrium points with the *actual* combinations of spending and output that are consistent with the current behavior of consumers and investors. That behavior, as we have seen, is described by the $C + I + G + (X - IM)$ line in Figure 26–3, which shows how total expenditure varies as income changes. Thus, *the economy will always be on the expenditure line* because only points on the $C + I + G + (X - IM)$ line describe the current spending plans of consumers and investors. Similarly, *if* the economy is in equilibrium, it *must* be on the 45° line. As Figure 26–3 shows, these two requirements together imply that the only viable equilibrium is at point $E$, where the $C + I + G + (X - IM)$ line intersects the 45° line. Only this point is consistent both with equilibrium and with people's actual desires to consume and invest.

Notice that to the left of the equilibrium point, $E$, the expenditure line lies above the 45° line. This means that total spending exceeds total output, as we have already noted in words and with numbers. Hence, inventories will be falling and firms will conclude that they should increase production. Thus, production will rise toward the equilibrium point, $E$. The opposite is true to the right of point $E$. Here spending falls short of output, inventories rise, and firms will cut back production—thereby moving closer to $E$.

In other words, whenever production is *above* the equilibrium level, market forces will drive output *down*. And whenever production is *below* equilibrium, market forces will drive output *up*. Thus, in either case, deviations from equilibrium will gradually be eliminated.

Diagrams like this one will recur so frequently in this and the next several chapters that it will be convenient to have a name for them. Let us therefore call them **income-expenditure diagrams** because they show how expenditures vary with income. Sometimes we shall also refer to them simply as **45° line diagrams.**

An **income-expenditure diagram,** also called a **45° line diagram,** plots total real expenditure (on the vertical axis) against real income (on the horizontal axis). The 45° line marks off points where income and expenditure are equal.

## ■ THE AGGREGATE DEMAND CURVE

Chapter 23 introduced aggregate demand and aggregate supply curves, which relate aggregate quantities demanded and supplied to the price level. The expenditure schedule graphed in Figure 26–3 is certainly *not* the aggregate demand curve, for we have yet to bring the price level into our discussion. It is now time to remedy this omission and derive the aggregate demand curve.

Fortunately, we require no further mechanical apparatus. To bring the price level into our income-expenditure analysis, just recall something we learned in the last chapter: At any given level of real income, higher prices lead to lower real consumer spending. The reason, you will recall, is that consumers own many assets whose values are fixed in money terms, and which therefore lose purchasing power when prices rise.[3] With lower real wealth, consumers spend less. Therefore, total spending in the economy falls *even with no change in real income.*

In terms of our 45° line diagram, a rise in the price level will pull down the consumption function depicted in Figure 26–2 and, hence, will pull down the total expenditure schedule, as well. Conversely, a fall in the price level will raise both the $C$ and $C + I + G + (X - IM)$ schedules in the diagram. The two parts of Figure 26–4 on the next page illustrate both of these shifts.

What, then, do changes in the price level do to the equilibrium level of real GDP on the demand side? Common sense says that, with lower spending, equilibrium GDP should fall, and Figure 26–4 shows that this conclusion is correct. Panel (a) shows that a rise in the price level, by shifting the expenditure schedule downward from $C_0 + I + G + (X - IM)$ to $C_1 + I + G + (X - IM)$ leads to a reduction in

---

[3] The money in your bank account is a prime example. If prices rise, it will buy less.

**The Effect of the Price Level on Equilibrium Aggregate Quantity Demanded**

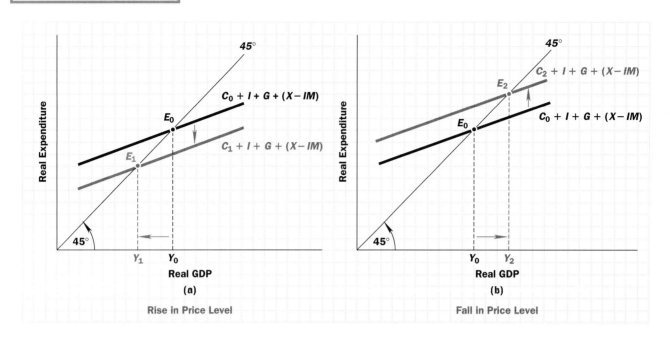

(a) Rise in Price Level

(b) Fall in Price Level

**The Aggregate Demand Curve**

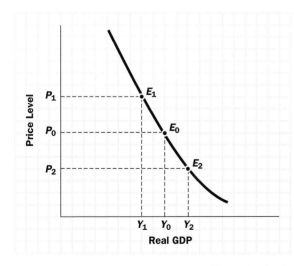

the equilibrium quantity of real GDP demanded from $Y_0$ to $Y_1$. Panel (b) shows that a fall in the price level, by shifting the expenditure schedule upward from $C_0 + I + G + (X - IM)$ to $C_2 + I + G + (X - IM)$, leads to a rise in the equilibrium quantity of real GDP demanded from $Y_0$ to $Y_2$. In summary:

A rise in the price level leads to a lower equilibrium level of real aggregate quantity demanded. This relationship between the price level and the equilibrium quantity of real GDP demanded is depicted in Figure 26-5 and is precisely what we called the *aggregate demand curve* in earlier chapters. It comes directly from the 45° line diagrams in Figure 26-4. Thus, points $E_0$, $E_1$, and $E_2$ in Figure 26-5 correspond precisely to the points bearing the same labels in Figure 26-4. Figure 26-5 shows that higher prices lead to lower aggregate quantity demanded; this relationship is called the *aggregate demand curve.*

The effect of higher prices on consumer wealth is just one of several reasons why the aggregate demand curve slopes downward. A second reason comes from international trade. In our discussion of the determinants of net exports (see pages 551–552), we pointed out that higher U.S. prices will depress exports ($X$) and stimulate imports ($IM$), provided that foreign prices are held constant. That means that, other things equal, a higher U.S. price level will reduce the ($X - IM$) component of total expenditure, thereby shifting the $C + I + G + (X - IM)$ line downward and lowering real GDP, as depicted in Figure 26-4(a).

Later in the book, after we have studied interest rates and exchange rates, we will encounter still more reasons for a downward-sloping aggregate demand curve. All of them imply that:

An income-expenditure diagram like Figure 26-3 can be drawn up only for a *specific* price level. At different price levels, the $C + I + G + (X - IM)$ schedule will be different and, hence, the equilibrium quantity of GDP demanded will also differ.

As we shall now see, this finding is critical to understanding the genesis of unemployment and inflation.

## ■ DEMAND-SIDE EQUILIBRIUM AND FULL EMPLOYMENT

We now turn to the second major question that we noted on page 554: Will the economy achieve an equilibrium at full employment without inflation, or will we see unemployment, inflation, or both? This is a crucial question surrounding government stabilization policy, for if the economy always gravitates toward full employment *automatically*, then the government should simply leave it alone.

In the income-expenditure diagrams used so far, the equilibrium level of GDP demanded has been shown as the intersection of the expenditure schedule and the 45° line, regardless of the GDP level that corresponds to full employment. However, as we will see now, when equilibrium GDP falls above potential GDP, the economy probably will be plagued by inflation, and when equilibrium falls below potential GDP, unemployment and recession will result.

This remarkable fact was one of the principal messages of Keynes's *General Theory of Employment, Interest, and Money*. Writing during the Great Depression, it was natural for him to focus on the case in which equilibrium falls short of full employment, so that some resources are unemployed. Figure 26–6 illustrates this possibility. A vertical line has been drawn at the level of *potential GDP*, which is assumed to be $7,000 billion in the example. We see that the $C + I + G + (X - IM)$ curve cuts the 45° line at point $E$, which corresponds to a GDP ($Y = \$6,000$ billion) below potential GDP. In this case, the expenditure curve is too low to lead to full employment. Such a situation characterized the U.S. economy in 1991–1993.

An equilibrium below potential GDP might arise because consumers or investors are unwilling to spend at normal rates, because government spending is low, because foreign demand is weak, or because the price level is "too high." Any of these would depress the $C + I + G + (X - IM)$ curve. Unemployment must then occur because not enough output is demanded to keep the entire labor force at work.

The distance between the *equilibrium* level of output demanded and the *full-employment* level of output (that is, potential GDP) is called the **recessionary gap**—and is shown by the horizontal distance from $E$ to $B$. Although Figure 26–6 is entirely hypothetical, real-world gaps of precisely this sort were shown shaded in blue in Figure 24–3. They are a pervasive feature of recent U.S. economic history.

Figure 26–6 clearly shows that full employment can be reached only by raising the total spending schedule to eliminate the recessionary gap. Specifically, the $C + I + G + (X - IM)$ schedule must move upward until it cuts the 45° line at point $F$. Can this happen without government intervention? We know that a sufficiently large drop in the price level can do the job. But is that a realistic prospect? We shall return to this question in Chapter 28 after we bring the supply side into the picture, for you cannot really discuss price determination without bringing in *both* supply *and* demand. But first let us consider the other case, when equilibrium GDP exceeds full employment.

Figure 26–7 illustrates this possibility, which many people believe characterized the U.S. economy in 1998 when jobs were abundant. Now the expenditure schedule intersects the 45° line at point $E$, where GDP is $8,000 billion. But this exceeds the full-employment level, $Y = \$7,000$ billion. A case like this can arise when consumer or investment spending is unusually buoyant, when foreign demand is particularly strong, when the government spends too much, or when a "low" price level pushes the $C + I + G + (X - IM)$ curve upward.

**FIGURE 26-6**

**A Recessionary Gap**

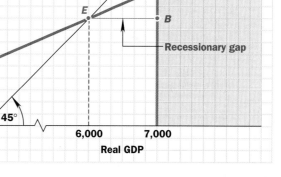

NOTE: Figures are in billions of dollars per year.

The **recessionary gap** is the amount by which the equilibrium level of real GDP falls short of potential GDP.

FIGURE 26-7

**An Inflationary Gap**

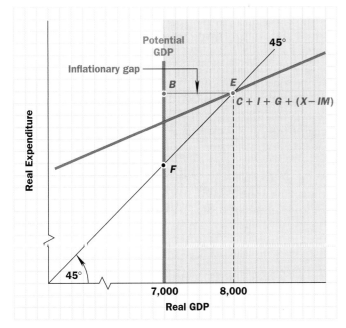

NOTE: Figures are in billions of dollars per year.

To reach an equilibrium at full employment, the price level would have to rise enough to drive the expenditure schedule *down* until it passed through point *F.* The horizontal distance *BE*—which indicates the amount by which the quantity of GDP demanded exceeds potential GDP—is called the **inflationary gap.** If there is an inflationary gap, a higher price level or some other means of reducing total expenditure is necessary to reach an equilibrium at full employment. Rising prices will eventually pull the $C + I + G + (X - IM)$ line down until it passes through point *F.* Real-world inflationary gaps were shown shaded in orange in Figure 24–3. In sum:

> The expenditure curve will intersect the 45° line precisely at full employment, so that neither a recessionary gap nor an inflationary gap occurs, only if the price level and spending plans are "just right."

Are there reasons to expect this outcome? Does the economy have a self-correcting mechanism that automatically eliminates recessionary or inflationary gaps and propels it toward full employment? And how is it that inflation and unemployment sometimes rise or fall together?

These are questions that we are not ready to address because we have not yet brought *aggregate supply* into the picture. However, it is not too early to get an idea about why things can go wrong, why the economy can find itself far away from full employment.

## THE COORDINATION OF SAVING AND INVESTMENT

FIGURE 26-8

**A Simplified Circular Flow**

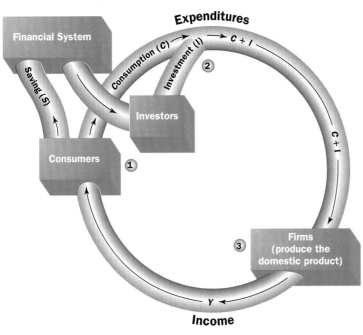

To understand what goes wrong during a recession, it is useful to pose the following question: Must the full-employment level of GDP be an equilibrium? Decades ago, economists thought the answer was yes. Since Keynes, most economists believe the answer is "not necessarily."

To see why, Figure 26–8 offers a simplified circular flow diagram that ignores exports, imports, and the government. In this version, income can "leak out" of the circular flow only at point 1, where consumers save some of their income. Similarly, lost spending can be replaced only at point 2, where investment enters the circular flow.

What happens if firms produce exactly the full-employment level of GDP at point 3 in the diagram? Will this income level be maintained as we move around the circle, or will it shrink or grow? The answer is that full-employment income will be maintained only if the spending by investors at point 2 exactly balances the saving done by consumers at point 1. In other words:

> The economy will reach an equilibrium at full employment only if the amount that consumers wish to save out of full-employment incomes happens to be equal to the amount that investors want to invest. If these two magnitudes are unequal, full employment will not be an equilibrium.

---

### ● UNEMPLOYMENT AND INFLATION AS COORDINATION FAILURES

The idea that unemployment stems from a *lack of coordination* between the decisions of savers and investors may seem abstract. But we encounter coordination failures all the time. The following familiar example may bring the idea down to earth. Picture a crowd watching a football game. Now something exciting happens and the fans rise from their seats. People in the front rows begin standing first, and those seated behind them are forced to stand if they want to see the game. Soon everyone in the stadium is on their feet.

But with everyone standing, no one can see any better than when everyone was sitting. And the fans are enduring the further discomfort of being on their feet. (Never mind that stadium seats are uncomfortable!) Everyone in the stadium would be better off if everyone sat down. Sometimes this happens. But the crowd rises to its feet again on every exciting play. There is simply no way to coordinate the individual decisions of tens of thousands of football fans.

Unemployment poses a similar coordination problem. During a deep recession, workers are unemployed and businesses cannot sell their wares. Figuratively speaking, everyone is "standing" and unhappy about it. If only the firms could agree to hire more workers, those newly employed people could afford to buy more of the goods and services the firms want to produce. But, as at the football stadium, there is no central authority to coordinate these millions of decisions.

The coordination failure idea also helps to explain why it is so hard to stop inflation. Virtually everyone prefers stable prices to rising prices. But now think of yourself as the seller of a product. If everyone else in the economy would hold their prices steady, you would happily hold yours steady, too. But, if you believe that others will continue to raise their prices at, say, 5 percent per year, you may find it dangerous not to increase yours apace. Hence, society may get stuck with 5 percent inflation even though everyone agrees that zero inflation is better.

Specifically, we can see from the circular flow diagram that if saving exceeds investment at full employment, then the total demand received by firms at point 3 will fall short of total output because the added investment spending will not be enough to replace the leakage to saving. With demand inadequate to support production at full employment, GDP must fall below potential. There will be a recessionary gap. Conversely, if investment exceeds saving when the economy is at full employment, then total demand will exceed potential GDP and production will rise above the full-employment level. There will be an inflationary gap.

Now, this discussion does nothing but restate what we already know in different words.[4] But these words provide the key to understanding why the economy can find itself stuck below full employment (or above it, for that matter), for *the people who invest are not the same as the people who save.* In a modern capitalist economy, investing is done by one group of individuals (primarily corporate executives and home buyers), whereas saving is done by another group.[5] It is easy to imagine that their plans may not be well coordinated. If they are not, we have just seen how either unemployment or inflation can occur.

The **inflationary gap** is the amount by which equilibrium real GDP exceeds the full-employment level of GDP.

---

[4] In symbols, our equilibrium condition without government or foreign trade is $Y = C + I$. If we note that $Y$ is also the sum of consumption plus saving, $Y = C + S$, it follows that $C + S = C + I$, or $S = I$, is a restatement of the equilibrium condition.

[5] In a modern economy, not only do households save; businesses save also in the form of retained earnings. Nonetheless, households are the ultimate source of the saving needed to finance investment.

"Go home, I tell you! The recession is over!"

Neither of these problems would arise if the acts of saving and investing were not separated in time or space. Imagine a primitive economy of farmers, each of whom invests only in his own farm. There is no borrowing or lending and no financial system. In this world, any farmer wanting to buy a new plow or tractor (that is, wanting to *invest*) would have to refrain from consuming part of his income (that is, he would have to *save*). Therefore, the amount that farmers planned to *save* out of full-employment income would by necessity be equal to the amount they planned to *invest*. Total spending and production would always have to be equal at full employment.

Almost the same holds true in a centrally planned economy. There, the state decides how much will be invested and the government exerts a great deal of leverage over how much saving people do. If the planners do their calculations correctly, they can force saving to be equal to investment at full employment. Consequently, business fluctuations were not historically major problems for the economies of China and the former Soviet Union. (Though, of course they had plenty of other problems!) However, as these two countries liberalized their economies, they found that they had to deal with the inflation and unemployment problems that have long plagued the West.

The analysis in the accompanying box "Unemployment and Inflation as Coordination Failures" raises a tantalizing possibility. If both high unemployment and high inflation arise from *coordination failures*, might the government be able to do something about it? Keynes suggested that it could, and we will examine this idea in detail in later chapters. But the football analogy reminds us that a central authority may not find it easy to solve the coordination problem.

## S U M M A R Y

1. *Investment* is the most volatile component of aggregate demand, largely because it is tied so closely to the state of business confidence and to expectations about the future performance of the economy.

2. Government policy cannot influence business confidence in any reliable way, so policies designed to alter investment spending are aimed at more objective, though possibly less important, determinants of investment. Among these are interest rates, the overall state of aggregate demand, and tax incentives.

3. *Net exports* depend on GDPs and relative prices both here and abroad.

4. The *equilibrium* level of national income on the demand side is the level at which total spending just equals the value of production (GDP). Because total spending is the sum of consumption, investment, government purchases, and net exports, the condition for equilibrium is $Y = C + I + G + (X - IM)$.

5. Income levels below equilibrium are bound to rise because, when spending exceeds output, firms will see their inventory stocks being depleted and will react by stepping up production.

6. Income levels above equilibrium are bound to fall because, when total spending is insufficient to absorb total output, inventories will pile up and firms will react by curtailing production.

7. The determination of the equilibrium level of GDP on the demand side can be portrayed on a convenient *income-expenditure diagram* as the point at which the *expenditure schedule*—defined as the sum of $C + I + G + (X - IM)$—crosses the 45° line. The 45° line is significant because it marks off points at which spending and output are equal—that is, at which $Y = C + I + G + (X - IM)$—and this is the basic condition for equilibrium.

8. An income-expenditure diagram can only be drawn up for a specific price level, however. Thus, the equilibrium GDP so determined depends on the price level.

9. Because higher prices reduce the purchasing power of consumers' wealth and hence reduce their spending, equilibrium real GDP demanded is lower when prices are higher. This downward-sloping relationship is known as the *aggregate demand curve*.

10. Equilibrium GDP can be above or below *potential GDP*, which is defined as the GDP that would be produced if the labor force were fully employed.

11. If equilibrium GDP exceeds potential GDP, the difference is called an *inflationary gap*. If equilibrium GDP falls short of potential GDP, the resulting difference is called a *recessionary gap*.

12. Such gaps can occur because the saving that consumers want to do at full-employment income levels may differ from the investing that investors want to do. This problem of *coordination failure* is not likely to arise in a planned economy or in a primitive economy.

## QUESTIONS FOR REVIEW

1. For almost 20 years now, imports have consistently exceeded exports in the U.S. economy. Many people consider this a major problem. Does this chapter give you any hints about why? (You may want to discuss this issue with your instructor. We will certainly learn more about it in later chapters.)

2. Why isn't any arbitrary level of GDP an equilibrium for the economy? (Do not give a mechanical answer to this question. Explain the economic mechanism involved.)

3. From the following data, construct an expenditure schedule on a piece of graph paper. Then use the income-expenditure (45° line) diagram to determine the equilibrium level of GDP.

| Income | Consumption | Investment | Government Purchases | Net Exports |
|---|---|---|---|---|
| $3,600 | $3,220 | $240 | $120 | $40 |
| 3,700 | 3,310 | 240 | 120 | 40 |
| 3,800 | 3,400 | 240 | 120 | 40 |
| 3,900 | 3,490 | 240 | 120 | 40 |
| 4,000 | 3,580 | 240 | 120 | 40 |

4. From the following data, construct an expenditure schedule on a piece of graph paper. Then use the income-expenditure (45° line) diagram to determine the equilibrium level of GDP. Compare your answer with your answer to Review Question 3.

| Income | Consumption | Investment | Government Purchases | Net Exports |
|---|---|---|---|---|
| $3,600 | $3,280 | $180 | $120 | $40 |
| 3,700 | 3,340 | 210 | 120 | 40 |
| 3,800 | 3,400 | 240 | 120 | 40 |
| 3,900 | 3,460 | 270 | 120 | 40 |
| 4,000 | 3,520 | 300 | 120 | 40 |

5. Suppose that investment spending is always $250, government purchases are $100, net exports are always $50, and consumer spending depends on the price level in the following way:

| Price Level | Consumer Spending |
|---|---|
| 90 | $740 |
| 95 | 720 |
| 100 | 700 |
| 105 | 680 |
| 110 | 660 |

On a piece of graph paper, use these data to construct an aggregate demand curve. Why do you think this example supposes that consumption declines as the price level rises?

6. Does the economy this year seem to have an inflationary gap or a recessionary gap? (If you do not know the answer from reading the newspaper, ask your instructor.)

7. Why were there no recessions in the former Soviet Union?

8. (More difficult)[6] Consider an economy in which the consumption function takes the following simple algebraic form:

$$C = 300 + 0.75DI$$

and in which investment (*I*) is always 900 and net exports are always –100. Government purchases are fixed at 1,300 and taxes are fixed at 1,200. Find the equilibrium level of GDP and compare your answer to Table 26–2 and Figure 26–3. (*Hint:* Remember that in this case disposable income is GDP minus taxes: $DI = Y - T = Y - 1,200$.)

9. (More difficult) An economy has a consumption function:

$$C = 200 + 0.8DI$$

The government budget is balanced with government purchases and taxes both fixed at 1,000. Net exports are 100. Investment is 600. Find equilibrium GDP.

---

● **APPENDIX**   ▌ **THE SIMPLE ALGEBRA OF INCOME DETERMINATION**

The model of demand-side equilibrium that the chapter presented graphically and in tabular form can also be handled with some simple algebra. Written as an equation, the consumption function in our example is as follows:

$$C = 300 + 0.75DI$$
$$= 300 + 0.75(Y - T)$$

---

[6] The answer to this question is provided in the appendix to this chapter.

because, by definition, $DI = Y - T$. This is simply the equation of a straight line with a slope of 0.75 and an intercept of $300 - 0.75T$. Because $T = 1,200$ in our example, the intercept is $-600$ and the equation can be written more simply as follows:

$$C = -600 + 0.75Y$$

Investment in the example was assumed to be 900, regardless of the level of income, government purchases were 1,300, and net exports were $-100$. So the sum $C + I + G + (X - IM)$ is as follows:

$$C + I + G + (X - IM)$$
$$= -600 + .075Y + 900 + 1,300 - 100$$
$$= 1,500 + .075Y$$

which describes the expenditure curve in Figure 26–3. Because the equilibrium quantity of GDP demanded is defined by

$$Y = C + I + G + (X - IM)$$

we can solve for the equilibrium value of $Y$ by substituting $1,500 + 0.75Y$ for $C + I + G + (X - IM)$ to get

$$Y = 1,500 + 0.75Y$$

To solve this equation for $Y$, first subtract $0.75Y$ from both sides to get

$$0.25Y = 1,500$$

Then divide both sides by 0.25 to obtain the answer:

$$Y = 6,000$$

This, of course, is precisely the solution we found by graphical and tabular methods in the chapter.

We can easily generalize this algebraic approach to deal with any set of numbers in our equations. Suppose that the consumption function is as follows:

$$C = a + bDI = a + b(Y - T)$$

(In the example, $a = 300$, $T = 1,200$, and $b = 0.75$.) Then the equilibrium condition that $Y = C + I + G + (X - IM)$ implies that

$$Y = a + bDI + I + G + (X - IM)$$
$$= a - bT + bY + I + G + (X - IM)$$

Subtracting $bY$ from both sides leads to

$$(1 - b)Y = a - bT + I + G + (X - IM)$$

and dividing through by $1 - b$ gives:

$$Y = \frac{a - bT + I + G + (X - IM)}{1 - b}$$

This formula, which is certainly *not* to be memorized, is valid for any numerical values of $a$, $b$, $T$, $G$, $I$, and $(X - IM)$ (so long as $b$ is between zero and 1).

---

## QUESTIONS FOR REVIEW

1. Find the equilibrium level of GDP demanded in an economy in which investment is always $300, net exports are always –$50, the government budget is balanced with purchases and taxes both equal to $400, and the consumption function is described by the following algebraic equation:

   $$C = 150 + 0.75DI$$

   (*Hint:* Do not forget that $DI = Y - T$.)

2. Do the same for an economy in which investment is $250, net exports are zero, government purchases and taxes are both $400, and the consumption function is

   $$C = 250 + 0.5DI$$

3. In each of these cases, how much saving is there in equilibrium? (*Hint:* Income not consumed must be saved.) Is saving equal to investment?

4. Imagine an economy in which consumer expenditure is represented by the following equation:

   $$C = 50 + 0.75DI$$

   Imagine also that investors want to spend 500 at every level of income ($I = 500$), net exports are zero ($X - IM = 0$), government purchases are 300, and taxes are 200.

   a. What is the equilibrium level of income?

   b. If the full-employment level of income is 3,000, is there a recessionary or inflationary gap? If so, how much?

   c. What will happen to the equilibrium level of income if investors become optimistic about the country's future and raise their investment to 600?

   d. Is there a recessionary or inflationary gap now? How much?

5. Fredonia has the following consumption function:

   $$C = 100 + 0.8DI$$

   Firms in Fredonia always invest $700 and net exports are zero, initially. The government budget is balanced with spending and taxes both equal to $500.

   a. Find the equilibrium level of GDP.

   b. How much is saved? Is saving equal to investment?

   c. Now suppose that an export-promotion drive succeeds in raising net exports to $100. Answer (a) and (b) under these new circumstances.

A definite ratio, to be called the *Multiplier,* can be established between income and investment.

John Maynard Keynes

# CHANGES ON THE DEMAND SIDE: MULTIPLIER ANALYSIS

In the last chapter, we derived the economy's *aggregate demand curve,* which shows how the equilibrium quantity of real gross domestic product (GDP) demanded depends on the price level—holding all other factors constant. But often these "other factors" do not remain constant, and, as a consequence, the entire aggregate demand curve shifts. This chapter is the first of several that are devoted to enumerating these "other factors" and explaining how and why they make the aggregate demand curve shift

This short chapter has only one central concept: the *multiplier*—the idea that an increase in spending will bring about an *even larger* increase in equilibrium GDP. We develop this remarkable result in several different ways, and then apply it to several issues.

### Would Cutting Taxes Work in Japan?

In early 1998, the Japanese economy, once one of the marvels of the world, seemed stuck in the mud. Japan's growth was anemic, and an outright recession seemed likely. (It was.) The Japanese economy was plainly suffering from a shortage of aggregate demand. The United States and other governments urged Japan to cut income taxes to give its economy a boost. But Japanese officials objected that the high level of economic anxiety among their citizens meant that a tax cut would not add much to aggregate demand. Instead, Japanese people would save the money rather than spend it. In the language of this chapter, the Japanese government argued that the multiplier was extraordinarily low at the time. Were the government officials right? We will revisit the issue at the end of the chapter.

## ■ THE MAGIC OF THE MULTIPLIER

Because it is subject to such abrupt swings, investment spending often causes business fluctuations in the United States and elsewhere. So let us ask what would happen to equilibrium income if firms suddenly decided to spend more on investment goods. As we shall see, such a decision would have a *multiplied* effect on GDP; that is, each $1 of additional investment spending would add *more* than $1 to GDP. The same should be true in Japan or in the United States.

For simplicity, we continue to use our fictitious economy as an example and to assume that the price level is fixed—an assumption that we will drop in the next chapter. Refer first to Table 27–1, which looks very much like Table 26–1. The only difference is that we assume here that, for some reason, firms now want to invest $200 billion more than they previously did—for a total of $1,100 billion. As indicated by the blue numbers, only income level $Y = \$6,800$ billion is an equilibrium on the demand side of the economy because only at this level is total spending, $C + I + G + (X - IM)$, equal to production ($Y$).

The **multiplier** principle says that GDP will rise by more than the $200 billion increase in investment. Specifically, the multiplier is defined as the ratio of the

> The **multiplier** is the ratio of the change in equilibrium GDP ($Y$) divided by the original change in spending that causes the change in GDP.

| TABLE 27–1 |
|---|

**Total Expenditure after a $200 Billion Increase in Investment Spending**

| (1)<br>Income<br>(Y) | (2)<br>Consumption<br>(C) | (3)<br>Investment<br>(I) | (4)<br>Government<br>Purchases<br>(G) | (5)<br>Net Exports<br>(X – IM) | (6)<br>Total<br>Expenditure |
|---|---|---|---|---|---|
| 4,800 | 3,000 | 1,100 | 1,300 | −100 | 5,300 |
| 5,200 | 3,300 | 1,100 | 1,300 | −100 | 5,600 |
| 5,600 | 3,600 | 1,100 | 1,300 | −100 | 5,900 |
| 6,000 | 3,900 | 1,100 | 1,300 | −100 | 6,200 |
| 6,400 | 4,200 | 1,100 | 1,300 | −100 | 6,500 |
| 6,800 | 4,500 | 1,100 | 1,300 | −100 | 6,800 |
| 7,200 | 4,800 | 1,100 | 1,300 | −100 | 7,100 |

NOTE: Figures are in billions of dollars per year.

change in equilibrium GDP (Y) to the original change in spending that causes GDP to change. In shorthand, when we deal with the multiplier for investment (I), the formula is:

$$\text{Multiplier} = \frac{\text{Change in } Y}{\text{Change in } I}$$

Let us verify that the multiplier is indeed greater than 1. Table 27–1 shows the construction of a new expenditure schedule by adding up C, I, G, and (X – IM) at each level of Y, just as we did in Chapter 26—only now I = $1,100 billion rather than $900 billion. If you compare the last column of Table 27–1 with that of Table 26–1, you will see that the new expenditure schedule lies uniformly above the old one by $200 billion.

**FIGURE 27–1**

**Illustration of the Multiplier**

Figure 27–1 illustrates this shift graphically. The schedule marked $C + I_0 + G + (X - IM)$ is derived from the last column of Table 26–1, while the higher schedule marked $C + I_1 + G + (X - IM)$ is derived from the last column of Table 27–1. The two expenditure lines are parallel and $200 billion apart.

So far no act of magic has occurred—things look just as you might expect. But one more step will bring the multiplier rabbit out of the hat. Let us see what the upward shift of the expenditure line does to equilibrium income. In Figure 27–1, equilibrium moves outward from point $E_0$ to point $E_1$, that is, from $6,000 billion to $6,800 billion. The difference is an increase in national income of $800 billion. All this from a $200 billion stimulus to investment? That is the magic of the multiplier.

Because the change in I is $200 billion and the change in equilibrium Y is $800 billion, by applying our definition, the multiplier is:

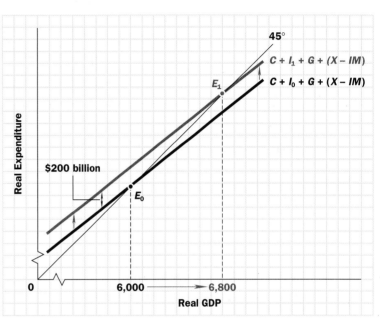

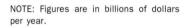

NOTE: Figures are in billions of dollars per year.

$$\text{Multiplier} = \frac{\text{Change in } Y}{\text{Change in } I} = \frac{\$800}{200} = 4$$

This tells us that, in our example, each additional dollar of investment demand will add $4 to equilibrium GDP!

This does indeed seem mysterious. Can something be created from nothing? Let's first check that the graph has not deceived us. The first and last columns of Table 27–1 show in numbers what Figure 27–1 shows graphically. Notice that equilibrium now comes at Y = $6,800 billion, because only here is total expenditure equal to production (Y). This equilibrium level of GDP is $800 billion higher than the $6,000 billion level found in the last chapter, when investment was only $900 billion. Thus, a $200 billion rise in investment does indeed lead to an $800 billion rise in equilibrium GDP. The multiplier really *is* 4.

## DEMYSTIFYING THE MULTIPLIER: HOW IT WORKS

The multiplier result seems implausible at first, but it loses its mystery once we remember the circular flow of income and expenditure and the simple fact that one person's spending is another person's income. To illustrate the logic of the multiplier and see why it is exactly 4 in our model economy, let us look more closely at what actually happens if businesses decide to spend an additional $1 million on investment goods.

Suppose that Microhard—a major corporation in this hypothetical country—decides to spend $1 million to build a new office building. Its $1 million expenditure goes to construction workers and owners of construction companies as wages and profits. That is, it becomes their *income*.

But the construction firm's owners and workers will not keep their $1 million in the bank. They will spend most of it. If they are "typical" consumers, their spending will be $1 million times the marginal propensity to consume (MPC). In our example, the MPC is 0.75. So let us assume that they spend $750,000 and save the rest. *This $750,000 expenditure is a net addition to the nation's demand for goods and services, exactly as Microhard's original $1 million expenditure was.* So, at this stage, the $1 million investment has already pushed GDP up some $1.75 million. But the process by no means stops here.

Shopkeepers receive the $750,000 spent by construction workers, and they in turn also spend 75 percent of their new income. This accounts for $562,500 (75 percent of $750,000) in additional consumer spending in the "third round." Next follows a fourth round in which the recipients of the $562,500 spend 75 percent of this amount, or $421,875, and so on. At each stage in the spending chain, people spend 75 percent of the additional income they receive, and the process continues. Consumption grows in each round.

Where does it all end? Does it all end? The answer is that it does, indeed, eventually end—with GDP a total of $4 million higher than it was before Microhard built the original $1 million office building. The multiplier, is, indeed, 4.

Table 27–2 displays the basis for this conclusion. In the table, "round 1" represents Microhard's initial investment, which creates $1 million in income for construction workers; "round 2" represents the construction workers' spending, which creates $750,000 in income for shopkeepers. The rest of the table proceeds accordingly; each entry in Column (2) is 75 percent of the previous entry. Column (3) tabulates the running sum of Column (2).

We see that after 10 rounds of spending, the initial $1 million investment has mushroomed to $3.77 million, and the sum is still growing. After 20 rounds, the total increase in GDP is over $3.98 million—near its eventual value of $4 million. Although it takes quite a few rounds of spending before the multiplier chain nears 4, we see from the table that it hits 3 rather quickly. If each income recipient in the chain waits, say, 2 months before spending his new income, the multiplier will reach 3 in only about 10 months.

Figure 27–2 provides a graphical presentation of the numbers in the last column of Table 27–2. Notice how the multiplier builds up rapidly at first and then tapers off to approach its ultimate value (4, in this example) gradually.

Although this is only a hypothetical example, the same thing occurs every day in the real world. For instance, a burst of new housing creates a multiplier effect on everything from appliances and furniture to carpeting and insulation. Similarly, when a large company like AT&T makes an investment in a developing country, the multiplier effect boosts business activity in many sectors.

## ALGEBRAIC STATEMENT OF THE MULTIPLIER

Figure 27–2 and Table 27–2 probably make a persuasive case that the multiplier eventually reaches 4. But for the remaining skeptics, we offer a simple algebraic proof.[1] Most of you learned about something called an *infinite geometric progression* in high school. This term refers to an infinite series of numbers, each one of which is a fixed fraction of the previous one. The fraction is called the *common ratio*. A geometric progression beginning with 1 and having a common ratio of 0.75 would look like this:

$$1 + 0.75 + (0.75)^2 + (0.75)^3 + \ldots$$

---

**TABLE 27-2**

**The Multiplier Spending Chain**

| (1) Round Number | (2) Spending in This Round | (3) Cumulative Total |
|---|---|---|
| 1 | $1,000,000 | $1,000,000 |
| 2 | 750,000 | 1,750,000 |
| 3 | 562,500 | 2,312,500 |
| 4 | 421,875 | 2,734,375 |
| 5 | 316,406 | 3,050,781 |
| 6 | 237,305 | 3,288,086 |
| 7 | 177,979 | 3,466,065 |
| 8 | 133,484 | 3,599,549 |
| 9 | 100,113 | 3,699,662 |
| 10 | 75,085 | 3,774,747 |
| ⋮ | ⋮ | ⋮ |
| 20 | 4,228 | 3,987,317 |
| ⋮ | ⋮ | ⋮ |
| "Infinity" | 0 | 4,000,000 |

**FIGURE 27-2**

**How the Multiplier Builds**

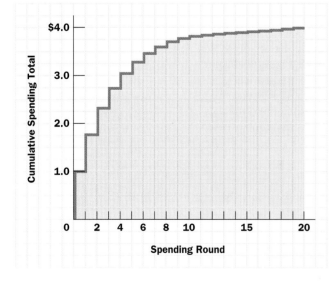

NOTE: Amounts are in millions of dollars.

---

[1] Students who blanch at the sight of algebra should not be put off. Anyone who can balance a checkbook (even many who cannot!) will be able to follow the argument.

More generally, a geometric progression beginning with 1 and having a common ratio $R$ would be:

$$1 + R + R^2 + R^3 + \ldots$$

A simple formula enables us to sum such a progression as long as $R$ is less than 1.[2] The formula is:[3]

**Sum of infinite geometric progression** $= \dfrac{1}{1 - R}$

Now we can recognize that the multiplier chain in Table 27–2 is just an infinite geometric progression, with 0.75 as its common ratio. That is, each \$1 that Microhard spends leads to a $(0.75) \times \$1$ expenditure by construction workers, which in turn leads to a $(0.75) \times (0.75 \times \$1) = (0.75)^2 \times \$1$ expenditure by the shopkeepers, and so on. Thus, for each initial dollar of investment spending, the progression is:

$$1 + 0.75 + (0.75)^2 + (0.75)^3 + (0.75)^4 + \ldots$$

Applying the formula for the sum of such a series, we find that:

$$\text{Multiplier} = \frac{1}{1 - 0.75} = \frac{1}{0.25} = 4$$

Notice how this result can be generalized. If we did not have a specific number for the marginal propensity to consume, but simply called it MPC, the geometric progression in Table 27–2 would have been:

$$1 + \text{MPC} + (\text{MPC})^2 + (\text{MPC})^3 + \ldots$$

which uses the MPC as its common ratio. Applying the same formula for summing a geometric progression to this more general case gives us the following general result:

**OVERSIMPLIFIED FORMULA FOR THE MULTIPLIER:**

$$\text{Multiplier} = \frac{1}{1 - \text{MPC}}$$

We call this formula "oversimplified" because it ignores many factors that are important in the real world. You can begin to appreciate just how unrealistic the "oversimplified" formula is by considering some real numbers for the U.S. economy. The marginal propensity to consume (MPC) has been estimated many times—it is about 0.9. From our oversimplified formula, then, it would seem that the multiplier should be:

$$\text{Multiplier} = \frac{1}{1 - 0.9} = \frac{1}{0.1} = 10$$

In fact, the actual multiplier for the U.S. economy is less than 2. That is quite a discrepancy!

But it does not mean that anything we have said about the multiplier so far is incorrect. Our story is simply incomplete. As we progress through this and subsequent

---

[2] If $R$ exceeds 1, nobody can possibly sum it—not even with the aid of a modern computer—because the sum is not a finite number.

[3] The proof of the formula is simple. Let the symbol $S$ stand for the (unknown) sum of the series:

$$S = 1 + R + R^2 + R^3 + \ldots$$

Then, multiplying by $R$,

$$RS = R + R^2 + R^3 + R^4 + \ldots$$

By subtracting $RS$ from $S$, we obtain:

$$S - RS = 1 \text{ or } S = \frac{1}{1 - R}$$

chapters, you will learn why the multiplier is below 2—even though the MPC is close to 0.9. One such reason is *international trade*—in particular, the fact that a country's imports depend on its GDP. We deal with this complication in Appendix B to this chapter. A second factor is *inflation*, a complication we will address in the next chapter. A third is *income taxation*, a point we will elaborate in Chapter 29. The last important influence arises from the *financial system* and, after we discuss money and banking in Chapters 30 and 31, we will explain how the financial system influences the multiplier in Chapter 32. As you will see, each of these factors *reduces* the size of the multiplier. So:

> Although the multiplier is larger than 1 in the real world, it cannot be calculated with any degree of accuracy from the oversimplified formula. The actual multiplier is *much lower* than the formula suggests.

## ■ THE MULTIPLIER: A GENERAL CONCEPT

Business firms that invest are not the only ones that can unleash the magic of the multiplier; so can consumers.

### THE MULTIPLIER EFFECT OF CONSUMER SPENDING

To see how the multiplier works when the process is initiated by an upsurge in consumer spending, we must distinguish between two types of change in consumer spending. To do so, it is helpful to bring back Figure 25–6, which we repeat here as Figure 27–3.

When $C$ rises because income rises—that is, when consumers move outward *along a fixed consumption function*—we call the increase in $C$ an **induced increase in consumption.** (See the red arrow in the figure.) However, if instead $C$ rises because the entire consumption function *shifts up* (such as from $C_0$ to $C_1$ in the figure), we call this an **autonomous increase in consumption.** The name indicates that consumption changes *independently* of income, and Chapter 25's discussion of the consumption function pointed out that a number of events, such as a change in the price level or in the value of the stock market, can initiate such a shift.

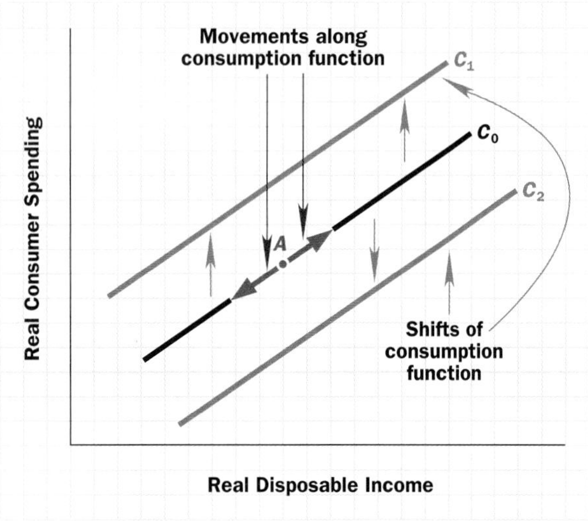

Let us suppose that, for some reason, consumer spending rises autonomously by $200 billion. In this case, we would revise our table of aggregate demand to look like Table 27–3. Comparing this to Table 27–1, we note that each entry in Column (2) is $200 billion *higher* than the corresponding entry in Table 27–1 (because consumption is higher), and each entry in Column (3) is $200 billion *lower* (because in this case investment is only $900 billion).

The equilibrium level of income is clearly $Y = \$6,800$ billion once again. Indeed, the entire expenditure schedule—Column (6)—is the same as it was in Table 27–1. The initial rise of $200 billion in consumer spending leads to an ultimate rise of $800 billion in GDP, just as it did in the case of higher investment spending. In fact, Figure 27–1 applies directly to this case once we note that the upward shift is now caused by an autonomous change in $C$ rather than in $I$. The multiplier for autonomous changes in consumer spending, then, is also 4 (=$800/$200).

The reason is straightforward. It does not matter who injects an additional dollar of spending into the economy, whether it is business investors or consumers. Wherever it comes from, 75 percent of it will be respent if the MPC is 0.75, and the recipients of this second round will, in turn, spend 75 percent of their additional income, and so on and on. And that is what constitutes the multiplier process.

**FIGURE 27-3**

**Shifts of the Consumption Function**

Real Consumer Spending

Movements along consumption function

$C_1$

$C_0$

$C_2$

$A$

Shifts of consumption function

Real Disposable Income

**Total Expenditure after Consumers Decide to Spend $200 Billion More**

TABLE 27-3

| (1) Income (Y) | (2) Consumption (C) | (3) Investment (I) | (4) Government Purchases (G) | (5) Net Exports (X – IM) | (6) Total Expenditure |
|---|---|---|---|---|---|
| 4,800 | 3,200 | 900 | 1,300 | −100 | 5,300 |
| 5,200 | 3,500 | 900 | 1,300 | −100 | 5,600 |
| 5,600 | 3,800 | 900 | 1,300 | −100 | 5,900 |
| 6,000 | 4,100 | 900 | 1,300 | −100 | 6,200 |
| 6,400 | 4,400 | 900 | 1,300 | −100 | 6,500 |
| 6,800 | 4,700 | 900 | 1,300 | −100 | 6,800 |
| 7,200 | 5,000 | 900 | 1,300 | −100 | 7,100 |

NOTE: Figures are in billions of dollars per year.

## OTHER MULTIPLIERS

What about the other two components of total spending, government purchases (G) and net exports (X – IM)? Because we now know that the multiplier process applies no matter who injects the additional dollar of spending into the economy, we conclude that G and X – IM must have the same multiplier as I and C. Figure 27–1 can again be used to illustrate the conclusion graphically—just think of the upward shift as being caused by a either a rise in G or a rise in X – IM this time.

The multipliers are identical because the logic behind them is identical. The multiplier spending chain set in motion when Microhard spent $1 million to build a factory could equally well have been kicked off by the government or foreign customers buying $1 million worth of software from Microhard. Thereafter, each recipient of additional income would spend 75 percent of it (the assumed marginal propensity to consume), until $4 million in new income had eventually been created.

The idea that changes in G have multiplier effects on GDP will play a central role in the discussion of government stabilization policy that begins in Chapter 29. So it is worth noting here that:

> Changes in the volume of government purchases of goods and services will change the equilibrium level of GDP in the same direction, and by a multiplied amount.

This is, more or less, the issue that faced the Japanese government in 1998. In the "first round," the government spent more money on road building and other public works. After that, however, it relied on construction workers to use most of their paychecks in a "second round" of spending on items like groceries, paint, and toys for their kids. In the third and subsequent rounds, yet more recipients of new income would have to purchase still different goods and services. The Japanese concern was that their people would save rather than spend, cutting the multiplier process short.

Application of multiplier analysis to foreign trade also teaches us an important lesson: *Booms and recessions tend to be transmitted across national borders.* Why is that? Suppose a boom abroad raises aggregate demand and GDP in foreign countries. With rising incomes, foreigners will buy more American goods—which means that U.S. exports will rise. But a rise in our exports will, via the multiplier, raise GDP in the United States. By this mechanism, rapid economic growth abroad contributes to rapid economic growth here.

Of course, the same mechanism also operates in the downward direction. Suppose some of the countries that trade with us slip into recession. As their GDPs decline, so do their *imports*. But this means that the United States will experience a decline in *exports* which, through the multiplier, will pull down GDP here. That is why the unhappy events in Asia in 1997 and 1998, which we will discuss more thoroughly in Chapters 36 and 37, were a drag on economic growth in the United States.

An **induced increase in consumption** is an increase in consumer spending that stems from an increase in consumer incomes. It is represented on a graph as a movement along a fixed consumption function.

An **autonomous increase in consumption** is an increase in consumer spending without any increase in incomes. It is represented on a graph as a shift of the entire consumption function.

Naturally, what foreign countries do to us, we also do to them. Thus, rapid economic growth in the United States tends to produce boom conditions in the countries from which we buy, and recessions here tend quickly to spill beyond our borders. In summary:

> The GDPs of the major economies are linked by trade. A boom in one country tends to raise its imports and hence push up exports and GDP in other countries. Similarly, a recession in one country tends to pull GDP down in other countries.

## ■ THE MULTIPLIER IN REVERSE

**FIGURE 27-4**

**The Multiplier in Reverse**

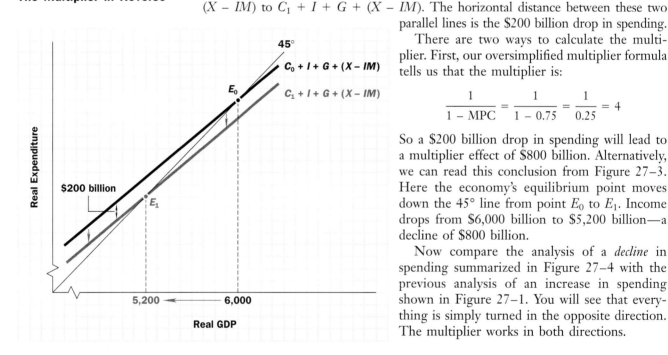

NOTE: Figures are in billions of dollars per year.

A good way to check your understanding of the multiplier process is to run it in reverse: What happens if, for example, consumers abruptly decide to spend less? For example, suppose a wave of thriftiness comes over the people of our hypothetical economy so that, no matter what their total income, they now want to spend $200 billion *less* than they did previously, rather than the $200 billion *more* assumed in Table 27–1.

A decision to spend $200 billion less out of any given level of income is, by definition, a *downward* shift of the total expenditure schedule by $200 billion. This is shown in Figure 27–4, where the $C + I + G + (X - IM)$ schedule falls from $C_0 + I + G + (X - IM)$ to $C_1 + I + G + (X - IM)$. The horizontal distance between these two parallel lines is the $200 billion drop in spending.

There are two ways to calculate the multiplier. First, our oversimplified multiplier formula tells us that the multiplier is:

$$\frac{1}{1 - MPC} = \frac{1}{1 - 0.75} = \frac{1}{0.25} = 4$$

So a $200 billion drop in spending will lead to a multiplier effect of $800 billion. Alternatively, we can read this conclusion from Figure 27–3. Here the economy's equilibrium point moves down the 45° line from point $E_0$ to $E_1$. Income drops from $6,000 billion to $5,200 billion—a decline of $800 billion.

Now compare the analysis of a *decline* in spending summarized in Figure 27–4 with the previous analysis of an increase in spending shown in Figure 27–1. You will see that everything is simply turned in the opposite direction. The multiplier works in both directions.

### THE PARADOX OF THRIFT

This last example of multiplier analysis teaches us an important theoretical and practical lesson: An increase in consumers' desire to save may lead to a cumulative fall in GDP. And, *because saving depends on income*, the resulting decline in national income will pull saving down. In consequence, saving may fail to rise despite an increase in the public's desire to save.

Let us be a bit more specific about this remarkable result. Before the upsurge in saving, consumers were spending $3,900 billion out of a total national income of $6,000 billion, as can be seen by referring back to Table 26–1. How much was being saved? Since taxes are assumed to be fixed at $1,200 billion, disposable income was:

$$DI = Y - T = \$6,000 - \$1,200 = \$4,800 \text{ billion}$$

Hence, saving was $900 billion (=$4,800 − $3,900).

In Figure 27–4, GDP falls to $5,200 billion, so disposable income drops to $4,000. Because investment, government purchases, and net exports are all unchanged, the

## ● THE PARADOX OF THRIFT IN ACTION

A decade ago, when Japan was considered economically mighty and the U.S. was struggling, many economists agreed that a big reason for the disparity was savings: The thrifty Japanese had plenty to invest in their future, the wanton Americans too little.

Today, the average Japanese family puts away more than 13 percent of its income, the average American family 4 percent. Yet Japan is in the tank while the U.S. prospers.

Is saving no longer an economic virtue and profligacy no longer a vice? Did Benjamin Franklin get it all wrong? Maybe not—but it isn't as simple as Franklin's Poor Richard's Almanac made it seem: An economy *can* save too much.

Japan is the first major developed country since World War II to confront the "paradox of thrift," the condition John Maynard Keynes worried about, where bad times lead individuals to save more, suppressing overall demand and making a country even worse off. . . . So the Japanese government nudges its citizens to live it up. . .

A cartoon in a magazine ad shows a father excitedly reading about the [tax] cuts in the newspaper, inspiring his two young kids to dream of cake and candy and his blushing wife to ask for a blouse. A poster plastered in subway stations pictures an aerial shot of a crammed neighborhood with words emanating from the homes. "I'll drink a toast with fine wine," says one. "I'll finally buy those golf clubs," says another. One implores: "Let's spend it all at once!"

SOURCE: Jacob Schlesinger and David Hamilton, "Thrift Shift: The More the Japanese Save for a Rainy Day, the Gloomier It Gets," the *Wall Street Journal*, July 21, 1998, p. A1.

entire $800 billion drop in GDP must come out of consumption, which therefore falls by $800 billion (to $3,100 billion). Thus, *DI* is down to $4,000 billion and *C* is down to $3,100 billion, leaving total saving still $900 billion. The effort to save more has been totally frustrated by the decline in GDP.[4]

This remarkable result is called the **paradox of thrift,** because it shows that while saving may pave the road to riches for an individual, if the nation as a whole decides to save more, the result may be a recession and the falling incomes that come with it. The paradox of thrift is important because it is contrary to most people's thinking, and it means that a greater desire to save may be a mixed blessing if it is not accompanied by greater desire to invest in homes, factories, or equipment.

The **paradox of thrift** is the idea that an effort by a nation to save more may simply reduce national income and fail to raise total saving.

### Tax Cutting in Japan

Japan in the late 1990s is a poignant case in point. (See the accompanying box, The Paradox of Thrift in Action.) Worried about their economic futures, Japanese consumers increased their already-high propensities to save. The result was a sharp decline in the sales of consumer products, which contributed mightily to the

[4] It is even possible to devise examples in which total saving goes *down* when people attempt to save more. This will happen, for example, if there is *induced investment*.

recession. Notice also from our oversimplified multiplier formula that a *lower* marginal propensity to consume leads to a *lower* multiplier. That was the Japanese government's concern. The government feared that the MPC had fallen so low that the multiplier, although above 1, would be extraordinarily small.

# ■ THE MULTIPLIER AND THE AGGREGATE DEMAND CURVE

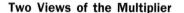

**FIGURE 27-5**

**Two Views of the Multiplier**

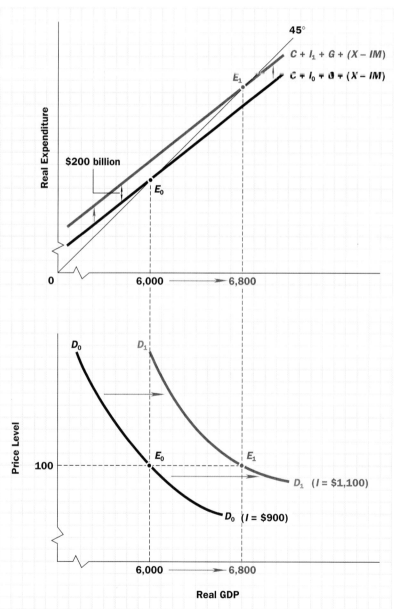

NOTE: Figures are in billions of dollars per year.

At this point, we must recall something we mentioned at the start of the chapter: Income-expenditure diagrams, such as Figures 27–1 and 27–4, can be drawn up only for a given price level. Different price levels lead to different total expenditure curves. This means that our oversimplified multiplier formula measures *the increase in real GDP demanded that would occur if the price level were fixed.* That is, it measures the *horizontal shift* of the economy's aggregate demand curve.

Figure 27–5 illustrates this conclusion by supposing that the price level that underlies Figure 27–1 is $P = 100$. The top panel simply repeats Figure 27–1 and shows how an increase in investment spending from $900 to $1,100 billion leads to an increase in GDP from $6,000 to $6,800 billion.

The bottom panel shows two downward-sloping aggregate demand curves. The first, labeled $D_0D_0$, depicts the situation when investment is $900 billion. Point $E_0$ on this curve indicates that, at the given price level $(P = 100)$, the equilibrium quantity of GDP demanded is $6,000 billion. It corresponds exactly to point $E_0$ in the top panel. The second aggregate demand curve, $D_1D_1$, depicts the situation after investment has risen to $1,100 billion. Point $E_1$ on this curve indicates that the equilibrium quantity of GDP demanded when $P = 100$ has risen to $6,800 billion, which corresponds exactly to point $E_1$ in the top panel.

As Figure 27–5 shows, the horizontal distance between the two aggregate demand curves is exactly equal to the increase in real GDP shown in the income-expenditure diagram—in this case, $800 billion. Thus:

An autonomous increase in spending leads to a horizontal shift of the aggregate demand curve by an amount given by the oversimplified multiplier formula.

So everything we have learned about the multiplier applies to *shifts of the economy's aggregate demand curve.* If businesses decide to increase their investment spending, or if the consumption function shifts up, or if the government or foreigners decide to buy more goods, the aggregate demand curve moves horizontally to the right—as indicated in Figure 27–5. If any of these variables move down instead, the aggregate demand curve moves horizontally to the left.

Thus, the economy's aggregate demand curve cannot be expected to stand still for long. Autonomous changes in one or another of the four components of total spending will cause the aggregate demand curve to move around. But to understand the consequences of shifts of aggregate demand, we must bring the aggregate supply curve into the picture. That is the task we take up in the next chapter.

## S U M M A R Y

1. Any autonomous increase in expenditure has a *multiplier* effect on GDP; that is, it increases GDP by more than the original increase in spending.

2. The reason for this multiplier effect is that one person's additional expenditure constitutes a new source of income for another person, and this additional income leads to still more spending, and so on.

3. The multiplier also works in reverse: An autonomous decrease in any component of aggregate demand leads to a multiplied decrease in national income.

4. The multiplier is the same for an *autonomous increase in consumption*, investment, government purchases, or net exports.

5. A simple formula for the multiplier says that its numerical value is $1/(1 - MPC)$. But this formula is too simple to give accurate results.

6. Rapid (or sluggish) economic growth in one country contributes to rapid (or sluggish) growth in other countries because one country's imports are other countries' exports.

7. If the nation as a whole decides to save more, that is, to consume less, the resulting decline in national income may serve to make everyone poorer. This possibility that thriftiness, although a virtue for the individual, may be disastrous for an entire nation is called the *paradox of thrift*.

## K E Y   T E R M S

The multiplier   566

Induced increase in consumption   570

Autonomous increase in consumption   570

Paradox of thrift   573

## Q U E S T I O N S   F O R   R E V I E W

1. Try to remember where you last spent a dollar. Explain how this dollar will lead to a multiplier chain of increased income and spending. (Who received the dollar? What will he or she do with it?)

2. Use both numerical and graphical methods to find the multiplier effect of the following shift in the consumption function in an economy in which investment is always $220, government purchases are always $100, and net exports are always −$40. (*Hint:* What is the marginal propensity to consume?)

| Income | Consumption before Shift | Consumption after Shift |
|--------|--------------------------|-------------------------|
| 1,080  | 880                      | 920                     |
| 1,140  | 920                      | 960                     |
| 1,200  | 960                      | 1,000                   |
| 1,260  | 1,000                    | 1,040                   |
| 1,320  | 1,040                    | 1,080                   |
| 1,380  | 1,080                    | 1,120                   |
| 1,440  | 1,120                    | 1,160                   |
| 1,500  | 1,160                    | 1,200                   |

3. Turn back to Review Question 3 in Chapter 26. Suppose investment spending rises to $260, and the price level is fixed. By how much will the equilibrium GDP increase? Derive the answer both numerically and graphically.

4. Explain the paradox of thrift. Why do you think it is called a paradox? Do you think it applies to contemporary Japan? What about the United States?

5. (More difficult) Suppose the consumption function is as given in Review Question 8 of Chapter 26:

$$C = 300 + 0.75DI$$

and investment ($I$) rises to 1,100 while net exports ($X - IM$) remain at −100, government purchases remain at 1,300, and taxes remain at 1,200. Use the equilibrium condition $Y = C + I + G + (X - IM)$ to find the equilibrium level of GDP. (In working out the answer, assume the price level is fixed.) Compare your answer to Table 27–1 and Figure 27–1. Now compare your answer to the answer to Review Question 8 of Chapter 26. What do you learn about the multiplier?

6. (More difficult) Look back at Review Question 9 of Chapter 26. What is the multiplier for this economy? If $G$ rises by 100, what happens to $Y$? What happens to $Y$ if both $G$ and $T$ rise by 100 at the same time?

---

● **APPENDIX A** ▌ **THE SIMPLE ALGEBRA OF THE MULTIPLIER**

---

The appendix to Chapter 26 presented a general expression for the equilibrium level of GDP when the price level is fixed, investment ($I$), government purchases ($G$), taxes ($T$), and net exports ($X - IM$) are all constant, and the consumption function is:

$$C = a + bDI = a + b(Y - T)$$

The answer obtained there (which can be found on page 564) was:

$$Y = \frac{a - bT + I + G + (X - IM)}{1 - b}$$

From this formula, it is easy to derive the oversimplified multiplier formula algebraically and to show that it applies equally well to a change in investment, autonomous consumer spending, government purchases, or net exports. To do so, suppose that any of the symbols in the numerator of the multiplier formula increases by 1 unit. In any of these cases, GDP would rise from the previous formula to:

$$Y = \frac{a - bT + I + G + (X - IM) + 1}{1 - b}$$

By comparing this with the previous expression for $Y$, we see that a 1-unit change in any component of spending changes equilibrium GDP by

$$\text{Change in } Y = \frac{a - bT + I + G + (X - IM) + 1}{1 - b}$$
$$- \frac{a - bT + I + G + (X - IM)}{1 - b}$$

or

$$\text{Change in } Y = \frac{1}{1 - b}$$

Recalling that $b$ is the marginal propensity to consume, we see that this is precisely the oversimplified multiplier formula.

---

● **APPENDIX B** ▌ **THE MULTIPLIER WITH VARIABLE IMPORTS**

---

In Chapters 26 and 27, we assumed that net exports were a fixed number. But in fact a nation's imports depend on its GDP. The reason is simple; higher GDP leads to higher incomes, some of which is spent on foreign goods. Thus:

**Our imports rise as our GDP rises and fall as our GDP falls.**

Similarly, our *exports* are the *imports* of other countries, so it is natural to assume that our exports depend on *their* GDPs, not on our own. Thus:

**Our exports are relatively insensitive to our own GDP, but are quite sensitive to the GDPs of other countries.**

This appendix derives the implications of these rather elementary observations. In particular, it shows that once we recognize the dependence of a nation's imports on its GDP:

**International trade lowers the value of the multiplier.**

To see why, we begin with Table 27–4, which adapts the example of our hypothetical economy to allow imports to depend on GDP. Columns (2) through (4)

---

| TABLE 27–4 | | | **Equilibrium Income with Variable Imports** | | | | |

| (1)<br>Gross<br>Domestic Product<br>(Y) | (2)<br>Consumer<br>Expenditures<br>(C) | (3)<br>Investment<br>(I) | (4)<br>Government<br>Purchases<br>(G) | (5)<br>Exports<br>(X) | (6)<br>Imports<br>(IM) | (7)<br>Net<br>Exports<br>(X − IM) | (8)<br>Total<br>Expenditure<br>[C + I + G + (X − IM)] |
|---|---|---|---|---|---|---|---|
| 4,800 | 3,000 | 900 | 1,300 | 650 | 570 | +80 | 5,280 |
| 5,200 | 3,300 | 900 | 1,300 | 650 | 630 | +20 | 5,520 |
| 5,600 | 3,600 | 900 | 1,300 | 650 | 690 | −40 | 5,760 |
| 6,000 | 3,900 | 900 | 1,300 | 650 | 750 | −100 | 6,000 |
| 6,400 | 4,200 | 900 | 1,300 | 650 | 810 | −160 | 6,240 |
| 6,800 | 4,500 | 900 | 1,300 | 650 | 870 | −220 | 6,480 |
| 7,200 | 4,800 | 900 | 1,300 | 650 | 930 | −280 | 6,720 |

NOTE: Figures are in billions of dollars per year.

**The Dependence of Net Exports on GDP**    | FIGURE 27-6 |

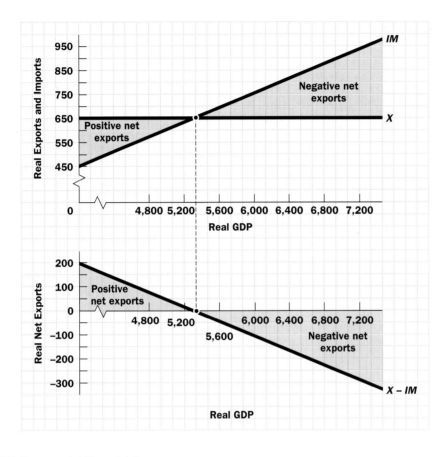

NOTE: Figures are in billions of dollars per year.

are the same as in Table 26–1; they show $C$, $I$, and $G$ at alternative levels of GDP. Columns (5) and (6) record revised assumptions about the behavior of exports and imports. Exports are fixed at $650 billion regardless of GDP. But imports are assumed to rise by $60 billion for every $400 billion rise in GDP, which is a simple numerical example of the idea that imports depend on GDP. Column (7) subtracts imports from exports to get net exports, $(X - IM)$, and Column (8) adds up the four components of total expenditure, $C + I + G + (X - IM)$. The equilibrium, you can see, occurs at $Y = $6,000$ billion, just as it did in Chapter 26.

Figures 27–6 and 27–7 display the same conclusion graphically. The upper panel of Figure 27–6 shows that exports are fixed at $650 billion regardless of GDP whereas imports increase as GDP rises, just as in Table 27–4. The difference between exports and imports, or net exports, is positive until GDP reaches around $5,300 billion and negative once GDP surpasses that amount. The bottom panel of Figure 27–6 shows the subtraction explicitly and makes it clear that:

**Net exports decline as GDP rises.**

Figure 27–7 carries this analysis over to the 45° line diagram. We begin with the familiar $C + I + G +$

| FIGURE 27-7 |

**Equilibrium GDP with Variable Imports**

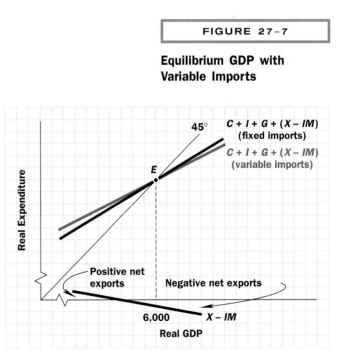

$(X - IM)$ line of Chapters 26 and 27 in black. There we simply assumed that net exports were fixed at –$100 billion regardless of GDP. Now that we have amended our model to note that net exports decline as GDP rises, the sum $C + I + G + (X - IM)$ rises more slowly than we

| TABLE 27-5 | | **Equilibrium Income after a $160 Billion Increase in Exports** | | | | | |
|---|---|---|---|---|---|---|---|
| (1)<br>Gross Domestic<br>Product<br>(Y) | (2)<br>Consumer<br>Expenditures<br>(C) | (3)<br>Investment<br>(I) | (4)<br>Government<br>Purchases<br>(G) | (5)<br>Exports<br>(X) | (6)<br>Imports<br>(IM) | (7)<br>Net<br>Exports<br>(X – IM) | (8)<br>Total<br>Expenditure<br>[C + I + G + (X – IM)] |
| 4,800 | 3,000 | 900 | 1,300 | 810 | 570 | +240 | 5,440 |
| 5,200 | 3,300 | 900 | 1,300 | 810 | 630 | +180 | 5,680 |
| 5,600 | 3,600 | 900 | 1,300 | 810 | 690 | +120 | 5,920 |
| 6,000 | 3,900 | 900 | 1,300 | 810 | 750 | +60 | 6,160 |
| 6,400 | 4,200 | 900 | 1,300 | 810 | 810 | 0 | 6,400 |
| 6,800 | 4,500 | 900 | 1,300 | 810 | 870 | −60 | 6,640 |
| 7,200 | 4,800 | 900 | 1,300 | 810 | 930 | −120 | 6,880 |

NOTE: Figures are in billions of dollars per year.

previously assumed. This is shown by the red line. Note that it is less steep than the black line.

Let us now consider what happens if exports rise by $160 billion while imports remain as in Table 27–4.

---

**FIGURE 27-8**

**The Multiplier with Variable Imports**

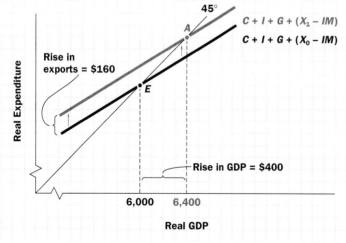

Table 27–5 shows that equilibrium now occurs at a GDP of $Y = \$6,400$ billion. Naturally, higher exports have raised domestic GDP. But consider the magnitude. A $160 billion increase in exports (from $650 billion to $810 billion) leads to an increase of $400 billion in GDP (from $6,000 billion to $6,400 billion). So the multiplier is 2.5 (=$400/$160).[5]

This same conclusion is shown graphically in Figure 27–8, where the line $C + I + G + (X_0 - IM)$ represents the original expenditure schedule and the line $C + I + G + (X_1 - IM)$ represents the expenditure schedule after the $160 billion rise in exports. Equilibrium shifts from point $E$ to point $A$, and GDP rises by $400 billion.

Notice that the multiplier in this example is 2.5, whereas in the chapter, with net exports taken to be a fixed number, it was 4. This simple example illustrates a general result: *International trade lowers the numerical value of the multiplier.* Why is this so? Because, in an open economy, any autonomous increase in spending is partly dissipated in purchases of foreign goods, which creates additional income for *foreigners* rather than for domestic citizens.

Thus, international trade gives us the first of what will eventually be several reasons why the oversimplified multiplier formula overstates the true value of the multiplier.

---

## SUMMARY

1. Because imports rise as GDP rises, while exports are insensitive to (domestic) GDP, net exports decline as GDP rises.

2. If imports depend on GDP, international trade reduces the value of the multiplier.

---

[5] *Exercise:* Construct a version of Table 27–4 to show what would happen if imports rose by $160 billion at every level of GDP while exports remained at $650 billion. You should be able to show that the new equilibrium would be $Y = \$5,600$.

1. Suppose exports and imports of a country are given by the following:

| GDP | Exports | Imports |
|-----|---------|---------|
| $2,500 | $400 | $250 |
| 3,000 | 400 | 300 |
| 3,500 | 400 | 350 |
| 4,000 | 400 | 400 |
| 4,500 | 400 | 450 |
| 5,000 | 400 | 500 |

Calculate net exports at each level of GDP.

2. If domestic expenditure (the sum of $C + I + G$ in the economy described in Review Question 1) is as shown on the following table, construct a 45° line diagram and locate the equilibrium level of GDP.

| GDP | Domestic Expenditures |
|-----|----------------------|
| $2,500 | $3,100 |
| 3,000 | 3,400 |
| 3,500 | 3,700 |
| 4,000 | 4,000 |
| 4,500 | 4,300 |
| 5,000 | 4,600 |

3. Now raise exports to $650 and find the equilibrium again. How large is the multiplier?

## CHAPTER

**28**

We might as well reasonably dispute whether it is the upper or the under blade of a pair of scissors that cuts a piece of paper, as whether value is governed by [demand] or [supply].

Alfred Marshall

# SUPPLY-SIDE EQUILIBRIUM: UNEMPLOYMENT *AND* INFLATION?

In Chapter 26, we learned that the position of the economy's total expenditure schedule governs whether the economy will experience a recessionary or an inflationary gap. If the $C + I + G + (X – IM)$ schedule is "too low," a *recessionary gap* will arise. A $C + I + G + (X – IM)$ schedule that is "too high" leads to an *inflationary gap*. Which sort of gap actually occurs is of considerable practical importance, because a recessionary gap translates into unemployment whereas an inflationary gap leads to inflation.

The tools provided in Chapter 26, however, are not sufficient to determine which sort of gap will arise because, as we learned there, the position of the expenditure schedule depends on the price level. And the price level is determined by *both* aggregate demand *and* aggregate supply.

Hence, the task of this chapter: to bring the supply side of the economy into the picture.

Doing this will put us in a position to deal with the crucial question raised in earlier chapters: Does the economy have an efficient self-correcting mechanism? We shall see that the answer is "yes, but"; yes, but it works slowly. It will also enable us to explain the vexing problem of *stagflation*—the simultaneous occurrence of high unemployment *and* high inflation—which plagued the economy in the 1980s.

### How Could Inflation Fall While the Economy Boomed?

For years, economists talked about the agonizing trade-off between inflation and unemployment—a notion that made its first appearance in Chapter 1's list of *Ideas for Beyond the Final Exam.* Very low unemployment was supposed to make the inflation rate rise. Yet the stunning success of the United States economy from 1997 through early 1999 seemed to belie this idea. The unemployment rate fell to as low as 4.2 percent of the labor force, which was the lowest rate recorded in almost 30 years. But inflation did not rise; in fact, it fell for much of this period. How can we explain this marvelous conjunction of events—extremely low unemployment coupled with falling inflation? Does it mean—as many critics said at the time—that standard economic theory did not apply to the "New Economy" of the late 1990s? Before this chapter is over, we shall have some answers.

*The Short Run Trade-off between Inflation and Unemployment*

## ■ THE AGGREGATE SUPPLY CURVE

In earlier chapters, we noted that aggregate demand is a schedule, not a fixed number. The quantity of real gross domestic product (GDP) that will be demanded depends on the price level, as summarized in the economy's *aggregate demand curve.* The same point applies to *aggregate supply:* The concept of aggregate supply does not refer to a fixed number, but rather to a schedule (a *supply curve*).

The volume of goods and services that profit-seeking enterprises will provide depends on the prices they obtain for their outputs, on wages and other production costs, on the state of technology, and on other things. The relationship between the price level and the quantity of real GDP supplied, *holding all other determinants of quantity supplied constant*, is called the economy's **aggregate supply curve.**

A typical aggregate supply curve is drawn in Figure 28–1. It slopes upward, meaning that, as prices rise, more output is produced, *other things held constant.* Let's see why.

### WHY THE AGGREGATE SUPPLY CURVE SLOPES UPWARD

Producers in the U.S. economy are motivated mainly by profit. The profit made by producing a unit of output is simply the difference between the price at which it is sold and the unit cost of production:

$$\text{Profit per unit} = \text{Price} - \text{Cost per unit}$$

**FIGURE 28–1**

**An Aggregate Supply Curve**

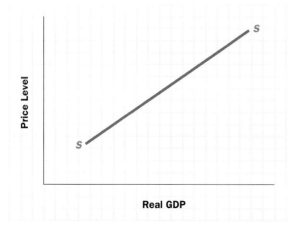

So the response of output to a rising price level—which is what the slope of the aggregate supply curve shows—depends on the response of costs.

Many of the prices that firms pay for labor and other inputs are relatively fixed for periods of time—though certainly not forever. Often, workers and firms enter into long-term labor contracts that set money wages up to three years in advance. Even where no explicit contracts exist, wage rates typically adjust only once a year. During the interim period, money wages are fixed. Similarly, a variety of material inputs are delivered to firms under long-term contracts at prearranged prices.

Why is this fact significant? Because firms decide how much to produce by comparing their selling prices with their costs of production, and production costs depend, among other things, on input prices. If the selling prices of the firm's products rise while its wages and other factor costs are fixed, production becomes more profitable, and firms will presumably increase output.

A simple example will illustrate the idea. Suppose a firm uses one hour of labor to manufacture a gadget that sells for $9. If workers earn $8 per hour, and the firm has no other costs, its profit per unit is:

$$\text{Profit per unit} = \text{Price} - \text{Cost per unit}$$
$$= \$9 - \$8 = \$1$$

Now what happens if the price of a gadget rises to $10 but wage rates remain constant? The firm's profit per unit becomes:

$$\text{Profit per unit} = \text{Price} - \text{Cost per unit}$$
$$= \$10 - \$8 = \$2$$

With production more profitable, the firm will likely supply more gadgets.

The same process operates in reverse. If selling prices fall while input costs are relatively fixed, profit margins will be squeezed and production cut back. This behavior is summarized by the upward slope of the aggregate supply curve: Production rises when the price level (henceforth, *P*) rises, and falls when *P* falls. In other words:

> The aggregate supply curve slopes upward because firms normally can purchase labor and other inputs at prices that are fixed for some period of time. Thus, higher selling prices for output make production more attractive.[1]

The phrase "for some period of time" alerts us to an important fact: The aggregate supply curve may not stand still for long. If wages or prices of other inputs change, as they surely will during inflationary times, then the aggregate supply curve will shift.

## SHIFTS OF THE AGGREGATE SUPPLY CURVE

We have concluded so far that, for given levels of wages and other input prices, there will be an upward-sloping aggregate supply curve relating the price level to aggregate quantity supplied. Now let's consider what happens when these input prices change.

**THE MONEY WAGE RATE** The most obvious determinant of the aggregate supply curve position is the *money wage rate*. Wages are the major element of cost in the economy, accounting for more than 70 percent of all inputs. Since higher wage rates mean higher costs, they spell lower profits at any given prices. That is why companies have been known to dig in their heels when unions demand large wage increases. For example, what started as a small strike in a parts plant in Flint, Michigan virtually closed down General Motors during the summer of 1998. But neither the company nor the union was inclined to yield.

The **aggregate supply curve** shows, for each possible price level, the quantity of goods and services that all the nation's businesses are willing to produce during a specified period of time, holding all other determinants of aggregate quantity supplied constant.

---

[1] There are both differences and similarities between the *aggregate* supply curve and the *microeconomic* supply curves studied in Chapter 5. Both are based on the idea that quantity supplied depends on how output prices move relative to input prices. But the aggregate supply curve pertains to the behavior of *the overall price level*, whereas a microeconomic supply curve pertains to the *price of some particular commodity*.

Returning to our example, consider what would happen to a gadget producer if the money wage rose to $8.75 per hour while the gadget's price remained $9. Profit per unit would decline from:

$$\$9 - \$8 = \$1$$

to

$$\$9.00 - \$8.75 = \$0.25$$

With profits squeezed, the firm would probably cut back on production.

This is the way firms in our economy typically react to a rise in wages. Therefore, a wage increase leads to a decrease in aggregate quantity supplied at current prices. Graphically, the aggregate supply curve shifts to the left (or inward), as shown in Figure 28–2. In this diagram, firms are willing to supply $6,000 billion in goods and services at a price level of 100 when wages are low (point *A*). But after wages increase these same firms are willing to supply only $5,500 billion at this price level (point *B*). By similar reasoning, the aggregate supply curve will shift to the right (or outward) if wages fall. Thus:

> A rise in the money wage rate makes the aggregate supply curve *shift inward,* meaning that the quantity supplied at any price level *declines.* A fall in the money wage rate makes the aggregate supply curve *shift outward,* meaning that the quantity supplied at any price level *increases.*

**PRICES OF OTHER INPUTS**    In this regard, wages are hardly unique. An increase in the price of *any* input that firms buy will shift the aggregate supply curve in the same way; that is:

> The aggregate supply curve is shifted *inward* by an increase in the price of any input to the production process, and it is shifted *outward* by any decrease.

Although producers use many inputs other than labor, the one that has attracted the most attention in recent decades is energy. Increases in energy prices, such as those that took place in the early 1980s and again during the 1991 Persian Gulf War, push the aggregate supply curve inward more or less as shown in Figure 28–2. By the same token, decreases in the price of imported oil, such as the ones we enjoyed in 1997–1998, should shift the aggregate supply curve in the opposite direction—that is, outward.

**TECHNOLOGY AND PRODUCTIVITY**    Another factor that determines the position of the aggregate supply curve is the state of technology. Suppose, for example, that a technological breakthrough increases the **productivity** of labor. If wages do not change, an improvement in productivity will *decrease* business costs, improve profitability, and encourage more production.

Once again, our gadget company will help us understand how this works. Suppose the price of a gadget stays at $9 and the hourly wage rate stays at $8, but gadget workers become much more productive. Specifically, suppose the labor input required to manufacture a gadget falls from one hour (which costs $8) to three-quarters of an hour (which costs $6). Then profit per unit rises from:

$$\$9 - \$8 = \$1$$

to

$$\$9 - \$6 = \$3$$

The lure of higher profits should induce gadget manufacturers to increase production—which is, of course, why manufacturers constantly strive to raise productivity. In brief, we have concluded that:

**FIGURE 28-2**

**A Shift of the Aggregate Supply Curve**

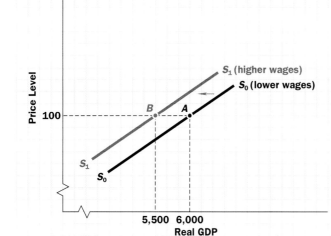

$S_1$ (higher wages)
$S_0$ (lower wages)

*B*     *A*

100

Price Level

$S_1$

$S_0$

5,500  6,000

**Real GDP**

NOTE: Amounts are in billions of dollars per year.

**Productivity** is the amount of output produced by a unit of input.

*Improvements in productivity shift the aggregate supply curve outward.*

We can therefore interpret Figure 28–2 as illustrating a *decline* in productivity. As we mentioned in Chapter 24, slow growth of productivity has been a persistent problem for the United States and other industrialized nations since the 1970s.

**AVAILABLE SUPPLIES OF LABOR AND CAPITAL**    The last determinant of the position of the aggregate supply curve is obvious. The bigger the economy—as measured by its available supplies of labor and capital—the more it is capable of producing. So:

> *As the labor force grows or improves in quality, and as investment increases the capital stock, the aggregate supply curve shifts* outward *to the right, meaning that more output can be produced at any given price level.*

So, for example, the investment boom of the 1990s, by boosting the supply of capital, has presumably left the U.S. economy with a greater capacity to produce goods and services—that is, has shifted the aggregate supply curve outward.

These, then, are the major "other things" that we hold constant when drawing up an aggregate supply curve: wage rates, prices of other inputs (such as energy), technology, labor force, and capital stock. Whereas a change in the price level moves the economy *along a given supply curve*, a change in any of the other determinants of aggregate quantity supplied *shifts the entire supply schedule*.

## ■ EQUILIBRIUM OF AGGREGATE DEMAND AND SUPPLY

Chapter 26 taught us that the price level is a crucial determinant of whether equilibrium GDP falls below full employment (a "recessionary gap"), precisely at full employment, or above full employment (an "inflationary gap"). We can now analyze which type of gap, if any, will actually occur in any particular case. By combining the aggregate supply analysis we just completed with the aggregate demand analysis from the last two chapters, we can determine *simultaneously* the equilibrium level of real GDP ($Y$) and the equilibrium price level ($P$).

Figure 28–3 displays the simple mechanics. Aggregate demand curve *DD* and aggregate supply curve *SS* intersect at point *E*, where real GDP is $6,000 billion and the price level is 100. As can be seen in the graph, at any higher price level, such as 120, aggregate quantity supplied would exceed aggregate quantity demanded. There would be a glut on the market as firms found themselves unable to sell all their output. As inventories piled up, firms would compete more vigorously for the available customers, thereby forcing prices down. Both the price level and production would fall.

At any price level lower than 100, such as 80, quantity demanded would exceed quantity supplied. There would be a shortage of goods on the market. With inventories disappearing and customers knocking on their doors, firms would be encouraged to raise prices. The price level would rise, and so would output. Only when the price level is 100 are the quantities of real GDP demanded and supplied equal. Therefore, only the combination of $P = 100$, $Y = \$6,000$ is an equilibrium.

Table 28–1 illustrates the same conclusion in another way, using a tabular analysis similar to the one in Chapter 26 (refer back to Table 26–2). Columns (1) and (2) constitute an aggregate demand schedule corresponding to the aggregate demand curve *DD* in Figure 28–3. Columns (1) and (3) constitute an aggregate supply schedule corresponding exactly to aggregate supply curve *SS* in the figure.

The table clearly shows that equilibrium occurs only at $P = 100$ and $Y = \$6,000$. At any other price level, aggregate quantities supplied and demanded would be

**FIGURE 28-3**

**Equilibrium of Real GDP and the Price Level**

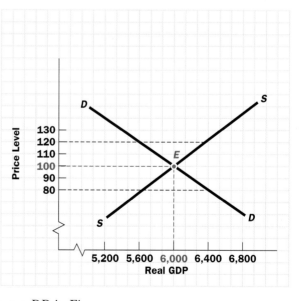

NOTE: Amounts are in billions of dollars per year.

| TABLE 28-1 |
|:----------:|

**Determination of the Equilibrium Price Level**

| (1)<br>Price Level | (2)<br>Aggregate<br>Quantity<br>Demanded | (3)<br>Aggregate<br>Quantity<br>Supplied | (4)<br>Balance of<br>Supply and<br>Demand | (5)<br>Prices<br>will be: |
|:---:|:---:|:---:|:---|:---|
| 80 | $6,400 | $5,600 | Demand<br>exceeds supply | Rising |
| 90 | 6,200 | 5,800 | Demand<br>exceeds supply | Rising |
| 100 | 6,000 | 6,000 | Demand<br>equals supply | Unchanged |
| 110 | 5,800 | 6,200 | Supply<br>exceeds demand | Falling |
| 120 | 5,600 | 6,400 | Supply<br>exceeds demand | Falling |

NOTE: Quantities are in billions of dollars.

unequal, with consequent upward or downward pressure on prices. For example, at a price level of 90, customers demand $6,200 billion worth of goods and services, but firms wish to provide only $5,800 billion. The price level is too low and will be forced upward. Conversely, at a price level of, say, 110, quantity supplied ($6,200 billion) exceeds quantity demanded ($5,800 billion), implying that the price level must fall.

## ■ RECESSIONARY AND INFLATIONARY GAPS REVISITED

Let us now reconsider a question we posed, but could not answer, in Chapter 26: Will equilibrium occur at, below, or beyond potential GDP, that is, the level of GDP corresponding to full employment?

We could not answer this question completely in Chapter 26 because we had no way to determine the equilibrium price level, and therefore no way to tell which type of gap, if any, would arise. The aggregate supply and demand analysis summarized in Figure 28–3 and Table 28–1 now gives us what we need. But we find that our answer is still the same: Anything can happen.

The reason is that Figure 28–3 tells us nothing about where potential GDP falls. It could be above the $6,000 billion equilibrium level or below it. Depending on the locations of the aggregate demand and aggregate supply curves, then, we can reach equilibrium *beyond* potential GDP (an inflationary gap), *at* potential GDP, or *below* potential GDP (a recessionary gap).

All three possibilities are illustrated in Figure 28–4. The three upper panels are familiar from Chapter 26. Remember, such income-expenditure diagrams consider *only* the demand side of the economy, and hold the price level fixed. As we move from left to right, the expenditure schedule rises from $C + I_0 + G + (X - IM)$ to $C + I_1 + G + (X - IM)$ to $C + I_2 + G + (X - IM)$, leading respectively to a recessionary gap, an equilibrium exactly at potential GDP, and an inflationary gap. In fact, the upper left-hand diagram looks just like Figure 26–6, and the upper right-hand diagram duplicates Figure 26–7. We emphasized in Chapter 26 that any one of the three cases is possible, depending on the price level and other determinants of the position of the expenditure schedule.

The three lower panels consider *both* aggregate demand *and* aggregate supply, and therefore determine *both* the equilibrium price level *and* equilibrium GDP at point *E* by the intersection of the aggregate supply curve *SS* and aggregate demand curve *DD*. But the same three possibilities nonetheless emerge.

**Recessionary and Inflationary Gaps Revisited**

FIGURE 28-4

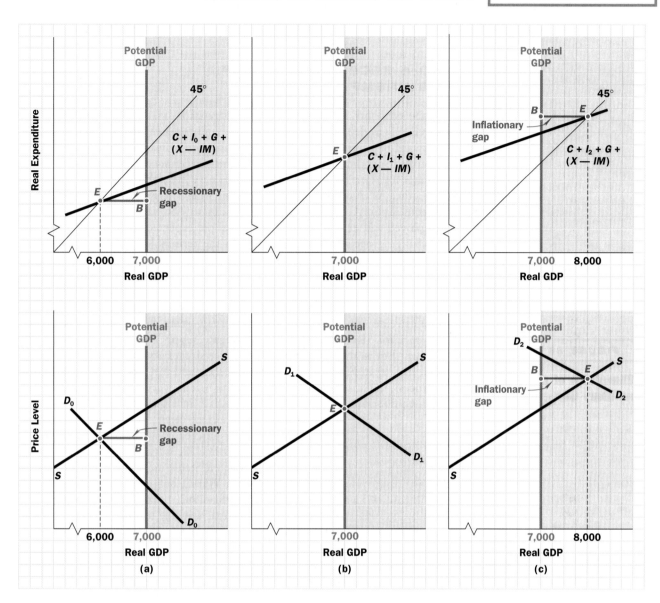

NOTE: Real GDP is in billions of dollars per year.

In the lower left-hand panel, aggregate demand is too low to provide jobs for the entire labor force, so there is a recessionary gap equal to distance *EB*, or $1,000 billion. This corresponds precisely to the situation depicted on the income-expenditure diagram immediately above it.

In the lower right-hand panel, aggregate demand is so high that the economy reaches an equilibrium well beyond potential GDP. An inflationary gap equal to *BE*, or $1,000 billion, arises, just as in the diagram immediately above it.

In the lower middle panel, the aggregate demand curve $D_1D_1$ is at just the right level to produce an equilibrium at potential GDP. Neither an inflationary nor a recessionary gap occurs, as in the diagram just above it.

It may seem, therefore, that we have done nothing but restate our previous conclusions. But, in fact, we have done much more. Because now that we have studied the determination of the equilibrium price level, we are able to examine how the economy adjusts to either a recessionary gap or an inflationary gap. Specifically, because wages are fixed in the short run, any one of the three cases depicted in

Figure 28–4 can occur. But, in the long run, wages will adjust to labor market conditions, and that will shift the aggregate supply curve. It is to that adjustment that we now turn.

# ADJUSTING TO A RECESSIONARY GAP: DEFLATION OR UNEMPLOYMENT?

Suppose the economy starts with a recessionary gap—that is, an equilibrium *below* potential GDP—as depicted in the lower left-hand panel of Figure 28–4. A situation like that might be caused, for example, by inadequate consumer spending or by anemic investment spending. Although we have not experienced such conditions in the United States for some years, recessionary gaps have been all too common recently in Japan and other Asian countries. What happens when there is a recessionary gap?

With equilibrium GDP below potential, jobs will be hard to find. The ranks of the unemployed will exceed the number of people expected to be jobless because of moving, changing occupations, and so on. In the terminology of Chapter 24, there will be a considerable amount of *cyclical unemployment.* Businesses, on the other hand, will have little trouble finding workers, and their current employees will be eager to hang on to their jobs.

In such an environment, it will be difficult for workers to win wage increases. Indeed, in extreme situations, wages may even fall—thus shifting the aggregate supply curve *outward.* (Remember that an aggregate supply curve is drawn for a *given* money wage.) But as the aggregate supply curve shifts outward—eventually moving from $S_0S_0$ to $S_1S_1$ in Figure 28–5—prices decline and the recessionary gap shrinks. By this process, deflation eventually erodes the recessionary gap—leading the economy to an equilibrium at potential GDP (point *F* in Figure 28–5).

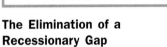

**FIGURE 28-5**

**The Elimination of a Recessionary Gap**

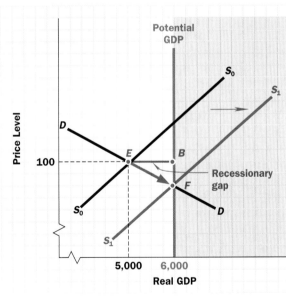

NOTE: Amounts are in billions of dollars per year.

But there is an important catch. In our modern economy, this adjustment process proceeds slowly—painfully slowly. Our brief review of the historical record in Chapter 23 showed that the history of the United States includes several examples of *deflation* before World War II but none since. Not even the severe recession of 1981–1982, during which unemployment climbed above 10 percent, was able to force average prices and wages down—though it certainly slowed their rates of increase.

Exactly why wages and prices rarely fall in our modern economy has been a subject of intense and continuing controversy among economists for years. Some economists emphasize institutional factors like minimum wage laws, union contracts, and a variety of government regulations that place legal floors under particular wages and prices. Because most of these institutions are of recent vintage, this theory successfully explains why wages and prices fall less frequently now than they did before World War II. However, only a small minority of the U.S. economy is subject to legal restraints on wage and price cutting. So it seems doubtful that legal restrictions take us very far in explaining sluggish wage-price adjustments in the United States. These institutional factors are, however, far more important in many European countries.

Other observers suggest that workers have a profound psychological resistance to accepting a wage reduction. This theory certainly has the ring of truth. Think how you would react if your boss announced he was cutting your hourly wage rate. You might quit, or you might devote less care to your job. If the boss suspects you will react this way, he may be reluctant to cut your wage. Nowadays, genuine wage reductions are rare enough to be newsworthy. But although no one doubts that wage cuts can be bad for morale, the psychological theory has one major drawback. It fails to explain why the psychological resistance to wage cuts apparently started only after World War II. Until a satisfactory answer to this question is provided, many economists will remain skeptical.

A third explanation is based on a fact we emphasized in Chapter 23—that business cycles have been less severe in the postwar period than they were in the pre-war period. Because workers and firms came to believe that recessions would not turn into depressions, the argument goes, they may have decided to wait out the bad times rather than accept wage or price reductions that they would later regret.

Yet another theory is based on the old adage, "you get what you pay for." The idea is that workers differ in productivity, but that the productivities of individual employees are hard to identify. Firms therefore worry that a general wage reduction will result in the loss of their best employees—because these workers have the best opportunities elsewhere in the economy. Rather than take this chance, the argument goes, firms prefer to maintain high wages even in recessions.

Other theories abound as well, but none of them commands a clear majority of professional opinion. But regardless of the cause, we may as well accept the fact that, in our modern economy, wages generally fall only sluggishly when demand is weak.

The implications of this rigidity are quite serious, for a recessionary gap cannot cure itself without some deflation. And if wages and prices will not fall, recessionary gaps like *EB* in Figure 28–5 will linger for a long time. That is:

> When aggregate demand is low, the economy may get stuck with a recessionary gap for a long time. If wages and prices fall very slowly, the economy will endure a prolonged period of production below potential GDP.

## DOES THE ECONOMY HAVE A SELF-CORRECTING MECHANISM?

Now a situation like this would, presumably, not last forever. As the recession lengthened, and perhaps deepened, more and more workers would be unable to find jobs at the prevailing "high" wages. Eventually, their need to be employed would overwhelm their resistance to wage cuts.

Firms, too, would become increasingly willing to cut prices as the period of weak demand persisted and managers became convinced that the slump was not merely a temporary aberration. Prices and wages did, in fact, fall during the Great Depression of the 1930s, and they are falling (slightly) now in Japan.

Nowadays, however, political leaders of both parties believe it is folly to wait for falling wages and prices to eliminate a recessionary gap. They agree that *some* government action is both necessary and appropriate under recessionary conditions. But there is still vocal—and highly partisan—debate over how much and what kind of intervention is warranted. One reason for the disagreement is that the *self-correcting mechanism* does operate—if only weakly—to cure recessionary gaps.

## AN EXAMPLE FROM RECENT HISTORY: DISINFLATION IN THE 1990s

As mentioned, recent U.S. history offers no examples of recessionary gaps. So we have to go back to the early 1990s. Recovery from the 1990–1991 recession was weak and long delayed, but it did eventually come. The unemployment rate peaked at 7.7 percent in June 1992 and then began a slow descent, which brought it down to 5.4 percent by December 1994. Meanwhile, the inflation rate fell from 6.1 percent in 1990 to 3.1 percent in 1991 and down to 2.7 percent in both 1993 and 1994. Qualitatively, this is just the sort of behavior the theoretical model of the self-correcting mechanism predicts. But it sure took a long time! Hence, the practical policy question is: How long can we afford to wait?

## ■ ADJUSTING TO AN INFLATIONARY GAP: INFLATION

Let us now consider what happens when the economy finds itself *beyond* full employment, that is, with an *inflationary* gap like that shown in Figure 28–6. When the aggregate supply curve is $S_0S_0$ and the aggregate demand curve is $DD$,

**FIGURE 28-6**

**The Elimination of an Inflationary Gap**

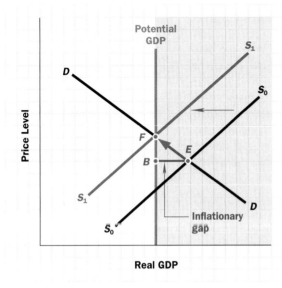

the economy will initially reach equilibrium (point *E*) with an inflationary gap, shown by the segment *BE*.

According to many economists, this is the sort of situation that described the U.S. economy in 1999. What should happen under such circumstances? As we shall see now, the tight labor market produces an inflation that eventually eliminates the gap, though perhaps in a slow and painful way. Let us see how.

When equilibrium GDP is above potential, jobs are plentiful and labor is in great demand. Firms are likely to have trouble recruiting new workers or even holding onto their old ones as other firms try to lure them away with higher wages.

Rising wages add to business costs, thus shifting the aggregate supply curve *inward*. As the aggregate supply curve shifts in from $S_0S_0$ to $S_1S_1$ in Figure 28–6, the size of the inflationary gap declines. In other words, inflation eventually erodes the inflationary gap and brings the economy to an equilibrium at potential (point *F*).

There is a straightforward way of looking at the economics underlying this process. Inflation arises because buyers are demanding more output than the economy is capable of producing at normal operating rates. To paraphrase an old cliché, there is too much demand chasing too little supply. Such an environment encourages price hikes.

But rising prices eat away at the purchasing power of consumers' wealth, forcing them to cut back on consumption, as explained in Chapter 25. In addition, exports fall and imports rise, as we learned in Chapter 27. Eventually, aggregate quantity demanded is scaled back to the economy's capacity to produce, and at this point the self-correcting process stops. In brief:

> If aggregate demand is exceptionally high, the economy may reach a short-run equilibrium above full employment (an *inflationary gap*). When this occurs, the tight situation in the labor market soon forces wages to rise. Because rising wages increase business costs, prices increase; there is inflation. As higher prices cut into consumer purchasing power and net exports, the inflationary gap begins to close.
>
> As the inflationary gap closes, output falls and prices continue to rise. When the gap is finally eliminated, a long-run equilibrium is established with a higher price level and with GDP equal to potential GDP.

This was precisely the scenario that many economists expected to be played out in 1998. Because they believed that the U.S. economy had an inflationary gap in 1997 and 1998, they expected inflation to rise. But it did not. Why not? We will have the answer in just a few more pages.

But first we repeat an important caveat: The self-correcting mechanism takes time because wages and prices do not adjust quickly. Thus, while an inflationary gap sows the seeds of its own destruction, the seeds germinate slowly. So, once again, policymakers may want to speed up the process.

## DEMAND INFLATION AND STAGFLATION

Simple as it is, this model of how the economy adjusts to an inflationary gap teaches us a number of important lessons about inflation in the real world. First, Figure 28–6 reminds us that the real culprit in this particular inflation is excessive aggregate demand—relative to potential GDP. The aggregate demand curve is initially so high that it intersects the aggregate supply curve well beyond full employment. The resulting intense demand for goods and labor pushes prices and wages higher. Although aggregate demand in excess of potential GDP is not the only possible cause of inflation, it certainly is the cause in our example.

However, business managers and journalists may blame inflation on rising wages. In a superficial sense, of course, they are right, because higher wages do indeed lead

---

● **THE GRADS OF 1998-1999 FACE THE HOTTEST JOB MARKET IN DECADES**

---

Recent college graduates—and their older, less fortunate siblings—can attest to the fact that timing matters in life. When the college graduates of the years 1991 and 1992 received their degrees, they faced a very tough job market. But their younger brothers and sisters, the graduating classes of 1998 and 1999, could hardly have asked for better luck. The unemployment rate dropped to 4.3 percent in April of 1998—the lowest reading in a generation—and employers were literally scrambling for new hires. Starting salaries rose, many graduating seniors had multiple job offers, and some firms were even offering $10,000–$20,000 bonuses to students who signed on the dotted line!

firms to raise product prices. But in a deeper sense they are wrong. Both rising wages and rising prices are symptoms of an underlying malady: too much aggregate demand. Blaming labor for inflation in such a case is a bit like blaming high doctor bills for making you ill.

Second, notice that output *falls* while prices *rise* as the economy adjusts from point *E* to point *F* in Figure 28–6. This is our first (but not our last!) explanation of the phenomenon of **stagflation**—the conjunction of inflation and economic stagnation. Specifically:

> A period of stagflation is part of the normal aftermath of a period of excessive aggregate demand.

It is easy to understand why. When aggregate demand is excessive, the economy will temporarily produce beyond its normal capacity. Labor markets tighten and wages rise. Machinery and raw materials may also become scarce and so start rising in price. Faced with higher costs, business firms quite naturally react by producing less and charging higher prices. That is stagflation.

**Stagflation** is inflation that occurs while the economy is growing slowly or having a recession.

## A RECENT EXAMPLE

The stagflation that follows a period of excessive aggregate demand is, you will note, a rather benign form of the dreaded disease. After all, while output is falling, it nonetheless remains above potential GDP, and unemployment is low. The U.S. economy last experienced such an episode about a decade ago.

The long economic expansion of the 1980s brought the unemployment rate down to 5.5 percent by mid-1988 and (briefly) to a 15-year low of 5.0 percent by March 1989. Almost all economists believe that 5.0 percent was below the full-employment unemployment rate at that time, that is, that the U.S. economy had an *inflationary gap* in 1989. As the theory suggests, inflation began to accelerate—from 4.4 percent in 1988 to 4.6 percent in 1989 and 6.1 percent in 1990.

In the meantime, the economy was stagnating. Real GDP growth fell from 3.5 percent during 1988 to 2.4 percent in 1989 and −0.2 percent in 1990. Inflation was eating away at the inflationary gap, which was virtually gone by mid-1990, when the recession started. Yet inflation remained high through the early months of the recession. The U.S. economy was in a *stagflation* phase.

Our overall conclusion about the economy's ability to right itself seems to run something like this:

> The economy does indeed have a self-correcting mechanism that tends to eliminate either unemployment or inflation. However, this mechanism works slowly and unevenly. In addition, its beneficial effects on either inflation or unemployment are sometimes swamped by strong forces (such as rapid increases or decreases in aggregate demand) pushing in the opposite direction. Thus, the self-correcting mechanism is not always reliable.

## ■ STAGFLATION FROM A SUPPLY SHOCK

We have just discussed the type of stagflation that follows in the wake of an inflationary boom. However, that is not what happened in the 1970s and early 1980s, when unemployment and inflation soared at the same time. What caused this more virulent strain of stagflation? Several things, but the principal culprit was rising energy prices.

In 1973, the Organization of Petroleum Exporting Countries (OPEC) quadrupled the price of crude oil. American consumers soon found the prices of gasoline and home heating fuels increasing sharply, and American businesses found that one important cost of doing business—energy prices—rose drastically. OPEC struck again in 1979 to 1980, this time doubling the price of oil. Then the same thing happened a third time, albeit on a smaller scale, when Iraq invaded Kuwait in 1990.

Higher energy prices, we observed earlier, shift the economy's aggregate supply curve *inward* in the manner shown in Figure 28–7. If the aggregate supply curve shifts inward, as it surely did in 1973–1974, 1979–1980, and again in 1990, production will decline. To reduce demand to the available supply, prices will have to rise. The result is the worst of both worlds: falling production and rising prices.

This conclusion is shown graphically in Figure 28–7, which superimposes an aggregate demand curve, *DD*, on the two aggregate supply curves of Figure 28–2. The economy's equilibrium shifts upward to the left, from point *E* to point *A*. Thus, output falls while prices rise—exactly our definition of stagflation. In brief:

> Stagflation is the typical result of adverse shifts of the aggregate supply curve.

The numbers used in Figure 28–7 are roughly indicative of what happened in the United States after the big "energy shock" of late 1973. Between 1973 (represented by supply curve $S_0 S_0$ and point *E*) and 1975 (represented by supply curve $S_1 S_1$ and point *A*), real GDP fell by about 1 percent, while the price level rose a stunning 19 percent. Thus, inflation soared and the economy weakened. The general lesson to be learned from the U.S. experience with supply shocks is both clear and important:

> The typical results of an adverse supply shock are a fall in output and an acceleration in inflation. This is one reason why the world economy was plagued by stagflation in the mid-1970s and early 1980s. And it can happen again if another series of supply-reducing events takes place.

---

**FIGURE 28-7**

**Stagflation from an Adverse Shift in Aggregate Supply**

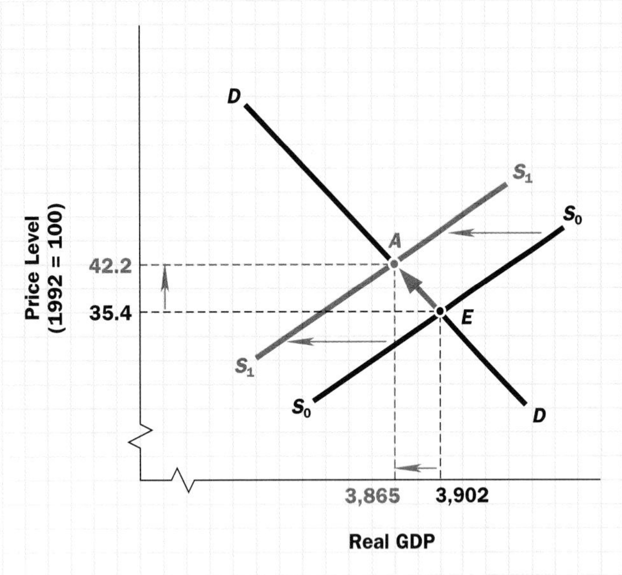

Price Level (1992 = 100)

42.2
35.4

*D*
*S₁*
*S₀*
*A*
*E*
*S₁*
*S₀*
*D*

3,865   3,902

**Real GDP**

NOTE: Amounts are in billions of dollars per year.

---

### Explaining the Roaring Nineties

Of course, the aggregate supply curve can shift in the other direction as well, and therein lies the key to understanding why the U.S. economy performed so marvelously in the late 1990s. As we observed at the start of this chapter, inflation *fell* while unemployment was extremely low, leading many observers to proclaim that some of the most basic precepts of macroeconomics no longer applied.

What really happened? Several things. First, the world oil market weakened in 1997 and 1998, and oil prices plummeted. Second, computer prices, which fall every year, started dropping at roughly twice their normal speed. Third, the rising value of the U.S. dollar made every imported input used by American businesses cheaper when foreign prices were translated into dollars[2]. Each of these three events can be thought of as a favorable supply shock that shifted the aggregate supply curve *outward,* thereby stimulating U.S. economic growth and curbing inflation. So we enjoyed the happy combination of falling unemployment and declining inflation at the same time.

Lucky? Yes. But mysterious? No. What was happening was that the economy's aggregate supply curve was shifting outward much faster than it normally does. As we know from turning our previous analysis of supply shocks in the opposite direction:

**Favorable supply shocks tend to push output up and reduce inflation.**

It was mainly a series of favorable supply shocks, not any strange new factors arising out of a "New Economy," that account for most of the surprisingly good news in the late 1990s.

## ■ INFLATION AND THE MULTIPLIER

When we introduced the concept of the multiplier in the previous chapter, we said that its actual value is smaller than suggested by the oversimplified multiplier formula for several reasons. One of these—variable imports—emerged in an appendix to the previous chapter. We are now in a position to understand the second:

**Inflation reduces the size of the multiplier.**

The basic idea is simple. In the previous chapter, we described a multiplier process in which one person's spending becomes another person's income, which leads to further spending by the second person, and so on. But this story was confined to the *demand* side of the economy. Let us therefore consider what is likely to be happening on the *supply* side as the multiplier process unfolds. Will the additional demand be taken care of by firms without raising prices?

If the aggregate supply curve slopes upward, the answer is no. More goods will be provided only at higher prices. Thus, as the multiplier chain progresses, pulling income and employment up, prices will also rise. This, as we know from earlier chapters, will reduce net exports and dampen consumer spending because rising prices erode the purchasing power of consumers' wealth. So the multiplier chain will not proceed as far as it would have in the absence of inflation.

How much inflation results from the rise in demand? How much is the multiplier chain muted by inflation? The answers depend on the slope of the economy's aggregate supply curve.

For a concrete example, let us return to the $200 billion increase in investment spending used early in the previous chapter. There we found (see especially Figure 27–1) that $200 billion in additional investment spending will eventually lead to *$800 billion in additional spending if the price level does not rise.* But that, as we now see, is unlikely to happen. To determine the actual quantity that will ultimately

---

[2] For example, a 1,000-yen electrical component costs $10 when the exchange rate is 100 yen = $1, but it costs only $8 when the exchange rate is 125 yen = $1. We will have much more to say about exchange rates in Chapter 36.

FIGURE 28-8

**Inflation and the Multiplier**

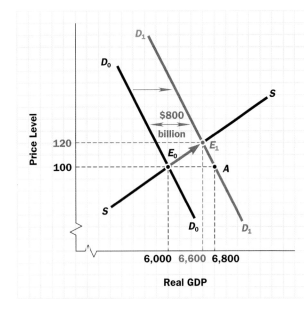

NOTE: Amounts are in billions of dollars per year.

be produced and the actual price level, we must bring the aggregate supply curve into the picture.

Figure 28–8 does precisely this. Here we show the $800 billion rightward shift of the aggregate demand curve, from $D_0D_0$ to $D_1D_1$, that we derived from the over-simplified multiplier formula in Chapter 27. Remember that this calculation ignored rising prices, that is, *it tacitly assumed that the aggregate supply curve was horizontal.* But that is not so. The slope of the aggregate supply curve, *SS*, tells us how any expansion of aggregate demand gets apportioned between higher output and higher prices.

We see in this example that, as the economy's equilibrium moves from point $E_0$ to point $E_1$, real GDP does not rise by $800 billion. Instead, prices rise, which cancels out part of the rise in quantity demanded. So output increases only from $6,000 billion to $6,600 billion—an increase of $600 billion. Thus, in our example, inflation reduces the multiplier from $800/$200 = 4 to $600/$200 = 3. In general:

As long as the aggregate supply curve slopes upward, any increase in aggregate demand will push up the price level. This, in turn, will drain off some of the higher real demand by eroding the purchasing power of consumer wealth and by reducing net exports. Thus, inflation reduces the value of the multiplier below that suggested by the oversimplified formula.

Notice also that the price level in this example has been pushed up (from 100 to 120, or 20 percent) by the rise in investment demand. This, too, is a general result:

As long as the aggregate supply curve slopes upward, any outward shift of the aggregate demand curve will cause some rise in prices.

The economic behavior behind these results is certainly not surprising. Firms faced with large increases in quantity demanded at their original prices respond to these changed circumstances in two natural ways: They raise production (so real GDP rises), and they raise prices (so the price level rises). But this rise in the price level reduces the purchasing power of the bank accounts and bonds held by consumers, and they too react in the natural way: They cut down on their spending. Such a reaction amounts to a movement *along* aggregate demand curve $D_1D_1$ in Figure 28–8 from point *A* to point $E_1$.

Figure 28–8 also shows us exactly where the oversimplified multiplier formula goes wrong. By ignoring the effects of the higher price level, the oversimplified formula erroneously supposes that the economy moves horizontally from point $E_0$ to point *A*—which it would do only if the aggregate supply curve was horizontal. As the diagram clearly shows, output does not actually rise this much, which is one reason why the oversimplified formula exaggerates the size of the multiplier.

## ■ A ROLE FOR STABILIZATION POLICY

Chapter 26 emphasized the volatility of investment spending, and Chapter 27 noted that changes in investment have multiplier effects on aggregate demand. This chapter took the next step by showing how shifts in the aggregate demand curve cause fluctuations in *both* real GDP growth *and* inflation—fluctuations that are widely decried as undesirable. It also suggested that the economy's self-correcting mechanism works, but slowly, thereby leaving room for government stabilization policy to improve the workings of the free market. Can the government really do this? If so, how? These are the questions for Part VII.

## SUMMARY

1. The economy's *aggregate supply curve* relates the quantity of goods and services that will be supplied to the price level. It normally slopes upward to the right because the costs of labor and other inputs are relatively fixed in the short run, meaning that higher selling prices make input costs relatively cheaper and therefore encourage greater production.

2. The position of the aggregate supply curve can be shifted by changes in money wage rates, prices of other inputs, technology, or quantities or qualities of labor and capital.

3. The *equilibrium price level* and the *equilibrium level of real GDP* are jointly determined by the intersection of the economy's aggregate supply and aggregate demand schedules. This intersection may come at full employment, below full employment (a recessionary gap), or above full employment (an inflationary gap).

4. The economy has a self-correcting mechanism that erodes a *recessionary gap*. Specifically, a weak labor market reduces wage increases and, in extreme cases, may even drive wages down. This shifts the aggregate supply curve outward. But it happens very slowly.

5. If there is an *inflationary gap*, the economy has a similar mechanism that erodes the gap through a process of inflation. Unusually strong job prospects push wages up, which shifts the aggregate supply curve to the left and reduces the inflationary gap.

6. One consequence of this *self-correcting mechanism* is that, if a surge in aggregate demand opens up an inflationary gap, part of the economy's natural adjustment to this event will be a period of stagflation—that is, a period in which prices are rising while output is falling.

7. An inward shift of the aggregate supply curve will cause output to fall while prices rise—that is, it will cause *stagflation*. Among the events that have caused such a shift are abrupt increases in the price of foreign oil.

8. Adverse supply shifts like this plagued our economy when oil prices skyrocketed in 1973–1974, 1979–1980, and again in 1990, leading to stagflation each time.

9. But things reversed in 1997–1998, when a series of favorable supply shocks shifted the aggregate supply curve out more rapidly than usual, thereby boosting real growth and reducing inflation at the same time.

10. Among the reasons why the oversimplified multiplier formula is wrong is the fact that it ignores the inflation that is caused by an increase in aggregate demand. Such *inflation decreases the multiplier* by reducing both consumer spending and net exports.

## KEY TERMS

Aggregate supply curve   582

Productivity   584

Equilibrium of real GDP and the price level   585

Recessionary gap   587

Inflationary gap   587

Self-correcting mechanism   589

Stagflation   591

Inflation and the multiplier   593

## QUESTIONS FOR REVIEW

1. In an economy with the following aggregate demand and aggregate supply schedules, find the equilibrium levels of real output and the price level. Graph your solution. If full employment comes at $2,800 billion, is there an inflationary or a recessionary gap?

| Aggregate Quantity Demanded | Price Level | Aggregate Quantity Supplied |
|---|---|---|
| $3,200 | 85 | 2,600 |
| 3,100 | 90 | 2,750 |
| 3,000 | 95 | 2,850 |
| 2,900 | 100 | 2,900 |
| 2,800 | 105 | 2,925 |

NOTE: Amounts are in billions of dollars.

2. Suppose a worker receives a wage of $18 per hour. Compute the real wage (money wage deflated by the price index) corresponding to each of the following possible price levels: 85, 95, 100, 110, 120. What do you notice about the relationship between the real wage and the price level? Relate this to the slope of the aggregate supply curve.

3. Explain why a decrease in the price of foreign oil shifts the aggregate supply curve outward to the right. What are the consequences of such a shift?

4. Comment on the following statement: "Inflationary and recessionary gaps are nothing to worry about because the economy has a built-in mechanism that cures either type of gap automatically."

5. Give *two* different explanations of how the economy can suffer from stagflation.

6. Why do you think wages tend to be rigid in the downward direction?

7. Add the following aggregate supply and demand schedules to the example in Review Question 3 of Chapter 26 to see how inflation affects the multiplier.

| (1) Price Level | (2) Aggregate Demand when investment is $240 | (3) Aggregate Demand when investment is $260 | (4) Aggregate Supply |
|---|---|---|---|
| 90 | $3,860 | $4,060 | $3,660 |
| 95 | 3,830 | 4,030 | 3,730 |
| 100 | 3,800 | 4,000 | 3,800 |
| 105 | 3,770 | 3,970 | 3,870 |
| 110 | 3,740 | 3,940 | 3,940 |
| 115 | 3,710 | 3,910 | 4,010 |

Draw these schedules on a piece of graph paper. Then:

a. Notice that the difference between Columns (1) and (3) (the aggregate demand schedule at two different levels of investment) is always $200. Discuss how this relates to your answer in the previous chapter.

b. Find the equilibrium GDP and the equilibrium price level both before and after the increase in investment. What is the value of the multiplier?

8. Explain in words why rising prices reduce the multiplier effect of an autonomous increase in aggregate demand.

9. Use an aggregate supply and demand diagram to show that multiplier effects are smaller when the aggregate supply curve is steeper. Which case gives rise to more inflation—the steep aggregate supply curve or the flat one? What happens to the multiplier if the aggregate supply curve is vertical?

# VII

---

## FISCAL AND MONETARY POLICY

Part VI developed a theoretical framework for undertanding the macroeconomy, based on aggregate demand and supply analysis. Part VII *uses* that framework to consider a variety of public policy issues—the sorts of things that make headlines in the newspapers and on television.

At several points in earlier chapters, we hinted that the government might be able to manage aggregate demand by using its *fiscal and monetary policies*. Chapters 29–31 pick up and develop that suggestion. You will learn how the government tries to promote rapid growth and low unemployment while simultaneously limiting inflation—and why its efforts do not always succeed. Then, in Chapters 32–34, we turn explicitly to a number of important controversies related to the government's *stabilization policy*. How should the Federal Reserve do its job? Why was the budget deficit considered to be such a serious national problem? Is there a tradeoff between inflation and unemployment?

By the end of Part VII, you will be in an excellent position to understand some of the most important debates over national economic policy—not only today, but also in the years to come.

Next, let us turn to the problems of our fiscal policy. Here the myths are legion and the truth hard to find.

John F. Kennedy

# MANAGING AGGREGATE DEMAND: FISCAL POLICY

In the model of the economy we constructed in Part VI, the government played an entirely passive role. It did some spending and collected a fixed amount of taxes, and that was about it. We concluded that such an economy has only a weak tendency to move toward an equilibrium with high employment and low inflation. Furthermore, we hinted that well-designed policies might improve the economy's performance. It is now time to pick up that hint—and to learn about some of the difficulties the government must overcome if it is to conduct a successful stabilization policy.

Traditionally, the government has used its taxing and spending powers to influence the demand side of

The government's **fiscal policy** is its plan for spending and taxation. It is designed to steer aggregate demand in some desired direction.

the economy. So this chapter begins there, in the domain of **fiscal policy.** The next three chapters take up the government's other main tool for managing aggregate demand: *monetary policy.*

### How to Stimulate Japan's Economy

The Japanese economy has been weak for years. By 1998, both consumers and investors had grown pessimistic and reduced their spending. The unemployment rate, which is traditionally quite low in Japan, rose ominously. To many observers, it looked like a classic case of an economy with a large—and growing—recessionary gap. Japan seemed to be suffering from inadequate aggregate demand. Because Japan's economy is the world's second largest, this situation set off a global debate over how Japan might use fiscal policy to stimulate its economy.

Many foreigners, especially Americans, urged the Japanese to cut income taxes. But Japanese officials resisted. They argued that income tax cuts would have unusually small multiplier effects in such depressed circumstances—much smaller than the mutiplier effects of additional government spending, which is the policy they favored.

In this chapter, we will learn the basis for the Japanese claim that tax cuts would have a smaller mutiplier than increased spending. And we will investigate other aspects of the choice between spending and taxes as stabilization tools. In the end, however, the Japanese government decided that its economy was so weak in 1998, and the need for fiscal stimulus was therefore so large, that *both* tax cuts *and* more spending were necessary.

## ■ INCOME TAXES AND THE CONSUMPTION SCHEDULE

**Fixed taxes** are taxes that do not vary with the level of GDP.

**Variable taxes** are taxes that do vary with the level of GDP.

To understand how taxes affect equilibrium gross domestic product (GDP), we must distinguish between **fixed taxes,** which are the only kind we have considered so far, and **variable taxes,** which are much more important in practice.

Most of the taxes collected by both the Japanese and American governments—indeed, by all national governments—rise and fall with GDP. In some cases, the reason is obvious: *Personal* and *corporate income tax* collections, for example, depend on how much income there is to be taxed. *Sales tax* receipts depend on GDP because consumer spending is higher when GDP is higher. On the other hand, some types of tax receipts—such as property taxes—do not vary with GDP. We call the first kind of tax *variable taxes* and the second kind *fixed taxes.*

Why is this distinction important? Remember that taxes ($T$) are the difference between gross domestic product ($Y$) and disposable income ($DI$):

$$DI = Y - T$$

Thus, when taxes increase, disposable income falls—and hence so does consumption—*even if GDP remains unchanged.* As a result:

An increase in taxes shifts the consumption schedule in our 45° line diagram *downward*. Similarly, a tax reduction shifts the consumption schedule *upward*.

But precisely *how* the consumption schedule shifts depends on the nature of the tax change. If a fixed tax is increased, disposable income falls by the *same* amount regardless of the level of GDP. Hence, the decline in consumer spending is the same. In a word, the $C$ schedule shifts downward in a parallel manner, as shown in Figure 29–1(a).

But many tax policies change disposable income by amounts that depend on income levels—normally the tax change is greater when incomes are higher. This is true, for example, whenever Congress alters the bracket rates in the personal income tax code, as it last did in 1993. Because higher tax rates decrease disposable income more when GDP is higher, the $C$ schedule shifts down more sharply at higher income levels than at lower ones. [See Figure 29–1(b).] The same relationships apply for tax decreases, as the upward shifts in both panels show.

The two parts of Figure 29–1 illustrate the first reason why the distinction between fixed and variable taxes is important. Figure 29–2 illustrates the second. Here we show two consumption lines, $C_1$ and $C_2$. $C_1$ is the consumption schedule used in previous chapters; it is constructed on the assumption that taxes are fixed at $1,200 billion regardless of GDP. $C_2$ depicts a more realistic case in which the government collects taxes equal to 20 percent of GDP. You will notice that $C_2$ is flatter than $C_1$. This is no accident. In fact:

Variable taxes such as the income tax flatten the consumption schedule in a 45° line diagram.

We can easily understand why. Column (1) of Table 29–1 shows alternative values of GDP ranging from $4.5 trillion to $7.5 trillion. Column (2) then indicates that taxes are always one-fifth of this amount. Column (3) subtracts Column (2) from Column (1) to arrive at disposable income ($DI$). Column (4) then gives the amount of consumer spending corresponding to each level of $DI$. The schedule relating $C$ to $Y$, which we need for our 45° diagram, is therefore found in Columns (1) and (4).

**FIGURE 29–1**

**How Tax Policy Shifts the Consumption Schedule**

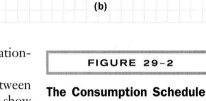

(a)

(b)

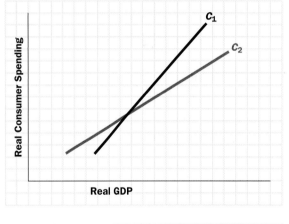

**FIGURE 29–2**

**The Consumption Schedule with Fixed and Variable Taxes**

**The Effects of an Income Tax on the Consumption Schedule**

**TABLE 29–1**

| (1) Gross Domestic Product | (2) Taxes | (3) Disposable Income (GDP minus taxes) | (4) Consumption |
|---|---|---|---|
| $4,500 | $900 | $3,600 | $3,000 |
| 5,000 | 1,000 | 4,000 | 3,300 |
| 5,500 | 1,100 | 4,400 | 3,600 |
| 6,000 | 1,200 | 4,800 | 3,900 |
| 6,500 | 1,300 | 5,200 | 4,200 |
| 7,000 | 1,400 | 5,600 | 4,500 |
| 7,500 | 1,500 | 6,000 | 4,800 |

NOTE: Figures are in billions of dollars per year.

| TABLE 29-2 |
| --- |

**The Relationship between Consumption and GDP**

| With Fixed Taxes (T = $1,200) (from Table 27-1) | | With a 20 Percent Income Tax (from Table 29-1) | |
| --- | --- | --- | --- |
| Y | C | Y | C |
| $4,800 | $3,000 | $4,500 | $3,000 |
| 5,200 | 3,300 | 5,000 | 3,300 |
| 5,600 | 3,600 | 5,500 | 3,600 |
| 6,000 | 3,900 | 6,000 | 3,900 |
| 6,400 | 4,200 | 6,500 | 4,200 |
| 6,800 | 4,500 | 7,000 | 4,500 |
| 7,200 | 4,800 | 7,500 | 4,800 |
| Line $C_1$ in Figure 29-2 | | Line $C_2$ in Figure 29-2 | |

Notice that, in Table 29–1, each $500 billion increase in GDP leads to a $300 billion rise in consumer spending. Thus, the slope of line $C_2$ in Figure 29–2 is $300/$500, or 0.60. But, in our examples in Chapter 27, consumption rose by $300 billion each time GDP increased $400 billion—making the slope $300/$400, or 0.75. (See the steeper line $C_1$ in Figure 29–2.) Table 29–2 compares the two cases explicitly. In Chapter 27, taxes were fixed at $1,200 billion and each $400 billion rise in $Y$ led to a $300 billion rise in $C$—as in the left-hand panel. But now, with taxes variable (equal to 20 percent of GDP), each $500 billion increment to $Y$ gives rise to a $300 billion increase in $C$—as in the highlighted right-hand panel.

All of this sounds terribly mechanical, but the economic reasoning behind it is both straightforward and vital to understanding tax policies. When taxes are fixed, as in line $C_1$, each additional dollar of GDP raises disposable income ($DI$) by $1. Consumer spending then rises by $1 times the marginal propensity to consume (MPC), which is 0.75 in our example. Hence, each additional dollar of GDP leads to 75 cents more spending. But when taxes vary with income, each additional dollar of GDP raises $DI$ by less than $1 because the government takes a share in taxes. In our example, taxes are 20 percent of GDP, so each additional $1 of GDP generates 80 cents more $DI$. With an MPC of 0.75, that means that spending rises by only 60 cents (75 percent of 80 cents) each time GDP rises by $1. Thus, the slope of line $C_2$ in Figure 29–2 is only 0.60, instead of 0.75.

Table 29–3 and Figure 29–3 take the next step by replacing the old consumption schedule with this new one in both the tabular presentation of income determination and the 45° line diagram. We see immediately that the equilibrium level of GDP is at point $E$. Here gross domestic product is $6,000 billion, consumption is $3,900 billion, investment is $900 billion, net exports are −$100 billion, and government purchases are $1,300 billion. As we know, full employment may occur above or below $Y = $6,000 billion. If below, an inflationary gap arises. Prices probably will start to rise, pulling the expenditure schedule down and reducing equilibrium GDP. If above, a recessionary gap results, and history suggests that prices will fall only slowly. In the interim, the economy will suffer a period of high unemployment.

| FIGURE 29-3 |
| --- |

**Income Determination with a Variable Income Tax**

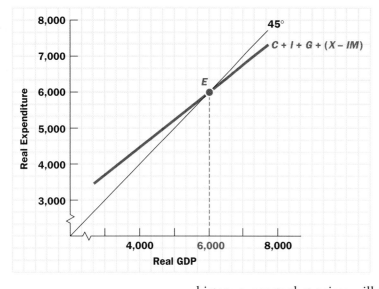

NOTE: Figures are in billions of dollars per year.

**Total Expenditure Schedule with a 20 Percent Income Tax**

TABLE 29-3

| (1) Gross Domestic Product Y | (2) Consumption C | (3) Investment I | (4) Government Purchases G | (5) Net Exports (X – IM) | (6) Total Expenditures C + I + G + (X – IM) |
|---|---|---|---|---|---|
| $4,500 | $3,000 | $900 | $1,300 | –$100 | $5,100 |
| 5,000 | 3,300 | 900 | 1,300 | –100 | 5,400 |
| 5,500 | 3,600 | 900 | 1,300 | –100 | 5,700 |
| 6,000 | 3,900 | 900 | 1,300 | –100 | 6,000 |
| 6,500 | 4,200 | 900 | 1,300 | –100 | 6,300 |
| 7,000 | 4,500 | 900 | 1,300 | –100 | 6,600 |
| 7,500 | 4,800 | 900 | 1,300 | –100 | 6,900 |

NOTE: Figures are in billions of dollars per year.

In short, once we adjust the expenditure schedule for variable taxes, the determination of national income proceeds exactly as before. The effects of government spending and taxation, therefore, are fairly straightforward and can be summarized as follows:

Government purchases of goods and services add to total spending *directly* through the G component of C + I + G + (X − IM). Taxes reduce total spending *indirectly* by lowering disposable income and thus reducing the C component of C + I + G + (X − IM). On balance, then, the government's actions may raise or lower the equilibrium level of GDP, depending on how much spending and taxing it does.

However, there is more to the story. As we will see next:

The multiplier is smaller in the presence of an income tax.

## THE MULTIPLIER REVISITED

We learned in Chapter 27 that the multiplier works through a chain of spending and respending, as one person's expenditure becomes another's income. But, if income is taxed, some of the additional income leaks out of the circular flow at each stage. Specifically, if the income tax rate is 20 percent, when Microhard spends $1 million on salaries, workers actually receive only $800,000 in *after-tax* (that is, disposable) income. If workers spend 75 percent of this amount (because the MPC is 0.75), spending in the next round will be only $600,000. Notice that this is only *60 percent* of the original expenditure, not *75 percent*—just as we observed in the last section.

Thus, the multiplier chain for each original dollar of spending shrinks from:

$$1 + 0.75 + (0.75)^2 + (0.75)^3 + \cdots = \frac{1}{1 - 0.75} = \frac{1}{0.25} = 4$$

to

$$1 + 0.6 + (0.6)^2 + (0.6)^3 = \cdots = \frac{1}{1 - 0.6} = \frac{1}{0.4} = 2.5$$

This is clearly a large reduction in the multiplier. We thus have a third reason why the oversimplified multiplier formula of Chapter 27 exaggerates the size of the multiplier: It ignores income taxes.

**Reasons Why the Oversimplified Multiplier Formula Is Wrong:**

1. It ignores variable imports, which reduce the size of the multiplier (see Appendix B to Chapter 27).

2. It ignores price-level changes, which reduce the multiplier (see Chapter 28).

3. It ignores income taxes, which also reduce the size of the multiplier (this chapter).

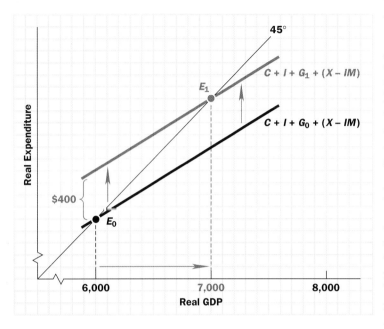

**FIGURE 29-4**

**The Multiplier in the Presence of an Income Tax**

NOTE: Figures are in billions of dollars per year.

The last of these three reasons is the most important in practice.

This conclusion about the multiplier is shown graphically in Figure 29–4, where we have drawn our $C + I + G + (X - IM)$ schedules with a slope of 0.6 rather than the 0.75 slope we used in earlier chapters. This new slope reflects an MPC of 0.75 and a tax rate of 20 percent. Figure 29–4 depicts the effect of a \$400 billion increase in government purchases of goods and services, which shifts the $C + I + G + (X - IM)$ schedule from $C + I + G_0 + (X - IM)$ to $C + I + G_1 + (X - IM)$. Equilibrium moves from point $E_0$ to point $E_1$—a GDP increase from $Y = \$6,000$ billion to $Y = \$7,000$ billion. Thus, if we ignore for the moment any increases in the price level (which would further reduce the multiplier), a \$400 billion increment in government spending leads to a \$1,000 billion increment in GDP. So, when taxes are included in our model, the multiplier is only \$1,000/\$400 = 2.5, just as we concluded before.

## AUTOMATIC STABILIZERS

The size of the multiplier may seem to be a rather abstract notion of little practical importance. But such is not the case. Fluctuations in one or another of the components of total spending—$C$, $I$, $G$, or $X - IM$—happen all the time. Some come unexpectedly; some are even hard to explain after the fact. We know from Chapter 27 that any such fluctuation will move GDP up or down by a multiplied amount. If the multiplier is smaller, GDP will be less sensitive to such shocks—that is, the economy will be more stable.

An **automatic stabilizer** is a feature of the economy that reduces its sensitivity to shocks, such as sharp increases or decreases in spending.

Features of the economy that reduce its sensitivity to shocks are called **automatic stabilizers.** The most obvious example is the one we have just been discussing: the personal income tax. This tax acts as a shock absorber because it makes disposable income, and thus consumer spending, less sensitive to fluctuations in GDP. As we have just seen, when GDP rises, disposable income (*DI*) rises less because part of the increase in GDP is siphoned off by the U.S. Treasury. This helps limit any increase in consumption spending. When GDP falls, *DI* falls less sharply because part of the loss is absorbed by the Treasury rather than by consumers. So consumption does not drop as much as it otherwise might. Thus, the much-maligned personal income tax is one of several features of our modern economy that helps ensure against a repeat performance of the Great Depression.

Our economy features many other automatic stabilizers. For example, Chapter 24 discussed the U.S. system of unemployment insurance. This program serves as an automatic stabilizer as well: When GDP drops and people lose their jobs, unemployment benefits prevent disposable incomes from falling as dramatically as earnings do. As a result, unemployed workers can maintain their spending better, and consumption fluctuates less than employment.

The list could continue. The basic principle is the same: Each automatic stabilizer serves, in one way or another, as a shock absorber, thereby lowering the multiplier. And each does so quickly, without the need for any decision maker to take action. In a word, they work *automatically*.

## MULTIPLIERS FOR TAX POLICY

Now let us turn our attention to multipliers for tax changes. These are more complicated than multipliers for spending such as $G$ or $I$, because they work indirectly via consumption. Tax multipliers must be worked out in two steps.

**Step 1.** Figure out how much any proposed or actual changes in the tax law affect consumer spending.

**Step 2.** Enter this vertical shift of the consumption schedule in the 45°line diagram and see how it affects output.

A reduction in income taxes provides a convenient example of this two-step procedure because we have already done Step 1 in Chapter 25, when we studied how consumer spending would respond to an income tax cut. There we concluded that, if consumers viewed the tax reduction as permanent, they would increase their spending by an amount equal to the tax cut times the marginal propensity to consume.

To create a simple and familiar numerical example, suppose income taxes fall by a fixed amount at each level of GDP—say by $400 billion, from $0.2Y$ (that is, 20 percent of GDP) to $0.2Y - \$400$ billion. Step 1 instructs us to multiply the $400 billion tax cut by the marginal propensity to consume (MPC), which is 0.75, to get $300 billion as the vertical shift of the consumption schedule.

Step 2 then instructs us to multiply this $300 billion increase in consumption by the multiplier—which is 2.5 in our example—giving $750 billion as the rise in GDP. Figure 29–5 verifies that this is so by entering a $300 billion vertical shift of the consumption function into the 45° line diagram and noting that GDP does indeed rise by $750 billion as a result—from $6,000 billion to $6,750 billion.

Notice something interesting here. The $400 billion tax cut raises GDP by $750 billion. Thus, the multiplier is $700/\$400 = 1.875$. But the multiplier for the $400 government purchases that we worked out on the previous page and depicted in Figure 29–4 was 2.5. What's going on here? Apparently:

The multiplier for changes in taxes is smaller than the multiplier for changes in government purchases.

The reason is no mystery. Although $G$ is a direct component of total expenditure, taxes are not. Taxes work indirectly, by first changing disposable income which then changes $C$ according to the MPC. Because some of the change in disposable income affects *saving* rather than *spending*, a $1 tax cut does not pack as much punch as $1 of $G$. That is why we must multiply the $400 billion change in taxes by 0.75 to get the $300 billion shift of the $C$ schedule shown in Figure 29–5.

The fact that the multiplier for taxes is smaller than the multiplier for $G$ has several interesting implications.

**The Multiplier for a Reduction In Fixed Taxes**

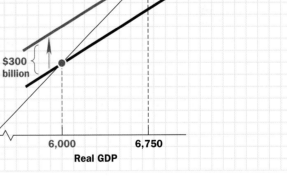

NOTE: Figures are in billions of dollars per year.

### The Japanese Economy

The first pertains to the debate over Japanese fiscal policy mentioned at the start of this chapter. It really is true that a tax cut should pack less punch than a spending increase of equal dollar (or yen) amount. How much less? That depends on the marginal propensity to consume. If the MPC in Japan in 1998 really was extremely low because consumers were insecure, then the tax-cut multiplier would have been much smaller than the expenditure multiplier—as the government of Japan claimed.

Second, different multipliers for government purchases and taxes imply that if the government raises $G$ and $T$ by equal amounts, the effects do not cancel out. Instead, the equilibrium level of GDP on the demand side rises. Similarly, if $G$ and $T$ fall by equal amounts, the equilibrium level of GDP on the demand side falls. For example, we have seen that a $400 billion increase in $G$ raises GDP by $1,000 billion, whereas a $400 billion cut in $T$ raises GDP by just $750 billion. Thus, if *both* $G$ and $T$ are *raised* by $400 billion, GDP will go up by $250 billion.

The moral of the story is that fiscal policies that seem to keep the deficit $(G - T)$ the same do not necessarily keep aggregate demand the same. A cut in government spending balanced by an equal cut in tax revenues can be expected to reduce $Y$—a lesson that policymakers frequently forget.

### GOVERNMENT TRANSFER PAYMENTS

Finally, we should mention the last major tool of fiscal policy: *government transfer payments.* Transfers, you will remember, are payments to individuals that do not compensate them for any direct contribution to production. How are transfers treated in our models of income determination—like purchases of goods and services $(G)$ or like taxes $(T)$?

The answer follows readily from the circular flow diagram back on page 553 or the accounting identity on page 600. The important thing to understand about transfer payments is that they intervene between gross domestic product $(Y)$ and disposable income $(DI)$ in precisely the *opposite* way from income taxes.

Specifically, starting with the wages, interest, rents, and profits that constitute national income, we *subtract* income taxes to calculate disposable income. We do so because these taxes represent the portion of incomes that consumers *earn* but never *receive.* But then we must *add* transfer payments because they represent sources of income that are *received* although they were not *earned* in the process of production. Thus:

**Transfer payments are basically negative taxes.**

So giving consumers $400 billion in the form of transfer payments is treated in the 45° line diagram as a $400 billion decrease in taxes. Thus, Figure 29–5, which we devised to illustrate a tax cut, also illustrates a rise in unemployment benefits, or in Social Security benefits, or any other such transfer payment. Similarly, the analysis of a decrease in transfer payments would proceed exactly like the analysis of a tax increase.

## ■ PLANNING EXPANSIONARY FISCAL POLICY

Now imagine you are a member of Congress (or the Japanese Diet) trying to decide whether to use fiscal policy to stimulate the economy—and, if so, by how much. Suppose the economy would have a GDP of $6,000 billion if the government simply reenacted last year's budget. Suppose further that your goal is to achieve a fully employed labor force and that staff economists tell you that this would require a GDP of approximately $7,000 billion. Finally, just to keep the calculations manageable, imagine that the price level is fixed. What sort of budget should you vote for?

This chapter has taught us that the government has three ways to raise GDP by $1,000 billion. Congress can close the recessionary gap between actual and potential GDP by:

- Raising government purchases
- Reducing taxes
- Increasing transfer payments

Figure 29–6 illustrates the problem and its cure through higher government spending, on our 45° line diagram. Figure 29–6(a) shows the equilibrium of the economy if no changes are made in the budget. Except for the full-employment line

**Fiscal Policy to Eliminate a Recessionary Gap**    FIGURE 29-6

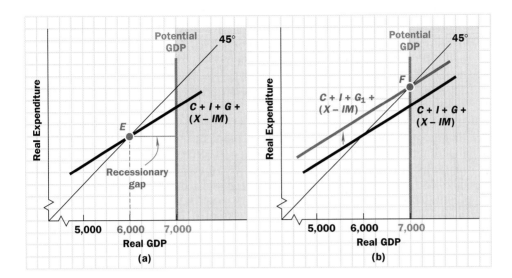

NOTE: Figures are in billions of dollars per year.

at $Y = \$7,000$ and the corresponding recessionary gap, it looks just like Figure 29–3. With an expenditure multiplier of 2.5, you can figure out that an additional $400 billion of government spending will be needed to push GDP up $1,000 billion and eliminate the gap ($400 × 2.5 = $1,000).

So you might vote to raise $G$ from $G_0 = \$1,300$ billion to $G_1 = \$1,700$ billion, hoping to move the $C + I + G + (X - IM)$ line in Figure 29–6(a) up to the position indicated in Figure 29–6(b), thereby achieving full employment. Or you might prefer to achieve this fiscal stimulus by lowering income taxes instead. Or you might opt for more generous transfer payments. The point is that there are a variety of budgets capable of increasing GDP by $1,000 billion. Figure 29–6 applies equally well to any of them.

*"I need some short-term economic stimulus."*

### ■  PLANNING CONTRACTIONARY FISCAL POLICY

The preceding example assumed that the basic problem of fiscal policy is to close a recessionary gap, as has been the case in Japan for years. Often this is so. But by 1999 many economists believed that the major macroeconomic problem in the United States was just the opposite: real GDP exceeded potential GDP, leading to an inflationary gap. In such a case, government would wish to adopt more restrictive fiscal policies to reduce aggregate demand.

It does not take much imagination to run our previous analysis in reverse. If an inflationary gap would arise from a continuation of current budget policies, contractionary fiscal policy tools can eliminate it. By cutting spending, raising taxes, or by some combination of the two, the government can pull the $C + G + I + (X - IM)$ schedule down to a noninflationary position and achieve an equilibrium at full employment.

Notice the difference between this way of eliminating an inflationary gap and the natural self-correcting mechanism that we discussed in the last chapter. There we observed that, if the economy were left to its own devices, a cumulative but self-limiting process of inflation would eventually eliminate the inflationary gap and return the economy to full employment. Here we see that we need not put the economy through the inflationary wringer. Instead, a restrictive fiscal policy can avoid inflation by limiting aggregate demand to the level the economy can produce at full employment.

### ■  THE CHOICE BETWEEN SPENDING POLICY AND TAX POLICY

In principle, fiscal policy can nudge the economy in the desired direction equally well by changing government spending or by changing taxes. For example, if the government wants to expand the economy, it can raise $G$ or lower $T$. Either policy would shift the total expenditure schedule upward, as depicted in Figure 29–6, thereby raising the equilibrium GDP on the demand side.

In terms of our aggregate demand and supply diagram, either policy shifts the aggregate demand curve outward, from $D_0D_0$ to $D_1D_1$ in Figure 29–7. As a result, the economy's equilibrium moves from point $E$ to point $A$. Both real GDP and the price level rise. As this diagram points out:

> Any combination of higher spending and lower taxes that produces the same aggregate demand curve leads to the same increases in real GDP and prices.

How, then, do policymakers decide whether to raise spending or to cut taxes? The answer depends mainly on how large a public sector they want to create: a long-running debate in the United States, which has become particularly contentious of late.

The small-government point of view, typically advocated by conservatives who gained the ascendancy in the 1990s, says that we are foolish to rely on the public sector to do things that private individuals and businesses can do better on their own. Conservatives believe that the growth of government interferes too much in our everyday lives, thereby curtailing our freedom. Those who hold this view can argue for *tax cuts* when macroeconomic considerations call for expansionary fiscal policy, and for *lower public spending* when contractionary policy is required.

An opposing opinion, expressed most often by liberals, holds that something is amiss when a country as wealthy as the United States has such an impoverished public sector. In this view, America's most pressing needs are not for more fast food and video games but rather for better schools, more efficient public transportation

**FIGURE 29–7**

**Expansionary Fiscal Policy**

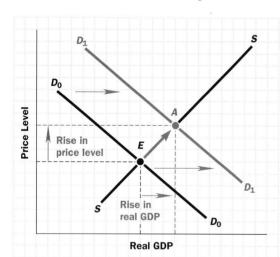

"Free gifts to every kid in the world?—
Are you a *Keynesian* or something?"

systems, and cleaner and safer city streets. People on this side of the debate believe that we should *increase* spending when the economy needs stimulus and pay for these improved public services by *increasing taxes* when it is necessary to rein in the economy.

The use of fiscal policy for economic stabilization is sometimes erroneously associated with a large and growing public sector—that is, with "big government." This need not be the case.

> Individuals favoring a smaller public sector can advocate an active fiscal policy just as well as those who favor a larger public sector. Advocates of bigger government should seek to expand demand (when appropriate) through higher government spending and contract demand (when appropriate) through tax increases. By contrast, advocates of smaller government should seek to expand demand by cutting taxes and reduce demand by cutting expenditures.

Ronald Reagan's presidency should have dispelled the myth that active fiscal policy spells big government, because President Reagan pursued an extremely activist fiscal policy that boosted the economy with tax cuts, not with more spending.

## ■ SOME HARSH REALITIES

The mechanics outlined so far in this chapter make the fiscal policy planner's job look rather simple. The elementary diagrams suggest, rather misleadingly, that policymakers can drive GDP to any level they please simply by manipulating spending and tax programs. It seems they should be able to hit the full-employment bull's eye every time. But, in fact, a better analogy is shooting through dense fog at an erratically moving target with an inaccurate gun and slow-moving bullets!

The target is moving because, in the real world, the investment, net exports, and consumption schedules constantly shift about as expectations, technology, events abroad, and other factors change. This means that the policies decided on today, which will take effect at some future date, may no longer be appropriate by the time that date rolls around.

The second misleading feature of our diagrams (the "inaccurate gun") is that we do not know multipliers with as much precision as our examples suggest. Thus, although our best guess may be that a $20 billion cut in government purchases will reduce GDP by $35 billion (a multiplier of 1.75), the actual outcome may be as little as $20 billion or as much as $50 billion. It is therefore impossible to "fine tune" every wobble out of the economy's growth path. Economic science is simply not that precise.

A third complication is that our target—full-employment GDP—may be only dimly visible, as if through a fog. For example, a lively debate has lately arisen over whether the unemployment rate that corresponds to full employment might be lower than mainstream economists have thought, perhaps even as low as 4.5 percent.

A final complication is that fiscal-policy "bullets" travel slowly: Tax and spending policies affect aggregate demand only after some time elapses. Consumer spending, for example, may take months to react to an income tax cut. Because of these *time lags*, fiscal policy decisions must be based on *forecasts* of the future state of the economy. And no one has yet discovered a foolproof method of economic forecasting. The combination of long lags and poor forecasts may occasionally leave the government fighting the last inflation just as the new recession gets under way.

In addition to all of these operational problems, legislators trying to decide whether to push the unemployment rate lower would like to know how large the inflation cost is likely to be. As we know, an expansionary fiscal policy that reduces a recessionary gap by increasing aggregate demand will lower unemployment. But it also tends to be inflationary. This undesirable side effect may make the government hesitant to use fiscal policy to combat recessions.

Is there a way out of this dilemma? Can we carry on the battle against unemployment without aggravating inflation? For more than 20 years, a small but influential minority of economists, journalists, and politicians have argued that we can. They call their approach "supply-side economics." The idea helped sweep Ronald Reagan to smashing electoral victories in 1980 and 1984. By 1992, however, Bill Clinton was able to win the presidency by running against it. Just what is supply-side economics?

## ■ THE IDEA BEHIND SUPPLY-SIDE TAX CUTS

The central idea of supply-side economics is that certain types of tax cuts can be expected to increase aggregate supply. For example, taxes can be cut in ways that raise the rewards for working, saving, and investing. *If people actually respond to these incentives*, such tax cuts will increase the total labor and capital supplies in the economy, thereby increasing aggregate supply.

Figure 29–8 illustrates the idea on an aggregate supply and demand diagram. If policy measures can shift the economy's aggregate supply to position $S_1S_1$, then prices will be lower and output higher than if the aggregate supply curve remained at $S_0S_0$. Policymakers will have reduced inflation and raised real output (lowering unemployment) at the same time—as shown by point $B$ in the figure. The trade-off between inflation and unemployment will have been defeated. This is the goal of supply-side economics.

What sorts of policies do supply siders advocate? Here is a small sample of their long list of recommended tax cuts:

**LOWER PERSONAL INCOME TAX RATES** Sharp cuts in personal taxes were the cornerstone of President Reagan's economic strategy. Tax rates on individuals were reduced in stages between 1981 and 1984, and then again in 1986. By 1987, the richest Americans were in the 28 percent tax bracket, and most taxpayers were in the 15 percent bracket. Such low tax rates, supply siders argued, augment the supplies of both labor and capital.

**REDUCE TAXES ON INCOME FROM SAVINGS** One extreme form of this proposal would simply exempt from taxation all income from interest and dividends. Since income must be either consumed or saved, this would, in effect, change our present personal income tax into a tax on consumer spending. Several such proposals for radical tax reform have been under serious consideration in Washington for years.

**REDUCE TAXES ON CAPITAL GAINS** When investors sell assets for a profit, that profit is called a *capital gain* on their investments. Supply siders argue that the

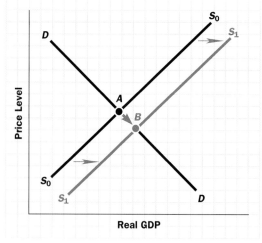

**FIGURE 29–8**

**The Goal of Supply-Side Tax Cuts**

government can encourage more investment by taxing capital gains at lower rates than ordinary income. This proposal, long favored by many Republicans, was enacted in 1997, when the top tax rate on capital gains was cut to 20 percent.

**REDUCE THE CORPORATE INCOME TAX** By reducing the tax burden on corporations, proponents argue, the government can provide both greater investment incentives (by raising the profitability of investment) and more investable funds (by letting companies keep more of their earnings). This advice was followed in 1986.

Let us suppose, for the moment, that a successful supply-side tax cut is enacted. Because *both* aggregate demand *and* aggregate supply increase simultaneously, the economy may be able to avoid the painful inflationary consequences of an expansionary fiscal policy shown in Figure 29–7.

Figure 29–9 illustrates this conclusion. The two aggregate demand curves and the initial aggregate supply curve $S_0S_0$ carry over directly from Figure 29–7. But we have introduced an additional supply curve, $S_1S_1$, to reflect the successful supply-side tax cut depicted in Figure 29–8. The equilibrium of the economy moves from $E$ to $C$, whereas with a conventional demand-side tax cut it would have moved from $E$ to $A$. As compared with point $A$, which reflects only the demand-side effects of a tax cut, output is higher and prices are lower at point $C$.

A good deal, you say! Indeed it is. The supply-side argument is extremely attractive in principle. The question is: Does it work in practice? Can we actually do what is depicted in Figure 29–9? Let us consider some difficulties.

**FIGURE 29-9**

**A Successful Supply-Side Tax Reduction**

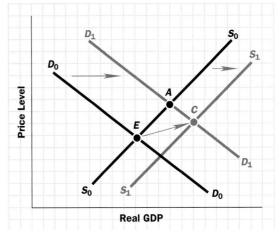

## ■ SOME FLIES IN THE OINTMENT

Critics of supply-side economics rarely question its goals or the basic idea that lower taxes improve incentives. They argue, instead, that supply-siders exaggerate the beneficial effects of tax cuts and ignore some undesirable side effects. Here is a brief rundown of some of the main objections to supply-side tax cuts.

**SMALL MAGNITUDE OF SUPPLY-SIDE EFFECTS** The first objection is that supply siders are simply too optimistic: we really do not know how to do what Figure 29–9 shows. Though it is easy, for example, to design tax incentives that make saving more *attractive* financially, people may not actually respond to these incentives. In fact, most of the statistical evidence suggests that we should not expect very much from tax incentives for saving. As economist Charles Schultze once quipped: "There's nothing wrong with supply-side economics that division by 10 couldn't cure."

**DEMAND-SIDE EFFECTS** The second objection is that supply siders underestimate the effects of tax cuts on aggregate demand. If you cut personal taxes, for example, individuals *may possibly* work more. But they *will certainly* spend more. If you reduce business taxes and thereby encourage expansion of industrial capacity, business firms will demand more investment goods.

The joint implications of these two objections appear in Figure 29–10. Here we depict a small outward shift of the aggregate supply curve (which reflects the first objection) and a large outward shift of the aggregate demand curve (which reflects the second). The result is that the economy's equilibrium moves from point $A$ (the intersection of $S_0S_0$ and $D_0D_0$) to point $E$ (the intersection of $S_1S_1$ and $D_1D_1$). Prices rise as output expands. The outcome differs only a little from the straight "demand-side" fiscal stimulus depicted in Figure 29–7.

**FIGURE 29-10**

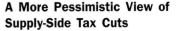

**A More Pessimistic View of Supply-Side Tax Cuts**

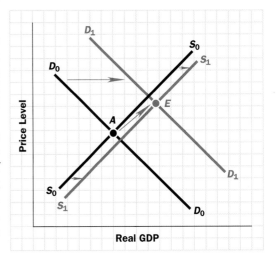

**PROBLEMS WITH TIMING**   The most promising types of supply-side tax cuts seek to encourage greater business investment. But the benefits from investment do not arrive by overnight mail. It may take years before we see any substantial increases in industrial capacity. Thus, the *expenditures* on investment goods almost certainly come before the *expansion of capacity*. In a word, supply-side tax cuts will have their primary short-run effects on aggregate demand. Effects on aggregate supply come later.

**EFFECTS ON INCOME DISTRIBUTION**   The preceding objections all pertain to the likely effects of supply-side policies on aggregate supply and demand. But a different problem bears mention: Most supply-side initiatives increase income inequality. Although raising the incomes of the wealthiest members of our society may not be their primary aim, most supply-side cuts cannot help but concentrate their benefits on the rich, simply because the rich own most of the capital.

Indeed, this tilt toward the rich is almost an inescapable corollary of supply-side logic. The basic aim of supply-side economics is to increase the incentives for working and investing, that is, to increase the gap between the rewards of those who succeed in the economic game (by working hard, investing well, or by just plain luck) and those who fail. It can hardly be surprising, therefore, that supply-side policies tend to increase economic inequality.

**LOSSES OF TAX REVENUE**   You can hardly help noticing that most of the policies suggested by supply siders involve cutting one tax or another. Thus, unless policymakers raise some other tax or cut spending, supply-side tax cuts are bound to raise the government budget deficit. This problem proved to be the Achilles' heel of supply-side economics in the United States in the 1980s. It left behind a legacy of budget deficits that took 15 years to overcome.

## TOWARD AN ASSESSMENT OF SUPPLY-SIDE ECONOMICS

On balance, most economists have reached the following conclusions about supply-side tax initiatives:

1. The likely effectiveness of supply-side tax cuts depends on what kinds of taxes are cut. Tax reductions aimed at stimulating business investment are likely to pack more punch than tax reductions aimed at getting people to work longer hours or to save more.

2. Such tax cuts probably will increase aggregate supply much more slowly than they increase aggregate demand. Thus, supply-side policies should not be thought of as a substitute for short-run stabilization policy, but rather as a way to promote (slightly) faster economic growth in the long run.

3. Demand-side effects of supply-side tax cuts are likely to overwhelm supply-side effects in the short run.

4. Supply-side tax cuts are likely to widen income inequalities.

5. Supply-side tax cuts are almost certain to lead to bigger, not smaller, budget deficits.

But this list does not close the books on the issue. It does not even tell us whether supply-side tax cuts are a good idea or a bad one. Some people will look over the list and decide that they favor supply-side tax cuts; others, perusing the same facts, will reach the opposite conclusion. We cannot say that either group is wrong because, like almost every economic policy, supply-side economics has its pros and cons and involves value judgments that color people's conclusions.

Why, then, did so many economists and politicians react so negatively to supply-side economics as preached and then practiced in the early 1980s? The main reason seems to be that the claims made by the most ardent supply-siders were clearly excessive. Naturally, these claims proved wrong. But showing that wild claims are wild does not dispose of the kernel of truth in supply-side economics: Reductions in marginal tax rates *do* improve economic incentives. Any specific supply-side tax cut must be judged on its individual merits.

---

● **POLICY DEBATE** ┃ SHOULD CONGRESS CUT TAXES?

---

As the federal budget swung from deficit into surplus, a new debate emerged in Washington: Should Congress "spend" some of the surplus by giving Americans a tax cut? The debate has many aspects—ideological, political, and economic.

Ideologically, conservatives see a tax cut as a way to shrink the size of government and to take money out of the hands of bureaucrats and return it to the people. But many liberals take a different view. After years on a starvation diet necessitated by huge budget deficits, they argue, many public needs are going unmet. The newfound surplus gives the country a chance to engage in some much-needed public spending.

Politically, a number of Republicans see cutting taxes as a way to rekindle the political spark lit by Ronald Reagan in 1980. Tax cutting, they argue, is their best election issue.

Curiously, however, virtually no politician in this debate seems to have paid any attention to the macroeconomics of the issue. In 1998, aggregate demand in the U.S. was plainly very high and growing rapidly. Although there was some controversy over whether America really had a large inflationary gap, as many economists claimed, no one argued that we had a recessionary gap. Adding to aggregate demand by cutting taxes in such an environment is not the usual recipe for macroeconomic stability.

---

## ■ TWO SIDES TO THE SUPPLY SIDE

As a candidate in 1992, Bill Clinton attacked the Reagan-Bush brand of supply-side economics as "trickle-down economics" and argued that it had failed. He emphasized, in particular, the last two items in our assessment: the effects on income inequality and on the budget deficit. The voters apparently agreed.

Ironically, however, President Clinton also ran on an avowedly supply-side platform—though of a different stripe. He emphasized building up the nation's resources of labor, capital, and technology so that our capacity to produce would be higher in the long run. This, of course, is precisely the goal of supply-side economics: to push the aggregate supply curve outward.

But, unlike Presidents Reagan and Bush, President Clinton did not propose to accomplish this mainly by cutting taxes. Although some tax cuts were included in the original Clinton plan, it featured more tax *increases* than cuts—in order to reduce the budget deficit. The real emphasis of Clintonomics was on improving the productivity of the American workforce through more and better education and training.

But programs like these cost money, money the federal government did not have at the time because of the huge budget deficit. So the focus of Clintonomics in practice became deficit reduction, not public spending designed to raise aggregate supply. As such, it was a highly successful. Although only modest sums were spent on improving labor force quality, the deficit fell rapidly and by fiscal year 1998 had turned into a substantial surplus—the first federal budget surplus since 1969.

The story of how this happened is a complicated one and cannot be told until we have gained some understanding of the government's other tool for managing aggregate demand—monetary policy. That is the task of the next three chapters.

1. The government's *fiscal policy* is its plan for managing aggregate demand through its spending and taxing programs. It is made jointly by the president and Congress.

2. The government's net effect on aggregate demand—and hence on equilibrium output and prices—depends on whether the expansionary effects of its spending are greater or smaller than the contractionary effects of its taxes.

3. Because consumer spending (C) depends on disposable income (DI), and DI is GDP minus taxes, any change in taxes will shift the consumption schedule on a 45° line diagram. The nature of this shift depends on whether *fixed taxes* or *variable taxes* are changed.

4. Such shifts in the consumption function caused by tax policy are subject to the same multiplier as autonomous shifts in G, I, or X − IM.

5. An income tax reduces the size of this common multiplier.

6. The multiplier for changes in taxes is smaller than the multiplier for changes in government purchases because each $1 of tax cut leads to less than $1 of increased spending.

7. *Government transfer payments* act like negative taxes, not like government purchases of goods and services, because they influence total spending only indirectly through their effect on consumption.

8. If the multipliers were known precisely, it would be possible to plan any of a variety of fiscal policies to eliminate either a recessionary or an inflationary gap. Recessionary gaps can be cured by raising G, cutting taxes, or increasing transfers. Inflationary gaps can be cured by cutting G, raising taxes, or reducing transfers.

9. Active stabilization policy can be carried out either by means that tend to expand the size of government (by raising either G or T when appropriate) or by means that reduce the size of government (by reducing either G or T when appropriate).

10. Expansionary fiscal policy can cure recessions, but it normally exacts a cost in terms of higher inflation. This dilemma has led to a great deal of interest in *"supply-side" tax cuts* designed to stimulate aggregate supply.

11. Supply-side tax cuts aim to push the economy's aggregate supply curve outward to the right. If successful, they can expand the economy and reduce inflation at the same time—a highly desirable outcome.

12. But critics point out at least five serious problems with supply-side tax cuts: They also stimulate aggregate demand, the beneficial effects on aggregate supply may be small, the demand-side effects occur before the supply-side effects, they make the income distribution more unequal, and large tax cuts lead to large budget deficits.

Fiscal policy   600

Fixed taxes   600

Variable taxes   600

Automatic stabilizer   604

Effect of income taxes on the multiplier   604

Government transfer payments   606

Supply-side tax cuts   610

1. America's defense budget has fallen since the end of the Cold War. How would GDP in the United States be affected if the reduced defense spending were used to:

   a. reduce the budget deficit, so that government purchases fell?

   b. free funds for other public purposes, so that government purchases remained the same?

2. Consider an economy in which tax collections are always $800 and in which the four components of aggregate demand are as follows:

| GDP | Taxes | DI | C | I | G | (X – IM) |
|---|---|---|---|---|---|---|
| $1,360 | $800 | $560 | $420 | $200 | $800 | $30 |
| 1,480 | 800 | 680 | 510 | 200 | 800 | 30 |
| 1,600 | 800 | 800 | 600 | 200 | 800 | 30 |
| 1,720 | 800 | 920 | 690 | 200 | 800 | 30 |
| 1,840 | 800 | 1,040 | 780 | 200 | 800 | 30 |

Find the equilibrium of this economy graphically. What is the marginal propensity to consume? What is the multiplier? What would happen to equilibrium GDP if government purchases were reduced by $60 and the price level were unchanged?

3. Now consider a related economy in which investment is also $200, government purchases are also $800, net exports are also $30, and the price level is also fixed. But taxes now vary with income, and as a result the consumption schedule looks like the following:

| GDP | Taxes | DI | C |
|---|---|---|---|
| $1,360 | $720 | $640 | $510 |
| 1,480 | 760 | 720 | 570 |
| 1,600 | 800 | 800 | 630 |
| 1,720 | 840 | 880 | 690 |
| 1,840 | 880 | 960 | 750 |

Find the equilibrium graphically. What is the marginal propensity to consume? What is the tax rate? Use your diagram to show the effect of a decrease of $60 in government purchases. What is the multiplier? Compare this answer to your answer to Review Question 2. What do you conclude?

4. Explain why G has the same multiplier as I, but taxes have a different multiplier.

5. Return to the hypothetical economy in Review Question 2 and suppose that *both* taxes and government purchases are increased by $120. Find the new equilibrium under the assumption that consumer spending continues to be exactly three-quarters of disposable income (as it is in Review Question 2).

6. If the government today decides that aggregate demand is excessive and is causing inflation, what options are open to it? What if it decides that aggregate demand is too weak instead?

7. Suppose that you are in charge of the fiscal policy of the economy in Review Question 2. There is an inflationary gap, and you want to reduce income by $120. What specific actions can you take to achieve this goal?

8. Now put yourself in charge of the economy in Review Question 3, and suppose that full employment comes at a GDP of $1,840. How can you push income up to that level?

9. Which of the proposed supply-side tax cuts appeals to you most? Draw up a list of arguments for and against enacting such a cut right now.

10. (More difficult) Advocates of lower taxes on capital gains argue that this type of tax cut will raise aggregate supply by spurring business investment. But, of course, any increase in investment spending will also raise aggregate demand. Compare the effects on aggregate supply, aggregate demand, and tax revenue of three different ways to cut the capital gains tax:

a. Reduce capital gains taxes on *all* investments, including those that were made before tax rates were cut.

b. Reduce capital gains taxes only on investments made after tax rates are cut.

c. Reduce capital gains taxes only on certain types of investments, such as corporate stocks and bonds.

Which of the three seems most desirable to you? Why?

---

| ● APPENDIX | ▌ ALGEBRAIC TREATMENT OF FISCAL POLICY AND AGGREGATE DEMAND |
|---|---|

In this appendix, we explain the simple algebra behind the fiscal policy multipliers discussed in the chapter. In so doing, we deal only with a simplified case in which prices do not change. Although it is possible to work out the corresponding algebra for the more realistic aggregate demand—aggregate supply analysis with variable prices—the analysis is rather complicated and is best left to more advanced courses.

We start with the example used in the chapter (especially on pages 603 and 604). The government spends $1,300 billion on goods and services ($G = 1,300$) and levies an income tax equal to 20 percent of GDP. So, if the symbol $T$ denotes tax receipts:

$$T = 0.20Y$$

Because the consumption function we have been working with is:

$$C = 300 + 0.75DI$$

where $DI$ is disposable income, and because disposable income and GDP are related by the accounting identity:

$$DI = Y - T$$

it follows that the $C$ schedule used in the 45° line diagram is described by the algebraic equation:

$$C = 300 + 0.75(Y - T)$$
$$= 300 + 0.75(Y - 0.20Y)$$
$$= 300 + 0.75(0.80Y)$$
$$= 300 + 0.60Y$$

We can now apply the equilibrium condition:

$$Y = C + I + G + (X - IM)$$

Because investment in this example is $I = 900$ and net exports are −100, substituting for $C$, $I$, $G$, and $(X - IM)$ into this equation gives:

$$Y = 300 + 0.60Y + 900 + 1,300 - 100$$
$$0.40Y = 2,400$$
$$Y = 6,000$$

This is all there is to finding equilibrium GDP in an economy with a government.

To find the multiplier for government spending, increase $G$ by 1 and solve the problem again:

$$Y = C + I + G + (X - IM)$$
$$Y = 300 + 0.60Y + 900 + 1,301 - 100$$
$$0.40Y = 2,401$$
$$Y = 6,002.5$$

So the multiplier is $6,002.5 - 6,000 = 2.5$, as stated in the text.

To find the multiplier for an increase in fixed taxes, change the tax schedule to:

$$T = 0.20Y + 1$$

Disposable income is then:

$$DI = Y - T = Y - (0.20Y + 1) = 0.80Y - 1$$

so the consumption function is:

$$C = 300 + 0.75DI$$
$$= 300 + 0.75(0.80Y - 1)$$
$$= 299.25 + 0.60Y$$

Solving for equilibrium GDP as usual gives:

$$Y = C + I + G + (X - IM)$$
$$Y = 299.25 + 0.60Y + 900 + 1,300 - 100$$
$$0.40Y = 2,399.25$$
$$Y = 5,998.125$$

So a $1 increase in fixed taxes lowers $Y$ by $1.875. The tax multiplier is $-1.875$.

Now let us proceed to a more general solution, using symbols rather than specific numbers. The equations of the model are as follows:

$$Y = C + I + G + (X - IM) \tag{1}$$

is the usual equilibrium condition:

$$C = a + bDI \tag{2}$$

is the same consumption function we have used in the appendixes of Chapters 26 and 27:

$$DI = Y - T \tag{3}$$

is the accounting identity relating disposable income to GDP:

$$T = T_0 + tY \tag{4}$$

is the tax function, where $T_0$ represents fixed taxes (which are zero in our numerical example) and $t$ represents the tax rate (which is 0.20 in the example). Finally, $I$, $G$, and $(X - IM)$ are just fixed numbers.

We begin the solution by substituting (3) and (4) into (2) to derive the consumption schedule relating $C$ to $Y$:

$$C = a + bDI$$
$$C = a + b(Y - T)$$
$$C = a + b(Y - T_0 - tY)$$
$$C = a - bT_0 + b(1 - t)Y \tag{5}$$

You will notice that a change in fixed taxes ($T_0$) *shifts the intercept* of the $C$ schedule whereas a change in the tax rate ($t$) changes its *slope*, as explained in the chapter (page 601).

Next substitute Equation (5) into Equation (1) to find equilibrium GDP:

$$Y = C + I + G + (X - IM)$$
$$Y = a + bT_0 + b(1 - t)Y + I + G + (X - IM)$$
$$[1 - b(1 - t)]Y = a - bT_0 + I + G + (X - IM)$$

or

$$Y = \frac{a - bT_0 + I + G + (X - IM)}{1 - b(1 - t)} \tag{6}$$

Equation (6) shows us that the multiplier for $G$, $I$, $a$, or $(X - IM)$ is

$$\text{Multiplier} = \frac{1}{1 - b(1 - t)}$$

To see that this is in fact the multiplier, raise any of $G$, $I$, $a$, or $(X - IM)$ by 1 unit. In each case, Equation (6) would be changed to read:

$$Y = \frac{a - bT_0 + I + G + (X - IM) + 1}{1 - b(1 - t)} \tag{6}$$

Subtracting Equation (6) from this expression gives the change in $Y$ stemming from a 1-unit change in $G$ or $I$ or $a$:

$$\text{Change in } Y = \frac{1}{1 - b(1 - t)}$$

We noted in Chapter 27 (page 569) that if there were no income tax ($t = 0$), a realistic value for $b$ (the marginal propensity to consume) would yield a multiplier of 10, which is much bigger than the true multiplier. Now that we have added taxes to the model, our multiplier formula produces much more realistic numbers. Approximate values for these parameters for the U.S. economy are $b = 0.90$ and $t = \frac{1}{3}$. The multiplier formula then gives

$$\text{Multiplier} = \frac{1}{1 - 0.90(1 - \frac{1}{3})}$$
$$= \frac{1}{1 - \frac{3}{5}} = \frac{1}{\frac{2}{5}}$$
$$= 2.50$$

which is not far from its actual estimated value—between 1.5 and 2.

Finally, we can see from Equation (6) that the multiplier for a change in fixed taxes ($T_0$) is:

$$\text{Tax multiplier} = \frac{-b}{1 - b(1 - t)}$$

For the example considered in the text and earlier in this appendix, $b = 0.75$ and $t = 0.20$, so the formula gives:

$$\frac{-0.75}{1 - 0.75(1 - 0.20)} = \frac{-0.75}{1 - 0.75(0.80)}$$
$$= \frac{-0.75}{1 - 0.60} = \frac{-0.75}{0.40} = -1.875$$

According to these figures, each $1 *increase* in $T_0$ reduces $Y$ by $1.875.

## QUESTIONS FOR REVIEW

1. Consider an economy described by the following set of equations:

$$C = 120 + 0.80DI$$
$$I = 320$$
$$G = 480$$
$$(X - IM) = -80$$
$$T = 200 + 0.25Y$$

Find the equilibrium level of GDP. Then find the multipliers for government purchases and for fixed taxes. If full employment comes at $Y = 1,800$, what are some policies that would get GDP there?

2. This is a variant of the previous problem that approaches things the way a fiscal policy planner might. In an economy whose consumption function and tax function are as given in Review Question 1, with investment fixed at 320 and net exports fixed at $-80$, find the value of $G$ that would make GDP equal to 1,800.

3. You are given the following information about an economy:

$$C = 0.90DI$$
$$I = 100$$
$$G = 540$$
$$(X - IM) = -40$$
$$T = (\tfrac{1}{3})Y$$

a. Find equilibrium GDP and the budget deficit.

b. Suppose the government, unhappy with the budget deficit, decides to cut government spending by precisely the amount of the deficit you found in Review Question 3(a). What actually happens to GDP and the budget deficit, and why?

4. (More difficult) In the economy considered in Review Question 3, suppose the government, seeing that it has not wiped out the deficit, keeps cutting $G$ until it succeeds in balancing the budget. What levels of GDP will then prevail?

[Money] is a machine for doing quickly and commodiously what would be done, though less quickly and commodiously, without it.

John Stuart Mill

# MONEY AND THE BANKING SYSTEM

The circular flow diagrams of earlier chapters had a "financial system" in the upper left-hand corner. (Look back, for example, at Figure 25–1.) Savings flowed into this system and investment flowed out. Something obviously goes on *inside* the financial system to channel the savings back into investment, and it is time we learned just what this something is.

There is another, equally important, reason for studying the financial system. The government exercises significant control over aggregate demand by manipulating *monetary policy.* Indeed, most observers nowadays see monetary policy as a far more important stabilization tool than fiscal policy. If we are to understand how monetary policy is conducted (the subject of Chapters 31 and 32), we must first acquire some understanding of the banking and financial system. By the end of this chapter, you will have this understanding.

## What Caused the Biggest "Bank Run" in History?

Beginning in Thailand in July 1997, a series of financial panics cascaded across the former "Tiger economies" of Southeast Asia: Thailand, Malaysia, Indonesia, the Philippines, and South Korea. Both domestic and foreign investors lost confidence in the currencies, stock markets, and banking systems of those countries, which had grown at astounding rates for years. By October, even Hong Kong, the pillar of financial strength in the region, was tottering.

Some observers likened what they were seeing to a series of ever-widening "bank runs"—instances when depositors get jittery about the security of their money and rush to cash in their accounts. Panicky investors first ran on the Thai banks, then on Thailand in general, then on Malaysian banks and Malaysia, and so on until much of Southeast Asia was hemorrhaging funds. These financial calamities threw the entire region into deep economic crisis—for several reasons.

First, banks started to (or threatened to) fail in large numbers, endangering the safety of depositors. In a free-enterprise system, new businesses are born and die every day; and no one other than the people immediately involved takes much notice. When a firm goes bankrupt, stockholders lose money and employees may lose their jobs. (The latter may not even happen if new management takes over the assets of the bankrupt firm.) But, except for the case of very large firms, that is about it.

But banking is different. If banks were treated like other firms, depositors would lose money whenever one went bankrupt. That is bad enough by itself, but the real danger comes in the case of a **run on a bank.** For reasons we will learn in this chapter, most banks cannot survive such a "run" and would be forced to shut their doors.

Worse yet, this disease is highly *contagious.* If one family hears that their neighbors just lost their life savings because their bank went broke, they are likely to rush to their own bank to withdraw their funds. In fact, that is precisely what happened throughout Southeast Asia in 1997 and 1998. Contagious panic spread from one nation to another as investors bolted for the exit doors. Then, when Russia defaulted on some of its debts in August 1998, the panic spread to Latin America and even to some U.S. financial markets.

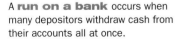

A **run on a bank** occurs when many depositors withdraw cash from their accounts all at once.

Last, but certainly not least, the main "output" of a nation's banking industry—the money supply—is an important determinant of aggregate demand—as we will see in the next chapter. Because the crisis in each country made the banking industry contract, it caused the money supply to shrink, thereby plunging each nation into recession. Economies that had grown accustomed to growing at 6 to 8 percent per year and more suddenly found themselves shrinking. It was, by some accounts, the most serious economic crisis since the Great Depression of the 1930s.

## ■ THE NATURE OF MONEY

Money is so much a part of our daily existence that we take it for granted and fail to appreciate all that it accomplishes. But money is in no sense "natural." Like the wheel, it had to be invented.

The most obvious way to trade commodities is not by using money, but by **barter**—a system in which people exchange one good directly for another. And the best way to appreciate what monetary exchange accomplishes is to imagine a world without it.

> **Barter** is a system of exchange in which people directly trade one good for another, without using money as an intermediate step.

### BARTER VERSUS MONETARY EXCHANGE

Under a system of direct barter, if Farmer Jones grows corn and has a craving for peanuts, he has to find a peanut farmer, say, Farmer Smith, with a taste for corn. If he finds such a person (called the "*double coincidence of wants*" by the classical economists), they make the trade. If this sounds easy, try to imagine how busy Farmer Jones would be if he had to repeat the sequence for every commodity he consumed in a week. For the most part, the desired double coincidences of wants are more likely to turn out to be double wants of coincidence. Jones gets no peanuts and Smith gets no corn. Worse yet, with so much time spent looking for trading partners, Jones would have far less time to grow corn. In brief:

Money greases the wheels of exchange, and thus makes the whole economy more productive.

Under a monetary system, Farmer Jones gives up his corn for money. He does so not because he wants the money per se, but because of what that money can buy. Money makes his shopping tasks much easier, allowing him simply to locate a peanut farmer who wants money. And what peanut farmer does not? For these reasons, monetary exchange replaced barter at a very early stage of human civilization, and only extreme circumstances, like massive wars and runaway inflations, have been able to bring barter (temporarily) back.

## THE CONCEPTUAL DEFINITION OF MONEY

**Money** is the standard object used in exchanging goods and services. In short, money is the **medium of exchange.**

The **unit of account** is the standard unit for quoting prices.

Monetary exchange provides an alternative to barter. With monetary exchange, people trade **money** for goods when they purchase something, and trade goods for money when they sell something, but they do not trade goods directly for other goods. This defines money's principal role as the **medium of exchange.** But once it has become accepted as the medium of exchange, whatever serves as money is bound to serve other functions as well. For one, it will inevitably become the **unit of account,** that is, the standard unit for quoting prices. Thus, if inhabitants of an idyllic tropical island use coconuts as money, they would be foolish to quote prices in terms of seashells.

A **store of value** is an item used to store wealth from one point in time to another.

Money may also come to be used as a **store of value.** If Farmer Jones's corn sales bring in more value than he wants to spend right away, he may find it convenient to store the difference temporarily in the form of money. He knows that money can be "sold" easily for goods and services at a later date, whereas land, gold, and other stores of value might not be. Of course, if money pays no interest and inflation is substantial, he may decide to forgo the convenience of money and store his wealth in some other form rather than see its purchasing power eroded. So money's role as a store of value is far from inevitable.

Because money may not always serve as a store of value, and because other commodities may act as stores of value, we will not include the store-of-value function as part of our conceptual definition of money. Instead, we simply label as "money" whatever serves as the medium of exchange.

## WHAT SERVES AS MONEY?

Anthropologists and historians can testify that a bewildering variety of objects have served as money in different times and places. Cattle, stones, candy bars, cigarettes, woodpecker scalps, porpoise teeth, and giraffe tails provide a few of the more colorful examples.

A **commodity money** is an object in use as a medium of exchange, but which also has a substantial value in alternative (nonmonetary) uses.

In primitive or less organized societies, the commodities that served as money generally held value in themselves. If not used as money, cattle could be slaughtered for food, cigarettes could be smoked, and so on. But such **commodity money** generally runs into several severe difficulties. To be useful as a medium of exchange, a commodity must be divisible. This makes cattle a poor choice because it's hard to keep the other 15/16ths of a cow fresh enough. It must also be of uniform, or at least readily identifiable, quality so that inferior substitutes are easy to recognize. This may be why woodpecker scalps never achieved great popularity. The medium of exchange must also be storable and durable, which presents a serious problem for candy-bar money. Finally, because people will carry and store commodity money, it is helpful if the item is compact, that is, if it has high value per unit of volume and weight.

All of these traits make it sensible that gold and silver have circulated as money since the first coins were struck about 2,500 years ago. Because they have high value in nonmonetary uses, a lot of purchasing power can be carried without too much weight. Pieces of gold are also storable, divisible (with a little trouble), and of identifiable quality (with a little more trouble).

The same characteristics suggest that paper would make an even better money. The Chinese invented paper money in the 11th century, and Marco Polo brought the idea to Europe. Because we can print any number on it that we please, we can make paper money as divisible as we like, and people can also carry a large value of

## ● DEALING BY WHEELING ON YAP

Primitive forms of money still exist in some remote places, as this extract from a newspaper article shows.

Yap, Micronesia—On this tiny South Pacific Island . . . the currency is as solid as a rock. In fact, it is rock. Limestone to be precise.

For nearly 2,000 years the Yapese have used large stone wheels to pay for major purchases, such as land, canoes and permission to marry. Yap is a U.S. trust territory, and the dollar is used in grocery stores and gas stations. But reliance on stone money . . . continues.

Buying property with stones is "much easier than buying it with U.S. dollars," says John Chodad, who recently purchased a building lot with a 30-inch stone wheel. "We don't know the value of the U.S. dollar."

Stone wheels don't make good pocket money, so for small transactions, Yapese use other forms of currency, such as beer. . . .

Besides stone wheels and beer, the Yapese sometimes spend *gaw,* consisting of necklaces of stone beads strung together around a whale's tooth. They also can buy things with *yar,* a currency made from large seashells. But these are small change.

The people of Yap have been using stone money ever since a Yapese warrior named Anagumang first brought the huge stones over from limestone caverns on neighboring Palau, some 1,500 to 2,000 years ago. Inspired by the moon, he fashioned the stone into large circles. The rest is history. . . .

By custom, the stones are worthless when broken. You never hear people on Yap musing about wanting a piece of the rock.

SOURCE: Adapted from Art Pine, "Hard Assets, or Why a Loan in Yap Is Hard to Roll Over," the *Wall Street Journal,* March 29, 1984, p. 1.

paper money in a lightweight and compact form. Paper is easy to store and, with a little cleverness, we can make counterfeiting hard (though never impossible).

Paper cannot, however, serve as commodity money because its value per square inch in alternative uses is so low. A paper currency that is repudiated by its issuer can, perhaps, be used as wallpaper or to wrap fish, but these uses will surely represent only a small fraction of the paper's value as money.[1] Contrary to the popular expression, such a currency literally *is* worth the paper it is printed on—which is to say that it is not worth much. Thus, paper money is always **fiat money.**

Money in the contemporary United States is almost entirely fiat money. Look at a dollar bill. Next to George Washington's picture it states: "This note is legal tender for all debts, public and private." Nowhere on the certificate is there a promise, stated or implied, that the U.S. government will exchange it for anything else. A dollar bill is convertible into, say, four quarters or 10 dimes—but not into gold, chocolate, or any other commodity.

Why do people hold these pieces of paper? Only because they know that others are willing to accept them for things of intrinsic value—food, rent, shoes, and so on. If this confidence ever evaporated, these dollar bills would cease serving as a medium of exchange and, given that they make ugly wallpaper, would become virtually worthless. (Indeed, as we mentioned in Chapter 5, that nearly happened to the Indonesian rupiah in 1997 and 1998, when it lost some 80 percent of its value.)

**Fiat money** is money that is decreed as such by the government. It is of little value as a commodity, but it maintains its value as a medium of exchange because people have faith that the issuer will stand behind the pieces of printed paper and limit their production.

---

[1] The first paper money issued by the federal government, the Continental dollar, was essentially repudiated. (Actually, the new government of the United States redeemed the Continentals for 1 cent on the dollar in the 1790s.) This gave rise to the derisive expression, "It's not worth a Continental."

---

● **REMAKING AMERICA'S PAPER MONEY**

---

The U.S. Treasury is currently replacing America's paper money with new notes designed to be much harder to counterfeit. Several of the new anticounterfeiting features are visible to the naked eye. By inspecting one of the new $20 bills—the ones with the big picture of Andrew Jackson on the front and lots of white space on the back, you can easily see two of them. (Others are much harder to detect.)

First hold the bill up to a light, with Jackson facing you. Near the left edge, you will see an embedded black vertical line. Look closer. The line consists of lettering and, if your eyesight is good, you will be able to read the words. But, if you were a counterfeiter, you would find this line devilishly hard to duplicate.

Next, put the bill down on a flat surface and inspect the numeral "20" in the lower right-hand corner. It appears green and shiny. Now pick up the bill and twist it to view the same number "20" from different angles. Notice how its color changes. At some angles, it even looks black! An optical illusion? No, a clever way to make life hard on counterfeiters.

But don't panic. This is hardly likely to occur in the United States. Our current monetary system has evolved over hundreds of years, during which *commodity* money was first replaced by *full-bodied paper money*—paper certificates that were backed by gold or silver of equal value held in the issuer's vaults. Then the full-bodied paper money was replaced by certificates that were only partially backed by gold and silver. Finally, we arrived at our present system, in which paper money has no "backing" whatsoever. Like a hesitant swimmer who first dips her toes, then her legs, then her whole body into a cold swimming pool, we have "tested the water" at each step of the way—and found it to our liking. It is unlikely that we will ever take a step back in the other direction.

## HOW THE QUANTITY OF MONEY IS MEASURED

Because the amount of money in circulation is profoundly important for the determination of national product and the price level, the government must know how much money there is. So we must devise some *measure* of the money supply.

Our conceptual definition of money describes it as the medium of exchange. But this raises difficult questions about just what items to include and exclude when we count up the money supply—questions that have long made the statistical definition of money a subject of dispute. In fact, the U.S. government has several official definitions of the money supply, two of which we will meet shortly.

Some components are obvious. All of our coins and paper money, the small change of our economic system, clearly should count as money. But we cannot stop there if we want to include the main vehicle for making payments in our society, for the lion's share of our nation's payments are made neither in metal nor in paper money, but by check.

Checking deposits are actually no more than bookkeeping entries in bank ledgers. Many people think of checks simply as a convenient way to pass coins or dollar bills to someone else. But that is not so. In fact, the volume of money held in the form of checkable deposits far exceeds the volume of currency. For example, when you pay the grocer $50 by check, dollar bills rarely change hands. Instead, that check normally travels back to your bank, where $50 is deducted from the bookkeeping entry that records your account and $50 added to the bookkeeping entry for your grocer's account. (If you and the grocer hold accounts at different banks, more books get involved; but still no coins or bills will likely move.)

## M1

Because households and businesses make so many transactions by check, it seems imperative that checkable deposits be included in any useful definition of the money supply. Unfortunately, this is not an easy task nowadays, because of the wide variety of ways to transfer money by check. Traditional checking accounts in commercial banks are the most familiar. But many people can also write checks on their savings accounts, on their deposits at credit unions, on their mutual funds, on their accounts with stockbrokers, and so on.

One popular definition of the money supply draws the line early and includes only coins, paper money, traveler's checks, conventional checking accounts, and certain other checkable deposits in banks and savings institutions. In the official U.S. statistics, this narrowly defined concept of money is called **M1**. The left-hand side of Figure 30–1 shows the composition of M1 as of March 1999.

The narrowly defined money supply, usually abbreviated **M1,** is the sum of all coins and paper money in circulation, plus certain checkable deposit balances at banks and savings institutions.[2]

**Two Definitions of the Money Supply, March 1999**          FIGURE 30–1

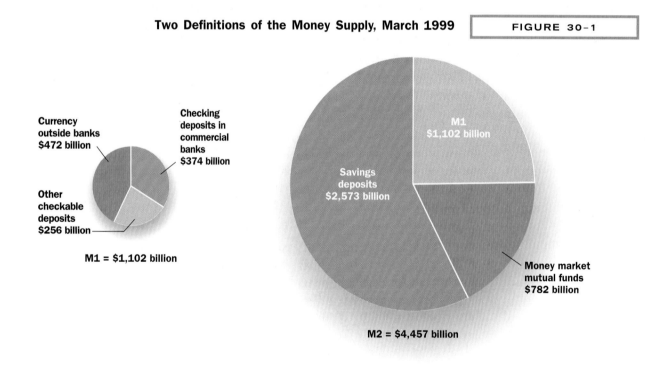

## M2

But other types of accounts allow withdrawals by check, so they are also candidates for inclusion in the money supply. Most notably, *money market deposit accounts* allow only a few checks per month but pay market-determined interest rates. Consumers have found these accounts extremely attractive vehicles for short-term investment, and balances in them now exceed all the checkable deposits included in M1.

In addition, many mutual fund organizations and brokerage houses offer *money market mutual funds*. These funds sell shares and use the proceeds to purchase a

[2] This includes travelers' checks and NOW (negotiable order of withdrawal) accounts.

variety of short-term securities. But the important point for our purposes is that owners of shares in money market mutual funds can withdraw their funds by writing checks. So depositors can—and sometimes do—use their holdings of fund shares just like checking accounts.

Finally, although you cannot write a check on a *savings account,* most economists feel that modern banking procedures have blurred the distinction between checking balances and savings balances. For example, most banks these days offer convenient electronic transfers of funds from one account to another, either by telephone or by pushing a button on an automated teller. Consequently, savings balances can become checkable almost instantly. For this reason, savings accounts are included—along with money market deposit accounts and money market mutual fund shares—in the broader definition of the money supply known as **M2.**

The composition of M2 as of March 1999 is shown on the right-hand side of Figure 30–1. You can see that savings deposits predominate, dwarfing M1. Figure 30–1 illustrates two points that are worth remembering. First, our money supply comes not only from banks, but also from savings institutions, brokerage houses, and mutual fund organizations. Second, however, banks still play a predominant role.

## OTHER DEFINITIONS OF THE MONEY SUPPLY

Supply economists do not want to stop counting at M2; they prefer still broader definitions of money (M3, and so on), which include more types of bank deposits and other closely related assets. The inescapable problem, however, is that there is no obvious place to stop, no clear line of demarcation between those assets that *are* money and those that are merely *close substitutes* for money—so-called **near moneys.**

If we define an asset's **liquidity** as the ease with which its holder can convert it into cash, there is a range of assets of varying degrees of liquidity. Everything in M1 is completely "liquid," the money market fund shares and passbook savings accounts included in M2 are a bit less so, and so on, until we encounter such things as short-term government bonds, which, while still quite liquid, would not normally be included in the money supply. Any number of different *M*s can be defined—and have been—by drawing the line in different places.

And still more complexities arise. For example, credit cards clearly serve as a medium of exchange. So should they be included in the money supply? Of course, you say. But how much money does your credit card represent? Is it the amount you currently owe on the card, which may well be zero? Or is it your entire line of credit, even though you may never use it all? Neither choice seems sensible, which is one reason why economists have so far ignored credit cards in their definitions of money. And soon Americans may start using electronic money instead of cash. Money will be transferred via computer hookups or by so-called smart cards with memory chips. (See the accompanying box, "Is There a Smart Card in Your Future?")

We could mention further complexities, but an introductory course in economics is not the place to get bogged down in complex definitional issues. So we will simply adhere to the convention that:

> "Money" consists only of coins, paper money, and checkable deposits.

The broadly defined money supply, usually abbreviated **M2,** is the sum of all coins and paper money in circulation, plus all types of checking account balances, plus most forms of savings account balances, plus shares in money market mutual funds.

**Near moneys** are liquid assets that are close substitutes for money.

An asset's **liquidity** refers to the ease with which it can be converted into cash.

## ■ THE BANKING SYSTEM

Now that we have defined money and seen how to measure it, we turn our attention to the principal creators of money—the banks. Banking is a complicated business—and getting more so. If you go further in your study of economics, you will probably learn more about the operations of banks. But for present purposes, a few simple principles will suffice. Let's start at the beginning.

---

## ● IS THERE A SMART CARD IN YOUR FUTURE?

In the 1990s, several banks and other companies began test-marketing new forms of high-tech electronic currency or "e-cash." One proposed form uses encrypted electronic messages to send balances from one computer to another, possibly bypassing banks entirely.

But the most commonly discussed form of e-cash, at least so far, is the so-called stored-value card. It works as follows. Soon you may be able to buy a "smart card" (which looks much like a credit card) with an embedded memory chip on which your initial payment is recorded. At this point, your conventional money is transformed into electronic currency. Thereafter, you can use the cash stored on the card to make purchases simply by inserting your card into specially designed slots in vending machines and stores. When the stored value on your card gets depleted, you can replenish it at an ATM.

Electronic currency raises several novel issues. For one thing, the federal government has long held a monopoly over currency issue; e-cash may erode that monopoly. For another, consumers and businesses may have privacy and safety concerns: Will their electronic transactions be safe from system errors and computer snoopers and hackers? Law enforcement agencies are also worried that large, untraceable electronic transfers of funds may be a draw to criminals and tax evaders.

Although futurists confidently predict that these new products represent the money of the future, skeptics note that we have heard such claims before—and they have never come true. Only time will tell if the new technologies will catch on.

---

## HOW BANKING BEGAN

When Adam and Eve left the Garden of Eden, they did not encounter a branch of Citibank. Banking had to be invented, and some time passed before it came to be practiced as it is today. With a little imagination, we can see how the first banks must have begun.

When money was made of gold or other metals, it was most inconvenient for consumers and merchants to carry it around and weigh and assay its purity every time they made a transaction. So the practice developed of leaving one's gold in a goldsmith's safe storage facilities and carrying in its place a receipt stating that John Doe did indeed own 5 ounces of gold. When people began trading goods and services for the goldsmiths' receipts, rather than for the gold itself, the receipts became an early form of paper money.

At this stage, paper money was fully backed by gold. Gradually, however, the goldsmiths began to notice that the amount of gold they were actually required to pay out in a day was but a small fraction of the total gold they had stored in their warehouses. Then one day some enterprising goldsmith hit upon a momentous idea that must have made him fabulously wealthy.

His thinking probably ran something like this. "I have 2,000 ounces of gold stored away in my vault, for which I collect storage fees from my customers. But I am never called upon to pay out more than 100 ounces on a single day. What harm could it do if I lent out, say, half the gold I now have? I'll still have more than enough to pay off any depositors who come in for withdrawals, so no one will ever know the difference. And I could earn 30 additional ounces of gold each year in interest on the loans I make (at 3 percent interest on 1,000 ounces). With this profit, I could lower my service charges to depositors and so attract still more deposits. I think I'll do it."

With this resolution, the modern system of **fractional reserve banking** was born. This system has three features that are crucially important to this chapter.

**BANK PROFITABILITY**  By getting deposits at zero interest and lending some of them out at positive interest rates, goldsmiths made profits. The history of banking as a profit-making industry was begun and has continued to this date. *Banks, like other enterprises, are in business to earn profits.*

> **Fractional reserve banking** is a system under which bankers keep as reserves only a fraction of the funds they hold on deposit.

---

## ● THE BANKING CRISIS IN SOUTHEAST ASIA: WHAT WENT WRONG?

When Asian stock markets and currencies crashed in 1997, it was not long before the international community realized that one of the root causes was weak and inadequately regulated banking systems. Similarly, when the International Monetary Fund began prescribing remedies for Thailand, Indonesia, and South Korea, one of its main objectives was to strengthen the banking systems and improve regulation.

As long as the good times rolled, none of the weaknesses in the banking systems of the Tiger economies received much attention. But, in retrospect, it was clear that Asian banks and governments made several grievous errors.

First, banks lent a great deal of money to local companies with little regard to risk, even though those companies were taking on mountains of debt. The dominant view in the Asian Tiger economies was one of great optimism. A booming economy would ensure that even seemingly risky loans would be repaid. Malaysia's leader, Mahatir Mohamed, captured the spirit of the day when he observed that, "In a river, high water takes you over the rocks."

Second, a great deal of favoritism, rather than sober assessments of creditworthiness, seems to have influenced banks' lending decisions. Often, governments would influence or even direct banks to lend money on political criteria. This system, which came to be called "crony capitalism," left the banks extremely vulnerable when things started falling apart.

Third, banks in several Asian nations took big gambles on exchange rates by borrowing U.S. dollars in international markets, converting them to domestic currencies, and then lending the proceeds locally. Here's how it worked. When 2,500 Indonesian rupiah could buy a dollar, an Indonesian bank might borrow $1 million in world markets and then lend 2.5 billion rupiah (the same amount of money) in Indonesia at a much higher interest rate. Such operations were highly profitable as long as the rupiah maintained its value. But when the rupiah tumbled to 10,000 to the dollar, the bank suddenly found itself needing 10 billion rupiah to repay its $1 million loan. Many banks simply could not pay.

All this was compounded by lax regulatory systems in which the government officials charged with the responsibility of supervising the banks often looked the other way when bankers assumed undue risks. The whole system was, in many respects, an accident looking for a time and a place to happen. It found both in Thailand in July 1997.

**BANK DISCRETION OVER THE MONEY SUPPLY** When goldsmiths decided to keep only fractions of their total deposits on reserve and lend out the balance, they acquired the ability to *create money.* As long as they kept 100 percent reserves, each gold certificate represented exactly 1 ounce of gold. So whether people decided to carry their gold or leave it with their goldsmiths did not affect the money supply, which was set by the volume of gold.

With the advent of fractional reserve banking, however, new paper certificates appeared whenever goldsmiths lent out some of the gold they held on deposit. The loans, in effect, created new money. In this way, the total amount of money came to depend on the amount of gold that each goldsmith felt compelled to keep in his vault. For any given volume of gold on deposit, the lower the reserves the goldsmiths kept, the more loans they could make, and therefore the more money would circulate.

Although we no longer use gold to back our money, this principle remains true today. *Bankers' business decisions influence the supply of money.* A substantial part of the rationale for modern monetary policy is, in fact, that profit-seeking bankers might not create the amount of money that is best for society. So governments have been unwilling to leave this important decision in private hands.

**EXPOSURE TO RUNS** A goldsmith who kept 100 percent reserves never had to worry about a run on his vault. Even if all his depositors showed up at the door at once, he could always convert their paper receipts back into gold. But as soon as the first goldsmith decided to get by with only fractional reserves, the possibility of a run on the vault became a real concern. If that first goldsmith who lent out half his gold had found 51 percent of his customers at his door one unlucky day, he would have had a lot of explaining to do. Similar problems have worried bankers for centuries. *The danger of runs on the bank has induced bankers to keep prudent reserves and to lend out money carefully.*

As we observed earlier, this danger turned into a harsh reality when an epidemic of bank runs swept several Asian countries in 1997 and 1998. It turned out that many bankers in these countries had been less than careful in their lending practices.

## PRINCIPLES OF BANK MANAGEMENT: PROFITS VERSUS SAFETY

Bankers have a reputation for conservatism in politics, dress, and business affairs. From what has been said so far, the economic rationale for this conservatism should be clear. Checking deposits are pure fiat money. Years ago, these deposits were "backed" by nothing more than a particular bank's promise to convert them into currency on demand. If people lost trust in that bank, it was doomed.

Thus, bankers have always relied on a reputation for prudence. This they did in two principal ways. First, they had to maintain a sufficiently generous level of reserves to minimize their vulnerability to runs. Second, they had to be somewhat cautious in making loans and investments, because any large losses on their loans would undermine their depositors' confidence.

It is important to realize that banking under a system of fractional reserves is an inherently risky business that is rendered safe only by cautious and prudent management. Not only the Asian financial crisis, but also America's long history of bank failures (see Figure 30–2), bears sober testimony to the fact that many bankers have been neither cautious nor prudent. Why? Because this is not a recipe for high profits. Bank profits are maximized by keeping reserves as low as possible, by making at least some risky investments, and by granting loans to borrowers with questionable credit standing who will pay higher interest rates.

**Bank Failures in the United States, 1915–1998**  **FIGURE 30-2**

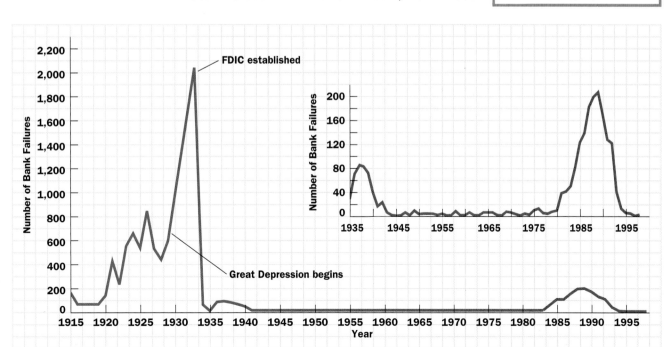

SOURCE: Federal Deposit Insurance Corporation.

The art of bank management is to strike the appropriate balance between the lure of profits and the need for safety. If a banker errs by being too stodgy, his bank will earn inadequate profits. If he errs by taking unwarranted risks, his bank may not survive at all.

## BANK REGULATION

Governments in virtually every society have decided that profit-minded bankers may not strike the balance between profits and safety where society wants it struck. So they have thrown up a web of regulations designed to insure depositors' safety and to control the money supply.

**Deposit insurance** is a system that guarantees that depositors will not lose money even if their bank goes bankrupt.

**DEPOSIT INSURANCE**    The principal innovation that guarantees the safety of bank deposits is **deposit insurance.** Today, most bank deposits are insured against loss by the *Federal Deposit Insurance Corporation (FDIC)*—an agency of the U.S. government. If your bank belongs to the FDIC, as almost all do, each of your accounts is insured for up to $100,000 regardless of what happens to the bank. Thus, while bank failures may spell disaster for the bank's stockholders, they do not cause many depositors concern. Deposit insurance eliminates the motive for customers to rush to their bank just because they hear some bad news about the bank's finances. Many observers give this innovation much of the credit for the pronounced decline in bank failures after the FDIC was established in 1933—which is apparent in Figure 30–2. Most of the Southeast Asian countries, unfortunately, do not have comparable insurance systems in place.

**BANK SUPERVISION**    In addition to insuring depositors against loss, the government takes steps to see that banks do not get into financial trouble. For one thing, various regulatory authorities conduct periodic *bank examinations* to keep tabs on the financial conditions and business practices of the banks under their purview. After a rash of bank failures in the late 1980s and early 1990s (see again Figure 30–2), U.S. bank supervision was tightened by legislation that permits the authorities to intervene early in the affairs of financially troubled banks. Other laws and regulations *limit the kinds and quantities of assets in which banks may invest.* For example, banks are permitted to own only limited amounts of common stock. Both of these forms of regulation are clearly aimed at keeping banks safe.

**Required reserves** are the minimum amount of reserves (in cash or the equivalent) required by law. Normally, required reserves are proportional to the volume of deposits.

**RESERVE REQUIREMENTS**    A final type of regulation also has some bearing on safety but is motivated primarily by the government's desire to control the money supply. We have seen that the amount of money any bank will issue depends on the amount of reserves it elects to keep. For this reason, most banks are subject by law to minimum **required reserves.** Although banks may (and sometimes do) keep reserves in excess of these legal minimums, they may not keep less. This regulation places an upper limit on the money supply. The rest of this chapter is concerned with the details of this mechanism.

## ■  THE ORIGINS OF THE MONEY SUPPLY

Our objective is to understand how the money supply is determined. But before we can fully understand the mechanics of modern banking and the process by which money is "created," we must acquire at least a nodding acquaintance with the way bankers keep their books.

### HOW BANKERS KEEP BOOKS

The first thing to know is how to distinguish assets from liabilities.

An **asset** of an individual or business firm is an item of value that the individual or firm owns.

An **asset** of a bank is something of value that the bank *owns.* This "thing" may be a physical object, such as the bank building or a computer, or it may be just a piece of paper, such as an IOU from a customer to whom the bank has made a loan.

---

**● POLICY DEBATE** ▮ **ABOLISH THE COMMUNITY REINVESTMENT ACT?**

---

Not all bank regulation is aimed at the safety of depositors. Some regulation is designed to protect borrowers from discriminatory practices by banks. One particularly controversial law is the Community Reinvestment Act (CRA), which was designed to combat "redlining"—the practice of delineating certain geographical areas, often minority neighborhoods, in which banks did not lend.

Bankers complain that CRA regulations bury them in paperwork and force them to make unprofitable loans. Such lending amounts to government-enforced allocation of credit, critics contend. Community advocacy groups counter that access to credit, which is inadequate in low-income and moderate-income areas, is crucial for economic success. A strong CRA keeps the pressure on banks to do better, they argue.

Because the statute is terse and somewhat vague, much depends on how bank regulators interpret it. So in 1993 President Clinton ordered the regulatory agencies to rewrite the CRA rules in ways that would focus more on *results* and less on *paperwork*. The lengthy and contentious rule-making process took more than two years. Then, after the 1994 elections, Republicans in Congress introduced several legislative proposals that would essentially repeal the CRA, thereby relieving banks of the regulatory burden and letting the market

work. President Clinton threatened to veto any such legislation, and the idea died in Congress in 1995.

But the controversy continues. Should the government pursue what some people consider an affirmative action policy for bank lending? Or should such matters be left to the market? What do you think?

---

A **liability** of a bank is something of value that the bank *owes*. Most bank liabilities take the form of bookkeeping entries. For example, if you have an account in the Main Street Bank, your bank balance is a liability of the bank. (It is, of course, an asset to you.)

An easy test shows whether some piece of paper or bookkeeping entry is a bank's *asset* or *liability*. Ask yourself whether, if this paper were converted into cash, the bank would receive the cash (if so, it is an asset) or pay it out (if so, it is a liability). This test makes it clear that loans to customers are bank assets (when loans are repaid, the bank collects), while customers' deposits are bank liabilities (when deposits are cashed in, the bank must pay). Of course, things are just the opposite to the bank's customers: The loans are liabilities and the deposits are assets.

When accountants draw up a complete list of all the bank's assets and liabilities, the resulting document is called the bank's **balance sheet.** Typically, the value of all the bank's assets exceeds the value of all its liabilities. (On the rare occasions when this is not so, the bank is in serious trouble.) In what sense, then, do balance sheets "balance"?

They balance because accountants have invented the concept of **net worth** to balance the books. Specifically, they define the net worth of a bank to be the difference between the value of all its assets and the value of all its liabilities. Thus, by definition, when accountants add net worth to liabilities, the sum they get must be the same as the value of the bank's assets. In short:

**Assets = Liabilities + Net Worth**

Table 30–1 illustrates this point with the balance sheet of a fictitious bank, Bank-a-mythica, whose finances are extremely simple. On December 31, 1999, it had only two kinds of assets (listed on the left-hand side of the balance sheet)—$1 million in cash, which it held as reserves, and $4.5 million in outstanding loans to its customers,

A **liability** of an individual or business firm is an item of value that the individual or firm owes. Many liabilities are known as *debts*.

A **balance sheet** is an accounting statement listing the values of all the assets on the left-hand side and the values of all the liabilities and *net worth* on the right-hand side.

**Net worth** is the value of all assets minus the value of all liabilities.

| TABLE 30-1 | **Balance Sheet of Bank-a-mythica, December 31, 1999** |

| Assets | | Liabilities and Net Worth | |
| --- | --- | --- | --- |
| **Assets** | | **Liabilities** | |
| Reserves | $1,000,000 | Checking deposits | $5,000,000 |
| Loans outstanding | $4,500,000 | | |
| Total | $5,500,000 | **Net Worth** | |
| | | Stockholders' | |
| **Addendum: Bank Reserves** | | equity | $500,000 |
| Actual reserves | $1,000,000 | Total | $5,500,000 |
| Required reserves | 1,000,000 | | |
| Excess reserves | 0 | | |

that is, in customers' IOUs. And it had only one type of liability (listed on the right-hand side)—$5 million in checking deposits. The difference between total assets ($5.5 million) and total liabilities ($5.0 million) was the bank's net worth ($500,000), shown on the right-hand side of the balance sheet.

## BANKS AND MONEY CREATION

Let us now turn to the process of deposit creation. Many bankers will deny that they have any ability to "create" money. The phrase itself has a suspiciously hocus-pocus sound to it. But they are not quite right. For although any individual bank's ability to create money is severely limited, the banking system as a whole can achieve much more than the sum of its parts. Through the modern alchemy of *deposit creation*, it can turn one dollar into many dollars. But to understand this important process, we had better proceed in steps, beginning with the case of a single bank, our hypothetical Bank-a-mythica.

### THE LIMITS TO MONEY CREATION BY A SINGLE BANK

According to the balance sheet in Table 30–1, Bank-a-mythica holds cash reserves of $1 million, equal to 20 percent of its $5 million in deposits. Assume that this is the minimum reserve ratio prescribed by law and that the bank strives to keep its reserves down to the legal minimum; that is, it strives to keep its **excess reserves** at zero.

**Excess reserves** are any reserves held in excess of the legal minimum.

Now let us suppose that on January 2, 2000, an eccentric widower comes into Bank-a-mythica and deposits $100,000 in cash in his checking account. The bank now has $100,000 more in cash reserves, and $100,000 more in checking deposits. But because deposits are up by $100,000, *required* reserves rise by only $20,000, leaving $80,000 in *excess* reserves. Table 30–2 illustrates the effects of this transaction on Bank-a-mythica's balance sheet. Tables such as this, which show *changes* in balance sheets rather than the balance sheets themselves, will help us follow the money-creation process.[3]

Bank-a-mythica is unlikely to be happy with the situation illustrated in Table 30–2, for it is holding $80,000 in excess reserves on which it earns no interest. So as soon as possible, it will lend out the extra $80,000—let us say to Hard-Pressed Construction Company. This loan leads to the balance sheet changes shown in Table 30–3: Bank-a-mythica's loans rise by $80,000 while its holdings of cash reserves fall by $80,000.

---

[3] Notice that in all such tables, which are called *T accounts*, the two sides of the ledger must balance. This is because changes in assets and changes in liabilities must be equal if the balance sheet is to balance both before and after the transaction.

### Changes in Bank-a-mythica's Balance Sheet, January 2, 2000

TABLE 30-2

| Assets | | Liabilities | |
|---|---|---|---|
| Reserves | +$100,000 | Checking deposits | +$100,000 |

**Addendum: Changes in Reserves**

| | |
|---|---|
| Actual reserves | +$100,000 |
| Required reserves | + $20,000 |
| Excess reserves | + $80,000 |

### Changes in Bank-a-mythica's Balance Sheet, January 3–6, 2000

TABLE 30-3

| Assets | | Liabilities | |
|---|---|---|---|
| Loans outstanding | +$80,000 | No change | |
| Reserves | −$80,000 | | |

**Addendum: Changes in Reserves**

| | |
|---|---|
| Actual reserves | −$80,000 |
| Required reserves | No change |
| Excess reserves | −$80,000 |

By combining Tables 30–2 and 30–3, we arrive at Table 30–4, which summarizes all the bank's transactions for the week. Reserves are up $20,000, loans are up $80,000, and, now that the bank has had a chance to adjust to the inflow of deposits, it no longer holds excess reserves.

Looking at Table 30–4 and keeping in mind our specific definition of money, it appears at first that the chairman of Bank-a-mythica is right when he claims not to have engaged in the nefarious practice of "money creation." All that happened was that, in exchange for the $100,000 in cash it received, the bank issued the widower a checking balance of $100,000. This does not change M1; it merely converts one form of money into another.

But wait. What happened to the $100,000 in cash that the eccentric man brought to the bank? The table shows that Bank-a-mythica retained $20,000 in its vault. Because this currency is no longer in circulation, it no longer counts in the official money supply, or M1. (Notice that Figure 30–1 included only "currency outside banks.") But the other $80,000, which the bank lent out, is still in circulation. It is held by Hard-Pressed Construction, which probably will redeposit it in some other bank. But even before this happens, the original $100,000 in cash

### Changes in Bank-a-mythica's Balance Sheet, January 2–6, 2000

TABLE 30-4

| Assets | | Liabilities | |
|---|---|---|---|
| Reserves | +$20,000 | Checking deposits | +$100,000 |
| Loans outstanding | +$80,000 | | |

**Addendum: Changes in Reserves**

| | |
|---|---|
| Actual reserves | +$20,000 |
| Required reserves | +$20,000 |
| Excess reserves | No change |

has supported a rise in the money supply: there is now $100,000 in checking deposits and $80,000 of cash in circulation, making a total of $180,000. The money creation process has begun.

## MULTIPLE MONEY CREATION BY A SERIES OF BANKS

Let us now trace the $80,000 in cash and see how the process of money creation gathers momentum. Suppose that Hard-Pressed Construction Company, which banks across town at the First National Bank, deposits the $80,000 into its bank account. First National's reserves increase by $80,000. But because deposits are up by $80,000, *required* reserves rise by only 20 percent of this amount or $16,000. If the management of First National Bank behaves like that of Bank-a-mythica, it will lend out the $64,000 of its excess reserves.

Table 30–5 shows the effects of these events on First National Bank's balance sheet. (We do not show the preliminary steps corresponding to Tables 30–2 and 30–3 separately.) At this stage in the chain, the original $100,000 in cash has led to $180,000 in deposits—$100,000 at Bank-a-mythica and $80,000 at First National Bank—and $64,000 in cash, which is still in circulation (in the hands of the recipient of First National's loan—Al's Auto Shop). Thus, from the original $100,000, a total of $244,000 has been added to the money supply ($180,000 in checking deposits plus $64,000 in cash).

But, to coin a phrase, the bucks do not stop here. Al's Auto Shop will presumably deposit the proceeds from its loan into its own account at Second National Bank, leading eventually to the balance sheet adjustments shown in Table 30–6 when Second National makes an additional loan of $51,200 rather than hold on to excess reserves. You can see how the money creation process continues.

Figure 30–3 summarizes these balance sheet changes of the first five banks in the chain (from Bank-a-mythica through the Fourth National Bank) graphically, on the assumptions that each bank holds exactly the 20 percent required reserves and that each loan recipient redeposits the proceeds in the next bank. But the chain does not end there. The Main Street Movie Theatre, which received a $32,768 loan from the Fourth National Bank, then deposits these funds into the Fifth National Bank. Fifth

| TABLE 30–5 |
|---|

**Changes in First National Bank's Balance Sheet**

| Assets | | Liabilities | |
|---|---|---|---|
| Reserves | +$16,000 | Checking deposits | +$80,000 |
| Loans outstanding | +$64,000 | | |

**Addendum: Changes in Reserves**

| | |
|---|---|
| Actual reserves | +$16,000 |
| Required reserves | +$16,000 |
| Excess reserves | No change |

| TABLE 30–6 |
|---|

**Changes in Second National Bank's Balance Sheet**

| Assets | | Liabilities | |
|---|---|---|---|
| Reserves | +$12,800 | Checking deposits | +$64,000 |
| Loans outstanding | +$51,200 | | |

**Addendum: Changes in Reserves**

| | |
|---|---|
| Actual reserves | +$12,800 |
| Required reserves | +$12,800 |
| Excess reserves | No change |

National has to keep only 20 percent of this deposit, or $6,553.60, on reserve and will lend out the balance. And so the chain continues.

Where does it all end? The running sums on the right-hand side of Figure 30–3 show what eventually happens to the entire banking system. The initial deposit of $100,000 in cash is ultimately absorbed in bank reserves, Column (1), leading to a total of $500,000 in new deposits, Column (2), and $400,000 in new loans, Column (3). The money supply rises by $400,000 because the nonbank public eventually holds $100,000 *less* in currency and $500,000 *more* in checking deposits.

So there really is some hocus-pocus. Somehow, an initial deposit of $100,000 leads to $500,000 in new bank deposits—a multiple expansion of $5 for every original dollar—and a net increase of $400,000 in the money supply. We had better understand why this is so. But first let us verify that the calculations in Figure 30–3 are correct.

If you look carefully at the numbers, you will see that each column forms a *geometric progression*; specifically, each entry is equal to exactly 80 percent of the entry before it. Recall that in our discussion of the multiplier in Chapter 27 we learned how to sum an infinite geometric progression, which is just what each of these chains eventually will be. In particular, if the common ratio is R, the sum of an infinite geometric progression is:

$$1 + R + R^2 + R^3 + \ldots = \frac{1}{1 - R}$$

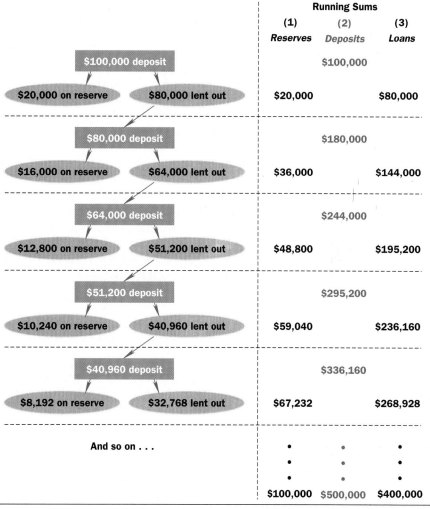

**FIGURE 30–3**

**The Chain of Multiple Deposit Creation**

SOURCE: This schematic diagram was suggested to us by Dr. Ivan K. Cohen, whom we thank.

By applying this formula to the chain of checking deposits in Figure 30–3, we get:

$$\$100,000 + \$80,000 + \$64,000 + \$51,200 + \ldots$$
$$= \$100,000 \times (1 + 0.80 + 0.64 + 0.512 + \ldots)$$
$$= \$100,000 \times (1 + 0.80 + 0.80^2 + 0.80^3 + \ldots)$$
$$= \$100,000 \times \frac{1}{1 - 0.80} = \frac{\$100,000}{0.20} = \$500,000$$

Proceeding similarly, we can verify that the new loans sum to $400,000 and that the new required reserves sum to $100,000. (Check these as exercises.) So the numbers in Figure 30–3 are correct. Let us, therefore, think through the logic behind them.

The chain of deposit creation can end only when there are no more *excess* reserves to be loaned out; that is, when the entire $100,000 in cash is tied up in *required* reserves. That explains why the last entry in Column (1) must be $100,000. But, with a reserve ratio of 20 percent, excess reserves disappear only when checking deposits expand by $500,000—which is the last entry in Column (2). Finally, because balance sheets must balance, the sum of all newly created assets (reserves plus loans) must equal the sum of all newly created liabilities ($500,000 in deposits). That leaves $400,000 for new loans—which is the last entry in Column (3).

More generally, if the reserve ratio is some number $m$ (rather than the one-fifth in our example), each dollar of deposits requires only a fraction $m$ of a dollar in reserves. So $R$, the common ratio in the above formula, is $R = 1 - m$, and deposits must expand by $1/m$ for each dollar of new reserves that are injected into the system. This suggests the general formula for multiple deposit creation when the required reserve ratio is some number $m$:

**Oversimplified Deposit Multiplier Formula**

If the required reserve ratio is some fraction, $m$, each $1 of reserves injected into the banking system can lead to the creation of $1/m$ in new deposits. That is, the so-called deposit multiplier is given by:

Change in deposits $= (1/m) \times$ Change in reserves

Notice that this formula correctly describes what happens in our example. The initial deposit of $100,000 in cash at Bank-a-mythica constitutes $100,000 in new reserves (Table 30–2). Applying a multiplier of $1/m = 1/0.20 = 5$ to this $100,000, we conclude that bank deposits will rise by $500,000—which is just what happens. Remember, however, that the expansion process started when some eccentric widower took $100,000 in cash and deposited it in his bank account. So the public's holdings of *money*—which includes both checking deposits *and cash*—increase by only $400,000 in this case: There is $500,000 *more* in deposits, but $100,000 *less* in cash.

## THE PROCESS IN REVERSE: MULTIPLE CONTRACTIONS OF THE MONEY SUPPLY

Let us now briefly consider how this deposit creation mechanism operates in reverse—as a system of deposit *destruction*. In particular, suppose that our eccentric widower came back to Bank-a-mythica to withdraw $100,000 from his checking account and return it to his mattress, where it rightfully belongs. Bank-a-mythica's *required* reserves would fall by $20,000 as a result of this transaction (20 percent of $100,000), but its *actual* reserves would fall by $100,000. The bank would be $80,000 short, as indicated in Table 30–7(a).

How does it react to this discrepancy? As some of its outstanding loans are routinely paid off, the bank will cease granting new ones until it has accumulated the necessary $80,000 in required reserves. The data for Bank-a-mythica's contraction are shown in Table 30–7(b), assuming that borrowers pay off their loans in cash.[4]

But where did the borrowers get this money? Probably by making withdrawals from other banks. In this case, let us assume it all came from First National Bank,

| TABLE 30-7 | | | Changes in the Balance Sheet of Bank-a-mythica | | | |
|---|---|---|---|---|---|---|
| **(a)** | | | | **(b)** | | |
| **Assets** | | **Liabilities** | | **Assets** | | **Liabilities** |
| Reserves | −$100,000 | Checking deposits | −$100,000 | Reserves | +$80,000 | No change |
| | | | | Loans outstanding | −$80,000 | |
| **Addendum: Changes in Reserves** | | | | **Addendum: Changes in Reserves** | | |
| Actual reserves | −$100,000 | | | Actual reserves | +$80,000 | |
| Required reserves | −$20,000 | | | Required reserves | No change | |
| Excess reserves | −$80,000 | | | Excess reserves | +$80,000 | |

[4] In reality, they would probably pay with checks drawn on other banks. Bank-a-mythica would then cash these checks to acquire the reserves.

| Changes in the Balance Sheet of First National Bank | TABLE 30-8 |
| --- | --- |

### (a)

| Assets | | Liabilities | |
| --- | --- | --- | --- |
| Reserves | −$80,000 | Checking deposits | −$80,000 |
| **Addendum: Changes in Reserves** | | | |
| Actual reserves | −$80,000 | | |
| Required reserves | −$16,000 | | |
| Excess reserves | −$64,000 | | |

### (b)

| Assets | | Liabilities |
| --- | --- | --- |
| Reserves | +$64,000 | No change |
| Loans outstanding | −$64,000 | |
| **Addendum: Changes in Reserves** | | |
| Actual reserves | +$64,000 | |
| Required reserves | No change | |
| Excess reserves | +$64,000 | |

which loses an $80,000 deposit and $80,000 in reserves. It finds itself short some $64,000 in reserves, as shown in Table 30–8(a), and therefore must reduce its loan commitments by $64,000, as in Table 30–8(b). This, of course, causes some other bank to suffer a loss of reserves and deposits of $64,000, and the whole process repeats just as it did in the case of deposit expansion.

After the entire banking system had become involved, the picture would be just as shown in Figure 30–3, except that all the numbers would have *minus signs* in front of them. Deposits would shrink by $500,000, loans would fall by $400,000, bank reserves would be reduced by $100,000, and the M1 money supply would fall by $400,000. As suggested by our deposit multiplier formula with $m = 0.20$, the decline in the bank deposits is $1/0.20 = 5$ times as large as the decline in excess reserves.

One of the authors of this book was a student in Cambridge, Massachusetts, during the height of the radical student movement of the late 1960s. One day a pamphlet appeared urging citizens to withdraw all funds from their checking accounts on a prescribed date, hold them in cash for a week, and then redeposit them. This act, the circular argued, would surely wreak havoc upon the capitalist system. Obviously, some of these radicals were well-schooled in modern money mechanics, for the argument was basically correct. The tremendous multiple contraction of the banking system and subsequent multiple expansion that a successful campaign of this sort could have caused might have seriously disrupted the local financial system. But history records that the appeal met with little success. Checking-account withdrawals are not the stuff of which revolutions are made.

## ■ WHY THE DEPOSIT CREATION FORMULA IS OVERSIMPLIFIED

So far, our discussion of the process of money creation has seemed rather mechanical. If everything proceeds according to formula, each $1 in new excess reserves will lead to a $1/m$ increase in new deposits. But in reality, things are not this simple. Just as in the case of the expenditure multiplier, the oversimplified formula for deposit creation is accurate only under very particular circumstances. These circumstances require that:

1. Every recipient of cash must redeposit the cash into another bank rather than hold it.

2. Every bank must hold reserves no larger than the legal minimum.

The "chain" diagram in Figure 30–3 shows clearly what happens if either of these assumptions is violated.

Suppose first that the business firms and individuals who receive bank loans decide to redeposit only a fraction of the proceeds into their bank accounts. Then, for example, the first $80,000 loan would lead to a deposit of less than $80,000—and similarly down the chain. The whole chain of deposit creation would therefore be reduced. Thus:

> If individuals and business firms decide to hold more cash, the multiple expansion of bank deposits will be curtailed because fewer dollars of cash will be available to be used as reserves to support new checking deposits. Consequently, the money supply will be smaller.

The basic idea here is simple. Each $1 of cash held by a bank can support several dollars (specifically, $1/m$) of money. But $1 of cash held by an individual is exactly $1 of money; it supports no bank deposits. Hence, any time cash leaves the banking system, the money supply will decline. And any time cash enters the banking system, the money supply will rise.

### The Asian Bank Run Explained

The application of this idea to bank runs in general, and to the recent spate of bank runs in Asia in particular, is apparent. When nervous depositors withdraw money from banks to hold it in cash instead, the money supply must contract. If the withdrawals are massive, so will be the contraction of the banking system.

Next, suppose bank managers become more conservative or that the outlook for loan repayments worsens because of a recession. Then banks might decide to keep more reserves than the legal requirement and lend out less than the amounts assumed in Figure 30–3. If this happens, banks further down the chain receive smaller deposits and, once again, the chain of deposit creation is curtailed. Thus:

> If banks wish to keep excess reserves, the multiple expansion of bank deposits will be restricted. A given amount of cash will support a smaller supply of money than would be the case if banks held no excess reserves.

This latter problem afflicted Japan in 1998, when the so-called bad loan problem made Japanese bankers super-cautious about lending money to any but their most creditworthy borrowers. Japanese businesses wound up starved for credit.

## ■ THE NEED FOR MONETARY POLICY

If we pursue these two points a bit further, we will see why government must regulate the money supply to maintain economic stability. We have just suggested that banks will wish to keep excess reserves when they do not foresee profitable and secure opportunities to make loans. This is most likely to happen during the downswing and around the bottom of a business contraction. At such times, the propensity of banks to hold excess reserves can turn the deposit creation process into one of deposit destruction, as happened recently in Japan. In addition, if depositors become jittery, they may decide to hold on to more cash. Thus:

> During a recession, profit-oriented banks would be prone to reduce the money supply by increasing their excess reserves and declining to lend to less credit-worthy applicants—if the government did not intervene. As we will learn in subsequent chapters, the money supply is an important influence on aggregate demand, so such a contraction of the money supply would aggravate the recession.

This is precisely what happened—with a vengeance—during the Great Depression of the 1930s. Although total bank reserves grew, the money supply contracted violently because banks preferred to hold excess reserves rather than make loans that might not be repaid.

On the other hand, banks will want to squeeze the maximum possible money supply out of any given amount of cash reserves by keeping their reserves at the bare minimum when the demand for bank loans is buoyant, profits are high, and secure investment opportunities abound. This reduced incentive to hold excess reserves in prosperous times means that:

> During an economic boom, profit-oriented banks will likely make the money supply expand, adding undesirable momentum to the booming economy and paving the way for a burst of inflation. The authorities must intervene to prevent this rapid money growth.

Regulation of the money supply, then, is necessary because profit-oriented bankers might otherwise provide the economy with a gyrating money supply that dances to and amplifies the tune of the business cycle. Precisely how the authorities keep the money supply under control is the subject of the next chapter.

## SUMMARY

1. It is more efficient to exchange goods and services by using *money* as a *medium of exchange* than by *bartering* them directly.

2. In addition to being the medium of exchange, whatever serves as money is likely to become the standard *unit of account* and a popular *store of value*.

3. Throughout history, all sorts of things have served as money. *Commodity money* gave way to full-bodied paper money (certificates backed 100 percent by some commodity, like gold), which in turn gave way to partially backed paper money. Nowadays our paper money has no commodity backing whatsoever; it is pure *fiat money*.

4. One popular definition of the U.S. money supply is *M1*, which includes coins, paper money, and several types of checking deposits. However, most economists prefer the *M2* definition, which adds to M1 other types of checkable accounts and most savings deposits. Much of M2 is held outside of banks by investment houses, credit unions, and other financial institutions.

5. Under our modern system of *fractional reserve banking*, banks keep cash reserves equal to only a fraction of their total deposit liabilities. This is the key to their profitability, because the remaining funds can be loaned out at interest. But it also leaves banks potentially vulnerable to *runs*.

6. Because of this vulnerability, bank managers are generally conservative in their investment strategies. They also keep a prudent level of reserves. Even so, the government keeps a watchful eye over banking practices.

7. Before 1933, bank failures were common in the United States, but they declined sharply when *deposit insurance* was instituted.

8. Because it holds only fractional reserves, the banking system as a whole can create several dollars of deposits for each dollar of reserves it receives. Under certain assumptions, the ratio of new deposits to new reserves will be $1/m$, where $m$ is the required reserve ratio.

9. The same process works in reverse, as a system of money destruction, when cash is withdrawn from the banking system.

10. Because banks and individuals may want to hold more cash when the economy is shaky, the money supply would probably contract under such circumstances if the government did not intervene. Similarly, the money supply would probably expand rapidly in boom times if it were unregulated.

## KEY TERMS

| | | |
|---|---|---|
| Run on a bank   620 | M1   625 | Required reserves   630 |
| Barter   621 | M2   626 | Asset   630 |
| Money   622 | Near moneys   626 | Liability   631 |
| Medium of exchange   622 | Liquidity   626 | Balance sheet   631 |
| Unit of account   622 | Fractional reserve banking   627 | Net worth   631 |
| Store of value   622 | Deposit insurance   630 | Deposit creation   632 |
| Commodity money   622 | Federal Deposit Insurance Corporation (FDIC)   630 | Excess reserves   632 |
| Fiat money   623 | | |

## QUESTIONS FOR REVIEW

1. If ours were a barter economy, how would you pay your tuition bill? What if your college did not want the goods or services you offered in payment?

2. How is "money" defined, both conceptually and in practice? Does the U.S. money supply consist of commodity money, full-bodied paper money, or fiat money?

3. What is fractional reserve banking, and why is it the key to bank profits? (*Hint:* What opportunities to make profits would banks lose if reserve requirements were 100 percent?) Why does fractional reserve banking give bankers discretion over how large the money supply will be? Why does it make banks potentially vulnerable to runs?

4. During the 1980s and early 1990s, there was a rash of bank failures in the United States. Explain why these failures did not lead to runs on banks. On the contrary, bank runs were common in Southeast Asia in 1997 and 1998. Why the difference?

5. Suppose that no banks keep excess reserves and no individuals or firms hold on to cash. If someone suddenly discovers $12 million in buried treasure, explain what will happen to the money supply if the required reserve ratio is 10 percent.

6. How would your answer to Review Question 5 differ if the reserve ratio were 25 percent? If the reserve ratio were 100 percent?

7. Each year during Christmas shopping season, consumers and stores increase their holdings of cash. Explain how this could lead to a multiple contraction of the money supply. (As a matter of fact, the authorities prevent this contraction from occurring by methods explained in the next chapter.)

8. Excess reserves make a bank less vulnerable to runs. Why, then, don't bankers like to hold excess reserves? What circumstances might persuade them that it would be advisable to hold excess reserves?

9. Use tables such as Tables 30–2 and 30–3 to illustrate what happens to bank balance sheets when each of the following transactions occurs:

   a. You withdraw $50 from your checking account to buy concert tickets.

   b. Sam finds a $50 bill on the sidewalk and deposits it into his checking account.

   c. Mary Q. Contrary withdraws $1,000 in cash from her account at Hometown Bank, carries it to the city, and deposits it into her account at Big City Bank.

10. For each of the transactions listed in Review Question 9, what will be the ultimate effect on the money supply if the required reserve ratio is one-eighth (12.5 percent)? Assume that the oversimplified deposit multiplier formula applies.

11. If the government takes over a failed bank with liabilities (mostly deposits) of $2.0 billion, pays off the depositors, and sells the assets for $1.5 billion, where does the missing $500 million come from? Why?

Victorians heard with grave attention that the Bank Rate had been raised. They did not know what it meant. But they knew that it was an act of extreme wisdom.

J. K. Galbraith

# MONETARY POLICY AND THE NATIONAL ECONOMY

Now that we understand the rudiments of banking, we are ready to bring money and interest rates into our model of income determination and the price level. In earlier chapters, we took investment (*I*) to be a fixed number. But this is a poor assumption. Not only is investment highly variable, it also depends on interest rates—which are, in turn, heavily influenced by *monetary policy*. The main task of this chapter is to explain how monetary policy affects interest rates, and thereby investment and aggregate demand. By the end of the chapter, we will have constructed a complete macroeconomic model, which we will use in the next few chapters to investigate a variety of important policy issues.

## Just Why Is Alan Greenspan So Important?

When Bill Clinton was elected president of the United States, one of his top economic advisers informed him that, where macroeconomic matters are concerned, he had just been elected to the *second-highest* position in the land! The first spot was already occupied by Alan Greenspan, the chairman of the Federal Reserve Board.

Greenspan is a taciturn and not very charismatic economist. But when he speaks, people in financial markets around the world listen. Listen? They scrutinize his remarks for nuances with an intensity that was once reserved for utterances from behind the Kremlin walls. Why? Because, in the view of many economists, the Federal Reserve's decisions on interest rates are the single most important influence on aggregate demand—and hence on economic growth, unemployment, and inflation.

Greenspan heads America's central bank, the *Federal Reserve System.* The "Fed," as it is called, is a very special kind of bank. Its customers are banks rather than individuals, and it performs some of the same services for them as your bank performs for you. Although it makes enormous profits, profit is not its goal. Instead, the Fed tries to manage the money supply and interest rates according to what it perceives to be best for the nation. This chapter will teach you how the Fed does its job, and why its decisions affect our economy so profoundly. In brief, it will teach you why people listen so intently when Alan Greenspan speaks.

ALAN GREENSPAN PONDERS HIS GROCERY LIST...

## ■ MONEY AND INCOME: THE IMPORTANT DIFFERENCE

But first we must get some terminology straight. The words *money* and *income* are used almost interchangeably in common parlance. This is a pitfall we must learn to avoid.

*Money* is a snapshot concept. It answers questions like "How much money do you have right now?" or "How much money did you have at 3:32 p.m. on Friday, November 5th?" To answer questions like these, you would add up the cash you are (or were) carrying and whatever checkable balances you have (or had), and answer something like: "I have $126.33," or "On Friday, November 5th, at 3:32 p.m., I had $31.43."

*Income*, by contrast, is more like a motion picture; it comes to you over a period of time. If you are asked "What is your income?" you must respond by saying "$200 *per week*," or "$800 *per month*," or "$10,000 *per year*," or something like that. Notice the unit of time attached to each of these responses. If you just answer "My income is $452," without indicating whether it is per week or per month or per year, no one will understand what you mean.

That the two concepts are very different is easy to see. A typical American family has an *income* of about $40,000 per year, but its *money* holdings at any point in time (using the M1 definition) may be less than $2,000. Similarly, at the national level, nominal GDP at the end of 1998 was more than $8.5 trillion, while the money stock (M1) was a little less than $1.1 trillion.

Although money and income are very different, they are certainly related. This chapter focuses on that relationship. Specifically, we will look at how the stock of *money* in existence at any moment of time influences the rate at which people will earn *income*, that is, *how money affects GDP.*

## ■ AMERICA'S CENTRAL BANK: THE FEDERAL RESERVE SYSTEM

When Congress established the *Federal Reserve System* in 1914, the United States joined the company of most other advanced industrial nations. Up until then, the United States, distrustful of centralized economic power, was almost the only important nation without a **central bank.** Britain's central bank, the Bank of England, for example, dates from 1694.

A **central bank** is a bank for banks. America's central bank is the *Federal Reserve System.*

### ORIGINS AND STRUCTURE

Some painful experiences with economic reality, not the power of economic logic, provided the impetus to establish a central bank for the United States. Four severe banking panics between 1873 and 1907, in which many banks failed, convinced legislators and bankers alike that a central bank that would regulate credit conditions was not a luxury but a necessity. The 1907 crisis led Congress to study the shortcomings of the banking system and, eventually, to establish the Federal Reserve System.

Although the basic ideas of central banking came from Europe, the United States made some changes when it imported the idea, making the Federal Reserve System a uniquely American institution. Owing to the vastness of our country, the extraordinarily large number of commercial banks, and our tradition of shared state-federal responsibilities, Congress decided that the United States should have, not one central bank, but 12.

Technically, each Federal Reserve bank is a corporation; its stockholders are its member banks. But your bank, if it is a member of the system, does not enjoy the privileges normally accorded to stockholders: It receives only a token share of the Federal Reserve's immense profits (the bulk is turned over to the U.S. Treasury), and it has virtually no say in corporate decisions. The private banks are more like customers of the Fed than like owners.

Who, then, controls the Fed? Most of the power resides in the seven-member board of governors of the Federal Reserve System in Washington, especially in its

## ● A MEETING OF THE FEDERAL OPEN MARKET COMMITTEE

Meetings of the Federal Open Market Committee are serious and formal affairs. All 19 members—7 governors and 12 reserve bank presidents—sit around a mammoth table in the Fed's cavernous but austere board room. A limited number of top Fed staffers join them at and around the table, for access to FOMC meetings is strictly controlled.

At precisely 9 A.M.—for punctuality is a high virtue at the Fed—the doors are closed and the chairman calls the meeting to order. No press is allowed and, unlike most important Washington meetings, nothing will leak. Secrecy is another high virtue at the Fed.

After hearing a few routine staff reports, the chairman calls on each of the members in turn to give their views of the current economic situation. Although he knows them all woll, ho addroccoc oach mombor formally as "Governor X" or "President Y." District bank presidents offer insights into their local economies, and all members comment on the outlook for the national economy. Disagreements are raised, but voices are not. There are no interruptions while people talk. Strikingly, in this most political of cities, politics is almost never mentioned.

Once he has heard from all the others, the chairman offers his own views of the economic situation. Then he usually recommends a course of action. Members of the

committee, in their turn, comment on the chairman's proposal. Most agree, though some note differences of opinion. After hearing all this, the chairman announces what he perceives to be the committee's consensus and asks the secretary to call the roll. Only the 12 voting members answer, saying yes or no. Negative votes are rare, for the FOMC tries to operate by consensus and a dissent is considered a loud objection.

The meeting adjourns, and at about 2:15 P.M. a Fed spokesman announces the decision to the public. Within minutes, financial markets around the world react.

chairman. The governors are appointed by the president of the United States, with the advice and consent of the Senate, for 14-year terms. The president also designates one of the members to serve a four-year term as chairman of the board, and thus to be the most powerful central banker in the world. Alan Greenspan has chaired the Fed since 1987.

The Federal Reserve stands *independent* of the rest of the government. As long as it stays within its statutory authority as delineated by Congress, it alone has responsibility for determining the nation's monetary policy. The power of appointment, however, gives the president some long-run influence over Federal Reserve policy.

Closely allied with the board of governors is the powerful *Federal Open Market Committee (FOMC)*, which meets eight times a year in Washington. For reasons to be explained shortly, FOMC decisions largely determine short-term interest rates and the size of the U.S. money supply. This 12-member committee consists of the seven governors of the Federal Reserve System, the president of the Federal Reserve Bank of New York, and, on a rotating basis, four of the other 11 district bank presidents.[1]

### THE INDEPENDENCE OF THE FED

Some people look upon the institutional independence of the Federal Reserve System as a source of pride, whereas others see it as an antidemocratic embarrassment.

---

[1] Alan Blinder was the vice chairman of the Federal Reserve Board and thus a member of the Federal Open Market Committee from 1994 to 1996.

## ● POLICY DEBATE | HOW INDEPENDENT SHOULD THE CENTRAL BANK BE?

The debate over central bank independence is somewhat "academic" in the United States, since the Fed's independence is widely respected and not under any serious threat. But the issue is a live one in many other countries.

Nations vary a great deal in how much independence they grant their central banks. At one extreme, the German Bundesbank and the Swiss National Bank are often cited as the world's most independent central banks, with the Fed not far behind. But in Australia, monetary policy is still set by the treasurer, not by the Reserve Bank of Australia.

Over the last decade or so, a large number of countries have moved toward greater central bank independence and no major country has moved in the other direction. Why? The main reason seems to be the desire to fight inflation. As the accompanying chart shows, countries with more independent central banks turn in better inflation performance, on average.

Under the terms of the Maastricht Treaty, which committed members of the European Union to move toward a single currency—the euro, each country must have an independent central bank. All member nations have made the switch, even though several (most notably, the United Kingdom) have not joined the monetary union.

In Latin America, several formerly high-inflation countries have found that giving their central banks more independence helped them reduce inflation dramatically. Some of the formerly socialist countries in Europe, finding themselves saddled with high inflation and "unsound" currencies, made their central banks more independent for the same reasons.

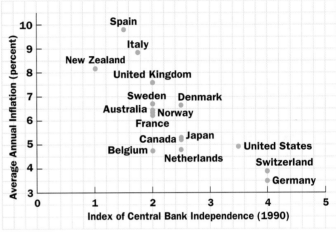

Proponents of Federal Reserve independence argue that it enables the FOMC to make monetary policy decisions on objective, technical criteria and keeps monetary control out of the "political thicket." Without this independence, they argue, politicians might try to force the Fed to expand the money supply too rapidly, thereby contributing to chronic inflation and undermining faith in America's financial system. They point to international evidence showing that countries with more independent central banks have lower inflation. (See the accompanying box, "How Independent Should the Central Bank Be?")

Opponents of this view counter that there is something profoundly undemocratic about letting a group of unelected bankers and economists make decisions that affect every American's well-being. Monetary policy, they argue, should be formulated by the elected representatives of the people, just as fiscal policy is. Those who argue for political control over the Fed can point to historical instances in which monetary and fiscal policy were at loggerheads—with the Fed undermining or even overwhelming the effects of fiscal policy decisions.

Plenty of middle ground exists between the two extremes. One far less drastic proposal would shift the Fed chairman's term to start shortly after that of the president of the United States. As things stand today, a newly elected president must retain the chairman that his predecessor appointed, whether or not he agrees with that chairman's policies. A second suggestion would let the president of the United States appoint the presidents of the 12 district banks; now they are chosen by their

*"I'm sorry, sir, but I don't believe you know us well enough to call us the Fed."*

## A CENTRAL BANK IS BORN

The Maastricht Treaty, which provides for a common currency for all members of the European Union, requires all member nations to follow the same monetary policy. That meant that authority over monetary policy had to be assigned to a single European-wide central bank. This new institution—called the European Central Bank (ECB)—officially opened for business on January 1, 1999.

The structure of the ECB is patterned on that of the Federal Reserve: Monetary policy is made by a committee consisting of six ECB officials headquartered in Frankfurt plus the heads of the 11 national central banks.* They meet monthly in Frankfurt to determine Europe's monetary policy.

After a nasty international squabble, the honor of being the first person selected to head the ECB was granted to Wim Duisenberg, a widely respected veteran central banker from The Netherlands. Because the ECB is not a creature of any national government, it is potentially the most independent central bank in the world.

*The European Union has 15 members, but the United Kingdom, Sweden, Denmark, and Greece are not part of the monetary union.

own boards of directors. A third proposal would take FOMC voting rights away from the bank presidents, who are not presidential appointees.

A much weaker proposed reform would simply require the Fed to announce its ultimate targets for unemployment and inflation and explain how it expects its monetary policy actions to promote these goals. In one version of this proposal, the Fed would have to adopt the goals of the administration or Congress. But a more moderate version would simply make the Fed announce its own goals and subject them to public scrutiny.

How people react to these and other reform proposals that would affect the Fed's independence depends partly on how they perceive the office. Are Federal Reserve governors like judges and therefore, at least in principle, best thought of as nonpartisan and independent technocrats? The 14-year term of office certainly suggests an analogy to the judiciary, but the board's role most assuredly involves making policy, not just interpreting the law. Or are the governors more like members of the cabinet, that is, policy-making officials who should properly serve only at the pleasure of the president? Because neither analogy fits precisely, the issue is a vexing one.

## CONTROLLING THE MONEY SUPPLY: OPEN MARKET OPERATIONS

**Open-market operations** refer to the Fed's purchase or sale of government securities through transactions in the open market.

When it wants to change the money supply and interest rates, the Fed normally relies on what are called **open-market operations.** Open-market operations either give banks more reserves or take reserves away from them, thereby triggering a multiple expansion or contraction of the money supply, as described in the previous chapter.

How does this work? If the Federal Open Market Committee decides that the money supply is too low, it can issue instructions to expand the money supply through open market operations. Specifically, the Federal Reserve System would then *purchase* U.S. government securities (generally short-term securities called *Treasury bills*) from any individual or bank that wished to sell, thus putting more reserves in the hands of the banks.

An example will illustrate the mechanics. Suppose the FOMC orders a purchase of $100 million worth of securities in the open market and that commercial banks sell those securities. *The Fed makes payment by giving the banks $100 million in new reserves.* So, if they held only their required reserves initially, the banks now have $100 million in excess reserves. The relevant transactions are shown in Table 31–1.

When the Fed buys $100 million worth of securities from the banks, the ownership of these securities shifts from the banks to the Fed. (See the black arrows in Table 31–1.) The Fed makes payment by adding $100 billion to the bookkeeping entries that represent the banks' accounts at the Fed—called "bank reserves" in the table. These reserves (shown in blue in the table) are liabilities of the Fed and assets of the banks. Because deposits have not increased at all, *required* reserves are unchanged by this transaction. But *actual* reserves are increased by $100 million, so there are now $100 million in *excess* reserves. This excess, we know from the previous chapter, will trigger a multiple expansion of the banking system.

Where does the Fed get the money that it turns over to the banks in exchange for the securities? It could pay in cash, but normally does not. Instead, it manufactures the funds out of thin air or, more literally, by punching the keyboard of a computer terminal. Specifically, the Fed pays the banks for the securities by adding the appropriate sums to the reserve accounts that the banks maintain at the Fed. Balances held in these accounts constitute bank reserves, just like cash in bank vaults.

Although this process of creating bookkeeping entries at the Federal Reserve is commonly referred to as "printing money," the Fed does not literally run any printing presses. Instead, it simply trades its IOUs for an existing asset (a government security). But unlike your IOUs, the Fed's IOUs constitute legal bank reserves and thus can support a multiple expansion of the money supply in the same way that cash does. The banks, not the Fed, actually increase the money supply; but the Fed's actions give the banks the ability to lend the additional funds that fuel the expansion.

Once excess reserves are created, multiple expansion of the banking system proceeds in the usual way. It is not hard for the Fed to estimate the ultimate increase in the money supply that will result from its actions. As we saw in the previous chapter, each dollar of excess reserves can support $1/m$ dollars of checking deposits, if $m$

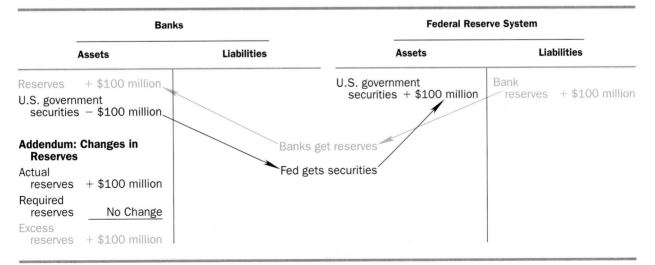

**Effects of an Open-Market Purchase of Securities on the Balance Sheets of Banks and the Fed**

TABLE 31–1

| Banks | | Federal Reserve System | |
|---|---|---|---|
| **Assets** | **Liabilities** | **Assets** | **Liabilities** |
| Reserves   + $100 million | | U.S. government securities + $100 million | Bank reserves   + $100 million |
| U.S. government securities − $100 million | | | |

**Addendum: Changes in Reserves**

| | |
|---|---|
| Actual reserves | + $100 million |
| Required reserves | No Change |
| Excess reserves | + $100 million |

Banks get reserves

Fed gets securities

---

If you read or listen to the financial press the next time the FOMC changes monetary policy, you will probably hear that the Fed has raised or lowered "the Federal funds rate." What in the world is that?

As we mentioned in the previous chapter, banks sometimes find themselves with either insufficient or excess reserves. Neither situation is satisfactory. Reserve deficiencies (actual reserves below required reserves) are not allowed. Excess reserves (actual reserves above requirements) are perfectly legal but earn the bank no interest. So an active market has developed in which banks with excess reserves lend their surpluses to banks with reserve deficiencies. The interest rate charged on such loans is called the *federal funds rate.*

When the Fed conducts an open-market operation, the federal funds rate reacts almost instantly. Why? Because the Fed's action alters the supply-demand balance in the federal funds market. An open-market purchase bolsters reserve *supply,* and therefore lowers the federal funds rate. An open-market sale adds new *demand,* and so pushes the funds rate higher. Although changes in the funds rate affect only certain banks *directly,* the effects soon ripple through the economy's entire interest rate structure.

Think of the federal funds market as the Archimedian lever that the Fed uses to move the giant U.S. economy.

---

is the required reserve ratio. In our example, $m = 0.20$; so \$100 million in new reserves can support $\$100/0.2 = \$500$ million in new money.

But *estimating* the ultimate monetary expansion is a far cry from *knowing it* with certainty. As we know from the previous chapter, the simple deposit multiplier formula is predicated on the assumptions that people will want to hold no more cash and that banks will want to hold no more excess reserves, as the monetary expansion proceeds. In practice, these assumptions are unlikely to be literally true. So to predict the eventual effect of its action on the money supply, the Fed must estimate both the amount that firms and individuals will add to their currency holdings and the amount that banks will add to their excess reserves. Neither of these can be estimated with utter precision. In summary:

> When the Federal Reserve System wants to increase the money supply, it purchases U.S. government securities in the open market. It pays for these securities by creating new bank reserves, and these additional reserves lead to a multiple expansion of the money supply. However, because of fluctuations in people's desires to hold cash and banks' desires to hold excess reserves, the Fed cannot predict the consequences of these actions with perfect accuracy. Thus, over short periods, control over the money supply must of necessity be imperfect.

The procedures followed when the FOMC wants to *contract* the money supply are just the opposite of those we have just explained. In brief, it *sells* government securities in the open market. This takes reserves *away* from banks, because banks pay for the securities by drawing down their deposits at the Fed.[2] A multiple *contraction* of the banking system ensues. The principles are exactly the same as when the process operates in reverse—and so are the uncertainties.

### OPEN-MARKET OPERATIONS, BOND PRICES, AND INTEREST RATES

When it offers more government bonds for sale on the open market, the Federal Reserve normally depresses bond prices. This process is illustrated by Figure 31–1, which shows a rightward shift of the (vertical) supply curve of bonds—from $S_0S_0$ to

---

[2] It is not important that *banks* be the buyers. Question 5 at the end of the chapter shows that the effect on the money supply is the same if bank *customers* purchase the securities.

"WHEN INTEREST RATES GO UP, BOND PRICES GO DOWN. WHEN INTEREST RATES GO DOWN, BOND PRICES GO UP. BUT PLEASE DON'T ASK ME WHY."

$S_1S_1$—with an unchanged demand curve, $DD$. The price of bonds falls from $P_0$ to $P_1$ as equilibrium in the bond market shifts from point $A$ to point $B$.

Falling bond prices translate directly into rising interest rates. Why is that? Most bonds pay a fixed number of dollars of interest per year. For concreteness, consider a bond that pays $90 each year. If the bond sells for $1,000, bondholders earn a 9 percent return on their investment (the $90 interest payment is 9 percent of $1,000). We say that *the interest rate on the bond is 9 percent.* Now suppose the price of the bond falls to $900. The annual interest payment is still $90, so bondholders now earn 10 percent on their money ($90 is 10 percent of $900). *The effective interest rate on the bond has risen to 10 percent.* This relationship between bond prices and interest rates is completely general:

> When bond prices fall, interest rates must rise because the purchaser of a bond spends less money than before to earn a given number of dollars of interest per year. Similarly, when bond prices rise, interest rates must fall.

In fact, the relationship amounts to nothing more than two ways of saying the same thing. Higher interest rates *mean* lower bond prices; lower interest rates *mean* higher bond prices.[3]

We thus see that the Fed, through its open-market operations, exercises direct influence over interest rates. Specifically:

> An open-market purchase of bonds by the Fed not only raises the money supply but also drives up bond prices and pushes interest rates down. Conversely, an open-market sale of bonds, which reduces the money supply, lowers bond prices and raises interest rates.

**FIGURE 31-1**

**Open-Market Sales and Bond Prices**

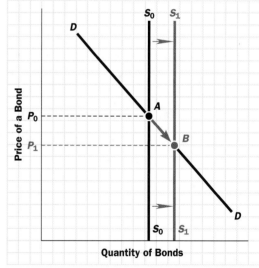

## OTHER METHODS OF MONETARY CONTROL

When the Federal Reserve System was first established, its founders did not intend it to pursue an active monetary policy to stabilize the economy. Indeed, the basic ideas of stabilization policy were foreign at the time. Instead, the Fed's

---

[3] For further discussion and examples, see Question 6 at the end of the chapter.

founders viewed it as a means of preventing the supplies of money and credit from drying up during economic contractions, as had happened so often in the pre-1914 period.

### LENDING TO BANKS

One of the principal ways in which Congress intended the Fed to provide such insurance against financial panics was to act as a "lender of last resort." When risky business prospects made commercial banks hesitant to extend new loans, or when banks were in trouble, the Fed would step in by lending money to the banks, thus inducing the banks to lend more money to their customers. The Fed last performed this role on a large scale in October 1987, when a stock market crash stunned the financial world. Its lending to banks helped avert a financial panic.

When the Fed extends borrowing privileges to a bank in need of reserves, that bank receives a credit in its deposit account at the Fed (see the blue entries in Table 31–2) Because bank deposits, and hence required reserves, have not increased, this addition to bank reserves creates *excess reserves*—$5 million in the example. This excess may lead to an expansion of the money supply; or it may eliminate a reserve deficiency and thereby prevent a multiple contraction of the banking system. In either case, the Fed eases monetary conditions by lending to banks.

The **discount rate** is the interest rate the Fed charges on loans that it makes to banks.

In principle, Federal Reserve officials can influence the amount banks borrow by manipulating the *rate of interest charged on these loans*. For historical reasons, this is called the **discount rate** in the United States. In foreign countries, it is often known as the *bank rate*. If the Fed wants banks to have more reserves, it can reduce the interest rate that it charges on loans, thereby tempting banks to borrow more. Alternatively, it can soak up reserves by raising its rate and persuading the banks to reduce their borrowings.

When it changes its discount rate, the Fed cannot know for sure how banks will react. Sometimes they may respond vigorously to a cut in the rate, borrowing a great deal from the Fed and lending a correspondingly large amount to their customers. At other times they may essentially ignore the change in the discount rate. So the link between the discount rate and the money supply is apt to be quite loose.

Some foreign central banks *actively* use their bank rate as the centerpiece of monetary policy. But in the United States, the Fed lends infrequently and in small amounts. Instead, it relies on open-market operations in conducting its monetary policy. The Fed normally adjusts its discount rate *passively*, to keep it in line with market interest rates.

| TABLE 31–2 | Balance Sheet Changes for Borrowings from the Fed |
| --- | --- |

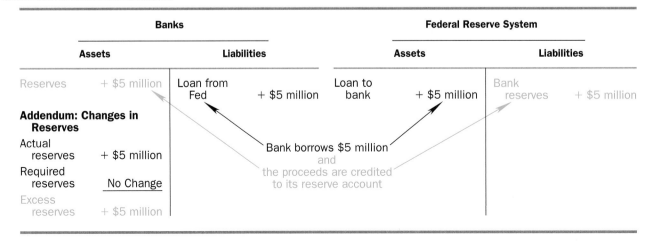

## CHANGING RESERVE REQUIREMENTS

The Fed has one final method of controlling the money supply: varying the minimum required reserve ratio. To see how this works, imagine that banks hold reserves that just match their required minimums. Excess reserves are zero.

If the Federal Reserve Board decides that the money supply needs to be increased, it can lower the required reserve ratio, thereby transforming some previously *required* reserves into *excess* reserves. Although no new money is created directly by this action, we know from the previous chapter that it will set in motion the wheels of a multiple expansion of the banking system. Similarly, raising the required reserve ratio will set off a multiple contraction of bank deposits. In point of fact, however, the Fed no longer uses the reserve ratio as a weapon of monetary control. Current law and regulations provide for a basic reserve ratio of 10 percent against transaction deposits—a figure that has not changed since 1992.

## ■ SUPPLY-DEMAND ANALYSIS OF THE MONEY MARKET

This completes our discussion of the Fed's three methods of controlling the money supply—open-market operations, lending policy, and reserve requirements—and the limitations of each. One point, however, merits further emphasis. We have noted that the Fed's control of the money supply is imperfect because banks can and do vary their excess reserve holdings. Because reserves earn no interest, banks will hold substantial *excess* reserves only when they feel that funds cannot be put to profitable uses without excessive risks. This may happen if shaky business conditions make loans to customers look unusually risky or if interest rates are very low. Conversely, banks will work hard to keep reserves to just the legal minimum when loans to customers look safe and when interest rates are high. Thus:

> As interest rates rise, banks normally find it more profitable to expand their volume of loans and deposits, thus increasing the money supply. However, the Fed can shift the relationship between the money supply and interest rates by employing any of its principal weapons of monetary control: open-market operations, changes in reserve requirements, or changes in lending policy to banks.

### THE MONEY SUPPLY MECHANISM

These ideas are depicted graphically in Figure 31–2. Panel (a) shows a typical money supply schedule, labeled *MS*, illustrating the fact that banks will supply more money as interest rates rise.[4] Notice that the sensitivity of the money supply to interest rates is rather weak in the diagram—a large increase in the rate of interest (from 3 percent to 5 percent) induces only a small increase in the money supply (from \$820 billion to \$830 billion). The drawing is deliberately constructed that way because that is what the statistical evidence shows.

The *MS* line in panel (a) shows the money supply schedule corresponding to some specific monetary policy. Panel (b) portrays how the money supply schedule responds to an *expansionary change in monetary policy*, such as an open-market purchase of government bonds. The money supply schedule shifts outward from the black line $M_0S_0$ to the red line $M_1S_1$, as indicated by the arrows. After banks have adjusted to the change, the money supply is greater at any given interest rate.

Panel (c) shows what happens in the reverse case—a *contractionary monetary policy* such as an open-market sale of securities. The money supply shifts inward from the black line $M_0S_0$ to the red line $M_2S_2$.

---

[4] There are many interest rates in the economy. However, they all tend to move up and down together. Hence, for present purposes, we can speak of "the" rate of interest.

| FIGURE 31-2 |
|---|

**The Supply Schedule for Money**

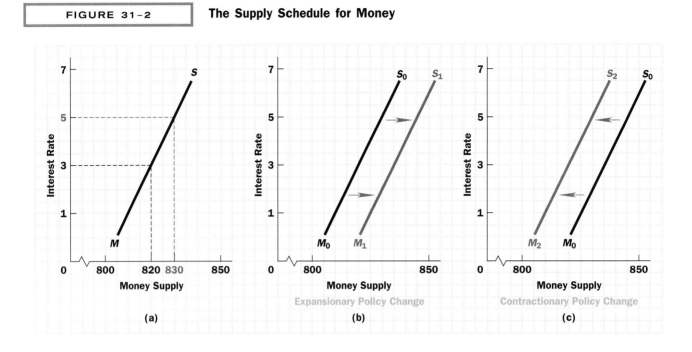

(a)

Expansionary Policy Change

(b)

Contractional Policy Change

(c)

As we have emphasized, the diagrams make things look rather more precise than they actually are. Because the Fed's control over the money supply schedule is imperfect in the short run, the actual *MS* schedule is obscured by a bit of fog. In what follows, we portray all the graphs as clean straight lines only for pedagogical simplicity. The Fed wishes things were so simple in the real world!

## THE DEMAND FOR MONEY

Just as we must know something about both the supply of and the demand for wheat before we can predict how much will be sold and at what price, we must know something about the *demand for money* if we are to understand the amount of money actually in existence and the prevailing interest rate.

The definition of *money* given in Chapter 30 suggests the most important reason why people hold money balances: The medium of exchange is needed to carry out purchases and sales of goods and services conveniently. More dollars are needed to conduct the nation's business if more purchases and sales are made or if each transaction takes place at a higher price. Because nominal gross domestic product (GDP) is normally considered to be the best measure of the money volume of goods and services traded in the economy, it seems safe to assume that the demand for money will rise as nominal GDP rises. Indeed, an impressive amount of statistical evidence supports this supposition.

But nominal GDP is not the only factor affecting the demand for money; interest rates influence money demand, too. At first, that may seem surprising because many forms of money pay either no interest or a fixed interest rate. Why, then, are interest rates relevant? They are relevant because money is only one of a variety of forms in which individuals can store wealth. Holders of money *give up* the opportunity to hold one of these other assets, such as government bonds, in order to gain the convenience of money. In so doing, they *give up* the interest that they could have earned on one of these alternative assets.

This is another example of the concept of *opportunity cost*.[5] On the surface, it seems virtually costless to hold money. But, *compared with the next best alternative*, this action is not costless at all. For example, if the best alternative to holding $100

---

[5] If you need to review this concept, see Chapter 4.

in cash is to put those funds into a government bond that pays 7 percent interest, then the opportunity cost of holding that cash is $7 per year (7 percent of $100).

Money holdings should therefore be lower when the rate of interest is higher. Why? Because, although people hold money to facilitate making transactions, this benefit comes at a cost. For example, holders of cash give up the potential interest they could earn by investing the funds in, say, government bonds. It is natural, therefore, to assume that higher interest rates induce households and firms to economize more on holding money balances. In a word, the demand to hold money should *decline* as the interest rate *rises*. Once again, careful analysis of the data shows this to be true. To summarize:

> People and businesses hold money primarily to finance their transactions. Therefore, the quantity of money demanded *increases* as nominal output rises. However, the quantity of money demanded *decreases* as the rate of interest rises because the rate of interest is the opportunity cost of holding money balances.

We can portray the demand for money by a graphical device, as shown in the three panels of Figure 31–3. In Panel (a), we show a downward-sloping demand schedule for money (the curve labeled *MD*)—the quantity of money demanded decreases as the rate of interest rises. But because the quantity of money demanded also depends on nominal GDP, we must hold nominal GDP constant in drawing such a curve. Changes in this variable will shift the *MD* curve in the manner indicated in the other two panels. At higher levels of nominal GDP, as illustrated in Panel (b), the demand for money is greater at any interest rate because more transactions occur and because the average transaction requires more money. At lower levels of nominal GDP, as illustrated in Panel (c), the demand for money is smaller.

**The Demand Schedule for Money** | FIGURE 31–3

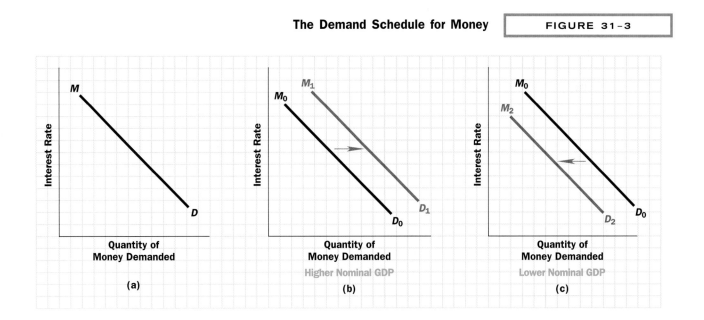

**EQUILIBRIUM IN THE MONEY MARKET**

As is usual in supply and demand analysis, it is useful to put both sides of the market together on a single graph. Figure 31–4 combines the money supply schedule of Figure 31–2(a) (labeled *MS*) with the money demand schedule of Figure 31–3(a) (labeled *MD*). Point *E* is the equilibrium of the money market. The diagram thus shows that *given* nominal GDP (which locates the *MD* curve) and *given* the Federal Reserve's monetary policy (which locates the *MS* curve), the money market is in equilibrium at an interest rate of 5 percent and a money stock of $830 billion.

FIGURE 31-4

**Equilibrium in the Money Market**

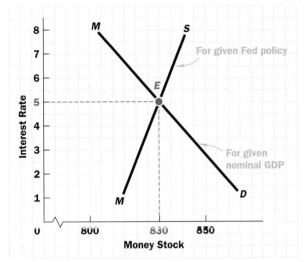

NOTE: Interest rates are in percent; money stock figures are in billions of dollars.

At any interest rate above 5 percent, the quantity of money supplied would exceed the quantity demanded and the interest rate—which is the price for renting money—would therefore decline. At any interest rate below 5 percent, more money would be demanded than supplied, and so the interest rate would rise. This is familiar ground.

Because the Fed can shift the *MS* curve, it can alter this equilibrium through its **monetary policy.** Purchasing government securities in the open market will provide additional excess reserves to the banking system, thus encouraging banks to increase their loans and deposits. As money becomes more plentiful, interest rates drop.

Our supply-demand analysis of the money market shows this process in Figure 31–5(a). By shifting the money supply schedule outward from $M_0S_0$ to $M_1S_1$, the Fed moves the market equilibrium from point $E$ to point $A$—thus forcing the interest rate down and the money supply up. Contractionary monetary policy actions, such as selling securities in the open market, have the opposite effect. They push interest rates up and the money supply down, as Figure 31–5(b) shows. Thus:

Monetary policies that expand the money supply normally lower interest rates. Monetary policies that reduce the money supply normally raise interest rates.

FIGURE 31-5

**The Effects of Monetary Policy on the Money Market**

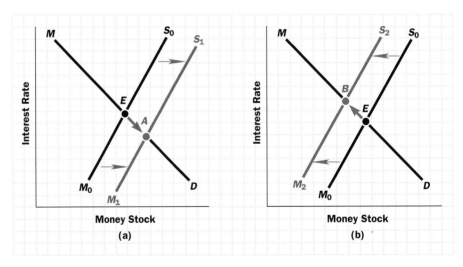

**Money Stock**
**(a)**

**Money Stock**
**(b)**

**Monetary policy** refers to actions that the Federal Reserve System takes in order to change the equilibrium of the money market; that is, to alter the money supply, move interest rates, or both.

## HOW MONETARY POLICY WORKS

We are now ready to see precisely how the Federal Reserve's monetary policy decisions affect unemployment, inflation, and the overall state of the economy. To begin, we go back to the analysis of Chapters 25 through 29, where we learned that aggregate demand is the sum of consumption spending (*C*), investment spending (*I*), government purchases of goods and services (*G*), and net exports (*X* − *IM*). We know that *fiscal policy* controls *G* directly, and influences both *C* and *I* through the tax laws. We now want to find out how *monetary policy* affects total spending.

Most economists agree that, of the four components of aggregate demand, investment and net exports are the most sensitive to monetary policy. We will study the effects of monetary and fiscal policy on net exports in detail in Chapter 37, after we have learned about international exchange rates. For now, we will assume that net exports $(X - IM)$ are fixed and focus on monetary policy's influence on investment $(I)$.

## INVESTMENT AND INTEREST RATES

*Business investment* in new factories and machinery is sensitive to interest rates for reasons that have been explained in earlier chapters.[6] Because the rate of interest that must be paid on borrowings is one part of the cost of an investment, business executives will find investment prospects less attractive as interest rates rise. Therefore, they will spend less. For similar reasons, higher interest rates may also deter some individuals from *investment in housing*. Because the interest cost of a home mortgage is the major component of the total cost of owning a home, fewer families will want to buy new homes when interest rates are high than when interest rates are low. We conclude that:

> Higher interest rates lead to lower investment spending. But investment $(I)$ is a component of total spending, $C + I + G + (X - IM)$. Therefore, when interest rates rise, total spending falls. In terms of the 45° line diagram of previous chapters, a higher interest rate leads to a lower expenditure schedule. Conversely, a lower interest rate leads to a higher expenditure schedule. All this is depicted in Figure 31–6.

## MONETARY POLICY AND TOTAL EXPENDITURE

The effect of interest rates on spending provides a mechanism through which monetary policy moves the macroeconomy. We know from our analysis of the money market that monetary policy can profoundly affect interest rates. Let us, therefore, outline how monetary policy works.

Suppose the Federal Reserve, seeing the economy stuck with unemployment and a recessionary gap, increases the money supply. It would normally do this by purchasing government securities in the open market, but the specific weapon that the Fed uses is not terribly important for present purposes. What matters is that the money supply schedule shifts outward, as shown by the shift from the black line $M_0 S_0$ to the red line $M_1 S_1$ in Figure 31–7.

With the demand schedule for money, $MD$, temporarily fixed, such a shift in the supply curve for money has the effect that an increase in supply always has in a free market: It lowers the price, as Figure 31–7 shows. In this case, the price of renting money is the rate of interest, $r$; so $r$ falls from 5 percent to 3 percent in the example.

Next, for reasons we have just outlined, investment spending $(I)$ rises in response to the lower interest rates. But, as we learned in Chapter 27, such an autonomous rise in investment kicks off a multiplier chain of increases in output and employment. Thus, finally, we have completed the links from the money supply to the level of aggregate demand. In brief, monetary policy works as follows:

> A higher money supply $(M)$ leads to lower interest rates $(r)$, and these lower interest rates encourage investment $(I)$, which has multiplier effects on aggregate demand.

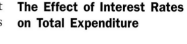

**FIGURE 31–6**

**The Effect of Interest Rates on Total Expenditure**

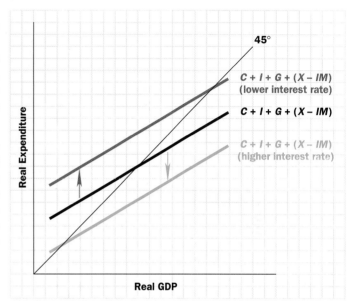

**FIGURE 31–7**

**The Effect of Expansionary Monetary Policy on the Money Supply and Rate of Interest**

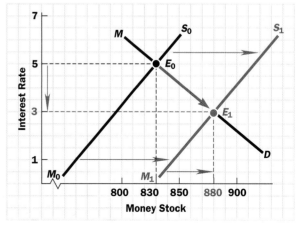

NOTE: Interest rates are in percent; money stock figures are in billions of dollars.

---

[6] See, for example, Chapter 26, page 550.

The process operates equally well in reverse. By contracting the money supply, the Fed can force interest rates up, causing investment spending to fall and pulling down aggregate demand via the multiplier mechanism. This, in outline form, is how monetary policy operates in the Keynesian model. Because the chain of causation is fairly long, the following schematic diagram may help clarify it:

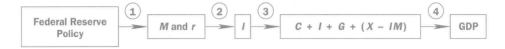

In this causal chain, Link 1 indicates that the Federal Reserve's actions affect money and interest rates. Link 2 stands for the effect of interest rates on investment. Link 3 simply notes that investment is one component of total spending. And Link 4 is the multiplier, relating an autonomous change in investment to the ultimate change in aggregate demand. Let us therefore review what we know about each of these links and fill in some illustrative numbers. In the process, we will see what economists must study if they are to estimate the effects of monetary policy.

Link 1 is the subject of this chapter. It was just depicted in Figure 31–7, which shows the money stock rising from $830 billion to $880 billion while the interest rate declines from 5 percent to 3 percent. Thus, the first thing an economist must know is how sensitive interest rates are to changes in the supply of money.

Link 2 translates the lower interest rate into higher investment spending. We take $I$ to rise by $200 billion in this example. To estimate this effect in practice, economists must study the sensitivity of investment to interest rates—a topic we took up in Chapter 26.

Link 3 instructs us to enter this $200 billion rise in $I$ as an autonomous shift in the $C + I + G + (X - IM)$ schedule of a 45° line diagram. Figure 31–8 carries out this step. The expenditure schedule rises from $C + I_0 + G + (X - IM)$ to $C + I_1 + G + (X - IM)$.

Finally, Link 4 applies multiplier analysis to this vertical shift in the expenditure schedule in order to predict the eventual increase in real GDP demanded. We have been using a multiplier of 2.5 in our examples, so multiplying $200 billion by 2.5 gives the final effect on aggregate demand—a rise of $500 billion. This change is shown in Figure 31–8 as a shift in equilibrium from $E_0$ (where GDP is $6,000 billion) to $E_1$ (where GDP is $6,500 billion). Of course, the size of the multiplier itself must also be estimated. To summarize:

**The effect of monetary policy on aggregate demand depends on the sensitivity of interest rates to the money supply, on the responsiveness of investment spending to the rate of interest, and on the size of the multiplier.**

## FIGURE 31-8

**The Effect of Expansionary Monetary Policy on Total Expenditure**

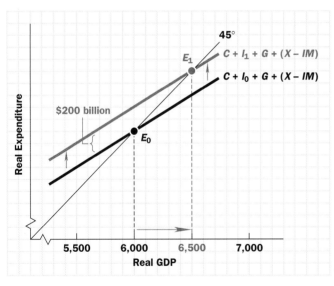

NOTE: Figures are in billions of dollars per year.

# MONEY AND THE PRICE LEVEL IN THE KEYNESIAN MODEL

Our analysis up to this point leaves one important question unanswered: What happens to the price level? To find the answer, we must simply remember once again that aggregate demand *and* aggregate supply jointly determine prices and output. Our analysis of monetary policy so far has shown us how an increase in the money supply boosts total spending, that is, increases the *aggregate quantity demanded at any given price level*. But to learn what happens to the price level and to real output, we must consider *aggregate supply* as well.

Specifically, in considering shifts in aggregate demand caused by *fiscal* policy in Chapter 29, we noted that an upsurge in total spending normally induces firms to increase output somewhat *and* to raise prices somewhat. This is just what an aggregate supply curve shows. Whether prices or real output respond more depends on the slope of the aggregate supply curve.

Because this analysis of output and price responses applies equally well to monetary policy or, for that matter, to any other factor that raises aggregate demand, we conclude that:

> Expansionary monetary policy causes some inflation under normal circumstances. But how much inflation it causes depends on the slope of the aggregate supply curve.

The effect of a rise in the money supply on the price level appears graphically on an aggregate supply and demand diagram in Figure 31–9. In the example we have been using, the Fed's actions raise the money supply by $50 billion, and this increases aggregate demand (through the multiplier) by $500 billion. We enter this increase as a horizontal shift of $500 billion in the aggregate demand curve of Figure 31–9, from $D_0D_0$ to $D_1D_1$. The diagram shows that this expansionary monetary policy pushes the economy's equilibrium from point $E$ to point $B$—the price level therefore rises from 100 to 103, or 3 percent. The diagram also shows that real GDP rises by only $400 billion, which is less than the $500 billion stimulus to aggregate demand. The reason, as we know from earlier chapters, is that rising prices stifle real aggregate demand.

By taking account of the effect of an increase in the money supply on the price level, we have completed our story about the role of monetary policy in the Keynesian model. We can thus expand our schematic diagram of monetary policy as follows:

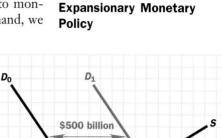

**FIGURE 31-9**

**The Inflationary Effects of Expansionary Monetary Policy**

NOTE: GDP figures are in billions of dollars per year.

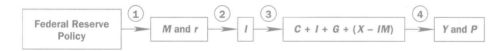

The last link now recognizes that *both* output *and* prices normally are affected by changes in the money supply.

## APPLICATION: WHY THE AGGREGATE DEMAND CURVE SLOPES DOWNWARD

This analysis of the effect of money on the price level puts us in a better position to understand why higher prices reduce aggregate quantity demanded; that is, why the aggregate demand curve slopes downward. In earlier chapters, we explained this phenomenon in two ways. First, we observed that rising prices reduce the purchasing power of certain assets held by consumers, especially money and government bonds, and that this in turn retards consumption spending. Second, we noted that higher domestic prices depress exports and stimulate imports.

There is nothing wrong with this analysis; it is just incomplete. Higher prices have another important effect on aggregate demand, through a channel that we can now understand.

Money is demanded primarily to conduct transactions and, as we have noted in this chapter, a rise in the *average money cost* of each transaction—that is, a rise in the price level—will increase the quantity of money demanded by pushing up nominal GDP. This means that when expansionary policy of any kind raises the price level, more money will be demanded at any given interest rate.

But if the money supply is *not* increased, an increase in the quantity of money demanded at any given interest rate must force

*"Ray Brown on bass, Elvin Jones on drums, and Alan Greenspan on interest rates."*

the cost of borrowing money—the rate of interest—to rise. As we know, increases in interest rates reduce investment and, hence, reduce aggregate demand. This is the main reason why the economy's aggregate demand curve has a negative slope, meaning that aggregate quantity demanded is lower when prices are higher. In sum:

> At higher price levels, the quantity of money demanded is greater. Given a fixed supply schedule, therefore, a higher price level must lead to a higher interest rate. Because high interest rates discourage investment, aggregate quantity demanded is lower when the price level is higher. That is, the aggregate demand curve has a negative slope.

## FROM MODELS TO POLICY DEBATES

You will no doubt be relieved to hear that we have now provided just about all the technical apparatus we need to analyze stabilization policy. To be sure, you will encounter many graphs in the next few chapters. But most of them repeat diagrams with which you are already familiar. Our attention now turns from *building* a theory to *using* that theory to understand important policy issues.

The next three chapters address a trio of important and controversial policy debates that surface regularly in the newspapers: the debate over the efficacy of monetary policy (Chapter 32), the continuing debate over the effects of fiscal and monetary policy on growth (Chapter 33), and the controversy over the trade-off between inflation and unemployment (Chapter 34).

---

## SUMMARY

1. A *central bank* is a bank for banks.

2. The *Federal Reserve System* is America's central bank. There are 12 Federal Reserve banks, but most of the power is held by the Board of Governors in Washington and by the *Federal Open Market Committee.*

3. The Federal Reserve acts independently from the rest of the government. There is controversy over whether this *independence* is a good idea, and a number of reforms have been suggested that would make the Fed more accountable to the president or to Congress.

4. The Fed has three major weapons for control of the money supply: *open-market operations,* reserve requirements, and its lending policy to banks. But only open-market operations are used frequently.

5. The Fed raises the money supply by purchasing government securities in the open market. When it pays banks for such purchases, the Fed provides banks with new reserves, which in turn lead to a larger money supply. Conversely, open-market sales of securities take reserves from banks and lead to a smaller money supply.

6. When the Fed buys bonds, bond prices rise and interest rates fall. When the Fed sells bonds, bond prices fall and interest rates rise.

7. The Fed can also increase the money supply by allowing banks to borrow more reserves, perhaps by reducing the interest rate it charges on such loans or by reducing reserve requirements.

8. None of these weapons, however, gives the Fed perfect control over the money supply in the short run, because it cannot predict perfectly how far the process of deposit creation or destruction will go.

9. The upward-sloping *money supply schedule* shows that more money is supplied at higher interest rates because, as interest rates rise, banks find it more profitable to expand their loans and saving account deposits. This schedule can be shifted by Federal Reserve policy.

10. The downward-sloping *money demand schedule* shows that less money is demanded at higher interest rates because interest is the opportunity cost of holding money. This schedule shifts when output or the price level changes, that is, when nominal GDP changes.

11. The *equilibrium* money stock ($M$) and the equilibrium interest rate ($r$) are determined by the intersection of the money supply and money demand schedules.

12. Federal Reserve policy can shift this equilibrium. Expansionary policies cause $M$ to rise and $r$ to fall. Contractionary policies reduce $M$ and increase $r$.

13. Investment spending ($I$), including business investment and investment in new homes, is sensitive to interest rates ($r$). Specifically, $I$ is lower when $r$ is higher.

14. This explains how *monetary policy* works in the Keynesian model. Raising the money supply ($M$) leads to lower $r$; the lower interest rates stimulate investment spending; and this investment stimulus, via the multiplier, then raises aggregate demand.

15. However, prices are likely to rise as output rises. The amount of inflation caused by increasing the money supply depends on the slope of the aggregate supply curve. There will be much inflation if the supply curve is steep, but little inflation if it is flat.

16. The main reason *why the aggregate demand curve slopes downward* is that higher prices increase the demand to hold money in order to finance transactions. Given the money supply, this pushes interest rates up; this, in turn, discourages investment.

## QUESTIONS FOR REVIEW

1. Why does a modern industrial economy need a central bank?

2. The chapter listed several current proposals for changing the structure of the Fed. Which, if any, of these provisions would you favor? Explain why.

3. Suppose there is $120 billion of cash and that half of it is held in bank vaults as *required* reserves (that is, banks hold no *excess* reserves). How large will the money supply be if the required reserve ratio is 10 percent? $12\frac{1}{2}$ percent? $16\frac{2}{3}$ percent?

4. Show the balance sheet changes that would take place if the Federal Reserve Bank of New York purchased an office building from the Chase Manhattan Bank for a price of $100 million. Compare this to the effect of an open-market purchase of securities shown in Table 31–1. What do you conclude?

5. Suppose the Fed purchases $5 billion worth of government bonds from Bill Gates, who banks at the Bank of America in San Francisco. Show the effects on the balance sheets of the Fed, Bank of America, and Gates. (*Hint:* What will Gates do with the $5 billion check he receives from the Fed?) Does it make any difference if the Fed buys bonds from a bank or from an individual?

6. Treasury bills have a fixed face value and pay interest by selling "at a discount." For example, if a 1-year bill with a $1,000 face value sells today for $950, it will pay $1,000 − $950 = $50 in interest over its life. The interest rate on the bill is therefore $50/$950 = 0.0526, or 5.26 percent.

   a. Suppose the price of the Treasury bill falls to $940. What happens to the interest rate?

   b. Suppose, instead, that the price rises to $960. What is the interest rate now?

   c. (More difficult) Now generalize this example. Let $P$ be the price of the bill and $r$ be the interest rate. Develop an algebraic formula expressing $r$ in terms of $P$. (*Hint:* The interest earned is $1,000 − P. What is the percentage interest rate?) Show that this formula illustrates the point made in the text: Higher bond prices mean lower interest rates.

7. Explain why the quantity of money supplied normally is higher and the quantity of money demanded normally is lower at higher interest rates.

8. In the fall of 1998, the Fed decided that interest rates were too high and took steps to lower them. How did the Fed cut interest rates? Illustrate on a diagram.

9. Explain why both business investments and purchases of new homes rise when interest rates decline.

10. Explain what a $50 billion increase in the money supply will do to real GDP under the following assumptions:

    a. Each $10 billion increase in the money supply reduces the rate of interest by 0.5 percentage point.

    b. Each 1 percentage point decline in interest rates stimulates $30 billion worth of new investment.

    c. The expenditure multiplier is 2.

    d. The aggregate supply curve is so flat that prices do not rise noticeably when demand increases.

11. Explain how your answer to Question 10 would differ if each of the assumptions were changed. Specifically, what sorts of changes in the assumptions would make monetary policy very weak?

12. Use graphs like those in Figures 31–4 and 31–6 to explain why the aggregate demand curve has a negative slope.

13. In recent years, the federal government has eliminated its budget deficit by reducing spending. If the Federal Reserve wanted to maintain the same level of aggregate demand in the face of large-scale deficit reduction, what should it have done? What would you expect to happen to interest rates?

14. (More difficult) Consider an economy in which government purchases, taxes, and net exports are all zero, the consumption function is:

$$C = 300 + 0.75Y$$

and investment spending ($I$) depends on the rate of interest ($r$) in the following way:

$$I = 1,000 − 100r$$

Find the equilibrium GDP if the Fed makes the rate of interest (a) 2 percent ($r = 0.02$), (b) 5 percent, (c) 10 percent.

The love of money is the root of all evil.

New Testament, I Timothy 6:10

Lack of money is the root of all evil.

George Bernard Shaw

# THE DEBATE OVER MONETARY POLICY

Up to now, our discussion of stabilization policy has been almost entirely objective and technical. In seeking to understand how the national economy works and how government policies affect it, we have mostly ignored the intense economic and political controversies that surround the actual conduct of stabilization policy. Chapters 32 through 34 cover precisely these issues.

We begin this chapter by introducing an alternative theory of how money affects the economy, known as *monetarism*. Although the monetarist and Keynesian views seem to contradict one another, we will see that the conflict is more apparent than real. In fact, the disagreement is akin to hearing a Briton say, "Yes," and a Frenchman say, "Oui." The uninitiated hear two different languages, but knowledgeable listeners understand that they mean the same thing.

However, although monetarist and Keynesian *theories* do not differ significantly, important differences *do* arise among economists over the appropriate design and execution of monetary *policy*. These differences are the central concern of the chapter. We will learn about the continuing debates over the nature of aggregate supply, over the relative virtues of monetary versus fiscal policy, and over whether the Federal Reserve should try to control the money stock or interest rates. As we shall see, the resolution of these issues is crucial for the proper conduct of monetary policy and, indeed, to the decision of whether the government should try to conduct any stabilization policy at all.

### Should We Forsake Stabilization Policy?

We have suggested several times in this book that well-timed changes in fiscal or monetary policy can mitigate fluctuations in inflation and unemployment. And we have devoted many pages, including most of Chapters 29 and 31, to explaining how this can be done. Although full examination of the complexities of such stabilization policy requires more advanced discussion, the basic principles are simple enough to learn in even an introductory course, as we hope you have done.

But some economists argue that these lessons are best forgotten. In practice, they claim, attempts at macroeconomic stabilization likely do more harm than good. Policymakers are therefore best advised to follow fixed rules rather than use their best judgment on a case-by-case basis.

Nothing we have said so far leads to this conclusion. But we have not yet told the whole story. By the end of the chapter you will have encountered several arguments in favor of rules, and hence you will be in a better position to make up your own mind on this important debate.

## ■ VELOCITY AND THE QUANTITY THEORY OF MONEY

In the previous chapter, we studied the Keynesian view of how money influences real output and the price level. But another, older model provides a different way to look at these matters. This model, known as the *quantity theory of money*, is easy to understand once we have introduced one new concept: **velocity.**

We learned in Chapter 30 that because barter is so cumbersome, virtually all economic transactions in advanced economies use money. This means that if there are, say, $5,000 billion worth of transactions in the economy during a particular year, and there is an average money stock of $1,000 billion during that year, then each dollar of money is used an average of five times during the year.

The number 5 in this example is called the *velocity of circulation*, or *velocity* for short, because it indicates the *speed* at which money circulates. For example, a particular dollar bill might be used to buy a haircut in January; the barber might use it to buy a sweater in March; the storekeeper might then use it to pay for gasoline

**Velocity** indicates the number of times per year that an "average dollar" is spent on goods and services. It is the ratio of nominal gross domestic product (GDP) to the number of dollars in the money stock. That is:

$$\text{Velocity} = \frac{\text{Nominal GDP}}{\text{Money stock}}$$

in May; the gas station owner could pay it out to the house painter in October; and the painter might spend it on a Christmas present in December. This would mean that the dollar was used five times during the year. If it were used only four times during the year, its velocity would be 4, and so on. Similarly, a $20 bill circulating with a velocity of 8 would be the monetary instrument used to finance $160 worth of transactions in that year.

No one has data on all the transactions in any economy. To make velocity an operational concept, economists must settle on a workable definition of transactions that they can actually measure. The most popular choice is nominal gross domestic product, even though it ignores many transactions that use money, such as sales of existing assets. If we accept nominal GDP as a measure of the money value of transactions, we are led to a concrete definition of velocity as the ratio of nominal GDP to the number of dollars in the money stock. Because nominal GDP is the product of real GDP times the price level, we can write this definition in symbols as follows:

$$\text{Velocity} = \frac{\text{Value of transactions}}{\text{Money stock}} = \frac{\text{Nominal GDP}}{M} = \frac{P \times Y}{M}$$

By multiplying both sides of the equation by $M$, we arrive at an identity called the **equation of exchange,** which relates the money supply and nominal GDP:

**Money supply × Velocity = Nominal GDP**

Alternatively, stated in symbols, we have the following:

**$M \times V = P \times Y$**

Here we have an obvious link between the stock of money, $M$, and the nominal value of the nation's output. But it is only an arithmetic link, not an economic one. For example, it does not imply that the Fed can raise nominal GDP by increasing $M$. Why not? Because $V$ might simultaneously fall by enough to prevent $M \times V$ from rising. In other words, if more dollar bills circulated than before, but each bill changed hands more slowly, total spending might not rise. Thus, we need an auxiliary assumption to change the arithmetic identity into an economic theory:

The **quantity theory of money** transforms the equation of exchange from an arithmetic identity into an economic model through the assumption that changes in velocity are so minor that velocity can be taken to be virtually constant.

You can see that if $V$ never changed, the equation of exchange would be a marvelously simple model of the determination of nominal GDP—far simpler than the Keynesian model. To see this, it is convenient to rewrite the equation of exchange in growth-rate form:

**$\%\Delta M + \%\Delta V = \%\Delta P + \%\Delta Y$**

If $V$ was constant (so its percentage change was always zero), this equation would say, for example, that if the Federal Reserve wanted to make nominal GDP grow by 8.7 percent per year, it need only raise the money supply by 8.7 percent per year. In such a simple world, economists could use the equation of exchange to *predict* nominal GDP growth simply by predicting the growth rate of money. And policymakers could *control* nominal GDP growth simply by controlling growth of the money supply.

In the real world, things are not so simple because velocity is not a fixed number. But this does not necessarily destroy the usefulness of the quantity theory. We explained in Chapter 1 why all economic models make assumptions that are at least mildly unrealistic: Without such assumptions, they would not be models at all, just tedious descriptions of reality. The question is really whether the assumption of constant velocity is a useful abstraction from annoying detail or a gross distortion of facts.

Figure 32–1 sheds some light on this question by showing the behavior of velocity since 1929. You will note that there are two different measures of velocity, labeled $V_1$ and $V_2$. Why? Recall from Chapter 30 that we can measure money in several

The **equation of exchange** states that the money value of GDP transactions must be equal to the product of the average stock of money times velocity. That is,

$M \times V = P \times Y$

The **quantity theory** of money assumes that velocity is (approximately) constant. In that case, nominal GDP is proportional to the money stock.

ways, the most popular of which are M1 and M2. Because velocity ($V$) is simply nominal GDP divided by the money stock ($M$), we get a different measure of $V$ for each measure of $M$. Figure 32–1 shows the velocities of both M1 and M2.

| FIGURE 32–1 | **Velocity of Circulation, 1929–1998** |

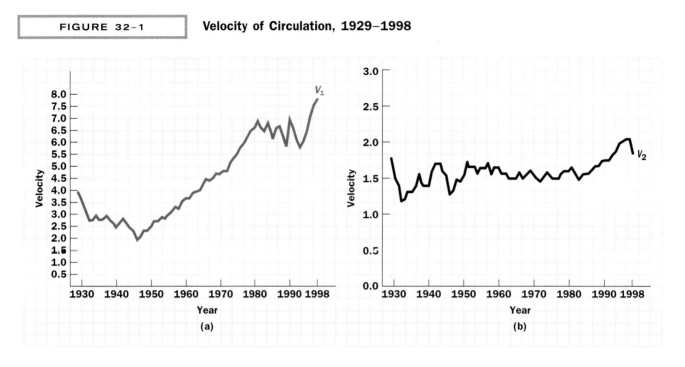

SOURCE: Constructed by the authors; data from Bureau of Economic Analysis, Federal Reserve Board, and Professor Robert Rasche.

Several features are apparent. You will undoubtedly notice the stark difference in the behavior of $V_1$ versus $V_2$. $V_1$ displays a clear downward trend from 1929 until 1946, a pronounced upward trend until 1981, and quite erratic behavior since then. Clearly, the velocity of M1 is not constant over long periods of time. The velocity of M2 is much closer to constant, but it has risen noticeably since the 1980s. Furthermore, closer examination of monthly or quarterly data on either $V_1$ or $V_2$ reveals some rather substantial fluctuations in velocity. Such fluctuations have led most economists to conclude that velocity is not constant in the short run. And predictions of nominal GDP growth based on assuming constant velocity have not fared very well, regardless of how $M$ is measured. It seems, then, that the strict quantity theory of money is not an adequate model of aggregate demand.

## THE DETERMINANTS OF VELOCITY

Because it is abundantly clear that velocity is a variable, not a constant, the equation of exchange is useful as a model of GDP determination only if we can explain movements in velocity. What factors decide whether $V_1$ or $V_2$ will be 4 or 5 or 6; that is, whether a dollar will be used to buy goods and services four or five or six times a year?

**FREQUENCY OF CASH INFUSIONS**    Perhaps the principal factor is the frequency with which people receive paychecks. We can best explain this idea through a numerical example. Consider a worker who earns $24,000 a year, paid to her in 12 monthly paychecks of $2,000 each. Suppose she spends the whole $2,000 over the course of each month and maintains a minimum balance in her checking account of $500. Each payday her bank balance will jump to $2,500 and then gradually decline as she withdraws funds to purchase goods and services. Finally, on the day before her next paycheck arrives, her checking balance will be just $500. Over the course of a typical month, then, her average checking account balance will be $1,500 (halfway between $2,500 and $500).

Now suppose her employer switches to a twice-a-month payroll. Her paychecks come twice as often, but are reduced to $1,000 each. There is no reason for her rate of spending to change, but her average cash balance will change. For now her checking balance will rise only to $1,500 on payday (the $500 minimum balance plus the $1,000 paycheck), and it will still be drawn down gradually to $500. Her average cash balance will therefore decline to $1,000 (halfway between $1,500 and $500). Why is this so? Because, with the next paycheck coming sooner than before, it is not necessary to keep as much cash in the bank in order to carry out a given quantity of transactions.

But what does this have to do with velocity? Notice that when she was on a monthly payroll, this worker's personal velocity was:

$$V = \frac{\text{Annual income}}{\text{Average cash balance}} = \frac{\$24,000}{\$1,500} = 16$$

When she switched to a semimonthly payroll, velocity rose to:

$$V = \frac{\text{Annual income}}{\text{Average cash balance}} = \frac{\$24,000}{\$1,000} = 24$$

The general lesson to be learned is that:

> More frequent wage payments mean that people can conduct their transactions with lower average cash balances. Because they will want to hold less cash, money will circulate faster. In other words, velocity will rise.

**EFFICIENCY OF THE PAYMENTS SYSTEM**    A second factor influencing velocity is the nature and efficiency of the payments mechanism, including how quickly checks clear banks, the use of credit cards, and other methods of transferring funds. It is easy to see how this works.

Our example assumed that the worker holds her entire paycheck in her checking account until she uses it to make a purchase. But, given that ordinary checking accounts pay little or no interest, this may not be sensible behavior. If it is possible to convert interest-bearing assets into money on short notice and at low cost, a rational individual might use her paycheck to purchase such assets and then use credit cards for most purchases, making periodic transfers to her checking account as necessary. For the same amount of total transactions, then, she would require lower money balances. This means that money would circulate faster: Velocity would rise.

The incentive to limit cash holdings depends on the ease and speed with which it is possible to exchange money for other assets. This is what we mean by the "efficiency of the payments system." As computerization has speeded up banks' bookkeeping procedures, as financial innovations have made it possible to transfer funds rapidly between checking accounts and other assets, and as credit cards have come to be used instead of cash, the need to hold money balances has declined. By definition, then, velocity has risen.

In practice, changes in the payments mechanism have posed severe practical problems for analysts interested in predicting velocity. A host of financial innovations, beginning in the 1970s and continuing to this day (some of which were mentioned in the Chapter 30 discussion of the definitions of money) have made forecasting velocity a hazardous occupation. In fact, many economists believe the task is impossible and should not even be attempted.

**INTEREST RATES**    A third determinant of velocity is the rate of interest. The basic motive for economizing on money holdings is that most money (at least M1) pays little or no interest, although many alternative stores of value pay higher rates. The higher these alternative rates of interest, the greater the incentive to economize on holding money. Therefore, as interest rates rise, people want to hold less money. So the existing stock of money circulates faster, and velocity rises.

> It is this factor that most directly undercuts the usefulness of the quantity theory of money as a guide for monetary policy. In the previous chapter, we learned that expansionary monetary policy, which increases *M*, normally also decreases the interest rate.

*But if interest rates fall, other things being equal, velocity (V) will also fall. Thus, when the Fed raises the money supply (M), the product M × V may go up by a smaller percentage than does M itself.*

One component of the interest rate is worth singling out for special attention: *the expected rate of inflation.* We explained in Chapter 24 why an "inflation premium" equal to the expected inflation rate often gets built into market interest rates.[1] Thus, in many instances, high inflation is the principal cause of high nominal interest rates. High rates of inflation, which erode the purchasing power of money, therefore lead both individuals and businesses to hold as little money as they can get by on—actions that increase velocity. To summarize this discussion of the determinants of velocity:

*Velocity is not a strict constant but depends on such things as the frequency of payments, the efficiency of the financial system, the rate of interest, and the rate of inflation. Only by studying these determinants of velocity can we hope to predict the growth rate of nominal GDP from knowledge of the growth rate of the money supply.*

## MONETARISM: THE QUANTITY THEORY MODERNIZED

**Monetarism** is a mode of analysis that uses the equation of exchange to organize and analyze macroeconomic data.

Adherents to a school of thought called **monetarism** try to do precisely this. Monetarists recognize that velocity changes, but they believe that such changes are fairly *predictable*—certainly in the long run and perhaps even in the short run. So they conclude that the best way to study economic activity is to start with the equation of exchange in growth-rate form:

$$\%\Delta M + \%\Delta V = \%\Delta P + \%\Delta Y$$

From here, careful study of the determinants of money growth (which we provided in the previous two chapters) and of changes in velocity (which we just completed) can be used to *predict* the growth rate of nominal GDP. Similarly, given an understanding of movements in $V$, control over $M$ gives the Fed *control* over nominal GDP.

These are the central tenets of monetarism. When something happens in the economy, monetarists ask two questions:

1. What does this event do to the growth rate of money?
2. What does this event do to velocity?

From the answers, they assert, they can predict how the growth rate of nominal GDP will be affected.

By comparing the monetarist approach with the Keynesian approach that we described in the previous chapter, we can put both theories into perspective and understand the limitations of each. As we mentioned earlier, they differ more in style than in substance. Keynesians divide economic knowledge into four neat compartments marked $C$, $I$, $G$, and $(X - IM)$ and unite them all with the equilibrium condition that $Y = C + I + G + (X - IM)$. In Keynesian analysis, money affects the economy by first affecting interest rates.

Monetarists, on the other hand, organize their knowledge into two alternative boxes labeled $M$ and $V$ and then use a simple identity that says $M \times V = P \times Y$ to bring this knowledge to bear in predicting aggregate demand. In the monetarist model, the role of money in the national economy is not necessarily limited to working through interest rates.

The bit of arithmetic that multiplies $M$ and $V$ to get $P \times Y$ is neither more nor less profound than the one that adds up $C$, $I$, $G$ and $(X - IM)$ to get $Y$, and certainly both are correct. The only substantive difference is that the monetarist equation leads to a prediction of *nominal* GDP, whereas the Keynesian equation leads to a prediction of *real* GDP.

Why, then, do we not simply mesh the two theories using the monetarist approach to study nominal GDP and the Keynesian approach to study real GDP? It seems that

---

[1] If you need review, turn back to page 516.

by doing so we could use the separate analyses of real and nominal GDP to predict the price level, which, of course, is the ratio of nominal GDP to real GDP.

The reason that this appealing procedure will not work helps point out the major limitation of each theory. *Taken by itself, either theory is incomplete.* Each gives us a picture of the *demand* side of the economy without saying anything about the *supply* side. To try to predict both the price level and real output solely from these demand-oriented models would be like trying to predict the price of peanuts by studying only consumer behavior and ignoring farmers' actions. It just will not work. In terms of our earlier aggregate supply and demand analysis:

> Both the monetarist and Keynesian analyses are ways of studying the *aggregate demand curve.* Neither approach allows us to learn anything about both output and the price level without also studying the *aggregate supply curve.*

Economists thus must choose between two alternative ways of predicting aggregate demand. Those who choose the monetarist route will use velocity and the money supply to study aggregate demand in nominal terms. But then they must turn to the supply side to estimate how any predicted change in nominal demand gets apportioned between changes in production and changes in prices. The schematic diagram on page 657 in Chapter 31, with its emphasis on interest rates, plays little role in the monetarist analysis of how monetary policy affects the economy.

On the other hand, an economist working with the Keynesian approach will start by using that same schematic diagram to predict how monetary policy affects aggregate demand in real terms, that is, real GDP. But then he will have to turn to the aggregate supply curve to estimate the inflationary consequences of this real demand.

Which approach works better? There is no generally correct answer for all economies in all periods of time. When velocity behaved predictably in the 1960s and early 1970s, monetarism won many converts—in the United States and around the world. But since then velocity has behaved so erratically here and in many other countries that most economists have abandoned monetarism.

## ■ FISCAL POLICY, INTEREST RATES, AND VELOCITY

We have now almost reconciled the Keynesian and monetarist views of how the economy operates. Because $G$ is a part of $C + I + G + (X - IM)$, Keynesian analysis lends itself naturally to the study of fiscal policy. But we learned in the previous chapter that Keynesian economics also provides a powerful and important role for monetary policy: An increase in the money supply reduces interest rates, which, in turn, stimulates the demand for investment.

Monetarist analysis provides an obvious and direct route by which monetary policy influences both output and prices. But can the monetarist approach also handle fiscal policy? It can, because fiscal policy has an important effect on the rate of interest. Let us see how this works.

What happens to real output and the price level following, say, a rise in government purchases of goods and services? We learned in Chapter 29 that both real GDP $(Y)$ and the price level $(P)$ rise, and so nominal GDP certainly rises. But the Chapter 31 analysis of the demand for money taught us that rising nominal GDP pushes the demand curve for money outward to the right. With no change in the supply curve for money, the rate of interest must rise. *So expansionary fiscal policy raises interest rates.*

If the government uses its spending and taxing weapons in the opposite direction, the same process works in reverse. Falling output and (possibly) falling prices shift the demand curve for money inward to the left. With a fixed supply curve for money, equilibrium in the money market leads to a lower interest rate. Thus:

> Monetary policy is not the only type of policy that affects interest rates. Fiscal policy also affects interest rates. Specifically, increases in government spending or tax

---

● **POLICY DEBATE**     ▊     **DOES MONEY GROWTH ALWAYS CAUSE INFLATION?**

---

Monetarists have long claimed that, in the famous words of Milton Friedman, "inflation is always and everywhere a monetary phenomenon." By this, Friedman means that changes in the growth rate of the money supply (%ΔM) are far and away the principal cause of changes in the inflation rate (%ΔP)—in all places and at all times.

Few economists question the dominant role of rapid money growth in accounting for extremely high rates of inflation. During the German hyperinflation of the 1920s, for example, money was being printed so fast that the printing presses had a hard time keeping up the pace! But most economists question the words "always and everywhere" in Friedman's dictum. Aren't many cases of moderate inflation driven by factors other than the growth rate of the money supply?

The answer appears to be yes. The accompanying charts use the past two decades of U.S. history as an illustration.

In the left-hand scatter diagram, each point records both the growth rate of the M2 money supply and the inflation rate (as measured by the Consumer Price Index) for a particular year between 1979 and 1998. Because of the years 1979–1981, there looks to be a weak positive relationship between the two variables. But no relationship at all appears for the years 1982–1998.

Monetarists often argue that this comparison is unfair because the effect of money supply growth on inflation operates with a lag of perhaps two years. So the right hand scatter diagram compares inflation with money supply growth *two years earlier*. It tells a pretty similar story. More sophisticated versions of scatter plots like these have led most economists to reject the monetarist claim that inflation and money supply growth are tightly linked.

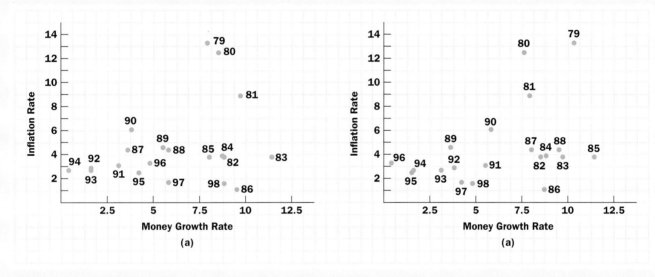

NOTE: All figures are in percent.

---

cuts normally push interest rates up, whereas restrictive fiscal policies normally pull interest rates down.

The fact that fiscal policy affects interest rates gives it a role in the monetarist model, despite the fact that the equation of exchange, $M \times V = P \times Y$, includes neither government spending nor taxation among its variables. Any fiscal policy that a Keynesian would call "expansionary"—higher spending, lower taxes, and so on—pushes up the rate of interest. And rising interest rates push up velocity, because people want to hold less money when the interest they can earn on alternative assets increases. So fiscal policy does its work in the monetarist framework through the $V$ term in $M \times V$. The equation of exchange then implies that nominal GDP must rise when, say, government spending increases, even if $M$ is fixed, because velocity is higher.

Conversely, restrictive fiscal policies like tax increases and expenditure cuts reduce the quantity of money demanded and lower interest rates. The consequent drop in velocity reduces income through the equation of exchange, because the money supply circulates more slowly.

The translation, then, is complete. We can tell the Keynesian story about how fiscal policy works in the monetarist dialect. And the monetarist tale about monetary policy can be told with a Keynesian accent. Furthermore, both modes of analysis only help to explain the mysteries of aggregate demand and must be supplemented by an analysis of aggregate supply to be complete. We must conclude, then, that:

> **The differences between Keynesians and monetarists have been grossly exaggerated by the news media. Indeed, when it comes to matters of basic economic theory, there are hardly any differences at all.**

The fact that changes in fiscal policy move interest rates up and down has two other important consequences that merit some discussion.

## APPLICATION: THE MULTIPLIER FORMULA REVISITED

We have just noted that expansionary fiscal policy raises interest rates. And we know that higher interest rates deter private investment spending. So when the government raises the $G$ component of $C + I + G + (X - IM)$, one notable side effect will be to reduce the $I$ component. Consequently, total spending will rise by *less* than simple multiplier analysis might suggest. The fact that a surge in government demand ($G$) discourages some private demand ($I$) provides another reason why the oversimplified multiplier formula, $1/(1 - MPC)$, exaggerates the size of the multiplier:

> **Because a rise in *G* (or, for that matter, an autonomous rise in any component of total expenditure) pushes interest rates higher, and hence deters some investment spending, the increase in the sum *C + I + G + (X − IM)* is smaller than what the oversimplified multiplier formula predicts.**

Combining this observation with our previous analysis of the multiplier, we now have the following complete list:

**Reasons Why the Oversimplified Multiplier Formula Is Wrong:**

1. It ignores variable imports, which reduce the size of the multiplier (see Appendix B to Chapter 27).

2. It ignores price-level changes, which reduce the size of the multiplier (see Chapter 28).

3. It ignores the income tax, which reduces the size of the multiplier (see Chapter 29).

4. It ignores the rising interest rates that accompany any autonomous spending increase, which also reduce the size of the multiplier (this chapter).

Notice that all four of these adjustments point to a reduction of the multiplier. No wonder the actual multiplier, which is estimated to be below 2 for the U.S. economy, is so much less than the oversimplified formula suggests.

## APPLICATION: DEFICIT REDUCTION AND INVESTMENT

We will discuss the government budget deficit in greater detail in the next chapter. But one major argument for reducing the deficit is that lower deficits should lead to higher levels of private investment spending. It is now simple to understand why. The government reduces its budget deficit by engaging in *contractionary* fiscal policies—lower spending or higher taxes. As we have just seen, any such measure should reduce real interest rates. These lower real interest rates should spur investment spending.

## ■ DEBATE: SHOULD STABILIZATION POLICY RELY ON FISCAL OR MONETARY POLICY?

We have seen that the Keynesian and monetarist approaches are more like two different languages than two different theories. However, it is well known that language influences attitudes in many subtle ways. For example, the Keynesian language biases things subtly toward thinking first about fiscal policy simply because $G$ is a part of $C + I + G + (X - IM)$, whereas $M$ works indirectly. Monetarists, on the other hand, think first about the equation of exchange, $M \times V = P \times Y$, which makes the effect of money on aggregate demand apparent and direct.

Years ago, economists engaged in a spirited debate in which extreme monetarists claimed that fiscal policy was futile, whereas extreme Keynesians argued that monetary policy was useless. But substantial evidence accumulated against both extreme positions, and these arguments are rarely heard today.

Instead of arguing over which type of policy is more *powerful*, economists nowadays debate which type of medicine—fiscal or monetary—cures the patient more *quickly*. Up to now, we have ignored questions of timing and pretended that the authorities noticed the need for stabilization policy instantly, decided on a course of action right away, and administered the appropriate medicine at once. In reality, each of these steps takes time.

First, delays in data collection mean that the most recent macroeconomic data describe the economy as it was a few months ago. Second, one of the prices of democracy is that the government often takes a distressingly long time to decide what should be done, to muster the necessary political support, and to put its decisions into effect. Finally, our $9 trillion economy is a bit like a sleeping elephant that reacts rather sluggishly to moderate fiscal and monetary prods. As it turns out, these *lags in stabilization policy*, as they are called, play a pivotal role in the choice between fiscal and monetary policy. Here's why.

The main policy tool for manipulating consumer spending ($C$) is the personal income tax, and Chapter 25 documented why the fiscal policy planner can feel fairly confident that each $1 of tax reduction will lead to about 90 to 95 cents of additional spending *eventually*. But not all of this happens at once.

First, consumers must learn about the tax change. Then they may need to be convinced that the change is permanent. Finally, there is simple force of habit: Households need time to adjust their spending habits when circumstances change. For all these reasons, consumers may increase their spending by only 30 to 50 cents for each $1 of additional income within the first few months after a tax cut. Only gradually will they raise their spending up to about 90 to 95 cents for each additional dollar of income.

Lags are much longer for investment ($I$), which provides the main vehicle by which monetary policy affects aggregate demand. Planning for capacity expansion in a large corporation is a long, drawn-out process. Ideas must be submitted and approved, plans must be drawn up, funding acquired, orders for machinery or contracts for new construction placed. And most of this occurs *before* any appreciable amount of money is spent. Economists have found that much of the response of investment to changes in interest rates or tax provisions takes several *years* to develop.

The fact that $C$ responds more quickly than $I$ has important implications for the choice among alternative stabilization policies. The reason is that the most common varieties of fiscal policy either affect aggregate demand directly—$G$ is a component of $C + I + G + (X - IM)$—or work through consumption with a relatively short lag, whereas monetary policy primarily affects investment. Therefore:

> Conventional types of fiscal policy actions, such as changes in *G* or in personal taxes, probably affect aggregate demand much more promptly than do monetary policy actions.

This important fact was once used to argue that fiscal policy should bear the major burden of economic stabilization. But such a conclusion is a bit hasty, for the lags we have just described, which are beyond policymakers' control, are not the only ones affecting the timing of stabilization policy. Further lags stem from the behavior of the policymakers themselves! We refer here to the delays that occur while the policymakers study the state of the economy, contemplate what steps they should take, and finally put their decisions into effect. Here monetary policy has a huge advantage, that is:

> Policy lags are normally much shorter for monetary policy than for fiscal policy.

The reasons are apparent. The Federal Open Market Committee (FOMC) meets eight times a year, more often if necessary. So monetary policy decisions are made frequently. Once the Fed decides on a course of action, it normally executes its plan immediately by buying or selling bonds on the open market.

In contrast, federal budgeting procedures operate on an annual budget cycle. Except in rare circumstances, *major* fiscal policy initiatives can occur only at the time of the annual budget. In principle, tax laws can be changed at any time, but the wheels of Congress grind slowly and are often gummed up by partisan politics. So it may take many months for Congress to change fiscal policy. Even President Clinton's first budget, which Congress passed in record time in 1993, took almost six months from introduction to enactment. In 1995–1996, Congress failed to pass any budget at all before the government's fiscal year began, leading to two partial shutdowns of the federal government. In sum, it takes extreme optimism to believe that the government can take important fiscal policy actions on short notice.

So where does the combined effect of expenditure lags and policy lags leave us? With nothing conclusive, we are afraid, at least in principle. In practice, however, most observers of contemporary America believe that active use of fiscal policy for stabilization purposes is quite difficult, given the unwieldy and often partisan nature of our political system. So for now, but not necessarily forever, monetary policy appears to be the only game in town.

## DEBATE: SHOULD THE FED CONTROL THE MONEY SUPPLY OR CONTROL INTEREST RATES?

Once we recognize that monetary policy must bear the current burden of stabilization policy, other questions arise. One major controversy, which raged for decades, was over how the Federal Reserve should conduct monetary policy. Some economists argued that the Fed should use its open-market operations to control the rate of interest ($r$) whereas others, especially monetarists, insisted that the Fed should concentrate on controlling some measure of the money supply ($M$). To understand the nature of this debate, we must first understand why the Fed cannot control both $M$ and $r$ at the same time.

Figure 32–2 will help us see why. It shows an initial equilibrium in the money market at point $E$, where money demand curve $M_0D_0$ crosses money supply curve $MS$. Here the interest rate is $r = 5$ percent and the money stock is $M = \$830$ billion. Let us assume that these are the Fed's targets for $M$ and $r$; it wants to keep the money supply and interest rates just where they are.

If the demand curve for money holds still, everything works out fine. But suppose the demand for money is not so obliging. Suppose, instead, that the demand curve shifts outward to the position indicated by the red line $M_1D_1$ in Figure 32–2. We learned in the previous chapter that this might happen because output increases or because prices rise. Or it might happen simply because people decide to hold more money. Whatever the reason, the Fed can no longer achieve both of its previous targets.

If the Fed takes no action, the outward shift in the demand curve will push up both the quantity of money ($M$) and the rate of interest ($r$). Figure 32–2 shows this graphically as the move from point $E$ to point $A$. If the demand curve for money shifts outward from $M_0D_0$ to $M_1D_1$, and monetary policy does not change (so the supply schedule does not move), the money stock rises to $\$840$ billion and the interest rate rises to 7 percent.

But suppose, first, that the Fed is targeting the money supply and is unwilling to let $M$ rise. In that case, it must use

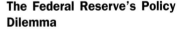

**FIGURE 32–2**

**The Federal Reserve's Policy Dilemma**

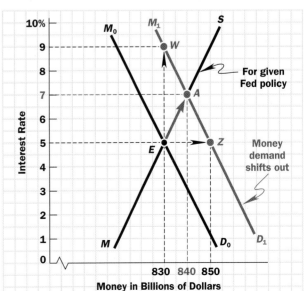

*contractionary* open-market operations to prevent $M$ from rising. But in so doing it will push $r$ up even higher, as Figure 32–2 shows. After the demand curve for money shifts out, point $E$ is unattainable. The Fed must choose from among the points on the red line $M_1D_1$, and point $W$ is the point on this line that keeps the money supply at \$830 billion. By pushing the supply curve inward so that it passes through point $W$, the Fed can hold $M$ at \$830 billion. (Pencil this shift in for yourself on the diagram.) But the interest rate will skyrocket to 9 percent.

Alternatively, if the Fed is pursuing an interest rate target, it might decide that a rise in $r$ is to be avoided. In this case, the Fed would be forced to engage in *expansionary* open-market operations to prevent the outward shift of the demand curve for money from pushing $r$ up. In terms of Figure 32–2, the interest rate can be held at 5 percent by shifting the supply curve outward to pass through point $Z$. But to do this, the Fed will have to let the money supply rise to \$850 billion. (Again, try penciling in the requisite shift of the money supply schedule.) To summarize this discussion:

When the demand curve for money shifts outward, the Fed must tolerate a rise in interest rates, a rise in the money stock, or both. It simply cannot control *both* the supply of money *and* the interest rate. If it tries to keep $M$ steady, then $r$ will rise sharply. Conversely, if it tries to stabilize $r$, then $M$ will shoot up.

## TWO IMPERFECT ALTERNATIVES

For years, economists have debated how the Fed should deal with its inability to control both the money supply and the rate of interest. Should it adhere rigidly to its target growth path for the money supply, regardless of the consequences for interest rates? Should it hold interest rates steady, even if that causes sharp gyrations in the money stock? Or is some middle ground more appropriate? Let us explore the issues first and then consider what has actually been done.

The main problem with rigid targets for the *supply* of money is that the *demand* for money does not cooperate by growing smoothly and predictably from month to month; instead it dances about quite a bit in the short run. This confronts the recommendation to control the money supply with two problems:

1.  It is almost impossible to achieve. Because the volume of money in existence depends on *both* the demand *and* supply curves, keeping $M$ on target in the face of significant fluctuations in the demand for money would require exceptional dexterity from the Fed.

2.  For reasons just explained, rigid adherence to money-stock targets might lead to wide fluctuations in interest rates, which could create an unsettled atmosphere for business decisions.

By the same token, even more powerful objections can be raised against exclusive concentration on interest rate movements. Because increases in nominal GDP shift the demand schedule for money outward (as shown in Figure 32–2), a central bank determined to keep interest rates from rising would have to expand the money supply in response. Conversely, when GDP sagged, it would have to contract the money supply to keep rates from falling. Thus, interest rate pegging would make the money supply expand in boom times and contract in recessions with potentially grave consequences for the stability of the economy. Ironically, this is precisely the sort of monetary behavior the Federal Reserve System was designed to prevent. Hence, if the Fed is to control interest rates, it had better formulate flexible targets, not fixed ones.

## WHAT HAS THE FED ACTUALLY DONE?

In the early part of the postwar period, the predominant Keynesian view held that the interest rate target was much the more important of the two. The rationale was that gyrating interest rates would cause abrupt and unsettling changes in investment spending, which in turn would make the whole economy fluctuate. Stabilizing interest rates

---

● **DISSENT AT THE FED**

In 1998, a number of observers worried that the U.S. economy was "overheating," that is, opening up a sizable inflationary gap. In the spring, two voting members of the Federal Open Market Committee—Cleveland's Jerry Jordan and St. Louis' William Poole—lodged formal dissents against Fed Chairman Alan Greenspan's recommended monetary policy—which was to hold rates steady. They believed that interest rates should rise in order to "cool down" the fast-growing U.S. economy and stave off inflation.

Although Greenspan's recommended policy passed by a 10–2 margin, the two negative votes raised many eyebrows, because dissent is rare on the Fed. Notably, the two men based their dissents on explicitly monetarist grounds: They argued that the money supply was growing too fast. The old monetarist versus Keynesian debate lingers on.

By the fall, however, worries about the world financial system and the prospective health of the U.S. economy led the Fed to *cut* rather than raise interest rates. Since then (up to this printing), the Fed has maintained unchanged interest rates, and the U.S. economy has continued to do well, growing rapidly with little inflation. It is hard to find fault with the Fed's recent decisions.

"Daddy's not mad at you, dear—Daddy's mad at the Fed."

SOURCE: by Baloo, January, 19, 1994. the *Wall Street Journal*.

---

was therefore believed to be the best way to stabilize GDP. If doing so required fluctuations in the money supply, so be it. Consequently, the Fed focused on interest rates and paid little attention to the money supply.

In the 1960s, this prevailing view came under attack by Professor Milton Friedman and other monetarists. They argued that the Fed's obsession with stabilizing interest rates actually *destabilized* the economy by making the money supply fluctuate too much. The monetarist prescription was simple: The Fed should stop worrying about fluctuations in interest rates and make the money supply grow at a constant rate from month to month and year to year.

Monetarism made important inroads at the Fed during the inflationary 1970s. Early in the decade, the central bank began to keep much closer tabs on the money stock than it previously had. More important, a major change in the conduct of monetary policy was announced by then-Chairman Paul Volcker in October 1979. Henceforth, he asserted, the Fed would stick more closely to its target for money-stock growth regardless of the implications for interest rates. Interest rates would go wherever the law of supply and demand took them.

According to our analysis, this change in policy should have led to wider fluctuations in interest rates. And it certainly did. Unfortunately, the Fed ran into some bad luck. The ensuing three years were marked by unusually severe gyrations in the demand for money, so the ups and downs of interest rates were far more extreme than anyone had expected. Figure 32–3 shows just how volatile interest rates were between late 1979 and late 1982. As you might imagine, this erratic performance provoked some heavy criticism of the Fed.

Then, in October 1982, Chairman Volcker announced that the Fed was temporarily abandoning its attempts to stick to a target growth path for the money supply. Although he did not say so, his announcement presumably meant that the Fed started once again to pay more attention to interest rate targets. As you can see in Figure 32–3, interest rates became much more stable after the change in policy. Most observers think this was no coincidence.

After 1982, the Fed gradually distanced itself from the position that the money supply should grow at a constant rate. Finally, in 1993, Chairman Alan Greenspan officially

**FIGURE 32-3**

**The Behavior of Interest Rates, 1979–1985**

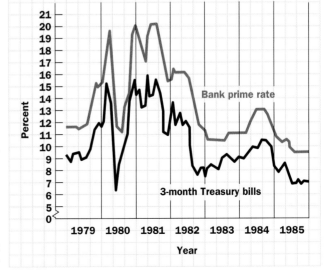

confirmed what many people already knew: that the Fed was no longer using the various $M$s to guide policy. He strongly hinted that the Fed was targeting interest rates, especially *real* interest rates, instead—a hint that has been repeated many times since then. In truth, the Fed had little choice. The demand curve for money behaved so erratically and so unpredictably in the 1980s and 1990s that stabilizing the money stock was probably impossible and certainly undesirable. Whether this situation will continue is anyone's guess. But as of this writing, the Fed has shown little inclination to return to trying to control the $M$s.

■    **DEBATE: THE SHAPE OF THE AGGREGATE SUPPLY CURVE**

Another lively debate over stabilization policy revolves around the shape of the economy's aggregate supply curve. Many economists think of the aggregate supply curve as quite flat, as in Figure 32–4(a), so that large increases in output can be achieved with little inflation. But other economists envision the supply curve as steep, as shown in Figure 32–4(b), so that prices respond strongly to changes in output. The differences for public policy are substantial.

| FIGURE 32-4 | **Alternative Views of the Aggregate Supply Curve** |

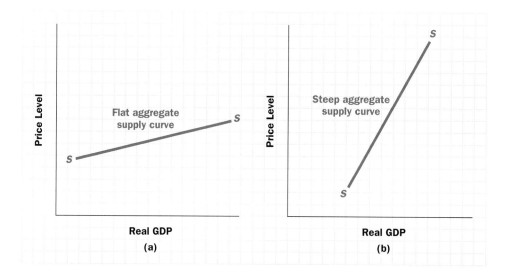

If the aggregate supply curve is flat, expansionary fiscal or monetary policy that raises the aggregate demand curve can buy large gains in real GDP at low cost in terms of inflation. In Figure 32–5(a), stimulation of demand pushes the aggregate demand curve outward from $D_0D_0$ to $D_1D_1$, thereby moving the economy's equilibrium from point $E$ to point $A$. The substantial rise in output ($400 billion in the diagram) is accompanied by only a pinch of inflation (1 percent). So the antirecession policy succeeds.

Conversely, when the supply curve is flat, a restrictive stabilization policy is not a very effective way to bring inflation down. Instead, it serves mainly to reduce real output, as Figure 32–5(b) shows. Here a leftward shift of the aggregate demand curve from $D_0D_0$ to $D_2D_2$ moves equilibrium from point $E$ to point $B$, lowering real GDP by $400 billion but cutting the price level by merely 1 percent. Fighting inflation by contracting aggregate demand is obviously quite costly in this example.

Things are just the reverse if the aggregate supply curve is steep. In that case, expansionary fiscal or monetary policies will cause a good deal of inflation without adding much to real GDP. This is apparent in Figure 32–6(a), where expansionary

**Stabilization Policy with a Flat Aggregate Supply Curve** | FIGURE 32-5

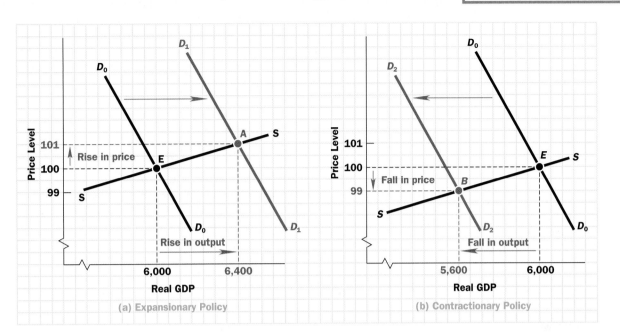

NOTE: Real GDP in billions of dollars per year.

policies shift the aggregate demand curve outward from $D_0D_0$ to $D_1D_1$, thereby moving the economy's equilibrium from $E$ to $A$. Output rises by only $100 billion, but prices shoot up 10 percent.

Similarly, contractionary policies are effective ways of bringing down the price level without much sacrifice of output, as shown by the shift from $E$ to $B$ in Figure 32–6(b). Here it takes only a $100 billion loss of output (from $6,000 billion to $5,900 billion) to "buy" 10 percent less inflation.

**Stabilization Policy with a Steep Aggregate Supply Curve** | FIGURE 32-6

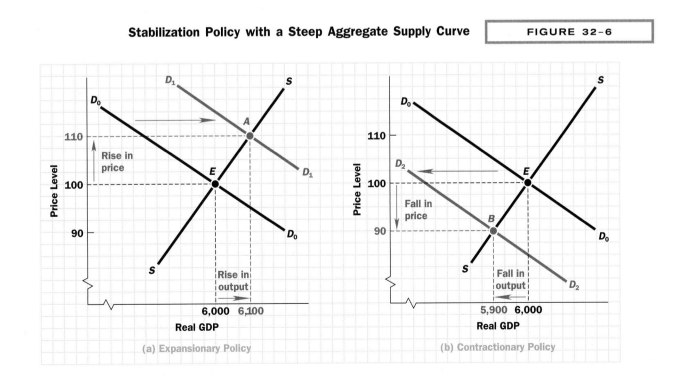

NOTE: Real GDP in billions of dollars per year.

So deciding whether the aggregate supply curve is steep or flat is clearly of fundamental importance to the proper conduct of stabilization policy. If the supply curve is flat, stabilization policy is much more effective at combating recession than inflation. If the supply curve is steep, precisely the reverse is true.

But why does the argument persist? Why can't economists determine the shape of the aggregate supply curve and stop arguing? The answer is that supply conditions in the real world are far more complicated than our simple diagrams suggest. Some industries may have flat supply curves, whereas others have steep ones. For reasons explained in Chapter 28, supply curves shift over time. And, unlike laboratory scientists, economists cannot perform controlled experiments that would reveal the shape of the aggregate supply curve directly. Instead, they must use statistical inference to make educated guesses.

Although empirical research continues, our understanding of aggregate supply remains less settled than our understanding of aggregate demand. Nevertheless, many economists believe that the outline of a consensus view has emerged. This view holds that *the steepness of the aggregate supply schedule depends on the time period under consideration.*

In the very short run, the aggregate supply curve is quite flat, making Figure 32–5 the more relevant picture of reality. Over short time periods, therefore, fluctuations in aggregate demand have large effects on output but only minor effects on prices. In the long run, however, the aggregate supply curve becomes quite steep, perhaps even vertical. In that case, Figure 32–6 is a better representation of reality, so that changes in demand affect mainly prices, not output.[2] The implication is that:

> Any change in aggregate demand will have most of its effect on *output* in the short run but on *prices* in the long run.

## ■ DEBATE: SHOULD THE GOVERNMENT INTERVENE?

We have yet to consider what may be the most fundamental and controversial debate of all—the issue posed as a puzzle at the beginning of the chapter. Is it likely that government policy can successfully stabilize the economy? Or are even well-intentioned efforts likely to be harmful, so that it would be better to adhere to fixed rules?

This controversy has raged for several decades, and there is no end in sight. It is partly a political or philosophical debate because economists, like other people, come with both liberal and conservative stripes. Liberal economists tend to be more intervention-minded and hence look more favorably on discretionary stabilization policy. Conservative economists are more inclined to keep the government's hands off the economy and hence advise adhering to fixed rules. Such political differences are not surprising. But more than ideology propels the debate. We need to understand the economics.

Critics of stabilization policy point to the lags and uncertainties that surround the operation of both fiscal and monetary policies—lags and uncertainties that we have stressed repeatedly in this and earlier chapters. Will the Fed's actions have the desired effects on the money supply? What will these actions do to interest rates and spending? Can fiscal policy actions be taken promptly? How large is the expenditure multiplier? The list could go on and on.

They look at this formidable catalog of difficulties, add a dash of skepticism about our ability to forecast the future state of the economy (discussed later), and worry that stabilization policy may do more harm than good. These skeptics advise both the fiscal and monetary authorities to pursue a passive policy rather than an active one—adhering to fixed rules that, although incapable of ironing out every bump in the economy's growth path, will at least keep it roughly on track in the long run.

---

[2] The reasoning behind the view that the aggregate supply curve is flat in the short run but steep in the long run will be developed in Chapter 34.

Advocates of active stabilization policies admit that perfection is unattainable. But they are much more optimistic about the prospects for success, and they are much *less* optimistic about how smoothly the economy would function in the absence of demand management. They therefore advocate discretionary increases in government spending (or decreases in taxes) and lower interest rates when the economy has a recessionary gap. Such policies, they believe, will help keep the economy closer to its full-employment growth path.

Naturally, each side can point to evidence that buttresses its own view. Activists look back with pride at the tax cut of 1964 and the sustained period of economic growth that it helped to introduce. They also point to the tax cut of 1975 (which was enacted at just about the trough of a severe recession), the Federal Reserve's switch to easy money in 1982, and especially the Fed's expert steering of the economy since 1992. Advocates of rules remind us of the government's refusal to curb what was obviously a situation of runaway demand during the 1966–1968 Vietnam buildup, its overexpansion of the economy in 1972, the monetary overkill that helped bring on the sharp recession of 1981–1982, and the inadequate antirecession policies of the early 1990s.

The historical record of fiscal and monetary policy is far from glorious. It shows that although the authorities have sometimes taken appropriate and timely action to stabilize the economy, at other times they either took inappropriate steps or did nothing at all. The question of whether the government should adopt passive rules or attempt an activist stabilization policy therefore merits a closer look. As we shall see, the lags in the effects of policy that we discussed earlier in this chapter play a pivotal role in the debate.

## LAGS AND THE RULES-VERSUS-DISCRETION DEBATE

The reason why lags lead to a fundamental difficulty for stabilization policy—a difficulty so formidable that it has led some economists to conclude that attempts to stabilize economic activity are likely to do more harm than good—can be explained best by referring to Figure 32–7. Here we chart the behavior of both actual and potential GDP over the course of a business cycle in a hypothetical economy with no stabilization policy. At point *A*, the economy begins to slip into a recession and does not recover to full employment until point *D*. Then, between points D and *E*, it overshoots potential GDP and enters an inflationary boom.

The case for stabilization policy runs like this. Policymakers recognize that the recession is a serious problem at point *B*, and they take appropriate actions. These actions have their major effects around point *C* and therefore curb both the depth and the length of the recession.

But suppose the lags are really longer and less predictable than this. Suppose, for example, that actions do not come until point *C* and that stimulative policies do not have their major effects until after point *D*. Then policy will be of little help during the recession and will actually do harm by overstimulating the economy during the ensuing boom. Thus:

In the presence of long lags, attempts at stabilizing the economy may actually succeed in destabilizing it.

**FIGURE 32–7**

**A Typical Business Cycle**

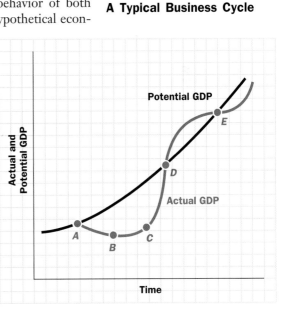

Because of this, some economists argue that we are better off letting the economy alone and relying on its natural self-corrective forces to cure recessions and inflations. Instead of embarking on periodic programs of monetary and fiscal stimulus or restraint, they advise policymakers to stick to fixed rules, that is, to rigid formulas that ignore current economic events.

For monetary policy, we have already mentioned the monetarist policy rule: The Fed should keep the money supply growing at a constant rate. For fiscal policy, proponents of rules often recommend that the government resist temptations to manage aggregate demand actively and rely instead on the economy's automatic stabilizers, which we discussed in Chapter 29 (see page 604).

## ■ DIMENSIONS OF THE RULES-VERSUS-DISCRETION DEBATE

Are the critics right? Should we forget about discretionary policy and put the economy on autopilot—relying on automatic stabilizers and the economy's natural, self-correcting mechanisms? As usual, the answer depends on many factors.

### HOW FAST DOES THE ECONOMY'S SELF-CORRECTING MECHANISM WORK?

We emphasized in Chapter 28 that the economy has a self-correcting mechanism. If recessions and inflations will go away by themselves, the case for intervention is weak. For if such problems typically last only a short time, then lags in discretionary stabilization policy mean that the medicine will often have its major effects only after the disease is over. In terms of Figure 32–7, this would be a case where point *D* comes very close to point *A*.

Although extreme advocates of rules argue that this is indeed what happens, most economists agree that the economy's self-correcting mechanism is slow and not terribly reliable, even when supplemented by the automatic stabilizers. On this count, then, a point is scored for discretionary policy.

### HOW LONG ARE THE LAGS IN STABILIZATION POLICY?

We just explained why long and unpredictable lags in the formulation or operation of stabilization make it unlikely that policy can do much good. Short, reliable lags point in the opposite direction. Thus, advocates of fixed rules emphasize the length of lags, whereas proponents of discretion discount them.

Who is right? It all depends on the circumstances. Sometimes policymakers take action promptly, and the economy receives much of the stimulus from expansionary policy within a year after slipping into a recession. Although far from perfect, such timely actions certainly would be felt soon enough to do some good. But, as we have seen, very slow policy responses may actually be destabilizing. Because history offers examples of each type, we can draw no general conclusion.

### HOW ACCURATE ARE ECONOMIC FORECASTS?

One way to cut down the policy-making lag enormously is to forecast economic events accurately. If we could see a recession coming a full year ahead of time (which we certainly *cannot* do), even a rather sluggish policy response would still be timely. In terms of Figure 32–7, this would be a case where the recession is predicted well before point *A*.

Over the years, economists in universities, government agencies, and private businesses have developed a number of techniques to assist them in predicting what the economy will do. But none of them are terribly accurate. To give a rough idea of magnitudes, forecasts of either the inflation rate or the real GDP growth rate for the year ahead typically err by plus or minus $\frac{3}{4}$ to 1 percentage point. But, in a bad year for forecasters, errors of 2 or 3 percentage points are common.

Is this record good enough? That depends on how the forecasts are used. It is certainly not good enough to support so-called *fine tuning*, that is, attempts to keep the economy always within a hair's breadth of full employment. But it probably is good enough for policymakers interested in using discretionary stabilization policy to close persistent and sizable gaps between actual and potential GDP.

### THE SIZE OF GOVERNMENT

One bogus argument that is nonetheless sometimes heard is that active fiscal policy must inevitably lead to a growing public sector. Because proponents of fixed rules tend also to oppose big government, they view this as undesirable. Of course, others think that a larger public sector is just what society needs.

This argument, however, is completely beside the point because, as we pointed out in Chapter 29: *One's opinion about the proper size of government should have nothing to do with one's view on stabilization policy.* For example, President Ronald Reagan was as conservative as they come and devoted to shrinking the size of the public sector. But his tax-cutting initiatives in the early 1980s constituted an extremely activist policy to spur the economy. Furthermore, most stabilization policy these days is monetary policy, which neither increases nor decreases the size of government.

## UNCERTAINTIES CAUSED BY GOVERNMENT POLICY

Advocates of rules are on stronger ground when they argue that frequent changes in tax laws, government spending programs, or monetary conditions make it difficult for firms and consumers to formulate and carry out rational plans. They argue that the authorities can provide a more stable environment for the private sector by adhering to fixed rules, so that businesses and consumers will know exactly what to expect.

No one disputes that a more stable environment is better for private planning. But supporters of discretionary policy emphasize that stability in the *economy* is more important than stability in the *government budget* (or in Federal Reserve operations). Stabilization policy aims to *prevent* gyrations in the pace of economic activity by *causing* timely gyrations in the government budget (or in monetary policy). Which atmosphere is better for business, they ask: one in which fiscal and monetary rules keep things peaceful on Capitol Hill and at the Federal Reserve while recessions and inflations rack the economy, or one in which government changes its policy abruptly on occasion but the economy grows more steadily? They think the answer is self-evident.

## A POLITICAL BUSINESS CYCLE?

A final argument used by advocates of rules is political rather than economic in nature. Fiscal policy, they note, is decided upon by elected politicians: the president and members of Congress. When elections are on the horizon (and for members of the House of Representatives, they *always* are), politicians may be as concerned with keeping their jobs as with doing what is right for the economy. This leaves fiscal policy subject to all sorts of "political manipulations," meaning that lawmakers may take inappropriate actions to attain short-run political goals. A system of purely automatic stabilization, its proponents argue, would eliminate this peril by replacing the rule of people by the rule of law.

It is certainly *possible* that politicians could deliberately *cause* economic instability to help their own reelection. And some observers of these "political business cycles" have claimed that several American presidents have taken full advantage of the opportunity. Furthermore, even without any insidious intent, politicians may take the wrong actions for perfectly honorable reasons. Decisions in the political arena are never clear cut, and it certainly is easy to find examples of grievous errors in the history of U.S. fiscal policy.

So, taken as a whole, the political argument against discretionary fiscal policy seems to have a great deal of merit. But what are we to do about it? It is unrealistic to believe that fiscal decisions could or should be made by a group of objective and nonpartisan technicians. Tax and budget policies require inherently *political* decisions which, in a democracy, should be made by elected officials.

This fact may seem worrisome in view of the possibilities for political chicanery. But it should not bother us any more (or any less!) than similar maneuvering in other areas of policy making. After all, the same problem besets international relations, national defense, formulation and enforcement of the law, and so on. Politicians make all these decisions for us, subject only to sporadic accountability at elections. Is there really any reason why fiscal decisions should be different?

But monetary policy *is* different. Because Congress was concerned that elected officials would focus on the short run, and therefore pursue monetary policies that are too inflationary, it long ago gave the unelected technocrats at the Federal Reserve

System day-to-day decision-making authority over monetary policy. Politics does influence monetary policy, but quite indirectly: The Fed must report to Congress, and the president has the power to appoint Federal Reserve governors to his liking.

## What Should Be Done?

So where do we come out on the question posed at the start of this chapter? On balance, is it better to pursue the best discretionary policy we can, knowing full well that we will never achieve perfection? Or is it wiser to rely on fixed rules and automatic stabilizers?

In weighing the pros and cons, your basic view of the economy is crucial. Some economists believe that the economy, if left unmanaged, would generate a series of ups and downs that are hard to predict, but that it would correct each of them by itself in a relatively short time. They conclude that, because of long lags and poor forecasts, our ability to anticipate whether the economy will need stimulus or restraint by the time policy actions have their effects is quite limited. So they advocate fixed rules.

Other economists liken the economy to a giant glacier with a great deal of inertia. This means that, if we observe an inflationary or recessionary gap today, it will likely still be there a year or two from now because the self-correcting mechanism works slowly. In such a world, accurate forecasting is not imperative, even if policy lags are long. If we base policy on a forecast of a 2 percent gap between actual and potential GDP a year from now, and the gap turns out to be only 1 percent, we still will have done the right thing despite the inaccurate forecast. So holders of this view of the economy tend to support discretionary policy.

There is certainly no consensus on this issue, either among economists or among politicians. After all, the question touches on political ideology as well as economics. And liberals often look to government to solve social problems, whereas conservatives consistently point out that many efforts of government fail despite the best intentions. A prudent view of the matter might be that:

The case for active discretionary policy is strong when the economy has a serious deficiency or excess of aggregate demand. However, advocates of fixed rules are right that it is unwise to try to iron out every little wiggle in the growth path of GDP.

But one thing seems certain: The rules-versus-discretion debate is likely to go on for quite some time.

---

## SUMMARY

1. Monetarist and Keynesian analyses are two different ways of studying the determination of aggregate demand. Neither is a complete theory of the behavior of the economy because neither addresses aggregate supply issues.

2. *Velocity* ($V$) is the ratio of nominal GDP to the stock of money ($M$). It indicates how quickly money circulates.

3. One important determinant of velocity is the rate of interest ($r$). At higher interest rates, people find it less attractive to hold money because money pays zero or little interest. Thus, when $r$ rises, money circulates faster, and $V$ rises.

4. *Monetarism* is a type of analysis that focuses attention on velocity and the money supply ($M$). Though monetarists realize that $V$ is not constant, they believe that it is predictable enough to make it a useful tool for policy analysis and forecasting.

5. Because it raises output and prices, and hence increases the demand for money, expansionary fiscal policy pushes interest rates higher. This is how a monetarist explains the effect of fiscal policy. Because higher $r$ leads to higher velocity, it leads to a higher product $M \times V$, even if $M$ is unchanged.

6. Because fiscal policy actions affect aggregate demand either directly through $G$ or indirectly through $C$, the expenditure lags between fiscal actions and their effects on aggregate demand are probably fairly short. By contrast, monetary policy operates mainly on investment, $I$, which responds slowly to changes in interest rates.

7. However, the policy-making lag normally is much longer for fiscal policy than for monetary policy. Hence, when the two lags are combined, it is not clear which type of policy acts more quickly.

8. Because it cannot control the demand curve for money, the Federal Reserve cannot control both $M$ and $r$. If the demand for money changes, the Fed must decide whether it wants to hold $M$ steady, hold $r$ steady, or adopt some compromise position.

9. Monetarists emphasize the importance of stabilizing the growth path of the money supply, whereas Keynesians put more emphasis on keeping interest rates on target.

10. In practice, the Fed has changed its views on this issue several times. For decades, it attached primary importance to interest rates. Between 1979 and 1982, it stressed its commitment to stable growth of the money supply. But lately the focus is clearly on interest rates again.

11. When the aggregate supply curve is very flat, increases in aggregate demand will add much to the nation's real output but little to the price level. Under those circumstances, stabilization policy works well as an antirecession device, but it has little power to combat inflation.

12. When the aggregate supply curve is steep, increases in aggregate demand increase real output rather little and succeed mostly in pushing up prices. In such a case, stabilization policy can do much to fight inflation but is not a very effective way to cure unemployment.

13. The aggregate supply curve is likely to be relatively flat in the short run but relatively steep in the long run. Hence, stabilization policy affects mainly output in the short run, but mainly prices in the long run.

14. When there are long and unpredictable lags in the operation of fiscal and monetary policy, attempts to stabilize economic activity may actually destabilize it.

15. Some economists believe that our imperfect knowledge of the channels through which stabilization policy works, the long lags involved, and the inaccuracy of forecasts make it unlikely that discretionary stabilization policy can succeed.

16. Other economists recognize these difficulties but do not believe they are quite as serious. They also place much less faith in the economy's ability to cure recessions and inflations on its own. They therefore think that discretionary policy is not only advisable, but essential.

17. Stabilizing the economy by fiscal policy need not imply a tendency toward "big government."

## KEY TERMS

Quantity theory of money  663

Velocity  662

Equation of exchange  663

Effect of interest rate on velocity  665

Monetarism  666

Effect of fiscal policy on interest rates  667

Lags in stabilization policy  670

Controlling $M$ versus controlling $r$  671

Rules versus discretionary policy  676

## QUESTIONS FOR REVIEW

1. How much money (including cash and checking account balances) do you typically have at any particular moment? Divide this into your total income over the past 12 months to obtain your own personal velocity. Are you typical of the nation as a whole?

2. In the following table, you will find data on nominal gross domestic product and the money supply (M1 definition) for selected years. Compute velocity in each year. Can you see any trend?

| Year | End-of-Year Money Supply (M1) | Nominal GDP |
|------|------|------|
| 1996 | $1,081 | $7,662 |
| 1997 | 1,075 | 8,111 |
| 1998 | 1,093 | 8,511 |

NOTE: Amounts are in billions.

3. Use the concept of opportunity cost to explain why velocity is higher at higher interest rates.

4. How does monetarism differ from the quantity theory of money?

5. Given the behavior of velocity shown in Figure 32–1, would it make more sense for the Federal Reserve to formulate targets for M1 or M2?

6. Distinguish between the expenditure lag and the policy lag in stabilization policy. Does monetary or fiscal policy have the shorter expenditure lag? What about the policy lag?

7. Explain why their contrasting views on the shape of the aggregate supply curve lead some economists to argue much more strongly for stabilization policies to fight unemployment and others to argue much more strongly for stabilization policies to fight inflation.

8. Use a supply and demand diagram similar to Figure 32–2 to show the choices open to the Fed following an unexpected decline in the demand for money. If the Fed is following a monetarist policy rule, what will happen to the rate of interest?

9. Explain why lags make it possible for policy actions intended to stabilize the economy actually to destabilize it.

10. Which of the following events would strengthen the argument for the use of discretionary policy, and which would strengthen the argument for rules?

    a. Structural changes make the economy's self-correcting mechanism work more quickly and reliably than before.

    b. New statistical methods are found that improve the accuracy of economic forecasts.

    c. A Democratic president is elected when there is an overwhelmingly Republican Congress. Congress and the president differ sharply on what should be done about the national economy.

11. Many observers think that the Federal Reserve succeeded in using deft applications of monetary policy to "fine-tune" the U.S. economy into the full-employment zone in the 1990s without worsening inflation. Use the data on money supply, interest rates, real GDP, unemployment, and the price level given on the inside back cover of this book to evaluate this claim. Ask your instructor what has happened since.

Blessed are the young, for they shall inherit the national debt.

Herbert Hoover

# DEFICITS, MONETARY POLICY, AND GROWTH

It's over! For more than a decade, the United States worried about its large federal budget deficit and debated how to get rid of it. The deficit was the No. 1 question on the national political agenda. Then, over the course of a remarkable five-year period (1993 to 1998), the deficit not only disappeared, but actually turned into a sizable surplus. Today, politicians in Washington argue over what to do with the large budget surpluses that loom in the future.

What was the economic substance of the long-running debate over reducing the budget deficit? What kinds of problems do large deficits pose for the economy, both now and in the future? Should we strive to balance the budget? These are some of the main questions for this chapter. Paradoxically, we shall see that the answers depend quite a bit on the stance of monetary policy.

## Are Smaller Deficits Good or Bad for Growth?

For years, critics of U.S. economic policy argued that large budget deficits created a drag on economic growth. We could grow faster, they said, if we reduced the deficit. Sure enough, growth did accelerate as the budget deficit disappeared in the mid-1990s. So reducing the budget deficit boosted growth in the United States. Right?

But wait a minute. In 1997, the Japanese government, alarmed at both its large budget deficit and its sluggish economic growth, raised taxes to reduce its deficit. Critics, especially American critics, warned against this policy. A tax hike in a weak economy, they argued, can bring on a recession. Sure enough, the Japanese economy began sinking like a stone right after the tax hike took effect. So, did reducing the budget deficit actually *slow* growth in Japan?

Confused? Then consider this. When several countries in Southeast Asia plunged into economic crises in the summer and fall of 1997, the International Monetary Fund (IMF) rode to the rescue with large infusions of funds. But the IMF attached many strings—including a requirement that the countries take steps to reduce their budget deficits. Critics of the IMF objected that raising taxes and cutting spending would slow economic recovery in Southeast Asia, just as it had in Japan, and it looks as if those critics were right.

So which is it? Does reducing its budget deficit help or hurt a country's chances for rapid economic growth? As we will see in this chapter, both claims contain elements of truth.

## ■ SHOULD THE BUDGET BE BALANCED?

Let us begin by reviewing the basic principles of fiscal policy that we have learned so far (especially in Chapter 29) and what they say about the goal of balancing the budget. They certainly do not imply that we should always maintain a balanced budget, much as that notion may appeal to our intuitive sense of good financial management. But neither do they lead to the conclusion that massive deficits should be the norm.

In brief, these principles tell us that we should focus fiscal policy not on *balancing the budget*, but rather on *balancing aggregate supply and aggregate demand.* They point to the desirability of budget *deficits* when private demand, $C + I + (X - IM)$, is too weak and budget *surpluses* when private demand is too strong. The budget should be balanced, according to these principles, only when $C + I + G + (X - IM)$ under a balanced-budget policy approximately equals full-employment levels of output. This may sometimes occur, but it will not necessarily be the norm.

The reason why a balanced budget is not always advisable should be clear from our earlier discussion of stabilization policy. Consider the fiscal policy that the government would follow if its goal were to maintain a rigorously balanced budget. If private spending sagged for some reason, the multiplier would pull GDP down. Because personal and corporate tax receipts fall sharply when GDP declines, the budget would automatically start swinging into the red. To bring the budget back into balance, the government would then be forced either to lower spending or raise taxes—exactly the opposite of the appropriate policy response. Thus:

> Attempts to balance the budget—as was done, say, during the Great Depression—will prolong and deepen recessions.

This is precisely what many observers feel happened to Japan and Southeast Asia in 1997 and 1998. In fact, Ryutaro Hashimoto, Japan's prime minister from 1996 to 1998, was once disparagingly called the "Herbert Hoover of Japan" because he sought to reduce the budget deficit despite Japan's sinking economy.

Budget balancing can also lead to inappropriate fiscal policy under boom conditions. If rising tax receipts induce a budget-balancing government to spend more or cut taxes, fiscal policy will "boom the boom"—with unfortunate inflationary consequences. This is one reason why few economists thought cutting taxes was a wise policy for the United States in 1999, despite the fact that the federal government was running a surplus.

"The 'Twilight Zone' will not be seen tonight, so that we may bring you the following special on the federal budget."

## THE IMPORTANCE OF THE POLICY MIX

Actually, the issue is even more complicated than we have indicated so far. As we learned in Chapter 31, fiscal policy is not the only way the government affects aggregate demand. The government also influences aggregate demand through its *monetary* policy. For this reason:

> The appropriate fiscal policy depends, among other things, on the current monetary policy stance. Although a balanced budget may be appropriate under one monetary policy, a deficit or a surplus may be appropriate under another monetary policy.

An example will illustrate the point. Suppose Congress and the president believe that the aggregate supply and demand curves will intersect approximately at full employment if the budget is balanced. Then a balanced budget would seem to be the appropriate fiscal policy.

Now suppose monetary policy turns contractionary, pulling the aggregate demand curve inward to the left, as shown by the red arrow in Figure 33–1, and creating a recessionary gap. If the fiscal authorities wish to restore real gross domestic product (GDP) to its original level, they must shift the aggregate demand curve back to its original position, $D_0D_0$, as indicated by the blue arrow. To do so, they must either raise spending or cut taxes, thereby opening up a budget deficit. Thus, the tightening of *monetary* policy changes the appropriate *fiscal* policy from a balanced budget to a deficit, because both monetary and fiscal policies affect the aggregate demand curve.

By the same token, a given target for aggregate demand implies that any change in *fiscal* policy will alter the appropriate *monetary* policy. For example, we can reinterpret Figure 33–1 as indicating the effects of reducing the budget deficit by cutting government spending. Then, if the authorities do not want real GDP to fall, the Fed must expand the money supply sufficiently to restore the aggregate demand curve to $D_0D_0$.

It is precisely this change in the *mix* of policy—a smaller budget deficit balanced by easier money—that the U.S. government managed to engineer in the 1990s. Congress and the administration raised taxes and cut spending, which subtracted from aggregate demand. But the Federal Reserve pursued a sufficiently expansionary policy to return this "lost" aggregate demand to the economy via lower interest rates.

So we should not expect a balanced budget to be the norm. How, then, can we tell whether any particular deficit is too large or too small? That is a good question, but a complicated one. Before attempting an answer, we need to get some facts straight.

**FIGURE 33–1**

**The Interaction of Monetary and Fiscal Policy**

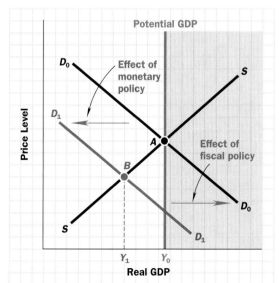

## ■ DEFICITS AND DEBT: TERMINOLOGY AND FACTS

The **budget deficit** is the amount by which the government's expenditures exceed its receipts during a specified period of time, usually a year.

The **national debt** is the federal government's total indebtedness at a moment in time. It is the result of previous deficits.

First, some critical terminology. People confuse two terms that have different meanings: *budget deficits* and the *national debt*. We must learn to distinguish between the two.

The **budget deficit** is the amount by which the government's expenditures exceed its receipts during some specified period of time, usually a year. If, instead, receipts exceed expenditures, we have a *budget surplus*. For example, during fiscal year 1998, the government raised about $1,720 billion in taxes but spent about $1,650 billion, resulting in a surplus of about $70 billion.[1]

The **national debt,** also called the *public debt*, is the total value of the government's indebtedness at a moment in time. Thus, for example, the national debt at the end of fiscal year 1998 was about $5.5 trillion.

These two concepts—deficit and debt—are closely related because the government accumulates *debt* by running *deficits* or reduces its debt by running surpluses. The relationship between the debt and the deficit can be explained by a simple analogy. As you run water into a bathtub ("run a deficit"), the accumulated volume of water in the tub ("the debt") rises. Alternatively, if you let water out of the tub ("run a surplus"), the level of the water ("the debt") falls. Analogously, budget deficits raise the national debt, whereas budget surpluses lower it.

But, of course, getting rid of the deficit (shutting off the flow of water) will not eliminate the accumulated debt (drain the tub). The U.S. government is a prime example. Although it now runs a sizable annual surplus, it still has a very large accumulated debt (though that debt is falling).

Having made this distinction, let us look first at the size and nature of the accumulated public debt and then at the annual budget deficit.

### SOME FACTS ABOUT THE NATIONAL DEBT

How large a public debt do we have? How did we get it? Who owes it? Is it growing?

To begin with the simplest question, the public debt is enormous. At the end of 1998, it amounted to about $20,200 for every man, woman, and child in America. But about 40 percent of this outstanding debt was owned by agencies of the U.S. government—in other words, one branch of the government owed it to another. If we deduct this portion, the net national debt was just about $3.3 trillion, or around $12,200 per person.

Furthermore, when we compare the debt with the gross domestic product—the volume of goods and services our economy produces in a year—it does not seem so large after all. With a GDP more than $8.5 trillion in late 1998, the net debt was well under one-half of the nation's yearly income. By contrast, many families who own homes owe *several years'* worth of income to the banks that granted them mortgages. Many U.S. corporations also owe their bondholders much more than one-half of a year's sales.

But before these analogies make you feel too comfortable, we should point out that simple analogies between public and private debt are almost always misleading. A family with a large mortgage debt also owns a home with a value that presumably exceeds the mortgage. A solvent business firm has assets (factories, machinery, inventories, and so forth) that far exceed its outstanding debt in value.

Is the same thing true of the U.S. government? No one knows for sure. How much is the White House worth? Or the national parks? And what about military bases, both here and abroad? Simply because these government assets are *not* sold on markets, no one really knows their value. However, a federal government estimate made a few years ago concluded that its assets were worth "only" about $2.3 trillion at the end of 1994—a number far less than the national debt.

Figure 33–2 charts the path of the *net* national debt from 1915 to 1998, expressing each year's net debt as a fraction of that year's nominal GDP. Looking at the

---

[1] *Reminder:* The fiscal year of the U.S. government ends on September 30. Thus, fiscal year 1999 ran from October 1, 1998, to September 30, 1999.

debt *relative to GDP* is important for two reasons. First, we must remember that everything grows in a growing economy. Private debt and business debt have grown rapidly since 1915; it would have been surprising indeed if the public debt did not grow while GDP expanded so enormously. In fact, federal debt grew more slowly than private debt for most of the period since World War II until about 1980. The years from 1980 to about 1995 stand out as an aberration.

**The U.S. National Debt Relative to GDP, 1915–1998**    FIGURE 33-2

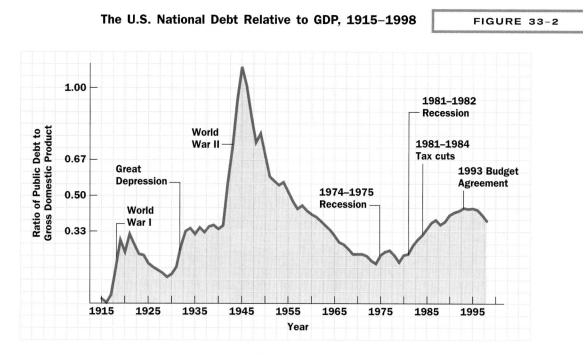

SOURCE: Constructed by the authors from data in *Historical Statistics of the United States* and *Economic Report of the President*.

**DISTORTED MEASUREMENTS**  Second, the debt is measured in dollars and, as long as there is any inflation, the amount of purchasing power that each dollar represents declines each year—as we pointed out in Chapter 1 in one of our *Ideas for Beyond the Final Exam*. Dividing the debt by nominal GDP, as done in Figure 33-2, adjusts for both real growth and inflation, and so puts the debt numbers in better perspective.

*Inflation Distorts Measurements*

The diagram shows us how and when the U.S. government acquired all this debt. Notice the sharp increases in the ratio of debt to GDP during World War I, the Great Depression, and especially World War II. Thereafter, you see an unmistakable downward trend until the recession of 1974–1975. In 1945, the national debt was the equivalent of 13 months' national income. By 1974, this figure had been whittled down to just two months' worth.

Thus, until the 1980s, the U.S. government acquired most of the debt either during wars or recessions. As we shall see later, the *cause* of the debt is quite germane to the question of whether or not the debt is a burden. So it is important to remember that:

Until about 1983, almost all of the U.S. national debt stemmed from financing wars and from the losses of tax revenues that accompany recessions.

But then things changed. From the early 1980s until 1993, the national debt grew faster than nominal GDP, reversing the pattern that had prevailed since 1945. And this happened with no wars and only one recession. By 1993, the debt exceeded five months' GDP—nearly triple its value in 1974. This disturbing development was a major reason why economists grew alarmed by continued large budget deficits.

Then, as we noted earlier, the government took decisive actions to reduce the budget deficit, and the ratio of debt to GDP has been falling ever since.

## ■ INTERPRETING THE BUDGET DEFICIT

We have observed that the federal government ran extremely large annual budget deficits from the early 1980s until the late 1990s. As Figure 33–3 shows, the budget deficit ballooned from the $40 to $80 billion range in fiscal years 1979 through 1981 up to $208 billion by fiscal year 1983—setting a record that was subsequently eclipsed several times. As late as fiscal year 1995, the deficit was still $164 billion. These are enormous, even mind-boggling, numbers. But what do they mean? How should we interpret them?

| FIGURE 33–3 | **Official Fiscal-Year Budget Deficits, 1979–1998** |
|---|---|

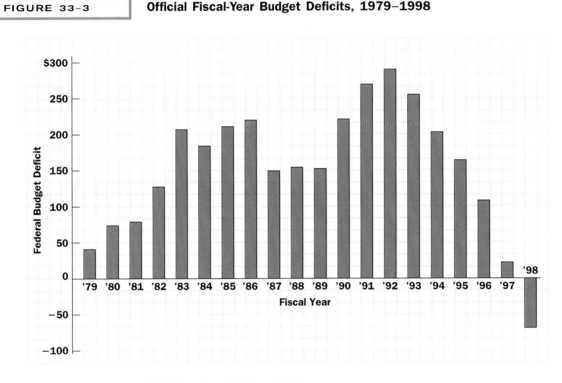

NOTE: Amounts are in billions of dollars.

SOURCE: *Economic Report of the President* (Washington, D.C.: U.S. Government Printing Office, 1999).

### THE STRUCTURAL DEFICIT

First, it is important to understand that the same fiscal program can lead to a large or small deficit, depending on the state of the economy. Failure to appreciate this point has led many people to assume that a larger deficit always signifies a more expansionary fiscal policy. But that is not always true.

Think, for example, about what happens to the budget during a recession. As GDP falls, the government's most important sources of tax revenue—income taxes, corporate taxes, and payroll taxes—all shrink because firms and people pay lower taxes when they earn less. Similarly, some types of government spending, notably transfer payments like unemployment benefits, rise when GDP falls, because more people are out of work.

Remember that the deficit is the difference between government expenditures, which are either purchases or transfer payments, and tax receipts:

Deficit = *G* + Transfers − Taxes = *G* − *T*

Because a falling GDP leads to higher expenditures and lower tax receipts:

**The deficit rises in a recession and falls in a boom, even with no change in fiscal policy.**

Figure 33–4 depicts the relationship between GDP and the budget deficit. The government's fiscal program is summarized by the blue and red lines. The horizontal blue line labeled *G* indicates that federal purchases of goods and services are approximately unaffected by GDP. The rising red line labeled *T* (for taxes minus transfers) indicates that taxes rise and transfer payments fall as GDP rises. Notice that the same fiscal policy (that is, the same two lines) can lead to a large deficit if GDP is $Y_1$, a balanced budget if GDP is $Y_2$, or a surplus if GDP is as high as $Y_3$. Clearly, the deficit itself is not a good measure of the government's fiscal policy.

To seek a better measure, many economists pay more attention to what is called the **structural budget deficit** or *surplus*. This hypothetical measure replaces both the spending and taxes in the *actual* budget by estimates of how much the government *would be* spending and receiving, given current tax rates and expenditure rules, if the economy were operating at some fixed, high-employment level. For example, if the high-employment benchmark in Figure 33–4 was $Y_2$, although actual GDP was only $Y_1$, the actual deficit would be *AB* although the structural deficit would be zero.

Because it is based on the spending and taxing the government *would be* doing at some fixed level of GDP, rather than on *actual* expenditures and receipts, the structural deficit is insensitive to the state of the economy. It changes *only* when policy changes, *not* when the GDP changes. That is why most economists view it as a better measure of the thrust of fiscal policy than the actual deficit.

This new concept helps us understand the changing nature of the large budget deficits of the 1980s and 1990s. Table 33–1 displays both the actual deficit and the structural deficit every second year since 1981. Because of recessions in 1983 and 1991, the difference between the two budgets was particularly large in those years. But it was negligible in 1987 and 1995, when the economy was near full employment.

Three interesting facts stand out when we compare the numbers in the first and last columns. First, even though the *official* deficit was smaller in fiscal 1995 than in fiscal 1983, the structural deficit was *actually* larger in 1995—despite years of budget "stringency." Second, the structural deficit rose between 1987 and 1993. It was this trend toward larger structural deficits that most alarmed keen students of the

| FIGURE 33-4 |

**The Effect of The Economy on the Budget**

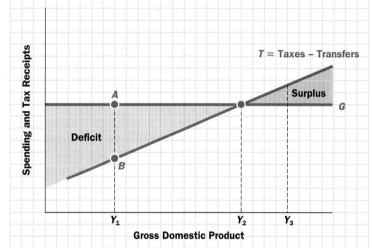

The **structural budget deficit** is the hypothetical deficit we *would have* under current fiscal policies if the economy were operating near full employment.

**Unemployment and the Deficit**          | TABLE 33-1 |

| Fiscal Year | Official Deficit | + | Adjustment to High Employment | = | Structural Deficit (−) or Surplus (+) |
|---|---|---|---|---|---|
| 1981 | −79 | | +28 | | −51 |
| 1983 | −208 | | +81 | | −127 |
| 1985 | −212 | | +14 | | −198 |
| 1987 | −150 | | +8 | | −142 |
| 1989 | −152 | | −24 | | −176 |
| 1991 | −269 | | +44 | | −225 |
| 1993 | −255 | | +43 | | −212 |
| 1995 | −164 | | −2 | | −166 |
| 1997 | −22 | | −34 | | −56 |
| 1998 | +69 | | −48 | | +21 |

NOTE: Amounts are in billions of dollars.
SOURCE: Congressional Budget Office.

federal budget. Third, the stunning $324 billion swing in the budget deficit from 1993 to 1998 (from a deficit of $255 billion to a surplus of $69 billion) exceeds the change in the structural deficit, which fell by $233 billion. This last number, which is still impressive, better indicates how much fiscal policy changed during this period.

## INFLATION ACCOUNTING FOR INTEREST PAYMENTS[2]

The next major problem is one of measurement rather than interpretation. Government accountants treat every dollar of interest payments as part of the government's spending. At first blush, that seems like the right thing to do, but it ignores the fundamental distinction between real and nominal interest rates that we emphasized in Chapter 24. To review that analysis:

> The real interest rate tells us the amount of purchasing power the borrower turns over to the lender for the privilege of borrowing. To this we must add an *inflation premium,* equal to the expected rate of inflation, to get the *nominal interest rate.* The inflation premium compensates the lender for the expected erosion of the purchasing power of her money and is best thought of as repayment of principal.[3]

The last sentence has important implications for the government budget—implications that few people understand.

From an economic point of view, the portion of the government's interest payments that merely compensates lenders for inflation should be counted as early *repayment of principal,* not as *interest,* because it simply returns to lenders the purchasing power of their original funds. Only the *real* interest that the government pays should be treated as an expenditure item in the budget. Breaking up interest payments in this way is called **inflation accounting.** Because so few people understand inflation accounting, it is worth taking the time to illustrate the idea with an analogy and a simple example.

**Inflation accounting** means adjusting standard accounting procedures for the fact that inflation lowers the purchasing power of money.

Imagine that you lend a roommate, who is enrolled in a chemistry course, a quantity of radium that you happen to own. Your roommate uses the radioactive material (carefully!) in experiments for a year and then returns it to you. Has your loan been repaid in full? Certainly not. Because of radioactive decay, what you get back is smaller than what you originally loaned. To pay you back in full, your roommate would have to give you enough additional radium to replace the portion that decayed during the year.

The analogy to interest rates on loans is straightforward: Inflation erodes the purchasing power of money just as radioactive decay erodes radium. So, in figuring out how many dollars constitute repayment of principal, we must take inflation into account. Let's illustrate this by a concrete example: comparing a loan made at zero inflation (no decay) with a loan made at 10 percent inflation (rapid decay).

First, suppose the government borrows $1,000 for a year when the inflation rate is zero, paying 2 percent interest. At the end of the year it must pay back $1,000 in principal and $20 in interest, for a total of $1,020. Of this, only $20—the interest payment—counts as expenditure in the budget. The repayment of principal is not counted as spending. The loan transaction is summarized simply in Column (1) of Table 33–2.

Now let us see how inflation (radioactive decay of money) complicates the accountant's job. Suppose the same transaction takes place when the rate of inflation is 10 percent. To compensate the lender for 10 percent inflation, the government must return $1.10 for each dollar originally borrowed. If the real interest rate is still 2 percent, the government must return 2 percent more than this, or $1.02 \times \$1.10 = \$1.122$ per dollar borrowed. Thus, each dollar of lending earns 12.2 cents in interest, meaning that the nominal interest rate is 12.2 percent.

So suppose the government borrows $1,000 at the start of the year and repays $1,122 at year's end. Conventional accounting procedures will treat $1,000 as repayment of principal (and hence not as an expenditure) and $122 as interest

---

[2] This section contains difficult material, which may be skipped in shorter courses.

[3] If you need review, see page 516.

**Accounting for a $1,000 Loan at a 2 Percent Real Interest Rate**

TABLE 33-2

| Item | (1) At Zero Inflation | (2) At 10% Inflation Conventional Accounting | (3) At 10% Inflation Inflation Accounting |
|---|---|---|---|
| **Interest** (included in budget) | $ 20 | $ 122 | $ 22 |
| plus | | | |
| **Principal** (excluded from budget) | 1,000 | 1,000 | 1,100 |
| equals | $1,020 | $1,122 | $1,122 |
| **Total payment** | | | |
| Addendum: Purchasing power of principal repayment | $1,000 | $ 909 | $1,000 |

(which *is* an expenditure). This conventional accounting treatment is indicated in Column (2) of Table 33–2.

But these numbers are misleading since $1,000 at the end of the year is not full repayment of principal because inflation has eroded the real value of money. In fact, it is worth just $909 in terms of beginning-of-the-year money. The correct inflation accounting treatment recognizes that it takes $1,100 at the end of the year to buy what $1,000 bought at the beginning of the year. So $1,100 is treated as repayment of principal, leaving only $22 ($1,122 − $1,100) to be treated as interest. The correct inflation accounting for the loan is shown in Column (3) of Table 33–2.

In general, the proper economic treatment of a loan in an inflationary environment must recognize that more dollars (in our example, $1,100) must be returned to the lender in order to give back the purchasing power of the original loan ($1,000). Only the excess of the nominal interest payment ($122) over any compensation for inflation ($100) should count as interest. Because conventional accounting does not recognize the difference between nominal and real interest:

**DISTORTED MEASUREMENTS**  Inflation distorts the government budget deficit under conventional accounting procedures by exaggerating interest expenses. This problem is yet another case in which inflation distorts economic measurements—one of our *Ideas for Beyond the Final Exam.* The example also suggests how this error can be corrected:

   To correct the deficit for inflation, we must subtract the inflation premium from the interest paid on the national debt, thereby counting only *real* interest payments.

*Inflation Distorts Measurements*

Table 33–3 shows that making the inflation adjustment to interest payments would have reduced reported deficits by $30 to $85 billion in recent years—a sizable adjustment.

## CONCLUSION: WHAT HAPPENED AFTER 1981?

Table 33–4 puts our two major adjustments—for unemployment via the structural deficit and for inflation accounting—together and compares the official deficits recorded since 1981—Column (1)—with the corresponding figures for the structural, inflation-corrected deficit—Column (4). The difference between the two columns is startling in some years. For example, in 1981 the economy was weak and inflation was high. So the apparently substantial budget deficit of 1981 was actually a surplus on a structural, inflation-corrected basis! But after 1983 even the structural, inflation-corrected budget was in substantial deficit.

Table 33–4 tells the following story about the recent evolution of the budget deficit. On a structural, inflation-corrected basis, the federal budget swung from a

| TABLE 33-3 |
|---|

**Inflation Accounting and the Deficit**

| Fiscal Year | Official Deficit | + Inflation Adjustment for Interest Paid | = Inflation-Adjusted Deficit (−) or Surplus (+) |
|---|---|---|---|
| 1981 | −79 | +67 | −12 |
| 1983 | −208 | +33 | −175 |
| 1985 | −212 | +39 | −173 |
| 1987 | −150 | +48 | −102 |
| 1989 | −152 | +77 | −75 |
| 1991 | −269 | +85 | −184 |
| 1993 | −255 | +70 | −185 |
| 1995 | −164 | +77 | −87 |
| 1997 | −22 | +67 | +45 |
| 1998 | +69 | +31 | +100 |

NOTE: Amounts are in billions of dollars.

SOURCE: Congressional Budget Office and authors' estimates.

| TABLE 33-4 |
|---|

**Actual and Adjusted Budget Deficits**

| Fiscal Year | (1) Official Deficit | + (2) Adjustment for Inflation | + (3) Adjustment to High Employment | = (4) Adjusted Deficit (−) or Surplus (+) |
|---|---|---|---|---|
| 1981 | −79 | +67 | +28 | +16 |
| 1983 | −208 | +33 | +81 | −94 |
| 1985 | −212 | +39 | +14 | −159 |
| 1987 | −150 | +48 | +8 | −94 |
| 1989 | −152 | +77 | −24 | −99 |
| 1991 | −269 | +85 | +44 | −140 |
| 1993 | −255 | +70 | +43 | −142 |
| 1995 | −164 | +77 | −2 | −89 |
| 1997 | −22 | +67 | −34 | +11 |
| 1998 | +69 | +31 | −48 | +52 |

NOTE: Amounts are in billions of dollars.

SOURCE: Congressional Budget Office and authors' estimates.

small surplus to an extremely large deficit in the first half of the 1980s—largely due to tax cuts under "Reaganomics." We made some progress toward reducing the deficit in the late 1980s, but the problem worsened after 1989 as government spending grew faster than tax receipts. Then, starting around 1993, a combination of tax hikes and rigorous spending controls eliminated the deficit, returning the nation by 1997 to approximately the same fiscal position as in 1981.

## ■ BOGUS ARGUMENTS ABOUT THE BURDEN OF THE DEBT

Having gained some perspective on the facts, let us now turn to some of the arguments advanced by those who claim that budget deficits place an intolerable burden on future generations.

---

● **POLICY DEBATE**   ▌ **A BALANCED-BUDGET AMENDMENT TO THE CONSTITUTION?**

---

Since 1995, both President Clinton and the Republican-dominated Congress have agreed that the federal government should move gradually toward a balanced budget. But in both 1995 and 1997, the two sides clashed sharply over a proposed constitutional amendment that would have required a balanced budget, with most Republicans in favor and the president and most Democrats opposed. (The amendment failed in the Senate by a single vote on both occasions.)

What's the difference? Why do many people who favor a balanced budget nonetheless oppose a constitutional amendment to require one? There are many reasons.

Let's start with stabilization policy. Establishing a balanced budget as a long-run norm is one thing. But a constitutional mandate to balance the budget every year is quite another—and might destabilize the economy. To understand why, remember that tax receipts decline and unemployment benefits rise automatically whenever economic activity weakens. No explicit government actions are necessary; it all happens before the government even recognizes that there is a

problem. Such automatic stabilizers cushion the decline in GDP, but they also increase the deficit.

If there were a constitutional amendment requiring a balanced budget, however, this process would not be allowed to run its course. Instead, as tax receipts fell, the government would be forced to raise taxes or cut spending even as the economy sagged—precisely the wrong fiscal policy.

Constitutional experts also raise legal questions about the amendment. For example, views on the advisability of balanced budgets have changed over the years, and likely will change again. Will we amend the Constitution as economic theories change? And who will enforce the amendment if the president and Congress fail to balance the budget? Do we want judges making fiscal policy?

**ARGUMENT 1**   Our children and grandchildren will be burdened by heavy interest payments. Higher taxes will be necessary to make these payments.

**ANSWER**   It is certainly true that a higher debt will necessitate higher interest payments and, other things being equal, this will force our children and grandchildren to pay higher taxes. But think who will own the bonds and therefore receive the higher interest payments as income: our children and grandchildren! Thus, one group of future Americans will be making interest payments to another group of future Americans. So we conclude that:

> As long as the national debt is owned by domestic citizens, as the bulk of the U.S. debt is, future interest payments transfer money from one group of Americans to another. These transfers may or may not be desirable, but they hardly constitute a burden on the nation as a whole.

However, this argument *is* valid—and worrisome—for the portion of our debt that is held by foreigners, a share that is up to 38 percent and has been growing rapidly. Paying interest on this portion of the debt will burden future Americans in a concrete way: In the 21st century, a portion of America's GDP will have to be sent abroad to pay interest on the debts we incurred in the 1980s and 1990s. For this reason, many thoughtful observers are becoming concerned that the United States is borrowing too much from abroad.[4]

Another valid element of the argument is that the taxes that will have to be raised to pay interest even to U.S. citizens may reduce the efficiency of the economy.

**ARGUMENT 2**   Repaying the enormous debt will ruin the nation.

**ANSWER**   A first answer to this argument merely rephrases the answer to the previous one: Most of America's debt is owed to Americans. But this argument raises an even more fundamental point. *Unlike a private family, the nation need never pay off*

---

[4] We will discuss the linkages between the federal budget deficit and foreign borrowing in greater detail in Chapter 37.

*its debt.* Instead, each time the principal is due, the U.S. Treasury simply "rolls it over" by floating more debt.

Is this a bit of chicanery? How can the U.S. government get away with making loans that it never intends to pay back? The answer lies in the fallacy of comparing the U.S. government to a family or an individual. People cannot borrow in perpetuity, because they will not live that long. Sensible lenders will not extend long-term credit to very old people because their heirs cannot be forced to pay up. But the U.S. government will never "die"; at least, we hope not! So this problem does not arise. In this respect, the government is in much the same position as a large corporation. AT&T never pays off its debt. It, too, rolls it over by floating new debt all the time.

**ARGUMENT 3**   Like any family or any business firm, a nation has a limited capacity to borrow. If it exceeds this limit, it is in danger of being unable to pay its creditors. It may go bankrupt with calamitous consequences for everyone.

**ANSWER**   This is another false analogy. For private debtors, this issue certainly applies. But the U.S. government need never fear defaulting on its debt. Why? First, because it has enormous power to raise revenues by taxation. If you had such power, you would never have to fear bankruptcy either.

But once again, the statement raises a more fundamental point—one that distinguishes the U.S. debt from that of most other nations. *The American national debt is an obligation to pay U.S. dollars:* Each debt certificate obligates the Treasury to pay the holder so many U.S. dollars on a prescribed date. But the U.S. government is the source of these dollars. It prints them! *No nation need default on debts that call for repayment in its own currency.*[5] If worse comes to worst, it can always print whatever money it needs to pay off its creditors. This option is not open to countries whose debts call for payment in U.S. dollars, as Mexico in 1995 and a number of Southeast Asian countries in 1997 learned in particularly painful ways.

It does not, of course, follow that acquiring more debt through budget deficits is necessarily a good idea for the U.S. government. Sometimes it is a very bad idea. As we know, printing money to pay the debt will expand aggregate demand and cause inflation. In addition, as we will learn in Chapter 37, printing more dollars will make the international value of the dollar fall. We may not relish either of these outcomes. The point is not that budget deficits are either good or bad; they can be either under the appropriate circumstances. Rather, the point is that worrying about a possible default on the national debt is unnecessary and even foolish. We have plenty of other economic issues to worry about.

Having cleared the air of these fallacious arguments about the national debt, we are now in a position to explore some genuine problems that may arise when the government spends more than it raises through taxation, that is, when it runs budget deficits.

## ■ BUDGET DEFICITS AND INFLATION

One indictment of deficit spending that certainly *is* valid under some circumstances is the charge that it is inflationary. Why? Because when government policy pushes up aggregate demand, firms may find themselves unwilling or unable to produce the higher quantities of their products that consumers are demanding at the going prices. Prices will therefore have to rise.

The aggregate supply and demand diagram in Figure 33–5 shows this analysis graphically. Initially, equilibrium is at point *A*—where demand curve $D_0D_0$ and supply curve *SS* intersect. Output is $7,000 billion, and the price index is at 100. The diagram indicates that the economy is operating at full employment, because the aggregate demand and supply curves intersect precisely at potential GDP.

---

[5] Russia astounded the financial world by defaulting on ruble-denominated debt in August 1998.

Now suppose the government raises its spending or cuts taxes enough to shift the aggregate demand schedule upward from $D_0D_0$ to $D_1D_1$. Equilibrium shifts from point A to point B, thereby raising the equilibrium price level to 106, or 6 percent. But that is not the end of the story because point B indicates an inflationary gap. We know from previous chapters that inflation will continue until the aggregate sup-

FIGURE 33-5

## The Inflationary Effects of Deficit Spending

ply curve shifts far enough upward to the left so that it passes through point C, at which point the inflationary gap disappears. In the long run, then, deficit spending will have raised the price level 12 percent in this example.

Although Figure 33–5 is entirely hypothetical, it illustrates how the Vietnam War started the inflation problem in the United States in the late 1960s. The U.S. economy was roughly at full employment in 1965 with very low inflation. Then government spending on the war soared, shifting the aggregate demand curve outward and opening up an inflationary gap. Inflation rose from 2.5 percent in 1965 to 5.0 percent in 1969.

Thus, the cries that budget

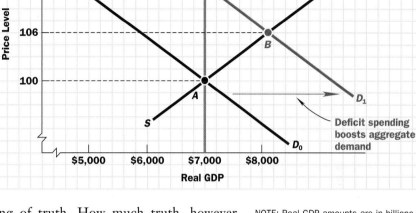

NOTE: Real GDP amounts are in billions of dollars.

deficits are "inflationary" have the ring of truth. How much truth, however, depends on several factors. One is the slope of the aggregate supply curve; Figure 33–5 clearly shows that a steep supply curve leads to more inflation than a flat one. A second factor is the degree of resource utilization. Deficit spending is more inflationary in a fully employed economy (like Figure 33–5) than in an economy with lots of slack.

Finally, we must remember that the Federal Reserve's monetary policy can always cancel out the potential inflationary effects of deficit spending by pulling the aggregate demand curve back to its original position. Once again, the policy *mix* is crucial.

The central bank is said to **monetize the deficit** when it purchases the bonds that the government issues.

## THE MONETIZATION ISSUE

But will the Federal Reserve always neutralize the expansionary effect of a higher budget deficit? This question brings up another reason why some people worry about the inflationary consequences of deficits. They fear that the Federal Reserve

FIGURE 33-6

## Fiscal Expansion and Interest Rates

may have to "monetize" part of the deficit, by which they mean that the Fed may feel compelled to purchase some of the newly issued government debt. Let us explain, first, why the Fed might make such purchases, and second, why these purchases are called **monetizing the deficit.**

Deficit spending, we have just noted, normally drives up both real GDP and the price level. As we have emphasized, such an economic expansion shifts the demand curve for money outward to the right—as depicted by the movement from $M_0D_0$ to $M_1D_1$ in Figure 33–6. The diagram shows that, if the Federal Reserve takes no actions to shift the money supply curve, interest rates will rise as equilibrium moves from point A to point B.

Suppose now that the Fed does not want interest rates to rise. What can it do? To prevent the incipient rise in *r*, it would have to engage in *expansionary monetary policies* that shift the supply curve for money outward to the right—as indicated in Figure 33–7. With the blue money

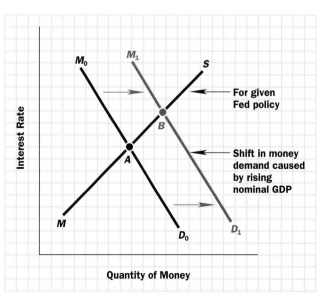

**FIGURE 33-7**

**Monetization and Interest Rates**

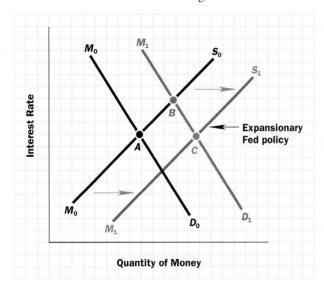

supply curve $M_1S_1$, equilibrium would be at point $C$ rather than at point $B$. So interest rates would be unchanged from point $A$. Because the Fed usually pursues expansionary monetary policies by purchasing government bonds in the open market, this means that deficit spending might induce the Federal Reserve to buy more government debt.

But why is this called *monetizing* the deficit? The reason is simple. As we learned in Chapter 31, open-market purchases of bonds by the Fed give banks more reserves, which leads, eventually, to an increase in the money supply. This is also shown in Figure 33–7: The outward shift of the money supply schedule from $M_0S_0$ to $M_1S_1$ leads to an increase in the quantity of money. By this indirect route, then, larger budget deficits may lead to a larger money supply. To summarize:

**If the Federal Reserve takes no countervailing actions, an expansionary fiscal policy that increases the budget deficit will raise real GDP and prices, thereby shifting the demand curve for money outward and driving up interest rates. If the Fed does not want interest rates to rise, it can engage in expansionary open-market operations, that is, purchase more government debt. If the Fed does this, the money supply will increase. In this case, we say that part of the deficit is *monetized*.**

**FIGURE 33-8**

**Monetized Deficit Spending**

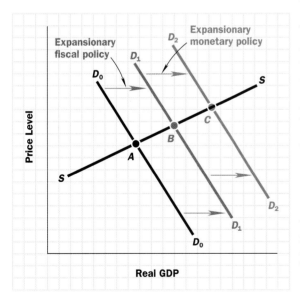

Monetized deficits are more inflationary than nonmonetized deficits for a simple reason: Expansionary monetary and fiscal policies *together* are more inflationary than expansionary fiscal policy *alone*. Figure 33–8 illustrates this simple conclusion. The aggregate supply curve and aggregate demand curves $D_0D_0$ and $D_1D_1$ correspond to those in Figure 33–5. The shift from $D_0D_0$ to $D_1D_1$ represents the effect of expansionary fiscal policy (raising the budget deficit). If, in addition, the Fed monetizes part of the deficit, the aggregate demand curve will shift out still further—perhaps to the position indicated by $D_2D_2$. Thus, the price level will rise even more (compare points $B$ and $C$).

Is this a real worry? Does the Fed actually monetize any substantial portion of the deficit? Normally, it does not. The clearest evidence is the fact that the Fed managed to *reduce* inflation during the 1980s and 1990s while the government ran unprecedented deficits. Nonetheless, many economists and business leaders are concerned about the long-run dangers of monetization when deficits are large and chronic. The reason is simple arithmetic. When budget deficits are extremely large, even a small percentage of monetization can lead to substantial increases in bank reserves and the money supply.

This last point has been amply illustrated by many countries' experiences. Although monetization of deficits has not been much of a problem for the United States, it has been a source of very rapid inflation at various times in a variety of Latin American countries, in Russia, in Israel, and elsewhere.

## ■ DEFICITS, INTEREST RATES, AND CROWDING OUT

So far we have been looking for possible burdens that the national debt might place on the *demand* side of the economy. But the real case for cutting the deficit probably comes on the *supply* side. In brief, large budget deficits discourage investment and therefore retard the growth of our nation's capital stock. The mechanism is easy to understand.

We have just seen that budget deficits tend to raise interest rates unless the Fed engages in substantial monetization. But the rate of interest ($r$) is a major determinant of investment spending ($I$). In particular, higher $r$ leads to lower $I$. And if we spend less on $I$ today, we will have a smaller capital stock tomorrow—and thus a smaller potential GDP. This, according to most economists, is the true sense in which a large national debt may burden future generations:

> Because of the large national debt, we may bequeath less physical capital to future generations. If they inherit less plant and equipment, these generations will be burdened by a lower productive capacity—a lower potential GDP. In a word, large deficits may retard economic growth.

Phrasing this point another way explains why it is often called the **crowding-out effect.** Consider what happens in financial markets when the government engages in deficit spending. When it spends more than it raises in taxes, the government must borrow the balance. It does so by selling bonds, which compete with corporate bonds and other financial instruments for the available supply of funds. If some savers decide to buy government bonds, the funds remaining to invest in private bonds must be smaller. Thus, some private borrowers will get "crowded out" of the financial markets as the government claims an increasing share of the economy's total saving.

Some critics of deficits have taken this lesson to its illogical extreme and argued that each $1 of deficit spending by the government crowds out exactly $1 of private spending, so that expansionary fiscal policy has no net effect on total demand. In their view, when $G$ rises, $I$ falls by the same amount, so the total of $C + I + G + (X - IM)$ is unchanged.

Under normal circumstances, we would not expect this to occur. Why? First, moderate budget deficits push up interest rates only slightly. Second, private spending appears only moderately sensitive to interest rates. Even at the higher interest rates that government deficits cause, most corporations will continue to borrow to finance their capital investments.

Furthermore, a counterforce arises that we might call the **crowding-in effect.** Deficit spending in times of economic slack presumably quickens the pace of economic activity; that, at least, is its purpose. As the economy expands, businesses find it both necessary and profitable to add to their capacity so as to meet the greater consumer demands. Because of this *induced investment*, as we called it in earlier chapters, any increase in $G$ tends to *increase* investment, rather than *decrease* it as the crowding-out hypothesis predicts.

The strength of the crowding-in effect depends on how much additional real GDP is stimulated by government spending (that is, on the size of the multiplier) and on how sensitive investment spending is to the improved profit opportunities that accompany rapid growth. It is even conceivable that the crowding-in effect can dominate the crowding-out effect in the short run, so that $I$ rises, on balance, when $G$ rises.

But how can this be true in view of the crowding-out argument? Certainly, if the government borrows more *and the total volume of private saving is fixed*, then private industry must borrow less. That's just arithmetic. The fallacy in the strict crowding-out argument comes in supposing that the economy's flow of saving is really fixed. If government deficits succeed in raising output, we will have more income and therefore more saving. In that way, *both* government *and* industry can borrow more.

Which effect dominates, crowding out or crowding in? Crowding out stems from the increases in interest rates caused by deficits, whereas crowding in derives from the faster real economic growth that deficits sometimes produce. In the short run, the crowding-in effect—which derives from the outward shift of the aggregate

**Crowding out** occurs when deficit spending by the government forces private investment spending to contract.

**Crowding in** occurs when government spending, by raising real GDP, induces increases in private investment spending.

"Would you mind explaining again how interest rates and the national deficit affect my allowance?"

demand curve—is often the more powerful, especially when the economy is performing below full employment.

In the long run, however, the supply side dominates because the economy's self-correcting mechanism pushes the growth rate of actual GDP toward the growth rate of potential GDP. Here the crowding-out effect takes over: With higher interest rates, the capital stock grows more slowly and, hence, so does potential GDP.

## THE BOTTOM LINE

Let us summarize what we have learned about the crowding-out controversy.

■ The basic argument of the crowding-out hypothesis is sound: *Unless the economy produces enough additional saving,* more government borrowing will force out those private borrowers who are discouraged by the high interest rates. This will reduce investment spending and cancel out some of the expansionary effects of higher government spending.

■ This crowding-out force is rarely strong enough to cancel out the *entire* expansionary thrust of government spending, however. Some net stimulus to the economy remains.

■ If deficit spending induces substantial GDP growth, then the crowding-in effect will lead to more saving. There might even be so much more that private industry can borrow *more* than before, despite the increase in government borrowing.

■ The crowding-out effect is likely to dominate in the long run or when the economy is operating near full employment. The crowding-in effect is likely to dominate in the short run, especially when the economy has a great deal of slack.

## THE TRUE BURDEN OF THE NATIONAL DEBT: SLOWER GROWTH

This analysis of crowding-out versus crowding-in helps us to understand whether or not budget deficits impose a burden on future generations:

When government budget deficits take place in a high-employment economy, the crowding-out effect will probably dominate. So deficits will exact a burden by leaving a smaller capital stock and hence lower potential GDP to future generations. However, deficits in a slack economy may well lead to *more* investment rather than *less.* In this case, where the crowding-in effect dominates, deficit spending increases growth and the new debt is a blessing rather than a burden.

Which case applies to the U.S. national debt? To answer this, let us go back to the historical facts and recall how we accumulated debt prior to the 1980s. The first cause was the financing of wars, especially World War II. Because this debt was contracted in a fully employed economy, it undoubtedly constituted a burden in the formal sense. After all, the bombs, ships, and planes that it financed were used up in the war, not invested and bequeathed as capital to future generations.

Yet today's Americans may not feel terribly burdened by the decisions of those in power in the 1940s, for consider the alternatives. We could have financed the entire war by taxation and thus placed the burden on consumption rather than on investment. But that would truly have been ruinous, and probably impossible, given the colossal wartime expenditures. Or we could have printed money. But that would have unleashed an inflation that nobody wanted. Or the government could have just spent much less money and perhaps not have won the war, leaving future generations a far more severe burden. Compared to these alternatives, opting for massive deficit spending in the 1940s looks like a sound decision.

A second major contributor to the national debt prior to 1983 was a series of recessions. But these are precisely the circumstances under which increasing the debt might prove to be a blessing rather than a burden. So, it was only in the 1980s that we had the type of deficits to which the valid burden-of-the-debt argument applies—deficits acquired in a fully employed, peacetime economy.

This sharp departure from historical norms is what made those budget deficits so worrisome. The tax cuts of 1981–1984 blew a large hole in the government budget, and the recession of 1981–1982 ballooned the deficit even further. By the late 1980s, the U.S. economy had recovered to full employment, but a structural deficit of around $150 billion per year remained. This was something that had never happened before. Then, in the early 1990s, the structural deficit ratcheted up again—to more than $200 billion per year. Such large structural deficits posed a real threat of crowding out and constituted a serious potential burden on future generations.

Let us now summarize our evaluation of the burden of the national debt and thereby clarify one of the *Ideas for Beyond the Final Exam* introduced in Chapter 1.

1. The arguments that a large national debt may lead the nation into bankruptcy, or unduly burden future generations who have to make onerous payments of interest and principal, are mostly bogus.

2. The national debt *will* be a burden if it is sold to foreigners or contracted in a fully employed, peacetime economy. In the latter case, it will reduce the nation's capital stock.

3. Under some circumstances, budget deficits are appropriate for stabilization-policy reasons.

4. Until the 1980s, the actual public debt of the U.S. government was mostly contracted as a result of wars and recessions—precisely the circumstances under which the valid burden-of-the-debt argument does not apply. However, the large deficits of the 1980s and 1990s were not mainly attributable to recessions, and were therefore worrisome.

*Why Was it Important to Reduce the Budget Deficit?*

## Resolving the Issue of Deficits and Growth

We are now in a position to answer the question posed at the start of this chapter: How can some economists argue that we should reduce the budget deficit as a way to speed economic growth, whereas others claim that reducing the deficit too quickly will imperil economic growth? The answer comes from distinguishing carefully between the short-run and long-run effects of smaller budget deficits.

In the short run, reducing the deficit means pursuing a contractionary fiscal policy: either cutting spending or raising taxes. Unless monetary policy turns sufficiently expansionary, we know from earlier chapters that such a fiscal contraction will pull the aggregate demand curve inward—as shown in Figure 33–9. So shrinking the deficit will reduce both real GDP and the price level as the economy's equilibrium moves from point *A* to point *B*.

A sufficiently strong dose of this contractionary fiscal medicine might even cause a recession. Those who warn of the dangers of overzealous deficit reduction are thinking about this short-run danger. For example, many critics of the IMF's prescription for Southeast Asia in 1997 argued that spending cuts and tax increases would deepen the economic crises in these countries.

In the long run, however, smaller budget deficits lead to lower real interest rates and hence to higher levels of private investment. That makes the nation's capital stock grow faster, thereby boosting the growth rate of *potential* GDP and shifting the aggregate supply curve outward at a faster pace. This is all depicted in Figure 33–10, which shows a smaller deficit leading to a potential GDP of $Y_1$ instead of $Y_0$. With the

**FIGURE 33–9**

**The Short-Run Effect of Deficit Reduction**

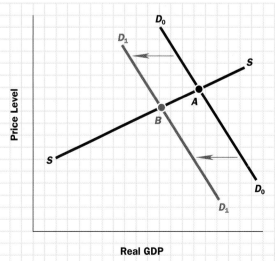

**FIGURE 33-10**

**The Long-Run Effect of Deficit Reduction**

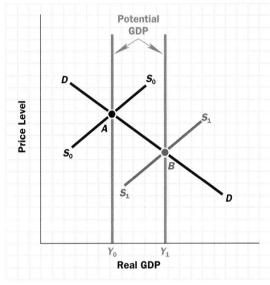

same aggregate demand curve, *DD*, the result is higher GDP—and also lower prices.

This was precisely the argument behind calls for sharp deficit reduction in the United States in the 1990s, and it focuses squarely on the long run. History suggests that it all worked out: Both investment and GDP growth accelerated as the structural deficit fell.

Which view is correct? Paradoxically, both are! In the short run, aggregate demand factors dominate economic performance and deficit reduction is therefore a contractionary force—unless it is offset by monetary policy. But, in the long run, output gravitates toward potential GDP no matter what is happening to aggregate demand, so aggregate supply rules the roost. And because smaller deficits spur investment spending, they increase the economy's potential growth rate.

## THE IMPORTANCE OF THE POLICY MIX

This analysis once again calls attention to the importance of the fiscal-monetary policy mix. Various combinations of fiscal and monetary policy can lead to the same level of aggregate demand, and hence the same real GDP and price level, in the short run. But the long-run consequences may be quite different.

A combination of larger budget deficits and tighter money should produce higher real interest rates and lower investment. It should therefore shift the composition of total expenditure, $C + I + G + (X - IM)$, toward more *G*, more *C* (from tax cuts), and less *I*.[6] The expected result? Slower growth of potential GDP. That policy mix, in a nutshell, is what the United States government chose in the early 1980s.

But the opposite policy mix—tighter budgets and looser monetary policy—should produce the opposite outcomes: lower real interest rates, more investment, and hence faster potential GDP growth. That, fortunately, is the direction American macroeconomic policy has taken in recent years—with excellent results.

Lowering the budget deficit (or running a surplus), economists believe, is one effective way to raise the investment share of GDP. The general point is:

The *composition* of aggregate demand is a major determinant of the rate of economic growth. If a larger fraction of GDP is devoted to investment rather than to consumption, government purchases, or net exports, then the nation's capital stock will grow faster and the aggregate supply schedule will shift more quickly to the right, accelerating growth.

International data likewise show a positive relationship between growth and the share of GDP invested. Figure 33–11 shows, for

**FIGURE 33-11**

**Growth and Investment in 24 Countries**

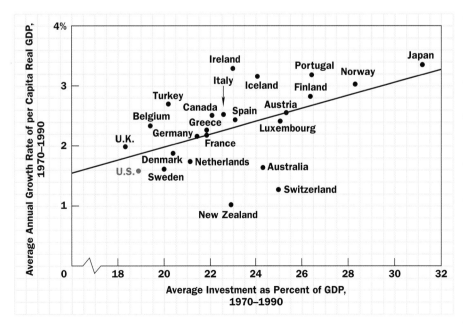

SOURCE: *Economic Report of the President* (Washington, D.C.: U.S. Government Printing Office, 1995), p. 28.

[6] We take up the consequences of the policy mix for $X - IM$ in Chapter 37.

a set of 24 countries on four continents, both investment as a share of GDP and growth in per-capita output over two decades (the 1970s and 1980s). Countries with higher investment rates clearly experienced higher growth, on average.

## ■ THE ECONOMICS AND POLITICS OF THE U.S. BUDGET DEFICIT

Given what we have learned in this chapter about the theory and facts of budget deficits, we can now address some of the issues that have been debated in the political arena for over a decade.

1. *How did we get such a large deficit?* Triple-digit deficits began in 1982. At first, the most important cause was the deep recession, not President Reagan's budget policies. As we saw in Table 33–1, the structural deficit was far smaller than the actual deficit in, say, 1983. But within a few years, the economy improved and the tax cuts became fully effective, leaving an enormous structural deficit.

   By the late 1980s, the economy was at or beyond full employment, so deliberate fiscal policy actions (and inactions) accounted for virtually all of the deficit. Then the budget deteriorated further as the government's interest bill mounted (because of past deficits) and spending on items like health care soared. Whether the blame for failing to address the deficit problem earlier rests with Presidents Reagan and Bush or with the Democratic Congress is a matter of politics, not economics. But the fact remains that little was done to solve the problem until Congress enacted the first large deficit-reduction package in 1990.

2. *Were the deficits really a problem?* Once again, the answer to the question was different in the early 1980s from what it was in the late 1980s and early 1990s. In 1981 and 1982, the economy suffered through a deep recession. And in 1983, the first year of recovery, unemployment was still extremely high. Under these circumstances, crowding out was not a serious problem and actions to close the deficit would have threatened the recovery. According to the basic principles of fiscal policy, a large deficit was probably appropriate.

   But things were much different by 1987. Crowding out became a more serious issue as the economy reached full employment. So budget deficits should have fallen. But the actual deficit did not fall, and the structural deficit actually rose. So worries about the burden of the national debt, once mostly myths, became all too realistic.

3. *How did we get rid of the deficit?* We did it the old-fashioned way: by raising taxes and reducing spending in three not-so-easy steps. Both the 1990 budget agreement and the 1993 deficit-reduction package, which turned out to be the decisive step, contained some of each. The smaller 1997 budget deal relied exclusively on spending cuts. But either choice—taxing more or spending less—produces a contractionary fiscal policy that reduces aggregate demand.

   Is that a problem? Not if fiscal and monetary policies are well-coordinated. If fiscal policy turns contractionary to reduce the deficit, monetary policy can turn expansionary to counteract the effects on aggregate demand. In this way, we can hope to shrink the deficit without shrinking the economy. Such a change in the policy mix should also bring down interest rates, because both tighter budgets and easier money tend to push interest rates down. That, indeed, was the policymakers' hope, and it appears to have worked extremely well. Interest rates fell, and the Fed made sure that aggregate demand was sufficient to keep the economy growing.

---

**THE AMAZING SHRINKING BUDGET DEFICIT**

Not so very long ago, budget experts were talking and fretting about the likelihood of mammoth federal deficits "as far as the eye can see." As recently as fiscal year 1994, the red ink exceeded $200 billion. Yet by fiscal 1997, the budget was nearly balanced (the deficit was just $22 billion), and in fiscal 1998 the government ran its first surplus in almost 30 years. How did it all happen so fast?

The answer is a happy combination of good policy and good luck. First, the large deficit-reduction package that President Clinton barely managed to get through Congress in August 1993 began to have major effects in 1996 and 1997. Second, Congress and the president agreed on another deficit-reduction plan, albeit a smaller one, in 1997. Third, the economy grew much faster than expected in 1996 through 1998. As we have learned in this chapter, stronger economic performance leads to smaller deficits.

But in addition to these three relatively well-understood factors, a fourth one still remains somewhat mysterious: Tax receipts came in surprisingly high, even given the high levels of income. No one is quite sure why, but the profits that Americans were making from the booming stock market are the leading suspect.

The numbers were impressive. Take fiscal year 1998 as an example. In March 1997, six months before FY98 started, the Congressional Budget Office (CBO) forecast a *deficit* of $122 billion. A year later, it was projecting a tiny $8 billion *surplus*. When the fiscal year finally ended in September 1998, the books showed an impressive $69 billion surplus. That's a swing of $191 billion in just 18 months! The pleasant surprise left many smiling faces in Washington.

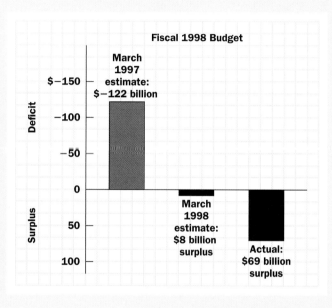

---

**SUMMARY**

1. Rigid adherence to budget balancing would make the economy less stable, by reducing aggregate demand (via tax increases and reductions in government spending) when private spending is low and raising aggregate demand when private spending is high.

2. Because both monetary and fiscal policy influence aggregate demand, the appropriate *budget deficit or surplus* depends on monetary policy. Similarly, the appropriate monetary policy depends on budget policy.

3. The same level of aggregate demand can be generated by different mixes of fiscal and monetary policy. But the composition of GDP will be different. Larger budget deficits and tighter money tend to produce higher interest rates, a smaller share of investment in GDP, and slower growth. Smaller budget deficits (or surpluses) and looser monetary policy lead to a larger investment share and faster growth.

4. One major reason for the large budget deficits of the early 1980s and early 1990s was the fact that the economy operated well below full employment. In those years, the *structural deficit*, which uses estimates of what the government's receipts and outlays would be at full employment to correct for business cycle fluctuations, was much smaller than the official deficit.

5. Inflation exaggerates the deficit because all *nominal interest payments* are counted as expenditures. Under *inflation accounting*, only *real interest payments* would count as expenditures, and the deficit would be seen to be much smaller.

6. If we correct the official deficit for inflation and use the structural deficit to correct for the business cycle, we find that budget deficits began only around 1983. Before that, there were balanced budgets or surpluses.

7. Arguments that the public debt will burden future generations, who will have to make huge payments of interest and principal, are mostly based on false analogies. In fact, most of these payments are simply transfers from one group of Americans to another. However, taxes must be raised to pay the interest, and there is a legitimate worry about the portion of the national debt that is owned by foreigners.

8. The bogus argument that a large national debt can bankrupt a country like the United States ignores the fact that our national debt consists entirely of obligations to pay U.S. dollars—a currency the government can raise by taxation or create by simply printing money.

9. Under many circumstances, budget deficits are inflationary because they expand aggregate demand. They are even more inflationary if they are *monetized*, that is, if the Federal Reserve buys some of the newly issued government debt in the open market.

10. Unless the deficit is substantially monetized, deficit spending forces interest rates higher and discourages private investment spending. This is called the *crowding-out effect*. If there is a great deal of crowding out, then deficits really do impose a *burden on future generations* by leaving them a smaller capital stock to work with.

11. But there is also a *crowding-in effect* from higher government spending (*G*). If expansionary fiscal policy succeeds in raising real output (*Y*), more investment will be induced by the higher *Y*.

12. Whether crowding out or crowding in dominates largely depends on the time horizon. In the short run, and especially when unemployment is high, crowding in is probably the stronger force; so higher *G* does not cause lower investment. But, in the long run, the economy will be near full employment, and the proponents of the crowding-out hypothesis will be right: High government spending mainly displaces private investment.

13. So larger deficits may spur growth (via aggregate demand) in the short run but deter growth (via aggregate supply and potential GDP) in the long run.

14. Whether or not deficits create a burden therefore depends on how and why the government ran these deficits in the first place. If the government runs deficits to fight recessions, more investment may be crowded in by rising output than is crowded out by rising interest rates. Deficits contracted to carry on wars certainly impair the future capital stock, though they may not be considered a burden for noneconomic reasons. Because these two cases account for most of the debt the U.S. government contracted until the mid-1980s, that debt cannot reasonably be considered a serious burden. However, the deficits between 1984 and 1996 were more worrisome on this score. This is one of our *Ideas for Beyond the Final Exam.*

---

### KEY TERMS

Mix of monetary and fiscal policy 685

Budget deficit 686

National debt 686

Structural deficit or surplus 689

Real versus nominal interest rates 690

Inflation accounting 690

Monetization of deficits 695

Crowding out 697

Crowding in 697

Burden of the national debt 698

---

### QUESTIONS FOR REVIEW

1. Explain the difference between the budget deficit and the national debt. If the deficit gets turned into a surplus, what happens to the debt?

2. Explain how the U.S. government managed to accumulate a debt of more than $5 trillion. To whom does it owe this debt? Can the debt be considered a burden on future generations?

3. Comment on the following: "Deficit spending paves the road to ruin. If we keep it up, the whole nation will go bankrupt. Even if things do not go this far, what right have we to burden our children and grandchildren with these debts while we live high on the hog?"

4. Calculate the budget deficit and the inflation-corrected deficit for an economy with the following data:

   Government expenditures other than interest = 1,400

   Tax receipts = 1,500

   Interest payments = 240

   Interest rate = 6 percent

   Inflation rate = 3 percent

   National debt at start of year = 4,000

   (*Note:* 6 percent interest on a $4,000 debt is $240.)

5. Explain in words why the *structural* budget might show a surplus while the *actual* budget is in deficit. Illustrate this with a diagram such as Figure 33–4.

6. If the Federal Reserve begins to increase the money supply more slowly than before, what will happen to the government budget deficit? (*Hint:* What will happen to tax receipts and interest expenses?) If the government wants to offset the effects of the Fed's actions on aggregate demand, what might it do? How will this affect the deficit?

7. Newspaper reports frequently suggest that the administration (regardless of who is president) is pressuring the Fed to lower interest rates. In view of your answer to Review Question 6, why do you think that might be?

8. Given the current state of the economy, what sort of fiscal-monetary policy mix seems most appropriate to you now? (*Note:* There is no one correct answer to this question. It is a good question to discuss in class.)

9. Explain the difference between crowding out and crowding in. Given the current state of the economy, which effect would you expect to dominate today?

CHAPTER

We must seek to reduce inflation at a lower cost
in lost output and unemployment.

Jimmy Carter

# THE PHILLIPS CURVE AND ECONOMIC GROWTH

It's nice to have everything you want, but in reality that is
an unattainable goal. Early in our discussion of macroeconomics (Chapter 24), we looked closely at the three
basic goals of macroeconomic policy: low unemployment,
low inflation, and rapid, sustained economic growth. But
the list of *Ideas for Beyond the Final Exam* in Chapter 1
noted a bothersome trade-off between inflation and unemployment: If we want lower inflation, we may have to
endure a period of high unemployment to get it. A statistical relationship called the *Phillips curve* seeks to summarize the quantitative dimensions of this trade-off.

The importance of the trade-off between inflation
and unemployment can hardly be overstated. This trade-
off is probably the macroeconomic issue where confusion

is most widespread. And because this confusion can have disastrous consequences for the conduct of stabilization policy, the trade-off merits the comprehensive examination that we give it in this chapter.

### Is the Trade-off between Inflation and Unemployment a Relic of the Past?

From 1996 to early 1999, unemployment in the United States fell to extremely low levels—the lowest in almost 30 years. Yet, in stark contrast to prior experience, inflation did not rise. In fact, it fell slightly. This pleasant conjunction of extremely low unemployment and falling inflation, nearly unprecedented in U.S. history, set many people talking about a "New Economy" in which there was no longer any trade-off between inflation and unemployment.

Is the long-feared trade-off really just a memory now? Can the modern U.S. economy speed along without fear of rising inflation? Or does faster growth eventually have inflationary consequences? These are the central questions for this chapter. Our answers, in brief, are: no, no, and yes, and we devote most of this chapter to explaining them.

## DEMAND-SIDE INFLATION VERSUS SUPPLY-SIDE INFLATION: A REVIEW

Because this chapter is the capstone of Part VII, we begin by reviewing some of what we learned about inflation in earlier chapters.

One major cause of inflation, though certainly not the only one, is *excessive growth of aggregate demand*. We know that any autonomous increase in spending—whether by consumers, investors, the government, or foreigners—will have a multiplier effect on aggregate demand. So each additional \$1 of $C$ or $I$ or $G$ or $X - IM$ will lead to more than \$1 of additional demand. We also know that firms normally find it profitable to supply additional output only at higher prices. Hence, a stimulus to aggregate demand will normally pull up *both* real output *and* prices.

Figure 34–1, which is familiar from earlier chapters, reviews this conclusion. Initially, the economy is at point $A$, where aggregate demand curve $D_0D_0$ intersects aggregate supply curve $SS$. Then something happens to increase spending, and the aggregate demand curve shifts horizontally to $D_1D_1$. The new equilibrium is at point $B$, where both prices and output are higher than they were at $A$. Thus, the economy has experienced some inflation along with increased output.

The slope of the aggregate supply curve measures the amount of inflation that accompanies any specified rise in output and therefore encapsulates the trade-off between inflation and economic growth. We observed in Chapter 32 that this trade-off looks rather different in the short run than in the long run because the aggregate supply curve is fairly flat in the short run but quite steep (perhaps even vertical) in the long run. Thus, a stimulus to demand mostly raises output (and thus lowers unemployment) in the short run but mostly raises prices in the long run.

**FIGURE 34–1**

**Inflation from the Demand Side**

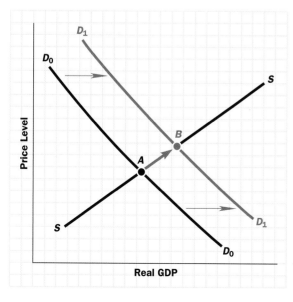

But we have learned in this book (especially in Chapter 28) that inflation does not always originate from the demand side. An impediment to the growth of aggregate supply—caused, for example, by an increase in the price of foreign oil—can shift the economy's aggregate supply curve inward. This sort of inflation is illustrated in Figure 34–2, where the aggregate supply curve shifts inward from $S_0S_0$ to $S_1S_1$. and the economy's equilibrium consequently moves from point $A$ to point $B$. Prices rise as output falls. We have *stagflation*.

Thus, although inflation can emanate from either the *demand* side or the *supply* side of the economy, a crucial difference arises between the two sources. Demand-side inflation is normally accompanied by rapid growth of real gross domestic product (GDP) (see Figure 34–1), whereas supply-side inflation may well be accompanied by falling GDP (see Figure 34–2). This is a distinction of major practical importance, as we shall see in this chapter.

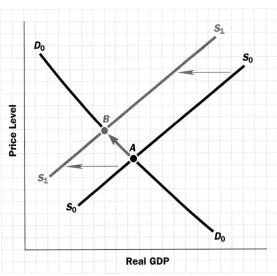

Inflation from the Supply Side

## APPLYING THE MODEL TO A GROWING ECONOMY

You may have noticed that since Chapter 23 we have been using the simple aggregate supply and aggregate demand model to determine the equilibrium *price level* and the equilibrium *level of real GDP*. But in the real world neither the price level nor real GDP remains constant for long. Instead, both normally rise from year to year.

The growth process is illustrated in Figure 34–3, which is a scatter diagram of the U.S. price level and the level of real GDP for every year from 1972 to 1998. The labeled points show the clear upward march of the economy through time—toward higher prices and higher levels of output.

The Price Level and Real GDP Output in the United States, 1972–1998

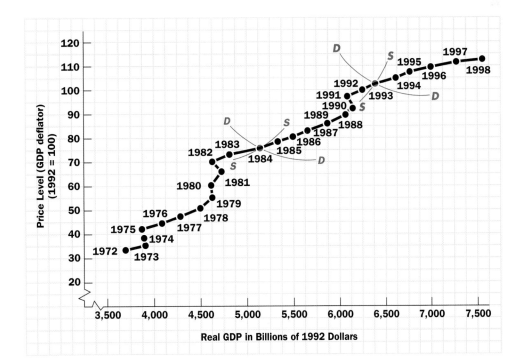

SOURCE: U.S. Department of Commerce, Bureau of Economic Analysis.

It is certainly no mystery why this occurs. As we have observed repeatedly, *both* the aggregate demand curve *and* the aggregate supply curve normally shift to the right each year. Aggregate supply grows because more workers join the workforce each year and because investment and technology improve productivity. Aggregate demand grows because a growing population generates more demand for both consumer and investment goods, because the government increases its spending, and because the Federal Reserve increases the money supply. We can think of each point in Figure 34–3 as the intersection of an aggregate supply curve and an aggregate demand curve for that particular year. To help you visualize this, the curves for 1984 and 1993 are sketched in the diagram.

Figure 34–4 is a more realistic version of a graph that we have been using since Chapter 23. It illustrates how our theoretical model of aggregate supply and demand applies to a growing economy. We have chosen the numbers so the black curves $D_0D_0$ and $S_0S_0$ roughly represent the year 1997, and the red curves $D_1D_1$ and $S_1S_1$ roughly represent 1998—except that we use nice round numbers to facilitate computations. Thus, the equilibrium in 1997 was at point *A*, with a real GDP of $8,000 billion (in 1997 dollars) and a price level of 100, whereas the equilibrium a year later was at point *B*, with real GDP at $8,320 billion and the price level at 102. The blue arrow in the diagram shows how equilibrium moved from 1997 to 1998. It points upward and to the right, meaning that both prices and output increased. In this case, the economy grew by 4 percent and prices rose 2 percent, which is roughly what happened in the United States. (In fact, real growth was 3.9 percent and inflation was only 1 percent.)

| | |
|---|---|
| **FIGURE 34-4** | |

**Aggregate Supply and Demand Analysis of a Growing Economy**

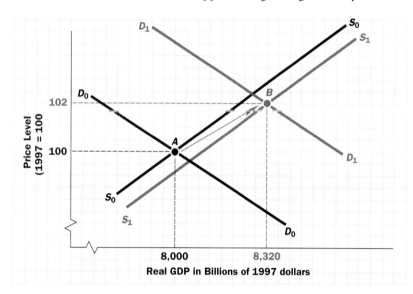

Real GDP in Billions of 1997 dollars

## DEMAND-SIDE INFLATION AND THE PHILLIPS CURVE

| | |
|---|---|
| **FIGURE 34-5** | |

**The Effects of Faster Growth of Aggregate Demand**

Let us now use our theoretical model to rerun history. Suppose that aggregate demand grew *faster* than it actually did between 1997 and 1998. What difference would this have made for the performance of the national economy? Figure 34–5 provides the answers. Here the black demand curve $D_0D_0$ is exactly the same as in the previous diagram, as are the two supply curves, showing a given rate of aggregate supply growth. But the red demand curve $D_2D_2$ lies farther to the right than the demand curve $D_1D_1$ in Figure 34–4. Equilibrium is at point *A* in 1997 and point *C* in 1998. Comparing point *C* in Figure 34–5 with point *B* in Figure 34–4, we see that output would have increased more over the year ($400 billion versus $320 billion) and prices would also have increased more (to 103 instead of 102); that is, the economy would have experienced more *inflation*. This is generally what happens when the growth rate of aggregate demand speeds up.

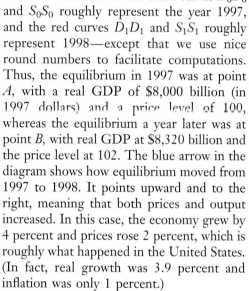

Real GDP in Billions of 1997 dollars

For any given rate of growth of the aggregate supply curve, a faster rate of growth of the aggregate demand curve will lead to more inflation and faster growth of real output.

Figure 34–6 illustrates the opposite case. Here, we imagine that the aggregate demand curve shifted out *less* than in Figure 34–4. That is, the red demand curve $D_3D_3$ in Figure 34–6 lies to the left of demand curve $D_1D_1$ in Figure 34–4. The consequence, we see, is that the shift of the economy's equilibrium from 1997 to 1998 (from point A to point E) would have entailed *less inflation* and *slower growth of real output* than actually took place. Again, such is generally the case when aggregate demand grows more slowly.

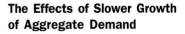

**FIGURE 34-6**

**The Effects of Slower Growth of Aggregate Demand**

> For any given rate of aggregate supply curve growth, a slower rate of growth of the aggregate demand curve will lead to less inflation and slower growth of real output.

If we put these two findings together, we have a clear prediction from our theory:

> If fluctuations in the economy's real growth rate from year to year arise primarily from variations in the rate at which aggregate *demand* increases, then the data should show the most rapid inflation occurring when output grows most rapidly and the slowest inflation occurring when output grows most slowly.

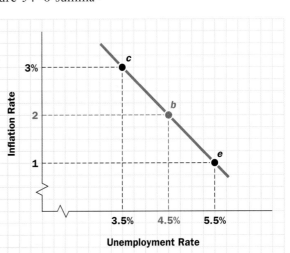

Does the theory fit the facts? We will put it to the test in a moment, but first let us translate this trade-off between inflation and *growth* into a corresponding trade-off between inflation and *unemployment*. Faster growth of real output naturally means faster growth in the number of jobs and, hence, *lower unemployment*. Conversely, slower growth of real output means slower growth in the number of jobs and, hence, *higher unemployment*. We conclude that, if business fluctuations emanate from the demand side, unemployment and inflation should move inversely: Unemployment should be low when inflation is high, and inflation should be low when unemployment is high.

Figure 34–7 illustrates this idea. The unemployment rate in the United States in 1998 averaged 4.5 percent, and the inflation rate in Figure 34–4 was 2 percent. Point *b* in Figure 34–7, which corresponds to equilibrium point *B* in Figure 34–4, records these two numbers. The faster growth rate of demand depicted by point *C* in Figure 34–5 would have led to higher inflation and lower unemployment. For the sake of a concrete example, we suppose that unemployment would have been 3.5 percent and inflation would have been 3 percent (as shown in Figure 34–5); this is point *c* in Figure 34–7. Point *E* in Figure 34–6 summarized the results of slower growth of aggregate demand: unemployment would have been higher and inflation lower. In Figure 34–7, these facts are represented by point *e*, with an unemployment rate of 5.5 percent and an inflation rate of 1 percent. This figure shows graphically the principal empirical implication of our theoretical model:

**FIGURE 34-7**

**Origins of the Phillips Curve**

> If fluctuations in economic activity are primarily caused by variations in the rate at which the aggregate demand curve shifts outward from year to year, then the data should show an inverse relationship between unemployment and inflation, as in Figure 34–7.

Now we are ready to look at real data. Do we actually observe such an inverse relationship between inflation and unemployment? More than 40 years ago, economist A. W. Phillips plotted data on unemployment and the rate of

FIGURE 34-8

## The Original Phillips Curve

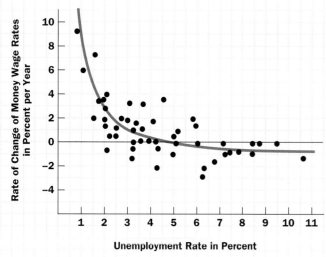

SOURCE: A. W. Phillips, "The Relation between Unemployment and the Rate of Change of Money Wages in the United Kingdom, 1861–1957," *Economica,* New Series, 25 (November 1958).

change of money *wages* (not prices) for several extended periods of British history on a series of scatter diagrams, one of which is reproduced as Figure 34–8. He then sketched in a curve that seemed to "fit" the data well. This type of curve, which we now call a **Phillips curve,** shows that wage inflation normally is high when unemployment is low and is low when unemployment is high. So far, so good. These data illustrate the short run trade-off between inflation and unemployment, one of our *Ideas for Beyond the Final Exam.*

Phillips curves have also been constructed for *price* inflation, and one such diagram for the postwar United States is shown in Figure 34–9. The curve appears to fit the data well. As viewed through the eyes of our theory, these facts suggest that economic fluctuations in Great Britain between 1861 and 1913 and in the United States between 1954 and 1969 probably arose primarily from changes in the growth of aggregate demand. The simple model of demand-side inflation really does seem to describe what happened.

During the 1960s and early 1970s, economists often thought of the Phillips curve as a "menu" of choices available to policymakers. In this view, policymakers could opt for low unemployment and high inflation—as in 1969. Or they might prefer higher unemployment coupled with lower inflation—as, for example, in 1961. The Phillips curve, it was thought, described the *quantitative* trade-off between inflation and unemployment, and for a number of years it seemed to work.

FIGURE 34-9

## A Phillips Curve for the United States, 1954–1969

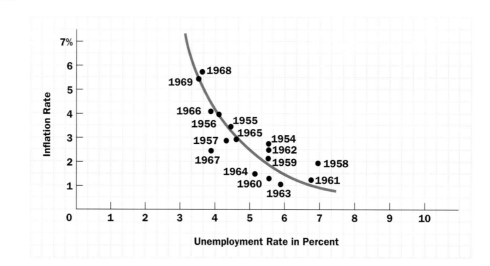

A **Phillips curve** is a graph depicting the rate of unemployment on the horizontal axis and either the rate of inflation or the rate of change of money wages on the vertical axis. Phillips curves are normally downward sloping, indicating that higher inflation rates are associated with lower unemployment rates.

Then something happened. The economy in the 1970s and early 1980s behaved far worse than the Phillips curve led economists to expect. In particular, given the unemployment rates in each of those years, inflation was astonishingly high by historical standards. This fact is shown in Figure 34–10, which simply adds to Figure 34–9 the points for 1970 to 1984. Clearly something had gone wrong with the old view of the Phillips curve as a menu for policy choices. But what?

## ■ SUPPLY-SIDE INFLATION AND THE COLLAPSE OF THE PHILLIPS CURVE

There are two major answers to this question, and a full explanation contains elements of each. We begin with the simpler answer, which is that much of the inflation of the period from 1972 to 1982 did not emanate from the demand side. Instead, the 1970s and early 1980s were full of adverse "supply shocks"—events such as the crop failures of 1972–1973 and the oil price increases of 1973–1974 and 1979–1980. These events pushed the economy's aggregate supply curve inward to the left. What kind of Phillips curve will be generated when economic fluctuations come from the supply side?

To find out, let us take the events of 1979 and 1980 as an example. In Figure 34–11, the black aggregate demand curve $D_0D_0$ and aggregate supply curve $S_0S_0$ represent the economic situation in 1979. Equilibrium was at point $A$, with a price level of 55 and real output of $4,631 billion. By 1980, the aggregate demand curve had shifted out to the position indicated by the red curve $D_1D_1$, and, under normal conditions, the aggregate supply curve would have shifted out as well. But 1979 to 1980 was anything but normal. The Iranian revolution led to a long shutdown of Iran's oil fields, and the price of oil doubled.

Thus, instead of shifting *outward* as it normally does from one year to the next, the aggregate supply curve shifted *inward* from 1979 to 1980, to the red curve $S_1S_1$. The equilibrium for 1980 (point $B$ in the figure) therefore wound up to the left of the equilibrium point for 1979. Real output declined slightly and prices—led by energy costs—rose rapidly.

Now, in a growing population with more people looking for jobs each year, a stagnant economy that does not generate new jobs suffers a rise in the unemployment rate. This is precisely what happened in the United States; the unemployment rate averaged 5.8 percent in 1979 and 7.1 percent in 1980. Thus, inflation and unemployment increased at the same time: The Phillips curve basically shifted upward. The general conclusion is:

> If fluctuations in economic activity emanate from the supply side, higher rates of inflation will be associated with higher rates of unemployment, and lower rates of inflation will be associated with lower rates of unemployment.

The major supply shocks of the 1970s stand out clearly in Figure 34–10. (Remember these are *real* data, not textbook examples.) Food prices soared from 1972 to 1974 and again in 1978. Energy prices skyrocketed in 1973–1974 and again in 1979–1980. Clearly, the inflation and unemployment data generated by the U.S. economy from 1972 to 1974, and again in 1978–1980, are consistent with our model of supply-side inflation. Many economists believe that supply shocks, rather than abrupt changes in aggregate demand, made the Phillips curve shift.

### EXPLAINING THE 1990s

Now let's stand this analysis of supply shocks on its head. Suppose the economy experiences a *favorable* supply shock, rather than an adverse one, so that the aggregate supply curve shifts *outward* at an unusually rapid rate. Any number of

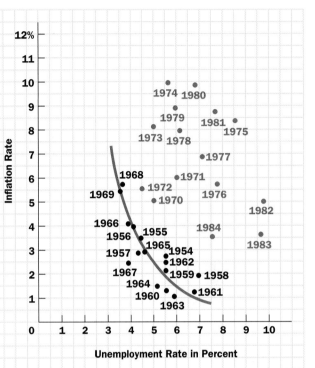

FIGURE 34–10

**A Phillips Curve for the United States?**

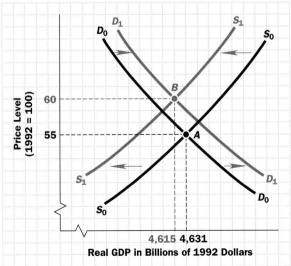

FIGURE 34–11

**Stagflation from an Adverse Supply Shock**

FIGURE 34-12

**The Effects of a Favorable Supply Shock**

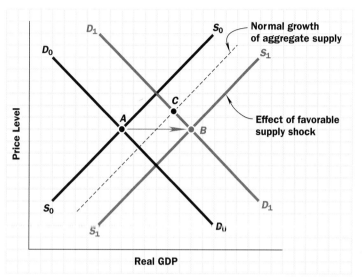

factors—such as a drop in oil prices, bountiful harvests, or exceptionally rapid technological advance—can have this effect.

Whatever the cause, Figure 34–12 depicts the consequences. The aggregate demand curve shifts out from $D_0D_0$ to $D_1D_1$ as usual, but the aggregate supply curve shifts all the way out to $S_1S_1$. (The dotted line indicates what would happen in a "normal" year.) So the economy's equilibrium winds up at point $B$ rather than at point $C$. Compared to $C$, point $B$ represents *faster economic growth* ($B$ is to the right of $C$) and *lower inflation* ($B$ is lower than $C$). In brief, the economy wins on both fronts: Inflation falls while rapid growth reduces unemployment.

Figure 34–12 more or less characterizes the experience of the U.S. economy from 1996 to 1998. Oil prices plummeted, lowering costs to American businesses and households. Stunning advances in technology made computer prices drop even more rapidly than usual. And the rising value of the U.S. dollar made imported goods cheaper to Americans.[1] Thus, we benefited from a series of favorable supply shocks, and the effects were just as depicted in Figure 34–12. The U.S. economy grew rapidly, and both inflation and unemployment fell at the same time.

**Why Inflation and Unemployment Both Declined**

So we now have the answer to the question posed at the start of this chapter. We need nothing particularly new or mysterious to explain the marvelous economic performance of the second half of the 1990s. According to the basic macroeconomic theory taught in this book, favorable supply shocks *should* produce rapid economic growth with falling inflation. The U.S. economy did so well because we were so fortunate.

## WHAT THE PHILLIPS CURVE IS NOT

So one view is that adverse supply shocks caused the stagflation of the 1970s and 1980s. But there is another view of what went wrong. This one holds that policymakers misinterpreted the Phillips curve and tried to pick combinations of inflation and unemployment that were simply unsustainable.

Specifically, the Phillips curve is a *statistical relationship* between inflation and unemployment that we expect to emerge *if business cycle fluctuations arise mainly from changes in the growth of aggregate demand.* But the curve was widely misinterpreted as depicting a number of *alternative equilibrium points* that the economy could achieve and from which policymakers could choose.

We can understand the flaw in this reasoning by quickly reviewing an earlier lesson. We know from Chapter 28 that the economy has a *self-correcting mechanism* that will cure both inflations and recessions *eventually*, even if the government does nothing. Why is this relevant here? Because it tells us that many combinations of output and prices cannot be maintained indefinitely. Some will self-destruct. Specifically, if the economy finds itself far away from the normal full-employment level of unemployment, forces will be set in motion that tend to erode the inflationary or recessionary gap.

---

[1] This point will be discussed in detail in Chapter 37.

Figure 34–13 depicts the case of a recessionary gap where aggregate supply curve $S_0S_0$ intersects aggregate demand curve $DD$ at point $A$. With equilibrium output well below potential GDP, the economy has unused industrial capacity and unsold output. So firms will not raise prices much. At the same time, the availability of unemployed workers eager for jobs limits the rate at which labor can push up wage rates. But wages are the main component of business costs, so when wages decline (relative to what they would have been without a recession) so do costs. And lower costs stimulate greater production. Figure 34–13 illustrates this idea as an outward shift of the aggregate supply curve—from $S_0S_0$ to the red curve $S_1S_1$.

As the figure shows, the outward shift of the aggregate supply curve brought on by the recession pushes equilibrium output up as the economy moves from point $A$ to point $B$. Thus, the size of the recessionary gap begins to shrink. This process continues until the aggregate supply curve reaches the position indicated by the blue curve $S_2S_2$ in Figure 34–13. Here wages have fallen enough to eliminate the recessionary gap, and the economy has reached a full-employment equilibrium at point $C$.[2]

We can relate this to our discussion of the origins of the Phillips curve with the help of Figure 34–14, which is a hypothetical Phillips curve. Point $a$ in Figure 34–14 corresponds to point $A$ in Figure 34–13: It shows the initial recessionary gap with unemployment (assumed to be 6.5 percent) above full employment, which we assume to occur at 5 percent.

But we have just seen that point $A$ in Figure 34–13—and therefore also point $a$ in Figure 34–14—is not sustainable. The economy tends to rid itself of the recessionary gap through the disinflation process we have just described. The adjustment path from $A$ to $C$ depicted in Figure 34–13 would appear on our Phillips curve diagram as a movement toward less inflation and less unemployment—something like the blue arrow from point $a$ to point $c$ in Figure 34–14.

Similarly, points representing inflationary gaps—such as point $d$ in Figure 34–14—are also not sustainable. They too are gradually eliminated by the self-correcting mechanism that we studied in Chapter 28. Wages are forced up by the abnormally low unemployment, and this in turn pushes prices higher. Higher prices deter investment spending by forcing up interest rates, and they deter consumer spending by lowering the purchasing power of consumer wealth. The inflationary process continues until the amount people want to spend is brought into balance with the amount firms want to supply at normal full employment. During such an adjustment period, unemployment and inflation both rise—as indicated by the blue arrow from point $d$ to point $f$ in Figure 34–14.

Putting these two conclusions together, we see that:

On a Phillips curve diagram such as Figure 34–14, neither points corresponding to an inflationary gap (like point $d$) nor points corresponding to a recessionary gap (like

FIGURE 34-13

**The Elimination of a Recessionary Gap**

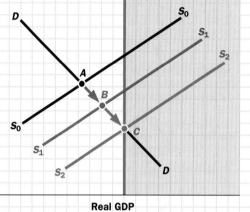

FIGURE 34-14

**The Vertical Long-Run Phillips Curve**

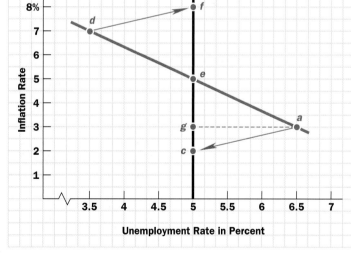

[2] This simple analysis assumes that the aggregate demand curve does not move during the adjustment period. If it is shifting to the right, the recessionary gap will disappear even faster, but inflation will not slow down as much. *Exercise:* Construct the diagram for this case by adding a shift of the aggregate demand curve to Figure 34–13.

point *a*) can be maintained indefinitely. Inflationary gaps lead to rising unemployment and rising inflation. Recessionary gaps lead to falling inflation and falling unemployment.

All the points that are sustainable in the long run (such as *c*, *e*, and *f*) correspond to the same rate of unemployment, which is therefore called the **natural rate of unemployment.** The natural rate corresponds to what we have so far been calling the "full-employment" unemployment rate.

> The economy's self-correcting mechanism always tends to push the unemployment rate back toward a specific rate of unemployment that we call the **natural rate of unemployment.**

Thus, the Phillips curve connecting points *d*, *e*, and *a* is not a menu of policy choices at all. Although we can move from a point like *e* to a point like *d* by stimulating aggregate demand sufficiently, the economy will not be able to stay at point *d*. We cannot keep unemployment this low indefinitely. Instead, policymakers must choose from among points like *c*, *e*, and *f*, all of which correspond to the same "natural" rate of unemployment. For obvious reasons, the line connecting these points has been dubbed the **vertical long-run Phillips curve.** It is this vertical Phillips curve, connecting points like *e* and *f*, that represents the true long-run menu of policy choices. We thus conclude:

> The **vertical (long-run) Phillips curve** shows the menu of inflation/unemployment choices available to society in the long run. It is a vertical straight line at the natural rate of unemployment.

**THE INFLATION-UNEMPLOYMENT TRADE-OFF** In the short run, it is possible to "ride up the Phillips curve" toward lower levels of unemployment by stimulating aggregate demand. (See, for example, point *d* in Figure 34–14.) Conversely, by restricting the growth of demand, it is possible to "ride down the Phillips curve" toward lower rates of inflation (like point *a* in Figure 34–14). Thus, there is a *trade-off between unemployment and inflation* in the short run. Stimulating demand will improve the unemployment picture but worsen inflation; restricting demand will lower inflation but aggravate the unemployment problem.

However, *there is no such trade-off in the long run.* The economy's self-correcting mechanism ensures that unemployment eventually returns to the "natural rate" no matter what happens to aggregate demand. In the long run, faster growth of demand leads only to higher inflation, not to lower unemployment; and slower growth of demand leads only to lower inflation, not to higher unemployment.

> *The Short-Run Trade-off between Inflation and Unemployment*

## FIGHTING UNEMPLOYMENT WITH FISCAL AND MONETARY POLICY

Now let us apply this analysis to a concrete policy problem, one that has troubled many U.S. presidents and the leaders of many foreign countries as well. Should the government's ability to manage aggregate demand through fiscal and monetary policy be used to combat unemployment? If so, how?

Because unemployment in the United States has been low since late 1994, we must go back to early 1993 for a real-world example. When President Clinton took office in January 1993, the inflation rate was about 3 percent and the unemployment rate was about 7 percent—a starting point quite similar to point *a* in Figure 34–14. The president considered 7 percent unemployment intolerably high. What were his options? Should he have adopted a policy of boosting the growth of aggregate demand by expansionary fiscal and/or monetary policies?

Suppose first that the government did nothing. The economy's self-correcting mechanism would have gradually eroded the recessionary gap that existed at point *a*. Both unemployment and inflation would have declined gradually as the economy moved along the blue arrow from point *a* to point *c* in Figure 34–14. Eventually, the diagram shows, the economy would have returned to its natural rate of unemployment (assumed here to be 5 percent) and inflation would have fallen—from 3 percent to 2 percent.

This eventual outcome is quite satisfactory—lower unemployment *and* lower inflation. But it may take an agonizingly long time to get there. Suppose now that the president was impatient and wanted to see unemployment decline much faster. A large dose of expansionary fiscal and monetary policy could have pushed the economy up the short-run Phillips curve from point *a* toward point *e* in Figure 34–14. The faster economic growth and lower unemployment would have made the president (and the voters) happy. But it would also have left us with higher inflation, roughly 5 percent in the example.

This, then, is the range of choices: Wait patiently while the economy's self-correcting mechanism pulls unemployment down to the natural rate—leading to a long-run equilibrium like point *c* in Figure 34–14. Or rush the process along with expansionary stabilization policy—and wind up with the same unemployment rate but higher inflation. In what sense, then, do policymakers face a *trade-off* between inflation and unemployment? The answer is:

> **The cost of reducing unemployment more rapidly by expansionary fiscal and monetary policies is a permanently higher inflation rate.**

## ■ WHAT SHOULD BE DONE?

Should the government pay the inflationary costs of fighting unemployment? When the transitory benefit (lower unemployment for a while) is balanced against the permanent cost (higher inflation), have we made a good bargain?

The United States opted for an intermediate strategy in 1993–1994. The Federal Reserve had embarked on an expansionary monetary policy to reduce unemployment well before President Clinton was elected, and it maintained this policy into early 1994. So two forces were at work simultaneously: The self-correcting mechanism was pulling the economy toward point *c* in Figure 34–14, and the Fed's expansionary policy was pushing it toward point *e*. The net result was an intermediate path (shown as the dotted line) leading to a point like *g*. By the end of 1994, the unemployment rate was down to about 5.5 percent and inflation remained around 3 percent. How do policymakers make such decisions? Our analysis highlights three critical issues on which the answer depends.

### THE COSTS OF INFLATION AND UNEMPLOYMENT

In Chapter 24 we examined the social costs of inflation and unemployment. Most of the benefits of lower unemployment, we concluded, translate easily into dollars and cents. Basically, we need only estimate the higher real GDP each year. However, the costs of the permanently higher inflation rate are harder to measure. So, there is considerable controversy over the costs and benefits of using demand management to fight unemployment.

Economists and political leaders who believe that inflation is extremely costly may deem it unwise to accept the inflationary consequences of reducing unemployment faster. As just noted, U.S. policymakers apparently disagreed with that view in 1993—they decided that reducing unemployment was more important. But many European countries made different decisions in the 1980s and 1990s. Their governments generally avoided expansionary stabilization policies rather than accept higher inflation.

### THE SLOPE OF THE (SHORT-RUN) PHILLIPS CURVE

The shape of the short-run Phillips curve is also critical. Look back at Figure 34–14, and now suppose that the Phillips curve connecting points *a* and *e* was much steeper than shown. In that case, the inflationary costs of using expansionary policy to reduce unemployment would be more substantial. On the other hand, if the short-run Phillips curve was much flatter than the one shown in Figure 34–14, unemployment could be reduced with little inflationary cost.

### THE EFFICIENCY OF THE ECONOMY'S SELF-CORRECTING MECHANISM

We have emphasized that, once a recessionary gap opens, the economy's natural self-correcting mechanism will eventually close it—even in the absence of any policy response. The obvious question is: How long must we wait? If the self-correcting mechanism—which works through reductions in the rate of wage inflation—is fast and reliable, high unemployment will not last very long so that the costs of waiting will be small. But if wage inflation responds only slowly to unemployment, the costs of waiting may be enormous. That has evidently been true in much of Europe, where unemployment has remained persistently high for years.

The efficacy of the self-correcting mechanism is also surrounded by controversy. Most economists believe that the weight of the evidence points to extremely sluggish wage behavior. Wage inflation appears to respond slowly to economic slack. In terms of our Figure 34–14, this means that the economy will traverse the path from *a* to *c* at an agonizingly slow pace, so that a long period of weak economic activity will be necessary to appreciably affect inflation.

But a significant minority opinion finds this assessment far too pessimistic. Economists in this group argue that the costs of reducing inflation are not nearly so severe and that the key to a successful anti-inflation policy is how it affects people's *expectations* of inflation. To understand this argument, we must first understand why expectations are relevant to the Phillips curve.

## ■ INFLATIONARY EXPECTATIONS AND THE PHILLIPS CURVE

Recall from Chapter 28 that the main reason why the economy's aggregate supply curve slopes upward—that is, why output increases as the price level rises—is that businesses typically purchase labor and other inputs under long-term contracts that fix input costs in *money* terms. (The money wage rate is the clearest example.) If such contracts are in force when prices of goods rise, then *real* wages fall. Labor therefore becomes cheaper in real terms, which persuades businesses to expand employment and output. Buying low and selling high is, after all, the mantra for higher profits.

Table 34–1 illustrates how this works in a concrete example. We suppose that workers and firms agree today that the money wage to be paid a year from now will be $10 per hour. The table then shows the real wage corresponding to each alternative inflation rate. For example, if inflation is 4 percent, the real wage a year from now will be $10.00/1.04 = $9.62. Clearly, the higher the inflation rate, the higher the price level at the end of the year and the lower the real wage.

Lower real wages provide an incentive for the firm to increase output, as we have just noted. But lower real wages also impose purchasing power losses on workers. Thus, workers are, in some sense, "cheated" by inflation if they sign a contract specifying a fixed money wage in an inflationary environment.

Many economists doubt that workers will sign such contracts *if they can see inflation coming.* Would it not be wiser, these economists ask, to insist on being compensated for inflation? After all, firms should be willing to offer higher money wages if they expect inflation, because they realize that higher money wages need not imply higher *real* wages.

| TABLE 34–1 | **Money and Real Wages under Unexpected Inflation** |

| Inflation Rate | Price Level 1 Year from Now | Wage per Hour 1 Year from Now | Real Wage per Hour 1 Year from |
|---|---|---|---|
| 0% | 100 | $10.00 | $10.00 |
| 2 | 102 | 10.00 | 9.80 |
| 4 | 104 | 10.00 | 9.62 |
| 6 | 106 | 10.00 | 9.43 |

NOTE: Each real wage figure is obtained by dividing the $10 nominal wage by the corresponding price level a year later and multiplying by 100. Thus, for example, when the inflation rate is 4 percent, the real wage at the end of the year is ($10.00/104) × 100 = $9.62.

TABLE 34-2

## Money and Real Wages under Expected Inflation

| Expected Inflation Rate | Expected Price Level 1 Year from Now | Wage per Hour 1 Year from Now | Expected Real Wage per Hour 1 Year from Now |
|---|---|---|---|
| 0% | 100 | $10.00 | $10.00 |
| 2 | 102 | 10.20 | 10.00 |
| 4 | 104 | 10.40 | 10.00 |
| 6 | 106 | 10.60 | 10.00 |

Table 34–2 illustrates how this can be done. For example, if people expect 4 percent inflation, the contract could stipulate that the wage rate be increased to $10.40 (which is 4 percent more than $10) at the end of the year. That would keep the real wage at $10 (since $10.40/1.04 = $10.00), the same as it would be under zero inflation. The other money wage figures in Table 34–2 are derived similarly.

If workers and firms behave this way, and if they forecast inflation accurately, then the real wage will not decline as the price level rises. Instead, prices and wages will go up together, leaving the real wage unchanged. Workers will not lose from inflation, and firms will not gain. (In Table 34–2, the expected future real wage is $10 per hour regardless of the expected inflation rate.) But then there would be no reason for firms to raise production when the price level rises. In a word, the aggregate supply curve would become *vertical*. In general:

> If workers can see inflation coming, and if they receive compensation for it, inflation does not erode *real* wages. But if real wages do not fall, firms have no incentives to increase production. So the economy's aggregate supply curve will not slope upward. It will, instead, be a vertical line at the level of output corresponding to potential GDP.

Such a curve is shown in Panel (a) of Figure 34–15. Because we derived the Phillips curve from the aggregate supply curve earlier in the chapter, it follows that even the *short-run* Phillips curve would be vertical under these circumstances, as in Panel (b) of Figure 34–15.[3]

If this analysis is correct, it has profound implications for the costs and benefits of fighting inflation. To see this, refer once again to Figure 34–14, but now use the graph to depict the strategy of fighting inflation by causing a recession. Suppose we start at point *e*, with 5 percent inflation. In order to move to point *c* (representing 2 percent inflation), the economy must take a long and unpleasant detour through point *a*. Specifically, contractionary policies must push the economy down the Phillips curve toward point *a* before the self-correcting mechanism takes over and moves the economy from *a* to *c*. In other words, we must endure a recession to reduce inflation.

But what if even the *short-run* Phillips curve were *vertical* rather than downward sloping? Then this unpleasant recessionary detour would not be necessary. It would be possible

FIGURE 34-15

**A Vertical Aggregate Supply Curve and the Corresponding Vertical Phillips Curve**

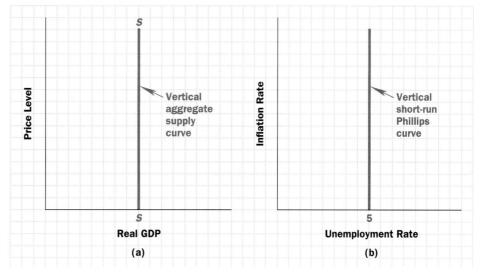

(a) Real GDP — Price Level — *S* — Vertical aggregate supply curve

(b) Unemployment Rate — Inflation Rate — Vertical short-run Phillips curve

---

[3] See Review Question 7 at the end of the chapter.

for inflation to fall without unemployment rising. The economy could jump directly from point *e* to point *c*.

Is this analysis correct? Can we really slay the inflationary dragon so painlessly? Not necessarily, for our discussion of expectations so far has made at least one unrealistic assumption: that businesses and workers can predict inflation accurately. Under this assumption, as Table 34–2 shows, real wages are unaffected by inflation—leaving the aggregate supply curve vertical, even in the short run.

But forecasts of inflation are often inaccurate. Suppose workers underestimate inflation. For example, suppose they expect 4 percent inflation but actually get 6 percent. Then real wages will decline by 2 percent. More generally, real wages will fall if workers underestimate inflation *at all*. The effect of inflation on real wages will be somewhere in between those shown in Tables 34–1 and 34–2.[4] So firms will retain some incentive to raise production as the price level rises. The aggregate supply curve will remain upward sloping. We thus conclude that:

> The short-run aggregate supply curve is *vertical* when inflation is predicted accurately but *upward sloping* when inflation is underestimated. Thus, only *unexpectedly* high inflation will raise output, because only unexpected inflation reduces real wages. (To see this, compare Tables 34–1 and 34–2.) Similarly, only an *unexpected* decline in inflation will lead to a recession.

Because people often fail to anticipate changes in inflation correctly, this seems to leave our earlier analysis of the Phillips curve almost intact. Indeed, most economists nowadays believe that the Phillips curve slopes downward in the short run but is vertical in the long run.

## ■ THE THEORY OF RATIONAL EXPECTATIONS

However, a vocal minority of economists—led by Nobel Prize winner Robert Lucas of the University of Chicago—disagrees. This group, believers in the hypothesis of *rational expectations*, insists that the Phillips curve is vertical even in the short run. To understand their point of view, we must first explain what rational expectations are. Then we will be in a position to see why rational expectations have such radical implications for the trade-off between inflation and unemployment.

### WHAT ARE RATIONAL EXPECTATIONS?

In many economic contexts, people must formulate expectations about what the future will bring. For example, those who invest in the stock market need to forecast the future prices of the stocks they buy and sell. And we have just discussed why workers and businesses may want to forecast future prices before agreeing on a money wage. **Rational expectations** is a controversial hypothesis about how such forecasts are made.

As used by economists, a forecast (an "expectation") of a future variable is considered rational if the forecaster makes *optimal* use of all *relevant* information that is *available* at the time of the forecast. Let us elaborate on the italicized words in this definition, using as an example a hypothetical stock market investor who has rational expectations.

First, proponents of rational expectations recognize that *information is limited*. An investor interested in buying Coca-Cola stock would like to know how much profit the company will make in the coming years. Armed with such information, she could predict the future price of Coke stock more accurately. But that information

**Rational expectations** are forecasts that, while not necessarily correct, are the best that can be made given the available data. Rational expectations, therefore, cannot err systematically. If expectations are rational, forecasting errors are pure random numbers.

---

[4] To make sure you understand why, construct a version of Table 34–2 based on the assumption that workers expect 4 percent inflation (and hence set next year's wage at $10.40 per hour), regardless of what the actual rate of inflation is. If you do this correctly, your table will show that higher inflation leads to lower real wages, as in Table 34–1.

is simply not available. Her forecast of the future price of Coke stock is not "irrational" just because she does not know Coca-Cola's future profits. On the other hand, if Coke stock normally goes down on Fridays and up on Mondays, she should be aware of this fact.

Next, we have the word *optimal.* As used by economists, this means using proper statistical inference to process all the relevant information that is available before making a forecast. In brief, to have rational expectations, your forecasts do not have to be correct, but they cannot have systematic errors that you could avoid by applying better statistical methods. This requirement, although exacting, is not quite as outlandish as it may seem. A good billiards player makes expert use of the laws of physics even without understanding the theory. Similarly, an experienced stock market investor may make good use of information even without formal training in statistics.

## RATIONAL EXPECTATIONS AND THE TRADE-OFF

Let us now see how some economists have used the hypothesis of rational expectations to deny any trade-off between inflation and unemployment—even in the short run.

Although they recognize that inflation cannot always be predicted accurately, proponents of rational expectations insist that workers will not make *systematic* errors. Our argument leading to a sloping short-run Phillips curve tacitly assumed that workers normally *under*estimate changes—they thus underestimate inflation when it is rising and *over*estimate inflation when it is falling. Many observers believe that this realistically describes human behavior. But advocates of rational expectations claim that it is fundamentally illogical. Workers, they argue, will always make the best possible forecast of inflation, using all the latest data and the best available economic models. Such forecasts will sometimes be too high and sometimes be too low, but they will not err systematically in one direction or the other. Consequently:

If expectations are rational, the difference between the *actual* rate of inflation and the *expected* rate of inflation (the forecasting error) must be a purely random number, that is:

Inflation = Expected inflation + A random number

Now recall that the argument in the section on inflationary expectations and the Phillips curve concluded that employment is affected by inflation only to the extent that inflation *differs* from what was expected. But, under rational expectations, no *predictable* change in inflation can make the *expected* rate of inflation deviate from the *actual* rate of inflation. Such deviations are purely random. Hence, according to the rational expectations hypothesis, unemployment will always remain at the natural rate—except for random, and therefore totally unpredictable gyrations due to forecasting errors. Thus:

If expectations are rational, the inflation rate can be reduced without a period of high unemployment because the short-run Phillips curve, like the long-run Phillips curve, will be vertical.

According to the rational expectations view, the government's ability to manipulate aggregate demand gives it no ability to control real output and unemployment because the aggregate supply curve is vertical—even in the short run. (To see why, experiment by moving an aggregate demand curve when the aggregate supply curve is vertical, as in Figure 34–15[a].) The government's manipulations of aggregate demand are planned ahead and are therefore predictable, and any *predictable* change in aggregate demand will change the *expected* rate of inflation. It will therefore leave real wages unaffected.

The government can influence output only by making *unexpected* changes in aggregate demand. But that is not easy to do if expectations are rational, because people will understand what policymakers are up to. If the monetary and fiscal authorities typically react to high inflation by reducing aggregate demand, people will soon come to anticipate this reaction. And anticipated reductions in aggregate demand do not cause *unexpected* changes in inflation.

## AN EVALUATION

Believers in rational expectations are optimistic that we can reduce inflation without losing any output, even in the short run. Are they right?

As a piece of pure logic, the rational expectations argument is impeccable. But as is common in economic policy, controversy arises over how best to apply the idea in practice. Although the theory has attracted some adherents, the evidence to date leads most economists to reject the extreme rational expectationist position in favor of the view that a trade-off between inflation and unemployment does exist in the short run. Here are some of the reasons.

**CONTRACTS MAY EMBODY OUTDATED EXPECTATIONS**   Many contracts for labor and other raw materials cover such long periods of time that the expectations on which they were based, although rational at the time, may appear quite irrational from today's point of view. For example, some three-year labor contracts were drawn up in 1980, when inflation was above 10 percent. It might have been rational then to expect the 1984 price level to be 30 percent above the 1981 price level and to have set 1984 wages accordingly. By late 1982, inflation had tumbled dramatically and such an expectation would have been plainly irrational. But it might already have been written into contracts. If so, real wages would have wound up much higher than intended, giving firms a powerful incentive to reduce output and therefore employment—even though no one behaved irrationally.

**EXPECTATIONS MAY ADJUST SLOWLY**   Many people believe that inflationary expectations do not adapt as quickly to changes in the economic environment as the rational expectations hypothesis assumes. If, for example, the government embarks on an anti-inflation policy, workers may continue to expect high inflation for a while. Thus, they may continue to insist on rapid money wage increases. Then, if inflation actually slows down, real wages will rise faster than anyone expected, and unemployment will result. Such behavior may not be strictly *rational*. But, to many observers, it seems realistic.

**WHEN DO WORKERS RECEIVE COMPENSATION FOR INFLATION?**   Some observers question whether wage agreements typically compensate workers for *expected* inflation *in advance*, as assumed by the rational expectations theory. More typically, they argue, wages catch up to *actual* inflation *after the fact*. If so, real wages will be eroded by inflation, as in the conventional view.

**WHAT THE FACTS SHOW**   The facts have not been kind to the rational expectations point of view. The theory suggests that unemployment should hover around the natural rate most of the time, with random gyrations in one direction or the other. Yet this does not seem to be the case. The theory also predicts that preannounced (and thus expected) anti-inflation programs should be relatively painless. Yet, in practice, fighting inflation has been very costly in virtually every country. Finally, many direct tests of the rationality of expectations have cast doubt on the hypothesis. For example, survey data on people's expectations rarely meet the exacting requirements of rationality.

But all these problems with rational expectations should not obscure a basic truth. In the long run, the rational expectations viewpoint should be more or less appropriate, because people will not cling to incorrect expectations indefinitely. As Abraham Lincoln said, you cannot fool all of the people all of the time.

## ■  WHY ECONOMISTS (AND POLITICIANS) DISAGREE

This chapter has now taught us some of the reasons why economists often disagree about the proper conduct of national economic policy. It also helps us understand some of the related political debates.

Should the government take stern actions to prevent or reduce inflation? You will say *yes* if you believe that (1) inflation is more costly than unemployment,

(2) the short-run Phillips curve is steep, (3) expectations react quickly, and (4) the economy's self-correcting mechanism works smoothly and rapidly. These views on the economy tend to be held by monetarists and rational expectationists and by the (generally conservative) politicians who listen to them.

But you will say *no* if you believe that (1) unemployment is more costly than inflation, (2) the short-run Phillips curve is flat, (3) expectations react sluggishly, and (4) the self-correcting mechanism is slow or unreliable. These views are held by many Keynesian economists, so it is not surprising that the (generally liberal) politicians who follow their advice often oppose using recession to fight inflation.

The tables turn, however, when the question is whether to use demand management to bring a recession to a rapid end. The Keynesian view of the world—that unemployment is costly, that the short-run Phillips curve is flat, that expectations adjust slowly, and that the self-correcting mechanism is unreliable—leads to the conclusion that the benefits of fighting unemployment are high whereas the costs are low. Keynesians are therefore eager to fight recessions. The monetarist and rational expectationist positions on these four issues are precisely the reverse, and so are the policy conclusions.

## ■ THE DILEMMA OF DEMAND MANAGEMENT

We have seen that the makers of monetary and fiscal policy face an unavoidable trade-off. If they stimulate aggregate demand to reduce unemployment, they will aggravate inflation. If they restrict aggregate demand to fight inflation, they will cause higher unemployment.

But wait. Early in the chapter we learned that when inflation comes from the supply side, inflation and unemployment are *positively* correlated: We suffer from more of both or enjoy less of each. Does this mean that monetary and fiscal policymakers can escape the trade-off between inflation and unemployment? Certainly not.

### THE TRADE-OFF BETWEEN INFLATION AND UNEMPLOYMENT

Adverse shifts in the aggregate supply curve can cause both inflation and unemployment to rise together, and thus can destroy the statistical Phillips curve relationship. Nevertheless, anything that monetary and fiscal policy can do will make unemployment and inflation move in *opposite* directions because monetary and fiscal policies give the government control only over the *aggregate demand* curve, not over the *aggregate supply* curve.

Thus, no matter what the source of inflation, and no matter what happens to the Phillips curve, the monetary and fiscal policy authorities must still face the disagreeable trade-off between inflation and unemployment. This is a principle that many policymakers have failed to recognize, and it is one of the *Ideas* that we hope you will remember well *Beyond the Final Exam*.

*The Short-Run Trade-off between Inflation and Unemployment*

Naturally, the unpleasant nature of this trade-off has led both economists and public officials to search for a way out of the dilemma. The rest of this chapter—including the accompanying Policy Debate box, "Should the Fed Concentrate Only on Reducing Inflation?"—considers some of these ideas, none of which are panaceas.

## ■ ATTEMPTS TO REDUCE THE NATURAL RATE OF UNEMPLOYMENT

One highly desirable approach—if only we knew how to do it—would be to reduce the natural rate of unemployment. Then we could enjoy lower unemployment without higher inflation. The question is: How?

The most promising approaches have to do with education, training, and job placement. The data clearly show that more educated workers are unemployed less

---

● **POLICY DEBATE**     **SHOULD THE FED CONCENTRATE ONLY ON REDUCING INFLATION?**

---

One disarmingly simple way to sidestep the dilemma of demand management is to eliminate one of the two traditional goals. In particular, some economists and politicians have proposed that the Federal Reserve be directed to devote itself to price stability and forget about trying to stabilize output and employment. The argument runs something like this.

Price stability is of overriding importance to the smooth functioning of a market economy.

The short-run trade-off between inflation and unemployment impedes the Fed's efforts to reduce inflation. (In extreme versions of the argument, this step denies the existence of any short-run trade-off.)

The Fed has failed in its efforts to stabilize output and employment and, in the process, it has lost ground in the war against inflation.

Let us briefly examine each step of the argument.

The first proposition is a matter of intense debate, as we have emphasized in this and earlier chapters. Someone who believes that inflation is a terrible problem and unemployment a minor one might very well want the Fed to concentrate on reducing inflation. But many other people hold just the opposite view.

The second proposition is undoubtedly true. Concerns about the unemployment consequences of its actions surely have tempered the Fed's inflation-fighting zeal on many occasions.

The third proposition is again debatable. As we learned in previous chapters, the Fed's stabilization policy has

sometimes been stunningly successful (such as since 1993) and sometimes has failed miserably (such as the 1930s and 1972–1973). Lately, however, most observers give the Fed exceptionally high marks.

In 1995, legislation was introduced that would direct the Fed to make price stability its primary goal. But the bill has yet to reach the floor of either house of Congress.

---

frequently than less educated ones. Vocational training and retraining programs, if successful, help unemployed workers with obsolete skills acquire abilities that are currently in demand. By so doing, they both raise employment and help alleviate upward pressures on wage rates in jobs where qualified workers are in short supply.

Government job placement and counseling services play a similar role. Such programs try to improve the match of workers to jobs by funneling information from prospective employers to prospective employees.

These ideas sound promising and sensible. But two big problems arise. First, training and placement programs often look better on paper than they do in practice, where they achieve only modest successes. Too often, people are trained for jobs that do not exist by the time they finish their training—if indeed those jobs ever existed.

The second problem is that the high cost of these programs restricts the number of workers that can be accommodated, even when they work. For this reason, publicly supported job training is done on a very small scale in the United States—much less, say, than in most European countries. The Clinton administration has vigorously promoted various retraining initiatives, but Congress has rejected most of them. Small expenditures can hardly be expected to make a large dent in the natural rate of unemployment.

But many observers believe the natural rate of unemployment has fallen in the United States nonetheless. Why? One reason is that work experience has much in common with formal training—workers become more productive by learning on the job. As the American workforce has aged, the average level of work experience has increased, which, according to many economists, has lowered the natural rate of unemployment.

<table>
<tr><td></td></tr>
</table>

## ■ INDEXING

**Indexing**—which refers to provisions in a law or contract which automatically adjust monetary payments whenever a specific price index changes—presents a very different approach to the inflation-unemployment dilemma. Instead of trying to improve the terms of the trade-off, indexing seeks *to reduce the social costs of inflation.*

The most familiar example of indexing is an *escalator clause* in a wage agreement. Escalator clauses provide for automatic increases in money wages—without the need for new contract negotiations—any time the price level rises by more than a specified amount. Such agreements thus partly protect workers from inflation. Nowadays, with inflation so low and stable, relatively few workers are covered by escalator clauses.

Interest payments on bonds or bank accounts can also be indexed, and the U. S. government began doing so with a small fraction of its bonds in 1997.[5] The most extensive indexing to be found in the United States today, however, appears in government transfer payments. Social Security benefits, for instance, are indexed so that retirees are not victimized by inflation.

Some economists believe that the United States should follow the example of several foreign countries and adopt a much more widespread indexing system. Why? Because, they argue, it would take most of the sting out of inflation. To see how, let us review some of the social costs of inflation that we enumerated in Chapter 24.

One important cost is the capricious redistribution of income caused by unexpected inflation. We saw that borrowers and lenders normally incorporate an *inflation premium* equal to the *expected rate of inflation* into the nominal interest rate. Then, if inflation turns out to be higher than expected, the borrower has to pay the lender only the agreed-upon nominal interest rate, including the premium for *expected* inflation; he does not have to compensate the lender for the (higher) *actual* inflation. Thus, the borrower enjoys a windfall gain and the lender loses out. The opposite happens if inflation turns out to be lower than expected.

But if interest rates on loans were indexed, none of this would occur. Borrowers and lenders would agree on a fixed *real* rate of interest, and then the borrower would compensate the lender for whatever *actual inflation* occurred. No one would have to guess what the inflation rate would be.[6]

A second social cost we mentioned in Chapter 24 stems from the fact that our tax system levies taxes on nominal interest and nominal capital gains. As we learned, this flaw in the tax system leads to extremely high effective tax rates in an inflationary environment. But indexing can cure this problem. We need only rewrite the tax code so that only *real* interest payments and *real* capital gains are taxed.

In the face of all these benefits, why do many economists oppose indexing? Probably the major reason is the fear that indexing will erode society's resistance to inflation. With the costs of inflation reduced so markedly, they argue, what will persuade governments to pay the price of fighting inflation? What will stop them from inflating more and more? They fear that the answer to these questions is: Nothing. Voters who stand to lose nothing from inflation are unlikely to pressure their legislators into stopping it. Opponents of indexing worry that a mild inflationary disease could turn into a ravaging epidemic in a highly indexed economy.

**Indexing** refers to provisions in a law or a contract whereby monetary payments are automatically adjusted whenever a specified price index changes. Wage rates, pensions, interest payments on bonds, income taxes, and many other things can be indexed in this way, and have been. Sometimes such contractual provisions are called *escalator clauses.*

---

[5] Some other countries, with much higher inflation than ours, do extensive indexing of interest rates. Brazil and Israel are notable examples.

[6] For example, an indexed loan with a 2 percent real interest rate would require a 5 percent nominal interest payment if inflation were 3 percent, a 7 percent nominal interest payment if inflation were 5 percent, and so on.

## SUMMARY

1. Inflation can be caused either by rapid growth of aggregate demand or by sluggish growth of aggregate supply.

2. When fluctuations in economic activity emanate from the demand side, prices will rise rapidly when real output grows rapidly. Because rapid growth means more jobs, unemployment and inflation will be inversely related.

3. This inverse relationship between unemployment and inflation is called the *Phillips curve*. U.S. data for the 1950s and 1960s display a Phillips-curve relation, but data for the 1970s and 1980s do not.

4. The Phillips curve is not a menu of *long-run* policy choices for the economy because the *self-correcting mechanism* guarantees that neither an inflationary gap nor a recessionary gap can last indefinitely.

5. Because of the self-correcting mechanism, the economy's true long-run choices lie along a *vertical long-run Phillips curve*, which shows that the so-called *natural rate of unemployment* is the only unemployment rate that can persist indefinitely.

6. In the short run, the economy can move up or down its short-run Phillips curve. *Temporary* reductions in unemployment can be achieved at the cost of higher inflation, and *temporary* increases in unemployment can be used to fight inflation.

7. Whether it is advisable to use unemployment to fight inflation depends on four principal factors: the relative social costs of inflation versus unemployment, the efficiency of the economy's self-correcting mechanism, the shape of the short-run Phillips curve, and how quickly inflationary expectations adjust.

8. If workers expect inflation to occur, and if they demand (and receive) compensation for inflation, output will be independent of the price level. Both the aggregate supply curve and the short-run Phillips curve are vertical in this case.

9. However, errors in predicting inflation will still change real wages and therefore the quantity of output that firms wish to supply. Thus, *unpredicted* movements in the price level will lead to a normal, upward-sloping aggregate supply curve.

10. According to the *rational expectations* hypothesis, errors in predicting inflation are purely random. This means that, except for some random (and uncontrollable) gyrations, the aggregate supply curve is vertical even in the short run.

11. Many economists reject the rational expectations view of the world. Some deny that expectations are "rational" and believe instead that people tend, for example, to underpredict inflation when it is rising. Others point out that contracts signed years ago cannot possibly embody expectations that are "rational" in terms of what we know today.

12. When fluctuations in economic activity are caused by shifts of the aggregate supply curve, output will grow slowly (causing unemployment to rise) when inflation speeds up. Hence, the rates of unemployment and inflation will be positively correlated. Many observers feel that this sort of *stagflation* is why the Phillips curve collapsed in the 1970s. Similarly, a series of favorable supply shocks help explain the excellent macroeconomic outcomes of the 1990s.

13. Even if inflation is initiated by supply-side problems, so that inflation and unemployment occur together, the monetary and fiscal authorities still face this trade-off: Anything they do to improve unemployment is likely to worsen inflation, and anything they do to reduce inflation is likely to aggravate unemployment. The reason is that monetary and fiscal policy mainly influence the aggregate demand curve, not the aggregate supply curve. This is one of our *Ideas for Beyond the Final Exam*.

14. Policies that improve the functioning of the labor market—including retraining programs and employment services—can, in principle, lower the natural rate of unemployment. To date, however, the U.S. government has had only modest success with these measures.

15. *Indexing* is another way to approach the trade-off problem. Instead of trying to improve the trade-off, it concentrates on reducing the social costs of inflation—perhaps eliminating them altogether. Opponents of indexing worry, however, that the economy's resistance to inflation may be lowered by indexing.

## KEY TERMS

Demand-side inflation    706

Phillips curve    710

Supply-side inflation    711

Stagflation caused by supply shocks    711

Self-correcting mechanism    712

Natural rate of unemployment    714

Vertical (long-run) Phillips curve    714

Trade-off between unemployment and inflation in the short run and in the long run    714

Rational expectations    718

Indexing (escalator clauses)    723

Real versus nominal interest rates    723

## QUESTIONS FOR REVIEW

1. When inflation and unemployment fell together in the 1990s, some observers claimed that policymakers no longer faced a trade-off between inflation and unemployment. Were they correct?

2. "There is no sense in trying to shorten recessions through fiscal and monetary policy because the effects of these policies on the unemployment rate are sure to be temporary." Comment on both the truth of this statement and its relevance for policy formulation.

3. Why is it said that decisions on fiscal and monetary policy are, at least in part, political decisions that cannot be made on "objective" economic criteria?

4. What is a Phillips curve? Why did it seem to work so much better in the period from 1954 to 1969 than it did in the 1970s?

5. Explain why expectations about inflation affect the wages that result from labor-management bargaining.

6. What is meant by "rational" expectations? Why does the hypothesis of rational expectations have such stunning implications for economic policy? Would believers in rational expectations want to shorten a recession by expanding aggregate demand? Would they want to fight inflation by reducing aggregate demand?

7. Show that, if the economy's aggregate supply curve is vertical, fluctuations in the growth of aggregate demand produce only fluctuations in inflation with no effect on output. Relate this to your answer to the previous question.

8. Long-term government bonds now pay approximately 5.5 percent *nominal* interest. Would you prefer to trade yours in for an indexed bond that paid a 3 percent *real* rate of interest? What if the real interest rate offered were 2 percent? What if it were 1 percent? What do your answers to these questions reveal about your personal attitudes toward inflation?

9. It is said that the Federal Reserve Board typically cares more about inflation and less about unemployment than the administration. If this is true, why might President Clinton have been worried about what Fed Chairman Alan Greenspan would do in early 1995, when inflation increased for a few months?

10. The year 1999 opened with the unemployment rate under 5 percent, real GDP growing moderately, inflation under 2 percent, and the federal budget showing a surplus of about $70 billion.

   a. Make an argument for engaging in contractionary monetary or fiscal policies under these circumstances.

   b. Make an argument for engaging in expansionary monetary or fiscal policies under these circumstances.

   c. Which argument do you find more persuasive?

# VIII

---

## THE UNITED STATES IN THE WORLD ECONOMY

As a recent popular book put it, we now live in one world—ready or not. What happens in the United States influences other countries, and events abroad reverberate in the United States. Trillions of dollars worth of goods and services—American computers, German machine tools, Japanese cars—are traded across international borders each year. A vastly larger volume of financial transactions—trade in stocks, bonds, and bank deposits, for example—take place in the global economy at lightning speed.

We have mentioned all these subjects before, but we have not emphasized them. Part VIII puts international factors at center stage.

Chapter 35 studies the factors that underlie *international trade,* and Chapter 36 takes up the determination of *exchange rates*—the prices at which the world's currencies are bought and sold. Then Chapter 37 integrates these international influences fully into our model of the macroeconomy.

If you want to understand why there has been so much economic turmoil in Southeast Asia, Russia, and Latin America in recent years, why our international trade policy is so controversial, or why many thoughtful observers think we need to overhaul the *international monetary system,* read these three chapters with care.

No nation was ever ruined by trade.

Benjamin Franklin

# INTERNATIONAL TRADE AND COMPARATIVE ADVANTAGE

International trade is vital to the health of any nation, so it is essential to our study of economics. The world's major economies have always been linked in various ways. But dramatic improvements in transportation, telecommunications, and international relations in recent decades have drawn the industrial nations of the world ever closer together. This process, called "globalization," is often portrayed as something new. But in fact it is not, as the box, "Is Globalization Something New?" points out on page 731.

Economic events in other countries affect the United States for both macroeconomic and microeconomic reasons. For example, we learned in Parts VI and VII that the level of net exports is one important determinant of a nation's output and employment. But we have not delved very deeply into the factors that determine a nation's exports and imports. Chapters 36 and 37 will take up these macroeconomic linkages in greater detail.

But, first, this chapter studies some of the microeconomic linkages among nations: How are patterns and prices of world trade determined? How and why do governments interfere with foreign trade? The central idea of this chapter is one we have encountered before (in Chapters 1 and 4): the law of comparative advantage.

## How Can Americans Compete with "Cheap Foreign Labor"?

Why do Americans (and the citizens of many other nations) often want their government to limit or prevent import competition? One major reason is the common belief that imports take bread out of American workers' mouths. According to this view, "cheap foreign labor" steals jobs from Americans and pressures U.S. businesses to lower wages.

But actually, the facts are not consistent with this story. For one thing, wages in industrialized countries that export to the United States have risen spectacularly during the past 25 years. Table 35–1 shows that wages in seven leading countries rose from an average of only 46 percent of American wages in 1970 to 110 percent by 1997.

By 1997, labor costs in Sweden, the Netherlands, western Germany, and Japan exceeded our own, and costs in France were about equal. Yet American imports of Toyotas from Japan, Volkswagens from Germany, and Volvos from Sweden grew as wages in those countries rose relative to American wages.

By comparison, when European and Japanese wages were far below those in the United States in the 1950s, American industries had no trouble marketing our products abroad. In fact, the main problem then was to raise their imports up to the level of our bountiful exports. Ironically, our position in the international marketplace deteriorated as wage levels in Europe and Japan began to rise closer to our own.

TABLE 35–1

**Labor Costs in Industrialized Countries as a Percentage of U.S. Labor Costs**

|  | 1970 | 1997 |
|---|---|---|
| France | 41% | 99% |
| United Kingdom | 35 | 85 |
| Italy | 42 | 92 |
| Japan | 24 | 106 |
| Netherlands | 51 | 113 |
| Sweden | 70 | 122 |
| (West) Germany | 56 | 155 |

NOTE: Data are compensation estimates per hour, converted at exchange rates, and relate to production workers in the manufacturing sector.
SOURCE: U.S. Bureau of Labor Statistics.

## ● IS GLOBALIZATION SOMETHING NEW?

Few people realize that the industrialized world was in fact highly globalized prior to World War I, before the ravages of two world wars and the Great Depression severed many international linkages. Furthermore, as the British magazine *The Economist* points out, globalization has not gone nearly as far as many people imagine.

Despite much loose talk about the "new" global economy, today's international economic integration is not unprecedented. The 50 years before the first world war saw large cross-border flows of goods, capital and people. That period of globalisation, like the present one, was driven by reductions in trade barriers and by sharp falls in transport costs, thanks to the development of railways and steamships. The present surge of globalisation is in a way a resumption of that previous trend. . . .

Two forces have been driving [globalization]. The first is technology. With the costs of communication and computing falling rapidly, the natural barriers of time and space that separate national markets have been falling too. The cost of a three-minute telephone call between New York and London has fallen from $300 (in 1996 dollars) in 1930 to $1 today. . . .

The second driving force has been liberalisation. . . . Almost all countries have lowered barriers to trade. . . . [T]he ratio of trade to output . . . has increased sharply in most countries since 1950. But by this measure Britain and France are only slightly more open to trade today than they were in 1913. . . .

Product markets are still nowhere near as integrated across borders as they are within nations. Consider the example of trade between the United States and Canada, one of the least restricted trading borders in the world. On average, trade between a Canadian province and an American state is 20 times smaller than domestic trade between two Canadian provinces, after adjusting for distance and income levels.

The financial markets are not yet truly integrated either. Despite the newfound popularity of international investing, capital markets were by some measures more integrated at the start of this century than they are now. . . . [And] labour is less mobile than it was in the second half of the 19th century, when some 60m people left Europe for the New World.

SOURCE: "Schools Brief: One World?" *The Economist,* October 18, 1997.

Clearly, then, cheap foreign labor must not be a major obstacle to U.S. sales abroad, as a "common sense" view of the matter suggests. In this chapter we will see what is wrong with that view.

## ■ WHY TRADE?

The earth's resources are not equally distributed across the planet. Although the United States can produce its own coal and wheat, it depends almost *entirely* on the rest of the world for such items as rubber and coffee. Similarly, Saudi Arabia has little land that is suitable for farming but sits atop a huge pool of oil. Because of the seemingly whimsical distribution of vital resources, every nation must trade with others to acquire what it lacks.

Even if countries had all the resources they needed, other differences in natural endowments such as climate, terrain, and so on would lead them to engage in trade. Americans *could*, with great difficulty, grow their own bananas and coffee in hothouses. But these crops grow much more efficiently in Honduras and Brazil, where the climates are appropriate.

The skills of a nation's labor force also play a role. If New Zealand has a large group of efficient farmers and few workers with industrial experience, while the opposite is true in Japan, it makes sense for New Zealand to specialize in agriculture and let Japan concentrate on manufacturing.

Finally, a small country that tried to produce every product would end up with many industries too small to utilize mass-production techniques and other methods that confer cost advantages on large-scale operations. For example, some countries operate their own international airlines for reasons that can only be described as political, not economic.

To summarize, the main reason why nations trade with one another is to exploit the many advantages of **specialization,** some of which we discussed back in Chapter 4. International trade greatly enhances living standards for all parties involved because:

**Specialization** means that a country devotes its energies and resources to only a small proportion of the world's productive activities.

1. Every country lacks some vital resources that it can get only by trading with others.

2. Each country's climate, labor force, and other endowments make it a relatively efficient producer of some goods and an inefficient producer of other goods.

3. Specialization permits larger outputs and can therefore offer economies of large-scale production.

## MUTUAL GAINS FROM TRADE

Many people have long believed that a nation can gain from trade only at the expense of another. After all, nothing new is produced by the mere act of trading. So if one country gains from a swap, it is argued, the other country must necessarily lose. One consequence of this mistaken belief was and continues to be a policy prescription calling for each country to try to take advantage of its trading partners on the (fallacious) grounds that one nation's gain must be another's loss.

Yet, as Adam Smith emphasized, and as we learned in Chapter 4, both parties must expect to gain something from any *voluntary exchange.* Otherwise, why would they agree to trade?

But how can mere exchange of goods leave both parties better off? The answer is that although trade does not increase the total output of goods, it does allow each party to acquire items better suited to its tastes. Suppose Scott has four cookies and nothing to drink, whereas William has two glasses of milk and nothing to eat. A trade of two of Scott's cookies for one of William's glasses of milk does not increase the total supply of either milk or cookies, but it almost certainly improves the welfare of both boys.

By exactly the same logic, both the United States and Mexico must be better off if Mexico voluntarily ships tomatoes to the United States in return for chemicals. In general, as we emphasized in Chapter 4:

*Trade Is a Win-Win Situation*

**VOLUNTARY EXCHANGE**   Both parties must expect to gain from any *voluntary exchange.* Trade brings about mutual gains by redistributing products so that both parties end up holding more preferred combinations of goods than they held before. This principle, which is one of our *Ideas for Beyond the Final Exam,* applies to nations just as it does to individuals.

## ■   INTERNATIONAL VERSUS INTRANATIONAL TRADE

The 50 states of the United States may be the most eloquent testimony to the gains from specialization and free trade. Florida specializes in growing oranges, Iowa in growing corn, Pennsylvania makes steel, and Michigan builds cars. All these states trade freely with one another and enjoy great material prosperity. Try to imagine how much lower your standard of living would be if you could consume only items produced in your own state.

The essential logic behind international trade is no different from that underlying trade among different states; the basic reasons for trade are equally applicable within a country or among countries. Why, then, do we study international trade as a special subject? There are at least three reasons.

## POLITICAL FACTORS IN INTERNATIONAL TRADE

First, domestic trade takes place under a single national government, whereas foreign trade always involves at least two governments. But a nation's government is normally much less concerned about the welfare of other countries' citizens than it is about its own. So, for example, the U.S. Constitution prohibits tariffs on trade among states, but it does not prohibit the United States from imposing tariffs on imports from abroad. One major issue in the economic analysis of international trade is the use and misuse of impediments to free international trade.

## THE MANY CURRENCIES INVOLVED IN INTERNATIONAL TRADE

Second, all trade within the borders of the United States is carried out in U.S. dollars. But trade across national borders almost always involves at least two currencies. Rates of exchange between different currencies can and do change. In 1985, it took about 250 Japanese yen to buy a dollar; now it takes only about 120. Variability in exchange rates brings with it a host of complications and policy problems.

## IMPEDIMENTS TO MOBILITY OF LABOR AND CAPITAL

Third, it is much easier for labor and capital to move about within a country than to move from one country to another. If jobs are plentiful in Michigan but scarce in West Virginia, workers can move freely to follow the job opportunities. Of course, personal costs like the financial burden of moving and the psychological cost of leaving friends and familiar surroundings may discourage mobility. But such relocations are not inhibited by immigration quotas, by laws restricting the employment of foreigners, or by the need to learn a new language.

There are also greater impediments to the transfer of capital across national boundaries than to its movement within a country. For example, many countries have rules limiting foreign ownership; even the United States limits foreign ownership of broadcast outlets and airlines. Foreign investment is also subject to special political risks, such as the danger of outright expropriation or nationalization after a change in government.

But even if nothing as extreme as expropriation occurs, capital invested abroad faces significant risks from exchange rate variations. An investment valued at 250 million yen will be worth $1.0 million to American investors if the dollar is worth 250 yen, but it is worth $2.5 million if the dollar is worth just 100 yen.

## ■ THE LAW OF COMPARATIVE ADVANTAGE

The gains from international specialization and trade are clear when one country is better at producing one item while its trading partner is better at producing another. For example, no one finds it surprising that Brazil sells coffee to the United States while the United States exports aircraft to Brazil. We know that coffee can be produced using less labor and other inputs in Brazil than in the United States. And the United States can produce airplanes at a lower resource cost than can Brazil.

We say that in such a situation Brazil has an **absolute advantage** in coffee production, and the United States has an absolute advantage in aircraft production. In such cases, it is obvious that both countries can gain by producing the item in which they have an absolute advantage and then trading with one another.

What is much less obvious, but equally true, is that these gains from international trade still exist *even if one country is more efficient than the other in producing everything.* This lesson, the principle of **comparative advantage,** is one we first learned in

One country is said to have an **absolute advantage** over another in the production of a particular good if it can produce that good using smaller quantities of resources than can the other country.

One country is said to have a **comparative advantage** over another in the production of a particular good relative to other goods if it produces that good less inefficiently as compared with the other country.

Chapter 4.[1] It is, in fact, one of the most important of our *Ideas for Beyond the Final Exam*, so we repeat it here for convenience.

> **COMPARATIVE ADVANTAGE**  Even if one country is at an absolute disadvantage relative to another country in the production of every good, it is said to have a *comparative advantage* in making the good at which it is least inefficient (compared with the other country).
>
> The great classical economist David Ricardo (1772–1823) discovered almost 200 years ago that two countries can still gain from trade, even if one is more efficient than the other in every industry—that is, even if one has an absolute advantage in producing every commodity.
>
> In determining the most efficient production patterns, it is *comparative* advantage, not *absolute* advantage, that matters. Thus, a country can gain by importing a good even if that good can be produced more efficiently at home. Such imports make sense if they enable the country to specialize in producing goods at which it is even more efficient.

## THE ARITHMETIC OF COMPARATIVE ADVANTAGE

Let's see precisely how this works using a hypothetical example first suggested in Chapter 4. Table 35–2 gives a somewhat exaggerated impression of the trading positions of the United States and Japan a few years ago. We imagine that labor is the only input used to produce computers and television sets in the two countries and that the United States has an absolute advantage in manufacturing both goods. In this example, a year's worth of labor can produce either 50 computers or 50 TV sets in the United States but only 10 computers or 40 televisions in Japan. So the United States is the more efficient producer of both goods. Nonetheless, as we shall now show, it pays for the United States to specialize and trade with Japan.

To demonstrate this conclusion, we begin by noting that the United States has a comparative advantage in computers, whereas Japan has a comparative advantage in producing TVs. Specifically, the numbers in Table 35–2 show that the United States can produce 50 televisions with a year's labor whereas Japan can produce only 40; so the United States is 25 percent more efficient than Japan in producing TV sets.

However, the United States is five times as efficient as Japan in producing computers: It can produce 50 per year of labor rather than 10. Because America's competitive edge is far greater in computers than in televisions, we say that the United States has a *comparative advantage* in computers.

From the Japanese perspective, these same numbers indicate that Japan is only slightly less efficient than the United States in TV production but drastically less efficient in computer production. So Japan's comparative advantage is in the television industry. According to Ricardo's law of comparative advantage, then, the two countries can gain if the United States specializes in producing computers, Japan specializes in producing TVs, and the two countries trade. Let's verify that this is true. Suppose Japan transfers 1,000 years of labor out of the computer industry and into TV manufacturing. According to the figures in Table 35–2, its computer output falls by 10,000 units while its TV output rises by 40,000 units. (See the middle column of Table 35–3.) Suppose, at the same time, the United States transfers 500 years of labor

| TABLE 35-2 | **Alternative Outputs from One Year of Labor Input** |

| | In the U.S. | In Japan |
|---|---|---|
| Computers | 50 | 10 |
| Televisions | 50 | 40 |

---

[1] To review, see page 62.

**Example of the Gains from Trade**

TABLE 35-3

|  | U.S. | Japan | Total |
|---|---|---|---|
| Computers | +25,000 | −10,000 | +15,000 |
| Televisions | −25,000 | +40,000 | +15,000 |

out of television manufacturing (thereby losing 25,000 TVs) and into computer making (thereby gaining 25,000 computers). Table 35–3 shows us that these transfers of resources between the two countries increase the world's production of both outputs. Together, the two countries now have 15,000 additional TVs and 15,000 additional computers—surely a nice outcome.

Was there some sleight of hand here? How did both the United States and Japan gain both computers and TVs? The explanation is that the process we have just described involves more than just a swap of a fixed bundle of commodities. It is also *a change in the production arrangements*, with some of Japan's inefficient computer production taken over by more efficient American makers, and with some of America's TV production taken over by Japanese television companies who are *less* inefficient at making TVs than Japanese computer manufacturers are at making computers. The underlying principle is both simple and fundamental:

> When every country does what it can do best, all countries can benefit because more of every commodity can be produced without increasing the amounts of labor and other resources used.

## THE GRAPHICS OF COMPARATIVE ADVANTAGE

The gains from trade can also be displayed graphically, and doing so helps us understand whether such gains are large or small.

The lines *US* and *JN* in Figure 35–1 are closely related to the production possibilities frontiers of the two countries, but they differ in that they pretend that each country has the same amount of labor available. In this case, we assume that each has 1 million person-years.[2] For example, Table 35–2 tells us that for each 1 million person-years of labor, the United States can produce 50 million TVs and no computers (point *U* in Figure 35–1), 50 million computers and no TVs (point *S*), or any combination between (the line *US*). Similar reasoning leads to line *JN* for Japan.

America's actual production possibilities frontier would be even higher, relative to Japan's, than shown in Figure 35–1 because the U.S. population is larger. But Figure 35–1 is more useful because it highlights the differences in efficiency that determine both absolute and comparative advantage. Let us see how.

The fact that line *US* lies *above* line *JN* means that the United States can manufacture more televisions and more computers than Japan with the same amount of labor. This reflects our assumption that the United States has an *absolute* advantage in both commodities.

America's comparative advantage in computer production and Japan's comparative advantage in TV production are shown in a different way by the relative *slopes* of the two lines. Look back to Table 35–2, which shows

FIGURE 35-1

**Per-Capita Production Possibilities Frontiers for Two Countries**

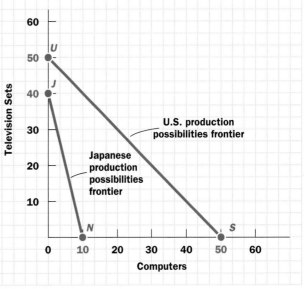

NOTE: Quantities are in millions.

---

[2] To review the concept of the production possibilities frontier, see Chapter 4.

that the United States can acquire a computer on its own by giving up one TV. Thus, the *opportunity cost* of a computer in the United States is one television set. This opportunity cost is depicted graphically by the slope of the U.S. production possibilities frontier in Figure 35–1, which is $OU/OS = 50/50 = 1$.

Table 35–2 also tells us that the opportunity cost of a computer in Japan is four TVs. This is depicted in Figure 35–1 by the slope of Japan's production possibilities frontier, which is $OJ/ON = 40/10 = 4$.

> A country's *absolute* advantage in production over another country is shown by its having a higher per-capita production possibilities frontier. The difference in the *comparative* advantages between the two countries is shown by the difference in the slopes of their frontiers.

Because opportunity costs differ in the two countries, gains are possible if the two countries specialize and trade with one another. Specifically, it is cheaper, in terms of real resources forgone, for *either* country to acquire its computers in the United States. By a similar line of reasoning, the opportunity cost of TVs is higher in the United States than in Japan, so it makes sense for both countries to acquire their televisions in Japan.[3]

Notice that if the slopes of the two production possibilities frontiers, *JN* and *US*, were equal, then opportunity costs would be the same in each country. In that case, no potential gains would arise from trade. Gains from trade arise from *differences* across countries, not from similarities. This is an important point about which people are often confused. Some argue that two very different countries, say the United States and Mexico, cannot gain much by trading with one another. In fact:

> Two very similar countries may gain little from trade. Large gains from trade are most likely when countries are very different.

How the two countries divide the gains from trade depends on the prices that emerge from world trade, which is the subject of the next section. But we already know enough to see that world trade must, in our example, leave a computer costing more than one TV and less than four. Why? Because, if a computer bought less than one TV (its opportunity cost in the United States) on the world market, the United States would produce its own TVs rather than buying them from Japan. And if a computer cost more than four TVs (its opportunity cost in Japan), Japan would prefer to produce its own computers rather than buy them from the United States.

We conclude, therefore, that if both countries are to trade, the rate of exchange between TVs and computers must be somewhere between 4 to 1 and 1 to 1. To illustrate the gains from trade in a concrete example, suppose the world price ratio settles at 2 to 1; that is, one computer costs the same as two televisions. How much, precisely, do the United States and Japan gain from world trade in this case?

Figure 35–2 is designed to help us see the answers. The blue production possibilities frontiers *US* in Panel (b) and *JN* in Panel (a) are the same as in Figure 35–1. But the United States can do better than line *US*. Specifically, with a world price ratio of 2 to 1, the United States can buy two TVs for each computer it gives up, rather than just one (which is the opportunity cost of a computer in the United States). Hence, if the United States produces only computers—point *S* in Figure 35–2(b)—and buys its TVs from Japan, America's *consumption possibilities* will be as indicated by the red line that begins at point *S* and has a slope of 2 indicating that each computer sold brings the United States two television sets. Because trade allows the United States to choose a point on *AS* rather than on *US*, trade opens up consumption possibilities that were simply not available before.

The story is similar for Japan. If the Japanese produce only television sets— point *J* in Figure 35–2(a)—they can acquire a computer from the United States for every two TVs they give up as they move along the red line *JP* (whose slope is 2). This is better than they can do on their own, because a sacrifice of two TVs in Japan

---

[3] As an exercise, provide this line of reasoning.

**The Gains from Trade** | FIGURE 35-2

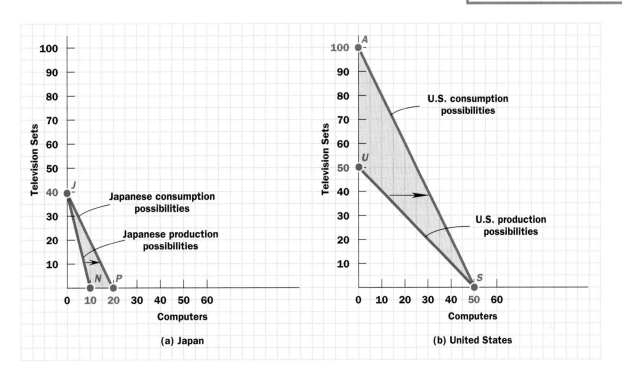

NOTE: Quantities are in millions.

yields only one-half of a computer. Hence, world trade enlarges Japan's consumption possibilities from *JN* to *JP*.

Figure 35–2 shows graphically that gains from trade arise to the extent that world prices (2 to 1 in our example) differ from domestic opportunity costs (4 to 1 and 1 to 1 in our example). So it is a matter of some importance to understand how prices in international trade are established. We shall do so shortly.

## Comparative Advantage Exposes the Fallacy of "Cheap Foreign Labor"

But first let us observe that the principle of comparative advantage takes us a long way toward uncovering the fallacy in the "cheap foreign labor" argument described at the start of this chapter. Given the assumed productive efficiency of American labor, and the inefficiency of Japanese labor, we would expect wages to be much higher in the United States. Indeed, they were until recent years.

In these circumstances, one might expect American workers to be apprehensive about an agreement to permit open trade between the two countries: "How can we hope to meet the unfair competition of those underpaid Japanese workers?" And Japanese laborers might also be concerned: "How can we hope to meet the competition of those Americans, who are so efficient in producing everything?"

The principle of comparative advantage shows us that both fears are unjustified. As we have just seen, when trade is opened between Japan and the United States, *workers in both countries will be able to earn higher real wages than before* because of the increased productivity that comes about through specialization.

As Figure 35–2 shows, once trade opens, Japanese workers should end up with more TVs and more computers than they had before. So their living standards should rise, even though they have been left vulnerable to competition from "superefficient" Americans. Workers in the United States should also end up with more TVs and with more computers, so their living standards should also rise even though they have been exposed to competition from "cheap" Japanese labor. These higher standards of living, of course, reflect the higher real wages earned by workers in both countries.

The lesson to be learned here is elementary:

**Nothing helps raise living standards more than a greater abundance of goods.**

## ■ SUPPLY-DEMAND EQUILIBRIUM AND PRICING IN WORLD TRADE

How parties share the gains from trade depends on the prices that emerge from world trade. As usual, price determination in a free market depends on supply and demand.

When applied to international trade, however, the supply-demand model runs into several new complications. First, it involves at least two demand curves: that of the exporting country and that of the importing country. Second, it may also involve two supply curves, because the importing country may produce part of its own consumption. Third, equilibrium does not take place at the intersection point of *either* pair of supply-demand curves. Why? Because if they trade at all, the exporting country must supply more than it demands, whereas the importing country demands more than it supplies.

These complications are illustrated in Figure 35–3, where we show the supply and demand curves of a country that exports wheat in Panel (a) and of a country that imports wheat in Panel (b). For simplicity, we assume that these countries do not deal in wheat with anyone else. Where will the two-country wheat market reach equilibrium?

| FIGURE 35–3 | **Supply-Demand Equilibrium in the International Wheat Trade** |

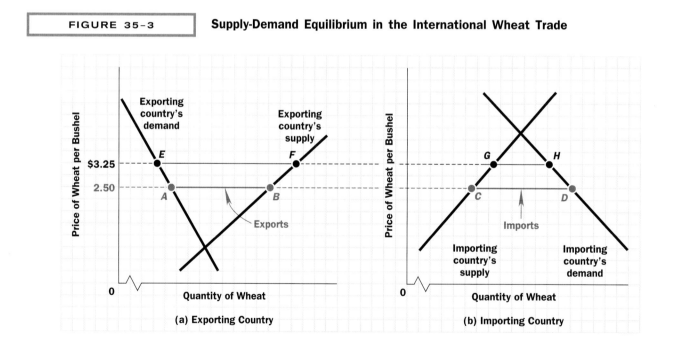

(a) Exporting Country          (b) Importing Country

If there is free trade, the equilibrium price must satisfy two requirements:

1. **The price of wheat must be the same in both countries.**

2. **The quantity of wheat exported must equal the quantity of wheat imported.**

In Figure 35–3, this happens at a price of $2.50 per bushel. At that price, the distance *AB* between what the exporting country produces and what it consumes equals the distance *CD* between what the importing country consumes and what it produces.

This means that, at a price of $2.50 per bushel, the amount the exporting country wants to sell exactly equals the amount the importing country wants to buy.

At any price above $2.50, producers in both countries will want to sell more and consumers in both countries will want to buy less. For example, if the price rises to $3.25 per bushel, the exporter's quantity supplied will rise from B to F whereas its quantity demanded falls from A to E, as shown in Figure 35–3(a). As a result, more wheat will be available for export—EF rather than AB. For exactly the same reason, the price increase will cause higher production and lower sales in the importing country, leading to a reduction in imports from CD to GH in Panel (b).

But this means that the higher price, $3.25 per bushel, cannot be sustained in a free and competitive international market. With export supply EF far greater than import demand GH, there must be downward pressure on price and a move back toward the $2.50 equilibrium price. Similar reasoning shows that prices below $2.50 also cannot be sustained. Thus:

> In international trade, the equilibrium price is the one that makes the exporting country want to export exactly the amount that the importing country wants to import. Equilibrium will thus occur at a price at which the horizontal distance AB in Figure 35–3(a) (the excess of the exporter's quantity supplied over its quantity demanded) is equal to the horizontal distance CD in Figure 35–3(b) (the excess of the importer's quantity demanded over its quantity supplied). At this price, the *world's* quantity demanded equals the *world's* quantity supplied.

## ■ TARIFFS, QUOTAS, AND OTHER INTERFERENCES WITH TRADE

Despite the mutual gains from international trade, nations often interfere with the operation of free international markets. In fact, until the rise of the free-trade movement about 200 years ago (with such economists as Adam Smith and David Ricardo as its vanguard), it was taken for granted that one of the essential tasks of government was to impede trade, presumably in the national interest!

Many argued then (and many still argue today) that the proper aim of government policy was to promote exports and discourage imports, for that would increase the amount foreigners owed the nation. According to this so-called **mercantilist** view, a nation's wealth consists of the amount of gold or other monies at its command.

**Mercantilism** is a doctrine that holds that exports are good for a country, whereas imports are harmful.

Obviously, governments can only pursue such a policy within certain limits. A country *must* import vital foodstuffs or critical raw materials that it cannot supply for itself. Moreover, it is mathematically impossible for *every* country to sell more than it buys, for one country's exports *must* be some other country's imports. If everyone competes in this game and cuts imports to the bone, then obviously exports must go the same way. The result will be that everyone is deprived of the mutual gains from trade—which is precisely what happens in a trade war.

After the protectionist 1930s, the United States moved away from mercantilist policies designed to impede imports and gradually assumed a leading role in promoting free trade. Over the past 50 years, tariffs and other trade barriers have been reduced dramatically. In recent years, the United States has led the world to complete the Uruguay Round of tariff reductions and has joined Canada and Mexico in the North American Free Trade Agreement (NAFTA). The latter caused a political firestorm in the United States in 1993 and 1994, with critic (and 1992 presidential contender) Ross Perot predicting a "giant sucking sound" as American workers lost their jobs to competition from "cheap Mexican labor." (Does that sound familiar?)

Modern governments use three main devices when seeking to control trade: tariffs, quotas, and export subsidies. A **tariff** is simply a tax on imports. An importer of wheat, for example, may be charged $1 for each bushel brought into the country. The United States is generally a low-tariff country, with only a few notable exceptions, such as the 25 percent tariff on light trucks. However, many other countries rely on heavy tariffs to protect their industries. Tariff rates of 100 percent or more are not uncommon.

A **tariff** is a tax on imports.

---

### ● HOW SWEET IT IS: THE U.S. SUGAR QUOTA

The United States has restricted sugar imports since 1934. But the current program, which many economists believe is the most egregious of all our agricultural subsidies, dates only from 1990. It is called a "tariff-rate quota," which most economists view as a fancy name for grotesque protectionism.

Each year a small amount of imported sugar is allowed to enter the United States under a negligible tariff. Beyond that, however, the U.S. government posts a tariff so high that no one wants to pay it in order to import sugar. In consequence, our domestic price of sugar is far above the world price.

This high price is, of course, a great boon to American producers of sugar and sugar-substitutes like corn syrup. But it costs U.S. consumers of sugar and manufacturers of candy and soft drinks between $1 billion and $2 billion per year. And it has also led to some bizarre

attempts to evade the quota, like importing sugar as an ingredient in chocolate and powdered drinks and then removing the sugar content in the United States.

---

A **quota** specifies the maximum amount of a good that is permitted into the country from abroad per unit of time.

A **quota** is a legal limit on the amount of a good that may be imported. For example, the government might allow no more than 25 million bushels of wheat to be imported in a year. In some cases, governments ban the importation of certain goods outright—a quota of zero. The United States now imposes quotas on a smattering of goods, including textiles, meat, and sugar. But most imports are free of quotas.

An **export subsidy** is a payment by the government to exporters to permit them to reduce the selling prices of their goods so they can compete more effectively in foreign markets.

An **export subsidy** is government payment to an exporter. By reducing the exporter's costs, such subsidies permit exporters to lower their selling prices and to compete more effectively in world trade. Although export subsidies are minor in the United States, some foreign governments use them extensively to assist their industries—a practice that provokes bitter complaints from American manufacturers about "unfair competition." For example, years of heavy government subsidies helped the European Airbus consortium take a sizable share of the world commercial aircraft market away from American manufacturers like Boeing and McDonnell-Douglas.

### HOW TARIFFS AND QUOTAS WORK

Both tariffs and quotas restrict supplies coming from abroad and drive up prices. A tariff works by raising prices, which in turn cuts the demand for imports, whereas the sequence associated with a quota is just the reverse—a restriction in supply forces prices up.

The supply and demand curves in Figure 35–4 illustrate how tariffs and quotas work. Just as in Figure 35–3, the equilibrium price of wheat under free trade is $2.50 per bushel (in both countries). At this price, the exporting country produces 125 million bushels—point *B* in Panel (a)—and consumes 80 million (point *A*). So its exports are 45 million bushels—the distance *AB*. Similarly, the importing country consumes 95 million bushels—point *D* in Panel (b)—and produces only 50 million (point *C*), so its imports are also 45 million bushels—the distance *CD*.

Now suppose the government of the importing nation imposes a quota limiting imports to 30 million bushels. The free-trade equilibrium with imports of 45 million bushels is no longer possible. Instead, the market must equilibrate at a point where both exports and imports are only 30 million bushels. As Figure 35–4 indicates, this requires different prices in the two countries.

**Quotas and Tariffs in International Trade**

FIGURE 35-4

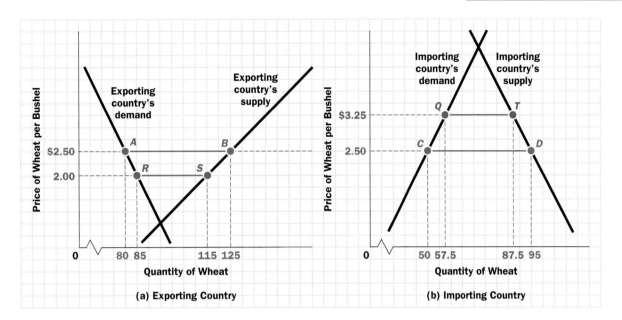

**(a) Exporting Country**

**(b) Importing Country**

NOTE: Quantities are in millions of bushels.

Imports in Panel (b) will be 30 million—the distance *QT*—only when the price of wheat in the importing nation is $3.25 per bushel, because only at this price will quantity demanded exceed domestic quantity supplied by 30 million bushels. Similarly, exports in Panel (a) will be 30 million bushels—the distance *RS*—only when the price in the exporting country is $2.00 per bushel. At this price, quantity supplied exceeds domestic quantity demanded by 30 million bushels in the exporting country. Thus, the quota *raises* the price in the importing country to $3.25 and *lowers* the price in the exporting country to $2.00. In general:

> An import quota on a product normally reduces the volume of that product traded, raises the price in the importing country, and reduces the price in the exporting country.

A tariff can accomplish the same restriction of trade. In our example, a quota of 30 million bushels led to a price that was $1.25 higher in the importing country than in the exporting country ($3.25 versus $2.00). Suppose that, instead of a quota, the importing nation posts a $1.25 per bushel tariff. International trade equilibrium then must satisfy the following two requirements:

> 1. The price that consumers in the importing country pay for wheat must exceed the price that suppliers in the exporting country receive by $1.25 (the amount of the tariff).
>
> 2. The quantity of wheat exported must equal the quantity of wheat imported.

By consulting the graphs in Figure 35–4, you can see exactly where these two requirements are met. If the exporter produces at *S* and consumes at *R*, while the importer produces at *Q* and consumes at *T*, then exports and imports are equal (at 30 million bushels), and the two domestic prices differ by exactly $1.25. (They are $3.25 and $2.00.) What we have just discovered is a general result of international trade theory:

> Any restriction of imports that is accomplished by a quota normally can also be accomplished by a tariff.

In this case, the tariff corresponding to an import quota of 30 million bushels is $1.25 per bushel.

### TARIFFS VERSUS QUOTAS

But although tariffs and quotas can accomplish the same reduction in international trade and lead to the same domestic prices in the two countries, some important differences arise between the two types of restrictions.

First, under a quota, profits from the price increases in the importing country usually go into the pockets of the foreign and domestic sellers of the product. Because supplies are limited by quotas, customers in the importing country must pay more for the product. So the suppliers, whether foreign or domestic, receive more for every unit they sell. For example, estimates showed that U.S. import quotas on Japanese cars in the early 1980s raised the profits of both American and Japanese automakers by billions of dollars per year.

On the other hand, when trade is restricted by a tariff, some of the profits go instead as tax revenues to the *government* of the importing country. In effect, the government increases its tax revenues partly at its own citizens' expense and partly at the expense of foreign exporters, who must accept a reduced price because of the resulting decrease in quantity demanded in the importing country. (Domestic producers again benefit, because they are exempt from the tariff.) In this respect, a tariff is certainly a better proposition than a quota from the viewpoint of the country that enacts it.

Another important distinction between the two measures arises from their different implications for productive efficiency. Because a tariff handicaps all foreign suppliers equally, it still awards sales to those firms and nations that are most efficient and can therefore supply the goods most cheaply. A quota, on the other hand, necessarily awards its import licenses more or less capriciously—perhaps in proportion to past sales or even based on political criteria. There is not the slightest reason to expect the most efficient suppliers to get the import permits.

The U.S. quota on Japanese cars in the 1980s illustrates all of these effects. Japanese automakers responded to the limit on the number of cars by shipping bigger models equipped with more optional equipment. The "stripped-down" Japanese car became a thing of the past. And the newer, smaller Japanese automakers—like Subaru and Mitsubishi—found it difficult at first to compete in the U.S. market because their quotas were so much smaller than those of Toyota, Nissan, and Honda.

If a country must inhibit imports, two important reasons support a preference for tariffs over quotas:

1. Some of the revenues resulting from tariffs go to the government of the importing country rather than to foreign and domestic producers.

2. Unlike quotas, tariffs offer special benefits to more efficient exporters.

## WHY INHIBIT TRADE?

To state that tariffs provide a better way to inhibit international trade than quotas leaves open a far more basic question: Why limit trade in the first place? It has been estimated that trade restrictions cost American consumers about $70 billion per year in the form of higher prices. Why should they be asked to pay these higher prices?

A number of answers are commonly given. Let's examine each in turn.

### GAINING A PRICE ADVANTAGE

A tariff forces foreign exporters to sell more cheaply by restricting their market access. If they do not cut their prices, they will be left with unsold goods. Suppose, as in Figure 35–4(b), that a $1.25 tariff on wheat raises the price in the importing country from $2.50 to $3.25 per bushel. This higher price drives down imports from an amount represented by the length of the red line *CD* to the smaller amount represented by the blue line *QT*. To the exporting country, this means an equal reduction in exports, as illustrated by the change from *AB* to *RS* in Figure 35–4(a).

As a result, the price at which the exporting country can sell its wheat is driven down—from $2.50 to $2.00 in the example. Meanwhile, producers in the importing country—being exempt from the tariff—can charge $3.25 per bushel. So, in effect, the tariff amounts to government intervention to rig prices in favor of domestic producers.

Not bad, you say. However, this technique works only as long as foreigners accept tariff exploitation passively—which they rarely do. Instead, they will probably retaliate by imposing tariffs or quotas of their own on imports from the country that first began the tariff game. Such tit-for-tat behavior can easily lead to a trade war in which no one gains more favorable prices but everyone loses through the resulting reductions in trade. Something like this happened to the world economy in the 1930s and helped prolong the worldwide depression.

**Tariffs or quotas can benefit particular domestic industries in a country that is able to impose them without fear of retaliation. But when every country uses them, everyone is likely to lose in the long run.**

## PROTECTING PARTICULAR INDUSTRIES

The second, and probably more frequent, reason why countries restrict trade is to protect particular industries from foreign competition. If foreigners can produce steel or shoes more cheaply, domestic businesses and unions in these industries are quick to demand protection, and their governments are often reluctant to deny them that support.

The "cheap foreign labor" argument is most likely to arise in this context. Protective tariffs and quotas are explicitly designed to rescue firms whose relative inefficiency does not permit them to compete with foreign exporters in an open world market. But it is precisely the harsh international competition to produce better products more efficiently that gives consumers the benefits of international specialization.

In our numerical example of comparative advantage, we can well imagine the complaints from Japanese computer makers as the opening of trade leads to increased importation of U.S. computers. At the same time, American TV manufacturers would probably express outrage over the flood of imported TVs from Japan. Yet Japanese specialization in televisions and U.S. specialization in computers is precisely what enables citizens of both countries to enjoy higher standards of living. If governments interfere with this process, consumers in both countries lose out.

Industries threatened by foreign competition often argue that some form of protection against imports is needed to prevent job losses. For example, the U.S. steel industry made exactly this argument recently when world steel prices plummeted and imports surged. (And the U.S. government delivered some protection!) But basic macroeconomics teaches us better ways to stimulate employment, such as raising aggregate demand.

A program that limits foreign competition will be more effective at preserving employment *in the particular protected industry*. But it will typically do so at a high cost to consumers and to the economy. Table 35–4 estimates some of the costs

### Estimated Costs of Protectionism to Consumers

TABLE 35–4

| Industry | Cost per Job Saved |
|---|---|
| Apparel | $139,000 |
| Costume jewelry | 97,000 |
| Shipping | 415,000 |
| Sugar | 600,000 |
| Textiles | 202,000 |
| Women's footwear | 102,000 |

SOURCE: Gary C. Hufbauer and Kimberly Ann Elliott, *Measuring the Costs of Protectionism in the United States* (Washington, D.C.: Institute for International Economics, January 1994), Table 1.3, pp. 12–13.

## ● HOW POPULAR IS PROTECTIONISM?

Although the world has been moving gradually toward freer trade, its citizens are not entirely persuaded that this trend is desirable. In 1998, a Canadian polling company asked almost 13,000 people in 22 countries the following question: "Which of the following two broad approaches do you think would be the best way to improve the economic and employment situation in this country—protecting our local industries by restricting imports, or removing import restrictions to increase our international trade?" By this measure, protectionism outnumbered free traders by a narrow margin—47 percent to 42 percent, with the rest undecided. But protectionist sentiment was stronger in the United States, where the margin was 56 percent to 37 percent.

SOURCE: *The Economist,* January 2, 1999, page 59.

to American consumers of using tariffs and quotas to save jobs in selected industries. In every case, the costs far exceed the wages of the workers in the protected industries—ranging as high as $600,000 per job for the sugar quota.

Nevertheless, complaints over proposals to reduce tariffs or quotas are justified unless something is done to ease the cost to individual workers of switching to the product lines that trade makes profitable.

> The argument for free trade between countries cannot be considered airtight if governments provide no adequate program to assist those few citizens in each country who are harmed whenever patterns of production change drastically—as would happen, for example, if governments suddenly reduced tariff and quota barriers.

Owners of television factories in the United States and of computer factories in Japan may see heavy investments suddenly rendered unprofitable. Workers in those industries would see their special skills and training devalued in the marketplace. And displaced workers also pay some intangible costs. They may need to move to new locations as well as to new industries, uprooting their families, losing old friends and neighbors, and so on. That the *majority* of citizens undoubtedly gain from free trade is no consolation to those who are its victims.

To mitigate these problems, the United States follows two basic approaches. First, our trade laws offer temporary protection from sudden surges of imports, on the grounds that unexpected changes in trade patterns do not give businesses and workers enough time to adjust.

**Trade adjustment assistance** provides special unemployment benefits, loans, retraining programs, and other aid to workers and firms that are harmed by foreign competition.

Second, the government has set up **trade adjustment assistance** programs to help workers and businesses who lose their jobs or their markets because of import increases. Firms may be eligible for technical assistance, government loans or loan guarantees, and permission to delay tax payments. Workers may qualify for retraining programs, longer periods of unemployment compensation, and funds to defray moving costs. Each form of assistance is designed to ease the burden on the victims of free trade so that the rest of us can enjoy its considerable benefits.

## ■ OTHER ARGUMENTS FOR PROTECTION

### NATIONAL DEFENSE AND OTHER NONECONOMIC CONSIDERATIONS

A third reason trade protectionists cite is the need to maintain national defense. For example, even if the United States were not the most efficient producer of aircraft, it might still be rational to produce our own military aircraft so that no foreign government could ever cut off supplies of this strategic product. The national defense argument is fine as far as it goes, but there is a clear danger: Even industries with the most peripheral relationship to defense are likely to invoke this argument on their behalf. For instance, for years the U.S. watchmaking industry argued for protection on the grounds that its skilled craftsmen would be invaluable in wartime!

Similarly, the United States has occasionally banned either exports to or imports from nations such as Cuba, Iran, and Iraq on political grounds. Such actions often have important economic effects, creating either bonanzas or disasters for particular American industries. But they are justified by politics, not by economics. Noneconomic reasons also explain quotas on importation of whaling products and on the furs of other endangered species.

### THE INFANT-INDUSTRY ARGUMENT

Yet a fourth common argument for protectionism is the so-called *infant-industry argument*. Promising new industries allegedly often need breathing room to flourish and grow. If we expose these infants to the rigors of international competition too soon, the argument goes, they may never develop to the point where they can survive on their own in the international marketplace.

The argument, although valid in certain instances, is less defensible than it seems at first. Protecting an infant industry is justifiable only if the prospective future gains are sufficient to repay the up-front costs of protectionism. But if the industry is likely to be so profitable in the future, why doesn't private capital rush in to take advantage of the prospective net profits? The annals of business are full of cases in which a new product or a new firm lost money at first, but profited handsomely later.

The infant-industry argument for protection stands up to scrutiny only if private funds are unavailable for some reason, despite a industry's glowing profit prospects. Even then it may make more sense to provide a government loan than to provide trade protection.

It is hard to think of legitimate examples where the infant-industry argument applies. But even if such a case were found, we would have to be careful that the industry not remain in diapers forever. In too many cases, industries were awarded protection when young and, somehow, never matured to the point where protection could be withdrawn. We must be wary of infants that never grow up.

### STRATEGIC TRADE POLICY

A stronger argument for (temporary) protection has substantially influenced U.S. trade policy. Advocates of this argument, including some top officials in the Clinton administration, agree that free trade for all is the best system. But they point out that we live in an imperfect world in which many nations refuse to play by the rules of the free-trade game. And they fear that a nation that pursues free trade in a protectionist world is likely to lose out. It therefore makes sense, they argue, to *threaten* to protect your markets unless other nations agree to open theirs.

The United States has followed this strategy in trade negotiations with several countries in recent years. One extremely prominent case arose in 1995, when the U.S. government threatened to impose 100 percent tariffs on imported Japanese luxury cars unless Japan agreed to open its domestic markets for automobiles and auto parts. A dangerous trade war was narrowly averted when the two countries struck

---

### ● CAN PROTECTIONISM SAVE FREE TRADE?

In this 1983 column, William Safire shook off his long-standing attachment to free trade and argued eloquently for retaliation against protectionist nations.

Free trade is economic motherhood. Protectionism is economic evil incarnate. . . . Never should government interfere in the efficiency of international competition.

Since childhood, these have been the tenets of my faith. If it meant that certain businesses in this country went belly-up, so be it. . . . If it meant that Americans would be thrown out of work by overseas companies paying coolie wages, that was tough. . . .

The thing to keep in mind, I was taught, was the Big Picture and the Long Run. America, the great exporter, had far more to gain than to lose from free trade; attempts to protect inefficient industries here would ultimately cost more American jobs.

While playing with my David Ricardo doll and learning nursery rhymes about comparative advantage, I was listening to another laissez-fairy tale: Government's role in the world of business should be limited to keeping business honest and competitive. In God we antitrusted. Let businesses operate in the free marketplace.

Now American businesses are no longer competing with foreign companies. They are competing with foreign governments who help their local businesses. That means the world arena no longer offers a free marketplace; instead, most other governments are pushing a policy that can be called *helpfulism.*

Helpfulism works like this: A government like Japan decides to get behind its baseball-bat industry. It pumps in capital, knocks off marginal operators, finds subtle ways to discourage imports of Louisville Sluggers, and selects target areas for export blitzes. Pretty soon, the favored Japanese companies are driving foreign competitors batty.

How do we compete with helpfulism? One way is to complain that it is unfair; that draws a horselaugh. Another way is

to demand a "Reagan Round" of trade negotiations under GATT, the Gentlemen's Agreement To Talk, which is equally laughable. Yet another way is to join the helpfuls by subsidizing our exports and permitting our companies to try monopolistic tricks abroad not permitted at home. But all that makes us feel guilty, with good reason.

The other way to deal with helpfulism is through—here comes the dreadful word—*protection.* Or, if you prefer a euphemism, *retaliation.* Or if that is still too severe, *reciprocity.* Whatever its name, it is a way of saying to the cut-throat cartelists we sweetly call our trading partners: "You have bent the rules out of shape. Change your practices to conform to the agreed-upon rules, or we will export a taste of your own medicine."

A little balance, then, from the free trade theorists. The demand for what the Pentagon used to call "protective reaction" is not demagoguery, not shortsighted, not self-defeating. On the contrary, the overseas pirates of protectionism and exemplars of helpfulism need to be taught the basic lesson in trade, which is: tit for tat.

SOURCE: William Safire, "Smoot-Hawley Lives," *The New York Times,* March 17, 1983. Copyright © 1983 by The New York Times Company. Reprinted by permission.

---

an agreement at the eleventh hour. At this writing, another such game of chicken is being played with the European Union over their restrictions on imports of hormone-treated beef.

The strategic argument for protection is a hard one for economists to deal with. Although it recognizes the superiority of free trade, it argues that threatening protectionism is the best way to achieve that end. Such a strategy might work, but it clearly involves great risks. If threats that the United States will turn protectionist induce other countries to scrap existing protectionist policies, then the gamble will have succeeded. But, if the gamble fails, protectionism increases.

> ● **UNFAIR FOREIGN COMPETITION**

Satire and ridicule are often more persuasive than logic and statistics. Exasperated by the spread of protectionism under the prevailing Mercantilist philosophy, French economist Frédéric Bastiat decided to take the protectionist argument to its illogical conclusion. The fictitious petition of the French candlemakers to the Chamber of Deputies, written in 1845 and excerpted below, has become a classic in the battle for free trade.

> We are subject to the intolerable competition of a foreign rival, who enjoys, it would seem, such superior facilities for the production of light, that he is enabled to inundate our national market at so exceedingly reduced a price, that, the moment he makes his appearance, he draws off all custom for us; and thus an important branch of French industry, with all its innumerable ramifications, is suddenly reduced to a state of complete stagnation. This rival is no other than the sun.
>
> Our petition is, that it would please your honorable body to pass a law whereby shall be directed the shutting up of all windows, dormers, skylights, shutters, curtains, in a word, all openings, holes, chinks, and fissures through which the light of the sun is used to penetrate our dwellings, to the prejudice of the profitable manufactures which we flatter ourselves we have been enabled to bestow upon the country. . . .
>
> We foresee your objections, gentlemen; but there is not one that you can oppose to us . . . which is not equally opposed to your own practice and the principle which guides your policy. . . . Labor and nature concur in different proportions, according to country and climate, in every article of production. . . . If a Lisbon orange can be sold at half the price of a Parisian one, it is because a natural and gratuitous heat does for the one what the other only obtains from an artificial and consequently expensive one. . . .
>
> Does it not argue the greatest inconsistency to check as you do the importation of coal, iron, cheese, and goods of foreign manufacture, merely because and even in proportion as their price approaches *zero,* while at the same time you freely admit, and without limitation, the light of the sun, whose price is during the whole day at *zero*?

SOURCE: F. Bastiat, *Economic Sophisms* (New York: G. P. Putnam's Sons, 1922).

## ■ CAN CHEAP IMPORTS HURT A COUNTRY?

One of the most curious—and illogical—features of the protectionist position is the fear of low import prices. Countries that subsidize their exports are accused of **dumping**—of getting rid of their goods at unjustifiably low prices. For example, Russia, Japan, and Korea have recently been accused of dumping steel on the U.S. market.

Economists find this argument strange. As a nation of consumers, we should be indignant when foreigners charge us *high* prices, not *low* ones. That commonsense rule guides every consumer's daily life. Only from the topsy-turvy viewpoint of an industry seeking protection are low prices seen as being against the public interest.

Ultimately, the best interests of any country are served when it imports as cheaply as possible. It would be ideal for the United States if the rest of the world were willing to provide us with goods at no charge. We could then live in luxury at the expense of the rest of the world.

But, of course, benefits to the United States as a whole do not necessarily inure to every single American. If quotas on, say, sugar imports were dropped, American consumers and industries that purchase sugar would gain from lower prices. But owners of sugar fields and their employees would suffer serious losses in the form of lower profits, lower wages, and lost jobs—losses they would fight hard to prevent. For this reason, politics often leads to the adoption of protectionist measures that we would likely reject on strictly economic criteria.

**Dumping** means selling goods in a foreign market at lower prices than those charged in the home market.

## ■ A LAST LOOK AT THE "CHEAP FOREIGN LABOR" ARGUMENT

The preceding discussion reveals the fundamental fallacy in the argument that American workers should fear cheap foreign labor. The average American worker's living standard must rise if other countries willingly supply their products to us more cheaply. As long as the government's monetary and fiscal policies succeed in maintaining high levels of employment at home, how can we possibly lose by getting world products at bargain prices? This is precisely what is happening to the U.S. economy as this book goes to print—imports are pouring in at low prices and U.S. unemployment is the lowest in a generation.

We must add, however, some important qualifications. First, our macroeconomic stabilization policy may not always be effective. If workers displaced by foreign competition cannot find new jobs, they will indeed suffer from international trade. But high unemployment reflects a shortcoming of the government's monetary and fiscal policies, not of its international trade policies.

Second, we have noted that an abrupt stiffening of foreign competition can hurt U.S. workers by not allowing them adequate time to adapt to the new conditions. If change occurs fairly gradually, workers can retrain and move on to the industries that now require their services. Indeed, if the change is slow enough, normal attrition may suffice. But competition that inflicts its damage overnight is certain to impose real costs on the affected workers, costs that are no less painful for being temporary. That is why our trade laws make provisions for people and industries damaged by import surges.

But these are, after all, only qualifications to an overwhelming argument. They call for intelligent monetary and fiscal policies and for transitional assistance to unemployed workers, not for abandonment of free trade. In general, the nation as a whole need not fear competition from cheap foreign labor.

In the long run, labor will be "cheap" only where it is not very productive. Wages will be high in countries with high labor productivity, and this high productivity will enable those countries to compete effectively in international trade despite high wages. It is thus misleading to say that the United States held its own in the international marketplace until recently *despite* high wages. Rather it is much more on point to note that the higher wages of American workers were a result of higher worker productivity, which gave the United States a heavy competitive edge.

Remember, in this matter it is absolute advantage, not comparative advantage, that counts. The country that is most efficient in every output can pay its workers more in every industry.

---

## SUMMARY

1. Countries trade because differences in their natural resources and other inputs create discrepancies in the efficiency with which they can produce different goods, and because *specialization* may offer them greater economies of large-scale production.

2. Voluntary trade will generally be advantageous to both parties in an exchange. This is one of our *Ideas for Beyond the Final Exam.*

3. International trade is more complicated than trade within a nation because of political factors, different national currencies, and impediments to the movement of labor and capital across national borders.

4. Two countries will gain from trade with one another if each exports goods in which it has a *comparative advantage.* Even

   a country that is inefficient across the board will benefit by exporting the goods in whose production it is *least inefficient.* This is another of the *Ideas for Beyond the Final Exam.*

5. When countries specialize and trade, each can enjoy consumption possibilities that exceed its production possibilities.

6. The prices of goods traded between countries are determined by supply and demand, but one must consider explicitly the demand curve and the supply curve of *each* country involved. Thus the equilibrium price must be where the excess of quantity supplied over quantity demanded in the exporting country is equal to the excess of quantity demanded over quantity supplied in the importing country.

7. The "cheap foreign labor" argument ignores the principle of comparative advantage, which shows that real wages

(which determine living standards) can rise in both importing and exporting countries as a result of specialization.

8. *Tariffs* and *quotas* aim to protect a country's industries from foreign competition. Such protection may sometimes be advantageous to that country, but not if foreign countries adopt tariffs and quotas of their own in retaliation.

9. Although the same trade restrictions can be accomplished by either a tariff or a quota, tariffs offer at least two advantages to the country that imposes them: some of the gains go to the government rather than to foreign producers, and they provide greater incentive for efficient production.

10. When a nation shifts from protection to free trade, some industries and their workers will lose out. Equity then demands that these people and firms be compensated in some way. The U.S. government offers protection from import surges and various forms of *trade adjustment assistance* to help those workers and industries adapt.

11. Several arguments for protectionism can, under the right circumstances, have validity. These include the national defense argument, the *infant-industry argument*, and the use of trade restrictions for *strategic* purposes. But each of these arguments is frequently abused.

12. *Dumping* will hurt certain domestic producers, but it benefits domestic consumers.

---

## KEY TERMS

Imports  730

Exports  730

Specialization  732

Mutual gains from trade  732

Absolute advantage  733

Comparative advantage  733

"Cheap foreign labor" argument  737

Mercantilism  739

Tariff  739

Quota  740

Export subsidy  740

Trade adjustment assistance  744

Infant-industry argument  745

Strategic trade policy  745

Dumping  747

---

## QUESTIONS FOR REVIEW

1. You have a dozen shirts and your roommate has six pairs of shoes worth roughly the same amount of money. You decide to swap six shirts for three pairs of shoes. In financial terms, neither of you gains anything. Explain why you are nevertheless both likely to be better off.

2. In the 18th century, some writers argued that one person in a trade could be made better off only by gaining at the expense of the other. Explain the fallacy in the argument.

3. Country A has a cold climate with a short growing season, but a highly skilled labor force. What sorts of products do you think it is likely to produce? What are the characteristics of the countries with which you would expect it to trade?

4. Upon removal of a quota on sugar, many U.S. sugar farms go bankrupt. Discuss the pros and cons of removing the quota in the short and long runs.

5. Country A's mercantilist government believes that it is always best to export more than it imports. As a consequence, it exports more to Country B every year than it imports from Country B. After 100 years of this arrangement, both countries are destroyed in an earthquake. What were the advantages or disadvantages of the surplus to Country A? To Country B?

6. The following table describes the number of yards of cloth and barrels of wine that can be produced with a week's worth of labor in England and Portugal. Assume that no other inputs are needed.

|  | In England | In Portugal |
|---|---|---|
| Cloth | 8 yards | 12 yards |
| Wine | 2 barrels | 6 barrels |

a. If there is no trade, what is the price of wine in terms of cloth in England?

b. If there is no trade, what is the price of wine relative to cloth in Portugal?

c. Suppose each country has 1 million weeks of labor available per year. Draw the production possibilities frontier for each country.

d. Which country has an absolute advantage in the production of which good(s)? Which country has a comparative advantage in the production of which good(s)?

e. If the countries start trading with each other, which country will specialize and export which good?

f. What can be said about the price at which trade will take place?

7. Suppose that the United States and Mexico are the only two countries in the world and that labor is the only productive input. In the United States, a worker can produce 12 bushels of wheat *or* 2 barrels of oil in a day. In Mexico, a worker can produce 2 bushels of wheat *or* 4 barrels of oil per day.

a. What will be the price ratio between the two commodities (that is, the price of oil in terms of wheat) in each country if there is no trade?

b. If free trade is allowed and there are no transportation costs, what commodity would the United States import? What about Mexico?

c. In what range would the price ratio have to fall under free trade? Why?

d. Picking one possible post-trade price ratio, show clearly how it is possible for both countries to benefit from free trade.

8. The following table presents the demand and supply curves for microcomputers in Japan and the United States.

| Price per Computer | Quantity Demanded in U.S. | Quantity Supplied in U.S. | Quantity Demanded in Japan | Quantity Supplied in Japan |
|---|---|---|---|---|
| 1 | 90 | 30 | 50 | 50 |
| 2 | 80 | 35 | 40 | 55 |
| 3 | 70 | 40 | 30 | 60 |
| 4 | 60 | 45 | 20 | 65 |
| 5 | 50 | 50 | 10 | 70 |
| 6 | 40 | 55 | 0 | 75 |

NOTE: Price and quanitity are in thousands.

   a. Draw the demand and supply curves for the United States on one diagram and those for Japan on another one.
   b. If the United States and Japan do not trade, what are the equilibrium price and quantity in the computer market in the United States? In Japan?
   c. Now suppose trade is opened up between the two countries. What will be the equilibrium price in the world market for computers? What has happened to the price of computers in the United States? In Japan?
   d. Which country will export computers? How many?
   e. When trade opens, what happens to the quantity of computers produced, and therefore employment, in the computer industry in the United States? In Japan? Who benefits and who loses *initially* from free trade?

9. Under current trade law, the president of the United States must report periodically to Congress on countries engaging in unfair trade practices that inhibit U.S. exports. How would you define an "unfair" trade practice? Suppose Country X exports much more to the United States than it imports, year after year. Does that constitute evidence that Country X's trade practices are unfair? What would constitute such evidence?

10. Suppose the United States finds Country X guilty of unfair trade practices and penalizes it with import quotas. So U.S. imports from Country X fall. Suppose, further, that Country X does not alter its trade practices in any way. Is the United States better or worse off? What about Country X?

Cecily, you will read your Political Economy in my absence. The chapter on the Fall of the Rupee you may omit. It is somewhat too sensational.

Miss Prism in Oscar Wilde's,
*The Importance of Being Earnest*

# THE INTERNATIONAL MONETARY SYSTEM: ORDER OR DISORDER?

Miss Prism, the Victorian tutor, may have had a point. In the summer of 1997, the rupiah fell and economic disaster in Indonesia quickly followed. The International Monetary Fund rushed to the rescue with billions of dollars and pages of advice. But its plan failed, and some say it may even have helped precipitate the bloody riots that led to the fall of the Indonesian government.

This chapter is not about such sensational political upheavals. Rather, it focuses on a seemingly mundane topic: how the market determines rates of exchange among different national currencies. But events in Southeast Asia in 1997 and 1998 amply demonstrated that dramatic exchange rate movements can have human as well as financial severe consequences. This chapter and the next will help us understand why.

### What Happened to the Asian Tigers?

As recently as the middle of 1997, a number of the so-called Asian Tiger economies were considered models of success. Hard work, high saving, market-friendly government policies, and a determined drive to export had raised living standards enormously in South Korea, Indonesia, Thailand, and Malaysia, to name a few. Southeast Asia was the fastest-growing region in the world, and international capital was pouring in.

Then, starting in Thailand in July 1997, the bottom fell out. With a suddenness that was both stunning and destructive, investors took fright and massive amounts of money started flowing out instead of flowing in. Thailand, Indonesia, Malaysia, the Philippines, and then Korea were all forced to abandon fixed exchange rates. Currency values plummeted, interest rates soared, and stock markets collapsed. The Thai currency, the baht, which had been fixed at about 4 cents, tumbled to less than 2 cents by the end of the year. The Indonesian rupiah dropped even more. In June 1997, about 2,500 rupiah could buy a U.S. dollar; by January 1998, it took more than 10,000. Soon inflation, which had been quite low in all these countries, was on the rise. Severe recessions quickly followed.

What went so badly wrong? What forced one Southeast Asian nation after another to abandon its fixed exchange rate? And why did that decision have such dire consequences? We will learn some of the answers in this and the following chapter. But first we need to understand what determines exchange rates.

## ■ WHAT ARE EXCHANGE RATES?

We noted in the previous chapter that international trade is more complicated than domestic trade. There are no national borders to be crossed when, say, California lettuce is shipped to Massachusetts. The consumer in Boston pays with *dollars*, just the currency that the farmer in Modesto wants. But if that same farmer ships his lettuce to Japan, consumers there will have only Japanese *yen* with which to pay, rather than the dollars the farmer in California wants. Thus, if international trade is to take place, there must be some way to convert one currency into another. The rates at which such conversions are made are called **exchange rates.**

The **exchange rate** states the price, in terms of one currency, at which another currency can be bought.

There is an exchange rate between every pair of currencies. For example, one British pound is currently the equivalent of about $1.60. The exchange rate between the pound and the dollar, then, may be expressed as roughly "$1.60 to the pound" (meaning that it costs $1.60 to buy a pound) or about "63 pence to the dollar" (meaning that it costs 63 British pence to buy a dollar).

Exchange rates vis-à-vis the United States have changed dramatically over time. In a nutshell, the dollar soared in the period from mid-1980 to early 1985, fell relative to most major currencies from early 1985 until early 1988, and has generally fluctuated—sometimes sharply—with no clear trend since. This chapter seeks to explain such currency movements.

Under our present system, currency rates change frequently. When other currencies become more expensive in terms of dollars, we say that they have **appreciated** relative to the dollar. Alternatively, we can look at this same event as the dollar buying less foreign currency, meaning that the dollar has **depreciated** relative to another currency.

> **What is a depreciation to one country must be an appreciation to the other.**

For example, if the cost of a pound rises from $1.60 to $2, the cost of a U.S. dollar in terms of pounds simultaneously falls from 63 pence to 50 pence. The United Kingdom has had a currency *appreciation*, whereas the United States has had a currency *depreciation*.

Notice also that, when many currencies are changing in value, the dollar may be appreciating with respect to one currency but depreciating with respect to another. Table 36–1 offers a selection of exchange rates prevailing in July 1980, February 1985, and June 1999, showing how many dollars or cents it cost at each of those times to buy each unit of foreign currency. You will note that, between February 1985 and June 1999, the dollar *depreciated* sharply relative to the Japanese yen and most European currencies. For example, the British pound rose from $1.10 to $1.60. Yet during that same period the dollar *appreciated* dramatically relative to the Mexican peso; it bought about 0.2 pesos in 1985 but over 9.5 in 1999.[1]

Although the terms "appreciation" and "depreciation" are used to describe movements of exchange rates in free markets, a different set of terms is used to describe decreases and increases in currency values that are set by government decree. When

A nation's currency is said to **appreciate** when exchange rates change so that a unit of its own currency can buy more units of foreign currency.

The currency is said to **depreciate** when exchange rates change so that a unit of its currency can buy fewer units of foreign currency.

## Exchange Rates with the U.S. Dollar

TABLE 36–1

| Country | Currency | Symbol | Cost in Dollars | | |
|---------|----------|--------|-----------|-----------|-----------|
| | | | **July 1980** | **Feb. 1985** | **June 1999** |
| Australia | dollar | $ | $1.16 | $0.74 | $0.66 |
| Canada | dollar | $ | 0.87 | 0.74 | 0.68 |
| France | franc | FF | 0.25 | 0.10 | 0.16* |
| Germany | mark | DM | 0.57 | 0.30 | 0.53* |
| Italy | lira | L | 0.0012 | 0.00049 | 0.00053* |
| Japan | yen | ¥ | 0.0045 | 0.0038 | 0.0083 |
| Mexico | new peso | $ | 44.0† | 5.0† | 0.10 |
| Sweden | krona | Kr | 0.24 | 0.11 | 0.12 |
| Switzerland | franc | S.Fr. | 0.62 | 0.36 | 0.65 |
| United Kingdom | pound | £ | 2.37 | 1.10 | 1.60 |
| — | euro | € | — | — | 1.03 |

NOTE: Exchange rates are in U.S. dollars per unit of foreign currency.

*These exchange rates were locked together at the start of the euro in January 1999.

†On January 1, 1993, the peso was redefined so that 1,000 old pesos were equal to one new peso. Hence, the numbers 44 and 5 listed for July 1980 and February 1985 were actually 0.044 and 0.005 on the old basis.

SOURCE: International Financial Statistics and *The Wall Street Journal*.

---

[1] In fact, the dollar bought about 200 pesos in February 1985, but that is because the old peso was replaced by a new peso in January 1993, which moved the decimal point three places.

A **devaluation** is a reduction in the official value of a currency.

A **revaluation** is an increase in the official value of a currency.

an officially set exchange rate is altered so that a unit of a nation's currency can buy *fewer* units of foreign currency, we say there has been a **devaluation** of that currency. When the exchange rate is altered so that the currency can buy *more* units of foreign currency, we say there has been a **revaluation.** We will say more about devaluation and revaluation shortly, but first let's look at how the free market determines exchange rates.

## EXCHANGE RATE DETERMINATION IN A FREE MARKET

**Floating exchange rates** are rates determined in free markets by the law of supply and demand.

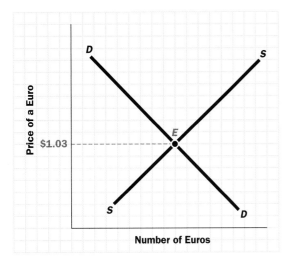

**FIGURE 36-1**

**Determination of Exchange Rates in a Free Market**

At the start of 1999, eleven European countries adopted a new common currency, the euro. Why is it that a euro now costs about $1.03 and not $0.93 or $1.13? In a world of **floating exchange rates,** with no government interferences, the answer would be straightforward. Exchange rates would be determined by the forces of supply and demand, just like the prices of apples, computers, and haircuts.

In a leap of abstraction, imagine that the dollar and the euro are the only currencies on earth, so the market need determine only one exchange rate. Figure 36–1 depicts the determination of this exchange rate at the point (denoted *E* in the figure) where demand curve *DD* crosses supply curve *SS*. At this price ($1.03 per euro), the number of euros demanded is equal to the number of euros supplied.

In a free market, exchange rates are determined by supply and demand. At a rate below the equilibrium level, the number of euros demanded would exceed the number supplied, and the price of a euro would be bid up. At a rate above the equilibrium level, quantity supplied would exceed quantity demanded, and the price of a euro would fall. Only at the equilibrium exchange rate is there no tendency for the exchange rate to change.

As usual, supply and demand determine price. But in this case, we must ask: From where do the supply and demand come? Why does anyone demand a euro? The answer has three parts:

■ *International trade in goods and services.* This was the subject of the previous chapter. If, for example, Jane Doe, an American, wants to buy a new BMW, she will first have to buy euros with which to pay the dealer in Munich.[2] So Jane's demand for a European car leads to a demand for European currency. In general, *demand for a country's exports leads to demand for its currency.*[3]

■ *International trade in financial instruments like stocks and bonds.* If American investors want to purchase Italian stocks, they will first have to acquire the euros that the sellers will insist on for payment. In this way, demand for European financial assets leads to demand for European currency. Thus, *demand for a country's financial assets leads to demand for its currency.*

■ *Purchases of physical assets like factories and machinery overseas.* If IBM wants to buy out a small French computer manufacturer, the owners will no doubt want to receive euros. So IBM will first have to acquire European currency. In general, *direct foreign investment leads to demand for a country's currency.*

Now, where does the supply come from? To answer this, just turn all of these transactions around. Europeans who want to buy U.S. goods and services, invest in U.S. financial markets, or make direct investments in the United States will have to

---

[2] Actually, she will not do this because banks generally handle foreign exchange transactions for consumers. An American bank probably will buy the euros for her. But the effect is exactly the same as if Jane had done it herself.

[3] See Review Question 2 at the end of this chapter.

offer their euros for sale in the foreign-exchange market (which is mainly run through banks) to acquire the needed dollars. To summarize:

> The *demand* for a country's currency is derived from the demands of foreigners for its export goods and services and for its assets—including financial assets, like stocks and bonds, and real assets, like factories and machinery. The *supply* of a country's currency arises from its imports, and from foreign investment by its own citizens.

To appreciate the usefulness of even this simple supply and demand analysis, think about how the exchange rate between the dollar and the euro would be changed by an economic boom in the United States. One important effect of such a boom would be to stimulate American demand for European products, such as machine tools, fashions, and wine. In terms of the supply-demand diagram shown in Figure 36–2, the increased desires of Americans for European goods would shift the demand curve for euros out from $D_1D_1$ (the black line in the figure) to $D_2D_2$ (the red line). Equilibrium would shift from point $E$ to point $A$, and the exchange rate would rise from $1.03 per euro to $1.12 per euro. Thus the increased demand for euros by U.S. citizens causes the euro to *appreciate* relative to the dollar.

**EXERCISE** Test your understanding of the supply and demand analysis of exchange rates by showing why each of the following events would lead to an appreciation of the euro (a depreciation of the dollar) in a free market:

1. A recession in Italy cuts Italian purchases of American goods.
2. American investors are attracted by prospects for profit on the German stock market.
3. Interest rates on government bonds rise in France but are stable in the United States. (*Hint:* Which country's citizens will be attracted to invest by high interest rates in the other country?)

**FIGURE 36-2**

**The Effect of an Economic Boom Abroad on the Exchange Rate**

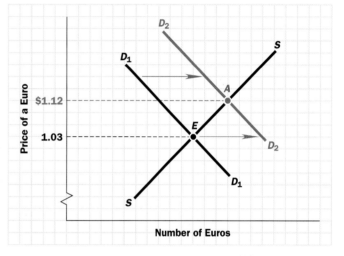

To say that supply and demand determine exchange rates in a free market is at once to say everything and to say nothing. If we are to understand the reasons why some currencies appreciate whereas others depreciate, we must look into the factors that move the supply and demand curves. Economists believe that the principal determinants of exchange rate movements differ significantly in the long, medium, and short runs. So we turn in the next three sections to the analysis of exchange rate movements over these three "runs," beginning with the long run.

## THE PURCHASING-POWER PARITY THEORY: THE LONG RUN

As long as goods can move freely across national borders, exchange rates should eventually adjust so that the same product costs the same amount of money, whether measured in dollars in the United States, euros in Germany, yen in Japan, and so on—except for differences in transportation costs and the like. This simple statement forms the basis of the major theory of exchange rate determination in the long run.

> The *purchasing-power parity theory of exchange rate determination* holds that the exchange rate between any two national currencies adjusts to reflect differences in the price levels in the two countries.

An example will bring out the basic truth in this theory and also suggest some of its limitations. Suppose German and American steel is identical and that these two nations are the only producers of steel for the world market. Suppose further that steel is the only tradable good that either country produces.

*Question:* If American steel costs $220 per ton and German steel costs 200 euros per ton, what must be the exchange rate between the dollar and the euro?

*Answer:* Because 200 euros or $220 each buys a ton of steel, they must be of equal value. Hence, each euro must be worth $1.10. Why? Any higher price for a euro, like $1.20, would mean that steel would cost $240 per ton (200 euros at $1.20 each) in Germany but only $220 per ton in the United States. In that case, all foreign customers would shop for their steel in the United States—which would increase the demand for dollars and decrease the demand for euros. Similarly, any exchange rate below $1.10 per euro would send all the steel business to Germany, driving the value of the euro up toward its purchasing-power parity level.

**EXERCISE**   Show why an exchange rate of $1.00 per euro is too low to lead to an equilibrium in the international steel market.

The purchasing-power parity theory is used to make long-run predictions about the effects of inflation on exchange rates. To continue our example, suppose that steel (and other) prices in the United States rise while prices in Europe are constant. The purchasing-power parity theory predicts that the euro will appreciate relative to the dollar. It also predicts the amount of the appreciation. After the inflation, American steel costs more, say $250 per ton, while German steel still costs 200 euros per ton. For these two prices to be equivalent, 200 euros must be worth $250, or one euro must be worth $1.25. The euro, therefore, must have risen from $1.10 to $1.25.

> According to the purchasing-power parity theory, differences in domestic inflation rates are a major cause of exchange rate movements. If one country has higher inflation than another, its exchange rate should be depreciating.

For many years, the theory seemed to work tolerably well. Although precise numerical predictions based on purchasing-power parity calculations were never very accurate (see the accompanying box, "Purchasing Power Parity and the Big Mac"), nations with higher inflation did at least experience depreciating currencies. But in the 1980s, even this rule broke down. For example, although the U.S. inflation rate was consistently higher than both Germany's and Japan's, the dollar nonetheless rose sharply relative to both the German mark and the Japanese yen from 1980 to 1985. The same thing happened again between 1995 and 1998. Clearly, the theory is missing something. What?

Many things. But perhaps the principal failing of the purchasing-power parity theory is that it focuses too much on trade in goods and services. Financial assets like stocks and bonds are also traded actively across national borders—and in vastly greater dollar volumes than goods and services. In fact, the astounding *daily* volume of foreign exchange transactions—more than $1.5 trillion—exceeds an entire *month's* worth of world trade in goods and services. The vast majority of these transactions are financial. If investors decide that, say, U.S. assets are a better bet than Japanese assets, the dollar will rise, even if our inflation rate is well above Japan's. For this and other reasons:

> Most economists believe that other factors are much more important than relative price levels for exchange rate determination in the short run. But in the long run, purchasing-power parity plays an important role.

## THE MEDIUM RUN: ECONOMIC ACTIVITY AND EXCHANGE RATES

Because consumer spending increases when income rises and decreases when income falls, the same is likely to happen to spending on imported goods. For this reason:

> A country's imports will rise quickly when its economy booms and rise only slowly when its economy stagnates.

We have already illustrated this point with Figure 36–2. There we saw that a boom in the United States would shift the demand curve for euros outward as Americans bought more European goods. And that, in turn, would lead to an appreciation of the euro (depreciation of the dollar) as Americans sold dollars to buy euros. However, if Europe was booming at the same time, Europeans would be buying

---

● **PURCHASING-POWER PARITY AND THE BIG MAC**

---

Since 1986, *The Economist* magazine has been using a well-known international commodity—the Big Mac—to assess the purchasing-power parity theory of exchange rates, or as the magazine once put it, "to make exchange-rate theory more digestible."

Here's how it works. In theory, the local price of a Big Mac, when translated into U.S. dollars by the exchange rate, should be the same everywhere in the world. The following numbers show that the theory does not work terribly well.

For example, although a Big Mac costs an average of $2.63 in the United States, it sold for just 4.3 ringgit in Malaysia. Using the exchange rate (at the time) of 3.8 ringgit to the dollar, that amounts to just $1.13. Thus, according to the hamburger parity theory, the ringgit was grossly undervalued.

By how much? The price in Malaysia was just 43 percent of the price in the United States ($1.13/$2.63 = 0.43). So the ringgit was 57 percent below its Big Mac parity—and therefore should appreciate. The other numbers in the table have similar interpretations.

True Big Mac aficionados may find these data helpful when planning international travel. But can deviations from Big Mac parity predict exchange rate movements? Surprisingly, they can.

When economist Robert Cumby studied Big Mac prices and exchange rates in 14 countries over a 10-year period, he found that deviations from hamburger parity were transitory. Their "half-life" was just a year, meaning that 50 percent of the deviation tended to disappear within a year. Thus the undervalued currencies in the accompanying table would be predicted to appreciate during 1999, whereas the overvalued currencies would be expected to depreciate.

**Deviations from Big Mac Purchasing Power Parity, December 1998**

| Country | Big Mac Prices | Percent Over (+) or Under (−) Valuation against dollar |
|---|---|---|
| United States | $2.63 | — |
| Venezuela | 3.33 | +27% |
| Israel | 3.25 | +24 |
| Germany | 2.99 | +14 |
| Chile | 2.66 | +1 |
| Japan | 2.39 | −9 |
| Mexico | 1.90 | −28 |
| South Africa | 1.44 | −45 |
| China | 1.20 | −54 |
| Malaysia | 1.13 | −57 |

NOTE: Prices are in U.S. dollars.

SOURCE: *The Economist*, December 19, 1998, p. 150 and Robert Cumby, "Forecasting Exchange Rates and Relative Prices with the Hamburger Standard: Is What You Want What You Get with McParity?" Georgetown University, May 1997.

---

more American exports, which would shift the supply curve of euros outward. On balance, the value of the dollar might or might not fall. What matters is whether exports are growing faster than imports. The general lesson is that:

> Other things equal, a country whose aggregate demand grows faster than the rest of the world's normally finds its imports growing faster than its exports. Thus, its demand curve for foreign currency shifts outward more rapidly than its supply curve, causing its currency to depreciate.

This is one reason why it is unwise to interpret a "strong currency" as an indication of a "strong economy." A nation that grows more rapidly than its trading partners is doing very well. Nonetheless, it may find itself with a depreciating currency.

## INTEREST RATES AND EXCHANGE RATES: THE SHORT RUN

Although economic activity is important for exchange rate determination in the medium run, "other things" often are not equal in the short run. Specifically, one factor that often seems to call the tune in determining exchange rate movements in the short run is *interest rate differentials*. A multitrillion dollar pool of so-called *hot money*—owned by banks, investment funds, multinational corporations, and wealthy individuals of all nations—travels rapidly around the globe in search of the highest interest rates.

Thus, suppose British government bonds pay a 5 percent rate of interest when yields on equally safe American government securities rise to 7 percent. British investors will be attracted by the high interest rates in the United States and will offer pounds for sale in order to buy dollars, planning to use those dollars to buy American securities. At the same time, American investors will find investing in the United States more attractive than ever, so fewer pounds will be demanded by Americans.

When the demand schedule shifts inward and the supply curve shifts outward, the effect on price is predictable: The pound will depreciate, as Figure 36–3 shows. In the figure, the supply curve of pounds shifts outward from $S_1S_1$ to $S_2S_2$ when British investors seek to sell pounds in order to purchase U.S. securities. At the same time, American investors wish to buy fewer pounds because they no longer wish to invest in British securities. Thus, the demand curve shifts inward from $D_1D_1$ to $D_2D_2$. The result, in our example, is a depreciation of the pound from $1.60 to $1.40. In general:

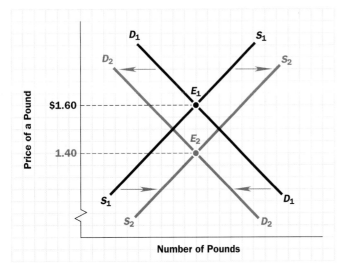

> Other things equal, countries that offer investors higher rates of return attract more capital than countries that offer lower rates. Thus, a rise in interest rates often will lead to an appreciation of the currency, and a drop in interest rates will lead to a depreciation.

Most experts in international finance agree that interest rates and financial flows are the major determinants of exchange rates in the short run. They certainly played a predominant role in the stunning movements of the U.S. dollar in the 1980s. In the early 1980s, American interest rates rose well above comparable interest rates abroad. In consequence, foreign capital was attracted here, American capital stayed at home, and the dollar soared. Similarly, a nation that suffers from capital flight, as the Southeast Asian countries did in 1997 and 1998, must offer extremely high interest rates to attract foreign capital.

## MARKET DETERMINATION OF EXCHANGE RATES: SUMMARY

We can summarize this discussion of exchange rate determination in free markets as follows:

1. Currency values generally will *appreciate* in countries with lower inflation rates than the rest of the world's, because buyers in foreign countries will demand their goods and thus drive up their currencies.

2. Exchange rates would also be expected to rise in countries where aggregate demand is growing more slowly than average, because these countries will be importing relatively little.

3. We expect to find appreciating currencies in countries that offer investors higher rates of return because these countries will attract capital from all over the world.

Reversing each of these, we expect that currencies will *depreciate* in countries with relatively high inflation rates, or rapid demand growth, or low interest rates.

## ■ FIXED EXCHANGE RATES AND THE BALANCE OF PAYMENTS

Some exchange rates today are truly floating, determined by the forces of supply and demand without government interference. But many are not. Furthermore, some people claim that exchange rate fluctuations are so troublesome that the world would be better off with fixed exchange rates. For these reasons, we turn next to a system of **fixed exchange rates,** or rates that are set by governments.

Naturally, under such a system the exchange rate, being fixed, is not closely watched. Instead, international financial specialists focus on a country's *balance of payments*—a term we must now define—to gauge movements in the supply of and demand for a currency.

To understand what the balance of payments is, look at Figure 36–4, which depicts a situation that might represent, say, Thailand just before the Asian crisis broke in the summer of 1997—an *overvalued* currency. Although the supply and demand curves for baht indicate an equilibrium exchange rate of 3 cents to the baht (point *E*), the Thai government is holding the rate at 4 cents. Notice that, at 4 cents per baht, more people supply baht than are demanding them. In the example, suppliers are offering to sell 800 billion baht per year, but purchasers want to buy only 400 billion.

This gap between the 800 billion baht that some people wish to sell and the 400 billion that others wish to buy is what we mean by Thailand's **balance of payments deficit**—400 billion baht (or about $16 billion) per year in this case. It appears as the horizontal distance between points *A* and *B* in Figure 36–4.

How can governments flout market forces in this way? Because sales and purchases on any market must be equal, as a simple piece of arithmetic, the excess of quantity supplied over quantity demanded—or 400 billion baht per year in this example—must be bought by the Thai government. To purchase these baht, it must give up some of the foreign currency that it holds as *reserves*. Thus, the Bank of Thailand would be losing about $16 billion in reserves per year as the cost of keeping the baht at 4 cents.

Naturally, this cannot go on forever, as the reserves eventually will run out. This is the fatal flaw of a fixed exchange rate system. Once speculators become convinced that the exchange rate can be held for only a short while longer, they will sell the overvalued currency in massive amounts rather than hold on to money whose value they expect to fall.

That is precisely what happened to Thailand in the summer of 1997. The supply curve of baht shifted outward drastically, as shown in Figure 36–5, causing a sharp rise in the balance of payments deficit—from 400 billion to 800 billion baht in the example. (The numbers are fictitious.) Lacking sufficient reserves, the Thai government had no choice but to let the baht fall to its equilibrium level, and this amounted to an even larger devaluation than would have been required before the speculative "run" on the baht.

For an example of the reverse case, a severely *undervalued* currency, let us go back in history to the case of West Germany in 1973. Figure 36–6 depicts demand and supply curves for marks that intersect at an equilibrium price of 50 cents per mark (point *E* in the diagram). Yet, in the example, we suppose that the German authorities are holding the rate at 33 cents. At this rate, the quantity of marks demanded (50 billion) greatly exceeds the quantity supplied (40 billion). The difference is Germany's **balance of payments surplus,** shown by the horizontal distance *AB*.

Germany can keep the rate at 33 cents only by providing the marks that foreigners want to buy: 10 billion marks per year in this example. In return, it receives U.S. dollars, British pounds, French francs, gold, and so on. All of this serves to increase Germany's reserves of

**Fixed exchange rates** are rates set by government decisions and maintained by government actions.

### FIGURE 36–4

## A Balance of Payments Deficit

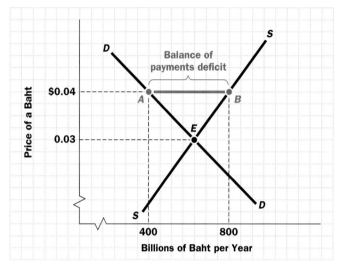

The **balance of payments deficit** is the amount by which the quantity supplied of a country's currency (per year) exceeds the quantity demanded. Balance of payments deficits arise whenever the exchange rate is pegged at an artificially high level.

### FIGURE 36–5

## A Speculative Run on the Baht

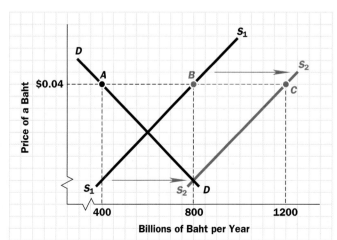

FIGURE 36-6

**A Balance of Payments Surplus**

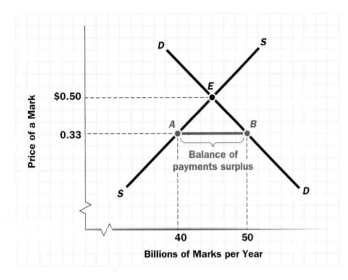

Billions of Marks per Year

The **balance of payments surplus** is the amount by which the quantity demanded of a country's currency (per year) exceeds the quantity supplied. Balance of payments surpluses arise whenever the exchange rate is pegged at an artificially low level.

The **current account balance** includes international purchases and sales of goods and services, cross-border interest and dividend payments, and cross-border gifts to and from both private individuals and governments.

The **capital account balance** includes purchases and sales of financial assets to and from citizens and companies of other countries.

foreign currencies. But notice one important difference between this case and the overvalued baht.

*The accumulation of reserves rarely will force a central bank to revalue in the way that losses of reserves can force a devaluation.*

This asymmetry is a clear weakness in a fixed exchange rate system. In principle, an exchange rate disequilibrium can be cured either by a *devaluation* by the country with a balance of payments deficit or by an upward *revaluation* by the country with a balance of payments surplus. In practice, though, only deficit countries are forced to act.

Why do surplus countries refuse to revalue? One reason is often a stubborn refusal to recognize some basic economic realities. They tend to view the disequilibrium as a problem that the deficit countries have created and thus believe that the deficit countries should take the corrective steps. This, of course, is nonsense in a worldwide system of fixed exchange rates. Some currencies are overvalued *because* some other currencies are undervalued. In fact, the two statements mean exactly the same thing.

The other reason why surplus countries resist upward revaluations is that such actions would make their exports more expensive to foreigners and thus cut into their sales. And export industries often have the political clout to make their views stick.

## DEFINING THE BALANCE OF PAYMENTS IN PRACTICE

The preceding discussion makes it look simple to measure a nation's balance of payments position: Just count up the private demand for and supply of its currency and subtract quantity supplied from quantity demanded. Conceptually, that is all there is to it. But in practice the difficulties are great because we never directly observe the number of dollars demanded and supplied.

Actual market transactions show that the number of, say, U.S. dollars *purchased* always equals the number of U.S. dollars *sold*. Unless someone has made a bookkeeping error, this must be so. How, then, can we recognize a balance of payments surplus or deficit? Easy, you say. Just look at the transactions of the central bank, whose purchases or sales must make up the difference between private demand and private supply. If the Federal Reserve is buying dollars, its purchases measure our balance of payments deficit. If the Fed is selling, its sales represent our balance of payments surplus. Thus, the idea is to measure the balance of payments by *excluding official transactions among governments.* That is, more or less, what is done.

In practice, the balance of payments accounts come in two main parts. The **current account** totes up exports and imports of goods and services, cross-border payments of interest and dividends, and cross-border gifts. The United States has been running large current account deficits for years.

But that represents only one part of our balance of payments, for it leaves out all purchases and sales of assets. Purchases of U.S. assets by foreigners bring foreign currency to the United States, and purchases of foreign assets cost us foreign currency. Netting the capital flows in each direction gives us our surplus or deficit on **capital account.** In recent years, this part of our balance of payments accounts has registered persistently large surpluses as foreigners have acquired U.S. assets.

In what sense, then, does the overall balance of payments balance? There are two possibilities. If the exchange rate is *floating*, all private transactions—current account plus capital account—must add up to zero (dollars purchased = dollars sold). But if, instead, the exchange rate is *fixed*, as shown in Figures 36–4 and 36–6, the two accounts need not balance one another. Government purchases or sales of foreign currency make up the surplus or deficit in the overall balance of payments.

# A BIT OF HISTORY: THE GOLD STANDARD AND THE BRETTON WOODS SYSTEM

It is hard to find examples of strictly fixed exchange rates in the historical record. About the only time exchange rates were truly fixed was under the old *gold standard*, at least when it was practiced in its ideal form.[4]

## THE CLASSICAL GOLD STANDARD

Under the gold standard, governments maintained fixed exchange rates by an automatic equilibrating mechanism that went something like this: All currencies were defined in terms of gold; indeed, some were actually made of gold. When a nation ran a balance of payments deficit, it had to *sell* gold to finance the deficit. Because the domestic money supply was based on gold, losing gold to foreigners meant that the money supply fell *automatically*—and that raised interest rates. The higher interest rates attracted foreign capital. At the same time, this restrictive "monetary policy" also pulled down output and prices, which discouraged imports and encouraged exports. The balance of payments problem quickly rectified itself.

This automatic adjustment process meant, however, that under the gold standard no nation had control of its domestic monetary policy. The same problem arises in any system of fixed exchange rates, regardless of whether it makes use of gold:

> Under fixed exchange rates, monetary policy must be dedicated to pegging the exchange rate. It cannot, therefore, be used to manage aggregate demand.

The gold standard posed one other serious difficulty: The world's commerce was at the mercy of gold discoveries. Major gold finds would mean higher prices and booming economic conditions, through the standard monetary-policy mechanisms that we studied in earlier chapters. When the supply of gold failed to keep pace with growth of the world economy, prices had to fall in the long run and employment had to fall in the short run.

## THE BRETTON WOODS SYSTEM

The gold standard faltered many times and finally collapsed amid the financial chaos of the Great Depression of the 1930s and World War II. Without it, the world struggled through a serious breakdown in international trade.

Then, as the war drew to a close, representatives of the industrial nations met at Bretton Woods, New Hampshire, in 1944. They sought to establish a stable monetary environment that would restore world trade. Because the United States held the lion's share of the world's reserves at the time, these officials naturally turned to the dollar as the basis for the new international economic order.

The Bretton Woods agreements reestablished fixed exchange rates based on the free convertibility of the U.S. dollar into gold. The United States agreed to buy or sell gold to maintain the $35 per ounce price that President Franklin Roosevelt had established in 1933. The other signatory nations, which had almost no gold in any case, agreed to buy and sell *dollars* to maintain their exchange rates at agreed-upon levels. Thus, all currencies were indirectly tied to gold. A holder of French francs, for example, could exchange these for dollars at (roughly) 5 francs per dollar and then exchange the dollars for gold at $35 per ounce. In this way, the value of the franc was fixed at 175 francs per ounce of gold (5 francs per dollar times $35 per ounce).

The *International Monetary Fund (IMF)*, which has been much in the news of late, was established in 1944 to police and manage the Bretton Woods system. Using funds contributed by member countries, the IMF was empowered to make loans to countries

---

[4] As a matter of fact, although the gold standard lasted (on and off) for hundreds of years, it was rarely practiced in its ideal form. Except for a brief period of fixed exchange rates in the late 19th and early 20th centuries, governments periodically adjusted exchange rates even under the gold standard.

that were running low on reserves. Letting the exchange rate adjust was viewed as a last resort, for it was believed that fixed exchange rates were essential to world trade.

The Bretton Woods system inherited the flaws of any fixed exchange rate system. A change in exchange rates was to be permitted only in the case of a "fundamental disequilibrium" in a nation's balance of payments—for it was believed that only relatively fixed exchange rates could provide the stable climate needed to restore world trade.

Of course, the Bretton Woods conferees did not define clearly what a "fundamental disequilibrium" was, nor could they have. As the system evolved, it came to mean a chronic *deficit* in the balance of payments of sizable proportions. Such nations would then *devalue* their currencies relative to the dollar. So the system was not really one of fixed exchange rates, but rather one where rates were "fixed until further notice." Since the IMF sanctioned devaluations only after a long run of balance of payments deficits had depleted the country's reserves, these devaluations (1) could be clearly foreseen and (2) normally had to be large. Speculators thus saw glowing opportunities for profit and would "attack" weak currencies with waves of selling.

This problem led many economists to question whether the system of fixed exchange rates really provided the stable climate for world trade that had been intended. Was a system where rates were constant for long periods and then altered by large amounts really more conducive to international trade than one in which overvalued currencies would gradually depreciate, as they would under a system of floating rates?

A second problem arose from the asymmetry mentioned in the previous section: Deficit nations could be forced to devalue while surplus nations could resist upward revaluations. Because the value of the U.S. dollar was fixed in terms of gold, the United States was the one nation in the world that had no way to devalue its currency. The only way exchange rates between the dollar and foreign currencies could change was if the surplus nations revalued their currencies upward relative to the dollar. They did not do this frequently enough, so the United States developed an overvalued currency and chronic balance of payments deficits.

The overvalued dollar finally destroyed the Bretton Woods system. By August 1971, the depletion of America's reserves and the accumulation of foreign debts forced President Richard Nixon to end fixed exchange rates—which he did by announcing that the United States would no longer buy or sell gold at $35 per ounce. After some futile attempts to reestablish fixed rates, the Bretton Woods system died in 1973.

## ADJUSTMENT MECHANISMS UNDER FIXED EXCHANGE RATES

The Bretton Woods system viewed devaluation as a last resort, to be used only after other methods of adjusting to payments imbalances had failed. What were these other methods?

We encountered most of them in our earlier discussion of exchange rate determination in free markets. Any factor that *increases the demand* for, say, U.S. dollars or that *reduces the supply* will push the value of the dollar upward—if it is free to adjust. But if the exchange rate is pegged, the balance of payments deficit will do the adjusting instead. Specifically, the U.S. balance of payments deficit will *shrink* if either the demand for dollars increases or the supply decreases.

The two panels of Figure 36–7 illustrate these adjustments. In each case, the United States has a payments deficit, because the official exchange rate (3 marks to the dollar) exceeds the equilibrium rate (2 marks). The deficit starts at *AB* in each diagram. Then either the demand curve moves outward, as in Panel (a), or the supply curve moves inward, as in Panel (b). With the exchange rate held at 3 marks to the dollar, the balance of payments deficit shrinks—to *CB* in Panel (a) or to *AC* in Panel (b).

Recalling our earlier discussion of the factors that underlie the demand and supply curves, we see that one way a nation can shrink its balance of payments deficit is to *reduce its aggregate demand*, thus discouraging imports and cutting down its demand for foreign currency. Another is to *lower its rate of inflation*, thus

**Adjusting to Balance of Payments Deficits** | FIGURE 36-7

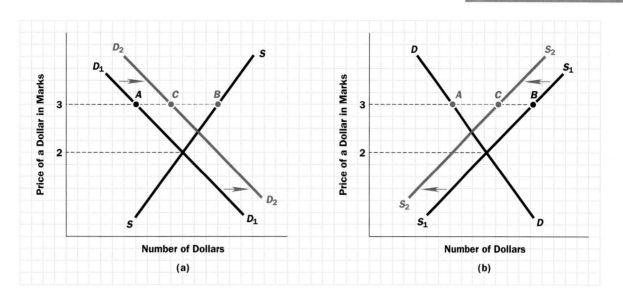

encouraging exports and discouraging imports. Finally, it can *raise its interest rates* to attract more foreign capital.

In other words, deficit nations are expected to follow restrictive monetary and fiscal policies *voluntarily*, just as they would have done *automatically* under the classical gold standard. However, just as under the gold standard, this medicine is often unpalatable.

A surplus nation could, of course, take the opposite measures: pursuing expansive monetary and fiscal policies to increase economic growth and lower interest rates. By increasing the supply of the country's currency and reducing the demand for it, such actions would reduce that nation's balance of payments surplus. But surplus countries often do not relish the inflation that accompanies expansionary policies, and so, once again, they leave the burden of adjustment to the deficit nations. The general point about fixed exchange rates is that:

> Under a system of fixed exchange rates, a country's government loses some control over its domestic economy. There may be times when balance of payments considerations force it to contract its economy in order to cut down its demand for foreign currency, even though domestic needs call for expansion. Conversely, there may be times when the domestic economy needs to be reined in, but balance of payments considerations suggest expansion.

Although we used the historical example of the dollar-mark exchange rate in Figure 36–7, this discussion helps us understand what several Southeast Asian governments would have needed to do in 1997 to stave off devaluations: raise interest rates and slow their economies.

But the authorities in Thailand, Indonesia, and the rest were accustomed to rapid growth and were naturally reluctant to risk the recessions that more restrictive monetary and fiscal policies probably would have brought on. So, instead of taking the bitter medicine, they sold their dollar reserves to buy their own currencies in an effort to maintain fixed exchange rates—a futile effort, as it turned out.

## ■ WHY TRY TO FIX EXCHANGE RATES?

In view of these and other problems with fixed exchange rates, why did the international financial community work so hard to maintain them for so many years? And why do some nations today still fix their exchange rates? The answer is that floating exchange rates also pose problems.

"Then it's agreed. Until the dollar firms up, we let the clamshell float."

Chief among these is the possibility that freely floating rates might prove to be highly variable rates, thereby adding an unwanted element of risk to foreign trade. For example, if the exchange rate is $1.10 to the euro, then a Parisian dress priced at 100 euros will cost $110. But should the euro appreciate to $1.50, that same dress would cost $150. An American department store thinking of buying the dress may need to place its order far in advance and will want to know the cost *in dollars*. It may be worried about the possibility that the value of the euro will rise, making the dress cost more than $110. And such worries might inhibit trade.

There are two responses to this concern. First, freely floating rates might prove to be fairly stable in practice. Prices of most ordinary goods and services, for example, are determined by supply and demand in free markets and do not fluctuate unduly. Unfortunately, experience since 1973 has dashed this hope. Exchange rates have proven to be extremely volatile, which is why some observers favor greater fixity in exchange rates.

A second possibility is that speculators might relieve business firms of exchange rate risks—for a fee, of course. Consider the department store example. If each euro costs $1.10 today, the department store manager can assure herself of paying exactly $110 for the dress several months from now by arranging for a speculator to deliver 100 euro to her at $1.10 per euro on the day she needs them. If the euro appreciates in the interim, the speculator, not the department store, will take the financial beating. Of course, if the euro depreciates, the speculator will pocket the profits. Thus, speculators play an important role in a system of floating exchange rates.

The widespread fears that speculative activity in free markets will lead to wild gyrations in prices, although occasionally valid, are often unfounded. The reason is simple. To make profits, international currency speculators must *buy* a currency when its value is low (thus helping to support the currency by pushing up its demand curve) and *sell* it when its value is high (thus holding down the price by adding to the supply curve). This means that successful speculators must come into the market as *buyers* when demand is weak (or when supply is strong) and come in as *sellers* when demand is strong (or supply is scant). In doing so, they help limit price fluctuations. Looked at the other way around, speculators can *destabilize* prices only if they are systematically willing to lose money.[5]

Notice the stark—and ironic—contrast to the system of fixed exchange rates in which speculation often leads to wild "runs" on currencies that are on the verge of devaluation—as happened in Southeast Asia in 1997. Speculative activity, which may well be *destabilizing* under fixed rates, is more likely to be *stabilizing* under floating rates.

We do not mean to imply that speculation makes floating rates trouble-free. At the very least, speculators will demand a fee for their services—a fee that adds to the costs of trading across national borders. In addition, speculators will not assume *all* exchange rate risks. For example, few contracts on foreign currencies last more than, say, a year or two. Thus, a business cannot easily protect itself from exchange rate changes over periods of many years. Finally, speculative markets can and do get carried away from time to time, moving currency rates in ways that are hard to understand, that frustrate the intentions of governments, and that devastate some people—as happened in Southeast Asia in 1997.

Despite all these problems, international trade has flourished under floating exchange rates. Perhaps exchange rate risk is not as burdensome as some people think.

## ■ THE CURRENT "NONSYSTEM"

The international financial system today is an eclectic blend of fixed and floating exchange rates, with no grand organizing principle. Indeed, it is so diverse that it is often called a "nonsystem."

---

[5] See Review Question 11 at the end of the chapter.

Some currencies are still pegged in the old Bretton Woods manner. Two examples are Argentina and Hong Kong, which maintain fixed values for their currencies by standing ready to buy or sell U.S. dollars as necessary. A few other countries employ a variation on this theme: They tie their currency to some other currency (say, the dollar), but let it depreciate gradually on a preannounced schedule. Brazil was perhaps the most prominent example of this "crawling peg" system until speculators destroyed it in January 1999. Other nations tie their currencies to a hypothetical "basket" of several currencies, rather than to a single currency.

More nations, however, let their exchange rates float, although not always freely. Such floating rates change slightly on a day-to-day basis, and market forces generally determine the basic trends, up or down. But governments do not hesitate to intervene to moderate exchange movements whenever they feel such actions are appropriate. Typically, interventions are aimed at ironing out what are deemed to be transitory fluctuations. But sometimes central banks oppose basic exchange rate trends. For example, the Federal Reserve and other central banks sold dollars aggressively in 1985 to push the dollar down, and they bought dollars in 1994 and 1995 to push the dollar up. The terms *dirty float* or *managed float* have been coined to describe this mongrel system.

## THE ROLE OF THE IMF

The role of the International Monetary Fund (IMF) in the current nonsystem is quite different from what it was under the old Bretton Woods system. No longer the police officer of fixed exchange rates, the Fund has evolved into a general-purpose international fire-and-rescue squad instead.

The IMF examines the economies of all its member nations on a regular basis. When a country runs into serious financial difficulties, it may turn to the Fund for help. The IMF typically provides loans, but with many strings attached. For example, if the country has a large current account deficit (as is normally the case when it comes to the IMF), the Fund will typically insist on contractionary fiscal and monetary policies to curb the country's appetite for imports. Often, this spells recession.

During the 1990s, the IMF found itself at the epicenter of several very visible economic crises: in Mexico in 1995, in Southeast Asia in 1997, in Russia in 1998, and in Brazil in 1999. While each case was different, they shared some common elements.

In each case, the crisis was precipitated by the collapse of a fixed exchange rate pegged to the U.S. dollar. In each case, the currency plummeted, with ruinous consequences. Questions were raised about the country's ability to pay its bills. In each case, the IMF arrived on the scene with both money and lots of advice, determined to stave off default. In the end, each country suffered through a severe recession—or worse.

The IMF's increased visibility has naturally brought it increased criticism. Some critics complain that the Fund sets excessively strict conditions on its client states, requiring them, for example, to cut their government budgets and raise interest rates in a recession—which just makes a bad domestic economic situation worse.

Other critics worry that the Fund is serving as a bill collector for banks and other financial institutions from the United States and other rich countries. These banks loaned money irresponsibly, these critics argue, and therefore deserve to lose it. By bailing them out of their losses, the IMF only encourages more reckless behavior in the future.

Suggestions for reform are everywhere (see the accompanying box, "Does the International Monetary System Need Reform?"), and major changes may be made in the international financial system in the coming years.

## THE VOLATILE DOLLAR

As mentioned earlier, floating exchange rates have not proven to be *stable* exchange rates. No currency illustrates this better than the U.S. dollar. (See Figure 36–8.)

In 1977 and 1978, the international value of the dollar plummeted until a concerted effort by central banks to buy dollars stopped the fall. The dollar then stabilized for

"Damn it! How <u>can</u> I relax, knowing that out there, somewhere, somehow, someone's attacking the dollar?"

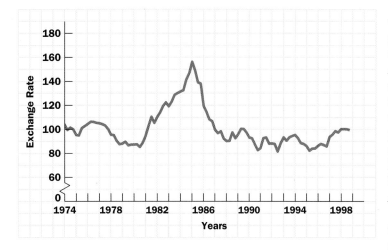

**FIGURE 36-8**

**The Ups and Downs of the Dollar**

NOTE: Exchange Rate in March 1973 = 100.

SOURCE: Federal Reserve System.

almost two years before rising like a rocket for a period of almost five years. As Table 36–1 showed, in July 1980 a U.S. dollar bought less than 2 German marks, about 4 French francs, and about 830 Italian lira. By the time it peaked in February 1985, the mighty dollar could buy more than 3 German marks, about 10 French francs, and over 2,000 Italian lira. Such major currency changes dramatically affect world trade.

The rising dollar was a blessing to Americans who traveled abroad or who bought foreign goods—because foreign prices, when translated to dollars by the exchange rate, looked cheap to Americans.[6] But the arithmetic worked just the other way around for U.S. firms seeking to sell their goods abroad; foreign buyers found everything American very expensive.[7] It was no surprise, therefore, that as the dollar climbed our exports fell, our imports rose, and many of our leading manufacturing industries were decimated by foreign competition. An expensive currency, Americans came to learn, is a mixed blessing.

From early 1985 until early 1988, the value of the dollar fell even faster than it had risen. The cheaper dollar curbed American appetites for imports and alleviated the plight of our export industries, many of which boomed. However, rising prices for imported goods and foreign vacations were a source of consternation to many American consumers.

Since 1988, the overall value of the dollar has not changed much—on average. But there have been quite a few appreciations and depreciations sharp enough to gain the attention of the world's financial markets and central banks. The international currency markets are anything but boring.

## THE DAWN OF THE EURO

As noted earlier, floating exchange rates are no magical cure-all. One particular problem confronted the members of the European Union (EU). As part of their long-range goal to create a unified market like that of the United States, they perceived a need to establish a single currency for all member countries—a monetary union.

---

[6] Example: How much does a 600-franc hotel room in Paris cost in dollars when the franc is worth 20 cents? 16 cents? 10 cents?

[7] Example: How much does a $55 American camera cost a German consumer when the mark is worth 55 cents? 44 cents? 33.33 cents?

Symbol for the euro.

The process of convergence to a single currency took place in steps, more or less as prescribed in the Treaty of Maastricht, over a period of years. Member nations encountered a number of serious obstacles along the way, including serious exchange rate crises in 1992 and 1993. But to the surprise of many skeptics, all such obstacles were overcome, and the euro is now a reality.

Since January 1999, electronic and checking transactions in 11 of the 15 EU nations have been denominated in euros rather than in national currencies. Three member nations—the United Kingdom, Sweden, and Denmark—have decided to opt out of the common currency project for now, and one country (Greece) has so far been unable to qualify because its inflation rate and budget deficit are too high.

In 2002, euro coins and paper money are scheduled to be introduced, after which French francs, German marks, Italian lira, and at least eight other national currencies will be withdrawn from circulation—and will become relics of the past. By that time, many observers believe, the U.K. will have joined the monetary union—although the British government has made no such commitment. If it all happens, every major European economy will be participating in what can only be called a grand experiment.

The establishment of the euro and the withdrawal of the other national currencies marks a giant step beyond mere fixed exchange rates. It actually means abolishing exchange rates among the participating nations. Just as there has long been no exchange rate between New York and New Jersey, there is now no exchange rate between Germany and France.

The difference between fixed exchange rates and a monetary union is consequential. A fixed exchange rate regime can be abolished at any time by decision of the relevant governments. And, as we have seen, speculators sometimes break fixed exchange rates even when governments want to maintain them. But Europe's monetary union was created by an international treaty and is more or less invulnerable to speculative attack. Monetary unions may create other problems, but exchange rate instability should not be one of them.

## The Fate of the Asian Tigers

So what have we learned so far about the causes of the currency crises in Southeast Asia?

First, the affected countries had chosen to peg their exchange rates to the U.S. dollar. They wound up with overvalued currencies for several reasons, but one important one was the sharp rise in the dollar's value starting in the spring of 1995 (see Figure 36–8). Countries like Malaysia and Thailand inadvertently hitched themselves to a rising star!

## ● POLICY DEBATE ▮ DOES THE INTERNATIONAL MONETARY SYSTEM NEED REFORM?

Robert Rubin, America's former Treasury secretary, wants to "modernize the architecture of the international financial markets." Eisuke Sakakibara, Japan's top international finance official, is thinking of a "Bretton Woods II." Alan Greenspan, chairman of the Federal Reserve, wants to review the "patchwork of arrangements" governing international finance. After East Asia's crisis, activism is in the air. . . .

It is easy to see why. . . . Policymakers worry that today's financial architecture, designed at Bretton Woods in 1944 for a world of limited capital mobility, may not be capable of dealing with an ever more global capital market. For international finance has been revolutionised. Formerly closed economies have cast off controls and embraced foreign funds. Better technology and financial innovation have made it easy to move money instantaneously.

The benefits are obvious: the expansion of private flows to developing countries. . . . But vast inflows can quickly become huge outflows. And financial crises can spread overnight between apparently unconnected markets. The five worst-affected Asian economies (South Korea, Indonesia, Thailand, Malaysia and the Philippines) received $93 billion of private capital flows in 1996. In 1997 they saw an outflow of $12 billion.

[One] reform to reinforce capital markets is better regulation. . . . Countless banking crises—in rich and poor countries alike—have shown that the combination of free capital flows and badly regulated banks is disastrous. . . . Others go much further, arguing that a global capital market needs global financial regulation, not a hotch-potch of national supervisors of varying quality. . . .

For many conservatives, particularly in America's Congress, the answer is to curb, or even eliminate, the IMF. It is the prospect of bail-outs, they argue, that encourages governments to profligacy and investors to recklessness. . . .

For those who see East Asia's crisis primarily as one of panic, . . . far more urgent is the need to control the capital flows themselves. . . . For those who are uneasy with the speed with which funds flow around the globe, the perennial idea of a tax on currency transactions has surfaced again. . . .

With such an array of possible reforms, it is hardly surprising that international officials are confused and uncertain [whereas] their political masters demand quick action.

SOURCE: "The Perils of Global Capital," *The Economist*, April 11, 1998.

Second, sizable current account deficits developed as a consequence of the overvaluations—as shown in Figure 36–4. But the governments of the countries were unwilling to adopt the contractionary monetary and fiscal policies that would have reduced or eliminated those deficits.

Third, both international speculators and domestic citizens saw something happening: The central banks of the Asian Tigers were losing reserves; it was only a matter of time until they ran out. That knowledge precipitated speculative attacks on one currency after another (as depicted in Figure 36–5), and Asia's fixed exchange rate systems crumbled.

There is more to be said about the Asian crisis, but that will have to wait until the next chapter—where we will study the macroeconomic impacts of exchange rates.

## SUMMARY

1. *Exchange rates* state the value of one currency in terms of others and thus translate one country's prices into the currencies of others. Exchange rates therefore influence patterns of world trade.

2. If governments do not interfere by buying or selling their currencies, exchange rates will be determined in free markets by the usual laws of supply and demand. Such a system is called *floating exchange rates*.

3. Demand for a nation's currency is derived from foreigners' desires to purchase that country's goods and services or to invest in its assets. Under floating rates, anything that increases the demand for a nation's currency will make its exchange rate *appreciate*.

4. Supply of a nation's currency is derived from the desire of that country's citizens to purchase foreign goods and services or to invest in foreign assets. Under floating rates, anything that increases the supply of a nation's currency will make its exchange rate *depreciate*.

5. Purchasing-power parity plays a major role in very long-run exchange rate movements. The *purchasing-power parity theory* states that relative price levels in any two countries determine the exchange rate between their currencies. Therefore, countries with relatively low inflation rates normally will have appreciating currencies.

6. Over shorter periods, purchasing-power parity has little influence over exchange rate movements. The pace of economic activity and the level of interest rates exert greater influence. In particular, short-term capital movements are typically the dominant factor.

7. An exchange rate can be fixed at a nonequilibrium level if the government is willing and able to mop up any excess of quantity supplied over quantity demanded, or provide any excess of quantity demanded over quantity supplied. In the first case, the country is suffering from a *balance of payments deficit* because of its overvalued currency. In the second, an undervalued currency has given it a *balance of payments surplus*.

8. The *gold standard* was a particular system of *fixed exchange rates* in which the value of every nation's currency was fixed in terms of gold. But this created problems because nations could not control their own money supplies and because the world could not control its total supply of gold.

9. After World War II, the gold standard was replaced by the *Bretton Woods system* under which exchange rates were fixed in terms of U.S. dollars, and the dollar was in turn tied to gold. This system broke up in 1971, when the dollar became chronically overvalued.

10. Since 1971, the world has moved toward a system of relatively free exchange rates, but with plenty of exceptions. We now have a thoroughly mixed system of *"dirty"* or *"managed" floating*, which continues to evolve and adapt.

11. Floating rates are not without their problems. For example, importers and exporters justifiably worry about fluctuations in exchange rates.

12. Under floating exchange rates, investors who speculate on international currency values provide a valuable service by assuming the risks of those who do not wish to speculate. Normally, speculators stabilize rather than destabilize exchange rates, because that is how they make profits.

13. The U.S. dollar rose dramatically in value from 1980 to 1985, making our imports cheaper and our exports more expensive. Then, from 1985 to 1988, the dollar tumbled, which had precisely the reverse effects. Since then the dollar has fluctuated in value with no clear trend.

14. The European Union has recently established a single currency, the euro, for most of its member nations.

## KEY TERMS

## QUESTIONS FOR REVIEW

1. What items do you own or routinely consume that are produced abroad? From what countries do these come? Suppose Americans decided to buy more of these things? How would that affect the exchange rates between the dollar and these currencies?

2. If the dollar depreciates relative to the euro, will the German camera you have wanted become more or less expensive? What effect do you imagine this will have on American demands for German cameras? Does the American demand curve for euros, therefore, slope upward or downward? Explain.

3. During the first half of the 1980s, inflation in (West) Germany was consistently lower than that in the United States. What, then, does the purchasing-power parity theory predict should have happened to the exchange rate between the mark and the dollar between 1980 and 1985? (Look at Table 36–1 to see what actually happened.)

4. Use supply and demand diagrams to analyze the effect of the following actions on the exchange rate between the dollar and the yen:

   a. Japan opens its domestic markets to more foreign competition.

   b. Investors come to fear that values on the Tokyo stock market will decline.

   c. The Federal Reserve lowers interest rates in the United States.

   d. The U.S. government, to help settle the problems of the Middle East, gives huge amounts of foreign aid to Israel and her Arab neighbors.

e. Japan has a recession while the United States booms.

f. Inflation in the United States exceeds that in Japan.

5. How are the problems of a country faced with a balance of payments deficit similar to those posed by a government regulation that holds the price of milk above the equilibrium level? (*Hint:* Think of each in terms of a supply-demand diagram.)

6. For each of the following transactions, indicate how it would affect the U.S. balance of payments if exchange rates were fixed:

   a. You spent the summer traveling in Europe.

   b. Your uncle in Canada sent you $20 as a birthday present.

   c. You bought a new Honda.

   d. You sold some stock you own on the Tokyo Stock Exchange.

7. Suppose each of the transactions listed in Review Question 6 was done by many Americans. Indicate how each would affect the international value of the dollar if exchange rates were floating.

8. Under the old gold standard, what do you think happened to world prices when there was a huge gold strike in California in 1849? What do you think happened when the world went without any important new gold strikes for 20 years or so?

9. Explain why the members of the Bretton Woods conference in 1944 wanted to establish a system of fixed exchange rates. What flaw led to the ultimate breakdown of the system in 1971?

10. Suppose you want to reserve a hotel room in London for the coming summer but are worried that the value of the pound may rise between now and then, making the rooms too expensive for your budget. Explain how a speculator could relieve you of this worry. (Don't actually try it. Speculators deal only in very large sums!)

11. We learned in this chapter that successful speculators buy a currency when demand is weak and sell it when demand is strong. Use supply and demand diagrams for two different periods (one with weak demand, the other with strong demand) to show why this will limit price fluctuations.

12. From the spring of 1995 through the fall of 1998, market forces generally reduced the international value of the Japanese yen. Why do you think the government of Japan was unhappy about this currency depreciation? What could the Bank of Japan (Japan's central bank) have done to try to prevent it? How could the Federal Reserve have helped? Why might the central banks have failed in this attempt?

# CHAPTER

**No man is an island, entire of itself.**

John Donne

# EXCHANGE RATES AND THE MACROECONOMY

Surveying the problems then afflicting a number of the world's economies in 1998, Federal Reserve Chairman Alan Greenspan famously declared that the United States could not long remain an "oasis of prosperity" in a troubled world. The nations of the world are indeed locked together in an uneasy economic union. Fluctuations in foreign growth, inflation, and interest rates profoundly affect the U.S. economy. Economic events that originate in our country reverberate around the globe. No one who ignores these international linkages can hope to understand the most important economic developments of our time.

The macroeconomic model we developed in earlier chapters does not go far enough. In particular, it ignores such crucial influences as exchange rates and international financial movements. The previous chapter showed how major macroeconomic variables such as

An **open economy** is one that trades with other nations in goods and services, and perhaps also trades in financial assets.

gross domestic product (GDP), prices, and interest rates affect exchange rates. In this chapter, we complete the circle by studying how changes in the exchange rate affect the domestic economy. Then we bring international capital flows into the picture and learn how monetary and fiscal policy work in an **open economy.**

### Should the Yen Rise or Fall?

From the spring of 1995 until the fall of 1998, the Japanese yen generally depreciated relative to the dollar. At its peak value in April 1995, it took only about 80 yen to buy a dollar. But by June 1998, it took more than 145—which meant that the yen had lost 55 percent of its value. Then, in a matter of two months from mid-August to mid-October 1998, the yen skyrocketed, rising as high as 111 yen to the dollar at one point before retreating.

This surprising development pleased some observers, who said it was just the tonic the world needed. The Japanese government also seemed delighted to see its currency rebound. But quite a few critics were dismayed by the rising yen. In their view, Japan—and perhaps the whole world—would have been better off with a cheaper yen. Clearly, these diametrically opposed views cannot both be right. Indeed, when the yen started rising again in January 1999, a front-page column in *The Wall Street Journal* posed the question, "Should Japan Cheer about a Strong Yen?" We will examine this question as the chapter progresses.

## INTERNATIONAL TRADE, EXCHANGE RATES, AND AGGREGATE DEMAND

We know from earlier chapters (especially Chapters 26 and 27) that a country's net exports, $(X - IM)$, are one component of its aggregate demand, $C + I + G + (X - IM)$. It follows that an autonomous increase in exports or decrease in imports has a multiplier effect on the economy, just like an increase in consumption, investment, or government purchases.[1] Figure 37–1 depicts this conclusion on an aggregate demand and supply diagram. A rise in net exports shifts the aggregate demand curve outward to the right, pushing equilibrium from point *A* to point *B*. Both GDP and the price level therefore rise.

But what increases net exports? One factor mentioned in Chapter 26 was a rise in foreign incomes. If foreign economies boom, their citizens are likely to spend more on a wide variety of products, some of which will be American exports. Thus, Figure 37–1 illustrates the effect on the U.S. economy of more rapid growth in foreign countries. Similarly, a recession abroad would reduce U.S. exports and shift the U.S. aggregate demand curve inward. Thus, as we learned in Chapter 27:

Booms or recessions in one country tend to be transmitted to other countries through international trade in goods and services.

---

[1] An appendix to Chapter 27 showed that international trade lowers the numerical value of the multiplier. But autonomous changes in *C, I, G,* or $(X - IM)$ all have the same multiplier.

One other important determinant of net exports was mentioned in Chapter 26, but not discussed in depth: the relative prices of foreign and domestic goods. The idea is a simple application of the law of demand: If the prices of the goods of Country X rise, then people everywhere will tend to buy fewer of them—and more of the goods of Country Y. As we shall see now, this simple idea holds the key to understanding how exchange rates affect international trade.

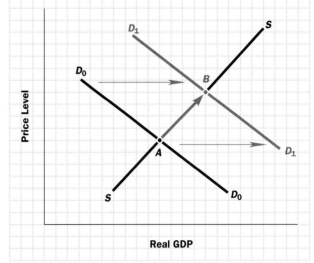

**FIGURE 37-1**

**The Effects of Higher Net Exports**

## RELATIVE PRICES, EXPORTS, AND IMPORTS

First assume—just for this short section—that exchange rates are *fixed*. What happens if the prices of American goods fall while, say, Japanese prices are constant? With U.S. products now less expensive *relative to Japanese products*, both Japanese and American consumers will probably buy more American goods and fewer Japanese goods. So America's exports will rise and imports will fall, adding to greater aggregate demand in this country—as shown in Figure 37–1. Conversely, a rise in American prices (relative to Japanese prices) will *decrease* U.S. net exports and aggregate demand. Thus:

A *fall* in the relative prices of a country's exports tends to *increase* that country's net exports and hence to raise its real GDP. Analogously, a *rise* in the relative prices of a country's exports will *decrease* that country's net exports and GDP.

Precisely the same logic applies to changes in Japanese prices. If Japanese prices rise, Americans will export more and import less. So $X - IM$ will rise, boosting GDP in the United States. Figure 37–1 applies to this case without change. By similar reasoning, falling Japanese prices decrease U.S. net exports and depress our economy. Thus:

Price increases abroad raise a country's net exports and hence its GDP. Price decreases abroad have the opposite effects.

## THE EFFECTS OF CHANGES IN EXCHANGE RATES

From here it is a simple matter to figure out how changes in *exchange rates* affect a country's net exports. For what do currency appreciations or depreciations accomplish? They change international relative prices.

Recall that the basic role of an exchange rate is to convert one country's prices into another country's currency. Table 37–1 uses two examples of U.S.-Japanese trade to remind us of this role. Suppose the dollar depreciates from 120 yen to 100 yen. Then, from the American consumer's viewpoint, a television set that costs ¥30,000 in Japan goes up in price from $250 (that is, 30,000/120) to $300. To Americans, it is just as if Japanese manufacturers had raised TV prices by 20 percent. Naturally, Americans react by purchasing fewer Japanese products. So American imports go down.

Now consider the implications for Japanese consumers interested in buying American personal computers that cost $1,000. When the dollar falls from 120 yen

### Exchange Rates and Home Currency Prices

**TABLE 37-1**

| Exchange Rate | ¥30,000 Japanese TV Set | | $1,000 U.S. Home Computer | |
| --- | --- | --- | --- | --- |
| | Price in Japan | Price in the U.S. | Price in the U.S. | Price in Japan |
| $1 = 120 yen | ¥30,000 | $250 | $1,000 | ¥120,000 |
| 1 = 100 yen | 30,000 | 300 | 1,000 | 100,000 |

to 100 yen, they see the price of these computers falling from ¥120,000 to ¥100,000. To them, it is just as if American producers had offered a 16.7 percent markdown. Under such circumstances, we expect U.S. sales to the Japanese to rise. So U.S. exports should increase. Putting these two findings together, we conclude that:

A currency *depreciation* should *raise* net exports and therefore *increase* aggregate demand. Conversely, a currency *appreciation* should *reduce* net exports and therefore *decrease* aggregate demand.

The aggregate supply and demand diagram in Figure 37–2 illustrates this conclusion. If the currency depreciates, net exports rise and the aggregate demand curve shifts outward from $D_0D_0$ to $D_1D_1$. Both prices and output rise as the economy's equilibrium moves from $E_0$ to $E_1$. If the currency appreciates, everything operates in reverse: Net exports fall, the aggregate demand curve shifts inward to $D_2D_2$, and both prices and output decline.

This simple analysis already helps us understand why the U.S. trade deficit grew so large in the 1980s. We learned in the previous chapter that the international value of the dollar soared in the first half of the 1980s. According to the reasoning we have just completed, such a stunning appreciation of the dollar should have raised U.S. imports and damaged U.S. exports. That is precisely what happened. In constant dollars, American imports soared by 60 percent between 1981 and 1986, while American exports rose a scant 8 percent. The result is that a $6 billion net export *surplus* in 1981 turned into a $164 billion *deficit* by 1986.

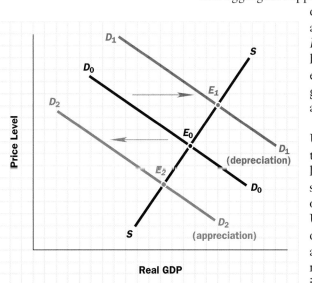

**FIGURE 37-2**

**The Effects of Exchange Rate Changes on Aggregate Demand**

## ■ AGGREGATE SUPPLY IN AN OPEN ECONOMY

So far we have concluded that a currency depreciation increases aggregate demand whereas a currency appreciation decreases it. To complete our model of macroeconomics in an open economy, we must now turn to the implications of international trade for *aggregate supply.*

Part of the story is familiar. As we know from previous chapters, the United States, like all economies, purchases some of its productive inputs from abroad. Oil is only the most prominent example. We also rely on foreign suppliers for metals like titanium, raw agricultural products like coffee beans, and thousands of other items used by American industry. When the dollar depreciates, these imported inputs become more costly in terms of U.S. dollars—just as if foreign prices had risen.

The consequence is clear: With imported inputs more expensive, American firms will be forced to charge higher prices at any given level of output. Graphically, this means that *the aggregate supply curve will shift inward* (to the left).

When the dollar *depreciates,* the prices of imported inputs rise. The U.S. aggregate supply curve therefore shifts *inward,* pushing up the prices of American-made goods and services. By exactly analogous reasoning, an *appreciation* of the dollar makes imported inputs cheaper and shifts the U.S. aggregate supply curve *outward,* thus pushing American prices down. (See Figure 37–3.)

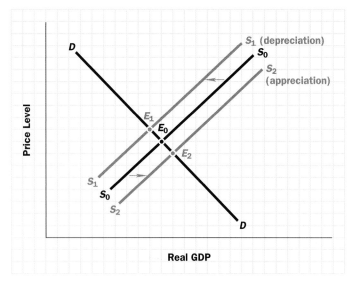

**FIGURE 37-3**

**The Effects of Exchange Rate Changes on Aggregate Supply**

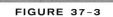

Beyond this, a depreciating dollar has further inflationary effects that do not show up on an aggregate demand and supply diagram, which shows on its vertical axis the price of *domestic product*. Most obviously, prices of imported goods are included in American price indexes like the Consumer Price Index (CPI). So when dollar prices of Japanese cars, French wine, and Swiss watches increase, the CPI goes up *even if no American prices rise*. For this and other reasons, the inflationary impact of a dollar depreciation is even greater than that indicated by Figure 37–3.

## THE MACROECONOMIC EFFECTS OF EXCHANGE RATES

**FIGURE 37–4**

**The Effects of a Currency Depreciation**

Let's now put aggregate demand and aggregate supply together and study the macroeconomic effects of changes in exchange rates.

First, suppose the international value of the dollar falls. Referring back to the red lines in Figures 37–2 and 37–3, we see that this will shift the aggregate demand curve *outward* and the aggregate supply curve *inward*. The result, as Figure 37–4 shows, is that the U.S. price level certainly rises. Whether real GDP rises or falls depends on whether the supply or demand shift is the dominant influence. The evidence strongly suggests that aggregate *demand* shifts are usually larger, so we expect GDP to rise. Hence:

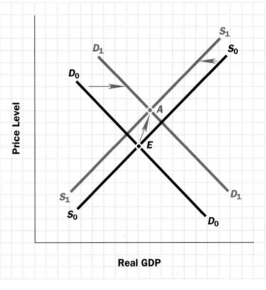

A currency depreciation is inflationary and probably also expansionary.

The intuitive explanation for this result is clear. When the dollar falls, foreign goods become more expensive to Americans. That effect is directly inflationary. At the same time, aggregate demand in the United States is stimulated by rising net exports. As long as the expansion of demand outweighs the adverse shift of the aggregate supply curve brought on by the depreciation, real GDP should rise.

But wait. By this reasoning, the massive depreciations of the Thai baht, the Indonesian rupiah, and other currencies in 1997 and 1998 should have given these economies tremendous boosts. Instead, the Asian Tigers suffered horrific slumps. Why? The answer is that our simple analysis of aggregate supply and demand omits a detail which, although unimportant for the United States, was critical in Southeast Asia.

Countries that borrow in foreign currency, as the Asian Tigers did, will see their debts increase whenever their currencies fall in value. For example, an Indonesian business that borrowed $1,000 in July 1997, when $1 was worth 2,500 rupiah, thought it owed 2.5 million rupiah. But when the dollar suddenly became worth 10,000 rupiah, the company's debt skyrocketed to 10 million rupiah. Many businesses found themselves unable to cope with their crushing debt burdens and simply went bankrupt.

Now let's reverse direction, and look at what happens when the currency *appreciates*. In this case, net exports *fall* so the aggregate demand curve shifts *inward*. At the same time, imported inputs become cheaper, so the aggregate supply curve shifts *outward*. Both of these shifts are shown in Figure 37–5. Once again, as the diagram shows, we can be sure of the movement of the price level: It falls. Output also falls if the demand shift is larger than the supply shift, as is likely. Thus:

A currency appreciation is certainly disinflationary and is probably contractionary.

**FIGURE 37–5**

**The Effects of a Currency Appreciation**

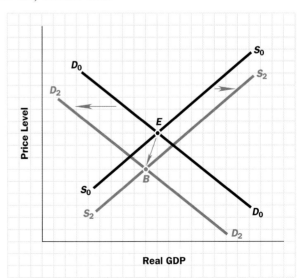

It was this fear that led many economists and financial experts to cringe when the yen appreciated sharply in the fall of 1998. The Japanese economy was already very weak. About the last thing it needed, they claimed, was a decrease in aggregate demand that would depress output further.

## INTEREST RATES AND INTERNATIONAL CAPITAL FLOWS

We have left one important piece out of our international economic puzzle so far. Although we have analyzed international trade in goods and services rather fully, we have ignored international movements of *capital.*

For some nations, this omission is of little consequence because they rarely receive or lend international capital. But things are quite different for the United States because the vast majority of international financial flows involve either buying or selling assets whose values are stated in U.S. dollars. In addition, we cannot hope to understand the Asian crisis of 1997–1998 without incorporating capital flows into our analysis. Fortunately, this is easy to do, given what we have just learned about the effects of exchange rates.

Recall from the previous chapter that interest rate differentials and capital flows are typically the most important determinants of exchange rate movements in the short run. Specifically, suppose interest rates in the United States rise while foreign interest rates remain unchanged. We learned in the previous chapter that this will attract capital to the United States and cause the dollar to appreciate. This chapter has just taught us that an appreciating dollar will, in turn, reduce net exports, prices, and output in the United States—as indicated in Figure 37–5. Thus:

> A rise in interest rates tends to contract the economy by appreciating the currency and reducing net exports.

Notice that this conclusion has a familiar ring. When we studied monetary policy in Chapter 31, we observed that higher interest rates deter investment spending and hence reduce the $I$ component of $C + I + G + (X - IM)$. Now, in studying an open economy with international capital flows, we see that higher interest rates also reduce the $X - IM$ component. Thus, *international capital flows strengthen the negative effects of interest rates on aggregate demand.*

If interest rates in the United States fall, or if those abroad rise, everything we have just said is turned in the opposite direction. The conclusion is:

> A decline in interest rates tends to expand the economy by depreciating the currency and raising net exports.

**EXERCISE**   Provide the reasoning behind this conclusion.

## FISCAL AND MONETARY POLICIES IN AN OPEN ECONOMY

Now we are ready to use our model to analyze how fiscal and monetary policies work when the exchange rate floats and capital is internationally mobile. Doing so will teach us how international economic relations modify the effects of stabilization policies that we learned about in earlier chapters. Fortunately, no new theoretical apparatus is necessary; we need only remember what we have learned in the chapter up to this point. Specifically:

- A rise in the domestic interest rate leads to capital inflows and makes the exchange rate appreciate. A fall in the domestic interest rate leads to capital outflows and makes the exchange rate depreciate.
- A currency appreciation reduces aggregate demand and raises aggregate supply (see Figure 37–5). A currency depreciation raises aggregate demand and reduces aggregate supply (see Figure 37–4).

## FISCAL POLICY REVISITED

With this in mind, suppose the government cuts taxes or raises spending. Aggregate demand increases, which pushes up both real GDP and the price level in the usual manner. This is shown as the shift from $D_0D_0$ to the red line $D_1D_1$ in Figure 37–6. In a **closed economy,** that is the end of the story. But in an *open economy* with international capital flows, we must add in the macroeconomic effects that work through the exchange rate. We do this by answering two questions.

First, what will happen to the exchange rate? We know from earlier chapters that a fiscal expansion pushes up interest rates. At higher interest rates, American securities become more attractive to foreign investors, who go to the foreign exchange markets to buy dollars with which to purchase American securities. This buying pressure drives up the value of the dollar. Thus:

> A fiscal expansion normally makes the exchange rate appreciate.

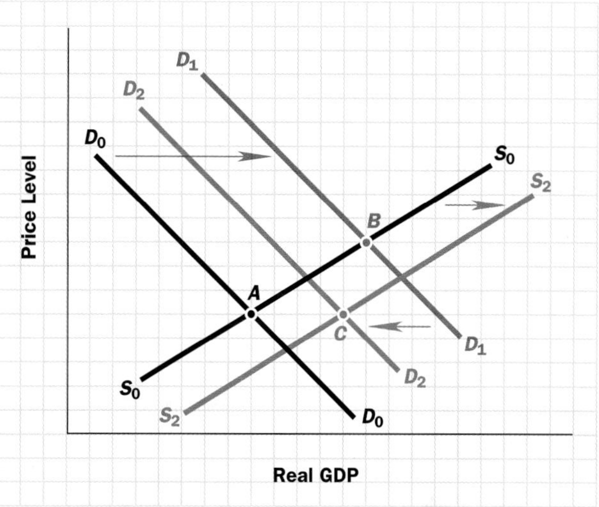

Second, what are the effects of a higher dollar? As we know, when the dollar rises in value, American goods become more expensive abroad and foreign goods become cheaper here. So exports fall and imports rise, driving down the $X - IM$ component of aggregate demand. The fiscal expansion thus winds up increasing both America's *capital account surplus* (by attracting foreign capital) and its *current account deficit* (by reducing net exports). In fact, the two must rise by equal amounts because, under floating exchange rates, it is always true that:[2]

> Current account surplus + Capital account surplus = 0

Because a fiscal expansion leads in this way to a trade deficit, many economists believe that the large U.S. trade deficits of the 1980s were a side effect of the large tax cuts made early in the decade. We will come back to that issue shortly.

But first note that the induced rise in the dollar will shift the aggregate supply curve *outward* and the aggregate demand curve *inward*, as we saw in Figure 37–5. Figure 37–6 adds these two shifts (in blue) to the effect of the original fiscal expansion (in red). The final equilibrium in an open economy is point *C*, whereas in a closed economy it would be point *B*. By comparing points *B* and *C*, we can see how international linkages change the picture of fiscal policy that we painted earlier in the book.

Two main differences arise. First, a higher exchange rate makes imports cheaper and thereby offsets part of the inflationary effect of a fiscal expansion. Second, a higher exchange rate reduces the expansionary effect on real GDP by reducing $X - IM$. Here we have a new kind of "crowding out," different from the one we studied in Chapter 33. There we learned that an increase in $G$ will crowd out some private investment spending by raising interest rates. Here a rise in $G$, by raising both interest rates and the exchange rate, crowds out *net exports.* But the effect is the same: The fiscal multiplier is reduced. Thus, we conclude that:

> International capital flows reduce the power of fiscal policy.

Table 37–2, which shows actual U.S. data, suggests that this new international variety of crowding out was much more important than the traditional type of crowding out in the early 1980s. Between 1981 and 1986, the share of investment in GDP barely changed despite the rise in the shares of both consumer spending and government purchases. Only the share of net exports, $X - IM$, fell—from 0.1 percent to −3.0 percent.

This was an important lesson that American economists learned in the 1980s. In 1981, many economists worried that large government budget deficits would crowd

**FIGURE 37–6**

**A Fiscal Expansion in an Open Economy**

A **closed economy** is one that does not trade with other nations in either goods or assets.

---

[2] If you need review, turn back to Chapter 36, page 760.

**TABLE 37-2**

**Percentage Shares of Real GDP in the United States, 1981 and 1986**

| Year | C | I | G | X − IM |
|------|------|------|------|------|
| 1981 | 64.5% | 14.6% | 20.1% | 0.1% |
| 1986 | 67.6 | 14.8 | 20.7 | −3.0 |
| Change | +3.1 | +0.2 | +0.6 | −3.1 |

NOTE: Totals do not add up because of rounding and deflation.

out private investment. By the end of the decade, most were more concerned that deficits were crowding out net exports and producing a massive trade deficit.

## MONETARY POLICY REVISITED

Now let us consider how *monetary policy* works in an open economy with floating exchange rates and international capital mobility. To remain consistent with the history of the 1980s, we consider a *tightening*, rather than a *loosening*, of monetary policy.

As we know from earlier chapters, contractionary monetary policy *reduces* aggregate demand, which lowers both real GDP and prices. This is shown in Figure 37–7 by the shift from $D_0D_0$ to the red line $D_1D_1$, and it looks like the exact opposite of a fiscal expansion. Without international capital flows, that would be the end of the story.

**FIGURE 37-7**

**A Monetary Contraction in an Open Economy**

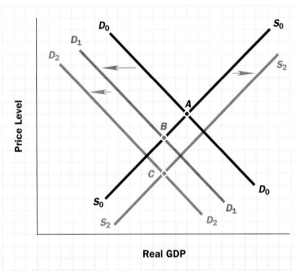

But in the presence of internationally mobile capital, we must think through the consequences for interest rates and exchange rates. As we know from previous chapters, a monetary contraction *raises* interest rates—just like a fiscal expansion. Hence, tighter money attracts foreign capital into the United States in search of higher rates of return. The exchange rate therefore *rises*. The appreciating dollar encourages imports and discourages exports; so $X − IM$ falls. America therefore winds up with capital flowing in and an increase in its trade deficit.

In Figure 37–7, the two effects of the exchange rate appreciation appear in blue: aggregate supply shifts *outward* and aggregate demand shifts *inward*. This time, as you can see in the figure:

**International capital flows increase the power of monetary policy.**

In a closed economy, higher interest rates *reduce* investment spending, *I*. In an open economy, these same higher interest rates also appreciate the currency and reduce net exports, $X − IM$. So the effect of monetary policy is enhanced.

It may seem puzzling that capital flows *strengthen* monetary policy but *weaken* fiscal policy. The resolution lies in their effects on interest rates. The main international repercussion of either a fiscal *expansion* or a monetary *contraction* is to raise interest rates and the exchange rate, thereby crowding out net exports. But that means that the initial effects of a fiscal expansion on aggregate demand are *weakened*, whereas the initial effects of a monetary contraction are *strengthened*.

## ■ INTERNATIONAL ASPECTS OF DEFICIT REDUCTION

This completes our theoretical analysis of the macroeconomics of open economies. Now let us put the theory to work by applying it to a question of current interest: Should reducing the budget deficit (or raising the surplus) strengthen or weaken the dollar?

**Expected Effects of Policy**

TABLE 37-3

| Variable | (1) Fiscal Contraction | (2) Monetary Expansion | (3) Combination |
|---|---|---|---|
| Real interest rate | − | − | − |
| Exchange rate | − | − | − |
| Net exports | + | + | + |
| Real GDP | − | + | ? |
| Inflation | − | + | ? |

As discussed in Chapter 33, the U.S. government transformed its mammoth budget deficit into a notable surplus during the 1990s by raising taxes and cutting expenditures. Column (1) of Table 37–3 reviews the predicted effects of a fiscal contraction: It should lower real interest rates, make the dollar depreciate, reduce real GDP, and be less disinflationary than normal because of the falling dollar. This information is recorded by entering + signs for increases and − signs for decreases.

Now let's consider the monetary policy that accompanied the fiscal contraction. Eliminating the budget deficit reduced aggregate demand. But the Federal Reserve restored the missing demand by lowering interest rates so that the economy would not suffer a slump. According to the analysis in this chapter, such a monetary expansion should lower real interest rates, make the dollar depreciate, raise real GDP, and be a bit more inflationary than usual because of the falling dollar. All this is recorded in Column (2).

Column (3) puts the two pieces together. We conclude that a policy mix of fiscal *contraction* and monetary *expansion* should reduce interest rates strongly, push down the value of the dollar, and strongly stimulate our foreign trade. The net effects on output and inflation are uncertain, however: The balance depends on whether the fiscal contraction overwhelms the monetary expansion or vice versa.

What actually happened? First, interest rates did fall, just as predicted. The rate on 10-year U.S. government bonds dropped from almost 7 percent in late 1992 to just over 4.5 percent in December 1998, and by 1998 American households were enjoying the lowest home mortgage rates since the 1960s. Second, the U.S. economy expanded rapidly between 1992 and 1998; apparently, the monetary stimulus overwhelmed the fiscal contraction. Third, inflation fell despite such rapid growth. As we explained in Chapter 28, one major reason was a series of favorable supply shocks that pushed inflation down.

But what about the exchange rate and international trade? Here the theory did less well. The dollar generally declined from 1993 to 1995, as the theory predicts. But then it turned around and rose sharply from 1995 to 1998, just when the budget deficit was turning into a surplus. America's trade performance was even more puzzling. According to the theory, a lower budget deficit should have led to a lower exchange rate, and therefore to a smaller trade deficit. But, in fact, America's real net exports sagged from just −$30 billion in 1992 to −$238 billion in 1998. What went wrong?

## THE LOOSE LINK BETWEEN THE BUDGET DEFICIT AND THE TRADE DEFICIT

To answer this question, let's explore the connection between the budget deficit and the trade deficit in more detail. To do so, we need one simple piece of arithmetic. Begin with the familiar equilibrium condition for GDP in an open economy:

$$Y = C + I + G + (X - IM)$$

Because GDP can either be spent, saved, or taxed away:[3]

$$Y = C + S + T$$

Equating these two expressions for $Y$ gives:

$$C + I + G + (X - IM) = C + S + T$$

Finally, subtracting $C$ from both sides and bringing the $I$ and $G$ terms over to the right-hand side, leads to an accounting relationship between the trade deficit and the budget deficit:

$$X - IM = (S - I) - (G - T)$$

Notice that this equation is a matter of accounting, not economics. It must hold in all countries at all times, and it has nothing to do with any particular economic theory. In words, it says that a trade deficit—a *negative* value of the trade surplus, $(X - IM)$—can arise from one of two sources: a government budget deficit ($G$ larger than $T$) or an excess of investment over saving ($I$ larger than $S$).

Now let's apply this accounting relationship to actual U.S. events in the 1990s. As we know, the government deficit, $G - T$, fell precipitously. Other things equal, that would have reduced the trade deficit. But other things were certainly not equal. The equation reminds us that the balance between saving and investment matters too. And business investment boomed while household saving declined from 1992 to 1998. So $S - I$ moved sharply in the negative direction. And that, as our equation shows, should raise the trade deficit (reduce net exports).

In brief, taken by itself, deficit reduction would have increased net exports. But sharp changes in private economic behavior—specifically, less saving and more investment—overwhelmed the government's actions and made net exports fall instead. The link from the budget deficit to the trade deficit can be a loose one!

## ■ IS THE TRADE DEFICIT A PROBLEM?

The preceding explanation suggests that America's large trade deficits over the past 15 to 20 years are a symptom of a deeper trouble: The nation as a whole—including both the government and the private sector—has been spending more than it has been producing for years. The United States has therefore been forced to borrow the difference from foreigners. The trade deficit is just the mirror image of the required capital inflows.

Those who worry about trade deficits point out that these capital inflows create debts on which interest and principal payments will have to be made in the future. In this view, Americans have been mortgaging their futures to finance higher consumer spending.

But there is another, quite different, interpretation of the trade deficit. Suppose foreign investors come to see the United States as an especially attractive place to invest their funds. Then capital would flow here, not because Americans need to *borrow* it, but because foreigners are eager to *lend* it. The desire of foreigners to acquire American assets would push the value of the dollar up, which would push America's net exports down. In that case, the trade deficit would still be the mirror image of the capital inflows. But it would signify America's economic *strength*, not its weakness.

Each view holds elements of truth. But the second raises a critical question: How long can it go on? As long as the United States continues to run large trade deficits,

---

[3] If you do not see why, recall that GDP equals disposable income ($DI$) plus taxes ($T$), $Y = DI + T$, and that disposable income can either be consumed or saved, $DI = C + S$. These two definitions together imply that $Y = C + S + T$.

foreign investors will continue to accumulate large amounts of U.S. assets. At some point, economists and financial experts fear, these investors may conclude that they have acquired about all the American assets they want. If and when that happens, the U.S. trade deficit must be eliminated. The only question is how.

## ■ ON CURING THE TRADE DEFICIT

How can we cure our foreign trade problem and end our addiction to foreign borrowing? There are four basic ways.

### CHANGE THE MIX OF FISCAL AND MONETARY POLICY

The fundamental equation:

$$X - IM = (S - I) - (G - T)$$

suggests an *increase in the budget surplus* ($T > G$) as one good way to reduce the trade deficit. According to the analysis in this chapter, a reduction in $G$ or an increase in $T$ would lead to lower real interest rates in the United States, a depreciating dollar, and, eventually, a shrinking trade deficit.

When the government curtails its spending or raises taxes, aggregate demand falls. If we do not want a larger budget surplus to slow economic growth, we must therefore compensate for it by monetary stimulus. Like contractionary fiscal policy, expansionary monetary policy lowers interest rates, depreciates the dollar, and should therefore help reduce the trade deficit. So the policy recommendation actually amounts to tightening *fiscal* policy and loosening *monetary* policy.

As we have noted, the U.S. government—after years of vacillation—finally changed the policy mix in this way in the 1990s. But our trade deficit did not fall. Why not? What else might work?

### MORE RAPID ECONOMIC GROWTH ABROAD

One factor behind the growing U.S. trade deficit is that many foreign nations—the customers for our exports—have been growing slowly or even shrinking in recent years. If foreign economies would grow faster, their residents would buy more American goods. That would raise American exports and reduce our trade deficit. So the U.S. government has been urging our major trading partners to stimulate their economies and to open their markets more to American goods—with only modest success.

### RAISE DOMESTIC SAVING OR REDUCE DOMESTIC INVESTMENT?

Our fundamental equation calls attention to two other routes to a smaller trade deficit: more saving or less investment.

The U.S. personal saving rate (saving as a share of disposable income) has been hitting new all-time lows in recent years. It actually fell to about zero in 1998 and 1999 for the first time since the Great Depression of the 1930s! If Americans would only save more, we would need to borrow less from abroad. This, too, would lead to a cheaper dollar and a smaller trade deficit.

The trouble is that no one has yet found a reliable way to induce Americans to save more. The government has tried a variety of tax incentives for saving, and more are suggested every year. But there is not much evidence that any of them have worked. Indeed, large increases in stock market wealth in recent years have convinced Americans that it is prudent to spend even more freely (and save even less) than they normally do.

If the other cures for our trade deficit fail to work in time, the deficit may cure itself in a particularly unpleasant way: by dramatically reducing U.S. domestic investment.

"But we're not just talking about buying a car—we're talking about confronting this country's trade deficit with Japan."

Let's see how this might happen. As our trade deficits and foreign borrowing persist, foreigners wind up holding more and more U.S. dollar assets. At some point, their willingness to acquire yet more dollar assets will begin to wear thin, and they will start demanding much higher interest rates. At best, higher interest rates lead to lower investment in the United States. At worst, foreigners cease lending to the United States, interest rates skyrocket, and we experience a severe recession. A recession, of course, would reduce our trade deficit substantially by curbing our appetite for imports. But that is a painful cure, indeed.

## PROTECTIONISM

We have saved the worst remedy for last. One seemingly obvious way to cure our trade deficit is to limit imports by imposing stiff tariffs, quotas, and other protectionist devices. We discussed protectionism, and the reasons why almost all economists oppose it, in Chapter 35. Despite the economic arguments against it, protectionism has an undeniable political allure. It seems, superficially, to "save American jobs," and it conveniently shifts the blame for our trade problems onto foreigners.

In addition to depriving us and other countries of the benefits of comparative advantage, protectionism might not even succeed in reducing our trade deficit. One reason is that other nations may retaliate. If we erect trade barriers to reduce our imports, *IM* will fall. But if foreign countries erect corresponding barriers to our exports, *X* will fall, too. On balance, our *net* exports, $X - IM$, may or may not improve. However, world trade will surely suffer. This is a game that may have no winners, only losers.

Even if other nations do not retaliate, tariffs and quotas may not improve our trade deficit much. Why? If they succeed in reducing American spending on imports, tariffs and quotas will thereby reduce the supply of dollars on the world market. That will push the value of the dollar up. A rising dollar, of course, would hurt U.S. exports and encourage more imports. The fundamental equation:

$$X - IM = (S - I) - (G - T)$$

reminds us that protectionism can raise $X - IM$ only if it raises the budget surplus, raises saving, or reduces investment.[4]

---

[4] Here tariffs, which raise revenue for the government, have a clear advantage over quotas, which do not.

## ■ CONCLUSION: NO NATION IS AN ISLAND

The poet John Donne wrote that "no man is an island." Similarly, no nation is isolated from economic developments elsewhere on the globe. Instead, we live in a world economy in which the fates of nations are intertwined. The major trading countries are linked by exports and imports, by capital flows, and by exchange rates. What happens to national income, prices, and interest rates in one country affects other nations. No event makes this point better than the crisis that erupted in Southeast Asia in the summer of 1997.

As we noted in the previous chapter, one root cause of the crisis was the Asian nations' decisions, several years previously, to fix their exchange rates to the U.S. dollar. Unfortunately for them, the dollar rose spectacularly from 1995 to 1997—for example, from about 80 yen in April 1995 to about 125 yen in March 1997. With their exchange rates tied to the dollar, the Thai baht, the Malaysian ringgit, the Indonesian rupiah, and the Korean won automatically appreciated relative to most other currencies. That, of course, made exports from the Tigers more costly to prospective foreign buyers. Soon these one-time export powerhouses found themselves in an unaccustomed position: running large trade deficits.

Then the crisis hit, and all four of these countries watched their currencies tumble in value. The sharp devaluation restored their international competitiveness, but it also ruined their economies and impoverished many of their citizens. Naturally, the shrinking Asian economies curbed their appetites for American goods, so our exports to the region fell—which contributed to further deterioration in the U.S. trade deficit.

Thus a primarily American development (the rise of the dollar) harmed the Asian economies, and then a primarily Asian development (deep recessions in the Asian tigers) hurt the U.S. economy.

### The Yen's Effect on Smaller Asian Economies

Recall the issue with which we began this chapter: Would it have been better for the Japanese yen to appreciate or depreciate in 1998? We have already mentioned the main argument for depreciation: Japan's sluggish economy desperately needed more aggregate demand, and a cheaper yen was one way to get it.

But many analysts worried about possible reverberations on the smaller Asia economies. For example, if the yen depreciated, Korea would find itself at a competitive disadvantage in export markets—and might be forced to devalue again. So, in this case, it was feared that a seemingly Japanese event (a depreciation of the yen) might inflict serious harm on neighboring economies.

For better or for worse, we all live in one world.

## SUMMARY

1. The nations of the world are linked together economically because national income, prices, and interest rates in one country affect those in another. They are thus *open economies*.

2. Because one country's *imports* are another country's *exports*, rapid (or sluggish) economic growth in one country contributes to rapid (or sluggish) growth in other countries.

3. A country's *net exports* depend on whether its prices are high or low relative to those of other countries. Because exchange rates translate one country's prices into the currencies of other countries, the *exchange rate* is a key determinant of net exports.

4. If the currency depreciates, net exports rise and aggregate demand increases, thereby raising both real GDP and the price level. A depreciating currency also reduces aggregate supply by making imported inputs more costly.

5. If the currency appreciates, net exports fall and aggregate demand, real GDP, and the price level all decrease. But an appreciating currency also increases aggregate supply by making imported inputs cheaper.

6. *International capital flows* respond strongly to interest rate differentials among countries. Hence, higher domestic interest rates lead to currency *appreciations*, and lower interest rates lead to *depreciations*.

7. Contractionary monetary policies raise interest rates and therefore make the currency appreciate. Both the higher interest rates and the stronger currency reduce aggregate demand. Hence, international capital flows make monetary policy more powerful than it would be in a *closed economy.*

8. Expansionary fiscal policies also raise interest rates and make the currency appreciate. But, in this case, the international repercussions cancel out part of the demand-expanding effects of the policies. Hence, international capital flows make fiscal policy less powerful than it would be in a closed economy.

9. Because eliminating the budget deficit in the 1990s combined tighter fiscal policy with looser monetary policy, it

lowered interest rates. That should have pushed the dollar down and led to a smaller trade deficit in the United States. However, changes in private economic behavior—specifically, lower saving and higher investment—offset the presumed international effects of deficit reduction.

10. *Budget deficits* and *trade deficits* are linked by the fundamental equation $X - IM = (S - I) - (G - T)$.

11. It follows from this equation that the U.S. trade deficit must be cured by some combination of lower budget deficits, higher savings, and lower investment.

12. Protectionist policies might not cure the U.S. trade deficit because (a) they will make the dollar appreciate and (b) they may provoke foreign retaliation.

---

### KEY TERMS

Net exports   772

Open economy   772

Exchange rate   773

Appreciation   774

Depreciation   774

Closed economy   777

International capital flows   777

Trade deficit   779

Budget deficits and trade deficits   779

$X - IM = (S - I) - (G - T)$   780

---

### QUESTIONS FOR REVIEW

1. For years, the U.S. government has been trying to get Japan to expand its economy faster. Explain how more rapid growth in Japan would affect the U.S. economy.

2. If inflation is higher in Italy than in Germany, and the exchange rate between the two countries is fixed, what is likely to happen to the balance of trade between the two countries?

3. Explain why a currency appreciation leads to a deterioration in a country's trade balance.

4. Explain why American fiscal policy is less powerful and American monetary policy is more powerful than indicated in the closed-economy model of the previous part of this book.

5. Use an aggregate supply-demand diagram to analyze the effects of a currency depreciation.

6. Explain why $X - IM = (S - I) - (G - T)$. Now multiply both sides of this equation by $-1$ to get:

$$IM - X = (I - S) + (G - T)$$

and remember that the trade deficit, $IM - X$, is the amount we have to borrow from foreigners to get:

Borrowing from foreigners $= (I - S) + (G - T)$

Explain the common sense behind this version of the equation.

7. Given what you now know, do you think it was a good idea for the United States to adopt a policy mix of tight money and large government budget deficits in the early 1980s? Why or why not? What were the benefits and costs of reversing that policy mix in the 1990s?

8. What, in your view, is the best way for the United States to reduce its trade deficit?

9. In late 1998, the international value of the yen rose sharply. This development worried many observers. Why? (*Hint:* The Japanese economy was in recession at the time.)

10. (More difficult) Suppose consumption and investment are described by the following:

$$C = 150 + 0.75DI$$
$$I = 300 + 0.2Y - 50r$$

Here $DI$ is disposable income, $Y$ is GDP, and $r$, the interest rate, is measured in percentage points. (For example, a 5 percent interest rate is $r = 5$.) Exports and imports are as follows:

$$X = 300$$
$$IM = -50 + 0.2Y$$

Government purchases are $G = 800$, and taxes are 20 percent of income. The price level is fixed and the central bank uses its monetary policy to peg the interest rate at $r = 8$.

a. Find equilibrium GDP, the budget deficit or surplus, and the trade deficit or surplus.

b. Suppose the currency appreciates and, as a result, exports and imports change to:

$$X = 250$$
$$IM = 0.2Y$$

Now find equilibrium GDP, the budget deficit or surplus, and the trade deficit or surplus.

**Ability-to-pay principle** The ability-to-pay principle of taxation refers to the idea that people with greater ability to pay taxes should pay higher taxes. (p. 441)

**Absolute advantage** One country is said to have an absolute advantage over another in the production of a particular good if it can produce that good using smaller quantities of resources than can the other country. (p. 773)

**Abstraction** Abstraction means ignoring many details in order to focus on the most important elements of a problem. (p. 11)

**Affirmative action** Affirmative action refers to active efforts to locate and hire members of underrepresented groups. (p. 399)

**Aggregate demand curve** The aggregate demand curve shows the quantity of domestic product that is demanded at each possible value of the price level. (p. 557)

**Aggregate demand** Aggregate demand is the total amount that all consumers, business firms, and government agencies are willing to spend on final goods and services. (p. 482, 529)

**Aggregate supply curve** The aggregate supply curve shows the quantity of domestic product that is supplied at each possible value of the price level. (p. 482)

**Aggregate supply curve** The aggregate supply curve shows, for each possible price level, the quantity of goods and services that all the nation's businesses are willing to produce during a specified period of time, holding all other determinants of aggregate quantity supplied constant. (p. 583)

**Aggregation** Aggregation means combining many individual markets into one overall market. (p. 481)

**Allocation of resources** Allocation of resources refers to the society's decisions on how to divide up its scarce input resources among the different outputs produced in the economy and among the different firms or other organizations that produce those outputs. (p. 60)

**Antitrust policy** Antitrust policy refers to programs and laws that preclude the deliberate creation of monopoly and prevent powerful firms from engaging in related "undesirable practices." (p. 420)

**Applied research** Applied research is research whose goal is to invent or improve particular products or processes, often for profit, though the military and health industries provide examples of not-for-profit applied research. (p. 304)

**Appreciate** A nation's currency is said to appreciate when exchange rates change so that a unit of its own currency can buy more units of foreign currency. (p. 753, 774)

**Asset** An asset of an individual or business firm is an item of value that the individual or firm owns. (p. 630)

**Automatic stabilizer** An automatic stabilizer is a feature of the economy that reduces its sensitivity to shocks, such as sharp increases or decreases in spending. (p. 604)

**Autonomous increase in consumption** An autonomous increase in consumption is an increase in consumer spending without any increase in incomes. It is represented on a graph as a shift of the entire consumption function. (p. 570)

**Average physical product (APP)** The average physical product (APP) is the total physical product (TPP) divided by the quantity of input. Thus, $APP = TPP/X$ where $X$ = the quantity of input. (p. 143)

**Average revenue (AR)** The average revenue (AR) is total revenue (TR) divided by quantity. (p. 173)

**Average tax rate** The average tax rate is the ratio of taxes to income. (p. 435)

**Balance of payments deficit** The balance of payments deficit is the amount by which the quantity supplied of a country's currency (per year) exceeds the quantity demanded. Balance of payments deficits arise whenever the exchange rate is pegged at an artificially high level. (p. 759)

**Balance of payments surplus** The balance of payments surplus is the amount by which the quantity demanded of a country's currency (per year) exceeds the quantity supplied. Balance of payments surpluses arise whenever the exchange rate is pegged at an artificially low level. (p. 759)

**Balance sheet** A balance sheet is an accounting statement listing the values of all the assets on the left-hand side and the values of all the liabilities and *net worth* on the right-hand side. (p. 631)

**Barter** Barter is a system of exchange in which people directly trade one good for another, without using money as an intermediate step. (p. 621)

**Basic research** Basic research refers to research that seeks to provide scientific knowledge and general principles rather than coming up with any specific marketable inventions. (p. 304)

**Beneficial or detrimental externality** An activity is said to generate a beneficial or detrimental externality if that activity causes incidental benefits or damages to others not directly involved in the activity and no corresponding compensation is provided to or paid by those who generate the externality. (p. 272)

**Benefits principle** The benefits principle of taxation holds that people who derive benefits from a service should pay the taxes that finance it. (p. 442)

**Bilateral monopoly** A bilateral monopoly is a market situation in which there is both a monopoly on the selling side and a monopsony on the buying side. (p. 372)

**Bond** A bond is simply an IOU by a corporation that promises to pay the holder of the bond a fixed sum of money at the specified *maturity* date and some other fixed amount of money (the *coupon* or the *interest payment*) every year up to the date of maturity. (p. 312)

**Bottleneck facility** A facility or service owned by a single firm and needed for the activities of rival firms is called a bottleneck facility (or, simply, a bottleneck). (p. 409)

**Budget deficit** The budget deficit is the amount by which the government's expenditures exceed its receipts during a specified period of time, usually a year. (p. 686)

**Bundling** Bundling refers to a pricing arrangement under which the supplier offers substantial discounts to customers if they buy several of the firm's products, so that the price of the bundle of products is less than the sum of the prices of the products if they were bought separately. (p. 427)

**Burden of a tax** The burden of a tax to an individual is the amount one would have to be given to be just as well off with the tax as without it. (p. 442)

**Capital account balance** The capital account balance includes purchases and sales of financial assets to and from citizens and companies of other countries. (p. 760)

**Capital gain** A capital gain is the difference between the price at which an asset is sold and the price at which it was bought. (p. 517)

**Capital good** A capital good is an item used to produce other goods and services in the future, rather than being consumed today. Factories and machines are examples. (p. 58)

**Capital** Capital refers to an inventory (*a stock*) of plant, equipment, and other (generally durable) productive resources held by a business firm, an individual, or some other organization. (p. 333)

**Capitalism** Capitalism is an economic system in which most of the production process is controlled by private firms operating in markets with minimal government control. The investors in these firms (called "capitalists") own the firms. (p. 293)

**Cartel** A cartel is a group of sellers of a product who have joined together to control its production, sale, and price in the hope of obtaining the advantages of monopoly. (p. 254)

**Central bank** A central bank is a bank for banks. America's central bank is the *Federal Reserve System.* (p. 642)

**Closed economy** A closed economy is one that does not trade with other nations in either goods or assets. (p. 34, 777)

**Closed shop** A closed shop is an arrangement that permits only union members to be hired. (p. 369)

**Closed** An economy is considered relatively closed if they constitute a small share. (p. 34)

**Commodity money** A commodity money is an object in use as a medium of exchange, but which also has a substantial value in alternative (nonmonetary) uses. (p. 622)

**Common stock** A common stock of a corporation is a piece of paper that gives the holder of the stock a share of the ownership of the company. (p. 312)

**Comparative advantage** One country is said to have a comparative advantage over another in the production of a particular good relative to other goods if it produces that good less inefficiently as compared with the other country. (p. 5, 61, 733)

**Complements** Two goods are called complements if an increase in the quantity consumed of one increases the quantity demanded of the other, all other things remaining constant. (p. 127)

**Concentration ratio** A concentration ratio is the percentage of an industry's output produced by its four largest firms. It is intended to measure the degree to which the industry is dominated by large firms. (p. 423)

**Consumer expenditure** Consumer expenditure, symbolized by the letter $C$, is the total amount spent by consumers on newly produced goods and services (excluding purchases of new homes, which are considered investment goods). (p. 529)

**Consumer's surplus** Consumer's surplus is the difference between the value to the consumer of the quantity of Commodity $X$ purchased and the amount that the market requires the consumer to pay for that quantity of $X$. (p. 103)

**Consumption function** The consumption function shows the relationship between total consumer expenditures and total disposable income in the economy, holding all other determinants of consumer spending constant. (p. 535)

**Consumption good** A consumption good is an item that is available for immediate use by households, one that satisfies people's wants without contributing directly to the economy's future production. (p. 58)

**Corporation** A corporation is a firm that has the legal status of a fictional individual. This fictional individual is owned by a number of persons, called its *stockholders*, and is run by a set of elected officers and a board of directors, whose chairman is often also in a powerful position. (p. 310)

**Correlated** Two variables are said to be correlated if they tend to go up or down together. But correlation need not imply causation. (p. 13)

**Credible threat** A credible threat is a threat that does not harm the threatener if it is carried out. (p. 263)

**Cross elasticity of demand** The cross elasticity of demand for Product X to a change in the price of another product, Y, is the ratio of the percentage change in quantity demanded of X to the percentage change in the price of Y that brings about the change in quantity demanded. (p. 128)

**Cross licensing** Cross licensing of patents occurs when each of two firms agrees to let the other use some specified set of its patents, either at a price specified in their agreement or in return for access to the other firm's patents. (p. 298)

**Cross-subsidization** Cross-subsidization means selling one product at a loss, which is balanced by higher profits on another product. (p. 412)

**Crowding in** Crowding in occurs when government spending, by raising real GDP, induces increases in private investment spending. (p. 697)

**Crowding out** Crowding out occurs when deficit spending by the government forces private investment spending to contract. (p. 697)

**Current account balance** The current account balance includes international purchases and sales of goods and services, cross-border interest and dividend payments, and cross-border gifts to and from both private individuals and governments. (p. 760)

**Cyclical unemployment** Cyclical unemployment is the portion of unemployment that is attributable to a decline in the economy's total production. Cyclical unemployment rises during recessions and falls as prosperity is restored. (p. 509)

**Deflation** Deflation refers to a sustained decrease in the general price level. (p. 489)

**Demand curve** A demand curve is a graphical depiction of a demand schedule. It shows how the quantity demanded of some product during a specified period of time will change as the price of that product changes, holding all other determinants of quantity demanded constant. (p. 71)

**Demand schedule** A demand schedule is a table showing how the quantity demanded of some product during a specified period of time changes as the price of that product changes, holding all other determinants of quantity demanded constant. (p. 70)

**Depletable** A commodity is depletable if it is used up when someone consumes it. (p. 276)

**Deposit insurance** Deposit insurance is a system that guarantees that depositors will not lose money even if their bank goes bankrupt. (p. 630)

**Depreciate** The currency is said to depreciate when exchange rates change so that a unit of its currency can buy fewer units of foreign currency. (p. 753, 774)

**Derived demand** The derived demand for an input is the demand for the input by producers as determined by the demand for the final product that the input is used to produce. (p. 332)

**Devaluation** A devaluation is a reduction in the official value of a currency. (p. 754)

**Direct taxes** Direct taxes are taxes levied directly on people. (p. 435)

**Discount rate** The discount rate is the interest rate the Fed charges on loans that it makes to banks. (p. 650)

**Discouraged worker** A discouraged worker is an unemployed person who gives up looking for work and is therefore no longer counted as part of the labor force. (p. 509)

**Disposable income** Disposable income is the sum of the incomes of all the individuals in the economy after all taxes have been deducted and all transfer payments have been added. (p. 530)

**Division of labor** Division of labor means breaking up a task into a number of smaller, more **specialized** tasks so that each worker can become more adept at a particular job. (p. 60)

**Dumping** Dumping means selling goods in a foreign market at lower prices than those charged in the home market. (p. 747)

**Economic discrimination** Economic discrimination occurs when equivalent factors of production receive different payments for equal contributions to output. (p. 389)

**Economic growth** Economic growth occurs when an economy is able to pro-duce more goods and services for each consumer. (p. 58)

**Economic model** An economic model is a simplified, small-scale version of some aspect of the economy. Economic models are often expressed in equations, by graphs, or in words. (p. 13)

**Economic profit** Economic profit equals net earnings, in the accountant's sense, minus the opportunity costs of capital and of any other inputs supplied by the firm's owners. (p. 170, 203)

**Economic profit** Economic profit is the total revenue of a firm minus all of its costs including the interest payments and opportunity costs of the capital it obtains from its investors. (p. 345)

**Economic rent** Economic rent is the portion of the earnings of a factor of production that exceeds the minimum amount necessary to induce any of that factor to be supplied. (p. 338, 363)

**Economies of scale** Economies of scale are savings that are obtained through increases in quantities produced. Scale economies occur when an X percent increase in input use raises output by *more than* X percent, so that the more the firm produces, the lower its per-unit costs become. (p. 406)

**Economies of scale** Production is said to involve economies of scale, also referred to as increasing returns to scale, if, when all input quantities are doubled, the quantity of output is *more* than doubled. (p. 155)

**Economies of scope** Economies of scope are savings that are obtained through simultaneous production of many different products and occur if a firm that produces many commodities can supply each good more cheaply than a firm that produces fewer commodities. (p. 409)

**Efficient allocation of resources** An efficient allocation of resources is one that takes advantage of every opportunity to make some individuals better off in their own estimation while not worsening the lot of anyone else. (p. 211)

**Entrepreneurship** Entrepreneurship is the act of starting new firms, introducing new products and technological innovations, and, in general, taking the risks that are necessary in seeking out business opportunities. (p. 330)

**Equation of exchange** The equation of exchange states that the money value of GDP transactions must be equal to the product of the average stock of money times velocity. That is,

$$M \times V = P \times Y. \text{ (p. 663)}$$

**Equilibrium** An **equilibrium** is a situation in which there are no inherent forces that produce change. Changes away from an equilibrium position will occur only as a result of "outside events" that disturb the status quo. (p. 78)

**Equilibrium** Equilibrium refers to a situation in which neither consumers nor firms have any incentive to change their behavior. They are content to continue with things as they are. (p. 553)

**Excess burden** The excess burden of a tax to an individual is the amount by which the burden of the tax exceeds the tax that is paid. (p. 443)

**Excess reserves** Excess reserves are any reserves held in excess of the legal minimum. (p. 632)

**Exchange rate** The exchange rate states the price, in terms of one currency, at which another currency can be bought. (p. 752, 773)

**Excludable** A commodity is excludable if someone who does not pay for it can be kept from enjoying it. (p. 276)

**Expenditure schedule** An expenditure schedule shows the relationship between national income (GDP) and total spending. (p. 555)

**Export subsidy** An export subsidy is a payment by the government to exporters to permit them to reduce the selling prices of their goods so they can compete more effectively in foreign markets. (p. 740)

**Externality** An activity is said to generate a beneficial or detrimental externality if that activity causes incidental benefits or damages to others not directly involved in the activity, and no corresponding compensation is provided to or paid by those who generate the externality. (p. 453)

**Factors of production** Factors of production are the broad categories, land, labor, capital, exhaustible natural resources, and entrepreneurship, into which we divide the economy's different productive inputs. (p. 32, 330)

**Fiat money** Fiat money is money that is decreed as such by the government. It is of little value as a commodity, but it maintains its value as a medium of exchange because people have faith that the issuer will stand behind the pieces of printed paper and limit their production. (p. 623)

**Final goods and services** Final goods and services are those that are purchased by their ultimate users. (p. 485)

**Fiscal federalism** Fiscal federalism refers to the system of grants from one level of government to the next. (p. 440)

**Fiscal policy** The government's fiscal policy is its plan for spending and taxation. It is designed to steer aggregate demand in some desired direction. (p. 600)

**Fixed cost** A fixed cost is the cost of an input whose quantity does not rise when output goes up, one that the firm requires to produce any output at all. The total cost of such indivisible inputs does not change when the output changes. Any other cost of the firm's operation is called a variable cost. (p. 141)

**Fixed exchange rates** Fixed exchange rates are rates set by government decisions and maintained by government actions. (p. 759)

**Fixed taxes** Fixed taxes are taxes that do not vary with the level of GDP. (p. 600)

**Floating exchange rates** Floating exchange rates are rates determined in free markets by the law of supply and demand. (p. 754)

**Flypaper theory of tax incidence** The flypaper theory of tax incidence holds that the burden of a tax always sticks where the government puts it. (p. 446)

**45° line** A 45° line is a ray through the origin with a slope of +1. It marks off points where the variables measured on each axis have equal values (assuming both variables are measured in the same units). (p. 22)

**Fractional reserve banking** Fractional reserve banking is a system under which bankers keep as reserves only a fraction of the funds they hold on deposit. (p. 627)

**Frictional unemployment** Frictional unemployment is unemployment that is due to normal turnover in the labor market. It includes people who are temporarily between jobs because they are moving or changing occupations, or are unemployed for similar reasons. (p. 509)

**Government purchases** Government purchases, symbolized by the letter *G*,

refer to the goods (such as airplanes and paper clips) and services (such as school teaching and police protection) purchased by all levels of government. (p. 530)

**Gross domestic product (gdp)** Gross domestic product (gdp) is a measure of the size of the economy or, rather, of the total amount it produces. It is, roughly speaking, the money value of all the goods and services produced in a year. (p. 32)

**Gross domestic product (GDP)** Gross domestic product (GDP) is the sum of the money values of all final goods and services produced in the domestic economy and sold on organized markets during a specified period of time, usually a year. (p. 482, 541)

**Horizontal equity** Horizontal equity is the notion that equally situated individuals should be taxed equally. (p. 441)

**Incidence of a tax** The incidence of a tax is an allocation of the burden of the tax to specific individuals or groups. (p. 446)

**Income elasticity of demand** Income elasticity of demand is the ratio of the percentage change in quantity demanded to the percentage change in income. (p. 127)

**Income-expenditure diagram** An income-expenditure diagram, also called a 45° line diagram, plots total real expenditure (on the vertical axis) against real income (on the horizontal axis). The 45° line marks off points where income and expenditure are equal. (p. 557)

**Index fund** An index fund, is a mutual fund that chooses a particular stock market index and then buys the stocks (or most of the stock) that are included in the index. The value of an investment in an index fund depends on what happens to the prices of all the stocks in that index. (p. 316)

**Indexing** Indexing refers to provisions in a law or a contract whereby monetary payments are automatically adjusted whenever a specified price index changes. Wage rates, pensions, interest payments on bonds, income taxes, and many other things can be indexed in this way, and have been. Sometimes such contractual provisions are called *escalator clauses*. (p. 723)

**Indirect taxes** Indirect taxes are taxes levied on specific economic activities. (p. 435)

**Induced increase in consumption** An induced increase in consumption is an in-

crease in consumer spending that stems from an increase in consumer incomes. It is represented on a graph as a movement along a fixed consumption function. (p. 570)

**Induced investment** Induced investment is the part of investment spending that rises when GDP rises and falls when GDP falls. (p. 555)

**Industrial Revolution** The Industrial Revolution is the stream of new technology and the resulting growth of output that began in England toward the end of the 18th century. (p. 293)

**Inferior good** An inferior good is a commodity whose quantity demanded falls when the purchaser's real income rises, all other things remaining equal. (p. 105)

**Inflation accounting** Inflation accounting means adjusting standard accounting procedures for the fact that inflation lowers the purchasing power of money. (p. 690)

**Inflation** Inflation refers to a sustained increase in the average level of prices. (p. 24, 482)

**Inflationary gap** The inflationary gap is the amount by which equilibrium real GDP exceeds the full-employment level of GDP. (p. 560, 587)

**Innovation** Innovation is the process by which new products or new methods of production are introduced, including all the steps from the inventor's idea to bringing the new item to market. (p. 292, 346)

**Input-output analysis** Input-output analysis is a mathematical procedure that takes account of the interdependence among the economy's industries and determines the amount of output each industry must provide as inputs to the other industries in the economy. (p. 218)

**Inputs or factors of production** Inputs or factors of production are the labor, machinery, buildings, and natural resources used to make outputs. (p. 32, 54)

**Interest** Interest is the payment for the use of funds employed in the production of capital; it is measured as a percentage per year of the value of the funds tied up in the capital. (p. 333)

**Intermediate good** An intermediate good is a good purchased for resale or for use in producing another good. (p. 485)

**Invention** Invention is the act of generating an idea for a new product or a new method for making an old product. (p. 346)

**Investment in human capital** Investment in human capital is any expenditure on an individual that increases that person's future earning power or productivity. (p. 355)

**Investment spending** Investment spending, symbolized by the letter *I*, is the sum of the expenditures of business firms on new plant and equipment and households on new homes. Financial "investments" are not included, nor are resales of existing physical assets. (p. 529)

**Investment** Investment is the *flow* of resources into the production of new capital. It is the labor, steel, and other inputs devoted to the *construction* of factories, warehouses, railroads, and other pieces of capital during some period of time. (p. 333)

**Invisible hand** The invisible hand is a phrase used by Adam Smith to describe how, by pursuing their own self-interests, people in a market system are "led by an invisible hand" to promote societal well-being. (p. 68)

**Labor force** The labor force is the number of people holding or seeking jobs. (p. 501)

**Labor productivity** Labor productivity refers to the amount of output a worker turns out in an hour (or a week or a year) of labor. It can be measured as gross domestic product (GDP) in a given year divided by the total number of paid work hours during that year. That is, labor productivity is defined as GDP per hour of labor. (p. 292, 502)

**Labor union** A labor union is an organization made up of a group of workers (usually with the same specialization, such as plumbing or costume design, or in the same industry). The unions represent the workers in negotiations with employers over issues such as wages, vacations, and sick leave. (p. 367)

**Laissez faire** Laissez faire refers to the practice of minimal government interference with the workings of the market system. The term means that people should be left alone in carrying out their economic affairs. (p. 215)

**"Law" of demand** The "law" of demand states that a lower price generally increases the amount of a commodity that people in a market are willing to buy. Therefore, for most goods, market demand curves have negative slopes. (p. 106)

**"Law" of diminishing marginal utility** The "law" of diminishing marginal utility asserts that additional units of a commodity are worth less and less to a consumer in money terms. As the individual's consumption increases, the marginal utility of each additional unit declines. (p. 96)

**Law of supply and demand** The law of supply and demand states that, in a free market, the forces of supply and demand generally push the price toward the level at which quantity supplied and quantity demanded are equal. (p. 79)

**Liability** A liability of an individual or business firm is an item of value that the individual or firm owes. Many liabilities are known as *debts*. (p. 631)

**Limited liability** Limited liability is a legal obligation of a firm's owners to pay back company debts only with the money they have already invested in the firm. (p. 310)

**Liquidity** An asset's liquidity refers to the ease with which it can be converted into cash. (p. 626)

**Long run** The long run is a period of time long enough for all of the firm's commitments to come to an end. (p. 140)

**M1** The narrowly defined money supply, usually abbreviated M1, is the sum of all coins and paper money in circulation, plus certain checkable deposit balances at banks and savings institutions. (p. 625)

**M2** The broadly defined money supply, usually abbreviated M2, is the sum of all coins and paper money in circulation, plus all types of checking account balances, plus most forms of savings account balances, plus shares in money market mutual funds. (p. 626)

**Marginal land** Marginal land is land that is just on the borderline of being used, i.e., any land the use of which would be unprofitable if the farmer had to pay even a penny of rent. (p. 339)

**Marginal physical product (MPP)** The marginal physical product (MPP) of an input is the increase in total output that results from a one-unit increase in the input, holding the amounts of all other inputs constant. (p. 143, 330)

**Marginal profit** Marginal profit is the addition to total profit resulting from one more unit of output. (p. 175)

**Marginal propensity to consume (MPC)** The marginal propensity to consume (MPC) is the ratio of changes in consumption relative to changes in disposable income that produce the change in consumption. On a graph, it appears as the slope of the consumption function. (p. 535)

**Marginal revenue product (MRP)** The marginal revenue product (MRP) of an input is the additional revenue that the producer earns from the increased sales when it uses an additional unit of the input. (p. 144, 330)

**Marginal revenue** Marginal revenue, often abbreviated MR, is the addition to total revenue resulting from the addition of one unit to total output. Geometrically, marginal revenue is the slope of the total revenue curve. Its formula is $MR_1 = TR_1 - TR_0$, and so on. (p. 173)

**Marginal social cost (MSC)** The marginal social cost (MSC) of an activity is the sum of its marginal private cost (MPC) plus the incidental cost (positive or negative) that is borne by others. (p. 273)

**Marginal tax rate** The marginal tax rate is the fraction of each *additional* dollar of income that is paid in taxes. (p. 435)

**Marginal utility** The marginal utility of a commodity to a consumer (measured in money terms) is the maximum amount of money that she or he is willing to pay *for one more unit* of that commodity. (p. 96)

**Market demand curve** A market demand curve shows how the total quantity of some product demanded by *all* consumers in the market during a specified period of time changes as the price of that product changes, holding all other things constant. (p. 105)

**Market system** A market system is a form of economic organization in which resource allocation decisions are left to individual producers and consumers acting in their own best interests without central direction. (p. 63)

**Maximin criterion** The maximin criterion requires you to select the strategy that yields the maximum payoff on the assumption that your opponent does as much damage to you as he or she can. (p. 261)

**Mercantilism** Mercantilism is a doctrine that holds that exports are good for a country, whereas imports are harmful. (p. 739)

**Merger** A merger refers to unification of two previously independent firms, as when one purchases the other or the two simply decide to combine into a single enterprise. (p. 427)

**Mixed economy** A mixed economy is one with some public influence over the workings of free markets. There may also be some public ownership mixed in with private property. (p. 49)

**Monetarism** Monetarism is a mode of analysis that uses the equation of exchange to organize and analyze macroeconomic data. (p. 666)

**Monetary policy** Monetary policy refers to actions that the Federal Reserve System takes in order to change the equilibrium of the money market; that is, to alter the money supply, move interest rates, or both. (p. 654)

**Monetize the deficit** The central bank is said to monetize the deficit when it purchases the bonds that the government issues. (p. 695)

**Money** Money is the standard object used in exchanging goods and services. In short, money is the medium of exchange. (p. 622)

**Monopolistic competition** Monopolistic competition refers to a market in which products are heterogeneous but which is otherwise the same as a market that is perfectly competitive. (p. 190, 248)

**Monopoly power** Monopoly power (or market power) is the ability of a business firm to raise the prices of its products above competitive levels and to keep those prices high for a substantial amount of time. (p. 406)

**Monopsony** A monopsony is a market situation in which there is only one buyer. (p. 372)

**Moral hazard** Moral hazard refers to the tendency of insurance to discourage policyholders from protecting themselves from risk. (p. 287)

**MRP$_L$, the marginal revenue product of labor** MRP$_L$, the marginal revenue product of labor, is the increase in the employer's total revenue that results when he hires an additional unit of labor. (p. 354)

**Multiplier** The multiplier is the ratio of the change in equilibrium GDP ($Y$) divided by the original change in spending that causes the change in GDP. (p. 566)

**Mutual fund** A mutual fund, in which individual investors can buy shares, is a private investment firm that holds a portfolio of securities. Investors can choose among a large variety of different mutual funds, such as stock funds, bond funds, and so forth. (p. 315)

**Nash equilibrium** A Nash equilibrium results when each player adopts the strategy that gives her the highest possible payoff if her rival sticks to the strategy he has chosen. (p. 262)

**National debt** The national debt is the federal government's total indebtedness at a moment in time. It is the result of previous deficits. (p. 686)

**National income** National income is the sum of the incomes that all individuals in the economy earned in the forms of wages, interest, rents, and profits. It excludes government transfer payments and is calculated before any deductions are taken for income taxes. (p. 530, 543)

**Natural monopoly** A natural monopoly is an industry in which advantages of large-scale production make it possible for a single firm to produce the entire output of the market at lower average cost than a number of firms each producing a smaller quantity. (p. 232)

**Natural rate of unemployment** The economy's self-correcting mechanism always tends to push the unemployment rate back toward a specific rate of unemployment that we call the natural rate of unemployment. (p. 714)

**Near moneys** Near moneys are liquid assets that are close substitutes for money. (p. 626)

**Net exports** Net exports, symbolized by ($X - IM$), is the difference between U.S. exports and U.S. imports. It indicates the difference between what we sell to foreigners and what we buy from them. (p. 530, 551, 572)

**Net worth** Net worth is the value of all assets minus the value of all liabilities. (p. 631)

**Nominal GDP** Nominal GDP is calculated by valuing all outputs at current prices. (p. 484)

**Nominal rate of interest** The nominal rate of interest is the percentage by which the money the borrower pays back exceeds the money that he borrowed, making no adjustment for any fall in the purchasing power of this money that results from inflation. (p. 516)

**Oligopoly** An oligopoly is a market dominated by a few sellers, at least several of which are large enough relative to the total market to be able to influence the market price. (p. 190)

**Open economy** An open economy is one that trades with other nations in goods and services, and perhaps also trades in financial assets. (p. 772)

**Open** An economy is called relatively open if its exports and imports constitute a large share of its GDP. (p. 34)

**Open-market operations** Open-market operations refer to the Fed's purchase or sale of government securities through transactions in the open market. (p. 646)

**Opportunity cost** The opportunity cost of any decision is the value of the next best alternative that the decision forces the decision maker to forgo. (p. 4, 203, 652)

**Opportunity cost** The **opportunity cost** of some decision is the value of the next best alternative that must be given up because of that decision (for example, working instead of going to school). (p. 53)

**Optimal decision** An optimal decision is one which, among all the decisions that are actually possible, is best for the decision maker. For example, if profit is the sole objective of some firm, the price that makes the firm's profit as large as possible is optimal for that company. (p. 168)

**Origin** The "0" point in the lower left-hand corner of a graph where the axes meet is called the origin. Both variables are equal to zero at the origin. (p. 18)

**Outputs** Outputs are the goods and services that consumers want to acquire. (p. 32, 54)

**Paradox of thrift** The paradox of thrift is the idea that an effort by a nation to save more may simply reduce national income and fail to raise total saving. (p. 573)

**Partnership** A partnership is a firm whose ownership is shared by a fixed number of proprietors. (p. 309)

**Perfect competition** Perfect competition occurs in an industry when that industry is made up of many small firms producing homogeneous products, when information is perfect, and when there is no impediment to the entry or exit of firms. (p. 192)

**Perfectly contestable** A market is perfectly contestable if entry and exit are costless and unimpeded. (p. 264)

**Phillips curve** A Phillips curve is a graph depicting the rate of unemployment on the horizontal axis and either the rate of inflation or the rate of change of money wages on the vertical axis. Phillips curves are normally downward sloping, indicating that higher inflation rates are associated with lower unemployment rates. (p. 710)

**Plowback** Plowback (or retained earnings) is the portion of a corporation's profits that management decides to keep and invest back into the firm's operations rather than paying dividends directly to stockholders. Corporations may also buy back shares from stockholders. (p. 314)

**Portfolio diversification** Portfolio diversification means including a number and variety of stocks, bonds, and other such items in an individual's portfolio. If the individual owns airline stocks, for example, diversification requires the purchase of a stock or bond in a very different industry, such as a breakfast cereal producer. (p. 315)

**Potential GDP** Potential GDP is the real GDP that the economy would produce if its labor and other resources were fully employed. (p. 501)

**Poverty line** The poverty line is an amount of income below which a family is considered "poor." (p. 382)

**Predatory pricing** Predatory pricing is pricing that threatens to keep a competitor out of the market. It is a price that is so low that it will be profitable for the firm that adopts it only if a rival is driven from the market. (p. 426)

**Price ceiling** A price ceiling is a legal maximum on the price that may be charged for a commodity. (p. 82)

**Price discrimination** Price discrimination is the sale of a given product at different prices to different customers of the firm, when there is no difference in the cost of supplying different customers. Prices are also discriminatory if it costs more to supply one customer than another, but they are charged the same price. (p. 239)

**(Price) elasticity of demand** The (price) elasticity of demand is the ratio of the *percentage* change in quantity demanded to the *percentage* change in price that brings about the change in quantity demanded. (p. 119)

**Price floor** A price floor is a legal minimum on the price that may be charged for a commodity. (p. 85)

**Price leadership** Under price leadership, one firm sets the price for the industry and the others follow. (p. 256)

**Price taker** Under perfect competition, the firm is a price taker. It has no choice but to accept the price that has been determined in the market. (p. 193)

**Price war** In a price war, each competing firm is determined to sell at a price that is lower than the prices of its rivals, usually regardless of whether that price covers the pertinent cost. Typically, in such a price war, Firm A cuts its price below Firm B's; then B retaliates by undercutting A, and so on and so on until one or more of the firms surrender and let themselves be undersold. (p. 257)

**Principle of increasing costs** The principle of increasing costs states that as the production of a good expands, the opportunity cost of producing another unit generally increases. (p. 55)

**Private good** A private good is a commodity characterized by both excludability and depletability. (p. 276)

**Process innovation** A process innovation is an innovation that changes the way in which a commodity is produced. (p. 303)

**Product innovation** A product innovation is the introduction of a good or service that is entirely new or involves major modifications of earlier products. (p. 303)

**Production function** The production function indicates the *maximum* amount of product that any particular collection of inputs is capable of producing. (p. 151)

**Production indifference map** A production indifference map is a graph whose axes show the quantities of two inputs that are used to produce some output. A curve in the graph corresponds to some given quantity of that output, and the different points on that curve show the different quantities of the two inputs that are enough to produce the given output. (p. 23)

**Production possibilities frontier** A production possibilities frontier shows the different combinations of various goods that a producer can turn out, given the available resources and existing technology. (p. 54)

**Productivity** Productivity is the amount of output produced by a unit of input. (p. 9, 43, 584)

**Progressive tax** A progressive tax is one in which the average tax rate paid by an individual rises as income rises. (p. 49)

**Progressive** A tax is progressive if the ratio of taxes to income rises as income rises. (p. 435)

**Proportional tax** A proportional tax is one in which the average tax rate is the same at all income levels. (p. 435)

**Proprietorship** A proprietorship is a business firm owned by a single person. (p. 309)

**Public good** A public good is a commodity or service whose benefits are *not depleted* by an additional user and from which it is generally difficult or *impossible to exclude* people, even if the people are unwilling to pay for the benefits. (p. 276)

**Purchasing power** The purchasing power of a given sum of money is the volume of goods and services that it will buy. (p. 512)

**Pure monopoly** A pure monopoly is an industry in which there is only one supplier of a product for which there are no close substitutes and in which it is very hard or impossible for another firm to coexist. (p. 190, 230)

**Quantity demanded** The quantity demanded is the number of units of a good that consumers want to buy over a specified period of time. (p. 70)

**Quantity supplied** The quantity supplied is the number of units that sellers want to sell over a specified period of time. (p. 73)

**Quantity theory** The quantity theory of money assumes that velocity is (approximately) constant. In that case, nominal GDP is proportional to the money stock. (p. 663)

**Quota** A quota specifies the maximum amount of a good that is permitted into the country from abroad per unit of time. (p. 740)

**Ramsey pricing rule** The Ramsey pricing rule is a rule for determining prices that promote consumer welfare while covering the producer's cost. (p. 414)

**Random walk** The time path of a variable such as the price of a stock is said to constitute a random walk if its magnitude in one period (say, May 2, 2000) is equal to its value in the preceding period (May 1, 2000) plus a completely random number. That is: Price on May 2, 2000 = Price on May 1, 2000 + Random number, where the random number (positive or negative) can be obtained by a roll of dice or some such procedure. (p. 313)

**Ratchet** A ratchet is an arrangement that permits some economic variable, such as investment or advertising, to increase, but prevents that variable from subsequently decreasing. (p. 301)

**Rational decision** A rational decision is one that best serves the objectives of the decision maker, whatever those objectives may be. Such objectives may include a firm's desire to maximize its profits, a government's desire to maximize the welfare of its citizens, or another government's desire to maximize its military might. The term *rational* connotes neither approval nor disapproval of the objective itself. (p. 53)

**Rational expectations** Rational expectations are forecasts that, while not necessarily correct, are the best that can be made given the available data. Rational expectations, therefore, cannot err systematically. If expectations are rational, forecasting errors are pure random numbers. (p. 718)

**Real GDP** Real GDP is calculated by valuing outputs of different years at common prices. Therefore, real GDP is a far better measure than nominal GDP of changes in total production. (p. 484)

**Real GDP** Real GDP is the value of all the goods and services produced by an economy in a year, evaluated in dollars of constant purchasing power. Hence, inflation does not raise real GDP. (p. 24)

**Real rate of interest** The real rate of interest is the percentage increase in purchasing power that the borrower pays to the lender for the privilege of borrowing. It indicates the increased ability to purchase goods and services that the lender earns. (p. 516)

**Real wage rate** The real wage rate is the wage rate adjusted for inflation. It indicates the volume of goods and services that money wages will buy. (p. 512)

**Recession** A recession is a period of time during which the total output of the economy falls. (p. 36, 482)

**Recessionary gap** The recessionary gap is the amount by which the equilibrium level of real GDP falls short of potential GDP. (p. 559, 587)

**Regressive tax** A regressive tax is one in which the average tax rate falls as income rises. (p. 435)

**Regulation** Regulation of industry is a process established by law that restricts or controls some specified decisions made by the affected firms, and is designed to protect the public from exploitation by firms with monopoly power. Regulation is usually carried out by a special government agency assigned the task of administering and interpreting the law. That agency also acts as a court in enforcing the regulatory laws. (p. 407)

**Relative price** An item's relative price is its price in terms of some other item rather than in terms of dollars. (p. 513)

**Rent seeking** Rent seeking refers to unproductive activity in the pursuit of economic profit—in other words, profit in excess of competitive earnings. (p. 285)

**Repeated game** A repeated game is one that is played over again a number of times. (p. 262)

**Required reserves** Required reserves are the minimum amount of reserves (in cash or the equivalent) required by law. Normally, required reserves are proportional to the volume of deposits. (p. 630)

**Research and development (R&D)** Research and development (R&D) is the activity of firms, universities, and government agencies that seeks to invent new products and processes and to improve those inventions so that they are ready for the market or other uses. (p. 295)

**Resources** Resources are the instruments provided by nature or by people that are used to create goods and services. Natural resources include minerals, the soil, water, and air. Labor is a scarce resource, partly because of time limitations (the day has only 24 hours) and partly because the number of skilled workers is limited. Factories and machines are resources made by people. These three types of resources are often referred to as *land*, *labor*, and *capital*. They are also called *inputs* or *factors of production*. (p. 52)

**Revaluation** A revaluation is an increase in the official value of a currency. (p. 754)

**Run on a bank** A run on a bank occurs when many depositors withdraw cash from their accounts all at once. (p. 620)

**Scatter diagram** A scatter diagram is a graph showing the relationship between two variables (such as consumer spending and disposable income). Each year is represented by a point in the diagram. The coordinates of each year's point show the values of the two variables in that year. (p. 532)

**Shift in a demand curve** A shift in a demand curve occurs when any variable other than price changes. If consumers want to buy *more* at any given price than they wanted previously, the demand curve shifts to the right (or outward). If they desire *less* at any given price, the demand curve shifts to the left (or inward). (p. 129)

**Short run** The short run is a period of time during which some of the firm's cost commitments will *not* have ended. (p. 140)

**Shortage** A shortage is an excess of quantity demanded over quantity supplied. When there is a shortage, buyers cannot purchase the quantities they desire. (p. 77)

**Specialization** Specialization means that a country devotes its energies and resources to only a small proportion of the world's productive activities. (p. 60, 732)

**Speculation** Individuals who engage in speculation deliberately invest in risky assets, hoping to obtain profits from future changes in the prices of these assets. (p. 319)

**Stabilization policy** Stabilization policy is the name given to government programs designed to prevent or shorten recessions and to counteract inflation (that is, to stabilize prices). (p. 494)

**Stagflation** Stagflation is inflation that occurs while the economy is growing slowly ("stagnating") or having a recession. (p. 492, 591)

**Statistical discrimination** Statistical discrimination is said to occur when the productivity of a particular worker is estimated to be low just because that worker belongs to a particular group (such as women). (p. 391)

**Stock price index** A stock price index, such as the S&P 500, is an average of the prices of a large set of stocks. These stocks are selected to represent the price movements of the entire stock market, or some specified segment of the market, and the chosen set is rarely changed. (p. 316)

**Store of value** A store of value is an item used to store wealth from one point in time to another. (p. 622)

**Structural budget deficit** The structural budget deficit is the hypothetical deficit we *would have* under current fiscal policies if the economy were operating near full employment. (p. 689)

**Structural unemployment** Structural unemployment refers to workers who have lost their jobs because they have been displaced by automation, because their skills are no longer in demand, or because of similar reasons. (p. 509)

**Substitutes** Two goods are called substitutes if an increase in the quantity consumed of one cuts the quantity demanded of the other, all other things remaining constant. (p. 128)

**Supply curve** A supply curve is a graphical depiction of a supply schedule. It shows how the quantity supplied of some product during a specified period of time will change as the price of that product changes, holding all other determinants of quantity supplied constant. (p. 75)

**Supply schedule** A supply schedule is a table showing how the quantity supplied of some product during a specified period of time changes as the price of that product changes, holding all other determinants of quantity supplied constant. (p. 73)

**Supply-demand diagram** A supply-demand diagram graphs the supply and demand curves together. It depicts the equilibrium price and quantity. (p. 77)

**Surplus** A surplus is an excess of quantity supplied over quantity demanded. When there is a surplus, sellers cannot sell the quantities they desire to supply. (p. 77)

**Takeover** A takeover is the acquisition by an outside group (the raiders) of a controlling proportion of a company's stock. When the old management opposes the takeover attempt, it is called a *hostile takeover attempt.* (p. 319)

**Tangent** The tangent to a curve at some point, *Z*, on that curve is a straight line that touches point *Z* but does not cross the curve at that point. (p. 21)

**Tariff** A tariff is a tax on imports. (p. 739)

**Tax deduction** A tax deduction is a sum of money that may be subtracted before the taxpayer computes his or her taxable income. (p. 436)

**Tax exempt** A particular source of income is tax exempt if income from that source is not taxable. (p. 436)

**Tax loophole** A tax loophole is a special provision in the tax code that reduces taxation below normal rates (perhaps to zero) if certain conditions are met. (p. 436)

**Tax shifting** Tax shifting occurs when the economic reactions to a tax cause prices and outputs in the economy to change, thereby shifting part of the burden of the tax onto others. (p. 446)

**Technology trading** Technology trading is an arrangement in which a firm voluntarily makes its privately owned technology available to other firms either in exchange for access to the technology of the second company or for an agreed-upon fee. (p. 298)

**Theory** A theory is a deliberate simplification of relationships used to explain how those relationships work. (p. 12)

**Time-series graph** A time-series graph is a type of two-variable diagram in which time is the variable measured along the horizontal axis. It shows how some variable changed as time passed. (p. 24)

**Total physical product (TPP)** The firm's total physical product (TPP) is the amount of output it obtains in total from a given quantity of input. (p. 143)

**Total profit** The total profit of a firm is its net earnings during some period of time. It is equal to the total amount of money the firm gets from sales of its products (the firm's total revenue) minus the total amount that it spends to make and market those products (total cost). (p. 170)

**Total utility** The total utility of a quantity of a good to a consumer (measured in money terms) is the maximum amount of money that he or she is willing to give in exchange for it. (p. 96)

**Trade adjustment assistance** Trade adjustment assistance provides special unemployment benefits, loans, retraining programs, and other aid to workers and firms that are harmed by foreign competition. (p. 744)

**Transfer payments** Transfer payments are sums of money that certain individuals receive as outright grants from the government rather than as payments for services rendered. (p. 49)

**Transfer payments** Transfer payments are sums of money that the government gives certain individuals as outright *grants* rather than as payments for services rendered to employers. Some common examples are Social Security and unemployment benefits. (p. 531)

**Unemployment rate** The unemployment rate is the number of unemployed people, expressed as a percentage of the labor force. (p. 505)

**Union shop** A union shop is an arrangement under which nonunion workers may be hired, but then must join the union within a specified period of time. (p. 369)

**Unit of account** The unit of account is the standard unit for quoting prices. (p. 622)

**Unlimited liability** Unlimited liability is a legal obligation of a firm's owner(s) to pay back company debts with whatever resources he or she owns. (p. 309)

**Variable taxes** Variable taxes are taxes that do vary with the level of GDP. (p. 600)

**Variable** A variable is something measured by a number; it is used to analyze what happens to other things when the size of that number changes (varies). (p. 18)

**Velocity** Velocity indicates the number of times per year that an "average dollar" is spent on goods and services. It is the ratio of nominal gross domestic product (GDP) to the number of dollars in the money stock. That is:

$$\text{Velocity} = \frac{\text{Nominal GDP}}{\text{Money stock.}} \text{ (p. 663)}$$

**Vertical (long-run) Phillips curve** The vertical (long-run) Phillips curve shows the menu of inflation/unemployment choices available to society in the long run. It is a vertical straight line at the natural rate of unemployment. (p. 714)

**Vertical equity** Vertical equity refers to the notion that differently situated individuals should be taxed differently in a way that society deems to be fair. (p. 441)

## Selected U.S. Macroeconomic Data, 1929–1998

| Year | (1) Gross Domestic Product | (2) Personal Consumption Expenditure | (3) Gross Private Domestic Investment | (4) Government Purchases | (5) Net Exports | (6) Gross Domestic Product | (7) Personal Consumption Expenditure | (8) Gross Private Domestic Investment | (9) Government Purchases | (10) Net Exports | (11) Real GDP per capita |
|---|---|---|---|---|---|---|---|---|---|---|---|
| | (in billions of dollars) | | | | | (in billions of chained 1992 dollars)[a] | | | | | (in chained 1992 dollars) |
| 1929 | 103.8 | 77.5 | 16.7 | 9.3 | 0.4 | 790.9 | 593.9 | 92.4 | 105.4 | −10.7 | 7,004 |
| 1933 | 56.2 | 45.9 | 1.7 | 8.6 | 0.1 | 577.3 | 484.8 | 16.4 | 112.8 | −11.2 | 4,592 |
| 1939 | 91.9 | 67.2 | 9.3 | 14.6 | 0.8 | 866.5 | 654.0 | 79.5 | 171.6 | −5.7 | 6,613 |
| 1945 | 223.2 | 119.9 | 10.9 | 93.3 | −0.9 | 1,626.7 | 808.4 | 68.8 | 1,012.0 | −29.0 | 11,624 |
| 1950 | 294.6 | 192.7 | 54.2 | 47.1 | 0.7 | 1,611.3 | 1,034.1 | 234.1 | 344.6 | −10.6 | 10,623 |
| 1955 | 415.1 | 259.1 | 69.0 | 86.7 | 0.4 | 2,001.1 | 1,242.6 | 261.9 | 541.3 | −16.7 | 12,107 |
| 1960 | 526.6 | 332.2 | 78.8 | 113.2 | 2.4 | 2,262.9 | 1,432.6 | 270.5 | 617.2 | −21.3 | 12,519 |
| 1965 | 719.1 | 444.3 | 118.0 | 153.0 | 3.9 | 2,881.1 | 1,799.1 | 397.2 | 737.6 | −27.4 | 14,825 |
| 1970 | 1,035.6 | 648.1 | 150.2 | 236.1 | 1.2 | 3,397.6 | 2,197.8 | 426.1 | 866.8 | −65.0 | 16,566 |
| 1971 | 1,125.4 | 702.5 | 176.0 | 249.9 | −3.0 | 3,510.0 | 2,279.5 | 474.9 | 851.0 | −75.8 | 16,900 |
| 1972 | 1,237.3 | 770.7 | 205.6 | 268.9 | −8.0 | 3,702.3 | 2,415.9 | 531.8 | 854.1 | −89.0 | 17,637 |
| 1973 | 1,382.6 | 851.6 | 242.9 | 287.6 | 0.6 | 3,916.3 | 2,532.6 | 595.5 | 848.4 | −63.0 | 18,479 |
| 1974 | 1,496.9 | 931.2 | 245.6 | 323.2 | −3.1 | 3,891.2 | 2,514.7 | 546.5 | 862.9 | −35.5 | 18,192 |
| 1975 | 1,630.6 | 1,029.1 | 225.4 | 362.6 | 13.6 | 3,873.9 | 2,570.0 | 446.6 | 876.3 | −7.2 | 17,936 |
| 1976 | 1,819.0 | 1,148.8 | 286.6 | 385.9 | −2.3 | 4,082.9 | 2,714.3 | 537.4 | 876.8 | −39.9 | 18,721 |
| 1977 | 2,026.9 | 1,277.1 | 356.6 | 416.9 | −23.7 | 4,273.6 | 2,829.8 | 622.1 | 884.7 | −64.2 | 19,400 |
| 1978 | 2,291.4 | 1,428.8 | 430.8 | 457.9 | −26.1 | 4,503.0 | 2,951.6 | 693.4 | 910.6 | −65.5 | 20,226 |
| 1979 | 2,557.5 | 1,593.5 | 480.9 | 507.1 | −24.0 | 4,630.6 | 3,020.2 | 709.7 | 924.9 | −45.3 | 20,571 |
| 1980 | 2,784.2 | 1,760.4 | 465.9 | 572.8 | −14.9 | 4,615.0 | 3,009.7 | 628.3 | 941.4 | 10.1 | 20,265 |
| 1981 | 3,115.9 | 1,941.3 | 556.2 | 633.4 | −15.0 | 4,720.7 | 3,046.4 | 686.0 | 947.7 | 5.6 | 20,524 |
| 1982 | 3,242.1 | 2,076.8 | 501.1 | 684.8 | −20.5 | 4,620.3 | 3,081.5 | 587.2 | 960.1 | −14.1 | 19,896 |
| 1983 | 3,514.5 | 2,283.4 | 547.1 | 735.7 | −51.7 | 4,803.7 | 3,240.6 | 642.1 | 987.3 | −63.3 | 20,499 |
| 1984 | 3,902.4 | 2,492.3 | 715.6 | 796.6 | −102.0 | 5,140.1 | 3,407.6 | 833.4 | 1,018.4 | −127.3 | 21,744 |
| 1985 | 4,180.7 | 2,704.8 | 715.1 | 875.0 | −114.2 | 5,323.5 | 3,566.5 | 823.8 | 1,080.1 | −147.9 | 22,320 |
| 1986 | 4,422.2 | 2,892.7 | 722.5 | 938.5 | −131.5 | 5,487.7 | 3,708.7 | 811.8 | 1,135.0 | −163.9 | 22,801 |
| 1987 | 4,692.3 | 3,094.5 | 747.2 | 992.8 | −142.1 | 5,649.5 | 3,822.3 | 821.5 | 1,165.9 | −156.2 | 23,264 |
| 1988 | 5,049.6 | 3,349.7 | 773.9 | 1,032.0 | −106.1 | 5,865.2 | 3,972.7 | 828.2 | 1,180.9 | −114.4 | 23,934 |
| 1989 | 5,438.7 | 3,594.8 | 829.2 | 1,095.1 | −80.4 | 6,062.0 | 4,064.6 | 863.5 | 1,213.9 | −82.7 | 24,504 |
| 1990 | 5,743.8 | 3,839.3 | 799.7 | 1,176.1 | −71.3 | 6,136.3 | 4,132.2 | 815.0 | 1,250.4 | −61.9 | 24,549 |
| 1991 | 5,916.7 | 3,975.1 | 736.2 | 1,225.9 | −20.5 | 6,079.4 | 4,105.8 | 738.1 | 1,258.0 | −22.3 | 24,060 |
| 1992 | 6,244.4 | 4,219.8 | 790.4 | 1,263.8 | −29.5 | 6,244.4 | 4,219.8 | 790.4 | 1,263.8 | −29.5 | 24,447 |
| 1993 | 6,558.1 | 4,459.2 | 876.2 | 1,283.4 | −60.7 | 6,389.6 | 4,343.6 | 863.6 | 1,252.1 | −70.2 | 24,750 |
| 1994 | 6,947.0 | 4,717.0 | 1,007.9 | 1,313.0 | −90.9 | 6,610.7 | 4,486.0 | 975.7 | 1,252.3 | −104.6 | 25,357 |
| 1995 | 7,269.6 | 4,953.9 | 1,043.2 | 1,356.4 | −83.9 | 6,761.7 | 4,605.6 | 996.1 | 1,254.5 | −96.5 | 25,691 |
| 1996 | 7,661.6 | 5,215.7 | 1,131.9 | 1,405.2 | −91.2 | 6,994.8 | 4,752.4 | 1,084.1 | 1,268.2 | −111.2 | 26,338 |
| 1997 | 8,110.9 | 5,493.7 | 1,256.0 | 1,454.6 | −93.4 | 7,269.8 | 4,913.5 | 1,206.4 | 1,285.0 | −136.1 | 27,138 |
| 1998 | 8,510.7 | 5,805.6 | 1,368.7 | 1,487.5 | −151.2 | 7,552.1 | 5,151.6 | 1,331.9 | 1,297.3 | −238.3 | 27,944 |

[a] Components do not add up to GDP due to chain method of deflation.
[b] Persons 14 years and older for 1929–1945; thereafter, persons 16 years and older.
[c] Moody's Aaa rating.
[d] Multilateral trade-weighted average of 10 currencies.
[e] National income and product accounts basis; calendar years.